JAPANESE
COLLEGES
and
UNIVERSITIES
1989

JAPANESE COLLEGES and UNIVERSITIES 1989

A GUIDE TO INSTITUTIONS OF HIGHER EDUCATION IN JAPAN

Supervised by
Monbusho
(The Ministry of Education, Science and Culture)

Compiled and Edited by
The Association of International Education, Japan

In Collaboration with
Association of National Universities, Association of Public Universities and
Federation of Private Colleges and Universities Associations

Published by
Maruzen Co., Ltd., Tokyo

Japanese Colleges and Universities 1989

© 1989 by the Association of International Education, Japan
5-29, Komaba 4-chome, Meguro-ku, Tokyo, 153 Japan
Published by MARUZEN COMPANY, LTD.
3-10, Nihonbashi 2-chome, Chuo-ku, Tokyo, 103 Japan
All Rights Reserved. Printed in Japan

Address orders to:
MARUZEN COMPANY, LTD.
Export & Import Department
P.O. Box 5050, Tokyo International, 100-31 Japan.

ISBN 4-621-03357-3 C1502

EDITOR'S PREFACE

The Association of International Education, Japan, provides for the welfare of foreign students, offers information on study in Japan and abroad, and administers examinations for the selection of foreign students at Japanese universities.

In 1983, the committee for encouraging foreign students to study in Japan expressed their desire to make painstaking efforts in accepting more students in "Policy for receiving foreign students toward 21st Century."

Currently, there are about 22,000 foreign students who are engaged in study at Japanese institutions of higher education. Even with this, useful information concerning higher education is still insufficient for those who desire to study here. To answer this growing need, in 1985, the first edition of this catalog was compiled containing a listing of national and public colleges and universities. To the second edition, a listing of private universities was added.

This updated edition gives more information of each individual institution, including details of faculty staff, number of students, description of undergraduate and graduate programs, admission requirements, and also a brief background of each institution's history and special characteristics to give the reader a broader understanding of the school atmosphere and academic environment.

It has been my privilege, along with the cooperation of participating institution, to have had the opportunity to edit this catalog of valuable information.

We sincerely hope this catalog will be of aid and assistance to the reader.

January, 1989

Shigeto Kawano

Shigeto Kawano
Director General
Association of International
Education, Japan

ACKNOWLEDGEMENTS

Appreciation is extended to all institutions listed herein for their cooperation in providing their program information.

In addition, Kokuritsu Daigaku Kyokai (Association of National Universities), Koritsu Daigaku Kyokai (Association of Public Universities) and Nihon Shiritsu Daigaku Dantai Rengokai (Federation of Japanese Private Colleges and Universities Associations) all gave their full support to the project and were most helpful in promoting their member institutions' cooperation in this undertaking.

CONTENTS

CONTENTS

PREFACE

Japan warmly welcomes young people from all over the world to come and study at its many colleges and universities.

In today's internationalized and interdependent world, for the harmonious development of all nations, it is important for young people of other countries and Japan to study together at the college and university level, to promote friendship, goodwill and mutual understanding.

The number of foreign students in Japan has increased each year. Japanese universities are making great strides to improve and expand with hopes of attracting students from around the world.

If you are presently planning to further your education abroad, we hope you will consider coming to Japan.

To begin with, you will need to select the proper institution where you can accomplish your goals. To make the right decision, it is necessary to get various information on undergraduate and graduate programs, faculties, departments, admission procedure, school fees, course outlines. Information on the educational system in Japan, scholarships and other special programs for foreign students, etc., is also helpful in making your decision before coming to Japan.

This catalog is designed to provide such information as much as possible. We hope this catalog will be useful to many people, and especially to those who have a strong desire to study in Japan.

In closing, we wish to extend our sincere appreciation to the Association of International Education, Japan, for undertaking the task of editing and publishing this catalog, and also to all the Japanese colleges and universities for their cooporation in providing information for compilation.

Tokyo, February 1989

Tsuneaki Kawamura
Director General
Science and International
Affairs Bureau
Ministry of Education, Science
and Culture

Higher Education in Japan

(1) Japanese education system

The Japanese school education system is generally broken down into six years elementary, three years lower secondary, three years upper secondary, four years university or college, and five years graduate school. In addition, there are kindergartens, colleges of technology which may follow lower secondary, and two-year junior colleges. Compulsory education is from age six through lower secondary, a total of nine years.

A general description of each of the different types of educational institution shown in the chart is presented below.

i) Kindergartens

Kindergartens are non-compulsory schools intended to help infants develop their minds and bodies by providing them with an appropriate educative environment. They cater for pre-school children aged three or above.

Kindergartens are under the supervision of national and local education authorities, while the legal standards for physical facilities and equipment, curriculum and other matters are set forth by the Minister of Education,

Japanese Education System

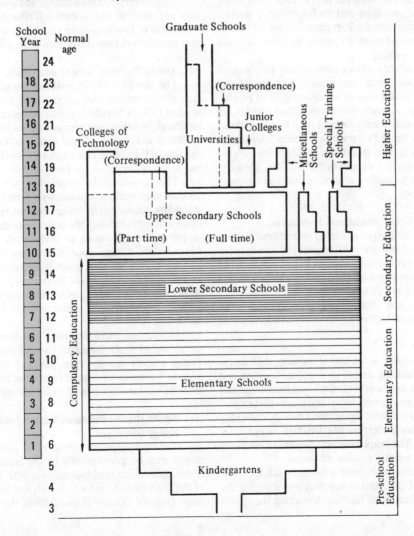

Science and Culture.

ii) *Elementary Schools*

All children who have reached the age of six are required to attend a six-year elementary school. The elementary school is intended to provide children between the ages of six and 12 with elementary general education suited to the stage of their mental and physical development.

iii) *Lower Secondary Schools*

All children who have completed the elementary school course are required to go on to a three-year lower secondary school. The lower secondary school aims to provide children between the ages of 12 and 15 with general secondary education suited to the level of their mental and physical development, on the basis of education provided in the elementary school.

iv) *Upper Secondary Schools*

Upper secondary schools are intended to offer lower secondary school graduates general and specialized secondary education suited to their level of mental and physical development, on the basis of education provided in lower secondary schools. There are three types of upper secondary school courses: full-time, part-time and correspondence. The full-time course lasts three years, while both the part-time and correspondence courses require four years or more. Part-time courses are further divided into day and evening courses, however, most are offered in the evening.

Upper secondary school courses may be classified broadly into two categories: general and specialized. General courses offer general education with an emphasis on academic subjects, while specialized courses are designed to provide vocational, technical or other education for those students who have chosen a particular vocational area as their future career. These courses are classified into several categories: agriculture, industry, business, fishery, home economics, nursing, science-mathematics, etc.

(2) Types of higher educational institutions

There are four types of higher educational institutions in Japan. They are: (i) *Daigaku* (university); (ii) *Tanki-daigaku* (junior college); (iii) *Kôtô-senmon-gakkô* (college of technology); and (iv) *Senshû-gakkô* (special training school) and others.

The legal and institutional frameworks of the respective types of higher education institutions are as follows:

i) *Universities*

"The University, as a center of learning, shall aim at teaching and studying deeply professional learning and technical arts as well as providing a broad knowledge and developing the intellectual, moral and practical abilities." (Article 52 of the School Education Law). A university has one or more undergraduate faculties, which offer courses lasting four years. However, medicine, dentistry and veterinary science require six years.

The university may have a graduate school. "The graduate school shall aim at teaching and studying the theory and application of learning, mastering the secrets

of it, and contributing to the development of culture." (Article 65 of the School Education Law)

In principle, those who have finished the whole course of upper secondary school or have completed 12 years of schooling under normal courses are qualified to apply for admission.

ii) *Junior Colleges*

Junior colleges offer two-year college level programs. The main aim of the junior colleges is "to conduct teaching and research in depth in specialized academic subjects and to cultivate such abilities as are required in vocations or practical life" (Article 69-2, paragraph 1, of the School Education Law).

Qualifications for entering a junior college are the same as those for the university.

iii) *Colleges of Technology*

Colleges of technology offers five years of integrated education to those who have completed the course of the first stage of secondary education (i.e. lower secondary school education). "A college of technology shall aim to teach specialized academic subjects in depth and to cultivate the abilities required for certain vocations" (Article 70-2 of the School Education Law).

The university, junior college and college of technology are part of the system of education in Japan. Graduates of junior colleges and colleges of technology may be admitted into universities as second or third year students.

iv) *Special Training Schools and Others*

The *senshû-gakkô* (special training school) is a new type of educational institution which was institutionalized in 1976. It "conducts systematic education to develop the abilities necessary for certain vocations or practical life, or to enhance cultural standards" (Article 82-2 of the School Education Law). Courses cover at least a year but many of them are for two years or more.

The *senshû-gakkô* may offer upper secondary courses open mainly to those who have finished lower secondary education, or college courses open mainly to those who have finished the upper secondary education, or general courses open to anybody. A *senshû-gakkô* which offers college courses is called *senmon-gakkô* (special training college), and is regarded as a higher education institution. However, there is no provision which allows those who have finished such college courses to transfer to universities, junior colleges or colleges of technology.

In addition there are many educational establishments called *Kakushu-gakkô* (miscellaneous schools). These schools mainly offer practical and vocational courses for those who have completed lower or upper secondary education as well as for the general public.

(3) Administrative and financing mechanism governing higher education

Universities, junior colleges and colleges of technology may be founded only by the State, local public bodies and educational foundations, with the exception of the University of the Air, which was founded by *the Hôsô Daigaku Gakuen* (University of the Air Foundation), an educational foundation having a special status and financed by the State.

If a local public body or an educational foundation wishes to establish a university, junior college or college of technology, authorization by the Minister of Education, Science and Culture must first be obtained. Prior to his granting authorization, the Minister must consult the University Chartering Council. The Council then deliberates the matter based on the standards of establishment as laid down in an Ordinance of the Ministry of Education, Science and Culture, and recommends to the Minister whether he should or should not give authorization.

In the case of private universities, junior colleges and colleges of technology, the Minister of Education, Science and Culture must also consult the Private University Council, which deliberates, inter alia, whether the educational foundation wishing to establish the institution in question has sufficient managerial ability to operate the institution.

(4) Number of colleges and universities, and student enrollment

As of 1988 there were 96 national, 36 public and 357 private four-year universities as well as 41 national, 54 public and 477 private two-year junior colleges. There is at least one national university in each prefecture with public and private schools well distributed throughout the country.

There were 1,994,615 students enrolled in universities as of May 1, 1988; of those 491,539 were in national, 59,217 in public and 1,443,859 in private universities. Out of the above figures, foreign students were 9,955 in national, 664 in public and 9,109 in private universities.

(5) Recent developments in higher education

Two major recent developments in Japanese higher education are, systematic planning-administration, and promotion of diversification.

Higher education in Japan has expanded rapidly since 1960's, and has proceeded to an age of mass higher education. In 1988, the ratio of enrollment at higher education institutions (i.e. the ratio of those who were admitted to universities and junior colleges plus fourth year students at technical colleges against the 18-year-old population) was as high as 36.7%.

(6) Faculties and departments

Universities generally consist of a number of faculties which are divided into various departments and/or courses depending on the subject, while graduate schools consist of various departments and courses.

(7) Qualifications for admission

Admission to Japanese universities is limited to those who have completed a normal 12 year school education or those who can show an equivalent education record. If a foreign student interested in entering a Japanese University and has not completed requisit 12 year education, he/she can compensate by attending the

International Students Institute in Tokyo (3-22-7, Kita-Sinjuku, Sinjuku-ku, Tokyo 160 ☎ 03-371-7265) or the Kansai International Students Institute in Osaka (8-3-13, Uehonmachi, Tennoji-ku, Osaka-shi 543 ☎ 06-774-0033).

Admission to a master's course is limited to those who have completed 16 years of education, i.e., university graduates, or those with an equivalent level of education.

(8) School calendar and curriculum

The academic year is from April to March. The number of class days in a year, including test days, is 210 days, or 35 weeks. Summer vacation varies according to the university, but in general is from the middle of July to the end of August. Winter vacation (December to January) is about two weeks. Spring vacation (March to April) is approximately 40 days. Most universities operate on a semester system.

In general, educational institutions in Japan are closed on Sundays and on the national holidays. No formal instruction is given on Saturday afternoon.

University curriculum is divided into General Education, Foreign Languages, Health and Physical Education, and Professional Education. Compulsory and elective subjects of study are regulated by the individual university.

General subjects, foreign languages and physical education classes are generally taken in the first and second years. These classes are usually large, and held in an auditorium or a large classroom. The student's major subjects are usually taken in the third and fourth years. These classes are relatively small. They are generally structured as seminars, labs, study projects, or practical application studies.

It should be understood that in principle, all classes in Japanese universities are conducted in Japanese. Except for some few graduate level courses, chances to take courses in English are virtually non-existent.

(9) Credits, exams and grades

Except for schools of medicine and dentistry, universities follow the credit system. Students must complete the required study and exams for each course in order to receive credit.

Since Japanese universities are on a semester system, exams are usually held in September or October, after summer vacation, and again in January or February after winter vacation. The exams are generally written, but reports or essays may be required in lieu of the exam.

Grades are based on the student's exam scores and paper results, with attendance also taken into consideration. Grades are broken down as excellent, good, passing, failing, i.e., A, B, C, D. Usually A=100–80%, B=79–70%, C=69–60%, D=59–0%. No credit is given for a D.

(10) Conferment of degrees

In order to graduate from a university it is necessary to complete four years (six years in the case of medicine, dentistry and veterinary science) of study, and obtain the credits as required by the university. Although the number of credits needed for graduation differs with the university, most schools require a minimum of 124 credits (except for medicine, dentistry and veterinary medicine).

A bachelor's is conferred only upon those who graduate from a university. It is not conferred to graduates of higher educational institutions other than universities. Thus it may be said that universities in Japan are medium which have the authority to confer bachelor's degrees. Graduates from junior colleges and colleges of technology may be admitted to universities as second or third year students. The master's degree is conferred upon those who have completed two years or more in the master's program, have accumulated at least 30 required credits in their major subjects, and have successfully passed their thesis exam and final exams. A doctorate degree requires five years of study (three years after the master's) (four years for those in medicine and dentistry), completion of the required units, and passing finals and thesis exams.

Graduate schools are not set up in all of the universities. In 1988, 59.9% of Japanese universities had graduate schools.

85.6% of all 1988 university graduates received their bachelor's degree after four years (the minimum period) of study.

In general, it is said that it is difficult to get a master's or doctorate degree in Japan, but for foreign students, it is much more encouraging. (see Table 1) Further, while graduate theses generally must be written in Japanese, recently, depending on the advising professor, theses submitted in English are also being accepted.

(11) Research students (*Kenkyusei*)

Kenkyusei are non-degree students attending graduate courses. They may apply for graduate programs by taking the necessary entrance exams. Research students, as such, do not receive degrees.

(12) Selection of Japanese applicants to universities

The ratio of successful applicants to universities and junior colleges has recently been stabilized at about a little over 65%. However, due partly to the differences in social evaluation, etc. of history, tradition, teaching and research activities among respective universities, there is a strong desire to enter specific universities. Thus, the struggle to pass the entrance examination to universities in Japan is a severe one.

In order to rectify this situation, measures are being taken, such as eliminating a general social trend of overestimating academic careers, developing the features of each university, and providing adequate guidance at upper secondary schools. In addition the method of selection of applicants itself needs to be improved. With this in mind, a selection method utilizing the Joint First-

Table 1   Master's and Doctrate Degrees Conferred on Foreign Students

Year	Category of Graduate Programs	Master's Course			Doctor's Course		
		Completed	Degree Conferred	*	Completed	Degree Conferred	*
1985	I	394	369	94%	53	19	36%
	II	562	554	99%	224	190	85%
	III	15	15	100%	8	8	100%
	Total	971	938	97%	285	217	76%
1986	I	429	413	96%	77	20	26%
	II	636	625	98%	244	201	84%
	III	40	40	100%	12	12	100%
	Total	1,105	1,078	98%	333	233	70%
1987	I	625	595	95%	96	25	26%
	II	817	806	99%	415	368	89%
	III	42	42	100%	16	16	100%
	Total	1,484	1,443	97%	527	409	78%

Note: Category of Graduate Programs
  I: Arts, Business Administration, Economics, Education, Law, Literature, Music, Mass Communication, Psychology, Sociology, etc.
  II: Agriculture, Animal Science, Chemistry, Computer Science, Engineering, Health Science, Library Science, Mathematics, Medical Science, Science, etc.
  III: Interdiciplinary Science, etc.
  * Percentage of students who upon completion of their graduation work received a degree

Stage Achievement Test program was adopted in 1979 for admission to national and public universities.

The Joint First-Stage Achievement Test program is conducted by national universities in cooperation with the National Center for University Entrance Examination. Questions posed in this test are designed to evaluate properly the degree of achievement of general and fundamental learning at upper secondary schools. In the secondary test, each of the universities makes innovative attempts by adding an interview, essay test, skills test, and evaluating school records submitted by upper secondary schools, and other factors.

Private universities and junior colleges are also making efforts to select applicants in such a way as to make the most of their academic tradition and other features unique to them.

Foreign Students in Japan

(1) Foreign students statistics

The 1988 figure for foreign students studying at Japanese universities, both undergraduate and graduate, junior colleges, colleges of technology and special training schools is approximately 25,000. Its breakdown by geography and major field of study indicates that there are a large number of those from Asia, the Middle East, and Central and South America in the natural sciences and engineering, while there is a tendency for those from Europe, North America and Oceania to major in the humanities and social sciences.

(2) Examinations for foreign students

i) All national and public universities, in cooperation with the National Center for University Entrance Examination give an achievement test. Students are judged on these results, together with the objective of determining candidate's scholastic level and suitability, holds its own separate entrance exam. Each university decides admission on the basis of these two exams and the student's high school transcript.

All Japanese applicants to national or public universities must take the JFSAT until 1989. However, starting 1990, new achievement test will take the place of JFSAT. Some private universities are also participating in this testing program.

This new test is designed to judge the applicants' level of achievement of study at the high school level. It is up to each university's judgement and creativity to utilize it properly to judge the applicants' ability and potential for receiving a university education. Contents of the test will be about the same level with JFSAT.

The Ministry of Education, Science and Culture has suggested that foreign students be exempted from this; schools and departments differ in procedure. Check the descriptions of each university for further details.

New test will be administered in January, 1990. For more detailed information on the new test, contact the person in charge of testing at one of the national or public universities.

ii) *General Examination for Foreign Students*

It is advisable for all foreign candidates for admission to regular undergraduate courses to take the General Examination for Foreign Students, and the Japanese Language Proficiency Test which is explained in section iii). The General Examination for Foreign Students is conducted by the Association of International Education, Japan (AIEJ) in Tokyo and Osaka at the beginning of December every year. The results of this Examination are sent to the applicants' prospective university in Japan. Most of the national universities as well as some private universities require foreign candidates to take this Ex-

Table 2   Foreign Students at Japanese Higher Educational Institutions   (as of May 1, 1988)

Level/Category / Area	University		Junior College	College of Technology	Senshu-gakko	Total	Percentage by Area
	Graduate	Undergraduate					
Africa	208	31	0	0	9	248	1.0%
America, North	219	797	9	0	20	1,045	4.1%
America, Central & South	858	186	13	0	20	577	2.3%
Asia	8,0551	8,977	673	172	4,931	22,808	88.9%
Europe	336	261	4	0	21	622	2.4%
Middle East	107	44	0	0	9	160	0.6%
Oceania	71	78	1	0	33	183	0.7%
Total	10,374	9,354	700	172	5,043	25,643	100.0%

Major Field of Applicants	Subject
Humanities, Social Sciences, Education, Arts, etc.	Mathematics World History English
Science, Engineering, Agriculture, Medicine, Dentistry, etc.	Mathematics Two of the following science subjects: Physics, Chemistry, Biology English

amination. Applicants may choose one of the two categories according to their major field.

iii) *The Japanese Language Proficiency Test*

The Japanese Language Proficiency Test is co-sponsored by AIEJ and the Japan Foundation. It is offered in Tokyo, Osaka and outside of Japan (40 cities in 20 countries/regions in 1988) at the beginning of December every year. This Test has four different levels as follows.

Level	Criteria		
	No. of Kanji	Vocabulary	Total Hours of Study
4 (Elementary I)	approx. 100	approx. 800	approx. 150
3 (Elementary II)	300	1,500	300
2 (Intermediate)	1,000	6,000	600
1 (Advanced)	2,000	10,000	900

Each level is made up of three categories: writing and vocabulary, listening comprehension, and reading comprehension and grammar.

Applicants to Japanese universities must choose Level 1 and the results are sent to their prospective universities. Certificates of proficiency will be sent to those who passed the Test.

Applicants in Japan should contact AIEJ (4-5-29 Komaba, Meguro-ku, Tokyo 153.)

Applicants who would like to take this Test outside of Japan should contact the Japan Foundation (Park Bldg., 3-6 Kioi-cho, Chiyoda-ku, Tokyo 102.)

(3) Tuition and fees

Students are required to pay a non-refundable application fee when they file an application and take the entrance examination. School expenses for the first-year students are; admission fee, tuition fee and other fees such as laboratory fee, facilities fee, student activities fee, etc. Fees in private and public schools vary according to the school and the faculty or department. Refer to Table (pp. 681).

Japanese Language Education

There are various Japanese language institutions to meet the various demands of foreign nationals interested in studying Japanese.

There are over 500 programs and courses for such students. These can be roughly categorized as follows; (1) university degree courses, (2) preparatory courses for university or graduate school attached to university, (3) preparatory courses for university, (4) Japanese language schools in general, (5) Japanese courses for technical trainees and (6) others.

At present, approximately 44,000 foreign nationals

are learning Japanese as a foreign language in Japan as of November 1, 1987 according to a report from the Agecy of Cultural Affairs.

From the educational viewpoint, Committee for research and investigation of the Ministry of Education, Science and Culture is in the process of setting up guidelines for the management of Japanese language Educational Institute to improve the quality of teaching and facilities so that foreign students may freely enjoy the benefits of such an opportunity.

Scholarships for Foreign Students

(1) Japanese Government Scholarships (Monbusho Scholarships) (pp. 698)

Those who have received scholarships to study or do research at higher educational institutions in Japan

from the Japanese Ministry of Education, Science and Culture are known as "Monbusho Scholarship Students."

This program is intended to give foreign students a

chance to study at higher educational institutions in Japan and at the same time, through their studies, help promote an international exchange in the field of education, science, and culture, thereby encouraging friendship and goodwill between Japan and other countries. As of May, 1988, a total of 4,118 students from approximately 110 countries around the world were studying under this program.

The Japanese Government Scholarship Programs are divided into six categories (p. 698).

Selection for the Monbusho Scholarships is made on the basis of recommendation by the Japanese Embassies. Detailed information may be obtained at each Japanese Embassy or Consulate-General.

(2) University Scholarships Available

Most universities have scholarships for the general student body as well as for foreign students. Selection standards are the same for foreign and Japanese students.

For further information, please contact the respective schools directly. There is a list of scholarships awarded by each university to foreign students on pp. 710–714.

(3) Scholarships awarded by private foundations

Generally, applicants should be currently enrolled in Japanese universities, graduate schools, or their affiliated research institutes as regular degree students. Some are open to non-degree students.

There are two ways to apply for a scholarship:
i) General Application: The individual may apply directly to the foundation.
ii) Application through University: Applications must be filed by the universities. Individual applications are not accepted. Application procedures differ with each university, and details as well as application forms should be obtained from the respective university.

How to Use This Book

The college/university profiles are presented in three sections: national, public and private colleges and universities, respectively. In each section, the colleges and universities are listed alphabetically, and the programs and courses are also arranged in alphabetical order.

The information contained is based on the manuscripts provided by the universities and colleges. Because of time constraints, the editor included only a brief list of programs for those universities whose manuscripts were not submitted by the publication deadline.

(1) Major Fields of Study

There are 105 fields of study listed on pp. 661–680. Each of these is listed alphabetically and the colleges and universities that offer such programs are also listed alphabetically with abbreviations B, M, and D, that stand for Bachelor's, Master's, and Doctor's degree programs in which he/she is interested and then turn to the descriptions of each institution. Graduate program listings are not given in detail but the reader may refer to the undergraduate course listings, which generally correspond to the fields of study students may pursue at the graduate level.

(2) Foreign Student Admission

The foreign student admission section gives detailed information on qualifications, what standardized tests, if any, are required, entrance examinations and documents to be submitted. "Standard Qualifications Requirement" and "Standard Documents Requirement" for each level of program are mentioned below. In addition, foreign students should note that Japanese language proficiency is very important for any level of study in Japan and that most of the forms to be filled out are in

Japanese and the documents must be prepared with Japanese or English translations.

Standard Qualifications Requirements

i) *Undergraduate Program*
1. Those who have completed 12 years of school education or the equivalent in countries other than Japan, or are expected to do so by the time of admission.
2. Those who are 18 years of age or older and have completed secondary education in less than 12 years but are eligible for admission to a university in their country, and have completed a preparatory Japanese language program at one of the institutions designated by the Ministry of Education, Science and Culture.
3. Applicants residing in Japan must be holders of one of the following visa status according to the Immigration-Control and Refugee-Recognition Act.
   (1) 4-1-6 (student)
   (2) 4-1-16-3 (to attend school)
   (3) 4-1-4 (temporary visitor) to take university entrance examinations
   (4) others with permission to stay for one year or more

ii) *Master's Program and One-Year Graduate Program*
1. Those who have completed 16 years of education and have obtained a Bachelor's degree or equivalent either in Japan or in countries other than Japan, or are expected to do so by the time of admission.
2. Applicants residing in Japan must be holders of an appropriate visa status as mentioned above.

iii) *Doctor's Program*
1. Those who have completed 18 years of education and have obtained a Master's degree or equivalent either in Japan or in countries other than Japan, or are expected to do so by the time of admission.
2. Applicants residing in Japan must be holders of an appropriate visa status as mentioned above.

Standard Documents Requirement
i) *Undergraduate Program*
1. Application form
2. Personal history
3. Certificate of Graduation or expected graduation from the high school attended. In the latter case, the presentation of the Certificate of Graduation should follow by the time of admission.
4. Official transcipt of record from the high school attended.
5. A letter of recommendation from the principal or teacher of the high school attended.
6. Certificate of physical examination
7. A letter of guarantee from a resident of Japan
8. A copy of Alien Registration if the applicant is residing in Japan.
9. Photos
10. Entrance examination fee

ii) *Transfer Students*
1. Application form
2. Personal history
3. Certificate of Graduation or expected graduation from the junior college attended, or a certificate of completion of two years or more of college level education.
4. Official transcript of record from the university/college attended.
5. A letter of recommendation from the dean or academic advisor of the university/college attended.
6. Certificate of physical examination
7. A letter of guarantee from a resident of Japan
8. A copy of Alien Registration Certificate if the applicant is residing in Japan.
9. Photos
10. Entrance examination fee

iii) *One-Year Graduate Program, Master's Program and Doctor's Program*
1. Application form
2. Personal history
3. Certificate of Graduation or expected graduation

from the university/college(s) attended.
4. Official transcript of record from the university/college(s) attended.
5. Research plan
6. A letter of recommendation from the dean or academic advisor of the university/college(s) attended.
7. Certificate of physical examination
8. A letter of guarantee from a resident of Japan
9. A copy of Alien Registration Certificate if the applicant is residing in Japan.
10. Photos
11. Entrance examination fee

(3) Research Institutes and Centers
Research institutes and centers are listed in alphabetical order regardless of their affiliations within the university. They are mostly attached to a faculty or school within each university, but in some cases they are independent institutions where different faculties and schools conduct co-research. In national universities some of these research organizations are jointly used by other national universities.

(4) Scholarships
Scholarships from the Ministry of Education, Science and Culture (Monbusho) and others from private foundations are listed on pp. 698–709. The University Scholarships section on pp. 710–714 gives information about the financial assistance programs given by each university. These programs are solely for foreign students and do not include those programs which apply to both Japanese and foreign students.

(5) Preparatory Japanese Language Programs associated with the Universities
These programs listed on pp. 715–716 are Japanese Language Programs associated with the Universities for the students who are seeking entrance into Universities in Japan.

(6) Study Abroad programs
This is a program where you can earn the credits which may be transferable at your home institution upon their evaluation. These programs are open to all students at the university level. However there are some programs only available to students of universities directly affiliated with universities in Japan. Programs for all the students are listed on pp. 717.

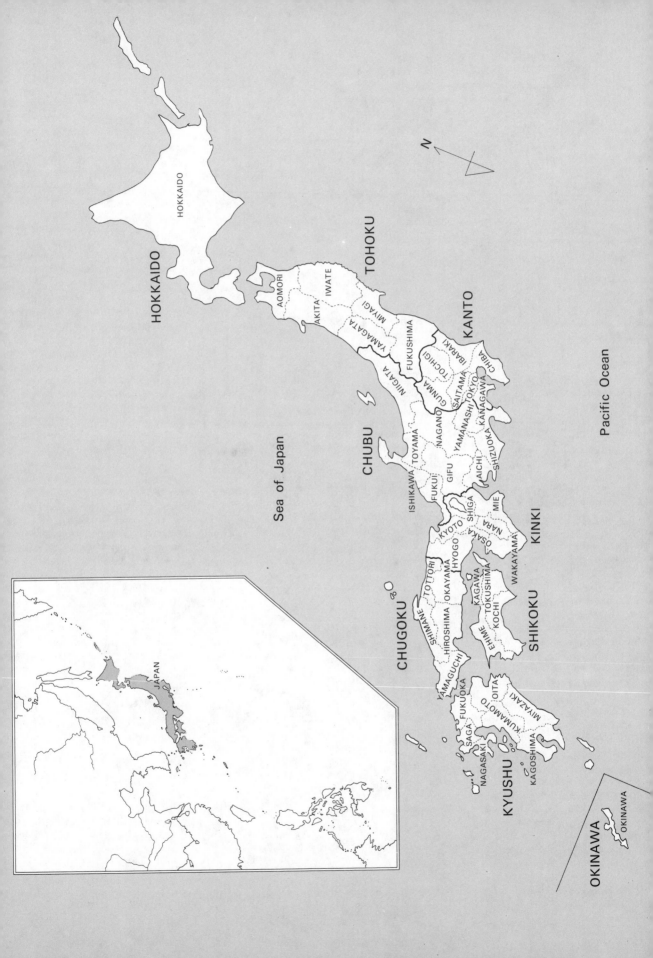

Descriptions of
the Colleges and Universities in Japan

National Colleges and Universities

1

Aichi University of Education
(Aichi Kyoiku Daigaku)

1 Hirosawa Igaya-cho, Kariya-shi, Aichi 448
☎ 0566-36-3111

Faculty
  Profs. 130   Assoc. Profs. 123
  Assist. Profs. Full-time 2; Part-time 213
  Res. Assocs. 20
Number of Students
  Undergrad. 4, 209   Grad. 153
Library 495, 716 volumes

Outline and Characteristics of the University

Aichi University of Education began as the Aichi Prefectural Academy in 1873, later developing into several Normal Schools over the period of three quarters of a century. In 1949 it became one of the new National Universities consolidating all the Normal schools in the area under the name of Aichi Gakugei University. A period of sustained development began in 1966 when the name Aichi University of Education was adopted.

The University's primary purpose has been to prepare elementary and junior high school teachers. Its expanded mission is to serve the needs of the region and of the nation in a variety of undergraduate and master's level graduate programs through instruction; to advance learning through research, and to prepare men and women for professional service in all educational areas and levels. It now offers additional courses to train special education, health science, and kindergarten as well as senior high school teachers. It also provides opportunities for one-year postgraduate study in selected areas.

The University has seven attached schools: two elementary schools, two junior high schools, a senior high school, a kindergarten, and a special education school for mentally retarded children.

Since 1987 six new departments of integrated arts and sciences (International Studies, Teaching Japanese as a Foreign Language, Human and Social Sciences, Information Science, Integrated Sciences, and Practicing Arts and Crafts) were established, reflecting the need of the nation to prepare people for a wide variety of professional fields beyond that of school teacher.

UNDERGRADUATE PROGRAMS

Faculty of Education (Freshmen Enrollment: 1, 035)
  Elementary School Teachers Course
Art, Career Guidance, Health and Physical Education, Home Economics, Japanese, Mathematics, Music, Science, Social Studies
  Health Science Teachers Course
Nursing in School

Junior High School Teachers Course
Art, Career Guidance, Engineering, Foreign Language, Health and Physical Education, Home Economics, Japanese, Mathematics, Music, Science, Social Studies
  Kindergarten Teachers Course
Early Childhood Education
  Teachers' Training Course in the Education of Mentally Handicapped Children
Special Education
  Teachers' Training Course in the Education of Physically Handicapped Children
Special Education
  Teachers' Training Course of Special Subjects of Senior High School
Calligraphy, Mathematics, Science
  Departments of Integrated Arts and Science
Human and Social Sciences, Information Science, Integrated Sciences, International Studies, Practicing Arts and Crafts, Teaching of Japanese as a Foreign Language

Foreign Student Admission
  Qualifications for Applicants
    Standard Qualifications Requirement
  Examination at the University
    Applicants should take the Joint First-Stage Achievement Test for all of the 5 subjects and the entrance examination of the University. The latter examination consists of scholastic tests; short essay or test of practical skills; it is given by each course entirely in Japanese.

The selective examination for graduates of foreign schools:
The qualifications are more rigorous than those-mentioned above. The entrance selection is chiefly determined by the personal merit report of the candidate, a short essay, and an individual interview. For more details, see the list of admission requirements which is available beginning in late July.
  Documents to be Submitted When Applying
    Standard Documents Requirement

ONE-YEAR GRADUATE PROGRAMS

One-Year Graduate Course in Education (Enrollment: 5)
Natural Sciences
One-Year Graduate Course in Special Education (Enrollment: 30)
Education of Mentally Handicapped Children

Foreign Student Admission
  Qualifications for Applicants
    Applicants should have finished 16 years of school education or the equivalent. They should also hold the regular credentials of teachers of kindergartens, primary schools, junior high schools, and senior high schools etc. , or they should be expected to acquire them.

Examination at the University

Admission is based on a scholastic test in Japanese, a health examination, and the personal merit report.

GRADUATE PROGRAMS

Graduate School of Education (First Year Enrollment : Master's 110)

Divisions

Art Education, Education of Handicapped Children, Engineering Education, English Education, Health and Physical Education, Home Economics Education, Japanese Education, Mathematics Education, School Education, Science Education, Social Studies Education

Foreign Student Admission

Qualifications for Applicants

Master's Program

Standard Qualifications Requirement

Examination at the University

Master's Program

The entrance examination consists of scholastic tests in Japanese related to the applicant's special field.

Documents to be Submitted When Applying

Standard Documents Requirement

*

Research Institutes and Centers

Center for Educational Technology, Center for Remedial Education, Center for Teaching Method Studies, Health Administration Center

Facilities/Services for Foreign Students

Accommodation: As we have no special accommodations set aside for foreign students at our university, private accommodations and student dormitories are made available through the University.

Lounge for Foreign Students: There is one cooperating lounge available in order to promote friendly social and academic communication amongst foreign students and between them and Japanese students.

Special Programs for Foreign Students

Supplemental lessons of Japanese language are offered four hours a week to students who are not proficient in Japanese. Moreover, we also offer a lecture course on Japanese education, a general lecture course on Japanese society and life, and observation study of educational institutions outside the university.

For Further Information

Undergraduate and Graduate Admission

Admissions Office, Aichi University of Education, 1 Hirosawa Igaya-cho, Kariya-shi, Aichi 448 ☎ 0566-36-3111 ext. 279

Akita University
(Akita Daigaku)

1-1 Tegata-Gakuen-cho, Akita-shi, Akita 010
☎ 0188-33-5261

Faculty
　　Profs.　123　　Assoc. Profs.　140
　　Assist. Profs.　Full–time　67; Part–time　276
　　Res. Assocs.　159
Number of Students
　　Undergrad.　3, 943　　Grad.　291
Library　383, 000 volumes

Outline and Characteristics of the University

Akita University was established in 1949 by combining the Akita Normal School, the Akita Youth Normal School and the Akita Mining College.

The College of Education was opened in 1949 together with the Mining College as one of the original two wings of Akita University. However the foundation of an old ancestral institution, the Akita Denshu Gakko (teacher training school), dates back to 1873. This makes the college one of the oldest colleges in Japan. It is primarily a four-year teacher training institution corresponding to a teachers college in the U.S.A. or in the United Kingdom. Secondly it provides all the students of the University with programs of general education courses as part of the faculty of liberal arts and sciences.

In 1910, The Mining College was established as the first mining college in Japan supported by the Government in Akita City, Akita Prefecture, which is famous for its mining industries. At the beginning, two departments of mining and metallurgy were opened, adopting the system of Freiberg Mining College in Germany. Since then, with the advancement of mining technology, the college has expanded greatly and enjoys a high reputation as a unique college for prospecting mining engineers. After the reformation of the educational system in 1949, the college was incorporated into Akita University. However, in appreciation of the tradition of the college and to maintain its uniqueness, the name "mining college" was preserved. But by adding new departments it has become a large college of 11 departments and one division concerned with the research and education of various engineering fields.

The School of Medicine was opened in 1970, adopting a very modern educational system which produced its first graduates in March of 1976. The total number of graduates reached 937 by March 1986. Most of them have gone on to serve their residency at the University Hospital or other general hospitals. The post-graduate course of the school of medicine was also founded in 1976. The School of Medicine and the University Hospital are located on the Hondo campus, three kilometers east of the main campus, and the campus itself forms a magnificent modern medical center.

Akita City is located on the western side of the North-Eastern district of Honshu (the Main Island). As the seat of the Akita Prefectural Government, it is one of the major cities of the district with a population of 290, 000. The city is situated at lat. 40°N. and long. 140°E. and enjoys a marked changing of the four seasons.

The University has also been promoting international programs. In 1983 the International Students Seminar was held here under the auspices of the Association of Internation Education, Japan. There have been 169 foreign students enrolled so far. At present the University has four overseas sister institutions and has exchanged staff and students.

UNDERGRADUATE PROGRAMS

Faculty of Education (Freshmen Enrollment: 320)
   Training Course for Elementary School Teachers
   Training Course for Junior High School Teachers
   Training Course for Kindergarten Teachers
   Training Course for Special Education
   Agriculture
Agricultural Chemistry, Agricultural Practice, Agronomy, Industry and Industrial Practice, Introduction to Industry, Vocational Guidance, Vocational Teaching, Zootechnical Science
   Educational Psychology
Abnormal Psychology, Adult Education, Clinical Psychology, Consulting Psychology, Criminal Psychology, Curriculum, Developmental Psychology, Education, Educational Administration and Finance, Educational Psychology, Educational Systems, Evaluation and Assessment, History of Education, Laws and Regulations, Methodology of Education, Philosophy of Education, Psychology of Learning, Psychology of Personality, Social Psychology, Sociology of Education, Supervision and Management of Schools
   English
British and American Literature, English Composition, English Grammar, English Linguistics, Modern French, Modern German, Teaching English as a Foreingn Language
   Fine Arts
Calligraphy, Construction and Theory of Construction, Craft and Theory of Design, Design, Drafting, Fine Arts Teaching, History of Calligraphy, History of Japanese Fine Arts, History of Western Fine Arts, Painting, Plastic Art, Theory of Art
   Home Economics
Child Care, Clothing and Textiles, Clothing Materials, Cooking, Domestic Machinery and Electricity, Family Relations, Food and Food Chemistry, Home Economics Teaching, Home Management and Economics, Housing and Interior Disign, Nutrition, Sewing
   Industrial Arts

Agronomy, Drafting, Electrical Engineering, Engineering Working Teaching, Mechanics, Metalwork, Woodwork
   Japanese
Calligraphy, Chinese Language and Literature, History of Calligraphy, Japanese Literature, Japanese Philology, Japanese Teaching Materials, Teaching of Japanese
   Kindergarten Education
Curriculum of Early Childhood Schools, Early Childhood Education, Infant Psychology
   Mathematics
Algebra, Analysis, Geometry, Mathematics Teaching, Statistics, Surveying, Teaching Materials of Elementary School Mathematics
   Music
Conducting, Instrumental Music, Musical Theory and History, Music Teaching, Solfeggio, Vocal Music
   Natural Sciences
Analytical Chemistry, Applied Physics, Astronomy, Biological Chemistry, Ecology, Electromagnetism, Field Study and Marine Practice, Fluid Mechanics, Genetics, Geology, Geophysics, Inorganic Chemistry, Mechanics, Mechanics of Elastic Bodies, Meteorology, Modern Physics, Morphology, Natural Sciences Teaching, Optics, Organic Chemistry, Petrology and Mineralogy, Physical Chemistry, Science Teaching Materials, Taxonomy
   Physical Education
Administration of Physical Education, Health Education for Schools, Hygienics, Physical Education, Physical Education Practice, Physical Education Teaching, Physiology
   Social Studies
Economics, Ethics, Geography, History of Ethical Thought, History of Europe and America, History of Philosophy, Japanese History, Jurisprudence, Logic, Oriental History, Philosophy, Politics, Public Law, Regional Geography, Social Studies Teaching, Social Studies Teaching Materials, Sociology
   Special School Education
Education of Mentally Handicapped Children, Health Education for Handicapped Children, Pathology of Mentally Handicapped Children, Practice in Teaching of Handicapped Children, Psychology of Mentally Handicapped Children
Faculty of Medicine (Freshmen Enrollment: 100)
   Department of Medicine
Anatomy, Anesthesiology, Biochemistry, Dermatology, Forensic Medicine, Hygiene, Internal Medicine, Microbiology, Neurosurgery, Obstetrics and Gynecology, Ophthalmology, Orthopedic Surgery, Otorhinolaryngology, Parasitology, Pathology, Pharmacology, Physiology, Psychiatry, Public Health, Radiology, Surgery, Urology
Faculty of Mining (Freshmen Enrollment: 451)
   Department of Chemical Engineering for Resources
   Department of Fuel Chemistry

Chemical Reaction Engineering, Chemistry, Coal Chemistry, Coal Technology, Combustion Chemistry, Conversion Process Engineering, Energy Engineering, Engineering, High Temperature, Instrumental Analysis and Material Design, Material Science, Micrometrics, Petroleum Chemistry, Petroleum Refinery Engineering, Physical Chemistry, Physical Organic Chemistry, Polymer Chemistry and Engineering, Process Control, Resource Cycling Engineering, Resource Recovery and Recycling, Synthetic Fuel Chemistry, Synthetic Organic Chemistry, Thermal Management, Unit Operation Transport Phenomena

Department of Civil Engineering
Bridge Engineering, Concrete Engineering, Construction Materials, Construction Methods for Engineering Works and Surveying, Dynamics of Elasticity, Harbor Engineering, Highway Engineering, Hydraulics, River Engineering, Soil Mechanics and Foundation Engineering, Statics and Dynamics of Structure, Transportation and Traffic Engineering

Department of Electrical Engineering
Automatic Control, Design of Electric Machinery, Electric Circuit, Electric Machinery, Electric Measurement and Measuring Apparatus, Electromagnetics, High Voltage Techniques and Measurement, Materials for Electrical Engineering and Applied Electrical Engineering, Power Station and Substation, Power Transmission and Distribution

Department of Electronic Engineering
Applied Electronics, Computer Science, Electrical and Electronic Communication, Electromagnetism, Electro-mechanical Transduction, Electronic Circuit, Electronic Measurements and Instruments, Information Processing, Medical Electronics and Applied Ultrasonics, Microwave Engineering, Quantum Dynamics, Semiconductor Engineering, Solid State Physics

Department of Mechanical Engineering
Department of Mechanical Engineering for Production
Air Conditioning, Automatic Control Engineering, Engineering Mechanics, Engineering of Plasticity, Fluid Machinery, Fluid Mechanics, Heat Transfer, Industrial Measurement, Internal Combustion Engineering, Kinematics of Machinery, Manufacturing Machinery, Material Engineering, Mechanical Engineering Design, Mechanical Technology, Mechanical Vibrations, Oil Hydraulics, Pneumatics, Steam Boiler and Turbine, Theory of Elasticity, Thermodynamics, Tribology

Department of Metallic Engineering for Materials
Chemical Metallurgy, Electrometallurgy, Ferrous Metallurgy, Foundry Metallurgy, Fuels and Furnaces in Metallurgical Industries, Mechanical Metallurgy, Metallic Materials, Nonferrous Production Metallurgy, Physical Metallurgy, Power Metallurgy, Welding and Metal Surface Engineering

Department of Metallurgy
Department of Mining Engineering
Coal Mining Engineering, Drilling, Engineering of Mine Safety, Metal Mining Engineering, Mineral Beneficiation Engineering, Mine Waste-Water Treatment Engineering, Petroleum Engineering, Reservoir Engineering, Rock Mechanics

Department of Mining Geology
Applied Geology, Exploration Geophysics (seismic, electric, magnetic and gravity methods), Geophysics, Mineral Deposit (metal and non-metal), Mineralogy, Paleontology, Petroleum and Coal Geology, Petrology, Stratigraphy, Structural Geology

Foreign Student Admission
Qualifications for Applicants
Standard Qualifications Requirement

An applicant who is totally color blind may not be admitted to the undergraduate schools.

Documents to be Submitted When Applying
Standard Documents Requirement

Those who have passed the Entrance Examinations should pay the entrance fee and the tuition fee for the first semester with the required documents including pledge on or before 25th of March.

Qualifications for Transfer Students
In the Faculty of Education and the Mining College, when a vacancy is available those who meet the following qualifications are sometimes admitted with the approval of the faculty conferences.

1. College graduates or those who leave college before graduation.
2. Those who have finished a 2-year course of teacher training college.
3. Those who have graduated from a junior college, technical college or the equivalent.

In the School of Medicine, when a vacancy occurs, those who meet the following qualifications are sometimes admitted with the approval of the faculty conference.

1. Those who have graduated from the medical courses or dental courses of other universities.
2. Those who have finished 14-year course schooling including pre-medical or pre-dental courses.

Examination for Transfer Students
To be conducted on request through the University Entrance Annoucement.

Documents to be Submitted When Applying
Standard Documents Requirement

ONE-YEAR GRADUATE PROGRAMS

One-Year Graduate Course of Education (Enrollment: 5)
Educational Sciences
One-Year Graduate Course of Special Education for the Mentally Handicapped (Enrollment: 30)
Special Education for the Mentally Handicapped

Foreign Student Admission
Qualifications for Applicants

Standard Qualifications Requirement
Examination at the University
The same examination as the Japanese students take.

GRADUATE PROGRAMS

Graduate School of Medicine (First Year Enrollment : Doctor's 56)
Basic Medical Course: Anatomy, Biochemistry, Microbiology and Parasitology, Pathology, Pharmacology, Physiology
Clinical Medicine Course: Dermatology, Internal Medicine, Neurosurgery, Obstetrics and Gynecology, Ophthalmology, Orthopedic Surgery, Otorhinolaryngology and Anesthesiology, Pediatrics, Psychiatry, Radiology, Surgery, Urology
Social Medicine Course: Hygiene, Public Health and Forensic Medicine
Graduate School of Mining (First Year Enrollment : Master's 86)
Divisions
Electrical Engineering, Electronic Engineering and Civil Engineering, Fuel Chemistry, Mechanical Engineering, Mechanical Engineering for Production, Metallic Engineering for Materials, Metallurgy, Mining Engineering, Mining Geology

Foreign Student Admission
Qualifications for Applicants
Master's Program
Standard Qualifications Requirement
An applicant who is totally color blind may not be admitted to the graduate schools.
Doctor's Program
Satisfactory completion of 18 years of education (the last part of the course must be in Medicine) is required.
An applicant who is totally color blind may not be admitted.
Examination at the University
Master's Program
For regular students, a satisfactory score in the entrance examination to graduate school is required.
Doctor's Program
Same as Master's program.
Documents to be Submitted When Applying
Standard Documents Requirement
Application forms are available on request at the Admissions Section of Student Office. Please inquire at the Admissions Section for details concerning due dates and dates of entrance examinations.

*

Research Institutes and Centers
Computer Center, Laboratory Center for Advanced Research, Mineral Industry Museum, The Center for Educational Technology, The Research Institute of Natural Resources
Facilities/Services for Foreign Students
Foreign Student House: Shared Facilities (Hall, Jap-

anese-Style Room) Accommodation (30 rooms: single 27, couple 3)
Special Programs for Foreign Students
Japanese language supplementary classes are available at the College of Education.
For Further Information
Undergraduate and Graduate Admission
Admissions Section of Student Office, Akita University, 1-1 Tegata Gakuen-cho, Akita-shi, Akita 010
☎ 0188-33-5261 ext. 256

Asahikawa Medical College
(Asahikawa Ika Daigaku)
4-5 Nishikagura, Asahikawa-shi, Hokkaido 078
☎ 0166-65-2111

Faculty
　　Profs.　38　　Assoc. Profs.　27
　　Assist. Profs.　Full-time　36; Part-time　49
　　Res. Assocs.　134
Number of Students
　　Undergrad.　756　　Grad.　58
Library　92, 792 volumes

Outline and Characteristics of the College
Asahikawa Medical College is a young college, located in Asahikawa, a bustling city with a population of about 364, 000. In the fresh climate of this northern city, there are 814 students, including graduate students, and about 900 staff members devoted to international medical research. The college takes an active part in local health and medical care. Also, it provides opportunities for the para-medical staff in the region to study.

Asahikawa Medical College was founded in September, 1973. Classes commenced in November of the same year. The Clinical Lecture Building, College Library, Gymnasium, and College Hospital were built in that order, and research facilities were added later. In April, 1979, a postgraduate course was established.

The mottos of the college are:
1. To train doctors and medical researchers to understand the medical code and medical ethics and to respect human life above all else.
2. To contribute to the advance of medical knowledge and social welfare.

The college aims to help students with their university life. One professor per grade is assigned as a counsellor. Professors of liberal arts are assigned for the first two years, professors of pre-clinical medicine for the third and the fourth years and professors of clinical medicine for the last two years of education. Also, there are staff members responsible for the health care of the students. Assistance in finding lodging and part-time jobs is also provided. Scholarships are available for those in need and extracurricular activities are many and various.

There are 30 sports clubs and 28 cultural clubs. For these activities, a Seminar Room, Chashitsu (tatami-matted room for tea ceremony), Gymnasium, Budo Gymnasium (gymnasium for Kendo, Judo and Karate), Kyudo Gymnasium, Athletic Sports Field, Baseball Field and Tennis Courts are provided.

UNDERGRADUATE PROGRAMS

Faculty of Medicine (Freshmen Enrollment: 120)
Department of Medicine

Foreign Student Admission
Qualifications for Applicants
Standard Qualifications Requirement
Examination at the College
In addition to the entrance exams taken by all applicants, foreign students are required to pass the Japanese Language Proficiency Test, the General Examination for Foreign Students, and the Joint First-Stage Achievement Test. Requirements and other details are under discussion.
Documents to be Submitted When Applying
Standard Documents Requirement

GRADUATE PROGRAMS

Graduate School of Medical Research (First Year Enrollment : Doctor's 30)
Divisions
Cells and Organs, Defense Mechanism, Human Ecology, Integrative Control of Biological Function

*

Research Institutes and Centers
Animal Experiment Center, Central Laboratory for Research and Education, College Hospital, College Library, Health Administration Center, Laboratory for Radio-active Isotope Research
For Further Information
Undergraduate and Graduate Admission
Instruction Section, Student Division, Asahikawa Medical College, 4-5 Nishikagura, Asahikawa-shi, Hokkaido 078 ☎ 0166–65–2111 ext. 2205

Chiba University
(Chiba Daigaku)

1-33 Yayoi-cho, Chiba-shi, Chiba 260
☎ 0472–51–1111

Faculty
Profs. 362   Assoc. Profs. 304
Assist. Profs. Full–time 113; Part–time 1, 163
Res. Assocs. 353
Number of Students
Undergrad. 11, 286   Grad. 1, 038
Library 1, 029, 000 volumes

Outline and Characteristics of the University

Chiba University was established in 1949 as a national comprehensive university by combining all national institutions of higher education then located in Chiba Prefecture, including Chiba Medical College (founded in 1923), Chiba Normal School (founded in 1874), Tokyo Industrial College (founded in 1921), and Chiba Prefectural School of Horticulture (founded in 1909).

Today, the University enrolls more than 13, 500 students, has a full-time faculty of some 1, 100, and is comprised of nine faculties (Letters, Education, Law and Economics, Science, Medicine, Pharmaceutical Sciences, Nursing, Engineering and Horticulture) which offer Master's or Doctor's programs, College of Arts and Sciences, a Research Center for Pathogenic Fungi and Microbial Toxicoses and other affiliated establishments.

The University is located in Chiba Prefecture, with Tokyo as its neighbor on the west, along the Bay of Tokyo. The campuses cover an area of 860, 000m^2 including two campuses in Chiba City and a campus in Matsudo City. About 50% of the students are from Chiba and Tokyo, with the rest coming from every other part of Japan. Some 300 foreign students from 27 countries are enrolled.

The School of Nursing and Faculty of Horticulture are unique among all the national universities in Japan and many divisions of the University, such as the Department of Behavioral Science (Faculty of Letters), Department of Image Science, Information Processing Center and Engineering (Faculty of Engineering) and Remote Sensing and Image Research Center are conducting special educational and research activities.

UNDERGRADUATE PROGRAMS

Faculty of Education (Freshmen Enrollment: 580)
Training Course for Elementary School Teachers
Training Course for Junior High School Teachers
English, Fine Arts, Health and Physical Education, Home Economics, Japanese Language and Literature, Mathematics, Music, Science, Social Studies, Technology and Vocational Education
Training Course for Teachers of Handicapped Children
Training Course for Kindergarten Teachers
Training Course for School Nurses
Faculty of Engineering (Freshmen Enrollment: 565, Evening Course 200)
Department of Applied Image Science and Technology
Applied Graphic Engineering, Graphic Engineering, Imaging Engineering, Imaging Materials, Imaging Systems, Imaging Technology, Plate-making Technology, Printing Technology
Department of Architectural Engineering
Disaster Prevention, Productive Process of Architecture, Structural Design, Structural Engineering
Department of Architecture

Architectural Design, Architectural History, Architectural Planning, Building Material, Methodology of Design, Residential Design

Department of Electrical Engineering

Electrical Power and Illuminating Engineering, Electrical Power Systems, Electric Machinery, Electric Materials and High Voltage Engineering, Electronic Circuits, Fundamentals of Electrical Engineering

Department of Electronic Engineering

Applied Information Science, Electrical Communication, Electronic Control Engineering, Fundamental Electronics, Image Information Engineering, Information Processing and System Science, Instrumentation and Measurements

Department of Image Science and Engineering

Applid Image Engineering, Image Instrumentation, Photographic Chemistry and Applied Photography, Photographic Engineering, Photographic Technology, Photo-sensitive Material Technology, Vision and Image Technology

Department of Industrial Chemistry

Chemical Engineering, Industrial Inorganic Chemistry, Industrial Organic Chemistry, Inorganic Material Chemistry, Organic Material Chemistry, Polymer Chemistry

Department of Industrial Design

Design Materials, Display Design and Sculpture, Ergonomics, Industrial Design, Philosophy and History of Design, Plastic Arts, Visual Communication Design and Painting, Visual Information and Design

Department of Mechanical Engineering I

Engineering for Precision Machining, Engineering Mechanics, Machine Elements, Manufacturing Technology, Metals and Alloys, Thermodynamics and Heat Engines

Department of Mechanical Engineering II

Automatic Control, Elasticity and Plasticity, Engineering of Plasticity, Fluids Engineering, Machine Design, Mechanical Engineering for Production

Department of Synthetic Chemistry

Chemical Measurements, Environmental Chemistry, Industrial Physical Chemistry, Synthetic Inorganic Chemistry, Synthetic Organic Chemistry, Synthetic Polymer Chemistry

Interdepartmental

Analytical Chemistry, Applied Physics, Information Processing Engineering, Mathematics for Engineering

Faculty of Horticulture (Freshmen Enrollment: 230)

Department of Agricultural Chemistry

Applied Microbiology, Biological Chemistry, Food and Nutritional Chemistry, Food Chemistry and Technology, Horticultural Plant Nutrition, Horticultural Soil Science

Department of Environmental Studies for Open Space

Botany for Landscaping, Environmental Biology, Nature Conservation, Planting Design, Plant Pathology

Department of Horticultural Economics

Agricultural Economics, Agricultural Information Science, Agricultural Marketing, Crop Production and Management, Farm Management

Department of Horticultural Science

Agricultural Meteorology, Floriculture and Ornamental Horticulture, Horticultural Engineering, Horticultural Machinery and Equipment, Plant Breeding, Pomology, Vegetable Science

Department of Landscape Architecture

Landscape Engineering, Landscape Gardening, Landscape Planning and Space Structure, Theory of Landscape Architecture and Landscape Planning, Town and Country Planning

Faculty of Law and Economics (Freshmen Enrollment: 440)

Department of Economics and Business Administration

Advanced Accounting, Business Administration, Commercial Policy, Comparative Economic Systems, Corporate Structure, Econometrics, Economic Policy, Economic Theory, History of Economic Thought, Industrial Organization, Interindustry Analysis, International Economics, International Finance, Introduction to Economic History, Introductory Accounting, Japanese Economic History, Management Theory, Modern Economic Analysis, Public Finance, Social Policy, Social Security, Statistics for Economic Analysis, Theory of Finance

Department of Law and Politics

Administrative Law, Anglo-American Law, Asian Legal History, Civil Law, Commercial Law, Comparative Politics, Constitutional Law, Criminal Law, Criminal Procedure, Criminology, Economic Law, European Legal History, History of Political Theory, International Law, Japanese Political History, Japanese Politics, Labor Law, Law of Civil Procedures, Philosophy of Law, Political History, Political Theory, Public Administration, Sociology of Law

Faculty of Letters (Freshmen Enrollment: 180)

Department of Behavioral Sciences

Applied Psychology, Applied Sociology, Behavioral Sociology, Behaviormetrics, Behavior Theory, Eastern Philosophy, Empirical Sociology, Ethics, Experimental Psychology, Foundations of Science, Human Behavior Sciences, Personality Psychology, Philosophy, Social Anthropology, Social Psychology, Sociology of Post-industrial Society

Department of Historical Sciences

Archaeology, Asian History, European History, Japanese Cultural History, Japanese History

Department of Literature

American Literature, Austrian Literature, Comparative Literature, Comparative Study of Culture, English Linguistics, English Literature, French Linguistics, French Literature, German Linguistics, German Literature, Japanese Classical Drama, Songs and Ballads, Japanese Classics, Japanese Dialectology, Japanese Legends, Japanese Linguistics, Japanese Literature, Linguistics (General, Historical and Applied), Literary Theory

School of Medicine (Freshmen Enrollment: 100)

Department of Medicine

Anatomy, Anesthesiology, Biochemistry, Dermatology, Hygiene, Internal Medicine, Legal Medicine, Microbiology, Neurological Surgery, Neurology Obstetrics and Gynecology, Ophthalmology, Oral Surgery, Orthopaedic Surgery, Otorhinolaryngology, Parasitology, Pathology, Pediatrics, Pharmacology, Physiology, Psychiatry, Public Health, Radiology, Surgery, Urology

School of Nursing (Freshmen Enrollment: 85)

Department of Nursing

Basic Health Science, Biophysics and Biochemistry, Child Nursing, Community Health Nursing, Fundamentals of Nursing, Maternity Nursing, Medical-Surgical Nursing, Nursing Education, Pathobiology, Psychiatric Nursing

Faculty of Pharmaceutical Sciences (Freshmen Enrollment: 80)

Department of Pharmaceutical Sciences

Drug Evaluation and Toxicological Sciences, Human Environmental Chemistry, Medicinal Materials, Pharmaceutics

Faculty of Science (Freshmen Enrollment: 185)

Department of Biology

Ecology, Morphology, Phylogeny, Physiology

Department of Chemistry

Biochemistry, Inorganic and Analytical Chemistry, Organic Chemistry, Physical Chemistry

Department of Earth Sciences

Applied Earth Sciences, Geology, Geophysics, Mineralogy

Department of Mathematics

Algebra, Applied Mathematics, Geometry, Mathematical Analysis, Statistics

Department of Physics

Atomic Physics, Experimental Physics, Solid State Physics, Theoretical Physics

Foreign Student Admission

Qualifications for Applicants

Standard Qualifications Requirement

Examination at the University

For each Faculty, applicants must take the Japanese Language Proficiency Test and General Examination for Foreign Students. They will be allowed to take each Faculty's special entrance examination consisting of written and oral exams and an interview.

Documents to be Submitted When Applying

Standard Documents Requirement

Application forms are available at the Academic Affairs Unit of each Faculty from December. All applicants are required to submit the specified application documents to the Admissions Office of each Faculty by early January.

GRADUATE PROGRAMS

Graduate School of Education (First Year Enrollment : Master's 60)

Divisions

Art Education, English Education, Health and Physical Education, Japanese Language Education, Mathematical Education, Music Education, School Education, Science Education, Social Studies Education, Technological Education

Graduate School of Engineering (First Year Enrollment : Master's 118)

Divisions

Applied Image Science and Engineering, Architectural Engineering, Architecture, Electrical Engineering, Electronic Engineering, Image Science and Engineering, Industrial Chemistry, Industrial Design, Mechanical Engineering, Synthetic Chemistry

Graduate School of Horticulture (First Year Enrollment : Master's 50)

Divisions

Agricultural Chemistry, Environmental Studies for Open Space, Horticultural Economics, Horticultural Science, Landscape Architecture

Graduate School of Human Science (First Year Enrollment : Master's 10)

Divisions

Behavioral Sciences, Euro-American Languages and Cultures, Historical Science, Japanese Literature

Graduate School of Medicine (First Year Enrollment : Doctor's 81)

Divisions

Internal Medicine, Pathological Sciences, Physiological Sciences, Social Medicine, Surgery

Graduate School of Nursing (First Year Enrollment : Master's 15)

Divisions

Clinical Nursing, Foundation of Nursing, Nursing Education and Nursing Administration

Graduate School of Pharmaceutical Sciences (First Year Enrollment : Master's 29, Doctor's 12)

Divisions

Drug Evaluation and Toxicological Sciences, Human Environmental Chemistry, Medicinal Materials, Pharmaceutics

Graduate School of Science (First Year Enrollment : Master's 40)

Divisions

Biology, Chemistry, Earth Sciences, Mathematics, Physics

Graduate School of Science and Technology (First Enrollment: Doctor's 48)

Divisions

Environmental Science (Doctor's 15)

Environmental Planning, Fundamental Science of Environment, Industrial Design, Planning and Design of Living Environment, Science of Environmental Dynamics

Mathematical and Materials Science (Doctor's 15)

Applied Science of Functional Materials, Fundamental Materials Science, Imaging Science, Material Structure and Differentiation, Mathematical Science

Production Science and Technology (Doctor's 18)

Biotechnology, Fundamentals of Bio-resources, Measurement and Information Science, Production Engineering, Production Science and Management of Bio-resources, Systems Engineering

Graduate School of Social Sciences (First Year Enrollment : Master's 10)

Divisions

Economics, Law

Foreign Student Admission

Qualifications for Applicants

Master's Program

    Standard Qualifications Requirement

Doctor's Program

    Standard Qualifications Requirement

Examination at the University

Master's Program

    Applicants must take the same entrance examination consisting of a written exam and an interview given to Japanese students.

Doctor's Program

    Same as Master's program

Documents to be Submitted When Applying

    Standard Documents Requirement

    Application forms are available at the Academic Affairs Unit of each Faculty from August (dependent on the Faculty). All applicants are required to submit the specified application documents to the Graduate Admissions Office of each Faculty by the fixed date.

*

Research Institutes and Centers

Attached schools (primary, lower secondary, handicapped) and a kindergarten, Center for Educational Technology, Center for Education and Research in Nursing Practice, Center for Neurobiology and Molecular Immunology, Chemical Analysis Center, Health Sciences Center, Information Processing Center Remote Sensing and Image Research Center, Institute for Training Midwives, Institute for Training Nurses, Institute for Training Radiological Technicians, Institute of Marine Ecosystem, Institute of Pulmonary Cancer Research, Laboratory Animal Center, Laboratory for Instrumental Analysis, Laboratory Waste Treatment Plant, Medical Plants Gardens, Regearch Center for Pathogenic Fungi and Microbial Toxicoses, Research and Guidance for Student Behavior Problems, University Farms, University Hospital

Facilities/Services for Foreign Students

Foreign Students' Dormitory

Accommodation: 164 rooms (115 for male, 49 for female)

Special Programs for Foreign Students

    The University provides classes in Japanese Language and Japanese Society for foreign students. The Faculty of Education provides a special course for teacher trainees from Asia and other countries.

For Further Information

Undergraduate Admission

Admissions Division, Student Bureau, Chiba University, 1-33 Yayoi-cho, Chiba-shi, Chiba 260 ☎ 0472-51-1111 ext. 2107, 2124

Graduate Admission

Graduate Schools of Education, Engineering, Human Science, Pharmaceutical Science, Science, Science and Technology, Social Science: Academic Affairs Unit of each Faculty, 1-33 Yayoi-cho, Chiba-shi, Chiba 260 ☎ 0472-51-1111 ext. 2575 (Education), 2918 (Engineering), 2359 (Human Science, Social Science), 2758 (Pharmaceutical Science), 2656 (Science), 2162 (Science and Technology)

Graduate Schools of Medicine, and Nursing: Academic Affairs Unit of each Faculty, 1-8-1 Inohana, Chiba- shi, Chiba 280 ☎ 0472-22-7171 ext. 2021 (Medicine), 4067 (Nursing)

Graduate School of Horticulture: Academic Affairs Unit, Faculty of Horticulture, 648 Matsudo, Matsudo-shi, Chiba 271 ☎ 0473-63-1221 ext. 212

Ehime University
(Ehime Daigaku)

10-13 Dogo-Himata, Matsuyama-shi, Ehime 790

☎ 0899-24-7111

Faculty

    Profs. 233   Assoc. Profs. 231

    Assist. Profs. Full–time 88; Part–time 632

    Res. Assocs. 220

Number of Students

    Undergrad. 7, 691   Grad. 420

Library 789, 099 volumes

Outline and Characteristics of the University

    Ehime University is one of Japan's national universities and has about 7, 700 undergraduate students and 420 graduate students, including 54 foreign students. The University consists of seven faculties and some attached schools and institutes, with a total staff of about 1, 900. The faculties are the Faculty of Law and Literature, Faculty of Education, Faculty of Science, School of Medicine, Faculty of Engineering, College of Agriculture, and Faculty of General Education.

    In accordance with the National School Establishment Law, Ehime University was established by the National Government in 1949, uniting four different National Schools: Matsuyama Higher School, Ehime Normal School, Ehime Youth's Normal School, and Niihama Technical College. It first consisted of three faculties, the Faculty of Literature and Science, the Faculty of Education, and the Faculty of Engineering. In 1954, Matsuyama Agricultural College, founded by Ehime Prefecture in 1949, was incorporated into Ehime University as the College of Agriculture. In 1968, the Faculty of Literature and Science was developmentally divided into three faculties: the Faculty of Law and Literature, the Faculty of Science, and the Faculty of General Education. In 1973, the School of Medicine was founded by the National Government as a branch of the University. Graduate School (leading to the master's degree) was started in 1967 in the Faculty of Engineering and the College of Agriculture. Subsequently, Graduate Schools of Science and Law were established in 1978 and 1981, respectively. The Graduate School of Medicine (leading to doctor's degree) was established in 1979. Advanced Courses (leading to diplomas) were founded in the Faculty of Education in 1963 and the Faculty of Law and Literature in 1973. A Special Course for Speech Defects was also established in 1967.

In 1985, the United Graduate School of Agricultural Sciences was established as an independent division of the Graduate School of Ehime University. Ehime University (primary university), Kagawa University (participating university) and Kochi University (participating university) were combined to establish a united graduate school.

Ehime University is situated in Matsuyama City, Ehime Prefecture, along the beautiful coast of the Seto Inland Sea and is the center of a famous citrus growing area of Japan. The population of Matsuyama is approximately 430,000 and it has a beautiful old castle and a famous hot spring spa named Dogo Onsen.

The University has three campuses, Johoku, Shigenobu and Tarumi Campuses. The main campus, Johoku, is in the center of Matsuyama. The Shigenobu campus is about half an hour away and the Tarumi campus about 10 minutes away by bus from the main campus. Public transportation is very convenient.

UNDERGRADUATE PROGRAMS

College of Agriculture (Freshmen Enrollment: 192)
School of Biological Resources
Course of Bioresource Production Science
Agricultural Biology, Biomechanical Systems, Bioresource Management
Course of Bioresource Utilization
Agricultural Chemistry
Course of Life Environment Sciences
Environmental Conservation, Forestry and Forest Seience, Rural Engineering
Faculty of Education (Freshmen Enrollment   355)
Course of School Teachers for the Deaf
Course of School Teachers for the Handicapped
Course of Junior High School Teachers
Course of Kindergarten Teachers
Course of Primary School Teachers
Course of Special Subject (Music) Teachers
Algebra and Geometry, Analysis and Applied Mathematics, Biology, Calligraphy, Carving and Modeling, Chemistry, Child Psychology, Chinese Classics, Chorus, Clothing Science, Composition, Concerted Music, Construction, Developmental Psychology,

Drawing and Painting, Earth Science, Economics, Educational Methods, Educational Psychology, Educational Sociology, Educational Systems, Education for Speech Defects, Education of Preschool Children, Education of the Handicapped, English and American Literature, English Linguistics, Ethics, Food Science, General Electricity and Electronics, General Metal Shop, Geography, History, History of Education, Home Management, Japanese Linguistics, Japanese Literature, Keyboard Instruments, Mechanical Engineering, Pathology of the Handicapped, Pedagogy, Pedology, Philosophy, Physical Training, Physics, Physiology and Hygiene, Psychology of Deafness, Psychology of the Handicapped, School Health, Social Education, Sociology, Speech Therapy, String Instruments, Studies of Kindergarten Education, Teaching of English, Teaching of Fine Arts, Teaching of Health and Physical Education, Teaching of Home Making, Teaching of Japanese, Teaching of Mathematics, Teaching of Music, Teaching of Science, Teaching of Social Studies, Teaching of Technology, Theory and History of Art, Theory and History of Music, Theory and History of Physical Education, Vocal Music, Wind Instruments
Faculty of Engineering (Freshmen Enrollment: 470)
Department of Civil Engineering
Hydraulic Engineering, Materials of Construction, Structural Engineering, Transportation Engineering
Department of Computer Science
Computer Engineering, Fundamentals of Computer Science
Department of Electrical Engineering
Applied Electrical Engineerig, Electric Machine Engineering, Electric Power Engineering, Fundamentals of Electrical Engineering
Department of Electronics Engineering
Applied Electronics, Communication Engineering, Electronic Instrument Engineering, Fundamental Electronics Engineering
Department of Industrial Chemistry
Chemical Engineering and Polymer Chemistry, Industrial Inorganic Chemistry, Industrial Organic Chemistry, Industrial Physical Chemistry
Department of Mechanical and Industrial Engineering
Analysis of Plastic Working, Applied Thermal Engineering, Control Engineering, Materials Science and Engineering
Department of Mechanical Engineering
Fluid Mechanical Engineering, Measuring Engineering, Mechanics of Machinery, Strength of Materials, Thermo-mechanical Engineering
Department of Metallurgy
Ferrous Metallurgy, Mechanical Metallurgy, Nonferrous Metallurgy, Physical Metallurgy, Welding Engineering
Department of Ocean Engineering
Coastal Oceanography, Marine Metrology, Marine Resources Engineering, Ocean Construction Engineering, Ocean Exploitation Engineering

Department of Resources Chemistry

Chemical Engineering, Marine Resources Chemistry, Material Chemistry, Organic Resources Chemistry

Faculty of Law and Literature (Freshmen Enrollment 490)

Department of Economics

Accounting, Book-keeping, Business Administration, Business Economics, Econometrics, Economic policy, History of Economic Thought, International Finance, Japanese Economic History, Labor Economics, Management, Marketing, Principles of Economics, Public Finance, Social Policy, World Economics

Department of Law

Administrative Law, Civil Law, Commercial Law, Constitutional Law, Criminal Law, Economic Law, History of Political Thought, International Law, International Relations, Labor Law, Law of Civil Procedure, Law of Criminal Procedure, Legal History, Philosophy of Law, Political History, Political Science, Public Administration

Department of Literature

Archaeology, Chinese Language and Literature, English Language and Literature, Euro-American Cultures, Geography, German Language and Literature, Human Sciences, Japanese and East-Asian Cultures, Japanese and Oriental History, Japanese Language and Literature, Linguistics, Occidental History, Philosophy, Psychology, Sociology

School of Medicine (Freshmen Enrollment: 100)

Department of Medicine

Anatomy, Anesthesiology, Biochemistry, Clinical Investigation, Dermatology, Hygiene, Internal Medicine, Legal Medicine, Microbiology, Neuropsychiatry, Neurosurgery, Obstetrics and Gynecology, Ophthalmology, Oral and Maxillofacial Surgery, Orthopedic Surgery, Otorhinolaryngology, Parasitology, Pathology, Pediatrics, Pharmacology, Physiology, Public Health, Radiology, Surgery, Urology

Faculty of Science (Freshmen Enrollment: 181)

Department of Biology

Developmental Biology, Ecology, Morphology, Physiology

Department of Chemistry

Analytical and Inorganic Chemistry, Organic Chemistry, Physical Chemistry, Structure Chemistry

Department of Earth Sciences

Geochemistry, Geology, Geophysics, Mineralogy

Department of Mathematics

Algebra and Geometry, Applied Mathematics, Mathematical Analysis, Topology

Department of Physics

Applied Physics, Electromagnetism, Quantum Physics, Solid State Physics

Foreign Student Admission

Qualifications for Applicants

Standard Qualifications Requirement

1. Applicants must have citizenship of a country other than Japan.

2. Those who have been granted an International Baccalaureate Diploma and is 18 years of age or older may also apply.

3. Applicants must take the Japanese Language Proficiency Test and the General Examination for Foreign Students.

Examination at the University

Foreign applicants are exempt from the Joint First-Stage Achievement Test. Their selection will be based on the results of the Japanese Language Proficiency Test, General Examination for Foreign Students, and an interview and will be decided by the appropriate faculty.

Documents to be Submitted When Applying

Standard Documents Requirement

Period for Application will be announced at the end of October.

GRADUATE PROGRAMS

United Graduate School of Agricultural Sciences (First Year Enrollment : Doctor's 16)

Divisions

Applied Bioresource Science, Bioresource Production Science, Life Environment Conservation Science

Graduate School of Agriculture (First Year Enrollment : Master's 62)

Divisions

Agricultural Business, Agricultural Chemistry, Agricultural Engineering, Agrobiology and Horticultural Science, Environment Conservation, Forestry

Graduate School of Engineering (First Year Enrollment : Master's 70)

Divisions

Civil Engineering, Electrical Engineering, Electronics Engineering, Industrial Chemistry, Mechanical and Industrial Engineering, Mechanical Engineering, Metallurgy, Ocean Engineering, Resources Chemistry

Graduate School of Law (First Year Enrollment : Master's 20)

Division

Law

Graduate School of Medicine (First Year Enrollment : Doctor's 30)

Divisions

Ecological Study, Functional Study, Morphological Study

Graduate School of Science (First Year Enrollment : Master's 40)

Divisions

Biology, Chemistry, Earth Sciences, Mathematics, Physics

Foreign Student Admission

Qualifications for Applicants

Master's Program

Standard Qualifications Requirement

Doctor's Program

Standard Qualifications Requirement
Examination at the University
Master's Program

The selection of applicants will be based on the results of the examination, an interview and the submitted documents.
Doctor's Program

Same as Master's program.

*

Research Institutes and Centers
Advanced Instrumentation Center for Chemical Analysis, Attached Institute of Agricultural Environmental Control, Center for Practical Studies of Education, Central Research Laboratory, Data Processing Center, Health Administration Center, Institiute for Comparative Medicine and Animal Experimentation, Marine Biological Station, University Farm, University Forest, University Hospital
Facilities/Services for Foreign Students
Dormitory (includes 10 rooms for foreign students)
Ehime University International House
Special Programs for Foreign Students

Japanese Course for In-service Training for Foreign Teachers, and Japanese language supplementary classes are available at the Student Bureau.
For Further Information
Undergraduate Admission
Admission Office, Ehime University, 3 Bunkyo-cho, Matsuyama-shi, Ehime 790 ☎ 0899–24–7111 ext. 2188
Graduate Admission
Student Section, College of Agriculture, Ehime University, 3-5-7 Tarumi, Matsuyama-shi, Ehime 790 ☎ 0899–41–4171 ext. 211
Each Student Section of Faculties of Engineering, and Law and Literature, Ehime University, 3 Bunkyo-cho, Matsuyama-shi, Ehime 790 ☎ 0899–24–7111 ext. 3621 (Engineering), 3026 (Law and Literature)
Student Section, School of Medicine, Ehime University, Shitsukawa, Shigenobu-cho, Onsen-gun, Ehime 791-02 ☎ 0899–64–5111 ext. 2021
Student Section, Faculty of Science, Ehime University, 2-5 Bunkyo-cho, Matsuyama-shi, Ehime 790 ☎ 0899–24–7111 ext. 3517

Fukui Medical School
(Fukui Ika Daigaku)

23 Shimoaizuki, Matsuoka-cho, Yoshida-gun, Fukui 910-11 ☎ 0776–61–3111

Faculty
    Profs. 38   Assoc. Profs. 35
    Assist. Profs. Full–time 25; Part–time 196
    Res. Assocs. 130
Number of Students
    Undergrad. 630   Grad. 58
Library 68, 860 volumes

Outline and Characteristics of the University

Fukui Medical School was founded by the Government in 1978 and matriculated its first students in April, 1980.

As a striking characteristic, the School offers radiation-related courses such as Experimental Radiology and Health Physics, which is rarely found in other medical education institutes in the country. This promises to make the School a unique center of radiological sciences and care. The background is greatly relevant: Fukui Prefecture where the School is located has a large proportion of the nuclear power plants in Japan. Therefore, research into and countermeasures against the nuclear influence on ecology are serious concerns of the prefecture.

The campus is situated to the east of Fukui City, which is flanked by the Sea of Japan, and is not far from Eiheiji Temple, a mecca for Zen Buddhism. The Kuzuryu River flowing nearby provides rich green fields and quiet and idyllic surroundings where students may spend a pleasant campus life.

The students, though few in number, come from almost every part of the country, contributing to the nation-wide prestige of the School.

UNDERGRADUATE PROGRAMS

Faculty of Medicine (Freshmen Enrollment: 100)
Department of Medicine
Anatomy, Anesthesiology, Biochemistry, Dentistry and Oral Surgery, Dermatology, Environmental Health, Experimental Radiology and Health Physics, Immunology, Internal Medicine, Legal Medicine, Microbiology, Neurosurgery, Obstetrics and Gynecology, Ophthalmology, Orthopedic Surgery, Otorhinolaryngology, Parasitology, Pathology, Pediatrics, Pharmacology, Physiology, Psychiatry, Radiology, Surgery, Urology

Foreign Student Admission
Qualifications for Applicants
    Standard Qualifications Requirement
Examination at the University

Foreign applicants as well as Japanese are required to take both the Joint First-Stage Achievement Test, which is held in late January of the relevant year, and the entrance examination for this school (written tests and an interview), which is given in early March.

No preferential treatment is accorded to any nationality.
Documents to be Submitted When Applying
    Standard Documents Requirement

Refer for application procedure to the Application Guide and forms which are available upon request from December of the previous year.

Successful applicants are announced in the middle of March and admission procedure is to be completed by the end of the same month.

GRADUATE PROGRAMS

Postgraduate Course of Medical Sciences (First Year Enrollment : Doctor's 30)
Divisions
Biochemistry, Ecology, Morphology, Physiology

Foreign Student Admission
Qualifications for Applicants
Doctor's Program
Standard Qualifications Requirement
Examination at the University
Doctor's Program
Selection is made through an overall assessment of the entrance examinations (written tests and an interview), the physical checkup, and the scholastic marks at college. The entrance examination is scheduled to be held in late February or early March.
Documents to be Submitted When Applying
Standard Documents Requirement
Refer for application procedure to the Application Guide and forms which are available upon request from December of the previous year. It is advisable to make prior contact with the professor of the intended course.

*

Research Institutes and Centers
Animal Laboratory, Radioisotope Laboratory, Research Institute for Joint Use (Microscope Division, Histology Division, Physiology Division, Biochemistry Division, Culture Division)
Facilities/Services for Foreign Students
The School offers no special accommodations for foreign students, but helps students, Japanese or foreign, find lodgings.
For Further Information
Undergraduate and Graduate Admission
Admissions Office, Student Division, Fukui Medical School, 23 Shimoaizuki, Matsuoka-cho, Yoshida-gun, Fukui 910-11 ☎ 0776-61-3111 ext. 2143

Fukui University
(Fukui Daigaku)

3-9-1 Bunkyo, Fukui-shi, Fukui 910
☎ 0776-23-0500

Faculty
    Profs.　105　　Assoc. Profs.　120
    Assist. Profs.　Full–time　13; Part–time　100
    Res. Assocs.　28
Number of Students
    Undergrad.　3, 076　　Grad.　177
Library　342, 658 volumes

Outline and Characteristics of the University
Fukui University is composed of two faculties: the Faculty of Education and the Faculty of Engi-

neering. It was organized in 1949 by uniting Fukui Normal School, Fukui Youth Normal School, and Fukui Technical College. Each of these schools had a respectable history of its own before unification.

The Faculty of Education originally consisted of a division of education and a division of liberal arts. At present, this Faculty offers teacher training courses exclusively. These courses include teacher training for elementary schools, lower secondary schools, and schools for the mentally handicapped. In the course of its development, the Faculty added special post-graduate courses in education and in education of the mentally handicapped; in addition, it established the Research and Guidance Center for Teaching Practice and four attached schools of various kinds and levels.

The Faculty of Engineering originally had three departments: Architecture, Textile Engineering (presently Polymer Engineering), and Fibers and Color Chemistry (presently Applied Chemistry). With time, it continued to grow by adding new departments, the newest being Information Science which opened in 1975. It now includes 9 departments. The Graduate Course of Engineering (master course) was organized in 1965. Today the Faculty, with its two research institutes, is one of the nation's largest schools of engineering.

Fukui University is rather small compared with the huge universities in major cities. It enrolls about 2, 900 students and has a full-time faculty of about 270. In recent years both Faculties have admitted foreign students, though the numbers vary from year to year. The campus is located in one of Japan's traditional provincial centers (the city population is 251, 576), close to the surrounding mountains and the Japan Sea coast. Students study, work, and relax in this peaceful and intimate atmosphere.

UNDERGRADUATE PROGRAMS

Faculty of Education (Freshmen Enrollment: 200)
Department of Education
Developmental Psychology, Educational Psychology, Educational System, Education of Handicapped Children, History of Education, Pathology of Handicapped Children, Pedagogy, Psychology of Handicapped Children, Social Education, Sociology of Education
Department of English
English and American Literature, English Linguistics and Philology, Methodology of Teaching English
Department of Fine Arts
Art Theory and Art History, Design, Methodology of Teaching Fine Arts, Painting, Sculpture
Department of Health and Physical Studies
Methodology of Teaching Health and Physical Education, Physiology and Hygiene, Technical Training in Physical Education, Theory and History of Physical Education
Department of Home Economics

Foods and Nutrition, Home Economics, Methodology of Teaching Home Economics, Textiles and Clothing

Department of Japanese

Japanese Literature, Japanese Philology, Methodology of Teaching Japanese, Sinology and Chinese

Department of Mathematics

Algebra and Geometry, Analysis and Applied Mathematics, Methodology of Teaching Mathematics

Department of Music

Composition, Instrumental Music, Methodology of Teaching Music, Vocal Music

Department of Natural Science

Biology, Chemistry, Geology, Methodology of Teaching Natural Science, Physics

Department of Social Science

Business Information Science, Economics, Ethics, Geography, History, Jurisprudence, Methodology of Teaching Social Studies, Philosophy, Political Science, Sociology

Department of Technological Studies

Agriculture, Electrical Engineering, Mechanical Engineering, Methodology of Teaching Technology, Wood Craft

Faculty of Engineering (Freshmen Enrollment: 540)

Department of Applied Chemistry

Biochemistry and Biochemical Processing, Colloid and Surface Chemistry, Functional Polymer Chemistry, Organic Chemical Reactions

Department of Applied Physics

Instrumentation Engineering, Physics of Materials, Quantum Physics, Solid State Physics

Department of Applied Science

Applied Mathematics, Chemistry, Environmental Engineering, Mathematical Physics, Physics

Department of Architecture

Building Construction, Planning of Architecture, Structural Analysis, Theory of Architecture

Department of Electrical and Electronics Engineering

Energy and Control (Power generation, Power conversion, Measurement and control), Materials and Devices (Quantum electronics, Opto-electronics, Condensed matter electronics), Systems and Informatics (Systems science and software, Communications systems, Knowledge based engineering)

Department of General Construction Engineering

Disaster Prevention Engineering, Environmental Planning, Geotechnics, Regional and Urban Planning, Structural Engineering

Department of Industrial Chemistry

Chemical Engineering, Inorganic Industrial Chemistry, Polymer Chemistry, Synthetic Organic Chemistry

Department of Information Science

Computer Systems, Information Processing, Information Systems

Department of Mechanical Engineering

Design and Manufacturing Engineering (Design and Manufacturing System, Machine Design, Manufacturing Processes), Materials Engineering (Materials Deformation, Materials for Machinery, Strength of Materials), System and Control Engineering (Control System, Instrumentation, Mechatronics, Mechanical Dynamics), Thermal and Fluid Engineering (Energy Conversion, Fluid Engineering, Thermal Engineering)

Department of Polymer Engineering

Materials Design, Polymer Materials, Polymer Physics, Polymer Processing

Foreign Student Admission

Qualifications for Applicants

Standard Qualifications Requirement

Faculty of Education: It is necessary to take the Japanese Language Proficiency Test. It is advisable to take the General Examination for Foreign Students.

Faculty of Engineering: Those who have taken the Japanese Language Proficiency Test and General Examination for Foreign Students (Science and Technology Major).

Examination at the University

Faculty of Education: Those applicants who have passed the screening of submitted documents must undergo an interview, a written exam, etc. about the middle of February.

Faculty of Engineering: Those applicants must undergo an interview, an oral exam, etc. about the middle of February.

Documents to be Submitted When Applying

Standard Documents Requirement

Application Deadline: End of January.

ONE-YEAR GRADUATE PROGRAMS

One-Year Graduate Course of Education (Enrollment: 5)

Education

One-Year Special Graduate Course of Education of Handicapped Children (Enrollment: 30)

Education of Mentally Handicapped

Foreign Student Admission

Qualifications for applicants

Standard Qualifications Requirement

Applicants for One-Year Special Graduate Course of Education of Handicapped Children must hold a teaching certificate.

Examination at the University

Foreign applicants must take the same examination as Japanese applicants, consisting of a written exam, an interview, and an essay.

GRADUATE PROGRAMS

Graduate School of Engineering (First Year Enrollment : Master's 88)

Divisions

Applied Chemistry, Applied Physics, Architecture,

Electrical Engineering, Electronics, General Construction Engineering, Industrial Chemistry, Information Science, Mechanical and Industrial Engineering, Mechanical Engineering, Textile Engineering

Foreign Student Admission
  Qualifications for Applicants
Master's Program
    Standard Qualifications Requirement
  Examination at the University
Master's Program
    Foreign applicants must take the same entrance examination as Japanese applicants, consisting of a written exam in basic subjects, one foreign language and specialized subjects, and an oral exam and interview in mid-September.
  Documents to be Submitted When Applying
    Standard Documents Requirement
    Application forms are available at Admissions Office from early July. Application documents should be submitted by August 31.

*

Research Institutes and Centers
Experimental Institute for Low Temperature Physics, Research and Guidance Center for Teaching Practice, Research Institute for Material Science and Engineering
Special Programs for Foreign Students
    The following courses are offered for foreign students:
First Semester: Japanese language 1-2, Japanese culture
Second Semester: Japanese language 3-4
For Further Information
  Undergraduate Admission
Admissions Office, Fukui University, 3-9-1 Bunkyo, Fukui-shi, Fukui 910 ☎ 0776–23–0500 ext. 248
  Graduate Admission
Graduate Admissions Office, Faculty of Engineering, Fukui University, 3-9-1 Bunkyo, Fukui-shi, Fukui 910 ☎ 0776–23–0500 ext. 608

Fukuoka University of Education
(Fukuoka Kyoiku Daigaku)

729 Akama, Munakata-shi, Fukuoka 811-41
☎ 0940-32-2381

Faculty
    Profs. 94   Assoc. Profs. 79
    Assist. Profs. Full–time 23; Part–time 196
    Res. Assocs. 14
Number of Students
    Undergrad. 3, 018   Grad. 89
Library 390, 712 volumes

Outline and Characteristics of the University
    Fukuoka University of Education was founded in 1949 as Fukuoka University of Liberal Arts in accordance with the National School Foundation Law. In addition to the main campus, it had four branches, Tagawa, Kokura, Fukuoka and Kurume—each of which had originally been a normal school. They were brought together at Akama in 1966, when the university's name was changed to Fukuoka University of Education.
    Since, the University has added of several departments. Graduate programs were added in 1983 to offer Master's degrees. Today the University enrolls 3, 100 students and has a full-time faculty of 210. It is comprised of 15 departments, 8 Graduate Schools, and 7 research centers.
    The University aims to train students to become outstanding teachers through broad cultivation of their knowledge and skills. It also provides them with abundant cultural opportunities and a rich program of special subjects, in order that they may contribute to the progress of civilization.

UNDERGRADUATE PROGRAMS

Faculty of Education (Freshmen Enrollment 710)
  Training Course for Elementary School Teachers
Educational Science and Psychology, Fine Arts, Health and Physical Education, Home Economics, Japanese, Mathematics, Music, Natural Science, Social Science
  Training Course for Junior High School Teachers
English, Fine Arts, Health and Physical Education, Home Economics, Industrial Arts, Japanese, Music, Natural Science, Social Science
  Training Course for Senior High School Teachers
Health and Physical Education, Japanese Calligraphy, Mathematics, Natural Science
  Training Course for Teachers of Deaf Children
  Training Course for Teachers of Kindergarten
  Training Course for Teachers of Mentally Handicapped Children
  Training Course for Teachers of Physically Handicapped Children

Foreign Student Admission
  Qualifications for Applicants
    Standard Qualifications Requirement
    1. Applicants must be foreign nationals.
    2. Applicants must have finished 12 years of school education their country or have obtained the legal Baccalaureate of the International Baccalaureate Office. They must be 18 years of age or older.
    3. Applicants should be those who have taken the Japanese Language Proficiency Test (the first class) and the General Examination For Foreign Students given by AIEJ.
  Examination at the University
    The selection of applicants is made by a combined evaluation of the Japanese Language Proficiency Test, the General Examination for Foreign Students, a written test in Japanese, and an interview

given by the University. Assessment will also cover past academic achievement, personal history, and applicant's health as given by the submitted documents.

Documents to be Submitted When Applying
Standard Documents Requirement
Applicants are also required to submit:
1. Photograph of certificate of graduation or record of course completed.
2. Identification card or letter of recommendation by the Japanese government or a foreign government recognized by the Japanese government. (Applicants may apply to the appropriate embassy or consulate in Japan.)

ONE-YEAR GRADUATE PROGRAMS

One-Year Graduate Course of Special Education
(Enrollment: 30)
Education of Physically Handicapped Children

Foreign Student Admission
Qualifications for Applicants
Standard Qualifications Requirement
Applicants must hold a teacher's license for kindergarten, elementary school, junior high school, or senior high school.
Examination at the University
Screening is based upon the following.
1. Test of education and educational psychology
2. Interview
3. Health certification form

GRADUATE PROGRAMS

Graduate School of Education (First Year Enrollment : Master's 41)
Divisions
Fine Art Education, Education for Handicapped Children, Foundations of School Education, Health and Physical Education, Home Economics Education, Mathematics Education, Music Education, Science Education

Foreign Student Admission
Qualifications for Applicants
Master's Program
Standard Qualifications Requirement
Examination at the University
Due to special screening (written test and interview, etc), applicants can be admitted without the written examination given to Japanese students.
Documents to be Submitted When Applying
Standard Documents Requirement
A Letter of Recommendation must be issued by the Japanese government, the applicant's government, or a professor (advisor) of the applicant's university/college.

*

Research Institutes and Centers
Center for Educational Technology, Center for Re-
medial Education, Health Center, Information Processing Center, Physical Education Research Center, Research Center for Dowa Education, Technical Center

Facilities/Services for Foreign Students
The Student Affairs Section helps foreign students in obtaining accommodations.

For Further Information
Undergraduate and Graduate Admission
Entrance Examination Section, Instruction Division of the Student Office , Fukuoka University of Education, 729 Akama, Munakata-shi, Fukuoka 811-41
☎ 0940–32–2381 ext. 233

Fukushima University
(Fukushima Daigaku)

2 Sugumichi, Asakawa, Matsukawa-machi,
Fukushima-shi, Fukushima 960-12

☎ 0245–48–5151

Faculty
Profs.   110   Assoc. Profs.   94
Assist. Profs.   Full–time   13; Part–time   88
Res. Assocs.   6
Number of Students
Undergrad.   3, 933   Grad.   45
Library   517, 479 volumes

Outline and Characteristics of the University
Fukushima University was founded in 1949 in accordance with the National School Establishment Law as a new-system national university, comprising two Faculties: the Faculty of Liberal Arts and Sciences and the Faculty of Economics. At the time of its foundation, two Normal Schools (Fukushima Normal School and Fukushima Normal School for Youth) and the Fukushima College of Economics were reorganized to form these two Faculties. In 1966, the Faculty of Liberal Arts and Sciences was renamed the Faculty of Education, which presently includes five Programs: Kindergarten Teachers Program, Elementary School Teachers Program, Junior High School Teachers Program, Teachers Program for Mentally and Physically Handicapped Children, Senior High School Teachers Program for Health and Physical Education. The Faculty of Education also offers a one-year graduate program in Health and Physical Education. The Faculty of Administration and Social Sciences was established in October, 1987. It admitted its first students in April, 1988. The Faculty of Administration and Social Sciences consists of two departments, Law and Administration and Applied Sociology. Each department has both a daytime course and an evening course. Included in the Faculty of Economics are two departments, Economics and Business Administration, each department having both a daytime course and an evening course.

Graduate Schools were opened in the Department of Economics in 1976, in the Faculty of Education in 1985 and in the Department of Business Administration in 1986.

In 1981 the University was moved to its present site approximately 10 km south of Fukushima City. The University intends further expansion on this new campus. In addition to the three existing faculties, a faculty of natural sciences is being planned. When the university is equipped with four faculties, it will be able to contribute even more to the development of the local community as a center of education, culture and academic research.

UNDERGRADUATE PROGRAMS

Faculty of Administration and Social Sciences (Freshmen Enrollment: 260)
Department of Applied Sociology
Regional Culture, Social Planning, Sociology
Department of Law and Administration
Fundamental Law for Administration, Local Administration, Public Administration, Social and Economic Law, Social Information
Faculty of Economics (Freshmen Enrollment: 340)
Department of Business Administration
Business, Business Administration, Financial Accounting, Management Accounting, Science of Commerce
Department of Economics
Dynamic Economics, Economic History of Europe and Asia, Economic Policy, Economic Statistics, Economic System, Finance, History of Economics, Industrial Economy, International Economy, Japanese Economy, Political Economy, Public Finance, Regional Economics, Regional Finance, Social Policy, Theoretical Economics
Faculty of Education (Freshmen Enrollment: 350)
Administration of Physical Education, Agriculture, Algebra and Geometry, Analysis and Applied Mathematics, Athletics, Child Care, Clothing Science, Construction, Dance, Electricity, Food Science, Gymnastics, Home Management, Hygiene, Instrumental Music, Judo, Machinery, Metal Processing and Craft, Methodology of Teaching Art, Methodology of Teaching Domestic Science, Methodology of Teaching English, Methodology of Teaching Japanese Language, Methodology of Teaching Mathematics, Methodology of Teaching Music, Methodology of Teaching Physical Education, Methodology of Teaching Science, Methodology of Teaching Social Studies, Methodology of Technical Education, Musical Composition, Musicology & Music History, Painting, Plastic Arts, Psychology of Physical Education, School Education, School Hygienics, Sports, Theory of Arts & Arts History, Theory of Physical Education & History of Physical Education, Vocal Music, Wood Processing and Craft

Foreign Student Admission

Qualifications for Applicants
Standard Qualifications Requirement
Those who have been awarded an International Baccalaureate Diploma may also apply.

Applicants are required to take the General Examination for Foreign Students and the Japanese Language Proficiency Test, First Grade, administered by the Association of International Education, Japan. Applicants to the Faculty of Economics, must take both the General Examination for Foreign Students and the Japanese Language Proficiency Test (First Grade), or must take the Joint First-Stage Achievement Test.
Examination at the University
The Second-Stage Test given by the University is required of all applicants. This Second-Stage Test includes an interview and a short essay. In the case of applicants for certain courses in the Faculty of Education, practical work or demonstration of knowledge may take the place of a short essay.
Documents to be Submitted When Applying
Standard Documents Requirement

ONE-YEAR GRADUATE PROGRAM

One-Year Graduate Program in Education (Enrollment: 5)
Health and Physical Education

Foreign Student Admission
Qualifications for Applicants
Standard Qualifications Requirement
Examination at the University
Applicants must take one foreign language out of the two, and one major subject out of the six.

GRADUATE PROGRAMS

Graduate School of Economics (First Year Enrollment : Master's 22)
Divisions
Business Administration, Economics
Graduate School of Education (First Year Enrollment : Master's 20)
Divisions
English Language Education, Japanese Language Education, School Education, Science Education, Social Studies Education

Foreign Student Admission
Qualifications for Applicants
Master's Program
Standard Qualifications Requirement
Examination at the University
Master's Program
Education: Applicants for each major course must take examinations in one foreign language (dictionaries may be used), two major subjects and an oral examination.
Economics: Applicants for each major course

must take examinations in one foreign language and two major subjects. Those who pass the written examinations must undergo an interview.

Documents to be Submitted When Applying
    Standard Documents Requirement

*

Research Institutes and Centers
Research and Guidance Center for Teaching Practice
Facilities/Services for Foreign Students
    Though we have no special facilities for foreign students, we can provide assistance in finding accommodation.
Special Programs for Foreign Students
    Though the Faculty of Education has no special programs for foreign students at present, it may be possible to arrange private lessons for those who do not have a sufficient command of Japanese. Two special subjects are offered to foreign students in the Faculty of Economics, "Japan and the Japanese"
For Further Information
    Undergraduate and Graduate Admissions
Faculty of Education: Chief of Academic Affairs, Faculty of Education, Fukushima University, 2 Sugumichi, Asakawa, Matsukawa-machi, Fukushima-shi, Fukushima 960-12 ☎ 0245-48-5151 ext. 2311
Faculty of Administration and Social Sciences: Dear of Students, Faculty of Administration and Social Sciences Fukushima University, 2 Sugumichi, Asakawa, Matsukawa-machi, Fukushima-shi, Fukushima 960-12 ☎ 0245-48-5151 ext. 2510
Faculty of Economics: Chief of Academic Affairs, Faculty of Economics, Fukushima University, 2 Sugumichi, Asakawa, Matsukawa-machi, Fukushima-shi, Fukushima 960-12 ☎ 0245-48-5151 ext. 2507

Gifu University
(Gifu Daigaku)

1-1 Yanagido, Gifu-shi, Gifu 501-11
☎ 0582-30-1111

Faculty
    Profs. 195   Assoc. Profs. 180
    Assist. Profs. Full-time 66; Part-time 372
    Res. Assocs. 196
Number of Students
    Undergrad. 4,670   Grad. 396
Library 647,489 volumes

Outline and Characteristics of the University
    Gifu University is composed of the Faculty of Education, School of Medicine, Faculty of Engineering, Faculty of Agriculture and Faculty of General Education. It also has a three-year College of Technology which was established with the cooperation of the Faculty of Engineering.
    The history of the Faculty of Education can be traced back 100 years when it was established as Gifu Prefectural Normal School. The School of Medicine

and the Faculty of Engineering with its 40 year history began as Gifu Prefectural Special Training School with a history of 40 years. The Faculty of Agriculture was first established as Gifu Higher Agricultural School 60 years ago. The College of Technology was established in 1959. All these institutions, based on the spirit of the Fundamental Law of Education, try to provide a wide range of knowledge and at the same time engage in research and educational activities in their various fields of specified subjects. Their prime objectives are the development of the intellectual, moral and practical abilities of the students and the nurturing of promising young people who can contribute to academic and cultural advancement.
    In 1984, all faculties and a college except the School of Medicine were integrated in a new campus in Yanagido. All the buildings are systematically located with the university library as its center. All former facilities have been renewed and new ones have been added. The integration of the separate campuses is expected to bring about closer cooperation among the institutions and as a result engender a new academic tradition at Gifu University.
    The city of Gifu has a population of 420,000. The city is located in the north-west area of the Nobi plain and is blessed with the changes of the four seasons. It is well qualified as a university city in view of its geographical and social environment.

UNDERGRADUATE PROGRAMS

Faculty of Agriculture (Freshmen Enrollment: 250)
    Department of Agricultural Chemistry
Applied Microbiology, Biological Chemistry, Natural Product Chemistry, Nutrition and Food Chemistry, Science of Agricultural Products Utilization, Soil and Manure Science
    Department of Agricultural Engineering
Agricultural Equipment and Machinery, Agricultural Hydraulic Engineering, Agricultural Land Engineering, Agricultural Structural Engineering, Farm Power Machinery, Irrigation and Drainage Engineering
    Department of Agricultural Science
Agricultural Economics, Crop Production, Entomology, Genetics and Plant Breeding, Horticultural Science, Physical Distribution of Agricultural Products, Plant Disease Science
    Department of Forestry
Forest Management, Forest Production, Tree Biochemistry, Tree Science, Wood Chemistry
    Department of Poultry and Animal Science
Animal Nutrition, Animal Products Technology, Livestock Farm Business Management, Poultry Breeding, Poultry Management, Zootechnical Chemistry
    Department of Veterinary Scienee
Theriogenocorogy, Veterinary Anatomy, Veterinary Bacteriology, Veterinary Internal Medicine, Veterinary Pathology, Veterinary Pharmacology, Veteri-

nary Physiology, Veterinary Public Health, Veterinary Surgery

Faculty of Education (Freshmen Enrollment: 340)

Training Course for Junior High School Teachers

Training Course for Primary School Teachers

Training Course for Teachers for Special Subject (*Science*)

Training Course for Teachers of School for the Handicapped

Faculty of Engineering (Freshmen Enrollment: 450)

Department of Cheminstry

Functional Chemistry, Material Chemistry and Process Engineering, Organic Chemistry, Physicochemistry of Materials, Polymer Chemistry

Department of Civil Engineering

Construction Materials and Structural Engineering, Geotechnical Engineering, Infrastructure Planning, Water Engineering

Department of Electronics and Computer Engineering

Condensed Matter Electronics, Electric Energy Engineering, Fundamentals of Computer Engineering, Information Systems, Solid State Electronics

Department of Mechanical Engineering

Control Engineering, Engineering Fluid Mechanics, Material Engineering, Production Engineering, Thermal Engineering

School of Medicine (Freshmen Enrollment: 80)

Department of Medicine

Anatomy, Anesthesiology, Bacteriology, Biochemistry, Dermatology, Forensic Medicine, Gynecology and Obsterics, Hygiene, Internal Medicine, Laboratory Medicine, Neurology and Psychiatry, Neurosurgery, Ophthalmology, Oral Surgery, Orthopedic Surgery, Oto-Rhino-Laryngology, Parasitology, Pathology, Pediatrics, Pharmacology, Physiology, Public Health, Radiology, Surgery, Urology

Foreign Student Admission

Qualifications for Applicants

Standard Qualifications Requirement

Examination at the University

For Faculty of Education, applicants must take the Second-Stage Admission Test by Gifu University, Some Departments will give a skill test besides it. Their selection is based upon the results of the above mentioned examinations and a health examination. For other faculties, applicants must have taken the Japanese Language Proficiency Test and General Examination for Foreign Students (Part of Science). Their selection is based on:

1. Scores of the above two examinations
2. Each faculty's separate entrance examination (achievement test, short essay test, interview)
3. Health examination

Documents to be Submitted When Applying

Standard Documents Requirement

Application forms are available at Entrance Examination Section, Admission Division, Student Office from November.

Applicants are required to submit the application documents to the Faculty Office by February 8.

ONE-YEAR GRADUATE PROGRAMS

Post-Graduate Course of Education (Enrollment: 5)
Education

GRADUATE PROGRAMS

Graduate School of Agriculture (First Year Enrollment : Master's 60)

Divisions

Agricultural Chemistry, Agricultural Engineering, Agricultural Science, Forestry, Poultry and Animal Science, Veterinary Science

Graduate School of Engineering (First Year Enrollment : Master's 76)

Divisions

Civil Engineering, Construction Engineering, Electrical Engineering, Electronic Engineering, Industrial Chemistry, Mechanical Engineering, Precision Engineering, Synthetic Chemistry, Textile Engineering

Graduate School of Medicine (First Year Enrollment : Doctor's 56)

Divisions

Internal Medicine, Morphology, Physiological Science, Social Medicine, Surgery

Foreign Student Admission

Qualifications for Applicants

Master's Program

Standard Qualifications Requirement

Doctor's Program

Standard Qualifications Requirement

Examination at the University

Master's Program

Each Graduate School holds a special examination for foreign students.

Doctor's Program

Graduate School of Medicine gives special examination containing a short essay and interview for foreign students.

Documents to be Submitted When Applying

Standard Documents Requirement

*

Research Institutes and Centers

Computing Center, Curriculum Research and Development Center, Experimental Farm, Experimental Forest, Institute for Development of Mountain Regions, Institute of Anaerobic Bacteriology, Institute of Equilibrium Research, Measurement Center, Radioisotope Co-operative Reseach Institution, Regional Research Center for Science and Technology, Veterinary Hospital

Facilities/Services for Foreign Students

Education: Office of International Education

Welfare: Student Counseling Room, Health Administration Center

Accommodations: Student Dormitory Kuronoryo and Gifu University International House

Special Programs for Foreign Students

Japanese language and culture classes are available at the Office of International Education.

For Further Information

Undergraduate Admission

Entrance Examination Section, Admission Division, Student Office, Gifu University, 1-1 Yanagido, Gifu-shi, Gifu 501-11 ☎ 0582–30–1111 ext. 2352, 2353

Graduate Admission

Educational Affairs Section, Administration Department, of each Graduate School, Gifu University, 1-1 Yanagido, Gifu-shi, Gifu 501-11 ☎ 0582–30–1111 Graduate School of Medicine: 40 Tsukasa-machi, Gifu-shi, Gifu 500 ☎ 0582–65–1241 ext. 2335

Gunma University
(Gunma Daigaku)

4-2 Aramaki-machi, Maebashi-shi, Gunma 371
☎ 0272–32–1611

Faculty
  Profs. 189   Assoc. Profs. 159
  Assist. Profs. Full–time 76; Part–time 843
  Res. Assocs. 215
Number of Students
  Undergrad. 3, 969   Grad. 273
Library 517, 632 volumes

Outline and Characteristics of the University

Gunma University was established on May 31, 1949, when the National School Establishment Law was enacted, and comprised of Gunma Normal School, Gunma Youth Normal School, the Maebashi Medical College, Maebashi College of Medical Science, and Kiryu Technical College.

At the beginning it consisted of the Faculty of Liberal Arts, the Faculty of Medicine, and the Faculty of Engineering, but it was expanded and reorganized many times up to the present to include the Faculty of Education, the Faculty of Medicine, the Faculty of Engineering, the Faculty of General Studies, the Institute of Endocrinology, University Library, University Hospital, the Kusatsu Branch of the University Hospital, the Administration Office, the Student Affairs Office, the Health Service Center, the College of Medical Care and Technology, and the College of Technology.

It also has graduate schools and offers postgraduate courses in several fields; a doctoral course in the Faculty of Medicine, a master's course in the Faculty of Engineering, and a One-Year Advanced Course in Education in the Faculty of Education.

The Faculty of Education has an attached kindergarten, a mentally handicapped children's school, an elementary school, and a junior high school.

The gross area of this university is about 680, 000 m², which is separated into three areas, the Aramaki Campus (about 290, 000 m²) and the Showa Campus (about 160, 000 m²) in Maebashi, and the Kiryu Campus (about 110, 000 m²) in Kiryu.

UNDERGRADUATE PROGRAMS

Faculty of Education (Freshmen Enrollment: 310)
  Course for Elementary School Teaching
  Course for Junior High School Teaching
  Course for Physically Handicapped or Mentally Handicapped Children's School Teaching
  Course for Training Senior High School Teachers of Science

Aesthetics, Agriculture, Algebra and Geometry, Analysis and Applied Mathematics, Applied Physics, Astronomy and Geophysics, Calligraphy, Chinese Classics, Clothing Science, Construction, Curriculum and Instruction Studies in Art Education, Curriculum and Instruction Studies in Domestic Science Education, Curriculum and Instruction Studies in Japanese Language and Literature Education, Curriculum and Instruction Studies in Mathematics Education, Curriculum and Instruction Studies in Music Education, Curriculum and Instruction Studies in Physical Education, Curriculum and Instruction Studies in Science Education, Curriculum and Instruction Studies in Social Science Education, Economics, Education of Handicapped Children, Electricity, English and American Literature, English Composition and Conversation, English Language, Ethics, Food Science, Fundamental Physics, Geography, Geological Mineralogy, History, History of Arts, History of Physical Education, Home Management, Hygiene of Handicapped Children, Inorganic Physical Chemistry, Instrumental Music, Japanese Language, Japanese Literature, Law, Machinery, Metal Processing and Craft, Methodology, Methodology in Teaching Japanese Language and Literature, Methodology of Teaching Art, Methodology of Teaching Domestic Science, Methodology of Teaching English, Methodology of Teaching Mathematics, Methodology of Teaching Music, Methodology of Teaching Physical Education, Methodology of Teaching Science, Methodology of Teaching Technical Education, Musical Composition, Musicology and Music History, Organic Chemistry, Painting, Pedagogy, Philosophy, Physical Education (Theory), Physical Education (Training), Physiological Ecology, Plastic Arts, Political Science, Psychology of Handicapped Children, School Hygienics, Social Education, Taxonomical Morphology, Vocal Music, Vocational Guidance, Wood Processing and Craft

Faculty of Engineering (Freshmen Enrollment: 506)
  Department of Applied Chemistry

Analytical Chemistry, Biochemistry, Bioorganic Chemistry, Crystal Chemistry, Geochemistry, Inorganic Chemistry, Organic Chemistry, Organometallic Chemistry, Organosilicon Chemistry, Physical

Organic Chemistry, Reaction Mechanism, Solid State Chemistry

Department of Chemical Engineering

Catalytic Chemistry, Combustion Process, Fluidization Engineering, Mass Transfer Operation, Reaction Engineering, Reactor Designing, Separation Process with Electricity, Solid-Liquid Separation Process, Transport Phenomena

Department of Civil Engineering

Bridge Engineering, Concrete Engineering, Environmental Engineering, Geotechnical Engineering, Hydraulics, Hydrology, Sanitary Engineering, Soil Mechanics

Department of Computer Science

Compiler Design Theory, Computer Algorithms, Computer Architecture, Computer Systems, Decision Theory, Graph Theory, Image Processing, Information Theory, Mathematical Programming, Numerical Analysis, Programming Languages

Department of Electrical Engineering

Control Engineering, Electric Machinery, Electric Power Engineering, Electroacoustics, Electromagnetic Theory, Electronic Measurement, Energy Conversion, Gaseous Discharge, Instrument Electronics, Wave Propagation

Department of Electronic Engineering

Antennas and Microwave Transmission, Communication Systems, Electric and Magnetic Materials, Electron Devices, Electronic Circuits, Plasma Physics, Semiconductor Engineering, Solid State Physics, Systems Engineering, Thin Film Physics

Department of Mechanical Engineering I

Dynamics of Machinery, Fluid Dynamics, Internal Combustion Engine, Laser Machining, Metal Machining, Plasma Physics, Strength of Materials, Theory of Elasticity, Thermal Power Engineering, Vibration

Department of Mechanical Engineering II

Diffusion in Metals, Heat and Mass Transfer, Instrument and Control Engineering, Material Processing, Plastic Working, Spray and Combustion System, Strength and Structure of Metals and Alloys

Department of Polymer and Textile

Applied Physics, Biophysics, Chemical Physics, Materials, Physical Chemistry, Polymer and Textile Science, Polymer Chemistry, Polymer Physics, Polymer Processing, Statistical Mechanics, Thermodynamics

Department of Polymer Chemistry

Ceramic Chemistry, Crystal Growth, Dyeing Chemistry, Photochemistry, Physical Chemistry, Physical Chemistry of Polymers, Polymer Reactions, Structure and Properties of Polymer, Synthetic Inorganic Materials, Textile Chemistry

Department of Synthetic Chemistry

Carbonization Engineering, Carbon Materials, Colloid Chemistry, Inorganic Materials, Organic Chemistry, Organosilicon Chemistry, Reaction Mechanism, Synthetic Inorganic Materials, Synthetic Organic Chemistry

Faculty of Medicine (Freshmen Enrollment: 100)

Department of Medicine

Anatomy, Anesthesiology, Biochemistry, Dermatology, Hygiene, Internal Medicine, Legal Medicine, Microbiology, Neuropsychiatry, Nuclear Medicine, Obstetrics and Gynecology, Ophthalmology, Oral Surgery, Orthopedic Surgery, Otorhinolaryngology, Parasitology, Pathology, Pediatrics, Pharmacology, Physiology, Public Health, Radiology, Surgery, Urology

Foreign Student Admission

Qualifications for Applicants

Standard Qualifications Requirement

Those who have an International Baccalaureate Diploma and are over 18 years old may also apply.

Examination at the University

Foreign applicants must sit for the Joint First-Stage Achivement Test and take the entrance examination for this university.

Applicants for the Faculty of Engineering may undergo a special selective examination; it is not necessary that they sit for the Joint First-Stage Achievement Test but instead must take the Science Course of the Genaral Examination for Foreign Students. A brief thesis and oral examination will be held in this special selective examination for the Faculty of Engineering.

Documents to be Submitted When Applying

Standard Documents Requirement

Following documents are also required.

1. Permit to study abroad issued by the government concerned, or recommendation of diplomatic establishment in Japan.
2. Certificate of Japanese proficiency adequate for undergraduate studies.

Application forms will be available in the middle of October and they must be submitted and completed appropriately, by the 15th of February. However, application for the special selective examination of the Faculty of Engineering will be accepted from the 1st to 7th of February.

GRADUATE PROGRAMS

Graduate School of Engineering (First Year Enrollment : Master's 88)

Divisions

Applied Chemistry, Chemical Engineering, Civil Engineering, Computer Science, Electrical Engineering, Electronic Engineering, Mechanical Engineering I & II, Polymer and Textile, Polymer Chemistry, Synthetic Chemistry

Graduate School of Medicine (First Year Enrollment : Doctor's 64)

Divisions

Clinical Medicine (Non-Surgical), Clinical Medicine (Surgical), Pathological Medical Sciences, Physiological Medical Sciences, Social Medicine

Foreign Student Admission

Qualifications for Applicants

Master's Program

Standard Qualifications Requirement

Doctor's Program

Standard Qualifications Requirement

Examination at the University

Master's Program

Applicants are to take the same entrance examination that Japanese students do.

Doctor's Program

Same as Master's program.

Documents to be Submitted When Applying

Standard Documents Requirement

Application forms will be handled similarly to undergraduate application forms. Requests for forms will be accepted at the Instruction Department of each Faculty.

Research Institutes and Centers

Behavior Research Institute, Center for Research and Instruction in Educational Practice, Hormone Assay Center, Institute of Endocrinology, Institute of Experimental Animal Research, Institute of Neurology and Rehabilitation, Laboratory of Drug Resistance in Bacteria, Research Institute of Composite Materials

For Further Information

Undergraduate and Graduate Admission

Instruction Section, Student Affairs Office, Gunma University, 4-2 Aramaki-machi, Maebashi-shi, Gunma 371 ☎ 0272–32–1611 ext. 306

Hamamatsu University School of Medicine

（Hamamatsu Ika Daigaku）

3600 Handa-cho, Hamamatsu-shi, Shizuoka 431-31
☎ 0534–35–2111

Faculty

    Profs. 37   Assoc. Profs. 31

    Assist. Profs. Full–time 27; Part–time 145

    Res. Assocs. 136

Number of Students

    Undergrad. 644   Grad. 80

Library 74, 601 volumes

Outline and Characteristics of the University

Hamamatsu University School of Medicine was founded by the government in 1974. The School's motto is to turn out both clinicians who will give the best care to patients as well as basic and clinical scientists who devote themselves to the study of the medical sciences for mankind. Since its foundation it has already sent out seven graduating classes into society. The percentage of successful students in the National Medical Licensure Examination has been more than 90 percent.

A Graduate School was opened to offer the Doctor's program in 1980. The program is quite unique in that the Graduate School is divided into four courses according to the way it approaches basic medical research—the human being and its phenomena of life. The program's principle is to train graduate students as independent, competent researchers by integrating basic and clinical medicine. The first 13 students who finished the Graduate School were conferred the degree of Doctor of Medical Science in March, 1984.

The School, still youthful and energetic, full of a pioneering atmosphere, celebrated its 10th anniversary in 1984. The faculty, generally young and therefore flexible and active, has a good rapport with students. The School provides undergraduate students with a six-year integrated curriculum. Classes are conducted with the above-mentioned objectives in mind.

The campus is located to the east of Lake Hamana which is noted for its fascinating view and marine products. Students study and relax among academic buildings and wooded glens, and enjoy sports in the playground overlooking the streets of Hamamatsu.

The majority of students are from Shizuoka and its neighboring prefectures, but the others come from virtually every part of Japan. In addition, a few foreign students study here at present: three supported by the Japanese government and nine by private funds. Enough rooming houses and apartments are available near the campus, though the School has no dormitory. Students seem to have an enjoyable life, cordially welcomed by the citizens of Hamamatsu.

UNDERGRADUATE PROGRAMS

Faculty of Medicine (Freshmen Enrollment: 100)

Department of Medicine

Foreign Student Admission

Qualifications for Applicants

Standard Qualifications Requirement

Those who hold an international baccalaureate awarded by the International Baccalaureate Office, a foundation by the Swiss Civil Code, and have reached the age of 18 are also eligible to apply.

Applicants must take both the Japanese Language Proficiency Test and General Examination for Foreign Students (all the subjects of Science), and must receive an "A" grade in the tests.

Documents to be Submitted When Applying

Standard Documents Requirement

Application forms are available at the Admissions Office from early December.

All applicants are required to submit the specified application documents to the Admissions Office from January 30 through Frebruary 8.

GRADUATE PROGRAMS

Graduate School of Medicine (First Year Enrollment : Doctor's 30)
Divisions
Biochemical-approach Course, Ecological-approach Course, Morphological-approach Course, Physiological-approach Course

Foreign Student Admission
Qualifications for Applicants
Doctor's Program
Standard Qualifications Requirement
Examination at the University
Doctor's Program
Applicants must take the same entrance examination consisting of a written exam and an interview that are given to Japanese students.
Documents to be Submitted When Applying
Standard Documents Requirement
Application forms are available at the Graduate Admissions Office from early December. All applicants are required to submit the specified application documents to the Graduate Addmissions Office from January 12 through January 30.

Research Institutes and Centers
Animal Laboratory, Equipment Center, University Hospital
For Further Information
Undergraduate and Graduate Admission
Student Division, Hamamatsu University School of Medicine, 3600 Handa-cho, Hamamatsu-shi, Shizuoka 431-31 ☎ 0534-35-2205

Hirosaki University
(Hirosaki Daigaku)

1 Bunkyo-cho, Hirosaki-shi, Aomori 036
☎ 0172-36-2111

Faculty
    Profs. 178   Assoc. Profs. 185
    Assist. Profs. Full–time 86; Part–time 589
    Res. Assocs. 156
Number of Students
    Undergrad. 4, 978   Grad. 294
Library 652, 511 volumes

Outline and Characteristics of the University
In 1949, Hirosaki Higher School (founded in 1920), Aomori Normal School (1943), Aomori Youth Normal School (1944), Aomori Medical School (1944), and Hirosaki Medical College (1948) were incorporated, in accordance with the National School Establishment Law, into a new university with three Faculties: Liberal Arts and Science, Education, and Medicine. In 1955, the Faculty of Agriculture was established. In 1965, the Faculty of Liberal Arts and Science was reorganized into separate Humanities and Science Faculties and the College of Liberal Arts was established that year as well. In 1958, the Graduate School of Medicine (Doctor's course) was opened, followed by the Graduate School of Agriculture (Master's course, 1971) and the Graduate School of Science (Master's course, 1977). In 1975, the School of Allied Medical Sciences was established as an annex to the University. Today the University enrolls more than 5, 000 students and is comprised of five Faculties, three Graduate Schools, the College of Liberal Arts and other affiliated establishments.

The campus is located in Hirosaki City (population about 176, 000), which until 1868 was the castle town of the Tsugaru Clan. The entire fief yielded approximately 145, 000 tons of rice per year. Hirosaki is the home of four private colleges (including junior colleges), the center of culture and education in the Tsugaru area. It is also noted for both its old shrines and temples built in the Edo period and for its western style buildings and churches of the Meiji period. Hirosaki is Japan's leading apple producer, as well.

UNDERGRADUATE PROGRAMS

Faculty of Agriculture (Freshmen Enrollment: 145)
Department of Agricultural Engineering
Agricultural Machinery, Agricultural Power, Agricultural Structures and Constructions Engineering, Irrigation and Drainage Engineering, Land Reclamation Engineering
Department of Agronomy
Agricultural Economics, Agricultural Managerial Economics, Agricultural Marketing, Crop Science, Plant Breeding, Zoo-Technical Animal Science
Department of Horticultural Chemistry
Biological Chemistry, Soil Science, Plant Nutrition and Utilization of Agricultural Products, Utilization of Horticultural Products
Department of Horticultural Science
Applied Entomology, Phytopathology, Pomology, Vegetable Crops and Floriculture
Faculty of Education (Freshmen Enrollment: 370)
Training Course for High School Teachers of Nursing
Training Course for Junior High School Teachers
Training Course for Kindergarten Teachers
Training Course for Special School Teachers of the Mentally Retarded
Training Course for Primary School Teachers
Training Course for School Nurse Teachers
Adult Education, Algebra and Geometry, Analysis and Applied Mathematics, Art Education, Basic Medical Science, Basic Nursing Science, Biology, Chemistry, Clinical Science, Clothing Science, Composition, Construction and Design, Developmental Psychology, Earth Science, Economics, Educational

Administration, Educational Psychology, Educational Sociology, Education of Handicapped Children, Education of Preschool Children, Electricity, English and American Literature, English Language, English Language Education, Food Science, Geography, History, History of Education, Homemaking Education, Instrumental Music, Japanese Language, Japanese Language Education, Japanese Literature, Law, Mathematics Education, Mechanics, Medical Nursing, Mother and Child Nursing, Music Education, Natural Science Education, Nursing Science, Painting, Pedagogy, Philosophy, Physical Education, Physics, Physiology and Hygiene, Psychology of Handicapped Children, Psychology of Preschool Children, pupil's Guidance, School Health, Sculpture and Plastic Art, Social Studies Education, Study of Material for Preschool Children Education, Surgical Nursing, Teaching of Health and Physical Education, Technical Education, Theory and History of Music, Theory and History of Physical Education, Vocal Music, Wood Processing

Faculty of Humanities (Freshmen Enrollment: 328)
  Department of Economics
Accounting, Business Administration, Business History, Economic History, Economic Policy, Economic Theory, Finance, International Economics,. Management Accounting, Management Theory, Private Law, Public Finance, Statistics, Theory of Business Enterprise
  Department of Humanities
Humane Studies, Japanese Studies, Oriental Studies, Social Studies, Western Studies

Faculty of Medicine (Freshmen Enrollment 120)
  Department of Medicine
Anatomy, Anesthesiology, Bacteriology, Biochemistry, Dental and Oral Surgery, Dermatology, Hygiene, Internal Medicine, Legal Medicine, Neuropsychiatry, Neurosurgery, Obstetrics and Gynecology, Ophthalmology, Orthopedic Surgery, Otorhinolaryngology, Parasitology, Pathology, Pediatrics, Pharmacology, Physiology, Public Health, Radiology, Surgery, Urology

Faculty of Science (Freshmen Enrollment: 216)
  Department of Biology
Cytology, Genetics and Physiological Chemistry, Environmental Biology, Physiology and Developmental Biology, Systematics and Morphology
  Department of Chemistry
Analytical Chemistry, Inorganic Chemistry, Organic Chemistry, Physical Chemistry
  Department of Earth Science
Geochemistry and Mineralogy, Geodynamics, Geology and Petrology, Seismology
  Department of Information Science
Fundamental Information, Information Processing
  Department of Mathematics
Algebra, Analysis, Applied Mathematics, Geometry
  Department of Physics
Atomic Physics, Electromagnetism, Quantum Physics, Solid State Physics

Foreign Student Admission
  Qualifications for Applicants
    Standard Qualifications Requirement
    Foreign applicants must take the Japanese Language Proficiency Test and General Examination for Foreign Students.
  Examination at the University
    Their selection will be based upon the results of the following examinations:
    1. The Japanese Language Proficiency Test and General Examination for Foreign Students
    2. Each Faculty's separate entrance examination (achievement test, skill test, interview and short essay examination)
    3. A health examination
    Selection methods differ from faculty to faculty.
  Documents to be Submitted When Applying
    Standard Documents Requirement
    Applicants must submit the required documents to the Admissions Office, Student Affairs Bureau by the appointed time.

ONE-YEAR GRADUATE PROGRAMS

One-Year Graduate Course of Humanities
(Enrollment 10)
Economics, Humanities
One-Year Graduate Course of of Education
(Enrollment 5)
Education

Foreign Student Admission
  Qualifications for Applicants
    Standard Qualifications Requirement
  Examination at the University
    The selection will be based upon the results of an achievement test, an examination of the official transcripts, an interview and a health examination.

GRADUATE PROGRAMS

Graduate School of Agriculture (First Year Enrollment : Master's 36)
  Divisions
Agricultural Engineering, Agronomy, Horticultural Chemistry, Horticultural Science
Graduate School of Medicine (First Year Enrollment : Doctor's 64)
  Divisions
Internal Medicine, Pathology, Physiology, Social Medicine, Surgery
Graduate School of Science (First Year Enrollment : Master's 40)
  Divisions
Biology, Chemistry, Earth Science, Mathematics, Physics

Foreign Student Admission
  Qualifications for Applicants

Master's Program
    Standard Qualifications Requirement
Doctor's Program
    Standard Qualifications Requirement
   Examination at the University
Master's Program
Graduate School of Science and Graduate School of Agriculture: The selection will be based upon the results of an achievement test, an examination of the official transcripts, an interview and a health examination.
Doctor's Program
Graduate School of Medicine: The selection will be based upon the results of an achievement test, an examination of the official transcripts, an interview and a health examination.
   Documents to be Submitted When Applying
    Standard Documents Requirement

Research Institutes and Centers
Center for Educational Research and Practice, Institute for Experimental Animals, Institute of Cerebrovascular Diseases, Seismological and Volcanological Observatory, University Hospital
Facilities/Services for Foreign Students
   There is no separate housing for foreign students, but the faculty in which they wish to study will help them find living accommodations near the campus.
   There is Health Administration Center on the campus, where a doctor is stationed for health care.
   The University holds a social meeting for foreign students, comprised of the President of the University and the staff members for the International programs.
Special Programs for Foreign Students
   In the Faculty of Education, some staff members teach Japanese language to foreign students. The class is also available for those foreign students in the other Faculties.
For Further Information
   Undergraduate and Graduate Admission
Admissions Office, Student Affairs Bureau, Hirosaki University, 1 Bunkyo-cho, Hirosaki-shi, Aomori 036 ☎ 0172–36–2111 ext. 2392

Hiroshima University
(Hiroshima Daigaku)

1-1-89 Higashisenda-machi, Naka-ku, Hiroshima-shi, Hiroshima 730 ☎ 082–241–1221

Faculty
   Profs. 471   Assoc. Profs. 408
   Assist. Profs.   Full–time 133; Part–time 897
   Res. Assocs. 573
Number of Students
   Undergrad. 12, 158   Grad. 1, 829
Library   2, 240, 000 volumes

Outline and Characteristics of the University
   Under the National School Establishment Law, Hiroshima University was founded in 1949 by combining eight institutions, such as Hiroshima University of Literature and Sciences (founded in 1929), Hiroshima Higher Normal School (1902), Hiroshima Normal School (originally in 1874), Hiroshima Higher Technical School (1923). Hiroshima Prefectural Medical College was added in 1953. Although these institutions suffered a great deal of damage due to the atomic bomb on August 6, 1945, they were reconstructed and combined to form the new Hiroshima University. It has risen from the ruins of the atomic bomb like a phoenix, which is in fact the University symbol.
   The University has, at present, 11 Faculties and Schools, 9 Graduate Schools, 11 Research Institutes and Centers, and 2 University Hospitals (Medical and Dental). Most of these institutions are located in Hiroshima City, which is now beautifully and completely reconstructed and has a population of 1, 059, 000.
   Since its foundation, Hiroshima University has strived to become one of the prominent, comprehensive universities in Japan, and is noted internationally for its high academic activities. More than three hundred foreign students from all over the world study at the University.
   In order to promote further growth of the University, the faculty and administration of the university decided to move most of the scattered faculties (except for Medical and Dental Schools) to a new site, which is located in the Saijo District of Higashi-Hiroshima City, 35 kilometers east from the main campus, and occupies approximately 280 hectares. The Faculty of Engineering completed its move to the new site in 1982 and the relocation and integration of the new campus is scheduled for completion in 1995.

UNDERGRADUATE PROGRAMS

Faculty of Applied Biological Science (Freshmen Enrollment: 130)
   Department of Applied Biological Science
Animal Science, Applied Biochemistry, Ecology and Plant Production, Farm Economics and Management, Food Science, Marine Biological Science, Microbiology and Hygiene
School of Dentistry (Freshmen Enrollment: 60)
   Department of Dentistry
Conservative Dentistry, Dental Materials, Dental Pharmacology, Oral Anatomy, Oral Bacteriology, Oral Biochemistry, Oral Pathology, Oral Physiology, Oral Radiology, Oral Surgery, Orthodontics, Pedodontics, Preventive Dentistry, Prosthodontics
Faculty of Economics (Freshmen Enrollment: 286)
   Department of Economics
Applied Economics, Economic Policy, Economic

Theory and Econometrics, Historical Economic Science, Management and Information

Faculty of Education (Freshmen Enrollment: 371)

Department of Curriculum and Instruction

English Language Education, Health and Physical Education, Home Economics Education, Japanese Language Education, Mathematics Education, Music Education, Science Education, Social Studies Education

Department of Education

Educational Administration and Finance, Educational Philosophy and History of Education, Educational Sociology and Educational Methodology

Department of Psychology

Educational Psychology, Experimental Psychology

Department of Teaching Japanese as a Foreign Language

Japanese Culture, Japanese Linguistics, Linguistics, Teaching Japanese as a Foreign Language

Faculty of Engineering (Freshmen Enrollment: 596)

Cluster I (Mechanical Engineering)

Design Engineering, Heat and Power Engineering, Mechanical Engineering, Power Generator Engineering, Precision Engineering, Production Engineering

Cluster II (Electrical and Industrial Engineering)

Circuit and Electrical System Engineering, Physical Electronics Engineering, Systems and Industrial Engineering

Cluster III (Chemical-and Bio-Engineering)

Applied Chemistry, Chemical Engineering, Fermentation Technology

Cluster IV (Structural Engineering and Architecture)

Architecture, Environmental Planning and Control, Ship Design, Ship Structure Engineering, Structural Engineering

Faculty of Integrated Arts and Sciences (Freshmen Enrollment: 170)

Department of Integrated Arts and Sciences

Asian Studies, Basic Sciences, Basic Studies of Information and Biology, British and American Studies, Comparative Cultural Studies, Environmental Studies, European Studies, Foreign Languages (Chinese, English, French, German, Russian), Human and Animal Behavior Studies, Information and Behavioral Sciences, Interdisciplinary Study of Natural Sciences, Japanese Studies, Physical Education, Social Sciences

Faculty of Law (Freshmen Enrollment: 285)

Department of Law

Civil Law, International Relations, Political Science, Public Law

Faculty of Letters (Freshmen Enrollment: 165)

Department of History

Archaeology, History of Ancient and Medieval Europe, History of Ancient and Medieval Japan, History of Asia, History of China, History of Modern and Contemporary Europe, History of Modern Japan, Human Geography and Regional Geography, Physical Geography and Regional Geography

Department of Literature

Ancient and Medieval Japanese Literature, British and American Literature, Chinese Language, Chinese Literature, English Language, English Literature, French Language and Literature, German Language, German Literature, Japanese Language, Linguistics, Modern Japanese Literature

Department of Philosophy

Ethics, History of Ancient and Medieval Chinese Thought, History of Philosophy, History of the Theory of Ethics, Indian Philosophy, Modern History of Chinese Thought, Philosophy

School of Medicine (Freshmen Enrollment: 180)

Department of Medicine

Anatomy, Anesthesiology, Bacteriology, Biochemistry, Dermatology, Hygienics, Internal Medicine, Neurology and Psychiatry, Neurosurgery, Obstetrics and Gynecology, Ophthalmology, Orthopedics, Oto-Rhino-Laryngology, Parasitology, Pathology, Pediatrics, Pharmacology, Physiology, Public Health, Radiology, Surgery, Urology

Department of Pharmaceutical Sciences

Analytical Chemistry, Medicinal Chemistry, Medicinal Chemistry of Natural Products, Pharmaceutics and Therapeutics, Pharmacobiodynamics, Public Health Chemistry

Faculty of School Education (Freshmen Enrollment: 350)

Training Course in Elementary School Teaching

Training Course in Teaching the Hearing Impaired

Training Course in Lower Secondary School Teaching

English, Fine Arts, Health and Physical Education, Home Economics, Industrial Arts, Japanese, Mathematics, Music, Science, Social Studies

Training Course in Teaching the Mentally Retarded

Training Course in Teaching the Visually Handicapped

Faculty of Science (Freshmen Enrollment: 260)

Department of Biology

Animal Morphology, Animal Physiology, Animal Taxonomy, Cytology and Cytogenetics, Ecology and Geography, Plant Morphology, Plant Physiology and Microbiology, Plant Taxonomy

Department of Chemistry

Analytical Chemistry, Biological Chemistry, Colloid Chemistry, Co-ordination Chemistry, Inorganic Chemistry, Natural Organic Chemistry, Organic Chemistry, Organic Reaction Chemistry, Physical Chemistry, Polymer Chemistry, Structural Chemistry

Department of Geology and Mineralogy

Historical Geology, Mineralogy, Petrology, Study of Ore Deposits

Department of Materials Science

Chemical Kinetics, Dielectrics, Magnetism, Metal Physics, Plasma Theory, Semiconductor Physics, Surface Science

Department of Mathematics

Algebra, Applied Analysis, Differential Equations, Functional Analysis, Function Theory, Geometry, Mathematical Statistics, Number Theory, Probability Theory, Topology

Department of Physics

Fluid Dynamics, Gaseous Electronics, Nuclear Physics, Nuclear Theory, Solid State Physics, Theory of Elementary Particles

Foreign Student Admission

Qualifications for Applicants

Standard Qualifications Requirement

Examination at the University

In general, applicants are required to take all subjects of the Joint First-Stage Achievement Test together with the entrance examination given by the University. Foreign students can, however, take all subjects of General Examination for Foreign Students and the Japanese Language Proficiency Test (First Level) instead of the Joint First-Stage Achievement Test.

Documents to be Submitted When Applying

Standard Documents Requirement

GRADUATE PROGRAMS

Graduate School of Biosphere Sciences (First Year Enrollment : Master's 61, Doctor's 12)

Divisions

Applied Biological Sciences, Biological Sciences , Environmental and Material Sciences

Graduate School of Dental Science (First Year Enrollment : Doctor's 30)

Divisions

Basic Dental Science, Clinical Dental Science

Graduate School of Education (First Year Enrollment : Master's 56, Doctor's 20)

Divisions

Child Study, Curriculum and Instruction, Education, Educational Administration, Educational Psychology, Experimental Psychology

Graduate School of Engineering (First Year Enrollment : Master's 138, Doctor's 45)

Divisions

Design Engineering, Engineering of Transport Phenomena, Environmental Science and Engineering, Industrial Chemistry, Information Engineering, Materials Engineering, Structural Engineering, Systems Engineering

Graduate School of Letters (First Year Enrollment : Master's 56, Doctor's 28)

Divisions

Archaeology, Chinese and Indian Philosophy, Chinese Language and Literature, English Language and Literature, Ethics, French Literature, Geography, German Language and Literature, Japanese History, Japanese Language and Literature, Linguistics, Oriental History, Western History, Western Philosophy

Graduate School of Medical and Pharmaceutical Sci- ences (First Year Enrollment : Master's 20, Doctor's 70)

Divisions

Clinical Medical Science, Clinical Surgical Science, Medical Biological Science, Molecular Pharmaceutical Science, Pathological Science, Pharmacobiodynamics, Social Medical Science

Graduate School of School Education (First Year Enrollment : Master's 60)

Divisions

Art Education, Education of the Handicapped, Health and Physical Education, Language Education, Mathematics Education, Music Education, School Education, Science Education, Social Studies Education, Special Course in Education of the Handicapped

Graduate School of Science (First Year Enrollment : Master's 96, Doctor's 50)

Divisions

Botany, Chemistry, Geology and Mineralogy, Material Science, Mathematics, Physics, Zoology

Graduate School of Social Sciences (First Year Enrollment : Master's 64, Doctor's 15)

Divisions

Economics, International and Regional Affairs, Law

Foreign Student Admission

Qualifications for Applicants

Master's Program

Standard Qualifications Requirement

Doctor's Program

Standard Qualifications Requirement

Applicants to the Doctoral Programs of the Graduate School of Medical and Pharmaceutical Sciences (a course of studying medical sciences) and the Graduate School of Dentistry must satisfy one of the following requirements.

1. Completion of 18 years of education in a foreign country where the last course has been a medical or dentistry course in the academic year before admission to the Graduate School.

2. Recognition by the Graduate School as being equivalent or superior to a graduate of a School of Medicine or a School of Dentistry in terms of scholastic achievement.

Examination at the University

Master's Program

The entrance examinations are usually given in September and/or the following February each year. Applicants must take their major subjects and two foreign languages selected from English, German, French or other approved languages by means of a written examination. An oral examination is given before final selection is made. Foreign students are sometimes permitted to choose Japanese as one of the Foreign Languages. Some Graduate Schools will permit foreign students to take the entrance examination in English.

The entrance requirements and application procedures for the Graduate School are somewhat different among the Graduate Schools. For further information applicants should direct their inquiries to the Graduate School concerned.

Doctor's Program

Same as Master's program.

*

Research Institutes and Centers

Center for Gene Science, Criogenic Center, Health Service Center, Information Processing Center, Institute for Fusion Theory, Institute for Peace Science, Institute for Waste Waters Treatment, Research Center for Integrated System, Research Institute for Higher Education, Research Institute for Nuclear Medicine and Biology, Research Institute for Theoretical Physics

Special Programs for Foreign Students

1.   Japanese Language and Japanese Culture

The University offers courses in Japanese as a foreign language in the Faculty of Education to foreign students, to make their period of study as rewarding as possible by developing their academic and social effectiveness in the use of spoken and written Japanese. Upon entry, all foreign students are required to take the Japanese Language Placement Test offered at the beginning of each semester. The test is designed to grade their ability in listening, speaking, reading, and writing Japanese. Permission or recommendation to enroll in the Japanese Language Courses is given on the basis of the test or by consent of the Director of the program. Depending on the result of this test, foreign students are classified into four groups; (1) those who are exempt from attending Japanese Language Classes, (2) those who are required to take Elementary Japanese Classes, (3) those who are required to take Intermediate Japanese Classes, (4) those who are required to take Advanced Japanese Classes. Intermediate and Advanced students may also be enrolled in courses in 'Elements of Japanese Culture and Customs.' Students may take a combination of the courses according to their specific needs with the consent of the Director. Regular foreign students enrolled in these courses will receive full University academic credit for work satisfactorily completed.

2.   Intensive Japanese Language Course for International Students

This is a 6 month course which is offered exclusively for the Mombusho Scholarship students who need to learn Japanese intensively before starting graduate work at national universities in the Chugoku and Shikoku areas of Japan.

For Further Information

Undergraduate and Graduate Admission

Foreign Student Section, Student Office, Hiroshima University, 1-1-89 Higashisenda-machi, Naka-ku, Hiroshima-shi, Hiroshima 730 ☎ 082–241–1221 ext. 3617, 3618

Hitotsubashi University
(Hitotsubashi Daigaku)
2-1 Naka, Kunitachi-shi, Tokyo 186
☎ 0425-72-1101

Faculty
   Profs.   147   Assoc. Profs.   64
   Assist. Profs.   Full–time   19; Part–time   138
   Res. Assocs.   88
Number of Students
   Undergrad.   4, 336   Grad.   335
Library   1, 237, 224 volumes

Outline and Characteristics of the University

Hitotsubashi University dates back to the Shoho Koshujo (Institute for Business Training) privately established in 1875. The institute came under government supervision in 1884, and became Tokyo Commercial School. Tokyo Commercial School developed into Higher Commercial School and then into Tokyo Higher Commercial School, and in 1920 it had its status raised and became Tokyo University of Commerce. With the introduction of the new university system in 1949, Tokyo University of Commerce was renamed Hitotsubashi University and restarted as a university with three faculties: the Faculty of Commerce, the Faculty of Economics, and the Faculty of Law and Social Studies. In 1951, the Faculty of Law and Social Studies was separated into the Faculty of Law and the Faculty of Social Studies, and in 1953 the master's course and the doctor's course were established. At present the university has 4, 700 students and a full-time faculty of 320. There are four faculties, graduate schools, two research institutes, and other facilities.

Hitotsubashi University has two campuses. One is in Kunitachi City (with a population of 63, 000) which is located 18 miles west of central Tokyo, and the other is in Kodaira City (with a population of 150, 000) which is located three miles north of Kunitachi City. Both campuses are located in quiet and verdant environments.

Our university is the only national university of social science in Japan and its academic excellence is highly rated. Especially in the field of commerce and economics, it has a long history of outstanding achievements.

The students of our university are very bright, and come from all over Japan. Some foreign students from more than 20 countries also study at our university. Many of the graduates work for banks, commercial firms, and insurance companies.

UNDERGRADUATE PROGRAMS

Faculty of Commerce (Freshmen Enrollment: 285)
Department of Business Management

Accounting, Auditing, Book-keeping, Business Management, Cost Accounting, Financial Management, Management Accounting, Management Information System, Management Science, Management Statistics, Personnel Management, Production Management

Department of Commerce

Banking System, Chemical Commodities, Energy Commodities, Foreign Exchange, Foreign Trade Practices, Foreign Trade Theory, History of Commerce and Business, Marine Insurance, Marketing, Money and Banking, Securities Market, Shipping, Social Insurance, Transportation and Warehousing

Faculty of Economics (Freshmen Enrollment: 285)

Applied Course

Basic Course

Economic Geography, Economic History, Economic Policy, Economic Principles, Economic Statistics, Public Economics, Regional Economy

Faculty of Law (Freshmen Enrollment: 245)

Course I (Public Law)

Course II (Private Law)

Course III (International Relations)

Administrative Law, Civil Law, Civil Procedure, Commercial Law, Comparative Constitutional Law, Comparative Legal Institutions, Conflict of Law, Constitutional Law, Criminal Law, Criminal Procedure, Criminology, Diplomatic History, Foreign Law, International Law, International Organizations, International Politics, Labor Law, Legal History, Philosophy of Law, Public Control of Business, Tax Law

Faculty of Social Studies (Freshmen Enrollment: 245)

Course in Studies of Civilizations and Social History

Course in Studies of Social Problems and Social Policies

Course in Social Theory

Educational Sociology, Politics, Social Anthropology, Social Geography, Social History, Social Policy, Social Psychology, Social Thought, Sociology

Foreign Student Admission

Qualifications for Applicants

A candidate of foreign nationality who fits one of the following categories.

1. A candidate of foreign nationality who has completed 12 years of education in a foreign country or equivalent as designated by the Minister of Education, Science and Culture.
2. A candidate who is awarded the qualification by the International Baccalaureate Office in Switzerland and has reached the age of 18.
3. A candidate of foreign nationality who has completed 9 years of education in a foreign country and has graduated from senior high school in accordance with the 41st Japanese School Education Law. (This includes the candidate who will graduate from senior high

school in March of the year of application.)

Examination at the University

Written examination and interview:

1. Date of written examination and interview: Early March
2. The subjects of the written examination are Japanese, English and Mathematics.
3. Announcement of results: Early March

Documents to be Submitted When Applying

Standard Documents Requirement

GRADUATE PROGRAMS

Graduate School of Commerce (First Year Enrollment : Master's 46, Doctor's 21)

Divisions

Business Management and Accounting, Commerce

Graduate School of Economics (First Year Enrollment : Master's 52, Doctor's 30)

Divisions

Economic History and Economic Policy, Theoretical Economics and Statistics

Graduate School of Law (First Year Enrollment : Master's 36, Doctor's 17)

Divisions

Law and Economy, Law and State

Graduate School of Social Studies (First Year Enrollment : Master's 28, Doctor's 28)

Divisions

Social Problems and Social Policies, Socio-Cultural Area Studies, Sociology

Foreign Student Admission

Qualifications for Applicants

Master's Program

Standard Qualifications Requirement

Doctor's Program

Standard Qualifications Requirement

Examination at the University

Master's Program

Written Examination (Mid-February). Subjects of examination: a. Graduate School of Commerce (1) An essay related to the candidate's specialized field of study (to be written in Japanese) (2) English (Japanese translation of English paragraphs) (3) Oral tests (languages, specialized field of study, etc.) b. Graduate School of Economics

The primary examination (1) Languages (written examination about Japanese, English) (2) An essay (select one subject among seven subjects).

The second examination (1) Oral tests (specialized field of study, etc), c. Graduate School of Law and Graduate School of Social Studies (1) An essay related to the candidate's specialized field of study (to be written in Japanese) (2) Oral tests (languages, specialized field of study, etc.)

Doctor's Program

Written Examination (March). Subjects of examination: a. Graduate School of Commerce and

Graduate School of Law (1) two foreign languages (2) Oral tests (languages, specialized field of study, etc.) b. Graduate School of Economics and Graduate School of Social Studies (1) Oral tests (languages, specialized field of study, etc.)
  Documents to be Submitted When Applying
  Standard Documents Requirement

*

Research Institutes and Centers
Center for Historical Social Science Literature, Information and Documentation Center for Japanese Economic Statistics, Institute of Business Research, Institute of Economic Research
For Further Information
  Undergraduate Admission
Admission Office, Hitotsubashi University, 2-1 Naka, Kunitachi-shi, Tokyo 186 ☎ 0425-72-1101 ext. 321
  Graduate Admission
Student Affairs Section, Hitotsubashi University, 2-1 Naka, Kunitachi-shi, Tokyo 186 ☎ 0425-72-1101 ext. 252

Hokkaido University
(Hokkaido Daigaku)

Nishi 5, Kita 8, Kita-ku, Sapporo-shi, Hokkaido 060
☎ 011-716-2111

Faculty
  Profs. 545   Assoc. Profs. 522
  Assist. Profs. Full-time 157; Part-time 820
  Res. Assocs. 775
Number of Students
  Undergrad. 10, 584   Grad. 2, 074
Library 2, 603, 679 volumes

Outline and Characteristics of the University
  Hokkaido University is one of the oldest and largest national universities in Japan. Originally established in 1876 as the Sapporo Agricultural College, it was renamed Hokkaido University in 1947. Previously, it was known as the Agricultural College of Tohoku Imperial University from 1907 to 1918 and as the Hokkaido Imperial University from 1918 to 1947. The University has experienced rapid growth in its more than 100 year history and is presently composed of 12 Faculties, 13 Graduate Schools, four major Institutes and a number of Institutions. Of these the Faculty of Agriculture is the oldest and the Graduate School of Environmental Science is the newest.
  The Faculties are Letters, Education, Law, Economics, Science, Medicine, Dentistry, Pharmaceutical Sciences, Engineering, Agriculture, Veterinary Medicine, and Fisheries. The Graduate Schools are Letters, Education, Law, Economics, Science, Medicine, Dentistry, Pharmaceutical Sciences, Engineer-

ing, Agriculture, Veterinary Medicine, Fisheries, and Environmental Science. With the exception of the Faculty of Fisheries and the Graduate School of Fisheries located at Hakodate (a historic seaport at the southern tip of Hokkaido Island), all Faculties, Graduate Schools, and Institutes are situated on the main University campus which covers an area of three square kilometers near the center of the City of Sapporo.
  As the Hokkaido University campus is one of the largest in Japan, it makes for an enjoyable learning environment and allows students to pursue a variety of extra-curricular activities on campus. Half of the students attending the University are from Hokkaido while the majority of the remainder are from all parts of Japan. Presently there are also 315 foreign students from over 39 countries enrolled at the University.
  Sapporo is the fifth largest city in Japan with a population of approximately 1, 613, 000 In spite of its size the city has retained much of its natural beauty. The Toyohira River, in which salmon can be observed in autumn, runs through the central part of the city. Mount Teine, on which the 1972 Winter Olympic slalom events were held, lies immediately west of the urban area of Sapporo.

UNDERGRADUATE PROGRAMS

Faculty of Agriculture (Freshmen Enrollment: 238)
  Department of Agricultural Biology
Applied Zoology, Crop Physiology, Entomology, Plant Pathology, Plant Virology and Mycology, Sericology
  Department of Agricultural Chemistry
Agriculutral Organic Chemistry, Applied Microbiology, Biochemistry, Food and Nutrition Science, Microbial Technology, Plant Nutrition, Soils, Utilization of Agricultural Products
  Department of Agricultural Economics
Agricultural Co-operation, Agricultural Development, Agricultural Marketing, Agricultural Policy, Farm Management
  Department of Agricultural Engineering
Agricultural Machinery, Agricultural Physics, Agricultural Prime Mover, Agricultural Process Engineering, Land Improvement, Soil Amelioration
  Department of Agronomy
Floriculture and Landscape Arichitecture, Food Crops, Horticulture (Fruit Trees and Vegetable Crops), Industrial Crops, Plant Breeding
  Department of Animal Science
Animal Breeding, Animal Nutrition and Feeding, Leather Science and Technology, Meat and Dairy Science and Technology
  Department of Forest Products
Chemical Technology of Forest Products, Timber Engineering, Wood Chemistry, Wood Physics
  Department of Forestry
Erosion Control Engineering, Forest Management,

Forest Policy, Silviculture

Faculty of Dentistry (Freshmen Enrollment: 80)

Department of Dentistry

Dental Materials and Engineering, Dental Radiology, Operative Dentistry, Oral Anatomy, Oral Biochemistry, Oral Microbiology, Oral Pathology, Oral Physiology, Oral Surgery, Orthodontics, Pediatric Dentistry, Periodontics and Endodontics, Pharmacology, Preventive Dentistry, Prosthetic Dentistry

Faculty of Economics (Freshmen Enrollment: 185)

Department of Business Administration

Accounting, Business Administration, Business Organization, Cost Accounting, Financial Management, Industrial Management, Marketing, Personnel Management

Department of Economics

Economic History, Economic Policy, Economic Statistics, History of Economic Doctrines, International Economics, Money and Banking, Principles of Economics, Public Finance, Social Policy

Faculty of Education (Freshmen Enrollment: 50)

Department of Education

Adult Education, Curriculum Making and Instruction Theory, Developmental Psychology, Didactics, Educational Administration, Educational Planning, Educational Sociology, History of Education, Industrial Education, Special Education and Clinical Psychology

Faculty of Engineering (Freshmen Enrollment: 691)

Department of Applied Chemistry

Cellulose Chemistry and Polymer Science, Ceramic Science, Chemical Engineering Unit Operations, Fuel Technology and Coal Chemistry, Industrial Inorganic Chemistry, Industrial Organic Chemistry

Department of Applied Physics

Applied Diffraction Crystallography, Applied Optics, Crystal Physics, Instrumentation Physics, Mathematical Physics, Molecular Engineering

Department of Architecture

Architectural Planning, Building Construction, Building Materials, Earthquake Engineering, Environmental Engineering of Building, Housing

Department of Chemical Process Engineering

Chemical Process Design, Chemical Process Instrumentation, Chemical Reaction Engineering, Materials Science, Organic Chemistry and Organic Synthesis, Polymer Chemistry

Department of Civil Engineering

Bridge Engineering, Concrete Engineering, Disaster Prevention Engineering, Foundation Engineering, Harbor Engineering, Highway Engineering, River Engineering, Soil Mechanics, Structural Engineering, Structural Mechanics, Transportation and Traffic Engineering, Transportation and Traffic Planning

Department of Electrical Engineering

Applied Electricity, Automatic Control, Electrical Machines, Electrical Materials Engineering, Electric Circuit, Electricity and Magnetism, Electric Power Engineering

Department of Electronic Engineering

Applications of Electromagnetic Waves, Computer and Signal Processing, Electromagnetic Waves and Transmission, Electronic Circuits, Electron Physics, Solid State Electronics

Department of Imformation Engineering

Applied Computer Engineering, Imformation Processing, Language and Imformation, Mathematical Science and Information Engineering, Systems Engineering

Department of Mechanical Engineering

Combustion Engineering, Fluid Mechanics, Heat Energy Conversion, Heat Engines, Materials Strenght, Mechanical Technology

Department of Mechanical Engineering II

Dynamics of Machines, Engineering Materials for Machinery, Fluid Mechanics, Heat Transfer, Machine Design, Plastic Working

Department of Metallurgical Engineering

Electrometallurgy, Ferrous Materials and Foundry Metallurgy, Ferrous Metallurgy, Fundamental Aspects of Physical Metallurgy, Mechanical Metallurgy Welding and Foundry, Nonferrous Extractive Metallurgy

Department of Mineral Resources Development Engineering

Economic Geology, Machinery for Engineering, Mineral Processing, Mining Engineering, Rock Mechanics, Safety Engineering

Department of Nuclear Engineering

Applied Radiation and Radioactivity, Energy Conversion Engineering, High Vacuum Engineering, Nuclear Reactor Safety, Quantum Instrumentation, Radiation Source

Department of Precision Engineering

Automatic Control Engineering, Engineering Physics, Precision Machining, Precision Mechanics

Department of Sanitary Engineering

Air Pollution Control, Industrial Health Engineering, Process Equipment for Sanitary Engineering, Sewage Works Engineering, Solid-Wastes Control, Urban Environmental Engineering, Water-Quality Engineering, Water Works

Faculty of Fisheries (Freshmen Enrollment: 219)

Department of Biology and Aquaculture

Embryology and Genetics, Fresh Water Fish Culture, Mariculture, Marine Botany, Marine Zoology, Physiology and Ecology, Planktology

Department of Chemistry

Analytical Chemistry, Biopolymer Chemistry, Chemical Engineering, Marine Chemistry, Marine Lipid Chemistry

Department of Fishing Science

Biology of Fish Population, Engineering of Fishing Boats, Fisheries Business Economics, Fishing Boat Seamanship, Fishing Gear Engineering, Fishing Navigation, Instrument Engineering for Fishing, Mechanical Engineering for Fishing, Oceanography and Meteorology, Operational Technology of Fishing, Principles of Fishing Grounds

Department of Food Science and Technology

Biochemistry, Food Chemistry, Marine Food Technology, Microbiology

Faculty of Law (Freshmen Enrollment: 231)

Education Division

Criminal Law Jurisprudence, Political Science, Private Law, Public Law, Social Law

Research Division

Comparative Law, History of Law, Philosophy of Law, Sociology of Law

Faculty of Letters (Freshmen Enrollment: 190)

Department of Behavioral Science

Cognitive Information Studies, Comparative Behavioral Studies, Dynamic Sociology, Mathematical Studies in Behavioral Science, Social Ecology, Social Psychology, Study of Social Behavior

Department of History

Asian History, Japanese History, Western History

Department of Literature

Chinese Literature, English & American Literature, English Linguistics, German Linguistics, German Literature, Japanese Linguistics, Japanese Literature, Linguistics, Russian Literature

Department of Philosophy

Chinese Philosophy, Ethics, Indian Philosophy, Religious Studies, Western Philosophy

Faculty of Medicine (Freshmen Enrollment: 120)

Department of Medicine

Anatomy, Anesthesiology, Biochemistry, Cardiovascular Medicine, Dermatology, Hygiene and Preventive Medicine, Internal Medicine, Laboratory Medicine, Legal Medicine, Microbiology, Neurosurgery, Nuclear Medicine, Obstetrics and Gynecology, Ophthalmology, Orthopedic Surgery, Otolaryngology, Pathology, Pediatrics, Pharmacology, Physiology, Plastic Surgery, Psychiatry and Neurology, Public Health, Radiology, Surgery, Urology

Faculty of Pharmaceutical Sciences (Freshmen Enrollment: 80)

Department of Pharmaceutical Chemistry

Biological Chemistry, Chemical Microbiology, Pharmaceutial Organic Chemistry, Pharmaceutical Synthetic Chemistry, Physical Chemistry and Biophysics, Plant Chemistry

Department of Pharmaceutical Sciences

Analytical Chemistry, Hygienic Chemistry, Pharmaceutical Chemistry, Pharmaceutics, Pharmacognosy, Pharmacology, Synthetic and Industrial Chemistry

Faculty of Science (Freshmen Enrollment: 290)

Department of Biology

Botany: Plant Morphology, Plant Physiology, Systematic Botany

Zoology: Animal Physiology, Morphology and Genetics, Systematics and Taxonomy

Department of Chemistry

Analytical Chemistry, Biological Chemistry, Environmental Chemistry, Inorganic Chemistry, Organic Chemistry, Physical Chemistry

Department of Chemistry II

Bioorganic Chemistry, Coordination Chemistry, Genetic Biochemistry, Liquid State Chemistry, Mechanistic Organic Chemistry, Quantum Chemistry, Solid Chemistry, Structural Chemistry

Department of Geology and Mineralogy

Coal and Petroleum Geology, Economic Geology, Mineralogy, Petrology, Stratigraphy

Department of Geophysics

Applied Geophysics, Hydrology, Meteorology, Physical Oceanography, Seismology and Volcanology

Department of Mathematics

Algebra, Applied Mathematics, Functional Analysis, Function Theory, Geometry, Number Theory, Theory of Manifolds, Theory of Partial Differential Operators

Department of Physics

Experimental Physics, Mathematical Physics, Solid State Physics, Theoretical Nuclear Physics, Theoretical Physics

Department of Polymer Science

Biopolymer Science, Polymer Chemistry, Polymer Physical Chemistry, Polymer Solution Physics, Solid Polymer Physics

Faculty of Veterinary Medicine (Freshmen Enrollment: 40)

Department of Veterinary Medicine

Comparative Pathology, Epizootiology, Laboratory Animal Science, Parasitology, Radiation Biology, Theriogenology, Veterinary Anatomy, Veterinary Biochemistry, Veterinary Hygiene and Microbiology, Veterinary Internal Medicine, Veterinary Pharmacology, Veterinary Physiology, Veterinary Public Health, Veterinary Surgery

Foreign Student Admission

Qualifications for Applicants

Standard Qualifications Requirement

1. Applicants must have Completed 12 years of education in foreign countries; or, be over 18 years old and hold the International Baccalaureát.

2. Applicants must take the Japanese Language Proficiency Test and the Standard Examination for Private Foreign Students.

Examination at the University

Applicants must take an entrance examination consisiting of a written exam and an interview.

Documents to be Submitted When Applying

Standard Documents Requirement

The following documents are also required.

1. Certificates of the Japanese Language Proficiency Test and the Standard Examination for Private Foreign Students.

2. A Certificate of Graduation from the Japanese language school the applicant attended.

Application forms are available at Forein Students Office in early December. All applicants are required to submit the specified application documents to Foreign Students Office in by January 31.

GRADUATE PROGRAMS

Graduate School of Agriculture (First Year Enrollment : Master's 81, Doctor's 41)
Divisions
Agricultural Biology, Agricultural Chemistry, Agricultural Economics, Agricultural Engineering, Agronomy, Animal Science, Forest Products, Forestry
Graduate School of Dentisty (First Year Enrollment : Doctor's 32)
Divisions
Basic Dentistry, Clinical Dentistry
Graduate School of Economics (First Year Enrollment : Master's 34, Doctor's 17)
Divisions
Business Administration, Economics
Graduate School of Education (First Year Enrollment : Master's 18, Doctor's 9)
Divisions
Education, Educational Systems
Graduate School of Engineering (First Year Enrollment : Master's 257, Doctor's 109)
Divisions
Applied Chemistry, Applied Physics, Architecture, Biomedical Engineering, Chemical Process Engineering, Civil Engineering, Electrical Engineering, Electronic Engineering, Information Engineering, Mechanical Engineering, Metallurgical Engineering, Mineral Resources Development Engineering, Nuclear Engineering, Precision Engineering, Sanitary Engineering
Graduate School of Environmental Science (First Year Enrollment : Master's 44, Doctor's 20)
Divisions
Environmental Conservation, Environmental Planning, Environmental Structure, Social Environment
Graduate School of Fisheries (First Year Enrollment : Master's 56, Doctor's 28)
Divisions
Biology and Aquaculture, Chemistry, Fishing Science, Food Science and Technology
Graduate School of Law (First Year Enrollment : Master's 38, Doctor's 18)
Divisions
Private Law, Public Law
Graduate School of Letters (First Year Enrollment : Master's 50, Doctor's 25)
Divisions
Asian History, Behaviral Scince, Chinese Literature, Eastern Philosophy, English and American Literature, German Literature, Japanese History, Japanese Literature, Linguistics, Philosophy, Western History
Graduate School of Medicine (First Year Enrollment : Doctor's 62)
Divisions
Internal Medicine, Pathology, Physiology, Social Medicine, Surgery
Graduate School of Pharmaceutical Sciences (First Year Enrollment : Master's 26, Doctor's 13)
Divisions
Pharmaceutical Chemistry, Pharmaceutical Sciences
Graduate School of Science (First Year Enrollment : Master's 117, Doctor's 66)
Divisions
Botany, Chemistry, Geology and Mineralogy, Geophysics, Mathematics, Physics, Polymer Science, Zoology
Graduate School of Veterinary Medicine (First Year Enrollment : Doctor's 13)
Divisions
Morphology-Function, Prophylaxis-Therapeutics

Foreign Student Admission
Qualifications for Applicants
Master's Program
Standard Qualifications Requirement
Doctor's Program
Standard Qualifications Requirement
Examination at the University
Master's Program
The dates and types of entrance examinations differ by division. The examination is usually given in September and/or in February or March. It consists of a written and oral exam plus an interview.
It is advisable for the applicant to enroll in this University or another university in Japan as a research student and then apply to the Graduate School of this University.
Doctor's Program
Same as Master's program.
Documents to be Submitted When Applying
Standard Documents Requirement
Application forms are available at the Graduate School Office. Applicants are required to submit the specified application documents to the Office.

*

Research Institutes and Centers
Center for Experimental Plants and Animals, Center for Information Processing Education, Center for Instrumental Analysis, Central Institute of Radioisotope Science, Institute of Immunological Science, Institute of Language and Culture Studies, Institute of Low Temperature Science, Research Institute for Catalysis, Research Institute of Applied Electricity, Slavic Research Center
Facilities/Services for Foreign Students
Foreign Students' House (Accommodation: 45 rooms, single, both sexes), Men's Dormitory (Accommodation: 40 rooms, single), Women's Dormitory (Accommodation: 15 rooms, single)
Special Programs for Foreign Students
The University offers courses in Japanese as a foreign language at the Institute of Language and Culture Studies. Students may take a course according to their specific needs. Classes are as follows: Elementary Japanese (6 months, Spring, Fall), Intermediate Japanese (6 months, Spring, Fall), Advanced Japanese (1 year, Spring, Fall)

For Further Information
Undergraduate and Graduate Admission
Foreign Students Office, International Affairs Section, Hokkaido University, Nishi 5, Kita 8, Kita-ku, Sapporo-shi, Hokkaido 060 ☎ 011–716–2111 ext. 2096, 3531

Hokkaido University of Education
(Hokkaido Kyoiku Daigaku)

1–3, Ainosato 5–3, Kita–ku, Sapporo–shi,
Hokkaido 002   ☎ 011–778–8811

Faculty
    Profs. 168   Assoc. Profs. 164
    Assist. Profs. Full–time 43; Part–time 394
    Res. Assocs. 31
Number of Students
    Undergrad. 5, 420   Grad. 6
Library 767, 009 volumes

Outline and Characteristics of the University

Hokkaido University of Education consists of five campuses, each located in a principal city of Hokkaido: Sapporo, Hakodate, Asahikawa, Kushiro, and Iwamizawa. In line with the postwar educational reforms, it was established as one of the national universities under the name of Hokkaido Gakugei Daigaku. This took place in May 1949, when Hokkaido First, Second, Third and Youth Normal Schools were restructured and promoted to the status of a higher level institution. The new Kushiro Campus was added at this time . Each of the four normal schools had long contributed to its own district and community in the field of teacher training, with several changes of names and organizations. Under the revision of the National School Establishment Law in 1966, the University changed its name to the present one, replacing the Faculty of Liberal Arts with the Faculty of Education.

The main objectives of the University are to conduct research and to educate students so that they may have the theoretical and practical understanding of the true meaning of education. Further, the University seeks to ensure that the students attain a comprehensive knowledge of the various fields, deep insights into human and social life, and professional capabilities for research in their own major subjects. The great majority of the graduates teach at schools of all levels from kindergarten to university, not only in Hokkaido but in other parts of Japan as well. Others work as education administrators.

The University offers training courses for those who wish to teach kindergarten, elementary school, junior high school , and schools for handicapped children. There are also courses for special subjects, and school nurses , Integrated arts and Sciences. It also has a one-year graduate study course in the fields of arts and crafts and education. Attached to the University are two kindergartens, four elementary schools, four junior high schools, a school for handicapped children, the Library, and the Educational Technology Research Center.

Hokkaido, which covers a fifth of the total area of Japan but makes up only five percent of its total population, is a land full of potential and energy in terms of the quality of life and the natural environment.

UNDERGRADUATE PROGRAMS

Asahikawa Campus
    Course for Elementary School Teachers
    Course for Junior High School Teachers
    Course for Kindergarten Teachers
    Course for School Nurses
Faculty of Education (Freshmen Enrollment 1, 330)
Hakodate Campus
    Course for Elementary School Teachers
    Course for Teachers of Schools for Handicapped Children
    Course of Integrated arts and Sciences
    Course for Junior High School Teachers
    Course for Kindergarten Teachers
I wamizawa Campus
    Course for Elementary School Teachers
Kushiro Campus
    Course for Elementary School Teachers
    Course for Junior High School Teachers
    Course for Kindergarten Teachers
Sapporo Campus
    Course for Teachers of Special Subjects: Arts and Crafts
    Course for Elementary School Teachers
    Course for Teachers of Schools for Handicapped Children
    Course for Junior High School Teachers
    Course for Teachers of Special Subjects: Music
    Course for School Nurses

Foreign Student Admission
    Qualifications for Applicants
        Standard Qualifications Requirement
    Examination at the University

No special entrance selection procedure is provided for foreign students. The selection is made on the basis of each applicant's results on the Joint First-Stage Achievement Test administered by the National Center for University Entrance Examination and the Second-Stage Examination given by the University, as well as the credentials of the student submitted by the upper secondary school, and other considerations.

An applicant who wants to be enrolled as an undergraduate research student to study a specific topic is required to have the scholastic attainments equivalent to at least two years of college education.

The applicant will be admitted, so far as educational circumstances permit.

Documents to be Submitted When Applying
Standard Documents Requirement

ONE-YEAR GRADUATE PROGRAMS

One-Year Graduate Study Course (Enrollment   15)
Hakodate Campus: Education
Sapporo Campus: Arts and Crafts, Education

Foreign Student Admission
Qualifications for Applicants
Standard Qualifications Requirement
Examination at the University
Entrants into the one-year graduate study course are selected on the basis of the results of the achievement test administered by the University, the health records, and interview. This procedure is applicable to both foreign and Japanese students.

Research Institutes and Centers
Educational Technology Research Center
For Further Information
Undergraduate Admission
School Affairs Division, Student Office , Hokkaido University of Education, 1–3, Ainosato 5–3, Kitaku, Sapporo–shi Hokkaido 002 ☎ 011–778–8811 ext. 254

Hyogo University of Teacher Education
(Hyogo Kyoiku Daigaku)

942-1 Shimokume, Yashiro-cho, Kato-gun, Hyogo
673-14   ☎ 0795–44–1101

Faculty
Profs.   70   Assoc. Profs.   71
Assist. Profs.   Full–time   4; Part–time   58
Res. Assocs.   21
Number of Students
Undergrad.   847   Grad.   503
Library   140, 180 volumes

Outline and Characteristics of the University
Taking into account the responsibility and humanity required of the teaching profession in this "age of education", it is particularly important that teachers be provided with a good educational background, a mastery of educational ideas and methods, and a deep understanding of the growth and development of human beings, as well as a sound professional knowledge of the various teaching subjects. In order to meet such social demands, Hyogo University of Teacher Education (Hyogo Kyoiku Daigaku) was founded on October 1, 1978.

The University offers both graduate and undergraduate programs. The former functions as "a university for practicing teachers" to enable them to pursue creative research in school education both in theory and practice, and as a center to enhance school education. The Undergraduate Program is designed to train students to become elementary-school teachers.

Within this concept the main objective of the Graduate School (Master Course in School Education) is to provide specialized professional knowledge, cultivate the ability for creative research in specified areas and also, from a wider point of view, develop the advanced skills necessary for a high-grade profession. About two-thirds of the graduate students admitted each year are in-service teachers who have at least three years of teaching experience. Since the first class of 1980, 1, 547 graduates of the School are now active in their local areas forming a nucleus for educational innovation. At any one time, about 500 graduate students from all parts of Japan, as well as some from abroad, are studying at the University.

Recognizing the importance of elementary education as the basis of human development, the University also provides undergraduate courses (Faculty of School Education). In this program the students are equipped with a broad perspective of the growth and development of children. Further, they are encouraged to familiarize themselves with the tasks of teachers by studying various subjects, undertaking teaching practice and observing school activities. The program started in 1982, and the number of students presently totals 847.

The University now plays a vital role as a center where members of the surrounding communities can enrich their cultural life. While it is conveniently located close to the large cities of Osaka and Kobe, the campus enjoys great scenic beauty, surrounded by green hills and woods.

UNDERGRADUATE PROGRAMS

Faculty of School Education (Freshmen Enrollment: 200)
Elementary School Teachers' Training Course
Early Childhood Education, School Education, School Subject Education (Fine Arts and Music, Language Education, Natural Sciences, Practical Life Studies, Social Sciences)

Foreign Student Admission
Qualifications for Applicants
Standard Qualifications Requirement
Examination at the University
All applicants must take the Joint First-Stage Achievement Test and the Faculty's Special Entrance Examination consisting of a short essay and aptitude tests for Fine Arts, Music, and Physical Education.
Documents to be Submitted When Applying
Standard Documents Requirement
Application forms are available at the Admis-

sions Office from early November prior to the year in which the examination is to be taken. All applicants are required to submit the specified application documents to the Admissions Office by the middle of January.

GRADUATE PROGRAMS

Graduate School of Education (First Year Enrollment : Master's 300)
Divisions
Early Childhood Education, Education for the Handicapped, School Education (Counseling and Guidance, Curriculum and Instruction, Educational Administration, Foundations of Education), School Subject Education (Fine Arts and Music, Language Studies, Natural Sciences, Practical Life Studies, Social Sciences)

Foreign Student Admission
Qualifications for Applicants
Master's Program
Standard Qualifications Requirement
Examination at the University
Master's Program
Applicants must take the entrance examination consisting of written and oral sections. Permission to register as a student of the Graduate School is given depending upon the results of the examination, the transcript from the applicant's previous university or college, and a satisfactory health certificate.
Documents to be Submitted When Applying
Standard Documents Requirement
Application forms are available at the Admissions Office from early June previous to the year in which entrance is sought. All applicants are required to submit the specified application documents to the Graduate Admissions Office by the end of July previous to the year in which entrance is sought.

*
Research Institutes and Centers
Center for Practical Skills Training, Center for School Education Research
For Further Information
Undergraduate and Graduate Admission
Admissions Office, Hyogo University of Teacher Education, 942-1 Shimokume, Yashiro-cho, Kato-gun, Hyogo 673-14 ☎ 0795–44–1101 ext. 261

Ibaraki University
(Ibaraki Daigaku)

2-1-1 Bunkyo, Mito-shi, Ibaraki 310
☎ 0292–26–1621

Faculty
Profs. 217   Assoc. Profs. 167
Assist. Profs. Full–time 31; Part–time 487
Res. Assocs. 69

Number of Students
Undergrad. 6, 300   Grad. 274
Library 620, 738 volumes

Outline and Characteristics of the University
In 1949, four eminent colleges, Mito College of Liberal Arts, Ibaraki Normal School, Ibaraki Normal School for Young Men, and Taga College of Technology, merged to form Ibaraki University consisting of the three faculties of Letters and Sciences, Education, and Technology. In 1952, the Faculty of Agriculture was added and in 1967, the University was reorganized into five Faculties (Agriculture, Education, Engineering, Letters and Social Science, Science) and the College of General Education. Graduate Courses (Master's) were established in the Faculties of Engineering, Agriculture, and Science in 1968, 1970, and, 1979 respectively. Since April 1, 1985 the Institution has participated as a collaborating school in starting the Union Graduate School for a Doctoral Course in Agricultural Science, Tokyo University of Agriculture and Technology.

The University is spread over three campuses in Ibaraki Prefecture. Three faculties and one college are on Mito Campus, only one hour and a half from Tokyo by train. Mito is an old city famous for its beautiful park, Kairakuen, and is a popular tourist center. It is very close to some of Japan's most attractive seaside and country resorts.

The Faculty of Engineering is located in Hitachi. Near the campus are the headquarters and many research centers of Hitachi Company, one of the biggest companies in Japan.

There is a very lively and spacious Ami Campus with the Faculty of Agriculture in Ami Town near the Lake of Kasumigaura an hour from Tokyo.

The University enrolls more than 6, 000 students and has more than 500 faculty members. The students are from every part of Japan.

UNDERGRADUATE PROGRAMS

Faculty of Agriculture (Freshmen Enrollment: 125)
Department of Agricultural Production
Agricultural and Environmental Engineering, Agricultural Economics and Management, Animal Production, Crop Production
Department of Resource Biology
Applied Biological Chemistry, Bio-technology, Sciences of Information Planning and Conservation of Resources
Faculty of Education (Freshmen Enrollment: 415)
Training Course for Elementary School Teachers
Training Course for Junior High School Teachers
Training Course for Teachers of Handicapped Children
Training Course for School Nurse Teachers
Agriculture, Algebra and Geometry, Analysis and Applied Mathematics, Art Education, Educational Health, Education for the Handicapped, Electrical

Engineering, English and American Literature, English Linguistics, Food Science, Health and Physical Education, Home Economics Education, Home Management, Instrumental Music, Mathematics Education, Mechanical Engineering, Metal Working, Music Education, Music Theory and History of Music, School Education, Science Education, Science of Clothing, Social Studies Education, Teaching of English, Teaching of Japanese, Technical Education, Vocal Music, Wood Working

Faculty of Engineering (Freshmen Enrollment: 405)

Department of Civil Engineering

Hydraulics and Environmental Engineering, Soil and Concrete Engineering, Structural Engineering, Transportation Engineering

Department of Electrical Engineering

Electrical Materials, Electric Machines and Instruments, Electric Power and Electrical Measurements, Fundamental Theories of Electrical Engineering

Department of Electronic Engineering

Applied Electronics, Basic Electronics, Electromagnetic System, Electronic Circuits

Department of Industrial Chemistry

Analytical Chemistry, Inorganic Chemistry, Organic Chemistry, Physical Chemistry

Department of Information Science

Foundation of Computer Science, Hardware, Software, System Engineering

Department of Mechanical Engineering

Fluid Dynamics, Heat Engine, Industrial Engineering, Mechanical Technology

Department of Mechanical Engineering II

Dynamics of Machines, Machine Design and Applied Mechanics, Manufacturing Technology, Thermal Engineering

Department of Metallurgy

Extraction Metallurgy, Ferrous Metallurgy, Mechanical Metallurgy, Metallic Materials, Non-ferrous Metallurgy, Physical Metallurgy, Physics of Metals and Physical Metallurgy, Process Metallurgy and Synthetic Materials

Department of Precision Engineering

Foundation and Design of Precision Engineering, Precision Instruments and Measurement , Precision Machining and Materials, Systems and Control

Faculty of Humanities (Freshmen Enrollment: 375)

Department of Humanities

Chinese Linguistics and Literature, English Linguistics and Literature, European History, French Linguistics and Literature, German Linguistics and Literature, International Relations, Japanese History, Japanese Literature, Oriental History, Philosophy, Psychology

Department of Social Science

Accounting, Administrative Law, Business Management, Civil Law, Commercial Law, Constitutional Law, Criminal Law, Economic History, Economic Policy, Economic Theory, Labor Law, Money and Banking, Political Science, Public Finance, Regional Study, Sociology

Faculty of Science (Freshmen Enrollment: 185)

Department of Biology

Cell Biology, Ecology, Physiology, Systematics

Department of Chemistry

Analytical Chemistry, Coordination Chemistry, Quantum Chemistry, Structural Chemistry, Synthetic Chemistry

Department of Earth Sciences

Earth and Planetary Physics, Geochemistry, Geology, Petrology and Mineralogy

Department of Mathematics

Algebra, Analysis, Applied Mathematics, Geometry

Department of Physics

Astrophysics, Atomic Physics, Solid-State Physics, Theoretical High Energy Physics

Foreign Student Admission

Qualifications for Applicants

Standard Qualifications Requirement

Examination at the University

Applicants must take the Japanese Language Proficiency Test and General Examination for Foreign Students. Each Faculty gives a special entrance examination consisting of a written test and/or an interview.

Documents to be Submitted When Applying

Standard Documents Requirement

Following documents are also required.

1. Letter of identification or recommendation by the applicant's government
2. Copies of the records of General Examination for Foreign Students and the Japanese Language Proficiency Test

Application forms are available at the Admissions Office from early October. All applicants are required to submit the documents described above to the Admissions Office by February 7.

Qualifications for Transfer Students

1. Graduate of a two-year college, or
2. Person who stayed not less than one year as a regular student at a four-year university.

Since those under above conditions are not necessarily admitted as transfer students, applicants are advised to make inquiries and submit their curriculum vitae.

Examination for Transfer Students

Applicants must undergo an examination and an interview.

Since subjects to be examined vary among faculties, applicants are advised to obtain and consult guidelines for enrollment of this university.

Documents to be Submitted When Applying

Standard Documents Requirement

Letter of identification or recommendation by the applicant's Government is also required.

Application forms are available at the Admissions Office from early June. Not all faculties (departments) admit transfer students. Applicants who wish to transfer are advised to make inquiries beforehand.

ONE-YEAR GRADUATE PROGRAMS

One-Year Graduate Course in Humanities (Enrollment: 10)
Humanities
One-Year Graduate Course in Education (Enrollment: 5)
Education
Special Course for Teachers of Handicapped Children (Enrollment: 30)
Education of Handicapped Children

Foreign Student Admission
Qualifications for Applicants
The applicant is required to have (or have the prospect of having within the academic year of application) a teacher's license of either elementary school, junior high school, senior high school, or kindergarten and meet one of the following requirements: (1) have graduated (or have the prospect of graduate within the academic year of the application) from a four-year university , (2) have completed 16 years of education abroad. One who does not fall under any of the categories above can apply for the course provided that he/she has a first-grade teacher's license of either elementary school, junior high school, or kindergarten or a teacher's license of senior high school.
Qualifications for applicants to Special Course for Teachers of Handicapped Children different from those of other courses.
Examination at the University
Applicants must undergo an examination and an interview.
Since subjects to be examined and test dates vary among graduate courses, applicants are advised to obtain and consult guidelines for enrollment.

GRADUATE PROGRAMS

Graduate School of Agriculture (First Year Enrollment : Master's 40, Doctor's 18)
Divisions
Agricultural Chemistry, Agricultural Engineering, Agriculture, Animal Science
Graduate School of Education (First Year Enrollment: Master's 25)
Divisions
Art Education, Education for the Handicapped, Health and Physical Education, School Education, Science Education, Social Studies Education, Teaching of Japanese
Graduate School of Engineering (First Year Enrollment : Master's 66)
Divisions
Civil Engineering, Information Science, Electrical Engineering, Electronic Engineering, Industrial Chemistry, Mechanical Engineering, Metallurgy, Precision Engineering
Graduate School of Science (First Year Enrollment : Master's 34)
Divisions
Biology, Chemistry, Earth Science, Mathematics, Physics

Foreign Student Admission
Qualifications for Applicants
Master's Program
Standard Qualifications Requirement
Examination at the University
Master's Program
Each Graduate School gives a special entrance examination consisting of a written test and/or an interview.
Documents to be Submitted When Applying
Standard Documents Requirement
A letter of identification or recommendation by the applicant's government is also required.
Application forms are available at the Admissions Office from late June. All applicants are required to submit the documents to the Admissions Office by the date specified by each graduate school. Since this deadline and the date for entrance examination vary among graduate schools, applicants are advised to obtain the guidelines for enrollment or consult the Office well in advance.

*

Research Institutes and Centers
Center for Educational Technology, Experimental Farm, Hydrobiological Station, Information Processing Center
Facilities/Services for Foreign Students
There is no special dormitory for foreign students. However, foreign students are allowed to live in ordinary dormitories. The university also provides assistance to foreign students in finding suitable off-campus housing.
There is a student health center on the Mito campus, where two full-time doctors advise students about their health.
There are a number of activities in the private sector, such as home stay and a friendship party, near the campuses. Foreign students may join these activities if they wish.
Special Programs for Foreign Students
Japanese Language and Japanese Studies Courses are offered for foreign students at the College of Liberal Arts.
For Further Information
Undergraduate Admission
Admissions Section, Ibaraki University, 2-1-1 Bunkyo, Mito-shi, Ibaraki 310 ☎0292-26-1621 ext. 253

Iwate University
(Iwate Daigaku)

3-18-8 Ueda, Morioka-shi, Iwate 020
☎ 0196–23–5171

Faculty
    Profs. 160   Assoc. Profs. 161
    Assist. Profs. Full–time 45; Part–time 205
    Res. Assocs. 58
Number of Students
    Undergrad. 5, 224   Grad. 231
Library 564, 084 volumes

Outline and Characteristics of the University

Iwate University was established on May 31, 1949 as a new-system university with the faculties of Agriculture, Engineering, and Liberal Arts by combining the Morioka Agricultural and Forestry College, the Morioka Technical College, the Iwate Normal School, and the Iwate Normal School for Youth when the National School Establishment Law came into force as a result of the postwar educational reform.

Since then the university has been incessantly ameliorated to attain its present-day scale replete with the Faculty of Agriculture, the Faculty of Engineering, the Faculty of Education, and the College of Liberal Arts and Social Sciences as well as the Graduate Schools for the Master's degree in Agriculture and Engineering. There are also a one-year course of advanced studies in Pedagogy and Special Education (Handicapped) for non-degree students of graduate level and a special course in Farming and Dairy Farming for intellectual young farmers who could not afford to pursue conventional undergraduate studies.

The Faculty of Agriculture has two experimental farms, two experimental forests, a veterinary hospital, Laboratory for Cell Biology and a botanical garden. The Center for Educational Technology, an elementary school, a junior high school, a school for the handicapped, and a kindergarten are affiliated with the Faculty of Education.

Iwate is now making tremendous progress as a bridgehead for the future development of Northern Japan through the revolutionary changes of high-speed mass transport systems, such as the bullet train of the Tohoku new stem-line inaugurated into regular service in 1982, the Tohoku superhighway expanding northward now at the Towada National Park, and the jetliner which entered service at the Hanamaki Airport in 1983. In fact, many industries including high-tech enterprises in electronics are moving to seek favorable locations in this prefecture .

On our campus, academic counselling is slways available through daily intercourse between teaching staff and students. An intimate relationship is promoted as a favorable environment as manifested in the teacher-to-student ratio of 1/10. Particulatly, students are allowed to use up-to-date facilities for learning and experiments in close partnership with the professor in charge of the laboratory. They are most helpful to students in advising in and out of the classroom, going as far as opening a ski school or a camp for ski training in winter.

Upon entering the front gate of Iwate University, you will most likely be surprised to find a clear stream drawn off the Takamatsu-pond which is famous for its scenic beauty especially with cherry blossoms in spring, running through the median strip of principal road. We have also a beautiful spray pond in the Botanical Garden, where red carps reflect the sunlight through the rippling water. Students can rest by a flock of sheep grazing on grass under lofty poplars.

One can see the austere shape of Mt. Iwate (Rocky-hand) as well as the graceful figure of Mt. Himekami (Young goddess) from the campus, " The whole campus strikes us as a wilderness park with woods and apple orchards around it where one often sees squirrels playing. It takes, however, only ten minutes to go downtown on foot. You will be able to enjoy a sense of fulfilment as a student, guaranteed by the best possible environment one can imagine in Northern Japan.

UNDERGRADUATE PROGRAMS

Faculty of Agriculture (Freshmen Enrollment: 210)
   Department of Agricultural Chemistry
Applied Microbiology, Biochemistry, Food Science of Agricultural Products, Nutritional Biochemistry, Plant Nutrition, Soil Science
   Department of Agricultural Engineering
Agricultural Construction Engineering, Agricultural Hydrotechnics, Agricultural Systems Engineering, Farm Land Reclamation Engineering, Land Improvement, Land Planning
   Department of Agricultural Machinery
Agricultural Environmental Engineering, Agricultural Process Engineering, Farm Land Reclamation Machinery, Farm Machinery
   Department of Agronomy
Agricultural Economics, Applied Entomology, Crop Science, Olericulture and Floriculture, Plant Breeding, Plant Pathology, Pomology
   Department of Animal Husbandry
Animal Breeding, Animal Nutrition and Management, Animal Reproduction, Feed, Grassland Improvement
   Department of Forestry
Erosion Control Engineering, Forest Management, Forest Operations and Techniques, Forest Policy, Silviculture, Wood Chemistry, Wood Technology
   Department of Veterinary Medicine
Veterinary Anatomy, Veterinary Internal Medicine, Veterinary Microbiology, Veterinary Parasitology,

Veterinary Pathology and Parasitology, Veterinary Pharmacology, Veterinary Physiology, Veterinary Public Health, Veterinary Surgery

Faculty of Education (Freshmen Enrollment: 350)
Department of Arts and Crafts Education
Department of Elementary Education
Department of Secondary Education
Department of Special Education
Agriculture, Algebra and Geometry, Analysis and Applied Mathematics, Biology, Calligraphy, Chemistry, Child Nursing, Chinese Classics, Composition of Music, Design, Developmental Psychology, Dietetics, Dyeing and Weaving, Earth Science, Economics, Educational Institutions, Educational Psychology, Educational Sociology, Education of the Handicapped, Electricity, English and American Literature, English Linguistics, Ethics, European Painting, Geography, Health Education, History, History of Education, Home Making, Home Management, Instrumental Music, Japanese Language, Japanese Literature, Japanese Painting, Mechanics, Metal Working, Method of Education, Musicology and History of Music, Oriental Painting, Pathology of the Handicapped, Pedagogy, Philosophy, Photography, Physical Exercise, Physics, Physiology and Hygiene, Political Science, Psychology of the Handicapped, Science of Clothing, Sculpture, Sociology, Teaching of Arts and Crafts, Teaching of English, Teaching of Japanese, Teaching of Mathematics, Teaching of Music, Teaching of Physical Education, Teaching of Science, Teaching of Social Studies, Teaching of Technology, Theory and History of Fine Arts, Theory and History of Physical Education, Vocal Music, Vocational Guidance, Wood Working

Faculty of Engineering (Freshmen Enrollment: 430)
Department of Applied Chemistry
Chemical Engineering, Industrial Inorganic Chemistry, Polymer Chemistry and Technology, Synthetic Organic Chemistry and Technology
Department of Civil Engineering
Hydraulic Engineering and Construction Materials, Planning in Civil Engineering, Sanitary Engineering, Structural Mechanics and Traffic Engineering
Department of Computer Science
Applied Computer Science, Computer Machinery, Computer Systems and Networks, Fundamentals of Computer Science
Department of Electrical Engineering
Basic Electricity, Electrical Communication Engineering, Electrical Power Application Engineering, Electrical Power Engineering
Department of Electronic Engineering
Applied Electronics, Electronic Materials and Measurements, Electron Tubes and Electronic Circuits, Fundamentals of Electronics
Department of Mathematics and General Natural Sciences
Analytical Chemistry, General Mechanical Engineering Mathematics, Mathematical Information Science, Physics

Department of Mechanical Engineering
Applied Mechanics, Fluid Engineering, Manufacturing Technology, Thermal Engineering
Department of Mechanical Engineering II
Designing of Machine Elements, Heat Power Engineering, Instrumentation and Control Engineering, Precision Engineering
Department of Metallurgical Engineering
Ferrous Metallurgy, Metallic Materials, Metallography, Nonferrous Metallurgy
Department of Mineral Development Engineering
Excavation Engineering, Geological Engineering, Mineral Engineering, Mineral Processing and Water Treatment
Department of Resource Chemistry
Applied Physical Chemistry, Chemical Reaction Engineering, Inorganic Resource Chemistry, Organic Resource Chemistry

College of Humanities and Social Sciences (Freshmen Enrollment: 210)
Department of Humanities and Social Sciences
Area Studies (Foundations in Area Studies, Occidental Studies, Oriental Studies), English, French, German, Philosophy of Science, Physical Education, Science, Social Sciences (Behavioral Science, Economics, Law)

Foreign Student Admission
Qualifications for Applicants
Standard Qualifications Requirement
Examination at the University
The process of screening is composed of the Joint First-Stage Achievement Test, (Second-Stage) Entrance Examination, General Examination for Foreign students, and the Japanese Language Proficiency Test. Tests required for each faculty or college other than the second-stage examination by the University are as follows.
Faculty of Agriculture: General Examination for Foreign Students and the Japanese Language Proficiency Test; Faculty of Engineering: General Examination for Foreign Students and the Japanese Language Proficiency Test (both referential); Faculty of Education: Joint First-Stage Achievement Test and General Examination for Foreign Students (the latter referential); College of Humanities and Social Sciences: General Examination for Foreign Students and the Japanese Language Proficiency Test.
Besides the Joint First-Stage Achievement Test, the University gives its own entrance examination on March 4 and 5. Foreign applicants seeking admission as regular students must take the examinations on an equal basis with Japanese applicants.
Documents to be Submitted When Applying
Standard Documents Requirement

ONE-YEAR GRADUATE PROGRAMS

Advanced Program in Pedagogy (Enrollment 10)
Arts and Crafts Education, Curriculum and Teaching

Special Advanced Program in Education of the Handicapped (Enrollment 30)
Education of the Mentally Handicapped

Foreign Student Admission
  Qualifications for Applicants
    Standard Qualifications Requirement
  Examination at the University
    The examination is usually held in either January or February of each year.

GRADUATE PROGRAMS

Graduate School of Agriculture (First Year Enrollment : Master's 96)
  Divisions
Agricultural Chemistry, Agricultural Engineering, Agricultural Machinery, Agronomy, Animal Husbandry, Forestry, Veterinary Medicine
Graduate School of Engineering (First Year Enrollment : Master's 72)
  Divisions
Applied Chemistry, Civil Engineering, Computer Science, Electrical Engineering, Electronic Engineering, Mechanical Engineering, Mechanical Engineering II, Metallurgical Engineering, Mineral Development Engineering, Resource Chemistry

Foreign Student Admission
  Qualifications for Applicants
Master's Program
    Standard Qualifications Requirement
  Examination at the University
Master's Program
    The entrance examination is usually given in the autumn previous to the school year of admission. If the students seats are not completely filled, additional applications will be accepted in January or February of the year of admission. Further information about the examinations can be obtained directly from the Student Services Section of the university.
    Applicants must take the same entrance examination conisisting of a written exam and an interview given to Japanese students.
  Documents to be Submitted When Applying
    Standard Documents Requirement
*

Research Institutes and Centers
Botanical Garden, Center for Information Processing, Cryogenic Laboratory, Electron Microscope Room, Environment Control Center, Experimental Farm, Experimental Forest, Laboratory for Cell Biology, Mass Spectrometer Laboratory, Memorial Hall of Agriculture, Natural Energy Greenhouse, Nuclear Magnetic Resonance Analysis Laboratory, Radioisotope Laboratory, Veterinary Hospital
Facilities/Services for Foreign Students
    Foreign students generally rent a room in town, either singly or with other students, at a minimum of about ¥25, 000 a month. It should be noted that the housing situation in Japan is tight, and foreign students must find suitable accommodations by themselves, although the Student Welfare Section of the university will be glad to cooperate. A suggested minimum monthly budget for living in Morioka is about ¥70, 000 to ¥100, 000.
    The university is always open to complaints from foreign student whenever he or she is in trouble. As a regular event, the Seminar for Cultural Exchange for foreign students is held once or twice a year, and this always includes a bus trip to a major industry and a famous sight of Japan.
Special Programs for Foreign Students
    In order to reinforce Japanese language skills, foreign students are allowed to take any of the Japanese classes among the modern language subjects in the general education program.
For Further Information
  Undergraduate and Graduate Admission
Student Division, Iwate University, 3-18-8 Ueda, Morioka-shi, Iwate 020 ☎ 0196–23–5171 ext. 2241

Joetsu University of Education
(Joetsu Kyoiku Daigaku)
1 Yamayashiki-machi, Joetsu-shi, Niigata 943
☎ 0255–22–2411

Faculty
  Profs. 56   Assoc. Profs. 74
  Assist. Profs. Full–time 17; Part–time 29
  Res. Assocs. 23
Number of Students
  Undergrad. 818   Grad. 390
Library 94, 657 volumes

Outline and Characteristics of the University
    Joetsu University of Education was founded in 1978 by the Japanese Government with the following in mind: promoting educational research, both theoretical and practical, into the problems of school education, and meeting the needs of society for school teachers who are highly competent and qualified for the profession.
    The University is composed of undergraduate and graduate divisions. The College of School Education, with its teacher training program for elementary education, aims to develop well-qualified school teachers who have a thorough knowledge of child development. In view of the importance of training teachers who are engaged in elementary education, which lays the foundation for human growth, some innovations have been made both in curriculum and method of training, such as emphasizing personality development of trainees, and extending practice hours for student teachers.
    The Graduate School of School Education (master's degree program), along with conducting scientific research on practical problems of elementary

and secondary education, intends to provide graduate students who are teachers in elementary and secondary schools with opportunities for higher learning and study towards their in-service growth in theoretical knowledge and practical application.

The campus is located at the foot of a gently-sloping hill to the south-east of Mt. Kasuga, a famous historic site in Joetsu, a city in the western part of Niigata prefecture. The campus area of about 356, 000m² is covered with rich greenery and provides us with surroundings favorable to education and research.

UNDERGRADUATE PROGRAMS

Faculty of School Education (Freshmen Enrollment: 200)
Teacher Education Program for Elementary Education

Foreign Student Admission
Qualifications for Applicants
At the present time no specific regulations have been established for foreign student admission. Foreign student applications are evaluated using the same criteria as those for Japanese students.

In addition to regular students, the University admits a limited number of research students from abroad, who are to study problems in their specialized field under the guidance of their professors. In this case, too, they are classified as research students in the same way as Japanese students. Applicants for admission as foreign research students to the College of Education are required to have a Bachelor's degree or equivalent.

Examination at the University
The applicants for admission as research students from abroad have to pass the examinations on their research papers, reports or results of their academic achievements, and their Japanese language proficiency.

GRADUATE PROGRAMS

Graduate School of School Education (First Year Enrollment : Master's 300)
Divisions
Early Childhood Education, Education in Schools (Foundations, Guidance and Moral Education, Method and Evaluation, Organization and Administration), Education of School Subjects (Art Education, Home Economics Education, Industrial Education, Language Education, Music Education, Physical Education, Science Education, Social Studies Education), Special Education

Foreign Student Admission
Qualifications for Applicants
Master's Program
Applicants are required to have a Master's de-

gree or equivalent.

*

Research Institutes and Centers
Center for Educational Research and Development, Center for Skills Training in Arts, Physical Education and Languages, attached to the College of Education

For Further Information
Undergraduate and Graduate Admission
Research-Cooperative Sub-section, Section of Academic Affairs, Joetsu University of Education, 1 Yamayashiki-machi, Joetsu-shi, Niigata 943 ☎ 0255–22–2411 ext. 277

Kagawa Medical School
(Kagawa Ika Daigaku)
1750-1 Ikenobe-oaza, Miki-cho, Kita-gun, Kagawa 761-07 ☎ 0878–98–5111

Faculty
Profs. 38   Assoc. Profs. 35
Assist. Profs. Full–time 38; Part–time 180
Res. Assocs. 121
Number of Students
Undergrad. 641   Grad. 87
Library 73, 206 volumes

Outline and Characteristics of the School
Kagawa Medical School was founded on October 1, 1978 by the Japanese government and opened its doors to 100 students in April, 1980. The Hospital attached to the School started admitting patients in October 1983, and other educational facilities were completed in 1985. The Graduate School of Medicine was established in 1986, and enrolled 29 students its first year. The School works always to keep pace with the times and to attract distinguished scholars and researchers from all over the country.

The campus is located on a low hill to the southeast of Takamatsu City. The central part of the city and the Seto Inland Sea can be seen in the distance from the campus, which is surrounded by beautiful ponds and verdant scenery rich with bird and insect life. The weather is mild throughout the year. The location of the campus itself presents a quiet and favorable environment for education and research.

The School's underlying principle is to establish a unique school of medicine in which medicine and its service are to be conducted through deeper consideration about their effects upon humanity. At the same time, medicine should correspond to developments in the larger community and render services to the improvement of local medicine as well as to the progress of medicine at large which will eventually contribute to the welfare of mankind.

Some Characteristics of Curricula:
1. General Education
Special emphasis is placed on:

(1) physical education in order to build up physical strength; (2) art education, such as painting and music, in order to cultivate artistic sensitivity; (3) human and social sciences lectures in order to promote social awareness. These courses furnish the humanitarian basis necessary for doctors who must have a broad knowledge of human nature.

2. Specialized Education

The department of endocrinology is unique in this country. The maternal and children's medical center integrating perinatogynecology with pediatric surgery is unusual and distinguished.

3. Graduate School Education

Graduate education develops graduate students' faculties for original research work in medical sciences and helps them mature in order to contribute to the progress of medical sciences.

4. The Medical School Hospital

The medical and surgical outpatient clinics provide practical primary-care medical training for students during their clinical year and for doctors during their clinical training. Anesthesiology and emergency medicine, and medical systems management with reference to primary care medicine are also distinguished units. A system of on-call night service has also been instituted. It aims at developing the spirit of autonomy, independence and cooperation through actual practice in the emergency department and the delivery room and develops an awareness that medicine is a 24-hour profession.

UNDERGRADUATE PROGRAMS

Faculty of Medicine (Freshmen Enrollment: 100)
Department of Medicine
Anatomy, Anestheology and Emergency Medicine, Biochemistry, Dermatology, Endocrinology, Forensic Medicine, Hygiene, Immunology Pharmacology, Internal Medicine, Medical Systems Management, Medical Zoology, Microbiology, Neuropsychiatry, Neurosurgery, Obstetrics and Gynecology, Ophthalmology, Orthopedics, Otorhinolaryngology, Pathology, Pediatrics, Pediatrics, Pediatric Surgery, Perinatology, Physiology, Plastic Surgery, Public Health, Radiology, Surgery, Urology

Foreign Student Admission
Qualifications for Applicants
Standard Qualifications Requirement
Applicants must also take the Joint First-Stage Achievement Test.
Documents to be Submitted When Applying
Standard Documents Requirement
Application forms are available at the Admissions Office early in December.
All applicants are required to submit the specified application documents to the Admissions Office by mail, between January 12 and 19.

GRADUATE PROGRAMS

Graduate School of Medicine (First Year Enrollment : 30)
Courses
Bio-Regulation, Ecology & Environment, Morphology & Cellular Function

Foreign Student Admission
Qualifications for Applicants
Doctor's Program
Standard Qualifications Requirement
Applicants must be graduates from medical or dental schools.
Examination at the School
(1) Foreign language test and oral examination.
a. Written examination in a foreign language (English, German, French)
b. oral examination of specialized subjects in medicine.
(2) Physical Examination

*

Research Institutes and Centers
Medical School Hospital, Research Equipment Center, R I Research Center, Experimental Animal Center
For Further Information
Undergraduate and Graduate Admission
Students Division, Department of School Affairs, Kagawa Medical School, 1750-1 Ikenobe, Miki-cho, Kita-gun, Kagawa 761-07 ☎ 0878-98-5111 ext. 2240

Kagawa University
(Kagawa Daigaku)

1-1 Saiwai-cho, Takamatsu-shi, Kagawa 760
☎ 0878-61-4141

Faculty
Profs. 160   Assoc. Profs. 121
Assist. Profs. Full-time 9; Part-time 163
Res. Assocs. 36
Number of Students
Undergrad. 4, 168   Grad. 54
Library 555, 109 volumes

Outline and Characteristics of the University

Kagawa University was founded in 1949 by the Japanese Government. At the time of its establishment the University consisted of two faculties: the Faculty of Liberal Arts and the Faculty of Economics. The former had developed from Kagawa Normal School and Kagawa Normal School for youths, and the latter from Takamatsu Higher School of Commerce, which was later renamed Takamatsu College of Economics. In 1955, Kagawa Prefectural College of Agriculture was transferred to the University and was added as the Faculty of Agriculture. The most recent addition was the Faculty of Law in 1981. In the meantime, the Faculty of Liberal Arts was renamed the Faculty of Education in 1966. The Graduate School of Agriculture (Master's Program) was added in 1968, the Graduate School of Economics (Master's Program) in 1979, the Graduate School of Law (Master's Program), and the United Graduate School of Agricultural Sciences (Doctor's Program) in 1985.

The campuses of the three faculties–Education, Law, and Economics–are conveniently situated in the center of the city of Takamatsu. The city of Takamatsu (population 320,000), often called the gateway to Shikoku Island, is situated very close to the great industrial and commercial areas of Osaka and Kobe. It is a very important port town with a long history of local culture, commerce, and tourism. The campus of the Faculty of Agriculture is in the countryside about ten kilometers away from the Takamatsu campus and is appropriately surrounded by a wide stretch of open fields and pastoral tranquility.

The city of Takamatsu and the surrounding areas in which the University is located are especially favored by natural beauty, mild climate, an abundance and variety of agricultural products. They are also free from natural disasters. This environment makes the life of students as well as that of its citizens extremely comfortable.

Being small in size, the University has the advantage of encouraging friendly relation between teachers and students. Among other important aspects of the University is the fact that it has always been on good terms with the local communities and has contributed to their cultural, educational, economic, and manufacturing activities.

UNDERGRADUATE PROGRAMS

Faculty of Agriculture (Freshmen Enrollment: 190)
Department of Agricultural Engineering
Agricultural Civil EngineeringAquatic Environment Engineering, Construction Material Engineering, Irrigation and Drainage Engineering, Irrigation Facility Engineering, Land Conservation Engineering, Land Reclamation Engineering, Oceanographical and Fisheries Engineering, Rural Regional Planning, Soil and Foundation Engineering, Structural Engineering, Water Conservation Engineering
Department of Agroindustrial Science
Agroecosystem ManagementAgricultural Marketing, Agrometeorology, Animal Husbandry, Applied Entomology, Controlled-environment Horticulture, Crop Science, Ecological Plant Protection, Environmental Ecology, Environment Control in Agricultural Structures, Farm Management, Feed Resources, Fruit Crops, Genetic Resources and Manipulation, Landscape Architecture, Ornamental Crops, Plant Breeding, Plant Pathology, Postharvest Horticulture, Seed and Nursery Production, Vegetable Crops
Department of Bioresource Science
Bioresource ChemistryApplied Enzyme Chemis-

try, Applied Microbial Genetics, Applied Microbiology, Biochemistry, Cell Technology, Chemistry of Agricultural Resources, Chemistry of Animal Resources, Chemistry of Marine Natural Resources, Food Chemistry, Food Hygiene, Food Physics, Food Processing and Preservation, Forest Products Chemistry, Marine Biochemistry, Marine Chemistry, Microbial Physiology, Nutritional Biochemistry, Phytochemistry, Plant Biochemistry, Plant Cell Physiology and Technology, Plant Nutritional Chemistry, Soil Science

Faculty of Economics (Freshmen Enrollment: 380)
Department of Business Administration
Accounting, Bookkeeping, Business and Society, Commodity Science, Economic Geography, General Theory of Business and Administration, Industrial Relations and Human Resources Management, Management and Organization Theory, Managerial Accounting, Marketing, Transportation and Insurance
Department of Economics
Economic History, Economic Policy, International Economics, Mathematical Economics, Money and Banking, Principles of Economics, Principles of Political Economy, Public Finance, Social Policy, Statistics
Department of Information Science
Applied Mathematics and Statistics, Economic Data Analysis, Information Processing, Information Science, Management Science

Faculty of Education (Freshmen Enrollment: 290)
Department of Elementary School Teacher Training
Department of Kindergarten Teacher Training
Department of Secondary School Teacher Training
Department of School Teacher Training for Special Education
Educational Studies (Educational Psychology and Pedagogy), English Linguistics and Literature, Fine Arts, Health and Physical Education, Home Economics, Industrial Arts, Japanese Linguistics and Literature, Mathematics, Music, Natural Sciences, Social Sciences
Department of Integrated Arts and Sciences
Basic Sciences, Human Culture, Information & Computer Science, Language

Faculty of Law (Freshmen Enrollment: 200)
Department of Law
Enterprise and Judicial Affairs Course
Judicial Administrative Course
Administrative Law, Administrative Science, Anti-Trust Law, Civil Law, Civil Procedure, Commercial Law, Company Law, Comparative Constitutional Law, Contracts Law, Criminal Law, Criminal Procedure, Criminology, Economic Law, English Legal History, Execution Law, Family Law, Foreign Law, Industrial Law, Insurance and Maritime Law, International Law, International Trade Law, Labor Law, Negotiable Instrument Law, Patent and Copyright Law, Philosophy of Law, Political History, Political Science, Private International Law, Socialist Law,

Social Law, Social Security Law

Foreign Student Admission
Qualifications for Applicants
Standard Qualifications Requirement
Examination at the University
Faculty of Agriculture: Applicants will be selected on the basis of the results of the science subjects in the General Examination for Foreign Students and the Japanese Language Proficiency Test. In addition, applicants must take the oral examination.
Faculty of Economics: Applicants are to be selected on the basis of the results of the General Examination for Foreign Students in all subjects and the Japanese Language Proficiency Test. In addition, applicants must take the oral examination.
Faculty of Education: Applicants are required to take the Japanese Language Proficiency Test and the oral examination. The results of the General Examination for Foreign Students, if taken, are used for reference.
Faculty of Law: No entrance requirements are prescribed and admission will be considered on a case-by-case basis.
Documents to be Submitted When Applying
Standard Documents Requirement
A document which attests to the applicant's ability to pay tuition and other necessary expenses is also required.
Application Period: January 12 to January 19.
Date of Oral Examination: Beginning March 5
Announcement of Successful Applicants: March 18.

ONE-YEAR GRADUATE PROGRAMS

One-Year Graduate Course of Education (Enrollment: 10)
Education, Natural Sciences
One-Year Graduate Course of Special Education (Enrollment: 30)
Education for the Mentally Handicapped

Foreign Student Admission
Qualifications for Applicants
Standard Qualifications Requirement
In addition, applicants for admission to the Course of Special Education must have a teaching certificate for elementary/lower secondary/upper secondary school or for kindergarten.
Examination at the University
Applicants must follow the same procedure as Japanese applicants and take a written examination, undergo an interview and have a medical examination.

GRADUATE PROGRAMS

United Graduate School of Agricultural Sci- ences (First Year Enrollment: Doctor's 16)
Divisions
Applied Bioresource Science, Bioresource Production Science, Life Environment Conservation Science
Graduate School of Agriculture (First Year Enrollment : Master's 58)
Divisions
Agricultural Chemistry, Agricultural Engineering, Agronomy, Food Science, Horticulture
Graduate School of Economics (First Year Enrollment : Master's 20)
Division
Economics
Graduate School of Law (First Year Enrollment : Master's 8)
Division
Law

Foreign Student Admission
Qualifications for Applicants
Master's Program
Standard Qualifications Requirement
Examination at the University
Master's Program
Applicants must follow the same procedure as Japanese applicants by taking a written examination, and undergoing an interview.
Doctor's Program
The entrance examinations are to be administered in late October. The successful applicants will be announced and individually notified. In the event that the number of successful applicants falls short of the prescribed number, additional applications will be invited, and application forms will be made available in early December.
Documents to be Submitted When Applying
Standard Documents Requirement
Application forms and other relevant forms are available at the Admissions Office of each Graduate School from early July (for the Graduate School of Agriculture and the United Graduate School of Agricultural Sciences) or from late July (for the Graduate Schools of Economics and of Law).
All the application documents must be submitted to the Admissions Office of each Graduate School by a specified date in September. The entrance examinations will be administered in late September and the successful applicants will be announced and individually notified in early October.

*
Special Programs For Foreign Students
Japanese language classes are offered at the College of General Education. The purpose of the classes is to help foreign students acquire language skill for daily communication and research activiites.
Courses are offered at three levels: Elementary 1, 2 Intermediate 3, 4 Advanced 5, 6. A Special lecture class on Japanese culture is also offered.
Classes are open to all foreign students (undergraduate, graduate and research students). Under-

graduate students can claim credits given in Japanese language classes in order to be officialy admitted.

Research Institutes and Centers

Center for Educational Research and Training attached to the Faculty of Education, Computation Center, Marine Environment Research Laboratory attached to the Faculty of Agriculture, University Extension Center, University Farm attached to the Faculty of Agriculture, University Library

For Further Information

Undergraduate Admission

Faculty of Education: Admissions Office, Faculty of Education, Kagawa University, 1-1 Saiwai-cho, Takamatsu-shi, Kagawa 760 ☎ 0878-61-4141 ext. 239

Undergraduate and Graduate Admission

Agriculture: Admissions Office, Faculty of Agriculture, Kagawa University, 2393 Ikenobe, Miki-cho, Kita-gun, Kagawa 761-07 ☎ 0878-98-1411 ext. 206

Law and Economics: Admissions Office, Faculties of Law and Economics, Kagawa University, 2-1 Saiwai-cho, Takamatsu-shi, Kagawa 760 ☎ 0878-61-4141 ext. 249

Kagoshima University
(Kagoshima Daigaku)

1-21-24 Korimoto, Kagoshima-shi, Kagoshima 890
☎ 0992-54-7141

Faculty
  Profs. 288   Assoc. Profs. 255
  Assist. Profs. Full-time 101; Part-time 546
  Res. Assocs. 324
Number of Students
  Undergrad. 8, 572   Grad. 444
Library 914, 238 volumes

Outline and Characteristics of the University

Kagoshima University was founded in 1949 in accordance with the National School Establishment Law with the fusion of five pre-war educational institutions: the Seventh Higher School, Kagoshima Normal School, Kagoshima Normal School for Youth Education, Kagoshima College of Agriculture and Forestry, and Kagoshima College of Fisheries. At the time of its foundation the university was composed of four faculties: Letters and Science, Education, Agriculture, and Fisheries. Since then the faculties were reorganized and new faculties were added and now the university consists of the following eight faculties: Law and Letters, Education, Science, Medicine, Dentistry, Engineering, Agriculture, and Fisheries, as well as the College of Liberal Arts.

The enrollment is about 9, 000 and there are about 80 foreign students from more than 20 countries. The faculties of Medicine, Dentistry and the United Graduate School of Agricultural Sciences offer a doctorate degree, and the faculties of Law and

Letters, Science, Engineering, Agriculture, and Fisheries offer a master's degree. Each faculty is proud of its well equipped facilities for education and research.

The University has promoted inter-faculty, inter-university, and international programs. In 1986, the Western Japan Conference on Foreign Students Programs was held here in Kagoshima under the auspices of the Ministry of Education, Science and Culture. At present, the University has many overseas sister institutions (the University of Georgia, University of Rhode Islands, University of Washington, University of South Carolina, Arizona State University, University of North Wales, the University of the South Pacific, Shotan University, and Institute Pertanian Bogor) and also works in cooperation with University Pertam Malaysia to strengthen their Ph. D. program in fisheries.

The Research Center for the South Pacific is a leading institution promoting research for the South Pacific in Japan, and is inter-faculty, inter-university, and internationally oriented. Using the research and training ship Kagoshima-Maru. (1, 292 GT), their research has been conducted in the South Pacific Ocean.

The campus is located in the center of Kagoshima City, which is the southern gateway of Japan. Having been a window to Chinese culture and European culture and technology in the olden days, Kagoshima was the first to import modern technology to Japan.

Kagoshima's natural environment—the waters in the southwest, with many islands—provides various subjects for academic research and study. Kagoshima University is a national university, which serves as the academic and cultural center of Southern Kyushu surrounded by a rich, natural environment and various historical remains and sites.

UNDERGRADUATE PROGRAMS

Faculty of Agriculture (Freshmen Enrollment: 235)

Department of Agricultural Chemistry

Applied Microbiology, Applied Starch Chemistry, Biochemistry and Nutritional Chemistry, Chemistry and Technology of Agricultural Products, Plant Nutrition and Fertilizers, Soil Science

Department of Agricultural Engineering

Agricultural Physics, Farm Land Engineering, Farm Power and Machinery, Food and Agricultural Process Engineering, Irrigation and Drainage Engineering

Department of Agronomy

Agricultural Economics and Policy, Agricultural Marketing, Crop Science, Entomology, Farm Management, Plant Breeding, Plant Pathology, Tropical Crop Science

Department of Animal Science

Animal Biochemistry, Animal Breeding, Animal Management, Animal Nutrition, Animal Products

Processing Research, Animal Reproduction

Department of Forestry

Forest Civil Engineering and Erosion Control, Forest Genetics and Protection, Forest Management, Forest Policy, Silviculture, Wood Technology and Forest Product Chemistry

Department of Horticulture

Fruit Science, Ornamental Horticulture and Floriculture, Postharvest Physiology and Preservation of Fruits and Vegetables, Vegetable Crops

Department of Veterinary Medicine

Veterinary Anatomy, Veterinary Medicine, Veterinary Microbiology, Veterinary Obstetrics and Gynecology, Veterinary Pathology, Veterinary Pharmacology, Veterinary Physiology, Veterinary Public Health, Veterinary Surgery

Faculty of Dentistry (Freshmen Enrollment: 80)

Department of Dentistry

Biochemistry, Dental Materials and Apparatus, Dental Radiology, Microbiology, Operative Dentistry, Oral Anatomy, Oral and Maxillofacial Surgery, Oral Physiology, Orthodontics, Pathology, Pedodontics, Periodontology, Pharmacology, Preventive Dentistry, Prosthetic Dentistry

Faculty of Education (Freshmen Enrollment: 360)

Health and Physical Education Course
Junior High School Education Course
Primary School Education Course
Special Education Course

Aesthetics and History of Arts, Agriculture, Algebra and Geometry, Analysis and Applied Mathematics, Ball Games, Biology, Business Management, Calligraphy, Chemistry, Childcare, Chinese Language, Dancing, Design, Developmental Psychology, Economics, Educational Psychology, Educational Sociology, Educational System, Education of Handicapped Children, Electricity, English and American Literature, English Linguistics, Ethics, Fine Arts Education, Food Science and Cooking, Geography, Geology, Grappling Sports, Gymnastics, History, History of Education, Home Economics Education, Home Management, Hygiene of Handicapped Children, Hygienics, Instrumental Music, Japanese Language, Japanese Literature, Law, Machinery, Management of Physical Education, Mathematics Education, Metal Processing and Craft, Musical Composition, Music Education, Musicology and History of Music, Painting, Pedagogy, Philosophy, Physics, Physiology, Plastic Arts, Political Science, Principles and History of Physical Education, Psychology of Handicapped Children, School Hygiene, Science Education, Social Education, Special Education, Sports Psychology, Teaching of English as a Foreign Language, Teaching of Health and Physical Education, Teaching of Japanese, Teaching of Social Subjects, Technical Education, Textiles and Clothing, Track and Field Sports, Vocal Music, Vocational Education, Wood Processing and Craft

Faculty of Engineering (Freshmen Enrollment: 390)

Department of Applied Chemistry

Applied Physical Chemistry, Industrial Inorganic Chemistry, Industrial Organic Chemistry, Organic Synthetic Chemistry

Department of Architecture

Architectural Planning, Building Equipment, Building Materials and Construction, History of Architecture and Architectural Design, Structural Engineering, Structural Mechanics

Department of Chemical Engineering

Chemical Reaction Engineering, Industrial Physical Chemistry, Transport Phenomena, Unit Operation

Department of Electrical Engineering

Electrical Communication, Electric Machinery, Electric Power Engineering, Fundamentals in Electrical Engineering

Department of Electronics Engineering

Electronic Circuits, Electronic Control Systems, Electronic Measurements, Fundamentals in Electronics, Information Processing

Department of Mechanical Engineering I

Hydraulic Engineering, Mechanics of Materials, Metallurgy and Production Engineering, Steam Engineering and Heat Transfer

Department of Mechanical Engineering II

Engineering Materials Science, Fluid Mechanics, Internal Combustion Engineering, Precision Engineering

Department of Ocean Civil Engineering

Coastal and Harbor Engineering, Fundamental Oceanography for Engineering, Marine Construction, Marine Structural Engineering, Planning of Marine Civil Engineering

Faculty of Fisheries (Freshmen Enrollment: 150)

Department of Fisheries

Aquacultural Physiology, Fisheries Business and Economics, Fisheries Environmental Sociology, Fisheries Resources, Fishing Gear, Fishing Technology, Fishing Vessel Navigation, Fishing Vessel Seamanship, Food Chemistry, Food Preservation Science, Food Quality Control and Analysis, International Marine Policy, Marine Biology, Marine Botany and Environmental Science, Marine Electronics, Marine Resource Biochemistry, Marine Resource Nutrition Chemistry, Microbiology, Physical Oceanography

Faculty of Law and Letters (Freshmen Enrollment: 390)

Department of Economics

Accounting and Cost Accounting, Economic History, Economic Policy, International Economics, Management, Money, Banking and Public Finance, Principles and History of Economics, Social Policy and History of Social Thought, Sociology and Social Survey

Department of Humanities

Archaeology, Cultural Anthropology, English and American Literature, English Linguistics, Human Geography, Japanese History, Japanese Linguistics, Japanese Literature, Occidental History, Oriental History, Philosophy, Psychology

Department of Law

Administrative Law, Civil Law, Commercial Law, Constitutional Law, Criminal Law and Criminal Procedure, International Law and Legal History and Philosophy of Law, Labor Law and Economic Law, Law of Civil Procedure, Political Science

Faculty of Medicine (Freshmen Enrollment: 100)

Department of Medicine

Anatomy, Anesthesiology, Bacteriology, Biochemistry, Dermatology, Hygiene, Internal Medicine, Laboratory Medicine, Legal Medicine, Medical Zoology, Neuro-Psychiathy, Neuro-Surgery, Obstetrics and Gynecology, Ophthalmology, Orthopedic Surgery, Otolaryngology, Pathology, Pediatrics, Pharmacology, Physiology, Public Health, Radiology, Rehabilitaion Medicine, Surgery, Urology, Virology

Faculty of Science (Freshmen Enrollment: 182)

Department of Biology

Biosystematics, Cell Biology, Environmental Biology, Physiology

Department of Chemistry

Biological Chemistry, Inorganic and Analytical Chemistry, Organic Chemistry, Physical Chemistry

Department of Earth Sciences

Applied Geology, Geology and Paleontology, Geophysics, Petrology and Mineralogy, Volcanology

Department of Mathematics

Algebra, Analysis, Geometry, Information Theory, Probability Theory and Statistics

Department of Physics

Applied Physics, Atomic Physics, Solid State Physics

Foreign Student Admission

Qualifications for Applicants

Standard Qualifications Requirement

Examination at the University

Applicants must have taken the General Examination for Foreign Students in their respective fields and the Japanese Language Proficiency Test. Applicants must also take the entrance examination by the University which includes an interview given by each faculty in addition to a written examination of three subjects: English, Mathematics, and one of Science (Biology, Chemistry, Geology, or Physics).

Documents to be Submitted When Applying

Standard Documents Requirement

Application forms are available from the Admissions Section, Student Bureau in late November. All applicants must submit the specified application documents to the Admissions Section between January 21 and February 1.

GRADUATE PROGRAMS

The United Graduate School of Agricultural Sciences (First Year Enrollment: Doctor's 18)

Divisions

Bioresource Production Science, Bioresource Science for Processing, Fishery Resources Science, Life Environment Conservation Science

Graduate School of Agriculture (First Year Enroll-

ment : Master's 68)

Divisions

Agricultural Chemistry, Agricultural Engineering, Agronomy, Animal Science, Forestry, Horticulture

Graduate School of Cultural Sciences (First Year Enrollment : Master's 10)

Divisions

Basis of Culture, Regional Culture

Graduate School of Dental Science (First Year Enrollment : Doctor's 18)

Division

Dental Science

Graduate School of Engineering (First Year Enrollment : Master's 70)

Divisions

Applied Chemistry, Architecture, Chemical Engineering, Electrical Engineering, Electronics Engineering, Mechanical Engineering I & II, Ocean Civil Engineering

Graduate School of Fisheries (First Year Enrollment : Master's 32)

Division

Fisheries

Graduate School of Law (First Year Enrollment : Master's 13)

Division

Law

Graduate School of Medical Science (First Year Enrollment : Doctor's 58)

Divisions

Internal Medicine, Pathology, Physiology, Social Medicine, Surgery

Graduate School of Science (First Year Enrollment : Master's 42)

Divisions

Biology, Chemistry, Geology, Mathematics, Physics

Foreign Student Admission

Qualifications for Applicants

Master's Program

Standard Qualifications Requirement

Doctor's Program

Standard Qualifications Requirement

Examination at the University

Master's Program

Applicants must take the entrance examination, consisting of a written examination and an interview. As a rule, the written examination consists of English and the applicants' respective special subjects given by each Graduate School. However, applicants in law are exempted from the written examination.

Doctor's Program

Applicants must take the entrance examination. For the Dental Science program, the examination consists of a written examination in English and an interview given by the Graduate School. For the Medical Science program, applicants must take the written examination in English, one of German or French, and their respective special subjects and an interview given by the Graduate School.

For The United Agricultural Sciences Program,

applicants must take the written examination in English and an interview given by the Graduate School.

Documents to be Submitted When Applying

Standard Documents Requirement

Application forms are available at the Admissions Section, Student Bureau from early July.

*

Research Institutes and Centers

Agricultural Experiment Stations (Ibusuki Plant Exp. St. , Iriki Livestock Exp. St. , Toso Orchard, On-campus Exp. St.,Sata Forest Exp. St.,and Takakuma Forest Exp. St.), Computing Center, Dental Hospital, Educational Experiment Stations (Elementary School, Junior High School, Kindergarten, Nursing School,On-Campus Exp. St.,and Terayama Exp. St.), Fisheries Research Laboratories (Kamoike Marine Production Lab. and Nagashima Marine Lab.), Health Center, Institute of Cancer Research, Institute of Laboratory Animal Science, Large-scale Running-water Laboratory, Reference Center for Scientific Research on the Southwest Pacific Area, Research and Training Ships (1, 292 GT Kagoshima-Maru, 860 GT Keiten-Maru, and 82 GT Nansei-Maru), Research Center for the South Pacific, School of Mid-wifery, School of Nursing, School of Nursing and Allied Medical Science, School of Public Health Nursing, Unversity Hospital

Facilities/Services for Foreign Students

Kagoshima Unversity Foreign Students Residence Hall

(Accommodations: 40 rooms-single 35, couple 3, and family 2; shared facilities: recreation room, lounge, Japanese-style room), personal services (administrators 2, student tutors 2, house-mother 1, foreign student advisors 2, academic staff for foreign students 2), committees (Committee for Foreign Student, Committee for Kagoshima University Foreign Students Residence Hall Administration, and Committee for Kagoshima University Foreign Affairs), associations (Kagoshima University Foreign Student Association: KUFSA), and many external supporting groups (Kagoshima Prefecture, Kagoshima City, Japanese Language Educator's Society, Kagoshima International Speaking Society, Rotary Clubs, International Soroptimist Club, Pilot Club, Kagoshima UNESCO Association, Japanese Association of University Women, Kagoshima International Forum, etc.)

On-campus health and legal aids are also available on request.

Special Programs for Foreign Students

Japanese and Japanese Studies courses are offered at the College of Liberal Arts for undergraduate students and at the Faculty of Fisheries for graduate students. Japanese language supplementary classes are offered by Foreign Students Section, Student Bureau. Limited graduate courses in fisheries are offered in English.

For Further Information

Undergraduate and Graduate Admission

Admissions Section, Student Bureau, Kagoshima University, 1-21-24 Korimoto, Kagoshima-shi, Kagoshima 890 ☎ 0992-54-7141 ext. 2441

Kanazawa University
(Kanazawa Daigaku)

1-1 Marunouchi, Kanazawa-shi, Ishikawa 920
☎ 0762-62-4281

Faculty
Profs.   325   Assoc. Profs.   261
Assist. Profs.   Full–time   101; Part–time   381
Res. Assocs.   271
Number of Students
Undergrad.   7, 185   Grad.   915
Library   1, 180, 349 volumes

Outline and Characteristics of the University

Kanazawa University was founded under the National School Establishment Law of 1949, when six existing institutions of higher learning (including Kanazawa Medical College which dates back to 1862) were incorporated and reorganized into the School of Medicine and five other Faculties: Education, Law and Letters, Pharmaceutical Sciences, Science, and Technology. The College of Liberal Arts was established in 1963 to offer general education courses. In 1980, the Faculty of Law and Letters was divided into independent Faculties of Economics, Law, and Letters.

Responding to the growing needs of the country, the University has continued to expand and now includes nine Graduate Schools, six research institutes and centers, and among other affiliated establishments, the Extension Institute which provides adult education programs and thus emphasizes the University's emerging role in the Learning Society.

The campuses are all situated in Kanazawa, an ancient city on the Japan Sea coast, which was already a center of learning in the Edo period when the ruling class, in an effort to make this province culturally invulnerable, set out to turn it into what has since been known as 'the Library of the Nation.' Numerous books were collected from all over the country and from overseas. Scholars and artists were brought here and offered patronage. This tradition of respect for academic and artistic activities has been handed down from generation to generation as a rich cultural heritage. This may account for the fact that in proportion to the city's population, natives of Kanazawa have received more Orders of Cultural Merit than those of any other city or region in Japan.

Today Kanazawa is a sizeable city with a population of 437, 723 but retains the character of a castle town both physically and spiritually. Located at the site of a feudal castle, that is, at the heart of the city, the main campus of the University is surrounded by moats and gardens, and provides a very tranquil setting for critical and creative pursuits.

UNDERGRADUATE PROGRAMS

Faculty of Economics (Freshmen Enrollment: 200)
Department of Economics
Applied Economics, Economic History, Economic Policy, Economic Theory and Econometrics, Information, Science of Management
Faculty of Education (Freshmen Enrollment: 295)
Training Course for Special School Teachers for the Deaf
Training Course for Elementary School Teachers
Training Course for Junior High School Teachers
Training Course for Special School Teachers for the Mentally Handicapped
Special Training Course for Physical Education Teachers
Training Course for Senior High School Physical Education Teachers
Training Course for Special School Teachers for the Speech-Handicapped
Faculty of Law (Freshmen Enrollment: 200)
Department of Law
International Relations, Jurisprudence, Politics, Private Law, Public Law
Faculty of Letters (Freshmen Enrollment: 155)
Department of Behavioral Sciences
Comparative Culture, Cultural Anthropology, Differential Psychology, Dynamic Sociology, Experimental Psychology, Foundations of Behavioral Sciences, Sociology of Human Behavior
Department of History
Archaeology, Geography, Japanese History, Oriental History, Regional Geography, Western History
Department of Literature
American Literature, Chinese Language and Literature, English Language, English Literature, French Language and Literature, German Language, German Literature, Japanese Language, Japanese Literature, Linguistics
School of Medicine (Freshmen Enrollment: 100)
Department of Medicine
Anatomy, Anesthesiology, Biochemistry, Dento-Oral Surgery, Dermatology, Forensic Medicine, Hygiene, Internal Medicine, Laboratory Medicine, Microbiology, Neurosurgery, Nuclear Medicine, Obstetrics and Gynecology, Ophthalmology, Orthopedics, Otorhinolaryngology, Parasitology, Pathology, Pediatrics, Pharmacology, Physiology, Psychiatry, Public Health, Radiology, Surgery, Urology
Faculty of Pharmaceutical Sciences (Freshmen Enrollment: 80)
Department of Pharmaceutical Sciences
Analytical Chemistry, Biochemistry, Chemistry, Hygiencic Chemistry, Microbiology, Pharmacognosy and Natural Products Chemistry, Pharmacology
Department of Pharmaceutical Technochemistry
Biology, Pharmaceutical Chemistry, Pharmaceutics, Physical Chemistry, Radiation Biology, Synthetic

Organic Chemistry
Faculty of Science (Freshmen Enrollment: 160)
Department of Biology
Animal Physiological Chemistry, Developmental Biology, Ecology, Plant Physiology and Biochemistry, Plant Taxonomy and Geobotany
Department of Chemistry
Analytical Chemistry, Biochemistry, Co-Ordination Chemistry, Inorganic Chemistry, Organic Chemistry, Radiochemistry, Theoretical Chemistry
Department of Earth Sciences
Mineralogy and Crystallography, Petrology and Chemical Geology, Stratigraphy and Paleontology, Structural Geology and Geophysics
Department of Mathematics
Algebra, Applied Mathematics, Functional Equations, Function Theory, Geometry, Mathematical Analysis
Department of Physics
Crystal Physics, Elementary Particle Physics, Molecular Physics, Nuclear Physics, Plasma Physics, Radio Frequency Spectroscopy, Solid State Physics
Faculty of Technology (Freshmen Enrollment: 515)
Department of Chemistry and Chemical Engineering
Chemical Engineering Fundamentals, Chemistry of Functional Materials, Energy and Environment, Physical and Analytical Chemistry, Separation and Mixing Processes, Synthesis of Materials
Department of Civil Engineering
Environmental Health Engineering, Geotecial Engineering, Hydraulic Engineering, Structural Engineering, Urban and Regional Facility Planning
Department of Electrical and Computer Engineering
Common Lectures (Engineering Science Class), Computer Engineering, Electronic Circuits, Electronic Devices, Electronic Materials, Energy Conversion and Power System, Information and Communication Engineering, Instrument and Control, Material Sciences, Mathematical Sciences
Department of Mechanical Systems Engineering
Automatic Mechanics, Electro-Mechanical Network, Energy Conversion Machinery for Energy Conversion, Engineering Materials, Production Engineering Manufacturing System, Solid Mechanics and Dynamics, Strength and Mechanism in Design

Foreign Student Admission
Qualifications for Applicants
Standard Qualifications Requirement
Those who hold the International Baccalauréat and are at least 18 years of age may also apply.
Examination at the University
It is preferable that applicants take the Japanese Language Proficiency Test and General Examination for Foreign Students. Although every applicant is required to take the entrance examination (written and oral exams and an interview) given by each Faculty, he/she will be screened by standards different from

those for Japanese applicants and may be admitted.
Documents to be Submitted When Applying
Standard Documents Requirement

GRADUATE PROGRAMS

Graduate School of Economics (First Year Enrollment : Master's 9)
Division
Economics
Graduate School of Education (First Year Enrollment : Master's 55)
Divisions
Education of Handicapped Children, English Education, Health and Physical Education, Japanese Education, Mathematics Education, Natural Science Education, School Education, Social Science Education
Graduate School of Law (First Year Enrollment : Master's 15)
Division
Law
Graduate School of Letters (First Year Enrollment : Master's 28)
Divisions
English Literature, German Literature, History, Japanese Literature, Philosophy
Graduate School of Medicine (First Year Enrollment : Doctor's 78)
Divisions
Internal Medicine, Pathology, Physiology, Social Medicine, Surgery
Gaduate School of Natural Science & Technology (First Year Enrollment: Doctor's 38)
Divisions
Life Sciences, Physical Sciences, System Science & Technology
Graduate School of Pharmaceutical Sciences (First Year Enrollment : Master's 26,)
Divisions
Pharmaceutical Sciences, Pharmaceutical Technochemistry
Graduate School of Science (First Year Enrollment : Master's 58)
Divisions
Biology, Chemistry, Earth Sciences, Mathematics, Physics
Graduate School of Technology (First Year Enrollment : Master's 88)
Divisions
Chemical Engineering, Civil Engineering, Construction and Environmental Engineering, Electrical Engineering, Electronic Engineering, Industrial Chemistry, Mechanical Engineering, Precision Engineering
Foreign Student Admission
Qualifications for Applicants
Master's Program
Standard Qualifications Requirement
Doctor's Program
Standard Qualifications Requirement
Documents to be Submitted When Applying

Standard Documents Requirement
*
Research Institutes and Centers
Applied Research Center of Composite Materials, Cancer Research Institute, Data Processing Center, Educational Technology Center, Environment Protection Center, Japan Sea Research Institute, Radioisotope Center
Facilities/Services for Foreign Students
There are no accommodations for foreign students only, but a limited number of rooms are available in the Residence Halls of the University.
Special Programs for Foreign Students
Japanese language and culture courses are offered for foreign students at the College of Liberal Arts.
For Further Information
Undergraduate and Graduate Admission
Office of Admissions, Student Affairs Section, Kanazawa University, 1-1 Marunouchi, Kanazawa-shi, Ishikawa 920 ☎ 0762-62-4281 ext. 282, 290

Kitami Institute of Technology
(Kitami Kogyo Daigaku)
165 Koen-cho, Kitami-shi, Hokkaido 090
☎ 0157-24-1010

Faculty
    Profs. 32   Assoc. Profs. 45
    Assist. Profs. Full-time 9; Part-time 10
    Res. Assocs. 28
Number of Students
    Undergrad. 1, 431   Grad. 32
Library   122, 206 volumes

Outline and Characteristics of the University
On April 1, 1960, Kitami Junior College of Technology (Mechanical Course and Applied Chemistry Course) was established in accordance with the National School Establishment Law. On April 1, 1962, the Electrical Course was established. On April 1, 1965, the Civil Course was established. On March 31, 1966, registration of students was discontinued. On April 1, 1966, Kitami Institute of Technology (Departments of Mechanical, Electrical and Civil Engineering and of Industrial Chemistry) was established in accordance with the National School Establishment Law. On June 1, 1967, Kitami Junior College of Technology was dissolved. On April 1, 1970, the Department of Developmental Engineering was established. On April 1, 1973, the Department of Electronic Engineering was established. On April 1, 1975, the Health Administration Center was established. On April 1, 1976, the Department of Environmental Engineering and the Post-graduate Courses in Engineering were established. On April 1, 1979, the Department of Applied Mechanical Engineering

was established. On March 31, 1984, the Post-graduate Courses in Engineering were dissolved. On April 12, 1984, the Graduate School of Engineering (Master's Course) was established in accordance with the National School Establishment Law.

UNDERGRADUATE PROGRAMS

Faculty of Engineering (Freshmen Enrollment: 360)
  Department of Applied Mechanical Engineering
Applied Mechanics, Fluid Machinery, Heat Engineering, Material Processing
  Department of Civil Engineering
Hydromechanics, Soil Engineering, Strength of Materials, Structural Engineering
  Department of Developmental Engineering
City Planning and Structural Engineering, Concrete and River Engineering, Excavation Engineering and Rock Mechanics, Geotechnics and Applied Geology
  Department of Electrical Engineering
Applied Electrical Engineering, Electrical Machinery, Electric Fundamentals, Electric Power System Engineering
  Department of Electronic Engineering
Electronic Apparatus, Electronic Application, Electronic Fundamentals, Physical Electronics
  Department of Environmental Engineering
Environmental Analysis, Environmental Control Engineering, Environmental Science, Reaction Chemistry
  Department of Industrial Chemistry
Chemical Reaction Engineering, Industrial Inorganic Chemistry, Industrial Organic Chemistry, Industrial Synthetic Chemistry
  Department of Mechanical Engineering
Fluid Mechanics, Mechanics of Materials, Metals Machining, Thermodynamics and Heat Transfer

Foreign Student Admission
  Qualifications for Applicants
    Standard Qualifications Requirement
    Foreign applicants must have taken the Japanese Language Proficiency Test (1st level) and General Examination for Foreign Students.
  Examination at the University
(1) First-stage selection:
    Candidates for the second-stage achievement test given by the University are selected on the basis of the results of the Japanese Language Proficiency Test and General Examination for Foreign Students.
(2) Second-stage selection:
    Applicants who have passed the first-stage selection must undergo the second-stage achievement test given by the University (February 29). The selection is made on the basis of a comprehensive judgement of the results of the achievement test, the oral test conducted in the Japanese language and the submitted health certificate form.
  Documents to be Submitted When Applying
    Standard Documents Requirement

Application forms are available at the Admissions Office in November. All applicants are required to submit a completed Kitami Institute of Technology School Career Form in addition to the specified application documents to the Admissions Office between January 18–25.
Entrance Procedure:
    The applicant is required to submit a document to show that he/she has sufficient funds to cover all the necessary expenses during his/her stay in Japan together with admission fee in March.

GRADUATE PROGRAMS

Graduate School of Engineering (First Year Enrollment : Master's 20)
  Divisions
Chemical Environmental Engineering, Developmental Civil Engineering, Electrical and Electronic Engineering, Mechanical Engineering

Foreign Student Admission
  Qualifications for Applicants
Master's Program
    Standard Qualifications Requirement
  Examination at the University
Master's Program
    Foreign applicants must undergo the same achievement and oral tests as Japanese applicants conducted in the Japanese language around in September. Selection of the students is made on the basis of a comprehensive judgment of the tests, University Report, and health examination.
  Documents to be Submitted When Applying
    Standard Documents Requirement
    Application forms are available at the Admissions Office in August. All applicants are required to submit a completed Kitami Institute of Technology School Career Form in addition to the specified application documents to the Admissions Office at about the end of August.
Entrance Procedure:
    The applicant is required to submit a document to show that he/she has sufficient funds to cover all the necessary expenses during his/her stay in Japan together with the admission fee in March.

＊

For Further Information
  Undergraduate and Graduate Admission
Entrance Examination Section, Student Office, School Affairs Division, Kitami Institute of Technology, 165 Koen-cho, Kitami-shi, Hokkaido 090
☎ 0157–24–1010 ext. 247

Kobe University
(Kobe Daigaku)

1-1 Rokkodai-cho, Nada-ku, Kobe-shi, Hyogo 657
☎ 078-881-1212

Faculty
    Profs. 389   Assoc. Profs. 283
    Assist. Profs.   Full-time 92; Part-time 559
    Res. Assocs. 359
Number of Students
    Undergrad. 10, 859   Grad. 1, 428
Library 2, 029, 586 volumes

Outline and Characteristics of the University

The inception of Kobe University goes back to March, 1902, when Kobe College of Commerce was founded by the Japanese Government. In April, 1924, the school was renamed Kobe University of Commerce, and in October, 1944, Kobe University of Economics. In May, 1949, the college was reorganized as a university by incorporating Hyogo Normal School, Hyogo Higher Normal School, Kobe College of Technology, and Himeji High School. Since then the University has developed with the times. Today, the University consists of the College of Liberal Arts, nine faculties with their respective graduate schools, two independent graduate schools, Research Institute for Economics and Business Administration, and other attached facilities.

The University is located in Kobe City, which, together with Kyoto and Osaka, is a principal city in the Kansai area, about 550km west of Tokyo. Kobe with a population of about 1. 4 milion is an international city which has prospered mainly through foreign trade. The city extends east and west, facing the Seto Inland Sea to the south and the Rokko mountains to the north. Thus sandwiched between mountains and a sea, it is one of the most beautiful cities in Japan. Moreover, because it offers various ways of enjoying leisure time in the mountains and on the sea, its way of life is very comfortable.

The University is one of the ten oldest and largest national universities in Japan, and enjoys a high academic reputation. Reflecting the cosmopolitan atmosphere of Kobe City, it has always placed a great emphasis on academic exchanges with foreign universities at various levels.

UNDERGRADUATE PROGRAMS

Faculty of Agriculture (Freshmen Enrollment: 185)
Department of Agricultural Chemistry
Biochemistry, Chemistry and Technology of Agricultural Products, Fermentation Technology, Food and Nutritional Chemistry, Plant Nutrition, Soil Science
Department of Agricultural Engineering
Agricultural Power, Agricultural Processing Machinery, Farm Machinery and Equipments, Land Use Engineering, Water Use Engineering
Department of Agriculture and Horticulture
Agricultural Economics, Crop Science, Farm Management, Floriculture and Olericulture, Plant Breeding, Pomology, Preservation Technology, Tropical Botany
Department of Plant Protection
Agricultural Entomology, Genetics, Pesticide Science, Plant Pathology
Department of Zootechnical Science
Animal Breeding, Animal Hygiene, Animal Management, Animal Nutrition, Animal Reproduction, Chemistry and Technology of Animal Products
Faculty of Business Administration (Freshmen Enrollment: 270, Evening Course 70)
Department of Accounting
Auditing, Bookkeeping, Cost Accounting, International Accounting, Managements Accounting, Principles of Accounting, Tax Accounting
Department of Business Administration
Administrative Management, Business Administration, Business Finance, Business Mathematics, Business Statistics, Industrial Administration, Labor Management, Public Utility Management
Department of Commercial Science
Distribution System, Financial Institutions, Foreign Trade, Insurance, Marketing, Ocean Transportation, Securities Analysis, Securities Market, Transportation
Faculty of Economics (Freshmen Enrollment: 270, Evening Course 80)
Department of Economics
Agricultural Policy, American Economy, Chinese Economy, Comparative Economics, Econometrics, Economic Geography, Economic History (Japan), Economic History (West Europe), Economic Statistics, Foreign Trade Policy, History of Economic Doctrines, Industrial Policy, International Economics, International Finance, Japanese Economy, Mathematical Economics, Money and Banking, National Economics, Principles of Economic Policy, Public Economics, Public Finance, Social Economics, Social Policy, Statistics, Theoretical Economics
Faculty of Education (Freshmen Enrollment: 420)
Special Course for Teachers of the Handicapped
Junior High School Teachers Training Course
Kindergarten Teachers Training Course
Primary School Teachers Training Course
Art, Art Education, Educational Technology, English Language Education, English Philology and English and American Literature, Health and Physical Education, Home Economics, Homemaking Education, Japanese Language Education, Japanese Philology and Literature, Mathematics, Mathematics Education, Method and Process of Education, Music, Music Education, Nurse Teachers Education, Physical Education, Human Movement and School Health, Science Education, Science II (Biology and Geology), Science I (Physics and Chemistry), Social

Studies Education, Social Studies I (History and Geography), Social Studies II (Ethics, Sociology, Law, Political Science and Economics), Studies in Human Development, System in Education, Technology, Technology Education

Faculty of Engineering (Freshmen Enrollment: 600)

Department of Applied Science

Applied Mathematics, Applied Physics

Department of Architecture

Applied Mechanics and Steel Structures, Architectural Design and Planning, Building Materials and Construction, History of Architecture, Structural Dynamics and Earthquake Resistant Design

Department of Chemical Engineering

Chemical Reaction Engineering, Diffusional Operation Engineering, High Pressure Chemical Engineering, Process Design and Control

Department of Civil Engineering

Civil Engineering Materials and Bridge Engineering, Hydraulic Engineering, Mountainous-Region Hydrology, Reclamation Engineering, Sanitary Engineering, Slope Condition, Soil Engineering, Structural Mechanics, Traffic Engineering

Department of Electrical Engineering

Circuit Theory, Information Science and Communication Systems Engineering, Electrical Machines and Control Engineering, Electric Power Engineering, Fundamental Electrical Engineering

Department of Electronics Engineering

Computer Engineering, Electronic Circuit Engineering, Fundamental Electronics, Semiconductor Electronics

Department of Environmental Planning

Analysis of Physical Environment, Disaster Prevention, Environmental Planning for Human Life, Physical Environmental Planning

Department of Industrial Chemistry

Industrial Inorganic Chemistry, Industrial Physical Chemistry, Polymer Chemistry, Synthetic Organic Chemistry

Department of Instrumentation Engineering

Applied Physics in Instrumentation Engineering, Automatic Control, Electronic Instrumentation, Mechanical Instrumentation

Department of Mechanical Engineering

Engineering Mechanics and Machine Design, Fluid Mechanics and Hydraulic Machinery, Steam Power Engineering, Strength of Materials, Thermodynamics and Internal Combustion Engine

Department of Production Engineering

Applied Kinematics, Material Research for Machinery, Production Engineering, Thermofluid Mechanics

Department of Systems Engineering

Systems Analysis, Systems Design, Systems Fundamentals, Systems Information

Faculty of Law (Freshmen Enrollment: 230, Evening Course 80)

Department of Law

Civil Law, Commercial Law, Criminal Law, International Law, International Relations, Legal Theory and History, Political Science, Public Law, Social Law, Sociology of Law

Faculty of Letters (Freshmen Enrollment: 120)

Department of History

Asian History, European History, Geography, Japanese History

Department of Literature

Chinese Literature, English and American Literature, French Literature, German Literature, Japanese Literature

Department of Philosophy

Art, Philosophy, Psychology, Sociology

Faculty of Medicine (Freshmen Enrollment: 120)

Department of Medicine

Anatomy, Anesthesiology, Biochemistry, Dermatology, Hygiene, Internal Medicine, Laboratory Medicine, Legal Medicine, Medical Zoology, Microbiology, Neurological Surgery, Neurology and Psychiatry, Obstetrics and Gynecology, Ophthalmology, Oral Surgery, Orthopedic Surgery, Otorhinolaryngology, Pathology, Pediatrics, Pharmacology, Physiology, Public Health, Radiation Biophysics, Radiology, Surgery, Urology

Faculty of Science (Freshmen Enrollment: 145)

Department of Biology

Cell Biology, Genetics, Microbial Biochemistry, Physiology, Systematics and Phylogeny

Department of Chemistry

Analytical Chemistry, Inorganic Chemistry, Molecular Structure and Dynamics, Organic Chemistry, Physical Chemistry

Department of Earth Science

Geochemistry, Geology, Geophysics, Marine Geophysics, Petrology and Mineralogy

Department of Mathematics

Algebra Topology, Analysis, Applied Mathematics, Geometry

Department of Physics

Cosmic Ray Physics, Elementary Particle Physics, High Energy Physics, Radio Frequency Spectroscopy, Solid State Physics

Foreign Student Admission

Qualifications for Applicants

Standard Qualifications Requirement

The faculties that accept special foreign student enrollment are: Faculties of Law, Economics Business Administration, and Engineering.

Examination at the University

Applicants must take the Japanese Language Proficiency Test and General Examination for Foreign Students, plus each faculty's special entrance examination consisting of written and oral exams and an interview.

Documents to be Submitted When Applying

Standard Documents Requirement

Additional documents to be submitted:

Faculty of Law, Faculty of Business Administration and Faculty of Engineering:

1. Certificate of Japanese language proficiency.

Faculty of Economics:

1. Letter of recommen-dation issued by the Japanese embassies and consulates abroad or embassies of the applicant's country in Japan.
2. Certificate of Japanese language proficiency.
   The period of application is as follows.

Application for admission: January-February
Examination: March

Applicants are requested to ask the respective faculties for the specific dates.

Qualifications for Transfer Students

Undergraduate transfer students are admitted only when there are vacancies. Applications, therefore, are not accepted every year.

Applicants for transfer must have graduated from a university or a four-year college.

Examination for Transfer Students

Examination procedures are specified by each faculty.

Documents to be Submitted When Applying
Standard Documents Requirement

GRADUATE PROGRAMS

Graduate School of Agriculture (First Year Enrollment : Master's 58)
Divisions
Agricultural Chemistry, Agricultural Engineering, Agriculture and Horticulture, Plant Protection, Zootechnical Science

Graduate School of Business Administration (First Year Enrollment : Master's 50, Doctor's 26)
Divisions
Accounting, Business Administration, Commercial Science

Graduate School of Economics (First Year Enrollment : Master's 51, Doctor's 26)
Divisions
Economics and Economic Policy, International Economics

Graduate School of Education (First Year Enrollment : Master's 70)
Divisions
Art Education, English Language Education, Japanese Language Education, Mathematics Education, Music Education, School Education, Science Education, Social Studies Education, Technology Education

Graduate School of Engineering (First Year Enrollment : Master's 150)
Divisions
Applied Science, Architecture and Environmental Planning, Chemical Engineering, Civil Engineering, Electrical Engineering and Electronics Engineering, Industrial Chemistry, Instrumentation Engineering, Mechanical Engineering and Production Engineering, Systems Engineering

Graduate School of Humanities and Social Sciences (First Year Enrollment : Doctor's 13)

Divisions
Culture and Society, Structure of Culture

Graduate School of Law (First Year Enrollment : Master's 50, Doctor's 23)
Divisions
Private Law, Public Law

Graduate School of Letters (First Year Enrollment : Master's 50)
Divisions
Art, Asian History, Chinese Literature, English and American Literature, European History, French Literature, Geography, German Literature, Japanese History, Japanese Literature, Philosophy, Psychology, Sociology

Graduate School of Medicine (First Year Enrollment : Doctor's 62)
Divisions
Medical Sciences, Pathological Sciences, Physiological Sciences, Social Medicine, Surgical Sciences

Graduate School of Science (First Year Enrollment : Master's 50)
Divisions
Biology, Chemistry, Earth Science, Mathematics, Physics

Graduate School of Science and Technology (First Year Enrollment : Doctor's 41)
Divisions
Environmental Science, Industrial Science, Science of Biological Resources, Science of Materials, System Science

Foreign Student Admission
Qualifications for Applicants
Master's Program
Standard Qualifications Requirement
Special foreign student enrollment is accepted at the Graduate Schools of Letters, Law, Education, Economics Science, Engineering, and Agriculture.
Doctor's Program
Standard Qualifications Requirement
Examination at the University
Master's Program
1. Written and oral examinations
2. Submitted documents
3. When judged appropriate, some students may be exempted from written or oral examinations.
Doctor's Program
1. Written and oral examinations
2. Submitted documents
Documents to be Submitted When Applying
Standard Documents Requirement
Additional documents to be submited:
1. Letter or recommendation issued by Japanese embassies and consulates abroad or foreign embassies in Japan
2. Certificate of Japanese proficiency.

The period of application is generally as follows.
Application for admission: August and the middle of January to the beginning of February.

Examination: September and the beginning of February to the beginning of March

The applicants are requested to ask each school for the specific dates.

The date of admission is April 1st (the beginning of the academic year). In special cases, when judged appropriate, students may be admitted in October (the beginning of the second semester).

*

Research Institutes and Centers
Center for Development of Coopertive Research, Cryogenic Center, Documentation Center for Business Analysis, Educational Technology Center, Environmental Quality Administration Center, Experimental Farm, Information Processing Center, Institute for Experimental Animals, International Center, International Center for Exchanging Medical Researches, Marine Biological Station, Medical Center for Student's Health Service, Radioactive Isotope Laboratory, Reclamation Engineering Research Institute, Research Institute of Economics and Business Administration, Scientific Instrument Center, University Hospital

Facilities/Services for Foreign Students
International Residence: Common use facilities (Conference Room, Library, Japanese-Style Room, Lobby), Accommodation (single 112, couple 10, family 4)

Foreign Student Counselling: The University offers counselling for foreign students to help them cope with difficulties in adapting themselves to the Japanese way of life.

Special Programs for Foreign Students
Japanese Language Classes for Foreign Students are offered at all levels: elementary, intermediate, and advanced. The main purpose of the courses offered is to prepare a foreign student for the university lectures and to train him in other Japanese language skills required for university studies.

At the time of entrance to the University, all foreign students are required to take a placement test. On the basis of the results of the test, each student will be counselled as to which Japanese courses are appropriate for him.

Appropriate certificates of attendance and credits are given upon request to those students upon the satisfactory completion of the courses.

Special Lectures on Japanese Culture are given three times a year.

In winter ski tour will be organized partly sponsored by the University.

For Further Information
Undergraduate and Graduate Admission
Student Affairs Section, Student Affairs Bureau, Kobe University, 1-1 Rokkodai-cho, Nada-ku, Kobe-shi, Hyogo 657 ☎ 078-881-1212 ext. 2624

Kobe University of Mercantile Marine
(Kobe Shosen Daigaku)
5-1-1 Fukaeminami-machi, Higashinada-ku, Kobe-shi, Hyogo 658 ☎ 078-453-2332

Faculty
    Profs. 36   Assoc. Profs. 45
    Assist. Profs.   Part-time 84
    Res. Assocs. 15
Number of Students
    Undergrad. 898   Grad. 51
Library 170, 613 volumes

Outline and Characteristics of the University
Kobe University of Mercantile Marine was established in 1952. It originated, however, from Kawasaki Merchant Marine School founded in 1917. In 1920, this school was nationalized and became Kobe Nautical College, and was put under the direct supervision of the Ministry of Education.

Later, in 1945, as one of the wartime measures of the Government, Kobe Nautical College and two other nautical colleges in Tokyo and Shimizu were combined into one new Nautical College, located in Shimizu. After the war, however, the economic independence of our country demanded the rapid development of the sea transportation industry. As one of the first steps toward that purpose, in 1952, Kobe University of Mercantile Marine started its glorious career as a national university with two departments under a new system, succeeding the old tradition of Kobe Nautical College.

Thereafter, the Department of Nuclear Engineering was founded in 1972, as the eighth department of nuclear engineering among the national universities. Subsequently two more departments were founded: Department of Transportation Science in 1979 and Department of Ocean Mechanical Engineering in 1980. This was done by separating and reorganizing the Departments of Nautical Science and Marine Engineering respectively.

The Sea Training Course was founded in 1980. In order to qualify as a merchant ship's officer or engineer, the graduate is required to attend this course in succession after graduation and undergo six months' sea training. However, graduates from the Departments of Transportation Science and Ocean Mechanical Engineering cannot take this course.

As our faculty has five departments, the graduate courses have a master's course in each of the five departments. Facing Osaka Bay, the school is situated in the eastern part of Kobe Port, the largest port in Japan.

UNDERGRADUATE PROGRAMS

Faculty of Mercantile Marine (Freshmen Enrollment: 210)

Department of Marine Engineering
Electrical Engineering, Fluid Mechanics, Heat Control, Internal Combustion Engines, Machine Design, Manufacturing Processes, Propulsion Management, Steam Power

Department of Nautical Science
Meteorology and Oceanography, Naval Architecture, Navigation, Navigational Instruments, Radio Navigation Systems, Safety of Ships and Seamen, Ship Handling

Department of Nuclear Engineering
Health Physics, Nuclear Heat Transport, Nuclear Power Engineering, Reactor Engineering

Department of Ocean Mechanical Engineering
Control Apparatus and Systems, Marine Equipment and Systems, Mechanics of Structures, Ocean Science

Department of Transportation Science
Physical Distribution Management and Logistics, Shipping Economics and Management, Traffic Science and Management, Transportation Systems Engineering

Foreign Student Admission
Qualifications for Applicants
Standard Qualifications Requirement
Examination at the University
For each Department, applicants must take the Japanese Language Proficiency Test and General Examination for Foreign Students. In addition, applicants must take the entrance examination held by the University (consisting of Mathematics, Physics and English) and an interview.
Documents to be Submitted When Applying
Standard Documents Requirement
Application forms are available at the Instruction Affairs Division from early August. All applicants are required to submit the specified application documents to the Instruction Affairs Division by February 15.

GRADUATE PROGRAMS

Graduate School of Mercantile Marine (First Year Enrollment : Master's 38)
Divisions
Marine Engineering, Nautical Science, Nuclear Engineering, Ocean Mechanical Engineering, Transportation Science

Foreign Student Admission
Qualifications for Applicants
Master's Program
Standard Qualifications Requirement
Examination at the University
Master's Program

Applicants must take the same entrance examination consisting of a written examination and an interview given to Japanese students.
The entrance examination is held twice annually, in October and March.
Documents to be Submitted When Applying
Standard Documents Requirement
Application forms are available at the Instruction Affairs Division from early August to early December. All applicants are required to submit the specified application documents to the Instruction Affairs Division by mid-September or mid-February.

*

Research Institutes and Centers
Awaji Marine Practice Center, Computer Center, Health Service Center, Research Institute for Cargo Transportation, Ship Model Basin, Ship Training Center, Training Ship "Fukae Maru"

Facilities/Services for Foreign Students
Undergraduate students are required to live in the dormitory for the 1st and 2nd year.

Special Programs for Foreign Students
Japanese Language (1st year and 2nd year)
Things Japanese (1st year and 2nd year)

For Further Information
Undergraduate and Graduate Admission
Entrance Examination Section, Instruction Affairs Division, Kobe University of Mercantile Marine, 5-1-1 Fukaeminami-machi, Higashinada-ku, Kobe-shi, Hyogo 658 ☎ 078–453–2332 ext. 244

Kochi Medical School
(Kochi Ika Daigaku)
Kohasu, Oko-cho, Nankoku-shi, Kochi 781-51
☎ 0888–66–5811

Faculty
Profs. 39   Assoc. Profs. 38
Assist. Profs. Full–time 31; Part–time 149
Res. Assocs. 127
Number of Students
Undergrad. 628   Grad. 93
Library 73, 930 volumes

Outline and Characteristics of the University
The School, composed of one faculty of medicine, was founded by the Government in October 1976, admitted its first undergraduate students in April 1978, and sent out its first graduates in March 1984. The School Hospital was opened in October 1981 for clinical education and public service. The Graduate School was opened and began to offer Doctor's programs (13 divisions of four courses) in April 1984.
The purpose of the School is to train students so that they may achieve a high level of medical knowledge and technique, and to cultivate excellent humanitarian practitioners and researchers of medicine.

The Graduate School aims at developing original and up-to-date researchers.

The School campus, surrounded by natural beauty, is located about 10 km to the east of Kochi, the main city in southern Shikoku. The area of the school and its hospital is about 204, 000 m².

UNDERGRADUATE PROGRAMS

Faculty of Medicine (Freshmen Enrollment: 100)
Department of Medicine
Anatomy, Anesthesiology, Biochemistry, Clinical Laboratory Diagnosis, Dentistry and Oral Surgery, Dermatology, Forensic Medicine, Geriatric Medicine, Hygiene, Immunology, Internal Medicine, Microbiology, Neuropsychiatry, Neurosurgery, Obstetrics and Gynecology, Ophthalmology, Orthopedics, Otorhinolaryngology, Parasitology, Pathology, Pediatrics, Pharmacology, Physiology, Public Health, Radiology, Surgery, Urology

Foreign Student Admission
Qualifications for Applicants
Standard Qualifications Requirement
Foreign applicants must take all the subjects of the Joint First-Stage Achievement Test conducted by the University Entrance Examination Center.
Examination at the University
Foreign applicants are selected using the same criteria as that used for Japanese applicants.
Documents to be Submitted When Applying
Standard Documents Requirement
If the applicant has completed courses at a Japanese language school in Japan and/or at an upper school abroad, official transcripts to so certify is also required.
A List of Application Requirements is made public at the beginning of December every year.
All applicants are required to submit the specified application documents to the School Administration Office by January 19.

GRADUATE PROGRAMS

Graduate School of Medicine (First Year Enrollment : Doctor's 30)
Divisions
Biological Function and Metabolism, Developmental and Biological Morphology, Etiopathogenesis, Regulatory System in the Body

Foreign Student Admission
Qualifications for Applicants
Doctor's Program
Standard Qualifications Requirement
Documents to be Submitted When Applying
Standard Documents Requirement
*

For Further Information
Undergraduate and Graduate Admission

School Affairs Section, School Administration Office, Kochi Medical School, Kohasu, Oko-cho, Nankoku-shi, Kochi 781-51 ☎ 0888-66-5811 ext. 2420

Kochi University
(Kochi Daigaku)
2-5-1 Akebono-cho, Kochi-shi, Kochi 780
☎ 0888-44-0111

Faculty
    Profs. 143   Assoc. Profs. 126
    Assist. Profs. Full–time 30; Part–time 132
    Res. Assocs. 32
Number of Students
    Undergrad. 3, 832   Grad. 139
Library   453, 362 volumes

Outline and Characteristics of the University
Kochi University was established in 1949 as a national university under the reformed system of education. The university now consists of four faculties: the Faculty of Agriculture, the Faculty of Education, the Faculty of Humanities and Economics, and the Faculty of Science. It also operates a Graduate School of Agriculture (Master's Degree,), a Graduate School of Science (Master's Degree), the Usa Marine Biological Institute, other research and educational institutes and affiliated schools. The United Graduate school of Agriculture (Doctor's Degree) was formed in 1985 by combining the Faculties of Agriculture of three universities, Kochi University, Kagawa University and Ehime University.

The university campuses are located in and around Kochi City, the capital of Kochi Prefecture. The Prefecture, on the south side of the Island of Shikoku, faces the Pacific Ocean to the south and the Shikoku Mountain Range to the north. The area is blessed with a mild climate and four distinct seasons, as well as a beautiful natural coastline and attractive local culture. Kochi City is rich in historic sites and has a population of approximately 320, 000 inhabitants. It can be reached From Osaka within five hours by train, one hour by air, or ten hours by ferry boat; from Tokyo it is less than two hours by air.

The main university offices are located on the Asakura campus. It is situated in the western section of Kochi City and includes the Administration Bureau, the Department of Student Affairs, the Faculty of Education, the Faculty of Humanities and Economics, the Faculty of Science, the Graduate School of Science, the University Library, the Health Administration Center, the Data Processing Center, and the Student Hall.

The Nissho Campus, is situated about 20 kilometers east of the main campus, near Kochi Airport houses the Faculty of Agriculture, the Graduate School of Agriculture, the University Farm, and other educational facilities.

The Usa Marine Biological Institute is located in Usa-cho, Tosa-shi. This town is on the Pacific coast 20 kilometers to the southwest of the Asakura Campus and is 40 minutes' ride by car.

UNDERGRADUATE PROGRAMS

Faculty of Agriculture (Freshmen Enrollment: 195)
  Department of Agricultural Chemistry
  Department of Agricultural Engineering
  Department of Cultural Fisheries
  Department of Forestry
  Department of Subtropical Agriculture
Faculty of Education (Freshmen Enrollment: 250)
  Teacher Training Course for Arts and Crafts
  Teacher Training Course for Elementary School
  Teacher Training Course in Health and Physical Education
  Teacher Training Course for Lower Secondary School
  Teacher Training Course in Teaching of the Mentally and Physically Handicapped
Faculty of Humanities and Economics (Freshmen Enrollment: 270)
  Department of Economics
  Department of Humanities
Faculty of Science (Freshmen Enrollment: 205)
  Department of Biology
  Department of Chemistry
  Department of Geology
  Department of Mathematics
  Department of Physics

Foreign Student Admission
  Qualifications for Applicants
  Standard Qualifications Requirement
  1. Applicants can not be Japanese nationals.
  2. Applicants must be 18 years of age or older and have obtained the legal baccalaureate of the International Baccalaureate Office authenticated by the Swiss Civil Code.
  3. Applicants must also be recommended by the embassy or legation of their country, or by an organization authorized by the university.
  Examination at the University

Applicants, Japanese or foreign, cannot be granted admission without passing the entrance examination given by the university. There is a special examination for foreign applicants, different from the one given to Japanese students. This special entrance examination varies with each faculty and graduate school. The number of foreign students to be admitted is not fixed, and they are admitted within the full number of students. It is advisable for applicants to have arrived in Japan by the time of application.
  1. Applicants are required to take the Japanese Language Proficiency Test and the General Examination for Foreign Students.
  2. Applicants must take the Japanese language examination and an oral test at Kochi University in February.
  Documents to be Submitted When Applying
  Standard Documents Requirement

Application forms and explanatory documents are sent to applicants from the university upon request.

The following specified forms and documents should be also submitted to the Department of Student Affairs by February 5.
  1. Certificate of Results of the Japanese Language Proficiency Test and the General Examination for Foreign Students.
  2. Letter of recommendation from the applicant's Embassy or Consulate in Japan, or by an organization authorized by the university.

The names of those who have passed the examination are announced at the university in the middle of March, and a written notice of admission is sent to each of the successful applicants. Prospe ctive applicants should contact the Department of Student Affairs regarding the admission procedures.

GRADUATE PROGRAMS

United Graduate School of Agricultural Sciences (First Year Enrollment : Doctor's 16)
  Divisions
Applied Bioresource Science, Bioresource Production Science, Life Environment Conservation Science
Graduate School of Agriculture (First Year Enrollment : Master's 58)
  Divisions
Agricultural Chemistry, Agricultural Engineering, Cultural Fisheries, Forestry, Subtropical Agriculture
Graduate School of Science (First Year Enrollment : Master's 15)
  Divisions
Biology, Chemistry, Geology, Mathematics, Physics

Foreign Student Admission
  Qualifications for Applicants
Master's Program
  Standard Qualifications Requirement
Doctor's Program
  Standard Qualifications Requirement
  Examination at the University
Master's Program

Applicants are selected on the basis of results of an examination and the submitted application documents. The applicants must take the same entrance examination (a written test, an interview on their specialized subject and, English test) as Japanese students. There is no special selection system for foreign applicants.
Doctor's Program

The selection is based on an examination, submitted documents, and a health examination. The entrance examination includes a written test on a specialized subject, English (foreign applicants have a choice of English essay or Japanese essay), and an interview on the applicant's Master's thesis, research report, or research plan.

Applicants must enter Japan by the date of application submission.

A written notice of admission is sent to successful applicants.

Those applicants who have passed the screening are granted admission to the graduate course and given a written permit. They must follow and complete all the necessary procedures for entering Japan as soon as possible, arrive at the university by the time of matriculation, and follow registration procedures for admission.

Documents to be Submitted When Applying
Standard Documents Requirement

Letter of recommendation by the government, embassy, or consulate of the applicant's country, or by the organization authorized by the university.

In addition to the above, a Master's thesis and other academic documents are required for application to the Doctoral Course.

Aapplication forms and other related documents are available at the Registrar's Office of each Graduate School beginning in June. All applicants are required to submit the specified application documents to the Dean of each Graduate School by August 31. Inquiries about details should be directed to the appropriate Graduate School Office.

Research Institutes and Centers
Usa Marine Biological Institute
Facilities/Services for Foreign Students
Accommodation: 3 rooms per family.
Special Programs for Foreign Students

Japanese language supplementary classes are available.
For Further Information
Undergraduate Admission
Department of Student Affairs, Kochi University, 2-5-1 Akebono-cho, Kochi-shi, Kochi 780 ☎ 0888–44–0111
Graduate Admission
Graduate School of Agriculture and United Graduate School of Agricultural Sciences: Division of Student Affairs, Graduate School of Agriculture, Kochi University, Otsu 200 Monobe, Nankoku-shi, Kochi 783 ☎ 0888–63–4141
Graduate School of Science: Registrar's Office, Graduate School of Science, Kochi University, 2–5–1 Akebono–cho, Kochi–shi, Kochi 780 ☎ 0888–44–0111

Kumamoto University
(Kumamoto Daigaku)
2-40-1 Kurokami, Kumamoto-shi, Kumamoto 860
☎ 096–344–2111

Faculty
    Profs. 272   Assoc. Profs. 222
    Assist. Profs. Full–time 110; Part–time 426
    Res. Assocs. 298
Number of Students
    Undergrad. 7, 655   Grad. 776
Library 955, 442 volumes

Outline and Characteristics of the University

Kumamoto University was established on May 31, 1949, under the National School Establishment Law that reformed the Japanese educational system after World War Ⅱ. The new University incorporated the following older institutions: Kumamoto Medical College (established 1896), The Fifth High School (1886), Kumamoto Technical College (1906), Kumamoto Normal School (1874), and Kumamoto Pharmaceutical College (1885). Today the University is composed of seven main specialized faculties: Letters, Education, Law, Science, Medicine, Pharmaceutical Sciences, Engineering, plus an eighth liberal arts faculty of General Education. Beginning with the establishment of a graduate program in medicine in 1955, the University now also offers graduate training and advanced degrees in pharmaceutical sciences, engineering, science, law, letters, and education.

Since the University's inception, a number of allied schools and facilities have been incorporated and developed within its structure. These include Aitsu Marine Biological Station; University Hospital; Institute for Medical Immunology; Institute for Medical Genetics; Laboratory Animal Research Center; Medicinal Plant Garden; Engineering Research Equipment Center; High Energy Rate Laboratory; Center for Educational Technology; and Kumamoto University College of Medical Science. In addition, the University operates a Kindergarten, Elementary School, Junior High School, and a School for Handicapped Children.

Kumamoto University is in the city of Kumamoto (population 568, 137) located in the middle of Kyushu, the southernmost main island of Japan. By air, Kumamoto is 90 minutes from Tokyo and 60 minutes from Osaka; by train it is 90 minutes from Fukuoka City. Nicknamed "City of Woods, " Kumamoto is one of Japan's oldest cities, and still has traces of its castle town past.

The University's main campus is located in the Kurokami district of the city, at the foot of Mt. Tatsuda, within easy access to all other parts of the city by bus. The main campus is the seat of the University main library, gymnasium, athletic grounds, central administrative offices, and the Letters, Education, Law, Science, Engineering, and General Education Faculties. Additional campuses include those of the Medical School, the University Hospital, and Kumamoto University College of Medical Science (at Honjo and Kuhonji), and the Faculty of Pharmaceutical Sciences (at Oe). They are two or three kilometers from the main campus.

UNDERGRADUATE PROGRAMS

Faculty of Education (Freshmen Enrollment: 390)
Elementary School Teachers' Training Course
High School Nurse Teachers' Training Course
Junior High School Teachers' Training Course
School Health Teachers' Training Course
Special Education Teachers' Training Course
Art, Domestic Science, Education, English, Health and Physical Education, Industrial Technology, Japanese, Mathematics, Music, Natural Science, Nursing, Psychology, School Health, Social Studies, Special Education

Faculty of Engineering (Freshmen Enrollment: 575)
Department of Applied Chemistry
Biorelated Chemistry, Chemistry of Industrial Meterials, Fundamental Industrial Chemistry
Derpartment of Architecture
Architectural Engineering, Architectural System Engineering, Architecture
Derpartment of Basic Engineering
Applied Mechanics, Engineering Mathematics
Derpartment of Civil and Environmental Engineering
Geo-environmental Engineering, Hydro-environmental Engineering, Infrastructural Engineering
Department of Electrical Engineering and Computer Science
Cicuits-Systems and Electronic Devices, Communication Systems, Electrical Energy, Information Processing Systems, Instrumentation and Control Engineering
Department of Machanical Engineering
Measurement and Control Systems, Mechanical Engineering Fundamentals, Precision and Production Engineering
Department of Materials Science and Resource Engineering
Materials Engineering, Process and System Engineering, Resourse Engineering.

Faculty of Law (Freshmen Enrollment: 260)
Department of Law
Civil Law, Criminal Law, Economics, Fundamentals of Law, Politics, Public Law, Social Law

Faculty of Letters (Freshmen Enrollment: 170)
Department of History
Archaeology, Cultural History, Japanese History, Occidental History, Oriental History
Department of Literature
Chinese Language and Literature, Comparative Literature, English Language, English Literature, French Language and Literature, German Language, German Literature, Japanese Language, Japanese Literature, Linguistics
Department of Philosophy
Aesthetics, Ethics, Philosophy, Philosophy of Science
Department of Regional Science
Anthropogeography, Folkore, Regional Sociology, Sociology

Faculty of Medicine (Freshmen Enrollment: 100)
Department of Medicine
Anatomy, Anesthesiology, Biochemistry, Dento-Oral Surgery, Dermatology, Forensic Medicine Hygiene, Internal Medicine, Microbiology, Neuropsychiatry, Neurosurgery, Obstetrics and Gynecology, Ophthalmology, Orthopedic Surgery, Otorhinolaryngology, Parasitology, Pathology, Pediatrics, Pharmacology, Physiology, Public Health, Radiology, Surgery, Urology

Faculty of Pharmaceutical Sciences (Freshmen Enrollment: 90)
Department of Pharmaceutical Sciences
Hygienic Chemistry (Biochemistry, Hygienic Chemistry, Pharmaceutical Analytical Chemistry, Radiochemistry), Medicinal Chemistry (Medicinal Chemistry, Pharmaceutical Chemistry, Pharmaceutical Engineering, Pharmacognosy), Pharmaceutics (Biopharmaceutics, Physical Pharmaceutics), Pharmacological Sciences (Medicinal Microbiology, Pharmaceutical Physical Chemistry, Pharmacology)

Faculty of Science (Freshmen Enrollment: 135)
Department of Biology
Animal Physiology and Biochemistry, Animal Systematics and Morphology, Plant Physiology and Biochemistry, Plant Systematics and Morphology
Department of Chemistry
Analytical Chemistry, Inorganic Chemistry, Organic Chemistry, Physical Chemistry
Department of Geology
Economic Geology, Geology and Paleontology, Geotectonics, Petrology and Mineralogy
Department of Mathematics
Algebra, Analysis, Applied Analysis, Geometry, Mathematical Statistics
Department of Physics
Atomic and Molecular Physics, Elementary Particle Physics, Radiation Physics, Solid State Physics

Foreign Student Admission
Qualifications for Applicants
Standard Qualifications Requirement
Those who have an International Baccalaureate Diploma and are 18 years of age or older may also apply.
Examination at the University
Achievement Test: Faculty of Education–Interview; Faculty of Engineering–Mathematics and Science; Faculty of Law–Japanese Language and Foreign Language (English, German or French) ; Faculty of Letters–Short Essay in Japanese; Faculty of

Medicine*–Mathematics, English, and Science; Faculty of Pharmaceutical Sciences–Mathematics and Science; Faculty of Science–Mathematics and Science

*The Faculty of Medicine does not adopt a special selection system for foreign applicants, and they must take the Joint First-Stage Achievement Test given in late January.

Documents to be Submitted When Applying
Standard Documents Requirement

A letter of recommendation or a statement of citizenship issued by the applicant's government or embassy in Japan is also required. The registration prospectus and application forms for admission will be available at the Admissions Section in early November. Application documents must be filed by the Admissions Section between January 12 and 19.

ONE-YEAR GRADUATE PROGRAMS

One-Year Graduate Course of Special Education (Enrollment 30)
Special Education for the Mentally Handicapped

GRADUATE PROGRAMS

Graduate School of Education (First Year Enrollment : Master's 25)
Divisions
School Education, School Subjects Education (Home Economics Education, Mathematics Education, Science Education, Social Studies Education), Special Education
Graduate School of Engineering (First Year Enrollment : Master's 98)
Divisions
Architecture, Civil Engineering, Electrical Engineering, Electronic Engineering, Environmental Construction Engineering, Industrial Chemistry, Information Engineering, Mechanical Engineering, Metallurgical Engineering, Production Engineering, Resource Development and Mechanical Engineering, Synthetic Chemistry
Graduate School of Law (First Year Enrollment : Master's 26)
Division
Law
Graduate School of Letters (First Year Enrollment : Master's 28)
Divisions
English Literature, German Literature, History, Japanese Literature, Philosophy, Regional Science
Graduate School of Medicine (First Year Enrollment : Doctor's 78)
Divisions
Internal Medicine, Pathology, Physiology, Social Medicine, Surgery
Graduate School of Pharmaceutical Sciences (First Year Enrollment : Master's 26, Doctor's 6)
Division
Pharmaceutical Sciences

Graduate School of Science (First Year Enrollment : Master's 40)
Divisions
Biology, Chemistry, Geography, Mathematics, Physics
Graduate School of Science and Technlogy (First Year Enrollment : Doctor's 30)
Divisions
Environmental Science, Industrial Science, System Science

Foreign Student Admission
Qualifications for Applicants
Master's Program
Standard Qualifications Requirement
Doctor's Program
Graduate School of Medicine: Those who have completed 18-year school course, or its equivalent (the last course must be medical or dental), or who have been recognized by Kumamoto University as having academic ability equivalent to that of a graduate from a Japanese college of medicine or dentistry.
Graduate School other than Medicine: Those who have been recognized by Kumamoto University as having academic ability equivalent to that of a person with master's degree from a Japanese university or college.
Examination at the University
Master's Program
Achievement Test:
1. Special Subject of Study
2. Foreign Language (English, German, or French)
3. Interviews
Doctor's Program
Achievement Test:
1. Special Subject of Study
2. Japanese Language (limited to Graduate School of Engineering)
3. Foreign Language (English, German, or French)
4. Interviews
Documents to be Submitted When Applying
Standard Documents Requirement
Following documents are also required.
1. A letter of recommendation or a statement of citizenship issued by the applicant's government or embassy in Japan.
2. Other papers required by the Graduate School.

Registration and examination dates vary according to the Graduate School and the year. Inquiries should be addressed to the appropriate Graduate School.

*

Research Institutes and Centers
Aitsu Marine Biological Station, Center for Educational Technology, Cooperative Resarch Center, Engineering Research Equipment Center, High Energy

Rate Laboratory, Institute for Medical Genetics, Institute for Medical Immunology, Laboratory Animal Research Center, Medicinal Plant Garden

Facilities/Services for Foreign Students

Foreign Student Study Room: Located in the Kumamoto University Alumni Association Building on the main campus, this room is offered for study and relaxation to foreign students.

International House:

Whenever space permitting, the accommodations are available for foreign guest scholars and foreign students.

Shared Facilities: Lobby, Conference Room, Seminar Room, Japanese-Style Room

Accommodation: 55 rooms (single 49, couple 3, family 3)

Special Programs for Foreign Students

Japanese Language I & II for first year students, Japanese Language III & IV for second year students, Japanese Studies I for first year students, Japanese Studies II for second year students, Japanese Studies III for third year students.

For Further Information

Undergraduate and Graduate Admission

Instruction Section, Student Division, Student Office, Kumamoto University, 2-40-1 Kurokami, Kumamoto-shi, Kumamoto 860 ☎ 096-344-2111 ext. 2117, 2118

Kyoto Institute of Technology
(Kyoto Kogei Sen-i Daigaku)

Hashigami-cho, Matsugasaki, Sakyo-ku, Kyoto-shi, Kyoto 606 ☎ 075-791-3211

Faculty
Profs. 91   Assoc. Profs. 81
Assist. Profs. Full-time 13; Part-time 144
Res. Assoc. 56
Number of Students
Undergrad. 2,535   Grad. 341
Library 258,200 volumes

Outline and Characteristics of the University

Kyoto Institute of Technology (KIT) was founded in May 1949, as a national university, in accordance with the National School Establishment Law, by incorporating two former national colleges : Kyoto College of Industry (established 1902) and Kyoto College of Textile Fibers (established 1899).

The Institute consists of the Faculty of Engineering and Design and the Faculty of Textile Science. Each faculty has an undergraduate school with a four-year program leading to the Bachelor's degree. The graduate school consists of a two-year program leading to the degree of Master of Engineering or Master of Agriculture and of a three-year program leading to the Ph. D. (Doctor of Engineering).

The undergraduate school and two-year gradu-

ate programs offer courses in the late afternoon and evening. The admission of veterans of society wish to increase their knowledge is heartily encouraged.

KIT has placed special emphasis on the basic theory and application of soft technology in order to educate students to become competent and promising scientists with sufficient ability to cope with the technology that has been rapidly innovated in recent years.

Detailed information concerning KIT will be found in a separate catalogue which may be obtained by writing to the Office of Student Admission.

UNDERGRADUATE PROGRAMS

Faculty of Engineering and Design (Freshmen Enrollment: 565)

Department of Architecture and Design
Design and Systems
Architectural Planning, Environmental Engineering, Environment Design, Product Design, Structural Engineering
Design and Theory
Architectural Design, Architectural/Design History and Theory, Housing, Space/Visual Design

Department of Chemistry and Materials Technology
Chemical Reaction of Materials, Function of Materials, Properties and Processing of Materials

Department of Electronics and Information Science
Computer/Communication and System, Electronics, Information Science and Technology

Department of Mechanical and System Engineering
Mechanical System Design
Algebraic Analysis, CAE, Fluid Mechanics, Materials for Machine, Mechanics of Materials, Mechatronics, Power Engineering, Strength and Fructure of Materials, Thermal Engineering
Mechanical System Development
Engineering Plasticity and Metal Forming Processes, Manufacturing Process and Systems, Mathematical Analysis, Non-Traditional Machining, Production Management Engineering, System and Control Engineering, Vibration Proof Engineering

Faculty of Textile Science (Freshmen Enrollment: 215)

Department of Applied Biology
Biochemistry Course
Biochemistry, Functional Biochemistry, Microbial Production, Protein and Nucleic Acid Chemistry
Life Science Course
Cell Biology, Genetics, Molecular Biology, Physiology
Sericultural Biology Course
Microbiology, Plant Physiology, Sericultural Production, Silkworm Pathology, Silkworm Physiology

Department of Polymer Science and Engineering
Industrial Biochemistry course

Biopolymer chemistry, Functional biophysics, Synthetic biochemistry
Polymer Chemistry course
Applied polymer chemistry, Instrumental analysis, Polymer reaction chemistry, Synthetic organic chemistry
Polymer Engineering course
Design of textile products, Molecular engineering of polymers, Polymer mechanics, Textile and polymer machinery
Polymer Material course
Fibrous materials, Functional materials, molecular design of polymers, Polymer physics

Foreign Student Admission
Qualifications for Applicants
Standard Qualifications Requirement
Proficiency in Japanese.
Examination at the University
Written and oral tests in early February.
Documents to be Submitted When Applying
Standard Documents Requirement
Appliciation forms are available at the Admissions Office in September. Application period : December 5-9 (Faculty of Engineering and Design) or November 30-December 5 (Faculty of Textile Science).

GRADUATE PROGRAMS

Graduate School of Technological Science (First Year Enrollment : Master's 120, Doctor's 26)
Divisions
Applied Biology, Applied Science for Functionality, Architecture and Design, Chemistry and Materials Technology, Electronics and Information Science, Information and Production Science, Materials Science, Mechanical and System Engineering, Polymer Science and Engineering

Foreign Student Admission
Examination at the University
Master's Program
Applicants must pass the special entrance examination consisting of written and oral tests, to be held in early February.
Doctor's Program
Same as Mater's programs
Documents to be Submitted When Applying
Standard Documents Requirement
Application forms will be available at the Admissions Office in September. All applicants are required to submit the specified application documents to the Admission Office between December 5-9.

*

Services for Foreign Students
Foreign Students' Common Room
Special Programs for Foreign Students
Special courses in Japanese Language are provided for foreign students : Japanese I–IV

For Further Information
Undergraduate Admission
Student Affairs Section, Engineering and Design/Textile Science, Kyoto Institute of Technology, Goshokaido-cho, Matsugasaki, Sakyo-ku, Kyoto-shi, kyoto 606 ☎ 075-791-3211 ext. 410, 412 (Engineering and Design) ; 708, 709 (Textile Science)
Graduate Admission
Chief, General Affairs Division, Technological Science, Kyoto Institute of Technology, Hashigami-cho, Matsugasaki, Sakyo-ku, Kyoto-shi, Kyoto ☎ 075-791-3211 ext. 220

Kyoto University
(Kyoto Daigaku)

Yoshida Honmachi, Sakyo-ku, Kyoto-shi, Kyoto 606
☎ 075-753-7531

Faculty
   Profs. 682   Assoc. Profs. 651
   Assist. Profs. Full-time 142; Part-time 965
   Res. Assocs. 1, 093
Number of Students
   Undergrad. 12, 219   Grad. 3, 903
Library 4, 670, 946 volumes

Outline and Characteristics of the University
Kyoto University was founded in 1897 by the Imperial Ordinance under the name of Kyoto Imperial University. Within ten years of the foundation of the University, the Colleges of Science and Engineering, Law, Medicine and Letters were opened. In 1914, the College of Science and Engineering was divided into the College of Science and the College of Engineering, giving the University five Colleges. In accordance with the revision of the Imperial University Law of 1919, the five Colleges were reorganized into five independent Faculties: Engineering, Law, Letters, Medicine and Science. In the same year the Faculty of Economics was established, and in 1923, the Faculty of Agriculture was established.
In 1947, the School Education Law was enacted, and the education system in Japan was greatly reformed. In the same year Kyoto Imperial University was renamed Kyoto University. In 1949, Kyoto University was recognized as a four-year university and the Faculty of Education was established. In 1953, the Graduate School under the new system was founded to promote and complete the Graduate School. This consisted of eight Graduate Schools: Agriculture, Economics, Education, Engineering, Law, Letters, Pharmaceutical Sciences and Science.
In 1954, the Bunko (The Branch School of the University) was renamed the College of Liberal Arts and Sciences, and in 1955, the Graduate School of Medicine was established. In 1960, the old Faculty of Medicine was divided into the Faculty of Medicine and the Faculty of Pharmaceutical Sciences. At pres-

ent, Kyoto University, one of the leading universities in Japan, is comprised of nine Faculties, the College of Liberal Arts and Sciences, the Graduate Schools, 13 Research Institutes, 14 Centers and the Junior College of Medical Technology.

The campus is located in the historical city of Kyoto, which was for many centuries the capital of Japan, and is a city where traditional Japanese culture has been preserved. Today, Kyoto Univesity enrolls about 16, 000 students and a fulltime faculty of 2, 600. About 350 researchers and 650 students come from more than 60 countries to the University every year.

Since its foundation in 1897, Kyoto University has been dedicated to the establishment of a tradition of academic freedom in higher education of Japan and has so far produced more than 123, 647 graduates who have made contributions in the academic, political, industrial, and other important aspects of society, both at home and abroad. As a result, the University now enjoys the reputation of "Kyoto School" in the Asian-oriented disciplines of the Humanities. Further, the University is proud to have produced leading scholars and shares in the glory of almost all of the Japanese Nobel Prize winners in the field of natural science.

UNDERGRADUATE PROGRAMS

Faculty of Agriculture (Freshmen Enrollment: 325)

Department of Agricultural and Forestry Economics

Agricultural History, Agricultural Policy, Farm Accounting, Farm Management, Forest Policy, The Principles of Agricultural Sciences

Department of Agricultural Biology

Applied Botany, Entomology, Genetics, Plant Pathology

Department of Agricultural Chemistry

Biochemistry, Biopolymer Chemistry, Fermentation Physiology and Applied Microbiology, Pesticide Chemistry, Plant Nutrition, Soil Science

Department of Agricultural Engineering

Agricultural Prime Mover, Agricultural Structure Engineering, Farm Machinery, Farm Processing Machinery, Irrigation and Drainage, Rural Planning, Water Use Engineering

Department of Agronomy and Horticultural Science

Crop Science, Plant Breeding, Pomology, Vegetable and Ornamental Horticulture, Weed Science

Department of Animal Science

Animal Breeding, Animal Nutrition, Animal Reproduction, Functional Anatomy of Farm Animals

Department of Fisheries

Aquatic Biology, Aquatic Microbiology, Fisheries Chemistry, Fisheries Physics

Department of Food Science and Technology

Analysis of Agricultural Products, Bioengineering, Enzyme Chemistry, Food Chemistry, Industrial Microbiology, Nutritional Chemistry

Department of Forestry

Erosion Control, Forest Ecology, Forest Management, Forestry Engineering, Landscape Architecture

Department of Wood Science and Technology

Chemical Processing of Wood, Forest Products Chemistry, Materials for Wood Improvement, Wood Structure, Wood Technology, Woodworking Machinery

Faculty of Economics (Freshmen Enrollment: 240)

Department of Business Administration

Business Administration, Business Policy, Marketing and Accounting Analysis

Department of Economics

Economic History, Economic Policy, Economic Theory, History of Social Thought, Industrial Economics, International Economics, Money and Banking, Public Finance, Social Policy, Statistics

Faculty of Education (Freshmen Enrollment: 60)

Department of Education

Comparative Education, Educational Anthropology, Educational Guidance, History of Education, Pedagogy, School Curriculum

Department of Educational Psychology

Audio-Visual Education, Clinical Psychology, Educational Psychology

Department of Educational Sociology

Adult Education, Educational Administration, Educational Sociology, Library Science

Faculty of Engineering (Freshmen Enrollment: 1, 030)

Department of Aeronautical Engineering

Airplane Construction, Fluid Dynamics, Gas Dynamics, Propulsion Engineering, Strength of Structures, Theory of Vibration

Department of Applied Mathematics and Physics

Applied Mathematics, Applied Mechanics, Control Theory, Engineering Mathematics, Engineering Mechanics, Logical Systems, Operations Research

Department of Architectural Engineering

Architectural Environment Control, Area Planning, Planning and Facilities Reinforced Concrete Construction, Soil and Foundation Engineering, Theory of Steel Structures

Department of Architecture

Architectural Design and Theory, Architectural Environment, Architectural Planning, Building Construction, Building Equipment, History of Architecture, Materials for Building Structures, Mechanics of Building Structures

Department of Chemical Engineering

Chemical Engineering Thermodynamics, Chemical Reaction Engineering, Diffusional Unit Operations, Equipments and Materials for Chemical Processes, Mechanical Unit Operations, Process Control and Process Systems Engineering, Transport Phenomena

Department of Civil Engineering

Bridge Engineering, Coastal Engineering, Construction Engineering, Construction Materials Engineering, Design in Civil Engineering, Hydraulics, Hydrology and water Resources Engineering, Regional Planning and Systems Analysis, River Engineering, Soil Mechanics, Structural Earthquake Engineering, Structural Mechanics

Department of Electrical Engineering

Applied Electrical Science, Electrical Discharge Engineering, Electrical Machinery, Electric Power Generation/Transmission and Distribution, Electromagnetic Theory, Measurement Instrumentation and Control

Department of Electrical Engineering II

Control Engineering, Digital Systems/Wire Communication Engineering, Electrical Power System Engineering, Electric Network Theory, Energy Conversion Devices, Radio Communication Engineering

Department of Electronics

Electron Devices, Electronic Circuit Engineering, Electron Physics, High Frequency Engineering, Quantum Electronics, Semiconductor Engineering

Department of Engineering Science

Atomic and Plasma Spectroscopy, Materials Science, Mechanical Behavior of Materials, Solid State Physics, Thermal Physics

Department of Environmental and Sanitary Engineering

Environmental Hygiene, Environmental Systems Engineering, Industrial Health Engineering, Radiological Health Engineering, Water Quality Control Engineering, Water Supply and Sewerage Engineering

Department of Hydrocarbon Chemistry

Catalyst Chemistry, Catalyst Engineering, Catalyst Physics, Hydrocarbon Chemistry Fundamentals, Hydrocarbon Physical Chemistry, Petrochemical Engineering, Petroleum Conversion Engineering

Department of Industrial Chemistry

General Analytical Chemistry, General Physical Chemistry, Industrial Analytical Chemistry, Industrial Biochemistry, Industrial Electrochemistry, Industrial Physical Chemistry, Industrial Solid-State Chemistry, Inorganic Structural Chemistry, Organic Chemistry of Natural Products, Organic Reaction Chemistry

Department of Information Science

Computer Software, Computer Sytsems, Information Processing, Information Science Fundamentals, Information Systems Engineering, Logic Circuits and Automata

Department of Mechanical Engineering

Applied Thermodynamics, Engineering Materials, Engineering Plasticity, Fluid Mechanics, Heat Transfer, Lubrication and Hydraulic Engineering, Mechanics of Materials, Power Engineering, Strength of Materials

Department of Metallurgy

Electrometallurgy, Extractive Metallurgy, Foundry and Mechanical Metallurgy, Process Metallurgy and Quality Control, Pyrochemical Metallurgy, Science of Metallic Materials

Department of Metal Science and Technology

Foundry Technology, Lattice Defects and Crystal Plasticity, Metal Physics, Science of Steels, Structural Metallurgy, Welding Engineering

Department of Mineral Science and Technology

Applied Geology, Applied Measurement Equipements for Iron-Steel Making/Continuous Casting and Plastic Working Systems, Exploration Geophysics and Technology, Mineral Processing and Particulate Technology, Rock Mechanics and Excavating Technology

Department of Nuclear Engineering

Atomic and Nuclear Physics, Atomic and Nuclear Reaction Engineering, Nuclear Fuel, Nuclear Materials, Nuclear Reactor Engineering, Nuclear Reactor Physics

Department of Polymer Chemistry

Fundamental Study of Polymer Chemistry, Material Science of Polymers/Radiation Polymer Chemistry. Molecular Properties of Polymers, Polymer Mechanics in the Solid-State, Polymer Physics, Polymer Synthesis, Structure of Polymers

Department of Precision Mechanics

Control Engineering, Exact Manufacturing Science, Machine Elements, Production Engineering, Systems Engineering, Vibration Engineering

Department of Synthetic Chemistry

Free Radical Chemistry, Organic and Bioorganic Catalysis, Organometallic Chemistry, Physical Organic Chemistry, Polymerlization Chemistry, Synthetic Organic Chemistry

Department of Transportation Engineering

Foundation Engineering, Structural Problems for Transportation Engineering, Terminal Facilities, Transportation and Traffic Planning, Transportation Facility Planning, Urban Transportation Engineering

Faculty of Law (Freshmen Enrollment: 400, Third Year Additional Enrollment 50)

Department of Law

Administrative Law, Civil Law, Commercial Law, Comparative Law, Comparative Politics, Constitutional Law, Contemporary Foreign Laws, Criminal Law, Criminal Procedure, Criminology, Diplomatic History, General Legal Theory of the State, Governmental Process, History of Political Ideas, International Law, International Politics, Japanese Legal History, Labour Law, Law of Bankruptcy, Law of Civil Procedure, Laws of International Trade and Transactions, Legal Philosophy, Maritime Law, Occidental Legal History, Political and Diplomatic History of Japan, Political History, Political Theory, Private International Law, Public Administration, Roman Law, Social Security Law, Sociology of Law, Tax Law

Faculty of Letters (Freshmen Enrollment: 220)

Department of History

Archaeology, Contemporary History, European History, Geography, Japanese History, Oriental History, West Asian History

Department of Literature

American Literature, Chinese Language and Literature, Classics (Greek and Latin), English Language and Literature, French Language and Literature, German Language and Literature, Indic Philology, Italian Language and Literature, Japanese Language and Literature, Linguistics

Department of Philosophy

Aesthetics and Art History, Buddhist Studies, Christian Studies, Ethics, History of Chinese Philosophy, History of Indian Philosophy, Philosophy, Psychology, Religion, Social Relations Sociology, Western Philosophy

Faculty of Medicine (Freshmen Enrollment: 120)

Department of Medicine

Anatomy, Anesthesiology, Cardiovascular-Surgery, Dermatology and Syphilology, Experimental Radiology, Geriatrics Medicine, Gynecology and Obstetrics, Hygiene, Internal Medicine, Laboratory Medicine, Legal Medicine, Medical Chemistry, Microbiology, Neurology, Neurosurgery, Nuclear Medicine, Ophthalmology, Oral and Maxillo-Facial Surgery, Orthopaedic Surgery, Otolaryngology, Pathology, Pediatrics, Pharmacology, Physiology, Plastic Surgery, Psychiatry, Public Health, Radiology, Surgery, Urology

Faculty of Pharmaceutical Sciences (Freshmen Enrollment: 80)

Department of Pharmaceutical Chemistry and Technology

Biological Chemistry, Molecular Microbiology, Pharmaceutical Manufacturing Chemistry, Physical Chemistry, Phytochemistry, Radiopharmaceutical Chemistry

Department of Pharmacy and Pharmacological Sciences

Analytical Chemistry, Health Chemistry, Organic Chemistry, Pharmaceutics, Pharmacognosy, Pharmacology, Structure Chemistry

Faculty of Science (Freshmen Enrollment: 306)

Department of Astronomy

Astrophysics, Galactic Astronomy

Department of Biophysics

Gene Expression and Regulation, Molecular Biology, Protoplasm Biophysics, Quantum Biology, Reactions of Biological Macromolecules, Structures of Biological Macromolecules, Theoretical Biophysics

Department of Botany

General Cytology, Plant Molecular Biology, Plant Physiology and Ecology, Plant Taxonomy

Department of Chemistry

Analytical Chemistry, Biochemistry, Chemistry of Aggregated Organic Molecules, Inorganic Chemistry, Metallurgy, Organic Chemistry, Physical Chemistry, Properties of Metals, Quantum Chemistry, Radiation Chemistry, Spectroscopic Chemistry, Structural Chemistry, Synthetic Organic Chemistry

Department of Geology and Mineralogy

Historical Geology and Paleontology, Mineralogy, Petrology, Stratigraphy and Sedimentology, Tectonophysics

Department of Geophysics

Applied Geophysics, Geomagnetism and Geoelectricity, Meteorology, Physical Oceanography, Physics of the Solid Earth

Department of Mathematics

Algebra, Applied Analysis, Complex Analysis, Functional Analysis, Geometry, Mathematical Analysis, Number Theory, Probability and Mathematical Statistics, Theory of Differential Equations, Topology

Department of Physics

Cosmic Ray Physics, Crystal Physics, Experimental High Energy Physics, Experimental Nuclear Physics, Fluid Physics, High Polymer Physics, Laser Spectroscopy and Magnetic Resonance, Low Temperature Physics, Neutron Physics, Nuclear Astrophysics, Nuclear Spectroscopy, Plasma Physics, Radiation Physics, Solid State Spectroscopy, Statistical Mechanics and Theory of Condensed Matter, Theoretical Nuclear Physics, Theory of Elementary Particles

Department of Zoology

Animal Ecology, Animal Systematics and Comparative Physiology, Developmental Biology, Human Evolution Studies, Physical Anthropology, Radiation Biology and Immunobiology

Foreign Student Admission

Qualifications for Applicants

Standard Qualifications Requirement

Examination at the University

For the Faculties of Economics, Pharmaceutical Science and Engineering, applicants must take the Japanese Language Proficiency Test and General Examination for Foreign Students. Those who receive a satisfactory grade will be allowed to take each Faculty's special entrance examination consisting of written exams and an interview. Also, the Faculty of Education allows entrance through a separate procedure. To enter other faculties the foreign applicants must take the same entrance examinations as are given to Japanese students.

Documents to be Submitted When Applying

Standard Documents Requirement

Applicants to the Faculties of Pharmaceutical Sciences and Engineering are required to submit a letter of recommendation from the diplomatic mission of their country in Japan. Also a letter of guarantee from a resident in Japan is required for applicants to the Faculty of Pharmaceutical Sciences.

Application forms are available at the respective faculty offices. All applicants are required to submit the specified application documents to their Faculty Office. The deadline for receiving applications is inflexible. Interested students should contact that faculty for further information.

Qualifications for Transfer Students

The Faculty of Law and the Faculty of Economics have a special procedure for entrance into the third year.

Faculty of Law:

1. Those possessing a bachelor's degree in a field other than law from a Japanese or foreign college or university.
2. Under certain condition, graduates from a junior college and those who have successfully completed two years of an undergraduate program outside Japan may be also eligible to apply for this special admission.

Faculty of Economics:

1. Those possessing a bachelor's degree from a Japanese or foreign university and those anticipating receipt of a bachelor's degree by March of each year.
2. Those who have completed a 16-year educational course abroad and those who anticipate completing such a course by March of each year.

Examination for Transfer Students

Applicants for the Faculty of Economics should pass the examination on foreign language, short essay and medical examination, while those who wish to apply for the Faculty of Law should pass the examination designed by the said faculty.

Documents to be Submitted When Applying

Standard Documents Requirement

GRADUATE PROGRAMS

Graduate School of Agriculture (First Year Enrollment : Master's 131, Doctor's 72)

Divisions

Agricultural and Forestry Economics, Agricultural Biology, Agricultural Chemistry, Agricultural Engineering, Agronomy and Horticultural Science, Animal Science, Fisheries, Food Science and Technology, Forestry, Tropical Agriculture, Wood Science and Technology

Graduate School of Economics (First Year Enrollment : Master's 52, Doctor's 23)

Divisions

Business Administration, Contemporary Economics, Economic Policy, Economic Theory and Economic History

Graduate School of Education (First Year Enrollment : Master's 34, Doctor's 13)

Divisions

Clinical Studies of Education, Education, Scientific Methods in Education

Graduate School of Engineering (First Year Enrollment : Master's 403, Doctor's 200)

Divisions

Aeronautical Engineering, Applied Mathematics and Physics, Applied Systems Science, Architectural Engineering, Architecture, Chemical Engineering, Civil Engineering, Electrical Engineering, Electrical Engineering II, Electronics Engineering Science, Environmental and Sanitary Engineering, Hydrocarbon Chemistry, Industrial Chemistry, Information Science, Mechanical Engineering, Metallurgy, Metal Science and Technology, Mineral Science and Technology, Molecular Engineering, Nuclear Engineering, Polymer Chemistry, Precision Mechanics, Synthetic Chemistry, Transportation Engineering

Graduate School of Law (First Year Enrollment : Master's 76, Doctor's 37)

Divisions

Basic Laws, Political Sciences, Private and Criminal Laws, Public Laws

Graduate School of Letters (First Year Enrollment : Master's 94, Doctor's 55)

Divisions

Aesthetics and Art History, Archaeology, Chinese Language and Literature, English Language, English and American Literature, French Language and Literature, Geography, German Language and Literature, Indic Philology, Japanese History, Japanese Language and Literature, Linguistics, Oriental History, Philosophy, Psychology, Religion, Sociology, Western History

Graduate School of Medicine (First Year Enrollment : Doctor's 90)

Divisions

Internal Medicine, Molecular Medicine, Pathology, Physiology, Social Medicine, Surgery

Graduate School of Pharmaceutical Sciences (First Year Enrollment : Master's 40, Doctor's 14)

Divisions

Pharmaceutical Chemistry and Technology, Pharmacy and Pharmacological Sciences

Graduate School of Science (First Year Enrollment : Master's 186, Doctor's 113)

Divisions

Astronomy, Biophysics, Botany, Chemistry, Geology and Mineralogy, Geophysics, Mathematical Sciences, Mathematics, Physics, Primatology, Zoology

Foreign Student Admission

Qualifications for Applicants

Master's Program

Standard Qualifications Requirement

Doctor's Program

Standard Qualifications Requirement

Examination at the University

Master's Program

Applicants must take the same entrance examination consisting of written exams and an interview as are given to Japanese students.

Doctor's Program

Same as Master's progrom

Documents to be Submitted When Applying

Standard Documents Requirement

One copy of applicant's graduation thesis and its summary from his previous university is necessary for admission to Doctor's program. In the case of Faculty of Letters, Education and Agriculture, this is also required for admission to Master's Program.

Application forms are available at each Graduate School Office. All applicants are required to submit the specified application documents to each Graduate School Office before the deadlines established by the individual Graduate Schools. Inquiries about details and deadlines should be directed to the appropriate Graduate School Office.

*

Research Institutes and Centers
Center for African Area Studies, Center for Archaeological Operations, Center for Moletular Biology and Genetics, Center for Southeast Asian Studies, Center for Student Health, Chest Disease Research Institute, Data Processing Center, Disaster Prevention Research Institute, Educational Center for Information Processing, Environment Preservation Center, Institute for Chemical Research, Institute for Virus Research, Institute of Atomic Energy, Institute of Economic Research, Plasma Physics Laboratory, Primate Research Institute, Radiation Biology Center, Radio Atmospheric Science Center, Radioisotope Research Center, Research Center for Medical Polymers and Biomaterials, Research Center for Sports Science, Research Institute for Food Science, Research Institute for Fundamental Physics, Research Institute for Humanistic Studies, Research Institute for Mathematical Sciences, Research Reactor Institute, Wood Research Institute

Facilities/Services for Foreign Students
Shugakuin International House: Shared Facilities (Lobby, Library/Conference Room, Lounge, Japanese-Style Room, Shower Rooms, Laundry Rooms, Cooking Rooms), Accommodation (76 rooms–single 45, couple 21, family 10)
Uji International House: Accommodation (13 rooms –single 6, couple 5, family 2)
Foreign Student Service: The Foreign Student Service was organized in 1960 for the purpose of advising students from abroad, and helping them with matters concerning language difficulties, financial problems, accommodations, medical treatment, and their studies, etc. The staff is also willing to assist foreign students in other matters that may arise, or to help them in any way possible during their stay at Kyoto University.

Foreign Student Advisor's office (Faculty of Agriculture) is also available for foreign students with problems concering study program, research work, etc.

Special Programs for Foreign Students
Japanese Language Courses: The Student Bureau of Kyoto University provides supplementary classes in Japanese language for foreign students who are currently registered at Kyoto University. These classes include: (1) elementary, (2) upper elementary and (3) intermediate. In addition to these classes, special classes in Japanese language for Chinese students registered at Kyoto University are available.

The main goal of these classes is to prepare a foreign student for university lectures and to train the foreign student in other Japanese language skills which might be required in conducting research at Kyoto University.

In the elementary level Japanese language classes, the teachers use English in explaining grammar and vocabulary. However, in the upper elementary and intermediate Japanese language classes, only Japanese is used.

Foreign students at Kyoto University who wish to learn the Japanese language, or to improve their abilities in Japanese, are invited to join one of these classes. Interested students should contact the Foreign Student Service office for information concerning registration.

For Further Information
Undergraduate and Graduate Admission
Registrar of each Faculty: (Letters, Education, Law, Economics, and Engineering) Yoshida Honmachi, Sakyo–ku, Kyoto 606; (Science and Agriculture) Kitashirakawa Oiwake–cho, Sakyo–ku, Kyoto 606; (Medicine) Yoshida Konoe–cho, Sakyo–ku, Kyoto 606; (Pharmaceutical Sciences) Yoshida Shimoadachi –cho, Sakyo–ku, Kyoto 606
For Further Information: Student Division, Student Bureau, Kyoto University, Yoshida Honmachi, Sakyo-ku, Kyoto-shi, Kyoto 606 ☎ 075–753–2513, 2514

Kyoto University of Education
(Kyoto Kyoiku Daigaku)
1 Fukakusa-Fujinomori-cho, Fushimi-ku, Kyoto-shi, Kyoto 612   ☎ 075–641–9281

Faculty
    Profs. 56   Assoc. Profs. 59
    Assist. Profs.   Full–time 8; Part–time 140
    Res. Assocs. 5
Number of Students
    Undergrad. 1, 824
Library   247, 430 volumes

Outline and Characteristics of the University
Kyoto University of Education was founded in 1949 under the name of Kyoto Gakugei University, comprising Kyoto Normal School (founded in 1876) and the Kyoto Teachers School for Youth Education (founded in 1944) as one of the 69 national universities under the new system of education. At that time, the Faculty of Liberal Arts was organized. In accordance with the revision of the National School Law in 1966 the University changed its name to Kyoto University of Education, as it is called today, and the Faculty became the Faculty of Education.

At the time of its founding the University was located at Murasakino, Kita-ku, Kyoto, the site of Kyoto Normal School. In 1957, the University moved to the present address where classrooms, faculty offices, laboratories, the administration building, the library, the student center, a physical training plant and other facilities were constructed, and in 1979 the auditorium was completed.

The campus at Fujinomori-cho is 140, 724 m² in area—about 35 acres. Moderately hilly and with a variety of tall shade trees, it affords a most favorable atmosphere for research and education.

The University has a full time faculty of approximately 130, which is an appropriate number of academic staff for the 1, 800 students in this environment. Since its foundation the University has made every effort to develop within the students a passion for research and education, and excellent results have been obtained at schools of primary and secondary education as well as in the University.

UNDERGRADUATE PROGRAMS

Faculty of Education (Freshmen Enrollment: 420)
  Junior High School Teachers' Training Course
  Kindergarten Teachers' Training Course
  Teachers' Training Course for Mentally Handicapped Instruction
  Primary School Teachers' Training Course
  Teachers' Training Course for Special Subjects (Fine Arts, Industrial Arts and Crafts)
  Teachers' Training Course for Special Subjects (Health and Physical Education)
  Teachers' Training Course for Special Subjects (Science)
  Course for Integrated Sciences

Foreign Student Admission
  Qualifications for Applicants
  Standard Qualifications Requirement
  Foreign applicants for undergraduate programs are those who are recommended by a Japanese mission abroad or a government agency of the applicant's country.
  Applicants must have received a grade of "B" or higher on the Japanese Language Proficiency Test and a grade of "C" or higher on the General Examination for Foreign Students.
  Examination at the University
  All applicants who have fulfilled the application requirements will be allowed to undergo a screening process consisting of an interview, an examination of the papers submitted, and a physical checkup. A written exam or an examination in technical skill may also be required for admission.
  Documents to be Submitted When Applying
  Standard Documents Requirement
  Letter of recommendation issued by a Japanese mission abroad or a government agency of the applicant's country is required.
  An information packet for applicants is available at the Admission Office (Student Division) at the end of July, and application forms are available in early December. All applicants are required to submit the specified application documents to the Ad-

mission Office (Student Division) by the date designated in the information packet.

*

Research Institutes and Centers
Center for Educational Research and Training
Special Programs for Foreign Students
Weekly Japanese language supplementary classes are under consideration.
For Further Information
  Undergraduate Admission
Admissions Office, Student Division, Kyoto University of Education, 1 Fukakusa-Fujinomori-cho, Fushimi-ku, Kyoto-shi, Kyoto 612 ☎ 075–641–9281 ext. 271

Kyushu Institute of Design
(Kyushu Geijutsukoka Daigaku)

4–9–1 Shiobaru, Minami-ku, Fukuoka-shi, Fukuoka
815 ☎ 092–541–1431

Faculty
  Profs. 32   Assoc. Profs. 20
  Assist. Profs. Full–time 4; Part–time 117
  Res. Assocs. 15
Number of Students
  Undergrad. 608   Grad. 61
Library 98, 824 volumes

Outline and Characteristics of the University

Kyushu Institute of Design, a national university, was established in 1968. At present the Institute is composed of one undergraduate school and one graduate school (master's course). The undergraduate school (Faculty of Design) has four departments: the Departments of Environmental, Industrial, Visual Communication, and Acoustic Design. The graduate school (Graduate School of Design) has two divisions: the Divisions of Living Environmental Studies and Audio and Visual Communication Studies.

The Institute has a full-time faculty of 80 members and each department accepts 40 first-year students annually. The proportion of academic staff to students is very high (about one to nine) and this is one of the characteristics of the Institute's education. The total number of graduates produced since the Institute's foundation is about 2, 100 and their abilities are highly esteemed by society.

The aim of the Institute is to study and develop technology which is based on a combination of art and science. To achieve this aim, the academic staff conducts research in various areas, such as science, engineering, art, and design. The Institute not only plays a leading role in the four research areas but trains students to have a practical as well as a scholarly knowledge in many fields from music and fine arts to engineering.

The campus (53, 000 square meters) is located in an urban area near the center of Fukuoka, which is the biggest city in Kyushu and is famous for its contribution to cultural exchange between Japan and countries overseas. The campus buildings and gardens are beautifully arranged.

UNDERGRADUATE PROGRAMS

Faculty of Design (Freshmen Enrollment: 160)
Department of Acoustic Design
Digital Signal Processing. , History of Music, Introduction of Musicology, Musical Instrument Lesson, Musicology, Noise Control Engineering, Psychology of Hearing, Sound Analysis and Synthesis, The oretical Acoustics, Training of Hearing Acoustic Devices and Instruments
Department of Environmental Design
Architectural Design, Building Environmental Engineering, Environmental Construction Processes, Historical Approach to Architectural Design, History of Environmental Design, Introduction to Environmental Degign, Landscape Planning and Design, Structural Analysis, Urban Design
Department of Industrial Design
Art and Design, General Ergonomics, Human Ergology, Interior Architectural Design Method, Interior Design, Machine Design, Product Design Methods, Strength of Material
Department of Visual Communication Design
Aesthetics of Image, Color Science, Image Construction, Image Display Planning, Image Information Engineering, Image Making, Image System Engineering, Marketing Communication Planning, Psychology of Visual Perception, video and Film Work Planning, Visual Design

Foreign Student Admission
Qualifications for Applicants
Standard Qualifications Requirement
Applicants must fulfill the standard qualification requirements or must have an International Baccalaureate Diploma (in this case the applicant must be 18 years of age or over).
Examination at the University
Applicants must take the Japanese Language Proficiency Test and the Science Course of the General Examination for Foreign Students. Those who fulfill the following requirements will be allowed to take the Institute's special entrance examination consisting of an interview and medical examinaition.
1. The score of the Japanese Language Proficiency Test is 50% or better.
2. Each score of Mathematics and Physics of the General Examination for Foreign Students is 50% or better, and the total score of all subjects is also 50% or better.

Applicants are required to select Physics and another in the science subjects.
Documents to be Submitted When Applying
Standard Documents Requirement
Following documents are also necessary if applicable.
1. International Baccalaureate Diploma and a transcript if the applicant has an International Baccalaureate.
2. A letter of recommendation from a consulate in Japan unless the applicant has a letter of recommendation from the principal of the senior high school from which the applicant graduated.

Information brochures on admission, including application forms, are available at the Instruction Section from early November. Applicants should inquire at the Instruction Section or refer to the brochure concerning the date of the Institute's special entrance examination and the deadline for application documents.

GRADUATE PROGRAMS

Graduate School of Design (First Year Enrollment : Master's 32)
Divisions
Audio and Visual Communication Studies, Living Environmental Studies

Foreign Student Admission
Qualifications for Applicants
Master's Program
Standard Qualifications Requirement
Examination at the University
Master's Program
The examination: oral or written tests in Japanese in a technical subjects, interview, and medical examination.
Documents to be Submitted When Applying
Standard Documents Requirement
Following documents are also required, if applicable.
1. Applicants advised to submit their graduation thesis or other academic thesis, if any.
2. A letter of recommendation from a consulate in Japan unless the applicant has a letter of recommendation from the president (or dean) of the university/college from which the applicant graduated.

Information brochures on admission, including application forms, are available at the Instruction Section from early November. Applicants should inquire at the Instruction Section or refer to the brochure concerning the date of the Institute's special entrance examination and the deadline for the application documents.

*
Research Institutes and Centers
Information Processing Center
Facilities/Services for Foreign Students
The Institute has no special dormitory for foreign students, but foreign undergraduate students (male only) can apply for admission into a dormitory for Japanese students.

For Further Information
Undergraduate and Graduate Admission
Instruction Section, Kyushu Institute of Design, 4-9-1 Shiobaru, Minami-ku, Fukuoka-shi, Fukuoka 815 ☎ 092–541–1431 ext. 243

Kyushu Institute of Technology
(Kyushu Kogyo Daigaku)

1-1 Sensui–cho, Tobata–ku, Kitakyushu–shi, Fukuoka 804 ☎ 093–871–1931

Faculty
    Profs. 98   Assoc. Profs. 74
    Assist. Profs. Full–time 29; Part–time 114
    Res. Assocs. 46
Number of Students
    Undergrad. 3, 556   Grad. 345
Library 312, 583 volumes

Outline and Characteristics of the University
In 1907, Baron Keiichiro Yasukawa and Mr. Kenjiro Matsumoto, prominent businessmen, began the work that led to the founding of a college aiming to enhance technical education and develop industry in Japan. Their efforts produced Meiji College of Technology which opened on April 1, 1909. Baron Kenjiro Yamakawa, Dr. Sc. , acting as advisor to the school, wanted to establish an institute not merely to impart knowledge and technical skills, but to build character. He placed great emphasis on the high ideals and standards of Kyushu Insitute of Technology (KIT). Dr. Chu Matoba became the first president and currently Dr. Shizuo Mukae is the 16th president.

Although begun as a private school, Meiji College of Technology was instituted as a national college in 1921, and renamed Kyushu Institute of Technology under the provisions of the National School Establishment Law on May 31, 1949. From the outset, KIT has enjoyed constant growth and development. From 420 in 1911 the number of students has grown to 3, 901 in 1988. KIT now has 2 faculties comprising 8 departmets for the undergraduate degree program and a Graduate School of Engineering for Master's and Doctor's degree programs.

The new Faculty of Computer Science and Systems Engineering was established in Iizuka in 1986. This faculty aims to produce high-level computer engineers who will contribute to Japan's future development.

During the past 79 years, KIT has not only graduated more than 19, 704 technical experts, but also produced able teachers and distinguished researchers for its own faculty as well as for other schools. Since it has achieved a nationwide reputation as a technological institution of high quality, KIT has atracted students from all sections of the nation and from many foreign countries. The number of students from abroad is now 36.

The campus of the Faculty of Engineering is located in Kitakyushu City (population 1, 060, 000), one of the largest industrial areas in the northern part of Kyushu Island. The new campus of the Faculty of Computer Science and Systems Engineering is in Iizuka City (population 80, 000), which lies in central Fukuoka Prefecture, nearly 45 kilometers southwest of Kitakyushu and about 40 kilometers east of Fukuoka City, the main city of Kyushu Island.

UNDERGRADUATE PROGRAMS

Faculty of Computer Science and System Engineering (Freshmen Enrollment: 320)
Department of Artificial Intelligence
Applied Artificial Intellignece, Computer Architecture, Fundamentals of Artificial Intelligence, Information Mathematics
Department of Biochemical Systems Engineering
Applied Biochemistry, Biochemical Catalysis Engineering, Biochemical Information, Biochemical Process Engineering
Department of Computer Science and Electronics
Applied Electronic System, Fundamentals of Information Science and Electronics, Information processing and Telecommunication, Integrated Circuit Technology
Department of Control Engineering and Science
Applied Control Systems, Control Systems, Fundamentals of Measurement and Control, Measurement Systems
Department of Mechanical Systems Engineering
Fundamentals of Mechanical Systems, Manufacturing Systems, Mechanical Systems Design, Precision Machine Systems
Faculty of Engineering (Freshmen Enrollment: 614)
Department of Applied Chemistry and Materials Science and Engineering
Material Processing and Chemical Engineering, Materials Chemistry, Metal Materials, Organic and Biological Chemistry
Department of Civil, Mechanical and Control Engineering
Applied Dynamics and Control Engineering, Construction Engineering, Fluid Engineering, Heat and Mass Transfer, Material Science, Production Engineering
Department of Electrical, Electronics and Computer Engineering
Computer Engineering, Electrical Engineering Fundamentals, Electric Power Engineering, Electron Device Engineering, Electronic Physics, Systems and Control
Faculty of Engineering Evening Course (Freshmen Enrollment: 90)
Department of Applied Chemistry and Materials Science and Engineeing
Department of Civil, Mechanical and Cntrol Engineering

Department of Electrical, Electronics and Computer Engineering

Foreign Student Admission
Qualifications for Applicants
Standard Qualifications Requirement
Examination at the University
For each Faculty, applicants must take the Japanese Language Proficiency Test and General Examination for Foreign Students, and later must take each Faculty's special entrance examination consisting of written and oral exams and an interview.
Documents to be Submitted When Applying
Standard Documents Requirement
The following documents are also required:
1. A letter of recommendation from the applicant's embassy or consular office in Japan.
2. A copy of the record of the Japanese Language Proficiency Test and General Examination for Foreign Students.

Application forms are available at the Admissions Office beginning in late November. The annual examination is given either in February or March, and the deadline for the application documents varies from year to year. For further information, inquire at the Admissions Office.

GRADUATE PROGRAMS

Graduate School of Engineering (First Year Enrollment : Master's 170, Doctor's 26)
Divisions
Applied Chemistry and Materials Science and Engineering, Civil, Mechanical and Control Engineering, Electrical, Electronics and Computer Engineering

Foreign Student Admission
Qualifications for Applicants
Master's Program
Standard Qualifications Requirement
Doctor's Program
Standard Qualifications Requirement
Examination at the University
Master's Program
Applicants must take the same entrance examination as Japanese applicants, consisting of a written exam and an interview.
Doctor's Program
Same as Master's Program.
Documents to be Submitted When Applying
Standard Documents Requirement
The following documents are also required:
1. A letter of recommendation from the applicant's embassy or consular office in Japan.
2. A copy of the record of the Japanese Language Proficiency Test and General Examination for Foreign Students.

Application forms are available at the Graduate Admissions Office. The examination is given in March and September. The deadlines for the applica-

tion documents vary from year to year.
For particulars, inquire at the Adimissions Office.

*

Research Institutes and Centers
Health Administration Center, Information Science Center
For Further Information
Undergraduate and Graduate Admission
Admissions Office, Kyushu Institute of Technology 1-1 Sensui, Tobata-ku, Kitakyushu-shi, Fukuoka 804 ☎ 093-871-1931 ext, 240

Kyushu University
(Kyushu Daigaku)
6-10-1 Hakozaki, Higashi-ku, Fukuoka-shi, Fukuoka 812   ☎ 092-641-1101

Faculty
    Profs.   522   Assoc. Profs.   467
    Assist. Profs. Full-time 115; Part-time 1, 287
    Res. Assocs.   952
Number of Students
    Undergrad.   10, 449   Grad.   2, 476
Library   2, 712, 152 volumes

Outline and Characteristics of the University
Kyushu University has a history of over 77 years since its establishment in 1911 as one of the seven Imperial Universities in Japan. During these years, various changes were introduced, such as the postwar educational system reform, expansion of the faculties and departments, etc. It is now a national university consisting of ten Faculties: Literature, Education, Law, Economics, Science, Medicine, Dentistry, Pharmaceutical Sciences, Engineering and Agriculture, besides the College of General Education, with approximately 13, 700 students and 4, 500 faculty and clerical members. Moreover, each faculty has a Graduate School; the Interdisciplinary Graduate School of Engineering Sciences has been established; and various Research Institutes and attached facilities have been completed. Thus, Kyushu University may be considered, nominally and virtually, as one of the highest academic institutions in Japan.

Foreign students have been accepted into Kyushu University since its establishment, chiefly in the Faculties of Medicine, Engineering and Agriculture. At present about 434 foreign students from about 42 countries, mainly from Asia, study at this university. The number has been increasing every year.

The basic organization for education and research in our university consists of faculties, each of which is further divided into departments according to the specialized fields. The shortest period of study is four years, except for the Faculties of Medicine and Dentistry, where it is six years. The first one and a half years after matriculation are called the general education course (but the pre-medical and pre-dental courses for the faculties of Medicine and Dentistry take two years). The College of General Education provides instruction in general culture, which is considered indispensable for producing competent citizens for the future, as well as basic subjects for specialized courses. For foreign students, the College offers special courses in the Japanese language and Japanese studies. (Details will be given later.)

Those who have completed the general education course (or the pre-medical/pre-dental course) proceed to specialized education in their respective subjects, and can be granted a Bachelor's Degree upon completion of the prescribed number of subjects and acquisition of credits required for graduation.

The Graduate Schools are for those who intend to pursue further studies and research after having graduated from a university. Each Graduate School is sub-divided into Divisions of special studies, according to their field. The course of study in each Graduate School is comprised of a two-year Master's Course and a three-year Doctor's Course, with the exception of the courses in the Graduate Schools of Medicine and Dentistry which offer a four year Doctor's Course only. The Degree of Master or Doctor can be granted to those who have acquired the prescribed number of credits upon completion of subjects, and have successfully submitted a thesis/dissertation after receiving research supervision.

In addition to the above-mentioned, the University offers such facilities as will meet the expectations of those who aspire to learning. Candidates may be accepted as research students, special students and auditors in each Faculty, the College of General Education, the Interdisciplinary Graduate School of Engineering Sciences, each Research Institute and Institute of Languages and Cultures. In these cases, the term of study should not exceed one year. However, it may be extended if the application for renewal is approved, following the prescribed procedure.

Kyushu University is located in the city of Fukuoka, a metropolis of Western Japan in the northern part of Kyushu Island. The main campuses of the University are situated in the eastern part of Fukuoka City, while the College of General Education is in the western part and the Interdisciplinary Graduate School of Engineering Sciences is in the southern part. Various types of research facilities are spread all over Kyushu Island, and the University Forests, attached to the Faculty of Agriculture, can be found even as far away as Hokkaido, the northernmost island of Japan.

UNDERGRADUATE PROGRAMS

Faculty of Agriculture (Freshmen Enrollment: 270)
Department of Agricultural Chemistry
Applied Microbiology, Biochemistry, Pesticide Chemistry, Plant Nutrition and Soil Fertility, Science of Soils, Sericultural Chemistry, Soil Microbiology and Biochemistry

Department of Agricultural Economics
Agricultural Economics, Agricultural Marketing, Agricultural Policy, Farm Management, Quantitative Analysis of Agriculture

Department of Agricultural Engineering
Agricultural Machinery, Agricultural Meteology, Agricultural Process Engineering, Drainage Engineering, Irrigation and Water Utilization Engineering, Soil Engineering

Department of Agronomy
Crop Husbandry, Crop Science, Entomology, Horticulture, Plant Breeding, Plant Pathology, Sericultural Science

Department of Animal Science
Animal Breeding and Reproduction, Chemistry and Technology of Animal Products, Forage Science, Functional Anatomy and Physiology of Domestic Animals, Zoology

Department of Fisheries
Fisheries Biology, Fisheries Chemistry, Fisheries Environmental Science, Fisheries Technology, Marine Biology

Department of Food Science and Technology
Food Analysis, Food Chemistry, Food Hygienic Chemistry, Food Technology, Microbial Technology, Nutrition Chemistry

Department of Forest Products
Industrial Chemistry of Wood, Polymer Chemistry of Woody Materials, Wood Chemistry, Wood Science, Wood Technology

Department of Forestry
Biophysics, Erosion Control, Forest Management, Forest Policy, Silviculture

Faculty of Dentistry (Freshmen Enrollment: 60)
Department of Dentistry
Conservative Dentistry, Dental Materials Engineering, Dental Pharmacology, Dental Radiology, Oral Anatomy, Oral Biochemistry, Oral Microbiology, Oral Pathology, Oral Physiology, Oral Surgery, Orthodontics, Pediatric Dentistry, Preventive Dentistry, Prosthetic Dentistry

Faculty of Economics (Freshmen Enrollment: 270)
Department of Business Economics
Business Accounting, Business Administration, Business Finance, Cost Accounting, Personnel Administration

Department of Economic Engineering
Econometrics, Economic Mathematics, Industrial Planning, Management Science

Department of Economics
Economic Analysis and Policy, Economic History of Japan, General Principles of Economics, History of Economic Thoughts

Faculty of Education (Freshmen Enrollment: 50)
Department of Education
Comparative Education, Educational Administration, Educational Sociology, History of Education, Methodology of Education, Philosophy of Education, Social Education

Department of Educational Psychology
Counselling, Educational Psychology, Group Dynamics, Science of Disabled Children

Faculty of Engineering (Freshmen Enrollment: 810)

Department of Aeronautical Engineering
Aerodynamics, Aero-Engines, Aircraft Dynamics-Performance and Propulsion, Aircraft Equipment Control and Guidance, Aircraft Strength and Vibration, Aircraft Strength and Vibration, Aircraft structures-Materials and Design

Department of Applied Chemistry
Chemical Reaction Engineering, Industrial Organic Chemistry, Polymer Chemistry I and Material Science of Polymers, Structural Inorganic Chemistry and High-Temperature Chemistry

Department of Architecture
Architectural Planning, Building Materials and Construction Methods, Earthquake and Wind Engineering, Environmental Engineering in Architecture, Environmental Planning in Architecture, History and Theory of Architecture, Reinforced Concrete Structures and Structural Mechanics, Steel Structure and Structural Mechanics, Urban Design and City Planning

Department of Chemical Engineering
Applied Physical Chemistry, Chemical Reaction Process, Design of Chemical Apparatus, Fluid Flow in Chemical Engineering, Heat Transfer in Chemical Engineering, Process Control, Unit Operations

Department of Civil Engineering
Bridge Engineering, Execution of Works and Concrete Engineering, Railway Engineering, Road Engineering, Structural Mechanics, Structures for Civil Engineering

Department of Computer Science and Communication Engineering
Computer and Communication Systems, Computer Hardware and Communication Devices, Computer Software, Electronic Elements in Computers and Communication Devices, Fundamentals of Information and Communication Networks, Information Processing, Wave Theory and Applications

Department of Electrical Engineering
Electrical Machinery, Electrical Measurement, Electrical System Control, Electric Discharge and Plasma Engineering, Electric Power Station and Substation; Electric Power Transmission and Distribution, Solid State Electrophysics, Theory of Electric Circuits, Theory of Electromagnetics

Department of Electronics
Electronic Circuits, Electronic Control Engineering, Electronic Measurement Engineering, Industrial Electronics, Information Processing System, Solid State Electronics

Department of Civil Engineering Hydraulics and Soil Mechanics
Applied Hydraulics, Coastal Engineering, River Engineering, Sewage Engineering, Soil Mechanics, Water Supply and Water Resources Engineering

Department of Iron and Steel Metallurgy
Ferrous Metallurgy, Material Science of Iron and Steel, Physical Chemistry of Melts, Surface Chemistry of Metals

Department of Mechanical Engineering
Combustion, Fluid Machinery, Fluid Mechanics, Gas Thermodynamics, Heat Transfer, Machine Design, Machine Structure and Strength, Mechanics of Machinery, Steam Thermodynamics

Department of Mechanical Engineering
Power Division
Air Science, Dynamics of Machinery, Internal Combustion Engine, Steam Power, Thermodynamics

Department of Mechanical Engineering
Production Division
Automatic Control, Design and Planning for Production, Machining, Metal Processing, Precision Surface Finishing, Tools and Machine Tools

Department of Metallurgy
Metallurgy of Less-Common Metals and Powder Metallurgy, Physical Metallurgy and Non-Ferrous Alloys, Technological Metallurgy, Technology of Metal Working

Department of Mining
Economic Geology, Exploration Geophysics, Geothermics, Mineral Processing, Mining, Mining Machinery

Department of Naval Architecture
Hydrodynamics and Dynamics of Ships, Resistance and Propulsion of Ships, Strength and Vibration of Ships, Structure of Ships; Design of Merchant Ships, Technical Theory of Shipbuilding; Equipments of Merchant Ships, Welding Engineering for Hull Construction; Design of Welding

Department of Nuclear Engineering
Nuclear Apparatus and Instrumentation, Nuclear Chemical Engineering, Nuclear Fuel Technology, Nuclear Mechanical Engineering, Radiation Measurement and Protection Engineering, Science and Technology of Radiation Effects

Department of Organic Synthesis
Chemical Process Design; Chemical Process Control, Chemistry of Enzyme and Catalysis, Organic Analytical Chemistry, Quantum Chemistry; Theoretical Organic Chemistry, Synthetic Chemistry of Low Molecular Compounds, Synthetic Macromolecular Chemistry

Faculty of Law (Freshmen Enrollment: 270)
Administrative Law, Anglo-American Law, Civil Law, Commercial Law, Comparative Theory of Constitution, Constitutional Law, Criminal Law, Criminal Policy, Economic Law, History of Political Science, International Law, International Politics, International Private Law, Japanese Legal History, Law of Civil Procedure, Law of Criminal Procedure, Philosophy of Law, Political History and Diplomatic History, Political Science, Science of Judicial Process, Social Law, Sociology of Law, Theory of Public Administration, Western Legal History

Faculty of Literature (Freshmen Enrollment: 160)
Department of History

Archaeology, Geography, Japanese History, Korean History, Occidental History, Oriental History
Department of Literature
Chinese Literature, English Literature, French Literature, German Literature, Japanese Literature
Department of Philosophy
Aesthetics and History of Fine Arts, Chinese Philosophy, Ethics, Indian Philosophy, Philosophy and History of Philosophy, Psychology, Science of Religion, Sociology
Faculty of Medicine (Freshmen Enrollment: 120)
Department of Medicine
Anatomy, Anesthesiology, Bacteriology, Biochemistry, Clinical Pharmacology, Dermatology, Experimental Radiology, Gynecology and Obstetrics, Hygiene, Internal Medicine, Legal Medicine, Neuro-Psychiatry, Ophthalmology, Orthopedic Surgery, Otorhinolaryngology, Parasitology, Pathology, Pediatrics, Pediatric Surgery, Pharmacology, Physiology, Psychosomatic Medicine, Public Health, Radiology, Surgery, Urology, Virology
Faculty of Pharmaceutical Sciences (Freshmen Enrollment: 80)
Department of Pharmaceutical Sciences
Analytical Chemistry, Chemistry of Microorganisms, Hygienic and Forensic Chemistry, Pharmaceutics, Pharmacognosy, Pharmacology, Physiological Chemistry
Department of Pharmaceutical Technology
Chemical Engineering and Technology, Pharmaceutical Chemistry, Pharmaceutical Synthetic Chemistry, Physical Chemistry, Plant Chemistry, Radio Pharmaceutical Chemistry
Faculty of Science (Freshmen Enrollment: 291)
Department of Biology
Animal Physiology, Biochemistry, Cytogenetics and Population Genetics, Developmental Biology, Ecology, Molecular Genetics, Physical Biology, Plant Physiology, Protein Chemistry, Theoretical Biology
Department of Chemistry
Analytical Chemistry, Biochemistry, Coordination Chemistry, Enzyme Chemistry, Inorganic Chemistry, Organic Chemistry, Physical Chemistry, Polymer Chemistry, Quantum Chemistry, Radiochemistry, Structural Chemistry, Synthetic Organic Chemistry, Theoretical Chemistry
Department of Geology
Coal Geology, Economic Geology, Mineralogy, Palaeontology, Petrology, Stratigraphy
Department of Mathematics
Algebra, Analysis, Computational Mathematics, Foundations of Mathematical Science, Functional Analysis, Geometry, Mathematical Programming and Control, Mathematical Statistics, Topology
Department of Physics
Applied Physics, Atmospheric Physics, Atomic Theory of Matter, Geophysics, Low Temperature Physics, Nuclear Reaction, Nuclear Spectroscopy, Physics of Magnetic Materials, Seismology, Semiconductor Physics, Theoretical Nuclear Physics, Theory of Elementary Particles, Upper Atmosphere Dynamics

Foreign Student Admission
Qualifications for Applicants
Standard Qualifications Requirement
1. Applicants are required not to possess Japanese nationality.
2. Those who are 18 years of age or older and have obtained the legal Baccalaureate of the International Baccalaureate Office authenticated by the Swiss Code are also eligible for application.
3. Applicants are required to have been recommended by the embassy or legation in Japan of the country concerned, or by an organization deemed proper by the university authorities.

Examination at the University
1. Applicants are required to take the Japanese Language Proficiency Test (in the year of application) and the General Examination for Foreign Students.
   *Those who apply for the Faculty of Engineering or Pharmaceutical Sciences are required to select both physics and chemistry in the field of science.
2. Applicants are required to take the examinations, conducted by the University, as follows: Japanese (Composition) –March 1, Interview –March 2, Detailed Physical Examination (applicable only to those who are judged to require one).

Documents to be Submitted When Applying
Standard Documents Requirement
Following documents are also required,
1. Letter of recommendation by the embassy or legation in Japan of the country concerned, or by an organization deemed proper by the university authorities
2. Letter of consent: applicable only to those who are currently enrolled in a university/college. In such a case, letter of consent by the president of the university/college concerned should be enclosed.

The application form and the prospectus of registration will be available from early December. All the documents must be sent to the Entrance Examination Section by registered mail.
Date of Application: February 1–10 (not later than 17: 00 hrs.)

GRADUATE PROGRAMS

Graduate School of Agriculture (First Year Enrollment : Master's 106, Doctor's 52)
Divisions
Agricultural Chemistry, Agricultural Economics, Agricultural Engineering, Agriculture Proper, Animal Science, Fishery Sciences, Food Science and Technology, Forestry, Technology of Forest Prod-

ucts

Graduate School of Dentistry (First Year Enrollment : Doctor's 30)
Divisions
Basic Science, Clinical Science

Graduate School of Economics (First Year Enrollment : Master's 40, Doctor's 16)
Divisions
Business Economics, Economic Engineering, Economics

Graduate School of Education (First Year Enrollment : Master's 24, Doctor's 12)
Divisions
Education, Educational Psychology

Graduate School of Engineering (First Year Enrollment : Master's 237, Doctor's 119)
Divisions
Applied Chemistry, Applied Mechanics, Applied Physics, Architecture, Chemical Engineering, Civil Engineering, Civil Engineering Computer Science and Communication Engineering, Electrical Engineering, Electronics, Iron and Steel Metallurgy, Mechanical Engineering, Mechanical Engineering-Power Division, Mechanical Engineering-Production Division, Metallurgy, Metallurgy, Mining Technology, Naval Architecture, Nuclear Engineering, Organic Synthesis

Interdisciplinary Graduate School of Engineering Sciences (First Year Enrollment : Master's 140, Doctor's 59)
Divisions
Energy Conversion Engineering, High Energy Engineering Science, Information Systems, Materials Science and Technology, Molecular Science and Technology, Thermal Energy System

Graduate School of Law (First Year Enrollment : Master's 46, Doctor's 23)
Divisions
Judicial Law, Legal Theory, Political Science, Public Law, Social Law

Graduate School of Literature (First Year Enrollment : Master's 48, Doctor's 24)
Divisions
Chinese Philosophy and Literature, English Language and Literature, French Literature, German Literature, History, Japanese Language and Literature, Linguistics, Philosophy and History of Philosophy, Psychology, Sociology

Graduate School of Medicine (First Year Enrollment : Doctor's 72)
Divisions
Internal Medicine, Molecular Biology, Molecular Medical Science, Pathological Science, Physiological Science, Social Medicine, Surgery

Graduate School of Pharmaceutical Sciences (First Year Enrollment : Master's 29, Doctor's 13)
Divisions
Pharmaceutical Sciences, Pharmaceutical Technology

Graduate School of Science (First Year Enrollment : Master's 98, Doctor's 46)
Divisions
Biology, Chemistry, Geology, Mathematics, Physics

Foreign Student Admission
Qualifications for Applicants
Master's Program
    Standard Qualifications Requirement
Doctor's Program
    Standard Qualifications Requirement
Examination at the University
1. In the Graduate Schools of Education, Law, Economics Science, Engineering and Interdisciplinary Graduate School of Engineering Sciences, a special selective examination system is adopted for foreign students.
2. In the Graduate Schools of Medicine, no special selection system is offered for foreign students; instead, the selection system is based on the same entrance examination for both foreign and Japanese students. Subsequently, applicants must be in Japan by the time application papers are due.
3. In the Graduate Schools of Literature, Dentistry, Pharmaceutical Sciences and Agriculture, as a general rule, a special selective examination is given only after accepting the applicants as research students first, instead of admitting them into the Graduate School from the start. This special examination is, however, not applicable to those foreign students who have graduated from a university in Japan; they must take the same entrance examination as Japanese students.

Documents to be Submitted When Applying
    Standard Documents Requirement
    Following documents are also required.
1. Letter of recommendation by the embassy or legation in Japan of the country concerned, or by an organization deemed proper by the university authorities
2. Essay or research project on the subject of specialization: Inquire at the respective Graduate School about particulars, since they vary according to the Graduate School.

All the above-mentioned documents should be written in Japanese.

The date and method of application vary according to the Graduate School. Inquiries should be made at the respective Graduate School about particulars.

Some graduate courses admit those who have a Master's Degree directly into the Doctor's Course. Even in this case, however, applicants must pass the selective examination. Candidates should refer to the Graduate School concerned for further details.

The prospectus of registration for the following year and the application form will be available upon request at each Graduate School in June.

＊

Research Institutes and Centers

Amakusa Marine Biological Laboratory, Biotron Institute, Center for Advanced Instrumental Analysis, Clinical Center for Disabled Children, Cobalt 60 Gamma-Ray Eradiation Laboratory, Computer Center, Educational Center for Information Processing, Education Center for Foreign Studeuts, Experimental Station for Medical Plant Studies, Fishery Research Laboratory, Geothermal Research Center, Hikosan Biological Laboratory, Institute of Advanced Material Study, Institute of Biological Control, Institute of Health Science, Institute of Languages and Cultures, Institute of Silkworm Genetics, Institute of Tropical Agriculture, Laboratory for Waste Water Treatment, Laboratory of Animal Experiments, Medical Institute of Bioregulation, Neurological Institute, Radioisotope Center, Research Center for Materials on Coal Mining, Research Institute for Applied Mechanics, Research Institute for Diseases of the Chest, Research Institute of Angiocardiology, Research Institute of Comparative Education and Culture, Research Institute of Fundamental Information Science, Research Institute of Kyushu Cultural History, Research Institute of Superconducting Magnet, Research Laboratory for Genetic Information, Research Laboratory of High Voltage Electron Microscope, Shimabara Volcano Observatory, Tsuyazaki Sea Safety Research Laboratory, University Computation Center, University Farm, University Forests, University Hospital Attached to the Faculty of Dentistry, University Hospital Attached to the Faculty of Medicine

Facilities/Services for Foreign Students

1. Education Center for Foreign Students

    The Center was inaugurated on April 1, 1985, as an educational and counseling institute for foreign students. The Center offers the preliminary Japanese Language Course from Monday to Saturday, total 31 hours, and counseling services for the recipients of Japanese Government Scholarship, Those students will engage in graduate studies at the universities in the Kyushu area after receiving a six-month training. The Center consists of five lecture rooms, a lounge, a library, a study room, a counseling room, five teacher's rooms and an office.

2. Kyushu University Foreign Students' Center

    Kyushu University foreign Students' Center was established in April, 1980, for the purpose of promoting mutual understanding between foreign students and Japanese students/faculty members, as well as fostering mutual friendship among foreign students themselves. The Center offers, among other things, special courses in the Japanese language for foreign students and guidance programs designed for the betterment of foreign students' living and studying conditions.

    The Center is a two-story concrete building with a floor space of 269 m^2, equipped with a lobby, a conference room, a counselling room, a library, a lounge and an office. A full-time advisor and a clerk are stationed there to offer guidance and management.

3. Kyushu University International House

    Kyushu University International House was established in March, 1984, for the purposes of providing living accommodations for foreign students and promoting international exchange programs with foreign students. The International House consists of six residential blocks of apartments (five-story concrete buildings) and a community building for common use (a two-story concrete building), comprising a total area of 7, 600 m^2.

    a) Residential facilities: Each apartment house is equipped with a desk, a wardrobe, a bed, a refrigerator, kitchen facilities, a washing machine, an air conditioner, a bath, a toilet, etc.

    b) Common facilities: Community Building (lounge, conference room, Japanese room, library, typing room), Blocks of apartments for single men/women (dining room with kitchenette, laundry room)

    Application for admission to Kyushu University International House should be submitted to the following: International House Section, Student Division, Student Office, Kyushu University, 4-5-5 Kashiihama, Higashi-ku, Fukuoka-shi 813

Special Programs for Foreign Students

1. Japanese Language Courses

    The following special courses in the Japanese language are offered for foreign students studying at the University.

    a) Undergraduate: As for foreign students in the General Education Course, general education subjects, foreign languages and physical education may be replaced, up to 26 credits, by the courses in "Japanese Language and Japanese Studies".

    b) Graduate/Research students: As for graduate/research students, the following courses in Japanese language and culture are offered as extracurricular activities at the Foreign Students' Center.

    Elementary O, Elementary, Intermediate A·B, Intermediate C·D, Advanced I, Advanced II, Japanese history and culture classes

2. Tutor System

    In order to help newly-enrolled foreign students reduce the possible difficulties in their study or research and in their daily lives, a Japanese-student tutor gives guidance in the Japanese language, the specialized field of study and life in general. The tutor will be selected through recommendations by the supervisor. You are advised to consult your supervisor and make the best use of this system.

The term of tutoring is two years after matriculation for the undergraduate, and one year for the graduate/research student.

3. Special Programs for Foreign Students

In order to promote cultural exchange between foreign students and the faculty/community members, the following programs are organized.

a) Organized by the University: Welcome Party for Foreign Students (May), Orientation for Freshmen and Newly-Promoted Faculty Students (May, October), Field Trip (July, October), Bus Hike (November), Farewell Party for Foreign Students (March).

b) Organized by the Foreign Students' Body and Off-Campus Organizations: Welcome Party for Freshmen (April, Kyushu University Foreign Students Association), River Fête (May, Amagi Youths' Chamber of Commerce), Home Stay (May, Yanagawa International Youth Lodge), Iris Fête (June, Dazaifu Shrine), Rice Planting (June, Amagi Youths' Chamber of Commerce), Karaoke Contest (July), Home Stay (August, Youths' Chambers of Commerce in various districts), Family Camp (August, Yanagawa International Youth Lodge), Ping-pong and Badminton Tournaments (October, Kyushu University Foreign Students Association), International Cooking Reception (October, Dazaifu Shrine), International Culture Exchange (October), Christmas Party (November, Women's Social Salon), Rice-cake Pounding (December, Kyushu University Foreign Students Association), New Year's Home Stay (January, Yame International Association of Youth Exchange), Home Stay (March, Yanagawa International Youth Lodge).

For Further Information

Undergraduate Admission

Entrance Examination Section, Admission Division, Student Office, Kyushu University, 6-10-1 Hakozaki, Higashi-ku, Fukuoka-shi, Fukuoka 812 ☎ 092–641–1101 ext. 2341, 2342

Graduate Admission

Graduate Schools of Economics, Education, Law and Literature: Student Section of each faculty, Kyushu University, 6-19-1 Hakozaki, Higashi-ku, Fukuoka-shi, Fukuoka 812 ☎ 092–641–1101 ext. Economics 3707, Education 3317, Law 3508, Literature 3114; Graduate Schools of Dentistry, Medicine and Pharmaceutical Sciences: Student Section of each faculty, Kyushu University, 3-1-1 Maidashi, Higashi-ku, Fukuoka-shi, Fukuoka 812 ☎ 092–641–1151 ext. Dentistry 4151, Medicine 3161, Pharmaceutical Sciences 6108; Graduate Schools of Agriculture, Engineering and Science: Student Section of each faculty, Kyushu University, 6-10-1 Hakozaki, Higashi-ku, Fukuoka-shi, Fukuoka 812 ☎ 092–641–1101 ext. Agriculture

6118, Engineering 5136, Science 4108; Interdisciplinary Graduate School of Engineering Sciences, Kyushu University, Kasugakoen, Kasuga-shi, Fukuoka 816 ☎ 092–573–9611 ext. 242

Mie University
(Mie Daigaku)

1515 Kamihama-cho, Tsu-shi, Mie 514
☎ 0592–32–1211

Faculty
Profs. 252   Assoc. Profs. 225
Assist. Profs. Full–time 58; Part–time 553
Res. Assocs. 178
Number of Students
Undergrad. 5, 458   Grad. 512
Library 610, 475 volumes

Outline and Characteristics of the University

Mie University dates from 1949, when, in accordance with the National School Establishment Law, Mie Normal School for Elementary School Teachers, Mie Normal School for Secondary School Teachers, and Mie Agricultural and Forestry School were merged and raised to the status of university. It was originally composed of two faculties: Liberal Arts and Agriculture. The Faculty of Liberal Arts changed its name to the Faculty of Education on April 5, 1966. In June 1969, the Faculty of Engineering was added, followed by the School of Medicine and the Faculty of Fisheries in May 1972, and the Faculty of Humanities and Social Sciences in April 1983.

In addition to the above undergraduate courses, Mie University now also offers a Postgraduate Program in the School of Medicine, Master's Programs in the faculties of Engineering, Bioresources, and one-year special programs for research students in Education, Special Education and Agriculture.

The University's educational and research facilities include a University library; a Kindergarten, elementary school, junior high school, school for handicapped children, and the Center for Educational Research and Practice, administered by the Faculty of Education. The School of Medicine maintains a hospital, a school of nursing, and the Animal Experimentation Facility. In addition, the Faculty of Bioresources maintains a form, an experimental Forest, the Facility for Fisheries Experimentation and a training ship, the Seisui-maru.

The campus is located in the northeastern part of Tsu, the capital of Mie Prefecture. It faces Ise Bay to the east and to the west, the peaks of the Suzuka Mountains can be seen from the campus. The climate in Mie Prefecture is mild throughout the year. The size of the campus is approximately 530, 000m².

UNDERGRADUATE PROGRAMS

Faculty of Bioresources (Freshmen Enrollment: 306)
Department of Bioresources
Agricultural Chemistry, and Bioscience, Aquatic Environment, Bioproduction and Machinery, Chemistry of Fishery Resources, Cultivation of Fishery Resources, Drainage and Reclamation, Economics of Rural- and Bio-resources, Exploitation of Fishery Resources, Forest Products, Forest Resources, Irrigation, Sciences for Agricultural Production

Faculty of Education (Freshmen Enrollment: 330)
Training Course for Junior High School Teachers
Training Course for Kindergarten Teachers
Training Course for Primary School Teachers
Training Course for Teachers of Schools for Handicapped Children
Agriculture, Algebra and Geometry, Analysis and Applied Mathematics, Art Education, Art of Handwriting, Biology, Chemistry, Child Nursing, Chinese Literature, Design, Developmental Psychology, Early Childhood Education, Earth Science, Economics, Educational Institutions, Educational Psychology, Educational Sociology, Education of the Handicapped, Electricity, English and American Literature, English Language Education, English Linguistics, Ethics, Geography, History, History of Education, Home Economics Education, Home Management, Instrumental Music, Japanese Literature, Japanese Philology, Jurisprudence, Mathematics Education, Mechanics, Metal Processing, Methodology of Health and Physical Education, Methodology of Language, Music Education, Painting, Pathology of the Handicapped, Pedagogy, Philosophy, Physical Exercise, Physics, Physiology and Hygiene, Political Science, Psychology of Infant, Psychology of the Handicapped, School Health, Science, Science Education, Science of Clothing, Science of Food, Sculpture, Social Education, Social Studies Education, Sociology, Technology Education, Theory and History of Art, Music, Physical Education, Theory of Nursery Program, Vocal Music, Wood Processing

Faculty of Engineering (Freshmen Enrollment: 330)
Department of Architecture
Architectual Design and Planning, Building Environment and Equipment, Regional Environmental Science, Structural Mechanics and Design
Chair in Common
Engineering Mathematics
Department of Chemistry of Industry
Inorganic, Organic Industrial Chemistry, Inorganic, Organic Material Chemistry
Department of Chemistry of Resources
Analytical Chemistry for Resources, Molecular Design, Physical Chemistry for Resources, Reaction Mechanism
Department of Electrical Engineering
Communications Engineering, Electric Power Engineering, Fundamentals of Electrical Engineering,

Physical Electronics
Department of Electronic Engineering
Electronic Devices, Electronic Materials, Information Processing, Measurements and System Control
Department of Mechanical and Materials Engineering
Design for Production, Material Processing, Materials Engineering for Mechanical Application, Strength of Materials
Department of Mechanical Engineering
Dynamics of Machinery, Fluid Engineering, Machineshop Technology, Thermal Engineering

Faculty of Humanities and Social Sciences(Freshmen Enrollment: 280)
Department of Humanities
American Studies, Asian and Oceanian Studies, Basic Studies of Culture, European and Mediterranean Studies, Japanese Studies
Department of Social Sciences
International Relations, Social Change, Social Management, Social Structure

Faculty of Medicine (Freshmen Enrollment: 100)
Department of Medicine
Anatomy, Anesthesiology, Biochemistry, Chest Surgery, Dermatology, Forensic Medicine, Hygiene, Internal Medicine, Laboratory Medicine, Medical Zoology, Microbiology, Neurosurgery, Obstetrics and Gynecology, Ophthalmology, Oral Surgery, Orthopaedic Surgery, Otorhinolaryngology, Pathology, Pediatrics, Pharmacology, Physiology, Psychiatry, Public Health, Radiology, Surgery, Urology

Foreign Student Admission
Qualifications for Applicants
Standard Qualifications Requirement
Since entrance examinations and instruction are given in Japanese, it is strongly recommended that applicants take the Japanese Language Proficiency Test and the General Examination for Foreign Students.
Examination at the University
Students from abroad are selected in the same way as Japanese students. Admission consideration is based on results in the Joint First-Stage Achievement Test, the Secondary Stage Examination given by Mie University, a report from the school which the applicant has attended most recently, and a medical examination.
Documents to be Submitted When Applying
Standard Documents Requirement
Students from abroad who have taken the Japanese Language Proficiency Test and the General Examination for Foreign Students are required to attach the results to the other documents.
Applicants are expected to obtain detailed information directly from the university as early as possible. A new list of the entrance requirements for the next academic year is officially published in October every year.
Qualifications for Applicants

Standard Qualifications Requirement
Examination at the University
Non-Japanese applicants must take the same entrance examination as Japanese students which consists of a written exam and interview.

ONE YEAR GRADUATE PROGRAM

One-year Graduate Course of Education (Enrollment: 5)
Education
One-year Graduate Course of Special Education (Enrollment: 30)
Education for the Mentally Handicapped

GRADUATE PROGRAMS

Graduate School of Bioresources (First Year Enrollment : Master's 80)
Divisions
Agricultural Engineering, Applied Chemistry and Biotechnology, Fisheries Science, Forestry and Forest Products, Science for Agricultural Production
Graduate School of Engineering (First Year Enrollment : Master's 48)
Divisions
Architecture, Chemistry for Resources, Chemistry of Industry, Electrical Engineering, Mechanical and Material Engineering, Mechanical Engineering
Graduate School of Medicine (First Year Enrollment : Doctor's 60)
Divisions
Internal Medicine, Morphological Medicine, Physiological Medicine, Social Medicine, Surgery

Foreign Student Admission
Qualifications for Applicants
Master's Program
Standard Qualifications Requirement
Doctor's Program
Standard Qualifications Requirement
Examination at the University
Master's Program
Students from abroad are selected in the same way as Japanese students. Admission consideration is based on results of the Scholastic Ability Test administered by each graduate school of Mie University, an interview, a report from the College which they have attended most recently, and a medical examination.
Doctor's Program
Applicants must take the same entrance examination as Japanese students which consists of a written exam and an interview.
Documents to be Submitted When Applying
Standard Documents Requirement
Applicants are expected to obtain detailed information directly from the graduate school as early as possible.

Research Institutes and Centers
Animal Experimentation Facility, Experimental Farm, Experimental Forest, Facility for Fisheries Experimentation, the Center for Educational Research and Practice
Special Programs for Foreign Students
Classes on Japanese Language and on the State of Affairs in Japan are provided for foreign students.
For Further Information
Undergraduate and Graduate Admission
Admission Section, Beureau of Student Affairs, Mie University, 1515 Kamihama–cho, Tsu–shi, Mie 514
☎ 0592–32–1211 ext. 2182, 2183

Miyagi University of Education
(Miyagi Kyoiku Daigaku)

Aramaki Aza Aoba, Sendai-shi, Miyagi 980
☎ 022–222–1021

Faculty
    Profs.   73   Assoc. Profs.   51
    Assist. Profs.   Full–time   3; Part–time   143
    Res. Assocs.   9
Number of Students
    Undergrad.   1, 803   Grad.   29
Library   235, 298 volumes

Outline and Characteristics of the University
Miyagi University of Education was founded by the Japanese government in 1965 by separating it from Tohoku University, for the purpose of fostering teachers At the time of its foundation, the University was composed of the Faculty of Education, Library, Junior High School, Elementary School, Kindergarten, and Research Institute for Science Education. Since that time, many courses, schools, divisions and centers have been added, such as the School for Retarded Children, the Health Service Center, and the Teacher's Center.

The University is well known for its effort and experimentation in educating active students with the individuality to become teachers. 80% of our graduates work as teachers in high schools, elementary schools, kindergartens, and schools for retarded handicapped children and youths all over the country.

The campus is located to the west of the town, on a hill surrounded by forests. Students study, take part in extracurricular activities, and relax among academic buildings, green woods and grounds of 211, 000 m² overlooking the city of Sendai.

The faculty covers almost all fields of studies: Japanese Linguistics, Japanese Literature, Chinese Classics, Literature, Calligraphy, Teaching of Japanese, Philosophy, Sociology, History, Geography, Jurisprudence, Political Science, Economics, Ethics, Teaching of Social Studies, Mathematics, Algebra,

Geometry, Topology, Analysis, Applied Mathematics, Mathematics Teaching, Physics, Fundamental Physics, Applied Physics, Chemistry, Inorganic and Physical Chemistry, Organic Chemistry, Biology, Taxonomy and Morphology, Physiology and Ecology, Geology, Astronomy and Earth Science, Geology and Mineralogy, Science Teaching, Vocal Music, Instrumental Music, Music Composition, Theory and History of Music, Music Teaching, Painting, Sculpture, Design, Theory and History of Art, Art Teaching, Physical Activities, Physiology and Hygiene, School Health, Theory and History of Physical Culture, Health and Physical Education, Teaching of Physical Culture, Wood Work, Electrology, Mechanical Engineering, Agriculture, Technology Teaching, Food Science, Science of Clothing, Household Management, Child Care, Teaching of Home Economics, English, German, French, English Linguistics, English and American Literature, English Teaching, Education of the Visually Disordered, Psychology of the Visually Disordered, Visual Physiology and Pathology, Education of the Mentally Handicapped, Psychology of the Mentally Handicapped, Pathology of the Mentally Handicapped, Psychology of Hearing and Speech Handicapped, Speech Clinic, Psychology of Children under Preschool Age, Child Care Studies, Pedagogy, History of Education, Educational Systems, Educational Sociology, Psychology, Educational Psychology, Developmental Psychology, Vocational Guidance, and Social Education. Students may receive instruction in any field they desire.

UNDERGRADUATE PROGRAMS

Faculty of Education (Freshmen Enrollment: 425)
   Course for Teachers of Elementary School
   Course for Teachers of Junior High School
Art, English, Health and Physical Education, Home Economics, Japanese Language and Literature, Mathematics, Music, Science, Social Studies, Technology
   Course for Teachers of Kindergarten
   Course for Teachers of Schools for the Handicapped
   Course for Teachers of Schools for the Speech Handicapped
   Course for Teachers of Schools for the Visually Handicapped
   Course for Teachers of Special Subject (Mathematics)
   Course for Teachers of Special Subject (Science)
Biology, Chemistry, Earth Science and Astronomy, Physics

Foreign Student Admission
   Qualifications for Applicants
   Standard Qualifications Requirement
   Examination at the University
   The official transcript from his/her high school,

results of the Japanese Language Proficiency Test (first level), General Examination for Foreign Students (GEFS), health certificate, and an interview (including a test with a given theme or under a given condition). The section of GEFS is designated according to the course or the major for which the student applies.
   Documents to be Submitted When Applying
   Standard Documents Requirement
   Application forms are available at the Admissions Office from the end of September.
   All applicants are required to mail the specified application documents to the Admissions Office during the period from January 12–19. This deadline for receiving applications is strictly observed.
   Research Student Program:
   This program is for those who wish to study independently under a particular instructor's guidance.
   Those who wish to apply for this program should contact the Training Program Section of the University at least 6 months before the starting date.

   Qualifications for Transfer Students
   Applicants must satisfy one of the following requirements.
   1. Applicants are required to have graduated from a university, or completed two years of study at a university or
   2. Applicants are required to have graduated from a junior college or a technical college.
   There may be special requirements according to the course or the major to which the student applies.
   Examination for Transfer Students
   Applications are received only when there is a vacancy. A prospectus is announced in December.
   Documents to be Submitted When Applying
   Standard Documents Requirement

ONE-YEAR GRADUATE PROGRAMS

One-Year Postgraduate Course for the Education of Handicapped Children (Enrollment: 30)
Education of Handicapped Children

GRADUATE PROGRAMS

Graduate School of Education (First Year Enrollment: Master's 25)
School Education, Education of Handicapped Children, Japanese Language Education, Science Education, Music Education, Health and Physical Education, English Education
   Qualifications for Applicanis
Master's Program
   Those applicants who have been recognized by this Graduate School to have the scholastic attainment equal to or better than applicants who have graduated from a university/college.
   Examination at the University
Master's Program

The decision to admit an applicaht is based on an overall estimation of the achievement test, the school report, and the health certificate. The entrance examination is given in three subjects: major field of study, foreign language, and personal interview.

Documents to be Submitted When Applying

Information leaflets on application for admission are available upon request in late July of every year.

Foreign Student Admission

Qualifications for Applicants

Standard Qualifications Requirement for

Applicants must have a teacher's certificate primary school, junior high school, senior high school, or kindergarten.

Examination at the University

Written test: Problems about education are asked.

Interview: Personal interview and group discussion.

Research Institues and Centers

Research Institute for Science Education (Biology, Physics and Chemistry Divisions), Teachers' Center

Facilities/Services for Foreign Students

Men's Dormitory

Accommodation: 120 double rooms

Shared Facilities: Japanese-style Room, etc.

Women's Dormitory

Accommodation: 68 double rooms

Shared Facilities: Japanese-style Room, etc.

Special Programs for Foreign Students

Special Japanese Language Supplementary Courses are available on request.

For Further Information

Undergraduate and Graduate Admission

Admissions Officer, Admissions Section, Miyagi University of Education, Aramaki Aza Aoba, Sendai-shi, Miyagi 980 ☎ 022–222–1021 ext. 247

Miyazaki Medical College
(Miyazaki Ika Daigaku)

5200 Kihara, Kiyotake-cho, Miyazaki-gun, Miyazaki 889-16 ☎ 0985-85-1510

Faculty

Profs. 33   Assoc. Profs. 29

Assist. Profs. Full–time 32; Part–time 131

Res. Assocs. 134

Number of Students

Undergrad. 647   Grad. 67

Library 84, 920 volumes

Outline and Characteristics of the College

Miyazaki Medical College was founded in June, 1974 by the Japanese Government. The College provides a consistent six year teaching system that includes courses for Liberal Arts, Basic Medical and Clinical Sciences. The Graduate School of Medicine (Doctor's Program) was opened in April, 1980. It contains four divisions of specialization and requires four years of study.

The Campus, covering 224, 271 square meters, with buildings of 93, 043 square meter total floor space, is located among the quiet hillsides of Kiyotake about 12 kilometers from the center of Miyazaki City.

UNDERGRADUATE PROGRAMS

Faculty of Medicine (Freshmen Enrollment: 100)

Department of Medicine

Basic Medical Sciences

Anatomy, Biochemistry, Forensic Medicine, Hygiene, Microbiology, Parasitology, Pathology, Pharmacology, Physiology, Public Health

Clinical Sciences

Anesthesiology, Dentistry and Oral Surgery, Dermatology, Internal Medicine, Neurosurgery, Obstetrics and Gynecology, Ophthalmology, Orthopedics, Otorhinolaryngology, Pediatrics, Psychiatry and Neurology, Radiology, Surgery, Urology

Foreign Student Admission

Qualifications for Applicants

Standard Qualifications Requirement

Examination at the College

No special selection is considered for foreign applicants. To obtain admission, applicants are required, like Japanese students, to pass the Joint First-Stage Achievement Test and the Second-Stage Entrance Examination conducted by the National Center for University Entrance and Miyazaki Medical College respectively. Application forms (printed in Japanese) are available at the student Division from early December.

GRADUATE PROGRAMS

Graduate School of Medicine (First Year Enrollment : Doctor's 30)

Divisions

Host-Defense Mechanisms, Morphology of Cells and Tissues, Regulations of Biological Functions, Social Medicine and Human Ecology

Foreign Student Admission

Qualifications for Applicants

Doctor's Program

A limited number of foreign students will be admitted each year.

The applicant must be a citizen of a country other than Japan and meet one of the following requirements.

1. Be a graduate of, or enrolled in the medical or dental school of a university or college established in Japan and scheduled to graduate in March of the year he or she is taking the en-

trance examination.

2. Have completed at least 18 years of education in a country other than Japan with a major in medicine or dentistry.

Examination at the College

Doctor's Program

Selection is based on total consideration of the results of written examinations on basic knowledge in the field of specialization and the English language, an oral examination, and a health examination.

Documents to be Submitted When Applying

Standard Documents Requirement

Required forms and materials must be prepared either in Japanese or English.   Letter of recommendation must be one of the followings: A letter of recommendation by the government of the country of which the applicant is a citizen or by its agencies in Japan; a letter of introduction by an overseas establishment of the Ministry of Foreign Affairs of Japan; or a letter of recommendation by a member of the university faculty, research facility, or the like with which the applicant is now, or has most recently been, affiliated.

Application forms are available at the Student Division. All applicants are required to submit complete application materials by January 31. Late applicants will not be considered.

✳

Research Institutes and Centers

Experimental Animal Center

For Further Information

Undergraduate and Graduate Admission

Student Division, Miyazaki Medical College, 5200 Kihara, Kiyotake-cho, Miyazaki-gun, Miyazaki 889–16 ☎ 0985–85–1510 ext. 2077

Miyazaki University
(Miyazaki Daigaku)

1–1 Gakuen Kibanadai Nishi, Miyazaki-shi, Miyazaki 889–21   ☎ 0985–58–2811

Faculty
 Profs. 95   Assoc. Profs. 123
 Assist. Profs. Full–time 38; Part–time 87
 Res. Assocs. 45
Number of Students
 Undergrad. 3,452   Grad. 173
Library 390, 440 volumes

Outline and Characteristics of the University

Miyazaki Univevsity was founded in May, 1949, by incorporating four special (vocational) schools Miyazaki Vocational School of Agriculture and Forestry (founded in 1924), Miyazaki Teachers' School (founded in 1942), Miyazaki Youth Teachers' School (founded in 1922) and Miyazaki Technical School (founded in 1944). Each of these schools had pro-

duced a number of respectable figures throughout its history. Since incorporation, the University has developed with the times; in 1966, the Faculty of Education set up a non-degree course for graduates; the Graduate Schools of Agriculture and Engineering were established in 1967 and 1976 respectively, offering Master's programs.

The University has three Faculties: the Faculty of Agriculture, the Faculty of Education, and the Faculty of Engineering. These faculties were initially located on separate campuses, but in order to integrate them, the University is now planning to move to the District of Kibana in the Miyazaki Urban Educational Area (840, 000 m^2). The Faculties of Agriculture and Engineering moved to the new campus area in 1984 and 1986, respectively. The Faculty of Education is scheduled to move there this summer.

The new campus is about 10 kilometers from the center of Miyazaki City and is located next to Miyazaki Medical College. Miyazaki Airport is also close to the campus. The new campus is a part of the National Designated Park of Nichinan Coast. This gives the campus an atmosphere worthy of legend, and a mild climate, with the natural beauty of the southern country. It is presumably one of the best places in Japan to study and conduct academic research.

UNDERGRADUATE PROGRAMS

Faculty of Agriculture (Freshmen Enrollment: 285)
 Department of Agricultural Chemistry
Agricultural Products Technology, Applied Microbiology, Biochemistry, Nutritional Chemistry, Soil Science and Plant Nutrition
 Department of Agricultural Engineering
Agricultural Land Engineering, Agricultural Structural Engineering, Agricutural Hydraulic Engineering, Farm Machinery, Farm Work Research
 Department of Agronomy
Applied Entomology, Crop Science, Farm Economics, Forcing Culture of Vegetable and Ornamental Plants, Plant Breeding, Plant Pathology, Pomology, Post-harvest Utilization of Horticultural Crop
 Department of Animal Science
Animal Breeding, Animal Management, Animal Nutrition and Feeding, Animal Products Science and Technology, Animal Reproduction
 Department of Fisheries
Aquaculture, Aquatic Biology, Aquatic Environment and Ecology, Diagnosis and Treatment of Fish Disease, Fish Disease Microbiology, Fish Nutrition and Biochemistry
 Department of Forestry
Forest Chemistry, Forest Engineering, Forest Management, Forest Policy, Forest Utilization, Silviculture
 Department of Grassland Science
Establishment of Grasslands, Forage Crops, Forage Utilization, Grassland Management
 Department of Veterinary Science

Veterinary Anatomy, Veterinary Hygiene, Veterinary Medicine, Veterinary Microbiology, Veterinary Pathology, Veterinary Pharmacology, Veterinary Physiology, Veterinary Public Health, Veterinary Surgery

Faculty of Education (Freshmen Enrollment: 280)
Training Course for Elementary School Teachers
Art, Crafts, Home Economics, Japanese, Mathematics, Music, Pedagogy, Physical Education, Physical Science, Psychology, Social Science
Training Course for Junior High School Teachers
Art, Crafts, English, Home Economics, Japanese, Mathematics, Music, Physical Education, Physical Science, Social Science
Training Course for Kindergarten Teachers
Training Course for Teachers of Physically or Mentally Handicapped Children
Training Course for Special Subject (*Music*) *Teachers*
Composition, Piano, Strings, Vocal Music, Wind Instruments
Training Course for Special Subject (*Physical Science*) *Teachers*
Biology, Chemistry, Earth Science, Physics

Faculty of Engineering (Freshmen Enrollment: 280)
Department of Applied Physics
Applied Mechanics and Thermodynamics, Applied Nuclear Physics, Applied Physics of Materials, Applied Solid State Physics
Department of Civil Engineering
Construction Materials and Methods, Hydraulic Engineering, Sanitation Engineering, Structural Engineering, Traffic and Geotechnical Engineering
Department of Electrical Engineering
Communication Engineering, Electrical Fundamentals, Electrical Machinery Engineering, Electrical Power Engineering
Department of Electronic Engineering
Electronic Circuit Engineering, Electronic Control Engineering, Electronic Information Engineering, Electronic Physics Engineering
Department of Industrial Chemistry
Inorganic Chemistry, Organic Chemistry, Physical Chemistry
Department of Mechanical Engineering
Applied Mechanics, Fluid Mechanics, Machining, Thermal Engineering

Foreign Student Admission
Qualifications for Applicants
Standard Qualifications Requirement
Examination at the University
If the Faculty Meeting admits that there is a special situation, there may be a special selection process different from the usual examination.
Documents to be Submitted When Applying
Standard Documents Requirement
A copy of a document showing the financial responsibility for expenses during the stay in Japan must also be submitted.

GRADUATE PROGRAMS

Graduate School of Agriculture (First Year Enrollment : Master's 76)
Divisions
Agricultural Chemistry, Agricultural Industry, Agricultural Science, Fisheries Science, Forestry, Grass and Soil Science, Stockbreeding, Veterinary Medicine

Graduate School of Engineering (First Year Enrollment : Master's 42)
Divisions
Applied Physics, Civil Engineering, Electrical Engineering, Industrial Chemistry, Mechanical Engineering

Foreign Student Admission
Qualifications for Applicants
Master's Program
Standard Qualifications Requirement
Examination at the University
Master's Program
An achievement test, an oral interview, and a health examination are required of all applicants. The President of the University determines admission based on these results together with the applicants' official transcripts.
The method and time of selection are specified by the graduate school concerned.
Documents to be Submitted When Applying
Standard Documents Requirement
＊
Research Institutes and Centers
Agricultural Museum, Analysis Center, Computer Center, Elementary and Junior High Schools, Fisheries Experimental Station, Health Care Center, Isotope Center, Stock Farm, University Farm, Veterinary Hospital
For Further Information
Undergraduate and Graduate Admission
Instruction Section, Student Division, Student Office, Miyazaki University, 1–1 Gakuen Kibanadai Nishi Miyazaki-shi, Miyazaki 889–21
☎ 0985–23–2811

Muroran Institute of Technology
(Muroran Kogyo Daigaku)

27-1 Mizumoto-cho, Muroran-shi, Hokkaido 050
☎ 0143–44–4181

Faculty
　　Profs. 62　　Assoc. Profs. 75
　　Assist. Profs. Full–time 3; Part–time 52
　　Res. Assocs. 41
Number of Students
　　Undergrad. 2, 631　　Grad. 230
· Library 218, 073 volumes

Outline and Characteristics of the University

Muroran Institute of Technology, an engineering college, was founded in 1949 by the Japanese Government. Its predecessors go back to the Civil Engineering School of Sapporo Agricultural College founded in 1897 and Muroran Higher Technical School founded in 1939. Ever since its foundation, the College has grown with the times. Today, the College consists of 11 departments belonging to the Faculty of Engineering I, two departments belonging to the Faculty of Engineering II (Evening Course) and the Graduate School (Master's Course) with 12 divisions. The freshmen enrollment is 540 at Faculty I, 90 at Faculty II and 100 at the Graduate School. There are over 2,600 students enrolled in the College.

The campus is located near Mt. Muroran (911m) in the city of Muroran. Muroran (population 130,000) is the largest industrial city in Hokkaido, where famous factories line the port. Students study, work and play sports among academic buildings and green hills overlooking the Pacific Ocean.

Since Muroran is blessed with the best of the four seasons, the citizens enjoy sea bathing and surfing in summer and skiing and skating in winter. Furthermore, Shikotsu-Toya National Park is located near the city and offers lovely views of Lake Shikotsu, Lake Toya, Mt. Usu and Mt. Tarumae.

The educational aim of the College is to train able engineers and intellectual specialists through the study of scientific and thchnical knowledge. University graduates play active roles in various fields internationally as well as domestically.

UNDERGRADUATE PROGRAMS

Faculty of Engineering I (Freshmen Enrollment: 540)

Department of Applied Materials Science
Applied Nonlinear Optics, Magnetism, Physics of Plasticity, Solid State Electronics

Department of Architecture and Building Engineering
Architectural Planning, Building Production Engineering, Building Structural Engineering, Building Structural Mechanics, Environmental Engineering for Buildings

Department of Chemical Engineering
Chemical Reaction Engineering, Diffusional Engineering, Process Control Engineering

Department of Civil Engineering
Highway and Traffic Engineering, River and Coastal Engineering, Sanitary Engineering and Soil Mechanics, Structural Engineering, Structural Mechanics

Department of Electrical Engineering
Electrical Applications, Electrical Machine Engineering, Electric Power Engineering, Fundamental Electrical Engineering

Department of Electronic Engineering

Electronic Application Engineering, Electronic Circuits Engineering, Electronic Control Engineering, Elementary Electronic Engineering

Department of Geotechnology
Applied Geology, Construction Machinery, Disaster Prevention Engineering, Mineral Dressing, Underground Development

Department of Industrial Chemistry
Industrial Analytical Chemistry, Industrial Physical Chemistry, Materials of Chemistry Industry, Organic Industrial Chemistry, Organic Quantum Chemistry

Department of Industrial Mechanical Engineering
Fluid Mechanics, Heat Transfer Engineering, Machining System Engineering, Metal Processing, System Control Engineering

Department of Mechanical Engineering
Combustion Engineering, Fluid Mechanics and Fluid Machinery, Mechanical Dynamics, Strength of Materials

Department of Metallurgical Engineering
Extractive Metallurgy, Metal Processing, Physical Metallurgy, Production of Metallic and Nonmetallic Compounds, Properties of Metals and Alloys

Faculty of Engineering II (**Evening Course**) (Freshmen Enrollment: 90)

Department of Electrical Engineering
Electrical Machinery, Electric Power Systems and Electrical Applications, Electronic Engineering, Elementary Electrical Engineering

Department of Mechanical Engineering
Fluid Mechanics, Machine Design and Machine Manufacture, Strength of Materials, Thermal Engineering

Foreign Student Admission

Qualifications for Applicants
Standard Qualifications Requirement
The results of the Japanese Language Proficiency Test (1st grade), the 1989 General Examination for Foreign Students (natural sciences).

Examination at the University
An interview in Japanese, and a medical inspection. The interview will examine the applicant's basic knowledge and ability IN mathematics and The natural sciences (physics or chemistry).

Documents to be Submitted When Applying
Standard Documents Requirement
All applicants are required to submit the specified application documents to the Admissions Office by September.

GRADUATE PROGRAMS

Graduate School of Engineering (First Year Enrollment: Master's 100)

Divisions
Applied Material Sciences, Applied Science for Energy, Architecture and Building Engineering, Chemical Engineering, Civil Engineering, Electrical Engineer-

ing, Electronic Engineering, Geotechnology, Industrial Chemistry, Industrial Mechanical Engineering, Mechanical Engineering, Metallurgical Engineering

Foreign Student Admission
Qualifications for Applicants
Master's Program
    Standard Qualifications Requirement
Examination at the University
Master's Program
    Applicants must take the same entrance examination, consisting of a written exam and an interview, given to Japanese students. The First Stage Entrance Examination is administered around September and the Second Stage Entrance Examination in March.
    Documents to be Submitted When Applying
    Standard Documents Requirement
    All applicants are required to submit the specified application documents to the Graduate Admissions Office by June (the First Stage) or by December (the Second Stage).

*

Research Institutes and Centers
Educational Center for Information Processing
Facilities/Services for Foreign Students
Housing for Foreign Students: 12 rooms
Special Programs for Foreign Students
    Upon admission to the College, private lessons in Japanese conversation may be arranged if necessary.
For Further Information
    Undergraduate and Graduate Admission
Student Office, Instruction Division, Instruction Section, Muroran Institute of Technology, 27-1 Mizumoto-cho, Muroran-shi, Hokkaido 050 ☎ 0143–44–4181 ext. 378

Nagaoka University of Technology
(Nagaoka Gijutsukagaku Daigaku)

1603-1 Kamitomioka-machi, Nagaoka-shi, Niigata 940-21   ☎ 0258–46–6000

Faculty
    Profs. 67   Assoc. Profs. 63
    Assist. Profs. Full–time 3; Part–time 96
    Res. Assocs. 34
Number of Students
    Undergrad. 916   Grad. 614
Library 65, 000 volumes

Outline and Characteristics of the University
    Recent rapid developments in science and technology have caused new problems about what science and technology should be in relation to human

beings and their society. In order to cope with this situation, the university seeks to produce practical and creative (leading) engineers who will make contributions toward the happiness and prosperity of mankind.
    Nagaoka University of Technology was established to suit these social needs providing the following:

1. Nagaoka University of *Technology* is a college of engineering emphasizing graduate level learning. The graduates of 3-year high schools and technical high schools are admitted to the university as freshmen (first year) and the graduates of 5-year technical colleges are admitted as juniors (third year). With almost all the undergraduate students continuing up to and through graduate school, the education system is consistent.

2. While the curriculum of the university is interdisciplinary, great importance is attached to practical experimentation and training. Fourth graders (seniors) undergo a five-month training period in public corporations or private industries. The aim of this practical experience is to foster responsible members of society who are knowledgeable and practical engineers.

3. The University is open for adult education. In response to the social demand for continual life-time education or retraining of adults, the university actively admits those who have once graduated from technical colleges or universities.

4. The university has ten joint research facilities (mentioned below) for original academic research.

    Nagaoka University of Technology was opened by the government in October 1976. In April 1978, the first freshmen and juniors were enrolled and in April 1980, the graduate school was opened offering a Master's Program, and Doctor's Program in April 1986. Today, the university is functioning as a newly-organized "University of Ideas".
    The university is in Nagaoka city located in the central part of Niigata prefecture. The campus is in a pleasant natural environment, surrounded by wooded hillsides, about 8. 5 kilometers from Nagaoka Railway Station.

UNDERGRADUATE PROGRAMS

Faculty of Engineering (Freshmen Enrollment: 90, Junior Enrollment: 240)
    Department of Civil Engineering
    Department of Electrical and Electronic Systems Engineering
    Department of Electronic Engineering
    Department of Materials Science and Technology
    Department of Mechanical Systems Engineering
    Department of Planning and Production Engineer-

ing

Foreign Student Admission
Qualifications for Applicants
Freshmen:
Foreign applicants for undergraduate programs must have completed 12 years of education or equivalent.
Juniors:
Foreign applicants for undergraduate programs must have completed 14 years of education or equivalent.
Examination at the University
1. Freshman year applicants must take the same entrance examination consisting of the written examination and the interview given to Japanese students. They must also take all the science subjects–mathematics, science, and a foreign language–of the General Examination for Foreign Students. Physics and chemistry are compulsory subjects. They must also take the Japanese Language Proficiency Test (Level 1)
2. Junior year applicants must take the same entrance examination consisting of the written examination and the interview given to Japanese students.
Documents to be Submitted When Applying
Standard Documents Requirement

GRADUATE PROGRAMS

Graduate School of Engineering (First Year Enrollment : Master's 300, Doctor's 18)
Doctor's Program:
Divisions
Energy and Environment Science, Information Science and Control Engineering, Materials Science
Master's program:
Divisions
Civil Engineering, Electrical and Electronic Systems Engineering, Electronic Engineering, Materials Science and Technology, Mechanical Systems Engineering, Planning and Production Engineering

Foreign Student Admission
Qualifications for Applicants
Master's Program
Standard Qualifications Requirement
Doctor's Program
Standard Qualifications Requirement
Examination at the University
Master's Program
Applicants must take the entrance examination of Japanese language including Japanese affairs, related subjects to his/her major including mathematics, and a written or oral examination of English/German/French (applicants should select one of these).
They must also undergo an interview in Japa-

nese which is similar to the interviews given to Japanese applicants.
Doctor's Program
Applicants must take a written or oral examination regarding his/her master's thesis and related subjects to his/her major. They must also undergo a written or oral language test.
Documents to be Submitted When Applying
Standard Documents Requirement
Applicants for the Doctor's program are also required to submit a copy of Master's thesis or equivalent.

＊

Research Institutes and Centers
Analysis and Instrumentation Center, Central machine shop, Department of Sciences and Mathematics, Information Processing Center, Laboratory of Beam Technology, Language Center, Physical Education and Medical Center, Radioisotope Center, Sound and Vibration Engineering Laboratory, Technological Development Center
Facilities/Services for Foreign Students
International House:
Shared Facilities; Lounge, Meeting Room, Japanese-Style Room
Accommodation; 20 Rooms (Single 16, Couple 2, Family 2)
Special Programs for Foreign Students
Japanese language supplementary classes are available, if necessary.
For Further Information
Undergraduate and Graduate Admission
Admissions Office, Educational Affairs Department, Nagaoka University of Technology, 1603-1 Kamitomioka-machi, Nagaoka-shi, Niigata 940-21 ☎ 0258–46–6000 ext. 2179

Nagasaki University
(Nagasaki Daigaku)

1-14 Bunkyo-machi, Nagasaki-shi, Nagasaki 852
☎ 0958–47–1111

Faculty
Profs. 220   Assoc. Profs. 196
Assist. Profs. Full–time 99; Part–time 640
Res. Assocs. 306
Number of Students
Undergrad. 6, 546   Grad. 438
Library 787, 924 volumes

Outline and Characteristics of the University
Nagasaki University aims at imparting a wide range of knowledge to students, encouraging them to develop their intellectual, moral, and practical abilities by promoting the study of arts and sciences, and to emerge as well-rounded graduates. Nagasaki, where Nagasaki University is located, boasts a long and illustrious history. During the Age of National

Exclusion it played an important role as the only prosperous window to foreign civilization and contributed greatly to the modernization of Japan. Having suffered an atomic bomb attack during World War II it has made strenuous efforts toward world peace and now prospers as a peace-loving city. It is also famous for its scenic beauty and enjoys a pleasantly warm climate.

Nagasaki University offers seven faculties (Dentistry, Economics, Education, Engineering, Fisheries, Medicine, and Pharmaceutical Sciences), the Department of Liberal Arts, the Institute of Tropical Medicine, the Graduate School of Marine Science and Engineering, the University Library, and a few other institutes. These and the Administration Office of Nagasaki University are in Nagasaki, which offers a quiet, academic atmosphere representative of its environment.

Ever since 1949, when it was founded as a part of the postwar educational reforms, Nagasaki University has developed into a well-equipped academic community with a large teaching staff and impressive facilities.

The University lays much stress on international exchange and has established institutional agreements with five universities abroad. Based on these agreements, the University promotes international collaboration in the field of education and the research.

Nagasaki is Japan's window to Asian countries and historically served as bridge for western civilization. Thus Nagasaki University is ideally placed for research in Japan's historic and academic ties with Europe and Asia. The location also favours research in such fields as marine science, medical science and tropical medicine. The Faculty of Fisheries, Institute of Tropical Medicine, School of Medicine, University Hospital, and other faculties offer unique opportunities for advanced research and training.

More than one hundred overseas students from seventeen countries are enrolled presently and study at the University. Foreign students are attracted to the University not only by its high academic reputation, but also because of its sympathetic and positive approach to the needs and problems of overseas students. The number of foreign students tends to increase rapidly year and year.

UNDERGRADUATE PROGRAMS

Faculty of Dentistry (Freshmen Enrollment: 60)
Department of Dentistry
Dental Materials, Dental Pharmacology, Endodontics and Operative Dentistry, Fixed Prosthodontics, Maxillofacial and Oral Surgery, Oral Anatomy, Oral Bacteriology, Oral Biochemistry, Oral Histology, Oral Pathology, Oral Physiology, Oral Radiology, Orthodontics, Pediatric Dentistry, Periodontics, Preventive Dentistry, Removable Prosthodontics
Faculty of Economics (Freshmen Enrollment: 305)

Department of Commerce
Commercial Communications in Foreign Language, Insurance, International Economics, International Finance, Trade Administration, World Economics
Department of Economics
Economic Geography, Economic Policy, Finance, History of Economics, Principles of Economics, Public Finance, Sociology, Statistics
Department of Management
Accounting, Business Administration, Business Enter-Prise Cost Accounting, Business Management, Commercial Science, History of Management, Information Processing
Faculty of Education (Freshmen Enrollment: 370)
Elementary School Teacher Training Course
Junior High School Teacher Training Course
Kindergarten Teacher Training Course
Training Course for Teachers of Mentally Handicapped Children
Algebra and Geometry, Analysis and Applied Mathematics, Biology, Calligraphy, Chemistry, Chinese Classics, Clothing, Composition of Music, Construction, Developmental Psychology, Economics, Education, Educational Psychology, Educational Sociology, Educational Systems Education, Education of Mentally Handicapped Children, Electricity, English and American Literature, English Philology, Ethics, Food, Geography, Gymnastics, History, History of Education, Home Management, Infant Education, Infant Psychology, Instrumental Music, Japanese Linguistics, Japanese Literature, Law, Mechanics, Metal Working, Nursing, Nursing Research, Paintings, Philosophy, Physical Exercise, Physical Geography, Physics, Psychology of Mentally Handicapped Children, School Hygiene, Sculpture, Social Education, Teaching, Teaching of Art, Teaching of English, Teaching of Hygiene, Teaching of Japanese, Teaching of Mathematics, Teaching of Music, Teaching of Science, Teaching of Social Studies, Teaching of Technology, Theory of Art and History of Art, Theory of Gymnastics and History of Physical Education, Theory of Music and History of Music, Vocal Music, Vocational Guidance, Woodcraft
Faculty of Engineering (Freshmen Enrollment: 420)
Department of Civil Engineering
Coastal Engineering, Hydrography Engineering, Soil Mechanics Engineering, Structural Engineering
Department of Electrical Engineering
Electrical Machinery, Electric Power, Fundamentals of Electricity, Instrument and Control
Department of Electronics
Communications, Computer Science, Controls, Fundamentals of Electronics
Department of Industrial Chemistry
Inorganic Chemistry, Organic Chemistry, Organic Synthesis, Physical Chemistry
Department of Materials Science and Engineering
Chemistry of Materials, Metal Science and Engineering, Physics of Materials, Polymer Science and Engineering

Department of Mechanical Engineering
Fluid Engineering, Product Engineering, Strength of Materials, Thermal Engineering
Department of Mechanical Engineering II
Automatic Control, Failure and Fracture of Materials, Machine Design, Thermal Fluid
Department of Structural Engineering
Design and Behavior of Concrete Structures, Design of Steel Structures and Fitting, General Dynamics of Structures, Welding Engineering and Structural Production
Faculty of Fisheries (Freshmen Enrollment: 120)
Department of Fisheries
Aquaculture Sciences, Fishery and Oceanographic Sciences, Marine Biological Sciences, Marine Chemical Sciences, Marine Food Sciences, Marine Information Sciences
Faculty of Medicine (Freshmen Enrollment: 100)
Department of Medicine
Anatomy, Anesthesiology, Bacteriology, Biochemistry, Dermatology, Forensic Medicine, Hygiene, Internal Medicine, Laboratory Medicine, Medical Oncology, Medical Zoology, Neurological Surgery, Obstetrics and Gynecology, Ophthalmology, Orthopedics, Otorhinolaryngology, Pathology, Pediatrics, Pharmacology, Physiology, Psychiatry, Public Health, Radiology, Surgery, Urology
Faculty of Pharmaceutical Sciences (Freshmen Enrollment: 80)
Department of Pharmaceutical Sciences
Clinical Pharmaceutics, Health Science, Medicinal Chemistry, Natural Product Chemistry and Biotechnology

Foreign Student Admission
Qualifications for Applicants
Standard Qualifications Requirement
Examination at the University
Applicants must take the General Examination for Foreign Students and the Japanese Language Proficiency Test (First Level) instead of the Joint First-Stage Achievement Test.
Those who receive the examination will be allowed to take each Faculty's special entrance examination consisting of written and oral exams and an interview at the University.
Documents to be Submitted When Applying
Standard Documents Requirement
Application forms are available at the Admissions Office from mid-September. All applicants are required to submit the specified application documents to the Admissions Office by February 8.

ONE-YEAR GRADUATE PROGRAMS

One-Year Graduate Program in Economics (Enrollment: 10)
Accounting, Management
One-Year Graduate Program in Education (Enrollment: 5)

Education
One-Year Graduate Program in Fisheries (Enrollment: 30)
Ocean Fishery

Foreign Student Admission
Qualifications for Applicants
Standard Qualifications Requirement
Examination at the University
Applications for the Education Program and the Fisheries Program will be accepted in January, and examinations will be held in February.
Applications for the Economics Program will be accepted in February, and examinations will be held in March.

GRADUATE PROGRAMS

Graduate School of Dentistry (First Year Enrollment : Doctor's 18)
Division
Dental Science
Graduate School of Engineering (First Year Enrollment : Master's 56)
Divisions
Civil Engineering, Electrical Engineering, Electronics, Industrial Chemistry, Material Science and Engineering, Mechanical Engineering, Mechanical Engineering II, Structural Engineering
Graduate School of Fisheries (First Year Enrollment : Master's 28)
Division
Fisheries
Graduate School of Marine Science and Engineering (First Year Enrollment: Doctor's 18)
Divisions
Marine Production Research and Development, Marine Resources Research and Development
Graduate School of Medicine (First Year Enrollment : Doctor's 61)
Divisions
Internal Medicine, Pathology, Physiology, Social Medicine, Surgery
Graduate School of Pharmaceutical Sciences (First Year Enrollment : Master's 26, Doctor's 6)
Divisions
Clinical Pharmaceutics, Health Science , Medicinal Chemistry, Natural Product Chemistry and Biotechnology

Foreign Student Admission
Qualifications for Applicants
Master's Program
Standard Qualifications Requirement
Doctor's Program
Standard Qualifications Requirement
Examination at the University
Master's Program
Applicants must take the same entrance examination, consisting of a written exam and an inter-

view, given to Japanese students.

Doctor's Program

Same as Master's program.

Documents to be Submitted When Applying

Standard Documents Requirement

Application forms for Graduate School of Dentistry Engineering, Fisheries, Marine Science and Engineering, and Pharmaceutical Sciences are available from June to July. Graduate School of Medicine application forms are available from December.

Applicants to Graduate School of Dentistry Engineering, Fisheries, Marine Science and Engineering, and Pharmaceutical Sciences are required to submit the specified application documents by September.

Graduate School of Medicine applicants are required to submit the specified application documents by February of the following year.

*

Research Institutes and Centers

Analysis and Treatment Center for Environmental Protection, Atomic Disease Institute, Botanical Garden for Medicinal Plants, Fisheries Experimental Station, Fishery Training Ship (Kakuyo Maru), Fishery Training Ship (Nagasaki Maru), Foreign Student Advising Office, Health Administration Center, Hospital of Dentistry, Information Processing Center, Institute for Tropical Medicine, Laboratory Animal Center for Biomedical Research, Medical Materials Center for Atomic Bomb Casualties, RI Center, The Center for Educational Research and Training, University Hospital

Facilities/Services for Foreign Students

International House

Shared Facilities: Lobby, Seminar Room

Accommodation: 38 Rooms (single 30, couple 4, family 4)

Special Programs for Foreign Students

"On Japan," a lecture given at the Department of Liberal Arts, is required of all foreign students. Supplementary Japanese language classes are available at the Faculty of Education.

For Further Information

Undergraduate Admission

Admissions Section, Student Division, Student Office, Nagasaki University, 1-14 Bunkyo-machi, Nagasaki-shi, Nagasaki 852 ☎ 0958–47–1111 ext. 2220

Graduate Admission

Student Affairs Section, Graduate School of Dentistry, Nagasaki University, 7-1 Sakamoto-machi, Nagasaki-shi, Nagasaki 852 ☎ 0958–47–2111 ext. 4050

School Affairs Section, Graduate School of Engineering, Nagasaki University, 1-14 Bunkyo-machi, Nagasaki-shi, Nagasaki 852 ☎ 0958–47–1111 ext. 2613

Student Affairs Section, Graduate School of Fisheries, Nagasaki University, 1-14 Bunkyo-machi, Nagasaki-shi, Nagasaki 852 ☎ 0958–47–1111 ext. 3110

Student Affairs Section, Graduate School of Science and Engineering, Nagasaki University, 1–14 Bunkyo-machi, Nagasaki-shi, Nagasaki, 852 ☎ 0958–47–1111 ext. 2613

School Affairs Section, Graduate School of Medicine, Nagasaki University, 12-4 Sakamoto-machi, Nagasaki-shi, Nagasaki 852 ☎ 0958–47–2111 ext. 2021

Student Affairs Section, Graduate School of Pharmaceutical Sciences, Nagasaki University, 1-14 Bunkyo-machi, Nagasaki-shi, Nagasaki 852 ☎ 0958–47–1111 ext. 2507

Nagoya Institute of Technology
(Nagoya Kogyo Daigaku)

Gokiso-cho, Showa-ku, Nagoya-shi, Aichi 466
☎ 052–732–2111

Faculty

Profs.   120   Assoc. Profs.   103

Assist. Profs.   Full–time   34; Part–time   115

Res. Assocs.   71

Number of Students

Undergrad.   5, 059   Grad.   477

Library   340, 032 volumes

Outline and Characteristics of the University

The Nagoya Institute of Technology was established in May 1949 as a national university under the program of educational reform after the second World War, merging the Nagoya College of Technology and the Aichi Prefectural College of Technology. The Nagoya College of Technology was originally founded in March 1905 as the Nagoya Higher Technical School. The College had turned out into society more than 12, 000 graduates by March 1951, when it was dissolved, leaving behind a respected history and tradition of 46 years. The Aichi Prefectural College of Technology, established in February 1943, had produced some 880 graduates by April 1951, when it was dissolved. The graduates of both Colleges have gone into various social fields, and are doing much for the advancement of various Japanese industries. In 1951, the Junior College with a three-year evening course was attached to the Institute. Since 1954, the Graduate School offered a one-year non-degree program for graduates in each department. In 1959, the status of the Junior College was promoted to that of university, and the Evening Course was expanded to a five-year program. In 1964, the Graduate School began a two-year Master's Course and discontinued the one year program.

In 1977, Ceramic Engineering Research Laboratory was established. In April 1985, reorganization from 14 to 6 Departments in the day courses took place: Applied Chemistry, Materials Science and Engineering, Mechanical Engineering, Production Systems Engineering, Electrical and Computer Engineering, and Architecture, Urban and Civil Engineering. Evening courses: Applied Chemistry, Mechanical Engineering, Electrical and Computer Engineering, and Architecture, Urban and Civil Engineering. The Master's Course of the Graduate School was reorganized as well. The Doctor's Courses with majors in Materials Science and Engineering and Production and Systems Engineering was established at this time. In April 1986, the Doctor's Courses in Electrical and Computer Engineering, and Architecture, Urban and Civil Engineering were established. In May 1987, Center for Instrumental Analysis was established.

The main academic buildings are located on Gokiso Campus, which neighbors famous Tsurumai Park, in the center of Nagoya City. It is favored with convenient transportation and suitable surroundings for study.

The Institute aims to cultivate persons who contribute to world peace and welfare through teaching and studying within industry, while promoting the technical development of local industry.

UNDERGRADUATE PROGRAMS

Faculty of Engineering (Freshmen Enrollment: 840)
Department of Applied Chemistry
Chemical Engineering, Inorganic Chemistry, Organic Chemistry and Biochemistry, Physical and Analytical Chemistry, Polymer Chemistry
Department of Architecture, Urban Engineering and Civil Engineering
Architectural Design & Urban Planning, Construction Materials & Environmental Management, Environmental & Disaster Engineering, Infrastructure Planning, Structural Engineering & Mechanics, Structural Planning & Construction Engineering
Department of Electrical and Computer Engineering
Circuit & Systems, Communication Systems, Computer Science, Electric Energy, Electron Devices, Information Processing, Solid State Physics
Department of Materials Science and Engineering
Ceramics Synthesis, Material Characterization, Material Fundamentals, Material Properties, Metallic Materials Design, Organic Materials Design
Department of Mechanical Engineering
Electronic-Mechanical Engineering, Fluid Mechanics, Mechanics, Production Technology, Thermal Energy
Department of Production Systems Engineering
Instrumentation System Engineering, Management Systems Engineering, Mathematics for System Science, Physical Instrumentation
Faculty of Engineering (**Evening Course**) (Freshmen Enrollment: 200)
Department of Applied Chemistry
Chemical Engineering, Inorganic Chemistry, Organic Chemistry, Physical and Analytical Chemistry
Department of Architecture, Urban Engineering and Civil Engineering
Environmental & Disaster Engineering, Infrastructure Planning, Materials & Construction Engineering, Structural Engineering & Mechanics
Department of Electrical and Computer Engineering
Circuits & Systems, Communication Systems, Electric Energy, Electronic Devices, Solid State Physics
Department of Mechanical Engineering
Fluid Mechanics, Production Technology, Strength of Materials, Thermal Engineering

Foreign Student Admission
Qualifications for Applicants
Standard Qualifications Requirement
Examination at the University
For each Department, applicants must take the Japanese Language Proficiency Test, General Examination for Foreign Students and the entrance examination of Nagoya Institute of Technology.
Documents to be Submitted When Applying
Standard Documents Requirement
Application forms are available at the Admissions Office from early November. All applicants are required to submit the specified application documents to the Admissions Office by January 19.

GRADUATE PROGRAMS

Graduate School of Engineering (First Year Enrollment : Master's 142, Doctor's 14)
Divisions
Architecture, Urban Engineering and Civil Engineering, Electrical and Computer Engineering, Materials Science and Engineering, Production and Systems Engineering

Foreign Student Admission
Qualifications for Applicants
Master's Program
Standard Qualifications Requirement
Doctor's Program
Standard Qualifications Requirement
Examination at the University
Master's Program
Applicants must take the same entrance examination, consisting of a written exam and an interview, given to Japanese students.
Doctor's Program
Same as Master's program.
Documents to be Submitted When Applying
Standard Documents Requirement
Application forms are available at the Admission Office from early July. All applicants are required to submit the specified application documents to the Admission Office by August 27.
Research Institutes and Centers
Center for Instrumental Analysis, Center of Information Processing Education, Ceramic Engineering Research Laboratory
Facilities/Services for Foreign Students
The Institute has no dormitory for foreign students. It is possible for students to stay at the Foreign

Student House of Nagoya University although accommodation may not be available for all applicants.

Special Programs for Foreign Students

The Institute offers Japanese language and culture classes.

Japanese 1, 2: The acquisition and enhancement of basic skills in Japanese language, with emphasis on grammar, speaking and hearing.

Japanese 3: An advanced course for those who have completed Japanese 1 & 2. Emphasis on the development and mastery of natural Japanese.

Japanology1, 2: Lectures on Japanese culture with special emphasis on the appreciation of Japanese arts as they influence Japanese life.

For Further Information

Undergraduate and Graduate Admission

Admission Office, Nagoya Institute of Technology, Gokiso-cho, Showa-ku, Nagoya-shi, Aichi 466
☎ 052–732–2111 ext. 2288

Nagoya University
(Nagoya Daigaku)

Furo-cho, Chikusa-ku, Nagoya-shi, Aich 464
☎ 052–781–5111

Faculty
    Profs. 460   Assoc. Profs. 406
    Assist. Profs. Full–time 140; Part–time 1, 416
    Res. Assocs. 655
Number of Students
    Undergrad. 8, 347   Grad. 2, 042
Library 2, 088, 615 volumes

Outline and Characteristics of the University

The history of the University dates back to 1871. After many vicissitudes, Nagoya Imperial University, consisting of the Faculty of Medicine and the Faculty of Science and Engineering combined, was founded in April 1939. In 1942, the latter was divided into two independent entities. In 1948, two new Faculties, the Faculty of Letters and the Faculty of Law and Economics combined, were opened. In the following year, 1949, the University saw a major reorganization under the new educational system and the Faculty of Education was opened. In 1951 the Faculty of Agriculture was added. In addition, Graduate Schools opened their doors in 1953. Today, the University comprises eight Faculties, the College of General Education, eight Graduate Schools, the University Library, four Research Institutes, seven other Centers for specialized study and research, and the College of Medical Technology.

The University is located in Nagoya, the largest city of Central Japan. The main campus (705, 000 square meters) is located in the Higashiyama district, one of the hilly areas to the east of the city, where the University Library, Toyota Auditorium, and many other buildings stand together in quiet surroundings. The Faculty of Medicine and affiliated hospital are located in Tsurumai, an area adjacent to Tsurumai Park, at some distance from Higashiyama. The College of Medical Technology and the attached hospital (a branch of the main University Hospital) are at Daiko.

Nagoya University is one of the leading universities in Central Japan: its academic achievements are highly esteemed both in Japan and internationally.

At present, the University has 413 foreign students from 41 countries.

UNDERGRADUATE PROGRAMS

Faculty of Agriculture (Freshmen Enrollment: 193)
Department of Agricultural Chemistry
Biological Chemistry, Microbiology, Nutritional Biochemistry, Pesticide Chemistry, Plant Nutrition and Fertilizer, Soil Science
Department of Agronomy
Applied Entomology and Nematology, Crop Science, Economics of Food Production, Horticultural Science, Plant Pathology, Sericultural Science, Theory of Agronomy and Plant Breeding
Department of Animal Science
Animal Genetics, Animal Nutrition, Animal Physiology, Animal Reproduction, Functional Comparative Anatomy
Department of Food Science and Technology
Bio-Reaction Technology, Chemistry of Animal Products, Chemistry of Plant Products, Fermentation Technology, Organic Chemistry, Physical Chemistry
Department of Forest Products
Chemical Technology of Wood, Chemistry of Forest Products, Wood Industrial Machinery, Wood Physics, Wood Technology
Department of Forestry
Forest Engineering, Forest Management, Silviculture, Soil and Water Conservation
Faculty of Economics (Freshmen Enrollment: 230)
Department of Business Administration
Accounting, Business Administration, Financial Management, Management Accounting, Production Management
Department of Economics
Agricultural Policy, Economic History, Economic Theory, History of Economic Thought, History of Social Thoughts, Industrial Organization and Industrial Policy, International Economics, Labor Economics, Money and Banking, Principles of Economic Policy, Public Finance, Statistics and Econometrics
Faculty of Education (Freshmen Enrollment: 70)
Department of Education
Adult Education, Curriculum, Educational Administration and System, History of Education, Methods of Education, Philosophy of Education, School Management, Sociology of Education, Technical and Technological Education

Department of Educational Psychology

Child Psychology, Educational Investigation and Statistics, Mental Developmental Disorders and Clinical Psychology, Psychology of Development and Learning, Psychology of Personality and Psychological Assessment, Social and Industrial Psychology

Faculty of Engineering (Freshmen Enrollment: 825)

Department of Aeronautical Engineering

Automatic Control, Engines, Flight Dynamics, Fluid Mechanics, Propulsion, Structure

Department of Applied Chemistry

Applied Chemistry of Oils, Chemistry of Industrial Inorganic Reactions, Chemistry of Industrial Organic Reactions, Chemistry of Inorganic Materials, Chemistry of Organic Materials

Department of Applied Physics

Applied Optics, Dielectric and Thermal Properties of Solids, Engineering of Plasticity, Industrial Solid State Physics, Theoretical Solid State Physics

Department of Architecture

Architectural Design, Architectural Environmental Engineering, Architectural Planning, Building Construction, Steel Structure, Structural Concrete Engineering

Department of Chemical Engineering

Catalysis Engineering, Chemical Thermodynamics and Chemical Reaction Engineering, Combustion and Heat Transmision, Design of Chemical Machinery and Equipment, Diffusional Unit Operation, Fluid Mechanics and Mechanical Unit Operation, Process System Engineering and Process Control, Transport Phenomena

Department of Civil Engineering

Civil Engineering Design, Civil Engineering Execution, Civil Engineering Planning, Hydraulics, Soil Mechanics, Structural Mechanics

Department of Electrical Engineering I

Electrical Machinery and Apparatus, Electric Power Applications, Electric Power Generation, Electroacoustics, Electromagnetic Waves, Fundamentals of Electrical Engineering, Transmission and Distribution Engineering

Department of Electrical Engineering II

Computation and System Engineering, Electrical Material Science and Devices, Electric Discharge, Electronic Control Engineering, Physical Electronics

Department of Electronic-Mechanical Engineering

Application and Design of Electronic Machinery, Fundamentals of Electronic-Mechanical Engineering, Integrated Mechanical Engineering, Precision Processing Technology, Sensor and Electric Instrumentation

Department of Electronics

Electronic Circuit Engneering, Electron Tubes, Fundamentals of Electronics, High Frequency Engineering, Industrial Electronics, Semiconductor Electronics

Department of Information Engineering

Computer Language, Fundamentals of Information Engineeing, Information Processing, Information System Engineering, Knowledge Information, Mathematical Software

Department of Iron and Steel Engineering

Applied Metal Physics, Metallic Materials, Metallurgical Engineering of Molten State, Plastic Working of Metals, Special Metallurgical Engineering, Strength of Metals

Department of Mechanical Engineering I

Dynamics of Machinery and Design, Fluid Mechanics, Machineshop Technology and Precision Processings, Strength of Materials, Thermodynamics and Heat Engines

Department of Mechanical Engineering II

Control Mechanics and Components, Deformation Processes and Die Engineering, Fluid Machinery, Internal-Combustion Engines and Gas Turbines, Materials Science and Machine Design

Department of Metallurgical Engineering

Chemical Metallurgy, Ferrous Metallurgy, Metal Casting, Metal Physics, Non-Ferrous Metallurgy, Welding Technology

Department of Nuclear Engineering

Applied Nuclear Chemistry, Nuclear Chemical Engineering, Nuclear Instruments, Radiation Detector Engineering, Radiation Safety

Department of Synthetic Chemistry

Applied Physical Chemistry of High Polymers, Catalysis and Catalytic Reaction, Chemistry of Polymerization, Industrial Analytical Chemistry, Petro-Chemistry, Synthetic Radiation Chemistry

Faculty of Law (Freshmen Enrollment: 190)

Department of Law

Civil Code, Commercial Law, Criminal Law and Procedure, Fundamental Sciences in Law, Public Law

Department of Political Science

International Politics, Political Theory and History, Public Administration

Faculty of Letters (Freshmen Enrollment: 150)

Department of History and Geography

Archaeology, Geography, Japanese History, Occidental History, Oriental History

Department of Literature

Chinese Literature, English Linguistics, English Literature, French Literature, German Literature, Japanese Linguistics, Japanese Literature, Linguistics

Department of Philosophy

Aesthetics and Art History, Comparative Sociology, History of Chinese Philosophy, History of Indian Philosophy, History of Occidental Philosophy, Philosophy, Psychology, Sociology

Faculty of Medicine (Freshmen Enrollment: 100)

Department of Medicine

Anatomy, Anesthesiology, Bacteriology, Biochemistry, Dermatology, Geriatrics, Hygiene, Immunology, Internal Medicine, Laboratory Medicine, Legal Medicine, Medical Zoology, Neurosurgery, Obstetrics and Gynecology, Ophthalmology, Oral Surgery, Orthopedic Surgery, Otorhinolaryngology, Pathology, Pediatrics, Pharmacology, Physiology, Preventive

Medicine, Psychiatry, Public Health, Radiology, Surgery, Thoracic Surgery, Urology

Faculty of Science (Freshmen Enrollment: 285)

Department of Biology

Cell Biochemistry, Gene Analysis and Plant Physiology, Insect Endocrinology, Molecular Genetics and Molecular Evolution, Physiological Genetics and Cell Biology, Physiological Zoology

Department of Chemistry

Analytical Chemistry, Biochemistry, Inorganic Chemistry, Isotope Chemistry, Organic Chemistry, Organic Reaction Chemistry, Physical Chemistry, Quantum Chemistry, Solid State Chemistry

Department of Earth Sciences

Geochemistry, Geophysics, Historical Geology, Petrology and Economic Geology, Seismology, Structural Geology

Department of Mathematics

Algebra, Analysis, Applied Mathematics, Computer Mathematics, Functional Analysis, Geometry, Mathematical Logic, Mathematical Programming, Mathematical Statistics

Department of Molecular Biology

Bioenergetics, Biological Response, Cell Motility, Cell Regulation, Genetic Analysis, Informational Macromolecules

Department of Physics I

Atomic Physics, Biophysics, Fundamental Theory of Physics, High Energy Physics, Nuclear Measurement, Nuclear Theory, Space Physics, Theory of Elementary Particles

Department of Physics II

Crystallography, Electromagnetic State, Fundamental Theory of Solid State, Molecular Structure, Polymer and Biophysics, Properties of Matter, Theory of Solid State

Foreign Student Admission

Qualifications for Applicants

Standard Qualifications Requirement

Applicants to the Faculty of Medicine must have taken all the subjects required of the Joint First-Stage Achievement Test, in addition to meeting the above requirements.

Examination at the University

Admission will depend on the results of an examination prepared by the University, the Japanese Language Proficiency Test, the General Examination for Foreign Students and a satisfactory health report. For applicants to the Faculty of Medicine, the Joint First-Stage Achievement Test will also be taken into account.

Documents to be Submitted When Applying

Standard Documents Requirement

All applicants are required to submit a copy of the report cards recording the results in the Japanese Language Proficiency Test and General Examination for Foreign Students.

Applicants to the Faculty of Medicine must write the identification numbers of the Joint First-Stage Achievement Test in the section marked "to be submitted to national, public or private university", detach the completed part and stick it onto the application form as directed.   Those who have not completed 12 years of regular education but become qualified for application by their success in a public examination or equivalent procedure, or by attending one of the designated Japanese language schools must submit a certificate showing that they have passed the examination or have completed the language program.

GRADUATE PROGRAMS

Graduate School of Agriculture (First Year Enrollment : Master's 72, Doctor's 38)

Divisions

Agricultural Chemistry, Agronomy, Animal Science, Biochemical Regulation, Food Science and Technology, Forest Products, Forestry

Graduate School of Economics (First Year Enrollment : Master's 32, Doctor's 16)

Divisions

Business Administration, Economics

Graduate School of Education (First Year Enrollment : Master's 26, Doctor's 26)

Divisions

Education, Educational Psychology

Graduate School of Engineering (First Year Enrollment : Master's 286, Doctor's 124)

Divisions

Aeronautical Engineering, Applied Chemistry, Applied Physics, Architecture, Chemical Engineering, Civil Engineering, Crystalline Material Science, Electrical Engineering, Electronic-Mechanical Engineering, Electronics, Geotechnical Engineering, Information Engineering, Iron and Steel Engineering, Mechanical Engineering, Metallurgy, Nuclear Engineering, Synthetic Chemistry

Graduate School of Law (First Year Enrollment : Master's 43, Doctor's 20)

Divisions

and Public Law, Political Science, Private and Criminal Law

Graduate School of Letters (First Year Enrollment : Master's 58, Doctor's 23)

Divisions

Chinese Literature, English Literature, French Literature, German Literature, History and Geography, Japanese Language and Culture (Master Course) Japanese Literature, Oriental Philosophy, Philology, Philosophy, Psychology, Sociology

Graduate School of Medicine (First Year Enrollment : Doctor's 80)

Divisions

Internal Medicine, Pathology, Physiology, Social Medicine, Surgery

Graduate School of Science (First Year Enrollment : Master's 126, Doctor's 76)

Divisions

Astrophysics, Biology, Chemistry, Earth Science, Mathematics, Molecular Biology, Physics I & II, Sciences of Atmosphere and Hydrosphere

Foreign Student Admission
Qualifications for Applicants
Master's Program
    Standard Qualifications Requirement
Doctor's Program
    Standard Qualifications Requirement
    In the case of applicants to the Graduate School of Medicine, schooling is to include undergraduate studies in medical or dental science.
Examination at the University
Master's Program
    Acceptance will depend on the results of an entrance examination and satisfactory health report.
Doctor's Program
    Same as Master's program.
Documents to be Submitted When Applying
    Standard Documents Requirement

*

Research Institutes and Centers
Center for Gene Research, Center for Linguistic and Cultural Research, Chemical Instrument Center, Computation Center, Education Center for Information Processing, Institute of Plasma Physics, Physical Fitness and Sports, Radioisotope Center, Research Center for Resource and Energy Conservation, Research Center of Health, Research Institute of Atmospherics, Research Institute of Environmental Medicine, Water Research Institute

Facilities/Services for Foreign Students
International Residence: Common Facilities (Library, Conference Room, Japanese-Style Room, Laundry and Lounge), Accommodation for students; 50 rooms (single 30, double 20), for visiting scholars; 20 rooms (all double)
Foreign Students House: Common Facilities (Library, Recreation Room, Japanese-Style Room, Dining Room and Kitchen for Residents' Use), Accommodation for students; 56 rooms (single for male 41, single for female 8, double 5, family 2)

Special Programs for Foreign Students
Training Coursees in Japanese: This is an intensive course intended for those going to study or conduct research at Nagoya University or other universities in this area. Participants should be research students or teachers undergoing training, and should be of postgraduate level.
Training Courses in Japanese Language: This is a course for those majoring in Japanese studies in their home universities, who have come here to attain proficiency in Japanese language, study the culture and play a full part in Japanese campus life.
Supplementary Japanese Course: This is designed to give graduate and research students an opportunity to learn Japanese.

For Further Information
Undergraduate Admission

Admission Office, Nagoya University, Furo-cho, Chikusa-ku, Nagoya-shi, Aichi 464–01 ☎ 052–781–5111 ext. 3672
Graduate Admission
Graduate Schools of Agriculture, Economics, Education, Engineering, Law, Letters and Science: The Curriculum and Student Section of each Graduate School, Furo-cho, Chikusa-ku, Nagoya-shi, Aichi 464–01 ☎ 052–781–5111 ext. 6207 (Agriculture), 2357 (Economics), 2607 (Education), 5860 (Engineering), 2317 (Law), 2206 (Letters), 2401 (Science)
Graduate School of Medicine: The Curriculum and Student Section, 65 Tsurumai-cho, Showa-ku, Nagoya-shi, Aichi 466 ☎ 052–741–2111 ext. 2135

Nara University of Education
(Nara Kyoiku Daigaku)
Takabatake-cho, Nara-shi, Nara 630
☎ 0742–26–1101

Faculty
    Profs.   63   Assoc. Profs.   49
    Assist. Profs.   Full–time   2
    Res. Assocs.   3
Number of Students
    Undergrad.   1, 287   Grad.   108
Library   230, 122 volumes

Outline and Characteristics of the University
    The campus of the university is located in the eastern part of Nara, the most ancient capital of Japan. It is referred to as the cradle of Japanese culture with its many old temples and shrines. Nara was the gateway through which Chinese civilization was introduced some 1, 200 years ago.
    The history of the university dates back to 1888 when Nara Prefectural Normal School was established, and to 1903 when Nara Prefectural Women's Normal School was founded. In 1949, Nara Gakugei Daigaku (Nara Liberal Arts College) was inaugurated, incorporating the aforesaid Normal Schools and the Nara Normal School for teachers of the Young Men's National Schools. This was in accordance with the reforms of the educational system of this country that had been under way step by step since 1945.
    The main objective of the university is to conduct research in education and various other fields of discipline, as well as to train students in the theory and practice of their respective fields of specialization. The university tries especially to prepare the students to be competent teachers as well as good citizens, and to contribute to the higher cultural features of the Nara community.
    Renamed Nara University of Education in 1966, the university has grown with the times. In 1983 the Graduate School was opened and started to offer Master's programs. This and other establishments

are based upon the idea that teacher training should be executed on a higher level of the university. At the same time Nara University of Education, with its academic excellence, is an ideal place for learning old Japanese culture and enjoying the beauty of nature. The number of students from foreign countries is and is expected to increase.

UNDERGRADUATE PROGRAMS

Faculty of Education (Freshmen Enrollment: 295)

Course for Calligraphy Teachers at Senior High Schools
History, Theory, and Skills of Calligraphy
Course for Elementary School Teachers
Art, Domestic Science, Health and Physical Education, Japanese, Mathematics, Music, Pedagogy, Psychology, Science, Social Studies
Course for Teachers of Schools for the Handicapped
Hygiene, Pedagogy, Psychology
Course for Junior High School Teachers
Art, Domestic Science, English, Handicrafts, Health and Physical Education, Japanese, Mathematics, Music, Science, Social Studies
Course for Kindergarten Teachers
Drawing and Painting, Health, Infant Education, Infant Psychology, Language, Musical Rhythm, Nature, Social Studies
Course for Science Teachers at Senior High Schools
Biology, Chemistry, Geology, Physics

Foreign Student Admission

Qualifications for Applicants
Standard Qualifications Requirement
Examination at the University
All applicants must take the Japanese Language Proficiency Test and the General Examination for Foreign Students. Those who receive satisfactory grades will be allowed to take each Department's special entrance examination consisting of written and oral examinations and an interview.
Documents to be Submitted When Applying
Standard Documents Requirement
Application forms are available at the Admissions Office from early November. All applicants are required to submit the specified application documents to the Admissions Office by January.

GRADUATE PROGRAMS

Graduate School of Education (First Year Enrollment : Master's 60)
Divisions
Art Education, English Language Education, Japanese Language Education, Mathematics Education, Music Education, Physical Education, School Education, Science Education, Social Studies Education

*

Research Institutes and Centers
Educational Technology Center, Experimental Farm and Forests, Health Administration Center, Institute for Education

Facilities/Services for Foreign Students
At the present time, our university has no facilities specifically for the use of foreign students. However, all university facilities may be shared with the Japanese students. These facilities include dormitories and the Student Hall.

Special Programs for Foreign Students
The University has one full-time teacher of Japanese language, and four part-time teachers, teaching Japanese and Japanese culture to undergraduate students and Asian and ASEAN teachers studying under the Japanese Government scholarship program started in 1983.

For Further Information
Undergraduate and Graduate Admission
Curriculum Section, Admissions Office, Nara University of Education, Takabatake-cho, Nara-shi, Nara 630 ☎ 0742–26–1101 ext. 262

Nara Women's University
(Nara Joshi Daigaku)

Kitauoyahigashi-machi, Nara-shi, Nara 630
☎ 0742–23–1131

Faculty
Profs.   75   Assoc. Profs.   62
Assist. Profs.   Full-time   4; Part–time   222
Res. Assocs.   32
Number of Students
Undergrad.   1, 676   Grad.   180
Library   366, 084 volumes

Outline and Characteristics of the University
Nara Women's University was originally established in 1908 as a girl's higher normal school, which aimed at training women instructors and teachers of women's normal schools and secondary schools. The present University was legally founded in 1949 during the post-war educational reforms. The University has cultivated many women students and sent them out into society since its establishment. It is located in Nara City, the former capital of Japan, surrounded by many cultural assets.

When the University was legally founded in 1949, it had two faculties, the Faculty of Letters and the Faculty of Science and Home Economics, along with attached primary and secondary schools, and a kindergarten. In 1953, the Faculty of Science and Home Economics was reformed and divided into two faculties, the Faculty of Science and the Faculty of Home Economics. The graduate school (master's course) was founded in the Faculty of Home Economics in 1964, in the Faculty of Science in 1965, and in the Faculty of Letters in 1968. The doctor's course was founded in the Faculty of Letters in 1980, but was reformed into the newly founded doctor's course, the Graduate Division of Human Culture, the following year.

At present, the University has three faculties, three graduate schools offering the master's course attached to each faculty, and one doctor's course. It enrolls about 1, 600 undergraduate students, and about 180 graduate students. The University also has a senior high school, a junior high school, a primary school, and a kindergarten, which are attached to the Faculty of Letters. About 340 faculty and staff members work at the University.

UNDERGRADUATE PROGRAMS

Faculty of Home Economics (Freshmen Enrollment: 145)
Department of Clothing Science
Clothing Care, Clothing Design, Clothing Life, Clothing Material, Clothing Physiology
Domestic Science Teacher's Training Course
Department of Dwelling Science
Dwelling Design, Dwelling Style and System, Living Environment, Supervision on Human Settlement
Department of Food Science and Nutrition
Cookery Science, Food Chemistry, Food Sanitation and Storage, Nutritional Chemistry, Nutritional Physiology
Department of Social Science of The Family
Ecological Studies and Welfare, Family Relations, Home Management, Household Economics
Faculty of Letters (Freshmen Enrollment: 165)
Department of Education
Education Method, Exercise Physiology and Biomechanics, Pedagogy, Physical Education, Physical Education Method, Psychology
Department of English Language and English and American Literature
American Literature, English Linguistics, English Literature, Linguistic Culture
Department of Geography
Human Geography, Physical Geography, Regional Geography
Department of History
Asian History, Japanese History, Western History
Department of Japanese and Japanese Literature
Ancient Japanese Literature, Chinese Language and Chinese Literature, Japanese Linguistics, Modern Japanese Literature
Department of Sociology
Empirical Sociology, Philosophy, Social Psychology, Theoretical Sociology
Faculty of Science (Freshmen Enrollment: 135)
Department of Biology
Animal Morphology, Animal Physiology and Ecology, Cytology and Genetics, Environmental Biology, Plant Morphology, Plant Physiology and Ecology
Department of Chemistry
Biochemistry, Inorganic and Analytical Chemistry,

Organic Chemistry, Physical Chemistry, Polymer Chemistry
Department of Mathematics
Algebra, Analysis, Functional Analysis, Geometry, Probability and Statistics
Department of Physics
Atomic Physics, Elementary Particle Physics, Experimental Solid State Physics, High Energy Physics, Radiation Physics, Theoretical Solid State Physics

Foreign Student Admission
Qualifications for Applicants
Standard Qualifications Requirement
All candidates for admission should know the University is not a coeducational institution. Applicants must be female. No male applicants are accepted.

Those who have an international baccalaureate and are at least 18 years of age are eligible to apply.
Examination at the University
In general, applicants are required to take Joint First-stage Achievement Test and the Entrance Examination given by the University. But foreign applicants can be exempted from "JFSAT, "taking instead the General Examination for Foreign Students, and the Japanese Language Proficiency Test.
Documents to be Submitted When Applying
Standard Documents Requirement
Brochures providing information concerning the entrance examinations given by the University are available at the Admissions Office in December. Application forms are included in the brochures.

Qualifications for Transfer Students
Applicants will be admitted only when there are vacancies and through screening by the Faculty Council.

GRADUATE PROGRAMS

Graduate Division of Home Economics (First Year Enrollment : Master's 34)
Courses
Clothing Science, Dwelling and Environmental Science, Food Science and Nutrition, Social Sciences of The Family
Graduate School of Human Culture (First Year Enrollment : Doctor's 13)
Courses
Comparative Culture, Human Life and Environmental Sciences
Graduate Division of Letters (First Year Enrollment : Master's 42)
Courses
English Literature, Geography, History, Japanese Literature, Pedagogy, Physical Education, Sociology
Graduate Division of Science (First Year Enrollment : Master's 44)
Courses
Biology, Chemistry, Mathematics, Physics

Foreign Student Admission

Qualifications for Applicants

Master's Program

Standard Qualifications Requirement

Doctor's Program

Standard Qualifications Requirement

Examination at the University

Master's Program

At the graduate level, there is no difference in the entrance examinations for both Japanese and overseas students.

Graduate Divisions of Home Economics, Letters, and Science: The entrance examinations are usually given twice a year in September or October, and January or February each year. An applicant is tested on her major subjects and one or two foreign languages selected from Chinese, English, French, German and Russian by means of a written examination. The transcript submitted will be checked carefully and an oral examination will be given before the final selection is made. For further information, applicants should consult with the department of the graduate school concerned.

Doctor's Program

Graduate School of Human Culture: The entrance examination is held in February each year. An applicant is tested on her major subjects and two foreign languages by means of a written examination. The thesis and transcript submitted will be checked carefully and an oral examination will be given before the final selection is made.

Documents to be Submitted When Applying

Standard Documents Requirement

Additional documents to be submitted.

Graduate Division of Home Economics, Letters, and Science:

1. If the applicant is employed, a certificate of permission from the office of her place of employment.

Graduate Division of Human Culture:

1. Master's thesis.
2. The subject the applicant plans to study.
3. If the applicant is employed, a certificate of permission from the office of her place of employment.

*

Research Institutes and Centers

Higashiyoshino Environment Study Institution

Facilities for Foreign Students

International house, Nara Women's University Shared Facilities (Lobby, Library/Conference Room, Japanese-style Room, Multiplepurpose Hall, Cooking Rooms, Laundry Rooms), Accommodation (44rooms-single40, couple2, family2)

For Further Information

Undergraduate and Graduate Admission

Student Welfare Division, Student Office, Nara Women's University, Kitauoyahigashi-machi, Nara 630 ☎ 0742–23–1131 ext. 234

Naruto University of Education
(Naruto Kyoiku Daigaku)

Takashima, Naruto-cho, Naruto-shi, Tokushima 772
☎ 0886–87–1311

Faculty
Profs. 73   Assoc. Profs. 40
Assist. Profs. Full–time 12; Part–time 43
Res. Assocs. 21
Number of Students
Undergrad. 555   Grad. 315
Library 79, 505 volumes

Outline and Characteristics of the University

Today, there is an urgent need for teachers to recognize the responsibilities and humanity required of the teaching profession. In response to this, the teacher should possess a good educational background, mastery of educational ideas and methods, and a deep understanding of the growth and development of human beings, as well as sound professional knowledge of the various teaching subjects.

In order to meet such social demands, Naruto University of Education (Naruto Kyoiku Daigaku) was founded on October 1, 1981. The University offers both graduate and undergraduate programs. It primarily serves to be an institution for practitioner-teachers in their post-experience programs in furthering both practical and theoretical research concerning school education. Its undergraduate program is designed to train students to become elementary or secondary school teachers.

The graduate school (Master of Education degree course), as its basic precept, provides specialized professional knowledge, possibilities for independent research, and at the same time opportunities to develop advanced skills necessary for an important profession with a wide perspective in mind. About two-thirds of the graduate students admitted each year are in-service teachers. They have experienced at least three years of teaching at the elementary or secondary school level.

The undergraduate program (Faculty of School Education) serves to train students to become familiar with and come to understand the growth and development of children in a broad perspective.

The History of Naruto University of Education:

October 1, 1981   Inauguration
April 1, 1984   Admission of Graduate Students (M. Ed. degree course in School Education
April 1, 1986   Admission of Undergraduate Students (Faculty of School Education)

UNDERGRADUATE PROGRAMS

Faculty of School Education (Freshmen Enrollment: 170)

Department of Early Childhood Education
Early Childhood Education

Department of Education of Subjects & Fields
Teaching of Fine Arts, Teaching of Japanese Language, Teaching of Music, Teaching of Natural Sciences, Teaching of Practical Life Sciences, Teaching of Social Sciences

Department of School Education
Educational Administration, Educational Method, Foundations of Human Development, Guidance & Counseling

Foreign Student Admission

Qualifications for Applicants
Standard Qualifications Requirement

Examination at the University
All applicants must take the Joint First–Stage Achievement Test and the Faculty's Special Entrance Examination consisting of (1) A Short Essay, (2) Aptitude tests or Skill Proficiency Examination (Fine Arts, Music and Physical Education only), (3) Written Examination (Specialized Subject).

Documents to be Submitted When Applying
Standard Documents Requirement

Qualifications for Transfer Students
The same as freshman applicants.
Examination for Transfer Students
The same as freshman applicants.
Documents to be Submitted When Applying
Standard Documents Requirement

GRADUATE PROGRAMS

Graduate School of School Education (First Year Enrollment : Master's 300)

Education for the Handicapped Course Education of Subjects & Fields Course *Divisions*
Teaching of Fine Arts, Teaching of Music, Teaching of Languages, Teaching of Natural Sciences, Teaching of Practical Life Sciences, Teaching of Social Sciences

School Education Course *Divisions*
Early Childhood Education, Educational Administration, Education Method, Foundations of Human Development, Guidance & Counseling

Foreign Student Admission

Qualifications for Applicants
Master's Program
Standard Qualifications Requirement

Examination at the University
Master's Program
1. Written Examination: (1) Teaching Fundamentals, (2) Foreign Language (English, German, or French), (3) Specialized Subject
2. Oral Examination

3. Skill Proficiency Examination (Fine Arts and Music only)
Documents to be Submitted When Applying
Standard Documents Requirement

*

Research Institutes and Centers
Center for Practical Skills Training Attached to Department of School Education, School Education Research Center

For Further Information
Undergraduate and Graduate Admission
Curriculum Division, Naruto University of Education, Takashima, Naruto-cho, Naruto-shi, Tokushima 772 ☎ 0886-87-1311 ext. 255.

National Institute of Fitness and Sports in Kanoya
(Kanoya Taiiku Daigaku)

1 Shiromizu-cho, Kanoya-shi, Kagoshima 891-23
☎ 0994-46-4111

Faculty
Profs. 19 Assoc. Profs. 13
Assist. Profs. Full–time 7; Part–time 19
Res. Assocs. 15
Number of Students
Undergrad. 651 Graduate 19
Library 37, 030 volumes

Outline and Characteristics of the University

Recent changes in lifestyle and living environment which have accompanied Japan's economic development have brought about a declining level of physical fitness and serious problems in the promotion and improvement of the nation's health. As a result, interest in health and fitness has grown considerably. Furthermore, additional leisure time and longer lifespans have significantly increased the need for sport, physical fitness, and recreation.

Therefore, it is now more important than ever to provide opportunities for fitness and sports for all people, ranging from children to the aged, as well as the handicapped. It has become a major task to train sports and physical recreation leaders and instructors for communities and industry. While educational programs for training physical educators for schools have already been established in Japan, little attention has been given to training programs for physical fitness and recreation instructors for communities and industry who are trained in scientific knowledge and health and physical fitness methods.

Budo, for example, which includes traditional martial arts such as Judo and Kendo, has contributed not only to the physical and mental development of children and adolescents but also to international understanding of the national heritage of Japan. Here there is a need for instructors of physical education in schools as well as in the community.

The establishment of the National Institute of Fitness and Sports in Kanoya is an ambitious answer to these needs.

The National Institute of Fitness and Sports in Kanoya is located in Kagoshima Prefecture in the southern part of Japan.

The city of Kanoya is the second largest city in Kagoshima with 75, 000 inhabitants and is situated in the central part of the Osumi Peninsula. Recently, Kanoya has been developing as the center of the eastern part of Kagoshima, in terms of politics, economy, culture, education, medical institutions and transportation

The National Institute of Fitness and Sports in Kanoya is located on a beautiful 370, 000 m² campus in the hilly district of the northwest section of the city of Kanoya.

The campus of the Institute provides high quality education and research facilities such as gymnasiums, an indoor swimming pool, a Budo-hall, athletic grounds, class room buildings, centers, a library, administration offices, and the Faculty of Physical Recreation.

The following is the Institute's Chronology: 1981, Establishement of the Institute; 1984, First school year, Physical Education and Sport, and Budo Courses, Faculty of Physical Recreation; 1985, Foreign Language Center; 1987, Marine Sport Center; 1988, Master's Program in Physical Recreation and Health Service Center.

UNDERGRADUATE PROGRAMS

Faculty of Physical Recreation (Freshmen Enrollment: 160)
Physical Education and Budo Course
Physical Education and Sports Course

Foreign Student Admission
Qualifications for Applicants
Standard Qualifications Requirement
Applicants must take the Japanese Language Proficiency Test and General Examination for Foreign Students. Examination at the University. Applicant must also take each faculty's special entrance examination consisting of a short essay, a practical test and an interview.
Documents to be Submitted When Applying
Standard Documents Requirement
Application forms are available at the Educational Affairs Division.

GRADUATE PROGRAMS

Graduate School of Physical Recreation (First Year Enrollment: Master's 18)
Divisions
Athletic Coaching, Fitness and Leisure Studies, Sports Science

Foreigh Student Admission
Qualifications for Applicants
Master's Program
Standard Qualifications Requirement
Examination at the University
Applicants must take the same entrance examination (consisting of written and oral test) that is given to Japanese applicants.
Documents to be Submitted When Applying
Standard Documents Requirement
Application forms are available at the Educational Affairs Division.
Foreign Language Center, Health Service Center, Marine Sport Center

*

For Further Information
Undergraduate and Graduate Admission
Educational Affairs Division, National Institute of Fitness and Sports in Kanoya, 1 Shiromizu-cho, Kanoya-shi, Kagoshima 891-23 ☎ 0994–46–4118 ext. 270

Niigata University
(Niigata Daigaku)

8050 Ikarashi 2–nocho, Niigata-shi, Niigata 950-21
☎ 025–262–6098

Faculty
Profs.   342   Assoc. Profs.   290
Assist. Profs.   Full–time   121; Part–time   444
Res. Assocs.   337
Number of Students
Undergrad.   9, 284   Grad.   619
Library   1, 029, 103 volumes

Outline and Characteristics of the University
It was under the National School Establishment Law that Niigata University was founded in 1949. Integration of Niigata Medical College with seven academic schools in the old system formed the original establishment of what is now known as Niigata University. At that time, it consisted of six faculties and some facilities. Ever since, Niigata University has steadily grown. At present, the University consists of nine faculties, nine graduate schools, two research institutes, two university hospitals, two junior colleges, and many other education and research facilities.

The University is situated in Niigata City. Niigata City, facing the Japan Sea, is the seat of Niigata Prefecture with a population of 472, 000, and can be reached in two hours by the super-express train from Tokyo. The City has an ideally quiet environment for study.

Ikarashi campus, one of two University campuses, is located in the western part of Niigata City and includes the Faculties of Humanities, Education,

Law, Economics, Science, Engineering, and Agriculture, as well as College of General Education, Graduate School of Science and Technology, Research Institute for Hazards in Snowy Areas and other facilities. Asahimachi campus, the other campus, is located in the central part of the City and includes the Schools of Medicine and Dentistry, University Hospitals (Medical and Dental), Brain Research Institute, the Junior College of Commerce, the College of Bio-Medical Technology and other facilities.

The University now enrolls approximately 11, 000 students and 2, 600 academic and administrative staff members. The majority of students are from Niigata Prefecture, but students come from many parts of Japan, and there are more than 60 foreign students from 17 countries.

The University aims to nurture capable persons of international sensibility. Thus, the University formed sister-university relationships with the University of Minnesota, U. S. A. in 1982, Heilongjiang University in the People's Republic of China in 1983 and the Agricultural University of Wageningen in the Netherlands in 1986 under an international faculty/student exchange program. The University intends to promote these close international relationships.

UNDERGRADUATE PROGRAMS

Faculty of Agriculture (Freshmen Enrollment: 166)
Department of Agricultural Chemistry
Agricultural Products Technology, Applied Microbiology, Biochemistry, Plant Nutrition and Fertilizer, Soil Science
Department of Agricultural Engineering
Agricultural Hydrotechnics, Agricultural Machinery, Agricultural Systems Engineering, Farm Land Engineering, Structural Engineering
Department of Agronomy
Crop Science, Farm Management, Horticultural Science, Plant Breeding, Plant Pathology
Department of Animal Husbandry
Animal Breeding and Reproduction, Animal Nutrition and Feeding, Biochemistry and Technology of Animal Products, Grassland Science, Livestock Management
Department of Forestry
Erosion Control Engineering and Logging Technology, Forest Management, Forest Mensuration, Silvics, Wood Technology
School of Dentistry (Freshmen Enrollment: 60)
Department of Dentistry
Dental Materials and Technology, Dental Pharmacology, Operative Dentistry and Endodontics, Oral Anatomy, Oral and Maxillofacial Surgery, Oral Biochemistry, Oral Microbiology, Oral Pathology, Oral Physiology, Oral Radiology, Orthodontics, Pedodontics, Periodontology, Preventive Dentistry, Prosthodontics
Faculty of Economics (Freshmen Enrollment: 230)

Department of Economics
Basic Theory and History, Economic Analysis, Economic Policy, Economic Systems, Management and Accounting
Faculty of Education (Freshmen Enrollment: 485)
Special Training Course for Calligraphy Teachers
Training Course for Elementary School Teachers
Training Course for Junior High School Teachers
Training Course for Kindergarten Teachers
Training Course for Teachers of Retarded Children
Art Education, Educational Psychology, Education of Domestic Science, Education of Handicapped Children, English Language Education, Health and Physical Education, Infant Education, Japanese Language Education, Mathematics Education, Music Education, School Education, Science Education, Social Studies Education
Special Training Course for Music Teachers
Faculty of Engineering (Freshmen Enrollment: 477)
Department of Applied Chemistry
Applied Analytical Chemistry, Applied Organic Chemistry, Applied Physical Chemistry, Industrial Inorganic Chemistry, Industrial Polymer Chemistry
Department of Architecture
Architectural Planning and Design, Building Materials and Structural Engineering, Disaster Protection Engineering and Urban Planning, Environmental and Sanitary Engineering
Department of Chemical Engineering
Diffusional Operations, Mechanical Operations, Process Control and Management, Reaction Engineering
Department of Civil Engineering
Concrete Engineering, Hydraulic Engineering, Soil Mechanics, Structural Mechanics
Department of Electrical Engineering
Applied Electrical Engineering, Electrical Communication, Electrical Measurements, Electric Power Engineering, Fundamental Electrical Engineering
Department of Electronic Engineering
Applied Electronics, Electronic Circuits, Electronic Materials, Fundamental Electronics
Department of Information Engineering
Biomedical Information, Information Processing, Information Processings Devices, Transmission of Information
Department of Mechanical Engineering
Fluid Engineering, Heat and Thermodynamics, Industrial Materials, Machine Element and Dynamics of Machinery, Production Engineering, Strength of Materials
Department of Precision Engineering
Control Engineering, Measurement Engineering, Precision Machining, Precision Mechanics
Faculty of Humanities (Freshmen Enrollment: 170)
Course of Culture and Civilization
English and American Culture and Civilization, European Culture and Civilization, Japanese Culture and Civilization, Oriental Culture and Civilization
Course of Science of Human Behavior

Behavioral Sciences, Philosophical Anthropology

Faculty of Law (Freshmen Enrollment: 250)

Department of Law

Criminal Law, Economic and Social Law, Political Science, Private Law, Public Law

School of Medicine (Freshmen Enrollment: 120)

Department of Medicine

Anatomy, Anesthesiology, Bacteriology, Biochemistry, Dermatology, Forensic Medicine, Hygiene, Internal Medicine, Laboratory Diagnosis, Medical Zoology and Immunology, Obstetrics and Gynecology, Ophthalmology, Orthopedic Surgery, Otorhinolaryngology, Pathology, Pediatrics, Pharmacology, Physiology, Psychiatry, Public Health, Radiology, Surgery, Urology, Virology

Faculty of Science (Freshmen Enrollment: 165)

Department of Biology

Animal Physiology and Biochemistry, Embryology and Genetics, Immunobiology, Plant Morphology and Cytology, Plant Physiology

Department of Chemistry

Analytical Chemistry, Biophysical Chemistry, Inorganic Chemistry, Organic Chemistry, Physical Chemistry

Department of Geology and Mineralogy

Applied Geology, Geology, Mineralogy, Mineralogy and Petrology

Department of Mathematics

Algebra, Functional Analysis, Geometry, Information Mathematics, Mathematical Analysis

Department of Physics

Crystal Physics, Molecular Physics, Nuclear Physics, Quantum Physics, Solid-State Physics, Statistical Physics

Foreign Student Admission

Qualifications for Applicants

Standard Qualifications Requirement

Foreign applicants for undergraduate programs must be of non-Japanese citizenship.

Those who have been granted an International Baccalaureate Diploma and are 18 years or older may also apply.

Examination at the University

Applicants to each faculty must take the Japanese Language Proficiency Test and General Examination for Foreign Students, and also must take each Faculty's special entrance examination. Applicants to the School of Medicine and the School of Dentistry must take the Joint First-Stage Achievement Test in addition to the above-mentioned examinations.

Documents to be Submitted When Applying

Standard Documents Requirement

A certificate of the Diploma is required if the applicant has been granted an International Baccalaureate Diploma.

Application forms are available at the Admission Office and each Faculty's Office from October.

All applicants are required to submit the specified application documents to each Faculty's Office by February 8. The deadline for receiving application is inflexible.

ONE-YEAR GRADUATE PROGRAMS

One-Year Advanced Course of Humanities (Enrollment: 10)

Economics

Foreign Student Admission

Qualifications for Applicants

Standard Qualifications Requirement

Foreign applicants must be of non-Japanese citizenship.

Examination at the University

Applicants will be selected based upon the evaluation of submitted documents and the score of the entrance examination consisting of written and/or oral examinations.

All applicants are required to submit the specified application documents within a fixed period. Applicants should inquire as to the period of submission for application to the Faculty of Economics.

GRADUATE PROGRAMS

Graduate School of Agriculture (First Year Enrollment : Master's 48)

Divisions

Agricultural Chemistry, Agricultural Engineering, Agronomy, Animal Husbandry, Forestry

Graduate School of Dentistry (First Year Enrollment : Doctor's 32)

Divisions

Basic Dental Science, Clinical Dental Science

Graduate School of Education (First Year Enrollment : Master's 34)

Divisions

School Education, School Subjects

Graduate School of Engineering (First Year Enrollment : Master's 80)

Divisions

Applied Chemistry, Architecture, Chemical Engineering, Civil Engineering, Electrical Engineering, Electronic Engineering, Information Engineering, Mechanical Engineering, Precision Engineering

Graduate School of Humanities (First Year Enrollment : Master's 10)

Divisions

Japanese and Oriental Culture and Civilization, Science of Human Behavior, Western Culture and Civilization

Graduate School of Law (First Year Enrollment : Master's 18)

Division

Law

Graduate School of Medicine (First Year Enrollment : Doctor's 70)

Divisions

Internal Medicine, Pathology, Physiology, Social

Medicine, Surgery
Graduate School of Science (First Year Enrollment :
Master's 50)
  Divisions
Biology, Chemistry, Geology and Mineralogy, Mathematics, Physics
Graduate School of Science and Technology (First
year Enrollment: Doctor's 36)
  Divisions
Biosystem Science, Environmental Science, Fundamental Science and Technology, Industrial Science

Foreign Student Admission
  Qualifications for Applicants
Master's Program
  Standard Qualifications Requirement
    Foreign applicants for graduate programs must
be of non-Japanese citizenship.
Doctor's Program
  Standard Qualifications Requirement
    Applicants for the Graduate Schools of Medicine and Dentistry must be graduates of a medical or
dental college.
  Examination at the University
Master's Program
    Applicants will be selected based upon the evaluation of submitted documents and the score of each
Graduate School's entrance examination consisting
of written and/or oral examinations.
Doctor's Program
    Same as Master's program.
  Documents to be Submitted When Applying
  Standard Documents Requirement
    Application forms are available at each Graduate School. Application procedures and requirements
may somewhat differ from school to school. All applicants are required to submit the specified application documents within a fixed period. Applicants
should inquire as to the application period, the deadline, the procedures and the requirements to each
Graduate School's Office.

*

Research Institutes and Centers
Analytical Instruments Laboratory, Attached
Schools and Kindergarten, Brain Research Institute,
Center for the Research and Instruction of Educational Practices, Data Processing Laboratory, Health
Administration Center, Institute for Laboratory Animals, Institute of Nephrology, Marine Biological
Station, Radioactive Isotope Laboratory, Research
Institute for Hazards in Snowy Areas, School for
Dental Technicians, Specimen Center for Nervous
Diseases, University Farm, University Forest, University Hospital (Dental), University Hospital (Medical), Waste Treatment Facilities
For Further Information
  Undergraduate and Graduate Admission
Head, Admissions Office, Niigata University,
8050 Ikarashi-2-nocho, Niigata-shi, Niigata 950-21
☎ 025-262-6079

Obihiro University of Agriculture and Veterinary Medicine
(Obihiro Chikusan Daigaku)

Nishi 2-11, Inada-cho, Obihiro-shi, Hokkaido 080
☎ 0155-48-5111

Faculty
  Profs. 46   Assoc. Profs. 45
  Assist. Profs. Full-time 10; Part-time 36
  Res. Assocs. 41
Number of Students
  Undergrad. 1, 127   Grad. 103
Library 125, 661 volumes

Outline and Characteristics of the University
  Obihiro University of Agriculture and Veterinary Medicine was founded in 1941 by the Government as the Obihiro Higher Technical School of Veterinary Medicine in response to a growing demand
for veterinary doctors at that time. Later the School
gradually expanded, adding related departments
such as Dairy Science and other departments in the
agricultural sciences. In 1949, the School became a
university level institution bearing the name Obihiro
Zootechnical University. Obihiro University of Agriculture and Veterinary Medicine became the new
English designation effective 1974.
  At present the University is composed of an undergraduate school and a graduate school for the
master's degree, each having seven departments with
necessary laboratories and one junior college level
course. The University has an enrollment of more
than 1, 200 students and a full time faculty of 140.
  Obihiro is located in central Hokkaido approximately 200 km east of Sapporo and about one and a
half hours by jet plane from Tokyo. With a population of about 160, 000, Obihiro is the center of the
rich Tokachi plain where diversified farming is the
main industry. The 200 ha. campus is located 7 km.
south of the center of the city with the beautiful Hidaka Mountain Range in the background.
  The University has many educational and research facilities within the campus including a large
university farm and veterinary hospital. The International House can accommodate 30 exchange professors and students from overseas. The University is
open to the international world and has student exchange programs with four sister universities in Asia
and one in Europe at present. The University also
participates in the international cooperation programs of the Japan International Cooperation Agency and renders services to the university in Latin
America.

UNDERGRADUATE PROGRAMS

Faculty of Agriculture and Veterinary Medicine (Freshmen Enrollment: 266)
Department of Agricultural Chemistry
Agricultural Processing Machinery, Applied Biochemistry, Food Chemistry, Forest Products Chemistry
Department of Agricultural Economics
Agricultural Economics and Marketing, Agricultural Policy and Development, Farm Accounting and Statistics, Farm Business Management
Department of Agricultural Engineering
Farm Power and Tractors, Field Machinery, Machinery for Animal Husbandry, Soil and Water Engineering
Department of Agro-Environmental Science
Environmental Botany, Environmental Chemistry, Environmental Entomology, Environmental Soil Science, Wildlife Management
Department of Animal Science
Animal Breeding, Animal Husbandry, Animal Nutrition, Dairy Chemistry, Meat Animal Production, Meat Animal Reproduction, Meat Preservation
Department of Grassland Science
Forage Crops, Grassland Ecology, Grassland Production, Grassland Utilization
Department of Veterinary Medicine
Veterinary Anatomy, Veterinary Internal Medicine, Veterinary Microbiology, Veterinary Obstetrics and Gynecology, Veterinary Pathology, Veterinary Pharmacology, Veterinary Physiology, Veterinary Public Health, Veterinary Radiology, Veterinary Surgery

Foreign Student Admission
Qualifications for Applicants
Standard Qualifications Requirement
Those who are qualified for the International Baccalaureat Diploma and are 18 years or older may also apply.
All applicants must take the General Examination for Foreign Students.
Examination at the University
Admission is based upon results of the General Examination for Foreign Students and the entrance examination held by the university, the health certificate and related documents.
The entrance examination is held on the date specified in the student recruitment publication.
Documents to be Submitted When Applying
Standard Documents Requirement
Necessary documents should be submitted by the February deadline prescribed in the student recruitment publication.

GRADUATE PROGRAMS

Graduate School of Agriculture and Veterinary

Medicine (First Year Enrollment : Master's 96)
Divisions
Agricultural Chemistry, Agricultural Economics, Agricultural Engineering, Agro-Environmental Science, Animal Science, Grassland Science, Veterinary Medicine

Foreign Student Admission
Qualifications for Applicants
Master's Program
Standard Qualifications Requirement
Examination at the University
Master's Program
Admission is based upon results of the entrance examination and an interview held by the university, health certificate, and related documents to be submitted. The entrance examination is held on the date specified in the student recruitment publication.
Documents to be Submitted When Applying
Standard Documents Requirement
All applicants are required to submit the necessary documents by the January deadline indicated in the student recruitment publication.

*

Research Institutes and Centers
Health Services, University Farm, Veterinary Hospital
Facilities/Services for Foreign Students
International House
Shared Facilities: Lobby, Conference Room, Library, Japanese-Style Room
Accommodation: 30 rooms (Single 12, Couple 12, Family 6)
Special Programs for Foreign Students
Japanese language supplementary classes are available at the International House.
For Further Information
Undergraduate and Graduate Admission
Dean of Students, Student Office, Obihiro University of Agriculture and Veterinary Medicine, Nishi 2-11, Inada-cho, Obihiro-shi, Hokkaido 080 ☎ 0155–48 –5111 ext. 445

Ochanomizu University
(Ochanomizu Joshi Daigaku)

2-1-1 Otsuka, Bunkyo-ku, Tokyo 112
☎ 03–943–3151

Faculty
Profs. 77   Assoc. Profs. 67
Assist. Profs. Full–time 14; Part–time 215
Res. Assocs. 36
Number of Students
Undergrad. 1, 941   Grad. 436
Library   452, 588 volumes

Outline and Characteristics of the University
Ochanomizu University is one of the two nation-

al universities for women in Japan. Its origin is traced to the Tokyo Women's Normal School which was founded in 1874 by the government for the purpose of training women teachers.

This was the first higher educational organization for women to be established in this country. In 1886, the School became the Department for Women of the Tokyo Higher Normal School, from which it separated itself in 1890 as the Tokyo Women's Higher Normal School. Since that time, the Attached Schools, the Special Courses and the Research Courses have been added to it.

Formerly, the School was located at Ochanomizu, after which the present University is named. But all the school buildings there were burnt down in the Great Earthquake of 1923. A new site was chosen at Otsuka and the reconstruction work was completed by 1930.

Soon after World War II, great changes were brought into the educational system of this country, and the School made its second start as Ochanomizu University.

Today the University proper is comprised of three faculties, three graduate courses, and a doctoral course. The three faculties are the Faculty of Letters and Education, the Faculty of Science, and the Faculty of Home Economics. The three graduate courses are the Research Course in the Humanities, in Science, and in Home Economics. The doctoral course is the Doctoral Research Course in Human Culture, which is characteristically interdisciplinary in character.

UNDERGRADUATE PROGRAMS

Faculty of Home Economics (Freshmen Enrollment: 157)

Department of Child Study
Department of Food and Nutrition
Department of Home Life Administration
Department of Textiles and Clothing

Faculty of Letters and Education (Freshmen Enrollment: 247)

Department of Dancing
Dancing, Music
Department of Education
Education, Psychology
Department of Foreign Literature
Chinese, English, French
Department of Geography
Department of History
Department of Japanese Literature
Department of Philosophy

Faculty of Science (Freshmen Enrollment: 114)

Department of Biology
Department of Chemistry
Department of Mathematics
Department of Physics

Foreign Student Admission

Qualifications for Applicants
Standard Qualifications Requirement

Each of the applicants is required to have taken the General Examination for Foreign Students, and the Japanese Language Proficiency Test.

Examination at the University

1. Applicants are required to take the subjects 'Japanese Language' and 'Foreign Languages' whether Japanese or alien; only, the questions in 'Foreign Languages' are different from those prepared for Japanese applicants.

2. As for the subjects, 'Japanese Language' 'Mathematics' and 'Sciences' the same questions as those for Japanese applicants are prepared; however, for Mathematics and Sciences, if necessary, explanations may be provided separately in written form, in order to enable foreign applicants to understand the questions more easily.

3. Practical exercises are examined using the same criteria as those for Japanese applicants.

4. After written tests have been completed, each of the applicants is interviewed by the department for which she is applying.

5. The Joint First-Stage Achievement Test is not required.

Documents to be Submitted When Applying
Standard Documents Requirement
Applicants are also required to submit:

1. A composition written in Japanese by the applicant herself; suggested themes including purpose of studying abroad, intended major, future plans for study, etc. The composition should be limited within 1, 000 words.

2. Testimonial of her capacity in Japanese

Application forms are accepted from the first of December.

GRADUATE PROGRAMS

Graduate School of Home Economics (First Year Enrollment : Master's 33)
Divisions
Child Study, Food and Nutrition, Home Life Administration, Textiles and Clothing

Graduate School of Human Culture (First Year Enrollment : Doctor's 35)
Divisions
Comparative Culture, Human Development, Human Environment

Graduate School of Humanities (First Year Enrollment : Master's 69)
Divisions
Chinese Literature, Dancing (including Music), Education, Geography, History, (including Psychology) English Literature, Japanese Literature, Philosophy

Graduate School of Science (First Year Enrollment : Master's 21)
Divisions

Biology, Chemistry, Mathematics, Physics

Foreign Student Admission

Qualifications for Applicants

Master's Program

Applicants are required to have completed 16 years of education or equivalent. They must have reached the age of 22, and have studied for more than 12 months in any Master's Program, or they need to be admitted by the standards of the Graduate School of our University.

Doctor's Program

Applicants must have studied for more than 12 months in any Doctor's Program, or they need to be admitted as equivalent by our Graduate School.

Examination at the University

Master's Program

In screening tests, applicants are required to take the same subjects and questions, whether Japanese or aliens. Foreign applicants, however, must also take the 'Japanese Language' test. Applicants for the Graduate School of Domestic Science are permitted to select one language under 'Foreign Languages'.

Doctor's Program

In screening tests, applicants are required to take the same subjects and questions, whether Japanese or aliens. Foreign applicants, however, must also take the 'Japanese Language' test.

Documents to be Submitted When Applying

Standard Documents Requirement

Application forms for the Graduate School of Humanities are accepted from the first of December, while the Graduate Schools of Science and Domestic Science will accept application forms from the tenth of July.

*

Research Institutes and Centers

Institute for Environmental Science for Human Life, Institute for Women's Studies, Tateyama Marine Laboratory

Special Programs for Foreign Students

Japanese Language supplementary classes are available at the University Language Center.

For Further Information

Undergraduate and Graduate Admission

Student Division, Ochanomizu University, 2-1-1 Otsuka, Bunkyo-ku, Tokyo 112 ☎ 03–943–3151 ext. 254

Oita Medical College
(Oita Ika Daigaku)

1-1506 Idaigaoka, Hazama-cho, Oita-gun, Oita 879-56 ☎ 0975-49-4411

Faculty
  Profs. 34   Assoc. Profs. 35
  Assist. Profs. Full-time 24; Part-time 9

Res. Assocs. 119
Number of Students
  Undergrad. 638   Grad. 97
Library 64, 343 volumes

Outline and Characteristics of the College

The Oita Medical College was founded on October 1, 1976. The first students were admitted on April 1, 1978. The Attached Hospital to the College was opened on April 1, 1981. The Graduate School of Medicine (the doctor's course) started on April 12, 1984.

In the decade since its foundation the college has undergone great expansion but it continues to be guided by its original precepts which are: (1) to present the most up-to-date medical technology; (2) to impart advanced technical knowledge to clinicians and researchers, and to inculcate in them a sense of morality based on the underlying principles of medicine, as consistent with the general culture; (3) to contribute effectively toward the progress of medicine, the maintenance and improvement of national health, and the welfare of the community through medical treatment and the preservation of public health.

The Undergraduate Program is a coherent six-year curriculum, during which students complete the first two-year course—consisting of general subjects, English, German, and physical education, together with some of the basic and specialized subjects in medicine—in order to work successfully in the specialized courses in the second four-year course.

The first Department of Clinical Pharmacology was established in Japan at this college. The Center for Clinical Pharmacology opened in April, 1983.

UNDERGRADUATE PROGRAMS

School of Medicine (Freshmen Enrollment: 100)

Department of Medicine

Anatomy, Anesthesiology, Biochemistry, Clinical Pharmacology, Dermatology, Internal Medicine, Legal Medicine, Microbiology, Neuropsychiatry, Neurosurgery, Obstetrics and Gynecology, Ophthalmology, Oral and Maxillo-Facial Surgery, Orthopaedics, Otorhinolaryngology, Pathology, Pediatrics, Pharmacology, Physiology, Public Health, Radiology, Surgery, Urology

Foreign Student Admission

Qualifications for Applicants

Standard Qualifications Requirement

Examination at the College

Applicants must take both the Joint First-Stage Achievement Test and this College's entrance examination, consisting of a written exam and an interview.

Documents to be Submitted When Applying

Standard Documents Requirement

Application forms are available at the Admissions Office from late November. All applicants are required to submit the specified application documents to the Admissions Office by the appointed date.

GRADUATE PROGRAMS

Graduate School of Medicine (First Year Enrollment : Doctor's 30)
Divisions
Biochemistry, Ecology, Morphology, Physiology

Foreign Student Admission
Qualifications for Applicants
Doctor's Program
    Standard Qualifications Requirement
Examination at the College
Doctor's Program
    Applicants must take the College's entrance examination, consisting of a written exam and an interview.
Documents to be Submitted When Applying
    Standard Documents Requirement
    Application forms are available at the Admissions Office from late November. All applicants are required to submit the specified application documents to the Admissions Office by the appointed date.

*

For Further Information
Undergraduate Admission
Admissions Office, Oita Medical College, 1-1506 Idaigaoka, Hazama-cho, Oita-gun, Oita 879-56 ☎ 0975-49-4411 ext. 2530
Graduate Admission
Entrance Examination Section, Admissions Office, Oita Medical College, 1-1506 Idaigaoka, Hazama-cho, Oita-gun, Oita 879-56 ☎ 0975-49-4411 ext. 2540

Oita University
(Oita Daigaku)

700 Dannoharu, Oita-shi, Oita 870-11
☎ 0975-69-3311

Faculty
    Profs. 100   Assoc. Profs. 106
    Assist. Profs. Full-time 30; Part-time 130
    Res. Assocs. 28
Number of Students
    Undergrad. 4, 184   Grad. 154
Library 404, 534 volumes

Outline and Characteristics of the University
    Oita University was established in May, 1949, as part of a new system for national universities in Japan under the National School Establishment Law, by joining together Oita Normal School, Oita Youth Normal School and Oita College of Economics of the old system.

The new Oita University was composed of the Faculty of Liberal Arts (renamed Faculty of Education in April, 1966) and the Faculty of Economics.

In May, 1972, the Faculty of Engineering was inaugurated.

In May, 1977, and in April, 1979, the Graduate Schools of Economics and Engineering respectively were opened and began to offer Master's Degrees.

Today, the university enrolls more than 4, 400 students and is comprised of three faculties, two graduate schools, one advanced course and other affiliated establishments.

The campus is located on a quiet mountain side on the outskirts of Oita City, about a 20-minute drive from downtown. Oita City, the prefectural capital, has a population of about 390, 000.

The area is characterized by a temperate climate with distinct seasons and provides an ideal environment for both study and recreation.

The period of undergraduate study is four years. The first two years are devoted to general education (economics, humanities, natural sciences, and physical sciences), foreign languages and physical education. In the second two years, students concentrate on their majors.

A student exchange program was established in 1972 with San Francisco State University, California, U.S.A.

Foreign students are welcome to study as regular students at Oita University. In addition, foreign students (either privately financed or on Japanese Government Scholarships) come from, India, Indonesia, Mexico, the Republic of Koreo, Zaire, Brazil, China, Malaysia, Papua New Guinea, Taiwan, the Philippines and the U.S.A.

As of May, 1988, the number of foreign students was 33. This number is expected to increase greatly in the years ahead.

UNDERGRADUATE PROGRAMS

Faculty of Economics (Freshmen Enrollment: 330)
Department of Business Management
Business Administration, Business Enterprises, Commerce, Computer Programming, Financial Accounting, Management, Management Science, Office Management, Principles of Transportation and Insurance
Department of Economics
Economic Engineering, Economic Geography, Economic History, Economic Policy, Economics, History of Economics, International Economics, Money and Banking, Public Finance, Social Policy, Statistics
Faculty of Education (Freshmen Enrollment: 290)
Training Course for Teachers of School for Handicapped Children
    Kindergarten Teachers Training Course
    Lower Secondary School Teachers Training Course

Primary School Teachers Training Course
Abnormal Psychology, Agriculture, Algebra and Geometry, Analytical and Applied Mathematics, Art Education, Biology, Chemistry, Child Rearing, Classic Chinese Literature, Clothing, Composition, Design and Construction, Developmental Psychology, Early Childhood Education, Early Childhood Psychology, Earth Sciences, Economics, Educational Psychology, Educational Sociology, Educational System, Electricity, English and American Literature, English Language Education, English Linguistics, Ethics, Food, Geography, Health and Physical Education, History, History of Education, History of Physical Education, Homemaking Education, Home Management, Industrial Arts Education, Instrumental Music, Japanese Calligraphy, Japanese Language Education, Japanese Linguistics, Japanese Literature, Law, Machines, Mathematics Education, Metalworking, Music Education, Nursery Education, Paintings, Pedagogy, Philosophy, Physical Training, Physics, Physiology and Hygienics, Science Education, Sculpture, Social Studies Education, Sociology, Special Education, Theory and History of Arts, Theory and History of Music, Theory of Physical Education, Vocal Music, Woodworking

Faculty of Engineering (Freshmen Enrollment: 350)
Department of Architectural Engineering
Architectural and Urban Planning, Disaster Prevention Engineering, Environmental Engineering, Structural Engineering
Department of Electrical Engineering
Communication Engineering, Electric Machine Engineering, Electric Power Engineering, Electromagnetic Fundamentals
Department of Electronic Engineering
Applied Electronics, Electronic Circuit, Electronic Control System, Physical Electronics
Department of Energy Engineering
Energy Conversion, Energy Resources, Energy Transfer, Fundamentals of Energy Engineering
Department of Environmental Chemistry and Engineering
Chemical Reaction Engineering and Biological Wastewater Treatment, Electrochemistry and Catalysis, Macromolecular Chemistry and Microbial Biochemistry, Physical Organic Chemistry and Chemistry of Wastewater Treatment
Department of Information Science and Systems Engineering
Computer Engineering, Computer Science Implementation, Control and Systems Engineering, Fundamentals of Information Science
Department of Mechanical Engineering
Fluid Mechanics, Mechanical Technology and Dynamics, Strength of Materials, Thermal Engineering

Foreign Student Admission
Qualifications for Applicants
Standard Qualifications Requirement
Examination at the University

For most Faculties, applicants must take the Japanese Language Proficiency Test and General Examination for Foreign Students. Applicants must also take each Faculty's specific entrance examination.
Documents to be Submitted When Applying
Standard Documents Requirement
Application forms are available at the Student Office in October. All applicants are required to submit the specified application documents to the Student Office by January 31. This deadline is strictly adhered to.

ONE-YEAR GRADUATE PROGRAMS

One-Year Graduate Course of Education (Enrollment: 5)
Education

GRADUATE PROGRAMS

Graduate School of Economics (First Year Enrollment : Master's 18)
Division
Economics
Graduate School of Engineering (First Year Enrollment : Master's 48)
Divisions
Architectural Engineering, Electrical Engineering, Electronic Engineering, Energy Engineering, Environmental Chemistry and Engineering, Information Science and System Engineering, Mechanical Engineering

Foreign Student Admission
Qualifications for Applicants
Master's Program
Standard Qualifications Requirement
Examination at the University
Master's Program
Applicants must take each Graduate School's specific entrance examination consisting of written and physical examinations and an interview.
Documents to be Submitted When Applying
Standard Documents Requirement
A letter of introduction or letter of recommendation by the embassy or consulate in Japan of the country concerned, or by the Japanese embassy or Japanese Consulate, in the student's home country, or by an organization deemed proper by the university authorities is also required.
Application forms are available at the Student Office from October. All applicants are required to submit the specified application documents to the Student Office by January 31. The deadline is strictly adhered to.

*

Research Institutes and Centers
Computer Center, Marine Science Laboratory, Research Institute of Economics, Solar Energy Thermal

Applications Laboratory, The Center for Industrial and Economic Research of the Seto Inland Sea Region, The Research and Guidance Center for Teaching Practice

Special Programs for Foreign Students

Japanese language classes and classes relating to life and culture in Japan are offered.

For Further Information

Undergraduate and Graduate Admission

Entrance Examination Section, Student Office, Oita University, 700 Dannoharu, Oita-shi, Oita 870-11 ☎ 0975–69–3311 ext. 259

Okayama University
(Okayama Daigaku)

1-1-1 Tsushimanaka, Okayama-shi, Okayama 700
☎ 0862–52–1111

Faculty
Profs. 359   Assoc. Profs. 297
Assist. Profs. Full–time 133; Part–time 750
Res. Assocs. 393
Number of Students
Undergrad. 9, 538   Grad. 1, 151
Library 1, 396, 863 volumes

Outline and Characteristics of the University

Okayama University was founded in 1949 as a national institute under the National School Establishment Law by incorporating five national schools and colleges which then existed in Okayama prefecture.

Ever since, the University has grown with the times, and now it is a national university composed of the college of general education and ten faculties (Agriculture, Dentistry, Economics, Engineering, Law, Letters, Medicine, Pharmaceutical Sciences, Science, Teacher Education) with two attached research institutes, two university hospitals and other affiliated establishments. The graduate schools offer eight master's programs (Agriculture, Economics, Engineering, Law, Letters, Pharmaceutical Sciences, Science, Teacher Education) and three doctor's programs (Dentistry, Medicine, Natural Science and Technology).

Today, the University has more than 10, 000 students and a teaching and administrative staff of about 2, 656.

The University lays much stress on international exchange, and many overseas students from more than 25 countries are enrolled presently. Foreign students are attracted to the University not only by its high academic reputation, but also because of its sympathetic and positive approach to the needs and problems of overseas students. The number of students from abroad is on the increase year by year.

The University is situated in Okayama city. The city is located 733 km west of Tokyo. It takes about four hours to Tokyo by "Shinkansen" (the bullet train). The climate of Okayama is comfortably mild, with an annual average temperature of 15°C. Okayama city boasts of having nine universities and colleges. Okayama is well-known for its people's enthusiasm and zeal for culture and education. Okayama University is the largest one among them.

The University, with its large and beautiful campus, is noted for its academic excellence, and can be called one of the leading universities in Japan.

UNDERGRADUATE PROGRAMS

Faculty of Agriculture (Freshmen Enrollment: 180)
   Geheral Agriculture Science
Agricultural Infrastructure Development and Conservation, Agricultural Products Technology, Agricultural Technology of Integrated Land Use, Animal Science, Biological Function and Genetic Resources Science, Bio-Resources Chemistry, Eco-Physiology of Crop Production, Environment and Resource Management

Dental School (Freshmen Enrollment: 60)
   Department of Dentistry
Dental Materials, Dental Pharmacology, Operative Dentistry, Oral Anatomy, Oral and Maxillo Facial Surgery, Oral Biochemistry, Oral Microbiology, Oral Pathology, Oral Physiology, Oral Radiology, Orthodontics, Pedodontics, Preventive Dentistry, Prosthodontics

Faculty of Economics (Freshmen Enrollment: 210)
   Department of Economics
Accounting, Applied Economics, Economic History, Economic Measurement, Economic Policy, Economic Theory, Industrial Administration

Faculty of Engineering (Freshmen Enrollment 520)
   Department of Applied Chemistry
Applied Organic Chemistry, Chemical Engineering, Electro-Reaction Chemistry, Materials Science
   Department of Biotechnology
Biochemical Regulation, Biofunctional Chemistry
   Department of Civil Engineering
Environmental Survey and Engineering, Mechanical Analysis and Construction
   Department of Electrical and Electronic Engineering
Applied Electronics, Electrical Engineering, Electronics
   Department of Engineering Sciences
Engineering Sciences
   Department of Information Technology
Artificial Intelligences, Computer Science, Foundations of Information Science, Information-Based Engineering Systems
   Department of Mechnical Engineering
Date Intenive Engineering, Design and Maunfacturing Technology, Energy Engineering, Material Engineering, Mechanical Systems Engineering

Faculty of Law (Freshmen Enrollment: 210)
   Department of Law

Civil Law, Criminal Law, Fundamental Sciences of Law, International Law, Politics, Public Law, Social Law

Faculty of Letters (Freshmen Enrollment: 175)

Department of History

Archaeology, Geography, History of Japanese Culture, Japanese History, Modern History, Occidental History, Oriental History

Department of Literature

American Literature, Chinese Language and Chinese Literature, English Language, English Literature, French Language, French Literature, German Language, German Literature, Japanese Classical Language, Japanese Language, Japanese Literature, Linguistics

Department of Philosophy

Aesthetics and Art History, Ethics, History of Philosophy, Philosophy, Psychology, Social Psychology

Faculty of Medicine (Freshmen Enrollment: 120)

Department of Medicine

Anatomy, Anesthesiology and Resuscitology, Biochemistry, Clinical Inspection Medicine Dermatology, Hygiene, Internal Medicine, Legal Medicine, Microbiology, Neurological Surgery, Neuropsychiatry, Obstetrics and Gynecology, Ophthalmology, Orthopedic Surgery, Otorhinolaryngology, Parasitology, Pathology, Pediatrics, Pharmacology, Physiology, Public Health, Radiation Medicine, Surgery, Urology, Virology

Faculty of Pharmaceutical Sciences (Freshmen Enrollment: 80)

Department of Pharmaceutical Science

Bioorganic Chemistry, Hygienic Chemistry, Pharmaceutical Chemistry, Pharmaceutics, Pharmacognosy, Pharmacology, Physiological Chemistry

Department of Pharmaceutical Technology

Environmental Hygiene, Immunochemistry, Medicinal Chemistry, Microbiology, Pharmaceutical Analytical Chemistry, Pharmaceutical Physical Chemistry

Faculty of Science (Freshmen Enrollment: 150)

Department of Biology

Animal Morphology, Animal Physiology, Genetics and Cytology, Plant Morphology, Plant Physiology

Department of Chemistry

Analytical Chemistry, High Polymer Chemistry, Inorganic Chemistry, Organic Chemistry, Physical Chemistry, Synthetic and Physical-Organic Chemistry

Department of Earth Sciences

Geochemistry, Geology, Geophysics, Mineralogy

Department of Mathematics

Algebra, Analysis, Applicable Mathematics, Geometry, Topology

Department of Physics

Magnetism, Mathematical Physics, Nuclear Physics, Plasma Physics, Solid State Physics, Theoretical Physics

Faculty of Teacher Education (Freshmen Enrollment: 420)

Special Training Course for Art and Craft Teachers

Training Course for Teachers of Handicapped Children

Training Course for Junior High School Teachers

Training Course for Kindergarten Teachers

Training Course for Nurse-Teachers

Training Course for Primary School Teachers

Algebra and Geometry, Analytical Mathematics and Applied Mathematics, Art and Craft, Art and Craft Education, Biology, Calligraphy, Chemistry, Chinese classical Literature, Clinical Medicine and Science of Nursing, Clothing, Composition and Conducting, Cubic Structure, Development Psychology, Domestic Science Education, Earth Science, Economics, Educational Psychology, Educational Sociology, Education of Handicapped Children, English and American Literature, English Language Education, English Linguistics, Ethics, Foods, Fundamental Medicine, Geography, Health and Physical Education, History, Home Management, Infant Psycology, Instrumental Music, Japanese Language Education, Japanese Linguistics, Japanese Literature, Kinematics, Law, Life Technology, Mathematics Education, Music Education, Natural Science Education, Painting, Pathology of Handicapped Children, Pedagogics Physical Education, Physics, Pre-school Education, Psychology of Handicapped Children, School and Public Hygiene, School Health, School Health Nurse, School Management, Sculpture, Social Education, Social Studies Education, Sociology, Study of Material for Pre-school Children Education, Vocal Music

Foreign Student Admission

Qualifications for Applicants

Standard Qualifications Requirement

Examination at the University

For each Faculty, except Faculties of Letters, Law, Economics, and Agriculture, applicants are required to take the Joint First-Stage Achievement Test.

Applicants for Faculties of Letters, Law, Economics and Agriculture are required to take the Japanese Language Proficiency Test.

Preliminary selection will be made on the basis of the documents submitted. Applicants who have successfully passed this initial screening will be notified to take the second stage test (oral or written examination) given by each faculty.

Documents to be Submitted When Applying

Standard Documents Requirement

Application forms are available at the Admission Office, Student Bureau.

GRADUATE PROGRAMS

Graduate School of Agriculture (First Year Enrollment : Master's 54)

Divisions

Agricultural Chemistry, Agricultural Engineering, Agronomy, Animal Science, Horticulture

Graduate School of Dental Sciences (First Year Enrollment : Doctor's 18)

Divisions

Dental Sciences

Graduate School of Economics (First Year Enrollment : Master's 18)

Divisions

Economics

Graduate School of Engineering (First Year Enrollment : Master's 66)

Divisions

Applied Mechanics, Civil Engineering, Electrical Engineering, Electronics, Industrial Chemistry, Industrial Science, Mechanical Engineering, Synthetic Chemistry

Graduate School of Law (First Year Enrollment : Master's 22)

Divisions

Civil and Criminal Laws, Public Law and Political Science

Graduate School of Letters (First Year Enrollment : Master's 42)

Divisions

English and American Literature, French Literature, German Literature, History, Japanese Literature, Philosophy, Psychology

Graduate School of Medicine (First Year Enrollment: Doctor's 76)

Divisions

Internal Medicine, Pathology, Physiology, Social Medicine, Surgery

Graduate School of Natural Science and Technology (First Year Enrollment: Doctor's 40)

Divisions

Science and Technology for Materials, Science for Engineering and Agricultural technology, Bioresources Science, Biopharmaceutical Science, System Science

Graduate School of Pharmaceutical Sciences (First Year Enrollment : Master's 26)

Divisions

Pharmaceutical Science, Pharmaceutical Technology

Graduate School of Science (First Year Enrollment : Master's 60)

Divisions

Biology, Chemistry, Earth Sciences, Mathematics, Physics

Graduate School of Teacher Education (First Year Enrollment : Master's 60)

Divisions

Domestic Science Education, English Language Education, Fine Arts Education, Japanese Language Education, Mathematics Education, Music Education, Physical Education, School Education, Science Education, Social Studies Education

School of Health Sciences (Freshmen Enrollment 160)

Department of Laboratory Technology

Department of Nursing

Department of Radiological Technology

Foreign Student Admission

Qualifications for Applicants

Master's Program

Standard Qualifications Requirement

Doctor's Program

Standard Qualifications Requirement

Examination at the University

Master's Program

The selective examination for graduate courses is carried out at each graduate school. The method of selection is different for each graduate course. Applicants are advised to refer to the student section of each graduate school.

Doctor's Program

Same as Master's program.

Documents to be Submitted When Applying

Standard Documents Requirement

*

Research Institutes and Centers

Cancer Institute Attached to Medical School, Center for Environmental Conservation Technology, Computer Center, Educational Technological Center Attached to Faculty of Teacher Education, Health and Medical Center, Herbal Garden Attached to Faculty of Pharmaceutical Sciences, Institute for Environment and Disease Attachend to Medical Institute for Neurobiology Attached to Medical School, Institute for Study of Kibi Culture, Institute for Study of the Earths Interior, Laboratory for Genetic Engineering, Observatory for Environmental Research, Radio-Isotope Laboratory, Research Farm Attached to Faculty of Agriculture, Research Forest Attached to Faculty of Agriculture, Research Institute for Bioresources Institute for Animal Experiment Attached to Medical School, Research Institute for Non-Crystalline Material Attached to Faculty of Engineering, Research Laboratory for Surface Science Attached to Faculty of Science, Teaching Practice Study Guidance Center Attached to Faculty of Teacher Education, University Hospital and Branch Hospitals Attached to Medical School, University Hospital Attached to Dental School, Ushimado Marine Laboratory Attached to Faculty of Science

Facilities/Services for Foreign Students

International House: Total Floor Area 1454 m^2; Number of rooms–28 rooms for male students, 16 rooms for Female students; room 14. 4 m^2 for single person. Each room is furnished with a bed, a desk, a shower and an air-conditioner.

Special Programs for Foreign Students

Japanese language supplementary classes are available at the College of General Education and the Faculty of Teacher Education for the Teacher Training Students.

For Further Information

Undergraduate and Graduate Admission

International Affairs Section, General Affairs Division, Administration Bureau, Okayama University, 1-1-1 Tsushimanaka, Okayama-shi, Okayama 700 ☎ 0862-52-1111 ext. 229, 278

Osaka Kyoiku University
(Osaka Kyoiku Daigaku)

4-88 Minami-Kawahori-cho, Tennoji-ku, Osaka-shi, Osaka 543   ☎ 06-771-8131

Faculty
    Profs.   137   Assoc. Profs.   113
    Assist. Profs.   Full–time   36; Part–time   242
    Res. Assocs.   32
Number of Students
    Undergrad.   4, 609   Grad.   187
Library   527, 995 volumes

Outline and Characteristics of the University

The history of the University dates back to 1875, when the Government established a school for training teachers in Osaka, one of the nation's commercial and industrial centers. The school developed in the course of time, undergoing a few changes in its name. Then, in 1949, a few years after the termination of World War II, Osaka Liberal Arts College was founded, incorporating Osaka First and Second Normal Schools, in line with the postwar educational reforms in this country.

The revision of the National School Law in 1966 led the University to change its name to Osaka Kyoiku University as it is called today.

At the time of its founding in 1949, the University offered only two courses, one for training elementary school teachers and one for training junior high school teachers, but it has grown with the times and now offers 11 courses as of 1985. In 1968, the Graduate School was opened and began to offer Master's programs.

The University is composed of three campuses with their respective functions and facilities for educational research and training: Tennoji Campus, Ikeda Campus and Hirano Campus, each conveniently located with an atmosphere suitable for study and research. The Main Administration Office is at Tennoji Campus.

The University's primary goal is to conduct research in various fields of education and train students in the theories and practices of teaching, preparing them to be good educators. This objective has been largely satisfied, and through its academic excellence, the University has made great contributions to the world of education in Japan, enjoying a high reputation.

UNDERGRADUATE PROGRAMS

Faculty of Education (Freshmen Enrollment: 980)

Department of Arts and Sciences
Teacher Training Course for The Handicapped
  Elementary School Teacher Training Course
  Kindergarten Teacher Training Course
  Lower Secondary School Teacher Training Course
  Nurse-Teacher Training Course
Faculty of Education (**Evening Course**) (Freshmen Enrollment: 50)
  Elementary School Teacher Training Course

Foreign Student Admission
  Qualifications for Applicants
    Standard Qualifications Requirement
Applicants are required to take both the Japanese Language Proficiency Test and the General Examination for Foreign Students.
  Examination at the University
    Permission to register as a student of the Faculty of Education is given depending upon the results of the Japanese Language Proficiency Test, the General Examination for Foreign Students, and the entrance examination given by the University, together with the contents of the documents submitted by the last school attended and a health certificate.
  Documents to be Submitted When Applying
    Standard Documents Requirement

ONE-YEAR GRADUATE PROGRAMS

One-Year Postgraduate Course in Education (Enrollment: 20)
Art and Craft Education, Mathematics Education, Music Education, Physical Education
One-Year Postgraduate Course in Education for the Handicapped (Enrollment: 30)
Education for the Speech Handicapped

Foreign Student Admission
  Qualifications for Applicants
    Standard Qualifications Requirement
One-Year Postgraduate Course in Education:
    Applicants for this course have any of the following first class licences for teachers of elementary school, junior high school or kindergarten; or the general licence for teachers of senior high school.
One-Year Postgraduate Course in Education for the Handicapped:
    Applicants must have the general licence for teachers of elementary school, junior high school, senior high school or kindergarten.
  Examination at the University
    Permission to register as a student of the Postgraduate Courses is given depending upon the results of the examination, the school record issued by the last school attended, and a satisfactory health certificate.

GRADUATE PROGRAMS

Graduate School of Education (First Year Enroll-

ment : Master's 124)
Divisions
Art Education, English Language Education, Health and Physical Education, Home Economics, Japanese Language Education, Mathematics Education, Music Education, School Education, Science Education, Social Studies, Special Education

Foreign Student Admission
Qualifications for Applicants
Master's Program
   Standard Qualifications Requirement
   Applicants from countries where 16 years' education is not necessary for graduation of a university must fill the following two requirements.
   1. Those who, after university education, have done more than one year's research as a researcher or a research student at a university.
   2. Those who will be 22 years of age before the 31st of March of the year of application.
Examination at the University
Master's Program
   Permission to register as a student of the Graduate School is given depending upon the results of the examination, a health certificate and the documents issued by the president (or the director) of the university attended. Those who have any research works (except a graduation thesis) can substitute the "research thesis" for the examination of their major subject among all other subjects. A foreign language test is given additionally.
   Documents to be Submitted When Applying
   Standard Documents Requirement
*

For Further Information
Undergraduate and Graduate Admission
Instructions Division, Entrance Examination Section, Osaka Kyoiku University, 4-88 Minami-Kawahori-cho, Tennoji-ku, Osaka-shi, Osaka 543
☎ 06–771–8131 ext. 326

Osaka University
(Osaka Daigaku)

1-1 Yamadaoka, Suita-shi, Osaka 565
☎ 06–877–5111

Faculty
   Profs. 514   Assoc. Profs. 458
   Assist. Profs. Full–time 212; Part–time 1, 172
   Res. Assocs. 995
Number of Students
   Undergrad. 10, 736   Grad. 2, 990
Library   2, 199, 336 volumes

Outline and Characteristics of the University
   Osaka University was established in 1931 as a national university with two faculties, Medicine and

Science. The Faculty of Engineering was added in 1933 and the Faculty of Law and Letters in 1948. In accordance with the National School Establishment Law of 1949, the four faculties were reorganized into ten independent faculties: Letters, Law (1953), Economics (1953), Science, Medicine, Engineering, Dentistry (1951), Pharmaceutical Sciences (1955), Engineering Science (1961), and Human Sciences (1972). The University has continued to keep pace voith the times. In 1953, Graduate Schools were opened in each faculty and both Master's and Doctor's programs were established. Today, the University enrolls more than 12, 500 students and has a full-time faculty of 2, 159. It is composed of 12 Faculties (those listed above plus Faculties of Language and Culture and Health and Sport Sciences), two Colleges, General Education and Bio-Medical Technology, ten Graduate Schools, five research institutes, ten Joint-use facilities and various other facilities.
   The University has three campuses in Osaka. Suita campus (992, 792m^2) is located in Suita City (population 347, 491), in the northeastern part of Osaka; Toyonaka campus (421, 434m^2) is in Toyonaka City (population 415, 831), in the northwestern part of Osaka; Nakanoshima campus (50, 243m^2) is in the central part of Osaka City (population 2, 647, 184).
   The University is internationally renowned for its academic excellence. Its faculty includes a Nobel prize recipient in physics and most departments are ranked number one in Japan.
   The quality of Osaka's student body complements the stature of its faculty. The majority of students are from the Kinki area, but others come from every part of Japan and about 50 foreign countries in order to study at Osaka.

UNDERGRADUATE PROGRAMS

Faculty of Dentistry (Freshmen Enrollment: 60)
   Department of Dentistry
Biochemistry and Calcified-Tissue Metabolism, Dental Anesthesiology, Dental Pharmacology, Dental Technology, Microbiology and Oral Microbiology, Operative Dentistry, Oral Anatomy, Oral and Maxillofacial Radiology, Oral and Maxillofacial Surgery, Oral Pathology, Oral Physiology, Orthodontics, Pedodontics, Periodontology and Endodontology, Preventive Dentistry, Prosthetic Dentistry
Faculty of Economics (Freshmen Enrollment: 225)
   Department of Business Administration
Management Science, Management Theory
   Department of Economics
Applied Economics, Economic History, Economic Policy, Economic Theory
Faculty of Engineering (Freshmen Enrollment: 860)
   Department of Applied Chemistry
Applied Physical Chemistry, Electrochemistry, Industrial Inorganic Chemistry and Rare Elements Chemistry, Industrial Organic Chemistry (Fatty

Oils - Surface Active Agents and Surface Coating Materials), Industrial Organic Chemistry (Fuel Chemistry and Coal Chemicals Industry), Natural and Synthetic Polymers - Organic Semiconductors

Department of Applied Fine Chemistry

Carbon Chemistry and Technology, Catalytic Organic Syntheses, Functional Polymer Chemistry, Inorganic Fine Chemistry, Methodological Chemistry, Molecular Design and Syntheses

Department of Applied Physics

Applied Mathematics - Computer and Computational Mathematics, Optical Instruments - Image Processing and Optical Measurement, Physical Optics and Spectroscopy, Scientific Measurement and Instrumentation, Solid State Physcis and Optical Properties of Solids, Solid State Physics of Metals-X-ray Crystallography and Electron Physics

Department of Architectural Engineering

Architectural Planning-Philosophy of Architecture-Town Planning and Exercise of Architectural Design, Human Engineering-Design Method of Architecture and Exercise on Architectural Design, Interior Environmental Control Engineering-Building Equipment-Finishing Materials and Insulation Materials, Steel Structure and Building Construction, Structural Mechanics-Soil Mechanics and Theory of Earthquake Resistant Structure, Theory of Building Structure and Structural Materials

Department of Civil Engineering

Applied Structural Engineering, Coastal and Harbor Engineering, Fundamental Structural Engineering, Hydraulics and River Engineering, Soil Mechanics and Foundation Engineering, Urban Transport Engineering

Department of Communication Engineering

Communication Technology-Information Theory-Noise Theory-Active and Digital Circuit Theory, Electromagnetic Theory-Electromagntic Waves and Applications-Quantum Electronics and Opto-Electronics-Lasers and Applications, Graphs-Network - Switching System and System Engineering, Information Processing Systems-Automation Theory-Data Communication and Pattern Recognition, Microwave Circuits-Microwave Communication Technology-Optical Circuits-and Microwave Measurements

Department of Electrical Engineering

Electrical Devices-Control Systems and System Theory, Electric Power Generation, Electric Power Transmission-Distribution and High Voltage Engineering, Electrophysics-Quantum Electrical and Material Engineering, Plasma Physics-Quantum Electronics and Gaseous Discharge Phenomena, Science and Technology of Electrical Engineering Materials, System Engineering and Bio-Engineering

Department of Electronic Engineering

Applied Combinatorics-Logic Design Switching Theory-Fault-Tolerant Computing, Basic Theories of Electronic Engineering, Computer - Aided Design-Design Automation-System Programs and Network Synthesis, High-Frequency Electron Devices-Laser

Information Processings-Application of Electron Beams and Lasers, Processor Architecture-Digital Communications-Electronic Circuits-Video Bandwidth Compression and Electronic Exchange,   Solid State Electronics-Physics-Application of Semiconductors and Opto-Electronics, System - Control Theory and Medical Electronics

Department of Environmental Engineering

Air Pollution Control, Environmental Design, Environmental Thermal Engineering, Planning of Environment, Water Conservation Engineering, Water Resources Engineering

Department of Fermentation Technology

Biochemical Process Design, Fermentation Chemistry, Fermentation Physiology and Fermentation Process Dynamics, Flavor Fermentation Technology, Food Preservation Technology, Industrial Microbiology and Genetics

Department of Materials Science and Englineering

Characterization and Design of Materials, Metallography and Structure of Materials, Physical Properties of Materials, Physics of Lattice of Defects, Plasticity and Mechanical Treatment of Materials, Properties and Technology of Powder Materials

Department of Materials Science and Processing

Environmental Materials and Surface Processing, Interface Science and Technology, Physical Chemistry of Metallurgy and Materials, Purification of Materials, Reaction Dynamics and Control in Material Processing, Solidification and Crystal Growth

Department of Mechanical Engineering

Combustion Engineering, Fluid Engineering, Machine Design, Machining and Production, Solid Mechanics, Thermohydrodynamics

Department of Mechanical Engineering for Computer-Controlled Machinery

Computer-Aided Manufacturing, Control Engineering, Information Processing, Machine Electronics, Modelling and Simulation

Department of Mechanical Engineering for Industrial Machinery and Systems

Industrial Equipment, Manufacturing Systems Engineering, Polymer Engineering, Safety Assessment of Structures, Systems Design Engineering, Transport Phenomena

Department of Naval Architecture

Ship Construction, Ship Design, Ship Motion, Ship Resistance and Propulsion, Ship Strength

Department of Nuclear Engineering

Neutronics, Nuclear Chemical Engineering, Nuclear Fuels, Nuclear Materials, Nuclear Reactor Engineering, Reactor Physics

Department of Precision Engineering

Computer - Control and Systems, Engineering Precision Measurements and Surface Physics, Materials Science for Precision Engineering, Precision Machining and Machine Tools, Scientific Instruments and Industrial Instrumentation, Unconventional Machining Processes

Department of Welding and Production Engineer-

ing

Fundamentals in Materials Processing for Welding and Production, Liquid State Materials Processing for Welding and Production, Materials Mechanics-Structural Behaviors for Welding and Production, Processes-Machines for Welding and Production, Reliability Accessment for Welding and Production, Solid State Materials for Welding and Production, Structural Design for Welding and Production, System Engineering for Welding and Production

Common Chairs

General Applications of Statistical Inferences and Operations Research, Mathematical Methods for Engineering, Mechanics in General-Statistical Mechanics of Gasses and Liquids, Mechanics of Materials and Engineering Mechanics, Physical Chemistry, Statistical Mechanics and Quantum Mechanics, System Engineering and Introduction to Electrical Engineering

Faculty of Engineering Science (Freshmen Enrollment: 385)

Department of Biophysical Engineering

Bioenergetics, Bio-Instruction and Mathematics, Information and Control in Biological System, Molecular Biology, Neurophysiology, Physics of Biomolecules

Department of Chemical Engineering

Basic Theory of Chemical Engineering, Catalysis and Surface Engineering, Chemical Process Engineering, Chemical Reaction Engineering, Molecular Engineering, Separation Engineering, Transport Engineering

Department of Chemistry

Inorganic Chemistry, Organic Chemistry, Physical Chemistry, Polymer Chemistry

Department of Control Engineering

Automatic Control Devices, Control System Synthesis, Intelligent Systems, Measuring Devices, Theory of Control Systems and their Application

Department of Electrical Engineering

Electronic Devices, Microwave Electronics, Microwave Transmission, Opto-Electronics, Semiconductor Electronics, Solid State Electronics

Department of Information and Computer Sciences

Analysis of Information Systems, ComputerAided Engineering, Computer Mechanism Network Architecture, Information Theory and Logics, Intelligent Information Processing, Programming Languages

Department of Material Physics

High Pressure Physics, Low Temperature Physics and Superconductivity, Metal Physics, Optical Properties of Solids, Semiconductor Physics, Statistical Physics, Theory of Magnetism, Theory of Solids and Solid Surfaces

Department of Mechanical Engineering

Applied Mechanics, Fluid Mechanics, Machining of Metals, Mechanical Science, Mechanics of Jet and Jet Engines, Plant Engineering, Plastic Working of Metals, Reciprocatory Machines, Rotary Machines,

Thermomechanics

Common Chairs

Applied Mathematics, Applied Mechanics, Statistical Inference

Faculty of Human Sciences (Freshmen Enrollment: 127)

Department of Human Sciences

Behavioral Engineering, Behavioral Physiology, Biological Anthropology, Comparative and Developmental Psychology, Comparative Study of Civilizations, Cultural Anthropology, Educational Organization and Administration, Educational Policy and Planning, Educational Psychology, Educational Technology, Empirical Sociology and Method in Social Research, Foundations of Human Sciences, General Psychology, Industrial Psychology, Philosophical Anthropology, Philosophy of Education, Social Group Theory and Organizational Sociology, Social Psychology, Sociology of Education, Theoretical Sociology and History of Sociological Thought, Theory of Communication, Theory of Out-of-School Education

Faculty of Law (Freshmen Enrollment: 210)

Department of Law

Administrative Law, Asian Law and Politics, Civil Law, Civil Procedure Law, Commercial Law, Comparative Legal Cultures, Constitutional Law, Criminal Law, Criminal Procedure Law, European and American Legal History, International Behavior, International Business Transactions, International Civil Procedure Law, International Economic Law, International Law, Japanese Legal History, Jurisprudence, Labor Law, Local Government Law and Tax Law, Political History, Political Science, Public Administration

Faculty of Letters (Freshmen Enrollment: 173)

Department of Aesthetics

Aesthetics, Art History, Musicology, Science of Literary Arts, Science of Theater and Performing Arts

Department of History

Archaeology, East Asian Studies, European History, History of Asian Peoples, History of Japanese Thought, History of Modern Europe, Japanese History

Department of Japanese Studies

Comparative Studies of Cultures, History of Cultural Exchange, Japanese Culture, Modern Japanese Linguistics, Sociolinguistics , Teaching of Japanese as a Foreing Language

Department of Literature

English Linguistics, English Literature, French Literature, German Literature, Japanese Linguistics, Japanese Literature

Department of Philosophy

Chinese Philosophy, Ethics, Indian Philosophy, Philosophy and History of Philosophy

Faculty of Medicine (Freshmen Enrollment: 100)

Department of Medicine

Anatomy, Anesthesiology, Bacteriology, Biochemistry, Dermatology, Environment Health and Hygiene,

Genetics, Internal Medicine, Laboratory Medicine, Legal Medicine, Medicine and Geriatrics, Molecular Pathology, Neuropsychiatry, Neurosurgery, Nutrition and Physiological Chemistry, Obstetrics and Gynecology, Ophthalmology, Orthopaedic Surgery, Otorhinolaryngology, Pathology, Pediatrics, Pharmacology, Physicochemical Physiology, Physiological Chemistry, Physiology, Public Health, Radiation Biology, Radiology, Surgery, Traumatology and Emergency Medicine, Urology

Faculty of Pharmaceutical Sciences (Freshmen Enrollment: 80)

Department of Pharmaceutical Chemistry

Analytical Chemistry, Medical Chemistry, Organic Chemistry, Pharmacognosy and Natural Products Chemistry, Physical Chemistry, Physico-Analytical Chemistry, Synthetic Organic Chemistry

Department of Pharmacy

Biochemical Engineering, Biochemistry, Environmental Science, Microbiology and Physiological Chemistry, Pharmaceutics, Pharmacology

Faculty of Science (Freshmen Enrollment: 215)

Department of Biology

Cell Physiology, Comparative Physiology, Enzyme Chemistry and Microbiology, Physical Biochemistry, Physiological Genetics, Radiation Biology

Department of Chemistry

Analytical Chemistry, Inorganic Chemistry, Organic Biochemistry, Organic Chemistry of Natural Products, Organic Reaction Mechanism, Physical Chemistry of Reaction Kinetics, Physical Chemistry of Solid State, Quantum Chemistry, Radiochemistry, Structual Organic Chemistry

Department of Macromolecular Science

Chemistry of Polymer Reactions, Chemistry of Polymer Synthesis, Macromolecular Physics, Polymer Solution Studies, Structure Studies of Solid-State Polymers

Department of Mathematics

Algebra, Applied Mathematics, Geometry, Information Theory, Mathematical Analysis, Mathematical Statistics

Department of Physics

Atomic Physics, Fundamental Physics, Molecular Physics, Nuclear Physics, Quantum Physics, Solid State Physics

Foreign Student Admission

Qualifications for Applicants

Standard Qualifications Requirement

Examination at the University

For the Faculties of Dentistry, Law, Medicine, and Pharmaceutical Sciences, applicants must take the Joint First-Stage Achievement Test. For the Faculty of Medicine, applicants must also take the Second-Stage Entrance Examination consisting of a written exam given by the faculty. For the others of those faculties, applicants must take the Examination consisting of oral exam given by each faculty. For the Faculties of Economics, Engineering, and Engineering Science, Human Sciences, Letters, applicants must take the Japanese Language Proficiency Test, the General Examination for Foreign Students and the Second-Stage Entrace Examination. For the Faculty of Science, applicants may take the Second-Stage Entrance Examination only.

Documents to be Submitted When Applying

Standard Documents Requirement

A Japanese proficiency certificate and a letter of recommendation from the applicant's embassy/consulate in Japan are also required.

Application forms are available at the Admission Office beginning in early October. All applicants are required to submit the specified application documents to the Office between December 20 and January 10 for the Faculties of Dentistry, Law, Medicine, and Pharmaceutical Sciences, and between February 1 and 8 for the Faculties of Economics, Engineering, and Engineering Science, Human Sciences, Letters, Science.

GRADUATE PROGRAMS

Graduate School of Dentistry (First Year Enrollment : Doctor's 34)

Divisions

Clinical Dentistry, Dental Science

Graduate School of Economics (First Year Enrollment : Master's 53, Doctor's 25)

Divisions

Business Administration, Economics, Public Economics

Graduate School of Engineering (First Year Enrollment : Master's 282, Doctor's 141)

Divisions

Applied Chemistry, Applied Fine Chemistry, Applied Physics, Architectural Engineering, Chemical Process Engineering, Civil Engineering, Communication Engineering, Electrical Engineering, Electromagnetic Energy Engineering, Electronic Engineering, Environmental Engineering, Fermentation Technology, Materials Science and Engineering, Mechanical Engineering, Mechanical Engineering for Industrial Machinery and Systems, Metallurgical Engineering, Naval Architecture, Nuclear Engineering, Precision Engineering, Welding Engineering

Graduate School of Engineering Science (First Year Enrollment : Master's 199, Doctor's 36)

Divisions

Chemical Sciences (Chemistry, Chemical Engineering), Mathematical Sciences, Physical Sciences (Mechanical Engineering, Electrical Engineering, Control Engineering, Material Physics, Biophysical Engineering, Information and Computer Sciences)

Graduate School of Human Sciences (First Year Enrollment : Master's 20, Doctor's 16)

Divisions

Anthropology, Education, Psychology, Sociology

Graduate School of Law (First Year Enrollment : Master's 38, Doctor's 19)

Divisions
Civil Law, Public Law
Graduate School of Letters (First Year Enrollment : Master's 59, Doctor's 28)
Divisions
English Literature, French Literature, German Literature, History, Japanese Literature, Japanese Studies, Philosophy and History of Philosophy, Science of Arts
Graduate School of Medicine (First Year Enrollment : Master's 20, Doctor's 86)
Divisions
Internal Medicine, Medical Science, Pathology, Physiology, Social Medicine, Surgery
Graduate School of Pharmaceutical Sciences (First Year Enrollment : Master's 26, Doctor's 13)
Divisions
Biological Pharmaceutical Sciences, Chemical Pharmaceutical Sciences
Graduate School of Science (First Year Enrollment : Master's 114, Doctor's 59)
Divisions
Biochemistry, Inorganic and Physical Chemistry, Macromolecular Science, Mathematics, Organic Chemistry, Physics, Physiology

Foreign Student Admission
Qualifications for Applicants
Master's Program
　　Standard Qualifications Requirement
Doctor's Program
　　Standard Qualifications Requirement
Examination at the University
Master's Program
Applicants must take an entrance examination consisting of written and/or oral exam prepared by each graduate program.
Doctor's Program
　　Same as Master's program.
Documents to be Submitted When Applying
　　Standard Documents Requirement
　　A Japanese proficiency certificate and a letter of recommendation from the applicant's embassy/consulate in Japan are also required.
　　Other documents will be prescribed by each Graduate School.
　　Application forms are available at the Academic Affairs Section, Administration Department of each Faculty. All applicants are required to submit the specified application documents to each Academic Affairs Section.

*
Research Institutes and Centers
Biomedical Research Center, Central Laboratory for Research and Education, Central Workshop, Chemical Thermodynamics Laboratory, Computation Center, Dental Technicians School, Education Center for Information Processing, Electron Beam Laboratory, Experimental Institute for Medicinal Plants and Herbal Garden, Health Administration Center, Hospital attached to the Faculty of Dentistry, Hospital attached to the Research Institute for Microbial Diseases, Institute for Molecular and Cellular Biology, Institute for Protein Research, Institute of Experimental Animal Sciences, Institute of Laser Engineering, Institute of Scientific and Industrial Research, Institute of Social and Economic Research, International Center of Cooperative Research in Biotechnology in Japan, Laboratory for Applied Superconductivity, Laboratory for Chemical Conversion of Solar Energy, Laboratory for Culture Collections, Laboratory of Ethological Studies, Laboratory of Nuclear Studies, Low Temperature Center, Material Analysis Center, Midwifery School, Molecular Genetics Laboratory, Oncogene Research Center, Plasma Physics Laboratory, Processing Research Center for High Performance Materials, Quarters for Experimentally Infected Animals, Radiation Laboratory, Radioisotope Research Center, Research Center for Extreme Materials, Research Center for High Energy Surface Processing, Research Center for Nuclear Physics, Research Center for Protein Engineering, Research Center for Ultra High Energy Density Heat Source, Research Center for Ultra High Voltage Electron Microscopy, Research Institute for Microbial Diseases, Sports Administration Center, University Hospital attached to the Faculty of Medicine, Welding Research Institute

Facilities/Services for Foreign Students
Osaka University Foreign Student House: Shared Facilities (Multipurpose Room, Library, Kitchenettes, Laundries, Shower Rooms), Accommodation (70 rooms for single male students)
Osaka University International House: Shared Facilities (Lobby, Conference Room, Library, Sky Lounge, Japanese-Style Room), Accommodation (40 rooms 24 for couples, 16 for families.

Special Programs for Foreign Students
Japanese language supplementary classes are available at the Faculty of Language and Culture, and the College of General Education gives a lecture on the culture and nature of Japan as a special subject.

For Further Information
Undergraduate Admission
Admission Division, Student Bureau, Osaka University, 1-1 Yamadaoka, Suita-shi, Osaka 565 ☎ 06–877–5111 ext. 2182
Graduate Admission
Graduate Schools of Economics, Engineering Science, Law, Letters, and Science: Academic Affairs Section of each Graduate School, 1-1 Machikaneyama-cho, Toyonaka-shi, Osaka 560 ☎ 06–844–1151 ext. 3515 (Economics), 4435 (Engineering Science), 3315 (Law), 3115 (Letters), 4015 (Science)
Graduate Schools of Engineering, Human Sciences, and Pharmaceutical Sciences: Academic Affairs Section of each Graduate School, Yamadaoka, Suita-shi, Osaka 565 ☎ 06–877–5111 ext. 4023 (Engineering), 6310 (Human Sciences), 6106 (Pharmaceutical Sciences)

Graduate School of Dentistry: Academic Affairs Section of the Graduate School , Yamadaoka, Suita-shi, Osaka 565 ☎ 06–876–5711 ext. 2123
Graduate School of Medicine: Academic Affairs Section of the Graduate School, 4-3-57 Nakanoshima, Kita-ku, Osaka-shi, Osaka 530 ☎ 06–443–5531 ext. 224

Osaka University of Foreign Studies

(Osaka Gaikokugo Daigaku)

8-1-1 Aomatani-higashi, Minoo-shi, Osaka 562
☎ 0727–28–3111

Faculty
    Profs. 64   Assoc. Profs. 68
    Assist. Profs. Full–time 24; Part–time 347
    Res. Assocs. 4
Number of Students
    Undergrad. 3, 866   Grad. 66
Library 409, 544 volumes

Outline and Characteristics of the University

Osaka University of Foreign Studies is one of the two Government universities dedicated to the cause of promoting international amity and understanding through the study of languages and related cultures of foreign countries. The University was first established in December 1921 as Osaka School of Foreign Languages, consisting of nine language departments—Chinese, Mongolian, Malaysian (now reorganized into Indonesian and Philippine), Hindustani (now reorganized into Hindi-Urdu), English, German, French, Spanish and Russian.

The school has continued to grow over the years. New departments were added one after another—Arabic (now reorganized into Arabic-Atrican) in 1940, Thai (now reorganized into Thai-Vietnamese) in 1949, Persian in 1961, Korean in 1963, Italian in 1964, Danish (now reorganized into Danish-Swedish) in 1966, Portuguese-Brazilian in 1979, Japanese in 1987. Thus, there are now 18 Language departments.

In May 1949, the school was promoted to the status of university according to the new school system, and in 1965 the Five-year Night School with six departments (Chinese, English, French, German, Russian and Spanish), which had started in 1958 as a Two-year Night Junior College, was incorporated into the University. Furthermore, in 1968, the Two-year Graduate School with nine divisions of studies (East Asian, South Asian, West Asian, English, French, German, Italian, Russian and Spanish) to confer the degree of M.A. was established.

In the meantime, in 1954, the Special Course for Foreign Students was attached to the University, and, in 1977, the Division of Japanese Studies, opened to foreign students as well as to Japanese students, was added to the Graduate School to meet the demands of the times. The University had outgrown its old campus at Uehonmachi, Osaka City, and so, in 1979, it moved to the present campus in Minoo City for more extensive academic pursuits.

UNDERGRADUATE PROGRAMS

Faculty of Foreign Language Studies (Freshmen Enrollment: 630)
    Department of Arabic-African
Arabic Culture, Arabic Linguistics, Swahili Linguistics
    Department of Burmese
Burmese Culture, Burmese Linguistics
    Department of Chinese
Chinese Culture, Chinese Linguistics, Chinese Literature, Chinese Politics and Economy
    Department of Danish-Swedish
Danish Culture, Danish Linguistics, Swedish Linguistics and Culture
    Department of English
American Literature, English and American Cultures, English Linguistics, English Literature
    Department of French
French Culture, French Linguistics, French Literature
    Department of German
German Culture, German Linguistics, German Literature
    Department of Hindi-Urdu
Hindi and Urdu Cultures, Hindi and Urdu Politics and Economy, Hindi Linguistics, Urdu Linguistics
    Department of Indonesian-Philippine
Indonesian Culture, Indonesian Linguistics, Philippine Linguistics and Culture
    Department of Italian
Italian Culture, Italian Linguistics
    Department of Japanese
Japanese Linguistics, Japanese Literature, Linguistics, Teaching of Japanese as a Foreign Language
    Department of Korean
Korean Culture, Korean Linguistics
    Department of Mongolian
Mongolian Culture, Mongolian Linguistics
    Department of Persian
Persian Culture, Persian Linguistics
    Department of Portuguese-Brazilian
Portuguese and Brazilian Culture, Portuguese and Brazilian Literature, Portuguese Linguistics
    Department of Russian
Russian and Soviet Culture, Russian and Soviet Literature, Russian Linguistics
    Department of Spanish
Practical Spanish, Spanish and Hispanic-American Cultures, Spanish and Hispanic-American Literatures, Spanish Linguistics
    Department of Thai-Vietnamese
Thai Culture, Thai Linguistics, Vietnamese Linguis-

tics and Culture
Faculty of Foreign Language Studies (Night School) (Freshmen Enrollment 225)
  Department of Chinese
Chinese Culture, Chinese Linguistics, Chinese Literature
  Department of English
American Literature, English and American Cultures, English Linguistics, English Literature
  Department of French
French Culture, French Linguistics, French Literature
  Department of German
German Culture, German Linguistics, German Literature
  Department of Russian
Russian and Soviet Culture, Russian and Soviet Literature, Russian Linguistics
  Department of Spanish
Spanish and Hispanic-American Cultures, Spanish and Hispanic-American Literatures, Spanish Linguistics

GRADUATE PROGRAMS

Graduate School of Foreign Language Studies (First Year Enrollment: 84)
  Divisions
East-Asian Language Studies, English Language Studies, French Language Studies, German Language Studies, Italian Language Studies, Japanese Language Studies, Russian Language Studies, South Asian Language Studies, Spanish Language Studies, West Asian Language Studies

Foreign Student Admission
  Qualifications for Applicants
Master's Program
    Standard Qualifications Requirement
  Examination at the University
    Applicants must take the same entrance examination (consisting of a written examination and an interview) that is given to Japanese applicants.
  Documents to be Submitted When Applying
    Standard Documents Requirement
    Application forms are available at the Graduate School Admission Office from early October. All applicants are required to submit the application documents to the Graduate Admission Office by December 12 (date subject to change).
                    ✻
Facilities/Services for Foreign Students
Foreign Students Hall: Accommodation: 84 rooms (single 78; double 6) with such shared facilities as Recreation Hall, Dining Hall, Lobby, Library, Laundries, Typing Room, Washrooms, Shower and Bath Room and Kitchenette.
Special Programs for Foreign Students
    The Special Course for Foreign Students accepts

eligible foreign students twice a year (April and October). (Enrollment: 219)
For Further Information
  Graduate Admission
Graduate Admission Office, Osaka University of Foreign Studies, 8-1-1 Aomatani-higashi, Minoo-shi, Osaka 562 ☎ 0727-28-311 ext. 105

Otaru University of Commerce
(Otaru Shoka Daigaku)
3-5-21 Midori, Otaru-shi, Hokkaido 047
☎ 0134-23-1101

Faculty
    Profs. 34   Assoc. Profs. 54
    Assist. Profs. Full-time 7; Part-time 41
    Res. Assocs. 10
Number of Students
    Undergrad. 1,735   Grad. 6
Library 291,865 volumes

Outline and Characteristics of the University
    Otaru University of Commerce was originally founded in 1910 as the Otaru High School of Commerce by the Japanese government with the intention of making it the center for economic development in northern Japan. In 1949, in accordance with the reformation of the education system, it was reorganized as a university consisting of the Faculty of Commerce, composed of the two Departments of Commerce and Economics. In 1952, a Junior College (three-year night course) was established and attached to the University. In 1953, Teacher's Training Courses in Commerce and English were added, followed in 1965 by the addition of the Department of Management Science. In 1971, the Graduate School was opened and offered a Master's program in Business Administration. In 1978, the Department of Commerce was divided into the two Courses of Commerce and Business Law. Today, the University has more than 2,000 students and a full-time faculty of 200, and is comprised of four Faculties, a Graduate School, three research and education institutes, and other affiliated establishments.
    The campus is located in the western highland of Otaru, an old sea-side city (population 180,000) on the Island of Hokkaido. Students study and relax within the academic facilities on a green hill that overlooks the beautiful harbor of Otaru.
    The University has long gained its renown as a gem in the north for its small size but excellent academic qualities. It has strong programs in liberal arts, including well-known foreign language training, and most of its departments are always ranked among the top ten in Japan. Students come from every part of the country and after graduation most enter the business world.

UNDERGRADUATE PROGRAMS

Faculty of Commerce (Freshmen Enrollment: 405)
Department of Commerce
Course of Business Law: Civil Affairs Law, Commercial Law, Economic Law, International Economic Law, International Law, Public Law, Social Law
Course of Commerce: Advanced Accounting, Business Administration, Business Management, Insurance, International Business Administration, International Marketing, Introductory Accounting, Managerial Accounting, Science of Commerce, Security Market, Transportation
Department of Economics
Economic History, Economic Policy, Finance, International Economics, International Finance, Public Finance, Statistics, Theoretical Economics
Department of Management Science
Applied Mathematics, Computer Sciences, Electronic Data Processing in Accounting, Management Sciences

Foreign Student Admission
Qualifications for Applicants
Standard Qualifications Requirement
Examination at the University
Applicants must take the General Examination for Foreign Students and the Japanese Language Proficiency Test. Upon satisfying these conditions, applicants will take the University's entrance examination (consisting of either Mathematics and English, or English and Japanese). This will be the same examination as taken by Japanese applicants. Those foreign applicants who take the two examinations are exempted from the Joint First-Stage Achievement Test.
Documents to be Submitted When Applying
Standard Documents Requirement
Application forms are available from the Admissions Office after December 1.

GRADUATE PROGRAMS

Graduate School of Commerce (First Year Enrollment : Master's 20)
Division
Business Administration

Foreign Student Admission
Qualifications for Applicants
Master's Program
Standard Qualifications Requirement
Examination at the University
Master's Program
Applicants must take the same entrance examination consisting of a written examination and an interview as given to Japanese applicants.
Documents to be Submitted When Applying
Standard Documents Requirement

Application forms are available from the Admissions Office beginning in early September. The entrance examination will be given in late October. The university may reinvite applications around January if there are still openings.

*

Research Institutes and Centers
Computer Center, Institute of Economic Research, Language Laboratory
Special Programs for Foreign Students
Japanese supplementary classes will be offered at the University Language Laboratory.
For Further Information
Undergraduate and Graduate Admission
Admissions Office, Student Division, Otaru University of Commerce, 3-5-21 Midori, Otaru-shi, Hokkaido 047 0134–23–1101 ext. 535

Saga Medical School
(Saga Ika Daigaku)

Nabeshima-Sanbonsugi, Nabeshima-machi, Saga-shi, Saga 840-01 ☎ 0952–31–6511

Faculty
Profs. 38   Assoc. Profs. 34
Assist. Profs. Full–time 29; Part–time 100
Res. Assocs. 136
Number of Students
Undergrad. 619   Grad. 34
Library 61, 820 volumes

Outline and Characteristics of the University
Saga Medical School was founded in 1976 by the Japanese Government under the policy of "a medical college for each and every prefecture." The School's first class, admitted in April 1978, graduated in March 1984.
The Graduate School was founded in 1984.
The campus, approximately 235, 000 m² in size, is located in the suburban northwest corner of the capital city of Saga Prefecture, and offers an atmosphere conducive to serious medical education and research with its pastoral environment free of urban cacophony.
The campus consists of a cluster of buildings which houses facilities for education and research; it also maintains a 600-bed hospital attached to the School.

UNDERGRADUATE PROGRAMS

Faculty of Medicine (Freshmen Enrollment 100)
Department of Medicine
Anatomy, Anesthesiology, Biochemistry, Communication Health Science, Forensic Science, Immunology and Serology, Internal Medicine, Microbiology, Obstetrics and Gynecology, Ophthalmology, Oral Surgery, Otorhinolaryngology, Pathology, Pediat-

rics, Pharmacology, Physiology, Psychiatry, Radiology, Surgery

Foreign Student Admission

Qualifications for Applicants

Standard Qualifications Requirement

Examination at the University

Saga Medical School does not have a special admissions procedure for foreign students; they are treated in the same way as their Japanese counterparts. Specifically, foreign applicants must take the Joint First-Stage Achievement Test given each year before they sit for the second and final round of Entrance Examinations given by the School. This final screening includes an interview and essay; no regular academic examinations are given.

Documents to be Submitted When Applying

Standard Documents Requirement

Application forms are available at the Student Division of the Administration Office beginning early October. All application documents should reach the Student Division during the period of January 22 through 31. No applications received after January 31 will be considered.

GRADUATE PROGRAMS

Graduate School of Medicine (First Year Enrollment : Doctor's 30)

Divisions

Bioregulation, Functional Anatomy and Pathology, Human Ecology

Foreign Student Admission

Qualifications for Applicants

Doctor's Program

1. Those who have graduated from a Japanese medical or dental college (including those who expect to graduate from such at the end of the academic year concerned).
2. Those who have successfully completed, in a foreign country, 18 years of regular schooling of which the last degree is in medicine or dentistry.
3. Those deemed to be at least equivalent to those in (1).

Examination at the University

Doctor's Program

As with Japanese nationals, foreign applicants must both take a written examination in foreign languages (English and German) and be interviewed.

Documents to be Submitted When Applying

Standard Documents Requirement

Application forms are available at the Student Division of the Administration Office beginning early November. All application documents should reach the Student Division during the period of January 22 through 27 (pending authorization). No applications received after January 27 will be considered.

*

For Further Information.

Undergraduate and Graduate Admission

Section in Charge of Entrance Examinations, Student Division, Saga Medical School, Nabeshima-Sanbonsugi, Nabeshima-machi, Saga-shi, Saga 840-01 ☎ 0952-31-6511 ext. 3130

Saga University
(Saga Daigaku)

1 Honjo-machi, Saga-shi, Saga 840
☎ 0952-24-5191

Faculty

Profs. 131   Assoc. Profs. 120

Assist. Profs. Full-time 46; Part-time 219

Res. Assocs. 54

Number of Students

Undergrad. 4,746   Grad. 215

Library 448,921 volumes

Outline and Characteristics of the University

Saga University was founded by the government in 1949 after the promulgation of the National School Establishment Law, reorganizing Saga National Higher School, Saga Normal School, and Saga Normal School for Youth Education into two Faculties: the Faculty of Humanities and Sciences and the Faculty of Education. Later in 1955, the Faculty of Agriculture was established, and in 1966 the Faculty of Humanities and Sciences was reorganized into three new independent Faculties: Economics, Science and Engineering, and Liberal Arts.

Ever since, the university has made remarkable progress. Graduate schools were opened in the Faculty of Agriculture and the Faculty of Science and Engineering in 1970 and 1975 respectively. Today the university enrollment is more than 4,950. It has a full-time faculty of 665, and is comprised of five Faculties (Education, Agriculture, Economics, Science and Engineering, and Liberal Arts), two graduate schools, postgraduate courses, and other attached schools and research centers.

Saga University lies in the center of Saga City, a city of history and tradition located in the northwestern part of Kyūshū. In the vicinity of the university are Ariake Sea and Sefuri Mountains which naturally contribute to the enhancement of the students' minds and bodies.

UNDERGRADUATE PROGRAMS

Faculty of Agricultural & Biological Sciences (Freshmen Enrollment: 165)

Department of Agricultural Sciences

Agricultural Environmental Engineering

Agricultural Construction Engineering, Agricultural Hydrotechnics, Agricultural Machinery, Agricultural Soil Engineering

Agricultural Information Science
Agricultural Land Information and Engineering, Agricultural System Information and Technology, Agricultural Water Supply and Management, Economics and Management of Food Production, Economics of Marketing and Information
Agrobiology Crop Science
Agricultural Production Engineering, Animal Production and Management, Animal Science, Crop Ecology, Improvement of Tropical Crops
  Department of Applied Biological Sciences
Biofunctional Chemistry
Applied Microbiology, Biochemistry, Life Chemistry, Microbial Genetics and Biotechnology
Biotechnology and Plant Breeding
Cell Engineering, Gene Engineering, Genetics and Plant Breeding, Plant Genetic Resources, Plant Propagation
Food Resource Science
Food Chemistry, Food Hygienics, Food Resource Chemistry, Food Science, Nutritional Biochemistry
Plant Protection and Soil Fertility
Entomology, Nematology, Plant Nutrition, Plant Pathology, Plant Virology, Soil Science
Faculty of Economics (Freshmen Enrollment   270)
  Department of Administrative Science
Administrative Science, Econometrics, Industrial Resouces, International Economics, Statistics
  Department of Business Economics
Accounting, Business Economics, Business Management, Business Organization, Management Accounting, Marketing
  Department of Economics
Business Law, Economic History, Economic Policy, Economic Theory, Finance, Industrial Economics Law, Public Finance, Public Law, Social Law, Social Policy
Faculty of Education (Freshmen Enrollment: 240)
  Teachers' Training Course for Elementary School
  Teachers' Training Course for Lower Secondary School
  Teachers' Training Course for Special Education
  Teachers' Training Course for Special Subjects (*Arts and Crafts*)
Arts and Crafts, Education, English, Home Economics, Japanese, Mathematics, Music, Physical Education, Psychology, Science, Social Studies, Special Education, Technical Education
Faculty of Science and Engineering (Freshmen Enrollment: 480)
  Department of Applied Chemistry
Applied Inorganic Chemistry Applied Physical Chemistry, Applied Organic Chemistry, Ceramics Engineering, Chemical Engineering
  Department of Chemistry
Analytical Chemistry, Inorganic Chemistry, Organic Chemistry, Physical Chemistry
  Department of Civil Engineering I
Construction Materials and Methods, Geotechnical Engineering, Hydraulic Engineering, Structural Engineering, Transportation
  Department of Civil Engineering II
Environment Planning, Geotechnical Engineering, Structural Engineering, Water Resources Engineering
  Department of Electrical Engineering
Electrical Machinery, Electric Power Engineering, Fundamentals of Electrical Engineering, Systems Control
  Department of Electronic Engineering
Applied Electronics, Communication Engineering, Fundamentals of Electronics, Information Processing and Electronic Circuit
  Department of Industrial Chemistry
Ceramic Engineering, Chemical Engineering, Industrial Physical Chemistry, Inorganic Industrial Chemistry, Organic Industrial Chemistry
  Department of Information Science
Applied Information Science, Computer Science, Fundamentals of Information Science, Mathematical Information Science
  Department of Mathematics
Algebra, Analysis, Applied Mathematics, Geometry
  Department of Mechanical Engineering
Fluid Engineering, Fundamentals of Mechanical Engineering, Machine Design and Manufacturing Technique, Thermal Engineering
  Department of Mechanical Engineering (*Production Division*)
Automatic Control Engineering, Heat and Mass Transfer Engineering, Metal Working Engineering, Precision Machinery
  Department of Physics
High Energy Physics, Mathematical Physics, Quantum Physics, Solid State Physics

Foreign Student Admission
  Qualifications for Applicants
    Standard Qualifications Requirement
    Applicants must take the Japanese Language Proficiency Test and the General Examination for Foreign Students.
  Examination at the University
    Individuals who have taken the tests specified above will be allowed to take the special entrance examination prepared by each Faculty. The examination consists of written tests (Japanese composition) and an interview.
  Documents to be Submitted When Applying
    Standard Documents Requirement
    Application forms are available at the Administration Office from late November. Applicants are required to submit the documents to the Administration Office not later than February 15. Incomplete or delayed applications will not be considered.

GRADUATE PROGRAMS

Graduate School of Agriculture (First Year Enrollment : Master's 38)

Divisions
United Graduate School of Agriculture (Doctoral Course in Agriculture) (Freshmen Enrollment: Doctor's 18)
Agricultural Chemistry, Agricultural Civil Engineering, Agronomy, Horticultural Science
Graduate School of Science and Engineering (First Year Enrollment : Master's 54)
Divisions
Applied Chemistry, Chemistry, Civil Engineering, Electrical Engineering, Electronic Engineering, Industrial Chemistry, Mathematics, Mechanical Engineering, Mechanical Engineering (Production Division), Physics

Foreign Student Admission
Qualifications for Applicants
Master's Program
   Standard Qualifications Requirement
Examination at the University
Master's Program
   Applicants have to pass the interview and/or the written examination
Documents to be Submitted When Applying
   Standard Documents Requirement
   Application forms are available at the office of admission of each Faculty from early July. Applicants are required to submit the documents to the office of admission of each Faculty by the middle of August. Incomplete or delayed applications will not be considered.

*

Research Institutes and Centers
Center for Practical Studies of Education, Computation Center, Experimental Farm, Health Administration Center, Laboratory of Ocean Thermal Energy Conversion, Laboratory of Radioactive Isotopes, Research Institute for Shallow Sea and Tidal Land
Facilities/Services for Foreign Students
   The dormitory is available for foreign students (although limited in number) for the first year only.
   International Friendship Room has just opened at a corner in the Faculty of Science and Engineering. All foreign students, together with Japanese students and university staff, may use it for seminars and other recreational purposes. This room is equipped with such items as a personal computor (usable as a word-processor), TV and video sets and others.
   Faculty wives voluntarily lend utensils and other goods necessary for starting out a new life in Japan.
For Further Information
Undergraduate and Graduate Admission
Guidance Section, Student Division, Student Office, Saga University, 1 Honjo-machi, Saga-shi, Saga 840
☎ 0952-24-5191 ext. 2163

Saitama University
(Saitama Daigaku)
255, Shimo-Okubo, Urawa-shi, Saitama 338
☎ 048-852-2111

Faculty
   Profs. 222   Assoc. Profs. 193
   Assist. Profs. Full-time 1; Part-time 461
   Res. Assocs. 48
Number of Students
   Undergrad. 6, 267   Grad. 333
Library 512, 618 volumes

Outline and Characteristics of the University
   Saitama University was established in 1949 as one of the new national universities, with two faculties: the Faculty of Liberal Arts and the Faculty of Education. The University has grown rapidly over the last three decades, both in size and scope. Today its undergraduate education includes the Faculties of Liberal Arts, Education, Economics, Science, and Engineering, as well as the College of Liberal Arts which provides students with a general education during the first two years. The Junior College of Economics offers a three-year associate degree program.
   In the graduate division, Saitama University offers four graduate programs: Cultural Science, Science, Engineering, and Policy Science, each leading to a master's degree.
   In addition, the Graduate School for Policy Science is preparing a special M.A. program in policy analysis in which all courses are to be taught in English. This program is scheduled to start in 1984, and is the first attempt on the part of Japanese universities to respond to international needs.
   Saitama University has a variety of specialized facilities to carry out its research mission. The Information Processing Center provides computing services to its faculty and students. The Institute for Policy Science is quickly becoming an international center for research in the field of science and technology policy. The Chemical Analysis Center maintains several large-sized analyzers and offers various programs to support research activities.
   Saitama University is located in the quiet suburban city of Urawa, which lies about 30 kilometers to the north of Tokyo. Japanese National Railway provides access to central Tokyo, an hour away from the University, enabling us to maintain active exchange programs in education and research with other universities around Tokyo.

UNDERGRADUATE PROGRAMS

Faculty of Economics (Freshmen Enrollment: 220)
Department of Business

Accounting, Auditing, Business Enterprise, Business History, Cost Accounting, General Theory of Business Enterprise and Organization, General Theory of Business Management, International Industries, Management Accountion

Department of Economics

Civil Law, Commercial Law, Economic History, Economic Theory, History of Economic Theory, Modern Economics, Money and Banking, Political History of Modern Japan, Politics, Principles of Economic Policy, Statistics, Theory of Public Finance

Faculty of Education (Freshmen Enrollment: 540)

Training Course for Teachers of Schools for the Handicapped (especially for the mentally handicapped)

Elementary Education Education for the Handicapped, Psychology of the Handicapped, and Physiology of the Handicapped, in addition to those courses offered in the Training Course for Primary School Teachers.

Secondary Education Education for the Handicapped, Psychology of the Handicapped, and Physiology of the Handicapped, in addition to those courses offered in the Training Course for Junior High School Teachers.

Training Course for Junior High School Teachers

Educational Psychology, Pedagogy, Specialized courses in one elected major subject in secondary education

Training Course for Kindergarten Teachers

Preschool Education, Psychology, of Preschool Children, and specialized courses in all areas of preschool education.

The Program for Adult Education

The program consists of five majors.

Adult Education Course provided three selective majors for adult education, sports and regional science in the community.

Counseling Course provided two selective majors for psychological counselor and welfare counselor.

Training Course for Primary School Teachers

Pedagogy and Eduational Psychology, Specialized courses in all the subjects in elementary education

Faculty of Engineering (Freshmen Enrollment: 400)

Department of Applied Chemistry

Industrial Inorganic Chemistry, Industrial Organic Chemistry, Industrial Polymer Chemistry, Introduction of Catalysis, Introduction to Inorganic Chemistry, Physical Chemistry, Physical Organic Chemistry, Synthetic Organic Chemistry

Department of Construction Engineering

Composite Materials Engineering, Construction Materials Engineering, Engineering Vibrations, Geophysical Prospecting, Mathematical Planning, Public Facility Planning, Reliability Analysis and Safety Engineering, Seismology, Transportation Engineering

Department of Electrical Engineering

Antenna Engineering, Electricity and Magnetism, Electric Machinery, Electric Power Engineering, High Frequency Engineering, High Frequency Measurement, High Voltage Engineering, Power Electronics, Power Transmission and Distribution Engineering, Theory of Electric Circuit

Department of Electronic Engineering

Design of Logic Circuits, Electronic Circuits, Electronic Solid State Physics, Magnetic Engineering, Measurement Theory, Numerical Calculus, Optoelectronics, Principles of Electronic Circuit

Department of Environmental Chemistry

Analytical Chemistry, Chemical Engineering Kinetics, Chemical Engineering Operations, Chemical Thermodynamics, Environmental Assessment, Environmental Chemistry, Instrumental Analysis, The Atmosphere, The Chemistry and Engineering of Environmental Purification

Department of Foundation Engineering

Foundation Engineering, Hydraulics, Hydrology, River Engineering, Rock Mechanics, Sedimentary Geology, Soil Mechanics, Structural Mechanics, Theory of Elasticity and Plasticity

Department of Information Engineering

Fundamental Information Engineering, Information Machinery Engineering, Information System Engineering, Knowledge Engineering

Department of Mechanical Engineering I & II

Applied Elasticity, Control Theory, Dynamics of Machinery, Engineering Material, Engineering Mechanics, Fluid Machinery, Fluid Mechanics, Fundamental Control Theory, Heat Transfer, Machine Design and Drawing, Manufacturing Engineering, Methods of Machine Design, Non-Ferrous and Non-Metallic Material, Precision Engineering, Strength of Materials, Theory of Mechanism, Thermodynamics

Faculty of Liberal Arts (Freshmen Enrollment: 140)

Department of Liberal Arts

American Studies, Anthropology, British Culture, Chinese Culture, Communications, French Linguistics and Literature, Geography, German Culture, History, International Relations, Japanese Culture, Modern Sociology, Philosophy and Thought, Social System Studies

Faculty of Science (Freshmen Enrollment: 200)

Department of Biochemistry

Biosynthesis, Cell Biochemistry, Enzymology, Metabolism and Bioenergetics, Molecular Biology, Structures and Functions of Biological Substances

Department of Chemistry

Analytical Chemistry, Chemistry of Natural Products, Inorganic Chemistry, Macromolecular Chemistry, Organic Chemistry, Physical Chemistry, Structural Chemistry

Department of Mathematics

Algebra, Analysis, Applied Mathematics, Geometry, Topology

Department of Physics

Electromagnetism, Mechanics, Nuclear Physics, Quantum Mechanics, Solid State Physics, Statistical Mechanics, Theory of Relativity

Department of Regulation Biology
Animal Physiology Developmental Biology, Endocrinology, Genetics, Plant Morphogenesis, Radiation Biology

Foreign Student Admission
Qualifications for Applicants
Standard Qualifications Requirement
Examination at the University
Applicants must take the same entrance examination given to the Japanese students in addition to an interview.

Applicants need not take the Joint First-Stage Achievement Test, but must take the Japanese Language Proficiency Test and General Examination for Foreign Students.
Documents to be Submitted When Applying
Standard Documents Requirement
Application forms are available at the Admissions Office from early October, and requests for information regarding admission and all application materials should be directed to the Head of the Admissions Office.

GRADUATE PROGRAMS

Graduate School of Cultural Science (First Year Enrollment : Master's 32)
Divisions
Science of Language Culture, Science of Social Culture
Graduate School of Engineering (First Year Enrollment : Master's 64)
Divisions
Applied Chemistry, Construction Engineering, Electrical Engineering, Electronic Engineering, Environmental Chemistry, Foundation Engineering, Mechanical Engineering I, Mechanical Engineering II
Graduate School of Policy Science (First Year Enrollment : Master's 25)
Division
Policy Science
Graduate School of Science (First Year Enrollment : Master's 46)
Divisions
Biochemistry, Chemistry, Mathematics, Physics, Regulation Biology

Foreign Student Admission
Qualifications for Applicants
Master's Program
Standard Qualifications Requirement
Examination at the University
Master's Program
For each Graduate School, applicants must take the same entrance examination given to the Japanese students. consisting of a written exam (both foreign languages and special subjects) and an interview (for some courses, an interview and an essay).
Documents to be Submitted When Applying

Standard Documents Requirement
Application forms are available from about July, so requests for information regarding admission and all application materials should be directed to the Head of the Admissions Office around that time.

Research Institutes and Centers
Health Service Center, The Chemical Analysis Center, The Institute for Policy Science
Facilities/Services for Foreign Students
Saitama University International House
Accommodation: 50 rooms (single 26, couples 16, family 8)
For Further Information
Undergraduate and Graduate Admission
Entrance Examination Section, Student Office, Saitama University, 255 Shimo-Okubo, Urawa-shi, Saitama 338 ☎ 048–852–2111 ext. 2186, 2187

Shiga University
(Shiga Daigaku)
1-1-1. Banba, Hikone-shi, Shiga 522
☎ 0749–22–5600

Faculty
    Profs. 79   Assoc. Profs. 94
    Assist. Profs. Full–time 11; Part–time 48
    Res. Assocs. 13
Number of Students
    Undergrad. 3, 251   Grad. 22
Library 394, 206 volumes

Outline and Characteristics of the University
Shiga University was established in 1949 as part of the new system of national universities in Japan. At present, Shiga University has two faculties on the undergraduate level, one graduate school division, two advanced courses and one junior college (the evening division). The Faculty of Education, which dates back to 1874, was established as a new Faculty to provide general education and applied education. The Faculty of Economics originated as the Hikone Commercial College, which was founded in 1922. In 1953, as a part of the Faculty of Economics, the Junior College Course of Economics was established with emphasis on training in practical management. The Graduate School of Economics (Master's Program) was established in September 1973. The University now has an enrollment of approximately 3, 200 students and employs 410 academic and administrative staff members.

The University campuses are located in Hikone City and Otsu City. Hikone City is a historic location with a population of approximately 95, 000 and can be reached in one hour by train from Kyoto City. Otsu City is a metropolitan city in Shiga Prefecture with a population of approximately 236, 000. It can be reached in half an hour by railway from Kyoto

City.

These cities both face Lake Biwa, which is the largest lake in Japan, and are characterized by a temperate climate with distinct seasons.

The main campus of the University is located on the west side of Hikone City and includes the principal buildings and facilities of the Administration Office, the Student Office, the Faculty of Economics, the Graduate School of Economics, the University Library, and the Health Administration Center as well as the Junior College of Economics. The Faculty of Education and the attached facilities of its schools are located at the Otsu campus, about 60km south of the main campus.

UNDERGRADUATE PROGRAMS

Faculty of Economics (Freshmen Enrollment: 410)
Department of Accounting
Accounting, Bookkeeping, International Accounting, Managerial Accounting
Department of Business Administration
Business Administration, Business History, Commerce and Marketing, Industrial Relations, Managerial Economics
Department of Economics
Economic History, Economic Policy, History of Economics Studies, Industrial Economics, International Economic Relations, Labor Economics, Money and Banking, Public Finance, Social Policy, Statistics, Theoretical Economics
Department of Management Science
Computing System, Industry Engineering, Information Processing, Information Retrieval, Mechanical Accounting
Faculty of Education (Freshmen Enrollment: 260)
Arts and Crafts, Education of the Mentally Handicapped, Foreign Languages, Household Technology, Japanese Language, Mathematics, Music, Natural Science, Pedagogy of Early Childhood, Physical Education and Health Preservation, Psychology, School Education, Social Studies, Technology, Vocational Guidance

Foreign Student Admission
Qualifications for Applicants
Standard Qualifications Requirement
Applicants must take the Japanese Language Proficiency Test and General Examination for Foreign Students.
Examination at the University
Faculty of Economics: English, Mathematics, Essay (1, 200 words), Oral Test
Faculty of Education: Those who wish to select the following chairs—Education of the Handicapped, English Language, Japanese Language, Pedagogy of Childhood, Psychology, School Education and Social Studies; Japanese Language, Oral Test
Those who wish to select the following chairs —Household Technology, Mathematics, Natural Science and Technology; Mathematics, Oral Test
Documents to be Submitted When Applying
Standard Documents Requirement
Applicants should inquire at each Faculty Office at the begining of December. The application form and explanatory documents are sent to applicants from each Faculty Office upon request. Required documents should be submitted to each Faculty, early in January (Faculty of Education), or late in January to early February (Faculty of Economics).

GRADUATE PROGRAMS

Graduate School of Economics (First Year Enrollment : Master's 40)
Divisions
Business Administration, Economics

Foreign Student Admission
Qualifications for Applicants
Standard Qualifications Requirement
Examination at the University
Preliminary selection will be made on the basis of the documents submitted. A foreign applicant must take the entrance examination (Written and Oral Examination) administered by the University.
Documents to be Submitted When Applying
Standard Documents Requirement
Applicants should inquire at the Office of the Graduate School late in December. Required documents should be submitted to the Office of the Graduate School in the begining of February.

*

Research Institutes and Centers
Archives Museum, Computing Center, Institute for Economics and Business Research, Institute of Lake Science, Institute of School Education
For Further Information
Undergraduate Admission
Admissions Office, Shiga University, 1-1-1Banba, Hikone-shi, Shiga 522 ☎ 0749-22-5600 ext. 302
Graduate Admission
Graduate Admissions Office, Shiga University, 1-1-1 Banba, Hikone-shi, Shiga 522 ☎ 0749-22-5600 ext. 259

Shiga University of Medical Science

(Shiga Ika Daigaku)

Seta-Tsukinowa-cho, Otsu-shi, Shiga 520-21
☎ 0775-48-2111

Faculty
    Profs. 34   Assoc. Profs. 35
    Assist. Profs. Full–time 29; Part–time 242
    Res. Assocs. 132
Number of Students

Undergrad. 615   Grad. 87
Library   83, 555 volumes

Outline and Characteristics of the University

Shiga University of Medical Science is located on 233, 017 m^2 of land on a hill in Otsu City, the capital of Shiga Prefecture. The city is near Kyoto, the ancient national capital, and has a warm climate with various seasonal changes. To the north, beautiful Lake Biwa, the largest lake in Japan, can be seen from the campus. It is located in a designated cultural zone along with a public library and the Shiga Museum of Modern Art.

The University was founded in October 1974 as one of the new national medical schools. The University aims to educate medical students and train newly graduated and research-minded doctors or investigators to enable them to contribute to the health care of the people.

Since then, the University has continued to expand. The University Hospital of 600 beds was opened in October 1978, followed by the University Library in March 1979. A graduate school was started in April 1981. The first students graduated from the Graduate School in 1985 and 90 persons received their doctorates by April 1988.

Shiga University of Medical Science is still making efforts to establish a firm foundation as a place for good education, creative research and excellent clinical medicine, the universal missions of any medical school.

UNDERGRADUATE PROGRAMS

Faculty of Medicine (Freshmen Enrollment: 100)
Department of Medicine
Anatomy, Anesthesiology, Biochemistry, Clinical Pathology, Dermatology, Experimental Radiology, Head and Neck Surgery, Health Care and Administration, Internal Medicine, Legal Medicine, Medical Biochemistry, Microbiology, Neurosurgery, Obstetrics and Gynecology, Ophthalmology, Oral and Maxillofacial Surgery, Orthopedic Surgery, Otolaryngology, Pathology, Pediatrics, Pharmacology, Physiology, Preventive Medicine, Psychiatry, Radiology, Surgery, Urology

Foreign Student Admission
Qualifications for Applicants
Standard Qualifications Requirement
Foreign applicants for undergraduate programs must take the Joint First-Stage Achievement Test given by the National Center for the University Entrance Examination.
Examination at the University
Those who wish to enter the undergraduate programs must pass the same entrance examination given to Japanese students.
Documents to be Submitted When Applying
Standard Documents Requirement

Application forms are available at the Student Division. Completed forms will be accepted within the appointed period in January.

GRADUATE PROGRAMS

Graduate School of Medicine (First Year Enrollment : Doctor's 30)
Divisions
Biological Defense Mechanism, Biological Information and Control, Biological Regulation of Metabolism, Development-Differentiation-Proliferation, Environment-Ecology

Foreign Student Admission
Qualifications for Applicants
Doctor's Program
Standard Qualifications Requirement
Those who wish to enter the Graduate School of Medicine must either, (1) present a certification of graduation from a faculty of medicine or dentistry, or (2) have completed a master's course in a faculty other than medicine, and be judged by this Graduate School to possess knowledge equivalent to that of graduates from faculties of medicine or dentistry.
Examination at the University
Doctor's Program
Those who wish to enter the Graduate School must pass the same entrance examination given to Japanese students. The examination consists of a written examination in English-German or English-French, or English-Japanese only for foreign applicants and an oral examination in their speciality.
Documents to be Submitted When Applying
Standard Documents Requirement
Application forms are available at the Student Division from the middle of December. All applicants are required to submit the specified application documents to the Student Division by the appointed day in February.

*

Research Institutes and Centers
Center for Anatomical Sciences, Central Research Laboratory, Institute for Experimental Animals, Radioisotope Research Center
Facilities/Services for Foreign Students
There is no special dormitory for foreign students, but the Student Division will help them to find a suitable lodging outside the university.
Health care service is available at the University Hospital.
For Further Information
Undergraduate and Graduate Admission
Student Division, Shiga University of Medical Science, Seta Tsukinowa-cho, Otsu-shi, Shiga 520-21 ☎ 0775-48-2071

Shimane Medical University
(Shimane Ika Daigaku)

89-1 Enya-cho, Izumo-shi, Shimane 693
☎ 0853-23-2111

Faculty
    Profs. 37   Assoc. Profs. 37
    Assist. Profs.   Full–time 28; Part–time 171
    Res. Assocs. 130
Number of Students
    Undergrad. 641   Grad. 82
Library 82, 745 volumes

Outline and Characteristics of the University

Shimane Medical University was established in October 1975, and its doors were opened for instruction in April of the following year. The aims of the institution are to produce doctors solidly grounded in medical ethics and thoroughly trained in scientific investigation, thereby contributing to the promotion of high medical standards and the provision of excellent medical services in the local area.

The University is located in Izumo City (population: 80, 000), which is developing rapidly as an important city in the San'in area and plans future expansion. The city is home to Japanese myth and legend and is well-known as the birthplace of *Ohkuninushi–no–mikoto*, the ancient god of healing; in addition there are many historical sites of great interest to tourists. The whole area is rich in beautiful scenery, and its people are known for their traditional warmth and friendliness.

The University is situated on the south side of the city about two kilometers away from Izumo City station on the San'in Line. It has a quiet rural atmosphere very suitable for outdoor activities as well as for academic pursuits. The campus has a total area of 220, 000m² and includes lecture and training facilities, research facilities, Library, University Hospital, Institute of Experimental Animals, Central Research Laboratories, Welfare Facilities, gymnasium, Budo gymnasium, baseball field, tennis courts, running track, and swimming pool.

The Graduate School was established in April, 1982 to offer Doctor's programs. The Graduate School consists of three courses: Biological Function, Human Ecology, and Morphology. Each course is divided into three units. The institution is set up in such a way that each member of faculty can give research guidance and education in his or her field in close cooperation with others, whether he or she is an instructor of basic medicine or of clinical medicine.

Shimane Institute of Health Science has been established in a neighboring building and is very active in the investigation of hypertension, brain, heart, circulation and similar fatal diseases. It works in close harmony with the university.

UNDERGRADUATE PROGRAMS

Faculty of Medicine (Freshmen Enrollment: 100)
    Department of Medicine
Anatomy, Anesthesiology, Biochemistry, Dermatology, Environmental Medicine, Internal Medicine, Legal Medicine, Microbiology & Immunology, Neurosurgery, Obstetrics & Gynecology, Ophthalmology, Oral & Maxillofacial Surgery, Orthopaedics, Otorhinolaryngology, Pathology, Pediatrics, Pharmacology, Physiology, Psychiatry, Radiology, Surgery, Urology

Foreign Student Admission
    Qualifications for Applicants
        Standard Qualifications Requirement
    Examination at the University
        The foreign applicants must take the Joint First-Stage Achievement Test, plus the same second-stage entrance examination given to Japanese students. The latter consists of a written examination, an essay and an interview. Admissions consideration is based on the results of the above-mentioned examinations, a transcript record from the institution most recently attended and a medical examination record. No special examination for foreign students is conducted at present.

        It is also recommended that applicants take the Japanese Language Proficiency Test and the General Examination for Foreign Students.
    Documents to be Submitted When Applying
        Standard Documents Requirement
        Refer to the Application Guide for a list of documents to be submitted when applying, the closing date for applicants and other details. The Application Guide is available at the Student Division of the College.

GRADUATE PROGRAMS

Graduate School of Medicine (First Year Enrollment : Doctor's 30)
    Divisions
Biological Function, Human Ecology, Morphology

Foreign Student Admission
    Qualifications for Applicants
Doctor's Program
        The applicants must have completed or be expected to complete a course of medicine or dentistry at a college or a university by the following March. The applicants must have completed or expect to complete 18 years of education or the equivalent abroad by the following March.
    Examination at the University
Doctor's Program
        Students from abroad are selected in the same way as Japanese students. Admission is based on the results of the Scholastic Ability Test administered by

the Graduate School of the university, a report from the college which they have most recently attended, and a medical examination.

It is also recommended that applicants take the Japanese Language Proficiency Test and the General Examination for Foreign Students.

∗

Research Institutes and Centers
Central Research Laboratories, Institute of Experimental Animals
For Further Information
Undergraduate and Graduate Admission
Student Division, Shimane Medical University, 89-1 Enya-cho, Izumo-shi, Shimane 693
☎ 0853–23–2111 ext. 2167

Shimane University
(Shimane Daigaku)
1060 Nishikawatsu-cho, Matsue-shi, Shimane 690
☎ 0852–21–7100

Faculty
    Profs. 140   Assoc. Profs. 124
    Assist. Profs. Full–time 26; Part–time 87
    Res. Assocs. 40
Number of Students
    Undergrad. 3, 990   Grad. 121
Library 559, 809 volumes

Outline and Characteristics of the University
Shimane University was founded in 1949 as a national university. It consists of four faculties, three graduate schools (Master's programs), and several other research centers and facilities. The main campus of Shimane University covers an area of some 200, 000 m².

The campus is located on the north-eastern edge of the city of Matsue (population 150, 000) which lies about 800 kilometers west of Tokyo and can be reached in about one hour by plane. Matsue, the seat of Shimane prefecture, plays the leading role in political, economic and cultural activities in this area. Since Matsue is rich in natural beauty and maintains its traditional appearance during these modern times, you will find the landscape in and around Matsue simply superb. The Irish-born writer, journalist and educator Lafcadio Hearn who taught here, wrote many stories and articles related, in some way or other, to Matsue bringing this city to the attention of the world.

Shimane University maintans the following educational/research centers and institutes: Multi-Grade Instruction and Educational Technology Center of Faculty of Education where fundamental and practical research and educational training of practice-teaching are conducted; Marine Biological Station Attached to Faculty of Science whose purpose is to do research and practice on living things in the Japan Sea and the ocean; Experimental Farms Attached to the Faculty of Agriculture, among which the computer-equipped Central Farm is unique in that vegerables, flowers and fruit-trees are grown by utilizing natural energies, such as solar heat and wind force, both of which are controlled by computer; Center for Studies of the San'in Region which operates in the four sections of the Ancient Culture, Farming Problems, Forest Resources, and Natural Environment. Each of these sections conducts investigations and research closely connected to the local area in its special field respectively.

During these past years Shimane University has been enthusiastically developing international exchanges with universities in the United States and mainland China. It is the University's belief that these efforts will promote international understanding and the advancement of learning on a world-wide scale.

UNDERGRADUATE PROGRAMS

Faculty of Agriculture (Freshmen Enrollment: 205)
    Department of Agricultural Chemistry
Agrochemical Engineering, Applied Microbiology, Biological Chemistry, Food Chemistry, Soil Physical Chemistry
    Department of Agricultural Economics
Agricultural Policy, Economics of Forestry, Eonomics of Agricultural Marketing, Farm Management, Rural Planning and Development
    Department of Agricultural Engineering
Agricultural Construction Engineering, Agricultural Machinery and Mechanization, Cultivation System Control Engineering, Irrigation and Drainage Engineering, Reclamation Engineering
    Department of Agriculture
Animal Science, Crop Science, Olericulture and Floriculture, Pomology
    Department of Environmental Preservation
Agro-environmental Preservation, Chemical Contamination Biology, Insect Management, Plant Pathology
    Department of Forestry
Chemical and Physical Processing of Wood, Forest Management, Silviculture, Wood Science and Engineering
Faculty of Education (Freshmen Enrollment: 300)
    Elementary School Teachers' Training Course
Art, Education, Educational Psychology, English, Health and Physical Education, Home Economics, Japanese, Mathematics, Music, Natural Science, Social Studies, Technology
    Junior High School Teacher's Training Course
Art, English, Health and Physical Education, Home Economics, Japanese, Mathematics, Music, Natural Science, Social Studies, Technology
    Training Course for Teachers of Handicapped children

Elementary School Teacher's Course

Junior High School Teacher's Course

Kindergarten Teacher's Training Course

Training Course for Teachers of Special Subject (*Music*)

Composition, Keyboard Instruments, Musicology, Stringed Instruments and Wind Instruments, Vocal Music

Training Course for Teachers of Subject (*Health and Physical Education*)

Health and Physical Education

Course of Social Education & Culture studies

Department of Social Education

Department of Regional Studies

Department of Intercultural Studies

Faculty of Law and Literature (Freshmen Enrollment: 280)

Department of Law

Economics, Political Science, Private Law, Public Law

Department of Literature

Area Studies, History, Oriental Language and Literature, Philosophy, Western Language and Literature

Faculty of Science (Freshmen Enrollment 205)

Department of Biology

Animal Morphology and Phylogeny, Animal Physiology, Plant Ecology, Plant Physiology

Department of Chemistry

Environmental Analytical Chemistry, Inorganic Chemistry, Organic Chemistry, Physical Chemistry

Department of Geology

Historical Geology, Mineral Resources Geology, Rock Mineralogy, Structural Geology

Department of Mathematics

Algebra, Applied Analysis, Geometry, Topology and Analysis

Department of Physics

Applied Physics, Condensed Matter Physics, Elementary Particle Theory, Solid State Physics

Common Program

Computer Aided Science

Foreign Student Admission

Qualifications for Applicants

Standard Qualifications Requirement

Examination at the University

All the foreign students are exempted from the Joint First-Stage Achievement Test, but must take the Japanese Language Proficiency Test and General Examination for Foreign Students, and the selection is made through the overall screening of the results of written examinations and physical examination.

All applicants must take the University administered Second-Stage Entrance Exmination. The required subjects to be taken for the General Examination for Foreign Students and the Second-Stage Entrance Examination vary with each Faculty/Department. The applicant should contact the concerned Faculty directly.

Documents to be Submitted When Applying

Standard Documents Requirement

Application Handbook is made available at the Entrance Examination Section in November.

ONE-YEAR GRADUATE PROGRAMS

One-Year Graduate Course of Education (Enrollment 15)

Education, Health and Physical Education, Music Education

One-Year Graduate Course of Literature (Enrollment 10)

Area Studies, History, Oriental Language and Literature, Philosophy, Western Language and Literature

Foreign Student Admission

Qualifications for Applicants

Standard Qualifications Requirement

Examination at the University

Literature Course

Literature Majors: Written examinations and an interview

Education Course

Education Majors: Written examinations and an interview.

Music Majors and Physical Education Majors: Written examination, an interview, and performance test

For details ask for the Application Handbook (in Japanese) to be published in December.

GRADUATE PROGRAMS

Graduate School of Agriculture (First Year Enrollment : Master's 50)

Divisions

Agricultural Chemistry, Agricultural Economics, Agricultural Engineering, Agriculture, Environmental Preservation, Forestry

Graduate School of Law (First Year Enrollment: Master's 6)

Division

Law

Graduate School of Science (First Year Enrollment : Master's 15)

Divisions

Biology, Chemistry, Geology, Mathematics, Physics

Foreign Student Admission

Qualifications for Applicants

Master's Program

Standard Qualifications Requirement

Examination at the University

Master's Program

Graduate School of Agriculture:

Written examinations (English and respective major subjects) and an interview.

Graduate School of Science:

Written examinations (English, basic major subjects and respective major subjects) and oral examinations.

Graduate School of Law:
Written examinations (Froreign languages and respective major subjects) and an interview.

For details ask for the Application Handbook.
Documents to be Submitted When Applying
Standard Documents Requirement

*

Research Institutes and Centers
Center for Studies of the San'in Region, Handicraft
and Engineering Work Center, Information Processing Center, Marine Biological Station Attached to
Faculty of Science, Multi-Grade Instruction and Educational Technology Center Attached to Faculty of
Education, Radioisotope Center, University Farm
Attached to Faculty of Agriculture, University Forests Attached to Faculty of Agriculture

Facilities/Services for Foreign Students
The Welfare and Guidance Section of each Faculty of the student's affiliation offers help in finding
off-campus housing for him/her.

Health care and consultation are taken care of
by two full-time physicians at the University Health
Center.

Special Programs for Foreign Students
Japanese teachers of the Department of Literature and Faculty of Education teach the "Japanese
language, and things Japanese" to foreign students
twice a week as outside-regular-classwork volunteer
teaching.

The contents of the teaching include "senryu"
(humorous or witty 17-syllable verse), mythology
and folklores of the local Izumo district, newspaper
reading, etc.

For Further Information
Undergraduate and Graduate Admission
Entrance Examination Section, Admission Office,
Shimane University, 1060 Nishikawatsu-cho, Matsue-
shi, Shimane 690 ☎ 0852–21–7100 ext. 245

Shinshu University
(Shinshu Daigaku)

3-1-1 Asahi, Matsumoto-shi, Nagano 390
☎ 0263-35-4600

Faculty
    Profs. 259   Assoc. Profs. 262
    Assist. Profs. Full–time 94; Part–time 291
    Res. Assocs. 242
Number of Students
    Undergrad. 8, 300   Grad. 541
Library 847, 328 volumes

Outline and Characteristics of the University
Following the 1949 revisions, the previous eight
Colleges were reorganized into six independent Fac-
ulties: Agriculture, Education, Engineering, Human-
ities and Sciences, Medicine, and Textile Science and
Technology.

In 1966, the Faculty of Humanities and Sciences
was reorganized into two Faculties—the Faculty of
Arts and the Faculty of Science. In addition, the Faculty of Liberal Arts was opened.

In 1983, the Faculty of Economics was opened.
In 1958, the Graduate School of Medicine was
opened.

Presently the University has six Graduate
Schools—Agriculture, Arts, Engineering, Medicine,
Science, and Textile Science and Technology.

Today the University has about 8, 850 students
and 857 full-time faculty members and is comprised
of eight specialist Faculties, six Graduate Schools
and the Faculty of Liberal Arts.

Nagano Prefecture is an area of great natural
beauty, and offers a good environment in which to
study.

UNDERGRADUATE PROGRAMS

Faculty of Agriculture (Freshmen Enrollment: 199)
    Department of Bioscience and Biotechnology
Agricultural Biotechnology, Biochemistry and Cell
Biology, Chemical Control
    Department of Crop and Animal Science
Animal Science, Ecology of Bio-Resources, Horticul-
ture and Food Economics
    Department of Forest Science
Forest Conservation, Forest Resources, Resources
Utilization
Faculty of Arts (Freshmen Enrollment: 150)
    Department of Arts
Chinese Literature, Comparative Literature, Com-
parative Philosophy, Cultural Anthropology, Eng-
lish and American Literature, English Linguistics,
European History, French Literature, German Lin-
guistics, German Literature, Japanese History, Japa-
nese Linguistics, Japanese Literature, Oriental History, Philosophy, Psychology, Social Psychology, Sociology
Faculty of Economics (Freshmen Enrollment: 220)
    Department of Economics
Accounting, Administrative Law, Administrative
Science, Business Administration, Business Policy,
Business Theory, Civil Law, Commercial Law, Comparative Study on Economic Systems, Constitutional
Law, Contemporary Economy, Contemporary Public Finance, Econometrics, Economic History, Economic Policy, Economics, Economic Statistics, Economic Theory, History of Economic Theories, Histo-
ry of Japanese Economy, Industrial Organizations,
International Economy, International Finance, Inter-
national Relations, Japanese Economy, Korean
Studies, Labor Law, Labor Relations, Law & Political Science, Locational Analysis, Macro Economics,
Money and Banking, Political History, Political Science, Public Finance, Social Policy, Social Security,
Statistics
Faculty of Education (Freshmen Enrollment: 320)
    Training Course for Elementary School Teachers

Training Course for Junior High School Teachers
Training Course for Kindergarten Teachers
Training Course for Teachers of Mentally Handicapped Children
Agriculture, Algebra and Geometry, Analysis and Applied Mathematics, Biology, British and American Literature, Calligraphy, Chemistry, Chinese Classics, Clothing Science, Curriculum Development, Developmental Psychology, Economics, Educational Administration, Educational Psychology, Education of Handicapped Children, Food and Nutrition, Geography, Geology, Graphic Design, History, History of Education, History of Music, History of Physical Education, Household Management, Infant Education, Infant Psychology, Instrumental Music, Japanese Language, Japanese Literature, Law, Lumber Processing, Mechanical Engineering, Metal Processing, Music Theory, Painting and Graphic Art, Pathology of Handicapped Children, Philosophy, Physical Education (Theory), Physical Education (Training), Physics, Physiology and Hygienics, Principles of Education, Psychology of Handicapped Children, Sculpture, Sociology, Teaching Methods and Materials (English, Fine Arts, Health and Physical Education, Homemaking, Infant Study, Japanese, Mathematics, Music, Social Science, Technical Education), Theory and History of Art, Vocal Music, Vocational Guidance

Faculty of Engineering (Freshmen Enrollment: 460)

Department of Architecture and Building Engineering
Architectural Equipment, Architectural Planning, Environmental Disaster Prevention Technology, Structural Engineering

Department of Civil Engineering
Bridge Engineering, Concrete Engineering, Earthquake Engineering, Highway Engineering, Hydraulic Engineering, Structural Mechanics

Department of Electrical Engineering
Electrical Fundamentals, Electric Machines, Electric Power Systems Engineering, Energy Engineering, Solid-State Electronics

Department of Electronic Engineering
Acoustic Engineering, Circuits and Systems, Electronic Circuits, Electronic Components and Materials, Fundamentals of Electronics, Radio Engineering

Department of Industrial Chemistry
Industrial Inorganic Chemistry, Industrial Organic Chemistry, Industrial Physical Chemistry, Organic Chemistry

Department of Information Engineering
Environment Information Engineering, Fundamental Information, Information Education, Information Machine, Information Processing

Department of Mechanical Engineering
Fluid Mechanics, Oil Hydraulics, Strength of Material, Thermodynamics

Department of Precision Engineering
Control Engineering, Engineering Metrology, Precision Instrument Design, Precision Machining and Materials Working

Department of Synthetic Chemistry
Industrial Catalytic Chemistry, Inorganic Synthetic Chemistry, Instrumental Analytical Chemistry, Organic Synthetic Chemistry

Faculty of Medicine (Freshmen Enrollment: 100)

Department of Medicine
Anatomy, Anesthesiology and Resuscitation Bacteriology, Biochemistry, Dental and Oral Surgery, Dermatology, Gerontology, Hygiene, Internal Medicine, Laboratory Medicine, Legal Medicine, Neuro Surgery, Obstetrics and Gynecology, Ophthalmology, Orthopaedics, Otorhinolaryngology, Parasitology, Pathology, Pediatrics, Pharmacology, Physiology, Psychiatry, Public Health, Radiology, Surgery, Urology

Faculty of Science (Freshmen Enrollment: 190)

Department of Biology
Altitudinal Biology, Developmental Biology, Ecology, Physiology

Department of Chemistry
Analytical Chemisty, Inorganic Chemisty, Organic Chemisty, Physical Chemisty

Department of Geology
Geochemistry, Geotectonics, Quaternarygeology, Stratigraphy

Department of Mathematics
Algebra, Analysis, Functional Analysis, Geometry, Topology

Department of Physics
Electronic Physics, Elementary Particle Physics, Solid State Physics, Statistical Physics

Faculty of Textile Science and Technology (Freshmen Enrollment: 275)

Department of Applied Biology
Applied Botany, Applied Ecology, Biological Production, Functional Physiology of Silkworm, Genetic Engineering, Silkworm Genetics and Pathology

Department of Fine Materials Engineering
Composite Materials Science, Fine Chemical Engineering, Interface Control Science, Mathematical Physics, Ultrafine Materials Science

Department of Functional Machinery and Mechanics
Applied Textile Mechanics, Electronic-Mechanical Engineering, Mathematical Engineering, Mechanical and Electronic Materials, Textile Machinery and Mechanics, Thermo-and Hydro-Dynamics

Department of Functional Polymer Science
Applied Polymer Chemistry, Biopolymers, Chemistry of Natural Resources, Functional Polymer Chemistry

Department of Materials Creation Chemistry
Inorganic Materials Chemistry, Materials Modification Chemistry, Molecular Designing, Structure Control of Materials, Synthetic Materials Chemistry

Department of Textile System Engineering
Fiber Materials, Information Systems and Management, System Design, Textile Manufacturing, Textile Processing and Design, Textile System Instrumenta-

tion Technology, Textile System Management

Foreign Student Admission
   Qualifications for Applicants
      Standard Qualifications Requirement
   Examination at the University
The Entrance Examination for foreign students varies with each Faculty.
   Documents to be Submitted When Applying
      Standard Documents Requirement
      List of the entrance requirements and application forms are available from the Admissions Office of each Faculty. All applicants are required to submit the specified application documents to the Admissions Office. Submission deadlines vary with each Faculty. For further information apply to the Admissions Office.

   Qualifications for Transfer Students
      Qualifications for transfer students vary with each Faculty. Applicants are required to contact the Admission Head in the Student Office for details.
   Documents to be Submitted When Applying
      Standard Documents Requirement

ONE-YEAR GRADUATE PROGRAMS

One-Year Advanced Course of Education (Enrollment: 5)
Education

GRADUATE PROGRAMS

Division of Agriculture (First Year Enrollment : Master's 50)
   Departments
Agricultural Chemistry, Agronomy and Horticultural Science, Animal Science, Forest Engineering, Forestry
Division of Arts (First Year Enrollment : Master's 10)
   Departments
Language and Literature, Regions and Cultures
Division of Engineering (First Year Enrollment : Master's 78)
   Departments
Architecture and Building Engineering, Civil Engineering, Electrical Engineering, Electronic Engineering, Industrial Chemistry, Information Engineering, Mechanical Engineering, Precision Engineering, Synthetic Chemistry
Division of Medicine (First Year Enrollment : Doctor's 54)
   Departments
Internal Medicine, Pathology, Physiology, Social Medicine, Surgery
Division of Science (First Year Enrollment : Master's 40)
   Departments
Biology, Chemistry, Geology, Mathematics, Physics
Division of Textile Science and Technology (First Year Enrollment : Master's 50)
   Departments
Functional Polymer Science. , Sericulture and Biological Production, Textile Chemical Engineering, Textile Engineering, Textile Industrial Chemistry, Textile Machinery and Mechanics

Foreign Student Admission
   Qualifications for Applicants
Master's Program
      Standard Qualifications Requirement
   Examination at the University
Master's Program
      The type of Entrance Examination varies according to the specific Graduate School.
   Documents to be Submitted When Applying
      Standard Documents Requirement
      The list of entrance requirements and application forms are available from the Graduate Admission Office of each Graduate School.
      All applicants are required to submit the specified application documents to the Admissions office.
      Submission deadlines vary according to each specific Graduate School. For further information apply to the Graduate Admissions Office.

*
Research Institutes and Centers
Health Administration Center, High Polymer Research Institute, Institute for Highland and Cool Zone Agriculture, Institute of Adaptation Medicine, University Farms, University Forests, University Hospital
Special Programs for Foreign Students
   Kyoyo-bu gives Japanese I, Japanese II and Japanese Studies. These courses are held once per week, two hours per class, for one academic year, and they are credit-transferable subjects.
   Japanese I is designed to foster reading and writing abilities.
   Japanese II is designed to train listening and presentation abilities. Oral presentation training includes from 2-to 15-minute periods of speaking Japanese.
   Japanese Studies: Faculty in the fields of humanities, social and natural sciences, and foreign languages participate in the course. Topics for 1989 academic year were the modernization of Japan, the medical treatment system, resources and energy, agriculture, literature, politics, economy, geography, social structure and others.
For Further Information
   Undergraduate and Graduate Admission
Head, Admission Division, Student Office, Shinshu University, 3-1-1 Asahi, Matsumoto-shi, Nagano 390
☎ 0263–35–4600 ext. 2274.

Shizuoka University
(Shizuoka Daigaku)

836 Ohya, Shizuoka-shi, Shizuoka 422
☎ 0542-37-1111

Faculty
  Profs. 277   Assoc. Profs. 239
  Assist. Profs. Full–time 26; Part–time 277
  Res. Assocs. 89
Number of Students
  Undergrad. 7, 238   Grad. 494
Library 788, 045 volumes

Outline and Characteristics of the University

Shizuoka University was founded in 1949 by the Japanese Government, consisting of three faculties: Faculties of Humanities and Science, Education, and Engineering. These were developed from five colleges under the old educational system. In 1951, the Faculty of Agriculture was added. In 1965, the Faculty of Liberal Arts was established to offer integrated general education to all students. Also, the faculties were modified and enlarged in number to comprise Humanities and Social Sciences, Education, Science, Engineering, Agriculture. The Research Institute of Electronics was also established. In 1964 the Graduate School of Engineering was opened offering a Master's Program. Since then Graduate Schools for Master's Programs were opened as follows: Agriculture in 1970 and Education in 1981. In addition, the Graduate School of Electronic Science and Technology was opened to offer a Doctor's Program in 1976. The University embraces a University Library, Health Service Center, University Farm and Forests, several research laboratories, attached schools of the Faculty of Education, and two Junior Colleges offering a three-year evening course in the departments of Law and Economics, and Engineering.

Shizuoka University has established a high reputation in education and research and continues to grow. The Campuses are located in Shizuoka and Hamamatsu, both situated along the Pacific coast in the center of the main island of Japan. The mild climate provides an ideal environment for study. Students organize the Student Autonomy Association of Shizuoka University which serves as the student spokesman in University affairs. The cultural activities group includes more than 40 circles, among which the music circles are very active. In sports activities, there are more than 40 groups, which are also traditionally active.

UNDERGRADUATE PROGRAMS

Faculty of Agriculture (Freshmen Enrollment: 165)
  Department of Agricultural Chemistry
Agricultural Geology, Applied Microbiology, Biological Chemistry, Food and Nutrition, Food Technology, Soil Science and Plant Nutrition
  Department of Agricultural Science
Agricultural Economics, Animal Production, Applied Entomology, Crop Science and Plant Breeding, Plant Pathology, Reproductive Physiology
  Department of Forest Products Science
Wood Adhesion, Wood Chemistry, Wood Industrial Chemistry, Wood Processing, Wood Technology
  Department of Forestry
Forest Conservation, Forest Engineering, Forest Management and Forest Policy, Silviculture
  Department of Horticultural Science
Citriculture, Plant Propagation, Postharvest Science, Protected Crop Cultivation

Faculty of Education (Freshmen Enrollment: 510)
  Elementary School Teacher Training Course
  Handicapped Children's School Teacher Training Course
  Junior High School Teacher Training Course
  Kindergarten Teacher Training Course
Aesthetics and Art History, Agriculture, Algebra and Geometry, Analytics and Applied Mathematics, Athletics, Biology, Calligraphy, Carving and Sculpture, Chemistry, Chinese Literature, Composition, Developmental Psychology, Economics, Electricity, English and American Literature, English Linguistics, Geography, Geology, History, History of Education, Home Economics, Instrumental Music, Japanese Language, Japanese Literature, Kinematics, Law, Mechanical Engineering, Metallurgical Technology, Painting, Pedagogical Psychology, Pedagogy, Philosophy and Ethics, Physics, School Hygienics, School Management, Science of Clothing, Science of Food, Social Education, Teaching for Handicapped Children, Teaching for Preschool Chidren, Teaching of English, Teaching of Fine Arts, Teaching of Health and Physical Education, Teaching of Home Economics, Teaching of Japanese Language, Teaching of Mathematics, Teaching of Music, Teaching of Science, Teaching of Social Studies, Teaching of Technical Education, Theory and History of Music, Visual Composition, Vocal Music, Wood Processing

Faculty of Engineering (Freshmen Enrollment: 501)
  Department of Applied Chemistry (Industrial Section)
Industrial Polymer Chemistry, Inorganic Industrial Chemistry, Organic Industrial Chemistry, Reaction of Organic Chemistry, Theoretical Inorganic Chemistry
  Department of Applied Chemistry (Synthetic Section)
Industrial Physical Chemistry, Organic Chemistry, Synthetic Inorganic Chemistry, Synthetic Organic Chemistry
  Department of Chemical Engineering
Bioengineering, Fluid Dynamics and Power Technology, Heat and Mass Transfer, Process Design and Development, Reaction Engineering

Department of Computer Science
Computer Systems, Information Mathematics, Information Processing, Information Systems
Department of Electrical Engineering
Applied Electrical Engineering, Fundamental Electrical Engineering
Department of Electronic Engineering
Digital Signal Processing, Electronic Applications, Electronic Circuits, Electronic Devices, Electron Physics, Opto-electronics
Department of Energy and Mechanical Engineering
Control Engineering, Heat and Mass Transfer, Hydraulic Engineering, Thermal Engineering
Department of Mechanical Engineering
Dynamics of Machine and Machine Design, Engineering Analysis, Engineering Materials, Strength of Materials
Department of Opto-Electronic and Mechanical Engineering
Application of Opto-Electronic and Mechanical Engineering, Fundamental Theory of Opto-Electronic and Mechanical Engineering
Department of Precision Engineering
Material Processing, Precision Machining and Machine Elements, Precision Measurements
Faculty of Humanities and Social Sciences(Freshmen Enrollment: 432)
Department of Economics
Accounting and Management Accounting, Business Economics and Management, Economic Policy, Economic Theory, History of Economics and Industries, Public Finance, Social Policy
Department of Humanities
History (Asian, Japanese, Occidental), Literature and Linguistics (American, British, Chinese, Comparative Literature, French, German, Japanese)
Department of Law
Civil Law, Legal and Political Science, Public Law, Social Law
Department of Sociology
Anthropology and Archaeology, Social Thought, Sociology
Faculty of Science (Freshmen Enrollment: 205)
Department of Biology
Cell Biology, Morphology, Physiological Chemistry, Physiology
Department of Chemistry
Biochemistry, Inorganic and Analytical Chemistry, Kinetic Physical Chemistry, Organic Chemistry, Structural Chemistry and Physical Chemistry
Department of Geosciences
Chemical Geoscience, Evolutionary Geoscience, Marine Geoscience, Physical Geoscience
Department of Mathematics
Analysis and Topology, Geometry and Algebra, Mathematical Logic and Applied Mathematics, Probability Theory and Statistics
Department of Physics
High Energy Physics including Nuclear Physics and Physics on Elementary Particles, Mathematical Physics, Physics on Polymers including Biophysics, Plasma Physics, Quantum Electronics, Solid State Physics

Foreign Student Admission
Qualifications for Applicants
Standard Qualifications Requirement
Examination at the University
For most Faculties, applicants must take the Japanese Language Proficiency Test and General Examination for Foreign Students. For some Faculties applicants are advised to take the examination mentioned above. Applicants must also take each Faculty's specific entrance examination consisting of written and oral examinations and an interview.
Documents to be Submitted When Applying
Standard Documents Requirement

ONE-YEAR GRADUATE PROGRAMS

One-Year Graduate Course of Humanities and Social Sciences (Enrollment   20)
Humanities (History, Literature and Linguistics, Sociology), Law and Economics (Economics and Accounting, Law, Political Science)

GRADUATE PROGRAMS

Graduate School of Agriculture (First Year Enrollment : Master's 50)
Divisions
Agricultural Chemistry, Agricultural Science, Forest Products, Forestry, Horticultural Science
Graduate School of Education (First Year Enrollment : Master's 55)
Divisions
English Language Education, Fine Arts Education, Health and Physical Education, Home Economics Education, Japanese Language Education, Mathematics Education, Music Education, School Education, Science Education, Social Studies Education, Technical Arts and Agriculture Education
Graduate School of Electronic Science and Technology (First Year Enrollment : Doctor's 21)
Divisions
Electronic Engineering, Electronic Material Science
Graduate School of Engineering (First Year Enrollment : Master's 99)
Divisions
Applied Chemistry (Industrial Section), Applied Chemistry (Synthetic Section), Chemical Engineering, Computer Science, Electrical Engineering, Electronic Engineering, Energy and Mechanical Engineering, Opto-Electronic and Mechanical Engineering, Precision Engineering
Graduate School of Science (First Year Enrollment : Master's 48)
Divisions
Biology, Chemistry, Geoscience, Mathematics, Phys-

ics

Foreign Student Admission
  Qualifications for Applicants
Master's Program
  Standard Qualifications Requirement
Doctor's Program
  Standard Qualifications Requirement
  Documents to be Submitted When Applying
  Standard Documents Requirement
  Applicants for the Doctor's program are required to submit a copy of Master's thesis or 800 word summary of their current research work along with reprints of papers, if any.

Research Institutes and Centers
Arid Land Agricultural Research Laboratory, Laboratory of Marine Biochemical Science, Radiochemistry Research Institute, Research Institute of Electronics, University Farm, University Forests
Facilities/Services for Foreign Students
International House
Shared facilities: Lobby, Conference Room, Lounge.
Accommodation: 34 rooms (single 30, couple 2, family 2)
For Further Information
  Undergraduate and Graduate Admission
Foreign Student Section, Student Affairs Bureau, Shizuoka University, 836 Ohya, Shizuoka-shi, Shizuoka 422 ☎ 0542-37-1111
Graduate School of Electronic Science and Technology, 3-5-1 Johoku, Hamamatsu-shi, Shizuoka 432 ☎ 0534-71-1171

Tohoku University
(Tohoku Daigaku)

2-1-1 Katahira, Sendai-shi, Miyagi 980
☎ 022-227-6200

Faculty
  Profs. 545   Assoc. Profs. 480
  Assist. Profs. Full-time 137; Part-time 1, 393
  Res. Assocs. 1, 113
Number of Students
  Undergrad. 10, 870   Grad. 2, 601
Library 2, 669, 091 volumes

Outline and Characteristics of the University
  Tohoku University is one of the largest and oldest universities in Japan, made up of ten faculties, ten graduate schools, two colleges, seven research institutes, five university libraries, four university hospitals, and other facilities for research and education.
  The faculties and graduate schools are those of Arts and Letters, Education, Law, Economics, Science, Medicine, Dentistry, Pharmacy, Engineering, and Agriculture. The University also operates the

following research institutes: Institute for Materials Research, Research Institute of Mineral Dressing and Metallurgy, Research Institute for Tuberculosis and Cancer, Research Institute for Science Measurements, Institute of High Speed Mechanics, Research Institute of Electrical Communication, and Chemical Research Institute of Non-Aqueous Solutions.
  The University staff is estimated to number 5, 200 and the number of studens totals 13, 000. Approximately 470 foreign students representing 39 countries are also enrolled, and there are more than 100 foreign researchers visting the University.
  The University was founded as Tohoku Imperial University in 1907, comprising the College of Science and the College of Agriculture and has been expanded gradually over 80 years.
  After World War II, the University was reorganized under the new academic system and took the present name of Tohoku University.
  Since its foundation, the University has been very progressive and liberal, with an "open-door" attitude to education. It was the first Japanese university to admit women students, and conferred degrees on foreign graduates as long ago as 1911.
  The University is also known for its "Research First" principle, believing that where there is good research, there is also good education.
  The main campuses of the University, covering about 240 hectares, are situated in Sendai City, which is about 300 kilometers north of Tokyo. With a population of about 800, 000, Sendai is one of Japan's most important cities. Called "the city of trees, " blessed by cultural as well as natural endowments, Sendai is an ideal surrounding for those devoted to study and research.

UNDERGRADUATE PROGRAMS

Faculty of Agriculture (Freshmen Enrollment: 180)
  Department of Agricultural Chemistry
Applied Biochemistry, Applied Microbiology, Biochemistry, Pesticide Chemistry, Plant Nutrition
  Department of Agronomy
Crop Science, Farm Management, Horticulture, Plant Breeding, Plant Pathology, Soil Science
  Department of Animal Science
Animal Breeding, Animal Morphology, Animal Nutrition, Animal Pathology, Animal Physiology, Animal Reproduction, Chemistry of Livestock Products
  Department of Fishery Science
Aquacultural Biology, Fisheries Biology, Fisheries Oceanography, Fish Genetics and Breeding, Marine Product Technology
  Department of Food Chemistry
Food Analysis, Food Hygiene, Food Reproduction, Food Science, Nutrition Chemistry
Faculty of Arts and Letters (Freshmen Enrollment: 210)
  Department of History
Archaeology, European History, History of Asian

and Japanese Fine Arts, History of Japanese Thought, Japanese History, Oriental History
Department of Japanese
Japanese Linguistics, Linguistics
Department of Literature
Chinese Literature, English Linguistics, English Literature, French Literature, German Literature, Japanese Literature
Department of Philosophy
Aesthetics and the History of Fine Arts, Chinese Philosophy, Contemporary Philosophy, Ethics, History of European Philosophy, History of Indian Buddhism, Indian Philosophy, Science and History of Religion
Department of Sociology
Applied Sociology, Behavioral Science, Psychology, Social Psychology, Theoretical Sociology
Faculty of Dentistry (Freshmen Enrollment: 60)
Department of Dentistry
Dental Material Science, Endodontics and Periodontics, Operative Dentistry, Oral Anatomy, Oral Biochemistry, Oral Diagnosis and Dental Radiology, Oral Microbiology, Oral Pathology, Oral Physiology, Oral Surgery, Orthodontics, Pedodontics, Pharmacology, Preventive Dentistry, Prosthetic Dentistry
Faculty of Economics (Freshmen Enrollment: 270)
Department of Business Management
Accounting, Business Administration, Business Policy, Management Sciences
Department of Economics
Contemporary Economy, Economic History, Economic Policy, Economic Statistics, Economic Theory
Faculty of Education (Freshmen Enrollment: 80)
Department of Educational Psychology
Mental Retardation Research, Psychology of Childhood and Adolescence, Psychology of Personality and Learning, Speech Pathology and Audiology, Visual Defectology
Department of Educational Science
Adult Education, Educational Administration, History of Education, Philosophy of Education, School Administration, School Curriculum and Teaching Method, Sociology of Education
Faculty of Engineering (Freshmen Enrollment: 915)
Department of Applied Physics
Applied Mathematical Physics, Low Temperature Physics, Magnetism and Magnetic Materials, Picosecond Spectroscopy, Piezoelectricity and Ferroelectrics, Solid State Physics (Theoretical)
Department of Architecture
Architectural History and Design, Architectural Planning, Building Environment and Equipment, Building Materials Science, Disaster Proof Engineering, Structural Engineering, Structural Mechanics, Urban Planning
Department of Biochemistry and Engineering
Bio-Process Engineering, Heterogeneous Catalysis, Molecular Thermodynamics, Organic and Bioorganic Synthesis, Process System Engineering, Reaction Engineering, Transport Phenomena

Department of Civil Engineering
Applied Hydraulics and Hydrodynamics, Bridge Engineering and Structures, Concrete Engineering, Fluvial and Coastal Engineering, Infrastructure Planning, Mechanics of Materials, Pollution Control Engineering, Road Engineering, Soil Engineering, Structural Engineering, Water Works Engineering
Department of Electrical Communications
Antennas and Optical Wave Transmission, Applied Radio Physics, Electrical Communication Systems, Electroacoustics, Instrumentation Electronics, Network Theory
Department of Electrical Engineering
Acoustic Measurements and Imaging, Applied Electrical Engineering, Control Systems Theory, Electric Power Engineering, Electromagnetics, Gravitational Waves and Radio Communication, High Voltage Engineering
Department of Electronic Engineering
Electron Devices, Electronic Circuits, Electronic Control Systems, Plasma Physics and Gaseous Electronics, Solid State Electronics, Solid State Physics
Department of Engineering Science
Chemistry Division
Basic Physical Chemistry, Inorganic and Physical Chemistry, Organic Chemistry
Physics Division
Applied Mathematics, Applied Mechanics, Electrical Engineering Science, Engineering Mechanics, Mathematics, Mechanical Engineering Science
Department of Information Engineering
Biological Information Systems, Computer Architecture and Systems, Foundation of Information Science, Information Systems Engineering, Information Transmission Systems, Knowledge Engineering, Linguistic Information Processing
Department of Materials Processing
Deformation Mechanics, Foundry Engineering, Materials Evaluation, Materials Systems, Powder Processing, Welding Engineering
Department of Materials Science
Applied Solid Physics, Electronics Materials, Microstructure Science, Solid Surface Science, Special Functional Materials, Structural Materials
Department of Mechanical Engineering
Combustion Engineering, Dynamics of Machines and Machine Design, Fluid Mechanics, Heat and Thermodynamics, Hydraulics Machinery, Instrument and Control Engineering, Materials and Manufacturing Engineering, Solid Mechanics, Supercomputer Architecture
Department of Mechanical Engineering II
Basic Thermodynamics and Heat Transfer, Elasticity and Solid Mechanics, Fluid Mechanics and Flow, Materials Science and Engineering, Plasticity and Plastic Working Robotics and Control Engineering, Science and Technology of Materials Working, Strength and Fracture of Materials, Theory of Machine and Mechanical Design Analysis
Department of Metallurgy

Applied Metallurgical Chemistry, Chemical Metallurgy, Extractive Metallurgy, Ferrous Process Metallurgy, Metallurgical Electrochemistry, Metallurgical Engineering

Department of Mining and Mineral Engineering
Applied Geology and Applied Mineralogy, Exploitation Machinery, Exploitation Plant Engineering, Mineral Processing Engineering, Mining and Excavation Engineering, Mining and Mineral Instrumentation Engineering, Resources Systems Engineering

Department of Molecular Chemistry and Engineering
Advanced Ceramic Materials, Analytical Chemistry, Applied Chemistry of Dimensionally Functional Materials, Biophysical Chemistry. Electrochemical Science and Technology, Fluid Materials Design, Industrial Inorganic Chemistry, Macromolecular Chemistry, Organic Resources Chemistry

Department of Nuclear Engineering
Nuclear Chemical Engineering, Nuclear Fuel Engineering, Nuclear Instruments and Measurements, Nuclear Materials Engineering, Plasma Physics, Reactor Engineering, Reactor Physics

Department of Precision Engineering
Automatic Control, Machine Elements, Measurement and Instrumentation, Plastic Forming, Precision Machinery, Precision Machining, Precision Measurement, Production Engineering, Workability and Strength of Materials

Faculty of Law (Freshmen Enrollment: 240)
Department of Law
Administrative Law, Anglo-American Law, Bankruptcy Law and Execution Law, Civil Law, Civil Procedure, Commercial Law, Comparative Constitutional Law, Comparative Politics, Constitutional Law, Criminal Law, Criminal Procedure, Criminology, European Legal History, History of Political Theory, International Law, International Politics, Japanese Legal History, Labor Law and Social Legislation, Legal Philosophy, Political Theory, Private International Law

Faculty of Medicine (Freshmen Enrollment: 120)
Department of Medicine
Anatomy, Anesthesiology, Applied Physiology, Bacteriology, Biochemistry, Clinical and Laboratory Medicine, Dermatology, Environmental Health, Forensic Medicine, Hospital and Medical Care Administration, Internal Medicine, Obstetrics and Gynecology, Ophthalmology, Orthopedic Surgery, Otorhinolaryngology, Pathology, Pediatrics, Pharmacology, Physiology, Psychiatry, Public Health, Radiation Research, Radiology, Surgery, Thoracic and Cardiovascular Surgery, Urology

Faculty of Pharmacy (Freshmen Enrollment: 80)
Department of Pharmaceutical Science
Analytical Chemistry, Hygienic Chemistry, Organic Chemistry, Pharmaceutical Chemistry, Pharmaceutics, Pharmacognosy, Pharmacology

Department of Pharmaceutical Technology
Biochemistry, Chemical Engineering, Heterocyclic Chemistry, Natural Products Chemistry, Physical Chemistry, Synthetic Organic Chemistry

Faculty of Science (Freshmen Enrollment: 314)
Department of Astronomy
Astrophysics, Theoretical Astronomy
Department of Biology
Cell and Plant Physiology, Developmental Biology and Genetics, Environmental Biology and Animal Ecology, Physiological Chemistry, Plant Ecology, Plant Taxonomy and Morphology
Department of Chemistry
Analytical Chemistry, Inorganic Chemistry, Organic Chemistry, Quantum Chemistry, Radiation Chemistry, Theoretical Chemistry
Department of Chemistry II
Analytical Organic Chemistry, Bio-organic Chemistry, Coordination Chemistry, Organic Reactions, Physical Chemistry, Synthetic Organic Chemistry
Department of Geography
Human Geography, Physical Geography
Department of Geology and Paleontology
Geology, Historical Geology, Paleontology
Department of Geophysics
Geomagnetism and Geoelectricity, Meteorology, Physical Oceanography, Seismology
Department of Mathematics
Algebra, Complex Analysis, Differential Equations, Functional Analysis, Geometry, Group Theory, Mathematical Statistics, Numerical Analysis, Real Analysis
Department of Mineralogy, Petrology and Economic Geology
Mineralogy, Petrology, Science of Metallic Deposits, Science of Petroleum Deposits
Department of Physics I
Applied Nuclear Physics, High Energy Physics, Nuclear Physics, Nuclear Structure Theory, Optical Properties of Solids, Physics of Iron and Steel, Solid State Physics, Theoretical High Energy Physics, Theory of Elementary Particles, X-ray, VUV Spectroscopy and Photo-electron Spectroscopy
Department of Physics II
Diffraction Physics, Low Temperature Physics, Magnetism and Solid State Physics, Neutron Scattering and Solid State Physics, Optical Properties of Solids and Solid State Spectroscopy, Semiconductor Physics, Statistical Physics and Solid State Physics, Theoretical Solid State Physics

Foreign Student Admission
Qualifications for Applicants
  Standard Qualifications Requirement
1. Applicants can not be of Japanese nationality.
2. The Applicants who have obtained the legal baccalaureate of the International Baccalaureate Office authenticated by the Swiss Code and are 18 years of age or older may also apply.
3. Applicants must take the Japanese Language Proficiency Test and the General Examination

for Foreign Students.

Examination at the University

Selection of students is made by a comprehensive judgement based on the results of the Japanese Language Proficiency Test, the General Examination for Foreign Students and special examinations given by the University in addition to the documents submitted.

Documents to be Submitted When Applying

Standard Documents Requirement

Application forms are available at the Admissions Office from August 1. All applicants are required to submit the specified application documents to the Admissions Office.

Qualifications for Transfer Students

In general, a foreign student cannot transfer directly, although completion of a 14-year course of formal education in his home country technically qualifies him to do so.

The Faculty of Economics and the Faculty of Engineering, however, have admitted a small number of foreign applicants through paper screening and other procedures.

Examination for Transfer Students

At the present, Faculty of Economics and Faculty of Engineering have admitted a small number of foreign applicants through paper screening, interviews and written examinations.

The Faculty of Economics accepts the applications for transfer students in November of every year and selects them using the same examination given on the same date as for Japanese students.

The Faculty of Engineering accepts applications and selects transfer students around October or November.

Documents to be Submitted When Applying

Standard Documents Requirement

For more detailed information, write directly to the office of the faculty concerned, describing the applicant's scholastic and professional history.

GRADUATE PROGRAMS

Graduate School of Agriculture (First Year Enrollment : Master's 60, Doctor's 32)

Divisions

Agricultural Chemistry, Agronomy, Animal Science, Fishery Science, Food Chemistry

Graduate School of Arts and Letters (First Year Enrollment : Master's 60, Doctor's 30)

Divisions

Aesthetics and the History of Fine Arts, Chinese Studies, English Literature/English Linguistics and Linguistics, European History, French Literature and Linguistics, German Literature and Linguistics, Indian Studies and the History of Buddhism, Japanese History, Japanese Literature/Linguistics and the History of Japanese Thought, Oriental History, Philosophy, Practical Philosophy, Psychology, Sociology

Graduate School of Dentistry (First Year Enrollment : Doctor's 34)

Divisions

Basic Dental Science, Clinical Dental Science

Graduate School of Economics (First Year Enrollment : Master's 42, Doctor's 21)

Divisions

Business Management, Economics

Graduate School of Education (First Year Enrollment : Master's 26, Doctor's 13)

Divisions

Educational Psychology, Pedagogy

Graduate School of Engineering (First Year Enrollment : Master's 329, Doctor's 192)

Divisions

Applied Chemistry, Applied Physics, Architecture and Building Engineering, Chemical Engineering, Civil Engineering, Electrical and Communication Engineering, Electronic Engineering, Information Engineering, Materials Chemistry, Materials Processing, Materials Science, Mechanical Engineering, Metallurgy, Mining and Mineral Engineering, Nuclear Engineering, Precision Engineering

Graduate School of Law (First Year Enrollment : Master's 50, Doctor's 23)

Divisions

Foundations of Law, Political Science, Private Law, Public Law

Graduate School of Medicine (First Year Enrollment : Doctor's 92)

Divisions

Internal Medicine, Medical Sciences, Pathology, Physiological Science, Social Medicine, Surgery

Graduate School of Pharmacy (First Year Enrollment : Master's 26, Doctor's 13)

Divisions

Pharmaceutical Science, Pharmaceutical Technology

Graduate School of Science (First Year Enrollment : Master's 155, Doctor's 84)

Divisions

Astronomy, Biology, Chemistry, Earth Science, Geophysics, Mathematics, Nuclear Physics, Physics

Foreign Student Admission

Qualifications for Applicants

Master's Program

Standard Qualifications Requirement

Doctor's Program

Standard Qualifications Requirement

Graduate Schools of Medicine and Dentistry: A student who has completed 18 years of formal education in a foreign country (the final course of which must have been in medicine or dentistry), or a student who has been recognized as being equal or superior in scholastic attainment to graduates from faculties of medicine or dentistry in Japan, may apply for this course.

Examination at the University

Master's Program

The date for application differs with each Graduate School. Some Graduate Schools accept applications in July or August and give entrance examinations in September. Other Graduate Schools, including those that invite students to fill vacancies, accept applications in January or February and give examinations in February or March. It is recommended that the applicant write to the office of the Graduate School concerned for further information well ahead of the time for application. In general, an applicant must take examinations on the subjects related to his major and in two foreign languages and have a personal interview. However, foreign students who the Graduate School Council considers constrained by unavoidable circumstances may be admitted not through the general selection procedure described above, but through special screening.

N.B. : In most cases, a foreign graduate of a foreign university who wishes to be admitted as a regular graduate student first registers as a research student, and later has his status changed to that of a regular graduate student, when he has proved himself to have the necessary research ability and has successfully passed specified screening.

Doctor's Program
Same as Master' program.
Documents to be Submitted When Applying
Standard Documents Requirement

*

Research Institutes and Centers
Chemical Research Institute of Non-Aqueous Solutions, Computer Center, Cryogenics Center, Cyclotron and Radioisotope Center, Education Center for Information Processing, Gene Research Center, Institute for High Speed Mechanics, Institute for Materials Research, Institute of Genetic Ecology, Research Center for Applied Information Science, Research Institute for Scientific Measurements, Research Institute for Tuberculosis and Cancer, Research Institute of Electrical Communication, Research Institute of Mineral Dressing and Metallurgy

Facilities/Services for Foreign Students
International House: Tohoku University's International House at Sanjo-machi was established in November 1983, as part of the University's international exchange program. It provides housing for foreign students and at the same time acts as a forum for intercultural communication in the region. The housing accommodation is as follows: Type A (48m^2, 11 apts.), Type B (46m^2, 22 apts.), Type C (18m^2, 84 apts.), Total: 117 apts.

Special Programs for Foreign Students
The University has designed a Japanese language program for foreign undergraduate students to reduce their study load and help them perfect their Japanese language skills. Some extracurricular courses in the Japanese language are available for graduate and research students from abroad.

Foreign students are also offered a special course which will help them to adapt to a new environment as well as to improve their Japanese language and basic academic skills. Supplementary lessons are given in three subjects: Japanese language, mathematics, and an orientation program.

For Further Information
Undergraduate and Graduate Admission
International Exchange Section, Division of General Affairs,
Tohoku University, 2-1-1 Katahira, Sendai-shi, Miyagi 980 ☎ 022-227-6200 ext. 2236

Tokyo Gakugei University
(Tokyo Gakugei Daigaku)
4-1-1 Nukuikita-machi, Koganei-shi, Tokyo 184
☎ 0423-25-2111

Faculty
    Profs. 143   Assoc. Profs. 155
    Assist. Profs. Full-time 32; Part-time 246
    Res. Assocs. 32
Number of Students
    Undergrad. 5, 114   Grad. 421
Library 733, 872 volumes

Outline and Characteristics of the University
Tokyo Gakugei University is a national university made up of a Faculty of Education, a Graduate School, Research Institutes, a Library, and other facilities. The University was established in May, 1949 absorbing all four normal schools that then existed in Tokyo area.

These four normal schools which preceeded the University had their own outstanding history and tradition. The oldest of them was founded in 1873 and the newest in 1937. Through their graduates, they contributed to the field of compulsory education not only in Tokyo area but throughout Japan. After the establishment of the University, the facilities of former normal schools were used as branch campuses until April, 1964, when these were closed and all branches were united on the present campus in Musashi-Koganei.

The campus is about a forty minute train ride from the heart of Tokyo, and transportation is very convenient. The campus has a vast area of 330, 000 square meters and is covered with greenery providing a pleasant environment for quiet studies. In spring, hundreds of cherry trees come into full bloom and provide a beautiful sight especially for the freshmen.

The University undertakes research in wide areas of learning and education, covering the humanities and the natural sciences, physical education and the arts. It provides students with both theory and practice in their specialized fields. One of the most important functions of the University is to give the students the necessary academic background and training to become competent teachers equipped with highly-specialized knowledge and ability. The founding of the Graduate School which confers the master's degree in education, in 1966 reflects the ever-increasing importance and responsibilities of the University. In 1988, the University added four new courses in the liberal arts in order to meet the demands of our information-oriented society in which international exchange and lifelong learning have become even more important.

UNDERGRADUATE PROGRAMS

Faculty of Education (Freshmen Enrollment: 1, 215)
Teacher Training Course
  Course for Teachers of Elementary School
Fine Art, Health and Physical Education, Home Economics, Japanese, Mathematics, Music, School Education, Science, Social Studies
  Course for Teachers of School for the Handicapped
Education for Deaf Children, Education for Mentally Handicapped Children, Education for Speech Handicapped Children
  Course for Teachers of Junior High School
Engineering, English, Fine Art, Health and Physical Education, Home Economics, Japanese, Mathematics, Music, Science, Social Studies, Vocational Education (At present, admission of freshman has been suspended.)
  Course for Teachers of Kindergarten
Kindergarten Education
  Courses for Liberal Arts
Art Course
Calligraphy, Fine Arts, Music
Educational and Environmantal Sciences Course
Cultural Asset Sciences, Educational Informatics, Environmental Sciences
Human Sciences Course
Counseling & Clinical Psychology, Integrated Social System, Lifelong Education, Lifelong Sports
International Education & Cultures Course
Asian Studies, European and American Studies, International Education, Japan Studies
  Course for Teachers of Special Subjects in Senior High School
Calligraphy, Fine Art, Health and Physical Education, Mathematics, Music, Science

Foreign Student Admission
  Qualifications for Applicants
  Standard Qualifications Requirement
  Applicants must:
  1.   have completed or will have completed 12 years of school education in a foreign country between April 1987 and March 31, 1989, or
  2.   have been granted the International Baccalaureate Diploma by the International Baccalaureate Office in 1987 or 1988 under the provisions of the Swiss Civil Code and be 18

years of age or older.
  Examination at the University
  The special screening exempting the Joint First-stage Achievement Test is given to foreign applicants. The screenrng consists of a short essay, and a Japanese proficiency test through a interview. Depending on circumstances, major subject or a performance test may be added
  Documents will be accepted in the middle of October.
  Documents to be Submitted When Applying
  Standard Documents Requirement
  A copy of the International Baccalaureate Diploma and an official transcript of the final test (or an official transcript of tests officially administered in countries other than Japan) must be submmited, if applicable.

ONE-YEAR GRADUATE PROGRAMS

Post Graduate Study Course for Special Education (Enrollment: 30)
Education for Mentally Handicapped Children

Foreign Student Admission
  Qualifications for Applicants
  Standard Qualifications Requirement
  The applicant must hold a Japanese teacher's licence by the time of entrance. Special screening for foreign students will not be given.
  Examination at the University
  Special screening for Foreign students will not be given.
  Documents to be Submitted when Applying
  Standard Documents Requirements
  Documents will be accepted in early February.
  Certrficate of Teacher's licence obtained in Japan

GRADUATE PROGRAMS

Graduate School of Education (First Year Enrollment : Master's 207)
  Divisions
Art Education (Calligraphy included), Education of Handicapped Children, Engineering Education, English Education, Health and Physical Education, Home Economics Education, Japanese Language Education, Mathematics Education, Music Education, School Education (Kindergarten Education included), Science Education, Social Studies Education

Foreign Student Admission
  Qualifications for Applicants
  Standard Qualifications Requirement
  Examination at the University
  Foreign applicants are exempt from the test on foreign languages and teaching related subjects and will be given instead a test on their major subject and an interview.

Documents to be Submitted When Applying
Standard Documents Requirement
Documents will be accepted in mid-July.

Application forms will be available at the Admissions Office from mid-June.

*

Research Institutes and Centers
Center for Educational Technology, Center for Education of Childeren Overseas, Pata Station, Radioisotope Laboratory, Research and Guidance Center for Teaching Practice, Research Institute for Education of Exceptional Children

For Further Information
Undergraduate and Graduate Admission
Admissions Office, Tokyo Gakugei University, 4-1-1 Nukuikita-machi, Koganei-shi, Tokyo 184 ☎ 0423-25-2111 ext. 2254 Research Student Admissions

Foreign Students Section, Student Affairs Section, Tokyo Gakugei University, 4-1-1, Nukuikita-machi, Koganei-shi, Tokyo 184 ☎ 0423-25-2111 ext. 2260

Tokyo Institute of Technology
(Tokyo Kogyo Daigaku)

2-12-1 Ookayama, Meguro-ku, Tokyo 152
☎ 03-726-1111

Faculty
    Profs. 234   Assoc. Profs. 237
    Assist. Profs. Full-time 7; Part-time 291
    Res. Assocs. 399
Number of Students
    Undergrad. 4, 326   Grad. 2, 143
Library 581, 467 volumes

Outline and Characteristics of the University
The Institute, originally called Tokyo Vocational School (Tokyo Shokko-Gakko), was founded by the Japanese Government in 1881. The aim was to produce engineers who would fulfill the urgent needs of our nation at the end of the 19th century. In 1890, Tokyo Vocational School was renamed Tokyo Technical School (Tokyo Kogyo Gakko), which subsequently developed into Tokyo Higher Technical School (Tokyo Kotokogyo Gakko) in 1901. In 1923, the School was seriously damaged by the Kanto earthquake, as buildings and equipment were totally destroyed by fire. Consequently, in 1924 it moved to the present site at Ookayama in the southwest suburbs of Tokyo from its birthplace in Kuramae, Tokyo. Tokyo Higher Technical School was promoted to university status in 1929 and called Tokyo Institute of Technology (Tokyo Kogyo Daigaku). After World War II, a Graduate School of Science and Engineering, offering a two-year master's program and a doctorate degree, was established in 1953. In 1975 the Nagatsuta Campus was opened, where one Graduate School consisting of ten interdisciplinary departments, and three Research Laboratories are located. They are the Research Laboratory of Resources Utilization, Research Laboratory of Precision Machinery and Electronics and Research Laboratory of Engineering Materials. The Ookayama campus and Nagatsuta campus are connected by an up-to-date 27 km long optical fiber cable, linking a pair of TV lecture rooms, a pair of TV conference rooms and many small advisory rooms. Tokyo Institute of Technology celebrated its centennial in 1981.

The Institute at present has two Faculties, two Graduate Schools, four Research Laboratories and other affiliated facilities, and enrolls more than 6, 000 students in undergraduate and post graduate programs with about 480 full-time faculty members. The Institute enjoys a high international reputation for its academic excellence and most of the departments are ranked highly in Japan.

UNDERGRADUATE PROGRAMS

Faculty of Engineering (Freshmen Enrollment: 992)
Department of Architecture and Building Engineering
Architectural Design and Drawing, Architectural Planning and Design, Building Materials, Environmental Engineering, History of Architecture, Structural Design, Structural Mechanics, Urban and Regional Planning
Department of Bioengineering
Biochemical Engineering, Bioelectronics, Biomimetic Chemistry and Biomaterial Science, Cytoengineering, Genetic Engineering and Protein Engineering, Molecular Bioprocess
Department of Biomolecular Engineering
Biomaterial Design, Biomolecular Processes, Biosystem, Enzyme Functions, Fundamentals of Biomolecules, Molecular Design of Biological Importance
Department of Chemical Engineering
Biochemical Reaction Engineering, Catalysis, Chemical Plant Materials and Design, Chemical Reaction Engineering, Chemistry, Electrochemistry, Fluid Process Engineering, Inorganic Industrial Chemistry, Mass Transfer Operations, Materials Science, Petrochemistry, Physical Chemistry, Plasma Processing, Process Dynamics, Reaction Kinetics, Surfac, Synthetic Organic Chemistry, Thermal System Engineering, Tribology
Department of Civil Engineering
Coastal Engineering, Concrete Engineering, Conputational Mechanics, Environmental Engineering, Geotechnical Engineering, Hydraulics and Hydrology, Structural Mechanics and Engineering, Transportation Planning and Systems Analysis
Department of Computer Science
Artificial Intelligence, Computer Architectures, Image Processing, Knowledge Engineering, Pattern Recognition, Software Engineering
Department of Control Engineering
Computer Control, Control Components, Control

Theory, Industrial Measurement, Mechatronics, Robotics, Systems Engineering

Department of Electrical and Electronic Engineering

Power and Electronics Course:
Communication Theory and Systems, Electric Machine Control, Electric Power Engineering, Electromagnetic Waves and Antennas, Electron Devices, Electronic Circuits, Integrated Circuits, Network Theory, Optoelectronics, Plasma Engineering, Power Electronics, Quantum Electronics, Signal Processing, Solid State Electronics

Department of Industrial Engineering and Management

Financial Management, Industrial Engineering, Industrial Management, Management Systems. , Process Analysis and Synthesis, Production Engineering, Production Management

Department of Inorganic Materials

Cement Chemistry, Ceramic Processing, Crystal Chemistry, Electroceramics, Engineering Ceamics, Glass Science and Technology, Materials Analysis, Mineralogy and Geology, Physics and Chemistry of Ceramics, Powder Technology, Solid State Chemistry

Department of Mechanical Engineering

Control of Mechanical Systems, Dynamics of Machinery, Fluid Mechanics, Machine Design, Machine Elements, Machine Tools and Machining, Mechanics of Plastic Solids, Strength of Materials, Thermal Engineering

Department of Mechanical Engineering for Production

Elasticity, Fatigue, Impact, Lubrication Engineering, Machine Tool Engineering, Material Science and Welding, Precision Engineering, Production System, Strength of Materials, Thermal Engineering, Tribology and Medical Engineering

Department of Mechanical Engineering Science

Biomechanics and Robotics, Engineering Analysis, Fracture Mechanics and Fatigue, Materials Processing and Applied Materials Science, Mechanical Vibrations, Thermo-fluid Dynamics

Department Metallurgical Engineering

Ferrous Metallurgy, Metal Chemistry, Metal Physics, Physical and Mechanical Metallurgy of Ferrous Materials, Physical and Mechanical Metallurgy of Nonferrous Materials

Department of Organic and Polymeric Materials.

Design of Polymeric Materials, Fiber and Polymer Processing, Physical Properties of Organic Materials, Physics of Organic Materials, Process Dynamics of Polymeric Materials, Rheology of Organic Materials, Solid State Physics of Organic Materials, Synthetic Chemistry of Polymeric Materials, Textile Physics

Department of Physical Electronics

Electron Devices, Electronic Circuits and Networks, Electronic Properties of Matter, Magnetic Materials, Microwave Engineering, Optoelectronics, Quantum Electronics

Department of Polymer Chemistry

Biopolymers, Chemical Processing of Polymers, Physical Chemistry of Polymers, Polymer Reactions, Polymer Syntheses, Properties of Polymers, Structures of Polymers

Department of Social Engineering

City Planning, Civil Systems, Environmental Systems, Landscape Planning, Learning Support Systems, Planning Theory and Artifical Intelligence Technology, Regional Planning, Socio-Economics, Tourism Planning, Urban System Analysis

Faculty of Science (Freshmen Enrollment 267)

Department of Applied Physics

Electromagnetism and Fluid Mechanics, Experimental Nuclear Physics, Experiment on the Properties of Matter, Geophysics, Low Temperature Physics and its Application, Material Science, Optical Properties of Matter, Physical Chemistry, Statistical Physics, Stochastic Processes and Applied Probability, Theory of Probabilities

Department of Biological Sciences

Biodynamics, Biological Physics, Biological Signal Recognition and Transduction, Developmental Biology, Molecular Evolution, Photobiology

Department of Chemistry

Analytical Chemistry, Chemistry of Catalysis, Geochemistry, Inorganic Chemistry, Molecular Spectroscopy, Organic Chemistry, Organic Chemistry of Natural Products, Photochemistry, Physical Inorganic Chemistry, Quantum Chemistry, Surface Chemistry, Synthetic Organic Chemistry

Department of Information Science

Applied Probability, Artificial Intelligence, Automata Theory, Combinatorial Topology, Computer Science, Formal Languages, Functional Analysis and its Applications, Game Theory, Information Theory, Mathematical Economics, Mathematical Programming, Mathematical Statistics, Operations Research, Probability Theory, Theory of Computation

Department of Life Science

Biochemical Genetics, Biochemistry, Biocontrol Mechanism, Bioorganic Chemistry, Chemistry of Biological Information, Developmetal Biology, Enzyme Biology, Enzyme Chemistry, Microbial Physiology, Molecular and Cellular Biology, Molecular Biophysics, Molecular Evolution, Molecular Physiology, Plant Physiology

Department of Mathematics

Algebra, Analysis, Differential Geometry, Functional Analysis, Functional Equations, Manifolds, Mathematical Statistics, Singularity and Geometry, Theory of Differential Equations, Theory of Functions, Theory of Functions of Several Variables, Topology

Department of Physics

Cosmic Ray Physics, Crystal and Surface Physics, Experimental High Energy Physics, Experimental Nuclear Physics, Experimental Solid State Physics, Ferroelectricity and Phase Transition, Low Temperature Physics, Magnetism and Magnetic Resonance,

Statistical Physics and Phase Transition, Theoretical High Energy and Particle Physics, Theoretical Nuclear Physics, Theoretical Solid State Physics

Foreign Student Admission
Qualifications for Applicants
Standard Qualifications Requirement
Examination at the University
Applicants must take the Japanese Language Proficiency Test and the General Examination for Foreign Students. The Institute will select from among those who score highly in the above tests and admit them to the Institute as regular students.
Documents to be Submitted When Applying
Standard Documents Requirement
Application forms are available at Student Office from early December. All applicants are required to submit the specified application documents to the Student Office.

GRADUATE PROGRAMS

Graduate School at Ookayama (Science and Engineering) (First Year Enrollment : Master's 397, Doctor's 136)
Divisions
Applied Physics, Architecture and Building Engineering, Chemical Engineering, Chemistry, Civil Engineering, Computer Science, Control Engineering, Electrical and Electronic Engineering, Industrial Engineering and Management, Information Science, Inorganic Materials, Mathematics, Mechanical Engineering, Mechanical Engineering for Production, Mechanical Engineering Science, Metallurgical Engineering, Nuclear Engineering, Physical Electronics, Physical Electronics, Physics, Polymer Chemistry, Social Engineering, Textile and Polymeric Materials
Graduate School at Nagatsuta (Interdisciplinary Science and Engineering) (First Year Enrollment: Master's 282, Doctor's 114)
Divisions
Applied Electronics, Electronic Chemistry, Energy Sciences, Environmental Chemistry and Engineering, Information Processing, Life Chemistry, Materials Science and Engineering, Precision Machinery Systems, Systems Science, Urban Planning, Environmental Engineering and Disater Engineering

Foreign Student Admission
Qualifications for Applicants
Master's Program
Standard Qualifications Requirement
Doctor's Program
Standard Qualifications Requirement
Examination at the University
Master's Program
Those who wish to be enrolled as regular students must either pass the entrance examinations on equal terms with Japanese applicants, or gain entrance by the special selection procedure for foreign

students.
Doctor's Program
Foreign applicants are subject to the same requirements as those for Japanese applicants, except that an examination of Japanese language may be imposed as one of the two foreign languages.
Documents to be Submitted When Applying
Standard Documents Requirement
The application form and further information are available at the Student Office.

*

Research Institutes and Centers
Center for Research and Development of Education Technology, Center for Research Cooperation and Information Exchange, Computer Center, Experimental Center for Very Low Temperature and Energy Technique, Imaging Science and Engineering Laboratory, International Cooperation Center for Science and Technology, Research Laboratory for Nuclear Reactors, Research Laboratory of Engineering Materials, Research Laboratory of Precision Machinery and Electronics, Research Laboratory of Resources Utilization
Facilities/Services for Foreign Students
Shofu Dormitory for Foreign Students: Shared Facilities (Lobby, Japanese-Style Room, Counselor Room), Accommodation (51 rooms—single 46 for men, couple 5)
Umegaoka Dormitory for Foreign Students: Shared Facilities (Lobby, Japanese-Style Room, Counselor Room), Accommodation (60 rooms—single 50, 31 for men, 19 for women, couple 10)
Special Programs for Foreign Students
Japanese language supplementary classes are available after enrollment.
For Further Information
Undergraduate and Graduate Admission
Students Affairs Section, Student Office, Tokyo Institute of Technology, 2-12-1 Ookayama, Meguro-ku, Tokyo 152 ☎ 03-726-1111 ext. 2053, 2048

Tokyo Medical and Dental University
(Tokyo Ikashika Daigaku)
1-5-45 Yushima, Bunkyo-ku, Tokyo 113
☎ 03-813-6111

Faculty
    Profs. 58   Assoc. Profs. 52
    Assist. Profs. Full–time 35; Part–time 247
    Res. Assocs. 173
Number of Students
    Undergrad. 989   Grad. 229
Library 251, 862 volumes

Outline and Characteristics of the University
    Tokyo Medical and Dental University was

founded as a national university in August, 1946.

Its predecessor was Tokyo Koto Shika Igakko (Tokyo School of Dentistry which is a governmental school) founded in October, 1928. The School was founded as the one and only governmental dental educational institution in Japan at that time, and contributed greatly to dental education, dental research and dental care delivery. In April, 1944, the School was re-organized to be Tokyo Igaku Shigaku Senmongakko (Tokyo Medical and Dental School) by setting up the Department of Medicine within its organization. Later, in April 1951, Tokyo Medical and Dental University under the then 'new' educational system was instituted through partial revision of the National School Foundation Law. In April 1955, the University was re-organized into the six-year system, consisting of the two-year medical preparatory, the two-year dentistry preparatory, the four-year medical specialized, and the four-year dentistry specialized courses. In April of the same year, the postgraduate course was instituted.

Tokyo Medical and Dental University consists of two Faculties of Medicine and Dentistry, and one Department of General Education. In addition, there is the Institute for Animal Research Center, Polyposis Center in the Faculty of Medicine, Institute of Stomatognathic Science in the Faculty of Dentistry as the peripheral research institute of the two Faculties, the Institute for Medical and Dental Engineering and Medical Research Institute as the research institutes of the University. Both Faculties also include hospitals. Affiliated educational institutions include the School of Nursing and the School of Medical Technology in the Faculty of Medicine; and the School for Dental Hygienists and the School for Dental Technicians in the Faculty of Dentistry.

The University Library consists of the main library and the annex, both of which are utilized by all students and the teaching staff of the University.

UNDERGRADUATE PROGRAMS

Faculty of Dentistry (Freshmen Enrollment: 80)
Department of Dentistry
Biochemistry, Conservative Dentistry, Dental Anesthesiology, Dental Pharamacology, Dental Radiology, Dental Technology, Oral Anatomy, Oral Microbiology, Oral Pathology, Oral Physiology, Oral Surgery, Orthodontics, Pedodontics, Preventive Dentistry and Public Health, Prosthodontics
Faculty of Medicine (Freshmen Enrollment: 80)
Department of Medicine
Anatomy, Anesthesiology and Critical care Medicine, Biochemistry, Dermatology, Forensic Medicine, Hygiene, Internal Medicine, Laboratory Medicine, Medical Zoology, Microbiology, Neurology, Neuropsychiatry, Neuro-Surgery, Obstetrics and Gynecology, Ophthalmology, Orthopedic Surgery, Otorhinolaryngology, Pathology, Pediatrics, Pharmacology, Physiology, Public Health, Radiology, Surgery, Thoracic-Surgery, Urology

Foreign Student Admission
Qualifications for Applicants
Standard Qualifications Requirement
For each Faculty, applicants must take the Japanese Language Proficiency Test and General Examination for Foreign Students. Those who receive an "A" grade will be allowed to take each Faculty's special entrance examination.
Examination at the University
Each Faculty's special entrance examination consists of a written and oral exams and interview.
Documents to be Submitted When Applying
Standard Documents Requirement
Application forms are available at the Admissions Office from early October. All applicants are required to submit the specified application documents to the Admissions Office by January 31.

GRADUATE PROGRAMS

Graduate School of Dentistry (First Year Enrollment : Doctor's 47)
Divisions
Dental Basic Science, Dental Clinics
Graduate School of Medicine (First Year Enrollment : Doctor's 64)
Divisions
Internal Medicine, Morphology, Physiology, Social Medicine, Surgery

Foreign Student Admission
Qualifications for Applicants
Doctor's Program
Standard Qualifications Requirement
Examination at the University
Doctor's Program
Applicants must take the same entrance examination consisting of a written exam and an interview given to Japanese students.
Documents to be Submitted When Applying
Standard Documents Requirement

*
Research Institutes and Centers
Animal Reseach Center, Health Service Center, Institute for Medical and Dental Engineering, Institute of Stomatognathic Science, Medical Research Institute, Polyposis Center
For Further Information
Undergraduate Admission
Student Division, Tokyo Medical and Dental University, 1-5-45 Yushima, Bunkyo-ku, Tokyo 113 ☎ 03–813–6111 ext. 2253
Graduate Admission
Department of Medical Office, Tokyo Medical and Dental University, 1-5-45 Yushima, Bunkyo-ku, Tokyo 113 ☎ 03–813–6111 ext. 3106
Department of Dental Office, Tokyo Medical and Dental University, 1-5-45 Yushima, Bunkyo-ku,

Tokyo 113 ☎ 03–813–6111 ext. 5514

Tokyo National University of Fine Arts and Music

(Tokyo Geijutsu Daigaku)

12-8 Ueno Koen, Taito-ku, Tokyo 110
☎ 03–828–6111

Faculty
    Profs. 78   Assoc. Profs. 64
    Assist. Profs. Full–time 16; Part–time 603
    Res. Assocs. 28
Number of Students
    Undergrad. 1, 940   Grad. 629
Library 400, 516 volumes

Outline and Characteristics of the University

Tokyo Geijutsu Daigaku was established in the year of 1949 in accordance with the National School Establishment Law by uniting Tokyo Fine Arts School (the predecessor of the present Faculty of Fine Arts) and Tokyo Music School (the predecessor of the present Faculty of Music). In the beginning there were the two Faculties of Fine Arts (Painting Course, Sculpture Course, Design and Crafts Course, Architecture Course and Aesthetics and Art History Course) and Music (Composition Course, Vocal Music Course, Instrumental Music Course, Conducting Course and Musicology Course) and the Library.

Briefly the history of the university since is as follows.

April 1950: the establishment of the Japanese Music Course in the Faculty of Music.

April 1951: the establishment of the Special Course in the Faculty of Music.

March 1952: the dissolution of Tokyo Fine Arts School and Tokyo Music School by revision of the National School Establishment Law.

April 1954: the establishment of the Senior High School of Music attached to the Faculty of Music at Kandasurugadai, Chiyoda-ku.

April 1963: the organization of the Graduate School with the Master's Courses in the Fine Arts Graduate Course and the Music Graduate Course.

April 1965: the establishment of the Institute of Ancient Art Researches attached to the Faculty of Fine Arts in Nara City.

April 1970: the establishment of the Art Museum.

April 1975: the reorganization of the Craft Course in the Faculty of Fine Arts into the Crafts Course and the Design Course, the establishment of the Training Center for Foreign Languages and Declamation.

April 1977: the organization of the Doctor's Courses in the Fine Arts Graduate Course and the Music Graduate Course. April 1988: the establishment of the Center for Foreign Students.

UNDERGRADUATE PROGRAMS

Faculty of Fine Arts (Freshmen Enrollment: 230)
    Department of Aesthetics and Art History
    Department of Architecture
    Department of Crafts
Ceramics, Lacquer Work, Metal Carving, Metal Casting, Metal Hammering, Weaving and Dyeing
    Department of Design
    Department of Painting
Japanese Painting, Oil Painting
    Department of Sculpture
Faculty of Music (Freshmen Enrollment: 247)
    Department of Composition
    Department of Conducting
    Department of Instrumental Music
Organ, Piano, Strings, Wind and Percussion
    Department of Japanese Music
Kiyomoto, Kiyomoto-Shamisen, Koto, Nagauta, Nagauta-Hayashi, Nagauta-Shamisen, No, Nogaku-Hayashi, Shakuhachi, Tokiwazu, Tokiwazu-Shamisen
    Department of Musicology
    Department of Vocal Music
Opera, Solo Vocal

Foreign Student Admission

Qualifications for Applicants
    Standard Qualifications Requirement

Those who have received the International Baccalaureate by the International Baccalaureate Association, a foundation based on the Swiss Civil Code, and are 18 years or older are also eligible to apply.

Examination at the University
    Applicants must take the General Examination for Foreign Students and the Japanese Language Proficiency Test. Our university has employed these aptitude examinations instead of the Joint First-Stage Achievement Test and our own examination for selecting students. Concerning application and selection, applicants should inquire at the Faculty administration office by the end of December or thereabout.

GRADUATE PROGRAMS

Graduate School of Fine Arts (First Year Enrollment : Master's 108, Doctor's 15)
    Divisions
Aesthetics and Art History, Architecture, Crafts, Design, Fine Arts, Painting, Sculpture
Graduate School of Music (First Year Enrollment : Master's 99, Doctor's 15)
    Divisions
Composition, Conducting, Instrumental Music, Japanese Music, Musicology, Vocal Music

Foreign Student Admission

Qualifications for Applicants
Master's Program

Standard Qualifications Requirement
Doctor's Program
Standard Qualifications Requirement
Examination at the University
Master's Program
All the applicants for the graduate school of our university are required to take an entrance examination.

It is advisable for an applicant to be enrolled in our university as a research student, and then apply to the graduate school.
Doctor's Program
Same as Master's program.
Documents to be Submitted When Applying
Standard Documents Requirement

*

Research Institutes and Centers
Institute of Ancient Art Researches (Faculty of Fine Arts), Photograph Research Center (Faculty of Fine Arts), The Training Center for Foreign Languages and Declamation, The University Art Museum
For Further Information
Undergraduate and Graduate Admission
Administration Office, Tokyo National University of Fine Arts and Music, 12-8 Ueno Koen, Taito-ku, Tokyo 110 ☎ 03–828–6111 ext. 312, 412

Tokyo University of Agriculture and Technology
(Tokyo Noko Daigaku)

3-8-1 Harumi-cho, Fuchu-shi, Tokyo 183
☎ 0423-64-3311

Faculty
    Profs.   134   Assoc. Profs.   111
    Assist. Profs.   Full–time   16; Part–time   286
    Res. Assocs.   109
Number of Students
    Undergrad.   3, 656   Grad.   575
Library   368, 310 volumes

Outline and Characteristics of the University
Tokyo University of Agriculture and Technology was reorganized as a national university in 1949 under the National School Establishment Law.

The foundation of this university can be traced back through the Tokyo College of Agriculture and Forestry and the Tokyo Textile College to the beginning of the Meiji Era.

Their prototypes were chartered by the Japanese Ministry of Home Affairs in 1872. After many alterations in name and system, the two colleges stated above were consolidated into Tokyo University of Agriculture and Technology.

The University consists of two schools, Agriculture and Technology. In 1949, there were only six departments in both Faculties, but due to the rapid development of modern science, the university has been greatly expanded to include 21 departments with a student enrollment of 3, 656. The graduate school offers programs leading to the master's degree.

In 1985, the Doctoral Course in Agricultural Science of the United Graduate School was established with the cooperation of the three Faculties of Agriculture, Ibaraki University, Utsunomiya University and this University.

The purpose of this university is to produce graduates who are not only highly qualified technically in agriculture and technology, but able to take an active part in every field of worldwide activities.

UNDERGRADUATE PROGRAMS

Faculty of Agriculture (Freshmen Enrollment: 345)
Department of Agricultural Chemistry
Animal Products Technology, Biological Chemistry, Bio-organic Chemistry, Enzymology and Microbial Chemistry, Food and Nutrition Chemistry Applied Microbiology
Department of Agricultural Engineering
Agricultural Construction Engineering, Agricultural Land Engineering, Farm Machines and Agricultural Processing, Farm Tractor and Farm Power, Irrigation and Drainage
Department of Agriculture
Agricultural Economics, Crop Science, Economics of Agricultural Production System, Horticultural Science, Plant Nutrition and Fertilizer Science, Soil Science, Zoo-technical Science
Department of Environmental Science and Conservation
Nature Conservation, Science of Pollution Environment, Science of Soil and Aquatic Environment, Science of Terrestrial Environment, Vegetation Management
Department of Forest Products
Forest Products Chemistry, Technology of Wood Improvement and Polymeric Materials Wood and Wood-based Materials, Wood Chemical Technology, Wood Processing
Department of Forestry
Forest Hydrology and Erosion Control Forest Engineering and Forest Machinery, Forest Landscape Science Forest Management, Silviculture
Department of Plant Protection
Applied Entomology, Biological Control, Pesticide Chemistry, Plant Pathology
Department of Sericulture
Biochemistry of Silkworm and Mulberry, Physiology and Ecology of Mulberry Plant, Sericultural Management, Silkworm Genetics and Embryology, Silkworm Physiology
Department of Veterinary Medicine
Animal Hygiene, Veterinary Anatomy, Veterinary Internal Medicine, Veterinary Microbiology, Veterinary Pathology, Veterinary Pharmacology, Veteri-

nary Physiology, Veterinary Reproduction, Veterinary Surgery

Faculty of Technology (Freshmen Enrollment: 555)

Department of Applied Chemistry for Resources
Applied Catalytic Chemistry, Chemical Process for Resources, Energy Chemical Engineering, Synthetic Chemistry for Resources

Department of Applied Physics
Applied Electromagnetics, Applied Mathematics, Applied Metrology, Applied Solid and Molecular Physics, Nonlinear Engineering

Department of Chemical Engineering
Chemical Reaction Engineering, Diffusional Unit Operations, Environmental Engineering, Mechanical Unit Operations, Process Engineering

Department of Electrical Engineering
Applied Electricity, Basic Electricity, Electrical Communication Engineering, Electrical Power Engineering, Electric Machines

Department of Electronic Engineering
Electron Devices, Electronic Circuit Engineering, Electronic Control Engineering, Physical Electronics

Department of Industrial Chemistry
Dyeing and Dye Chemistry, Industrial Inorganic Chemistry, Industrial Material Chemistry, Industrial Organic Chemistry, Polymer Chemistry

Department of Industrial Mechanical Engineering
Control Engineering, Material Science for Machinery, Plastic Working, Precision Engineering

Department of Information Science
Automatic Programming, Computer Applications, Devices and Equipment for Information Science, Fundamental Studies

Department of Material Systems Engineering
Material Systems Analysis, Material Systems Design, Material Systems Development, Material Systems Instrumentation, Material Systems Processing

Department of Mechanical Engineering
Applied Dynamics, Applied Kinematics, Engineering Fluid Mechanics, Heat Engineering, Machine Element and Mechanical Technology

Department of Mechanical Systems Engineering
Engineering Analysis, Measurements and Control System, Mechanical Systems Design, Production Engineering System

Department of Polymer Engineering
Biopolymer Engineering, Biopolymer Physics, Polymer Processing and Industrial Management, Synthetic Polymer Chemistry

Foreign Student Admission

Qualifications for Applicants
  Standard Qualifications Requirement
  Those who have International Baccalaureate Diploma and are at least 18 years old may also apply. Foreign applicants should be of non-Japanese nationality.

Examination at the University
  Foreign applicants need not sit for the Joint First-Stage Achievement Test. However, they must take the Japanese Language Proficiency Test and the General Examination for Foreign Students.

  Foreign applicants taking the Second Entrance Examination are evaluated using the same criteria as those for Japanese students. (Full details are provided in the Guide to Application.)

GRADUATE PROGRAMS

Graduate School of Agriculture (First Year Enrollment : Master's 82)

Divisions
Agricultural Chemistry, Agricultural Engineering, Agriculture, Environmental Science and Conservation, Forest Products, Forestry, Plant Protection, Sericulture

United Graduate School (Doctoral Course in Agricultural Science) (First Year Enrollment : Doctor's 18)

Divisions
Agricultural Engineering, Animal Production, Applied Biological Chemistry, Environmental Science, Forest and Wood Science, Management and Economics of Agriculture and Forestry, Plant Production, Plant Protection, Utilization of Biological Resources

Graduate School of Technology (First Year Enrollment : Master's 108)

Divisions
Applied Chemistry for Resources, Applied Physics, Chemical Engineering, Electrical Engineering, Electronic Engineering, Engineering Mechanical System Polymer Engineering, Industrial Chemistry, Industrial Mechanical Engineering, Information Science, Material Systems Engineering, Mechanical Engineering

Foreign Student Admission

Qualifications for Applicants
Master's Program
  Standard Qualifications Requirement
Doctor's Program
  Standard Qualifications Requirement
Examination at the University
Master's Program
  Foreign applicants are evaluated using the same criteria as those for Japanese students.
Doctor's Program
  Same as Master's program.

*

Research Institutes and Centers
Fiber and Textile Museum, Health Service Center, Information Processing Center, Institute for Agricultural Research on Rolling Land, Scleroprotein and Leather Research Institute, Surface Multiphase Engineering Research Laboratory, University Farm, University Forests, Veterinary Clinic

Special Programs for Foreign Students
  Tokyo University of Agriculture and Technology has a tutorial system in which the academic staff

and graduate students guide foreign students in their studies including Japanese language learning.

For Further Information

Undergraduate Admission

Faculty of Agriculture: Admissions Office, 3-5-8 Saiwai-cho, Fuchu-shi, Tokyo 183, ☎ 0423–64–3311 ext. 320

Faculty of Technology: Admissions Office, 2-24-16 Naka-cho, Koganei-shi, Tokyo 184, ☎ 0423–81–4221 ext. 220

Graduate Admission

Graduate School of Agriculture: Graduate Admissions Office, 3-5-8 Saiwai-cho, Fuchu-shi, Tokyo 183, ☎ 0423–64–3311 ext. 320

Graduate School of Technology: Graduate Admissions Office, 2-24-16 Naka-cho, Koganei-shi, Tokyo 184 ☎ 0423–81–4221 ext. 220

United Graduate School of Agricultural Science: Graduate Admissions Office, 3-5-8 Saiwai-cho, Fuchu-shi, Tokyo 183 ☎ 0423-64-3311 ext. 577

Tokyo University of Fisheries
(Tokyo Suisan Daigaku)

5-7 Konan4, Minato-ku, Tokyo 108
☎ 03–471–1251

Faculty
    Profs. 55   Assoc. Profs. 43
    Assist. Profs. Full–time 12; Part–time 71
    Res. Assocs. 42
Number of Students
    Undergrad. 1, 279   Grad. 80
Library 217, 312 volumes

Outline and Characteristics of the University

The Tokyo University of Fisheries was first established as a private school known as the Fisheries Institute (Suisan Denshujo) in Tokyo in 1888 by the Japanese Association of Fisheries (Dai-Nippon Suisankai). It was reorganized as the Imperial Fisheries Institute (Suisan Koshujo) in 1897 by the Ministry of Agriculture and Commerce. Under the most recent reorganization after World War II, the present Tokyo University of Fisheries (Tokyo Suisan Daigaku) was established in 1949-50.

Originally, the institution consisted of three undergraduate departments of fishing technology, food processing and aquaculture. It has now been expanded into seven departments and a division of general education, Which have been reorganized into four departments and a division of general education.

The University has a graduate school offering the Master's and Doctor's Programs in three courses, Marine Science and Technology, Aquatic Biosciences, and Food Science and Technology. The University also has an advanced school for seamanship apprentices.

The University works in cooperation with a research organization which consisting of the Radioisotope Laboratory, the Water-temperature Controlled Aquarium, the Computation Center, the University Library, and the University Museum, as well as the Research and Training Station and Research and Training Vessels.

During its 100-year history, the institution has fully contributed to the exploitation and constructive utilization of the sea and inland waters, not only domestically but also internationally. Its contributions range from the introduction of modern fisheries techniques at the end of the last century to our present cooperation with developing countries in the development of fisheries.

Today, when it is important that all the products of the ocean be shared among the world's nations as common property, Japan's fisheries must cooperate internationally. Based on such an understanding, the Tokyo University of Fisheries is open to students from all over the world, teaching them advanced technology, and thus contributing to the development of world fisheries science. This University is one of the few in the wrold which is solely devoted to the research and education of fisheries science.

UNDERGRADUATE PROGRAMS

Faculty of Fisheries (Freshmen Enrollment: 320)
    Department of Aquatic Bioscience
Aquaculture, Aquatic Biology, Sea-farming Biology
    Department of Fisheries Resources Management
Ecology and Economics of Fisheries Resources, Fisheries Resources Management System
    Department of Food Science and Technology
Food Chemistry, Food Engineering, Food Processing and Preservation, Food Safety and Preservation
    Department of Marine Science and Technology
Fisheries Oceanography, Fishing Science and Technology, Fishing Technology and Engineering, Marine Environmental Science

Foreign Student Admission
    Qualifications for Applicants
    Standard Qualifications Requirement
    Examination at the University
    1. Japanese and English (required subjects)
    2. Two of the following: Mathematics, Physics, Chemistry or Biology
    3. Confidential school reports, medical certificates
    4. An interview.
    Documents to be Submitted When Applying
    Standard Documents Requirement
    JLPT and GEFS scores
    Application period: January 30 to February 8, 1989

GRADUATE PROGRAMS

Graduate School of Fisheries (First Year Enrollment : Master's 68, Doctor's 12)

Courses

Aquatic Biosciences, Food Science and Technology, Marine Science and Technology

Foreign Student Admission

Qualifications for Applicants

Master's Program

Standard Qualifications Requirement

Doctor's Program

Standard Qualifications Requirement

Examination at the University

Master's Program and Doctor's Program

A written examination on their specialized subject, Interviews, confidential school reports, and medical certificates.

Examination Date: Master's-in September

Doctor's-in March

Documents to be Submitted When Applying

Standard Documents Requirement

Master's Program

Application period: in August.

(Application for the second-round entrance examination is accepted in January and is administered in February.)

Doctor's Program

Application period: in February

*

Research Institutes and Centers

Computation Center, Electron Microscope Laboratory, Hydraulic Basin, Laboratory of Gas Chromatograph-Mass Spectrometer, Radioisotope Laboratory, Research and Training Stations (Banda, Oizumi, Tateyama and Yoshida), Research and Training Vessels (Umitaka Maru, Shin'yo Maru, Seiyo Maru), Water-temperature Controlled Aquarium

For Further Information

Undergraduate and Graduate Admission

Admission Section, Student Division, Student Office, Tokyo University of Fisheries, 5-7 Konan 4, Minato-ku, Tokyo 108 ☏ 03–471–1251

Tokyo University of Foreign Studies

(Tokyo Gaikokugo Daigaku)

4-51-21 Nishigahara, Kita-ku, Tokyo 114
☎ 03–917–6111

Faculty

Profs. 65   Assoc. Profs. 43

Assist. Profs. Full–time 15; Part–time 270

Res. Assocs. 9

Number of Students

Undergrad. 2, 988   Grad. 118
Library 373, 415 volumes

Outline and Characteristics of the University

The history of the university goes back more than a century to the Tokyo School of Foreign Languages established in 1873. Even though the school was dissolved in 1885, it was restored in 1897 as a foreign language school affiliated with the Tokyo School of Commerce, predecessor to the present Hitotsubashi University.

When it became an independent institution, the Tokyo School of Foreign Languages, it offered three-year courses for middle school graduates. It was promoted to a four-year-course school during the 1927-43 period. Due to the national emergency, it offered only three-year courses under the altered name of Tokyo College of Foreign Affairs in 1944. Then in 1949, under the postwar educational reform, the College again became a four-year institution accepting qualified high-school graduates, called the Tokyo University of Foreign Studies.

It was an undergraduate institution with 12 area-study departments in 1943, which has developed into 16 departments at present. In 1964, the Institute for the Study of the Languages and Cultures of Asia and Africa was affiliated with the Universtity as a facility to be used by personnel from all national institutions of higher learning. Another affiliated institution of the Faculty of Foreign Studies was established in 1970: the Japanese Language School, which was to become the only national facility providing preparatory Japanese language training for students from abroad. The Graduate School of Language Studies was begun in 1966, offering a Master's degree program. The Graduate School of Area Studies was set up in 1977, also offering programs leading to the Master's degree.

The comprehensive research and educational programs in foreign languages, cultures, and international affairs, as well as in the Japanese language, make the University a central institution of importance in the field of foreign studies.

UNDERGRADUATE PROGRAMS

Faculty of Foreign Studies (Freshmen Enrollment: 721)

Department of Anglo-American Studies

American Literature, Anglo-American Affairs, Anglo-American Language, English Literature

Department of Arabic Studies

Arabic Affairs on Various Provinces, Arabic Language and Literature

Department of Chinese Studies

Chinese Affairs, Chinese Language, Chinese Literature

Department of French Studies

French Affairs, French Language, French Literature

Department of German Studies

German Affairs, German Language, German Literature

Department of Indochinese Studies

Burmese Language and Literature, Indochinese Affairs, Thai Language and Literature, Vietnamese Language and Literature

Department of Indonesian-Malaysian Studies

Dutch Language and Literature, Indonesian and Malaysian Affairs, Indonesian Language and Literature, Malaysian Language and Literature

Department of Indo-Pakistani Studies

Hindi Language and Literature, Indian Affairs, Pakistani Affairs, Urdu Language and Literature

Department of Italian Studies

Italian Affairs, Italian Language, Italian Literature

Department of Japanese Studies

Japanese Affairs, Japanese Culture, Japanese Language, Japanese Language Education, Linguistics

Department of Korean Studies

Korean Affairs, Korean Language and Literature

Department of Mongolian Studies

Mongolian Affairs, Mongolian Language and Literature

Department of Persian Studies

Persian Affairs, Persian Language, Persian Literature

Department of Portuguese-Brazilian Studies

Portuguese and Brazilian Affairs, Portuguese Language and Literature

Department of Russian Studies

Russian Affairs, Russian Language, Russian Literature

Department of Spanish Studies

Latin America Affairs, Spanish Affairs, Spanish Language, Spanish Literature

Foreign Student Admission

Qualifications for Applicants

Standard Qualifications Requirement

Foreign Student Admission to Department of Japanese Studies*

Qualifications for Entrance: Those eligible for entrance are persons without Japanese nationality who fall in either of the following two categories: (1) a person who finished education of 12 years in a foreign country or countries or a person recognized by the Minister of Education of Japan as having the corresponding qualification. (2) a person who is designated as such by the Education Minister of Japan.

Examination at the University

The decision on admission of an applicant will be made based on the overall estimation of the results of an achievement test, the school report and the health certificate. The entrance examination will be given here at this university in the three subjects of Japanese, Japanese History, and Foreign Languages.

Documents to be Submitted When Applying

Standard Documents Requirement

Applicants currently enrolled in other universities in Japan must submit a Permission of Applica-

tion from the Dean of the Faculty concerned.

Information leaflets on admission procedure and application forms will be distributed upon request in late summer of every year. Application, Examination, etc. : Application—January; Entrance Examination—February; Announcement of Admission—February; Registration—March

*N.B. Foreign students are also eligible for other departments.

GRADUATE PROGRAMS

Graduate School of Area Studies (First Year Enrollment : Master's 48)

Divisions

Asian and Pacific Area Studies , European Area Studies

Graduate School of Language Studies (First Year Enrollment : Master's 66)

Divisions

Asian Languages I (Chinese, Korean, Mongolian), Asian Languages II (Arabic, Hindi, Persian, Urdu), Asian Languages III (Burmese, Indonesian, Thai, Vietnamése), Germanic Languages (English, German), Japanese Language, Romance Languages (French, Italian, Portuguese, Spanish), Slavic Languages

Foreign Student Admission

Qualifications for Applicants

Master's Program

Standard Qualifications Requirement

Examination at the University

Master's Program

The decision on admission of an applicant will be made based on the overall estimation of the results of an achievement test (written and oral), the school report, and the health certificate. Details of the written test are as follows:

Language Studies: (A) one language of specialization, (B) linguistics, (C) a second foreign language.

Area Studies: (A) choice of one or two out of several questions concerning the area of specialization; (B) one subject out of international relations, international economy and comparative culture; (C) two foreign languages including English.

Documents to be Submitted When Applying

Standard Documents Requirement

A summary of the applicant's graduation thesis is also required.

Information leaflets on admission procedure and application forms will be distributed upon request in late summer of every year. Application, Examination, etc. : Application—November; Entrance Examination—February; Announcement of Admission—February; Registration—March

*

Research Institutes and Centers

Audio-Visual Education Center, Center for Development of Educational Materials for Foreign Students, Health Administration Center, Institute for the Study of Languages and Cultures of Asia and Africa, Institute of Foreign Affairs, Institute of Language Researches

Facilities/Services for Foreign Students
International Hall
Shared Facilities: Hall, Conference Room, Library, Japanese-Style Room
Accommodation: 80 rooms (single 70, couple 5, family 5)

Special Programs for Foreign Students
Japanese Language School
   The Japanese Language School attached to the Faculty of Foreign Languages, Tokyo University of Foreign Studies, was established on April 1, 1970, as an educational institution for undergraduate students sponsored under the Japanese Government (Monbusho) Scholarship Program.

For Further Information
   Undergraduate and Graduate Admission
Admissions Office, Tokyo University of Foreign Studies, 4-51-21 Nishigahara, Kita-ku, Tokyo 114
☎ 03–917–6111 ext. 315

Tokyo University of Mercantile Marine
(Tokyo Shosen Daigaku)

2-1-6 Etchujima, Koto-ku, Tokyo 135
☎ 03–641–1171

Faculty
   Profs. 42   Assoc. Profs. 33
   Assist. Profs. Full–time 6; Part–time 27
   Res. Assocs. 20
Number of Students
   Undergrad. 737   Grad. 35
Library 153, 635 volumes

Outline and Characteristics of the University
   Under the National School Establishment Law, Tokyo University of Mercantile Marine was established on November 30th, 1949. The origin of this University can be traced back to the Mitsubishi Nautical School (Mitsubishi Shosen Gakko) which was established in November 1875 for the purpose of training merchant marine officers for the emerging new nation of Japan.
   The purpose of this University is to study and offer instruction in a variety of sciences related to the navigation of ships. The special aims of this University make it quite unique among all the national universities of Japan.

UNDERGRADUATE PROGRAMS

Faculty of Mercantile Marine Science (Freshmen En-

rollment: 180)
   Department of Control Engineering
   Department of Engineering
   Department of Navigation
   Department of Transportation Engineering

Foreign Student Admission
   Qualifications for Applicants
   Standard Qualifications Requirement
   It is desirable that applicants take the Japanese Language Proficiency Test and the General Examination for Foreign Students.
   Documents to be Submitted When Applying
   Standard Documents Requirement
   Identification certificate or letter of recommendation issued by an overseas agency of the Foreign Ministry or by the diplomatic establishment of the applicant's country in Japan is also required.
   Application and other forms are available at the Admissions office towards the end of November. All applicants are required to submit the specified application documents to the Admissions office between January 30 and February 8.

GRADUATE PROGRAMS

Graduate School of Mercantile Marine Science (First Year Enrollment : Master's 30)
   Divisions
Control Engineering, Engineering, Navigation, Transportation Engineering

Foreign Student Admission
   Qualifications for Applicants
Master's Program
   Standard Qualifications Requirement
   Documents to be Submitted When Applying
   Standard Documents Requirement
   Identification certificate or letter of recommendation issued by an overseas agency of the Foreign Ministry of Japan or by the diplomatic establishment of the applicant's country in Japan is also required.

✳

Research Institutes and Centers
Research Institute of Maritime Science
Special Programs for Foreign Students
Japanese supplementary classes are available and may be substituted for some of the required courses within the school curriculum.
For Further Information
   Undergraduate and Graduate Admission
Admissions Office, Tokyo University of Mercantile Marine, 2-1-6 Etchujima, Koto-ku, Tokyo 135
☎ 03–641–1171 ext. 265

Toyama Medical and Pharmaceutical University
(Toyama Ikayakka Daigaku)

2630 Sugitani, Toyama-shi, Toyama 930-01
☎ 0764-34-2281

Faculty
    Profs. 60   Assoc. Profs. 57
    Assist. Profs. Full–time 38; Part–time 34
    Res. Assocs. 159
Number of Students
    Undergrad. 1, 094   Grad. 168
Library 127, 937 volumes

Outline and Characteristics of the University

Toyama Medical and Pharmaceutical University was founded in October, 1975. It was composed of a new Faculty of Medicine and the already established Toyama University Faculty of Pharmaceutical Sciences, formerly known as Kyoritsu Toyama Pharmaceutical School, a non-governmental college begun in 1893.

In June 1978, the Research Institute for Wakanyaku (oriental medicines) was transferred from Toyama University to our present location, thus giving the University a full complement of two faculties and one research institute.

Graduate programs offering Doctor's degrees were officially begun by the Graduate Schools of Pharmaceutical Sciences and of Medicine in June, 1978 and April, 1982, respectively. These Graduate Schools were set up for the purpose of nurturing highly-talented persons who will play an active role in the fields of medicine and pharmaceutical sciences based on the integration of oriental and occidental medicine, as well as the cooperation of medicine and pharmacy.

With the opening of the University Hospital in October, 1979 and the final completion of the Graduate Schools in 1982, the entire scheme of the University facilities was accomplished.

A marked characteristic of our University's curriculum is that general and professional education is offered as an integrated unit for four years in the pharmaceutical course and six years in the medical course.

We have no separate department of general education or independent liberal arts course for medical students. Rather, to promote education based on the integration of medicine and pharmacy, we offer some common courses to both medical and pharmaceutical students.

Furthermore, with the cooperation of the staff of the Research Institute for Wakan'yaku, students receive instruction in the science of oriental medicines.

The campus is located in a hilly area on the outskirts of Toyama City. It covers a rather vast area of 320, 000 m². With its modern facilities for education and research, together with the convenience of sporting activities and concern for their welfare, this can be called an ideal environment for students. One can also enjoy the rich natural setting, as well as warm hospitality found only in this district of Hokuriku.

Students come from all parts of Japan, with a slight majority of Toyama-ites. About 18 students attend from overseas countries. They study and research under an excellent teaching staff.

UNDERGRADUATE PROGRAMS

Faculty of Medicine (Freshmen Enrollment: 100)
    Department of Medicine
Anatomy, Anesthesiology, Bacteriology & Immunology, Biochemistry, Biology, Chemistry, Community Medicine, Dermatology, Internal Medicine, Legal Medicine, Mathematics, Neuropsychiatry, Neurosurgery, Obstetrics & Gynecology, Ophtalmology, Oral & Maxillofacial Surgery, Orthopedics, Otorhinolaryngology, Pathology, Pediatrics, Pharmacology, Physiology, Public Health, Radiology, Surgery, Urology, Virology

Faculty of Pharmaceutical Sciences (Freshmen Enrollment: 105)
    Department of Pharmaceutical Sciences
Biological Chemistry, Biology, Clinical Chemistry, Medicinal Chemistry, Natural Products Chemistry, Pharmacy & Pharmacology, Philosophy, Physics

Foreign Student Admission
    Qualifications for Applicants
    Standard Qualifications Requirement
    Documents to be Submitted When Applying
    Standard Documents Requirement
    JLPT and GEFS scores.
    Application forms are available at the Student Division from early December.

GRADUATE PROGRAMS

Graduate School of Medicine (First Year Enrollment : Doctor's 30)
    Divisions
Biochemistry and Related Sciences, Environmental Medicine, Morphology and Related Sciences, Physiology and Related Sciences

Graduate School of Pharmaceutical Sciences (First Year Enrollment : Master's 33, Doctor's 14)
    Division
Medicinal Sciences

Foreign Student Admission
    Qualifications for Applicants
Master's Program
    Standard Qualifications Requirement
Doctor's Program

Standard Qualifications Requirement
Documents to be Submitted When Applying
Standard Documents Requirement
Application forms are available at the Student Division Office from early August.

*

Research Institutes and Centers
Health Care Center, Herbal Garden, Laboratory Animal Research Center, Radioisotope Laboratory, Research Institute for Wakan'yaku, Scientific Instrument Center

For Further Information
Undergraduate and Graduate Admission
Student Division, Toyama Medical and Pharmaceutical University, 2630 Sugitani, Toyama-shi, Toyama 930-01 ☎ 0764-34-2281 ext. 2148 (Undergraduate), 2157 (Graduate)

Toyama University
(Toyama Daigaku)

3190 Gofuku, Toyama-shi, Toyama 930
☎ 0764-41-1271

Faculty
    Profs. 149   Assoc. Profs. 160
    Assist. Profs. Full-time 40; Part-time 176
    Res. Assocs. 55
Number of Students
    Undergrad. 5, 773   Grad. 207
Library 655, 175 volumes

Outline and Characteristics of the University

Toyama University is a national university composed of five faculties: Humanities, Education, Economics, Science and Engineering and the Department of Liberal Arts. It was founded in 1949 in accordance with the National School Establishment Law by integrating Toyama Higher School, Toyama Normal School, Toyama Young Men's Normal School, Toyama Pharmaceutical College and Takaoka Technical College. It started with four faculties: Humanities and Science, Education, Pharmacy and Engineering.

The Faculty of Economics was instituted in 1953 by making the Department of Economics independent from the Faculty of Humanities and Science. The Department of Liberal Arts was instituted in 1967 with the reorganization of the Faculty of Humanities and Science. The Faculty of Pharmacy was transferred with the establishment of Toyama Medical and Pharmaceutical College in 1976. The Faculty of Humanities and Science was reorganized into the present Faculty of Humanities and Faculty of Science in 1977. In 1986 the department of Economics was reorganized into two courses, a day course and a night course.

As for graduate school, there are three: Graduate School of Engineering (established in 1967), Graduate School of Science (established in 1978), and Graduate School of Humanities (established in 1986), all of which offer master's programs. As for special courses, we provide two: education and economics.

Four years are required to graduate from the university. In the first year and a half, students take general education courses in the Department of Liberal Arts and thereafter receive special education in their respective faculties. Graduate school requires two years and the special course may be completed in one year.

The university operates a Tritium Research Center, where advanced studies are conducted on tritium, which is a prospective fuel for the nuclear fusion reactor.

In the Faculty of Education, facilities for the Center for Research and Training in Teacher Education have been completed recently, where up-to-date electronic equipment displays great power in the laboratory and field work of the students who intend to become teachers. Moreover, keeping in step with the rapid advancement of information processing techniques in recent years, the Information Processing Center was established in order to cope with academic research and information processing education.

In the Faculty of Humanities, the study of the Japan Sea Economy and other studies dealing with East Asian Culture are actively being pursued by the concerned departments. With this in mind, an agreement enabling the friendly interchange of teachers and students was concluded between our university and Chinese universities in May 1984.

UNDERGRADUATE PROGRAMS

Faculty of Economics (Freshmen Enrollment: 430)
    Department of Business Management
    Department of Economics
    Department of Management Laws
Applied Economics, Applied Management, Civil Law, Comparative Economic Theory, Control Science, Corporate Law, Economic Theory, Fundamental Law, Management, Political Science

Faculty of Education (Freshmen Enrollment 240)
    Course in Informatics and Education
    Kindergarten Teachers Course
Early Childhood Education
    Lower Secondary School Teachers Course
English, Fine Arts, Health and Physical Education, Homemaking, Industrial Arts, Japanese Language, Mathematics, Music, Science, Social Studies
    Primary School Teachers Course
Arts and Handicrafts, Educational Psychology, Homemaking, Japanese Language, Mathematics, Music, Pedagogy, Physical Education, Science, Social Studies
    Special Education Teachers Course
Special Education (for mentally handicapped children)

Faculty of Engineering (Freshmen Enrollment: 342)

Department of Chemical Engineering
Diffusional Unit Operation, Mechanical Unit Operations, Reaction Engineering, Transport Phenomena
Department of Electric Engineering
Applied Electronics, Electronic Circuits, Electronic Device Engineering, Fundamental Electronics
Department of Electronic Engineering
Communication Engineering, Concepts and Methods of Electrical Engineering, Control Engineering, Electric Machinery and Apparatus, Electric Power Engineering
Department of Industrial Chemistry
Applied Physical Chemistry, Environmental Chemistry, Industrial Inorganic Chemistry, Industrial Organic Chemistry, Organic Synthetic Chemistry
Department of Mechanical Engineering
Dynamics of Machines, Fluid Engineering, Internal Combustion Engine, Strength of Materials, Thermomechanics
Department of Mechanical Engineering for Production
Control Machinery, Industrial Measurement, Metal Cutting, Plastic Forming
Department of Metallurgical Engineering
Ferrous Metallurgy, Materials Science, Nonferrous Metallurgy, Physical Metallurgy
Faculty of Humanities (Freshmen Enrollment 190)
Department of Humanities
Archaeology, Cultural Anthropology, Humanistic Geography, Japanese History, Linguistics, Occidental History, Oriental History, Philosophy, Structural Study of Culture Traits
Department of Language and Literature
Chinese Linguistics and Literature, Comparative Literature, English Linguistics and English and American Literature, German Linguistics and Literature, Japanese Linguistics and Literature, Korean Linguistics and Literature, Russian Linguistics and Literature
Faculty of Science (Freshmen Enrollment 200)
Department of Biology
Cell Biology, Environmental Biology, Genaral Physiology and Plant Physiology, Morphology and Systematics
Department of Chemistry
Analytical Chemistry, Natural Products Chemistry, Organic Chemistry, Physical Chemistry, Structural Chemistry
Department of Earth Science
Geochemistry, Geology, Geophysics, Glaciology, Hydrology
Department of Mathematics
Algebra and Geometry, Analysis, Applied Analysis and Computer Science, Mathematical Statistics
Department of Physics
Crystal Physics, Laser Physics, Molecular Physics, Quantum Physics, Radio and Microwave Physics, Solid State Physics

Foreign Student Admission

Qualifications for Applicants
Standard Qualifications Requirement
Applicants must take the Japanese Language Proficiency Test and General Examination for Foreign Students.
Examination at the University
Successful applicants will be selected on the basis of the results of Japanese Language Proficiency Test, General Examination for Foreign Students, scholastic ability examination which is performed by our university, the records of scholastic attainments prepared by the final schools, and the certificate of medical examination.
The subjects of the scholastic ability examination conducted by our university varies by faculty. Foreign applicants shall take the same examination as Japanese applicants.
Documents to be Submitted When Applying
Standard Documents Requirement
A letter recommendation from the diplomatic and consular office of his country in Japan is also required.
A guide for foreign applicants is available toward the end of October. Applicaion will be accepted between January 30 and February 8.

ONE-YEAR GRADUATE PROGRAMS

One-Year Special Graduate Course of Economics (Enrollment 10)
Economics
One-Year Special Graduate Course of Education (Enrollment 5)
Education

GRADUATE PROGRAMS

Graduate School of Engineering (First Year Enrollment : Master's 62)
Divisions
Chemical Engineering, Electrical Engineering, Electronic Engineering, Industrial Chemistry, Mechanical Engineering, Mechanical Engineering for Production, Metallurgical Engineering
Graduate School of Humanities (First Year Enrollment : Master's 10)
Divisions
Japanese, Oriental Culture, Occidental Culture
Graduate School of Science (First Year Enrollment : Master's 42)
Divisions
Biology, Chemistry, Earth Science, Mathematics, Physics

Foreign Student Admission
Qualifications for Applicants
Standard Qualifications Requirement
Examination at the University
Scholastic ability examination (written and oral), certificate of medical examination and the re-

port from the university graduated from.

Documents to be Submitted When Applying

Standard Documents Requirement

An application guide is available to ward the end of June, and in January for the Graduate School of Humanities.

Research Institutes and Centers

Center for Research and Training in Teacher Education attached to the Faculty of Education, Information Processing Center, Research and Development Center, Tritium Research Center

For Further Information

Undergraduate Admission

Entrance Examination Section, Student Division, Student Office, Toyama University, 3190 Gofuku, Toyama-shi, Toyama 930 ☎ 0764–41–1271 ext. 497

Graduate Admission

Graduate School of Humanities: Educational Affairs Section, Faculty of Humanities, Toyama University, 3190 Gofuku, Toyama-shi, Toyama 930 ☎ 0764–41–1271 ext. 286

Graduate School of Science: Educational Affairs Section, Faculty of Science, Toyama University, 3190 Gofuku, Toyama-shi, Toyama 930 ☎ 0764–41–1271 ext. 285

Graduate School of Engineering: Educational Affairs Section, Faculty of Engineering, Toyama University, 3190 Gofuku, Toyama-shi, Toyama 930 ☎ 0764–41–1271 ext. 719

Toyohashi University of Technology

(Toyohashi Gijutsukagaku Daigaku)

1-1 Hibarigaoka, Tenpaku-cho, Toyohashi-shi, Aichi 440   ☎ 0532–47–0111

Faculty
        Profs. 60   Assoc. Profs. 54
        Assist. Profs. Full–time 13; Part–time 66
        Res. Assocs. 43
Number of Students
        Undergrad. 940   Grad. 591
Library   75, 860 volumes

Outline and Characteristics of the University

Toyohashi University of Technology (TUT) was founded in 1976 by the Japanese government. The graduate school was inaugurated in 1980 with the Master's program, followed by the addition of the Doctor's program in 1986. This is a new type of institution for higher education established with priority placed on graduate courses. Its specific goal is to meet the urgent social need for a new breed of engineers able to meet the challenges of today and tomorrow.

The main body of our students consists of stu-

dents from technical colleges. They start their study here from the junior (third-year) level and finish the undergraduate courses in two years. This is followed by another two years of graduate education. A small number of students (about 20%) are admitted from both regular non-technical and technical high schools into our freshman class. They must attend for six years to complete the whole course of their education.

At TUT all students are expected to enroll in the Master's program. Some of the undergraduate students choose to begin their careers in industries after completing their undergraduate program, but such students are the exception.

Practicability is emphasized in our education. It is for that reason that our students spend two full months at on-the-job training at factories or research facilities in industries, where they are given a research theme and guided by industrial personnel.

TUT recognizes the importance of promoting international exchange. The university is prepared to open its doors as wide as possible and accommodate students and researchers from abroad. In fact, foreign students from 15 different countries have already started their study in our university. The number of foreign students is expected to increase steadily in the near future.

UNDERGRADUATE PROGRAMS

Faculty of Engineering (First Year Enrollment: 100, Third Year Enrollment: 330)

Department of Electrical and Electronic Engineering

Electric System Engineering, Electronic Devices, Fundamental Research

Department of Energy Engineering

Design Engineering of Energy Systems and Components, Energy Conversion Engineering, Thermal and Fluid Engineering

Department of Information and Computer Sciences

Computer Engineering, Information Processing Engineering, Information Systems Engineering

Department of Knowledge-based Information Engineering

Chemical Information Science, Computer Science, Function-related Information Engineering

Department of Materials Science

Industrial Analytical Chemistry, Industrial Inorganic Chemistry, Industrial Organic Chemistry

Department of Production Systems Engineering

Fabrication Engineering, Materials Science and Engineering, Production Systems Design and Control

Department of Regional Planning

Environment Engineering, Planning and Design, Structural Engineering

Foreign Student Admission

Qualifications for Applicants

Standard Qualifications Requirement
Examination at the University
Same as Japanese applicants
Documents to be Submitted When Applying
Standard Documents Requirement
JFSAT score

GRADUATE PROGRAMS

Graduate School of Engineering (First Year Enrollment : Master's 300, Doctor's 18)
Doctor's Program: *Divisions*
Comprehensive Energy Engineering, Materials System Engineering, Systems and Information Engineering
Master's Program: *Divisions*
Electrical and Electronic Engineering, Energy Engineering, Information and Computer Sciences, Materials Science, Production Systems Engineering, Regional Planning

Foreign Student Admission
Qualifications for Applicants
Master's Program
Standard Qualifications Requirement
Examination at the University
Master's Program
1. Written and Oral Examinations
   (a) Area examination: This examination is to ascertain whether or not the applicant is prepared for the advanced program in the intended area of study.
   (b) Language examination: Each applicant must demonstrate a proficiency in Japanese and one of the following languages: English, German, and French. (Chosen language must be shown on the application form.)
2. Medical Inspection
   Medical Inspection is, in general, made by a review of medical certificate. Some applicants, however, may be asked to undergo a detailed examination during the test period.
Doctor's Program
1. Written Examinations:
   (a) Subjects related to the intended area of research
   (b) Language: Japanese and English
2. Oral Examination: Tests by interview on the Master's thesis (or the equivalent), subjects of the areas studied, and the outline of the research intended for the Doctor's program.
Documents to be Submitted When Applying
Standard Documents Requirement
*
Research Institutes and Centers
Computer Center, Language Center, Manufacturing Technology Center, Research Center for Chemometrics, Research Center of Physical Fitness, Sports and Health, Technology Development Center

Facilities/Services for Foreign Students
International House
Shared Facilities; Lounge, Meeting Room, Japanese-Style Room
Accommodation; 46 Rooms (Single 40, Couple 6)
Special Programs for Foreign Students
Japanese language supplementary classes for overseas students are available as part of formal undergraduate education.
For Further Information
Undergraduate and Graduate Admission
Entrance Examination Section, Office of Admission, Toyohashi University of Technology, 1-1 Hibarigaoka, Tenpaku-cho, Toyohashi-shi, Aichi 440 ☎ 0532–47–0111 ext. 333

The University of Electro-Communications
(Denki-tsushin Daigaku)
1-5-1 Chofugaoka, Chofu-shi, Tokyo 182
☎ 0424–83–2161

Faculty
Profs. 93   Assoc. Profs. 77
Assist. Profs. Full–time 21; Part–time 192
Res. Assocs. 66
Number of Students
Undergrad. 3, 342   Grad. 367
Library 278, 747 volumes

Outline and Characteristics of the University
Denki-tsushin Daigaku, the University of Electro-Communications, was founded originally as the Technical Institute for Wireless Communications in 1918.

It is now one of 95 national universities in Japan. The university, comprising a single faculty, the Faculty of Electro-Communications, emerged in 1949 when the authority of the Institute was transferred from the Ministry of Communications to the Ministry of Education, Science, and Culture. Since then the campus has moved from its original site in Meguro to its present location in Chofu, some 30 kilometers west of downtown Tokyo. A number of departments have been added, and the University has grown into a center for research and instruction in the broader areas of science and engineering.

Today, the University offers courses leading to the Bachelor of Engineering, Masters of Engineering and Doctor of Engineering degrees in all 5 academic Departments: Electronic Engineering, Communications and Systems, Computer Science and Information Mathematics, Mechanical and Control Engineering, Applied Physics and Chemistry.

Denki-tsushin Daigaku promotes research actively and also provides educational leadership through teaching in the fields of science and engineering.

UNDERGRADUATE PROGRAMS

Faculty of Electro-Communications (Freshmen Enrollment 980)

Department of Applied Physics and Chemistry
Atomic Physics and its Applications, Condensed Matter Physics and its Applications, Molecular Engineering

Department of Communications and Systems
Communication Engineering, Electronics Systems, Industrial and Systems Engineering, Information Systems

Department of Computer Science and Information Mathematics
Computer Application, Computer Science, Information Mathematics, Software Engineering

Department of Electronic Engineering
Electron Devices, Electronic Measurements and Control Engineering, Information and Wave Transmission, Optelectronics and Wave Engineering

Department of Mechanical and Control Engineering
Design and Manufacturing System Engineering, Engineering Analysis, Robotic Engineering

Foreign Student Admission

Qualifications for Applicants
Standard Qualifications Requirement
Examination at the University
A written examination and interview.
Documents to be Submitted When Applying
Standard Documents Requirement
JLPT and GEFS scores

Application forms are available at the Admissions Office from early November. All applicants are required to submit the specified application documents to the Admissions Office by late January.

GRADUATE PROGRAMS

Graduate School of Electro-Communications (First Year Enrollment : Master's 104, Doctor's 24)

Divisions
Applied Physics and Chemisty, Communications and Systems, Computer Science and Information Mathematics, Electronic Engineering, Mechanical and Control Engineering

Foreign Student Admission

Qualifications for Applicants
Master's and Doctor's Program
Standard Qualifications Requirement
Examination at the University
Master's and Doctor's Program
Applicants residing in Japan must take the entrance examination consisting of a written examination and interview.

Documents to be Submitted When Applying
Standard Documents Requirement

Application forms are available at the Admissions Office from July. All applicants are required to submit the specified application documents to the Admissions Office by late September.

＊

Research Institutes and Centers
Institute for Laser Science, Sugadaira Space Wave Observatory

Facilities/Services for Foreign Students
The University offers a two–day field trip each year to increase foreign students' understanding and appreciation of Japan. In addition, social gatherings are held twice a year to promote mutual friendship between foreign students, academic advisers, adminstrative staff and Japanese students.

Special Programs for Foreign Students
The University offers Japanese language classes as compulsory, subjects to increase the undergraduate foreign students proficiency in understanding, speaking, reading and writing Japanese. The University also offers some subjects related to Information Processing by using peripheral devices for the exclusive use of foreign students.

Graduate foreign students are permitted to attend advanced Japanese language covrses.

For Further Information
Undergraduate and Graduate Admission
Admission Office, the University of Electro-Communications, 1-5-1 Chofugaoka, Chofu-shi, Tokyo 182
☎ 0424–83–2161 ext. 2544

The University of Library and Information Science
(Toshokan Joho Daigaku)

1-2 Kasuga, Tsukuba-shi, Ibaraki 305
☎ 0298–52–0511

Faculty
Profs.　24　　Assoc. Profs.　15
Assist. Profs.　Full–time　5; Part–time　36
Res. Assocs.　10
Number of Students
Undergrad.　613　　Grad.　25
Library　99, 577 volumes

Outline and Characteristics of the University
The University of Library and Information Science (ULIS) was founded in 1979 in order to promote the new field of Library and Information Science.

The goals of the university are to carry out research and educational activities to contribute to the development of the discipline and to prepare students for professions which require well-balanced knowledge and specialized technology to meet the demands of society. Each academic year since 1980, 120 students have been accepted and the number increased to 140 in 1986 and to 150 in 1987, while 20 transfer students have also been admitted since 1982. Furthermore, a graduate school offering a Master of Arts degree was started in 1984. Graduates have entered various other fields, as well as the information industry and libraries. Part of the educational facilities as well as some specialized courses are open to the public.

The campus is located near the center of Tsukuba Science City, and occupies a flat-site of 113, 419 m² where steel-and-concrete buildings are erected with a total floor area of 21, 261 m². On the site stands an auditorium where lectures and events for up to 600 participants can be held, and a gymnasium where indoor sports such as volleyball and basketball can be played, together with an outdoor swimming pool, four all-weather tennis courts, and an athletic field.

UNDERGRADUATE PROGRAMS

Library and Information Science (Freshmen Enrollment: 150, Junior Enrollment: 20)
Department of Library and Information Science

Foreign Student Admission
Qualifications for Applicants
Standard Qualifications Requirement
Examination at the University
Special entrance examinations are arranged in February for qualified foreign students who essentially have been educated outside of Japan. Applicant must have taken the Japanese Language Proficiency Test and General Examination for Foreign Students. He/she must also take an interview at the University.
Documents to be Submitted When Applying
Standard Documents Requirement

GRADUATE PROGRAMS

Graduate School of Library and Information Science (First Year Enrollment : Master's 16)
Division
Library and Information Science

Foreign Student Admission
Qualifications for Applicants
Master's Program
Standard Qualifications Requirement
Examination at the University
Master's Program
Special tests on English, mathematics and specialized subjects, and an interview in February
Documents to be Submitted When Applying
Standard Documents Requirement

*
Research Institutes and Centers

Foreign Language Education Center, Physical Education and Health Center
Facilities/Services for Foreign Students
International House: Lobby, Conference Room, Study room.
Accommodation: 20 Rooms (Single 16, Couple 2, Family 2).
For Further Information
Undergraduate and Graduate Admission
Administration Office (Educational Division), University of Library and Information Science, 1-2 Kasuga, Tsukuba-shi, Ibaraki 305 ☎ 0298-52-0511 ext. 233

University of the Ryukyus
(Ryukyu Daigaku)
1 Senbaru, Nishihara-cho, Okinawa 903-01
☎ 09889-5-2221

Faculty
    Profs.   223   Assoc. Profs.   203
    Assist. Profs.   Full–time   84; Part–time   381
    Res. Assocs.   208
Number of Students
    Undergrad.   5, 669   Grad.   237
Library   602, 929 volumes

Outline and Characteristics of the University
The University of the Ryukyus was founded in 1950 by the United States Civil Administration of the Ryukyu Islands, the first public institution for higher education to be established on Okinawa. The University represents a response to the people's need for such facilities and the realization of a long standing dream that originated in the first quarter of the present century. Following a period of administration under the Government of the Ryukyu Islands, during which time a three-year Junior College and the College of Health Sciences were added to the original six colleges, the University acquired its present status as a national institution upon the reversion of Okinawa to Japan in 1972. Faculty of Medicine was established in 1979 and incorporated the previously existing College of Health Sciences in 1981.

At present the University is comprised of the Faculties of Agriculture, Education, Engineering, Law and Letters, Medicine, and Science, as well as the Division of General Education and the Junior College. In addition to the undergraduate programs, courses of study leading to the master's degree are offered by the Faculties of Agriculture, Engineering, and Science, and the School of Health Sciences.

The more than 70 islands that make up Okinawa Prefecture extend south from Kyushu to Taiwan between the Pacific Ocean and the East China Sea. The University campus, with an area of over 1. 25 million m² is situated in a hilly region of the main Okinawa island, commanding a view of the sea that mirrors the myriad shades of blue of the ever-changing subtropical sky.

Okinawa is Japan's window to Southeast Asia, and thus the University is ideally placed for research in Japan's historical and cultural ties with the south. The location also favors research in such fields as marine science, tropical agriculture, and tropical medicine. The Marine Research Laboratory, the Tropical Agricultural Research Institute, the University Hospital, and other facilities offer unique opportunities for advanced research and training.

The founders' wish to make this University "a cultural dynamo from which will flow a new force and a new light into every village in the Ryukyu Islands" has been inherited by their successors, who in turn wish this new force and light to flow even farther. Thus, the University aspires to be genuinely international in posture, building on its earlier close ties with such institutions as Michigan State University in the United States. Presently, under the Student Exchange Program, a select number of students receive scholarships for study overseas. Approximately 40 foreign studennts are admitted each year from abroad as research students, auditors, and regular undergraduates. Through various programs, including the "Invitation of Foreign Scientists" sponsored by the Japan Society for the Promotion of Science, approximately 20 foreign researchers visit the University each year. Institutional agreement has recently been reached with two Thai universities, Chulalongkorn University and Thammasat University. Under the agreement with Chulalongkorn University, researchers in the field of science participate in joint projects, while the agreement with the latter university facilitates scientific and scholarly exchange in the humanities and social sciences.

UNDERGRADUATE PROGRAMS

Faculty of Agriculture (Freshmen Enrollment: 155)
Department of Agricultural Chemistry
Agricultural Processing and Pesticide Chemistry, Applied Microbiology, Biological Chemistry and Nutritional Chemistry, Soil Science and Plant Nutrition, Sugar Technological Chemistry
Department of Agricultural Engineering
Agricultural Land Engineering, Agricultural Process Engineering, Farm Machinery, Hydraulic Structures Engineering, Irrigation Engineering and Agricultural Hydrology
Department of Agriculture
Crop Science, Entomology, Farm Management, Horticultural Science, Phytopathology, Plant Breeding
Department of Animal Husbandry
Animal Anatomy and Physiology, Animal Breeding and Reproduction, Animal Environmental Science and Hygiene, Chemistry and Technology of Animal Products and Tropical Grassland Science, Livestock Feeding and Management

Department of Forestry
Forest Management and Policy, Forest Products Processing, Forest Protection and Engineering, Tropical Silviculture
Faculty of Education (Freshmen Enrollment: 220)
Department of Arts and Crafts
Art Education, Ceramic Art, Design, Painting, Sculpture, Textile Arts
Department of Education
Educational System, History of Education, Pedagogics, School Library, Social Education
Department of Educational Psychology
Developmental Psychology, Educational Psychology
Department of English
English and American Literature, English Language, Teaching of English
Department of Health and Physical Education
History and Theory of Physical Education, Physical Exercise, Physiology and Hygiene, Teaching Method of Health and Physical Education
Department of Home Economics
Clothing and Textiles, Cooking, Food Science, Home Economics Education, Nutrition
Department of Japanese
Chinese Classical Literature, Japanese Language, Japanese Literature, Teaching of Japanese
Department of Mathematics
Algebra and Geometry, Analysis and Applied Mathematics, Teaching of Mathematics
Department of Music
Instrumental Music, Music Theory and History of Music, Teaching of Music, Vocal Music
Department of Natural Sciences
Biology, Chemistry, Physical Geography, Physics, Teaching of Natural Sciences
Department of Social Sciences
Economics, Geography, History, Law, Philosophy, Social Science Education
Department of Special Education
Education of Handicapped Children, Psychology of Handicapped Children
Department of Technical Education
Electrical Engineering, Mechanical Engineering, Metal Work, Technical Education, Wood Work
Faculty of Engineering (Freshmen Enrollment: 295)
Department of Architectural Engineering
Architecture and Planning, Disaster Prevention Engineering, Environmental Engineering, Structural Engineering
Department of Civil Engineering
Hydraulic Engineering, Soil and Sanitation Engineering, Structural Engineering, Traffic and Bridge Engineering
Department of Electrical Engineering
Communication Engineering, Electronics, Eletrical Machinery and Power Systems, Fundamental Electrical Engineering
Department of Electronics and Information Engineering
Electronic Computer Systems, Electronics and Foun-

dations of Computer Science, Information Processing, Systems Engineering

Department of Energy and Mechanical Engineering

Energy Conversion, Material Science, Mechanical System Design, Thermo-Fluid System

Department of Mechanical Engineering

Engineering Materials and Manufacturing Processes, Fluid Engineering, Mechanics and Machine Elements, Subdivisions, Thermal Engineering

Faculty of Law and Letters (Freshmen Enrollment: 365)

Department of Economics

Business Administration Course

Accounting, Business Administration, Information Management, Management Policy

Economics Course

Economic Policy, International Economics, Public Finance and Monetary Theory, Social Policies and Economic History

Department of History

Geography Course

Descriptive Geography, Geographic Description

History Course

European History, Japanese History, Oriental History

Department of Law and Political Science

Administration and History of Political Ideas, Civil Law, Civil Procedure Law, Commercial Law, Constitutional Law and Labor Law, Criminal Law and Criminal Procedure Law, International Law and Philosophy of Law, International Politics and Diplomatic History, Political Science and Political History

Department of Literature

English Language and Literature Course

American Literature, English Language, English Literature, German Language and Literature, Linguistics, Philosophy

Japanese Language and Literature Course

Chinese Literature and Ryukyuan Literature, Japanese Language, Japanese Literature

Department of Sociology

Education and Psychology Course

Educational Sociology, Social Psychology

Sociology Course

Public Information, Social Anthropology, Social Welfare, Sociology

Faculty of Medicine (Freshmen Enrollment: 170)

Department of Health Sciences

Basic Health Sciences, Health Administration, Health Care, Health Technology

Department of Medicine

Anatomy, Bacteriology, Biochemistry, Dermatology, Internal Medicine, Legal Medicine, Obstetrics, Gynecology, Ophthalmology, Orthopedics, Otorhinolaryngology, Parasitology, Pathology, Pediatrics, Pharmacology, Physiology, Preventive Medicine, Radiology, Surgery

Faculty of Science (Freshmen Enrollment: 185)

Department of Biology

Ecology, Physiology and Biochemistry, Phytotaxonomy and Phytomorphology, Structural Zoology

Department of Chemistry

Analytical Chemistry, Inorganic Chemistry, Organic Chemistry, Physical Chemistry

Department of Marine Science

Coral Reef Studies, Geology, Marine Biology, Marine Environmental Science, Sedimentology

Department of Mathematics

Algebra, Analysis, Applied Mathematics, Geometry

Department of Physics

Electromagnetics, Mechanics, Quantum Physics, Solid State Physics

Foreign Student Admission

Qualifications for Applicants

Standard Qualifications Requirement

Examination at the University

Examination Date: in March.

Documents to be Submitted When Applying

Standard Documents Requirement

JLPT and GEFS scores

Application forms are available at the Office of Student Affairs, University of the Ryukyus. All respective applicants are required to submit the specified application documents to the Office of Student Affairs by the end of November.

GRADUATE PROGRAMS

Graduate School of Agriculture (First Year Enrollment : Master's 40)

Divisions

Agricultural Chemistry, Agricultural Engineering, Agriculture, Animal Husbandry, Forestry

Graduate School of Engineeing (First Year Enrollment : Master's 15)

Divisions

Architectural and Civil Engineering, Elctronics and Information Engineering, Mechanical Engineeing

Graduate School of Health Sciences (First Year Enrollment : Master's 10)

Divisions

Health Administration, Health Care, Health Technology

Graduate School of Law (First Year Enrollment: Master's 10)

Divisions

Law

Graduate School of Medicine (First Year Enrollment: Doctor's 30)

Divisions

Bioregulation Study, Environmental Medicine-Ecology, Morphology-Function Study

Graduate School of Science (First Year Enrollment : Master's 21)

Divisions

Biology, Chemistry, Marine Science, Mathematics, Physics

Foreign Student Admission
Qualifications for Applicants
Master's Program
    Standard Qualifications Requirement
Examination at the University
Master's Program
    A written examination and an interview.
Doctor's Program
    A written examination and an interview.
Documents to be Submitted When Applying
    Standard Documents Requirement
    Application forms are available at the Academic Affairs Section of the Office of the respective Graduate School. The specified application documents should be submitted in September to the same place.

Research Institutes and Centers
Agricultural Experiment Station, Computer Center, Engineering Manufacture Laboratory, Experimental Forest, Health Administration Center, Radioisotope Laboratory, Research Institute of Tropical Agriculture, Sesoko Marine Science Center, University Hospital

Facilities/Services for Foreign Students
    In addition to the regular courses they take for university credit in the Division of General Education, foreign students may receive special instruction through the "tutor" system organized by the Student Office. This "tutor" system, offered on a regular basis and adaptable to individual student needs, provides assistance in Japanese language and other subjects.
    International House:
Shared Facilities: Lobby, Conference Room, Library, Japanese-style Room
Accommodation: 60 Rooms (54 single, 4 for married couples, and 2 for larger families)

Special Programs for Foreign Students
    The Division of General Education offers courses in Japanese language at the elementary, intermediate, and advanced levels, as well as courses treating the history, culture, and geography of Japan.

For Further Information
Undergraduate and Graduate Admission
International Affairs Section, Administration Office, University of the Ryukyus, 1 Senbaru, Nishihara-cho, Okinawa 903-01 ☎ 09889-5-2221 ext. 2125

The University of Tokushima
(Tokushima Daigaku)

2-24 Shinkura-cho, Tokushima-shi, Tokushima 770
☎ 0886-22-5131

Faculty
    Profs.   221   Assoc. Profs.   174
    Assist. Profs.   Full-time   88; Part-time   699
    Res. Assocs.   272

Number of Students
    Undergrad.   4, 601   Grad.   385
    Library   542, 882 volumes

Outline and Characteristics of the University
    The University of Tokushima, a large national university in the southwest of Japan, is located in the old castle town of Tokushima, at the foot of the gentle, rolling hill of Bizan. In the background are the Shikoku Mountains called the Tibet of Shikoku Island; in the foreground is the fertile delta of the Yoshino River through which the Yoshino flows into the Kii Straits.
    The University was established on May 31, 1949 in accordance with the National School Establishment Law. It then consisted of three faculties: the Faculty of Education and Liberal Arts, the School of Medicine and the Faculty of Engineering.
    In the 1950's, the University expanded to include the annexed University Hospital with its affiliated schools, the Faculty of Pharmaceutical Sciences, two branches of the University Library, and the Graduate School of Medicine. The Technical College offering evening courses subsequently opened its doors to the public.
    In the 1960's, the Graduate Schools of Engineering, Pharmaceutical Sciences, and Nutrition were added. The Institute for Enzyme Research was also organized in the School of Medicine.
    The Medicinal Plant Graden of the Faculty of Pharmaceutical Sciences and the Health Service Center were founded in 1975.
    The School of Dentistry was founded in 1976, its hospital and Graduate School in 1979 and 1983 respectively. In 1986, the Faculty of Education was reorganized into the Faculty of Integrated Arts and Sciences.
    Most of the main institutions are located in two sections of Tokushima city. Josanjima Campus is comprised of the Faculty of Integrated Arts and Sciences, the Faculty of Engineering and the College of General Education, and Kuramoto Campus is comprised of the School of Medicine, the School of Dentistry and the Faculty of the Pharmaceutical Sciences. The history of the University of Tokushima is a thing alive, always growing.

UNDERGRADUATE PROGRAMS

School of Dentistry (Freshmen Enrollment: 60)
Course in Dentistry
Biochemistry, Dental Engineering, Fixed Prosthodontics, Microbiology, Operative Dentistry, Oral Anatomy, Oral and Maxillofacial Surgery, Oral Pathology, Oral Radiology, Orthodontics, Pedodontics, Periodontology and Endodontology, Pharmacology, Physiology, Preventive Dentistry, Removable Prosthodontics
Faculty of Engineering (Freshmen Enrollment: 475)
Department of Applied Physics and Mathematics

Mathematics and Applied Mathematics, Solid State Physics

Department of Biological Science and Technology
Biological Science, Biological Technology

Department of Chemical Science and Technology
Chemical Process Engineering, Physicochemical and Material Science, Synthetic and Polymer Chemistry

Department of Civil Engineering
Disaster Prevention and Environmental Engineering, Geotechnical Engineering, Structural Engineering and Design, Transportation and Urban Planning

Department of Electric and Electronic Engineering
Circuits, Communications, Controls and Computer Science, Electric Energy Engineering, Material Science and Device Engineering

Department of Information Science and Intelligent System
Information and Computer Science, Intelligent Systems Engineering

Department of Mechanical Engineering
Intelligent Mechanics, Mechanical Science, Mechanical System

Faculty of Integrated Arts and Sciences (Freshmen Enrollment: 250)

Department of Integrated Arts and Sciences
Arts
Calligraphy, Construction, Instrumental Music and Ensemble, Musicology, Painting and Science of Art, Sculpture, Vocal Music and Chorus
Behavioral Sciences
Applied Psychology, Basic Psychology, Sociology
Economics and Management
Economic Policy, Economic Theory and Economic History, Industrial Technology, Law, Management
Health Sciences
Medical Science, Method of Physical Education, Nutrition and Health Administration, Physiological Regulation, Physiological Sciences, Science of Living, Science of Physical Education, Studies of Physical Education
Humanities
Archaeology, Chinese Literature, English Linguistics, English Literature, Geography, German Linguistics and German Literature, History of Asia, History of Europe, History of Japan, Japanese Literature, Japanese Philology, Pedagogy, Philosophy
Natural Sciences
Applied Materials Science, Applied Mathematical Science, Fundamental Materials Science, General Materials Science, Information and Systems, Mathematics, Solid State Physics

School of Medicine (Freshmen Enrollment: 150)

Course in Medicine
Anatomy, Anesthesiology, Bacteriology, Biochemistry, Dermatology, Forensic Medicine, Gynecology and Obstetrics, Hygiene, Internal Medicine, Laboratory Medicine, Neurosurgery, Ophthalmology, Orthopedic Surgery, Otorhinolaryngology, Parasitology, Pathology, Pediatrics, Pharmacology, Physiology, Psychiatry and Neurology, Public Health, Radiology, Surgery, Urology, Virology

Course in Nutrition
Applied Nutrition, Clinico-Pathological Nutrition, Food Science, Hygiene of Foods, Nutritional Chemistry, Nutritional Physiology, Nutrition of Particular Status

Faculty of Pharmaceutical Sciences (Freshmen Enrollment: 80)

Department of Pharmaceutical Sciences
Pharmaceutical Life Science (Biochemistry, Health Chemistry, Microbial Chemistry), Pharmacodynamics and Pharmaceutics (Chemical Pharfmacology, Pharmaceutical Analytical Chemistry, Pharmaceuti-tical Physical Chemistry, Pharmaceutics)

Department of Pharmaceutical Technochemistry
Medicinal Chemistry (Chemical and Pharmaceutical Technology, Physical Pharmacy, Synthetic Pharmaceutical Chemistry), Medicinal Material and Natural Product Chemistry (Medicinal Biochemistry, Pharmaceutical Chemistry, Pharmacognosy)

Foreign Student Admission

Qualifications for Applicants
Standard Qualifications Requirement
Examination at the University
A written exam.
Faculty of Pharmaceutical Sciences,
Faculty of Engineering: special exam and an interview.
Documents to be Submitted When Applying
Standard Documents Requirement
JFSAT score
Application forms are available at the Bureau of Student Affainrs at the office of each Faculty from early December. All applicants are required to submit the specified application documents to the Bureau of Students Affairs by February 15.

Faculty of Engineering; Same as those for Japanese applicants

Statements of qualification for forein applicants are under consideration at present.

GRADUATE PROGRAMS

Graduate School of Dentistry (First Year Enrollment : Doctor's 18)

Division
Dentistry

Graduate School of Engineering (First Year Enrollment : Master's 74)

Divisions
Applied Chemistry, Chemical Enigineering, Civil Engineering, Construction Engineering, Electrical Engineering, Electronic Engineering, Information Science and Systems Engineering, Mechanical Engineering, Precision Mechanics

Graduate School of Medicine (First Year Enrollment : Doctor's 56)

Divisions
Basic Medicine (pathological fields), Basic Medicine

(physiological fields), Clinical Medicine (internal medicine), Clinical Medicine (surgical fields), Social Medicine

Graduate School of Nutrition (First Year Enrollment : Master's 14, Doctor's 7)
Division
Nutrition

Graduate School of Pharmaceutical Sciences (First Year Enrollment : Master's 26 Doctor's 6)
Division
Pharmaceutical Sciences

Foreign Student Admission
Qualifications for Applicants
Master's Program
Standard Qualifications Requirement
Doctor's Program
Standard Qualifications Requirement
Examination at the University
Master's Program
Applicants must take an entrance examination consisting of a written exam (as follows) and an interview on the subjects of intended research.
Graduate School of Nutrition: Nutritional Science, English or German
Graduate School of Pharmaceutical Sciences: Pharmaceutical Science, English or German
Graduate School of Engineering:
Course in Applied Chemistry; Mathematics or Physics, English and Japanese, Three subjects out of Inorganic Chemistry, Organic Chemistry, Physical Chemistry, Chemstry of High Polymers, Analytical Chemistry, Electrochemistry
Course in Information Science and Systems Engineering; Mathematics, English and Japanese, Three subjects out of Information Theory, Algorithms and Data Structures, Mathematical Programming, Linear System Theory, Electronic Circuits, Computer Engineering, Numerical Analysis and Programming
Course in Mechanical Engineering, and Precision Mechanics; Mathematics or Physics, English or Japanese, Statics and Dynamics
Course in Chemical Engineering; Mathematics, English or Japanese, Chemical Engineering of High Pressure, Chemical Reaction Engineering, Unit Operation, Chemical Plants and Chemical Engineering Materials
Course in Civil Engineering, and Construction Engineering; Mathematics, English or Japanese, One subject out of Structural Mechanics, Hydraulics, Soil Mechanics, Concrete Technology, Planning Theory of Civil Engineering
Course in Electrical Engineering, and Electronic Engineering; Mathematics, English and Japanese, Electromagnetic Theory and Circuit Theory, Four subjects out of Electrical Machines, Electric Power Engineering, Communicantion Engineering, Materials Science and Engineering, Electronic Device, Electronic Circuits, Control Engineering
Doctor's Program

Applicants must take an entrance examination consisting of a written exam (as follows) and an interview on the subjects of intended research.
Graduate School of Medicine: The subject which the applicant is going to study and two foreign languages (English, German or French)
Graduate School of Dentistry: English
Graduate School of Nutrition: English or German.
Documents to be Submitted When Applying
Standard Documents Requirement
Any further inquiries regarding application procedure should be made to the respective office of the Graduate School concerned.

*

Research Institutes and Centers
Institute for Animal Experimentation, Institute for Enzyme Research, Institute for University Extension, Medicinal Plant Garden
For Further Information
Undergraduate Admission
Admission Office, University of Tokushima, 2-24 Shinkura-cho, Tokushima-shi, Tokusihima 770 ☎ 0886-22-5131 ext. 653
Graduate Admission
Graduate School of Medicine and Nutrition: Section of School Affairs, School of Medicine, University of Tokushima, 3-18-15 Kuramoto-cho, Tokushima-shi, Tokushima 770 ☎ 0886-31-3111 ext. 2121
Graduate School of Dentistry: Section of School Affairs, School of Dentistry, Univerity of Tokushima, 3-18-15 Kuramoto-cho, Tokushima-shi, Tokushima 770 ☎ 0886-31-3111 ext. 5126
Graduate School of Pharmaceutical Sciences: Section of School Affairs, Faculty of Pharmaceutical Sciences, Univertity of Tokushima, 1-78 Sho-machi, Tokushima-shi, Tokushima 770 ☎ 0886-31-3111 ext. 6130
Graduate School of Engineering: Section of School Affairs, Faculty of Engineering, University of Tokushima, 2-1 Minamijosanjima-cho, Tokushima-shi, Tokushima 770 ☎ 0886-23-2311 ext. 4152

The University of Tokyo
(Tokyo Daigaku)
7-3-1 Hongo, Bunkyo-ku, Tokyo 113
☎ 03-812-2111

Faculty
Profs.   881   Assoc. Profs.   798
Assist. Profs.   Full-time   223
Res. Assocs.   1, 757
Number of Students
Undergrad.   14, 785   Grad.   5, 158
Library   5, 901, 899 volumes

Outline and Characteristics of the University
The University of Tokyo is the oldest national university, founded in 1877. It then consisted of four

Colleges: Law, Science, Literature and Medicine.

Since then the University has added new academic fields such as engineering, agriculture and economics and by 1919 the shape of the present University had essentially been formed with the exception of various research institutes and centers.

The Graduate School system started in 1886, but the present form of the graduate school was established in 1953.

Today the University has a student enrollment of about 19, 900 and a full-time faculty of 3, 700. It has ten Faculties, Graduate School with 11 divisions, 13 research institutes and other affiliated institutions.

The campus is centrally located at Hongo in Tokyo and occupies about 56 hectares of a former estate belonging to feudal lords. Parts of the landscaping of the original estate have been preserved and provide greenery and open space much needed in an otherwise crowded campus.

The University enjoys the highest reputation as an institution of higher learning and is known for the excellence of its faculty and students, and many of its graduates have always been leaders in the government, private and academic sectors.

There are about 1250 foreign students from 56 countries. More than 1, 700 foreign scholars come to the University for short as well as extended visits yearly.

UNDERGRADUATE PROGRAMS

Faculty of Agriculture (Freshmen Enrollment: 244)
Department of Agricultural Chemistry
Analytical Chemistry, Applied Microbiology, Biochemistry, Bioorganic Chemistry, Chemistry and Technology of Animal Products. Food Chemistry, Enzymology, Food Engineering, Microbiology, Microbiology and Fermentation, Nutritional Biochemistry and Animal Nutrition, Organic Chemistry, Pesticide Chemistry, Plant Nutrition and Fertilizer, Radiation Microbiology, Soil Science
Department of Agricultural Economics
Agricultural Economics, Agricultural Finance, Agricultural History, Agricultural Policy, Farm Management
Department of Agricultural Engineering
Agricultural Process Engineering and Processing, Agricultural Water Engineering, Conservation and Rural Engineering, Energy and Machinery, Environmental Engineering, Farm Power, Land Reclamation, Soil Physics and Soil Hydrology
Department of Agrobiology
Applied Entomology, Biometrics, Crop Science, Horticultural Science, Landscape Architecture, Plant Breeding and Genetics, Plant Ecology and Morphogenesis, Plant Pathology, Radiation Genetics, Sericultural Science
Department of Fisheries
Aquaculture Biology, Biochemistry of Aguatic Organisms, Fisheries Biology, Fisheries Oceanography, Fish Physiology, Technology of Marine Products
Department of Forest Products
Chemistry of Polymeric Materials, Forest Chemistry, Pulp and Paper Science, Woodbased Materials, Wood Chemistry, Wood Physics
Department of Forestry
Forest Botany, Forest Hydrology and Erosion Control, Forest Management, Forest Policy, Forest Utilization, Forest Zoology, Landscape Planning, Silviculture
Department of Veterinary Medical Sciences
Animal Breeding, Animal Management and Hygiene, Blomedical Science, Veterinary Anatomy, Veterinary Medicine and Parasitology, Veterinary Microbiology, Veterinary Pathology, Veterinary Pharmacology, Veterinary Physiology, Veterinary Surgery and Obstetrics
College of Arts and Sciences (Freshmen Enrollment: 157)
Department of Liberal Arts
American Studies, Asian Studies, British Studies, Classical Philology, Comparative Literature and Culture, Cultural Anthropology, Currents of World Thought, French Studies, German Studies, History and Philosophy of Science, Human Geography, International Relations, Latin American Studies, Russian Studies, Science of Human Behavior, Social Studies, Theory of Art
Department of Natural and Artificial Systems
Astrophysical Systems, Biological Systems, Ecological System Planning, Energy System Planning, Environmental Planning, Global System Planning, Information Science, Mathematical Science, Systems Science
Department of Pure and Applied Science
Applied Material Science, Chemical Physics, Chemistry of Inorganic Materials, Coordination Biology, Instrumentation for Physical Research, Mathematical Analysis, Physical Organic Chemistry, Polymer Chemistry, Solid State Physics, Theoretical Physics
Faculty of Economics (Freshmen Enrollment 376)
Department of Business Administration
Department of Economics
Accounting, Agricultural Economics, Asian Studies, Business Administration, Business Economics, Business History, Developing Economics, Econometrics, Economic Dynamics, Economic History, Economic History of Japan, Economic Policy, Economic Theory, Financial Management, Income Distribution, Industrial Organization, Industrial Relations, International Economics, International Finance, International Trade, Japanese Economy, Labor Economics, Mathematical Statistics, Money and Banking, Public Finance, Statistics, Transportation Economics, Western Economic History
Faculty of Education (Freshmen Enrollment: 82)
Department of Educational Administration
Adult Education and Youth Services, Educational Administration, Library Science
Department of Educational Psychology

Clinical Psychology, Educational Measurement, Educational Psychology

Department of Foundations of Education
Educational Sociology, History of Education, Science of Education

Department of Physical and Health Education
Health Education, Physical Education, Sports Sciences

Department of School Education
Comparative Education, Method of Education Curriculum

Faculty of Engineering (Freshmen Enrollment: 866)

Department of Aeronautics
Aerodynamics, Aeroengine, Aeronautics, Aircraft Materials, Astronautics, Combustion, Gas Dynamics, Propulsion, Structural Dynamics

Department of Applied Physics
Applied Mathematics and Fluid Dynamics, Applied Physics, Atomic and Molecular Physics, Metal Physics, Optics, Physics of Polymers and Liquid Crystals, Plasma Physics, Polymer Physics and Biophysics, Quantum Electronics, Semiconductor Materials, Solid State Physics, Surface Physics, Vacuum Physics

Department of Architecture
Architectural Planning and Design Welding, Building Construction, Building Equipment, Building Materials, Environment Engineering, Fire Protection, History of Architecture, Steel Structure, Structural Engineering

Department of Chemical Engineering
Chemical Engineering Kinetics and Reactor Design, Chemical Process Engineering, Chemical Reaction Engineering, Heat-Transfer Operations, Mass Transfer Operations, Mechanical Operations, Powder Technology and Sciences, Transport Phenomena

Department of Civil Engineering
Bridge and Structural Engineering, Concrete and Reinforced Concrete Engineering, Harbour and Coastal Engineering, Hydraulics, Regional Planning, River Engineering, Soil Mechanics and Foundation Engineering, Structural Dynamics, Transportation Engineering and Planning

Department of Electrical Engineering
Applied Electrics, Applied Electrostatic and Air Pollution Control, Communication Systems Design and Switching Engineering, Computer Engineering, Control Engineering, Electronic Devices, Electron Systems Engineering, High Voltage Engineering, Information Processing, Information Theory and Communication Engineering, Power Electronics, Power System Engineering, Transmission and Processing of Cognitive Information

Department of Electronic Engineering
Electronic Circuit Engineering, Electronic Systems, Information Theory and Communication Systems, Microwaves and Optoelectronics, Physical Electronics, Plasma and Superconducting Engineering, Semiconductor Electronics, Solid State Electronics, Speech and Optical Information Processing

Department of Industrial Chemistry
Analytical Chemistry, Applied Physical Chemistry, Ceramic Science, Chemistry of Engineering Materials, Crystal Chemistry, Energy Chemistry, Energy Chemistry, Industrial Organic Chemistry, Polymer Chemistry, Spectrochemical Analysis, Thermodynamics of Solid, X-ray Spectroscopy

Department of Marine Engineering
Controls and Propulsion, Dynamics of Machines, Gas Dynamics, Heat Transfer, Marine Gas Turbines, Steam Power Engineering, Strength of Materials

Department of Material Science
Applied Solid State Physics, Iron and Steel Materials, Nonferrous Metals and Alloys, Strength of Materials, Structure of Metals, Surface Technology

Department of Mathematical Engineering and Information Physics
Biocybernetics, Biological Engineering, Continuum Physics, Control Engineering, Industrial Instrumentation, Information Theory, Language Information Processing, Mathematical and Applied Statistics, Pattern Recognition, Precision Measurement, Remote Sensing, Software Engineering, Statistical Engineering

Department of Mechanical Engineering
Fluid Machinery, Fluid Mechanics, Heat Engineering, Heat Transfer, Information Systems, Internal Combustion Engines, Machine Design, Mechanics of Machines, Steam Power Engineering

Department of Mechanical Engineering for Production
Automatic Control, Automobile and Railway Vehicle Engineering, Casting, Machine Structure, Mechanical Vibrations, System Engineering and Industrial Management, Welding and Plastic Working of Metals

Department of Metallurgy
Electrometallurgy, Hydrometallurgy, Iron and Steelmaking, Mechanical Metallurgy, Metal Casting, Metallurgical, Nonferrous Extractive Metallurgy, Reaction

Department of Mineral Development Engineering
Fire Jet Technology, Marine Geology, Mineral Processing, Mining Geology, Petroleum Geology, Petroleum Reservoir Engineering, Rocket Mechanics

Department of Naval Architecture
Dynamics of Ships, Fatigue Strength of Materials, Fracture and Strength of Materials, Merchant Ship Design, Ship Hydrodynamics, Ship Resistance and Propulsion, Strength of Ships, Structural Design with Composites, Structure of Ships and Welding Dynamics

Department of Nuclear Engineering
Applied Radiation and Reactor Chemistry, Nuclear Chemical Engineering, Nuclear Fuels and Metallurgy, Nuclear Fusion Engineering, Nuclear Propulsion and Structural Engineering, Nuclear Radiation Measurements, Nuclear Reactor Engineering, Nuclear Reactor Heat Transfer, Nuclear Reactor Materials

Department of Precision Machinery Engineering
Automatic Assembly, Automation Engineering, Au-

tomation in Production Engineering and Electrical Machining, Bio-Engineering, Computer Aided Design and Manufacturing Man-machine Systems, Dynamics of Machine Elements, Elements of Precision Machinery, Engineering Metrology, Finite Element Method, Image Technology and High Speed Photography, Integrated Manufacturing System with Robot, Manufacturing System and Terotechnology, Material Processing, Materials for Precision Machinery and Plastic Working, Precision Machinery and Vibration Engineering, Theory of Machine Design Production

Department of Reaction Chemistry

Chemistry of Hazardous Materials, Chemistry of Reaction Materials, Detonation, Gas Phase Chemical Kinetics, Hydrocarbon Chemistry, Process Analysis, Quality Control, Safety Engineering

Department of Synthetic Chemistry

Bioorganic Chemistry, Biopolymer Chemistry, Catalysis, Catalytic Chemistry, Computer Chemistry, Electrochemistry, Fuel Chemistry, Organic Synthetic Chemistry, Photochemistry, Polymer Chemistry, Solid State Organic Reaction

Department of Urban Engineering

City Planning, Housing, Sanitary Engineering, Urban Design, Urban Disaster Prevention Program, Urban Traffic Planning, Urban Transportation Planning

Faculty of Law (Freshmen Enrollment: 655)

Department of Political Science

Department of Private Law

Department of Public Law

Administrative Law, American Political and Diplomatic History, Anglo-American Law, Asian Political and Diplomatic History, Civil Law, Civil Procedure, Commercial Law, Comparative Constitutional Law, Comperative Government, Constitutional Law, Criminal Law, Criminal Procedure, Criminology, European Political History, French Law, German Law, History of International Politics, History of Japanese Political Thought, History of Political Theory, Industrial Law, International Law, International Politics, Japanese Legal History, Japanese Political and Diplomatic History, Judicial Administration, Labor Law, Law of International Organization, Legal History of Modern Japan, Occidental Legal History, Oriental Legal History, Patent and Copyright Law, Philosophy of Law, Political Process, Political Science, Principles of Comperative Law, Private International Law, Roman Law, Science of Public Administration, Sociology of Law, Soviet Law, Tax Law

Faculty of Letters (Freshmen Enrollment: 340)

Department of History

Archaeology, History of Art, Japanese History, Occidental History, Oriental History

Department of Language and Literature

Chinese Language and Literature, English Language and Literature, French Language and Literature, German Language and Literature, Greek and Latin Classics, Italian Language and Literature, Japanese Language, Japanese Literature, Linguistics, Modern European and American Language and Literatures, Russian Language and Literature, Sanskrit Language and Literature

Department of Philosophy

Aesthetics, Chinese Philosophy, Ethics, Indian Philosophy and Buddhist Studies, Is lamic Studies, Philosophy, Science of Religion and History of Religion

Department of Psychology and Sociology

Psychology, Social Psychology, Sociology

Faculty of Medicine (Freshmen Enrollment 103)

School of Health Sciences

Adult Health, Epidemiology, Health Administration, Health Sociology, Human Ecology, Maternal and Chilld Health, Mental Health, Nursing, Nutrition

School of Medicine

Anatomy, Anesthesiology, Bacteriology, Biochemistry, Clinical Tests, Clinical Tests, Dermatology, Forensic Medicine, Geriatrics, Hygiene and Preventive Medicine, Immunology, Internal Medicine, Neurology and Psychiatry, Neurosurgery, Nutrition and Physiological Chemistry, Obstetrics and Gynecology, Ophthalmology, Oral Surgery, Orthopedic Surgery, Otorhinolaryngology, Pathology, Pediatrics, Pharmacology, Physical Therapy and Medicine, Physiology, Plastic Surgery, Plastic Surgery, Public Health, Radiation Biophysics, Radiological Health, Radiology, Surgery, Thoracic Surgery, Urology Immunology

Faculty of Pharmaceutical Sciences (Freshmen Enrollment 69)

Department of Pharmaceutical Life Science

and Medicinal Chemistry Chemical Toxicology and Immunochemistry, Bioorganic Chemistry, Toxicolgy and Pharmacology

Department of Pharmaceutical Sciences

Chemical Pharmacology, Hygienic and Forensic Chemistry, Pharmaceutical Analytical Chemistry, Pharmaceutical Chemistry, Pharmaceutics, Pharmacognosy and Plant Chemistry, Physiological Chemistry

Department of Pharmaceutical Technochemistry

Microbial Chemistry, Pharmaceutical Technochemistry, Physical Chemistry, Physico-chemical Analysis, Physico-chemical Technology

Faculty of Science (Freshmen Enrollment: 281)

Department of Anthropology

Human Genetics, Physical Anthropology, Primate Ecology

Department of Astronomy

Astrophysics and Stellar Astronomy, Celestial Mechanics, Radio Astronomy, Theoretical Astrophysics

Department of Biophysics and Biochemistry

Biochemistry, Bioorganic Chemistry, Biophysical Chemistry, Biophysics, Cell Biology, Cell Physiology, Molecular Biology, Physical Chemistry of Proteins

Department of Botany

Cell Physiology, Cellular Biochemistry, Developmental Biology, Eco-physiology, Genetics, Membrane Biochemistry, Molecular Biology, Plant Biochemistry, Plant Physiology

Department of Chemistry

Analytical Chemistry, Chemical Reactions, Inorganic Cemistry, Organic Chemistry, Physical Chemistry, Radiochemistry

Department of Geography

Human Geography, Physical Geography

Department of Geology

Historical Geology and Structural Geology, Mineral Deposits and Chemical Geology, Palaentology, Petrology, Sedimentary Petrology

Department of Geophysics

Geodynamics, Geomagnetism and Geochronology, Meteorology, Physical Oceanography, Seismology, Solar Terrestrial Physics

Department of Information Science

Computer Architecture and Operating System, Computer Science, Discrete Mathematics and Programming Languages, Formal Language and Kanji, Theory of Automata

Department of Mathematics

Algebra, Algebraic Geometry, Algebraic Groups, Algebraic Topology, Differential Equations, Functional Analysis, Geometry, Lie Groups, Number Theory, Probability, Topology

Department of Mineralogy

Crystallography, Mineralogy, X-ray Crystallography

Department of Physics

Biophysics, Electromagnetism and Relativity, Experimental Physics, Fluid Dynamics, High Energy Physics, Laboratory Work, Laser Spectroscopy and Chemical Physics, Low Temperature Physics, Magnetism, Mechanics, Microwave Physics and Quantum Electronics, Molecular Spectroscopy, Physical Optics, Plasma Physics, Quantum Mechanics, Solid State Physics, Solid State Spectoroscopy, Statistical Physics, Theoretical Nuclear Physics, Theory of Elementary Particles

Zoological Institute

Behavioral Biology, Developmental Biochemistry, Endocrinology, Experimental Embryology, Physiological Chemistry, Physiology, Radiation Biology

Foreign Student Admission

Qualifications for Applicants

Standard Qualifications Requirement

Examination at the University

Submitted documents, an essay test and an interview.

Documents to be Submitted When Applying

Standard Documents Requirement

JLPT and GEFS scores

GRADUATE PROGRAMS

Graduate School of Agriculture (First Year Enrollment: Master's 142, Doctor's 107)

Divisions

Agricultural Chemistry, Agricultural Economics, Agricultural Engineering, Agrobiology, Biotechnology, Fisheries, Forest Products, Forestry, Veterinary Medicine and Animal Sciences

Graduate School of Economics (First Year Enrollment : 5-year Doctor's 25)

Divisions

Applied Economics, Business Administration, Economic Theory and Economic History

Graduate School of Education (First Year Enrollment : Master's 36, Doctor's 31)

Divisions

Educational Administration, Educational Psychology, Foundation of Education, Physical Education, School Education

Graduate School of Engineering (First Year Enrollment : Master's 511, Doctor's 175)

Divisions

Aeronautics, Applied Physics, Architecture, Chemical Energy Engineering, Chemical Engineering, Civil Engineering, Electrical Engineering, Electronic Engineering, Industrial Chemistry, Information Engineering, Marine Engineering, Material Science, Mathematical Engineering and Information Physics, Mechanical Engineering, Mechanical Engineering for Production, Metallurgy, Mineral Development Engineering, Naval Architecture, Nuclear Engineering, Precision Machinery Engineering, Reaction Chemistry, Synthetic Chemistry, Urban Engineering

Graduate School of Humanities (First Year Enrollment : Master's 139, Doctor's 82)

Divisions

Aesthetics, Archaeology, Chinese Language and Literature, Chinese Philosophy, Classical Philology, English Language and Literature, Ethics, French Language and Literature, German Language and Literature, History of Fine Arts, Indian Philosophy, Japanese History, Japanese Language and Literature, Linguistics, Occidental History, Oriental History, Philosophy, Psychology, Russian Language and Literature, Science and History of Religion

Graduate School of International and Interdisciplinary Studies (First Year Enrollment : Master's 37, Doctor's 23)

Divisions

Area Studies, Comparative Literature and Culture, General Systems Studies, International Relations, Social Relations

Graduate School of Law and Politics (First Year Enrollment : Master's 17, Doctor's 10)

Divisions

Basic Science of Law, Civil and Criminal Law, Political Science, Public Law

Graduate School of Medical Sciences (First Year Enrollment : Doctor's 52)

Divisions

Basic Medicine, Clinical Medicine, Health Sciences

Graduate School of Pharmaceutical Sciences (First Year Enrollment : Master's 62, Doctor's 28)

Divisions
Pharmaceutical Life-Science, Pharmaceutical Sciences, Pharmaceutical Technochemistry
Graduate School of Science (First Year Enrollment : Master's 253, Doctor's 185)
Divisions
Anthropology, Astronomy, Biophysics and Biochemistry, Botany, Chemistry, Coordinated Sciences, Geography, Geology, Geophysics, History and Philosophy of Science, Information Science, Mathematics, Mineralogy, Physics, Zoology
Graduate School of Sociology (First Year Enrollment : Master's 17, Doctor's 11)
Divisions
Cultural Anthropology, Social Psychology, Sociology

Foreign Student Admission
Qualifications for Applicants
Master's Program
   Standard Qualifications Requirement
Doctoral Program
   Standard Qualifications Requirement
Examination at the University
Master's Program
   Same as for Japanese (a written exam and an interview)
Doctoral Program
   Same as Master's program.
Documents to be Submitted When Applying
   Standard Documents Requirement
   Admission procedures and requirements may differ slightly according to each school.

＊

Research Institutes and Centers
Computer Center, Cryogenic Center, Earthquake Research Institute, Educational Computer Center, Environmental Science Center, Historiographical Institute, Instite of Applied Microbiology, Institute for Cosmic Ray Research, Institute for Nuclear Study, Institute for Solid State Physics, Institute of Industrial Science, Institute of Journalism and Communication Studies, Institute of Medical Science, Institute of Oriental Culture, Institute of Social Science, Japanese Language Center for Foreign Students, Molecular Genetics Research Laboratory, Ocean Research Institute, Radioisotope Center, Research Center for Advanced Science and Technology, Research Center for Nuclear Science and Technology, Univesity Museum
Facilities/Services for Foreign Students
International Lodge: Shared Facilities (Lobby, Conference Room, Library, Japanese Style Room), Accommodation (108 apartments for families, couples and single people)
   The apartments are available to visiting scholars and students from abroad when space permitting.
Special Programs for Foreign Students
Japanese language supplementary classes are available at the Univesity.

For Further Information
Undergraduate Admission
Admissions Office, The University of Tokyo, 7–3–1 Hongo, Bunkyo–ku, Tokyo 113 ☎ 03–812–2111
Graduate Admission
Graduate Admissions Office, The Univesity of Tokyo, 7–3–1 Hongo, Bunkyo–ku, Tokyo 113 ☎ 03–812–2111

University of Tottori
(Tottori Daigaku)
4-101 Koyama-cho Minami, Tottori-shi, Tottori 680
☎ 0857–28–0321

Faculty
   Profs. 187   Assoc. Profs. 156
   Assist. Profs. Full–time 77; Part–time 207
   Res. Assocs. 198
Number of Students
   Undergrad. 4, 376   Grad. 394
Library 497, 366 volumes

Outline and Characteristics of the University
   University of Tottori was founded in 1949 by the Government. At the time of its foundation, the University was composed of three faculties: Education, Medicine and Agriculture. In 1965, the Faculty of Engineering was added. The Faculties of Education, Engineering and Agriculture moved to become united on Koyama Campus in 1966. In 1967, the Faculty of General Education was opened. In 1968, the Doctor's Program was established in the graduate course of Medicine, followed by Agriculture Master's Program in 1967 and Engineering Master's Program in 1974.
   Today, University of Tottori is comprised of five faculties, admitting 935 students annually, with three graduate schools, admitting 209 students annually, and enrolls a total number of about 4, 500 students. The University also has three research institutes attached to two Faculties and several other educational institutes, all of which contributing widely to society.
   The University is situated in Tottori Prefecture (population 617, 000), endowed with a rich and beautiful natural environment such as the grand sand dune in a nearby national park. The Faculties of Education, Engineering, Agriculture and General Education are on Koyama Campus, which is on the broad flat top of a hill overlooking Koyama Lake (area 6. 8 km²), located in the western part of Tottori City (population 138, 000). The School of Medicine is near Minatoyama Park in Yonago, a city (population 132, 000) by the Japan Sea and about 90 kilometers west of Tottori City. Both Campuses, Koyama and Yonago, are located conveniently so as to satisfy one's needs for seasonal recreation. The students may enjoy swimming in the Japan Sea in summertime

and skiing at Mt. Daisen in wintertime, and also are proud of the ideal environment provided for study and extracurricular activities.

Nearly half of the students are natives of Tottori Prefecture and the others are from every other part of Japan. At present eleven foreign students are enrolled in the University.

UNDERGRADUATE PROGRAMS

Faculty of Agriculture (Freshmen Enrollment: 280)
Cluster of Agriculture and Forestry Sciences
Agricultural Aroduction, Agricultural Chemistry, Agricultural Engineering, Agricultural Information Science, Bio-resource Science, Environmental Science, Farm Business Management, Forestry Science
Cluster of Veterinary Science
Animal Science, Veterinary Anatomy, Veterinary Internal Medicine, Veterinary Microbiology, Veterinary Pathology, Veterinary Pharmacology, Veterinary Physiology, Veterinary Public Health, Veterinary Surgery
Faculty of Education (Freshmen Enrollment   180)
Elementary School Teachers' Training Course
Handicapped Children's School Teachers' Training Course
Department of Interdisciplinary Studies
Humanities Division, Sciences Division
Secondary School Teachers' Training Course
Algebra and Geometry, Analysis and Applied Mathematics, Art Education, Biology, Calligraphy, Chemistry, Child-Care, Chinese Literature, Citizenship Education, Clothing, Composition, Design, Developmental Psychology, Earth Sciences, Economics, Education Methodology, Education Psychology, Education Sociology, Education System, Electrical Engineering, English and American Literature, English Language Education, English Linguistics, Ethics, Food and Nutrition, Geography, Handicapped Child Education, Handicapped Child Pathology, Handicapped Child Psychology, History, History of Education, Home Economics, Home Economics Education, Instrumental Music, Japanese Language Education, Japanese Linguistics, Japanese Literature, Law, Mathematics Education, Mechanical Engineering, Music Education, Painting, Pedagogy, Philosophy, Physical Education and School Health Education, Physics, Physiology and Hygiene, School Health, Science Education, Sculpture, Social Studies Education, Technical Training in Physical Education, Theory and History of Fine Arts, Theory and History of Music, Theory and History of Physical Education, Vocal Music
Faculty of Engineering (Freshmen Enrollment: 440)
Department of Civil Engineering
Geotechnical Engineering, Hydraulic Engineering, Structural Engineering, Structural Materials
Department of Electrical Engineering
Applied Electrical Engineering, Communication Engineering, Electric Power Engineering, Fundamental

Electrical Engineering
Department of Electronics
Applied Electronics, Electronic Devices and Circuits, Electron Physics, Solid State Electronics
Department of Environmental Chemistry and Technology
Chemical Reaction Engineering, Environmental Biotechnology, Inorganic Resources Utilization, Organic Resources Utilization
Department of Industrial Chemistry
Inorganic Industrial Chemistry, Organic Industrial Chemistry, Physical Chemistry, Synthetic Organic Cheristry
Department of Mechanical Engineering I
Applied Mechanics, Fluid Engineering, Heat Engineering, Machine Elements and Design
Department of Mechanical Engineering II
Control Engineering, Materials Science, Precision Engineering, Thermal Fluid Engineering
Department of Ocean Civil Engineering
Coastal and Ocean Engineering, Ocean Construction Engineering, Ocean Geotechnics, Ocean Structural Materials
Department of Social System Engineering
Applied Mathematics, Applied Physics, Basic System Theory, Information Processing
Faculty of Medicine (Freshmen Enrollment: 100)
Department of Medicine
Anatomy, Anesthesiology, Bacteriology, Biochemistry, Clinical Laboratory Medicine, Clinical Pharmacology, Dermatology, Hygiene, Internal Medicine, Legal Medicine, Medical Zoology, NeuroPsychiatry, Obstetrics and Gynecology, Ophthalmology, Oral Surgery, Orthopedic Surgery, Otorhinolaryngology, Pathology, Pediatrics, Pharmacology, Physiology, Public Health, Radiology, Surgery, Urology, Virology

Foreign Student Admission
Qualifications for Applicants
Standard Qualifications Requirement
Examination at the University
Applicants for the School of Medicine must take the same test as the Japanese applicants. Faculties of Education, Engineering and Agriculture will give a specific test for foreign applicants. That is, applicants for the Faculties of Education and Agriculture must take a personal interview, and those for the Faculty of Engineering must take both an achievement test (written) and a personal interview.
Documents to be Submitted When Applying
Standard Documents Requirement
JLPT and GEFS scores

ONE-YEAR GRADUATE PROGRAMS

One-Year Graduate Course of Education (Enrollment   5)
Education

Foreign Student Admission

Qualifications for Applicants

Standard Qualifications Requirement

Examination at the University

Applicants must take the same entrance examination consisting of a written exam and an interview as given to Japanese students.

GRADUATE PROGRAMS

Graduate School of Agriculture (First Year Enrollment : Master's 95)

Divisions

Agricultural Chemistry, Agricultural Engineering, Agronomy, Farm Economics, Forestry, Veterinary Science

Graduate School of Engineering (First Year Enrollment : Master's 56)

Divisions

Civil Engineering, Electrical Engineering, Electronics, Environmental Chemistry and Technology, Industrial Chemistry, Mechanical Engineering, Ocean Civil Engineering

Graduate School of Medicine (First Year Enrollment : Doctor's 58)

Divisions

Internal Medicine, Pathology, Physiology, Social Medicine, Surgery

Foreign Student Admission

Qualifications for Applicants

Master's Program

Standard Qualifications Requirement

Applicants for the graduate courses of Engineering and Agriculture must have completed 16 years of education or equivalent and the course of a university/college.

Doctor's Program

Standard Qualifications Requirement

Applicants for the doctor's program of Medicine must have completed 18 years of education or equivalent and the course of a university/college (the last course must be medical).

Examination at the University

Master's Program

Applicants must take the same entrance examination consisting of a written exam and an interview as given to Japanese students.

Doctor's Program

Same as Master's program.

Documents to be Submitted When Applying

Standard Documents Requirement

✳

Research Institutes and Centers

Health Service Center, Institute of Neurological Science, Institute of Steroid Research, Sand Dune Research Institute, University Farms, University Forests, University Hospital, University Veterinary Hospital

For Further Information

Undergraduate and Graduate Admission

Admission Section, Student Office, University of Tottori, 4-101 Koyama-cho Minami, Tottori-shi, Tottori 680 ☎ 0857–28–0321 ext. 2480

University of Tsukuba
(Tsukuba Daigaku)

1–1–1 Tennodai, Tsukuba-shi, Ibaraki 305

☎ 0298–53–2111

Faculty

Profs. 555   Assoc. Profs. 487

Assist. Profs. Full–time 400   470; Part–time

Res. Assocs. 58

Number of Students

Undergrad. 8, 296   Grad. 2, 419

Library 1, 518, 919 volumes

Outline and Characteristics of the University

University of Tsukuba, the 78th Japanese national university, was founded in 1973 as a part of the nation-wide effort to remodel the existing national university system in Japan.

The history of the University of Tsukuba goes far back to the Normal School founded in 1872, the only school of higher education in Japan at that time. Due to the successive changes in the national educational system since that period, the school has been reorganized several times; Tokyo Normal School in 1983, Tokyo Higher Normal School in 1903, Tokyo University of Literature and Science in 1929. Finally, it became the Tokyo University of Education in 1949, combining the Tokyo College of Agricultural Education (1937), and Tokyo College of Physical Education (1941).

In accordance with the plan for the relocation of a number of governmental research institutes to the present Tsukuba Science City in 1963, it was decided to move the Tokyo University of Education from the overcrowded Tokyo area to the present location in 1967. After ten years of planning, University of Tsukuba was finally founded by the National Diet on October 1st, 1973.

University of Tsukuba, the pioneer institution of the new Japanese university system, has adopted entirely new structures and administrative systems to ensure the progress of future generations and to promote advanced scientific and cultural achievements.

One of the most important aspects of the University of Tsukuba is the separation of the educational system from the research system, rather than implementing the departmental faculty systems adopted largely in conventional universities. This system treats research and education as structurally separate, but functionally interdependent endeavors.

In this system, the education of students place in the Clusters of Colleges, Schools, and ¡raduate School; and the research organizations consists of Institutes and Special Research Projects.

The administration is carried out by the President, Vice Presidents, University Senate and Councils.

Internationalization of higher education in Japan is another goal of the University of Tsukuba. The university currently has posts for 32 foreign faculty members and is trying to adopt many other features to promote internationalization in research, education and university operation. However, foreign applicants should be aware of the fact that most courses are taught in Japanese.

UNDERGRADUATE PROGRAMS

First Cluster of Colleges (Freshmen Enrollment: 460)
College of Humanities
Archaeology and Folklore, History, Linguistics, Philosophy
College of Natural Sciences
Chemistry, Geoscience, Mathematics, Physics
College of Social Sciences
Economics, Law, Political Science, Sociology
Second Cluster of Colleges (Freshmen Enrollment: 530)
College of Agriculture and Forestry
Applied Biochemistry, Biological Environment Creation, Biological Resources and Production, Organization of Biological Production
College of Biological Sciences
Applied Biology, Basic Biology
College of Comparative Culture
Comparative and Area Culture Studies, Comparative Literature, Modern Thought
College of Human Sciences
Education, Psychology, Special Education
College of Japanese Language and Culture
Third Cluster of Colleges (Freshmen Enrollment: 520)
College of Engineering Sciences
Applied Physics, Engineering Mechanics, Material and Molecular Engineering, Transformation Engineering
College of Information Sciences
Information Science, Information Technology
College of International Relations
College of Socio-Economic Planning
Management Studies, Socio-Economic Planning, Urban Planning
School of Art and Design (Freshmen Enrollment: 100)
Department of Art and Design
Aesthetics, Constructive Art, Design, History and Philosophy of Arts
School of Health and Physical Education (Freshmen Enrollment: 240)
Department of Health and Physical Education
Group Sports, Individual Sports, Martial Arts
School of Medicine (Freshmen Enrollment: 100)
Department of Medicine

Foreign Student Admission
Qualifications for Applicants
Standard Qualifications Requirement
Foreign applicants for undergraduate programs must take the Japanese Language Proficiency Test (first level) and General Examination for Foreign Students.
Examination at the University
Only applicants whose academic records have been screened by the University are eligible to take the examination.
The entrance examination consists of an interview and written test in academic subjects or a practical test.
Documents to be Submitted When Applying
Standard Documents Requirement
Following documents are also required.
1. Records of the Japanese Language Proficiency Test (first level) and General Examination for Foreign Students
2. Applicants from the United States of America who took the Scholastic Aptitude Test (SAT) are required to submit the record of the examination.
3. Applicants from the U. S. A. who are not native English speakers and took the SAT and Test of English as a foreign Language (TOEFL) are required to submit both records of the examinations.
4. Applicants from all other countries who took a certificate examination to enter a university in accordance with the regulations of their native countries are also required to submit the record of the examination.

Application forms are available in November and will be accepted at the beginning of February of the following year.

Qualifications for Transfer Students
Transfer students for undergraduate programs must have attended university for two years or more and obtained more than 62 credits or expect to obtain more that 62 credits.
In the case of transfer students for Medical School, they must have obtained more than 62 credits in specific subjects.
Examination for Transfer Students
The examination for transfer students is conducted only if there is a vacancy in the fixed number of students in the specified grade of Clusters (colleges) /schools.
The examination consists of an interview and a written examination in academic subjects or a practical test.

GRADUATE PROGRAMS

Graduate School of Agricultural Sciences (First Year Enrollment : Doctor's 20)

Divisions

Agricultural and Forestry Engineering, Agriculture and Forestry, Applied Biochemistry

Graduate School of Area Studies (First Year Enrollment : Master's 40)

Division

Area Studies

Graduate School of Art and Design (First Year Enrollment : 5-year Doctor's 7)

Division

Graduate School of Art and Design (First Year Enrollment : Master's 30)

Divisions

Art and Design, Design, Fine Arts

Graduate School of Biological Sciences (First Year Enrollment : 5-year Doctor's 10)

Divisions

Biology, Biophysics and Biochemistry

Graduate School of Chemistry (First Year Enrollment : 5-year Doctor's 10)

Division

Chemistry

Graduate School of Education (First Year Enrollment : 5-year Doctor's 14)

Division

Graduate School of Education (First Year Enrollment : Master's 125)

Divisions

Education, Education of Handicapped Children, Secondary Education

Graduate School of Engineering (First Year Enrollment : 5-year Doctor's 32)

Divisions

Applied Physics, Electronics and Information Sciences, Engineering Mechanics, Materials Science

Graduate School of Environmental Sciences (First Year Enrollment : Master's 90)

Division

Environmental Sciences

Graduate School of Geoscience (First Year Enrollment : 5-year Doctor's 10)

Divisions

Geography and Hydrology, Geology

Graduate School of Health and Physical Education (First Year Enrollment : Master's 60)

Divisions

Athletic Coaching, Health Education, Methodology of Physical Education

Graduate School of Health and Sports Sciences (First Year Enrollment : 5-year Doctor's 10)

Division

Health and Sports Sciences

Graduate School of History and Anthropology (First Year Enrollment : 5-year Doctor's 10)

Divisions

Cultural Anthropology, History

Graduate School of Literature and Linguistics (First Year Enrollment : 5-year Doctor's 26)

Divisions

Area Literature, Linguistics, Literature

Graduate School of Management Sciences and Public Policy Studies (First Year Enrollment : Master's 50)

Division

Management Sciences and Public Policy Studies

Graduate School of Mathematics (First Year Enrollment : 5-year Doctor's 12)

Division

Mathematics

Graduate School of Medical Sciences (First Year Enrollment : Master's 20)

Division

Graduate School of Medical Sciences (First Year Enrollment : 5-year Doctor's 30)

Division

Medical Sciences, Medicine

Graduate School of Philosophy (First Year Enrollment : 5-year Doctor's 6)

Divisions

Ethics, Philosophy, Religion and Comparative Thought

Graduate School of Physics (First Year Enrollment : 5-year Doctor's 18)

Division

Physics

Graduate School of Psychology (First Year Enrollment : 5-year Doctor's 8)

Division

Psychology

Graduate School of Scientific Technology (First Year Enrollment : Master's 120)

Division

Scientific Technology

Graduate School of Social Sciences (First Year Enrollment : 5-year Doctor's 9)

Divisions

Economics, Law, Sociology

Graduate School of Socio-Economic Planning (First Year Enrollment : 5-year Doctor's 13)

Divisions

Quantitative Policy Analysis, Urban and Regional Planning

Graduate School of Special Education (First Year Enrollment : 5-year Doctor's 8)

Division

Special Education

Foreign Student Admission

Qualifications for Applicants

Master's Program

Standard Qualifications Requirement

Doctor's Program

Standard Qualifications Requirement

Examination at the University

Master's Program

Selection of candidates will be based on the results of the student's records of past performance, test of scholastic ability, and physical examination.

Doctor's Program

Same as Master's program.

Documents to be Submitted When Applying
Standard Documents Requirement
Procedures for Application:
Collect and submit the required application forms before the deadlines specified below.
Deadlines for Submitting Applications:
The deadlines for submission of applications for the Master's programs are in the beginning of October except for the Scientific Technology and the Medical Science Programs, which are due at the end of August.
For the Doctoral Programs in the sciences and the liberal arts, the deadlines are at the end of August and the end of January, respectively.
Doctoral Programs in sciences; end of August
Doctoral Programs in liberal arts; end of January
Master's Programs in Scientific Technology and in Medical Science; end of August
All other Master's Programs; beginning of October

✳

Research Institutes and Centers
Agricultural and Forestry Research Center, Chemical Analysis Center, Cryogenics Center, Educational Media Center, Education Center for Foreign Students, Environmental Research Center, Foreign Language Center, Gene Experiment Center, Health Center, Laboratory Animal Research Center, Particle Radiation Medical Science Center, Plasma Research Center, Radioisotope Center, School Education Center, Science Information Processing Center, Shimoda Marine Research Center, Sports and Physical Education Center, Sugadaira Montane Research Center, Tandem Accelerator Center, University Hospital, University Instrument and Tool Shop, University Research Center

Facilities/Services for Foreign Students
Education Center for Foreign Students: (Shared Facilities–Lobby, Lounge and Classrooms)
Student Dormitories: The student dormitories are located at the northern and southernmost parts of the campus, for both single and married students. Each dormitory area has a dormitory office, dining halls, public baths, bookstores, dry-cleaning stores, barbershops and minimarkets in the Community Centers. (All rooms are furnished with a bed, desk, chair, bookshelf and locker.)
Off-Campus Housing: Students who would like to live off-campus in a private apartment or boarding house are advised to contact the Student Affairs Section of the Branch of the Secretariat for information. When renting a private apartment in Japan, it is customary to pay deposit and/or key money equivalent to two months rent. Most Japanese apartments are unfurnished.
Counseling Services: The Education Center for Foreign Students provides counseling services to all foreign students. Students may discuss, in confidence, any issues concerning academic, personal, social, emotional and other related matters.
Health Care: Because of changes in environment and

food, and problems of communication, many foreign students experience ill effects to their health after coming to Japan.
a) Health Examination: Toward the middle of April each year, all regular undergraduate, graduate students and research students (kenkyusei) are required to have an annual physical examination.
b) General Medical Care: Students may have medical consultation with and/or receive simple medical treatment from doctors in internal medicine, orthopedics, ophthalmology, psychiatry, gynecology, and dentistry at the Health Center.
c) Counseling at the Health Center: Doctors at the Health Center may be consulted for advice on various problems encountered by students. Of course, foreign students may consult with counselors at the Education Center for Foreign Students. Their academic advisors, and the staff members in charge of student affairs at the Division of International Relations are willing to advise them on any problems.
Home Visits and Overnight Stays: To help foreign students gain an understanding of the daily life of Japanese families, the Division of International Relations organizes home visits and short stays with families in the Tsukuba area.
Special Programs for Foreign Students
Japanese language supplementary classes are available at the Education Center for Foreign Students of the University.
For Further Information
Undergraduate Admission
Admission's Office, 2nd Division of Academic Affairs, Department of Academic Affairs, University of Tsukuba, 1-1-1 Tennodai, Tsukuba-shi, Ibaraki 305 ☎ 0298–53–2208
Graduate Admission
Administractive Office of Instruction, Division of Graduate Academic Affairs, Department of Academic Affairs, University of Tsukuba, 1-1-1 Tennodai, Tsukuba-shi, Ibaraki 305 ☎ 0298–53–2230

University of Wakayama
(Wakayama Daigaku)

930 Sakaedani, Wakayama-shi, Wakayama 640
☎ 0734–54–0361

Faculty
    Profs. 70   Assoc. Profs. 63
    Assist. Profs. Full–time 14; Part–time 55
    Res. Assocs. 6
Number of Students
    Undergrad. 2, 552   Grad. 19
Library 560, 000 volumes

Outline and Characteristics of the University
Wakayama University was established in May, 1949, at the time of the Educational Reform which ushered in the 6-3-3 graded educational system. On

that occasion, three schools were united: Wakayama Teachers' Training School, Wakayama Teachers' Training School for the Youth and Wakayama Economics College.

As the only national university in Wakayama Prefecture, it was originally composed of the Faculty of Economics and the Faculty of Liberal Arts. Later, the Economics Junior College (night school) and Graduate School of Economics (advanced course in economics and Master's Degree program) were added, and the Faculty of Liberal Arts changed its name to the Faculty of Education.

In 1966, a new undergraduate course in Economics (Industrial Engineering) was added to the Faculty of Economics. And, in 1987, the University finished to move to new campus which commands a fine view of Wakayama City.

Faculty of Education: Students must remain for four years or more in order to earn a B. A. degree in Education and to obtain the necessary qualifications for a teaching certificate, accumulating 136 credits in the following fields: General Education, Foreign Languages, Health and Physical Education, and Major Subjects (including Teacher Training Courses). The purpose of study in the field of General Education, which is divided into Humanities, Social Sciences, Natural Sciences, Foreign Languages and Health and Physical Education, is to give the student, before he or she specializes, an enriched cultural background with broad, humane knowledge.

The purpose of study in the major fields is to transmit special knowledge and skills and provide a deep academic and artistic education.

In the Teachers' Training Courses, students study the theory and methods of education related to their major, and develop the knowledge and skill necessary to lead their pupils as teachers.

Faculty of Economics: Its purpose is to provide future leaders in the economic and industrial fields with a basic knowledge of Economics, Business Administration, Industrial Engineering, and Law, along with the practical application of such knowledge. Students must remain in school for four years or more, earning 136 required credits in General Education, Foreign Languages, Health and Physical Education, and Major Subjects, in order to obtain a B.A. degree in Economics.

Also, the Faculty has a Training Course for Commercial Teachers which provides the education necessary for teaching high school commercial subjects and also provides the qualifications for obtaining a second-class certificate for senior high school teaching (commercial subjects). Students completing this course are not obligated to find positions in the educational field.

Department of Business Administration: The emphasis in this department is to teach the theory, history, and practice of commerce, management, and accounting. Further, it provides special knowledge and skills and at the same time, through related sub-jects, deepens the education and training those who will be active in society with broad perspectives.

Department of Economics: Students in this department study economic theory, history and politics, economic trends of the world, and methods of statistical and econometric analysis.

Department of Industrial Engineering: The purpose of this department is to research and teach from a new angle various problems of Business Administration, Economics and the connected Social Sciences especially through computers.

Graduate School of Economics: This is a program through which students will be awarded the Master's degree in Economics. Graduate students, with their fundamental knowledge of economics, are expected to do further research with a broader point of view and to cultivate a better understanding of their subject enough to continue their research in the future. Graduate students are required to earn 32 credits in a minimum term of two years. They must submit a dissertation and pass a graduate examination.

UNDERGRADUATE PROGRAMS

Faculty of Economics (Freshmen Enrollment: 340)
Department of Business Administration
Business History, Financial Accounting, International Finance, Management of Business, Managerial Accounting, Managerial Economics, Marketing
Department of Economics
Agricultural Policy, Economic Administration, Economic History, Economic Policy, Economic Statistics, Japanese Economic History, Principles of Economics, Public Finance, Social Policy, Theoretical Economics, Western Economic History, World Economy
Department of Industrial Engineering
Business Mathematics, Industrial Engineering, Industrial Planning, Information Processing System, Office Automation
Faculty of Education (Freshmen Enrollment 270)
Elementary School Teachers' Training Course
Junior High School Teacher's Training Course
Teachers' Traing Course for Special Subjects (Science)
Teachers' Training Course for the Handicapped
Art, Biology, Chemistry, Domestic Science, Earth Science, Education for the Handicapped, Engineering and Agriculture, English and American Literature and Language, French Literature and Language, Geography, German Literatute and Language, Health and Physical Education, History, Japanese Literature and Language, Language, Law and Social Studies, Mathematics, Music, Pedagogy, Philosophy, Physics, Psychology, Sociology

Foreign Student Admission
Qualifications for Applicants
Standard Qualifications Requirement

Examination at the University
Faculty's special entrance examination.
Documents to be Submitted When Applying
Standard Documents Requirement
JLPT and GEFS scores
Identity Card and Recommendation issued by diplomatic and/or consular offices to Japan are also required.

GRADUATE PROGRAMS

Graduate School of Economics (First Year Enrollment : Master's 36)
Divisions
Business Administration, Economics

Foreign Student Admission
Qualifications for Applicants
Master's Program
Standard Qualifications Requirement
Applicants must obtain a recommendation from either the Ministry of Education in Japan or the diplomatic and/or consular offices to Japan.
Examination at the University
Master's Program
Applicants will be admitted to the program, based upon the results of their submitted documents, the written examination, the interview, and health inspection.
The written examination and so forth will be administered in March and October.
Documents to be Submitted When Applying
Standard Documents Requirement
A letter of recommendation from the diplomatic and/or consular offices to Japan is also required.

*

For Further Information
Undergraduate and Graduate Admission
Student Division, Admissions Office, Student Bureau, University of Wakayama, 930 Sakaedani, Wakayama-shi, Wakayama 640 ☎ 0734-54-0361

Utsunomiya University
(Utsunomiya Daigaku)

350 Mine-machi, Utsunomiya-shi, Tochigi 321
☎ 0286-36-1515

Faculty
Profs. 142   Assoc. Profs. 128
Assist. Profs. Full-time 21; Part-time 288
Res. Assocs. 48
Number of Students
Undergrad. 4, 104   Grad. 267
Library 390, 646 volumes

Outline and Characteristics of the University
By the proclamation of the National School Establishment Law of 1949, Utsunomiya University, incorporating Utsunomiya Agriculture and Forestry Special School (founded in 1922), Tochigi Normal School (founded in 1943) and Tochigi Youth Normal School (founded in 1944), was founded. Under the new system, it was composed of the Faculty of Liberal Arts (renamed the Faculty of Education in 1966) and the Faculty of Agriculture. In 1964 the Faculty of Engineering, originally Utsunomiya Technological Junior College, was added, followed by the Faculty of General Education as the general curricula in 1968.

In 1966, the Graduate School of Agriculture (Master's Program) was opened, followed in 1973 by the Graduate School of Engineering (Master's Program), and in 1984 by the Graduate School of Education (Master's Program).

Today, the University enrolls more than 4, 000 students and a full-time faculty of 750 and is composed of three Faculties, the Faculty of General Education, Graduate Schools, four research institutes and other affiliated establishments.

The campus is divided into two areas: Mine area (the administrative building, the Faculty of Education, the Faculty of Agriculture, the Faculty of General Education) and Ishii area (the Faculty of Engineering). They are both located in the eastern part of the city of Utsunomiya (population about 400, 000), with a north-west command of Mt. Nantai and the Nikko mountain ranges in the distance. It is surrounded by the wonderful scenery overlooking the Kinu River to the east.

The students come from every part of Japan and half of them are graduates of senior high schools in Tochigi Prefecture. There are also some foreign students in the University.

UNDERGRADUATE PROGRAMS

Faculty of Agriculture (Freshmen Enrollment 273)
Department of Agricultural Chemistry
Applied Microbiology, Biochemistry, Chemurgy, Food Chemistry, Plant Nutrition and Science, Soil Science
Department of Agricultural Economics
Agricultural Economics, Agricultural History and Agricultural Location, Agricultural Policy, Agricultural Statistics and Farm Accounting, Science of Farm Management
Department of Agricultural Engineering
Agricultural Construction, Agricultural Hydrotechnics, Agricultural Machinery, Agricultural Structures and Equipments, Agricultural Technology, Land Reclamation, Power in Farming
Department of Agriculture
Agronomy, Applied Entomology, Comparative Agriculture, Horticultural Science, Plant Breeding, Plant Pathology, Sericultural Science
Department of Forestry
Forest Engineering, Forest Management, Forest Policy, Forest Products Processing, Silviculture and Soil

Conservation, Technology of Wood Improvement
Department of Zootechnical Science
Animal Breeding and Reproduction, Animal Disease, Animal Feeding, Chemistry and Technology of Animal Products
Faculty of Education (Freshmen Enrollment 310)
Elementary School Teacher Education Course
Art, Education, Educational Psychology, Health and Physical Education, Home Economics, Japanese, Mathematics, Music, Natural Science, Social Studies
Junior High School Teacher Education Course
English, Fine Arts, Health and Physical Education, Home Economics, Japanese, Mathematics, Music, Natural Science, Social Studies, Technical Education
Teacher of Mentally and Physically Handicapped Course
Division of Elementary School Teacher Education, Division of Junior High School Teacher Education
Faculty of Engineering (Freshmen Enrollment: 415)
Department of Applied Chemistry
Environmental Protection Chemistry, Material Chemistry, Synthetic Chemistry
Department of Architecture and Civil Engineering
Architecture, Civil Engineering
Department of Electrical Engineering and Electronic Engineering
Electromagnetic Energy, Electronic Material-Science, Information and Communication Systems
Department of Information Science
Information Processing, Mathemtical information Science
Department of Mechanical Systems Engineering
Mechanical Engineering, Precision Engineering

Foreign Student Admission
Qualifications for Applicants
Standard Qualifications Requirement
Examination at the University
A written exam and an interview or oral exam, a health certificate and a result certificate.
Documents to be Submitted When Applying
Standard Documents Requirement
JLPT and GEFS scores
Application period: January 28-February 3.
Refer to the Private Expense Foreign Students Registration at Utsunomiya University which is distributed late July every year.

GRADUATE PROGRAMS

Graduate School of Agriculture (First Year Enrollment : Master's 70)
Divisions
Agricultural Chemistry, Agricultural Economics, Agricultural Engineering, Agriculture, Forestry, Zootechnical Science
Graduate School of Education (First Year Enrollment : Master's 32)
Divisions
Art Education, Educational Science, English Litera-

ture and Language Education, Health and Physical Education, Japanese Literature and Language Education, Music Education, Natural Science Education, Social Science Education, Technological Education
Graduate School of Engineering (First Year Enrollment : Master's 64)
Divisions
Architecture, Civil Engineering, Electrical Engineering, Electronic Engineering, Environmental Chemistry, Industrial Chemistry, Information Science, Mechanical Engineering, Precision Engineering

Foreign Student Admission
Qualifications for Applicants
Master's Program
Standard Qualifications Requirement
Examination at the University
Master's Program
Faculty's entrance examination: a written exam and an interview, a health certificate and a result certificate provided by the president of the university from which the applicant graduated.
In certain cases applicants may be chosen by documentary screening.
Documents to be Submitted When Applying
Standard Documents Requirement
Following documents are also required.
1. A certificate proving ability in the Japanese language.
2. An identification issued by the Japanese Government or the Foreign Government, approved by the Japanese government or diplomatic establishments in Japan.
The deadline for application differs among Graduate Schools, so applicants are requested to inquire at the school desired.

*

Research Institutes and Centers
Experimental Forest, Information Processing Center, Institute of Weed Control, Research and Guidance Center of Teaching Practice, University Farms
Special Programs for Foreign Students
Special classes about Japanese history, culture and nature and Japanese language supplementary classes are available at the Faculty of General Education.
For Further Information
Undergraduate Admission
Entrance Examination Section, Student Division, Student Office, Utsunomiya University, 350 Mine-machi, Utsunomiya-shi, Tochigi 321 ☎ 0286–36–1515 ext. 621
Graduate Admission
Graduate School of Agriculture: Student Section, the Faculty of Agriculture, Utsunomiya University, 350 Mine-machi, Utsunomiya-shi, Tochigi 321 ☎ 0286–36–1515 ext. 408
Graduate School of Education: Student Section, the Faculty of Education, Utsunomiya University, 350 Mine-machi, Utsunomiya-shi, Tochigi 321 ☎ 0286–36–1515 ext. 258, 259

Graduate School of Engineering: Student Section, the Faculty of Engineering, Utsunomiya University, 2753 Ishii-machi, Utsunomiya-shi, Tochigi 321 ☎ 0286-61-3401 ext. 212

Yamagata University
(Yamagata Daigaku)

1-4-12 Kojirakawa-machi, Yamagata-shi, Yamagata 990 . ☎ 0236-31-1421

Faculty
Profs. 214   Assoc. Profs. 215
Assist. Profs. Full-time 91; Part-time 354
Res. Assocs. 204
Number of Students
Undergrad. 7, 365   Grad. 350
Library 772, 351 volumes

Outline and Characteristics of the University

Yamagata University was founded in May 1949 in accordance with the National School Establishment Law, bringing together various institutions of higher learning to form the core of the new University. These institutions were the National Yamagata Higher School, the Yamagata Normal School, the Yamagata Youth Normal School, the Yonezawa Higher Technical School, and the Yamagata Prefectural Tsuruoka Higher Agricultural and Forestry School. At the time of its founding, the University was composed of four Faculties: Liberal Arts, Education, Engineering, and Agriculture.

In June 1967, the Faculty of Liberal Arts was reorganized into three independent Faculties: the Faculty of Literature and Social Sciences, the Faculty of Science, and the Faculty of General Education. In September 1973, the School of Medicine was added.

In April 1964, the Graduate School of Engineering (Master Course) was opened, followed by the Graduate School of Agriculture (Master Course) in April 1970, the Graduate School of Science (Master Course) and the Graduate School of Medicine (Doctor Course) in April 1979.

In April 1959, the Graduate Course of Education was established, followed by the Graduate Course of Literature and Social Sciences in April 1972, the Nursing Teacher Training Course in April 1975, and the Evening Course at the Faculty of Engineering in April 1983.

The University has four campuses. The Faculty of Literature and Social Sciences, the Faculty of Education, the Faculty of Science, and the Faculty of General Education are located at the Kojirakawa campus in Yamagata City. The Iida campus in Yamagata City is used exclusively by the School of Medicine. Yamagata City, the capital, is located at the foot of fabulous Mt. Zao and is the center of culture and commerce for the surrounding region.

The Yonezawa campus is known for its Faculty of Engineering. Yonezawa City is located at the foot of Mt. Azuma, the source of the Mogami River, and is well known as the castle town of the famous Lord Uesugi. The city has flourished with the production of luxurious silk fabrics.

The Faculty of Agriculture is located at the Tsuruoka campus. Tsuruoka City is located in the Shonai Plain on the Japan Sea coast. This plain is especially famous for its rice production and the views of Mt. Chokai and Mt. Gassan from the campus are extremely beautiful.

Each of the campuses is surrounded by magnificent mountains and clean, clear rivers. They are blessed by beautiful natural surroundings which make them ideal for physical fitness as well as for the concentration academics demand.

UNDERGRADUATE PROGRAMS

Faculty of Agriculture (Freshmen Enrollment: 170)
Department of Agricultural Chemistry
Applied Microbiology, Biological Chemistry, Chemistry of Agricultural Products, Food and Nutritional Chemistry, Soil Science and Fertilizer Science
Department of Agricultural Engineering
Agricultural Machinery, Irrigation and Drainage, Reclamation and Melioration, Soil Mechanics
Department of Agriculture
Agricultural Economics, Applied Zoology, Crop Breeding, Crop Science and Farm Management, Phytopathology, Zootechnical Science
Department of Forestry
Forest Engineering, Forest Management, Forest Policy, Forest Utilization and Chemical Technology of Forest Products, Silviculture
Department of Horticulture
Horticultural Breeding and Propagation, Pomology, Post-harvest Horticulture, Vegetable Crop Science
Faculty of Education (Freshmen Enrollment: 320)
Elementary School Teacher Training Course
Junior High School Teacher Training Course
Special School Teacher Training Course
Special Subject (Music) Teacher Training Course
Agriculture, Algebra and Geometry, Analysis and Applied Mathematics, Biology, Calligraphy, Chemistry, Child Study, Chinese Classics, Chorus, Clothing Science, Composition, Conducting, Continuing Education, Design, Developmental Psychology, Earth Sciences, Economics, Education, Educational Psychology, Educational Sociology, Educational System, Education of Handicapped Children, Electrical Engineering, English and American Literature, English Linguistics, English Teaching, Ensemble, Ethics, Fine Arts Education, Food Science and Nutrition, Geography, Health and Physical Education, Health of Handicapped Children, History, History of Education, Home Economics Education, Home Management, Japanese Language Teaching, Japanese Linguistics, Japanese Literature, Keyboard Musical Instruments, Law, Mathematics Education, Mechanical

Engineering, Metal Machining, Music Education, Painting, Physics, Physiology and Hygiene, Practice of Physical Education, Psychology of Handicapped Children, School Health, School Health Care, Science Education, Sculpture, Social Studies, Stringed Instruments, Technical Education, Theory and History of Fine Arts, Theory and History of Music, Theory and History of Physical Education, Vocal Music, Wind Instruments

Faculty of Engineering (Freshmen Enrollment: 700)

Department of Applied Chemistry

Dyestuff Chemistry, Industrial Inorganic Chemistry, Industrial Organic Chemistry, Inorganic Material Chemistry, Organic Material Chemistry, Synthetic Chemistry, Technical Analytical Chemistry

Department of Basic Technology

Applied Mathematics, Applied Physics, Electrical Engineering, Management Engineering, Mechanical Engineering, Physical Chemistry

Department of Chemical Engineering

Chemical Reaction Engineering, Fluid Flow and Heat Transfer, Mass Transfer, Mechanical Operation, Process Control and Instrumentation

Department of Electrical Engineering

Applied Electricity, Electric and Electronic Machinery, Electric Energy Engineering, Electric Power Engineering, Information and Computer Engineering, Theory of Electricity, Transmission and Communication Engineering

Department of Electronic Engineering

Applied Electronics, Electronic Circuits, Electronic Devices, Instrument and Control Engineering, Physical Electronics

Department of Information Engineering

Applied Informatics, Computer Engineering, Fundamental Informatics, Information Processing, Information System, Intelligence System

Department of Mechanical Engineering

Engineering Materials, Engineering Thermodynamics and Heat Transfer, Fluid Mechanics and Fluid Machinery, Mechanism and Machine Design, Production Machine System, Strength of Materials, Thermal Engineering

Department of Polymer Chemistry

Applied Polymer Chemistry, Fundamental Polymer Chemistry, Polymer Synthesis, Structural Properties and Processing of Polymers, Technology of Dyeing and Finishing

Department of Polymer Materials Engineering

Applied Polymer Physics, Functional Polymer Materials, Fundamental Polymer Materials, Materials Application, Materials Design, Materials Dynamics

Department of Precision Engineering

Control Engineering, Materials and Processes of Precision Manufacturing, Precision Instrument and its Design, Precision Measurement, Technology of Plasticity

Faculty of Literature and Social Sciences (Freshmen Enrollment: 285)

Department of Economics

Business Administration and Accounting, Economic History, Economic Policy, Economic Theory, Principles of Political Economy, Public Finance, Social Policy, Statistics

Department of Law

Civil Law, Commercial Law, Constitutional Law and Administrative Law, Criminal Law, International Law, Labor Law and Social Security Law, Politics and Sociology

Department of Literature

Chinese Literature, English Linguistics, English Literature, Ethics, German Literature and Linguistics, Japanese History, Japanese Linguistics, Japanese Literature, Oriental History, Philosophy, Western History

School of Medicine (Freshmen Enrollment: 100)

Department of Medicine

Anatomy, Anesthesia, Bacteriology, Biochemistry, Dentistry and Oral Surgery, Dermatology, Forensic Medicine, Hygiene and Preventive Medicine, Internal Medicine, Molecular and Pathological Biochemistry, Neuropsychiatry, Obstetrics and Gynecology, Ophthalmology, Orthopaedics, Otolaryngology, Parasitology, Pathology, Pediatrics, Pharmacology, Physiology, Public Health, Radiology, Surgery, Surgical Neurology, Urology

Faculty of Science (Freshmen Enrollment: 181)

Department of Biology

Cytology, Embryology, Environmental Biology, Physiology

Department of Chemistry

Analytical Chemistry, Inorganic Chemistry, Organic Chemistry, Physical Chemistry

Department of Earth Sciences

Applied Geology, Crustal Evolution, Petrology and Mineralogy, Physical Geology

Department of Mathematics

Algebra, Analysis, Applied Mathematics, Geometry

Department of Physics

Applied Physics, Classical and Quantum Mechanics, Electromagnetism, Solid State Physics

Foreign Student Admission

Qualifications for Applicants

Standard Qualifications Requirement

For each Faculty/School, foreign applicants are exempted from the Joint First-Stage Achievement Test but must take the Japanese Language Proficiency Test and General Examination for Foreign Students.

Examination at the University

Examination Date: February 22–March 1.

Documents to be Submitted When Applying

Standard Documents Requirement

Application forms are available at the Admissions Office of each Faculty/School from November, 1988. Application period: January 30 through February 8, 1989.

Qualifications for Transfer Students

Undergraduate Programs (excluding the School of Medicine)

1. Applicants who hold a B. A.
2. Applicants who are enrolled or have been enrolled in another university/college.
3. Applicants who have graduated from a junior/technical college or who have finished the two-year course of a teacher training college.
4. Applicants wishing to re-enroll in the same Faculty/School that he/she has previously left.

Premedical Course of the School of Medicine

1. Applicants who have finished the premedical course of either the Faculty of Medicine or the Faculty of Dentistry of another university/college.
2. Applicants who have finished 14 years of education in a foreign country, including a course equivalent to the Japanese premedical course of either the Faculty of Medicine or the Faculty of Dentistry.

Examination for Transfer Students

Examinations for transfer students are administered by each Faculty/School.

Documents to be Submitted When Applying
Standard Documents Requirement

ONE-YEAR GRADUATE PROGRAMS

One-Year Graduate Course of Literature and Social Sciences (Enrollment: 5)
Literature
One-Year Graduate Course of Education (Enrollment: 10)
Education, Music

Foreign Student Admission
Qualifications for Applicants
Standard Qualifications Requirement
Examination at the University
The same tests as Japanese applicants.

GRADUATE PROGRAMS

Graduate School of Agriculture (First Year Enrollment : Master's 48)
Divisions
Agricultural Chemistry, Agricultural Engineering, Agriculture, Forestry, Horticulture
Graduate School of Engineering (First Year Enrollment : Master's 90)
Divisions
Applied Chemistry, Chemical Engineering, Electrical Engineering, Electronic Engineering, Mechanical Engineering, Polymer Chemistry, Precision Engineering, Textile and Polymer Technology
Graduate School of Medicine (First Year Enrollment : Doctor's 30)
Division
Medicine

Graduate School of Science (First Year Enrollment : Master's 40)
Divisions
Biology, Chemistry, Earth Sciences, Mathematics, Physics

Foreign Student Admission
Qualifications for Applicants
Master's Program
Standard Qualifications Requirement
Doctor's Program
Standard Qualifications Requirement
Examination at the University
Master's Program
A written exam and an interview (Same as Japanese Students)
Doctor's Program
The same entrance examination given to Japanese applicants, which consists both of an oral or written test in their specialized field and of a test in two foreign languages (either English and German or English and French).
Documents to be Submitted When Applying
Standard Documents Requirement
Application forms are available at the Graduate Admissions Office from the middle of August. All applicants are required to submit the specified application documents to the Graduate Admissions Office by the prescribed date.

*

Research Institutes and Centers
Central Laboratory for Research and Education, Laboratory Animal Center, Macromolecular Research Laboratory, The Computation Laboratory, The Radioisotope Laboratory, The Research and Guidance Center for Teaching Practice, University Farm, University Forest

Facilities/Services for Foreign Students
Student Housing: Five dormitories and off-campus living quarters.
Health Services: the Health Administration Center offer various types of consultation and service.

For Further Information
Undergraduate Admission
Admissions Office, Yamagata University, 1-4-12 Kojirakawa-machi, Yamagata-shi, Yamagata 990 ☎ 0236-31-1421 ext. 2095
Graduate Admission
Graduate School of Agriculture: Admissions Office, Graduate School of Agriculture, Yamagata University 1-23 Wakaba-cho, Tsuruoka-shi, Yamagata 997 ☎ 0235-23-1521 ext. 216
Graduate School of Engineering: Admissions Office, Graduate School of Engineering, Yamagata University, 4-3-16 Jonan, Yonezawa-shi, Yamagata 992 ☎ 0238-22-5181 ext. 304
Graduate School of Medicine: Admissions Office, Graduate School of Medicine, Yamagata University, 2-2-2 Iida Nishi, Yamagata-shi, Yamagata 990-23 ☎ 0236-33-1122 ext. 2635

Graduate School of Science: Admissions Office, Graduate School of Science, Yamagata University, 1-4-12 Kojirakawa-machi, Yamagata-shi, Yamagata 990 ☎ 0236–31–1421 ext. 2508

Yamaguchi University
(Yamaguchi Daigaku)

1677-1 Yoshida, Yamaguchi-shi, Yamaguchi 753
☎ 0839–22–6111

Faculty
    Profs. 231   Assoc. Profs. 190
    Assist. Profs.   Full–time 92; Part–time 668
    Res. Assocs. 201
Number of Students
    Undergrad. 7, 538   Grad. 423
Library   1, 133, 084 volumes

Outline and Characteristics of the University

The origins of Yamaguchi University go back to various separate Colleges and Schools founded from the 19th century onwards. These were consolidated to form Yamaguchi University in 1949, with Faculties of Literature and Science, Education, Economics, Engineering, and Agriculture. The Yamaguchi Medical College merged in 1964 to form the Faculty of Medicine, with the University Hospital and two training colleges added later. Science and Humanities were established as separate Faculties in 1978. From 1964, post-graduate courses and research divisions have been gradually created. Yamaguchi University has grown to become a sizable university of 7, 538 students, with a staff of 1, 789 including 231 full professors. The University is well equipped, with good research and library facilities.

The University, originally situated in the center of Yamaguchi-city, moved to a spacious new campus on the outskirts of the city in 1970. However, Yamaguchi is quite a small city (population 120, 000) and the present campus is only about 15 minutes from the center by bicycle, the usual student form of transport. Yamaguchi City has figured prominently in certain periods of Japanese history. It was an important cultural and political center in the 16th century, and as such was visited by Francis Xavier. In the 19th century, it played an important role in the Meiji Restoration. Yamaguchi remains a rather traditional Japanese city; an administrative and educational center with little industry. Students generally commend it for its natural beauty and clean air. Yamaguchi City may lack some of the attractions and distractions of a big city, but it has all the facilities of a modern city. This fact perhaps allows for a more relaxed and intimate student life than is possible in a big city.

The Faculties of Engineering and Medicine are located in the neighboring city of Ube, about 40 km away from Yamaguchi City. Ube is a city of similar size (170, 000 population) but has a more industrial character.

The student body is drawn from Yamaguchi prefecture (37%) and a wide area of central and western Japan. The number of overseas students is small but growing.

At present there are 32 non-Japanese students, from eleven countries, mainly in Asia. In 1983 an exchange program was inaugurated with Shandong University in China.

UNDERGRADUATE PROGRAMS

Faculty of Agriculture (Freshmen Enrollment: 125)
    Department of Agricultural Chemistry
Applied Microbiology, Biochemistry, Food Chemistry, Food Science and Technology, Soil Science and Plant Nutrition
    Department of Agronomy
    Environmental Sciences Course
Agricultural Environmental Science, Applied Entomology, Irrigation Drainage and Reclamation Engineering, Plant Pathology
    Food Production Course
Agricultural Marketing, Agricultural Resource Accounting, Animal Science, Crop Science, Horticultural Science
    Department of Veterinary Medicine
Veterinary Anatomy, Veterinary Hygiene, Veterinary Internal Medicine, Veterinary Microbiology, Veterinary Pathology, Veterinary Pharmacology, Veterinary Physiology, Veterinary Reproduction, Veterinary Surgery
Faculty of Economics (Freshmen Enrollment: 375)
    Department of Economics
Economic History, Economic Policy, Economics, Economic Statistics, History of Economics, Public Finance, Theory of Economic Fluctuation
    Department of International Economics
Commodity Science, Foreign Trade, Foreign Trade Policy and Practice, International Economics, International Finance, World Economy
    Department of Law and Economics
Business Law, Civil Law, Economic Law, Public Law, Social Law
    Department of Management
Accounting, Bookkeeping, Business Administration, Business History, Commerce, Industrial Engineering, Insurance and Transportation, Management, Management Accounting, Money and Banking
    Course for Commerce Teachers
Faculty of Education (Freshmen Enrollment: 310)
    Course for Elementary School Teachers
    Course for High School Teachers
Art Education, English as a Foreign Language Education, Home Making Education, Japanese Language and Literature Education, Mathematics Education, Music Education, Physical and Health Education, Science Education, Social Studies Education,

Technical Education, Vocational Education
  Course for Kindergarten Teachers
  Course for Teachers of the Handicapped
Faculty of Engineering (Freshmen Enrollment: 420)
  Department of Applied Science
Applied Mathematics, Applied Physics, Materials Science, Numerical Analysis
  Department of Chemical Engineering
Chemical Reaction Engineering, Industrial Physical Chemistry, Transport Phenomena, Unit Operations and Water Treatment Engineering
  Department of Civil Engineering
Concrete Engineering, Environmental Engineering, Hydraulic Engineering, River and Coastal Engineering, Sanitary Engineering, Soil Dynamics, Soil Mechanics, Structural Engineering
  Department of Construction Engineering
Bridge Engineering, Earthquake Engineering, Foundation Engineering, Geotechnical Engineering, Rock Mechanics, Soil Conservation and Water Control Engineering, Steel Structural Engineering, Transportation Engineering
  Department of Electrical Engineering
Biomedical Engineering, Electrical Communication Systems, Electric Machines, Electric Power System, Magnetic Recording Technology, Measuring Electronics, Plasma Engineering, Power Electronics
  Department of Electronics Engineering
Computer Science and Technology, Control and Instrumentation, Pattern Analysis and Information Processing, Solid State Electronics
  Department of Industrial Chemistry
Analytical Chemistry, Catalysis, Electrochemistry, Hydrocarbon Chemistry, Inorganic Chemistry, Physical Chemistry, Physical Organic Chemistry, Synthetic Organic Chemistry
  Department of Industrial Mechanical Engineering
Control Engineering, Dynamics of Machinery, Machinery Engineering and Metal Cutting, Material Science and Fracture Dynamics, Vibration and Strength of Gears
  Department of Mechanical Engineering
Boundary Layer, Elasto-Plasticity, Fracture Mechanics, Heat Transfer, Internal Combustion Engine, Material Testing, Noise Control, Strength of Materials, Thermodynamics, Turbulence
  Department of Mining and Mineral Engineering
Beneficiation of Potential Resources, Ceramic Engineering, Characterization of Ceramics, Economic Geology, Fracture Mechanics of Rock, Geotechnical Engineering, Mineral Processing, Synthetic Mineralogy
Faculty of Humanities (Freshmen Enrollment: 190)
  Department of Humanities
Aesthetics and Art History, Archeology, Chinese Philosophy, Ethics, History of Japanese Thought, Japanese History, Occidental History, Oriental History, Philosophy, Social Anthropology, Social Psychology, Sociology
  Department of Language and Literature

Chinese Language, Chinese Literature, English and American Literature, English Language, French Language and Literature, German Language and Literature, Japanese Language, Japanese Literature, Linguistics
School of Medicine (Freshmen Enrollment: 100)
  Department of Medicine
Anatomy, Anesthesiology-Resuscitology, Biochemistry, Clinical Laboratory Science, Dermatology, Forensic Medicine, Hygiene, Internal Medicine, Microbiology, Neurological Surgery, Neuropsychiatry, Obstetrics and Gynecology, Ophthalmology, Oral and Maxillofacial Surgery, Orthopedics, Otolaryngology, Pathology, Pediatrics, Pharmacology, Physiology, Public Health, Radiology, Surgery, Urology, Virology and Parasitology
Faculty of Science (Freshmen Enrollment: 196)
  Department of Biology
Biological Chemistry, Cell Biology, Developmental Biology, Environmental Biology
  Department of Chemistry
Analytical Chemistry and Inorganic Chemistry, Organic Chemistry, Physical Chemistry, Synthetic Chemistry
  Department of Mathematics
Algebra, Analysis, Applied Mathematics, Geometry
  Department of Mineralogical Sciences and Geology
Economic Geology, Historical Geology, Mineralogy, Petrology
  Department of Physics
Applied Physics, Crystal Physics, Quantum Physics, Solid State Physics

Foreign Student Admission
  Qualifications for Applicants
    Standard Qualifications Requirement
    Those who have the International Baccalaureate Diploma may also apply.
  Examination at the University
    Examinations for Foreign Students by the University; Faculty of Agr.: Dept. of Agricultural Chemistry (Chemistry, Japanese Composition, Interview in Japanese), Depts. of Agronomy, Veterinary Med. (Biology, Interview in Japanese), Faculty of Economics (English excluding English speakers, Japanese), Faculty of Education (Same exam as Japanese students), Faculty of Engineering (Essay in Japanese, Interview in Japanese), Faculty of Humanities (Same exam as Japanese students), Faculty of Medicine (Same exam as Japanese students), Faculty of Science (Same exam as Japanese students)
  Documents to be Submitted When Applying
    Standard Documents Requirement
    JFSAT, JLPT and GEFS Scores
    Application forms are available at the Student Division, Student Office of the University from November. All applicants are required to submit the specified application documents to the Student Section of each Faculty at the listed address by January 26 (Enginnering) and by February 15 (other Facul-

ties).

Faculties of Agriculture, Economics, Education, Humanities, Science: 1677-1 Yoshida, Yamaguchi-shi, Yamaguchi 753

Faculty of Engineering: 2557 Tokiwadai, Ube-shi, Yamaguchi 755

Faculty of Medicine: 1144 Kogushi, Ube-shi, Yamaguchi 755

ONE-YEAR GRADUATE PROGRAMS

One-Year Graduate Course of Education (Enrollment: 5)
Education

GRADUATE PROGRAMS

Graduate School of Agriculture (First Year Enrollment : Master's 54)
Divisions
Agricultural Chemistry, Agronomy, Veterinary Medicine
Graduate School of Economics (First Year Enrollment : Master's 13)
Division
Economics
Graduate School of Engineering (First Year Enrollment : Master's 68)
Divisions
Applied Science, Chemical Engineering, Civil Engineering, Construction Engineering, Electrical Engineering, Electronics Engineering, Industrial Chemistry, Industrial Mechanical Engineering, Mechanical Engineering, Mining and Mineral Engineering
Graduate School of Humanties (First Year Enrollment : Master's 8)
Divisions
Linguistic and Literary Culture, Regional Culture
Graduate School of Medicine (First Year Enrollment : Doctor's 56)
Divisions
Internal Medicine, Pathology, Physiology, Sociological Medicine, Surgery
Graduate School of Science (First Year Enrollment : Master's 40)
Divisions
Biology, Chemistry, Mathematics, Mineralogical Sciences and Geology, Physics

Foreign Student Admission
Qualifications for Applicants
Master's Program
Standard Qualifications Requirement
Doctor's Program
Standard Qualifications Requirement
Examination at the University
Master's Program
Applicants must take the entrance examination given by each Graduate School consisting of a written (and oral) examination and an interview.

Doctor's Program
Same as Master's program.
Documents to be Submitted When Applying
Standard Documents Requirement
Additional documents required differ according to the Graduate School. For further information write to the Student Section of the relevant Graduate School.

*

Research Institutes and Centers
Animal Research Center, Information Processing Center, Institute of East Asian Economics, Radioisotope Laboratory
Special Programs for Foreign Students
Japanese language classes are available at the College of General Education. Foreign students can also get guidance in the Japanese language, the specialized field of study and life in general from Japanese tutors.
Facilties/Services for Foreign Student
International House, Common facilities: Lobby, Conference Room, Lounge, Accommodation: 42 rooms (single 36, couple 4, family 2)
For Further Information
Undergraduate and Graduate Admission
Student Division, Student Office, Yamaguchi University, 1677-1 Yoshida, Yamaguchi-shi, Yamaguchi 753 ☎ 0839–22–6111 ext. 275

Yamanashi Medical College
(Yamanashi Ika Daigaku)

1110 Tamaho, Nakakoma-gun, Yamanashi 409-38
☎ 0552–73–1111

Faculty
Profs. 34 Assoc. Profs. 36
Assist. Profs. Full–time 32; Part–time 227
Res. Assocs. 128
Number of Students
Undergrad. 604 Grad. 71
Library 64, 995 volumes

Outline and Characteristics of the College

Yamanashi Medical College is a national college founded in October, 1978.

Since its inauguration, it has been the aim of the College to establish a medical school with an outstanding teaching staff and faculties that meet international standards. The first students were admitted in April, 1980.

In October 1983, an affiliated hospital was opened. The college is thus equipped to deal with education, research and medical services.

The first commencement was held in March 1986, and a graduate school for medical research was opened in April of the same year.

The environment of the college is ideal for education and research. The school is surrounded by views of Mt. Fuji, the Southern Alps and the Yatsu-gatake Mountains. An aerial view shows the many facilities provided for the students.

This college was established to provide education to future doctors based on the ideal of respect for human life. The goals are to teach the students moral ethics as doctors, develop a deep love for mankind and promote a broad view of life with the hope that they will be motivated to be open to the future. It is also hoped the staff will contribute toward better education and improved medical services in this area. The ultimate goal is international medical participation.

UNDERGRADUATE PROGRAMS

Faculty of Medical Science (Freshmen Enrollment: 100)
Department of Medical Science

Foreign Student Admission
Qualifications for Applicants
Standard Qualifications Requirement
Examination at the College
Written tests and an interview.
Documents to be Submitted When Applying
Standard Documents Requirement
The Application Guide and forms for the next year are available upon request from December.

GRADUATE PROGRAMS

Graduate School of Medical Research (First Year Enrollment : Doctor's 30)
Divisions
Biochemical Research, Ecological Research, Morphological Research, Physiological Research

Foreign Student Admission
Qualifications for Applicants
Doctor's Program
Standard Qualifications Requirement
Examination at the College
Doctor's Program
A written exam and an interview (same as Japanese applicants)
Documents to be Submitted When Applying
Standard Documents Requirement
Application forms are available at the Graduate Admissions Office from early December. All applicants are required to submit the specified application documents to the Graduate Admissions Office.

*

Research Institutes and Centers
College Hospital, Radioisotope and Animal Laboratory
For Further Information
Undergraduate and Graduate Admission
Subsection of Student Guidance, Section of Student Affairs, Divsion of School Affairs, Yamanashi

Medical College, 1110 Tamaho, Nakakoma-gun, Yamanashi 409-38 ☎ 0552–73–1111 ext. 2095, 2096

Yamanashi University
(Yamanashi Daigaku)
4-4-37 Takeda, Kofu-shi, Yamanashi 400
☎ 0552–52–1111

Faculty
Profs. 107   Assoc. Profs. 111
Assist. Profs. Full–time 27; Part–time 97
Res. Assocs. 54
Number of Students
Undergrad. 3, 263   Grad. 236
Library 388, 658 volumes

Outline and Characteristics of the University
Yamanashi University is a national university established in 1949 under the National School Establishment Law. It now includes the Faculty of Education, the Faculty of Engineering, the Graduate School, and several attached schools and research institutes. In terms of the number of faculties and students enrolled, Yamanashi University is a small national university. Each of its faculties, however, is larger and better-equipped than those at most other national universities in Japan.

The campus of Yamanashi University is in a quiet residential district of Kofu City, capital of Yamanashi Prefecture, which can be reached in two hours from Tokyo by express train. The University is situated in a scenic natural environment, with the famous Mt. Fuji to the south and snow-capped peaks of the Southern Alps of Japan to the west. The vicinity is rich in historic sites with relics of ancient and medieval Japan.

When established in 1949, Yamanashi University combined and integrated three national institutions of higher education which had been in existence for some time: Yamanashi Normal School, Yamanashi Technical College, and Yamanashi Normal School for Youth. These incorporated institutions enjoyed special distinctions. Yamanashi Technical College had achieved a high academic reputation since its foundation in 1924; Yamanashi Normal School, established as a teacher training school in 1874, had in fact grown out of a national institution of higher learning founded in the eighteenth-century.

Graduates of Yamanashi University have a reputation for integrity, sincerity, and enterprise, which has given opportunities for many of them to attain leading positions in education and industry circles in Japan. Such a reputation and the high academic standard of the University seem to have attracted a gradually increasing number of students from abroad. Yamanashi University now has more than 33 foreign students from six countries.

UNDERGRADUATE PROGRAMS

Faculty of Education (Freshmen Enrollment: 230)
Elementary School Teachers Training Course
Art and Handicrafts, Art and Handicrafts Education, Domestic Science, Domestic Science Education, Education, Japanese, Japanese Language Education, Mathematics, Mathematics Education, Music, Music Education, Physical Education, Psychology, Science, Science Education, Social Studies, Social Studies Education
Course of Integrated Arts and Sciences
Japanese Language and Culture, Low, Mathematics and Natural Sciences, Politcal Science and Economics
Kindergarten Teachers Training Course
Art and Handicrafts, Child Psychology, Mathematics Education, Music, Physical Education, Pre-school Education, Social Studies Education
Secondary School Teachers Training Course
Art, Domestic Science, English, Health and Physical Education, Industrial Arts, Japanese, Mathematics, Music, Science (Biology, Chemistry, Geology, Physics), Social Studies (Economics, Geography, History, Law and Political Science, Philosophy and Ethics, Sociology)
Training Course for Teachers of Mentally Handicapped Children
Faculty of Engineering (Freshmen Enrollment: 550)
Department of Applied Chemistry
Analytical Chemistry, Industrial Electrochemistry, Industrial Inorganic Chemistry, Industrial Organic Chemistry, Industrial Polymer Chemistry
Department of Basic Engineering
Analytical Chemistry, Applied Mathematics, Arithmetic and Programming for Computers, Differential Equations, Electricity, Fundamental Thermodynamics, General Chemistry, General Mechanics, Material Science, Mechanics of Solids, Physical Chemistry
Department of Civil Engineering
Construction Materials, Hydraulic Engineering, Soil Engineering, Structural Engineering, Transportation Engineering
Department of Computer Science
Graphic and Image Processing, Hardware and Computer Architecture, Numerical Mathematics and Operations Research, Programming and Software Systems, Speech and Image Understanding, Statistical and Quality Engineering, Theoretical Aspects of Computer Science
Department of Electrical Engineering
Electrical Communication, Electrical Machinery, Electric Circuits, Electric Power Engineering, Electromagnetics, Information Engineering
Department of Electronic Engineering
Electronic Circuits, Electronic Materials, Information Processing, Quantum Electronics, Semiconductor Devices
Department of Environmental Engineering

Environmental Biology, Environmental Chemistry, Environmental Planning, Sanitary Engineering, Water Resources Engineering
Department of Fermentation Technology
Applied Microbiology, Fermentation and Food Chemistry, Fermentation Technology, Industrial Biochemistry
Department of Mechanical Engineering
Dynamics of Machinery, Fluid Engineering and Fluid Machine, Heat Transfer and Thermal Engineering, Manufacturing Technology, Strength of Materials, Structure and Property of Materials
Department of Precision Engineering
Control Engineering, Design Engineering, Materials for Precision Engineering, Measurement and Instrumentation, Precision Machining

Foreign Student Admission
Qualifications for Applicants
Standard Qualifications Requirement
Examination at the University
Departmental exam: A written exam and an interview
Documents to be Submitted When Applying
Standard Documents Requirement
JLPT and GEFS Scores
Application forms are available at the Admissions Office from early December. All applicants are required to submit the specified application documents to the Admissions Office by the deadline indicated in the notes on the application form.

ONE-YEAR GRADUATE PROGRAMS

One-Year Graduate Course (Enrollment: 35)
Educational Psychology, Education of Mentally Handicapped Children, Pedagogy

GRADUATE PROGRAMS

Graduate School of Engineering (First Year Enrollment : Master's 102)
Divisions
Applied Chemistry, Civil Engineering, Computer Science, Electrical Engineering, Electronic Engineering, Environmental Engineering, Fermentation Technology, Mechanical Engineering, Precision Engineering

Foreign Student Admission
Qualifications for Applicants
Master's Program
Standard Qualifications Requirement
Examination at the University
Master's Program
A written exam and an interview (same as Japanese applicants)
Documents to be Submitted When Applying
Standard Documents Requirement
Application forms are available at the Graduate

Admissions Office from early July. All applicants are required to submit the specified application documents to the Graduate Admissions Office by the deadline indicated in the notes on the application form.

∗

Research Institutes and Centers
Computer Center, Institute of Enology and Viticulture, Institute of Inorganic Synthesis, Machine Laboratory, Technical Center for Material Research
Special Programs for Foreign Students
Japanese Language and Culture Ⅰ・Ⅱ (4 credits)

The credits earned in the above two courses can be counted towards the fulfillment of the requirements either for Humanities or Social Science in General Education. In addition, Japanese Language supplementary lessons (tutorials) can be arranged by the Student Division if considered necessary.
For Further Information
Undergraduate and Graduate Admission
Student Division, Yamanashi University, 4-4-37 Takeda, Kofu-shi, Yamanashi 400 ☎ 0552-52-1111 ext. 2415

Yokohama National University
(Yokohama Kokuritsu Daigaku)

156 Tokiwadai, Hodogaya-ku, Yokohama-shi, Kanagawa 240 ☎ 045-335-1451

Faculty
　　Profs.　225　　Assoc. Profs.　164
　　Assist. Profs.　Full–time　24; Part–time　488
　　Res. Assocs.　88
Number of Students
　　Undergrad.　7,910　　Grad.　620
Library　831,812 volumes

Outline and Characteristics of the University

Yokohama National University was established in 1949, under the National School Establishment Law, by amalgamation of Kanagawa Normal School, Kanagawa Youth Normal School, Yokohama College of Economics and Yokohama Institute of Technology. The University's three initial faculties of Liberal Arts & Education, Economics, and Engineering, were later joined by the Faculty of Business Administration, which branched off from the Faculty of Economics in 1967. The University's four faculties now have an enrollment of 7,106; in addition, 804 working students attend the evening courses in Business Administration and Engineering that have been offered since 1964 and 1967, respectively. The University has also established Master's Degree program in Engineering (1962), Economics (1972), Business Administration (1972), and Education (1979).

In 1985, Faculty of Engineering was reorganized into four Divisions, namely, Division of Materials Science and Chemical Engineering, Division of Me-

chanical Engineering and Materials Science, Division of Civil Engineering, Architecture and Marine Technology, and Division of Electrical and Computer Engineering, from 12 former departments (Dept. of Applied Chemistry, Dept. of Architecture and Building Science, Dept. of Chemical Engineering, Dept. of Civil Engineering, Dept . of Computer Engineering, Dept. of Electrical Engineering, Dept. of Material Chemistry, Dept. of Mechanical Engineering I, Dept. of Mechanical Engineering II, Dept. of Metallurgical Engineering, Dept. of Naval Architecture and Ocean Engineering and Dept. of Safety Engineering).

In the same year, Doctor's Degree Programs were newly established in the Division of Mechanical Engineering and Materials Science and Division of Materials Science and Chemical Engineering, Faculty of Engineering. The other two Divisions of the same Faculty established Doctor's Degree Courses in 1986. At present 569 candidates for the master's degree and 51 for the doctor's degree are enrolled.

The campus is located near the center of Yokohama City, the seat of the Kanagawa Prefectural Office. The City of Yokohama, with Tokyo and its satellite cities, forms a vast industrial area and is one of the largest megalopolises in the world.

As for international exchange, Yokohama National University has established sister-university agreements with seven universities abroad: San Diego State University (U.S.A.) in 1978; Saarland University (West Germany) in 1981, Shanghai Jiao Tong University (China) in 1982, São Paulo University (Brazil) in 1983, Ecole Centrale des Arts et Manufactures (France) in 1985, Rheinisch–Westfälische Technische Hochschule Aachen (West Germany) in 1986, and University of Georgia (U. S. A.) in 1988. Based on these agreements, the University promotes international exchange in the field of education and research. The major items of agreement include the exchange of faculty members and students (both undergraduate and graduate), cooperation in academic research and exchange of scientific information.

At present 267 foreign students from 22 countries study at the University and the number increases rapidly every year.

UNDERGRADUATE PROGRAMS

Faculty of Business Administration (Freshmen Enrollment: 250)
Department of Accounting
Bookkeeping, Cost Accounting, Ecological Accounting, Management Accounting, Principles of Accounting
Department of Business Administration
Business Administration, Business Behavior, Commercial Law, Insurance, Personnel Management, Principles of Marketing, Science of Commodities
Department of Management Science
Business Information, Environmental Management,

Human Science, Management Science, Mathematics of Business
Faculty of Business Administration (Evening Course) (Freshmen Enrollment: 100)
Department of Business Administration
Accounting, Business Administration, Economics, International Trade, Law, Principles of Marketing, Statistics
Faculty of Economics (Freshmen Enrollment: 260)
Department of Economics
Econometrics, Economic History, Economic Policy, Economics, Economic Statistics, History of Economics, Money and Banking, Public Finance, Social and Public Policy
Department of International Economics
Export Industry, History of International Economy, International Economics, International Finance, International Relations, International Trade Business, World Economy
Department of Law and Economics
Basic Law, Environmental and Public Law, International Economic Law, Japanese Economic Law
Faculty of Education (Freshmen Enrollment: 530)
Course for Elementary School Teachers
Course of Humanities and Social Science
Course for Junior High School Teachers
Course of Life -long Integrated Education
Course of Natural Science
Course for Teachers of Handicapped Children
Agriculture, Algebra and Geometry, Analytical and Applied Mathematics, Biology, Calligraphy, Chemistry, Chinese Classics, Clothing, Composition, Conducting of Music, Construction, Developmental Psychology, Economics, Education, Educational History, Educational Psychology, Educational Sociology, Educational System, Education of Handicapped Children, Electricity, English and American Literature, English Linguisitics, Ethics, Food Chemistry, Geography, Geology, History, Instrumental Music, Japanese Language, Japanese Literature, Kinematics, Law, Machine, Management of Family Life, Mathematical Education, Musicology, Painting, Pathology of Handicapped Children, Philosophy, Physical Education, Physics, Physiology and Hygiene, Politics, Psychology of Handicapped Children, School Health, Science Education, Sculpture, Sociology, Teaching of English, Teaching of Fine Arts, Teaching of Home Economics, Teaching of Japanese, Teaching of Japanese as a Foreign Language, Teaching of Music, Teaching of Physical Education, Teaching of Social Studies, Teaching of Technology, Theory of Art, Vocal Music, Wood Working and Carpentry
Faculty of Engineering (Freshmen Enrollment: 665)
Division of Civil Engineering/ Architecture and Marine Technology
Architecture and Building Science, Civil Engineering, Naval Architecture and Ocean Engineering, Regional, Urban and Environmental Planning
Division of Electrical and Computer Engineering

Electrical Systems, Electronic Engineering, Information Systems
Division of Materials Science and Chemical Engineering
Chemical Process Engineering, Energy Engineering, Materials Chemistry, Physical Chemistry, Safety Engineeing, Synthetic Chemistry
Division of Mechanical Engineering and Materials Science
Materials Processing, Materials Science, Mechanical Design and Systems Engineering, Thermodynamics and Fluid Mechanics
Faculty of Engineering (Evening Course) (Freshmen Enrollment: 60)
Division of Materials Science and Chemical Engineering
Division of Mechanical Engineering and Materials Science
See listing in Day Course.

Foreign Student Admission
Qualifications for Applicants
Standard Qualifications Requirement
Foreign applicants who have graduated or will graduate from Japanese senior high school will be treated just as a Japanese applicant.
The evening course neither in Faculty of Business Administration nor in Faculty of Engineering accept foreign students.
Examination at the University
According to his or her chosen faculty, the applicant must take a combination of the following examinations.
As the type of examination varies each academic year, applicants are advised to write to the faculties concerned and obtain detailed information.
The types of examinations for the 1988 academic year are as follows:
Faculty of Education: Either (A) and (B)
Faculty of Economics; (A) and (B)
Faculty of Business Administration: (A) and (B)
Faculty of Engineering: (B), in case the applicant has taken (A), the results of (A) will be used as reference data.
N. B.   Examination (A) indicates both the "General Examination for Foreign Students" and the "Japanese Language Proficiency Test". Examination (B) indicates the examinations given by each faculty concerned. For further information, contact the faculty.
Documents to be Submitted When Applying
Standard Documents Requirement
The results of the Japanese Language Proficiency Test and the General Examination for Foreign Students.
The applicant must submit the documents to the Dean of the Faculty in which he or she wishes to study by mid-February.
An applicant registered at a Japanese univerity should submit an agreement to sit for the examination from the president of the university at which he

or she is registered.

ONE-YEAR GRADUATE PROGRAMS

One-Year Graduate Course of Special Education (Enrollment: 60)
Education of the Mentally Handicapped, Education of the Multihandicapped

Foreign Student Admission
Qualifications for applicants
    Standard Qualifications Requirement
1. Those who graduated from universities (excluding junior colleges) and who qualified for the general certificate for teachers of kindergarten, elementary, junior high or senior high school.
2. Those who qualified (or are expected to qualify) for the first class general certificate for teachers of elementary school, junior high school, or kindergarten or who qualified (or are expected to qualify by March of the year of entrance) for the general certificate for senior high school teachers.

Examination at the University
    The examination is usually held in early March. The applicant must take written examinations of the following nature
1. Education
2. Educational Psychology
3. Short Essay

GRADUATE PROGRAMS

Graduate School of Business Administration (First Year Enrollment : Master's 26)
    Division
Business Administration
Graduate School of Economics (First Year Enrollment : Master's 22)
    Divisions
Economics, International Economics
Graduate School of Education (First Year Enrollment : Master's 85)
    Divisions
Art Education, Health and Physical Education, Home Economics Education, Mathematics Education, Music Education, School Education, Science Education, Social Studies Education, Special Education, Teaching Japanese Language and Literature, Teaching of English as a Foreign Language, Technical Education
Graduate School of Engineering (First Year Enrollment : Master's 126, Doctor's 26)
    Divisions
Civil Engineering, Architecture and Marine Technology, Electrical and Computer Engineering, Materials Science and Chemical Engineering, Mechanical Engineering and Materials Science

Foreign Student Admission
    Qualifications for Applicants
Master's Program
    Standard Qualifications Requirement
Doctor's Program
    Standard Qualifications Requirement
    Examination at the University
Master's Program
    Graduate School of Business Administration: The examination is usually held in early October, and involves: 1) Essays on two subjects (one is basic Business Administration, and the other is on some area of Business Administration and Accounting), 2) English, and 3) Interview. Applicants may be required to take an additional physical examination.
    Graduate School of Economics: The examinations is usually held in early October, and covers 1) one foreign language among English, German, French, Chinese and Russian, 2) Economics and Economic History for an hour respectively, and Applied Economics. Those who pass the above-mentioned examinations will take an interview later.
    Graduate School of Education: The examination is usually held in late September, and includes 1) one or two specific subjects in accordance with the course the applicant wishes to study, (Those who major in the Division of Art Education or Division of Music Education perform instead of taking the above-mentioned written examination.), 2) a foreign language (in most divisions English is required, dictionaries allowed), 3) Essays and 4) Interview.
    Graduate School of Engineering: The examination is usually held in the beginning of September. The applicant for Division of Electrical and Computer Engineering, for Division of Materials Science and Chemical Engineering and for Division of Mechanical Engineering and Materials Science should take 1) Mathematics and either Physics or Chemistry (These subjects are not required to the applicant for Division of Civil Engineering, Architecture and Marine Technology.), 2) two foreign languages; English and another language chosen among French, German and Japanese, 3) Major Subjects I, 4) Major Subjects II, and 5) Interview.
Doctor's Program
    Graduate School of Engineering: The examination is usually held in early September, and includes 1) two foreign languages; English and Japanese, 2) Subjects related to the applicant's major, and 3) Interview.
    Documents to be Submitted When Applying
    Standard Documents Requirement
    If the applicant is employed, permission for the applicant to sit for the examination from the president of the establishment where he or she is employed must be submitted.
    Applicants to the doctoral program are required to submit the following documents.
1. Official transcript of university attended (both undergraduate and graduate)

2. Letter stating why the applicant chose a Japanese university, and why he or she especially chose the particular Division of this University

3. The tittle and an abstract of the applicant's Master's Thesis

4. Research and Publication, Curriculum Vitae (If the publications are available, copies should be sent.)

5. An applicant registered at the graduate school of another Japanese university should submit permission to sit for the examination.

*

Research Institutes and Centers

Center for Educational Research and Practice, Center for International Trade Studies, Computer Center, Health Service Center, Institute of Environmental Science and Technology, Manazuru Marine Laboratory for Science Education, Radio Isotope Center

Facilities/Services for Foreign Students

Foreign Student House

The Foreign Student House was established in 1981 attached to Yokohama National University for the purpose of providing accommodations for foreign students who are studying at this University as well as other national universities in the Tokyo area. It also seeks to contribute towards international relations based on mutual understanding and intellectual exchange. The House is a three-story reinforced concrete building with 5, 009m² floor area and has 130 single rooms, 10 double rooms and 10 family rooms. The House also has a lounge, library, study rooms and Japanese style room for common use. At present more than 135 students from around 15 countries inhabit the House. Further information is available at the Section of Foreign Student House, Student Office of this University.

Special Programs for Foreign Students

In-Service Students for Teachers Training, one and a half year regular students, are required to include Japanese in their special curricula for the first six months. General foreign students may take Japanese (Grammar 2 credits, Reading 2 credits per year) as their second language. In addition, there is another chair for foreign students—Japan Affairs.

For Further Information

Undergraduate and Graduate Admission

Business Administration: Registrar's Office, Faculty of Business Administration, Yokohama National University, 156 Tokiwadai, Hodogaya-ku, Yokohama-shi, Kanagawa 240 ☎ 045-335-1451 ext. 2506

Economics: Registrar's Office, Faculty of Economics, Yokohama National University, 156 Tokiwadai, Hodogaya-ku, Yokohama-shi, Kanagawa 240 ☎ 045-335-1451 ext. 2406

Education: Registrar's Office I, Faculty of Education, Yokohama National University, 156 Tokiwadai, Hodogaya-ku, Yokohama-shi, Kanagawa 240 ☎ 045-335-1451 ext. 2111

Engineering (Undergraduate): Registrar's Office I, Faculty of Engineering, Yokohama National University, 156 Tokiwadai, Hodogaya-ku, Yokohama-shi, Kanagawa 240 ☎ 045-335-1451 ext. 2612

Engineering (Graduate): Graduate School of Engineering Office, Faculty of Engineering, Yokohama National University, 156 Tokiwadai, Hodogaya-ku, Yokohama-shi, Kanagawa 240 ☎ 045-335-1451 etx. 2632

Descriptions of
the Colleges and Universities in Japan

Local Public Colleges
and
Universities

2

Aichi Prefectural University
(Aichi Kenritsu Daigaku)

3-28 Takada-cho, Mizuho-ku, Nagoya-shi, Aichi 467
☎ 052-851-2191

Faculty
  Profs. 50   Assoc. Profs. 50
  Assist. Profs. Full–time 12; Part–time 165
Number of Students
  Undergraduates 1, 561
Library 310, 000 volumes

Outline and Characteristics of the University

Aichi Prefectural University was established in 1966, by reorganizing and expanding Aichi Prefectural Women's College and Aichi Prefectural Women's Junior College, which had been the leading institutions of higher education for women in central Japan since 1947. The University now comprises three Faculties of four-year co-educational courses: the Faculty of Literature, the Faculty of Foreign Studies, and the Night Division of the Faculty of Foreign Studies.

Although it is a comparatively small university, admitting only 360 students each year, Aichi Prefectural University has a good reputation as one of the few public universities for liberal arts majors and attracts students from all areas of the country. It is noted for its excellent teaching staff, including many active and leading members of academic circles. One prominent feature of education at Aichi Prefectural University is small classes in which students' individual work is encouraged and the teacher-student relationship is close.

Most of the students at this University are said to be modest, steady, and hardworking. Two-thirds of the student body of 1, 500 are female, and the general atmosphere on campus is relaxed and cheerful. Although intent on their studies, students nevertheless find time to enjoy the various extra-curricular or off-campus activities. Graduates from Aichi Prefectural University stand high in public estimation. In the 1988 academic year, eight foreign students are enrolled and are working for B. A. 's.

The campus is conveniently located in the southeastern part of the city of Nagoya, where it forms a school zone with adjacent high schools and Nagoya City University. Not far from campus are Nagoya City Museum and Mizuho Stadium. The University athletic grounds are outside of the city limits, with a new gymnasium at their center.

UNDERGRADUATE PROGRAMS

Faculty of Foreign Studies (Freshmen Enrollment: 120)
  Department of British and American Studies

Culture and Thought, History, Language, Literature, Politics and Diplomacy, Society and Economy
  Department of French Studies
History, Language, Literature and Fine Arts, Politics and Law, Society and Economy, Thought and Philosophy
  Department of Spanish Studies
  Latin American Studies
  Spanish Studies
History, Language and Literature, Society and Economy, Thought and Politics
Faculty of Foreign Studies (**Night Division**) (Freshmen Enrollment: 80)
  Department of British and American Studies
  Department of French Studies
(Roughly correspond to the programs of the day course departments)
Faculty of Literature (Freshmen Enrollment: 160)
  Department of Childhood Education
Cerebral Physiology, Child Care and Nursing, Child Psychology, Clinical Studies of Education, Contents of Early Childhood Education, Contents of Education, Educational Evaluation, Educational History, Educational Sociology, Method of Education, Moral Education, School Management, Science of Education, Studies of Childhood Education, Teaching Practice
  Department of English Literature
British and American Studies, Business English, Classical Languages, Creative Writing, Current English, English Linguistics, European Literature, History of American Literature, History of English, History of English Literature, Japanese Language and Literature, Linguistics, Studies of English and American Literature, Theory of Literature
  Department of Japanese Literature
Calligraphy, Chinese Literature, Chinese Philosophy, History of Japanese Culture, History of Japanese Literature, Japanese Grammar, Japanese Language, Japanese Literature, Linguistics, Theory of Literature
  Department of Social Welfare
Clinical Psychology, History of Social Welfare Work, Legislation for Social Welfare, Mental Hygienics, Method of Social Research, Method of Social Welfare, Modern Society, Practice in Social Research, Public Hygienics, Social Pathology, Social Security, Sociology of Family, Studies of Communities, Survey of Social Sciences, Survey of Social Welfare
Classes in Intermediate Japanese are offered for foreign students.

Foreign Student Admission

Qualifications for Applicants
  Standard Qualifications Requirement
Examination at the University
  Foreigners who have entered Japan for the purpose of receiving a college education and who want to enter Aichi Prefectural University without sitting

for its regular entrance examinations may apply for admission as Special Foreign Students.

Documents to be Submitted When Applying

Standard Documents Requirement

A certificate confirming the applicant's nationality or citizenship is also required.

Instructions for application procedure and application forms are available at the Student Division of the Student Office. All applicants are required to submit the specified application documents to the Student Division between January 5 and January 20. Selection and the results will be sent to the applicant by February 28.

*

For Further Information

Undergraduate Admission

Instruction Section, Student Division, Student Office, Aichi Prefectural University, 3-28 Takada-cho, Mizuho-ku, Nagoya-shi, Aichi 467 ☎ 052–851–2191

Aichi Prefectural University of Fine Arts

(Aichi Kenritsu Geijutsu Daigaku)

1-1 Sagamine, Yazako, Nagakute-cho, Aichi-gun, Aichi 480-11 ☎ 05616–2–1180

Faculty
    Profs. 31   Assoc. Profs. 22
    Assist. Profs. Full–time 14; Part–time 188
    Res. Assocs. 7
Number of Students
    Undergrad. 609   Grad. 90
Library 70, 331 volumes

Outline and Characteristics of the University

The university was founded on April 1, 1966 in order to contribute to the estabilshment and promotion of the unique local culture of the Chubu area. This area is situated between Tokyo and Osaka areas with Aichi Prefecture as its center, and it has made remarkable progress in its economy and industry. Four years after the foundation of our school, on April l, 1970, our two graduate schools were established.

Aichi Prefectural University of Fine Arts includes two Faculties: Art and Music. The School of Art is comprised of the Department of Japanese Painting, the Department of Oil Painting, the Department of Sculpture and the Department of Design, and the Department of Ceramics. The School of Music is comprised of the Department of Composition, the Department of Vocal Music, and the Department of Instruments (Piano and Strings and Winds and Parcussion). The Graduate Schools each have the same departments.

Our 400, 000m² campus is located in a suburban area to the east of the city of Nagoya, with the build-

ings and facilities beautifully harmonizing with the natural setting. The campus was designed by Junzo Yoshimura, professor emeritus of Tokyo National University of Fine Arts and Music, and consists of the following buildings: Lecture Buildings, School of Art Buildings, School of Music Buildings, University Hall, Library, Women's Dormitory, Administration Building, Concert Hall and Auditorium, Gymnasiums, Art Gallery, School of Art Faculty Building—a total of 31, 000m².

We have 691 materials stored in the Art Gallery.

UNDERGRADUATE PROGRAMS

Faculty of Art (Freshmen Enrollment: 90)
    Department of Ceramics
    Department of Design
    Department of Japanese Painting
    Department of Oil Painting
    Department of Sculpture
Faculty of Music (Freshmen Enrollment: 100)
    Department of Composition
    Department of Instruments (Winds and Parcussion)
    Department of Instruments (Piano)
    Department of Instruments (Strings)
    Department of Vocal Music

GRADUATE PROGRAMS

Graduate School of Art (First Year Enrollment : Master's 20)
    Divisions
Design, Painting (Japanese Painting), Painting (Oil Painting), Sculpture
Graduate School of Music (First Year Enrollment : Master's 16)
    Divisions
Composition, Instrumental Music (Piano), Instrumental Music (Strings), Vocal Music

*

For Further Information

Undergraduate and Graduate Admission

Aichi Prefectural University of Fine Arts, 1-1 Sagamine, Yazako, Nagakute-cho, Aichi-gun, Aichi 480-11 ☎ 05616–2–1180

Fukuoka Women's University

(Fukuoka Joshi Daigaku)

1-1-1 Kasumigaoka, Higashi-ku, Fukuoka-shi, Fukuoka 813 ☎ 092–661–2411

Faculty
    Profs. 23   Assoc. Profs. 16
    Assist. Profs. Part–time 72
    Res. Assocs. 11
Number of Students

Undergrad. 699
Library 99, 980 volumes

Outline and Characteristics of the University

The predecessor of the present Fukuoka Women's University is Fukuoka Women's College (Fukuoka Joshi Senmon Gakko), which was established in 1923 by Fukuoka Prefecture as the only professional school for women in the western area of Japan and the very first women's public college sponsored by a local government. The College held its first graduation in 1926 and by 1951 had graduated 2, 292 women (the 26th year). In 1950, in accordance with the educational system reform, the school restarted as a four-year college with a single department of liberal arts. In 1954, it established the present two Faculties of Literature and Home Life Science. The new-system Fukuoka Women's University turned out 4, 869 graduates from 1954 to 1987 (the 32nd year), who are very active not only in junior and senior high schools but also in various levels of governmental offices, research institutes, and companies in general.

This campus is located on Kasumigaoka, in the north-east section of Fukuoka City, and commands a good view of Hakata Bay. The University is well organized and the intimacy between faculty and students is well known.

UNDERGRADUATE PROGRAMS

Faculty of Home Life Science (Freshmen Enrollment: 90)
Department of Home Economics
Food and Nutrition, Textile and Clothing
Department of Living Science
Faculty of Literature (Freshmen Enrollment: 90)
Department of English and American Literature
Department of Japanese Literature

Foreign Student Admission

Qualifications for Applicants
Standard Qualifications Requirement
Applicants are required to take the Japanese Language Proficiency Test and the General Examination for Foreign Students.
Examination at the University
Applicants must take the entrance examination specially prepared for foreign applicants. The results of the Japanese Language Proficiency Test and General Examination for Foreign Students are also taken into consideration in selecting successful applicants.
Documents to be Submitted When Applying
Standard Documents Requirement
Instructions for application procedure and application form are available at the Division of Academic Affairs and the Office of Students Life. All applicants are required to submit the specified application documents to the Division of Academic Affairs within a fixed period in February.
There are two other short-term (1 year) pro-

grams, Auditor's program and Research Student's program. Ask the Division of Academic Affairs about these programs.

*

For Further Information

Undergraduate Admission
Division of Academic Affairs and Office of Students Life, Fukuoka Women's University, 1-1-1 Kasumigaoka, Higashi-ku, Fukuoka-shi, Fukuoka 813 ☎ 092-661-2411 ext. 220~222

Fukushima Medical College
(Fukushima Kenritsu Ika Daigaku)

1 Hikarigaoka, Fukushima-shi, Fukushima 960-12
☎ 0245-48-211

Faculty
Profs. 34   Assoc. Profs. 36
Assist. Profs. Full-time 37; Part-time 83
Res. Assocs. 132
Number of Students
Undergrad. 540   Grad. 37
Library 112, 190 volumes

Outline and Characteristics of the College

Fukushima Medical College was founded in 1944 as Fukushima Women's Medical School, maintained by Fukushima Prefecture. In 1947, under the prewar system of education, it became Fukushima Medical College open to both sexes. Following a nationwide educational reform in 1952, the college was reorganized into a six-year institution. The graduate school was then established, and the Central Research Laboratories (the Cell Science Laboratory and the Environmental Pollution Research Laboratory), the Institute of Physical Medicine and Rehabilitation, and the RI-Laboratory were subsequently added. The college, which is the only prefectural medical school in the northeastern region of the main island, is responsible for educating physicians who care for the residents of the prefecture. The college hospital serves as the medical center for the whole prefecture.

The campus is in the hills nine kilometers south of the center of Fukushima City. The college hospital moved there from the former campus near the center of the city in June 1987, and the college and its other related facilities moved in March 1988.

UNDERGRADUATE PROGRAMS

Faculty of Medicine (Freshmen Enrollment: 80)
Department of Medicine
Anatomy, Anesthesiology, Bacteriology, Biochemistry, Dermatology, Hygiene, Internal Medicine, Legal Medicine, Neuropsychiatry, Neurosurgery, Obstetrics and Gynecology, Ophthalmology, Orthopaedic Surgery, Otorhinolaryngology, Pathology, Pediat-

rics, Physiology, Public Health, Radiology, Surgery, Urology

Foreign Student Admission
Qualifications for Applicants
Standard Qualifications Requirement
Foreign applicants must take the Joint First-Stage Achievement Test.
Examination at the College
Applicants are required to take the second-stage entrance examination for this medical college given in early March.
Documents to be Submitted When Applying
Standard Documents Requirement
Information concerning application procedures and application forms are described in the brochure "Instructions for Filing an Application" which is available at the Student Affairs Office beginning in mid-October.

GRADUATE PROGRAMS

Graduate School of Medicine (First Year Enrollment : Doctor's 27)
Divisions
Internal Medicine, Pathological Studies, Physiological Studies, Social Medicine, Surgery

Foreign Student Admission
Qualifications for Applicants
Doctor's Program
Standard Qualifications Requirement
Applicants must have completed 18 years of education, the last part of which must be medical or dental education, or have achieved its equivalent.
Examination at the College
Doctor's Program
Foreign applicants must take the same entrance examination (given in early March) as Japanese applicants.
Documents to be Submitted When Applying
Standard Documents Requirement
Information concering application procedures and application forms are described in the brochure "Instructions for Filing an Application" which is available at the Student Affairs Office beginning in December.

*

Research Institutes and Centers
Central Research Laboratories, Hospital, Institute of Physical Medicine and Rehabilitation, RI-Laboratory

For Further Information
Undergraduate and Graduate Admission
Student Affairs Office, Fukushima Medical College, 1 Hikarigaoka, Fukushima-shi, Fukushima 960-12 ☎ 0245-48-2111 ext. 2043

Gifu Pharmaceutical University
(Gifu Yakka Daigaku)

5-6-1 Mitahora-higashi, Gifu-shi, Gifu 502
☎ 0582-37-3931

Faculty
Profs. 14   Assoc. Profs. 19
Assist. Profs. Full–time 4; Part–time 23
Res. Assocs. 25
Number of Students
Undergrad. 539   Grad. 58
Library 43, 386 volumes

Outline and Characteristics of the University
Gifu Pharmaceutical University started its history with the Gifu College of Pharmacy in 1932 at the site of Kokonoe-cho (Gifu City) under the financial administration of Gifu Municipal Government, and celebrated its golden jubilee in 1982.
Meanwhile, the University has grown with the times. In 1949, the College was reorganized into Gifu Pharmaceutical University in accordance with the reformation of the school system. The University opened a Graduate School offering Master's program in 1953 and Doctor's program in 1965 respectively. In 1965, the University campus was shifted to the present site, Mitahora.
At present, the University enrolls about 600 graduate and undergraduate students, possesses more than 80 academic staffs for education and research purposes, and consists of a faculty including two Departments and an Institute, Graduate School, the Instrumental Center and other affiliated establishments.
The Mitahora campus is located in the north of Gifu City (population 413, 000), which is the capital city of Gifu Prefecture and is adjacent to Nagoya City. The city and surroundings enjoy beautiful scenery and places of historical importance. In particular, the traditional cormorant fishing on the Nagara River is well known all over the world.
The University has produced 7, 234 graduates so far, who have occupied important places in various fields such as the industrial, the academic, the medical and the civil service. The University is internationally noted for its academic excellence. In 1982, it established the academic relationship with China Pharmaceutical University (the People's Republic of China) for the promotion of research in the fields of pharmaceutical science.

UNDERGRADUATE PROGRAMS

Faculty of Pharmacy (Freshmen Enrollment: 120)
Department of Manufacturing Pharmacy
Biochemistry, Pharmaceutical Analytical Chemistry, Pharmaceutical Chemistry, Pharmaceutical Engi-

neering, Pharmaceutical Physical Chemistry, Pharmaceutical Synthetic Chemistry

Department of Public Health Pharmacy

Hygienic Chemistry, Medicinal Chemistry, Pharmaceutics, Pharmacognosy, Pharmacology, Public Health

Foreign Student Admission

Qualifications for Applicants

Standard Qualifications Requirement

Foreign applicants are required to take the Joint First-Stage Achievement Test.

Examination at the University

The University entrance examination consists of a written exam and an interview. Results of both the Joint First-Stage Achievement Test and the University examination are considered for final selection. No distinction is made between Japanese and foreign applicants in this matter.

Documents to be Submitted When Applying

Standard Documents Requirement

Result-enquiry card on the Joint First-Stage Achievement Test must be submitted with other required documents.

Application forms are available at the Admissions Office from middle November. All applicants are required to submit the application documents to the Admissions Office during a particular period of time at the beginning of February.

GRADUATE PROGRAMS

Graduate School of Pharmacy (First Year Enrollment : Master's 24, Doctor's 8)

Division

Pharmacy

Foreign Student Admission

Qualifications for Applicants

Master's Program

Standard Qualifications Requirement

Doctor's Program

Standard Qualifications Requirement

Examination at the University

Master's Program

Applicants must take the same entrance examination consisting of a written exam and an interview given to Japanese students.

Doctor's Program

Same as Master's program.

Documents to be Submitted When Applying

Standard Documents Requirement

Applicants to the Doctor's program must submit a summary of his/her Master's thesis as well.

Application forms are available at the Graduate Admissions Office from early July for the Master's program and from December for the Doctor's program. All applicants are required to submit the application documents to the Graduate Admissions Office during the particular period of time in August for

Master's and in January for Doctor's respectively.

Research Institutes and Centers

Center for Education and Research, Center for Laboratory Animal Resources, Herbal Garden, Instrumental Center, Nenohara-Kawashima Memorial Experimental Farm, Pharmaceutical Research Institute (Biopharmaceutical Chemistry, Botanical Ecology, Microbiology, Radiochemistry), Radioisotope Laboratory

For Further Information

Undergraduate and Graduate Admission

Admissions Office, Student Affairs Bureau, Gifu Pharmaceutical University, 5-6-1 Mitahora-higashi, Gifu-shi, Gifu 502 ☎ 0582-37-3931 ext. 212

Gunma Prefectural Women's College

(Gunma Kenritsu Joshi Daigaku)

1395-1 Kaminote, Tamamura-machi, Sawa-gun, Gunma 370-11   ☎ 0270-65-8511

Faculty

Profs. 18   Assoc. Profs. 20

Assist. Profs. Full-time 4; Part-time 32

Res. Assocs. 8

Number of Students

Undergrad. 605

Library 83, 000 volumes

Outline and Characteristics of the College

Gunma Prefectural Women's College, founded in 1980 by Gunma Prefecture, consists of three departments: Aesthetics and Art History, English Literature and Japanese Literature, all of which belong to the faculty of Letters. This newly-founded college is devoted to the cultivation of artistic sentiments, emphasizing a sense of internationality. The institution enrolls approximately 605 students and maintain 51 full-time faculty members. This ratio provides close communication between professors and students. There is a wide range of classes in each major course. The liberal arts consist of various subjects in the humanities, social sciences and natural sciences so that students may afford to make their own choices.

The location of this college is fairly close to Maebashi, seat of Gunma Prefectural Office. The majority of students are from Gunma Prefecture while the others are from all over the country. The environments surrounding the college and the college premises are quite suitable for higher education.

UNDERGRADUATE PROGRAMS

Faculty of Letters (Freshmen Enrollment 130)

Department of Aesthetics and Art History

Aesthetics, History of Arts

Department of English Literature
American Literature, British Literature, English Language
Department of Japanese Literature
Chinese Literature, Japanese Language, Japanese Literature

Foreign Student Admission
Qualifications for Applicants
This college accepts foreign female students and will provide applicants with further information upon request.

*

For Further Information
Undergraduate Admission
Instruction Division, Gunma Prefectural Women's College, 1395-1 Kaminote, Tamamura-machi, Sawa-gun, Gunma 370-11 ☎ 0270–65–8511 ext. 209

Himeji Institute of Technology
(Himeji Kogyo Daigaku)

2167 Shosha, Himeji-shi, Hyogo 671-22
☎ 0792–66–1661

Faculty
    Profs. 45   Assoc. Profs. 44
    Assist. Profs. Full–time 20; Part–time 41
    Res. Assocs. 34
Number of Students
    Undergrad. 1, 362   Grad. 137
Library 136, 926 volumes

Outline and Characteristics of the University
Himeji Institute of Technology was founded as a Technical College in 1944 by Hyogo Prefecture. At the time of its foundation, the college was composed of three departments: Electrical Engineering, Mechanical Engineering, and Industrial Chemistry. In accordance with the revision of the University Law, the College was reorganized into the Himeji Institute of Technology, and at the time the Institute was composed of three departments: Electrical Engineering, Mechanical Engineering, and Applied Chemistry. In 1962 the Department of Chemical Engineering was added, followed by the Department of Electronic Engineering in 1965, and the Department of Material Engineering in 1966.

Ever since, the Institute has grown with the times. In 1968 the Graduate School was opened offering a Master's Program in the departments of Applied Chemistry and Chemical Engineering.

In 1973 two Master's Programs were added: Electricity and Electronics, and Material Science, and in 1975 one more Master's Program was added: Mechanical Engineering. In 1981, a Doctor's Program was started: Productive Engineering Course.

Today, the Institute enrolls more than 1, 400 students, has a full-time faculty of 143, and is comprised of six Departments, Graduate School, and other affiliated establishments.

The campus is located to the northwest of Himeji City (population 450, 000) and is at the foot of the famous Mt. Shosha. Students can study and relax among academic buildings and a quiet wooded campus.

Himeji Institute of Technology is the only prefectural university of engineering in the Kansai area in Japan, and provides a number of diverse and unique programs that have gained national recognition. The graduates are noted for their nation-wide reputation. Himeji Institute of Technology is expected to be one of the centers of Technopolis, a comprehensive high-technology-industrial district, which is planned for construction.

The majority of students (85%) are the sons and daughters of residents of Hyogo Prefecture, but others come from every part of Japan and foreign countries (Thailand and China) to study at Himeji Institute of Technology.

UNDERGRADUATE PROGRAMS

Faculty of Engineering (Freshmen Enrollment: 300)
Department of Applied Chemistry
Environmental Chemistry, Industrial Inorganic Chemistry, Industrial Organic Chemistry, Natural Polymer Chemistry, Physical Chemistry, Synthetic Polymer Chemistry
Department of Chemical Engineering
Design and Materials Science, Mass-transfer and Reaction Engineering, Material Forming Engineering, Powder Technology, Thermal Engineering, Transport Phenomena
Department of Electrical Engineering
Electrical Instrumentation and Energy, Electrical Physics, Electric Power and Control, Electric Power Application, Electromagnetic Conversion, Fundamental Electricity
Department of Electronic Engineering
Electromagnetic-Waves Engineering, Electron Devices and Electronic Materials, Electronic Circuits, Electron Physics, Information and Transmission Engineering
Department of Material Engineering
Metallic Materials, Metallography, Metal Surface Engineering, Physical Chemistry of Metals, Plasticity and Mechanical Working of Metals, Strength and Fracture of Materials
Department of Mechanical Engineering
Engineering Dynamics, Fluid Dynamics, Machine Design, Manufacturing Engineering, Solid Mechanics, Thermodynamics

Foreign Student Admission
Qualifications for Applicants
  Standard Qualifications Requirement
  Additional requirements are as follows.
1. Applicants must be non-Japanese and recom-

mended by the embassy or the consulate.

2. Applicants (for the sciences) must take the General Examination for Foreign Students and must receive an "A", or "B" or "C" grade. They must be recommended by the headmaster of the Japanese Language School of the International Students Institute or its equivalent.

Examination at the University

The applicants must take each Department's special entrance examination consisting of written and oral examinations and an interview.

1. Foreign Language (English IIB, IIC)
2. Short Essay in Japanese
3. Mathematics: algebra, geometry, elementary analysis, differential calculus, integral calculus, probability, statistics of probability and statistics, the following items are excluded. (1) descriptive study of data, (2) probability distribution and (3) statistical inference
4. Oral Examination

Documents to be Submitted When Applying

Standard Documents Requirement

Following documents are also required.

1. Official transcripts of the Japanese Language School of the International Students Institute or its equivalent, showing the grade and the certificate or diploma awarded to the applicant.
2. A letter of recommendation from the embassy or the consulate.
3. A letter of recommendation issued by the headmaster of the Japanese Language School of the International Students Institute or its equivalent.

Application forms are available at the Admissions Office from September. All applicants are required to submit the specified application documents to the Admissions Office by February 1.

GRADUATE PROGRAMS

Graduate School of Engineering (First Year Enrollment : Master's 52, Doctor's 6)

Divisions

Applied Chemistry, Chemical Engineering, Electricity and Electronics, Material Science, Mechanical Engineering, Productive Engineering

Foreign Student Admission

Qualifications for Applicants

Master's Program

Standard Qualifications Requirement

Applicants must be recommended by the embassy or the consulate.

Doctor's Program

Standard Qualifications Requirement

Applicants must be recommended by the embassy or the consulate.

Examination at the University

Master's Program

Admission is granted on the basis of paper-test, oral examination, personal documents, linguistic knowledge in English, and a Health Certificate.

Doctor's Program

Same as Master's program.

Documents to be Submitted When Applying

Standard Documents Requirement

A letter of recommendation from the embassy or the consulate is also necessary. Application forms are available at the Admissions Office from September. All applicants are required to submit the specified application documents to the Admissions Office by February 1.

＊

Research Institutes and Centers

Basic Research Laboratory, Information Processing Center

For Further Information

Undergraduate and Graduate Admission

Registrar's Office, Himeji Institute of Technology, 2167 Shosha, Himeji-shi, Hyogo 671-22 ☎ 0792-66-1661 ext. 220

Hiroshima Women's University
(Hiroshima Joshi Daigaku)

1-1-71 Ujina-higashi, Minami-ku, Hiroshima-shi, Hiroshima 734 ☎ 082-251-5178

Faculty

    Profs. 27   Assoc. Profs. 17

    Assist. Profs.   Full-time 7; Part-time 75

    Res. Assocs. 14

Number of Students

    Undergrad. 940

Library 139, 639 volumes

Outline and Characteristics of the University

The university started in 1914 as the advanced course of the Hiroshima Prefectural Girls' High School. In 1928 its status was raised to that of college and was named Hiroshima Women's College. During the prewar days, when there were very few colleges for women in Japan, it made great contributions to the education of women, attracting students from all over the Chugoku-Shikoku region.

As a result of the reform following the end of World War II, the college was reorganized as Hiroshima Women's Junior College in 1950. Fifteen years later in 1965, it became Hiroshima Women's University, comprising the Faculty of Letters and the Faculty of Home Economics.

Students can benefit from the advantages of a small institution both in academic work and in extracurricular activities. Two important features are guidance by advisers and in-depth teaching in seminars, which are aimed at encouraging student initiative. Students enjoy a friendly and liberal atmosphere on campus and acquire a positive attitude toward studies and pursuit of truth.

The majority of students come from Hiroshima prefecture, but some come from other prefectures in western Japan. The University has had a few foreign students from China, Taiwan, Korea, and South America. As a prefectural university for women, we are proud of the important role our institution has played in the education of women.

The University is situated in a quiet district of Hiroshima. Students can participate in many kinds of athletic and cultural club activities outside of classes. The campus is not far from the downtown area, Peace Memorial Park, and Atomic Park. They can visit the museum and art gallery as well as go to concerts, movies, art exhibitions and other cultural events. Near the campus are hills and parks, where they can jog or go for walks.

UNDERGRADUATE PROGRAMS

Faculty of Home Economics (Freshmen Enrollment: 150)

Department of Child Study

Art, Child Health, Childhood Education, Child Psychology, Music, Physical Education, Study of Child Culture

Department of Food and Nutrition

Applied Nutrition, Cookery, Food Science, General Nutrition

Department of Science of Living

Science of the Environment, Science of the Human Body, Technology of Life Sciences

Department of Textiles and Clothing

Arrangement of Clothing, Clothing Construction, Clothing Design, Clothing Materials, Hygienics of Clothing

Faculty of Letters (Freshmen Enrollment: 100)

Department of Japanese Language and Literature

Chinese Literature and Philosophy, History of Japanese Literature, Japanese Language, Japanese Literature, Japanese Philology

Department of Social Welfare

Field of Social Work, Field Work, Methods of Social Work

Foreign Student Admission

Qualifications for Applicants

Standard Qualifications Requirement

Examination at the University

The applicant need not take the Japanese Language Proficiency Test or the General Examination for Foreign Students. But if she has taken either or both, the results will be considered.

The applicant will be examined in the following subjects and/or interview.

Faculty of Letters: Dept. of Japanese Language and Literature—Japanese, Japanese Literature and interview, Dept. of Social Welfare—Japanese, English and interview. Faculty of Home Economics:

Dept. of Child Study—interview, Dept. of Food and Nutrition—interview, Dept. of Science of Living—interview, Dept. of Textiles and Clothing—interview

Documents to be Submitted When Applying

Standard Documents Requirement

Applicants are also required to submit an official document issued by the government of their home country or other public agency certifying that she is a citizen, or a copy of her family register.

*

For Further Information

Undergraduate Admission

Admissions Office, Hiroshima Women's University, 1-1-71 Ujina-higashi, Minami-ku, Hiroshima-shi, Hiroshima 734 ☎ 082-251-5178

Kanazawa College of Art

(Kanazawa Bijutsu Kogei Daigaku)

5-11-1 Kodatsuno, Kanazawa-shi, Ishikawa 920
☎ 0762-62-3531

Faculty
Profs. 23   Assoc. Profs. 25
Assist. Profs. Full–time 5; Part–time 118
Res. Assoc. 1
Number of Students
Undergrad. 570   Grad. 42
Library 45, 458 volumes

Outline and Characteristics of the College

Kanazawa College of Art was founded in 1946 by the municipal government. At the time of its foundation, the college was named Professional School of Arts and Crafts and was composed of six courses: Oil Painting, Japanese Painting, Sculpture, Pottery, Metalwork and Lacquerware. In 1955, in accordance with the revision of its constitution, the college was reorganized into the present faculty system comprising two departments, Fine Arts and Industrial Arts. They are divided into six independent courses: Aesthetics & Art History, Painting, Sculpture, Industrial Design, Visual Design and Craft Design.

Ever since, the college has grown with the times. In 1972, the college buildings and campus were newly built at its present site in Kodatsuno, and the Research Institute of Art and Craft which has been recently expanded was founded. In 1979 the Graduate School opened and began to offer a Master's program. In 1983 the Aesthetics & Art History course was added to the Fine Arts Department. Today the college enrolls approximately 600 students including graduate students, foreign students and auditors.

The campus is located in the most academic and scenic area in Kanazawa (population 430, 000). Students study, work and enjoy many traditional cultural heritages surrounded by natural beauty.

The college is noted for its artistic excellence, especially in the field of traditional craft work as well as modern art. The majority of students are from the Hokuriku district-Ishikawa, Toyama and Fukui, but people come from all parts of Japan and many foreign countries to study in Kanazawa.

UNDERGRADUATE PROGRAMS

Faculty of Art (Freshmen Enrollment: 130)
  Department of Fine Arts
Aesthetics and Art History, Japanese Painting, Oil painting, Sculpture
  Department of Industrial Art
Craft Design (Lacquer Ware, Metal-Casting, Metal-Hammering, Pottery, Textile Printing, Weaving), Industrial Design, Visual Design

Foreign Student Admission
  Qualifications for Applicants
    Standard Qualifications Requirement
    Foreign applicants must take the Joint First-Stage Achievement Test and the Japanese Language Proficiency Test. The number of foreign student accepted varies according to the facilities available in each course.
  Examination at the College
    Those who receive a reasonable grade in the tests mentioned above will be allowed to take the Department's special entrance examination consisting of presentations and an interview in Japanese.
Foreign Student Admission to Auditor's Programs: Foreign students sponsored by certain authorized institutions will be admitted without entrance examination, upon submitting the necessary documents. They may receive a diploma of completion after a one-year course.
  Documents to be Submitted When Applying
    Standard Documents Requirement
    Applicants are also required to submit a piece of work done in recent years.
    Application forms are available at the Admissions Office from early November. All applicants are required to submit the specified application documents to the Admissions Office by December 15. This deadline for receiving application is inflexible.

GRADUATE PROGRAMS

Graduate School of Art (First Year Enrollment : Master's 18)
  Divisions
Industrial Design, Painting, Sculpture

Foreign Student Admission
  Qualifications for Applicants
Master's Program
    Standard Qualifications Requirement
  Examination at the College
Master's Program

Applicants must take the same entrance examination consisting of practical presentations, a written exam and an interview, as given to Japanese students.
  Documents to be Submitted When Applying
    Standard Documents Requirement
    Application forms are available at the Graduate Admissions Office from early November. All applicants are required to submit the specified application documents to the Graduate Admissions Office by December 15.

*

Research Institutes and Centers
Research Institute of Kanazawa College of Art
Special Programs for Foreign Students
  Japanese language supplementary classes are available at the Institute Language Center.
For Further Information
  Undergraduate and Graduate Admission
Admissions Office, Kanazawa College of Art, 5-11-1 Kodatsuno, Kanazawa-shi, Ishikawa 920 ☎ 0762–62–3531 ext. 225

Kitakyushu University
(Kitakyushu Daigaku)

4-2-1 Kitagata, Kokuraminami-ku, Kitakyushu-shi, Fukuoka 802   ☎ 093–962–4436

Faculty
    Profs. 74   Assoc. Profs. 43
    Assist. Profs. Full–time 10; Part–time 118
Number of Students
    Undergrad. 3, 773   Grad. 39
Library 284, 110 volumes

Outline and Characteristics of the University
    Located in and supported by Kitakyushu city, a city with a population of over one million, Kitakyushu University is developing into one of the nation's largest municipal institutions for instruction, research and public service. Despite its rapid growth over the past 40 years, the University is establishing a proud and rich tradition of service to the nation, with particular emphasis on the communities in and around northern Kyushu.
    The idea of establishing the school was promoted immediately after World War II by the then mayor, Ryosuke Hamada and the local citizens. Their hard work led to its founding in 1946 as a college for foreign studies which holds educating young people the pioneering spirit and internationalism as ideal. The school achieved university status in 1950 under the name of Kitakyushu University of Foreign Languages, but it was renamed Kitakyushu University with the establishment of the Faculty of Economics and Business Administration in 1953. The evening program was instituted in 1957 within the Faculty of Foreign Studies to meet the needs of many working

people in the area. In 1959, the Kitakyushu Institute of Regional Studies was established as an affiliated institution. The University is a unique institution where the staff and its affiliated members research various problems closely related to the immediate needs of the Kitakyushu region.

The Faculty of Literature was founded in 1966, and with the establishment of the Faculty of Law in 1973, the institution has now grown into a university consisting of four faculties and eight departments.

Kitakyushu city is one of the most advanced and industrial areas in Japan. To meet the challenge and expectations of the community, the University in close partnership with the city established its first program in business administration in 1980. This was followed two years later by the graduate program in foreign studies, and by the Master's program in Law in 1984.

The University maintains high standards and academic excellence in all areas of studies. However, the Faculty of Foreign Studies is perhaps best known because it is the oldest and most intense, with regard to academic experience, of the University's Faculties.

The University views study abroad as an important component of its language and cultural studies curriculum, and has recently concluded an academic exchange program with Old Dominion Universtity in Norfolk, Virginia, U. S. A. When detailed arrangements to insure systematic and regular exchanges between the students and the faculties of the two institutions have been worked out in the near future, both universities will benefit to a great extent.

UNDERGRADUATE PROGRAMS

Faculty of Economics and Business Administration (Freshmen Enrollment: 300)

Department of Business Administration
Accounting, Advertising, Auditing, Bookkeeping, Business Administration, Business Management, Financial Administration, Industrial Management, Insurance, International Trade, Japanese Business History, Japanese Economic History, Marketing Management, Marketing Research, Merchandising, Personnel Administration, Production Control

Department of Economics
Agricultural Policy, Commercial Policy, Econometrics, Economic Geography, Economic Mathematics, Economic Policy, Economics, Economics of Japan, Economic Statistics, History of Social Thought, Industrial Policy, International Economics, International Monetary Economics, Japanese Economic History, Monetary Economics, Money and Banking, Public Finance, Regional Economics, Taxation

Faculty of Foreign Studies (Freshmen Enrollment: 180)

Department of Anglo-American Studies
American Culture, American Diplomacy, American History, American Literature, Comparative Literature, English Culture, English Grammar, English History, English Linguistics, English Literature, English Phonetics, English Writing, International Relations

Department of Chinese Studies
Chinese Culture, Chinese Grammar, Chinese History, Chinese Linguistics, Chinese Literature, Chinese Phonetics, Chinese Studies, Chinese Thoughts, Chinese Writing, Classical Chinese Usage, Comparative Literature, Oriental History

Faculty of Law (Freshmen Enrollment: 200)

Department of Law
Administrative Law, Bankruptcy, Civil Law, Civil Procedure, Commercial Code, Constitutional Law, Criminal Law, Criminal Procedure, Criminology, Economic Law, History of Legal System, International Law, Legal Philosophy, Local Government, Local Government Law, Management in the Public Services, Political Science, Private International Law, Public Administration, Social Law, Western Legal History

Department of Political Science
Administrative Law, Constitutional Law, Diplomatic History, History of Political Thought, International Law, International Politics, Japanese Political History, Political Science, Public Administration, Western Political History

Faculty of Literature (Freshmen Enrollment: 160)

Department of English Literature
American Novels, American Poetry and Drama, English Drama, English Grammar, English Linguistics, English Novels, English Phonetics, English Poetry, History of American Literature, History of English Literature, Medieval English Literature

Department of Japanese Literature
Asian History, Chinese Literature, History of Asian Philosophy, History of Japanese Thought, History of the Japanese Language, Japanese Ancient Literature, Japanese Classics, Japanese History, Japanese Literary History, Japanese Medieval Literature, Japanese Philosophy, Modern Japanese Works

Foreign Student Admission

Qualifications for Applicants
Standard Qualifications Requirement
Applicants must take the Japanese Language Proficiency Test and General Examination for Foreign Students.

Examination at the University
The applicant will be given examinations, written or oral, in the Japanese language and a subject designated by the department.

Documents to be Submitted When Applying
Standard Documents Requirement
Additional documents required are as follows.
1. A statement of purpose for his/her wish to be admitted (written by the applicant in Japanese)
2. A personal history (written by the applicant in Japanese)
3. A certificate or a report of an acceptable score

of the Japanese Language Proficiency Test

4. A copy of the certificate showing the results of the General Examination for Foreign Students

Application forms are available at the Admissions Office from mid-December. All applicants are required to submit the specified application documents to the Admissions Office by March 3. The deadline for receiving application is inflexible.

GRADUATE PROGRAMS

Graduate School of Anglo-American Languages and Cultures (First Year Enrollment : Master's 6)
Divisions
American Literature, American Studies, British Studies, English Linguistics, English Literature
Graduate School of Business Administration (First Year Enrollment : Master's 10)
Divisions
Accounting, Auditing, Bookkeeping, Business Administration, Business Management, Corporation, Enterprise, Financial Management, Industrial Control, International Business, Marketing, Personnel Management
Graduate School of Chinese Studies (First Year Enrollment : Master's 4)
Divisions
Chinese Linguistics, Chinese Literature, Chinese Studies
Graduate School of Law (First Year Enrollment : Master's 10)
Divisions
Administrative Law, Civil Law, Civil Procedure, Constitutional Law, Criminal Procedure, Criminology, International Law, Social Law, The Commercial Code

Foreign Student Admission

Qualifications for Applicants
Master's Program
    Standard Qualifications Requirement
Examination at the University
Master's Program
    Applicants shall be admitted to the University according to different requirements from the usual entrance examinations.
Documents to be Submitted When Applying
    Standard Documents Requirement
    As for the documents that applicants must submit, see the items described in the undergraduate programs for foreign applicants.
    Application forms are available at the Graduate Admissions Office from August. All applicants are required to submit the specified application documents to the Graduate Admissions Office by early October. Graduate applicants may be also accepted between mid-December and early February when there are openings. In such cases all the procedures and examinations must be completed during this pe-

riod.

*

Research Institutes and Centers
Computer Center, The Kitakyushu Institute of Regional Studies
For Further Information
    Undergraduate and Graduate Admission
Academic Affairs Section II, Admissions Office, Kitakyushu University, 4-2-1 Kitagata, Kokuraminami-ku, Kitakyushu-shi, Fukuoka 802
☎ 093–962–4436

Kobe City University of Foreign Studies

(Kobe-shi Gaikokugo Daigaku)

9-1 Gakuen-higashi-machi, Nishi-ku, Kobe-shi, Hyogo 673   ☎ 078–794–8121

Faculty
    Profs.   43   Assoc. Profs.   31
    Assist. Profs.   Full–time 9; Part–time   130
    Res. Assoc.   1
Number of Students
    Undergrad. 1, 678   Grad.   17
Library 218, 320 volumes

Outline and Characteristics of the University

The Kobe Municipal College of Foreign Affairs, with three original departments of English, Russian and Chinese was founded on June 1, 1946 as a municipal government-supported educational institution. The institution broadened its status into a full four-year university curriculum in 1949 as a result of the new Education Reform Plan, and assumed the name of Kobe City University of Foreign Studies. In 1962, the Spanish Department was added and in 1967, a graduate program was established in each department.

The university is committed to responsible scholarship in promoting the study and teaching of foreign languages in a framework of cross-cultural communications. Students are encouraged to acquire an intimate understanding of international affairs which will help prepare them for a positive role in the international community of nations. At the same time students are not expected merely to be trained as linguists, but to become cultured men and women with an international knowledge of world affairs.

Kobe City University of Foreign Studies is coeducational, and approximately 65% are women and 35% men, with enrollment totaling about 1, 700. Since its founding, 10, 000 students have been graduated from the university. About a quarter have gone into advanced studies in Japan and abroad. Others have entered a broad spectrum of positions in commerce and industry, education, the communications media, government and international agencies, cultural and research organizations, and social institutions.

Over the past several years, Kobe City has designed a unique international university and community center to accommodate the growing needs of its citizens. The new center became the home of Kobe City University of Foreign Studies from April, 1986. The 850 acre site is located in the tranquil mountain range of the western part of Kobe about a twenty-minute train ride from downtown Kobe.

UNDERGRADUATE PROGRAMS

Faculty of Foreign Studies (Freshmen Enrollment: 440)
Department of Chinese
Department of English-American
Department of English-American (*evening course*)
Department of International Relations
Department of Russian
Department of Spanish

GRADUATE PROGRAMS

Graduate School of Foreign Studies (First Year Enrollment : Master's 25)
Divisions
Chinese Linguistics, English Linguistics, Russian Linguistics, Spanish Linguistics
*
Research Institutes and Centers
Research Institute for Foreign Studies
For Further Information
Undergraduate and Graduate Admission
Administration Office, Kobe City University of Foreign Studies, 9–1 Gakuen-higashi-machi, Nishi-ku, Kobe-shi, Hyogo 673 ☎ 078–794–8121

Kobe University of Commerce
(Kobe Shoka Daigaku)

4–3–3 Seiryodai, Tarumi–ku, Kobe–shi, Hyogo 655
☎ 078–707–6161

Faculty
    Profs. 46   Assoc. Profs. 36
    Assist. Profs. Full–time 12; Part–time 49
    Res. Assocs. 10
Number of Students
    Undergrad. 1, 971   Grad. 43
Library 302, 673 volumes

Outline and Characteristics of the College
It was founded in 1929 under the prewar educational system as Hyogo Prefectural Kobe College of commerce. In 1948 it became Kobe University of Commerce in line with the new postwar education system. Since then, the University has enjoyed fur-

ther development, and two Graduate schools have been established.

At the undergraduate level, the University offers four-year courses in economics, business administration, management science, marketing and international business; at the postgraduate level, two master's and two doctoral courses are offered. (See Undergraduate and Graduate Programs.)

From its early days of Kobe College of Commerce, the University has maintained the ideal that the pursuit of education does not merely consist of the acquisition of knowledge, but instead builds and develops individual character. In Order to fulfill this ideal, Kobe University of Commerce encourages personal communication between student and instructor, and uses the seminar system for all specialized courses and in part for general education. The University is run on a small, personal scale, in which the student is aided in establishing his identity by the friendly and relaxed atmosphere on campus. This atmosphere facilitates a happier social relationship between student and instructor. In short, an important factor in the University's policy of education is to stimulate the student to build his character and to help him develop into a talented and creative individual.

UNDERGRADUATE PROGRAMS

Faculty of Economics and Business Administration (Freshmen Enrollment: 430)
    Department of Business Administraion
Accounting Organization and System, Business Law, Business Organization and Administration, Civil Law, Financial Accounting, Management Accounting, Management of Small Business, Personnel Management, Principles of Management, Public Law and Public Sector Accounting
    Department of Economics
Econometrics, Economic Geography, Economic History, Economic Policy, Economic Theory, History of Economics, International Economics, Monetary Economics, Public Finance, Social Policy
    Department of Management Science
Applied Mathematics, Electronic Data Processing, Management Information System, Mathematical Statistics, Operations Research, Production Engineering
    Department of Marketing and International Business
Comparative Sudies of Economy, International Business Management, Marketing, Theory of Consumer Economy, Theory of International Trade, Theory of Transportation and Insurance

Foreign Student Admission
    Qualifications for Applicants
    Standard Qualifications Requirement
    Applicants are also required to pass the Japanese Language Proficiency Test and the General Examination for Foreign Students.

Examination at the University

Applicants are required to take a set of written examinations in English, Japanese, and Mathematics. The examination is held every year in mid-February. An interview is also required. Admission is granted on the basis of the candidate's examination results, the interview, and his state of health.

Documents to be Submitted When Applying

Standard Documents Requirement

A Letter of Recommendation from the applicant's embassy or consulate in Japan or from an institute which is acceptable to the University.

GRADUATE PROGRAMS

Graduate School of Business Administration (First Year Enrollment : Master's 10, Doctor's 5)
Divisions
Business Administration
Graduate School of Economics (First Year Enrollment : Master's 10, Doctor's 5)
Divisions
Economics

Foreign Student Admission

Qualifications for Applicants
Master's Program
Standard Qualifications Requirement
Doctor's Program
Standard Qualifications Requirement
Examination at the University
Master's Program
Applicants are required to take a set of written and oral examinations, either in September or February.
Doctor's Program
Applicants are required to take a set of written and oral examinations, which are given every year in February.

Documents to be Submitted When Applying
Standard Documents Requirement
The following documents are also required:
1.   A Letter of Introduction from the applicant's foreign office, from his foreign legation, or from his foreign embassy or consullate in Japan.
2.   A certificate from an accredited language school or teacher which certifies that the applicant has a sufficient and working knowledge of Japanese to pursue his post-graduate studies.

Applicants are required to submit the required documents in person or by mail, with the necessary Application Fee, to the Section of Academic Affairs, Kobe University of Commerce. The deadlines for the September and the February applications are August 15 and January 15, respectively.

*
Research Institutes and Centers
Data Processing Education Center, Institute of Economic Research

For Further Information
Undergraduate and Graduate Admission
Section of Academic Affairs, Kobe Universitiy of Commerce 4-3-3 Seiryodai, Tarumi–ku, Kobe–shi, Hyogo 655 ☎ 078–707–6161 ext. 274

Kochi Women's University
(Kochi Joshi Daigaku)

5-15 Eikokuji-cho, Kochi-shi, Kochi 780
☎ 0888–73–2156

Faculty
    Profs.   34   Assoc. Profs.   17
    Assist. Profs.   Full–time   4; Part–time   125
    Res. Assocs.   11
Number of Students
    Undergrad.   718
Library   84, 235 volumes

Outline and Characteristics of the University

Kochi Women's University was established in 1949 by Kochi Prefecture on the foundation laid by its predecessors, Kochi Prefectural Women's Medical College founded in 1944 and Kochi Prefectural Women's College founded in 1947.

At the time of its establishment, it had only one Faculty containing a single Department. But it has grown rapidly with the times, supported by an ardent desire for higher education for women. The University is now composed of two Faculties, the Faculty of Home Economics and the Faculty of Literature, the former consisting of four Departments: Home Economics, Food and Nutrition, Science of Living, and Nursing; and the latter consisting of two Departments: Japanese and English, together with the Course of Liberal Education.

Along with the bachelor's degree granted to the graduate, the University provides the student with courses for various licenses and professional qualifications so that she can be an active member of her community equipped with expert knowledge and economic independence.

Today, the University enrolls more than 700 students and a full time faculty of 66. This is the only prefectural women's university in the Shikoku district. The greater part of the students come from the four prefectures of Shikoku, but there are some who come all the way from the Chugoku and Kyushu districts and many other remote parts of Japan.

The campus is located right in the heart of Kochi City (population 309, 789), the seat of the prefectural government. It is small and compact, conveniently situated many public facilities and shopping centers as well as the students' living quarters.

UNDERGRADUATE PROGRAMS

Faculty of Home Economics (Freshmen Enrollment: 80)

Department of Food and Nutrition

Cookery, Food Chemistry, Food Hygiene, Nutritional Chemistry, Nutritional Physiology, Nutrition Guidance

Department of Home Economics

Clothing Construction, Clothing Materials, Cookery, Family Relationships, Field Work of Home Economics, Home Management

Department of Nursing

Adult Nursing, Maternity Nursing, Nursing, Pediatric Nursing, Psychiatric Nursing

Department of Science of Living

Applied Physics, Biology, Chemistry, Computer Science, Earth Science (including Environmental Problems), Mathematics, Physical Science

Faculty of Literature (Freshmen Enrollment: 80)

Department of English

American Literature, English Linguistics, English Literature

Department of Japanese

Chinese Literature, Japanese Linguistics, Japanese Literature

*

For Further Information

Undergraduate Admission

Head of General Affairs Division, Administration Office, Kochi Women's University, 5-15 Eikokuji-cho, Kochi-shi, Kochi 780 ☎ 0888-73-2156

Kumamoto Women's University
(Kumamoto Joshi Daigaku)

2432-1 Mizuarai, Kengun, Kumamoto-shi,
Kumamoto 862 ☎ 096-383-2929

Faculty
Profs. 21   Assoc. Profs. 20
Assist. Profs. Full–time 2; Part–time 68
Res. Assocs. 10
Number of Students
Undergrad. 849
Library 114, 000 volumes

Outline and Characteristics of the University

Kumamoto Women's University developed into its present form in 1949 out of its predecessor, Kumamoto Women's College, which was founded in 1947 by Kumamoto Prefecture. The university at the time was composed of four departments—Japanese Language and Literature, English Language and Literature, Domestic Science and Food and Nutrition Science. It was the first university for women in the Kyushu district, established at the start of the new education system.

Ever since, the university, as the only public women's university in Southern Kyushu, has contributed a great deal to educating women not only from the region but also from different parts of the country.

In April of 1980, the university underwent a restructuring of the departments, reorganizing its four departments into two independent faculties—Letters and Living Science; with five departments—Japanese Language and Literature, English Language and Literature, Living Management, Science of Living Environment and Food and Nutrition Science. At the same time, the university was moved to the present campus which is located in the eastern part of Kumamoto city, at the former site of an airport. On 67, 000 m² of land there stands a complex of ivory-white buildings, in vivid contrast to the brick color of the pavement. The new campus, built as part of an urban development project, offers an ideal environment for university education.

During its 38 year history, Kumamoto Women's University has graduated some 6, 400 students, many of whom are playing an active role in the fields of education, culture, and industry.

UNDERGRADUATE PROGRAMS

Faculty of Letters (Freshmen Enrollment: 80)

Department of English Language and Literature

English, Literature and Linguistics

Department of Japanese Language and Literature

Faculty of Living Science (Freshmen Enrollment: 120)

Department of Food and Nutrition Science

Department of Living Management

Department of Science of Living Environment

Design and Housing, Textiles and Clothing

Foreign Student Admission

Qualifications for Applicants

Standard Qualifications Requirement

Applicants must take the Japanese Language Proficiency Test and General Examination for Foreign Students. They are, however, exempted from the Joint-First Stage Achievement Test.

Examination at the University

Admission will be determined by both application materials the student submits and the Faculty's entrance examination consisting of a written exam and an interview. The entrance examination is scheduled for March 6.

Written Examination for Foreign Students

Department of Japanese Language & Literature: short essay (in Japanese) and English

Department of English Language & Literature: short essay (in Japanese or English) and English

Department of Food & Nutrition Science: mathematics and science (physics, chemistry, or biology)

Department of Living Management: short essay (in Japanese or English)

Department of Science of Living Environment: mathematics and short essay (in Japanese)

Documents to be Submitted When Applying

Standard Documents Requirement

Those candidates who have been granted admission to the University must complete admission procedure on March 31.

*

Facilities/Services for Foreign Students

The University has no facilities for foreign students. It can, however, assist students in finding accommodations near campus.

For Further Information

Undergraduate Admission

Admissions Assistant, Instruction Department, Kumamoto Women's University, 2432-1 Mizuarai, Kengun, Kumamoto-shi, Kumamoto 862 ☎ 096–383–2929 ext. 221

Kushiro Public University of Economics
(Kushiro Koritsu Daigaku)

4-1-1 Ashino, Kushiro–shi, Hokkaido 085
☎ 0154–37–3211

Faculty
    Profs. 14   Assoc. Profs. 7
    Assist. Profs. Full–time 8; Part–time 5
Number of Students
    Undergrad. 266
Library 21, 824 volumes

Outline and Characteristics of the University

Kushiro Public University of Economics was inaugurated April 1, 1988 in order to meet the needs of Kushiro region for higher education and research. This intitute, founded by a special public organization of ten local municipalities, including Kushiro city, has, at present, only the Department of Economics.

The school's ideal of university education, namely to encourage an international ways of thinking and to put theories of economics into practice, appealed to young students throughout the country and brought more than 2, 300 applicants in its first year.

The magnificent campus is situated in the suburbs of Kushino city and faces Kushiro Marshland National Park to the north-east. Students can enjoy its splendid academic institution in a wonderful natural environment.

Kushiro City continues to develop into the industrial, adminisfrative, and cultural center of the eastern part of Hokkaido, with its major industries such as fisheries and paper-manufacturing, its role as an entrepot of various commodities, and a location close to the USSR, the USA, and Canada. It is not too much to say that the foundation of the university will be one of the most important factors to develop the Kushiro region.

The university which had an enrollment of only 266 freshmen in its first year will be able to enroll 1, 000 students within four years. Procedures for admitting foreign students are now under consideration.

UNDERGRADUATE PROGRAMS

Faculty of Economics (Freshmen Enrollment: 250)

Department of Economics

Accounting, Econometrics, Economic History, Economic Policy, Money and Banking, Principles of Economics, Public Finance, Regional Economics, Social Policy, Statistics

*

For Further Information

Undergraduate Admission

Administration Office, Kushiro Public University of Economics, 4–1–1 Ashino, Kushiro-shi, Hokkaido 085 ☎ 0154–37–3211

Kyoto City University of Arts
(Kyoto Shiritsu Geijutsu Daigaku)

13-6 Kutsukake-cho, Ooe, Nishikyo-ku, Kyoto-shi, Kyoto 610-11 ☎ 075–332–0701

Faculty
    Profs. 46   Assoc. Profs. 29
    Assist. Profs. Full–time 9
    Res. Assocs. 2
Number of Students
    Undergrad. 757   Grad. 136
Library 69, 137 volumes

Outline and Characteristics of the University

History:

July 1880	The establishment of Kyoto-fu Gagakko in Kyoto Gyoen as the temporary schoolhouse.
Dec. 1889	Transfer of control to Kyoto City and changing of its name to Kyoto-shi Gagakko.
Apr. 1891	Changing of its name to Kyoto-shi Bijutsu Gakko.
Aug. 1894	Changing of its name to Kyoto-shi Bijutsu Kogei Gakko.
May 1901	Changing of its name to Kyoto-shiritsu Bijutsu Gakko.
Apr. 1909	Authorized by the Ministry of Education; changing of its name to Kyoto-shiritsu Kaiga Senmon Gakko.
June 1926	The move to Higashiyama-ku, Imakumano Hiyoshi-cho.
Apr. 1945	The re-establishment as Kyoto-shiritsu Bijutsu Senmon Gakko.

Apr. 1950   The raising of status to Kyoto-shiritsu Bijutsu Daigaku.

Apr. 1952   The establishment of Kyoto-shiritsu Ongaku Tanki Daigaku at Kita-ku, Izumoji Tatemoto-cho.

Apr. 1953   The establishment of the post-graduate course of Fine Arts.

Sep. 1956   The moving of Kyoto-shiritsu Ongaku Tanki Daigaku to Sakyo-ku, Shogo-in Entonbi-cho.

Apr. 1963   The establishment of the post-graduate course of Music.

Apr. 1969   Changing of its name to Kyoto City University of Arts and the establishment of the Faculty of Music.

Mar. 1971   The abolition of Kyoto-shiritsu Ongaku Tanki Daigaku.

Aug. 1977   The start of construction of new school united Arts and Music at Nishikyo-ku, Ooe Kutsukake-cho.

Mar. 1980   The move to new schoolhouse at Nishikyo-ku, Ooe Kutsukake-cho

Apr. 1980   The establishment of Graduate School of Arts.

Mar. 1982   The abolition of the post-graduate course of Fine Arts.

Apr. 1986   The establishment of Graduate School of Music

Outline:

This university consists of Faculties of Fine Arts and Music. The former has a history of over 100 years since the time of Kyoto-fu Gagakko. The latter, which was preceded by Kyoto-shiritsu Ongaku Tanki Daigaku, has a history of 30 years. In 1969, they were combined into Kyoto City University of Arts, and moved to the present location in 1980. The university commands a very high place in the educational world of arts as a synthetic arts university.

The Faculty of Fine Arts, which was established earlier than Tokyo Fine Arts School (now Faculty of Fine Arts in Tokyo University of Fine Arts and Music), has produced many talented persons who were pioneers of Modern Fine Arts in Japan, such as Kagaku Murakami and Bakusen Tsuchida. The Faculty of Music sent out to the world young, spirited players and composers on the basis of a liberal and vivid educational policy.

Though only several years have passed since moving to the vast new campus in verdurous Rakusai of Kyoto, this university is expected to take an active part as a leader in the educational world of arts on the basis of its special curriculum which can adapt to every aspect of intricate modern arts—adapt its strengths and abandon its weaknesses.

The Graduate School of Arts, which originated as the post-graduate course of Fine Arts, was established in April 1980 for the purpose of teaching and studying art theories and their adaptation, and contributing to the development of culture.

This university participates actively in international cultural exchange by accepting Foreign Students (Graduate School of Arts) and holding lectures by professionals from various fields.

UNDERGRADUATE PROGRAMS

Faculty of Arts (Freshmen Enrollment: 125)
Department of Crafts
Ceramics, Dyeing and Weaving, Urushi Laquering
Department of Design
Environment Design, Product Design, Visual Design
Department of Fine Arts
Conceptual Planning, Art and Photography, Graphic Art, Japanese Painting, Oil Painting, Sculpture
Faculty of Music (Freshmen Enrollment: 60)
Department of Music
Composition, Conducting, Piano, Strings, Vocal Music, Winds and Percussions

GRADUATE PROGRAMS

Graduate School of Arts (First Year Enrollment : Master's 47)
Divisions
Crafts, Design, Painting, Science of Arts, Sculpture
Graduate School of Music (First Year Enrollment : Master's 20)
Divisions
Composition (including Musicology), Instrumental Music, Vocal Music

Foreign Student Admission
Qualifications for Applicants
Master's Program
Those who have studied as a research student (non-degree) for one year in our university can apply for this course.
Examination at the University
Master's Program
Admission is determined by the examination of the special studies (including works and papers), papers, the examination of the academic subjects, interview, writtern investigation and health certificate.
Documents to be Submitted When Applying
Standard Documents Requirement
Letter of recommendation is not required of the graduates of Kyoto City University of Arts. (Form is issued by the University).
Written permission of application: those who are employed in public agencies, offices and so on must have their superior fill in this form. Those who are attending other graduate schools need written permission for application from that university.

*

For Further Information
Undergraduate and Graduate Admission
General Affairs Division, Kyoto City Univerity of Arts, 13-6 Kutsukake-cho, Ooe, Nishikyo-ku, Kyoto-

shi, Kyoto 610–11 ☎ 075–332–0701 ext. 204

Kyoto Prefectural University
(Kyoto Furitsu Daigaku)

1-5 Shimogamo-Hangi-cho, Sakyo-ku, Kyoto-shi,
Kyoto 606   ☎ 075–781–3131

Faculty
    Profs. 50   Assoc. Profs. 56
    Assist. Profs. Full–time 14; Part–time 102
    Res. Assocs. 21
Number of Students
    Undergrad. 1, 185   Grad. 69
Library 216, 922 volumes

Outline and Characteristics of the University

Kyoto Prefectural University was founded in 1949. At the time of its foundation, the University was called Saikyo University and was composed of two faculties: Faculty of Letters and Domestic Science and Faculty of Agriculture. These faculties were originally two independent colleges: Kyoto Prefectural College for Women and Kyoto Prefectural College of Agriculture and Forestry. The University was given the present name in 1959.

The Faculty of Letters and Domestic Science was reorganized in 1970 into two faculties: Faculty of Letters and Faculty of Domestic Science. The latter changed its name to Faculty of Living Science in 1977. In 1970, the Graduate School of Agriculture was opened and offered a Master's program and 1983 it began to offer a Doctor's program as well. The most recent addition is the Graduate School of Living Science in 1986. It offers a Master's program only. In both its faculty and facilities the University has undergone a complete transformation since its foundation.

Furthermore, a junior college for women was founded in 1951 as an affiliated establishment of the University offering a higher education for women.

The two colleges which form the basis of the University were both colleges of high reputation with a distinguished history. Kyoto Prefectural College of Agriculture and Forestry traced its origin to Kyoto Prefectural School of Agriculture founded in 1895, and Kyoto Prefectural College for Women which was founded in 1927, known all over the country as an established and recognized institution of higher education for women.

The campus is located on the side of the Kamo river, the symbol of Kyoto, next to the Prefectural Botanical Garden and the Prefectural Reference Library and extends across 131, 130 m² forming quiet and green-shrouded surroundings, in which students who gather from all over Japan study and work.

UNDERGRADUATE PROGRAMS

Faculty of Agriculture (Freshmen Enrollment: 110)
    Department of Agricultural Chemistry
Biological Chemistry, Biopolymer Chemistry, Fermentation Physiology and Applied Microbiology, Food and Nutrition, Soil Science and Plant Nutrition
    Department of Agronomy
Animal Science, Entomology, Farm Management, Plant Breeding and Crop Science, Plant Pathology, Pomology, Vegetable Horticulture
    Department of Forestry
Erosion and Forestry Engineering, Forest Management, Silviculture, Wood Based Material, Wood Technology

Faculty of Letters (Freshmen Enrollment: 120)
    Department of History
Archaeology, Cultural History, History of Fine Arts, Japanese History, Japanese Paleography, Occidental History, Oriental History
    Department of Literature
Japanese and Chinese Literature Course Chinese Language and Literature, Japanese Language and Literature
Western Literature Course American Literature, English Language and Literature, German Language and Literature
    Department of Social Welfare
Clinical Psychology, History of Social Welfare Work, Labor Hygienics, Regional Sociology, Social Pedagogy, Social Research, Social Security, Social Welfare Legislation

Faculty of Living Science (Freshmen Enrollment: 50)
    Department of Food Science and Nutrition
Cookery Science, Environmental Healthy, Food Chemistry, Food Safety, Nutritional Physiology & Biochemistry
    Department of Housing and Living Design
House Design, House Environment, Housing Management, Housing Policy, Housing Problem, Housing Safety, Living Design

Foreign Student Admission
    Qualifications for Applicants
    Standard Qualifications Requirement
    Examination at the University
    Ordinary entrance examination or the special screening test for foreign applicants.
    Documents to be Submitted When Applying
    Standard Documents Requirement
    JLPT and GEFS scores
    Statement of Reasons for Application
    All applicants are required to submit the specified application documents to the Student Office between February 2 and February 7.

GRADUATE PROGRAMS

Graduate School of Agriculture (First Year Enroll-

ment : Master's 34, Doctor's 7)
Divisions
Agricultural Chemistry, Agronomy, Forestry
Graduate School of Living Science (First Year Enrollment : Master's 8)
Divisions
Food Science and Nutrition, Housing and Planning

Foreign Student Admission
Qualifications for Applicants
Master's Program
　Standard Qualifications Requirement
Doctor's Program
　Standard Qualifications Requirement
Examination at the University
　The ordinary entrance examination or the special screening test for foreign applicants.
Documents to be Submitted When Applying
　Standard Documents Requirement
　Statement of Reasons for Application
　Application period: Feb. 9-Feb. 15.

*

Research Institutes and Centers
Experimental Farm, University Forests
For Further Information
Undergraduate and Graduate Admission
Student Office, Kyoto Prefectural University, 1-5 Shimogamo-Hangi-cho, Sakyo-ku, Kyoto-shi, Kyoto 606 ☎ 075-781-3131

Kyoto Prefectural University of Medicine
(Kyoto Furitsu Ika Daigaku)

465 Kajii-cho, Kawaramachi-dori Hirokoji-agaru,
Kamigyo-ku, Kyoto-shi, Kyoto 602

☎ 075-251-5111~8

Faculty
　Profs.　38　　Assoc. Profs.　29
　Assist. Profs.　Full–time　47; Part–time　240
　Res. Assocs.　178
Number of Students
　Undergrad.　628　　Grad.　149
Library　198, 608 volumes

Outline and Characteristics of the University

　The University is one of the oldest medical schools in Japan, its foundation dating back to 1872, when a small hospital was opened for the purpose of treating the sick and training prospective physicians in accordance with Western medical knowledge. This embryonic forerunner became Kyoto Prefectural University of Medicine in 1921 after several stages of development. Meanwhile, a school of nursing was attached to the University in 1889. Two of the remarkable events in the recent history of the University are the establishment of the Graduate School in 1957 and the opening of Children's Research Hospital in 1982. The University now enrolls more than 1, 000 students including those of the nursing school, and approximately 1, 200 interns, research students and research workers, with a full time faculty of nearly 300.

　The buildings of the University, except those of the Premedical Course and the Branch Hospital, are located on a site of roughly 57, 500 m² in the central part of Kyoto City, in an environment particularly noted for its scenic beauty. The Premedical Course, which has its campus of about 9, 500 m² in the western part of the City, and the Branch Hospital occupying an area of about 7, 100 m² in the southern part, are easily accessible from the main campus, both being within half an hour's drive. On the main campus reconstruction is now under way, and by 1990, when the work is expected to reach completion, both the University and the Hospital will have been entirely renovated, with their facilities and equipment updated.

　The University Hospital has 17 clinical departments and 811 beds, while an average of 1, 494 patients visit the outpatient departments every day. The number of the operations performed in the Hospital is close upon 3, 600 annually. It has an eye bank, and ranks near the top among all the hospitals in Japan in the number of kidney transplants performed. Other features of the University Hospital worth mentioning include two CT scanners, ICU's, and a Rehabilitation Center. With the completion of the reconstruction, the total floor area will be 63, 000 m², and the number of beds will be increased to 1, 000.

　Throuhgout its history of over 110 years, it has been part of the University's ethos to make a point of trying to understand the feelings of the sick and afflicted and giving humanitarian care to them, and this has endeared its Hospital to local inhabitants. The University has been active in the fields of education and research also, and turned out more than 8, 000 researchers and practitioners, who have been engaged in medical work throughout Japan and in foreign countries, too. Not only is the University old enough to have great stability and time-honored tradition, but it is distinguished by the superior intellectual ability of its students complemented by the caliber of its faculty, whose academic achievements are highly appraised abroad as well as at home.

UNDERGRADUATE PROGRAM

Faculty of Medicine (Freshmen Enrollment: 100)
Department of Medicine

Foreign Student Admission
Qualifications for Applicants
　Standard Qualifications Requirement
　Only those students who have successfully completed the Premedical Course of the University are qualified to enter the Medical Course.
Examination at the University

Date: in March.

Documents to be Submitted When Applying

Standard Documents Requirement

JFSAT score

Application forms and detailed information concerning the entrance examination are available at the Student Division from the middle of November.

GRADUATE PROGRAMS

Graduate School of Medicine (First Year Enrollment : Doctor's 216)

Divisions

Course I (Anatomy, Biochemistry, Pharmacology, Physiology), Course II (Microbiology, Medical Zoology, Pathology), Course III (Hygiene, Legal Medicine, Preventive Medicine), Course IV (Internal Medicine, Dermatoloty, Pediatrics, Psychiatry, Radiology, Laboratory Medicine), Course V (Anesthesiology, Neurosurgery, Obstetrics and Gynecology, Ophthalmology, Orthopaedic Surgery, Otorhinolaryngology, Surgery)

Foreign Student Admission

Qualifications for Applicants

Doctor's Program

It is required that applicants have completed 18 years of school education of which the last course is medicine or dentistry. If they have not completed the required education, they must complete the remaining years as research students at the University.

A Japanese medical license is required of those who apply for Course IV or V.

Examination at the University

Doctor's Program

(1) a written or oral test in the Course for which they are applying, and (2) a written or oral test in the Japanese language and in one other language which must be other than their mother tongue and chosen out of English, German and French. The first test is conducted in the Japanese language or the English language.

Documents to be Submitted When Applying

Standard Documents Requirement

A recommendation from his Government or from one of the Government agencies of his country stationed in Japan, or a reference from one of the Japanese Government agencies stationed in his country.

Application forms and more complete information concerning the entrance examination are available at the Student Division from the beginning of July.

*

Research Institutes and Centers

Research Center for Children's Disease

For Further Information

Undergraduate and Graduate Admission

Instruction Section, Student Division, Kyoto Prefectural University of Medicine, 465 Kajii-cho,

Kawaramachi-dori Hirokoji-agaru, Kamigyo-ku, Kyoto-shi, Kyoto 602 ☎ 075-251-5227

Kyushu Dental College
(Kyushu Shika Daigaku)

2-6-1 Manazuru, Kokurakita-ku, Kitakyushu-shi, Fukuoka 803　☎ 093-582-1131

Faculty

　　Profs.　27　　Assoc. Profs.　20

　　Assist. Profs.　Full-time　22; Part-time　68

　　Res. Assocs.　58

Number of Students

　　Undergrad.　712　　Grad.　66

Library　71, 302 volumes

Outline and Characteristics of the College

The predecessor of the present Kyushu Dental College was Private Kyushu School of Dentistry, which was founded by Masaomi Kuninaga in Fukuoka City in 1914. The school was raised to college status in 1921. The majority of students came from western Japan with some from Taiwan.

Schoolhouses were built at its present location, Kitakyushu City in 1936. Since then, the faculty, staff, and educational facilities have improved over the years. The school has long had the reputation of being an excellent institute of dental education in western Japan.

The school administration was transferred to Fukuoka Prefecture in 1944, and at the same time, a medical course was established. Consequently, the school was renamed Fukuoka Prefectural College of Medicine and Dentistry.

After World War II, in accordance with the reforms of the educational system, the medical course was discontinued in 1947, and the college returned to its previous curriculum. The college was developed into Kyushu Dental College under the new six-year system in 1949.

In 1958, a pre-dental course was added, and in 1966 the graduate school was opened. During this term, the Faculty Building, College Hospital and Anatomy Center were reconstructed into modern buildings.

As an attached institute to the college, the School of Dental Hygiene was founded to train dental hygienists in 1950.

Kyushu Dental College has the most distinguished tradition and the best achievement record of all public colleges and universities of dentistry in Japan. The college has contributed to the dental care of the residents in and around Kitakyushu.

The dental education consists of a two-year pre-dental course and subsequent four-year dental course. About 25 percent of the students are female. The majority of students come from western Japan but also come from other various areas of Japan,

Taiwan, Iran, and the Republic of Korea. Approximately 7, 000 graduates are active in every field of dentistry.

The campus is surrounded by residential area in the center of Kitakyushu City (population ca. 1, 060, 000) and very accessible. Kitakyushu City, located in northern Kyushu, is the gateway to Kyushu Island linking the main island of Honshu by a long suspension bridge, undersea railroad, and undersea highway. The city is an amalgamation of five formerly independent cities, forming a thriving and progressive Kitakyushu Industrial Area. There are many large factories representing Japan's industries community and also many natural sights to see. The urban monorail for efficient intra-city transportation is one of the outstanding features of the city. The night scene of sparkling lights is excellent, particularly the illumination of the great suspension bridges reflected on the waves. Cultural institutions are nearby and working environment is very nice. All this contributes to the pleasure of studying at the college, providing an interesting and stimulating atmosphere.

UNDERGRADUATE PROGRAMS

Faculty of Dentistry (Freshmen Enrollment: 95)
Department of Dentistry
Basic Dentistry Biochemistry, Dental Pharmacology, Material Science, Oral Anatomy, Oral Bacteriology, Oral Neuroscience, Oral Pathology, Oral Physiology
Clinical Dentistry Dental Anesthesiology, Dental Radiology, Internal Medicine, Operative Dentistry, Oral Surgery, Orthodontics, Pedodontics, Periodontics and Endodonitics, Preventive Dentistry, Prosthetic Dentistry, Surgery

Foreign Student Admission
Qualifications for Applicants
Standard Qualifications Requirement,
1. must not be of Japanese nationality.
2. must be recommended by a diplomatic establishment or organization which is recognized by Kyushu Dental College.
Examination at the College
A written examination (English, Mathematics and Science 《 select one: Physics, Chemistry, Biology 》.) and an interview.
Documents to be Submitted When Applying
Standard Documents Requirement
JLPT and GEFS scores
Application forms are available at the Student Office in early December.
Approximately two foreign students are admitted as freshmen annually.

GRADUATE PROGRAMS

Graduate School of Dentistry (First Year Enrollment : Doctor's 17)

Divisions
Basic Dentistry, Clinical Dentistry

Foreign Student Admission
Qualifications for Applicants
Doctor's Program
Foreign applicants for graduate programs must have completed 18 years of education and have graduated from a dental or medical course in a university or college in his/her country. Applicants graduated from a five-year course in a university or college must spend one year as a research student of the research faculty in the college. Applicants graduated from a medical course are able to elect a subject (department) from basic dentistry and oral surgery in clinical dentistry.
Examination at the College
Doctor's Program
Foreign lauguage (select two : English, German, French), subject of special study in Japanese and interview. Date: mid-October.
Documents to be Submitted When Applying
Standard Documents Requirement
1. JLPT score or a cassette tape recording the applicant's spoken Japanese.
2. A certificate of license as dentist or doctor in applicant's country.
3. A written oath (designated form) promising to follow the rules of Kyushu Dental College.
Application forms are available at the Student Office in September.

*

Research Institutes and Centers
Central Research Laboratory, College Hospital
For Further Information
Undergraduate and Graduate Admission
Student Office, Kyushu Dental College, 2-6-1 Manazuru, Kokurakita-ku, Kitakyushu-shi, Fukuoka 803 ☎ 093–582–1131 ext. 208

Nagasaki Prefectural University of International Economics
(Nagasaki Kenritsu Kokusai Keizai Daigaku)

123 Kawashimo-cho, Sasebo-shi, Nagasaki 858
☎ 0956–47–2191

Faculty
　　Profs.　13　　Assoc. Profs.　12
　　Assist. Profs.　Full–time　9; Part–time　43
　　Res. Assoc.　1
Number of Students
　　Undergrad.　961
Library　87, 431 volumes

Outline and Characteristics of the University
This institution was established in 1951 as a pre-

fecture-supported two-year commercial college. The English course was added in 1957. The addition provided the basis for establishing this four-year college in 1967.

As the name suggests, this institution offers programs with primary emphasis on economics as well as foreign languages and thereby aims to educate students so that they can play an active role in the social and economic scenes in Japan or abroad.

This institution has an enrollment of 961 and a full-time teaching staff of 35.

The 60, 000m² campus is located in the northern part of Nagasaki Prefecture. It is geographically very close to the Chinese Continent and the other Asian countries and has had a historical role as the most important point of entry of foreign civilization to Japan. The Saikai National Park, dotted with numerous picturesque isles, is not very far from the campus and the vast, well-equipped municipal sports stadium is just across the road. In short, this campus is favored by ideal surroundings. For these reasons, perhaps, this university attracts students not only from the Nagasaki area but from many other parts of Japan and even from a few Asian countries.

UNDERGRADUATE PROGRAMS

Faculty of Economics (Freshmen Enrollment: 200)
Department of Economics

Foreign Student Admission
Qualifications for Applicants
Standard Qualifications Requirement
Examination at the University
A written examination and an interview in Japanese.
Documents to be Submitted When Applying
Standard Documents Requirement
1. Verification of Japanese Proficiency.
2. Identification card issued by a Japanese embassy or legation abroad or a foreign government.

Application forms are available at the Administration Office from November and the completed forms are accepted at the same office from December 16 to 25.

*

Research Institutes and Centers
Culture and Economy Research Institute
For Further Information
Undergraduate Admission
Administration Office, Nagasaki Prefectural University of International Economics, 123 Kawashimocho, Sasebo-shi, Nagasaki 858 ☎ 0956–47–2191

Nagoya City University
(Nagoya Shiritsu Daigaku)

1 Kawasumi, Mizuho-cho, Mizuho-ku, Nagoya-shi, Aichi 467 ☎ 052–851–5511

Faculty
  Profs. 89   Assoc. Profs. 84
  Assist. Profs. Full–time 38; Part–time 152
  Res. Assocs. 206
Number of Students
  Undergrad. 1, 711   Grad. 161
Library 353, 921 volumes

Outline and Characteristics of the University

Nagoya City University was founded in 1950 through the consolidation of Nagoya Women's Medical College and Nagoya College of Pharmacy. Therefore, at the time of its foundation the University was composed of two Faculties: the Medical School and the Faculty of Pharmaceutical Sciences. The Faculty of Economics was added in 1964, and the University came to be comprised of the Medical School, the Faculty of Pharmaceutical Sciences, the Faculty of Economics and the College of General Education. Three Graduate Schools (of Medicine, Pharmacy and Economics) were later opened, offering both Master's and Doctor's programs.

Nagoya City University is located in the southeastern part of the city and has three separate campuses—Kawasumi (the Medical School), Tanabe-Dori (the Faculty of Pharmaceutical Sciences) and Yamanohata (the Faculty of Economics and the College of General Education). Every campus is conveniently situated for commutation. Each of the three campuses has its own Student Hall or Welfare House, which is available for students' activities such as meetings of the sport and the cultural clubs.

The University's affiliated facilities include the Hospital and the Nursing School attached to the Medical School, three libraries and the Computation Center. Moreover, in 1982, the Seminar House named Ryomei-so, was built in Tateshina, Nagano Prefecture, for the extracurricular activities of the students.

The University enrolls approximately 1, 900 students including graduate students and auditors. The University opened its doors to foreign students in 1983, and today 14 foreign students study at the University.

UNDERGRADUATE PROGRAMS

Faculty of Economics (Freshmen Enrollment: 200)
  Department of Economics
Business and Accounting (Business Administration, Bookkeeping, Business Organization Theory, Marketing Theory, Theory of Film, Managerial Finance,

Accounting, Financial Statement, Managerial Accounting), Economic Policy I (Economic Policy, Economic History, Japanese Economic History, European Economic History, Public Economics, Economics of Transportation, Labor Economics, Social Security, Industrial Economics, Agricultural Economics), Economic Policy II (Public Finance, International Economics, Economic Development, Monetary Theory, Monetary Policy, Local Public Finance), Economic Theory (Economics, Mathematics of Economics, Statistics, Marxian Economics, Operations Research, Microeconomic Theory, Contemporary Economic Theory, Information Processing, Mathematical Statistics, History of Economic Thought, History of Social Thought, Econometrics, Quantitative Economics)

Faculty of Medicine (Freshmen Enrollment: 80)
Department of Medicine
Anatomy, Anesthesiology, Bacteriology, Biochemistry, Dermatology, Hygiene, Internal Medicine, Legal Medicine, Medical Zoology, Neurosurgery, Obstetrics and Gynecology, Ophthalmology, Orthopedic Surgery, Otorhinolaryngology, Pathology, Pediatrics, Pharmacology, Physiology, Psychiatry, Public Health, Radiology, Surgery, Urology

Faculty of Pharmaceutical Sciences (Freshmen Enrollment: 100)
Department of Pharmaceutical Sciences
Biological Chemistry, Biopharmaceutics, Chemical Hygiene and Nutrition, Chemical Pharmacology, Pharmaceutical Analytical Chemistry, Pharmaceutical Chemistry, Pharmacognocy
Department of Pharmaceutical Technology
Chemical Reaction Engineering, Microbial Chemistry, Pharmaceutical Industrial Chemistry, Pharmaceutics, Physical Chemistry, Physico-Analytical Chemistry, Synthetic Organic Chemistry

Foreign Student Admission
Qualifications for Applicants
Standard Qualifications Requirement
Examination at the University
Written and oral exams and an interview.
Documents to be Submitted When Applying
Standard Documents Requirement
JLPT and GEFS scores
Submit the documents to the Student Affairs Section.

GRADUATE PROGRAMS

Graduate School of Economics (First Year Enrollment : Master's 10, Doctor's 5)
Division
Economic Policy

Graduate School of Medicine (First Year Enrollment : Doctor's 27)
Divisions
Internal Medicine, Pathology, Physiology, Social Medicine, Surgery

Graduate School of Pharmaceutical Sciences (First Year Enrollment : Master's 26, Doctor's 13)
Division
Pharmaceutical Sciences

Foreign Student Admission
Qualifications for Applicants
Master's Program
Standard Qualifications Requirement
Doctor's Program
Standard Qualifications Requirement
Documents to be Submitted When Applying
Standard Documents Requirement
Submit the documents to the Student Affairs Section.

*

Research Institutes and Centers
Computation Center
Special Programs for Foreign Students
A tutorial system in which a Japanese student acts as an advisor to each foreign student throughout his/her campus life is available.
For Further Information
Undergraduate and Graduate Admission
Admission Office, Nagoya City University, 1 Kawasumi, Mizuho-cho, Mizuho-ku, Nagoya-shi, Aichi 467 ☎ 052–851–5511 ext. 2128

Nara Medical University
(Nara Kenritsu Ika Daigaku)

840 Shijo-cho, Kashihara-shi, Nara 634
☎ 07442–2–3051

Faculty
Profs. 41   Assoc. Profs. 29
Assist. Profs. Full–time 36; Part–time 242
Res. Assocs. 171
Number of Students
Undergrad. 631   Grad. 43
Library 125, 000 volumes

Outline and Characteristics of the University
The University was originally established as a medical college in 1945 and became a medical university following the revision of the educational system. In 1958, the liberal arts department was established as a premedical course and in 1960 the graduate school was opened. The University is located in Nara, where the nation's capital was situated from the 6th to 8th century. The district is rich with historical sites and relics. The University is supported by Nara Prefecture and has played a leading role in the health and welfare of its people, in cooperation with other medical groups. Efforts are being made to further medical service, research and education in the district.

UNDERGRADUATE PROGRAMS

Faculty of Medicine (Freshmen Enrollment: 100)
Department of Medicine
Basic Medicine
Anatomy, Bacteriology, Biochemistry, Hygiene, Legal Medicine, Oncological Pathology, Parasitology, Pathology, Pharmacology, Physiology, Public Health
Clinical Medicine
Anesthesiology, Clinico-Laboratory Diagnostics, Dermatology, Internal Medicine, Neurology, Obstetrics and Gynecology, Ophthalmology, Oral and Maxillofacial Surgery, Orthopedics, Otorhinolaryngology, Pediatrics, Psychiatry, Radiology, Surgery, Tumor Radiology, Urology

Foreign Student Admission
Qualifications for Applicants
Standard Qualifications Requirement
JFSAT score

GRADUATE PROGRAMS

Graduate School of Medicine (First Year Enrollment : Doctor's 24)
Divisions
Internal Medicine, Pathology, Physiology, Social Medicine, Surgery

Foreign Student Admission
Qualifications for Applicants
Doctor's Program
Standard Qualifications Requirement
Applicants must have completed 18 years of education, the final course being in medicine or dentistry.

*

For Further Information
Undergraduate and Graduate Admission
Instruction Section, Student Division, Student Office, Nara Medical University, 840 Shijo-cho, Kashihara-shi, Nara 634 ☎ 07442-2-3051 ext. 2213

Okinawa Prefectural College of Arts

(Okinawa Kenritsu Geijutsu Daigaku)

1-4 Tonokura Shuri, Naha-shi, Okinawa 903
☎ 0988-31-5000

Faculty
    Profs. 16   Assoc. Profs. 8
    Assist. Profs. Full-time 11; Part-time 17
    Res. Assocs. 7
Number of Students
    Undergrad. 205

Library 21, 509 volumes

Outline and Characteristics of the College
Okinawa Prefectural College of Arts was founded in 1986 as one of five public colleges and universities of arts in Japan. The college, situated in the southernmost part of Japan and recognizes itself as a higher educational institution for the learning of the artistic traditions and heritages of Okinawa, which have been cultivated basically in the natural and cultural environment of Okinawa, and which have been influenced by various Asian arts and cultures. The college is also designed to further the continuity and the development of the tradition of Okinawan art and culture. From the view point of research and teaching, therefore, the college attaches great importance to the relationship between Okinawa and various areas in Asia, especially East and Southeast Asia, concerning the actual conditions of artistic traditions and heritages.

The college is presently composed of one Faculty, the Faculty of Art and Design, and one affiliated research institute. The Faculty primarily places emphasis on the traditional Okinawan arts and crafts as well as fine arts and design. The Faculty offers not only a professional and technical education, but also a liberal arts education by placing importance on the basic aesthetic and philosophical theories in the fields of fine arts and design.

The college consists of the First Campus, the Second Campus, and the Third Campus, all located in Shuri, the ancient capital of the Kingdom of the Ryukyus, only 9. 8 kilometers from Naha Airport. The educational environment of the three campuses is excellent. The affiliated research institute, which is designed to research and spread the traditional Okinawan art and culture, is situated on the First Campus.

UNDERGRADUATE PROGRAMS

Faculty of Arts and Design
Department of Craft & Design
Dyeing & Weaving, Pottery, Product Design & Visual Design
Department of Fine Arts
Japanese Painting & Oil Painting, Sculpture

Foreign Student Admission
Qualifications for Applicants
Standard Qualifications Requirement
The Japanese Language Proficiency Test and the General Examination for Foreign Students.
Examination at the University
A practical examination and an interview.
Documents to be Submitted When Applying
Standard Documents Requirement
The certificate of General Examination for Foreign Students and the certificate of the Joint First-Stage Achievement Test.

*

Research Institutes and Centers
The Affiliated Reserch Institute of Okinawan Art
and Culture
For Further Information
  Undergraduate Admission
Head of the office of Academic Affairs, Okinawa
Prefectural College of Arts, 1-4 Tonokura, Shuri,
Naha, Okinawa 903 ☎ 0988-31-5000

Osaka City University
(Osaka Shiritsu Daigaku)

3-3-138 Sugimoto, Sumiyoshi-ku, Osaka-shi, Osaka
558 ☎ 06-605-2131

Faculty
  Profs. 233   Assoc. Profs. 195
  Assist. Profs. Full-time 153; Part-time 459
  Res. Assocs. 274
Number of Students
  Undergrad. 6, 343   Grad. 767
Library 1, 509, 462 volumes

Outline and Characteristics of the University
  When the Osaka University of Commerce, one
of the former bodies of the present Osaka City University, was founded in March 1928, Hajime Seki,
the Mayor of Osaka at that time, made the following
statement: the Osaka University of Commerce
should have unique characteristics apart from those
of a national university. As a municipal university, it
should maintain close relationships with the City of
Osaka and its citizens, devoting itself to research and
education. This idea has been carried on by the present Osaka City University.
  Osaka City University aims to cultivate educated persons of character with advanced knowledge
and skill so they may contribute to the economic,
cultural and social development of the citizens.
  Since the foundation of Osaka University of
Commerce, Osaka City University celebrated its centennial anniversary in November, 1980 and held various kinds of events and projects to commemorate it.
  After the Second World War, Osaka City University has grown to become the greatest municipal
university in Japan, having eight Faculties: Business,
Economics, Law, Letters, Science, Engineering,
Medicine, and Science of Living. There are eight
Graduate Schools with Master's and Doctor's pro-
grams.
  Among the teaching staff of each Faculty are
many internationally well-known scholars.
  The majority of students are in-city dwellers,
but people come from almost every part of Japan
and more than 11 foreign countries to study at the
University.

UNDERGRADUATE PROGRAMS

Faculty of Business (Freshmen Enrollment: 180)
  Department of Business
Accounting, Business Administration, Business Sci-
ences
Faculty of Economics (Freshmen Enrollment: 180)
  Department of Economics
Economic History, Economic Policy, Economic The-
ory, Industrial Enonomics, International Economics,
Statistics
Faculty of Engineering (Freshmen Enrollment: 245)
  Department of Applied Chemistry
Chemical Reaction Engineering, Inorganic Industrial
Chemistry, Polymer Chemistry, Synthetic Chemistry
  Department of Applied Physics
Engineering for Quantum Matters, Laser Engineer-
ing, Mathematical Physics, Optical Propertics of Sol-
id, Scientific Instruments, Vacuum Science
  *Department of Architecture and Building Engi-
neering*
Architectural History, Architectural Planning and
Design, Disaster Prevention for Building and Struc-
ture, Environmental Engineering for Architecture,
Structural Engineering for Architecture, Structural
Materials, Urban Planning and Design
  Department of Civil Engineering
Bridge Engineering, Construction Materials, Envi-
ronmental Engineering, Infrastructure Planning,
River and Coastal Engineering, Soil Engineerng,
Structural Engineering, Transportation Engineering
  Department of Electrical Engineering
Electrical Communication Engineering, Electrical
Machinery Engineering, Electromagnetic Theory,
Electronic Circuit Theory, Electronic Materials and
Measurement, Information and Computer Science
  Department of Mechanical Engineering
Fluid Engineering, Internal Combustion Engine and
Measurement Engineering, Machine Design Engi-
neering and Textile Machines, Mechanical Working
and Materials for Machine, Strength of Materials,
Thermal Engineering and Chemical Machinery
Faculty of Law (Freshmen Enrollment: 170)
  Department of Law
General Studies of Law, Political Science, Private
Law, Public Law
Faculty of Letters (Freshmen Enrollment: 130)
  Department of History and Geography
Geography Course
Regional Geography, Systematic Geography
  History Course
Asian History, Japanese History, Theory of History,
Western History
  Department of Human Relations
Psychology Course
Applied Psychology, Experimental Psychology, Hu-
man Relations, Psychology, Psychometrics
  Sociology Course
Applied Sociology, Human Relations, Methodology

of Sociology, Specialized Fields of Sociology
Department of Japanese and Chinese History
Chinese Course
Chinese Literary History, Chinese Literature, Chinese Philology, History of Chinese Thought
Japanese Course
Japanese Literary History, Japanese Literature, Japanese Philology
Department of Philosophy
Ethics, History of Philosophy, Philosophy Religion
Department of Western Literature
English Course
English and American Literary History, English and American Literature, English Philology
French Course
French Literary History, French Literature, French Philology
German Course
German Literary History, German Philology. German Literature
Faculty of Medicine (Freshmen Enrollment: 80)
Department of Medicine
Anatomy, Anesthesiology, Bacteriology, Biochimistry, Dermatology, Internal Medicine, Laboratory Medicine, Legal Medicine, Medical Zoology, Neuropsychiatry, Neurosurgery, Obstetrics& Gynecology, Ophthalmology, Orthopedic Surgery, Otorhinolaryngology, Pathology, Pediatrics, Pharmacology, Physiology, Public Health, Radiology, Surgery, Urology
Faculty of Science (Freshmen Enrollment: 110)
Department of Biology
Cell Biology, Developmental Biology, Enzyme Chemisty, General Physiology, Microbiological Chemistry, Plant Physiology
Department of Chemistry
Inorganic Chemistry, Organic Chemistry, Physical Chemistry
Department of Geosciences
Engineering Geology, Mineralogy, Stratigraphy, Tectonic Geology
Department of Mathematics
Algebra, Analysis, Geometry
Department of Physics
Experimental Physics, Theoretical Physics
Faculty of Science of Living (Freshmen Enrollment: 121)
Department of Child Developments
Child Education, Child Health, Child Psychology
Department of Clothing and Textiles
Textile Materials, Theory of Construction of Clothing System, Theory of Laundering and Conservation of Fabrics
Department of Food and Nutrition
Food Chemistry, Nutritional Biochemistry, Nutritional Physiology, Science of Food Processing
Department of Housing and Design
Housing Design, Physical Environmental Analysis, Theory of Housing
Department of Social Welfare

Family Sociology, Social Welfare, Welfare Economics

Foreign Student Admission
Qualifications for Applicants
Standard Qualifications Requirement
Examination at the University
Written and oral exams by Each Faculty (except Medicine)
Documents to be Submitted When Applying
Standard Documents Requirement
JLPT and GEFS scores
Application deadline: January 31.
Application forms are available at the office of Education Bureau from early December.

Qualifications for Transfer Students
Applicants must have completed 16 years of education or equivalent, and have graduated from a university/college.
The faculties that accept transfer students are as follows: Faculty of Business, Faculty of Economics, Faculty of Law, Faculty of Letters.
Examination for Transfer Students
Same as Japanese students. (written and oral exams)
Documents to be Submitted When Applying
Standard Documents Requirement

GRADUATE PROGRAMS

Graduate School of Business (First Year Enrollment : Master's 25, Doctor's 10)
Divisions
Business Administration, Business Sciences
Graduate School of Economics (First Year Enrollment : Master's 30, Doctor's 14)
Divisions
Economic Policy, Economic Theory and Economic History
Graduate School of Engineering (First Year Enrollment : Master's 66, Doctor's 33)
Divisions
Applied Chemistry, Applied Physics, Architecture and Building Engineering , Civil Engineering, Electrical Engineering, Mechanical Engineering
Graduate School of Law (First Year Enrollment : Master's 25, Doctor's 8)
Divisions
Private Law, Public Law
Graduate School of Letters (First Year Enrollment : Master's 48, Doctor's 24)
Divisions
Asian History, Chinese, Education, English, French, Geography, German, Japanese, Japanese History, Philosophy, Psychology, Sociology
Graduate School of Medicine (First Year Enrollment : Doctor's 62)
Divisions
Internal Medicine, Pathological Science, Physiologi-

cal Science, Social Medicine, Surgical Medicine
Graduate School of Science (First Year Enrollment :
Master's 58, Doctor's 25)
  Divisions
Biology, Chemistry, Geology, Mathematics, Physics
Graduate School of Science of Living (First Year En-
rollment : Master's 42, Doctor's 21)
  Divisions
Design and Environmental Analysis, Human Devel-
opment, Human Nutrition and Health Sciences, So-
cial Welfare

Foreign Student Admission
  Qualifications for Applicants
Master's Program
  Standard Qualifications Requirement
Doctor's Program
  Standard Qualifications Requirement
  Examination at the University
Master's Program
  Same as Japanese students (a written exam and
an interview)
Doctor's Program
  Same as Master's program.
  Documents to be Submitted When Applying
  Standard Documents Requirement
              ✳
Research Institutes and Centers
Botanical Garden, Center for Cultural Exchange,
Computer Center, Cosmic Ray Institute, Division of
Health Science and Physical Education, Documenta-
tion Center for Urban Studies, Dowa Problems, In-
stitute for Economic Research, Institute of Organic
Chemistry, Nursing School, Research Institute for
Atomic Energy, Toneyama Institute for Tuberculosis
Research, Univeristy Hospital
Facilities/Services for Foreign Students
  A small hall is provided for foreign students,
and the University gives an annual party where for-
eign students meet the President and Deans.
For Further Information
  Undergraduate and Graduate Admission
Education Bureau, Osaka City University, 3-3-138
Sugimoto, Sumiyoshi-ku, Osaka-shi, Osaka 558
☎ 06–605–2131

Osaka Women's University
(Osaka Joshi Daigaku)

2-1 Daisen-cho, Sakai-shi, Osaka 590
☎ 0722–22–4811

Faculty
  Profs. 27   Assoc. Profs. 20
  Assist. Profs. Full–time 11; Part–time 78
  Res. Assocs. 10
Number of Students
  Undergrad. 718   Grad. 20
Library 206, 444 volumes

Outline and Characteristics of the University
  Osaka Women's University is a small yet prestigious instiuttion of higher education founded by
Osaka Prefecture in 1949, with a history dating back
to 1924 when Osaka Prefectural Women's College
was established. The University is made up of the
Faculty of Arts and Sciences with four departments:
the Department of Japanese Language and Literature, the Department of English Language and Literature, the Department of Human Relations, and the
Department of Natural Science: and the Graduate
Scool (established in 1977) with programs leading to
the degree of Master of Arts. Admission to the College is limited to 160, and to the Graduate Scool to
15. Current enrollment is 718 and teaching staff totals 68.
  The University Campus (66, 828m²) is located in
Sakai City, adjacent to the tomb of Emperor Ninto-
ku, the largest tomb in the world, and Sakai City
Library. The City Museum and Daisen Park are located nearby.
  The University, with its long and outstanding
history as a public women's university, has provided
a wide scope of study and experience for 60 years. In
1984 the University began accepting students from
abroad. We believe that through a course of study at
this University, students will gain not only advanced
academic knowledge, but also the intellectual ability,
decision-making power and active temperament to
become self-reliant members of society both as individuals and as women.

UNDERGRADUATE PROGRAMS

Faculty of Arts and Sciences (Freshmen Enrollment:
160)
  Department of English Language and Literature
American Literature, Comparative Literature, Eng-
lish Grammar, English Language, English Literature, English Phonetics, History of American Literature, History of England, History of English Literature, History of the English Language, Old English
and Middle English, Philology
  Department of Human Relations
Abnormal Psychology, Community Studies, Cultural Sociology, Developmental Psychology, Educational Administration, Educational Psychology, Experimental Psychology, Family Studies, History of Education, Human Relations, Human Sciences, Methodology of Human Sciences, Methods of Psychological
Experiments, Pedagogical Anthropology, Pedagogy,
Philosophical Anthropology, Psychology, Social
History, Social Problems, Sociology
  Department of Japanese Language and Literature
Chinese Classics, History of Chinese Literature, History of Japanese Arts, History of Japanese Literature, Japanese Archive, Japanese Language, Japanese Literature, Modern Chinese Language, Philology

Department of Natural Science
Algebra, Analytical Chemistry, Biochemistry, Cell Biology, Ecology, Electro–magnetism, Environmental Science, Fundamental Physics, Geometry, Inorganic Chemistry, Macromolecular Science, Mathematical Analysis, Organic Chemistry, Physical Chemistry, Physiology, Quantum Mechanics, Solid–state Physics, Statistics

Foreign Student Admission
Qualifications for Applicants
Standard Qualifications Requirement
Those who have received an International Baccalaureate Diploma conferred by the International Baccalaureate Office and are 18 years of age or older are also eligible to apply.
Examination at the University
Written and oral examinations.
Documents to be Submitted When Applying
Standard Documents Requirement
Those who have an International Baccalaureate Diploma must submit a copy of International Baccalaureate Diploma and transcripts of records for six courses of a final examination.
Application period: January 6-19.
Application forms are available from late October

GRADUATE PROGRAMS

Graduate School of Literature (First Year Enrollment : Master's 15)
Divisions
English Language and Literature, Japanese Language and Literature, Social Welfare

Foreign Student Admission
Qualifications for Applicants
Master's Program
Standard Qualifications Requirement
Examination at the University
Master's Program
Written and oral examinations.
Documents to be Submitted When Applying
Standard Documents Requirement
English Language and Literature:
Graduation thesis (in English or Japanese) or its equivalent.
Japanese Language and Literature:
Graduation thesis or its equivalent (written in Japanese by the applicant; for reference purposes, a copy of the thesis written in the applicant's own language may be attached.) and its summary (written in Japanese by the applicant herself).
Social Welfare:
Graduation thesis or its equivalent, and summary (in Japanese), to be attached.
*
Facilities/Services for Foreign Students
Dormitory for Foreign Students (operated jointly

with Osaka Prefectural University)
Shared Facilities: Assembly Room
Accommodation: 15 rooms (single 10, couple or family 5)
For Further Information
Undergraduate and Graduate Admission
Instruction Department, Osaka Women's University, 2-1 Daisen-cho, Sakai-shi, Osaka 590—0722-22-4811 ext. 215

Sapporo Medical College
(Sapporo Ika Daigaku)
Minami 1, Nishi 17 , Chuo-ku, Sapporo-shi, Hokkaido 060   ☎ 011-611-2111

Faculty
　　Profs.   40   Assoc. Profs.   45
　　Assist. Profs.   Full–time   58; Part–time   125
　　Res. Assocs.   158
Number of Students
　　Undergrad.   639   Grad.   71
Library   140, 194 volumes

Outline and Characteristics of the College
Sapporo Medical College was founded in 1950 by Hokkaido Prefectural Government, based on the former Hokkaido Prefectural Women's School of Medicine. In 1956 the Graduate School was opened and started to offer the Doctor's Program.
Today, the College enrolls approximately 700 students with the full time faculty of 300 and is composed of the Faculty, the Graduate School, the College Hospital, two research institutes and other affiliated establishments.
The campus is located within easy access to the downtown center and is within a short-walking distance of various cultural institutions.
Students study, work, and relax in an excellent environment.
The College is internationally noted for its academic excellence. The Faculty includes quite a few scholars with advanced achievements in their areas of study.
The College is now promoting international medical interchange, exchanging medical scholars between our college and other countries, and also providing technical cooperation to certain countries.
The majority of students of Sapporo Medical College are from Hokkaido, and some from other parts of Japan.

UNDERGRADUATE PROGRAMS

School of Medicine (Freshmen Enrollment: 100)
Anatomy, Anesthesiology, Biochemistry, Dermatology, Hygiene, Internal Medicine, Legal Medicine, Microbiology, Neurological Surgery, Neuropsychiatry, Obstetrics and Gynecology, Ophthalmology,

Oral Surgery, Orthopedic Surgery, Otolaryngology, Pathology, Pediatrics, Pharmacology, Physiology, Public Health, Radiology, Surgery, Urology

Foreign Student Admission

Qualifications for Applicants

Standard Qualifications Requirement

Examination at the College

Foreign applicants must take the Japanese Language Proficiency Test and the General Examination (of science course) for Foreign Students.

Applicants must then take the same entrance examination as Japanese applicants do. This examination is administered by the college.

Documents to be Submitted When Applying

Standard Documents Requirement

Application documents are available at the Student Affairs and Research Section from early November.

Those who fall under any of the following categories as the result of a medical examination will not be admitted:

1. those who have a severe handicap in hearing,
2. those who have a severe handicap in sight,
3. those who have some other physical or mental handicap which may prevent them from attending lectures at the medical college.

GRADUATE PROGRAMS

Graduate School of Medicine (First Year Enrollment : Doctor's 31)

Divisions

Internal Medicine, Pathological Medicine, Physiological Medicine, Social Medicine, Surgery

Foreign Student Admission

Qualifications for Applicants

Doctor's Program

Standard Qualifications Requirement

Applicants must have completed or be expected to complete a medical or dental course in the preceding year of his or her expected admission.

It is desirable that those who wish to be admitted into an internal or surgical medical course should have acquired or be expected to acquire a medical practitioner's (doctor's) license in Japan within a year after his or her admission. Those who wish to be admitted into oral surgery should have acquired or be expected to acquire a dentist's license in Japan within a year after his or her admission.

Examination at the College

Doctor's Program

Same as for Japanese students (a written exam and interview)

Documents to be Submitted When Applying

Standard Documents Requirement

Applicants are required to submit a copy of his/her doctor's licence as well.

The directions for applicants and application forms are available at the Student Affairs and Research Section from early January.

In addition, applicants are required to make a preliminary arrangement with the professor in charge of his or her medical research.

✳

Research Institutes and Centers

Cancer Research Institute, College Hospital, Marine Biomedical Institute

For Further Information

Undergraduate and Graduate Admission

Student Affairs and Research Section, Sapporo Medical College, Minami 1, Nishi 17, Chuo-ku, Sapporo-shi, Hokkaido   060   ☎ 011-611-2111 ext. 2154

Shimonoseki City College
(Shimonoseki Shiritsu Daigaku)

2-1-1 Daigaku-cho, Shimonoseki-shi, Yamaguchi 751
☎ 0832-52-0288

Faculty
    Profs.   14   Assoc. Profs.   16
    Assist. Profs.   Full-time   5; Part-time   45
Number of Students
    Undergrad.   1, 547
Library   93, 119 volumes

Outline and Characteristics of the College

Shimonoseki City College was founded in 1956 as Shimonoseki Junior College of Commerce by the Local Government of Shimonoseki. In 1962, it became a four-year college and was renamed Shimonoseki City College. At that time, the College consisted only of the Department of Economics, but in 1983, the Department of International Commerce was added in order to meet the needs of changing world conditions.

Today, the College enrolls over 1, 000 students and has a full-time faculty of 45. A research institute and an affiliated association for intellectual studies are attached to the College.

The campus is located in Shimonoseki on the western end of the island of Honshu. The city is surrounded by the sea on three sides and is rich in historic spots. New school buildings and campus area enhance the study and living environment at the College.

In addition to economics and commerce, the College offers many areas of study covering various subjects. It especially puts emphasis on the learning of foreign languages, including East Asian languages, to cultivate graduates who may later enter international society.

The College attracts students from every part of Japan, although many of them come from the western half of the country. At present the College has two foreign students, both from china.

UNDERGRADUATE PROGRAMS

Faculty of Economics (Freshmen Enrollment: 400)
Department of Economics
Department of International Commerce

Foreign Student Admission
Qualificatious for Applicants
The Japanese Language Proficiency Test and the General Examination for Foreign Students results.
Examination at the College
Japanese (composition), a physical examination and an interview.

Research Institutes and Centers
The Shimonoseki City College Association for Intellectual Studies, the Shimonoseki Institute of Industry and Culture
For Further Information
Undergraduate Admission
Instruction Office, Shimonoseki City College, 2-1-1 Daigaku-cho, Shimonoseki-shi, Yamaguchi 751
☎ 0832–52–0288

Shizuoka Prefectural University
(Shizuoka Kenritsu Daigaku)

395 Yada, Shizuoka 422　☎ 0542–64–5102

Faculty
　　Profs. 62　　Assoc. Profs. 41
　　Assist. Profs. Full–time 26; Part–time 32
　　Res. Assocs. 53
Number of Students
　　Undergrad. 969　　Grad. 54
Library 108, 084 volumes

Outline and Characteristics of the University
　Inaugurated on April 1, 1987, the goal of Shizuoka Prefectural University is to develop talented individuals who can cope with the many changes in our society, such as the rapidly increasing number of older people and the internationalized and infomation-oriented world we are developing. To meet these needs, the University has established the Faculty of International Relations and the School of Adminsitration and Informatics, in addition to the School of Pharmaceutical Scinece and the School of Food and Nutritional Sciences, which had already existed at other colleges. The new faculty and school are the first to be establishded at a Japanese prefectural univeristy, making the university truly distinct.
　The aim of the university is to provide special study of arts and sciences develop intellectual, moral, and applied abilities. It also attempts to foster useful talents which can respond to the demands of the times and the community. Furthermore, it seeks re-turn education and study back to the communtiy, by contributing to the advancement of culture and the develoment of society.
　Shizuoka Prefecture lies in the midlle part of Japan. Conviniently situated, it takes about one hour to travel to Tokyo by bullet train. It is also blessed with a mild climate and a beautiful natural environment. The University of Shizuoka lies on the north side of the Nihonadaira Plateau, which rises to 307 meters above sea level and is one of most prominent scenic spots in Japan.
　School of Pharmaceutical Science
　The purpose of this school is to train talented men and women with well-rounded personalities who can make a contribution to society through special pharmaceutical knowledge and techniques. The school is composed of two courses, Pharmaceutical Sciences and Medicine Manufacture. The former puts emphasis on chemistry, medical treatment, and hygiene as they pertains to medical ingredients, and the latter emphasizes chemistry and the production of medicine.
　School of Food and Nutritional Sciences
　The school has two departments which offer slightly different teaching programs, the Department of Food Science and the Department of Nutrition Science. In the former, more emphasis is placed on chemistry of the food ingredients, food production and processings, but a fundametal knowledge of biochemistry, physiology, and nutrition is also offered to students taking this program.
　Faculty of International Relations
　The goal of the Faculty of International Relations is to cultivate students who have an understanding of international ways of thinking and excellent language abilities. Our faculty makes much of traditional studies such as politics, economics, but we attach importance to inter-disciplined and multi-disciplined Fields. Most importantly, we try to train pepole who can think from an international viewpoint and have a good command of languages.
　School of Administration and Informatics
　The school curriculum is based on the three main subjects of Administration and Accounting, Mathematics and Model-building, and Computers and Communications. These topics are not considered separately but are integrated into a core program.

UNDERGRADUATE PROGRAMS

School of Administration and Informatics (Freshmen Enrollment: 100)
Department of Administration and Infomatics
School of Food and Nutritional Sciences (Freshmen Enrollment: 50)
Department of Food Science
Department of Nutriton Secince
Faculty of International Relations (Freshmen Enrollment: 180)

Department of International Languages and Cultures

Department of International Relations

School of Pharmaceutical Science (Freshmen Enrollment: 120)

Department of Pharmacetics

Bio-organic Chemistry, Industrial Hygiene, Medicinal Chemistry, Pharmaceutical Chemistry of Natural Products, Pharmaceutical Engineering, Pharmaceutic Analytics, Radio Pharmaceutics

Department of Pharmacy

Advanced Organic Chemistry, Biochemistry, Hygienic Science, Microbiology, Pharmaceutic Analytics, Pharmaceutics, Pharmacognosy, Pharmacology

Foreign Student Admission

Documents to be Submitted When Applying

Standard Documents Requirement

The application for admission of foreign students will be sent at the end of October 1988, at the student's expense. applocation for examination will be acceted at the end of February 1989.

GRADUATE PROGRAMS

Graduate School of Pharmaceutical Sciences (First Year Enrollment : Master's 30, Doctor's 15)

Divisions

Pharmaceutical Sciences, Pharmaceutical Technology

*

Research Institutes and Centers

Institute for the Science of Living

For Further Information

Undergraduate and Graduate Admission

Student Affairs Department, University of Shizuoka, 395 Yada, Shizuoka 422 ☎ 0542-64-5007

Takasaki City University of Economics

(Takasaki Keizai Daigaku)

1300 Kaminamie-machi, Takasaki-shi, Gunma 370
☎ 0273–43–5417

Faculty
 Profs. 31   Assoc. Profs. 14
 Assist. Profs. Full–time 6; Part–time 67
 Res. Assoc. 1
Number of Students
 Undergrad. 2, 114
Library 111, 850 volumes

Outline and Characteristics of the University

Takasaki City Junior College, founded in 1952, was reorganized as Takasaki City University of Economics in 1957 with the warmth and support of the people in Takasaki City. As a community college, the University has met the expectations of the citizens of Takasaki, which is the center of commerce in the northern part of the Kanto plain, and boasts a long history.

As the number of students rapidly increased, the University moved to its new campus located on the outskirts of the city. Ever since, Takasaki City University of Economics has grown with the times. In 1964 the Department of Business Management was added, and today the University, consisting of two departments, has a total enrollment of nearly 2, 000 students from every part of Japan. Presently, there are about 20 foreign students from over ten countries enrolled at the University.

Takasaki City, surrounded by mountain ranges, is blessed with a rich natural environment. With a glorious heritage of the past, Takasaki continues to develop into a modern city of this new age. In step with the City, the University has the prospects of a great future.

The majority of students live in apartments near the campus. Warmly received by the people in the city, they study, work, and enjoy college life in Takasaki. The University has provided opportunities for foreign students to study. The State University of West Texas, is a sister college and has had active cultural, as well as academic, exchanges.

UNDERGRADUATE PROGRAMS

Faculty of Economics (Freshmen Enrollment: 400)

Department of Business Management

Department of Economics

Foreign Student Admission

Qualifications for Applicants

Standard Qualifications Requirement

Examination at the University

A written test in Japanese and an interview.

Documents to be Submitted When Applying

Standard Documents Requirement

JLPT score

Application deadline: January 31.

Application forms are available at the Admissions Office from early October.

*

Research Institutes and Centers

Institute for Research of Regional Economy

For Further Information

Undergraduate Admission

Admissions Office, Takasaki City University of Economics, 1300 Kaminamie-machi, Takasaki-shi, Gunma 370 ☎ 0273–43–5417

Tokyo Metropolitan Institute of Technology
(Tokyo Toritsu Kagaku Gijutsu Daigaku)

6-6 Asahigaoka, Hino-shi, Tokyo 191
☎ 0425–83–5111

Faculty
Profs. 29   Assoc. Profs. 19
Assist. Profs. Full–time 3; Part–time 21
Res. Assocs. 19
Number of Students
Undergrad. 720
Library 55, 446 volumes

Outline and Characteristics of the Institute

Tokyo Metropolitan Institute of Technology, financed by the Metropolitan Government, was inaugurated April 1, 1986 to meet the needs of the Tokyo Metropolitan Community for higher education and research in these times of rapid industrial growth. The predecessor of the institute was the Metropolitan College of Technology, a junior college for learning and research in the field of science and technology, which was started 1972 at the present campus.

A great number of the most advanced electronics, mechatronics, aerospace engineering and other related industries are located around the Metropolitan area. In order to secure the future, therefore, it is the mission of the institute to cultivate frontier sciences, develop new technologies, and foster creative minds and practical skills among the younger generation. To this end, the educational policy of the institute can be summed up by the following features:

1. Theoretical learning and technical training in electronics are particularly stressed in the curriculum. Students also recieve extensive training in the use of computers, and practice on their own using the computer aided learning system.
2. The institute places a great deal of importance on maintaining solidarity with the technical high schools and the technical junior colleges organized by the Metropolis.
3. The institute makes its services available to the community by giving public lectures and disseminating informations to the people and companies in the Metropolitan area.
4. International exchange programs are actively conducted by the institute, as have been exemplified by its affiliation with sister-college Hocking Technical College, Ohio, U. S. A. , and with the Department of Technical and Further Education in New South Wales, Australia.

UNDERGRADUATE PROGRAMS

Faculty of Engineering (Freshmen Enrollment: 180)
Department of Aero-space System Engineering
Department of Electronic System Engineering
Department of Management Engineering
Department of Mechanical System Engineering

Foreign Student Admission
Qualifications for Applicants
Standard Qualifications Requirement
General Examination for Foreign Students and the Japanese Language Proficiency Test
Examination at the Institute
Mathematics and English.
Documents to be Submitted When Applying
Standard Documents Requirement
Application date: January.

*

For Further Information
Undergraduate Admission
Division of Instruction and Research, Tokyo Metropolitan Institute of Technology, 6-6 Asahigaoka, Hino-shi, Tokyo 191 ☎ 0425–83–5111ext. 204

Tokyo Metropolitan University
(Tokyo Toritsu Daigaku)

1-1-1 Yakumo, Meguro-ku, Tokyo 152
☎ 03–717–0111

Faculty
Profs. 164   Assoc. Profs. 160
Assist. Profs. Full–time 13; Part–time 237
Res. Assocs. 248
Number of Students
Undergrad. 3, 808   Grad. 709
Library 871, 556 volumes

Outline and Characteristics of the University

Tokyo Metropolitan University represents the pinnacle of a group of institutions of higher learning financed exclusively by the Tokyo Metropolitan Government. It was founded in April, 1949 under the Post-War Educational Reform, with the consolidation of six schools operated by the Tokyo City Government: one college, one women's college, and four institutes of technology.

Starting out as a relatively small operation with three faculties, the University has grown, through subsequent partitions and additions, to include five faculties plus a General Education Committee.

The General Education Committee was established in 1958 with representation from all five faculties for the purpose of improving the quality and efficiency of the general education for first and second year students.

Graduate courses for the master's degree started

in 1953 with Humanities, Social Sciences, Science and Technology, and doctorate courses in 1955 with the same divisions.

Primarily an institution of higher learning and advanced research in specialized fields, Tokyo Metropolitan University also places special emphasis on general education to cultivate well-educated and responsible citizens. Thus, several interdisciplinary courses are currently available in addition to the more conventional undergraduate offerings.

The University also works towards contributing to the human environment of the Metropolis. For example, the Center for Urban Studies, a comprehensive research institute for urban problems, is projected as an affiliated and integral part of the University. Open university forums are also organized for the citizens each year.

Instruction is given in both day and evening classes and the curricula are so organized that working students can fulfill the graduation requirements solely by evening attendance. Provisions have been made for selected municipal civil servants to receive in-service training at the University.

Despite its short history, Tokyo Metropolitan University has consistently maintained a high academic standing and has recruited an excellent faculty. With a teaching staff of nearly 600 and a total enrollment of slightly over 4, 500, the student-teacher ratio at Tokyo Metropolitan University is probably one of the best in Japan. Due to these factors, together with the low tuition and entrance fee, there is strong competition for admission year by year.

Aim of the University: (Tokyo Metropolitan University Regulations, Article 1)

As a central institution of higher learning in the metropolis of Tokyo, the University shall disseminate knowledge, conduct research and instruction in advanced fields of academic enquiry, and promote intellectual, moral, and practical abilities, thereby contributing to the life and culture of the citizens of Tokyo.

UNDERGRADUATE PROGRAMS

Faculty of Economics (Freshmen Enrollment : Day 126, Evening 24)
Department of Economics
Accounting, Business Administration, Economic History, Economic Policy, Economic Policy (on specified subject), Economics, Economic Theory, Financial Theory, Municipal Finance, Public Enterprise, Public Finance, Social Policy, Statistics
Faculty of Law (Freshmen Enrollment : Day 120, Evening 51)
Department of Law
Civil Law, Civil Procedure, Commercial Law, Constitutional Law, Criminal Law, Criminal Procedure, Jurisprudence, Law of Economical Affairs, Social Law, Sociology of Law
Department of Politics

Administrative Law, History of Political Thought, International Law, International Politics, Political History, Political Science, Tax Law, Urban Administration
Faculty of Science (Freshmen Enrollment : Day 118, Evening 39)
Department of Biology
Biochemistry, Developmental Biology, Ecology, General Biology, Genetics, Microbiological Chemistry, Morphology, Plant Physiology
Department of Chemistry
Analytical Chemistry, Bio-Chemistry, General Chemistry, Inorganic Chemistry, Organic Chemistry, Physical Chemistry, Radio Chemistry
Department of Geography
Climatology and Biogeography, Geomorphology and Quaternary Geology, Human Geography, Regional Geography, Urban Geography
Department of Mathematics
Algebra, Analysis, Applied Mathematics, Geometry, Mathematics, Statistics
Department of Physics
Applied Physics, Chemical Physics, Fluid Mechanics, High Energy Physics, Nuclear Physics, Polymer Physics, Solid State Physics
Faculty of Social Sciences and Humanities (Freshmen Enrollment : Day 95, Evening 29)
Department of Language and Literature
Chinese Language and Literature Course
Chinese Culture, Chinese Language, Chinese Literature
English Language and Literature Course
American Literature, English Linguistics, English Literature, General Linguistics, Language and Culture in English-speaking Communities, Philology and Linguistics
French Language and Literature Course
French Culture, French Language, French Literature
German Language and Literature Course
Austrian and Swiss Culture, Comparative Culture, German Culture, German Language, German Linguistics, German Literature
Japanese Language and Literature Course
Japanese Linguistics, Japanese Literature
Department of Social Sciences and Humanities
History Course
History, History of Civilization, History of Urban Society, Methodology of Historical Science, Social History
Pedagogy Course
Adult Education, Educational Psychology, Pedagogy
Philosophy Course
Ethics, History of Philosophy, Philosophy, Philosophy of Science and History of Science
Psychology Course
Applied Psychology, Experimental Psychology, General Psychology
Social Welfare Course
Methodology of Social Welfare, Social Welfare Ad-

ministration, Theory of Social Welfare
  Sociology Course
General Sociology, Social Anthropology, Theory of Sociology, Urban Sociology
Faculty of Technology (Freshmen Enrollment: Day 214, Evening 48)
  Department of Architecture and Building Science
Architectural Design and Planning, Building Materials and Construction, City Planning, Earthquake Engineering, Environmental Engineering, Structural Analysis, Structural Engineering
  Department of Civil Engineering
Applied Mechanics for Civil Engineering, Civil Engineering for Disaster Prevention, Hydraulic Engineering, Infrastructure Planning, Material Science for Civil Engineering, Sanitary Engineering, Structure of Civil Engineering
  Department of Electrical Engineering
Communication Engineering, Electrical Energy Application, Electric Machinery, Electromagnetic Theory, Electronics, Emergency-oriented Information Engineering, Network Theory, Power System Engineering
  Department of Industrial Chemistry
Chemical Engineering, Electrochemistry, Industrial Analytical Chemistry, Industrial Inorganic Chemistry, Industrial Organic Chemistry, Industrial Physical Chemistry, Materials Science and Engineering, Polymer Chemistry, Synthetic Organic Chemistry
  Department of Mechanical Engineering
Applied Mechanics for Mechanical Engineering, Control Engineering, Fluid Engineering, Material Engineering, Material Science for Mechanical Engineering, Power Engineering, Precision Engineering, Precision Machining and Machine Tools, Thermal Engineering

Foreign Student Admission
  Qualifications for Applicants
  Standard Qualifications Requirement
  Examination at the University
  For each Faculty, applicants must take the Japanese Language Proficiency Test (First level) and General Examination for Foreign Students; or applicants must take all subjects of the Joint First-Stage Achievement Test. Those who receive the Faculty's fixed grade will be allowed to take each Faculty's special entrance examination consisting of a written test and an interview.
  Documents to be Submitted When Applying
  Standard Documents Requirement
  Information Sheet of grades of the Japanese Language Proficiency Test (First level) and General Examination for Foreign Students or Bill of grades of Joint First-Stage Achievement Test.
  Application forms are available at the Admissions Office from October.
Application period : January 26 and 27 (Mail not acceptable).

GRADUATE PROGRAMS

Graduate School of Humanities (First Year Enrollment : Master's 44, Doctor's 27)
  Divisions
Language and Literature (Chinese, English, French, German, Japanese), Pedagogy, Philosophy, Psychology
Graduate School of Science (First Year Enrollment : Master's 61, Doctor's 31)
  Divisions
Biology, Chemistry, Geography, Mathematics, Physics
Graduate School of Social Science (First Year Enrollment : Master's 18, Doctor's 10)
  Divisions
Economic Policy, Law, Political Science, Social Anthropology, Sociology
Graduate School of Technology (First Year Enrollment : Master's 79, Doctor's 4)
  Divisions
Architecture, Civil Engineering, Electrical Engineering, Industrial Chemistry, Mechanical Engineering

Foreign Student Admission
  Qualifications for Applicants
Master's Program
  Standard Qualifications Requirement
Doctor's Program
  Standard Qualifications Requirement
  Examination at the University
Master's Program
  The same entrance examination with Japanese students consisting of written and oral exams.
Doctor's Program
  Same as Master's program.
  Documents to be Submitted When Applying
  Standard Documents Requirement
Note: Applicants for Humanities must submit some additional documents.

*

Research Institutes and Centers
Center for Urban Studies
For Further Information
  Undergraduate Admission
General Education Division, Tokyo Metropolitan University, 1-1-1 Yakumo, Meguro-ku, Tokyo 152 ☎ 03-717-0111 ext. 2212
  Graduate Admission
Graduate School Office of each Graduate School, Tokyo Metropolitan University, 1-1-1 Yakumo, Meguro-ku, Tokyo 152 ☎ 03-717-0111 ext. 2306 (Humanities), 2505 (Social Sciences), 3022 (Science), 4021 (Technology)

Tsuru University
(Tsuru Bunka Daigaku)

3-8-1 Tahara, Tsuru-shi, Yamanashi 402
☎ 0554-43-4341

Faculty
    Profs.   44   Assoc. Profs.   23
    Assist. Profs.   Full-time 5; Part-time   136
Number of Students
    Undergrad.   2, 488
Library   110, 911 volumes

Outline and Characteristics of the University

Tsuru University was originally founded in 1953 as a provisional institute for training teachers for primary schools. In 1955, this institute developed into the municipal junior college of Tsuru City, and added a department of commerce which in 1960 was abolished. The junior college was promoted in 1960 to a four-year college composed of two departments: Elementary Education and Japanese. In 1963, the Department of English was establised and in 1982, the Department of Sociology was established.

The campus is located in Tsuru City (population 33, 000) in the southeastern part of Yamanashi Prefecture. It can be reached within two hours from Tokyo by train or a little over one hour by car via the Chuo Highway.

This area is blessed with the magnificent and noble Mt. Fuji and the clear water of Fuji Five Lakes. The campus is surrounded by rolling foothills. Here, students can enjoy a fine view of nature and relax within this tranquil and beautiful environment.

The university is noted for having sent out many capable teachers all over the nation. This reputation has brought many students from every part of Japan, from Hokkaido to Okinawa. In the spirit of friendship and harmony, they study and work together during their four years of school life, after which they return to their home town or city to become instructors.

UNDERGRADUATE PROGRAMS

College of Humanities (Freshmen Enrollment: 400)
Department of Elementary Education
Art, Japanese Language and Literature, Mathematics, Music, Natural Science, Philosophy, Physical and Health Education, Psychology, Science of Education, Social Science
Department of English
English Linguistics, English Literature
Department of Japanese
Japanese Linguistics, Japanese Literature
Department of Sociology
Culture, Economics, Environment, Politics, Synthetic Study and Education of Society

*
Research Institutes and Centers
Attached Primary School
For Further Information
Undergraduate Admission
Admission Office, Tsuru University, 3-8-1 Tahara, Tsuru-shi, Yamanashi 402 ☎ 0554-43-4341 ext. 208

University of Osaka Prefecture
(Osaka Furitsu Daigaku)

4-804 Mozu-Umemachi, Sakai-shi, Osaka 591
☎ 0722-52-1161

Faculty
    Profs.   159   Assoc. Profs.   146
    Assist. Profs.   Full-time 142; Part-time   164
    Res. Assocs.   205
Number of Students
    Undergrad.   4, 300   Grad.   552
Library   834, 430 volumes

Outline and Characteristics of the University

University of Osaka Prefecture was founded under the name of Naniwa University by Osaka Prefecture in 1949. At the time of its foundation, the University was composed of three Faculties: Agriculture, Education, and Engineering, reorganized from seven colleges under the old system. After that, Faculty of Economics was added in 1954, Faculty of Integrated Arts and Sciences in 1978, and Faculty of Social Welfare in 1981. During these years, the name of the University was changed to University of Osaka Prefecture in 1955, and Faculty of Education was dissolved in 1957. Regarding Graduate Schools, Graduate School of Engineering was opened in 1953, followed by Graduate School of Agriculture in 1955, Graduate School of Economics in 1959, and Graduate School of Integrated Arts and Sciences in 1982.

Since its foundation, the University has developed remarkably in scale, its fame has steadily increased, and its graduates have greatly contributed to the expansion of industry and the promotion of general welfare. Today, the University enrolls more than 4, 800 students including about 80 foreign students and a full-time faculty of about 660, and is comprised of five Faculties: Agriculture, Economics, Engineering, Integrated Arts and Sciences, and Social Welfare, four Graduate Schools: Agriculture, Economics, Engineering, and Integrated Arts and Sciences, and other affiliated organizations.

The University has the campus, in Osaka Prefecture. The Nakamozu Campus, is located in the suburb of Sakai City, and houses five Faculties and affiliated organizations. The buildings are orderly arranged with lawns or avenues among them on a campus occupying 430, 000 square meters. On campus, students enjoy their student life to the fullest.

UNDERGRADUATE PROGRAMS

Faculty of Agriculture (Freshmen Enrollment: 165)
Department of Agricultural Chemistry
Animal Nutrition, Applied Microbiology, Biochemistry, Biophysical Chemistry, Chemistry of Natural Products, Fermentation Chemistry, Food Chemistry, Pesticide Chemistry, Soil Science and Plant Nutrition
Department of Agricultural Engineering
Agricultural Machinery, Agrometeorological Environment, Environment Control in Agriculture, Land Development Engineering, Urban Landscape Design, Utilization of Water in Agriculture
Department of Horticultural Science and Agronomy
Agricultural Politics, Crop Science, Entomology, Farm Management Economics, Floriculture, Genetics and Plant Breeding, Landscape Architecture, Plant Pathology, Pomology, Post-harvest Physiology of Horticultural Products, Vegetable Crop Science
Department of Veterinary Science
Veterinary Anatomy, Veterinary Internal Medicine, Veterinary Microbiology, Veterinary Pathology, Veterinary Pharmacology, Veterinary Physiology and Animal Feeding, Veterinary Public Health, Veterinary Reproduction, Veterinary Surgery
Faculty of Economics (Freshmen Enrollment: 250)
Department of Business Administration
Business Economics and Administration, Financial Accounting, Industrial Law, Management Accounting, Management Science, Marketing, Personnel Management and Industrial Relations
Department of Economics
Civil Law, Commercial Law, Economic History, Economic Policy, Economic Statistics, Fiscal Economics, History of Economic Thought, Industrial Economics, International Economics, Labor Economics and Social Policy, Mathematical Economics, Monetary Economics, Principles of Economics, Public Law
Faculty of Engineering (Freshmen Enrollment: 435)
Department of Aeronautical Engineering
Aerodynamics, Aero-space Systems Engineering, Instrumentation and Control, Power Plant and Propulsion, Structural Mechanics
Department of Applied Chemistry
Analytical Chemistry, Electrochemistry, Industrial Organic Chemistry, Inorganic Chemistry, Organic Chemistry, Physical Chemistry, Physical Chemistry of Polymer, Polymer Chemistry, Synthetie Organic Chemistry
Department of Chemical Engineering
Chemical Reaction Engineering, Diffusional Mass Transfer, Mechanical Separation Processes, Plant Design and Engineering, Process Engineering
Department of Electrical Engineering
Electrical Engineering Materials, Electrical Machinery, Electromagnetic-Wave Communication and Information, Fundamental Theory of Electrical Engineering, Information and Communication Systems, Information Processing Theory, Material Physics, Power Engineering
Department of Electronics
Computers and Data Processing, Electronic Circuit Engineering, Electronic Control Engineering, Physical Electronics, Solid-State Electronics, Vacuum and Gaseous Electronics
Department of Industrial Engineering
Production Control, Production Engineering, Statistical Engineering, Systems Engineering
Department of Mathematical Sciences
Applied Analysis, Applied Mechanics, Mathematical Statistics, Numerical Analysis, Quantum Mechanics, Solid-State Physics
Department of Mechanical Engineering
Control Engineering, Engineering Design, Fluid Mechanics, Heat and Mass Transfer, Internal Combustion Engine, Machine Tools, Manufacturing Processes of Machine, Measurement Engineering, Strength of Materials, Thermal Energy Engineering
Department of Metallurgical Engineering
Crystal Plasticity, Extractive Metallurgy, Ferrous Materials, Nonferrous Materials, Physical Chemistry of Metals, Physical Metallurgy, Technology of Metal Working
Department of Naval Architecture
Construction of Ships: Theory of Special Vessels, Ship Hydrodynamics, Strength of Ships, Theory of Ship Design
Interdisciplinary Subject: Environmental Chemistry, Environmental Engineering
Faculty of Integrated Arts and Sciences (Freshmen Enrollment: 70)
Department of Integrated Arts and Sciences
English, German and French, Human Science, Instrument Science, Japanology, Life Science, Materials Science, Mathematics and Related Fields, Physical Education and Health Science, Western Studies
Faculty of Social Welfare (Freshmen Enrollment: 50)
Department of Social Welfare
Basic Theories, Methodology of Social Work, Specific Studies of Social Work Fields
Foreign Student Admission
Qualifications for Applicants
Standard Qualifications Requirement
Examination at the University
For Faculties of Agriculture, Engineering, and Social Welfare, applicants must take the Japanese Language Proficiency Test and General Examination for Foreign Students. Each Faculty's entrance examination generally consists of written and oral exams and an interview.
Documents to be Submitted When Applying
Standard Documents Requirement
The applicant's curriculum vitae must be in Japanese in his/her own handwriting.
Application forms and other necessary items are contained in "Outline of the Admission of Foreign

Students" published by University of Osaka Prefecture, and is available at the School Affairs Division. All applicants are required to submit the specified application documents and pay entrance examination fee to the School Affairs Division within the term for application (usually late February). For further particulars, refer to "Outline of the Admission of Foreign Students".

GRADUATE PROGRAMS

Graduate School of Agriculture (First Year Enrollment : Master's 92, Doctor's 35)
Divisions
Agricultural Chemistry, Agricultural Engineering, Horticultural Science and Agronomy, Veterinary Science

Graduate School of Economics (First Year Enrollment : Master's 36, Doctor's 13)
Division
Economics

Graduate School of Engineering (First Year Enrollment : Master's 132, Doctor's 66)
Divisions
Aeronautical Engineering, Applied Chemistry, Chemical Engineering, Electrical Engineering, Electronics, Industrial Engineering, Mathematical Sciences, Mechanical Engineering, Metallurgical Engineering, Naval Architecture

Graduate School of Integrated Arts and Sciences (First Year Enrollment : Master's 15)
Divisions
Culturology, Materials Science, Mathematics and Information Sciences

Foreign Student Admission
Qualifications for Applicants
Master's Program
Standard Qualifications Requirement
Doctor's Program
Standard Qualifications Requirement
Examination at the University
Master's Program
Written and oral exams and an interview.
Doctor's Program
Same as Master's program.
Documents to be Submitted When Applying
Standard Documents Requirement
The applicant's curriculum vitae must be in Japanese in his/her own handwriting.

As other documents to be submitted differ with Graduate Schools, apply to each Graduate School Office for further information. Application forms and other necessary items are available at each Graduate School Office. All applicants are required to submit the specified application documents and pay the entrance examination fee to each Graduate School Office within the term for application determined by each Graduate School. For further information, inquire at each Graduate School Office.

*
Research Institutes and Centers
Computer Center, Engineering Laboratory and Workshop, University Farm, Veterinary Hospital
Facilities/Services for Foreign Students
Dormitory for Foreign Students: Shared facilities (Assembly-Room), Accommodation (15 rooms: 9 twin-bed rooms for single students and 6 rooms for couples or families), Conversation Room for Foreign Students (in Student Hall)
Special Programs for Foreign Students
Courses in Japanese Language and Things Japanese are available, and those credits can be substituted for credits under General Education and foreign languages.
For Further Information
Undergraduate Admission
School Affairs Division, University, of Osaka Prefecture 4-804 Mozu-Umemachi, Sakai-shi, Osaka 591 ☎ 0722–52–1161 ext. 2785
Graduate Admission
Each Graduate School Office, University of Osaka Prefecture, 4-804 Mozu-Umemachi, Sakai-shi, Osaka 591 ☎ 0722–52–1161 ext. 2410 (Agriculture), 2510 (Economics), 2210 (Engineering), 2609 (Integrated Arts and Sciences)

Wakayama Medical College
(Wakayama Kenritsu Ika Daigaku)

27 Kyuban-cho, Wakayama-shi, Wakayama 640
☎ 0734–31–2151

Faculty
Profs. 42　Assoc. Profs. 25
Assist. Profs. Full–time 38; Part–time 121
Res. Assocs. 155
Number of Students
Undergrad. 376　Grad. 38
Library 71, 436 volumes

Outline and Characteristics of the College
In 1945, Wakayama Medical School (five-year school) was established by the Prefectural Government. Three years later, Wakayama Medical College was founded and recognized as the college of medicine in 1948. Ever since, the College has grown with the times. In 1960, the Graduate School of Medicine was inaugurated and started to offer a Doctor's program. Today, the College enrolls 400 students and a full-time faculty of 250, and is comprised of two hospitals in affiliation, one research institute, and one attached student nurses' training school.

The principal buildings of the College, the main hospital with 811 beds, and the research institute are located in the center of Wakayama City (population approximately 400, 000). The medical preparatory course is located to the east of the City, and the Kihoku Branch Hospital (220 beds) and the student nurses' training school (freshmen enrollment 20) are situated in the town of Katsuragi-cho, Wakayama Prefecture.

The College is both nationally and internationally noted for its advanced medical research and other academic services. While seeking to meet the growing demand for excellent and reliable doctors, the College holds firmly to its traditional role as the core and center of advanced medical treatment in this region.

UNDERGRADUATE PROGRAMS

Faculty of Medicine (Freshmen Enrollment: 60)
Department of Medicine
Basic Medical Sciences and Social MedicineAnatomy, Biochemistry, Hygiene, Legal Medicine, Microbiology, Pathology, Pharmacology, Physiology, Public Health
Clinical Sciences Anesthesiology, Dentistry and Oral Surgery, Dermatology, Internal Medicine, Laboratory Medicine, Neuropsychiatry, Obstetrics and Gynecology, Ophthalmology, Orthopedic Surgery, Otolaryngology, Pediatrics, Radiology, Surgery (Gastroenterological Surgery, Neurosurgery, Thoracic Surgery), Urology

Foreign Student Admission
Qualifications for Applicants
Standard Qualifications Requirement
Examination at the College
In principle, applicants are primarily required to take the Joint First–Stage Achivement Test in all subjects.

After taking this Test, applicants are expected to sit for the entrance examination (including the essay –writing examination and an interview) administered by the College. Those who achieve satisfactory scores on the examinations are finally admitted to the College after the qualifications of each applicant with regard to character, intellectual ability and professional promise are individually considered by the Committee of the College Entrance Examination.

GRADUATE PROGRAMS

Graduate School of Medicine (First Year Enrollment : Doctor's 31)
Divisions
Internal Medicine, Pathology, Physiology, Social Medicine, Surgery

Foreign Student Admission
Qualifications for Applicants
Doctor's Program
Standard Qualifications Requirement
Examination at the College
Doctor's Program
Applicants are admitted to the Graduate School of Medicine on condition that they achieve satisfacto-
ry scores in the written and oral examinations.
Documents to be Submitted When Applying
Standard Documents Requirement
*
Research Institutes and Centers
Research Institute for Medical Sciences
For Further Information
Undergraduate and Graduate Admission
Admissions Office, Wakayama Medical College, 27 Kyuban-cho, Wakayama-shi, Wakayama 640 ☎ 0734–31–2151 ext. 306

Yamaguchi Women's University
(Yamaguchi Joshi Daigaku)

3-2-1 Sakurabatake, Yamaguchi-shi, Yamaguchi 753
☎ 0839–28–0211

Faculty
    Profs. 29   Assoc. Profs. 17
    Assist. Profs. Full–time 4; Part–time 53
    Res. Assocs. 12
Number of Students
    Undergrad. 670
Library 110, 700 volumes

Outline and Characteristics of the University
The opening article of the University regulations reads as follows: Yamaguchi Women's University aims at teaching and studying up-to-date high-level art and science. It also aims to develop women's intellectual, moral and applied abilities, so they may contribute much to cultural betterment and social improvement.

Based on this definite policy, the University opened in 1941 as Yamaguchi Prefectural Professional School for Women. In 1950 the University grew to Yamaguchi Women's Junior College (departments of Japanese Literature and Home Science). It has since grown to become Yamaguchi Women's University. Today, the University has two faculties (Literature and Home Science) and enrolls about 670 students.

The campus is located in the suburbs of Yamaguchi City, which is called 'the Kyoto of Western Japan' and is famous for its long history and beautiful nature. The housing quarters are surrounded by greenery.

UNDERGRADUATE PROGRAMS

Faculty of Home Science (Freshmen Enrollment: 80)
Department of Food and Nutrition
Cuisine, Food Hygiene, Food Science, Nutrition Guidance, Nutrition Science, Public Hygiene
Department of Textile and Clothing Science
Clothing Design, Clothing Formation, Clothing Hygiene, Clothing Management, Clothing Materials, Dyeing Chemistry

Faculty of Literature (Freshmen Enrollment: 80)
Department of Child and Culture
Arts and Crafts, Child Studies, Music, Pedagogy, Psychology, Sociology, Sport Science
Department of Japanese Literature
Calligraphy, Chinese Literature, Japanese Language, Japanese Literature

Foreign Student Admission
Qualifications for Applicants
Standard Qualifications Requirement
Examination at the University
Selection of applicants is made through examination of their documents and a personal interview. Successful applicants are required to submit a written oath, and a letter of guarantee (in which the names of two resident guarantors in Japan must be mentioned).
Documents to be Submitted When Applying
Standard Documents Requirement

*

For Further Information
Undergraduate Admission
Student Office, Yamaguchi Women's University, 3-2-1 Sakurabatake, Yamaguchi-shi, Yamaguchi 753
☎ 0839–28–0211 ext. 314

Yokohama City University
(Yokohama Shiritsu Daigaku)

22-2 Seto, Kanazawa-ku, Yokohama-shi, Kanagawa 236   ☎ 045–787–2311

Faculty
    Profs. 101   Assoc. Profs. 90
    Assist. Profs. Full–time 43; Part–time 472
    Res. Assocs. 106
Number of Students
    Undergrad. 3, 106   Grad. 107
Library 387, 976 volumes

Outline and Characteristics of the University
Yokohama City University began as a school of commercial law in 1885. In 1949, it became Yokohama City University following the reform of the educational system after World War II.
In 1952, the School of Medicine based on Yokohama Municipal Medical College and Yokohama University School of Medicine, and the Faculty of Liberal Arts and Science were established. In 1955, the Premed school was integrated into the University, thus completing the major parts of the University. Two Graduate Schools were opened: the first, in 1961, to create a doctoral course in Medical Science; the second, in 1970, to create a master's course in Economics and Business Administration. In 1963, the General Education Department was established for the purpose of improving general education.
In 1949 the Economic Research Institute and in 1984 the Kihara Biology Research Institute were annexed to the University.
The campus is located in the southern part of Yokohama City, between Yokohama port to the south and the citizen's forest of Kamariya and Hitorizawa to the north, and thus students study and enjoy sports in comfortable surroundings.
The University contributes to the improvement of the city's culture as the academic center of Yokohama City (population 3, 000, 000) and it contributes to the cause of world peace and the welfare of mankind.
The quality of Yokohama City University's student body complements the stature of its faculty. The majority of students are Hamakko (Children of Yokohama), but people come from every part of Japan and eight foreign countries to study at YCU.

UNDERGRADUATE PROGRAMS

Faculty of Economics and Business Administration (Freshmen Enrollment: 350)
Department of Business Administration
Business Administration, Commerce and Accounting
Department of Economics
Applied Economics, Economic History, Economic Theory, History of Economic Thought
Faculty of Liberal Arts and Science (Freshmen Enrollment: 300)
Department of Liberal Arts
Foreign Languages, Humanities, International Relations, Social Science
Department of Science
Biology, Chemistry, Mathematics, Physics
School of Medicine (Freshmen Enrollment: 60)
Department of Medicine
Anaesthesiology, Anatomy, Bacteriology, Biochemistry, Cell Biology, Chemical Pharmacology, Dermatology, Hygiene, Internal Medicine, Legal Medicine, Medical History, Medical Parasitology, Neurological Surgery, Obsterics and Gynecology, Ophthalmology, Oral Surgery, Orthopedics, Otorhinolaryngology, Pathology, Pediatrics, Pharmacology, Physiology, Psychiatry, Public Health, Radiology, Surgery, Urology

Foreign Student Admission
Qualifications for Applicants
Standard Qualifications Requirement
For each Faculty applicants must take the Japanese Language Proficiency Test and General Examination for Foreign students.
Examination at the University
Foreign applicants, as Special Foreign Students, may take the entrance examination consisting mainly of an essay and an interview (except for School of Medicine).
Documents to be Submitted When Applying
Standard Documents Requirement

Following documents are also required.

1. A certificate or letter of recommendation from the applicant's government or some diplomatic establishment in Japan.
2. Certificates of the results of the Japanese Language Proficiency Test and the General Examination for Foreign Students.

Application forms are available at the Admission Office from early October. All applicants are required to submit the specified application documents to the Admission Office by January.

GRADUATE PROGRAMS

Graduate School of Business Administration (First Year Enrollment : Master's 10)
 Division
Business Administration
Graduate School of Economics (First Year Enrollment : Master's 10)
 Division
Economics
Graduate School of Medicine (First Year Enrollment : Doctor's 29)
 Divisions
Internal Medicine, Pathology, Physiology, Social Medicine, Surgery

Foreign Student Admission
 Qualifications for Applicants
Master's Program
 Standard Qualifications Requirement
Doctor's Program
 Standard Qualifications Requirement
 Examination at the University
Master's Program
 Applicants must take the same entrance examination consisting of written and oral exams given to Japanese students.
Doctor's Program
 Same as Master's program.
 Documents to be Submitted When Applying
 Standard Documents Requirement
 Application forms are available at the Admission Office from early July.

*

Research Institutes and Centers
Economic Research Institute, Kihara Biology Research Institute.
Facilities/Services for Foreign Students
The Foreign Student's Domitory of Yokohama City University
Shared Facilities: Conference Room, Locker Room, Japanese–style Room
Accommodation: 13 rooms (all single rooms)
For Further Information
 Undergraduate and Graduate Admission
Educational Affairs Section of each Faculty, Yokohama City University, 22–2 Seto, Kanazawa–ku, Yokohama–shi, Kanagawa 236 ☎ 045–787–2311

Descriptions of
the Colleges and Universities in Japan

Private Colleges
and
Universities

3

Aichi Gakuin University
(Aichi Gakuin Daigaku)

12 Araike, Iwasaki, Nisshin-cho, Aichi-gun, Aichi
470-01 ☎ 05617-3-1111

Faculty
    Profs. 141   Assoc. Profs. 67
    Assist. Profs. Full–time 76; Part–time 288
    Res. Assocs. 127
Number of Students
    Undergrad. 10, 670   Grad. 187
Library 490, 229 volumes

Outline and Characteristics of the University

Aichi Gakuin University has four faculties including eight departments, each faculty having graduate doctoral courses. The student enrollment is over 11, 000 and the faculty and administrative staff number over 1, 000. The University has three campuses; Nisshin, Kusumoto and Suemori. The facilities, which include a dental hospital, occupy about 150, 000 m² of the total university property of 600, 000 m². It is one of the leading universities in Central Japan.

It was founded as a Sotoshu special school for training Soto sect priests in 1876. Within its history of over 100 years, it has changed its name and experienced rapid growth. In 1953, Aichi Gakuin became a university with the addition of Faculty of Commerce. Later Faculties of Law, Dentistry and Letters were added, the latest addition being the Department of International Culture in the Faculty of Letters in 1986.

Based on the spirit of Buddhism, especially on the spirit of Zen Buddhism, "learning through experience" and "showing gratitude for blessings through kindness to others" are the founding philosophy of Aichi Gakuin University. It has produced responsible persons contributing greatly to the local society, the welfare of human beings and the development of culture.

Aichi Gakuin University is the only university that has an independent Zen meditation hall on campus. It places emphasis on cultivating aesthetic sentiments through, for example, worship services in the auditorium, and visits to the Eiheiji Temple to practice Zen meditation to experience a priest's life.

Nisshin Campus has a splendid environment and complete facilities for Commerce, Law, and Letters students, while the Faculty of Dentistry with its hospital located in the center of Nagoya City is a unique facility in this district. The graduates are sought after from many fields of employment, and those of the Faculty of Dentistry enjoy the highest passing percentage in the national dental examination among private universities in Japan each year.

UNDERGRADUATE PROGRAMS

Faculty of Commerce (Freshmen Enrollment: 1, 000)
Department of Commerce
Accounting, Advertising, Auditing, Banking, Commerce, Commodity Science, Cost Accounting, Foreign Trade, History of Commerce, Information Management, Insurance, Management Analysis, Marketing, Physical Distribution, Securities Market
Department of Management
Accounting, Auditing, Cost Accounting, Financial Management, History of Management, Information Management, Management, Management Analysis, Management Theory and Policy, Marketing Management, Office Practices, Personal Management, Production Management, Psychology of Management
Faculty of Dentistry (Freshmen Enrollment: 160)
Department of Dentistry
Anatomy, Anesthesiology, Biochemistry, Dental Materials Science, Microbiology, Operative Dentistry, Oral Hygiene, Oral Surgery, Orthodontics, Pathology, Pedodontics, Pharmacology, Physiology, Prosthetic Dentistry, Radiology
Faculty of Law (Freshmen Enrollment: 500)
Department of Law
Administrative Law, Anti-trust Law, Bankruptcy Law, Bills of Exchange and Cheques, Civil Law, Civil Procedure, Commercial Law, Company Law, Constitutional Law, Contracts, Criminal Law, Criminal Procedure, Criminology, Family Law and Succession, Foreign Law, Intellectual Property Law, International Law, International Politics, Labor Law, Law of Property, Legal History, Legal Philosophy, Political History, Politics, Private International Law, Religious Law, Sociology of Law, Tax Law, Torts
Faculty of Letters (Freshmen Enrollment: 440)
Department of Buddhist and Religious Studies
Anthropology of Religion, Chinese Buddhism, History of Buddhism, History of Chinese Thought, History of Indian Thought, History of Japanese Buddhism, History of Japanese Thought, Indian Buddhism, Japanese Buddhism, Missionary Method, Philosophy of Religion, Religious Doctorines, Science of Religion, Sociology of Religion, Zen-Buddhism, Zen-Scripture
Department of History
Archaeology, Comparative Culture, Cultural Anthropology, Geography, Historiography, History of East-West Relations, History of International Relations, Japanese History, Occidental History, Oriental History, Physical Geography, Topography
Department of International Culture
American Studies, British Studies, Buddhist Culture, Comparative Culture, Comparative Thought, Cultural Area Studies (East Asia, South Asian, the Pan Pacific Area), Cultures of English-Speaking Societies, English and American Literature, History of English and American Langauge, History of English

and American Literature, International Communication, International Culture, International Relations, Japanese Culture and History, Peace Studies, Zen Culture

Department of Japanese Culture

Asian arts, Buddhism and Culture, Buddhist Culture, Calligraphy-based Culture, Classical Chinese Literature, Classical Japanese Literature-ancient and Medieval, Community Study, Contemporary Japanese Society, Creative Writing, Cultural Anthropology, Culture of everyday life, Cultures shaped by Chinese Characters, Dialects of Japanese, English, Graduation Thesis, History of Calligraphy, History of Japanese Culture with Focus on Modern Japanese Culture, History of Japanese Thought, Intermediate and Advanced Courses, Introduction to Linguistics, Intruduction to History of Japanese Literature and Modern Japanese Literature, Japanese, Japanese as a Foreign Language-basic, Japanese Culture in the Asian Setting, Japanese Culture in the Global Setting, Japanese Ethnology, Japanese Grammar, Japanese Literature-literature Review, Japanese Phonemics, Japanese Style Management, Linguistic Culture, Methodology for Japanese as a Foreign Language with Focus on Teaching Materials, Research Design and Methodology, Seminars, Sociology of Family, Vocabulary of Japanese, Zen and Japanese Culture

Department of Psychology

Cognitive and Behavioral Psychology, Developmental and Educational Psychology, Education of Handicapped Children, General Psychology, History of Psychology, Managerial Psychology, Personality and Social Psychology, Psychological Statistics, Psychology of Handicapped Children, Psychometrics, Religious Psychology, Social Psychology

Foreign Student Admission

Qualifications for Applicants
    Standard Qualifications Requirement
Examination at the University
A written exam and an interview with regard to their proficiency in Japanese.
    Documents to be Submitted When Applying
    Standard Documents Requirement
    A copy of Certificate of Japanese Language Proficiency, if possible.

GRADUATE PROGRAMS

Graduate School of Commercial Science (First Year Enrollment : Master's 20, Doctor's 3)
    Division
Commercial Science
Graduate School of Dentistry (First Year Enrollment : Doctor's 18)
    Division
Dentistry
Graduate School of Law (First Year Enrollment : Master's 20, Doctor's 4)

Division
Private Law
Graduate School of Letters (First Year Enrollment : Master's 22, Doctor's 13)
    Divisions
History, Psychology, Religion & Buddhism

Foreign Student Admission

Qualifications for Applicants
Master's Program
    Standard Qualifications Requirement
Doctor's Program
    Standard Qualifications Requirement
Examination at the University
Master's Program
Graduate School of Letters:
1.   Written Exam concerning major subjects
2.   Foreign Language: (Course of Religion and Buddhism) one from English, German, French or Chinese, (Course of Psychology) one from English, German or French.
Graduate Schools of Commerce and Law:
1.   Thesis Exam concerning major subjects.
2.   Foreign Language: one from English, German or French.
3.   Interview.
Doctor's Program
Graduate Schools of Letters, Commerce and Law:
1.   Thesis concerning major subjects.
2.   Foreign Languages: English and one other from German or French.
    The following are exceptions: In the course of Religion and Buddhism, English and translations of special books written in languages other than English. In the course of history, English and one other from German, French or Chinese. In the course of Japanese or Oriental History, English and one other from the above languages, including Chinese Classics.
Graduate School of Dentistry:
1.   Written Exam concerning major subjects.
2.   Foreign Language:
    (A) English I (English concerned with major subjects.)
    (B) English II (general English) and one other from German or French.
3.   Interview.
Documents to be Submitted When Applying
    Standard Documents Requirement
    Detailed Family Information Card is required to all applicants.
    The applicant for the Master's Program in the Graduate School of Letters is required to submit a copy of his or her Bachelor's Thesis.
    The applicant for the Doctoral Program in the Graduate School of Letters, Commerce, and Law is required to submit his or her Master's Thesis and its synopsis.

*

Research Institutes and Centers

Data Processing Center of Aichi Gakuin University, Electronic Data Processing Education Center, Institute for Cultural Studies, Institute for Legal Systems of Religions, Institute of Business Administration, Institute of Foreign Languages, Institute of Zen, Marketing Reseach Institute

Facilities/Services for Foreign Students

The International Exchange Committee and Scientific Exchange Committee have been recently organized, and services for foreign students are now under consideration.

Special Programs for Foreign Students

The following lectures of the Department of International Culture in the Faculty of Letters are open to foreign students.

Special Japanese: Fundamental, Intermediate, Advanced,

Study of Japan I: An Introduction to the State of Affairs in Japan

For Further Information

Undergraduate Admission

The Admissions Office, Aichi Gakuin University, 12 Iwasaki, Nisshin-cho, Aichi-gun, Aichi 470-01 ☎ 05617-3-1111 ext. 170

Graduate Admission

Graduate Schools of Commerce, Law and Literature: Assistant Head, Graduate School Office, Aichi Gakuin University, 12 Iwasaki, Nisshin-cho, Aichi-gun, Aichi 470-01 ☎ 05617-3-1111 ext. 460

Graduate School of Dentistry: Administrative Head, Faculty of Dentistry, Aichi Gakuin University, 1-100 Kusumoto-cho, Chikusa-ku, Nagoya-shi, Aichi 464 ☎ 052-751-2561 ext. 304

Aichi Gakusen University
(Aichi Gakusen Daigaku)

28 Kamikawanari, Hegoshi-cho, Okazaki-shi, Aichi 444   ☎ 0564-31-6587

UNDERGRADUATE PROGRAMS

Faculty of Business Administration (Freshmen Enrollment: 200)

Department of Business Administration

Faculty of Domestic Science (Freshmen Enrollment: 50)

Department of Home Economics

American and European Culture Course   Clothing Science Course   Food and Nutrition Course

Aichi Institute of Technology
(Aichi Kogyo Daigaku)

1247 Yachigusa, Yakusa-cho, Toyota-shi, Aichi 470-03   ☎ 0565-48-8121

Faculty
    Profs. 76   Assoc. Profs. 49
    Assist. Profs. Full–time 44; Part–time 170
    Res. Assocs. 8

Number of Students
    Undergrad. 5, 697   Grad. 42

Library   205, 000 volumes

Outline and Characteristics of the University

The goal of Aichi Institute of Technology is to produce graduates who are well–rounded human beings with competent technological skills. The total educational program is geared toward this aim with the hope and expectation that its graduates will contribute both to technological advancement and to society as a whole.

Students receive a practical technological course using the latest available resources and equipment possible. Students are encouraged to be creative in their studies and to develop habits of continual searching for new truths as they prepare to adapt to the ever-changing technological world around them.

1912   Nagoya Training School of Electricity was founded.

1949   Nagoya Electricity High School was established.

1954   Nagoya Junior College of Electrical Engineering was established.

1959   Nagoya Institute of Electricity Department of Electrical Engineering was established.

1960   The name was changed to Aichi Institute of Technology. Electronic Engineering and Applied Chemistry were added.

1962   Mechanical Engineering and Industrial Engineering were added.

1963   Evening courses in Electrical Engineering and Mechanical Engineering were added.

1965   The Civil Engineering Department was added.

1966   Electrical Engineering and Applied Chemistry advanced courses were added.

1968   The Architecture Department was added.

1973   Civil Engineering advanced course was added.

1976   The Architecture Engineering Department was added. Mechanical Engineering and Architecture advanced courses were added.

1988   Information Network Engineering was added.

UNDERGRADUATE PROGRAMS

Faculty of Engineering (Freshmen Enrollment: 1000)

Department of Applied Chemistry

Analytical Chemistry, Biochemistry, Catalyst Chemistry, Chemical Engineering, Environmental Chemistry, Food Chemistry, Industrial Inorganic Chemistry, Industrial Organic Chemistry, Industrial Physical Chemistry, Inorganic Chemistry, Instrumental Analysis, Organic Chemistry, Organic Reaction Mechanism, Physical Chemistry, Polymer Chemistry, Quantum Chemistry

Department of Architectural Engineering
Aesthetic Design, Architectural Design and Drawing, Architectural Planning, Building Administration, Building Construction, Building Disaster Prevention, Building Equipment, Building Equipment Control Engineering, Building Management, Building Materials, Building Structural Design and Drawing, Construction of Building Equipment, Drawing of Building Equipment, Dynamics of Structure, Electrical Equipment of Building, Environmental Engineering, Graphics and Perspective Drawing, Planning of Building Equipment, Urban Design

Department of Architecture
Architectural Design and Drawing, Architectural History, Architectural Planning, Building Construction, Building Disaster Prevention, Building Equipment, Building Materials, Building Structure, Environmental Engineering of Building, Formative Design, Ground Engineering, Landscape Gardening, Structural Mechanics, Urban Planning & Design

Department of Civil Engineering
Bridge Engineering, City Planning, Civil Engineering Construction, Civil Engineering Planning, Coastal Engineering, Concrete Technology, Construction Equipments, Disaster Prevention Engineering, Earthquake Engineering, Electric Power Engineering, Environmental Engineering, Finite Element Method, Foundation Engineering, Harbor Engineering, Hydraulics, Railway Engineering, Reinforced Concrete Engineering, River Engineering, Soil Mechanics, Steel Structures, Traffic Engineering, Traffic Planning

Department of Electrical Engineering
Communication Engineering, Control Engineering, Design of Electrical Machinery, Electrical Engineering, Electrical Machinery, Electric Applications, Electric Circuits, Electric Measurements, Electric Power Engineering, Electrochemistry, Electromagnetism, High Voltage Engineering, Nuclear Engineering, System Engineering

Department of Electronics
Acoustic Engineering, Circuit Theory, Electronic Circuit Design, Electronic Circuits, Electronic Computer, Electronic Materials, Electronic Measurements, Electronics, Gas Electronics, Image Engineering, Information Theory, Instrumental Drawing, Microwave Engineering, Radio Communication Engineering, Semiconductor Engineering, Telephonic Transmission

Department of Industrial Engineering
Accounting, Business Administration, Business Law, Computer Science, Cost Accounting, Engineering Economy, Engineering Economy, Ergonomics, Financial Management, Industrial Accounting, Industrial Engineering, Industrial Psychology, Information Science, Marketing, Material Management, Office Management, Operations Research, Personnel Management, Production Control and Factory Planning, Production Management, Quality Control, Systems Engineering, Technical Drawing

Department of Information Network Engineering
Artificial Intelligence, Communication Systems, Computer Architectures, Computer Programming, Database Theory, Electromagnetic Waves, Electronic and Communication Measurements, Image Processing, Information and Communication Networks, Information Theory, Operating Systems, Operations Research, Optoelectronics, Signal Processing, Software Engineering, Speech and Acoustics, Theory of Transmission Networks

Department of Mechanical Engineering
Air Conditioning Engineering, Automatic Control, Automobile Engineering, Chemical Machinery, Elasticity and Plasticity, Electro-Mechanical Engineering, Engineering Mechanics, Fluid Dynamics, Fluid Machinery, Heat Engine, Heat Transfer, Hydrodynamics, Machine Design and Drafting, Machine Tools, Materials Engineering, Materials Handling Machinery, Mechanical Technology, Precise Measurement, Strength of Materials, Theory of Mechanism, Thermodynamics

Faculty of Engineering (Evening Course) (Freshmen Enrollment: 80)

Department of Electrical Engineering
Circuit Theory, Electric Applications, Electric Materials, Electric Power Engineering, Electrochemistry, Electromagnetism, Electronic Circuits, Electronic Computer, Electronics, High Voltage Engineering, Radio Communication Engineering, Telephonic Transmission

Department of Mechanical Engineering
Air Conditioning Engineering, Automatic Control, Automobile Engineering, Engineering Mechanics, Factory Management, Hydrodynamics, Instrumentation Engineering, Machine Design and Drafting, Machine Element, Machine Tool, Mechanical Drawing, Mechanical Technology, Plasticity, Precise Measurement, Quality Control, Strength of Materials, Strength of Materials, Theory of Mechanism, Thermodynamics

Foreign Student Admission
Qualifications for Applicants
   Standard Qualifications Requirement
   All applicants must be 18 years old or older by March in the year of application.
Examination at the University
1.   An oral test
2.   Written examinations
3.   Foreign students living in Japan are encouraged to take the General Examination for Foreign Students.

Documents to be Submitted When Applying
Standard Documents Requirement

A statement giving the applicant's reasons for wanting to study at Aichi Institute of Technology, and a document showing that the applicant has adequate funds to meet school expenses are also required. These documents can be in Japanese, English, German, French or Chinese.
Application Deadline: January 31
Documents to be Submitted When Applying
Standard Documents Requirement

ONE-YEAR GRADUATE PROGRAMS

One-Year Graduate Course of Industrial Engineering (Enrollment 10)
Industrial Engineering

GRADUATE PROGRAMS

Graduate School of Engineering (First Year Enrollment : Master's 25)
Divisions
Applied Chemistry, Architecture, Civil Engineering, Electrical Engineering, Mechanical Engineering

Foreign Student Admission
Qualifications for Applicants
Master's Program
Standard Qualifications Requirement
Applicants must have an undergraduate degree in Engineering.
Examination at the University
Master's Program
1. Personal interview.
Documents to be Submitted When Applying
Standard Documents Requirement
Proof of Finacial Support is also required.
Research Institutes and Centers
Computer Center, EarthquakeResearch Center
Facilities/Services for Foreign Students
The Office of Admissions assists foreign students who apply. Foreign graduate students from sister institutions in China stay at the International Center.
For Further Information
Undergraduate and Graduate Admission
Office of Admissions, Aichi Institute of Technology, 1247 Yachigusa, Yakusa-cho, Toyota-shi, Aichi 470-03 ☎ 0565-48-8121 ext. 122

Aichi Medical University
(Aichi Ika Daigaku)

21 Yazako Karimata, Nagakute-cho, Aichi-gun, Aichi 480-11 ☎ 05616-2-3311

Faculty
Profs. 41   Assoc. Profs. 47

Assist. Profs. Full–time 58; Part–time 108
Res. Assocs. 207
Number of Students
Undergrad. 706   Grad. 72
Library 112, 484 volumes

Outline and Characteristics of the University
Aichi Medical University was founded in 1972 with the intention of fostering excellent medical doctors and leaders with up-to-date knowledge and techniques in medicine who would render service to human beings by helping to maintain a healthy life. The University is situated at Nagakute-cho, Aichi prefecture, which retains much of its natural beauty, making it one of the finest sites for education, study, and medical care.

The University consists of the Faculty of Medical Science, the Graduate School of Medical Science and the Nursing School. The University has a Hospital, a Library, Institute for Medical Science of Aging, Institute for Molecular Science of Medicine, Information Processing Center, and Laboratory Animal Research Center on campus, and the Medical Clinic at the central part of Nagoya, the third largest city of Japan. The University Hospital retains 1, 271 beds, 265 doctors, 542 nurses, and 19 clinical departments. These are planned to be increased in the near future.

The University offers a six year integrated education—general education, basic medicine and clinical medicine. It strives for human medical science based on respect for the dignity of human life and humanism, and expects the spontaneous academic efforts of the students. The atmosphere of the University is harmonious; the students receive education from an excellent academic staff who enhance their sense of mission as medical doctors and leaders, preparing themselves to be doctors able to face the challenges of the 21st century.

Today, seven students from Taiwan are enrolled in the University, and are working hard on learning and enjoying sports in company with more than 700 Japanese students.

UNDERGRADUATE PROGRAMS

Faculty of Medicine (Freshmen Enrollment 100)
Department of Medicine
Anatomy, Anesthesiology&Emergency Medicine, Biochemistry, Dermatology, Hygiene, Internal Medicine, Legal Medicine, Microbiology, Neurosurgery, Obstetrics and Gynecology, Ophthalmology, Orthopedic Surgery, Otorhinolaryngology, Parasitology, Pathology, Pediatrics, Pharmacology, Physiology, Psychiatry and Neurology, Public Health, Radiology, Surgery, Urology

Foreign Student Admission
Qualifications for Applicants
Standard Qualifications Requirement

Japanese Language Proficiency Test and General Examination for Foreign Students.

Examination at the University
A written exam and an interview.

Documents to be Submitted When Applying
Standard Documents Requirement
Following documents are also required.

1. Certificates of the Japanese Language Proficiency Test and General Examination for Foreign Students if the applicant has taken the exams.
2. A recommendation of the Ministry of Foreign Affairs or the diplomatic establishment of one's own country, abroad or in Japan.

Application forms are available at the Admission Office, Student Division in September.

Application deadline: January 31.

GRADUATE PROGRAMS

Graduate School of Medicine (First Year Enrollment : Doctor's 30)

Divisions
Internal Medicine, Pathology, Physiology, Social Medicine, Surgery

Foreign Student Admission

Qualifications for Applicants
Doctor's Program
Standard Qualifications Requirement

Examination at the University
Doctor's Program
The entrance examination is given in October and March. It consists of a written and oral exam plus an interview.

Documents to be Submitted When Applying
Standard Documents Requirement

*

Research Institutes and Centers
Center for Physical Fitness, Center for Radioisotope Science, Information Processing Center, Institute for Medical Science of Aging, Institute for Molecular Science of Medicine, Laboratory Animal Research Center, Sports Medicine and Rehabilitation

Special Programs for Foreign Students
Tutorial system for foreign students: three tutors in charge of foreign students guide and advise in study and daily life.

For Further Information

Undergraduate Admission
Admission Office, Student Division, Aichi Medical University, 21 Yazako Karimata, Nagakute-cho, Aichi-gun, Aichi 480-11 ☎ 05616-2-3311

Graduate Admission
Research Promoting Division, Aichi Medical University, 21 Yazako Karimata, Nagakute-cho, Aichi-gun, Aichi 480-11 ☎ 05616-2-3311

Aichi Shukutoku University
(Aichi Shukutoku Daigaku)

9 Katahira, Nagakute, Nagakute-cho, Aichi-gun, Aichi 480-11   ☎ 05616-2-4111

Faculty
   Profs.   38   Assoc. Profs.   8
   Assist. Profs.   Full–time   6; Part–time   39
Number of Students
   Undergrad.   1, 514
Library   60, 000 volumes

Outline and Characteristics of the College
Aichi Shukutoku University (A. S. U.) was established in 1975 as the highest seat of learning of Aichi Shukutoku Educational Institution, founded in 1905. It started with two departments, Japanese Language and Literature, and English Language and Literature. A third department, Library and Information Science, was added in 1985 to meet the needs of the times and the future as well. And now the University has grown to become one of the best-known institutions of higher education for women in the local communities.

Based on the long tradition of Aichi Shukutoku Educational Institution, A. S. U. aims to carry out research and educational activities, and to train young women for four years to be outstanding citizens who can contribute to society. The students are not only provided with a well-balanced intellectual, moral and physical training, but also prepared for professions which require specialized knowledge and technical skills. They are further trained to be able to endure hardships and to be considerate to others as well as being encouraged to be simple and modest, cheerful and graceful in their daily lives.

Being small in size, the University has a friendly atmosphere promoting close relationships bewteen students and professors and other staff members. Moreover, ever since its establishment, A. S. U. has always been on good terms with the local communities and has done its fair share in cultural and sports activities. Every year it provides them with several special courses. Some of its facilities are open to the public.

The campus of A. S. U. is conveniently situated on the southeastern outskirts of Nagoya. Woodland adjoining its three sides, the grounds are covered with greenery and planted with cherry trees, pines, maples, and many other trees. The air is clean and refreshing, and everything is kept immaculate and beautiful. On this wonderful site stand a modern library, a spacious gymnasium-auditorium, a uniquely-structured students' hall-cafeteria and a cross-shaped main building, the east wing of which accommodates the well-equipped Educational Center for Information Science. Near the gymnasium are six tennis courts and further northeast lies a large running track and sports field. All this makes for a most suitable environment for research, learning and other campus activities.

The majority of the students commute from their own homes, which are mainly in Aichi, Gifu, and Mie Prefectures, while a few students from more distant places live in rooming houses or apartments as well as the dormitory. They all enthusiastically participate in extracurricular activities—the Anniversary Sports Festival in May, the Summer Seminar held off campus during the vacation and the College Festival in the fall, as well as their own club activities.

UNDERGRADUATE PROGRAMS

Faculty of Arts (Freshmen Enrollment: 300)
Department of English Language and Literature
American Literature, Creative Writing, Current of Thought in Western Literature, English Linguistics, English Literature, English Phonetics, History of American Literature, History of English Literature, Interlingual Communication
Department of Japanese Language and Literature
Buddhist Literature, Chinese Classics, History of Japanese Literature, Japanese Calligraphy, Japanese Linguistics, Japanese Literature, Regional Literature
Department of Library and Information Science
Information Media, Information Processing, Information Science, Information Storage and Retrieval, Information Systems, Library and Information Science, Management of Information Systems, Museum Science, Organization of Recorded Materials, Programming, Selection of Recorded Materials, Social Education

Foreign Student Admission
Qualifications for Applicants
Standard Qualifications Requirement
No entrance requirements are stipulated and admission is to be considered on a case-by-case basis.

*

For Further Information
Undergraduate Admission
Dean of Students, Student Office, Educational Affairs Division, Aichi Shukutoku University, 9 Katahira, Nagakute, Nagakute-cho, Aichi-gun, Aichi 480-11 ☎ 05616-2-4111 ext. 230

Aichi University
(Aichi Daigaku)

1-1 Machihata-machi, Toyohashi-shi, Aichi 440
☎ 0532-45-0441

Faculty
    Profs. 98   Assoc. Profs. 60
    Assist. Profs. Full–time 18; Part–time 221

Number of Students
    Undergrad. 8, 722   Grad. 39
Library   752, 067 volumes

Outline and Characteristics of the University
Aichi University was inaugurated as an institution of law and economics under the Old System of Education in the City of Toyohashi in November, 1946, shortly after the end of World War II. The core of the University was the professors and students repatriated from Towa Dobun Shoin University at Shanghai, China, Taihoku Imperial University at Taipei, Formosa, and Keijo Imperial University at Seoul, Korea. In November, 1946 the preparatory postgraduate course was first instituted, and in April, 1947 the Law and Economics Departments of the Faculty of Law and Economics were established, the first faculty ever set up in the field of social sciences in the Chubu District of Japan.

The Inauguratory University Prospectus formulated at that time states that bearing in mind the events of World War II, Japan should endeavor to render herself a true democracy and contribute to the promotion of world peace and culture. Further, the University selected the City of Toyohashi as its site in the hope that it would produce men and women of international culture and outlook, prevent centralization of learning in big cities, and promote the development of local cities and towns. This increasingly significant idea is as keenly alive today as it was at that time, and underlies the trend and direction of education and research at this University.

With the Educational Reform in 1949, which reorganized this institution into a new system university, the Department of Sociology of the Faculty of Letters was instituted, and in April, 1950, the Department of Letters was added to the same Faculty. In 1953, the master's program in law and economics was organised. In 1956, the Faculty of Letters instituted the Department of History, and in the same year the University established an evening course in law and economics on the Nagoya campus. In 1957, the Junior College, devoted to the education of young women in Japanese literature, English literature and domestic science, was inaugurated on the Toyohashi campus.

In 1963 the Faculty of Law and Economics opened the Department of Management and added a doctor's course in private law to its graduate program. The Faculty again added to its program a master's course in management in 1977, a doctor's course in economics in 1978, and a doctor's course in management in 1979.

Thus, Aichi University has carried on its education and research both on the Toyohashi and Nagoya campuses in a free, academic atmosphere based on its founding spirit. Among the programs provided here is Chinese Studies, one of the characteristics of this University not found in other institutions of higher learning. The Chinese Studies Courses belonging to the Faculty of Economics and the Faculty of Law and the Faculty of Letters offer a variety of unique lectures. This University is well known for the research conducted at its Institute for Chinese Studies, the compilation of *the Grand Chinese-Japanese Dictionary*, cultural exchange programs with Chinese universities, and other academic activities in the field of Chinese Studies.

UNDERGRADUATE PROGRAMS

Faculty of Economics (Freshmen Enrollment: 400)
Agricultural Economics, Business Cycles, Chinese Economics, Chinese Market, Econometrics, Economic History (Japanese, European, American and Chinese), Economic Planning, Economic Policy, Economic Theory, Economic Theory of Socialism, Financial Capital, History of Economic Thought, History of Social Thought, Industrial Economics, International Economics, Japanese Economy, Labor Problems, Mathematical Statistics, Money and Banking, National Income Analysis, Public Finance, Social Policy, Social Statistics, Soviet Economy, U. S. Economy

Faculty of Economics (**Evening Course**)
(Freshmen Enrollment: 200)
Agricultural Economics, Business Administration, Chinese Economics, Commerce, Econometrics, Economic History, Economic Policy, Economic Theory, Economic Theory of Socialism, History of Economic Thought, History of Social Thought, Industrial Economics, International Economics, Japanese Economy, Labor Problems, Management, Money and Banking, National Income Analysis, Public Finance, Social Policy, Statistics

Faculty of Law (Freshmen Enrollment: 300)
  Law Major
Administrative Law, Civil Law, Commercial Law, Comparative Law, Constitutional Law, Criminal Law, Criminal Policy, Economic Law, Foreign Legal Systems, International Law, Labor Law, Law of Civil Procedure, Law of Criminal Procedure, Legal History (Japanese, European and Chinese), Philosophy of Law, Private International Law, Public Administration, Sociology of Law, State and Law
  Politics Major
Chinese Constitutional Law, Chinese Law, Contemporary Chinese Politics, History of Political Thought (Japanese, European and Chinese), International Politics, Oriental Diplomatic History, Political History (Japanese, European and Chinese), Political Science, Politics in India

Faculty of Law (**Evening Course**) (Freshmen Enrollment: 200)
Administrative Law, Civil Law, Commercial Law, Comparative Law, Constitutional Law, Criminal Law, History of Political Thought, International Law, International Political History, Labor Law, Law of Civil Procedure, Law of Criminal Procedure, Legal History, Philosophy of Law, Political

History, Political Science, Sociology of Law
Faculty of Letters (Freshmen Enrollment: 300)
  Department of History
Archaeology, Asian History, Cartography, Historical Geography, History of Japanese Thought, Human Geography, Japanese Folk-lore, Japanese History, Palaeography, Social History of Asia, Theory of History, Western History, World History
  Department of Letters
Chinese Classics, Chinese Language, Chinese Literature, Comparative Literature, Drama and Cinema, English and American Literature, English Linguistics, French Linguistics, French Literature, German Linguistics, German Literature, History of Art, History of European Civilization, Japanese Classics, Japanese Linguistics, Japanese Literature, Juvenile Literature, Phonetics, World Literature
  Department of Philosophy
Aesthetics, Contemporary Philosophy, Eastern Philosophy, Ethics, History of Philosophical Thought in Japan, Indian Philosophy, Logic and Science, Science of Religion, Western Philosophy
  Department of Sociology
Contemporary Society, Educational Sociology, Family Sociology, History of Sociology, Industrial Sociology, Marketing, Mass Communication, Psychoanalysis, Social Anthropology, Social History of Japan, Social Pathology, Social Welfare, Urban-Rural Region Sociology
Faculty of Management (Freshmen Enrollment: 400)
Accounting, Auditing, Banking, Business Administration, Business History, Business Statistics, Chinese Management, Commerce, Cost Accounting, Distribution, Enterprise, Financial Management, Foreign Exchange, Foreign Trade, Insurance, Management, Management Accounting, Marketing, Merchandise, Money and Banking, Organization and Management, Personal Management, Production Management, Security Market, Tax Accounting, Transportation

Foreign Student Admission
  Qualifications for Applicants
    Standard Qualifications Requirement
  Examination at the University
    An essay in Japanese and an interview.
  Documents to be Submitted When Applying
    Standard Documents Requirement
    Pledge of School Life and Letter of Guarantee of School Fees are also required.
Application Period: February 6 to February 23
Date of Selection: March 5
Announcement of Results: March 10
Period for Entrance Procedures: by March 20

GRADUATE PROGRAMS

Graduate School of Economics (First Year Enrollment : Master's 25, Doctor's 5)
  Division

Economics
Graduate School of Law (First Year Enrollment :
Master's 30, Doctor's 5)
Divisions
Private Law, Public Law
Graduate School of Management (First Year Enroll-
ment : Master's 15, Doctor's 5)
Division
Management

Foreign Student Admission
Qualifications for Applicants
Master's Program
    Standard Qualifications Requirement
Doctor's Program
    Standard Qualifications Requirement
Examination at the University
Master's Program
    Application Period:
The first reception = August 29 to September 3
The second reception = January 30 to February 4
(A student can apply to either.)
    Preliminary Selection: paper screening
    Entrance Examination:
The first reception = September 19 to September 21
The second reception = March 1 to March 3
    Announcement of Results:
The first reception = September 22
The second reception = March 4
    Period for Entrance Procedures: by March 13
Doctor's Program
    Same as the procedures for the Master's Pro-
gram.
    Documents to be Submitted When Applying
    Standard Documents Requirement
    Certificate of Japanese language proficiency
and Letter of Guarantee of School Fees.
                    *
Research Institutes and Centers
Computer Center, Foreign Language Institute, Insti-
tute for Chinese-Japanese Dictionary Compilation,
Institute of Community Research, Institute of Inter-
national Affairs, Institute of Management and Ac-
counting Research, Research Institute of Industry in
The Chubu District
Facilities/Services for Foreign Students
    The study room for Foreign Students.
Special Programs for Foreign Students
    As for foreign students in the General Educa-
tion Course, general education subjects, foreign lan-
guages and physical education may be replaced by
the courses in "Japanese Language and Japanese
Studies".
For Further Information
    Undergraduate Admission
Entrance Examination Office, Aichi University, 1-1
Machihata-machi, Toyohashi-shi, Aichi 440 ☎ 0532-
45-0441 ext. 250
    Graduate Admission
Graduate School Office, Aichi University, 1-1

Machihata-machi, Toyohashi-shi, Aichi 440 ☎ 0532-
45-0441

Akita University of Economics and Law

(Akita Keizai Hoka Daigaku)

46-1 Morisawa, Sakura, Shimokitate, Akita-shi,
        Akita 010   ☎ 0188-35-6627

UNDERGRADUATE PROGRAMS

Faculty of Economics (Freshmen Enrollment: 200)
Department of Economics
Faculty of Law (Freshmen Enrollment: 200)
Department of Law

Aomori University

(Aomori Daigaku)

248 Abeno, Kohata, Aomori-shi, Aomori 030
        ☎ 0177-38-2114

UNDERGRADUATE PROGRAMS

Faculty of Business Administration (Freshmen En-
rollment: 100)
Department of Business Administration
Faculty of Sociology (Freshmen Enrollment: 100)
Department of Sociology

Aoyama Gakuin University

(Aoyama Gakuin Daigaku)

4-4-25 Shibuya, Shibuya-ku, Tokyo 150
        ☎ 03-409-8111

Faculty
    Profs.   270   Assoc. Profs.   70
    Assist. Profs. Full-time 29; Part-time 686
    Res. Assocs.   44
Number of Students
    Undergrad. 18, 468   Grad. 401
Library   809, 012 volumes

Outline and Characteristics of the University
    Aoyama Gakuin University is a private, coedu-
cational institution of higher learning that began
with the merger of two institutions in 1927. Both institutions were affiliated with the Methodist Church
of the United States and shared the same campus.
One was a school established in 1878, and the other

was a girls' school founded in 1874. In 1949, Aoyama Gakuin University was reorganized into a new system university under the educational reform act of the same year.

At present Aoyama Gakuin University has two campuses in Tokyo: one is the Aoyama Campus in Shibuya which is located in the central part of Tokyo, and the other is the Setagaya Campus, 13 km south-west of the Aoyama Campus. The Setagaya Campus houses the College of Science and Engineering. More than 18, 000 students attend the University where there are two undergraduate divisions--the day division and the evening division--and six graduate divisions. The day division consists of four colleges and two schools and the evening division has two colleges and a school. Each college or school consists of one to five departments.

The University has another compus at Atsugi, 45 km south-west of the Aoyama Campus. Students who enter the University will receive their first two years of education on the Atsugi Campus. However, science or engineering majors will attend courses there only during their freshman year.

Those who are enrolled in the evening division courses and graduate division courses will study during their entire years on the Aoyama Campus after they enter the University.

THE EDUCATIONAL POLICY OF AOYAMA GAKUIN

Aoyama Gakuin has as its aim education based upon the Christian faith and as its purpose the building up of persons who live in sincerity before God, who seek for truth with humility, and who actively take responsibility for all men and for society in a spirit of love and service.

UNDERGRADUATE PROGRAMS

School of Business Administration (Freshmen Enrollment: 500)

Department of Business Administration
Accounting, Administrative Management, Advertising, Auditing, Banking, Budgetary Control, Business Administration, Business History, Business Statistics, Circulation and Distribution, Commercial Business, Commercial Policy, Corporate Evaluation, Corporate Strategy and Policy, Financial Management, Foreign Exchange, Foreign Trade, Insurance, International Marketing, Management Analysis, Management Information Systems, Management Psychology, Management Sociology, Marine Transportation and Port Economics, Marketing Management, Organization Theory, Personnel Management, Production Management, Stock Market
School of Business Administration (**Evening Division**) (Freshmen Enrollment   200)
Department of Business Administration
See the listing for Day Course.
College of Economics (Freshmen Enrollment: 500)
Department of Economics

Agricultural Economics, Bookkeeping, Developmental Economics, Econometrics, Economic Geography, Economic History, Economic Policy, Economic Statistics, Economic Theory, Financial Accounting, History of Economics, Industrial Organization, International Economics, International Monetary Theory, Labor Economics, Local Finance, Monetary Theory, Planned Economics, Public Finance, Regional Economics, Social Security
College of Economics (**Evening Division**) (Freshmen Enrollment   250)
Department of Economics
See the listing for Day Course.
School of International Politics, Economics and Business (Freshmen Enrollment: 225)
Department of International Business
Area Studies, Business Management in Japan, Industrial Systems, International Financial Management, International Management, International Marketing, International Personnel Management, International Transportation, Management, Management Analysis, Multinational Business Management, Organization Theory, Principles of Marketing, Systems and Decision Science
Department of International Economics
Area Studies, Comparative Industrial Relations, Economic Policy, Economics of Developing Economies, International Development Policy, International Economic Order, International Economics, International Economic Statistics, International Finance, International Trade, Japanese Economy, Principles of Economics, World Resource Management
Department of International Politics
Area Studies, Comparative Cultures, Comparative Political Systems, Diplomatic History, History of International Relations, Interantional Security policy, International Law, International Mass Communications, International Organizations, International Politics, Japanese Politics, Laws Relating to International Relations, Political Science
College of Law (Freshmen Enrollment: 460)
Department of Private Law
Department of Public Law
Administrative Law, Anglo-American Law, Bankruptcy Law, Civil Law, Civil Procedure, Commercial Law, Constitutional Law, Copyright Law, Criminal Law, Criminal Procedure, Criminology, Doctrine of Political Science, Economic Relations Law, European Legal History, French Law, German Law, History of Legal Thought, History of Political Thought, International Law, Japanese Legal History, Labor Law, Law of Banking and Law of Security Exchanges, Law of Communications, Law of Education, Law of Industrial Property, Law of Leaselands, Dwellings and Buildings, Law of Socialist States, Local Government Law, Philosophy of Law, Political History, Private International Law, Public Administration, Roman Law, Social Security Law, Sociology of Law, Tax Law, Theory of Political Process

College of Literature (Freshmen Enrollment: 900)

Department of Education

Administration and Management of Education and Teacher Training Course, Curriculum and Teaching Methods, Educational Psychology, Social Education and Educational Sociology, Study of Philosophy and History of Education

Department of English

American Literature, American Thoughts and Cultures, Bible in English, British Thoughts and Cultures, Communication, English Linguistics, English Literature, English Phonetics, History of American Literature, History of English Literature, History of the English Language, Methods of Teaching English

Department of French

French Culture and Society, French Grammar, French Language, French Literature, French Phonetics, History of French Literature, History of the French Language, Methods of Teaching French

Department of History

Archaeology, Historical Science, Japanese History, Museology, Oriental History, Study of Ancient Manuscripts, Western History

Department of Japanese

Calligraphy, Chinese Classics, History of Japanese Literature, Japanese Grammar, Japanese Language, Japanese Literature

College of Literature (**Evening Division**) (Freshmen Enrollment: 300)

Department of Education

Department of English

See the listing for Day Course.

College of Science and Engineering (Freshmen Enrollment: 510)

Department of Chemistry

Analytical Chemistry, Biochemistry, Bioorganic Chemistry, Chemical Engineering, Chemical Thermodynamics, Co-ordination Chemistry, Electrochemistry, Inorganic Chemistry, Physical Chemistry, Polymer Chemistry, Quantum Chemistry, Radiochemistry, Structural Chemistry, Synthetic Organic Chemistry

Department of Electronics and Electrical Engineering

Applied Electrochemistry, Applied Electronics, Communication Engineering, Computer and Digital Systems, Control Engineering, Electrical Circuits, Electrical Engineering, Electrical Machine Design, Electrical Materials, Electrical Measurements, Electric Machinery, Electric Power and Its Application, Electroacoustics, Electromagnetics, Electromagnetic Waves, Electronic Circuits, Electronic Communications, Heat Engines, High Frequency Electronics, High Voltage Engineering, Information Processing, Integrated Circuit Engineering, Magnetics, Power Generation and Transmission, Quantum Electronics

Department of Industrial and Systems Engineering

Behavioral Science, Computer Architecture, Computer Data Structures, Data Communication, Engineering Economy, Human Engineering, Industrial Engineering, Industrial Psychology, Management Systems Analysis, Operations Research, Production Engineering, Production Management, Quality Control, Software Engineering, Systems Approach, Systems Engineering, Systems Simultation, Work System Design

Department of Mechanical Engineering

Automotive Engineering, Control Engineering, Energy Technology, Engineering Materials, Engineering Mechanics, Engineering Plasticity, Environmental Engineering, Fluid Dynamics, Heat and Mass Transfer, Heat Engines, Hydraulics, Machine Design, Machine Dynamics, Machine Tool, Materials Science, Mechanical Engineering, Piping Engineering, Powder Engineering, Project Engineering, Robotics, Thermodynamics, Tool Engineering, Transportation Machines, Tribology, Vacuum Engineering

Department of Physics

Applied Electromagnetism, Applied Physics, Astrophysics, Computer and Digital Systems, Computer Architecture, Diffraction Physics, Elasticity, Electromagnetic Wave, Electromagnetism, Fluid Dynamics, Geophysics, High Energy Physics, Magnetics, Nuclear Physics, Nuclear Radiation Measurements, Physical Metrology, Physics of Semiconductor Devices, Quantum Physics, Solid State Physics, Statistical Physics, Thermal Physics

Foreign Student Admission

Qualifications for Applicants

1. Those who have completed a 12-year course of study in school education in a foreign country, or those who have completed a course equivalent to the aforementioned and who have been approved by the Minister of Education of Japan. This includes those who will complete a required course of study by the end of the March prior to entrance. As to those who have studied in a Japanese high school, the period of their study must be less than one year.

2. Those who have completed a required course of study in a school for foreign high-school students which is located in Japan but is not run under Art. 1, Chapt. 1 of the School Education Law of Japan may not apply.

3. Those who hold the Diploma granted by the International Baccalaureate Office, and who are over 18 years old.

4. (a) Those who apply for admission from abroad are not required to take the Japanese Language Proficiency Test (JLPT) and the General Examination for Foreign Students (GEFS).

   (b) Those who reside in Japan and apply for admission to the College of Science and Engineering are required to take both the JLPT and the GEFS on Science, whereas those who apply for admission to the Colleges or Schools other than the College of Science and Engineering are required to take only the JLPT, prior to submission of applications.

(c) Those who have studied the final year in a Japanese high school are exempeted from JLPT and GEFS.

5. The College of Economics of the Evening Division and the School of International Politics, Economics and Business do not accept applications from foreign students.

6. The Evening Division offers courses mainly for students working in the daytime. Hence, a student visa will not be issued to those who are admitted to study at the Evening Division. The applicants for examinations for admission to the Evening Division are limited to persons who have a likely possibility of obtaining permission to renew their residential status in Japan for more than four consecutive years at the time of taking the examinations.

Examination at the University

Admission of foreign students to the University will be made by the following method. A preliminary selection will be a review of the application documents. Those who pass the preliminary selection will take a second examination consisting of an interview in Japanese and, if necessary, a written examination in other fields related to the candidate's fields of interest. In the case of those residents in Japan, and for the College of Science and Engineering, there is no preliminary examination.

A bulletin for Information for Foreign Students with application forms will be available at the Admissions Office in mid-August. Specific information on examinations, test dates, examination fees and tuition are given in this bulletin.

Application Procedures:

1. Applications for the preliminary selection from among those nationals applying for admission to the University from abroad will be accepted only if they are mailed to the Admissions Office. Applications must reach the office no later than early October. Those residents in Japan should reach the office no later than early December. Those residents in Japan and for the College of Science and Engineering should submit applications in person on specified date in January.

2. The applicants from abroad will be notified of the results of their first examination, and the date for the second examination will be advised by mail to those who pass the first examination by late October. Those who have passed the first examination are required to come to Japan by the appointed application period of the second examination, and submit applications in person for the second examination to the Admissions Office.

3. For applicants residing in Japan, the results of their first examination will be posted on the campus bulletin board in late January. Those who have passed the first examination should submit in person applications (which will be given at the time of the announcement of the results of the first examination) with a specified fee of postal money order for the second examination to the Admissions Office on specified date in January.

4. Specific information on the test date and the testing places for the second examination will be given to those who have passed the first examination.

5. The results of the second examination will be announced on the bulletin board between late February and early March.

Admission Procedures:

Admission procedures will be conducted during the appointed period for admission procedures in mid-March.

Those admitted should file registration forms after paying the prescribed tuition and fees within the period of admission procedures.

The payment of the various fees required at the time of admission procedures should be made in Japanese currency. and cannot be postponed or made by installment.

Documents to be Submitted When Applying

1. Application for Admission to Aoyama Gakuin University (Foreign Students)

2. Application Form for Entrance Examination.

3. Letter of Recommendation.

4. Proficiency in Japanese Form.

5. Letter of Guarantee.

6. Statement of Physical Condition.

7. The Certificate of Graduation or Diploma, or an official letter stating expectation of graduation either in Japanese or in English. In the case of those who hold the Diploma granted by the International Baccalaureate Office they should present official transcripts of six .subjects on the final examination.

8. Official transcripts from all schools which the applicants have attended in foreign countries or their native country either in Japanese or in English. Those who have studied in a Japanese high school are required to present official transcripts from that school in addition to the documents mentioned above.

9. Applicants from abroad should mail a document certifying their identity, such as a copy of their passport. Applicants residing in Japan should send their Alien Registration Certificate stating their residential status in Japan.

Those who reside in Japan and apply for admission to the College of Science and Engineering are required to use the Application Form for Entrance Examination for the College of Science and Engineering.

GRADUATE PROGRAMS

Graduate School of Business Administration (First Year Enrollment : Master's 15, Doctor's 3)
Division
Business Administration

Graduate School of Economics (First Year Enrollment : Master's 15, Doctor's 3)
Divisions
Economic Policy (Doctor's), Economics (Master's)

Graduate School of International Politics, Economics and Business (First Year Enrollment : -year Doctor's 9)
Divisions
International Business, International Economics, International Politics

Graduate School of Law (First Year Enrollment : Master's 20, Doctor's 4)
Divisions
Private Law, Public Law

Graduate School of Literature (First Year Enrollment : Master's 52, Doctor's 15)
Divisions
Education, English and American Literature, French Language and Literature, History, Japanese Language and Literature, Psychology

Graduate School of Science and Engineering (First Year Enrollment : Master's 40, Doctor's 20)
Divisions
Chemistry, Electronics and Electrical Engineering, Industrial and Systems Engineering, Mechanical Engineering, Physics

Foreign Student Admission
Qualifications for Applicants
Master's Program
    Standard Qualifications Requirement
    Applicants to the following Courses must satisfy the specific requirements.
Education Course: Those who have taken more than 20 credits in Education including Educational Psychology, or those who have the equivalent qualification.
Psychology Course: Those who have majored in Psychology, or taken more than 32 credits in the field of Psychology.
English and American Literature Course: Those who have majored in English Literature, American Literature or English Linguistics.
Doctor's Program
    Standard Qualifications Requirement
    Examination at the University
Master's Program
Education Course:
1. Writing test in special knowledge of Education
2. Essay-writing on a given subject
3. Japanese translation from English scholarly books
4. Interview

Psychology Course:
1. Writing test in special knowledge of Psychology (A)
2. Writing test in special knowledge of Psychology (B)
3. Japanese translation from English scholarly books
4. Interview

English and American Literature Course:
1. Japanese translation from English scholarly books
2. Writing an essay in English on a given subject
3. Writing test in special knowledge of English Literature, American Literature or English Linguistics
4. Foreign language other than English: French, German and Spanish
5. Interview

French Language and Literature Course:
1. French language and literature (I)
2. French language and literature (II)
3. Foreign language other than French: English or German
4. Interview

Japanese Language and Literature Course:
1. Writing test in special knowledge of Japanese language and literature
2. Foreign language: English, French or German
3. Interview

History Course:
1. Foreign language: English
2. Foreign language other than English: Chinese, French, German, Russian or Spanish
3. Writing test in special knowledge of Japanese history, Oriental history, European history or Archaeology
4. Interview

Economics Course:
1. Foreign language: English
2. Writing test in special knowledge of Economics. Applicants must choose two subjects out of: (1) Economic history, (2) Economic policy, (3) Money and finance, (4) Public finance, (5) Regional economics and (6) Theoretical Economics
3. Interview

Private Law Course and Public Law Course:
1. Foreign language: English, French or German
2. Writing test in special knowledge of law. Applicants must choose two subjects out of: (1) Administrative law, (2) Civil law, (3) Civil procedure law, (4) Commercial law, (5) Constitution, (6) Criminal law, (7) Criminal policy, (8) Criminal procedure law, (9) Economic law, (10) European legal history, (11) Labor law, (12) Legal philosophy, (13) Political history, (14) Politics, (15) Private International law, (16) Public International law.
3. Interview

Business Administration Course:

1. Foreign language: English
2. Writing test in special knowledge of Business Administration, Accounting or Commerce
3. Writing test in special knowledge of the field in which an applicant is expected to major after admission
4. Interview

Chemistry Course:
Electronics and Electrical Engineering Course:
Industrial and Systems Engineering Course:
Mechanical Engineering Course:
Physics Course:
1. Mathematics
2. Japanese translation from English scholarly books
3. Special subject (Written examination)
4. Interview

Doctor's Program
Education Course:
1. Japanese translation from English scholarly books
2. Japanese translation from French or German scholarly books
3. Examination of master's thesis
4. Interview

Psychology Course:
1. Japanese translation from English scholarly books
2. Japanese translation from French or German scholarly books
3. Examination of master's thesis
4. Interview

English Language and Literature Course:
1. Japanese translation from English scholarly books
2. Writing an essay in English on a given subject
3. Writing test in special knowledge of English Literature, American Literature or English Linguistics
4. Foreign language other than English: French or German
5. Examination of master's thesis
6. Interview

French Language and Literature Course:
1. French language and literature (I)
2. French language and literature (II)
3. Foreign language other than French: English or German
4. Examination of master's thesis
5. Interview

Japanese Language and Literature Course:
1. Writing test in special knowledge of Japanese language and literature
2. Foreign language: Applicants must choose two languages from English, French or German
3. Examination of master's thesis
4. Interview

History Course:
1. Foreign language: English
2. Foreign language other than English: Chinese,

French, German, Russian or Spanish
3. Examination of master's thesis
4. Interview

Economic Policy Course:
1. First foreign language: English
2. Second foreign language (French and German) or Mathematics
3. Examination of master's thesis
4. Interview

Private Law Course and Public Law Course:
1. Foreign language: Applicants must choose two languages from English, French and German
2. Examination of master's thesis
3. Interview

Business Administration Course:
1. First foreign language
2. Second foreign language
3. Examination of master's thesis
4. Interview

Note: Applicants must choose two languages from English, French, German and Russian besides their mother tongue, and decide one of the two as a first foreign language and the other as a second one. Those whose mother tongue is not Japanese may take Japanese as a second foreign language.

Chemistry Course:
Electronics and Electrical Engineering Course:
Industrial and Systems Engineering Course:
Mechanical Engineering Course:
Physics Course:
1. Japanese translation from English scholarly books
2. Foreign language: English, French or German
3. Special subject (Written examination)
4. Interview

International Politics Course:
1. Foreign language: Chinese, English, French, German or Russian
2. Writing test in special knowledge of Politics
3. Interview

International Economics Course:
1. Foreign language: Chinese, English, French, German or Russian
2. Writing test in special knowledge of Economics
3. Interview

International Business Course:
1. Foreign language: Chinese, English, French, German or Russian
2. Writing test in special knowledge of Business
3. Interview

Documents to be Submitted When Applying
  Standard Documents Requirement
  Following documents are also required.
1. Applicants must submit a Proficiency in Japanese form.
2. Applicants for Doctor's Program must submit a copy of their master's thesis either in Japanese or English translation in case that the thesis is not written in either of these languages.

*

Research Institutes and Centers
Information Science Research Center, Institute for Economic Research, Institute for Judicial Research, Institute for Research for Business Administration, Institute for Research in International Politics and Economics

Facilities/Services for Foreign Students
Support Systems for Foreign Students:
To enable foreign students at Aoyama Gakuin University to adjust to their environment and to pursue their studies effectively, the following support systems have been established.

Foreign Student Adviser:
A faculty member will be assigned to each foreign student upon arrival on campus. The student may consult the adviser on any academic or personal matters.

Foreign Student Tutor:
A graduate or undergraduate Japanese student will be assigned to each foreign student to assist the foreign student in all possible ways, including the latter's attempt in overcoming the language and cultural barriers.

International Exchange Office (Gaiji-ka):
This office will assist foreign students on matters beyond the help of the foreign student advisers and tutors, such as the technicalities of the immigrations regulations.

Health Administration Center:
This Center exists for the purpose of prevention and early detection of student illness and the promotion of good health. It provides periodical health cheek-ups in the spring and the fall and also vaccinations of various kinds. Emergency treatment and ambulance service to outside hospitals are also a part of its responsibilities.

Student Counseling Center:
Students may make use of the Counseling Center where counselors will talk with students on problems related to academic work, personality, human relations, adaptability, mental health, etc., in an attempt to resolve the problems so that students will be able to function satisfactorily.

For Further Information
Undergraduate Admission
Admissions Office, Aoyama Gakuin University, 4-4-25 Shibuya, Shibuya-ku, Tokyo 150 ☎ 03-409-8111 ext. 2150

Graduate Admission
Graduate School Division, Department of Academic Affairs, Aoyama Gakuin University, 4-4-25 Shibuya, Shibuya-ku, Tokyo 150 ☎ 03-409-8111 ext. 2146
Science and Engineering: Registrar's Office, College of Science and Engineering, Aoyama Gakuin University, 6-16-1 Chitosedai, Setagaya-ku, Tokyo 157 ☎ 03-307-2888 ext. 310

Asahikawa University
(Asahikawa Daigaku)

3-23, Nagayama, Asahikawa-shi, Hokkaido 079
☎ 0166-48-3121

Faculty
Profs. 19   Assoc. Profs. 12
Assist. Profs. Full-time 1; Part-time 42
Number of Students
Undergrad. 1, 106
Library 120, 000 volumes

Outline and Characteristics of the University
Asahikawa University was originally founded as a girls' sewing school in 1898, but the present institution was established as a four-year University in 1968. The board of regents of Asahikawa University administers not only the four-year college but also a kindergarten, a high school and a junior college for women. All institutions are located in Nagayama area of Asahikawa. Asahikawa University is divided into two programs: the daytime program and the evening program. The daytime program has two departments: the Department of Economics and the Department of Trade and Commerce. The Department of Economics has two courses: Economics, and Law and Administration. The Department of Trade also has two courses: the Language Course with the option of either English or Russian, and the Business, Management and Commerce Course. Each of these courses maintains its own curriculum. The Faculty of Economics of the evening course offers chances of retraining and acquiring various specialities to working members of the community. Asahikawa University also has a research institute, the Regional Research Institute.

Asahikawa University aims at being liberal and international in its character, and at the same time open to members of the local community as much as possible. The University's educational target is nurturing a pioneer spirit and the individual quality of each student. Each student is required to take a seminar and it is our policy to maintain small classes. This facilitates intimate communication between the instructors and the students as well as the communication among the students themselves.

Therefore, one of the main characteristics of this University "small is beautiful"--can be said to be its most attractive point, making Asahikawa University an ideal place to further one's education.

UNDERGRADUATE PROGRAMS

Faculty of Economics (Freshmen Enrollment 150)
Department of Economics
American Economy, Economic History, Economic History of Hokkaido, Economic Policy, Economics,

Finance, History of Economic Theory, International Economy, Japanese Economy, Socialist Economy

Department of Trade and Commerce

Accounting, Business Administration, International Finance, International Relations, Management and Information system, Marketing, Trade

Faculty of Economics (Evening Course) (Freshmen Enrollment 70)

Department of Economics

American Economy, Economic History, Economic History of Hokkaido, Economic Policy, Economics, Finance, History of Economic Theory, International Economy, Japanese Economy, Socialist Economy

Foreign Student Admission

Qualifications for Applicants

Standard Qualifications Requirement

Examination at the University

Faculty of Economics (Day Course)

1. For the applicants recommended by a high school principal: Short Essay and Interview
2. For general admission: Japanese (Classics not included) and English

However, the University takes into consideration the foreign linguistic background of the overseas applicants.

Documents to be Submitted When Applying

Standard Documents Requirement

*

Research Institutes and Centers

Asahikawa University Regional Research Institute

Facilities/Services for Foreign Students

The Counselling Section extends its counselling services to all students who require it in the areas of academic and general student life.

For Further Information

Undergraduate Admission

General Affairs Section, Asahikawa University 3-23, Nagayama, Asahikawa-shi, Hokkaido 079 ☎ 0166-48-3121

Asahi University
(Asahi Daigaku)

1851 Hozumi, Hozumi-cho, Motosu-gun, Gifu 501-02 ☎ 05832-6-6131

Faculty
    Profs. 57   Assoc. Profs. 39
    Assist. Profs. Full-time 45; Part-time 282
    Res. Assocs. 98
Number of Students
    Undergrad. 2, 525   Grad. 2, 278
Library 143, 750 volumes

Outline and Characteristics of the University

Asahi University is a unique private university in Japan. It consists of a School of Dentistry a School of Business Administration and a School of Law. Originally established as the Gifu College of Dentistry in 1971, it was reorganized into Asahi University with the addition of the School of Business Administration in 1985. The School of Law opened in 1987, and so its uniqueness as a professional university is clearly estblished.

The ideal of the University is to educate competent gentlemen; promising dentists who have the ambition to continue research as well as the humanity to share a patient's sufferings; successful businessmen who have the will to open the community of nations for future business in the world; and full-fledged members of society with sufficient theoretical and practical knowledge of law, bravely advancing with the diversified and ever-changing needs of the world.

The University has four Schools--School of Liberal Arts, School of Dentistry, School of Business Administration-and school of Law-and Graduate School of Dentistry.

The campus is conveniently situated in the rural town of Hozumi-cho, near Gifu city. The environment is especially favored by a quiet natural beauty, which inspires students to greater efforts in their studies, and helps to cultivate their minds.

Being rather small in size, the University has the unique advantage of maintaining cordial and friendly relationships between teachers and students. This is one of the greatest merits of the University.

One of the important aspects of the University is the fact that it has always been on good terms with local communities through its activities in dental treatments at the Hospital attached to the University.

UNDERGRADUATE PROGRAMS

School of Business Administration (Freshmen Enrollment: 200)

Department of Business Administration

Accounting, Business Administration, Business History, Finance Economics, Firm Management, Hospital Management, Management, Management Science

School of Dentistry (Freshmen Enrollment: 140)

Department of Dentistry

Anatomy, Dental Materials and Engineering, Endodontics, Internal Medicine, Operative Dentistry, Oral Anatomy and Histology, Oral and Maxillofacial Surgery, Oral Biochemistry, Oral Microbiology, Oral Pathology, Oral Pharmacology, Oral Physiology, Oral Radiology and Diagnosis, Orthodontics, Pedodontics, Periodontics, Preventive Dentistry, Prosthetic Dentistry, Surgery

School of Law (Freshmen Enrollment: 200)

Department of Law

Administrative Law, Anglo-American Law, Bankruptcy Law, City Planning, Civil Law, Commercial Law, Constitutional Law, Corporate Accounting Law, Criminal Law, Criminal Policy, Economic Law, German Law, Housing and Land Legislation, Housing and Land Policy, International Law, International Private Law, Labor Law, Law of Civil Procedure, Law of Criminal Procedure, Law of International Business, Law of Trade and Transactions, Legal History, Medical Law, Patent and Copyright Law, Philosophy of Law, Political Science, Real Estate Appraisal, Real Estate Legislation, Real Estate Management, Real Property, Social Law, Tax Law, Urban Problem, Western Legal History

Foreign Student Admission

Qualifications for Applicants
Standard Qualifications Requirement
Those who have received the International Baccalaureate and are 18 years or older may also apply.
Examination at the University
Same examination as that for Japanese applicants.
Documents to be Submitted When Applying
Standard Documents Requirement
Certificates of the Japanese Language Proficiency Test and General Examination for Foreign Students.

Application form and other necessary document forms are available at the Admission Office of Asahi University early in January. Applicants are required to submit the specified application documents to the Admission Office by January 31.

GRADUATE PROGRAMS

Graduate School of Dentistry (First Year Enrollment : Doctor's 18)
Division
Dental Science

Foreign Student Admission

Qualifications for Applicants
Doctor's Program
Standard Qualifications Requirement
Applicants must be graduates of School/Faculty of Dentistry.
Examination at the University
Doctor's Program
Entrance examination: (1) a foreign language (mainly English), (2) the applicant's majoring subject and (3) personal interview.
Documents to be Submitted When Applying
Standard Documents Requirement

*

Research Institutes and Centers
PDI Research Center
Special Programs for Foreign Students
Japanese Language, Japanese Cultural Affairs
For Further Information
Undergraduate and Graduate Admission
Admission Office, Asahi University, 1851 Hozumi, Hozumi-cho, Motosu-gun, Gifu 501-02 ☎ 05832-6-6131 ext. 305

Ashikaga Institute of Technology
(Ashikaga Kogyo Daigaku)
268-1 Omae-cho, Ashikaga-shi, Tochigi 326
☎ 0284-62-0605

Faculty
   Profs. 48   Assoc. Profs. 32
   Assist. Profs. Full-time 33; Part-time 60
   Res. Assocs. 10
Number of Students
   Undergrad. 2, 445
Library 86, 442 volumes

Outline and Characteristics of the University

Ashikaga Institute of Technology (AIT) was initially established in 1967 with three departments within the Faculty of Engineering—Department of Mechanical Engineering, Department of Electrical Engineering, and Department of Architecture. Later in 1973, Department of Civil Engineering and Department of Planning Technology were added.

One of the characteristics of AIT resides in the course of Religious Studies. The course reflects AIT's background. It was established by a religious organization founded by 17 leading Buddhist temples in the city of Ashikaga. Thanks to its rather small size, AIT has been able to promote informal and friendly relationships between faculty members and students.

The city of Ashikaga where AIT has its campus is about 80 kilometers north of Tokyo. In the 15th century, the Ashikaga area was famous throughout the nation as the site of Ashikaga School, Japan's oldest school which is said to have had an enrollment of as many as 3, 000 students. Present-day Ashikaga is the second largest city in Tochigi Prefecture with a population of approximately 170, 000 and is widely known for its textile industry.

AIT's campus, located in the western suburb of Ashikaga and covering an area of about 170, 000 m², provides an ideal learning environment rich in natural beauty. The majority of AIT students are from the Tokyo metropolitan area and its neighboring prefectures. Presently, however, three students from Southeast Asia are also enrolled. As part of its educational exchange program with foreign countries, AIT is affiliated with a Chinese equivalent—Zhejiang Institute of Technology, in Hangzhou City of Zhejiang Province. The affiliation has been promoting various academic activities among the faculty members of both institutes.

Although it is one of the newer universities in Japan, AIT is making its utmost efforts to enhance its resources for research and education to provide the world with scientists and engineers with enriched mind and wisdom.

UNDERGRADUATE PROGRAMS

Faculty of Engineering (Freshmen Enrollment: 550)
Department of Architecture
Architectural History, Architectural Material, Architectural Planning, Environmental Engineering, Structural Mechanics in Architecture, Urbanism
Department of Civil Engineering
Concrete Engineering, Hydraulics, Sanitation Engineering, Soil Mechanics, Steel Structures, Structural Mechanics, Surveying, Traffic Engineering
Department of Electrical Engineering
Digital Circuits, Electrical Engineering, Electric Circuits, Electromagnetics, Electronic Circuits
Department of Mechanical Engineering
Engineering Mechanics, Fluid Mechanics, Machine Tools, Metal Materials, Strength of Materials, Thermodynamics
Department of Planning Technology
Computer Science and Applications, Industrial Psychology, Managerial Economics, Measurement Engineering, Planning, Reliability Engineering, System Engineering

Foreign Student Admission
Qualifications for Applicants
Standard Qualifications Requirement
Examination at the University
Screening by documents submitted by applicants, plus interviews in Japanese.
Documents to be Submitted When Applying
Standard Documents Requirement
Application period: Nov. 6-Nov. 26
Interviews: Dec.
Announcement of successful applicants: Jan.

*
For Further Information
Undergraduate Admission
Section of Instructional Affairs, Ashikaga Institute of Technology, 268-1 Omae-cho, Ashikaga-shi, Tochigi 326 ☎ 0284-62-0605 ext. 215

Ashiya University
(Ashiya Daigaku)

13-22 Rokurokuso-cho, Ashiya-shi, Hyogo 659
☎ 0797-23-0661

Faculty
　　Profs.　42　　Assoc. Profs.　19
　　Assist. Profs.　Full-time　23; Part-time　49
Number of Students
　　Undergrad.　881　　Grad.　48
Library　142, 249 volumes

Outline and Characteristics of the University
Ashiya University is a private coeducational institution. Since its foundation on April 1, 1964, the University has continuously grown, with the Faculty of Education as the main field of concentration. The Faculty is based on the theoretical as well as practical studies of vocational guidance, which is the life work of Dr. Shigekazu Fukuyama, founder and president of Ashiya University.

Education is meant to guide students in discovering their life's ambitions and vocations, and acquiring the ability to achieve these vocations and serve society constructively. Thus, vocational guidance constitutes an integral part of education. To fulfill these needs, in 1966 the Department of Industrial Education was added. In 1968, the Graduate School of Education became accredited offering a Master's degree and Doctorate in Education. In 1972, the Faculty of Education was expanded to include the Department of English and English Literature. In the following year, the Department of Child Education was added to the curricula. The Graduate School was expanded in 1985, offering a Master's degree in English & English Literature, and again in 1986 to include a Master's degree in Technical Education. This broadening range of course offerings gives students a sufficient knowledge of the range of occupational alternatives.

The university is internationally acclaimed for its biennial International Conference on Vocational Guidance, supported by the Ministry of Education, Science and Culture of Japan. Dr. Fukuyama has projects implemented internationally. One such subject is a survey called the Test for Appraising the Ability to Choose Methodically Among Occupations, commonly known as the F-Test. The F-Test has been conducted in Hawaii since 1973, and in New York City since 1984. Application has expanded to include England, France, Switzerland, West Germany, and the Soviet Union. Comparative studies based on the findings derived from the F-Test have provided new information useful in planning school programs for vocational guidance internationally.

The University is located in a mountainous residential area of Ashiya City, a cosmopolitan center located on the edge of Rokko National Park. The beautiful trees, ponds, gardens, as well as the view of Osaka Bay, exquisitely harmonize with the excellent scenery of the surrounding mountains.

UNDERGRADUATE PROGRAMS

Faculty of Education (Freshmen Enrollment: 250)
Department of Child Education
Child Education, Child Physical Education, Child Psychology, Children's Dietetics, Children's Formative Art, Children's Health, Child Welfare, Developmental Psychhology, Early Childhood Education, Home Education Theory, Juvenile Culture, Juvenile Literature, Learning Psychology, Mental Hygienics, Pediatric Nursing, Pediatrics

Department of Education

Broadcasting Education, Counseling, Educational Administration, Educational Curriculum, Educational Philosophy, Educational Psychology, Educational Sociology, Educational Systems, Health Education, History of Education, Measurement & Evaluation in Education, Methods in Education, Methods in Educational Survey, Pedagogy, School Management, Social Education, Social Education, Social Psychology, Vocational Guidance

Department of English and English Literature Education

American Culture, British Culture, Engilsh Education, English & American Literature, English Grammar, English Language, History of English & American Literature, History of English Education, History of English Language, Linguistics, Western Classical Literature

Department of Industrial Education

Automotive Engineering, Counseling, Electrical Engineering, Electronic Engineering, Engineering, Health Education, History of Industrial Education, Hospital Management, Hotel Management, Human Engineering, Human Relations, Industrial Design, Industrial Hygienics, Industrial Organization Theory, Industrial Psychology, Industrial Welfare, Information Science, Labor Management, Mechanical Engineering, Organization & Administration of Vocational Guidance, Productivity Education, Safety Education, Techniques in Vocational Guidance, Vocational Guidance

Foreign Student Admission

Qualifications for Applicants

Standard Qualifications Requirement

Examination at the University

No entrance requirements are prescribed and admission is considered on an individual basis, evaluating the learning ability of each applicant.

Documents to be Submitted When Applying

Standard Documents Requirement

GRADUATE PROGRAMS

Graduate School of Education (First Year Enrollment : Master's 20, Doctor's 5)

Divisions

Education, English and English Literature Education, Technical Education

Foreign Student Admission

Qualifications for Applicants

Master's Program

Standard Qualifications Requirement

Doctor's Program

Standard Qualifications Requirement

Examination at the University

Same as Undergraduate.

Documents to be Submitted When Applying

Standard Documents Requirement

*

Research Institutes and Centers

Computation Center, Japanese Culture Center for Japanese Classical Music, Technical Research Institute, Video Theater

For Further Information

Undergraduate and Graduate Admission

Admissions Office, Ashiya University, 13-28 Rokurokuso-cho, Ashiya-shi, Hyogo 659 ☎ 0797-23-0661 ext. 2115

Asia University

(Ajia Daigaku)

5-24-10 Sakai, Musashino-shi, Tokyo 180

☎ 0422–54–3111

Faculty

Profs. 92   Assoc. Profs. 36

Assist. Profs. Full–time 18; Part–time 266

Res. Assocs. 2

Number of Students

Undergrad. 6, 020   Grad. 134

Library   361, 386 volumes

Outline and Characteristics of the University

Asia University is a relatively new university. Koa Senmon Gakko, the parent school of Asia University, was established in 1941. At the end of World War II in 1945, the school name was changed to Nihon Keizai Senmon Gakko. In 1950, there was a reform in the Japanese school system which resulted in another name change, to the Nihon Junior College of Economics.

By 1954, Japan had recovered from the wartime devastation and entered into an age of relative stability. A Foreign Student Department was initiated in this same year in an effort to reopen relations with other Asian countries. Nihon Junior College of Economics was the first university in post-war Japan to accept a large number of foreign students. Asia University has admitted many foreign students into the regular faculties as well as into the "Special Course for Foreign Students" (Japanese Language Course) since those early years.

In 1955, Asia University was established. During academic year 1976, Asia University established an International Relations Department in the Faculty of Economics. At present, the University is composed of three faculties: Business Administration, Economics, and Law. Each faculty has a graduate school which offers both the Master's and the Doctoral degrees. There are over 6, 000 students, including 350 foreign students from 10 countries, enrolled at the University.

The mission or goal of the University is to foster a spirit of self-help and cooperation among its students, to assist the student in developing a feeling of independence, to bring forth a student's maximum potential, and to help the student find fulfillment through cooperation and mutual understanding. The major objective of Asia University is to provide the finest educational program possible for its students so that upon graduation they may make a positive contribution to society, Asia, and the world.

Asia University is blessed with a quiet, natural environment as well as with a convenient means of commuter transportation. It takes only 25 minutes by train from the central part of Tokyo to reach Musashino-shi where the University is located.

UNDERGRADUATE PROGRAMS

Faculty of Business Administration (Freshmen Enrollment: 532)

Department of Business Administration

Accounting, Advertising, Auditing, Bookkeeping, Business Analysis, Business Finance, Business History, Business Management, Business Marketing, Business Organization, Business Policy, Business Psychology, Business Statistics, Cost Accounting, Distribution Economics, History of Business Management, Industrial Organization, Industrial Relations, International Accounting, International Marketing, Japanese Business History, Japanese Industry, Management Planning, Management Science, Management Systems, Managerial Marketing, Marketing, Modern Corporation, Product Planning, Retail and Wholesale Management, Small Business Management

Faculty of Economics (Freshmen Enrollment: 537)

Department of Economics

Agricultural Economics, Econometrics, Economic Fluctuations, Economic Geography, Economic History, Economic Planning, Economic Policy, Economics, Economics of Japan, Economics of Public Utilities, Fiscal Policy, History of Economic Thought, Industrial Economics, Industrial Organization, Labor and Industrial Relations, Labor Economics, Macroeconomics, Mathematical Economics, Mathematics for Economics, Microeconomics, Monetary Economics, Public Economics, Public Finances, Resource Economics, Statistics, Statistics, Theory of Economic Systems

Department of International Relations

Area Studies, Comparative Culture, Comparative Economic Systems, Comparative Religion, Contemporary Japanese Economy, Economic Policy, Economic Theory, History of International Relations, International Communication, International Development, International Economics, International Finance, International Management, International Organization, International Politics, International Relations, International Trade

Faculty of Law (Freshmen Enrollment: 487)

Department of Law

Administrative Law, Anglo-American Law, Bankruptcy Law, Civil Law, Commercial Law, Comparative Constitutional Law, Constitutional Law, Criminal Law, Criminal Procedure, Criminal Psychology, Diplomatic History, Economical Law, French Law, German Law, History of Legal Thoughts, Japanese Legal History, Jurisprudence, Labor Law, Law of Accounting for Taxation, Law of Civil Procedure, Law of Industrial Property, Private International Law, Public International Law, Sociology of Law, Tax Law

Foreign Student Admission

Qualifications for Applicants

Standard Qualifications Requirement

Examination at the University

A written exam, Japanese and English, and an interview.

Date: January

Documents to be Submitted When Applying

Standard Documents Requirement

"Certificate of Japanese Proficiency" and "Written Pledge".

Application forms are available at the Office for International Affairs in early July of each year. Applicants may request application forms either by mail or by telephone. Application filing procedure: All applicants and/or guarantors should submit the specified documents in person to the Center for International Affairs by the prescribed date in January. The application filing period will be announced in an information bulletin attached to the application forms.

Several days after the announcement of screening, necessary procedures should be made by the admitted students, during the announced period, in order to obtain a Certificate of Admission, a document necessary for acquiring a student visa. The new academic year starts with the Entrance Ceremony held on April 1 every year.

Qualifications for Transfer Students

Transfer student applicants are eligible for admission to the third year upon completion of at least two full academic years at an accredited college or university (either completed terms, or in attendance).

Examination for Transfer Students

A written exam, an English language exam, an exam in a specialized subject, and a personal interview.

Date: mid-March.

Since the Special Entrance Examination for Foreign Students is not applicable to the transfer students, foreign student applicants will have to sit for the same examination that Japanese applicants take.

Documents to be Submitted When Applying

Standard Documents Requirement

Information bulletin is available from the beginning of December.

GRADUATE PROGRAMS

Graduate School of Business Administration (First Year Enrollment : Master's 20, Doctor's 5)

Division

Business Administration

Graduate School of Economics (First Year Enrollment : Master's 20, Doctor's 5)
Division
Economics

Graduate School of Law (First Year Enrollment : Master's 20, Doctor's 5)
Division
Law

Foreign Student Admission
Qualifications for Applicants
Master's Program
      Standard Qualifications Requirement
Doctor's Program
      Standard Qualifications Requirement
Examination at the University
Master's Program
   Examination Date:
   The Entrance Examination for Foreign Students is held twice each year: in December (first sitting) and in March (second sitting). The detailed schedule of examination dates is announced in an information bulletin attached to the application forms which are available beginning at the end of July each year.
   Subjects:
   The examination consists of a written exam, a Japanese and basic aptitude test in a specialized field, and a personal interview.
   Announcement of Results of Examinations:
   An announcement of screening results will be posted on the main campus bulletin board, together with notification to the addressee.
Doctor's Program
   Examination Date:
   The Entrance Examination for Foreign Students is held during March each year. The fixed dates are announced in an information bulletin attached to the application forms which are available beginning at the end of July each year.
   Subjects:
   The examination consists of a written exam, a Japanese and basic aptitude test in a specialized field, and a personal interview.
   Announcement of Results of Examinations:
   An announcement of screening results will be posted on the main campus bulletin board, together with notification to the addressee.
Documents to be Submitted When Applying
   Standard Documents Requirement
   Asia University requests an applicant to submit the following items, in addition to the standard application documents: Certificate of Japanese Language Proficiency, Personal Information Sheet, and Statement (Oath).
   Application Procedures for Master's Progam:
   The specified documents should be submitted to the Asia University Academic Affairs Division either in person or by mail during the fixed period in September, for the first sitting, or in February, for the

second sitting.
   Application Procedures for Doctor's Program:
   The specified documents should be submitted to the Academic Affairs Division either in person or by mail during the fixed period in February each year.

∗

Research Institutes and Centers
The Institute for Asian Studies
Facilities/Services for Foreign Students
1. Office for International Affairs
   Originally named the Foreign Students Center in 1974, the Office for International Affairs (as it became known in 1985) assists foreign students in admission, registration, academic counseling, and the handling of special problems. It concerns itself with all foreign students studying at Asia University.
2. Foreign Student Club
   The University sponsors the Foreign Student Club which provides an opportunity for foreign students to intermix with Japanese students, and to relax in a social setting when classes are not in session.
3. Academic Guidance
   Personal academic guidance is given to all new foreign students (freshmen) at the start of each academic year so that the new students may better understand the various academic programs and arrange their own study schedules.
4. Freshmen Orientation
   A three-day-long freshmen orientation is held by the University for the mutual benefit of all entering students. During the freshmen orientation a master plan is arranged for each student's academic life. The master plan is plotted out by means of informal talks with Asia University faculty members and senior students.
Special Programs for Foreign Students
   There are some courses specifically provided for foreign students in the Liberal Arts Area. In addition, there is a course in the Japanese Language designed exclusively for foreign students. This course fulfills the requirement for a second language (i.e., the language normally chosen by the student in addition to English).
For Further Information
   Undergraduate Admission
Office for International Affairs, Asia University, 5-24-10 Sakai, Musashino-shi, Tokyo 180 ☎ 0422-54-3111 ext. 253
   Graduate Admission
Registrar's Office, Asia University, 5-24-10 Sakai, Musashino-shi, Tokyo 180 ☎ 0422-54-3111 ext. 300

Atomi Gakuen Women's College
(Atomi Gakuen Joshi Daigaku)

1-9-6 Nakano, Niiza-shi, Saitama 352
☎ 0484-78-3333

UNDERGRADUATE PROGRAMS

Faculty of Literature (Freshmen Enrollment: 400)
Department of Aesthetics and Art History
Department of Culture Studies
Department of English Literature
Department of Japanese Literature

Azabu University
(Azabu Daigaku)

1–17–71, Fuchinobe, Sagamihara–shi, Kanagawa 229
☎ 0427–54–7111

Faculty
    Profs. 52   Assoc. Profs. 40
    Assist. Profs. Full–time 33; Part–time 42
    Res. Assocs. 16
Number of Students
    Undergrad. 1, 669   Grad. 152
Library 92, 066 volumes

Outline and Characteristics of the University

Azabu University developed out of Tokyo Veterinary Training School, which was established at Honmura-cho, Azabu-ku, Tokyo in 1890. The school was founded as part of a plan developed by Masayoshi Matsukata, then Minister of Agriculture and Commerce. He formulated a threefold plan to improve Japanese livestock. First, fine breeds of livestock from advanced countries would be imported. Second, Japanese veterinarians would be taught the new science of veterinary medicine. Thirdly this new science would be applied to native Japanese breeds.

In 1990 the university will celebrate its centenary. During the past century the school has gone through many changes. The campus has moved to Fuchinobe since then. But the founding spirit of the school, to apply new science to industry and to contribute to the advancement of human life, has continued to thrive until today. Today the School of Veterinary Medicine with its staff of 27 tenured professors is one of the most substantial veterinary schools in Japan.

Throughout its long history, while maintaining a strict academic attitude, the school has fostered an earnest and liberal tradition in which teachers and students have grown to trust and rely upon each other.

In 1976 an Animal Environment and Production Program was started. This program focuses great attention on the environment of livestock.

In 1978 the college of Environmental Health was founded. The aim of the college is to make systematic researches into the relationship between animals, including human beings, and their environment. The college hopes to eventually make contributions to the overall improvement of human health.

Toward the 21st century rapid progress is expected in the area of Life Science. The sciences of Veterinary Medicine, Animal Environment and Production, and Environmental Health are expected to make great progress in the future.

Azabu University will sustain its efforts to maintain the highest academic standards possible and to contribute the results of its research to society and human welfare.

UNDERGRADUATE PROGRAMS

College of Environmental Health
  Faculty of Environmental Health
Analytical Chemistry, Environmental Biology, Environmental Hygiene, Environmental Microbiology, Environmental Technology, Food Hygiene, Public Health Administration
  Faculty of Hygienic Technology
Biochemistry, Bioorganic Chemistry, Environmental Pathology, Environmental Physiology, Hygiene, Immunology
School of Veterinary Medicine
  Animal Environment and Production Program
Animal Economics, Animal Environment and Management, Grassland Science, Science of Animal Products
  Veterinary Medicine Program
Animal Breeding, Animal Health, Animal Nutrition, Infectious Diseases, Laboratory Animal Science, Molecular Biology, Theriogenology, Veterinary Anatomy, Veterinary Biochemistry, Veterinary Internal Medicine, Veterinary Microbiology, Veterinary Parasitology, Veterinary Pathology, Veterinary Pharmacology, Veterinary Physiology, Veterinary Public Health, Veterinary Radiology, Veterinary Surgery

Foreign Student Admission
  Qualifications for Applicants
    Standard Qualifications Requirement
    All applicants from foreign countries must understand Japanese language sufficiently to join classes and attend lectures.
  Examination at the University
    Same as for Japanese. (Either a written examination together with a short essay in Japanese and an interview, or an examination on documents.)
  Documents to be Submitted When Applying
    Standard Documents Requirement
      1.   Adequate proof of ability in Japanese language.
      2.   A letter of recommendation from the applicant's Embassy in Japan or from an equivalent office representing that applicant's country in Japan.

GRADUATE PROGRAMS

Graduate School of Veterinary Medicine (First Year Enrollment : Master's 120, Doctor's 10)

Divisions
Veterinary Medicine

Foreign Student Admission
Examination at the University
Doctor's Program
A written examination, an oral examination, an official transcript from the Graduate School where the applicant received his/her Master's degree, a Master's thesis and a health certificate.
Documents to be Submitted When Applying
Standard Documents Requirement
1. Certification of the applicant's Japanese language ability by his/her adviser or any other qualified person.
2. A letter of recommendation from the applicant's Embassy in Japan.

Research Institutes and Centers
Science Information Center
For Further Information
Undergraduate Admission
Admissions Office, Azabu University, 1-17-71, Fuchinobe, Sagamihara-shi, Kanagawa-ken
☎ 0427-54-7111 ext. 312
Graduate Admission
Office of the Graduate School, Azabu University 1-17-71, Fuchinobe, Sagamihara-shi, Kanagawa
☎ 0427-54-7111 ext. 316

Baika Women's College
(Baika Joshi Daigaku)

2-19-5 Shukunosho, Ibaraki-shi, Osaka 567
☎ 0726-43-6221

Faculty
    Profs. 28   Assoc. Profs. 27
    Assist. Profs. Full-time 2; Part-time 105
Number of Students
    Undergrad. 1, 776   Grad. 9
Library 170, 000 volumes

Outline and Characteristics of the College
Baika Women's College, a small Christian liberal arts college, lies on a wooded hillside in the outskirts of Ibaraki City, Osaka Prefecture, and is within convenient commuting distance of Osaka (Japan's second largest city), Kyoto (the ancient capital and home of many cultural treasures) and Kobe (a port city noted for its cosmopolitan atmosphere).
Though the college opened in 1964, its history dates back to 1878, when Baika Girls' School was established as the first girls' school in Osaka. With the support of members of the Umemoto-cho Church and the Naniwa Church in Osaka, Rev. Paul Sawayama, a pioneer of the Christian world in those days, founded the school. The name Baika, meaning "plum blossom" is a combination of parts of the two churches' names. Missionaries of the Congregational Church's American Board of Commissioners for Foreign Missions played an important role as teachers from the very beginning, and to this day missionaries from various denominations have served on the faculty.
Over the years, the school developed as an integral institution, now comprising kindergarten, junior high school, senior high school, junior college, four-year college, and graduate school.
Baika Women's College aims to educate young women to be independent and creative and to develop a broad academic outlook through study and research. In addition to a stimulating academic atmosphere and spiritually refreshing environment, Baika provides rich character building based on Christianity while fostering a sense of freedom through various autonomous activities.
The college offers three academic majors: Japanese Literature, English and American Literature, and Children's Literature. Students wishing to pursue further studies in Japanese literature or English and American literature may apply for admission to the Graduate Course (M. A.) which opened in 1977. Total student enrollment is approximately 1, 700.
Overseas tours to England and America help to bring alive academic studies. Baika's sister college affiliation with Mount Union College (Alliance, Ohio, U. S. A.) makes it possible for students and teachers to participate not only in special summer studies there but also in longer study programs. Exchange teachers from Mount Union have stimulated both students and faculty.
To promote character building based on Christianity, the college provides a variety of religious activities including worship, social service, study programs, retreats, and fellowship events.
On-campus facilities include language labs, with VTR (video tape recorder) and CAI (computer aided instruction) equipment, an excellent library of almost 150, 000 volumes, special classrooms for calligraphy practice, two cafeterias, a gymnasium, a newly-built Sawayama Memorial Hall (a chapel plus an auditorium, dedicated in 1988), tennis courts, an archery court, and club houses for cultural and sports clubs. Academic and social events are planned by such autonomous organizations as the Japanese Literature Society, the English and American Literature Society, the Children's Literature Society, and many other student groups.
The academic program, extra-curricular activities, and Christian education program enable students to have a variety of experiences which are mentally, socially, and spiritually enriching.

UNDERGRADUATE PROGRAMS

Faculty of Literature (Freshman Enrollment: 330)
Department of Children's Literature
Child Psychology, Children's Culture, Children's

Language, Child Welfare, History of Children's Literature, Individual Authors and Works
Department of English and American Literature
Creative Writing, Drama, English and American Authors and Works, English Fiction, English Grammar, English Phonetics, History of American Literature, History of English Language, History of English Literature, Linguistics, Poetry
Department of Japanese Literature
Calligraphy, Chinese Literature, History of Chinese Literature, History of Japanese Literature, Japanese Grammar, Japanese Linguistics, Japanese Literature

Foreign Student Admission
Qualifications for Applicants
Standard Qualifications Requirement
Applicants must be alien females.
Examination at the College
Documents screening, written exams (Japanese and English) and an interview.
Documents to be Submitted When Applying
Standard Documents Requirement
1. Personal history, including educational background.
2. Statement written in Japanese by the applicant, giving the reason for wishing to enter this college.
3. Certificate of the Japanese Language Proficiency Test or, a statement from a qualified teacher of the Japanese language or issued by an officer of a Japanese overseas diplomatic agency, indicating the applicant's degree of proficiency in the Japanese language.

Qualifications for Transfer Students
Applicants must be alien females and have finished 14 years of education recognized as standard in their own countries, or equivalent.
Examination for Transfer Students
Same as freshman applicants.
Documents to be Submitted When Applying
Standard Documents Requirement
Additional documents to be submitted are the same as those for freshman applicants.

GRADUATE PROGRAMS

Graduate School of Literature (First Year Enrollment : Master's 10)
Divisions
English and American Literature, Japanese Literature

Foreign Student Admission
Qualifications for Applicants
Master's Program
Standard Qualifications Requirement
Applicants must be alien females.
Examination at the College
Master's Program

Documents screening,
Written exams in their major fields and a foreign language.
Applicants to the Japanese Literature Course will be examined in Japanese Linguistics, Japanese Literature, and English or French or German.
Applicants to the English and American Literature Course will be examined in English Linguistics, English and American Literature, and French or German.
An interview is also required of all applicants.
Documents to be Submitted When Applying
Standard Documents Requirement
1. Personal history, including educational background.
2. Statement written in Japanese by the applicant, describing her undergraduate study program and indicating plans for academic study and research at this graduate school. (Applicants to the English and American Literature Course may write in English).
3. Certificate of the Japanese Language Proficiency Test, or a statement from a qualified teacher of the Japanese language or issued by an officer of a Japanese overseas diplomatic agency, indicating the applicant's degree of proficiency in the Japanese language.

*

Facilities/Services for Foreign Students
Dormitory, Home stay program.
Meetings for international students for discussion, fellowship, and counseling sponsored by The International Affairs Committee
Special Programs for Foreign Students
A training course for the teaching of Japanese to foreigners, cultural events and field trips organized by the literature societies of each department.
Tutorial instruction for students needing special help is now under consideration.
For Further Information
Undergraduate and Graduate Admission
Admission Division, Baika Women's College, 2-19-5 Shukunosho, Ibaraki-shi, Osaka 567 ☎ 0726-43-6221 ext. 202

Baiko Jo Gakuin College
(Baiko Jo Gakuin Daigaku)

365 Yoshimi Myoji–cho, Shimonoseki–shi, Yamaguchi 759–65 ☎ 0832–86–2221

Faculty
Profs. 22 Assoc. Profs. 8
Assist. Profs. Full–time 8; Part–time 45
Number of Students
Undergrad. 824 Grad. 21
Library 103, 860 volumes

Outline and Characteristics of the College

Acceptance of international studens has been the prominent feature of the Christian education of Baiko Jo Gakuin College. Founded in 1872 by American missionary teachers, Baiko Jo Gakuin Institute, the oldest Christian school in the western part of Japan, has always kept her doors wide open to students from other lands of Asia. The proximity of the Shimonoseki school to the Continent of Asia had greatly facilitated the realization of its ideal of internationalism. In more recent years, Baiko's Internationalism has been reinforced by increasing number of her international students as the junior college (1964), four year college (1967) and its graduate program for Master's degree (1976), and Doctor's degree (1978) have been established.

Baiko Jo Gakuin Institute maintains an integrated system of education composed of a kindergarten, junior and senior high schools, junior college, and a senior college and graduate school. International students are eligible for admission at each level. Baiko Jo Gakuin College has a small enrollment and consists of one Faculty of Letters with three departmants of Japanese Literature, English and American Literature, and English and American Language. It has a distinguished tradition of accepting foreign students on the following basis: (1) Individual application with some form of financial aid according to the need of each applicant. (2) Established exchange programs with American universities. (3) Grants of fellowship consisting of tution waiver, free furnished housing, and stipend to meet living expernses.

The Christian education of Baiko Jo Gakuin College has been guided by the principle of "Walk as children of light" (Ephesians V: 8), and this ideal is reflected in the light of the college's internationalism as it strives to realize the ideal of brotherhood of all peple in the world.

UNDERGRADUATE PROGRAMS

Faculty of Letters (Freshmen Enrollment: 160)
Department of English and American Language
Area Studies of China, Area Studies of English and America, British and American Cultural History, Business English, Childern's Literature, Classcial Languages, Comparative Literature, Cultural Anthropology, Cultural History of China, Current Usages of English, English Composotion, English Conversation, English grammar, English Language of the Bible, English Phonetics, English Speech, Finance, History of England and America, History of English Language, History of English Literature History of American Literature, History of European Thought, History of the Arts of Asia, International Economics, International Law, Introduction to Lingusitics, Introduction to Studies in the English Language, Japanese as a Second Language, Reading in English and American Literature, Seminar in Business English, Seminar in English and American Language, Special Lecture on the English Language, Studies in European Cultures, Studies in the English Language, Womanlogy

Department of English and American Literature
Area Studies of China, Bushiness English, Children's Literature, Classical Languages, Comparative Literature, Cultural Anthropology, Cultural History of China, Current Usage of English, English Compostition, English Conversation, English Grammar, English Phonetics, History of American Literature, History of Christian Thoughts, History of English Literature, History of the arts of Asia, History of the English Languge, Introduction to American Culture, Introduction to Linguitstics, Introduction to Studies in English Language, Introduction to Western Literature, Introudctin to English Culture, Japanese as a Second Language, Seminar in Business English, Seminar in English and American Language, Seminar in English and American Literature, Special Lecture on American Literature, Special lecture on English Literature, Special Lecture on Psychology, Special Lecture on the English Language, Special Studies in the English Language, Studies in English and American Literature, The Bible as Literature, Womanlogy

Department of Japanese Literature
Advanced Studies in Thinking and Writing, Area Studies of China, Basic Survey of Japanese Literature, Calligraphy, Calligraphy in Block Style, Calligraphy in Cursive Style, Calligraphy in Sealing Print Style, Calligrphy in Kana style, Children's Literature, Comparative Literature, Cultral History of Japan, Cultural Anthropology, Cultural History of China, Hisotry of Japanese Literature of Medieval and Recent Past Periods, History of Chinese Calligraphy, History of Christian Thought, History of Janapese Literature of the Modern Period, History of Japanese Calligraphy, History of Japanese Language, History of Japanese Literature of The Ancient Period, History of the Arts of Asia, Human Science, Introduction of Japanese Literature, Japanese as a Second Language, Japanese Grammar, Japanese Language, Japanese Literature, Linguistics Chinese Classics, Literary Works of the Medieval Period, Literary Works of the Modern Period, Literary Works of the Recent Past Period, Reading in Foreign Reseaech Materiasl, Readings in Chinese Classics, Research Methods of Japanese Literature, Special Lecture on Japansese Literature, Special Lecture on Psychlogy, Studies of Literary Works of the Ancient Period, Studies of Thinking and Writing, The Bible as Literature, Thesis for B. A. degree. , Western Literature, Womanology

Foreign Student Admission
Qualifications for Applicants
Standard Qualifications Requirement
Examination at the University
The screening/admission system for international student is different from that used for Japanese applicants.
Documents to be Submitted When Applying

Standard Documents Requirement
Qualifications for Transfer Students
Standard Qualifications Requirement
Examination for Transfer Students
Written and oral examinations plus an interview.
Documents to be Submitted When Applying
Standard Documents Requirement

GRADUATE PROGRAMS

Graduate School of Literature (First Year Enrollment : Master's 24, Doctor's 6)
Divisions
English Literature, Japanese Literature

Foreign Student Admission
Qualifications for Applicants
Master's Program
Standard Qualifications Requirement
Doctor's Program
Standard Qualifications Requirement
Examination at the University
Master's Program
Date: October and between February and March.
Subjects: a written and oral examination plus an interview.
Doctor's Program
Same as for the Master's Program.
Documents to be Submitted When Applying
Standard Documents Requirement
＊
Research Institutes and Centers
Area Culture Research Center
Services for Foreign Students
Dormitory accomodations, Academic advisory assistance, On-and-off campus job placement
Special Programs for Foreign Students
Courses in Japanese as a second language
For Further Information
Undergraduate and Graduate Admission
Head, Genaral Management Office, Baiko Jo Gakuin College, 365 Yoshimi Myoji–cho, Shimonoseki–shi, Yamaguchi 759–65 ☏ 0832–86–2221

Beppu University
(Beppu Daigaku)

82 Kita-ishigaki, Beppu-shi, Oita 874-01
☏ 0977-67-0101

Faculty
　　Profs.　20　　Assoc. Profs.　12
　　Assist. Profs.　Full–time　10; Part–time　17
Number of Students
　　Undergrad.　1, 050
Library　111, 000 volumes

Outline and Characteristics of the University

Beppu University is a private, coeducational college which started as the Beppu Women's Special School in 1946. Under the new Education Law, it was renamed Beppu Women's College in 1950. In 1954, the name Beppu University was adopted and coeducation was introduced. At the same time the Junior College was established.

The university is situated in the northern part of Beppu City in Oita Prefecture. (Beppu is a world-famous hot spring resort on the northeastern coast of Kyushu Island.)

This university, established soon after the World War II, has followed the ideal of President Yoshiaki Sato which is well expressed in the university motto "Veritas Liberat. " Foreign students have been accepted into Beppu University since its establishment.

One of the important characteristics of Beppu University in terms of international educational exchange is its strong tie with the University of Hawaii. The University has continued to send its students to the sister university to participate in summer sessions ever since 1980. The formal "sister college" relationship was established in 1983. In 1986, 22 students from Hawaii came to Beppu University to participate in B. I. S. S. (Beppu-Daigaku International Summer Seminar). The Seminar covered Japanese archaeology, history, religion, with a focus on Kyushu. Conversational Japanese was also taught. Special lectures were given on Japanese art, Japanese literature and Japanese poetry. Besides the lectures in classrooms, field trips led by Beppu University professors to sites in Beppu, Usa, Kunisaki, Usuki, Kumamoto, Nagasaki, and Fukuoka helped the students from Hawaii study Kyushu as the cradle of Japanese civilization.

In addition to the University of Hawaii, Beppu University enjoys a sister college relationship with Szechwan University of Foreign Languages in the People's Republic of China since 1984 and with Lamar Uinversity in Beaumont in Texas, U. S. A since 1975.

UNDERGRADUATE PROGRAMS

Faculty of Literature (Freshmen Enrollment: 190)
Department of Aesthetics and History of Fine Arts
Carving and Modeling, Dramatic Theory, General Survey of the Arts, History of Aesthetics, History of Calligraphy, History of Fine Arts, Oil painting
Department of English Literature
American Literature, British Literature, English Linguistics, Teaching Method of English
Department of History
Archaeology, History of Japan, History of the Orient, History of the West
Department of Japanese Literature
Classical Chinese Literature, Classical Japanese Literature, Japanese Linguistics, Japanese Poetry, Modern Japanese Literature

Foreign Student Admission
Qualifications for Applicants
Standard Qualifications Requirement
Applicants must be non-Japanese.
Examination at the University
Japanese composition and an interview.
Date of the Entrance Exam: February 13, 1989
Announcement of Successful Applicants: February 21, 1989
Documents to be Submitted When Applying
Standard Documents Requirement
Application Period: Jan. 17-Feb. 8, 1989
Deadline of Entrance Procedures: Mar, 3, 1989

*

Research Institutes and Centers
Beppu University Museum, Research Institute for Asian History and Culture

For Further Information
Undergraduate Admission
Admission Office, Beppu University, 82 Kita-ishigaki, Beppu-shi, Oita 874-01 ☎ 0977-67-0101

Bukkyo University
(Bukkyo Daigaku)

96 Kitahananobo-cho, Murasakino, Kita-ku,
Kyoto-shi, Kyoto 603   ☎ 075-491-2141

Faculty
    Profs. 75   Assoc. Profs. 28
    Assist. Profs. Full-time 20; Part-time 239
    Res. Assocs. 5
Number of Students
    Undergrad. 5, 361   Grad. 116
Library 367, 403 volumes

Outline and Characteristics of the University
    Bukkyo University dates back to a Jodo Sect institution named Juhachi Danrin, which was opened in Edo (present-day Tokyo) early in the 17th century with a view to disseminating widely the faith of Honen Shonin, the founder of Japanese Pure Land Buddhism. In 1934, it was moved to its present location. In 1949, under a new system, it was renamed Bukkyo University. At first, the University consisted of Faculty of Buddhist Studies for the purpose of training Jodo Sect priests. In 1965, it was reorganized into the Faculty of Letters with three departments: Buddhist Studies, Japanese Literature, and Social Welfare. In 1966, the University instituted the Department of History, and in 1967 instituted the Faculty of Sociology and established the Department of Sociology. The Department of Social Welfare was then integrated into the Faculty of Sociology. The University established the Department of Education in 1968, the Department of English Literature in 1975, and the Department of Chinese Literature in 1986. At present, Bukkyo University has two facul-

ties with eight departments and graduate schools.
    The Correspondence Program, established in 1953, was the first university program of its kind in the Kansai area. It has opened the gates of the University to those who wish to receive higher education. The Special Buddhist Program was established in 1977.

UNDERGRADUATE PROGRAMS

Faculty of Letters (Freshmen Enrollment: 680)
Department of Buddhist Studies
Buddhism, Buddhist Culture, History of Buddhism, History of Chinese Buddhism, History of Indian Buddhism, History of Japanese Buddhism, History of Religion, History of the Pure Land Sect, History of Thought, Indian Philosophy, Mahayanist Buddhism, Pure Land Studies, Science of Religion
Department of Chinese Literature
Chinese Language, Chinese Literature, Chinese Philosophy, History of Chinese Literature, History of Chinese Philosophy, History of Cultural Exchange between Japan and China, History of Oriental Culture
Department of Education
Buddhist Pedagogy, Child Pedagogy, Education, Educational Administration, Educational Business Administration, Educational Philosophy, Educational Psychology, Educational Sociology, History of Education in Japan, History of Education in the West, Moral Education, Pedagogy, Primary Education Principles, Religious Education
Department of English Literature
English and American Literature, English Linguistics, English Phonetics, History of American Literature, History of English Literature, History of Occidental Literature, History of the English Language, Linguistics
Department of History
Archaeology, Folklore, Historical Geography, Historical Science, History of Japanese Thought, History of Oriental Thought, Japanese History, Occidental History, Oriental History, Science of Old Manuscripts, Topography
Department of Japanese Literature
Buddhist Literature, Chinese Literature, History of Japanese Literature, Japanese Grammar, Japanese Language Studies, Japanese Literature, *Tanka* Literature

Faculty of Sociology (Freshmen Enrollment: 470)
Department of Social Welfare
Buddhist Welfare, History of the Growth of Social Welfare, Social Science, Social Security, Social Welfare Law, Welfare of the Aged
Department of Sociology
Educational Sociology, History of Social Thought, History of Sociology, Industrial Psychology, Sociological Studies in Religion, Sociology, Sociology of Communities, Sociology of the Family, Theory of Modern Society, Theory of Social Surveys

Foreign Student Admission

Qualifications for Applicants

Standard Qualifications Requirement

Examination at the University

The same written examinations and personal interviews as Japanese students. In special circumstances, however, he, she can gain admission by submitting appropriate documents.

An applicant must undergo an interview concerning choice of major and management of life after entering the university.

Documents to be Submitted When Applying

Standard Documents Requirement

Qualifications for Transfer Students

1. Graduation from a university;
2. The completion of some work at a university; or
3. Graduation from a junior college.

Examination for Transfer Students

Same procedure as freshman applicants.

Documents to be Submitted When Applying

Standard Documents Requirement

ONE-YEAR GRADUATE PROGRAMS

Special Buddhist Program (Enrollment: 20)
Pure Land Sect Priests Training

Foreign Student Admission

Qualifications for Applicants

Standard Qualifications Requirement

Examination at the University

Same procedure as freshman applicants.

GRADUATE PROGRAMS

Graduate School of Letters (First Year Enrollment : Master's 55, Doctor's 11)

Divisions

Buddhist Studies, English and American Literature, Japanese History, Japanese Literature, Oriental History, Pure Land Buddhism

Graduate School of Sociology (First Year Enrollment : Master's 20, Doctor's 3)

Divisions

Social Welfare, Sociology

Foreign Student Admission

Qualifications for Applicants

Master's Program

Standard Qualifications Requirement

Applicants must have mastered the fundamentals in the chosen major field.

Doctor's Program

Standard Qualifications Requirement

Examination at the University

Master's Program

The same written examinations and personal interviews as Japanese students do. In special circum-

stances, however, he or she can gain admission by submitting appropriate documents.

Doctor's Program

Same procedure as the Master's program.

Documents to be Submitted When Applying

Standard Documents Requirement

*

Research Institutes and Centers

The Institute of Buddhist Cultural Studies, The Institute of Historical Research, The Institute of Psychological Research, The Institute of Sociological Research, The Jodo Buddhism Literature Center, The Research Institute for Buddhist Social Welfare Services

Facilities/Services for Foreign Students

1. The Bukkyo University Shijo Center.
2. The study room.
3. Advisors to foreign students introduce them to Japanese culture and society and help them to deal with practical problems in adjusting to life in Japan.

For Further Information

Undergraduate and Graduate Admission

Planning Section, General Affairs Division, Bukkyo University, 96 Kitahananobo-cho, Murasakino, Kita-ku, Kyoto-shi, Kyoto 603 ☎ 075-491-2141 ext. 2021

Bunka Women's University
(Bunka Joshi Daigaku)

3-22-1 Yoyogi, Shibuya-ku, Tokyo 151
☎ 03-370-3111

Faculty

Profs. 32 Assoc. Profs. 23

Assist. Profs. Full–time 21; Part–time 39

Res. Assocs. 11

Number of Students

Undergrad. 1, 749 Grad. 24

Library 135, 000 volumes

Outline and Characteristics of the University

Bunka Women's University started as Bunka Women's Junior College in 1950, its origins linked to the Bunka Gakuen Institute which was founded in 1919. Later in 1964, Bunka Women's University was established in addition to the junior college. With the two additions of the Fashion Department and the Living Arts Department both the university and the junior college have enjoyed further development. They have also strengthened their organization as a synthetic educational group by setting up the graduate course of the university, the extended study course of the junior college, Muroran Women's Junior College with its attached kindergarten, and the Fashion Information Science Institute (currently, an application is being filed for the establishment of an international culture department).

The Fashion Department aims at the comprehensive study of clothing versus human actions. The main feature of the department is the overall observation of clothing from a scientific, aesthetic and social viewpoint. The department also aims at the development of the potentials of the clothing science and obtaining the basic theory and technique of clothing construction. The Living Arts Department aims at developing the students' ability to create living art which will contribute greatly to consumer life through aesthetic sensibilities.

Bunka Women's University and the Junior College have always emphasized the students' attitudes toward rational research and intellectual harmony in creating and considering the beauty of the world. This has become the unique principles of Bunka Women's University and Junior College; to educate modern women whom Bunka is proud of with advanced knowledge and culture, always creating a new, beautiful world to live in.

UNDERGRADUATE PROGRAMS

Faculty of Domestic Economy (Freshmen Enrollment: 400)
Department of Fashion
Clothing Construction, Clóthing Science, Costume History, Fashion Design, Sociology of Costume and Fasion
Department of Living Arts
Ceramics, Craft Design, Dyeing, Interior Design, Metal work, Textile Design, Weaving

Foreign Student Admission
Qualifications for Applicants
Standard Qualifications Requirement
Examination at the University
Overall judgement of application documents, interview and short thesis. Examination is given in December.
Documents to be Submitted When Applying
Standard Documents Requirement
Certificate of Japanese language ability.
application Period: Nov. 8-25

Qualifications for Transfer Students
Those who have qualifications (a) and (c) or (b) and (c):
(a) Those who have finished or are going to finish their sophomore's year of the university.
(b) Those who have graduated or are going to graduate from a junior college.
(c) Those who studied in the same department as the one they wish to enter.
Examination for Transfer Students
Overall judgement of application documents, written examinations and a short thesis.
1. Examination subjects:
Fashion Dept.: clothing construction, costume design theory, study of clothing materi-

als, study of clothing maintenance, hygienics of clothing, history of Japanese costume, history of European costume, sociology of costume and fasion (Students are to pick one of these as their major subjects.)
Living Arts Dept.: basic formation (horizontal or vertical)
2. Foreign language: English or French
3. Short thesis
4. Interview
Examination is given in February.
Documents to be Submitted When Applying
Standard Documents Requirement
Period of application: Jan. 20-Feb. 3

GRADUATE PROGRAMS

Graduate School of Domestic Economy (First Year Enrollment: Master's 6)
Division
Fashion

Foreign Student Admission
Qualifications for Applicants
Master's Program
Standard Qualifications Requirement
Examination at the University
Master's Program
Students are accepted for admission by overall judgement of application documents, written examinations, short thesis and interview.
1. Examination subjects: select two of the following four categories and pick one subject each from the selected two.
(1) study of clothing materials, study of clothing maintenance, hygienics of clothing
(2) costume design
(3) history of Japanese costume, history of European costume, sociology of costume and fashion
(4) clothing construction
2. Foreign language: English, French or German
3. Short thesis
4. Interview
Documents to be Submitted When Applying
Standard Documents Requirement
*
Research Institutes and Centers
Fashion Information Science Research Institute
Facilities/Services for Foreign Students
Special guidance, welcome party for new students, training excursion, Christmas party, farewell party sponsored by the Foreign Student Committee Personal interviews and counseling.
Special Programs for Foreign Students
Subject of general education: Japanese Culture and Life
For Further Information
Undergraduate and Graduate Admission
Clerk in Charge of Examination, Educational Af-

fairs Department, Bunka Women's University, 3-22-1 Yoyogi, Shibuya-ku, Tokyo 151 ☎ 03-370-3111 ext. 2360

Bunkyo University
(Bunkyo Daigaku)

3337 Minami-Ogishima, Koshigaya-shi, Saitama 343
☎ 0489-74-8811

Faculty
    Profs. 87   Assoc. Profs. 43
    Assist. Profs. Full–time 23; Part–time 259
    Res. Assocs. 15
Number of Students
    Undergrad. 3, 127
Library 180, 000 volumes

Outline and Characteristics of the University

In keeping with the nation's fundamental statutes on education, which declare the love of truth and justice to be the central pillar of postwar Japanese education, Bunkyo University main educational goal is compassion and concern for other human beings. We make every effort to ensure that the learning we offer achieves a concrete and meaningful purpose for our individual students and for the society in which they live. We emphasize a relaxed atmosphere of contact between faculty and students. We also believe that our program gives birth to young men and women who possess a critical attitude toward learning and scholarship all and an all-embracing compassion with respect for human beings.

The Faculty of Education was the first of its kind among the nation's private universities to require all of its students to earn a teaching certificate in order to graduate. This requirement has naturally led to the assembly of a group of young people whose fondest hope is to become teachers. Through years of accumulated effort they have imbibed the learning and technique necessary to become successful teachers when they will actually take their places behind the podium. This unique position among Japan's private universites is a source of particular pride for us.

In our Faculty of Human Sciences our educational and research efforts are advancing toward timely answers to the fundamental question of how best to realize a comprehensive program of learning centered on human beings and their pursuit of happiness. Once again, among private universities this faculty is unique in its efforts to nurture scholars who can unite and develop the fields of psychology, sociology, and education as well as to train practitioners in clinical psychology, social work, and lifelong education.

In April of 1980, we established the Faculty of Information and Communication which moved five years later to its new campus in the lovely rolling hills around Chigasaki City. This faculty is the first of its kind in all of Japan. It was created, in response to the pressing contemporary need to comprehend the problems of the 'information boom' in today's society. It also aims to provide a comprehensive educational program to prepare young men and women to understand this major problem and how to organize and fully utilize the flood of new information inundating us daily.

The Faculty of Language and Literature was founded in April 1987 to respond to the needs of the rapid internationalization of our society. We are now expected to contribute to the world a great deal, and it is important to further understanding. The underlying aim of this faculty to understand foreigners by learning foreign languages, literature, and culture. In addition, we hope to gain a deeper understanding of our own tradition and culture through the study of the Japanese language. We encourage foreign students to form the same understanding through the study of Japanese language and culture.

Bunkyo University has come a long way since its humble beginnings as a small women's school in 1927 and the dark days of war when all of its facilities were destroyed. In 1977 it became co-educational and today its students and faculty enjoy the use of extensive facilities on two continually developing campuses.

UNDERGRADUATE PROGRAMS

Faculty of Information and Communication (Freshmen Enrollment: 300)
    Deparment of Information Systems
    Department of Management Information Science
    Department of Mass Communication
Faculty of Education (Freshmen Enrollment: 250)
    Elementary School Teachers' Training Course
    Junior High School Teachers' Training Course
Home Economics, Music
Faculty of Human Science (Freshmen Enrollment: 150)
    Department of Human Science
Faculty of Language and Literature (Freshmen Enrollment: 300)
    The Course of British and American Language and Literature
    The Course of Chinese Language and Literature
    The Course of Japanese Language and Literature

*

For Further Information
    Undergraduate Admission
Entrance Examination Section, Bunkyo University, 3337 Minami-Ogishima, Koshigaya-shi, Saitama 343
☎ 0489-74-8811

Chiba Institute of Technology
(Chiba Kogyo Daigaku)

2-17-1 Tsudanuma, Narashino-shi, Chiba 275
☎ 0474-75-2111

Faculty
    Profs. 108   Assoc. Profs. 51
    Assist. Profs. Full-time 40; Part-time 173
    Res. Assocs. 33
Number of Students
    Undergrad. 5, 959   Grad. 50
Library 108, 460 volumes

Outline and Characteristics of the University

In 1942, Chiba Institute of Technology was founded for the purpose of teaching students as excellent engineers, in response to the national demand. The foundation of our college was based on two principles: one is that the students should be able to study independently and display self-restraint; the other that the teachers and students should work and study together harmoniously. The priniciples have been upheld for 46 years and graduated more than 33, 000 students since the Institute's foundation. What Chiba Intitute of Technology is today has resulted from not only these principles but from the great efforts given by the leading authorities in every technological field of the teaching staffs as well.

Our college consists of eleven departments in the daytime course, and four departments in the evening course. Each department is highly specialized. It is a major premise that every area of technological investigation should have an organic relationship with each other. Consequently, it is required of the students to be concerned about the whole field of technology and to develop their decision-making abilities.

Shibazono campus for general education was opend in April, 1986. It is located on the seaside area to the southwest, at a distance of 3. 5 kilometers from Tsudanuma campus which is for senior and graduate education. Both campuses are easily accessible because each is adjacent to its own station and is a 30 minute train ride from Tokyo. The environment about our college is magnificent, since a number of schools and colleges are situated here in the city.

There are two agreements with Harbin Institute of Technology and Jilin University since 1983 respectively in People's Republic of China to exchange professors and students.

UNDERGRADUATE PROGRAMS

Faculty of Engineering (Freshmen Enrollment: 1, 040)
    Department of Architecture

Architectural and Environmental Planning, Architectural Structural Engineering, Environmental Engineering, Materials Execution and Fireproofing, Regional Facility Planning and Architectural Planning, Steel Structures, Steel Structures and Disaster Prevention
    Department of Civil Engineering
Construction Methods and Materials, Environmental and Sanitary Engineering, River and Harbor Engineering, Soil Mechanics and Foundation Engineering, Structural Engineering, Traffic and Transportation Engineering
    Department of Computer Sciences
Artificial Intelligence, Basic Computer Sciences, Basic Electronics, Computer-Aided Measurements, Information Systems
    Department of Electrical Engineering
Communication Engineering, Electrical Machinery and Apparatus, Electrical Materials, Electronic Engineering, Elements of Electrical Engineering, Power Engineering
    Department of Electronics
Applied Electronics, Electronic Circuit, Information Theory, Solid-State Electronics, Telecommunication Engineering
    Department of Industrial Chemistry
Applied Catalytic Chemistry, Ceramic Chemistry, Chemical Engineering, Inorganic Industrial Chemistry, Material Science, Organic Industrial Chemistry, Synthetic Organic Chemistry
    Department of Industrial Design
Basic Design, Environmental Design, Ergonomics & Materials Planning, Graphic Design, Interior Design, Product Design
    Department of Industrial Management
Engineering Science, Human Engineering, Managerial Economics, Mathematical and Information Engineering, Production Engineering
    Department of Mechanical Engineering
Applied Mechanics, Dynamics of Machinery, Fluid Engineering, Mechanical Processing, Thermal Engineering
    Department of Metallurgical Engineering
Iron and Steel Making, Iron and Steel Materials, Metal Casting, Non-Ferrous Extractive Metallurgy, Non-Ferrous Metals and Alloys, Plastic Working of Metals
    Department of Precision Engineering
Automatic Control, Precision Machine Elements, Precision Machining Technology, Process Instrumentation, Strength of Materials
Faculty of Engineering (**Evening Course**) (Freshmen Enrollment: 280)
    Department of Electrical Engineering
    Department of Industrial Management
    Department of Mechanical Engineering
    Department of Metallurgical Engineering
See the listing for Day Course.

Foreign Student Admission

Qualifications for Applicants
Standard Qualifications Requirement
Examination at the University
The same exam as the Japanese.
Documents to be Submitted When Applying
Standard Documents Requirement

Qualifications for Transfer Students
Those who have college degrees or junior college degrees and those who have completed sophomore courses.
Examination for Transfer Students
The same exam as the Japanese.
Documents to be Submitted When Applying
Standard Documents Requirement

GRADUATE PROGRAMS

Graduate School of Engineering (First Year Enrollment : Master's 24)
Divisions
Civil Engineering, Industrial Chemistry, Metallurgical Engineering

Foreign Student Admission
Qualifications for Applicants
Master's Program
Standard Qualifications Requirement
Examination at the University
Master's Program
Foreign languages (English and German or France), basic science (Mathematics), specialized subject (Metallurgical Physical Chemistry and Metal Engineering, Inorganic Chemistry or Organic Chemistry or Physical Chemistry or Chemical Fundamentals and Inorganic Industrial Chemistry or Organic Industrial Chemistry or Material Science or Chemical Engineering, Applied Mechanics and Structural Engineering or Soil Mechanics or Environmental Engineering or Engineering Systems Analysis or Hydraulic Engineering) and an oral test. Date: in mid-October and early in April. Fee: ¥25, 000.
Documents to be Submitted When Applying
Standard Documents Requirement

*

Research Institutes and Centers
Computer Center
For Further Information
Undergraduate Admission
Admissions Section, Academic Affairs Division, Chiba Institute of Technology, 2-17-1 Tsudanuma, Narashino-shi, Chiba 275 ☎ 0474-75-2111 ext. 357
Graduate Admission
Admission Section, Academic Affairs Division, Chiba Institute of Technology, 2-17-1 Tsudanuma, Narashino-shi, Chiba 275 ☎ 0474-75-2111 ext. 357

Chiba Keizai University
(Chiba Keizai Daigaku)
3-59-5, Todoroki-cho, Chiba-shi, Chiba 260
☎ 0472-53-9111

Faculty
Profs. 12   Assoc. Profs. 3
Assist. Profs. Full-time 2; Part-time 8
Res. Assoc. 1
Number of Students
Undergrad. 251
Library 19, 830 volumes

Outline and Characteristics of the University
Chiba Keizai University (economics) started in April, 1988 with the goal of producing professional economists of practical ability in an age of ever-increasing in ternationalism. Inheriting the motto of its predecessor, Chiba Keizai College (economics), established in 1968, the University Promotes "good sense and ingenuity" so that graduates may make real contributions in the cultural and economic realms of this new global society. The University pursues the cultivation of practical language ability through compulsory classes in the English and Chinese languages: classes are given to strengthen English language abilities in aural comprehension and practical handling of the language used in the worlds of economics, commerce and journalism. Lectures on international affairs are also held in the general education and professional progrms including lectures or seminars in international economics, world economics, Asian economics, economic development, international trade policies, international finance, multinational corporations and international relationships. To provide students with the technical ability necessary for an increasingly information-oriented society, C. K. U. offers a survey course in information science in the general education program and in the professional education program courses in information systems, managemant technology, information correspondence and basic, intermediate and advanced courses in computer field work. The University takes full advantage of its small size in providing the students with the opportunity for close contact with the faculty through their full participation in seminars on economics. Students take preliminary economics seminars in the second year to preapare for more advanced seminars in their third and fourth years.

The University encourages students to develop their own personalities and autonomy in research so that they may be come well adjusted and productive persons in their various fields. The University also strives to meet the increasing professional needs of the local community.

UNDERGRADUATE PROGRAMS

Faculty of Economics (Freshmen Enrollment: 200)
Department of Economics

*

For Further Information
Undergraduate Admission
Admission Office, Chiba Keizai University, 3–59–5, Todoroki–cho, Chiba–shi, Chiba 260
☎ 0472–53–9111ext. 507

Chiba University of Commerce
(Chiba Shoka Daigaku)

1-3-1 Konodai, Ichikawa-shi, Chiba 272
☎ 0473–72–4111

Faculty
Profs. 74   Assoc. Profs. 16
Assist. Profs. Full–time 10; Part–time 110
Number of Students
Undergrad. 6, 875   Grad. 24
Library 307, 798 volumes

Outline and Characteristics of the University

Chiba University of Commerce is located in Chiba Prefecture which is next to the capital city of Tokyo, and in the immediate vicinity of the Tokyo-Chiba Industrial belt and the New Tokyo International Airport at Narita.

With a history spanning half a century, the school has as its aim the teaching of vocational arts and sciences, both theory and practice, for cooperative research in the various scientific fields broadly related to industrial economics. It is our mission to contribute to society highly educated and knowledgeable individuals with capabilities essential to the world of economics.

Established in 1928 by Ryukichi Endo as Sugamo College of Commerce, the school was originally located in Tokyo. In 1944 the name of the school was changed to the Sugamo College of Economics. The School was destroyed in 1945 as a result of the air raids in Tokyo, and was relocated at the present site in Ichikawa, Chiba.

In the 1950 educational system reform, the school was redesignated "university", and renamed Chiba University of Commerce. Beginning with a single Department of Commerce in the Faculty of Commerce, in 1955 the Department of Economics was added, and the Faculty changed to Faculty of Commerce and Economics. In view of the public demand, the faculty added a Department of Business Administration in 1964. In 1977, Graduate School of Commerce was established, followed by Graduate School of Economics in 1979, each offering a Master's degree program.

UNDERGRADUATE PROGRAMS

Faculty of Commerce and Economics (Freshmen Enrollment: 1, 350)
Department of Business Administration
Accounting, Bookkeeping, Business Administration, Business Management, Enterprise Structure, Financial Management, History of Management, Labor Management, Management, Management History, Marketing Management, Production Management, Theory of Organization
Department of Commerce
Accounting, Auditing, Bookkeeping, Business Administration, Commerce, Commercial Policy, Cost Accounting, Financial Reporting, History of Commerce, Marketing Economics, Marketing Management, Study of Merchandise
Department of Economics
Economic History, Economic Policy, Economics, Economic Statistics, Finance, History of Economics, History of European Economy, History of Japanese Economy, International Economics, National Income, Public Finance, Social Policy

Foreign Student Admission
Qualifications for Applicants
Standard Qualifications Requirement
Examination at the University
Date: in mid-February. Results are announced 10 days later.
Documents to be Submitted When Applying
Standard Documents Requirement
Application period: January 17-30.
Deadline of entrance procedure: the end of February.

GRADUATE PROGRAMS

Graduate School of Commerce (First Year Enrollment : Master's 10)
Division
Commerce
Graduate School of Economics (First Year Enrollment : Master's 10)
Division
Economics

Foreign Student Admission
Qualifications for Applicants
Master's Program
Standard Qualifications Requirement
Examination at the University
Master's Program
Entrance examinations are held twice a year in October and March, but in either case, the school year begins in April. Exams are written and oral.
Documents to be Submitted When Applying
Standard Documents Requirement

*

For Further Information
Undergraduate and Graduate Admission
General Affairs Section, (Attention: Entrance Examination), Chiba University of Commerce, 1-3-1 Konodai, Ichikawa-shi, Chiba 272 ☎ 0473-72-4111 ext. 211

Chikushi Jogakuen College
(Chikushi Jogakuen Daigaku)

Ishizaka 2–12–1, Dazaifu-shi, Fukuoka 818–01
☎ 092–925–3511

Faculty
    Profs. 13   Assoc. Profs. 10
    Assist. Profs. Full–time 2; Part–time 22
Number of Students
    Undergrad. 160
Library 26, 247 volumes

Outline and Characteristics of the College
Chikushi Jogakuen College, founded in 1988, is the latest addition to the Chikushi Jogakuen Group, which has a history of more than 80 years as a Buddhist school dedicated to the education of women.

The College has two Departments: The Department of English offers an advanced program in English language and linguistics.

The Department of Japanese Language and Literature offers an advanced program in Japanese language and literature and also a special program in teaching Japanese as a foreign language.

In either department, overseas candidates are required to have a command of the Japanese language, both spoken and written.

The College is situated in Dazaifu, a small historic town to the south of Fukuoka City. The nearest railway station is Nishitetsu Dazaifu or Gojo.

UNDERGRADUATE PROGRAMS

Faculty of Arts (Freshmen Enrollment: 160)
Department of English
Department of Japanese Language and Literature

Foreign Student Admission
Qualifications for Applicants
    Standard Qualifications Requirement
Examination at the University
A writtern examination, An interview The examination tests the applicant's command of the Japanese language, both spoken and written.

*

For Further Information
Undergraduate Admission
Admission Section, School Affairs Division, Chikushi Jogakuen College, Ishizaka 2–12–1, Dazaifu–shi, Fukuoka 818–01 ☎ 092–925–3511

Chubu University
(Chubu Daigaku)

1200 Matsumoto-cho, Kasugai-shi, Aichi 487
☎ 0568-51-1111

Faculty
    Profs. 101   Assoc. Profs. 74
    Assist. Profs. Full–time 48; Part–time 155
    Res. Assocs. 7
Number of Students
    Undergrad. 5, 320   Grad. 57
Library 231, 000 volumes

Outline and Characteristics of the University
Chubu University was established in 1964 as a technical college for the purpose of training the techno–scientific engineers demanded by the nation's rapidly expanding economy. Since then, the institution has undergone many phases of innovative expansion. Throughout the 25 years of its history, "Technology is Personality" and "Trustworthy Engineers" have been the goals of our education. The institution has achieved excellence in its seven undergraduate engineering disciplines and five graduate (doctoral) programs and produced many capable techno-scientific engineers.

In recent years, however, the intertwining of political, economical, sociological and technological problems now make the single-discipline point of view insufficient for a comprehensive grasp of the world situation. The new requirement is for the development of interdiscipline and intercultural points of view capable of generating appropriate responses to new, complex phenomena.

Our institution has, therefore, expanded beyond its original focus on technology and the natural sciences to include the disciplines of the social sciences and humanities. In 1984, the institution grew into a full-fledged university: Chubu University, with the addition of the new College of International Studies (with Department of International Relations and of International Cultures) and College of Business Administration and Information Science.

The present era has been called the Post-Industrial and Information Era. This has greatly sharpened the demand for people trained to handle computers creatively, and for management personnel disciplined in both the behavioral sciences and in the new quantitative and computer sciences. Needs such as these have created a new field of study, addressed directly by our College of Business Administration and Information Science. Rather than the traditional approach which stresses a grounding in the theory of business management, this department aims to provide the student with a practical knowledge of how the business world works and how to operate within it with maximum efficiency.

The College of International Studies takes as its general aim the training of a sound, academically-based "international perspective. " The curriculum emphasizes rigorous training in two foreign languages, with the goal of a genuine proficiency in at least one of these languages. After surveying the general principles of politics, economics, sociology and anthropology, the student selects one particular region and engages in the specialized study of its features and problems. In addition to regularly scheduled classes, students participate actively in voluntary seminars and research trips.

The main campus of Chubu University is situated about a half hour's drive from Nagoya on a wooded hill overlooking the broad Nobi Plain. The new high rise offices and classroom buildings command an expansive view of metropolitan Nagoya to the south, and mountain vistas to the northeast and west. The quiet suburban atmosphere of the campus provides an ideal setting for study and research activities. Excellent transportation facilities make the campus easily accessible from anywhere in Japan.

Chubu University also operates a satellite campus in Ena at the southern tip of the Japan Alps. The Ena campus functions to provide athletic and supplemental research facilities for university students and faculty.

UNDERGRADUATE PROGRAMS

College of Business Administration and Information Science (Freshmen Enrollment: 200)
Department of Business Administration and Information Science
Accounting, Business Administration, Business Management, Computer Science, History of Business Enterprise, Industrial Engineering, Information Science, System Science, Theory of Business Enterprise
College of Engineering (Freshmen Enrollment: 700)
Department of Architecture
Architecture, Building Construction, Building Materials, Building Services, Environmental Engineering, Execution of Building Works, Structural Design, Structural Mechanics
Department of Civil Engineering
Civil Engineering, Concrete Engineering, Construction Method, Geotechnical Engineering, Hydraulic Engineering, Infrastructure Planning, Materials, Structural Engineering
Department of Electrical Engineering
Circuits Engineering, Electrical Engineering, Electrical Machinery, Materials Engineering, Power Engineering
Department of Electronic Engineering
Application Systems of Electronics, Circuits Engineering, Communication Engineering, Computer Engineering, Electronics, Materials Engineering
Department of Engineering Physics
Applied Electricity and Magnetism, Applied Nuclear Physics, Applied Solid State Physics, Engineering

Physics, Precision Measurements, Systems Control
Department of Industrial Chemistry
Chemical Engineering, Industrial Analytical Chemistry, Industrial Chemistry, Industrial Inorganic Chemistry, Industrial Organic Chemistry, Industrial Physical Chemistry, Synthetic Chemistry
Department of Mechanical Engineering
Applied Mechanics, Fluid Engineering, Heat Engineering, Machine Design, Manufacturing Technology, Mechanical Engineering, Mechanical Engineering Materials
College of International Studies (Freshmen Enrollment: 160)
Department of Comparative Cultures
Comparative Cultures, Cultural Anthropology, Regional Languages, Regional Studies, Sociology
Department of International Relations
Economics, International Relations, Law, Political Science, Regional Languages, Regional Studies

Foreign Student Admission
Qualifications for Applicants
Standard Qualifications Requirement
or those who have acquired the legal Baccalalureate and to be 18 years of age or older.
Examination at the University
A simple written test and an interview.
Documents to be Submitted When Applying
Standard Documents Requirement
The copy of International Baccalaureate Diploma and the certificate of the IB final examination

GRADUATE PROGRAMS

Graduate School of Engineering (First Year Enrollment : Master's 50, Doctor's 24)
Divisions
Applied Physics, Construction Engineering, Electrical Engineering, Industrial Chemistry, Mechanical Engineering

Foreign Student Admission
Qualifications for Applicants
Master's Program
Standard Qualifications Requirement
Doctor's Program
Standard Qualifications Requirement
Examination at the University
Master's Program
An interview and a written test on specialized subjects, if necessary. The same academic standard as Japanese students is required.
Date: in October
Doctor's Program
Same as the Master's program.
Documents to be Submitted When Applying
Standard Documents Requirement
＊
Research Institutes and Centers
Center for International Programs, Center for Phys-

ical Education and Cultural Activities, Central Experimental Facility for Materials, Computer Center, Educational Center for Information Processing, Experimental Facility for Constructional Materials and Structure, Innovation Center for Production Engineering, Learning Resources Center, Research Institute for Industry and Economics, Research Institute for International Studies, Research Institute for Science and Technology

Facilities/Services for Foreign Students

Department of Student Affairs. Center for International Programs. Foreign Student Adviser system. Dormitory

Special Programs for Foreign Students

The Japanese language course.

For Further Information

Undergraduate and Graduate Admission

Center for International Programs, Chubu University, 1200 Matsumoto-cho, Kasugai-shi, Aichi 487 ☎ 0568-51-1111 ext. 2234

Chukyo University
(Chukyo Daigaku)

101-2 Yagoto Honmachi, Showa-ku, Nagoya-shi, Aichi 466 ☎ 052-832-2151

Faculty
Profs. 162 Assoc. Profs. 69
Assist. Profs. Full–time 21; Part–time 322
Res. Assocs. 6
Number of Students
Undergrad. 10, 783 Grad. 102
Library 502, 321 volumes

Outline and Characteristics of the University

Founded in 1956, the School of Commercial Sciences is the oldest school at the university, followed by the School of Physical Education, which opened its doors to students three years later. The School of Letters, which comprises the Departments of Japanese Language and Literature, English Language and Literature, and Psychology, and the School of Law were added in 1966, and the School of Sociology in 1986. Graduate studies were inaugurated in 1969, when the School of Commercial Sciences instituted a course leading to the master's degree. At present the School of Commercial Sciences, Letters, Law , and physical Education all possess post-graduate courses leading both to the master's degree and to the doctorate. In 1987, the School of Economics was newly established.

UNDERGRADUATE PROGRAMS

School of Commercial Sciences (Freshmen Enrollment: 400)

Department of Business Administration

Accounting, Bookkeeping, Financial Management,

Industrial Sociology, Management Science, Production Management

Department of Commercial Sciences

Commodity Science, Economics, Marketing Research, Money and Banking, Statistics

School of Economics (Freshmen Enrollment: 300)

Department of Economics

Economic History, Economic Policy, International Economics, Modern Economics, Monetary and Financial Theory

School of Law (Freshmen Enrollment: 400)

Department of Law

Fundamental Law, Political Science, Private Law, Public Law

School of Letters (Freshmen Enrollment: 380)

Department of English Language and Literature

American Literature, English Literature, English Philology

Department of Japanese Language and Literature

Calligraphy, Japanese Linguistics, Japanese Literature

Department of Psychology

Animal Behavior, Applied Experimental and Industrial Psychology, Psychology of Sensation, Perception and Cognition, Psychotherapy and Personality Assessment

School of Physical Education (Freshmen Enrollment: 430)

Department of Martial Arts (Budo)

but with special emphasis on the martial arts. , Mainly the same as for the Department of Physical Education

Department of Health Education

Health Care, Health Guidance, Public Hygiene, Safety Education

Department of Physical Education

Health Sciences, Methodology of Sports Physiology, Sports Prychology, Sports Sociology

School of Sociology (Freshmen Enrollment: 250)

Department of Sociology

Culture, Folklore and Language, Mankind and Education, Mass Communication, Social Welfare, Sociology

GRADUATE PROGRAMS

Graduate School of Commercial Sciences (First Year Enrollment : Master's 10, Doctor's 3)

Division

Commerce

Graduate School of Law (First Year Enrollment : Master's 10, Doctor's 3)

Division

Law

Graduate School of Letters (First Year Enrollment : Master's 15, Doctor's 6)

Divisions

English Language and Literature, Japanese Language and Literature, Psychology

Graduate School of Physical Education (First Year Enrollment : Master's 12, Doctor's 4)
  Division
Physical Education and Sports Sciences

*

Research Institutes and Centers
Audio-Visual Center, Institute for Research in Economics, Institute for Research in Physical Education, Institute for Research in Social Science, Institute for Research in the Humanities, Institute for Research into Small and Medium-Sized Enterprises

For Further Information
  Undergraduate and Graduate Admission
Department of International Affairs Section, Chukyo University, 101-2 Yagoto Honmachi, Showa-ku, Nagoya-shi, Aichi 466 ☎ 052-832-2151 ext. 305

Chukyo Women's University
(Chukyo Joshi Daigaku)

55 Nadaka-Yama, Yokone-machi Obu-shi, Aichi 474
☎ 0562-46-1291

Faculty
  Profs. 18   Assoc. Profs. 9
  Assist. Profs. Full-time 12; Part-time 29
  Res. Assocs. 2
Number of Students
  Undergrad. 746
Library 82, 582 volumes

Outline and Characteristics of the University
  Chukyo Women's University is a four-year University created to offer higher education to motivated women. Its origin goes back to 1905 when Tamae Naiki founded a small girls' school. In those days, any education above the primary level was virtually non-existent for girls in the Tokai area, a section of Honshu with Nagoya as its central city, except for a few girls who were born to rich families. Naiki, supported by her strong conviction, thus created one of the oldest private educational institute for girls in the city of Nagoya. Her efforts enabled this school to become an accredited women's junior college in 1950 when women were given equal rights by the Constitution of Japan. Chukyo Women's University started its four-year programs in Physical Education and Home Economics (with department of Children's Study and Food and Nutrition Science), in 1963.
  The goal of Chukyo Women's University since its very early days has been to create women with self-assurance and self-control whose positive participation in society and the home should enrich their own environment. Much attention is given to the development of health in body, mind and environment through the curriculum and the research. Moreover, the importance of close relations among students, faculty and administrative members are emphasized.

UNDERGRADUATE PROGRAMS

Faculty of Home Economics (Freshmen Enrollment: 100)
  Department of Child Studies
  Child Education Course Child Studies CourseChid Health, Child Education, Child Education Methods, Child Education Theories, Child Welfare, Developmental Psychology, Infants Care, Physical Education of Children
  Department of Food and Nutrition
Clinical Physiology, Environmental Health, Food Chemistry, Food Economics, Food Material , Food Physiology, Food Processing, Health Management, Home Economics Education, Microbiology, Nutrition, Organic Chemistry, Public Health, School Lunch Management

Faculty of Physical Education (Freshmen Enrollment: 50)
  Department of Physical Education
Adolescent Psychology, Dance, Education Theories, Health Education, Health Management, History of Physical Education, Management of Physical Education, Physiology of Physical Education, Psychology of Physical Education, Recreation, Sociology of Physical Education, Swimming, Team Sports, Theories of Sports, Training Theories

Foreign Student Admission
  Qualifications for Applicants
    Standard Qualifications Requirement
  Examination at the University
    Same as Japanese applicants.
  Documents to be Submitted When Applying
    Standard Documents Requirement

  Qualifications for Transfer Students
  No specific prodedures for transfer students. However, each applicant will be considered for admission on a case by case basis. Please contact the Admissions Office for detail.

*

Facilities/Services for Foreign Students
  Scholarships
For Further Information
  Undergraduate Admission
Administration Office, Chukyo Women's University, 55 Nadaka-Yama, Yokone-machi, Obu-shi, Aichi 474 ☎ 0562-46-1291 ext. 152

Chuo Gakuin University
(Chuo Gakuin Daigaku)
451 Kujike, Abiko-shi, Chiba 270-11
☎ 0471-82-1311

Faculty
    Profs. 46   Assoc. Profs. 19
    Assist. Profs. Full–time 22; Part–time 46
    Res. Assoc. 1
Number of Students
    Undergrad. 2, 278
Library 120, 000 volumes

Outline and Characteristics of the University

Chuo Gakuin University, from its beginnings in 1900 as Nihonbashi Business School offering night classes to businessmen, has always been a leader in defining society's needs and then offering that pertinent, applicable instruction essential for the advancement of an even better, fairer society. That it was truly answering a contemporary demand was proved two years later, when, with the rapid increase in student numbers it was necessary to expand, establishing Chuo Business School in 1902. True to its traditions, Chuo Business School continued to grow, until in 1951 it was recognized as the Chuo Gakuin Educational Foundation. From there, it grew into university status in 1966, and recently added a law department, in 1985.

Building on this 86 year tradition, Chuo Gakuin University is continuing to seek new ways to afford the kind of education essential to today's world. Recognizing the importance of international understanding, Chuo Gakuin University has ongoing sister-school programs with Memphis State University in Memphis, Tennessee, U. S. A., and Tamkang University in Taipei, Taiwan, R. O. C. Through these avenues student and faculty exchanges, dual research, and overseas seminars are made possible on an international scale.

At its campus in Abiko city, among its Commerce and Law faculties a variety of courses are available to students. The Commerce department is divided into three different programs of study: the Business program, the Economics program, and the Information Systems program. Respectively, these programs offer far-ranging emphases: from the scientific analysis of management and trade practices, and systematic investigation of economic theories, to the acquirement of information management skills using the latest in computers.

The Law department consists of two programs of study, the Judicial program and the Administrative program. The former offers a thorough grounding in the orthodox legal curriculum, along with a special sub course for those interested in pursuing a professional career in the judicial field. The Adminis-

trative program of study offers another example of an innovative response to today's needs. The emphasis here is on the specialized legal knowledge and training necessary for those interested in becoming Public Service employees. Also, special classes have been added here to offer a curriculum in regional administration that is unique among Japanese Law departments.

Through instruction and research in Commerce and Law, Chuo Gakuin University's faculty and staff are dedicated to continuing a nearly century long tradition of preparing students to contribute to the betterment of Japan and the world of today and tomorrow.

UNDERGRADUATE PROGRAMS

Faculty of Commerce (Freshmen Enrollment: 340)
Department of Commerce
Accounting, Advertising, Auditing, Banking, Book-keeping, Business, Business History, Business Management, Business Policy, Commodities, Consumer Economics, Economic Geography, Economic Policy, Economics, Finance, History of Economics, Industrial Psychology, Information Management, Insurance, International Economics, International Finance, International Management, International Marketing, Japanese Economic History, Management, Management Analysis, Management Controls, Management Finance, Management Personnel, Marketing Information, Office Management, Security Economics, Security Markets, Small-Medium Enterprises, Socialist Economics, Trade Policy, Transportation Economics, Trusts, Warehousing

Faculty of Law (Freshmen Enrollment: 200)
Department of Law
Administrative Law, Business Law, Civil Law, Civil Suits, Comparative Law, Constitutional Law, Consumer Protection Law, Criminal Law, Economic Law, Education Law, Environmental Law, Foreign Law, History of Legal Systems, History of Politics, Intangible Assets Law, International Law, International Private Law, International Relations, Journalism, Labor Law, Local Jurisdiction, Penal Policies, Political Science, Political Sociology, Private Law, Public Administration, Public Finance Law, Public Information, Public Law, Public Policy, Social Security Law, Tax Law, The Philosophy of Law

Foreign Student Admission
Qualifications for Applicants
    Standard Qualifications Requirement
Examination at the University
1. Examination: Japanese or English
2. Written Report: Japanese, English, French, Chinese or German
3. Interview in Japanese
Documents to be Submitted When Applying
    Standard Documents Requirement
                *

Research Institutes and Centers
Comparative Cultures Center, Information Science Research Center, Research Institute of Chuo Gakuin University, The Local Public Entities Study Organization

For Further Information
Undergraduate Admission
International Affairs Office, Chuo Gakuin University, 451 Kujike, Abiko-shi, Chiba 270-11 ☎ 0471-82-1311

Chuo University
(Chuo Daigaku)

742-1 Higashinakano, Hachioji–shi, Tokyo 192-03
☎ 0426-74-2111

Faculty
    Profs. 403   Assoc. Profs. 98
    Assist. Profs. Full–time 59; Part–time 951
    Res. Assocs. 5
Number of Students
    Undergrad. 30, 112   Grad. 546
Library 1, 158, 676 volumes

Outline and Characteristics of the University
    Chuo University was founded as the English Law School in 1885 by a group of 18 young attorneys and scholars in central Tokyo. The founders endeavored to establish a university which would teach in the spirit of English law and democracy, a courageous effort reflecting their resolve to modernize the Japanese legal system through progressive legal education. The founders desired to provide practical education and opportunities for personal maturity and growth to all qualified and willing students, an alternative to the national institutions which at that time were designed to educate only the élite. This spirit, manifest at Chuo over its long history, is very much alive today. The philosophy Chuo has developed and attempts to further can be summarized in the following four premises: a practical and liberal education; respect for freedom and independence of the individual; preservation of democracy through responsibility; and flexibility based on a dynamic understanding of the development of society and law.
    After its start as the English Law School, the University was reorganized and renamed Chuo (Central) University in 1905, expressive of its role as a center of education and research. Through far-sighted and careful planning, Chuo has grown to have five Faculties and five Graduate Schools—Law, Economics, Commerce, Science and Engineering, and Literature—as well as seven Research Institutes, four centers and three affiliated senior high schools.
    In 1985 Chuo celebrated its centennial on two newly built campuses designed to meet all the needs of its students and faculty. The Faculty of Science and Engineering is located at the Korakuen Campus in central Tokyo. The four other faculties enjoy the new spacious Tama Campus in the western suburbs of Tokyo. Both campuses are equipped with modern technological facilities, and they provide a favorable environment for education and research.
    International academic activities at Chuo University are carried out by each faculty, graduate school or research institute. The International Center was founded in 1981, in order to promote international programs systematically and effectively. The Center coordinates international academic activities, provides the budget and makes the necessary arrangements. At present the University has cooperative arrangements with l'Université de Droit, d'Economie et des Sciences d'Aix-Marseille (France), l'Ecole Supérieure de Commerce de Paris (France), Carleton College (U. S. A.), Thammasat University (Thailand), Tulane University School of Law (U. S. A.), Illinois Benedictine College (U. S. A.), Maryville College (U. S. A.), Bayerische Julius-Maximilians-Universität Würzburg (West Germany) and Univerzitet U Beogradu (Yugoslavia).
Chuo University accepts foreign students through a special entrance examination for foreign applicants. In the academic year 1988-89, foreign students totalled about 150, from 15 countries representing, Asia, Europe and the U. S. A.

UNDERGRADUATE PROGRAMS

Faculty of Commerce (Freshmen Enrollment: Day 900, Evening 300)
    Department of Accounting
Accounting Information Systems, Advanced Bookkeeping, Auditing, Bookkeeping, Commercial Law, Cost Accounting, Financial Accounting, Financial Statement Analysis, Management Accounting, Tax Accounting
    Department of Business Administration
Business Administration, Business History, Business Sociology, Business Theories, Financial Management, Management Information Systems, Management of Computerized Information Systems, Management Planning, Marketing Management, Multinational Enterprises, Personnel Management & Labor Relations, Principles of Management, Production Management
    Department of Marketing and Trade
Advertisement, Business English, Consumer Behavior Theory, Export and Import Marketing, Foreign Trade, History of Commerce, Insurance, International Finance, International Trade Policy, Marketing, Marketing Information Systems, Marketing Management, Non-Life Insurance, Stock Market, System of Money and Finance, Transportation and Communication
Faculty of Economics (Freshmen Enrollment: Day 900, Evening 300)
    Department of Economics

Economic Mathematics, Economic Planning, Economic Statistics, History of Labor Movements, History of Social Thought, Labor Economics, Linear Economics, Public Economics, Public Finance and Local Government, Theory of Money

Department of Industrial Economics

Business Management, Business Organization, Corporate Strategy, Cost Accounting, Industrial Demography, Industrial Economics, Industrial Locations, Industrial Sociology, Labor Economics, Labor Law, Modern Technology, Principles of Bookkeeping, Public Enterprise, Securities and Capital Market, Small and Medium Business Policy

Department of International Economics

Current English, Development Economics, Foreign Economic Affairs (Advanced Countries, Asia, Socialist Countries, Others), Foreign Exchange, International Economics, International Law, International Marine Transportation, International Monetary Circulation, International Relations, International Trade Policy, International Trade Practices, Japanese International Trade, Marine Insurance, Multinational Corporations, The World Economy

Faculty of Law (Freshmen Enrollment: Day 1, 100, Evening 500)

Department of Law

Administrative Law, Anglo-American Law, Bankruptcy Law, Civil Law, Civil Procedure, Commercial Law, Constitutional Law, Creditor's Rights, Criminal Law, Criminal Policy, Criminal Procedure, Criminology, Economic Law, Industrial Property Law, International Law, Judicial Process, Philosophy of Law, Private International Law, Roman Law, Tax Law, Trade Union Law

Department of Political Science

Communications, Comparative Politics, Financial Management in Local Government, History of International Politics, History of Japanese Political Thought, History of Social Movements, History of Social Thought, History of Western Political Thought, International Politics, Japanese Political History, Occidental Political History, Political Sociology, Politics in China, Politics in the U. S. A., Politics in the U. S. S. R., Public Administration, Readings on Political Science in English, Regional Politics, The Fundamentals of Political Science, The Political Process

Faculty of Literature (Freshmen Enrollment: Day 800, Evening 150)

Department of History

Japanese History Course

History of Japanese Culture, History of Japanese Socio-Economics, History of Japanese Thought, Japanese History, Japanese Legal & Political History, Japanese Paleography

Occidental History Course

Ancient Occidental History, Contemporary Occidental History, History of Occidental Countries, Occidental History, Occidental History in the Middle Ages, Occidental History in the Modern Age

Oriental History Course

Ancient Oriental History, Early Modern Oriental History, Historiography of Asia, History of Regional Ages, Medieval Oriental History, Modern Oriental History

Department of Literature

English and American Literature Course

Contemporary American Writers & Their Works, English and American Cultural Sociography, English Phonetics, History of English and American Literature, Modern English Writers & Their Works

French Literature Course

Classic & Enlightenment French Literature, Contemporary French Literature, French Cultural Sociography, French Linguistics, History of French Literature, Medieval & Renaissance French Literature

German Literature Course

German Culture, German Linguistics, German Literature, History of German Literature, History of German Thought

Japanese Literature Course

Chinese Classics, History of Japanese Literature, Japanese Calligraphy, Japanese Literature, Japanese Literature and Language, Japanese Philology

Department of Philosophy

Education Course

Education, Educational Administration & Finance, Educational Methodology, Educational Philosophy, Educational Psychology, Educational Sociology, History of Educational Thought

Philosophy Course

History of Chinese Philosophy, History of Ethical Thought, History of Occidental Philosophy, Modern Logic, Philosophy of Science

Psychology Course

Educational Psychology, Industrial Psychology, Labor Science, Psychological Research, Psychological Statistics, Socio-Cultural Psychology

Sociology Course

Comparative Sociology, History of Social Thought, History of Sociology, Regional Sociology, Social Pathology, Social Psychology

Faculty of Science and Engineering (Freshmen Enrollment: Day 870, Evening 240)

Department of Civil Engineering

Applied Mechanics, Coastal Engineering, Concrete Engineering, Environmental Engineering, Highway Engineering, Hydraulics, Hydrology, Railway Engineering, River Engineering, Soil Engineering, Strength of Materials, Surveying, Traffic Planning

Department of Electrical Engineering

Control Theory, Electrical & Electronic Materials, Electrical Machinery, Electric Discharge, Electromagnetic Field, Electronic Circuits, Guided Wave Engineering, Information Processing, Introduction to Digital System Theory, Introduction to Electromagnetic Theory, Network Theory, Semiconductor Devices, Seminar in Computer Programming

Department of Industrial Chemistry

Biochemistry, Chemical Engineering Thermodynamics, Coordination Chemistry, Environmental Chemistry, Fermentation Engineering, Inorganic Material Chemistry, Organic Material Chemistry, Polymer Chemistry, Powder Technology, Quality Control, Surface Chemistry, Transport Phenomena

Department of Industrial Engineering

Cost Control, Engineering Economics, Experiments in Industrial Engineering, Human Engineering, Introduction to Information Processing, Mathematical Statistics, Methods Engineering, Operations Research, Production Control, Programming Languages, Quality Control, Reliability Engineering, Systems Engineering

Department of Mathematics

Algebra, Analysis, Applied Statistics, Computer Science, Functional Analysis, Geometry, Introduction to Information Processing, Introduction to Mathematics, Linear Algebra, Statistics, Topology

Department of Physics

Applied Analysis, Computational Physics, Condensed Matter Physics, Electricity and Magnetism, Experiments in Physics, Introduction to Contemporary Physics, Mechanics, Methods of Experimental Physics, Quantum Mechanics, Quantum Physics, Seminar in Physics, Solving Problems in Physics, Thermodynamics and Statistical Mechanics

Department of Precision Mechanical Engineering

Control Engineering, Data Analysis, Design of Precision Instruments, Dynamics of Machinery, Engineering Thermodynamics, Introduction to Information Processing, Machine Design, Machine Elements, Materials Science, Mechanics, Mechanics of Materials, Precision Machining, Precision Measurements

Foreign Student Admission

Qualifications for Applicants

Standard Qualifications Requirement

Foreign students who, at the time of examinations, have been in Japan over two years or have been registered in a Japanese college or university for more than one year as a regular student, must take the same entrance examination as Japanese students.

Applicants to the Faculties of Law, Economics and Literature are required to take the Japanese Language Proficiency Test (Level 1). Applicants to the Faculty of Law are required to take the General Examination for Foreign Students as well.

Examination at the University

Submitted documents, written examinations and an interview. Examination Subjects vary according to Faculty as follows:

Faculties of Law, Economics, Commerce and Literature: Japanese Language and English Language.

Faculty of Science and Engineering: Japanese Language, English Language, Mathematics and Science (Physics or Chemistry).

Documents to be Submitted When Applying

Standard Documents Requirement

Certificate of Japanese Language Proficiency.

Foreign students are accepted only in the day course.

Application forms are available at the International Center from late July. Applications must be submitted at the International Center personally by the applicant. Applications by mail cannot be accepted.

Application Period: Early December

Dates of Examination: Early February

Announcement of Results: Early February

Registration Period for Admission: Late February–Early March

GRADUATE PROGRAMS

Graduate School of Commerce (First Year Enrollment : Master's 25, Doctor's 5)

Division

Commerce

Graduate School of Economics (First Year Enrollment : Master's 25, Doctor's 5)

Division

Economics

Graduate School of Law (First Year Enrollment : Master's 110, Doctor's 18)

Divisions

Anglo–American Law, Criminal Law, Political Science, Private Law, Public Law

Graduate School of Literature (First Year Enrollment : Master's 45, Doctor's 24)

Divisions

Asian History, English and American Literature, European History, French Literature, German Literature, Japanese History, Japanese Literature, Philosophy, Sociology

Graduate School of Science and Engineering (First Year Enrollment : Master's 55, Doctor's 12)

Divisions

Civil Engineering, Electrical Engineering, Industrial Chemistry, Physics, Precision Mechanical Engineering

Foreign Student Admission

Qualifications for Applicants

Master's Program

Standard Qualifications Requirement

Overseas applicant needs a guarantor in Japan.

Doctor's Program

Standard Qualifications Requirement

Overseas applicant needs a guarantor in Japan.

Foreign students who have an undergraduate or graduate degree from a Japanese university must take the same entrance examination as Japanese students.

Examination at the University

Master's Program

The selection is based on submitted documents (including a thesis) and an interview. Applicants to the Graduate School of Commerce are required to take a written examination as well.

Doctor's Program

Same as Master's program.
Documents to be Submitted When Applying
Standard Documents Requirement
1. Certificate of Japanese Language Proficiency
2. Thesis
    The theme of the thesis can be freely chosen according to the applicant's major. in Japanese, English, German, French or Chinese. A summary in the Japanese language must be attached
    Application forms are available at the International Center from late July. Applications must be submitted at the International Center personally by the applicant or guarantor. Applications by mail cannot be accepted.
Application Period: Mid October
Dates of Examination: Late November—Early December
Announcement of Results: Mid December
Registration Period for Admission: Mid February– Mid March

*

Research Institutes and Centers
Audio–Visual Laboratory, Computer Center, Institute of Accounting Research, Institute of Business Research, Institute of Comparative Law in Japan, Institute of Cultural Science, Institute of Economic Research, Institute of Health and Physical Science, Institute of Social Science
Facilities/Services for Foreign Students
Orientation for freshmen; arrangements for scholarships; arrangements for medical fee reimbursement by AIEJ; summer seminar; friendly get–togethers with faculty and administrative members; follow–up communication with graduates in the form of campus news magazines by The International Center.
    A service introducing private lodgings near the campuses.
Special Programs for Foreign Students
    The following Japanese language courses.
1. Undergraduate:
    Faculties of Law, Economics, Commerce and Literature: Japanese language and Japanese studies for credit are required.
2. Graduate:
    A non–credit, extra–curricular Japanese language course is available.
For Further Information
    Undergraduate and Graduate Admission
International Center, Chuo University,
742-1 Higashinakano, Hachioji–shi, Tokyo 192-03
☎ 0426-74-2212

Daido Institute of Technology
(Daido Kogyo Daigaku)
2-21 Daido-cho, Minami-ku, Nagoya-shi, Aichi 457
☎ 052-612-6111

Faculty
    Profs. 42   Assoc. Profs. 32
    Assist. Profs. Full–time 21; Part–time 104
    Res. Assocs. 10
Number of Students
    Undergrad. 2, 477
Library 110, 000 volumes

Outline and Characteristics of the University
    Daido Institute of Technology is a private four-year college offering professional degrees in Engineering and Architecture. Since its founding in 1939, as a technical training school for industrial workers, under the auspices of Daido Steel Company, one of the world's largest manufacturers of specialty steel, the institution has grown to become a reliable source of talented, internationally-minded civil, electrical and mechanical engineers and architects for companies both large and small, throughout the Chubu District of central Japan.
    As the name Daido, "the Exalted Way", implies in Japanese, the school was originally founded with the intention of applying the principles of a humane education to the practical needs of society, especially in the technological and industrial sectors, for the general benefit of all mankind. In the early years, as Daido Gakuen Educational Foundation progressed from its humble beginnings, through a brief tenure as a junior college, and on to full accreditation in 1964 as a four–year college, the faculty and administration of the college adhered strictly to this fundamental creed of service to society through humane education in technological subjects.
    In addition to the humanistic ideals that have guided the college from the outset, Daido Institute of Technology has, in recent years, made a firm commitment to the principle of international educational exchange through the implementation of academic affiliations with the University of Oregon and Oregon State University. Daido students have been making annual study tours to these American campuses since 1979, and members of the faculties of all three institutions have enjoyed the crosscultural benefits of extended research visits, on both the Japanese and American campuses.
    The city of Nagoya, fourth largest in Japan, and sixth largest seaport in the world, is situated in the traditional heartland of the country, midway between Tokyo and Osaka, along the largely urbanized Pacific coast of Japan. The students and faculty of Daido Institute of Technology are fortunate to enjoy direct and easy access to the sea, as well as the year-

round recreational potential of the Central Japan Alps, world-famous for skiing and hiking.

Located in the southern section of the city, the college has, during the past few years, been expanding and beautifying its campus, while aggressively working to improve research, classroom and computer facilities. Other developments include the recent accreditation of a new undergraduate major in Applied Electronics, and currently scheduled expansions within the Mechanical and Construction Engineering Departments. A new state-of-the-art library is also on the drawing boards as the college gears up not merely to meet, but to surpass the challenges of excellence and internationalization that will increasingly confront the Japanese education system in years to come.

UNDERGRADUATE PROGRAMS

Faculty of Engineering (Freshmen Enrollment: 420)
  Department of Applied Electronics
Electromagnetic Waves and Control, Electronic Applications, Electronic Circuits and Computers, Semiconductor Electronics
  Department of Construction Engineering
  Architecture Course
Architectural Design and History, Architecture and City Planning, Building Materials and Building Construction, Environmental Engineering, Structural Mechanics for Buildings
  Civil Engineering Course
Hydraulics, Materials and Construction Engineering, Soil Mechanics and Foundation Engineering, Structural Engineering, Traffic Engineering and Planning
  Department of Electrical Engineering
Applied Electricity, Basic Electrical Engineering, Electric Machinery and Apparatus, Electric Power Engineering
  Department of Mechanical Engineering
Fluid Engineering, Machine Design, Machine Dynamics, Machine Manufacture, Machine Materials, Materials Dynamics, Mechanical Electronics, Production and Information Engineering, Thermal Engineering

Foreign Student Admission
  Qualifications for Applicants
  Standard Qualifications Requirement
  Examination at the University
  Japanese Language Proficiency Test, General Examination for Foreign Students and the entrance examination.
  Documents to be Submitted When Applying
  Standard Documents Requirement
  Following documents are also required.
  1. Official transcripts of the Japanese Language School of the International Students Institute or its equivalent, showing the grade and the certificate or diploma awarded to the applicant.

  2. A letter of recommendation from the embassy or the consulate.
  3. A letter of recommendation issued by the head-master of the Japanese Language School of the International Students Institute or its equivalent.

Application forms are available at the Admissions Office from September. Submission deadline: the end of November.

*

Research Institutes and Centers
Information Processing Center, Materials Engineering Laboratory
For Further Information
  Undergraduate Admission
Admissions Office, Daido Institute of Technology, 2-21 Daido-cho, Minami-ku, Nagoya-shi, Aichi 457
☎ 052-612-6111

Daiichi College of Commerce and Industry
(Daiichi Keizai Daigaku)

3-11-25 Gojo, Dazaifu-shi, Fukuoka 818-01
☎ 092-922-5131

UNDERGRADUATE PROGRAMS

Faculty of Economics (Freshmen Enrollment: 500)
  Department of Business Administration
  Department of Economics
  Department of Trade

Daiichi College of Pharmaceutical Sciences
(Daiichi Yakka Daigaku)

22-1 Tamagawa-cho, Minami-ku, Fukuoka-shi, Fukuoka 815   ☎ 092-541-0161

Faculty
  Profs. 26   Assoc. Profs. 6
  Assist. Profs. Full–time 11; Part–time 21
  Res. Assocs. 37
Number of Students
  Undergrad. 1, 450
Library 51, 531 volumes

Outline and Characteristics of the College
  The Daiichi College of Pharmaceutical Sciences was established in 1960 by the late Chancellor, Yorisuke Tsuzuki and Mrs. Sadae Tsuzuki, Chairman of the Board of Directors at present.
  This college has experienced rapid growth in the

short history of a quarter century, and is presently composed of two Departments, Pharmacy and Industrial Pharmacy, with more than 1, 260 students.

Faculty members are divided into 15 chairs according to each major, and make for an enjoyable studying environment. The Bachelor's degree, qualification for candidate registered pharmacist and a number of other qualifications for hygienic and environmental works are offered. Both departments are situated on the same campus at the southern educational district of the city of Fukuoka.

Fukuoka is a metropolitan city in western Japan. It is also said to be one of the oldest city in the country. Hakata Harbor has maintained its fame as the largest gateway to the Asian continent, through its more than 1, 500 years history.

UNDERGRADUATE PROGRAMS

Faculty of Pharmaceutical Sciences (Freshmen Enrollment: 260)
Department of Industrial Pharmacy
Department of Pharmacy
Analytical Pharmacy, Biochemistry, Biology, Hygienic Chemistry, Microbiology, Pharmaceutical Chemistry, Pharmacognosy, Pharmacology, Pharmacy, Physical Analysis, Physical Chemistry, Physical Pharmaceutics, Radio Chemistry, Synthetic Medicinal Chemistry

Foreign Student Admission
Qualifications for Applicants
Standard Qualifications Requirement
Examination at the College
Applicant must take an entrance examination consisting of a written exam and an interview in Japanese, conducted by the College, as follows: English, Chemistry and Mathematics, on either Feburuary 3, or March 12, 1987.
Documents to be Submitted When Applying
Standard Documents Requirement
Application forms are available at the Admission Office from October. All applicants are required to submit the specified application documents to the Admission Office by January 28 or March 9.

Qualifications for Transfer Students
Standard Qualifications Requiremeut
Examination for Transfer Students
Candidate must take the same entrance examination as freshman applicants under the same conditions.
Documents to be Submitted When Applying
Standard Documents Requirement
Candidates for admission as transfer students with second-year standing must have credit for the courses in the first-year curriculum in this college, and is required to submit official transcripts showing courses taken and grades received at all academic institutions in addition with normal application documents.

*

Research Institutes and Centers
Instrumental Analyses Center, Medicinal Plants Garden, Radio Isotope Center
Facilities/Services for Foreign Students
Female Students' Dormitory
For Further Information
Undergraduate Admission
Admission Office, Daiichi College of Pharmaceutical Sciences, 22-1 Tamagawa-cho, Minami-ku, Fukuoka-shi, Fukuoka 815 ☎ 092-541-0161 ext. 333, 362

Dai Ichi University, College of Technology
(Dai Ichi Kogyo Daigaku)
1-10-2 Chuo, Kokubu-shi, Kagoshima 899-43
☎ 0995-45-0640

Faculty
Profs. 40　Assoc. Profs. 26
Assist. Profs. Full–time 23; Part–time 57
Number of Students
Undergrad. 3, 198
Library 29, 430 volumes

Outline and Characteristics of the College
Dai Ichi University, College of Technology is in Kokubu City, which is located approximately in the center of Kagoshima Prefecture, and can be reached in 20 minutes from Kagoshima International Airport. Kokubu City, with its neighboring town, was selected as a"Technopolis", a highly technologically developed city.

The college is the only private college of technology in southern Kyushu, and is generally acknowledged as an important institute to help develop the Technopolis. The college, along with the help of expert specialists chosen from the industrial world, plays a leading role in educating promising students. The college specializes in training students who will later participate in the engineering world by placing emphasis on laboratory work and practice rather than on theoretical lectures.

The college curriculum consists of five departments: Aeronautic Engineering, Electronic Engineering, Mechanical Engineering, Civil Engineering, and Architecture. The five departments have 19 courses, so that students can choose a suitable course for their ability and capacity.

Surrounded by the beautiful scenery of Kirishima National Park, the college is eager to improve the educational equipment and research laboratories, so that in the 21st century the students can contribute to the industrial world. The whole college is striving for the realization of an ideal scientific education.

UNDERGRADUATE PROGRAMS

Faculty of Technology (Freshmen Enrollment: 360)
Department of Aeronautic Engineering
Aeronautic Engineering Course
Aircraft Maintenance Course
Aircraft Pre-flight Course
Department of Architecture
Architectural Design Course
Architectural Engineering Course
Building Maintenance Course
Real Estate Management Course
Residential Housing Course
Department of Civil Engineering
City Planning Course
Civil Engineering Course
Environmental Engineering Course
Landscape Gardening Course
Department of Electronic Engineering
Aeronautic Electronic Engineering Course
Electronic Engineering Course
Information Engineering Course
Department of Mechanical Engineering
Automotive Mechanical Course
Industrial Machine Course
Mechanical Electronics Course
Mechanical Engineering Course

*

For Further Information
Undergraduate Admission
Admission Office, Dai Ichi University, College of Technology, 1-10-2 Chuo, Kokubu-shi, Kagoshima 899-43 ☎ 0995-45-0640

Daito Bunka University
(Daito Bunka Daigaku)

1-9-1 Takashimadaira, Itabashi–ku, Tokyo 175
☎ 03-935-1111

Faculty
    Profs. 186   Assoc. Profs. 72
    Assist. Profs. Full–time 53; Part–time 314
    Res. Assocs. 4
Number of Students
    Undergrad. 11, 727   Grad. 99
Library 544, 786 volumes

Outline and Characteristics of the University
    Daito Bunka University was founded in 1923 under the name of Daito Bunka Gakuin. This period in Japanese history is noted for its great confusion in social, ideological and moral terms, resulting in serious social unrest and disturbances. Gravely concerned with this state of affairs, leaders in political, financial, industrial and academic circles conferred a number of times and finally presented a bill to the National Diet providing the establishment of a university which would "promote the national school of literature and philosophy and the Chinese studies as the essential elements of Japanese culture, enhance prestige and morals, educate able persons to work both at home and abroad, attain peace and stability in the citizens' thoughts and firmly establish national independence, all in order to contribute to national prosperity and world civilization." The bill passed the Diet, begetting this University.

    The university has seen a half century of numerous and sometimes violent changes. Always adhering to the founding principles, the university has been engaged in steady and expanding educational activities in the art and social sciences of the East and West, producing many able graduates.

    In 1949, Daito Bunka Gakuin became a private university under the new system of education introduced by the government at that time. It was renamed Tokyo Bunsei University. In 1953, the name was changed to Daito Bunka University, and in 1961 the University moved to Takashimadaira, Itabashi–ku, Tokyo, where it is now located. In 1967, a new campus was opened in Higashi–Matsuyama City, Saitama Prefecture. The general studies program for freshmen and sophomores is carried out there.

    The University now has eleven departments under five faculties and has become a university of the study of culture and social sciences. In addition to the undergraduate program, the graduate schools and postgraduate courses, there are educational institutes and centers.

    The University has a special program for overseas students. This is the Japanese Language Program and a one-year course open to those students who wish to enter the University (undergraduate program, graduate school and postgraduate course) and need to learn the Japanese language for this purpose.

    Through these institutions, men and women are being educated in the ideals of the founders of the University.

UNDERGRADUATE PROGRAMS

Faculty of Economics (Freshmen Enrollment: 1, 000)
Department of Business Administration
Accounting, Bookkeeping, Business Analysis, Cost Accounting, Financial Management, General Theory and History of Business Administration, Human Resources Management, Management Statitsics, Management Thought and Theory, Marketing Management, Production Control
Department of Economics
Economic History, Economic Policy, Economics, International Economics, Money and Banking, Public Finance, Social Policy, Statistics
Faculty of Foreign Languages (Freshmen Enrollment: 450)
Department of Chinese Language

Chinese Language, Chinese Literature, Chinese Studies
Department of English Language
Anglo–American Literature, Anglo–American Studies, English Phonetics and Grammar, History of English Language
Faculty of International Relations (Freshmen Enrollment: 200)
Department of International Cultures
Arts, Culture and History of East, South, Southeast and West Asia, Asian Studies, Languages (Arabic, Chinese, Hindi, Indonesian, Persian, Thai, Urdu and Vietnamese)
Department of International Relations
Asian Studies, Comparative Culture and Religion, Economics, International Relations, Languages (Arabic, Chinese, Hindi, Indonesian, Persian, Thai, Urdu and Vietnamese), Politics and Societies of East, South, Southeast and West Asia
Faculty of Law (Freshmen Enrollment: 350)
Department of Law
Administrative Law, Civil Law Commercial Law, Civil Procedure, Constitutional Law, Corporation Law, Criminal Law and Procedure, Family Law, International Law, Labor Law, Law of Inheritance, Philosophy of Law, Political Science, Private Law, Social Security Law
Faculty of Literature (Freshmen Enrollment: 630)
Department of Anglo–American Literature
Anglo–American Literature, Comparative Literature, English Phonetics, History of Anglo–American Literature, Linguistics
Department of Chinese Literature
Calligraphy, Chinese Classics in Japan, Chinese Literature and Philosophy, Japanese Literature
Department of Education
Education, Educational Administration and Finance, Educational Curriculum, Educational Law System, Educational Psychology, History of Education, Methodology of Education, Pedagogy, Sociology in Education
Department of Japanese Literature
Calligraphy, Chinese Literature and Philosophy, History of Japanese Literature, Japanese Linguistics and Grammar, Japanese Literature

Foreign Student Admission
Qualifications for Applicants
Standard Qualifications Requirement
Applicants must stay in Japan at the time of the entrance examination.
Examination at the University
Japanese, English and Japanese Composition: January 11, 1989
Interview: January 12, 1989
Documents to be Submitted When Applying
Standard Documents Requirement
The application forms and the prospectus of registration will be available from June, 1988. Relative's agreement (Prescribed form) is to be submitted along with other documents.

All the required documents must be delivered to the International Division between November 28 and December 19, 1988. The result of the entrance examination (January 11 and 12) will be announced on January 25, 1989 on the notice board in the campus. The written admission and registration forms will be directly handed over to the applicant or the guarantor between 9: 00 a. m and noon on the same day. The registration period is between January 26 and February 13, 1989.

ONE-YEAR GRADUATE PROGRAMS

One-Year Graduate Course of Literature (Enrollment: 20)
Chinese Language and Literature, Chinese Philosophy, Japanese Language and Literature
One-Year Graduate Course of Economics (Enrollment: 10)
Economics

Foreign Student Admission
Qualifications for Applicants
Standard Qualifications Requirement
1. Those who have graduated or are expected to graduate in March 1988 a Japanese university or college, or
2. An applicant with qualifications equivalent to a graduate of this University.
Date of Application: February 25–March 6.
Examination at the University
The same entrance examination as Japanese students: a written and oral examination.
Date of Examination: March 10
The result will be announced on March 20.
Registration Period: March 23–28

GRADUATE PROGRAMS

Graduate School of Economics (First Year Enrollment : Master's 10, Doctor's 5)
Division
Economics
Graduate School of Jurisprudence (First Year Enrollment : Master's 10)
Division
Law
Graduate School of Literature (First Year Enrollment : Master's 20, Doctor's 7)
Divisions
Chinese Literature and Philosophy, English Literature, Japanese Literature

Foreign Student Admission
Qualifications for Applicants
Master's Program
Standard Qualifications Requirement
Doctor's Program
Standard Qualifications Requirement

Examination at the University

Master's Program

The same entrance examination as the Japanese students: a written and oral examination and an interview.

Date of Examination: February 19 and 20

Announcement of the Result: March 2

Registration Period: March 3–10

Doctor's Program

Same as the Master's Program

Documents to be Submitted When Applying

Standard Documents Requirement

Application forms are available at the Admission Center. Applicants are required to submit the specified application documents to the Center.

Application Period: January 20–February 6

*

Research Institutes and Centers

Calligraphy Culture Center, Data Processing Center, Institute of Business Research, Institute of Language Education, Institute of Legal Studies, Institute of Oriental Studies, Sports Center

Facilities/Services for Foreign Students

A "Tutor System for Overseas Students "was set up for the purpose of improving their study of Japanese Language, promoting mutual understanding between overseas students and Japanese students as well as fostering mutual friendship among overseas students themselves. A field trip to an industrial plant in spring, a three–day tour of cultural explorations in autumn for overseas students and the International Exchange Program sponsored by Takahagi–City, Ibaraki Prefecture in May in order to experience a homestay and apppreciate Japanese culture have been welcomed by them.

Special Programs for Foreign Students

As for overseas students in the General Education Course (two years after matriculation for the undergraduate), general education subjects may be replaced, up to 26 credits, by the courses in"Japanese Language and Japanese Studies". This helps them improve their Japanese ability.

The University offers the Japanese Language Program for those foreign students desiring to enter a Japanese university. 31. 5 lesson hours a week are given throughout the year. The number of students is limited to 20. Because of the small number, a student can become familiar with an instructor and pave the way for the undergraduate program. An excellent student can be recommended to the undergraduate program with the exception of Faculties of Economics and Law without examination.

For Further Information

Undergraduate Admission

Chief Clerk in Charge of Overseas Students, International Division, Daito Bunka University, 1-9-1 Takashimadaira, Itabashi-ku, Tokyo 175 ☎ 03-935-1111 ext. 292

Graduate Admission

Chief Clerk in Charge of Graduate Admission, Division of General Educational Affairs, Daito Bunka University, 1-9-1 Takashimadaira, Itabashi-ku, Tokyo 175 ☎ 03-935-1111 ext. 265

Doho University
(Doho Daigaku)

7-1 Inabaji-cho, Nakamura-ku, Nagoya-shi, Aichi 453 ☎ 052-411-1111

Faculty
    Profs.   27   Assoc. Profs.   11
    Assist. Profs.   Full–time   6; Part–time   70
    Res. Assoc.   1
Number of Students
    Undergrad.   1, 066
Library   150, 000 volumes

Outline and Characteristics of the University

Doho University was originally founded in 1827 by Rakumon Aoki as a research institute for Buddhism. The education of this institution is based on Buddhist teachings, especially in the spirit of reverential friendship which was preached by Shinran during the Kamakura period.

Doho University aims to ultimately contribute to the promotion of the welfare of human beings in the contemporary world. In order to fulfill this mission, the University is deeply devoted to an academic and practical education that approaches studies from the point of view of self-enlightenment of True Pure Land Buddhism.

The predecessor of the present University was the College of True Pure Land Buddhism established in 1921. It was subsequently renamed Tokai Doho College in 1950, and finally Doho University in 1957.

Doho University has experienced rapid growth in its short 65 years history. At present, it is comprised of two faculties, Literature and Social Welfare, with three departments, Buddhism, Japanese Literature, and Social Welfare. And one-year program of Shin-Buddhism study started in 1986. Doho University is the primary institution of the Doho Educational Foundation which also consists of four other institutions. They are the Nagoya College of Music, the Nagoya Junior College of Creative Arts, Doho High School, and Doho Kindergarten.

UNDERGRADUATE PROGRAMS

Faculty of Literature (Freshmen Enrollment: 100)

Department of Buddhism

Buddhism, Buddhist Culture, History of Shin-Buddhism, Shin-Buddhism, Shin-Buddhism Scriptures, Study of Enlightenment

Department of Japanese Literature

Chinese Literature, History of Japanese Literature, Japanese Language and Linguistics, Japanese Literature

Faculty of Social Welfare (Freshmen Enrollment: 100)

Department of Social Welfare

Buddhist Social Welfare, Child Welfare, Comunity Organization, Family and Regional Sociology, Family Social Welfare, Foster Child Care, History of Social Welfare, International Social Welfare, Judicial Welfare, Medical Welfare, Public Assistance, Regional Community, Social Education, Social Pathology, Social Research, Social Security, Social Welfare, Social Welfare Facility Administration, Social Welfare Law, Theory of Social Welfare Practice, Welfare for the Aged, Welfare for the Handicapped, Welfare for Women

Foreign Student Admission

Qualifications for Applicants

Standard Qualifications Requirement

Examination at the University

The examination is usualy given in February. It mainly consists of a written and an interview concerning the submitted documents.

Documents to be Submitted When Applying

Standard Documents Requirement

A document attesting to the applicant's proficiency in Japanese is also required.

*

Research Institutes and Centers

Doho Gakuen Buddhist Culture Institute

For Further Information

Undergraduate Admission

Student Affairs Section, Bureau of Student Affairs, Doho University, 7-1 Inabaji-cho, Nakamura-ku, Nagoya-shi, Aichi 453 ☎ 052-411-1111 ext. 315

Dohto University
(Dohto Daigaku)

7 Ochiishi-cho, Mombetsu-shi, Hokkaido 094
☎ 01582–4–8101

Faculty
    Profs. 12   Assoc. Profs. 19
    Assist. Profs.   Full–time 15; Part–time 9
    Res. Assocs. 2
Number of Students
    Undergrad. 1, 000
Library 34, 353 volumes

Outline and Characteristics of the University

Dohto University originally started as Hokkaido Professional School of Industry, which was established in 1964 by the educational foundation, Hokkaido Industrial Institution. Jun Sakurai, who is presently the Chancellor of Dohto University, was the leader in this movement for establishment of a new institution. Sakurai, in cooperation with several knowledgeable persons, initiated an educational foundation for the purpose of establishing a universi-

ty while he was still serving the City Council of Sapporo. Through their efforts the Professional School of Industry, which was to develop later into Dohto University, came into being. The educational idea was to bring up a "backboned industrial man." In the process of fulfilling this idea, Hokkaido College of Industry was established. It was comprised of the Department of Management and the Department of Architecture. Thus, the Institution developed functionally as one that produced the competent talent needed in society.

In 1970, the educational foundation obtained the new name Hokkaido Sakurai Institution of Industry, and Hokkaido College of Industry was renamed Dohto College, and Jun Sakurai took up the duties of Chairman of the Board of Trustees.

In 1978, Dohto University was established, the product of the endeavor to create a four-year college for higher education and to train a "backboned industrial man." Dohto University consists of two faculties for professional courses, the Faculty of Social Welfare and the Faculty of Fine Arts, and one for liberal arts, the Faculty of Liberal Arts. The educational ideal of Dohto University is, of course, to train students to become a "backboned industrial man," and this ideal has been supported by others since the university foundation.

These ideals of "ever onward" and of "service to others, " are carried on by the students as a valued tradition. Learning has no limit. The spirit of the university foundation is to breed those young people who go forward coping with every difficulty with a spirit that never gives up.

UNDERGRADUATE PROGRAMS

Faculty of Fine Arts (Freshmen Enrollment: 100)

Department of Architecture

Computer Structural Design, Fine Arts Architectural Engineering

Department of Design

Computer Graphic Design, Environmental Plastic Design

Faculty of Social Welfare (Freshmen Enrollment: 150)

Department of Social Welfare

Child Welfare, Social Administration, Social Information, Social Work

Foreign Student Admission

Qualifications for Applicants

Standard Qualifications Requirement

Documents to be Submitted When Applying

Standard Documents Requirement

*

Research Institutes and Centers

Marine Biological Research Institute, Northern Welfare Research Institute

For Further Information

Undergraduate Admission

Instruction Second Section, Instruction Division, Bureau of Administrative Affairs, Dohto University, 7 Ochiishi-cho, Mombetsu-shi, Hokkaido 094 ☎ 01582-4-8101 ext. 225

Dokkyo University
(Dokkyo Daigaku)
1-1 Gakuen-cho, Soka-shi, Saitama 340
☎ 0489-42-1111

Faculty
    Profs. 138   Assoc. Profs. 35
    Assist. Profs. Full-time 24; Part-time 253
Number of Students
    Undergrad. 8, 583   Grad. 48
Library   480, 266 volumes

Outline and Characteristics of the University

The Dokkyo Educational Foundation (Dokkyo Gakuen), first known as the German Association School (Doitsu-gaku Kyokai Gakko), was founded in 1883 shortly after the Meiji Restoration. The institute was established as a center for research and study of German civilization and culture by Amane Nishi and Hiroyuki Kato, eminent intellectual leaders of the period. German politics and law were taught at the school. In 1963, on the occasion of the 80th anniversary of the institute, it was decided to found a university. In the following year Dokkyo University was established by Teiyu Amano (1887-1980), a renowned philosopher and former Minister of Education, who with the unique ideal—"Easy to enter, hard to graduate"—wanted to reform the current higher educational system in Japan; to effect, in his words, "a Copernican turn in Japanese higher education." The University was to be "a place for the development of personality through learning." Since then we continued to make Dokkyo University unique, and its unique humanistic curriculum is widely known. The ideal, an education with an international orientation, initiated by the German Association School over 100 years ago, is still animatedly alive in the spirit of the University.

The University's ultimate goal is the fostering of healthy, creative, practical, and emotionally mature individuals; men and women competent in foreign languages who can make significant contributions to the international community, thus enhancing peaceful and friendly relations between Japan and all nations. Hence, all students, no matter what their major, are required not only to gain practical ability in foreign languages but also to study and cultivate a philosophy of their own in the Liberal Arts Course. All students must complete the two year Liberal Arts Course before entering the third year studies of their chosen faculties. This course offers many programs which satisfy the general education requirements. For upper division specialization, the University provides a uniquely structured curriculum of core requirements and small compulsory seminars. There are also optional programs relating to Teachers Training Courses and Library Science Courses.

All Faculties, Graduate Schools and subsidiary institutions are situated on the University's garden-like campus which covers an area of 169, 148 m^2 in the city of Soka (Saitama Prefecture), a suburb of Tokyo.

UNDERGRADUATE PROGRAMS

Faculty of Economics (Freshmen Enrollment: 700)
    Department of Economics
Accounting, Agricultural Economy, Bookkeeping, Commercial Economy, Community Finance, Econometrics, Economic Geography, Economic History, Economic Planning, Economic Policies, Economics, Economic Statistics, History of Economics, Industrial Economy, Insurance, International Economy, International Finance, Japanese Economy, Modern Economics, Monetary Theory (Banking), Public Economy, Public Finance, Transportation
    Department of Management Science
Accounting, Advertising, Auditing, Bookkeeping, Budgetary Control, Business Administration, Business Analysis, Business History, Business Organization, Commercial Science, Enterprise, Financial Administration, Industrial Sociology, Insurance, International Trade, Management, Management in Labor-relations, Managerial Engineering, Managerial Finance, Marketing, Marketing Research, Mathematics for Management, Statistics, Stock Marketing, Transportation
Faculty of Foreign Languages (Freshmen Enrollment: 600)
    Department of English
American Literature, British and American Studies, British Literature, English Language, English Linguistics, English Phonetics, History of the English Language
    Department of French
French Language, French Linguistics, French Literature, French Studies, History of the French Language
    Department of German
German Language, German Linguistics, German Literature, German Studies, History of the German Language
Faculty of Law (Freshmen Enrollment: 350)
    Department of Law
Administrative Law, Anglo-American Law, Bankruptcy Law, Civil Law, Civil Procedure, Commercial Law, Comparative Law and Politics, Copyright Law, Criminal Law, Criminal Policy, Criminal Procedure, Diplomatic History, Economic Law, Educational Law, German Law, History of Law, History of Political Thought, Industrial Property Law, International Business Law, International Law, International Politics, Labour Law, Landlord and Tenant

Law, Law of Banking, Law of Local Government, Legal Sociology, Legal Systems, Local Government, Philosophy of Law, Political Science, Private International Law, Public Administration, Social Security Law, Tax Law

Foreign Student Admission

Qualifications for Applicants

Standard Qualifications Requirement

Examination at the University

The President of Dokkyo University will determine the admission of students after deliberation with the General Meeting of Faculty Members. His decision will be based on the students' academic abilities, interview performance, and a medical examination.

Required examinations include:

(a) written or oral examination in the Japanese language.

(b) a subject required by the Faculty concerned.

The latter examination will be conducted in Japanese. If there are special circumstances, however, the General Meeting of Faculty Members can decide otherwise.

Overseas candidates will take the above examinations when they are in Japan, after having been previously accepted by the University as provisional students on the basis of the submitted documents.

Documents to be Submitted When Applying

Standard Documents Requirement

Registration Period: the beginning of the academic year. Under exceptional circumstances, however, overseas students and nondegree students may be accepted in the middle of the academic year upon the recommendation of the Committee for International Academic Exchange.

ONE-YEAR GRADUATE PROGRAMS

One-year Graduate Course of Foreign Languages (Enrollment: 7)

French

One-Year Graduate Course of Economics (Enrollment: 20)

Economics, Management Science

Foreign Student Admission

Qualifications for Applicants

Standard Qualifications Requirement

Examination at the University

Same as undergraduate program except examination subject.

Details of the applicant requirements are as follows:

(a) academic reference from a University President, Dean of the Faculty, or a professor/lecturer who knows their work well.

(b) performance in the Japanese language, or an essay on a subject required by the Committee on Graduate Studies. The essay should be written either in Japanese or in a specified foreign language.

GRADUATE PROGRAMS

Graduate School of Foreign Languages (First Year Enrollment : Master's 14)

Divisions

English Linguisitcs and Literature, German Linguistics and Literature

Graduate School of Law (First Year Enrollment : Master's 10)

Division

Law

Foreign Student Admission

Qualifications for Applicants

Master's Program

Standard Qualifications Requirement

Examination at the University

Master's Program

Same as undergraduate program except examination subject.

Details of the applicant's requirements are as follows:

(a) academic reference from their University President, Dean of the Faculty, or a professor/lecturer who knows their work well.

(b) performance in the Japanese language, or an essay on a subject required by the Committee on Graduate Studies. The essay should be written either in Japanese or in a specified foreign language.

Documents to be Submitted When Applying

Standard Documents Requirement

Applicants may also be asked to submit certificates issued by their own governments or by the Japanese government, if necessary.

*

Research Institutes and Centers

Center for Data-processing and Computer Science, Research Institute of Foreign Language Teaching

Facilities/Services for Foreign Students

We have prepared eight rooms for foreign students near the University and are also preparing to arrange home stays in Soka City.

Special Programs for Foreign Students

Overseas students who have been admitted to Dokkyo University may, if necessary, take special courses instead of, or in addition to, some of the courses regularly taken as graduation requirements, or the Master of Arts degree reguirements, including Japanese language and area knowledge of Japan.

The General Meeting of Faculty Members (or the Committee on Graduate Studies) will determine any such special courses after deliberations with the Committee for International Academic Exchange.

For Further Information

Undergraduate and Graduate Admission

Center for International Academic Exchange,

Dokkyo University, 1-1 Gakuen-cho, Soka-shi, Saitama 340 ☎ 0489-42-1111 ext. 2000

Dokkyo University School of Medicine
(Dokkyo Ika Daigaku)

880 Kitakobayashi, Mibu-machi, Shimotsuga-gun, Tochigi 321-02 ☎ 0282-86-1111

Faculty
    Profs. 68   Assoc. Profs. 57
    Assist. Profs. Full-time 130; Part-time 144
    Res. Assocs. 314
Number of Students
    Undergrad. 720   Grad. 78
Library   147, 381 volumes

Outline and Characteristics of the University

Dokkyo University School of Medicine is an enterprising university. It is one of the five institues of Dokkyo Gakuen, Dokkyo Educational Foundation, which was originally founded in 1883 as Doitsugaku Kyokai, the Society of Germanology. The Society set up a school named Doitsugaku Kyokai Gakko as one of its educational actvities. After many changes, the Society changed its official name to Dokkyo Gakuen in 1948, and its school became Dokkyo Junior High School and Dokkyo Senior High School.

In 1952, the late Teiyū Amano, an alumnus of the school and ex-minister of Education, became the principal of the schools and devoted himself to the restoration of his alma mater. Being solicited for his assistance, Minato Seki took office in 1964 as Chairman of the Board of Directors and, through strenuous efforts, he opened Dokkyo University to realize Amano's educational ideals of bringing up the student's character through comprehensive education from junior high school to the university.

The Gakuen has been producing from among its graduates a great number of competent doctors and scholars in the medical world as well as prominent personages in the world of government, politics, diplomacy, and education. The Gakuen now enjoys a high reputation and is readily recognized in Japan by simply referring to it as "Dokkyo."

In 1970, on its 88th anniversary, the Dokkyo Gakuen set about realizing its long-cherished project of establishing a medical school, and finally succeeded in opening Dokkyo University School of Medicine in April, 1973. In 1974, the university opened its Affiliated Hospital with 26 clincal departments and 993 beds on the campus. In 1984, the Koshigaya Hospital with 13 clinical departments and 637 beds was opened in Saitama Prefecture. Both hospitals are equipped with up-to-date medical facilities and carry out their successful mission as a regional medical center.

The graduate school founded in 1979 offers high-level lectures and practical training. The students are encouraged to carry out active studies. The school has already produced many excellent medical doctors.

The educational philosophy of the university is to educate students to be humanitarian doctors and scholars, to cultivate to the full extent the student's competency in medicine, to fulfill the misssion of the medical center for the community, and to promote the study of medical science through international exchanges.

The university is located in Mibu-machi, about 100km north of Tokyo and 35km south of Nikko. Mibu-machi is a comparatively small town adjacent to Utsunomiya City, the capital of Tochigi Prefecture. The campus, surrounded with abundant greenery and alive with a scholastic atmosphere, provides an ideal environment for the study of medicine.

UNDERGRADUATE PROGRAMS

Faculty of Medicine (Freshmen Enrollment: 100)
   Department of Medicine
Allergology, Anatomy, Anesthesiology, Biochemistry, Bronchoesophagology, Clinical Pathology, Dermatoloty, Endocrinology, Hygiene, Hypertension and Cardio-renal Disease, Internal Medicine, Legal Medicine, Medical Zoology, Microbiology, Neurology, Neurosurgery, Obstetrics and Gynecology, Ophthalmology, Oral and Maxillo-Facial Surgery, Orthopedic surgery, Otorhinolaryngology, Pathology, Pediatrics, Pharmacology, Physiology, Psychiatry, Public Health, Radiology, Rehabilitation, Surgery, Urology

Foreign Student Admission
   Qualifications for Applicants
     Standard Qualifications Requirement
   Examination at the University
     One foreign language (chosen from among English, German, French), two subjects (chosen from among Mathematics, Physics, Chemistry, Biology), Japanese (composition), an interview, and a physical examination.
   Documents to be Submitted When Applying
     Standard Documents Requirement

GRADUATE PROGRAMS

Graduate School of Medicine (First Year Enrollment : Doctor's 39)
   Divisions
Internal Medicine, Morphology, Physiology, Social Medicine, Surgery

Foreign Student Admission
   Qualifications for Applicants
Doctor's Program
     Standard Qualifications Requirement

Applicants for Rehabilitation in Social Medicine Course, Internal Medicine Course, and Surgery Course, are expected to have finished the clinical training required by the Medical Act, Sub-Section 2, Section 16, or to have finishd an equivalent training.

Examination at the University

Doctor's Program

Two foreign languages and specialized subject, an interview and a physical examination.

Documents to be Submitted When Applying

Standard Documents Requirement

Following documents are also required.

1. Copy of the doctor's license if the applicant is licensed.
2. Certificate of the clinical training when applying for Rehabilitation in Social Medicine Course, Medical Course, and Surgical Course.

*

For Further Information

Undergraduate and Graduate Admission

Instruction Office, Dokkyo University School of Medicine, 880 Kitakobayashi, Mibu-machi, Shimotsuga-gun, Tochigi 321–02 ☎ 0282–86–1111 ext. 2019

Doshisha University
(Doshisha Daigaku)

Imadegawa-dori, Karasuma-Higashiiru, Kamigyo-ku, Kyoto-shi, Kyoto 602　☎ 075-251-3223

Faculty
　　Profs. 288　　Assoc. Profs. 94
　　Assist. Profs. Full–time 29; Part–time 668
　　Res. Assocs. 3
Number of Students
　　Undergrad. 19, 669　　Grad. 552
Library 1, 183, 000 volumes

Outline and Characteristics of the University

On the morning of November 29, 1875 Doshisha Eigakko (Doshisha College) started with an earnest prayer-meeting in a small house east of the Imperial Palace, Kyoto. There were eight students and two teachers. A century later it has become one of Japan's leading private universities and has expanded into a separate Women's College, four senior high schools, one of which is international and designated for children of Japanese employed abroad, four junior high schools and a kindergarten totalling close to 30, 000 students on five campuses. Students in the university number near 20, 000 with 414 full–time faculty and 668 lecturers. Doshisha was the first university in Japan to admit women, in 1923.

Doshisha is fortunate in having many ties abroad. The United Church Board for World Ministries, successor to the Congregational Mission Board, has given Doshisha constant help by aug-menting the faculty. Amherst College has long been represented in the faculty and has sponsored representatives since 1922. In 1932, it sponsored "Amherst House" on the Doshisha campus as a social center and student dormitory, and in 1962 a handsome Guest House.

The Associated Kyoto Program starting in 1973, now includes thirteen liberal arts colleges (Amherst, Bucknell, Carleton, Colby, Connecticut Middlebury, Mount Holyoke, Oberlin, Smith, Wesleyan, Whitman, Williams, Pomona) which send about 50 students to Kyoto for a junior-year-abroad under the guidance of a directing professor. Headquartered on the Doshisha campus, with home-stays in Kyoto the AKP students pursue Japanese Studies at first hand.

Governance of Doshisha University falls on the shoulders of the President, who, by law, is responsible for overall finances and personnel. A Council of Deans and a larger University Council divide the decisionmaking responsibilities. The autonomy of each Faculty, within its own fields, for curriculum and faculty selection and promotion has been traditionally recognized and maintained. There is a Board of Trustees of the "juridical person" which carries final fiscal and property responsibility for all the schools comprising the Doshisha including Doshisha University which is its major component. Fourteen Trustees and three Auditors serve three-and two-year terms respectively. As required by Japanese law there is also a larger Council of the juridical person.

UNDERGRADUATE PROGRAMS

Faculty of Commerce (Freshmen Enrollment: 700)
Accounting, Advertising, Auditing, Bookkeeping, Business Administration, Business Analysis, Business Statistics, Commercial History of Japan, Commercial Management, Commodity Science, Financing and Stock Market, Foreign Exchange, History of Commerce, Insurance, International Finance, International Trade, Marine Insurance, Marine Transportation, Marketing Systems, Money and Banking, Operations Research, Small and Medium-Sized Firms, Tourist Business

Faculty of Economics (Freshmen Enrollment: 700)
Business Economics, Econometrics, Economic History, Economics of Distribution Systems, Economics of the Open Economy, Economic Statistics, Environmental Economics, History of Economic Doctrine, International Economics, International Finance, Labor Economics, Macroeconomics, Microeconomics, Quantitative Economics, Statistics, Transportation Economics, Urban and Regional Economics

Faculty of Engineering (Freshmen Enrollment: 720)

Department of Applied Chemistry

Analytical Chemistry, Applied Inorganic Chemistry, Applied Organic Chemistry, Chemical Approach to Biological Systems, Chemical Refining, High Polymers, Industrial Inorganic Chemistry, Industrial Organic Chemistry, Inorganic Chemistry, Organic

Chemistry, Physical Chemistry
Department of Chemical Engineering
Chemical Engineering, Chemical Engineering Stoichiometry, Chemical Physics, Chemical Plant Elements and Design, Chemical Refining, Fuel Chemistry, High-Pressure Chemical Engineering, High-Temperature Chemical Engineering, Stereo-Chemistry, Vacuum Chemical Engineering
Department of Electrical Engineering and Electronics
Acoustics, Analog Circuits, Application of Electric Motors, Computer Analysis, Computer Programming, Design of Electrical Machines, Digital Circuits, Digital Signal Processing, Electrical Energy Engineering, Electrical High Tension Engineering, Electrical Machinery, Electrical Materials, Electrical Measurement, Electric Discharge Phenomena, Electric Power Engineering, Electrochemistry, Electromagnetic Theory, Electromagnetic Wave, Electronic Communication Measurement, Electronic Computers, Microwave Engineering, Power Electronics, Systems Engineering
Department of Mechanical Engineering
Construction Statics, Control Engineering, Dynamics for Machines, Elasticity Mechanics, Engineering Materials, Heat Engines, Heat Transmission, Hydraulic and Pneumatic Mechanics, Hydraulic Machines, Hydraulics, Machine Design, Machine Manufacture, Mechanical Design and Drawing, Mechanics, Metal Processing, Metrology, Nuclear Engineering, Plasticity Mechanics, Productive Engineering, Quantum Mechanics, Strength of Materials, Thermodynamics

Faculty of Law (Freshmen Enrollment: 700)
Department of Law
Administrative Law, Anglo-American Law, Bankruptcy and Corporate Reorganization, Civil Procedure, Commercial Law, Comparative Constitutional Law, Constitutional Law, Criminal Law, Criminal Procedure, Family Law, History of Legal Thought, Industrial Property Law, Insurance Law, International Law, Labor Law, Law of Trade Regulations, Legal Systems, Philosophy of Law, Private Law, Property Law, Sociology of Law, Tax Law
Department of Political Science
Diplomatic History, History of Political Thought, International Politics, Japanese Political History, Local and Municipal Governments, Political Psychology, Political Science, Political Sociology, Politics, Public Administration, Theory of the State, Western Political History

Faculty of Letters (Freshmen Enrollment: 900)
Department of English
American Cultural History, American Literature, American Studies, Anglo-American Culture, British and American Business Affairs, British and American Intellectual History, British Studies, Christian Literature, Comparative Literature, English and American Education, English Language Teaching, English Literature, English Philology, History of

American Literature, History of English Literature, History of the English Language, Linguistics Studies
Department of Humanities
Aesthetics and Theory of Arts Program
Aesthetics, Cinema, Design Theory, History of Japanese Art, History of Oriental Art, History of Western Art, Musicology, Theater, Theory of Arts
Cultural History Program
American Cultural History, American Social History, Archaeology, Classical Official Documents, Cultural History, Folklore, Historiography of Japan, History of Japanese Art, History of Japanese Society, History of Japanese Thought, History of Western Society, History of Western Thought, Japanese Cultural History, Oriental Cultural History, Provincial History, Western Cultural History
Education Program
Comparative History of Educational Thought, Education, Educational Administration, Educational Curriculum, Educational Materials, Educational Psychology, Educational Sociology, History of Education, Library and Information Science, Pedagogy, Philosophy of Education, Social Education, Teaching Methods
Japanese Literature Program
Calligraphy, Chinese Literature, Classical Chinese, Folklore, History of Japanese Language, History of Japanese Literature, Japanese Literature, Japanese Philology, Methods in Teaching Japanese Language and Literature
Philosophy Program
Buddhism, Contemporary Philosophy, Ethics, History of Chinese Ethical Thought, History of Christian Thought, History of Japanese Ethical Thought, History of Western Ethics, History of Western Philosophy, Philosophy, Philosophy of Education, Philosophy of History, Philosophy of Law, Philosophy of Religion, Philosophy of Science, Social Ethics, Social Philosophy
Psychology Program
Adolescent Psychology, Child Psychology, Clinical Psychology, Educational Psychology, Experimental Psychology, Industrial Psychology, Personality, Psychological Statistics, Psychological Testing, Psychology of Learning, Social Psychology
Department of Sociology
Industrial Relations Program
Industrial Hygiene and Medical Protection of Labor, Industrial Organization, Industrial Psychology, Industrial Relations, Industrial Research and Statistics, Industrial Sociology, Industrial Structure, Industrial Technology, Labor Law, Labor Problems, Personnel Management
Journalism Program
Advertising, Broadcasting, Community Theory, Foreign Journalism, History of Journalism, Journalism, Research Methods in Mass Communication, Theory of Communication
Social Welfare Program
Casework, Child Welfare, Community Organiza-

tion, Community Theory, Mental Hygiene, Public Assistance, Public Hygiene, Social Policy, Social Problems, Social Security, Social Welfare, Social Welfare Administration, Social Welfare Law

Sociology Program

Contemporary Urban Problems, Cultural Anthropology, Educational Sociology, Family Sociology, History of Social Thought, Industrial Sociology, Political Sociology, Social Psychology, Social Survey, Sociology, Structures of Living, Theory of Contemporary Society

Faculty of Theology (Freshmen Enrollment: 40)

Christian Churches and Denominations, Christian Ethics, Christianity and Child Education, Christianity and Culture, Christianity in Japanese Society, Church Music and Liturgies, Comparative Study of Religious Rituals, Contemporary American Christianity, Contemporary Philosophical Thought and Theology, Dogmatics, Exegesis of the Old Testament, History of Christianity, History of Christianity in America, History of Church Doctrine, History of the Reformation, Phenomenology of Religion, Theology of the Prophets in the Exilic Period.

Foreign Student Admission

Qualifications for Applicants

Standard Qualifications Requirement

Examination at the University

For applicants residing abroad

1. Applicants for regular student status will be selected by the following procedure:

    (1) First step: Consideration of application forms

    (2) Second step: Those applicants accepted in the first step will be given an oral examination or a written examination before the end of March. The results of the examinations will determine whether an applicant is accepted as a regular student or as a special student.

2. Selection of applicants for Special Student status will be based upon application forms only.

3. The applicant will be notified of the results of the consideration of his/her application forms by the end of December at the latest.

For applicants residing in Japan

1. Selection will be on the basis of:

    (1) The forms presented

    (2) An interview

    (3) A written examination if deemed necessary.

2. The dates for an interview and written examination will be designated after the forms arrive at the University.

3. Selection and notification will be made by the end of February.

The selection is made by the appropriate Faculty.

Documents to be Submitted When Applying

Standard Documents Requirement

Prescribed form on Proficiency in Japanese is

required for overseas applicants.

Applicants already in Japan must take the Japanese Language Proficiency Test and submit the test score to the International Liaison Office.

Deadline for overseas applicants: From October 1 to the end of October of the preceding year.

Deadline for applicants already in Japan: From December 21 of the preceding year to January 20 of the year entrance is sought.

Applications should be sent to International Liaison Office.

Qualifications for Transfer Students

Third year transfers: those who have certificates of completion of 14 years of education abroad or expect to do so before the end of March of the year entrance is sought.

Examination for Transfer Students

The same as for freshman application.

Documents to be Submitted When Applying

Standard Documents Requirement

Other necessary documents are the same as for freshman application.

GRADUATE PROGRAMS

Graduate School of Commerce (First Year Enrollment : Master's 40, Doctor's 5)

Division

Commerce

Graduate School of Economics (First Year Enrollment : Master's 50, Doctor's 5)

Divisions

Applied Economics, Economic Policy, Economic Theory

Graduate School of Engineering (First Year Enrollment : Master's 60, Doctor's 9)

Divisions

Applied Chemistry, Electrical Engineering, Mechanical Engineering

Graduate School of Law (First Year Enrollment : Master's 75, Doctor's 15)

Divisions

Political Science, Private Law, Public Law

Graduate School of Letters (First Year Enrollment : Master's 80, Doctor's 18)

Divisions

Aesthetics & Theory of Arts, Cultural History, English Literature, History of Philosophy, Japanese Literature, Journalism, Philosophy, Psychology, Social Welfare

Graduate School of Theology (First Year Enrollment : Master's 25, Doctor's 5)

Divisions

Biblical Theology, Historical Theology, Systematic Theology

Foreign Student Admission

Qualifications for Applicants

Master's Program

Standard Qualifications Requirement
Doctor's Program
Standard Qualifications Requirement
Examination at the University
Master's Program
The same as undergraduate applicants.
Doctor's Program
The same as undergraduate applicants.
Documents to be Submitted When Applying
Standard Documents Requirement
Other necessary documents are the same as for freshman application.

∗

Research Institutes and Centers
Institute for the Study of Humanities and Social Sciences, Science and Engineering Research Institute, The Center for American Studies.
Facilities/Services for Foreign Students
International Student Center.
Association of International Students.
Society for the Support of International Students.
Special Programs for Foreign Students
1. Introduction to Japanese Language (Humanity and Science): 4 credits
2. Japanese Literature (Humanity and Science): 4 credits
3. Japanese Language I (Humanity and Science): 4 credits
4. Japanese Language II (Humanity and Science): 4 credits
5. Contemporary Japan I (Social Science): 4 credits
6. Contemporary Japan II (Humanity and Science): 4 credits
7. Japanese Language and Culture: 4 credits

For Further Information
Undergraduate and Graduate Admission
The International Liaison office, Doshisha University, Imadegawa-dori, Karasuma-Higashiiru, Kamigyo-ku, Kyoto 602 ☎ 075-251-3223

Doshisha Women's College of Liberal Arts
(Doshisha Joshi Daigaku)

Imadegawa-dori, Teramachi-Nishiiru, Kamikyo-ku, Kyoto-shi, Kyoto 602   ☎ 075-251-4110

Faculty
Profs. 56   Assoc. Profs. 13
Assist. Profs.   Full–time 6; Part–time 268
Res. Assocs. 5
Number of Students
Undergrad. 2,932   Grad. 24
Library 190,000 volumes

Outline and Characteristics of the College
Doshisha Women's College was founded in 1876 by Joseph Hardy Neeshima. In his youth, Neeshima sought to find a way to help his country reach the level of development of the more advanced nations of the West, and, in 1864, he violated the national policy of isolation and fled Japan to realize his ambition. His destination was Boston, Massachusetts, where he pursued an education in the liberal arts and in the specialized fields of the natural sciences, history and theology, mostly at Amherst College. While studying, he was deeply impressed by Christianity, and was eventually converted to the faith.

After ten long years of study abroad he returned to Japan with a dream to establish a Christian university. In 1875, he established the Doshisha Eigakko (Doshisha College), the present Doshisha University, and in the following year, 1876, founded the Doshisha Girls School with the firm belief that the development of Japan was dependent, to a great extent, on the development of women's education. This was the beginning of the present Doshisha Women's College. With its 100 year history and tradition, it is counted among the oldest colleges and universities in Japan.

The founder, Neeshima, believed that "the merits of the private university are its ability to nourish the spirit of self-reliance in the students and to train a self-governing people." With these words as its foundation, the private institution of Doshisha was established. Today it is a composite educational institution, consisting of a kindergarten, three junior high schools, three senior high schools, two universities and two graduate schools. Each school works in cooperation with the others, and all share the goal of developing the character of their students in accordance with Christian principles.

As a part of this educational structure and particularly as a liberal arts institution, this college emphasizes not only the development of skills in scholarship and research but also the development of well-rounded personalities based on the Christian ideal, so that young women may live constructively and responsibly in an international, democratic society. Guided by these principles, Doshisha Women's College is a dominant institution in the Japanese educational world.

UNDERGRADUATE PROGRAMS

Faculty of Home Economics (Freshmen Enrollment: 220)

Food Studies Department

Biochemistry, Culinary Science, Science of Cooking, Food Chemistry, Nutrition, Social Welfare

Home Economics Department

Child Health, Child Care and Nursing, Home Economics, Home Education, Home Management, Textile Material

Faculty of Liberal Arts (Freshmen Enrollment: 400)

English Department

Backgrounds of English and American Literature, History of American Literature, History of English Literature, Language Studies, Literary Studies

Music Department

Counterpoint, Harmony, Music History, Solfege, Techniques of Composition

Foreign Student Admission

Qualifications for Applicants

Standard Qualifications Requirement

Examination at the College

1. Test of Japanese Reading and Writing Ability.
2. Interview Test of Speaking Ability.

Documents to be Submitted When Applying

Standard Documents Requirement

A document attesting the applicant's ability in Japanese should be submitted.

GRADUATE PROGRAMS

Graduate School of Home Economics (First Year Enrollment : Master's 8)

Division

Food Studies

Graduate School of Letters (First Year Enrollment : Master's 8, Doctor's 4)

Division

English Literature

Foreign Student Admission

Examination at the University

In September, October or in March. A written exam and an interview.

Documents to be Submitted When Applying

Standard Documents Requirement

Application forms are available at the Graduate Admissions Office. Applicants are required to submit the specified application documents to the Office.

✳

Research Institutes and Centers

Institute for Interdisciplinary Studies of Culture

For Further Information

Undergraduate and Graduate Admission

Admissions Office, Doshisha Women's College of Liberal Arts, Imadegawa-dori, Teramachi-Nishiiru, Kamikyo-ku, Kyoto-shi, Kyoto 602 ☎ 075-251-4123

Eichi University
(Eichi Daigaku)

2-18-1 Nakoji, Amagasaki-shi, Hyogo 661
☎ 06-491-5000

Faculty
  Profs. 26   Assoc. Profs. 16
  Assist. Profs. Full–time 15; Part–time 29
Number of Students
  Undergrad. 1, 079
Library 115, 000 volumes

Outline and Characteristics of the University

Eichi University is a Catholic university founded by the late Cardinal Paul Y. Taguchi, Archibishop of Osaka in 1963. The University is a Liberal Arts school consisting of four departments: Theology, English, Spanish and French Literature. At the present, Approximately 1, 000 students are currently enrolled. Eichi University is one of many outstanding universities in and around Osaka, the second largest city in Japan.

At Eichi, even in teaching literature, the question of "how to live" is brought out in conjunction with the question of "how to live eternally. " Furthermore, students are free to meet with priest-teachers to discuss problems of life or personal affairs. Eichi Unlversity campus is internationally diverse. Among the professors are many foreigners, from the United States, West Germany, France, Ireland, Hungary, Belgium, Spain, Sweden and Italy. This is an unusual opportunity for the students come to understand the cultures and languages of various countries, thereby widening their appreciation of world civilization. Moreover, Students benefit from, classes and seminars conducted in a family-like atmosphere.

Students enjoy the privilege of studying abroad at Loras College, Dubuqne, Iowa, with which Eichi has a sister-school relationship. The credits they obtain there are automatically acknowleged at Eichi, so a number of students take a year at Loras, and they return with a new sense of confidence. Moreover, a member of Eichi's faculty has spent a year at Loras as a Japanese instructor, and Loras instructors plan to teach at Eichi in the future. Also, every year teachers take a group of students to England, Spain, France and to Loras College to study for a short period; many students start preparing for this overseas travel shortly after they enter the university.

Eichi University provides students with an opportunity to visit with counselors and discuss their problems. Besides priest-counselors living full time on campus, there are professional counselors who are available to listen to the students and encourage them in their studies.

UNDERGRADUATE PROGRAMS

Faculty of Liberal Arts (Freshmen Enrollment: 277)
Department of English Literature
English and American Literature, English Linguistics, English Phonetics, History of American Literature, History of the English Language, Histroy of English Literature
Department of French Literature
French Linguistics, French Literature, French Literature and Christianity, History of French Literature
Department of Spanish Literature
Economy of Spain, History of Iberoamerica, History of Iberoamerica Literature, History of Spain, History of Spanish Art, History of Spanish Language, History of Spanish Music, Histroy of Spanish Literature, Spanish Language, Spanish Linguistics
Department of Theology
Biblical Theology, Christian Arts, Comparative Religion, History of Religion, Medieval Studies, Moral Theology, Sacred Scripture, Systematic Theology

*

For Further Information
Undergraduate Admission
Dean of Academic Affairs, Admission Office, Eichi University, 2-18-1 Nakoji, Amagasaki-shi, Hyogo 661 ☎ 06-491-5000 ext. 208

Elisabeth University of Music
(Erizabeto Ongaku Daigaku)

4-15 Nobori-cho, Naka-ku, Hiroshima-shi, Hiroshima 730   ☎ 082-221-0918

Faculty
    Profs. 24   Assoc. Profs. 18
    Assist. Profs. Full–time 4; Part–time 78
Number of Students
    Undergrad. 531   Grad. 9
Library 74, 000 volumes

Outline and Characteristics of the University

Elisabeth University of Music traces its roots back to the Hiroshima Evening Music School, a small Quonset hut built in September, 1947 on the ruins of a town still bleeding from the wounds of the atomic holocaust. Ernest Goossens, S. J., the founder of the school, set out on this new venture in the chaos of post-war Japan, when all sense of direction seemed to have been lost. He saw in the school a unique tool to give the young a new élan in their quest for beauty and attainment of truth through the arts.

In April, 1948 the new institution received early official recognition as the Hiroshima School of Music, and following a thorough academic revision, be-

came in 1952 a full-fledged junior college, under the patronage of Queen Elisabeth of Belgium, who kindly gave it her name. In answer to a widely felt need, the school was given formal recognition by the Ministry of Education as a four-year college in April, 1963, becoming the present Elisabeth University of Music. Subsequent developments have included the creation in 1967 of an independent Department of Sacred Music, the only such department in Japan, and the establishment in 1980 of a one-year graduate diploma program. Since December, 1961 it has been affiliated with the Vatican's Istituto Pontifizio di Musica Sacra; it is the only institution in East Asia to have been honored with such a distinction.

Elisabeth University of Music is now a coeducational institution consisting of an undergraduate Faculty of Music with four Departments —Sacred Music, Music Theory, Voice, and Instrumental Music—and a one-year graduate diploma program.

The Society of Jesus, the Catholic order which is the parent organization of Elisabeth University of Music, has a long educational tradition spanning over 400 years, and presently maintains nearly 100 institutions of higher education throughout the world. Integral formation of the human person, based on the Christian educational values of the Society of Jesus, and the university's international dimension as a meeting-place of Eastern and Western culture constitute the core of Elisabeth University's identity and tradition, and give it a meaningful place among the music schools of Japan. The importance of humanities, sciences and foreign languages is stressed in all programs of musical training and, as a distinguishing characteristic of the general music curriculum, all students receive a basic orientation in Gregorian chant and Renaissance polyphony. The very low student-teacher ratio creates a family atmosphere based on mutual trust and openness. The library's holdings provide abundant resources for original music research: the more than 74, 000 items include 15, 600 books on music, 31, 700 music scores, 9, 200 recordings, and about 430 music periodicals from around the world. Finally, while seeking to deepen the bonds between East and West in a spirit of universality and internationalism (seven of the 46 full-time faculty members are non-Japanese), Elisabeth University of Music sets as its ultimate goal that music become a life path leading students along the ways of the human spirit to God.

UNDERGRADUATE PROGRAMS

Faculty of Music (Freshmen Enrollment: 125)
Department of Instrumental Music
Instrumental Courses
Instrumental Performance (Strings, Winds, Percussion, Harp, Classical Guitar), Orchestral Ensemble
Piano Course
Accompaniment, Analysis, Interpretation, Performance

Department of Music Theory
Composition Course
Advanced Music Theory, Applied Music, Composition, Instrumentation
Music Education Course
Applied Music, Composition, History of Music Education, Methods, Music Education, Music Therapy
Musicology Course
Advanced Music Theory, Ethnomusicology, Historical Musicology, Source Readings (English, German)
Department of Sacred Music
Pipe Organ Course
Improvisation, Keyboard Harmony, Pipe Organ, Pipe Organ Organology
Sacred Music Musicology Course
Gregorian Chant, Sacred Music History (Baroque, Classical, Romantic, Modern), Sacred Music Practice (Choir), Sacred Polyphony
Sacred Vocal Music Course
Diction Courses, Sacred Music Practice (Choir), Solo Sacred Vocal Music
Department of Vocal Music
Diction Courses
Ensemble Singing, French Art Song, German Art Song, Japanese Art Song, Voice

Foreign Student Admission

Qualifications for Applicants
Standard Qualifications Requirement
All foreign applicants must take the Japanese Language Proficiency Test within the year prior to their entrance examinations.
Examination at the University
The examinations are given during the first two weeks of February. Details may be found in the Entrance Examination Prospectus and Application Form, available from the Office of Academic Affairs from early July.
I.   Basic Subjects
  1.   Japanese Language
  2.   Fundamental Music Theory and Solfège
  3.   Keyboard Proficiency ("minor"piano)
II.   Other subjects according to area of specialization ("major")
III.   Interview
Documents to be Submitted When Applying
Standard Documents Requirement
All documents must be submitted before the middle of January; the precise dates are specified in the Entrance Examination Prospectus and Application Form.

Qualifications for Transfer Students
The following are eligible to apply for admission as transfer students to undergraduate programs:
  1.   Graduates of a two or three year junior college program in music, or those who will complete requirements for graduation by March of the same year.
  2.   Graduates of four-year college-level programs

in music, or those who will complete requirements for graduation by March of the same year.
  3.   Students in four-year college-level programs in music who completed their second year of study or will do so by March of the same year.
All foreign transfer students must obtain the requisite residence status (visa), and they should have passed the Japanese Language Proficiency Test.
Examination for Transfer Students
Entrance examinations for foreign transfer students are the same as for Japanese transfer students. Details may be found in the Entrance Examination Prospectus, available from the Office of Academic Affairs.
I.   Basic Subjects
  1.   Harmony
  2.   Western Music History
  3.   Solfège (Dictation, Sight Singing)
  4.   Short written essay
  5.   Keyboard Proficiency ("minor"piano)
II.   Other subjects according to area of specialization ("major")
III.   Interview
Documents to be Submitted When Applying
Standard Documents Requirement
Documents and procedures for foreign transfer students are the same as freshman application.

ONE-YEAR GRADUATE PROGRAMS

One-Year Graduate Diploma Program of Music (Enrollment 10)
Composition, Instrumental Music, Music Education, Musicology, Piano, Pipe Organ, Sacred Music, Sacred Vocal Music, Vocal Music

Foreign Student Admission

Qualifications for Applicants
Only graduates of four-year college-level programs in music, or those who will complete requirements for graduation by March of the same year, are eligible to apply.
All foreign students must obtain the requistite residence status (visa), and they should have passed the Japanese Language Proficiency Test.
Applications are accepted during the last week of September and the first week of October; precise dates are specified in the One-Year Graduate Program Entrance Examination Prospectus, available from the Office of Academic Affairs from early June of each year.
Examination at the University
The same as for the Japanese. Date: during October at dates specified annually. Details may be found in the One-Year Graduate Program Entrance Examination Prospectus. The subjects examined vary accordingly to the area of specialization.
*
For Further Information

Undergraduate and Graduate Admission
Office of Academic Affairs, Elisabeth University of Music, 4-15 Nobori-cho, Naka-ku, Hiroshima-shi, Hiroshima 730 ☎ 082-221-0918 ext. 208

Ferris Women's College
(Ferisu Jogakuin Daigaku)

37 Yamate–cho, Naka–ku, Yokohama–shi, Kanagawa 231   ☎ 045–662–4521

Faculty
  Profs. 21   Assoc. Profs. 10
  Assist. Prfos. Full–time 10; Part–time 80
  Res. Assocs. 11
Number of Students
  Undergrad. 1, 187
Library   118, 000 volumes

Outline and Characteristics of the College
   Ferris Girl's School, the first school for women in Japan, was founded in 1870 by Mary Kidder, a missionary of the Reformed Church in America. Ferris is a Protestant Christian school dedicated to teaching young women to live responsibly in today's world. The school's motto is: "Let each of you look not only to her own interests, but also to the interests of others."
   The Junior College had its beginning in 1950 with the Departments of English and Domestic Science (Home Economics). A Music Department was added in 1951. In 1965 the Senior College with Faculty of Literature was begun. Majors are in either English Linguistics and Literature or Japanese Linguistics and Literature. In 1988 the Department of Asian and European Cultures was instituted in the Faculty of Literature.
   Ferris Women's College has an enrollment of around 1, 200 students. Most classes are small so there is ample opportunity for students to interact with faculty members on a personal level.
   The campus is located in the Bluff area of Yokohama, Japan's second largest city, and its largest port. In 1988 the 2nd Campus was opened in a new suburb of Yokohama. It takes about 45 minutes between the Campus by train.

UNDERGRADUATE PROGRAMS

Faculty of Literature (Freshmen Enrollment: 360)
  Department of Asian and European Cultures
  Department of English Literature
  Department of Japanese Literature
*
For Further Information
  Undergraduate Admission
Resistrar's Office, Ferris Women's College, 37 Yamate–cho, Naka–ku, Yokohama–shi, Kanagawa

231 ☎ 045–662–4521 ext. 331, 311

Fuji College
(Fuji Daigaku)

450-3 Shimoneko, Hanamaki-shi, Iwate 025
☎ 0198–23–6221

UNDERGRADUATE PROGRAMS

Faculty of Economics (Freshmen Enrollment: 100)
  Department of Economics

Fujita-Gakuen Health University
(Fujita-Gakuen Hoken'eisei Daigaku)

1-98 Dengakugakubo, Kutsukake-cho, Toyoake-shi, Aichi 470-11   ☎ 0562-93-2000

Faculty
  Profs. 92   Assoc. Profs. 44
  Assist. Profs. Full–time 104; Part–time 420
  Res. Assocs. 99
Number of Students
  Undergrad. 1, 515   Grad. 213
Library   134, 263 volumes

Outline and Characteristics of the University
   Fujita-Gakuen Health University School of Medicine opened in 1972 in Toyoake, southeast of the city of Nagoya. It is a private university and was the first medical school in the Chubu district of Japan. It is a school dealing with all branches of the medical profession. Fujita-Gakuen's unique "Health University" concept was conceived in 1964, nine years before the OECD Center for Educational Research and Innovation announced similar suggestions for improving medical education in 1973. Its unique buildings are especially designed for maximum efficiency in each section.
   The University also has a School of Hygiene, opened in 1968, where medical auxiliaries and nurses are educated. The primary objectives are to promote cooperation between the two schools in training professional health personnel, with the emphasis on community medicine. Graduate School of Medicine was opened in 1978 on the same campus.
   Faculty staff have been recruited according to a basic policy by which no more than 30 percent of the recruited should be graduates from any single school thereby preventing the formation of academic cliques.
   Educational objectives emphasize the development in the students of a comprehensive approach, and research is being undertaken to find the most effective methods for implementing this concept. To

this end, a special hour (called "assembly"), during which specific personality development is emphasized, is included in the curriculum of each academic year.

The medical curriculum extends over six years, integrating premedical and medical subjects. Applied anatomy, pathophysiology, pathobiochemistry, and immunology are examples of the integrated subjects taught in small group presentations and by joint lectures. Laboratories for the basic sciences are well equipped with multidisciplinary rooms, which are used for most practical exercises. Four hospitals are available for clinical training. The teaching hospital, with 1,673 beds, attached to the school, and three affiliated hospitals which are located in downtown Nagoya, in Hisai, Mie and in Toyoake, the city in which the University is located.

In accordance with its concepts and aims for future development, the University has included comprehensive medicine for senior students as a mandatory subject in its unique curriculum. It has, moreover, established Institute for Comprehensive Medical Science consisting of research divisions in the form of project-teams, which we hope will develop into a spearhead of modern medical research. The Institute's aims are to fill the gaps left in the curricula of traditional schools of medicine and hygiene, and to unify research in the basic and clinical sciences. The various departments which form this Institute are dedicated to biomedical research on those illnesses which at present most threaten humanity and for which it most urgently requires new forms of diagnosis, prevention and treatment.

UNDERGRADUATE PROGRAMS

School of Hygiene (Freshmen Enrollment: 200)
  Department of Hygiene
Biochemistry, Biostatistics, Clinical Chemistry, Clinical Pathology, Clinical Physiology, Epidemiology, Hematology, Industrial Medicine, Laboratory Animal Science, Medical Electronics, Microbiology, Organic Chemistry, Parasitology, Pathology, Physiology, Public Health, Radio Isotope Techniques, Serology, Virology
  Department of Nursing
Clinical Psychology, General Nursing, Geriatric Nursing, Health Administration and Welfare, Obstetric Nursing, Pediatric Nursing, Psychiatric Nursing, Public Health, Radio Medicine, Surgical Nursing
  Department of Radiological Technology
Electrical Engineering, Electromagnetics, Electronics, Instrumentation, Nuclear Medicine, Radio Biology, Radio Chemistry, Radio Diagnosis, Radio Hygiene, Radio Physics
School of Medicine (Freshmen Enrollment: 100)
  Department of Medicine
Anatomy, Anesthesiology, Biochemistry, Dermatology, Forensic Medicine, Hygiene, Internal Medicine,

Microbiology, Obstetrics and Gynecology, Ophthalmology, Orthopedic Surgery, Otorhinolaryngology, Parasitology, Pathology, Pediatrics, Pharmacology, Physiology, Psychiatry, Public Health, Radiology, Surgery, Urology

Foreign Student Admission
  Qualifications for Applicants
    Standard Qualifications Requirement
  Examination at the University
    A written exam and an interview (the same as Japanese applicants)
    Date: in December and/or between February and March.
  Documents to be Submitted When Applying
    Standard Documents Requirement

GRADUATE PROGRAMS

Graduate School of Medicine (First Year Enrollment : Doctor's 68)
  Divisions
Functional Science, Health & Hygiene, Internal Medicine, Molecular Medicine, Morphology, Surgery

Foreign Student Admission
  Qualifications for Applicants
Doctor's Program
    Standard Qualifications Requirement
    Applicants for Internal Medicine and Surgery are required to have at least two years' clinical training.
  Examination at the University
Doctor's Program
    Date: March.
    written tests on specialized subjects and two foreign languages, and an interview (same as Japanese applicants)
  Documents to be Submitted When Applying
    Standard Documents Requirement
                    *
Research Institutes and Centers
Institute for Comprehensive Medical Science
For Further Information
  Undergraduate and Graduate Admission
Director of Admission of each School, Fujita-Gakuen Health University, 1-98 Dengakugakubo, Kutsukake-cho, Toyoake-shi, Aichi 470-11
☎ 0562-93-2600 (School of Medicine), 0562-93-2502 (School of Hygiene)

Fuji Women's College
(Fuji Joshi Daigaku)
Nishi 2, Kita 16, Kita-ku, Sapporo-shi, Hokkaido 001
☎ 011-736-0311

Faculty
  Profs.   23

Assist. Profs.   Full–time   1
Number of Students
Undergrad.   571
Library   165, 000 volumes

Outline and Characteristics of the College

Fuji Women's College is the only four-year Catholic college in Hokkaido. It was founded in 1961 by the Sisters of St. Francis of the Martyr St. George, following Fuji Girls' Highschool (1925) and Fuji Women's Junior College (1950).

The College has the single Faculty of Letters. The main campus lies near the center of the City of Sapporo, and students enjoy the urban campus life. The large second campus is in the suburbs of Sapporo, where the newly-built beautiful Seminar House is available for various activities. The College offers a friendly, small-campus atmosphere, with a faculty and staff which give truly personal attention to every student. The College is also proud of its high quality student body, with clear motivation for academia and serious commitment to education.

The philosophy of the College is based on Catholicism to envision the full personal development of each student, with the hope that each grows in staunch independence of mind and in generous commitment to service of God, society, and fellow humans; a dedication to the life of study and reflection, but always with an eye for human and spiritual values, and for involvement in the things of this world; openness of mind and heart for what is beautiful and wonderful in nature and in human nature.

The City of Sapporo is a big, beautiful city, with a population of 1, 560, 000, rich in the natural beauties of mountains, forests, and rivers. Students can enjoy various kinds of summer and winter sports.

UNDERGRADUATE PROGRAMS

Faculty of Letters (Freshmen Enrollment: 100)
Department of English Literature
Bible as Literature, English and American Literature, English Grammar, English Linguistics, English Literature, English Philology, History of American Literature, History of English Language, History of English Literature, Linguistics, Modern English, Phonetics
Department of Japanese Literature
Art History, Calligraphy, Chinese Classics, Chinese Literature, History of Calligraphy, History of Japanese Language, History of Japanese Literature, Japanese Linguistics, Japanese Literature, Literary Expression

Foreign Student Admission

Qualifications for Applicants
Standard Qualifications Requirement
A few guarantors in Japan.
Examination at the College
1.   Overseas   applicants: the   submitted   docu-

ments.
2.   Applicants in Japan: written examination and interview.
Documents to be Submitted When Applying
Standard Documents Requirement
Application forms are available at the Admissions Office early December. Application dead line: Jan. 15.

*

For Further Information
Undergraduate Admission
Admissions Office, Fuji Women's College, Nishi 2, Kita 16, Kita-ku, Sapporo-shi, Hokkaido 001
☎ 011–736–0311 ext. 103

Fukui Institute of Technology
(Fukui Kogyo Daigaku)
3-6-1 Gakuen, Fukui-shi, Fukui 910
☎ 0776-22-8111

Faculty
Profs.   90   Assoc. Profs.   20
Assist. Profs.   Full–time   34; Part–time   75
Res. Assocs.   2
Number of Students
Undergrad.   2, 917   Grad.   21
Library   101, 825 volumes

Outline and Characteristics of the University

The Fukui Institute of Technology was founded in 1965 by Kenzo Kanai. At the time of its foundation the Institute consisted of two departments: the Department of Electrical Engineering and the Department of Mechanical Engineering. The former had developed from Hokuriku Electrical School, and the latter from Fukui High School, which was later attached to the Fukui Institute of Technology in 1978. In 1966, the Institute added the Department of Construction Engineering and in 1973 the Department of Applied Physics, which was renamed the Department of Safety Environment Engineering in 1979; It was renamed the Department of Applied Physics and Chemistry in 1988. The Graduate Schools of Mechanical, Construction and Safety Environment Engineering were added in 1985 and the Graduate School of Electrical Engineering in 1986. The most recent addition is the Department of Management Science of 1987.

Fukui Campus is located in a quiet residential area aptly named "Gakuen" (academy), 10 minutes by car to the northwest of Fukui Station on the Hokuriku Main Line of the Japanese Railways. It is a relaxed district, with mountains to the east and the Japanese Sea to the west.

The Awara Campus, located at Awara, Fukui prefecture, is set in the beautiful environment of the Echizen Kaga National Designated Park and Lake Kitagata. In addition to the lecture halls and seminar house, a baseball ground, facilities for field and track sports, a golf course, ball game ground and other facilities are in process of being built.

UNDERGRADUATE PROGRAMS

Faculty of Engineering (Freshmen Enrollment: 848)
Department of Applied Physics and Chemistry
Analytical Chemistry, Anti-destruction Inspection, Concept of Combution, Dynamics, Environmental Facility Design and Drawing, Environment Safety Engineering, Equipment Analysis, Facility Construction, Facility Regulation, Inorganic Chemistry, Organic Chemistry, Physical Chemistry, Physical Chemistry, Pollution Disposition, X-ray Management Engineering
Department of Architecture and Civil Engineering
Architecture Course
Architecture Environment Engineering, Life Space Planning, Plan Theory, Stress Exercise, Structure Analysis, Wooden Architecture Produce, Wooden Architecture Structure, Wooden Structure
Civil Engineering Course
Bridge Engineering, City Design, Concept of Architecture, Geology, Landscaping-gardening, Road Engineering and Drawing, Sea-river Engineering, Seismology, Space Management, Traffic Computation, Water Engineering Computation
Department of Electrical Engineering
Electrical Engineering Course
Electrical Circuitry, Electrical Design Drawing, Electrical Machinery, Electrical Magnetics, Electrical Material, Electrical Measurement, Electronic Computer Language, Laser Engineering, Ultra High Frequency Engineering
Electronics Engineering Course
Electrical Circuitry, Electrical Magnetism, Electronic Computer Language, Electronic Computer System, Electronic Medical Equipment, Electronics, Electronics Circuitry, Information Engineering, Living Body Electronic Measurements, Ultra-sonic Waves
Department of Management Science
Bookkeeping Science of Statistics, Business Management, Cost Accounting, Human Technology, Information processing, Introduction to Electronic Computer, Labor Control Management, Management of Production, Marketing, Operationsressarch, Quality Control, Outline of system Engineering, Programming, Theory of Industry Diagnosis, Theory of minor Enterprises, Theory of Sall Management
Department of Mechanical Engineering
Electronic Mechanical Engineering Course
Boiler Turbine, Fusion Engineering, Hydrodynamics, Machinery Elements and Design, Mesurement Engineering, Metalic Systems, Oil Pressure Engineering, Robot Engineering, Thermodynamic Engineering
Mechanical Engineering Course
Automobile Engineering, Automobile Maintenance, Hydrodynamics, Machine Construction, Machinery

Material, Material Dynamics, Metalic Surface Engineering, Thermodynamics Engineering, Water Dynamics

Foreign Student Admission
Qualifications for Applicants
Standard Qualifications Requirement
Examination at the University
Written exam and an interview.
Documents to be Submitted When Applying
Standard Documents Requirement

GRADUATE PROGRAMS

Graduate School of Engineering (First Year Enrollment : Master's 20)
Divisions
Construction Engineering, Electrical Engineering, Mechanical Engineering, Safety and Environment Engineering

Foreign Student Admission
Qualifications for Applicants
Master's Program
Standard Qualifications Requirement
Examination at the University
Master's Program
A written and oral exam plus an interview.
Date: between February and March.
Documents to be Submitted When Applying
Standard Documents Requirement

∗

Research Institutes and Centers
Electronic Computer Center, Institute of Industrial Research
Facilities/Services for Foreign Students
Kanai Kaikan (Accommodation: 5 single rooms)
For Further Information
Undergraduate and Graduate Admission
Admissions Office, Fukui Institute of Technology, 3-6-1 Gakuen, Fukui-shi, Fukui 910 ☎ 0776-22-8111 ext. 327

Fukuoka Dental College
(Fukuoka Shika Daigaku)

700 Ta, Sawara-ku, Fukuoka-shi, Fukuoka 814-01
☎ 092-801-0411

UNDERGRADUATE PROGRAMS

Faculty of Dentistry (Freshmen Enrollment: 120)
Department of Dentistry

GRADUATE PROGRAMS

Graduate School of Dentistry (First Year Enrollment : Doctor's 18)
 Division
Dentistry

Fukuoka Institute of Technology
(Fukuoka Kogyo Daigaku)

3-30-1 Wajirohigashi, Higashi-ku, Fukuoka-shi, Fukuoka 811-02 ☎ 092-606-3131

Faculty
    Profs. 47   Assoc. Profs. 23
    Assist. Profs. Full-time 23; Part-time 68
    Res. Assocs. 27
Number of Students
    Undergrad. 3, 381
Library 123, 340 volumes

Outline and Characteristics of the University

Fukuoka Institute of Technology consists of six departments centered around the field which has shown the greatest development in recent years: electronics. Research and education are constantly progressing in the departments of Electronics, Electronic Materials, Electronic Machinery, Management, Electricity, and Communications. Special attention is paid to the area of computer education to accommodate the ever-increasing shift to an information society. One of the features of our university is the fostering of application capabilities.

Currently, the advancement of electronic engineering is directed towards the development of fifth generation computers, aimed at the development of artificial intelligence. In the field of robotics, the development of intelligent robots is proceeding with some difficulty in harmonizing these robots with society.

Automation is spreading from factory to office and now to home, and all types of information systems including new media, are having a strong influence on everyone.

What is required from engineers in this type of society is the humanity to keep the happiness of mankind in mind and the wisdom to make the proper decisions.

Our education constantly aims at developing the character of our students so that they are first educated and trustworthy human beings and next excellent engineers.

Another goal of our education is to make students develop technology which is new to Japan, contributing to the international society by supplying new standards of culture. In order to fulfill this goal, it is most important to cultivate engineers who are brimming with creativity. The educational policy of this institution places special emphasis on the "nurturing of creativity".

At the same time, it is increasingly becoming inconceivable in our ever changing society that people will continue to work in the same field for many years. Creativity, a broad vision, and adaptability are necessary for opening up any job and taking full advantage of one's abilities. For this reason, our specialized education is aimed at deepening the understanding between actual industry and society — in other words, the education of engineers with a broad view who can contribute to society in many fields.

This institution which has departments of electronic engineering and electronic machinery, prepares individuals for their role in society by utilizing good teachers with good facilities. To cultivate highly capable engineers, we have plans to add new members to our already strong teaching staff each year. Buildings and facilities are of course necessary for fulfilling these educational goals. One of the slogans of this institution is to provide superior facilities. We are also engaged in campus planning which will provide the spacious campus necessary for a meaningful and pleasant student life.

In addition to the realization of better facilities, we have other plans in the works. In 1986, we will be increasing the staff for each department and are considering the addition of a graduate school and the addition of new departments to our institution. The addition of a new graduate school is expected to greatly improve the quality of research and education at Fukuoka Institute of Technology.

UNDERGRADUATE PROGRAMS

Faculty of Engineering (Freshmen Enrollment: 660)
 Department of Communication and Computer Engineering
Communication and Transmission Engineering, Communication System Engineering, Electronic Communications, Hardware Engineering, Software Engineering
 Department of Electrical Engineering
Electrical and Electronic Devices, Electrical Material Science, Electrical Power Engineering, Electricity, Instrumentation and Control Engineering
 Department of Electronic and Mechanical Engineering
Automation Machinery, Control and Instrumentation, Electronic Mechanics, Functional Materials, Precision Cutting
 Department of Electronic Materials Engineering
Applied Electronics, Electricity, Electronic Materials, Material Development Engineering
 Department of Electronics
Electricity, Electronic Communication Devices, Electronics, Instrumentation and Control Engineering, Material Engineering
 Department of Management Engineering
Information System Engineering, Management, Social System Engineering, Software Engineering

Foreign Student Admission

Qualifications for Applicants
    Standard Qualifications Requirement
Examination at the University
    Screening
Documents to be Submitted When Applying
    Standard Documents Requirement
    Proof of the student's proficiency in the Japanese language. Guarantor form
Application Deadline: October 30 (Overseas applicants), October 30 and January 31 (Applicants in Japan)

*

Research Institutes and Centers
Computer Center, Electronics Research Laboratory
For Further Information
Public Relations, office section Fukuoka Institute of Technology, 3-30-1 Wajirohigashi, Higashi-ku, Fukuoka-shi, Fukuoka 811-02
☎ 092-606-3131 ext. 228, 242

Fukuoka University
(Fukuoka Daigaku)

8-19-1 Nanakuma, Jonan-ku, Fukuoka-shi, Fukuoka 814-01   ☎ 092-871-6631

Faculty
    Profs. 264   Assoc. Profs. 169
    Assist. Profs. Full–time 95; Part–time 418
    Res. Assocs. 309
Number of Students
    Undergrad. 21, 341   Grad. 271
Library 941, 573 volumes

Outline and Characteristics of the University

Fukuoka University, originally established in 1934 as Fukuoka Higher Commercial School under the pre-World War II Educational System, was reestablished as Fukuoka College of Commerce in 1949 in accordance with the post-war educational system reformation. When the college of Law & Economics was established in 1956, the name was changed to Fukuoka University.

Located on 125 acres in the foothills of the Sefuri Mountains in the suburbs of Fukuoka City, Kyushu, Fukuoka University presently comprises nine faculties subdivided into 25 departments and offers academic work leading to Doctorate degrees in 13 major fields. University facilities include several complete libraries, a computer center and laboratories for language training, biological experimentation and radioisotope research. The on-campus work is supported by affiliated research centers with facilities covering practically all fields of research and educational programs in both the sciences and the humanities. To cope with the rapid growth of scientific and technical research, Fukuoka University is in the midst of building advanced facilities to provide complete resources and support services to faculty members and students.

Fukuoka University is constantly striving to continue as one of the leading private institutions for higher education in Japan. The student enrollment now numbers more than 20, 000.

UNDERGRADUATE PROGRAMS

Faculty of Commerce (Freshmen Enrollment: Day 800, Evening 200)
    Department of Commerce
Accounting, Advertising, Bookkeeping, Commerce, Commercial History, Cost Accounting, Foreign Trade, Management, Monetary Theory, Security Market
    Department of Commerce (Evening Course)
Accounting, Bookkeeping, Business Management, Commerce, Commercial History, Foreign Trade, Management, Marketing, Monetary Theory, Personal Management
    Department of International Trade
Commerce, Foreign Exchange, Foreign Trade, Foreign Trade Management, International Economics, International Finance, Management
Faculty of Economics (Freshmen Enrollment: 800)
    Department of Economics
Circulation of Money, Economic Dynamics, Economic History, Economic Policy, History of Economic Doctrine, International Economics, Macroeconomics, Marxian Economics, Microeconomics
    Department of Industrial Economics
Business Economics, Economic Statistics, Industrial Economy, Macroeconomics, Marxian Economics, Microeconomics, Quantitative Economic Analysis
Faculty of Engineering (Freshmen Enrollment: 660)
    Department of Architecture
Architectural Design, Building Construction, Building Materials, Construction Methods, Environmental Engineering, History of Architecture, Steel Structure, Strength of Materials, Structural Mechanics
    Department of Chemical Engineering
Chemical Engineering, Chemical Process Design, Chemical Reaction Engineering, Design and Drawing of Chemical Apparatus, Engineering Analytical Chemistry, Heat Transfer in Chemical Engineering, Industrial Physical Chemistry, Inorganic Chemistry, Organic Chemistry
    Department of Civil Engineering
Applied Mathematics, Bridge Engineering, Concrete Engineering, Construction Methods, Elasticity, Environmental Engineering, Fluid Mechanics for Civil Engineering, Harbor Engineering, Hydraulics, Reinforced Concrete Design
    Department of Electrical Engineering
Control Engineering, Electrical Discharges, Electrical Instrumentation, Electrical Instrumentation and Apparatus, Electric Circuit, Electric Transmission and Distribution, Electromagnetics, Generation and Transformation of Electric Energy, Material Science
    Department of Electronic Engineering

Computer Engineering, Differential Equations, Electric Circuit Analysis and Synthesis, Electromagnetic Theory, Electronic Circuits, Electronic Engineering, Information Theory, Semiconductor Engineering, Theory of AC Circuits

Department of Mechanical Engineering

Design of Machine Elements, Engineering Thermodynamics, Hydraulics, Kinematics, Machine Works, Mechanical Dynamics, Metallic Materials, Strength of Materials, Test of Materials

Faculty of Humanities (Freshmen Enrollment: 280)

Department of Culture

Ancient Thought, Archaeology, Current Thought, Historical Science, History of Oriental Culture, Medieval Thought, Methodology of Cultural Sciences, Modern Thought, Philosophy, Sociology

Department of English Language

British and American Literature, British and American Studies, English Grammar, English Language, English Linguistics, English Phonetics, Speech Communication

Department of French Language

French Grammar, French Language, French Linguistics, French Literature, French Phonetics, French Studies, History of French Literature

Department of German Language

German Grammar, German Language, German Linguistics, German Literature, German Phonetics, German Studies, History of German Literature

Department of History

Diplomatic History, History of International Relations, History of Japan, History of the East, History of the West, Introduction to Regional History, Readings in Japanese, Western and Eastern Historical Texts

Department of Japanese Language and Literature

History of Japanese Literature, Intruduction to Comparative Studies in Literature, Linguistic History of Japanese, Method of Bibliographical Survey, Readings in Japanese Literature, Studies in Regional Culture, Teaching Methods in the Japanese Language

Faculty of Law (Freshmen Enrollment: 800)

Department of Business Law

Bankruptcy, Business Law, Commercial Law, Economic Law, Labor Law, Registration Law, Tax Law

Department of Jurisprudence

Administrative Law, Civil Law, Civil Procedure, Constitutional Law, Criminal Law, International Public Law, Jurisprudence

School of Medicine (Freshmen Enrollment: 100)

Department of Medicine

Anatomy, Anesthesiology, Biochemistry, Cardiac Surgery, Dental Surgery, Dermatology, Health Care, Hygiene, Internal Medicine, Legal Medicine

Faculty of Pharmaceutical Sciences (Freshmen Enrollment: 180)

Department of Pharmaceutical Chemistry

Biochemistry, Instrumental Analysis, Organic Pharmaceutical Chemistry, Pharmaceutical Physical Chemistry, Pharmaceutical Synthetic Chemistry, Pharmacognosy, Pharmacology, Phytochemistry

Department of Pharmaceutics

Biochemistry, Forensic Chemistry, Hygienic Chemistry, Organic Pharmaceutical Chemistry, Pharmacognosy, Pharmacology, Pharmacy, Phytochemistry

Faculty of Physical Education (Freshmen Enrollment: 250)

Department of Physical Education

Administration of Physical Education, Anatomy, Coaching, History of Physical Education, Method of Athletic Training, Physical Education, Physiology of Athletic Training, Psychology of Physical Education, Public Hygiene, Social Physical Education

Faculty of Science (Freshmen Enrollment: 180)

Department of Applied Mathematics

Applied Analysis, Computer Programming, Differential Equations, Geodesy, Geometry, Integral Calculus, Linear Algebra, Mathematical Logic, Mathematics, Topological Space

Department of Applied Physics

Analytical Dynamics, Crystallography, Electricity and Magnetism, Metrology, Oceanophysics, Properties of Matter, Quantum Mechanics, Quantum Physics, Semiconductor Engineering, Thermodynamics

Department of Chemistry

Analytical Chemistry, Bio and High Molecular Chemistry, Biochemistry, Chemical Thermodynamics, Coordination Chemistry, Inorganic Chemistry, Organic Chemistry, Quantum Chemistry, Radio-Chemistry, Statistical Thermodynamics

Foreign Student Admission

Qualifications for Applicants

Standard Qualifications Requirement

1. Applicants must be 18 years of age or older as of April 2 of the year of enrollment.
2. or Those who have obtained the legal Baccalaureate, and to be 18 years of age or older as of April 2 of the year of enrollment.

Persons with abnormal color-perception (color-blindness, color-weakness) are ineligible to apply for Faculty of Pharmaceutical Sciences. Handicapped applicants are required to consult with the International Exchange Office at the University by letter (a certificate of diagonosis with specification of the condition to be attached).

Examination at the University

1. Written examination: School of Medicine—the written essay (in Japanese).
2. Interview

Faculty of Physical Education: physical proficiency test and the sports test in the individual specialty.

School of Medicine: medical examination.

Documents to be Submitted When Applying

Standard Documents Requirement

JLPT and GEFS scores

GRADUATE PROGRAMS

Graduate School of Commerce (First Year Enrollment : Master's 10, Doctor's 10)
Division
Commerce

Graduate School of Economics (First Year Enrollment : Master's 10, Doctor's 10)
Division
Economics

Graduate School of Engineering (First Year Enrollment : Master's 30)
Divisions
Chemical Engineering, Electrical Engineering, Mechanical Engineering

Graduate School of Humanities (First Year Enrollment : Master's 12)
Divisions
English, French

Graduate School of Law (First Year Enrollment : Master's 20, Doctor's 20)
Divisions
Civil and Criminal Law, Public Law

Graduate School of Medical Science (First Year Enrollment : Doctor's 60)
Divisions
Human Biology, Pathogenic Biology, Pathological Biochemistry, Pathological Bio-dynamics, Pathomorphology, Social Medicine and Environmental Health

Graduate School of Pharmaceutical Sciences (First Year Enrollment : Master's 10, Doctor's 10)
Division
Pharmaceutical Sciences

Graduate School of Science (First Year Enrollment : Master's 28, Doctor's 20)
Divisions
Applied Mathematics, Applied Physics, Chemistry

Foreign Student Admission

Qualifications for Applicants
Master's Program
　Standard Qualifications Requirement
Doctor's Program
　Standard Qualifications Requirement
Examination at the University
Master's Program
　First Screening: The documents.
　Second Screening: Japanese, some subjects of their major field (foreign languages included), personal interview
Doctor's Program
　Same as Master's Program.
Documents to be Submitted When Applying
　Standard Documents Requirement
1. Copy of documents that prove the solvency of tuition and other fees.
2. Register of Foreign Students to the Graduate Schools at Fukuoka University.

∗

Research Institutes and Centers
The Animal Care Unit, The Central Research Institute, The Computer Center, The Fukuoka University Chikushi Hospital, The Fukuoka University Hospital, The Language Training Center, The Medical School Radioisotope Center, The Radioisotope Center

Facilities/Services for Foreign Students
　Services for Foreign Students are offered on an equal basis with Japanese Students.

Special Programs for Foreign Students
　Japanese Language Training Course is offered for 15 hours a week. (This is applied for foreign exchange students from sister relationship institutes only.)

For Further Information
　Undergraduate Admission
International Exchange Office, Fukuoka University, 8-19-1 Nanakuma, Jonan-ku, Fukuoka-shi, Fukuoka 814-01 ☎ 092-871-6631 ext. 2160
　Graduate Admission
Office of Graduate Divisions, Fukuoka University, 8-19-1 Nanakuma, Jonan-ku, Fukuoka-shi, Fukuoka 814-01 ☎ 092-871-6631 ext. 2910

Fukuyama University
(Fukuyama Daigaku)

985 Sanzo, Higashimura-cho, Fukuyama-shi, Hiroshima 729-02 ☎ 0849-36-2111

Faculty
　Profs. 100　　Assoc. Profs. 37
　Assist. Profs. Full–time 24; Part–time 56
　Res. Assocs. 37
Number of Students
　Undergrad. 3, 994　　Grad. 31
Library 129, 524 volumes

Outline and Characteristics of the University
　Fukuyama University was founded in 1975 by Shigeru Miyachi, former Director of the Bureau of Higher Education and Scinence in the Ministry of Education. It is a comprehensive private university with three faculties: Economics, Engineering, and Pharmaceutical Sciences. It also includes a College of Liberal Arts and Graduate Schools of Engineering, Pharmacy, and Pharmaceutical Sciences. The three faculties, covering the Social, Natural, and Medical Sciences, lend the diversity that allows the school to claim that is indeed a full university.
　Fukuyama University aims at educating and preparing students to be refined and well-rounded humanists and to become qualified professionals in their chosen occupations, which may require higher knowledge and specialized thechnology in an increasingly international environment.
　The large campus is surrounded by beautiful scenery which harmonizes with the ideal of our univer-

sity: that students should contribute actively, and as members, to democratic society.

UNDERGRADUATE PROGRAMS

Faculty of Economics (Freshmen Enrollment: 300)
  Department of Economics
Accounting, Economic Fluctuation, Economic Geography, Economic History, Economic Policy, Economics, Economics of Finance, Economic Statistics, Financial Policy, History of Economics, International Economics, International Trade, Management, Money and Banking, Quantitative Economics
Faculty of Engineering (Freshmen Enrollment: 420)
  Department of Architecture
Base Construction, Building Design, Building Planning, Construction and City Planning, Construction Material, History of Architecture, Reinforced Concrete Construction, Steel Construction, Structural Mechanics
  Department of Biotechnology
Animal Cell Technology, Enzyme Technology, Fermentation Technology, Gene Technology, Molecular Genetics, Plant Cell Technology
  Department of Civil Engineering
Bridge Engineering, Environment Engineering, Foundation Mechanics, Hydraulics and Hydrology, Infrastructure Planning, Mechanical Engineering, Prestressed-Concrete Engineering, Railway Engineering, Reinforced-Concrete Engineering, River Engineering, Road Engineering, Soil Mechanics, Surveying, Transportation Engineering, Urban Design and Regional Planning, Vibration Engineering, Water Quality Management
  Department of Electronic and Electrical Engineering
Communication Engineering, Electrical Applied Engineering, Electrical Chemical Engineering, Electrical System Engineering, Electrical Transient Phenomena Theory, Electric and Electronic Measurement, Electric Circuit Theory, Electric Machine and Apparatus, Electric Power Engineering, Electro-Magnetic Theory, Electronic and Electrical Control Engineering, Electronic and Electric Material Engineering, Electronic Sensor Engineering, Environment Engineering, Factory Management Engineering, High Voltage Engineering, Microwave Engineering, Optoelectronics, Picture and Image Engineering, Radio Wave Engineering, Semiconductor Theory
  Department of Information Processing Engineering
Coding Theory, Computer Graphics, Computer Software, Data Base Systems, Image Processing, Industrial Information Systems, Information Processing, Information Transmitting Engineering
Faculty of Pharmacy and Pharmaceutical Sciences (Freshmen Enrollment: 120)
  Department of Biological Pharmacy
Bio-Organic Chemistry, Bio-Pharmaceutics, Immu-

nology, Microbiology, Molecular Biology, Pathological Biochemistry
  Department of Pharmacy
Applied Pharmacology, Legal Chemistry, Medicinal Chemistry, Natural Products, Nuclear Pharmacy, Organic Synthetic Chemistry, Oriental Medicine, Physical Pharmacy

GRADUATE PROGRAMS

Graduate School of Engineering (First Year Enrollment : Master's 16)
  Divisions
Civil Engineering, Electronic & Electrical Engineering
Graduate School of Pharmacy and Pharmaceutical Sciences (First Year Enrollmet: Master's 20)

*

Research Institutes and Centers
Institute of Industrial Science, Research Center for Human Science
For Further Information
  Undergraduate and Graduate Admission
Academic Bureau, Administrative Office, Fukuyama University, 985 Sanzo, Higashimura-cho, Fukuyama-shi, Hiroshima 729-02 ☎ 0849-36-2111 ext. 2117

Gakushuin University
(Gakushuin Daigaku)

1-5-1 Mejiro, Toshima-ku, Tokyo 171
☎ 03-986-0221

Faculty
  Profs.   131   Assoc. Profs.   32
  Assist. Profs.   Full–time   8; Part–time   381
  Res. Assocs.   36
Number of Students
  Undergrad.   7, 143   Grad.   320
Library   806, 531 volumes

Outline and Characteristics of the University

The origin of Gakushuin dates back to the middle of the nineteenth century. Successive emperors of Japan took great interest in education and encouraged learning. Emperor Kokaku (1780-1816) had aspired to establish a school for the children of court officials, which was realized during the reign of Emperor Komei (1846-1866). An institution called Gakushuin was founded in 1847 for the education of the children of the court nobility in Kyoto. In October 1877, Gakushuin was reopened as a private school under the national educational system at Kanda, Tokyo for the peerage. In 1884, it came under the management of the Imperial Household for the education of the children of the Royal Family and the peerage. After World War II, in 1947, Gakushuin was reorganized and became independent of the Imperial Household, supported by the Gakushuin Foundation and open to all. Thus, Gakushuin is one of the oldest schools in Japan and has contributed to the education of numerous persons who have made great contributions to the advancement of society.

The undergraduate division has four faculties and 14 departments; the graduate division has six graduate schools and 14 departments. Details of these faculties and divisions are described in the following section. While many universities and colleges have increased their capacity to admit a greater number of students, Gakushuin University holds to its ideal of "the broadest education for a select number of gifted students". Men students number a little less 4, 000 and women a little over than 3, 000.

The Gakushuin campus is located in the heart of metropolitan Tokyo, one of the most congested cities in the world, but enjoys a quiet atmosphere on 20 hectares covered with wide-leaf deciduous trees, conifers and evergreens and some 80 other species, providing splendid scenery for those who stroll through the campus the year round. It is a rare sanctuary in Tokyo. The class room buildings, buildings for the faculty, laboratories, seminars and all the other facilities under the trees including those for students' extracurricular activities are accessible in 30 to 60 minutes from almost any point in Tokyo.

UNDERGRADUATE PROGRAMS

Faculty of Economics (Freshmen Enrollment: 500)
Department of Business Administration
Accountancy, Business Administration, Business Behavior, Business History, Business Organization, Cost Accounting, Economics of Industry, Financial Management, Labor Management, Management, Management Science, Managerial Accounting, Marketing, Production Management
Department of Economics
Business Cycles, Econometrics, Economic History, Economic Policy, History of Economics, History of Economy, Industrial Organization, International Economics, International Monetary Economics, Japanese Economy, Labor Economics, Monetary Economics, Public Finance, Statistics
Faculty of Law (Freshmen Enrollment: 500)
Department of Law
Administrative Law, Anglo-American Law, Civil Law, Commercial Law, Comparative Study of Constitutions, Constitutional Law, Criminal Law, Criminology, French Law, German Law, History of European Law, History of Japanese Law, International Law, Labor Law, Law of Bankruptcy, Law of Civil Procedure, Law of Criminal Procedure, Law of Intangible Property, Laws of Economy, Philosophy of Law, Private International Law, Tax Law
Department of Politics
Comparative Politics, History of International Politics, History of Political Ideas in Japan, History of Politics and Diplomacy in Japan, History of Politics and Diplomacy in the Orient, History of Western Political Thought, International Politics, Mass Communication, Newspaper Journalism, Political and Diplomatic History of the U. S. A., Political History of Europe, Political Process of Japan, Political Psychology, Political Science, Public Administration and Politics
Faculty of Literature (Freshmen Enrollment: 600)
Department of English and American Literature
English and American Literature, English Language, English Language, History of American Literature, History of English Literature, Shakespeare
Department of French Literature
French Language, French Literature, History of French Drama, History of French Literature, History of French Thought
Department of German Literature
German Language, German Literature, History of German Drama, History of German Literature, Medieval German Grammar
Department of History
Archaeology, History, Japanese History, Occidental History, Oriental History, Palaeography
Department of Japanese Literature
History of Japanese Literature, History of the Japanese Language, Japanese Grammar, Japanese Language, Japanese Language Teaching Method, Japanese Literature
Department of Philosophy
Aesthetics, Comparative Culture, Comparative Study of Art, History of Art, History of Education, History of Philosophy, History of Thought, Humanities, Pedagogy, Philosophy
Department of Psychology
Clinical Psychology, Developmental Psychology, History of Psychology, Industrial Psychology, Psychology, Psychology of Learning, Psychology of Perception, Psychology of Personality, Psychology of Thinking, Social Psychology, Vocational Guidance and Management
Faculty of Science (Freshmen Enrollment: 150)
Department of Chemistry
Advanced Physical Chemistry, Analytical Chemistry, Applied Chemistry, Biochemistry, Geochemistry, Inorganic Chemistry, Organic Chemistry, Physical Chemistry, Polymer Chemistry, Radiochemistry
Department of Mathematics
Algebra, Analysis, Calculus, Geometry, Mathematical Science, Probability and Statistics, Topology
Department of Physics
Acoustics Electronics, Atomic Physics, Atoms and Molecules, Biophysics, Electricity and Magnetism, Fluid Dynamics, Geophysics, Laboratory Physics, Linear Algebra, Mechanics, Nuclear Physics, Optics, Physical Mathematics, Physics of Measurements, Physics of Waves, Quantum Mechanics, Solid State Physics, Thermodynamics and Statistical Mechanics, Wave Optics

Foreign Student Admission

Qualifications for Applicants

Standard Qualifications Requirement

Examination at the University

The same entrance examination requirements as Japanese students.

Documents to be Submitted When Applying

Standard Documents Requirement

Application forms are available at the Admissions Office in early December. Application deadline: Jan. 27.

GRADUATE PROGRAMS

Graduate School of Business Administration (First Year Enrollment : Master's 10, Doctor's 3)

Division

Business Administration

Graduate School of Economics (First Year Enrollment : Master's 10)

Division

Economics

Graduate School of Humanities (First Year Enrollment : Master's 52, Doctor's 18)

Division

English and American Literature, French Literature, German Literature, History, Japanese Literature, Philosophy, Psychology

Graduate School of Law (First Year Enrollment : Master's 10, Doctor's 3)

Division

Law

Graduate School of Political Science (First Year Enrollment : Master's 10, Doctor's 5)

Division

Political Science

Graduate School of Science (First Year Enrollment : Master's 18, Doctor's 9)

Divisions

Chemistry, Mathematics, Physics

Foreign Student Admission

Qualifications for Applicants

Master's Program

Standard Qualifications Requirement

Doctor's Program

Standard Qualifications Requirement

Examination at the University

Master's Program

Same as Japanese students.

Doctor's Program

Same as Master's program.

Documents to be Submitted When Applying

Standard Documents Requirement

Research Institutes and Centers

Biology Laboratory, Computer Center, Language Institute, Radiocarbon Laboratory, The Institute of Oriental Studies, University Archives

For Further Information

Undergraduate and Graduate Admission

The Admissions Office, Gakushuin University, 1-5-1 Mejiro, Toshima-ku, Tokyo 171 ☎ 03–986–0221 ext. 272

Gifu College of Economics
(Gifu Keizai Daigaku)

Kitagaracho 5–50, Ohgaki-shi, Gifu 503
☎ 0584–74–5151

Faculty

Profs.   38   Assoc. Profs   11

Assist. Profs.   Full–time   13; Part–time   74

Res. Assoc.   1

Number of Students

Undergrad.   2, 882

Library   14, 000 volumes

Gifu Women's University
(Gifu Joshi Daigaku)

80 Taromaru, Gifu-shi, Gifu 501-25
☎ 0582-29-2211

Faculty

Profs.   25   Assoc. Profs.   8

Assist. Profs.   Full–time   13; Part–time   47

Res. Assocs.   5

Number of Students

Undergrad.   911

Library   64, 260 volumes

Outline and Characteristics of the University

Originally established as Kayo Women's School in 1946 (permitted by Gifu Prefectural government in 1947), Gifu Women's University started as a four-year college with the Faculty of Home Economics in 1968. Two years later, in 1970, the Faculty of Literature was added.

In 1983, the Local Culture Research Institute was established and annexed to the University, aiming at comprehensive research on various aspects and different problems concerning the culture and life of Gifu and neighboring prefectures.

The campuses of the two faculties and the Institute are located at the beautiful northern tip of Gifu City, surrounded by green hills. Gifu is a medium-sized city in Central Japan with a population of approximately 410, 000. It has both urban convenience and rural natural beauty. The Nagara River, one of the most beautiful rivers in Japan, runs through the city halfway encircling the downtown area. Cormorant fishing of world-wide fame is a popular event on this river in summer.

With the School Slogan "Be humane, be womanly, and, above all, be yourself" in mind, the faculty concentrates its efforts on educing the particular abilities of each student as much as possible through small-group education. The University aims to prepare students for the demands of the society of the 21st century. This requires well-balanced knowledge and an international outlook. Further, the University induces students to cultivate qualities such as fraternity and motherly love which are needed to lead a happy domestic life.

UNDERGRADUATE PROGRAMS

Faculty of Home Economics (Freshmen Enrollment: 90)
Department of Home Economics
Child Behavioral Development and Education, Clothing Construction, Clothing Materials and Clothing Performance, Consumer Problems, Costume Design, Family Budgets, Family Relation, Home Management, Human Development, Life Design
Department of Housing and Design
Environmental Engineering, Execution of Work, Housing Equipment, Housing History, Housing Management, Housing Planning & Drawing, Housing Policy & Problems, Housing Structure, Human Engineering, Interior Design, Life of Dwelling
Department of Nutrition and Food Science
Analysis of Food Products, Community Nutrition, Dietetics, Food Chemistry, Food Microbiology, Food Processing, Food Service System Management, Meal Management, Nutrition and Human Development, Nutrition and Metabolism, Principles of Human Nutrition, Therapeutic Nutrition
Faculty of Literature (Freshmen Enrollment: 100)
Department of English Literature
English, English Phonetics, History of American Literature, History of English Language, History of English Literature
Department of Japanese Literature
Calligraphy, Classical Chinese Literature, History of Calligraphy & Fine Arts, History of Japanese Literature, Japanese Philology, Teaching Method of Japanese
Foreign Student Admission
Qualifications for Applicants
Standard Qualifications Requirement
Examination at the University
An interview in Japanese.
Documents to be Submitted When Applying
Standard Documents Requirement

Qualifications for Transfer Students
Persons who have completed the course of junior college in Japan or are due to do so by March of the year of application are qualified for application.
Examination for Transfer Students
A written test and an essay in the field concerned, an interview and the application documents submitted.
Documents to be Submitted When Applying
Standard Documents Requirement
Research Institutes and Centers

Local Culture Research Institute
Facilities/Services for Foreign Students
A dormitory.
For Further Information
Undergraduate Admission
Department of Educational Affairs, Administrative Office, Gifu Women's University, 80 Taromaru, Gifu-shi, Gifu 501-25 ☎ 0582-29-2211 ext. 22

Hachinohe Institute of Technology
(Hachinohe Kogyo Daigaku)
88-1 Obiraki, Myo, Hachinohe-shi, Aomori 031
☎ 0178-25-3111

Faculty
Profs. 36   Assoc. Profs. 42
Assist. Profs. Full-time 17; Part-time 30
Res. Assocs. 4
Number of Students
Undergrad. 2, 535
Library 58, 107 volumes

Outline and Characteristics of the University
Hachinohe Institute of Technology was founded in 1972 and is located in the new industrial city of Hachinohe, in the northern part of Honshu. It has been strongly supported by the local community since it was built.

By providing the fundamental knowledge and research techniques of the engineering disciplines, the college aims are: to train students to use applied technology, to display superior character as proficient technical leaders in our society, to contribute to the development of local society and of our nation and, finally, to be dedicated to world peace and the cultural prosperity of mankind.

UNDERGRADUATE PROGRAMS

Faculty of Engineering (Freshmen Enrollment: 400)
Department of Architectural Engineering
Architectural Planning and Design, Building Engineering, Building Equipment, Building Execution, Building Materials, City Planning, Environmental Engineering, History of Architecture, Regional Planning, Structural Mechanics, Surveying
Department of Civil Engineering
Bridge Engineering, Concrete Engineering, Construction Engineering, Design and Drawing, Geotechnical Engineering, Highway Engineering, House Planning, Hydraulics, Mechanics of Materials, Planning of Public Building, Planning of Residential District, Port and Harbor Engineering, River Engineering, Structural Analysis, Surveying, Transportation Engineering, Water Supply and Urban Sanitation
Department of Electrical Engineering

Computer, Control Engineering, Design of Electrical Machinery, Electrical Circuit, Electrical Communication, Electrical Engineering Materials, Electrical Measurement, Electric Power Applications, Electromagnetism, Electronic Circuits, Electronic Measurements and Their Applications, Energy Conversion Engineering, High Voltage Engineering, Informatics, Theory of Transient Phenomena

Department of Energy Engineering
Automatic Controls for Energy Systems, Chemical Energy, Electric Power Systems, Energy Management, Energy of Nature, Engineering Fluid Mechanics, Fossil Resources and Utilization, Heat and Mass Transfer, Materials Science, Measurement and Instrumentation, Nuclear Energy, Plant Engineering, Strength of Materials, Thermal Engineering, Utillizations of Thermal Energy

Department of Mechanical Engineering
Automatic Control, Computer Science and Engineering, Fluid Machinery, Fluid Mechanics, Heat Transfer, Industrial Materials, Machine Design, Machine Elements, Manufacturing Technology, Measurement and Instrumentation, Mechanism, Plastic Forming, Precision Machining, Production Control Technology, Strength of Materials, Thermal Engineering, Thermodynamics

Foreign Student Admission
Qualifications for Applicants
Standard Qualifications Requirement
Examination at the University
Same as Japanese applicants.
Documents to be Submitted When Applying
Standard Documents Requirement

Qualifications for Transfer Students
Applicants must be graduates of a university or community college, or be students who attended more than a year in college and acquired appropriate credits.
Examination for Transfer Students
The entrance examinations and the oral test.
Documents to be Submitted When Applying
Standard Documents Requirement
Special Programs for Foreign Students
Japanese language and Japanese culture programs.
For Further Information
Undergraduate Admission
Admissions Office, Hachinohe Institute of Technology, 88-1 Obiraki, Myo, Hachinohe-shi, Aomori 031
☎ 0178-25-3111 ext. 350

Hachinohe University
(Hachinohe Daigaku)

13–98 Mihono, Hachinohe-shi, Aomori 031
☎ 0178-25-2711

Faculty

Profs.   16   Assoc. Profs.   5
Assist. Profs.   Full–time   8; Part–time   19
Number of Students
Undergrad.   609
Library   31, 302 volumes

Outline and Characteristics of the University
Hachinohe University was established in 1981 by the late Joseph Yoshitaro Nakamura, the first Chairman of the Board of Directors for the Kosei Gakuin Foundation for Education. The Foundation now has eleven educational institutions in all including a junior college, high school, and kindergartens in and around Hachinohe City. Among them, Kosei Gakuin High School was first established in 1956.

Hachinohe University is located about ten kilometers to the east of the center of the city (pop. about 240, 000), and has a large campus of 250, 000 square meters. Located at the campus of Hachinohe University are Hachinohe Junior College, a gymnasium, electronic computer centre and various outdoor facilities. There is also a well-equipped campsite, a special feature of the campus. In summer, the junior high school boys and girls as well as college students gather here in great number. The Foundation also operates many buses which cover the areas that lie within fifty kilometers from the center of the city, and the students from kindergarten through college utilize this service. Not far from the university lies Towada National Park and Sanriku National Designated Park noted for its sawtooth coastline. Our students can also enjoy surfing all year round at the nearby seashore.

The city of Hachinohe was nominated by the government as a "New City of Industry" in 1964. Since then, it has developed as a leading port for fishing, a base for both southern and northern ocean fishing, and a trading port as well as a trading center for agricultural products.

Hachinohe University was established upon the principles of Catholicism. Its aim of education is to produce young men and women of high intelligence, refined culture and a keen moral sense. It is these students who will answer the demand of the future age, contributing at the same time to the local culture and economy.

UNDERGRADUATE PROGRAMS

Faculty of Commerce (Freshmen Enrollment: 150)
Department of Commercial Science
Accounting, Administrative Management, Commerce, Industrial Studies, Law and Political Economy

*

For Further Information
Undergraduate Admission
Entrance Examination Section, Admission Division, Hachinohe University, 13–98 Mihono, Hachinohe-shi, Aomori 031 ☎ 0178-25-2711 ext. 15

Hakodate University
(Hakodate Daigaku)

51–1 Takaoka-cho, Hakodate-shi, Hokkaido 042
☎ 0138–57–1181

Faculty
　　Profs. 8　　Assoc. Profs. 5
　　Assist. Profs.　Full–time 15; Part–time 23
Number of Students
　　Undergrad. 1,003
Library 81,645 volumes

Outline and Characteristics of the University

Hakodate University was established in 1965 as a 4-year college under the Nomata Schools Organization. Its origins begin with the Hakodate Keiri school. Thus, the University is proud of its 50 years of offering a meaningful tradition of international education to this historic city, one of the first three ports to be opened to the west.

The number of students in the 4-year program totals 800. Through a small college atmosphere, the University can offer a personalized approach in a curriculum that offers a wide variety of courses. Among these, from which students are free to select, are commercial science, business administration, bookkeeping, accounting, law, economics, and managerial information resources.

The founding spirit and principles of education have been to exert a true education with an emphasis on business education. That is, to foster intelligence, emotion, and drive in the comprehensive acquisition of a well-balanced education. Thus, we believe that we can contribute to the local community and to human society as a whole while producing ideal students.

The characteristics of our school are as follows: an education which emphasizes human relations; an atmosphere to cultivate independence in the students; a dedication to adaptation to an international society; a program which strives to be open to the public; a campus with the attractive surroundings of nature and a romantic city.

UNDERGRADUATE PROGRAMS

Faculty of Commerce (Freshmen Enrollment: 200)
　Department of Commerce
　　　　　　*

Research Institutes and Centers
Business Administration Institute, Industrial Development Research Institute
For Further Information
　Undergraduate Admission
Academic Affairs Department, Hakodate University, 51-1 Takaoka-cho, Hakodate-shi, Hokkaido 042
☎ 0138–57–1181 ext. 209

Hakuoh University
(Hakuoh Daigaku)

117 Daigyoji, Oyama–shi, Tochigi 323
☎ 0285–22–1111

Faculty
　　Profs. 15　　Assoc. Profs. 5
　　Assist. Profs.　Full–time 13; Part–time 48
　　Res. Assocs. 2
Number of Students
　　Undergrad. 800
Library 22,906 volumes

Outline and Characteristics of the University

Hakuoh University is located in Oyama City, which is north of Tokyo. Hakuoh University grew out of Hakuoh Women's Junior College, which was founded in 1974 by the late Mrs. Tatsu Kamioka, who was the first president. There were two departments at that time, and a total of 149 students. The department of Early Childhood education had one hundred students, while the department of English Language consisted of 49 students. Two years after the junior college was established, Mrs. T. Kamioka died, and Dr. Kazuyoshi Kamioka became president. In 1982, the Department of Business was added to the junior college, and in April, 1987 Hakuoh University was established. Hakuoh is a four-year, co-educational university. At the present time it consists of only the Department of Business.

Education goals are as follows.

A. To produce specialists in computer science to meet the demands of present business conditions.

B. To produce competent managers of small and medium-sized industries. There is now a shortage of competent managers in this field, which we consider the backbone of our industrial prosperity.

C. To educate internationally-minded business leaders. We are now living in an age of "internationalization" where it is no longer possible to live in isolation. We must establish various types of joint management with business leaders throughout the world. To enjoy our mutual prosperity, it is necessary for us to develop a broad-minded business elite who can cooperate with other nations. For this purpose we encourage the study of foreign languages, especially English. German, French, Spanish and Chinese are also taught.

UNDERGRADUATE PROGRAMS

Faculty of Business Management (Freshmen Enrollment: 200)
　Department of Business Management
Company Management Program
Computer Workshop (BASIC), Financial Management, Organizational Sciences, Production Manage-

ment
Computer Program
Accounting, Accounting-Information Systems, Business Analysis, Data-Communication Systems, Information Management
International Management Program
Computer Science, International Accounting, International Business, International Relations, Marketing

Foreign Student Admission

Qualifications for Applicants
Standard Qualifications Requirement
1.   Those who have received the International Baccalaureate and are 18 years or older are also eligible to apply.
2.   Applicants must take the Japanese Language Proficiency Test and the General Examination for Foreign Students.

Examination at the University
Japanese and English, and an interview.
Date: Jan. 23
Documents to be Submitted When Applying
Standard Documents Requirement
The following documents are also required:
1.   Certification of the Japanese Language Proficiency Test and the General Examination for Foreign Students.
2.   Certification from the Japanese Language school attended by the applicant.
Application deadline: January 19.
Qualifications for Transfer Students
The University accepts any transfer students who have finished 2 years of college or graduated from any Junior college. Those who have received an urdergraduate degree may also enroll for up to 2 years.
Examination for Transfer Students
A written examination in English, write an essay in Japanese and an interview.
Documents to be Submitted When Applying
Same as freshman applicants.

*

Research Institutes and Centers
Hakuoh Computer Center.
Services for Foreign Students
Scholarships are available to qualified applicants. Government financial aid is also given to qualified students.
Special Programs for Foreign Students
Japanese Language Lessons. Fellowship Circle Group for better understanding of one another and the world.
For Further Information
Undergraduate Admission
Admissions Office, Hakuoh University, 1117 Daigyoji, Oyama-shi, Tochigi 323 ☎ 0285-22-1111 ext. 514

Hanazono College
（Hanazono Daigaku）
8-1 Tsubonouchi-cho, Nishinokyo, Nakagyo-ku, Kyoto-shi, Kyoto 604   ☎ 075-811-5181

Faculty
Profs.   32   Assoc. Profs.   17
Assist. Profs.   Full–time 8; Part–time   111
Number of Students
Undergrad. 1,898   Grad.   14
Library   144,317 volumes

Outline and Characteristics of the College
One could characterize Hanazono College as"an infant hanging hair down as white as silk"[The Record of Chan Master Linji], that is, something at once extremely unripe and ripe—unripe from the worldly point of view and ripe in that it lives the life that goes beyond maturity and immaturity.

Affiliated with the Myoshin-ji branch of the Rinzai sect of Zen, Hanazono College with a single department of Buddhism started in 1949. In 1964 the department of Buddhist Welfare was added. The present system of four departments—Buddhism, History, Japanese Literature, and Social Welfare—started only in 1966.

Hanazono College is a coeducational institution consisting of only the Faculty of Letters that confers a Bachelor of Arts degree. Freshmen enrollment has increased from 150 in 1966, to 280 in 1976 (when the campus moved to its present site), and to 400 in 1980. In 1970, One-Year Graduate Course of Letters was established.

Hanazono College originated from Rinzai-shu Daigaku, a school for novice Rinzai Zen monks operating from 1911 onto 1932. It was renamed Rinzai Gakuin Senmon Gakko in 1934, and continued just before Hanazono College started, based on the new educational system of the country.

Although Rinzai-shu Daigaku, its successor Rinzai Gakuin Senmon Gakko, and Hanazono College differ in their educational system, they have shared one common point: a qualified Zen master (a *roshi*) has always been appointed for their presidents.

Appointing a Zen master as president signifies that this educational institution embodies the life of ultimate ripeness that goes beyond maturity and immaturity, that is, the self-awareness of true humanity.

The educational system of Hanazono College, except for the course of Zen studies in the Department of Buddhism, is not exclusively dedicated to the education of future Zen monks.

Hanazono College emphasizes what is most meaningful in the modern age through the radical criticism of todays world in order to come to an understanding of this post-modern way of life. Certainly this is a task not limited to a particular institution but the failure of the modern world to address such issues because of the lack of awakening to true humanity, provides Hanazono College with something to say to the world. However, what is demanded of those concerned with the college is that they should have self-realization of their college's historical significance; they should not and can not have it linger in the state of unripeness in the worldly sense, either. Through this kind of realization efforts have begun to be made toward working out the worldwide task in co-operation with all humanity.

UNDERGRADUATE PROGRAMS

Faculty of Letters (Freshmen Enrollment: 400)
Department of Buddhism
Buddhist Studies Course
Buddhism, Buddhist Culture, Chinese Buddhism, History of Buddhism, History of Chinese Buddhist Thought, History of Indian Buddhist Thought, History of Japanese Buddhist Thought, Indian Buddhism, Japanese Buddhism
Zen Studies Course
Buddhism, Buddhist Culture, History of Chinese Zen School, History of Japanese Zen School, Zen Culture, Zen Studies (China, Korea, Japan)
Department of History
Ancient History, Archaeology, Document Study, Historical Geography, History, History of Japanese Buddhism, History of Japanese Zen Schools, Japanese Ethnology, Japanese History, Medieval History, Modern History, Oriental History, Western History
Department of Japanese Literature
Ancient Literature, Buddhist Literature, Classical Chinese Literature, Early Modern Literature, History of Chinese Literature, History of Japanese Literature, Japanese Grammar, Japanese Linguistics, Japanese Philology, Literature, Medieval Literature, Mid-Ancient Literature, Modern Literature
Department of Social Welfare
Casework, Children's Welfare Legislation, Clinical Psychology, Community Organization, Developmental Psychology, Education of Handicapped Children, Family Sociology, Groupwork, History of Social Work, Juvenile Delinquents, Medical Social Work, Problems of Discrimination, Psychology of Handicapped Children, Social Pathology, Social Research, Social Security, Social Welfare, Social Welfare Legislation, Teaching Method for Handicapped Children, Welfare for the Aged, Welfare for the Handicapped

Foreign Student Admission
Qualifications for Applicants
Standard Qualifications Requirement
Examination at the College
An interview and a written examination concerning the major field of study.

Documents to be Submitted When Applying
Standard Documents Requirement

ONE-YEAR GRADUATE PROGRAMS

One-Year Graduate Course of Letters (Enrollment 15)
Buddhism, History, Japanese Literature

Foreign Student Admission
Qualifications for applicants
Standard Qualifications Requirement
Examination at the College
1. Interview
2. Written examination.

*

Research Institutes and Centers
Hanazono College International Zen Research Institute
Special Programs for Foreign Students
1. A course of the Japanese language
2. A course of practical composition
For Further Information
Undergraduate and Graduate Admission
Entrance Examination Office, Department of College Curriculum Affairs, Hanazono College, 8-1 Tsubonouchi-cho, Nishinokyo, Nakagyo-ku, Kyoto-shi, Kyoto 604 075-811-5181 ext. 224, 225

Higashi Nippon Gakuen University
(Higashi Nippon Gakuen Daigaku)

1757 Kanazawa, Tobetsu–cho, Ishikari–gun, Hokkaido 061–02 ☎ 01332–3–1211

Faculty
    Profs. 45   Assoc. Profs. 34
    Assist. Profs. Full–time 17; Part–time 106
    Res. Assocs. 115
Number of Students
    Undergrad. 1, 527   Grad. 27
Library 90, 814 volumes

Outline and Characteristics of the University

Higashi Nippon Gakuen University, established in 1974, is among the newest universities in Hokkaido. In the past 15 years the university has grown in scope and size with two Faculties, Pharmaceutical Sciences and Dentistry, two Graduate Schools, a Dental Hygienist School for secondary dental care, a Dental Hospital and various other institutes attached to the university. Higashi Nippon Gakuen University is still developing itself as a base for general medical services. All facilities are located on a sprawling campus of 28, 300 square meters, just 20 kilometers from Sapporo.

In Hokkaido, medical services are not yet fully developed in all communities. It was for this reason that the founder initiated Higashi Nippon Gakuen University to further develop medical services in Hokkaido. As a young university, it is always looking toward the future. The university campus is located on the outskirts of Tobetsu town, County of Ishikari, Hokkaido, and commands a splendid view of the Ishikari Plain and the Taisetsu Mountain range. There is a JR (Japan Railroad Co. Ltd.) station, "DAIGAKU-MAE" meaning University Station, just in front of the campus gate.

The university welcomes young men and women who share the goal of expanding excellent and considerate medical care in the 21st century. Students who aim to be pharmacists and dentists will benefit by the excellent instruction at Higashi Nippon Gakuen University.

UNDERGRADUATE PROGRAMS

School of Dentistry (Freshmen Enrollment: 96)
Department of Dentistry
Dental Materials and Engineering, Dental Radiology, Operative Dentistry, Oral Anatomy, Oral Biochemistry, Oral Microbiology, Oral Pathology, Oral Physiology, Oral Surgery, Orthodontics, Pediatric Dentistry, Periodontics and Enodontics, Pharmacology Prosthetic Dentistry
Faculty of Pharmaceutical Sciences (Freshmen Enrollment: 120)
Department of Hygienic Pharmaceutical Sciences
Biochemistry, Chemical Hygiene, Enviromental Chemistry and Hygiene, Microbiology, Pharmaceutical Analytical Chemistry
Department of Pharmaceutical Sciences
Biopharmaceutics, Pharmaceutical Chemistry, Pharmaceutical Physical Chemistry, Pharmaceutics, Pharmacogsy, Pharmacology, Radio Pharmacy, Synthetic and Pharmaceutical Chemistry, Toxicology

GRADUATE PROGRAMS

Graduate School of Dentistry (First Year Enrollment : Doctor's 72)
Divisions
Basic Dentistry, Clinical Dentistry
Graduate School of Pharmaceutical Sciences (First Year Enrollment : Master's 32, Doctor's 12)
Divisions
Biochemical Pharmacology and Biopharmaceutics, Environmental and Chemical Hygiene, Industrial and Pharmaceutical Chemistry

*

Research Institutes and Centers
Center for Experimental Animals, Center for Radioisotope Studies, Medical Plants Garden
Services for Foreign Students
Admission Office, Higashi Nippon Gakuen University, 1757 Kanazawa, Tobetsu-cho, Ishikari-gun, Hokkaido 061-02 ☎ 01332-3-1211 ext. 214, 215

Himeji Dokkyo University
(Himeji Dokkyo Daigaku)
7-2-1, Kamiohno, Himeji-shi, Hyogo 670　☎ 0792-23-2211120

Faculty
　Profs.　38　　Assoc. Profs　17
　Assist. Profs.　Full-time　19; Part-time　36
　Res. Assocs.　10
Number of Students
　Undergrad.　1, 479
Library　34, 167 volumes

Outline and Characteristics of the University
Dokkyo Gakuen (Dokkyo Educational Institutions) began with the founding of the Doitsu-gaku Kyokai (German Studies Association) in Tokyo in 1881. Doitsu-gaku Kyokai's founders included some of the Meiji Era's most important leaders: Amam Nishi, Chairman of the Imperial Academy; Taro Katsura, Prime Minister; and Yajiro Shinagawa, Envoy Extraordinary and Minister Plenipotentiary to Germany. Their goal was to promote Japan's modernization by introducing German culture and sophisticated technology to the young minds of the period.

The German Association became the Doitsu-gaku Kyokai Gakko in 1883, eventually evolving into today's Dokkyo Junior and Senior High Schools. The Doitsu-gaku Kyokai was the forerunner of the six educational institutions which today make up Dokkyo Gakuen and maintain the proud tradition of more than 100 years. In 1952, Dr. Amano, an alumnus of Dokkyo Junior High School, an eminent scholar of Kant, one of Japan's greatest educators, and former Minister of Education, was inaugurated as the thirteenth principal of Dokkyo Junior and Senior High Schools. Dr. Amano expanded Dokkyo Gakuen by establishing Dokkyo University in 1964. Dr. Amano's philosophy that a university should be "a place for the development of personality through learning, " underlies Dokkyo University's goal to educate the whole individual by integrating intellectual, physical, and ethical education. Dokkyo Gakuen continued its growth by adding Dokkyo Medical College in 1973, and a second senior high school, Dokkyo Saitama Senior High School, near Tokyo, in 1980. The most recent addition to Dokkyo Gakuen is Himeji Dokkyo University, founded in 1987 in Himeji City, Hyogo Prefecture.

The campus of Himeji Dokkyo University with Dr. Suda as president is located in the northern part of Himeji City. H. D. U. , based on Dokkyo Gakuen's tradition and Dr. Amano's philosophy, aims at producing graduates with high language proficiency and a deep knowledge of their special fields who can play important roles in the international society of today.

The University has three faculties and college of Foreign Languages, Law, and Economics & Informatics.

The College of Foreign Languages includes four Departments of German, English, Chinese and Japanese. In the Department of Japanese, half the number of students are reserved for foreign students and "returnees"Japanese students who have long lived abroad.

After two years of intensive course of Japanese, these students join the rest of the students for their later two years of study.

By contact with students from other countries all of the university's students also have the opportunity to learn about different cultures and to gain insight into their own culture. This kind of international contact will help to foster international understanding and to develop a new generation of active participants in the world community.

UNDERGRADUATE PROGRAMS

College of Foreign Languages (Freshmen Enrollment: 300)

Department of Chinese
Chinese, Chinese Culture, Chinese Culture, Chinese Expression, Chinese Linguistics, Chinese Literature, History of Chinese Language, Reading and Interpretation of Chinese Literature

Department of English
English, English and American Cultures, English and American Literature, English Expression, English Linguistics, History of English Language, Reading and Interpretation of English Literature

Department of German
German, German Culture, German Expression, German Linguistics, German Literature, History of the German Language, Reading and Interpretation of German Literature

Department of Japanese
History of the Japanese Language, Introduction to Japanese Linguistics, Japanese Culture, Japanese Culture, Japanese Literature, Reading and Interpretation of Japanese Literature, Study of Japanese Expression

Subject Courses common to all department
Linguistics and Culture Course
Applied Linguistics, Audio–Visual Education, Classical Language, Comparative Culture Study, Comparative Folklore, Comparative Linguistics, Comparative Literature, Comparative Religion, Critical Study of the Japanese Language, History of Japanese Thought, History of Occidental Thought, History of Oriental Thought, Introduction to Linguistics, Japanese Expressions Japanese Culture, Japanese Literature, the Japanese Language

Communication Courses
Advertising, Communication, Human Sciences, Intercultural Communication, Marketing Research, Simultaneous Interpretation Methods, Social Psychology, Social Research Methods

Computer Science Course
Cybernetics, Education Engineering, Human Engineering, Information Processing, Information Sociology, Information Systems, Linguistics Engineering, Neurobiology

International Relations Course
Area Sudies-America, -Asia, -Europe, History of Int'l Relations, Int'l Economics, Int'l Law, Int'l Management, Int'l Mechanism, Int'l Organization, Int'l Politics, Int'l Relations, Oceania

Faculty of Law (Freshmen Enrollment   300)
Administrative Law, Anglo-American Law, Civil Law, Civil Procedure, Commercial Law, Communication and Law, Comparative History of Law, Comparative Legal Cultures, Constitutional Law, Criminal Law, Criminal Procedure, Economic Law, English in Law and Politics, French Law, History of Asian Politics and Diplomacy, History of Japanese Political Thought, History of Japanese Politics and Diplomacy, History of Western Political Thought, History of Western Politics and Diplomacy, Int'l Business Law, Int'l Law, Int'l Politics, Int'l Private Law, Int'l Tax Law, Labor Law, Legal Problems, Local Government, Political Culture, Political Problems, Political Process, Political Science, Public Administration, Seminar, Social Security Law, Tax Law, The Third World

Foreign Student Admission
Qualifications for Applicants
Standard Qualifications Requirement

For October admission to the Japanese Department proficiency in the Japanese language is not required provided the applicant is capable of understanding classes in English.

Examination at the University
Applicants to the Japanese Department; Japanese and English and an interview. Applicants for October admission; transcripts and other documents.

The same entrance examinations with the Japanese students to the other departments (English, German, Chinese) of the College of Foreign Languages and to the Faculty of Law.

Documents to be Submitted When Applying
Standard Documents Requirement
Admission for April: Standard Documents Requirement.
Deadline: January 31.
Admission for October to The Japanese Department: Standard Documents Requirement.
Deadline: May 31.

*

Research Institutes and Centers
Area Research, Center for Computer Science, Human Science Center, International Center

Services for Foreign Students
Housing: The University does not have dormitory facilities, but it can assist students from overseas in

finding home-stay residences or apartments.

Health Care: Health insurance for students is available. At the University Health Aministration Center, doctors and nurse can administer first aid, give medical advice, and when necessary, help students find appropriate hospitals.

Counseling: Students can receive counseling for school-related and private concerns at the International Center and the student-counseling room. Students can also visit their faculty advisers during office hours to ask for assistance.

Special Programs for Foreign Students

The Department of Japanese includes a section for foreign students.

For Further Information

Undergraduate Admission

Admission Section, Instruction Division, Himeji Dokkyo University, 7-2-1, Kamiohno, Himeji-shi, Hyogo 670 ☎ 0792-23-2210 ext. 265

Hirosaki Gakuin College
(Hirosaki Gakuin Daigaku)

13-1 Minori-cho, Hirosaki-shi, Aomori 036
☎ 0172-34-5211

Faculty
      Profs. 5   Assoc. Profs. 9
      Assist. Profs. Full-time 5; Part-time 48
Number of Students
      Undergrad. 359
Library 54, 471 volumes

Outline and Characteristics of the College

In 1886 Hirosaki Gakuin was founded as part of Hirosaki Church by the Rev. Yoichi Honda. This was to become one of the first institutions for women's general education in northern Japan. The church began a program of education and called upon Christian missionary help in this work. In this way the Methodist Church has had a long-standing influence upon the several levels of education. A large portion of the funds was contributed by Madame Wright of the U. S. A. The school was originally called "Raito" Women's School named after Madame Wright. At all times, the education program has been an entirely Japanese one.

At Hirosaki Gakuin College, B. A. degrees are awarded in the areas of English and Japanese Literature.

The Department of English has two tracks to choose from: Literature and Linguistics. The literature courses cover all periods of English and American Literature. The linguistics track offers courses in the latest linguistic theories as well as in traditional grammar. In addition to these tracks, emphasis is placed upon "practical English."

The Department of Japanese has two areas of study. Literature courses include works of ancient

times as well as those of today. Studies of such famous local authors as Osamu Dazai and Yojiro Ishizaka are also encouraged. The linguistics studies offer keen insight into the Japanese language.

The college has an exchange program with North Central College, Naperville, Illinois, U. S. A.

UNDERGRADUATE PROGRAMS

Faculty of Literature (Freshmen Enrollment: 100)
      Department of English
American Literature, American Studies, English Drama, English Linguistics, English Literature, English Novels, English Poetry, Essay, History of the English Language, Phonetics
      Department of Japanese
Ancient Manuscripts, Calligraphy, Children's Literature, Chinese Literature, Comparative Literature, Folklore, History of Chinese Literature, History of Japanese Literature, Japanese Literature, Japanese Phonetics, Local Writers in Japanese Literature, The Japanese Language

Foreign Student Admission
      Qualifications for Applicants
      Standard Qualifications Requirement
      Examination at the College
      Foreign students are accepted individually on the basis of their overall academic preparation, character, and potential for success at the College. Special admission is granted on the basis of involvement in extracurricular activities, or any other evidence that indicates that the student can benefit from and contribute to an experience at the College.
      Documents to be Submitted When Applying
      Standard Documents Requirement

*

Research Institutes and Centers
Research Center for Historical and Cultural Studies
For Further Information
      Undergraduate Admission
Admissions Office, Hirosaki Gakuin College, 13-1 Minori-cho, Hirosaki-shi, Aomori 036 ☎ 0172-34-5211 ext. 01

Hiroshima Bunkyo Women's College
(Hiroshima Bunkyo Jyoshi Daigaku)

1-2-1 Kabe-higashi, Asakita-ku, Hiroshima-shi, Hiroshima 731-02   ☎ 08266-4-3191

Faculty
      Profs. 22   Assoc. Profs. 15
      Assist. Profs. Full-time 1; Part-time 48
      Res. Assoc. 1
Number of Students
      Undergrad. 662   Grad. 12

Library 80,000 volumes

Outline and Characteristics of the College

Hiroshima Bunkyo Women's College is situated in Kabe, about ten miles north of the center of Hiroshima city. It is a quiet residential town with the river Ota flowing nearby. With green hills behind and a stream in front, Bunkyo enjoys a most favorable educational environment.

Hiroshima Bunkyo Women's College was founded in 1966 by Miki Takeda, President of the College and Chairman of Board of Directors of the Takeda Educational Institution. The institution itself dates from 1948, when it opened as Kabe Girls' Professional School. It developed into Kabe Girls' High School in 1957, and five years later added Kabe Women's Junior College which offered a program in clothing science. Three more programs, the Food and Nutrition Course, Japanese Literature Course and English Literature Course were added within the following three years. On this basis a four-year college was created with two departments, Japanese Literature and English Literature, in 1966. Recent additions to the institution have been the Infant Education Course to the junior college (1970), the Primary School Teacher Training Department to the senior college (1981) and a kindergarten (1971). In 1986 the Graduate School of Japanese Literature was established and to this Graduate School was added the Course of Pedagogics in 1987.

As embodied in the three school mottos, (1) Strive after truth, be just and love diligence, (2) Be a woman of principle and practice, and (3) Be both modest and elegant, the founder's educational aims are to produce well-mannered, cultivated and trustworthy students. As the college is small in size, classes are also small. This enables the teachers to give thorough instruction. Moreover, a close and friendly relationship is constantly maintained between the teachers and the students, which benefits both the students' academic work and personal characters.

UNDERGRADUATE PROGRAMS

Faculty of Letters (Freshmen Enrollment: 130)
Department of English Literature
Department of Japanese Literature
Department of Primary School Teacher Training

Foreign Student Admission
Qualifications for Applicants
  Standard Qualifications Requirement
Examination at the College
1. Applicants are required to take the Japanese language proficiency test and the general examination conducted by the college.
2. Applicants are required to sit for an interview.
Documents to be Submitted When Applying
  Standard Documents Requirement

Application forms and entrance examination fee should be submitted to the Admissions Office by January 27.

GRADUATE PROGRAMS

Graduate School of Japanese Literature (First Year Enrollment : Master's 10)
  Division
Japanese Literature, Pedagogics

Foreign Student Admission
Qualifications for Applicants
Master's Program
  Standard Qualifications Requirement
Examination at the College
Master's Program
1. Applicants for the Japanese Literature Course must take the Japanese language and literature test and those who apply for the Pedagogics Course must take the pedagogics and psychology test. In addition, applicants for either course must take one foreign language (English, French, German or Chinese) test conducted by the college.
2. Applicants must sit for an oral examination.
3. The examinations are usually given in October and the following March.
Documents to be Submitted When Applying
  Standard Documents Requirement
  Application forms and entrance examination fee must be submitted together to the Admissions Office one week before each examination.

*

For Further Information
Undergraduate and Graduate Admission
Admissions Office, Hiroshima Bunkyo Women's College, 1-2-1 Kabe-higashi, Asakita-ku, Hiroshima-shi, Hiroshima 731-02 ☎ 08266-4-3191 ext. 207

The Hiroshima-Denki Institute of Technology
(Hiroshima Denki Daigaku)

6-20-1 Nakano, Aki-ku, Hiroshima-shi, Hiroshima 739-03 ☎ 082-893-0381

Faculty
  Profs. 28   Assoc. Profs. 20
  Assist. Profs. Full–time 13; Part–time 39
  Res. Assoc. 1
Number of Students
  Undergrad. 1,675
Library 49,980 volumes

Outline and Characteristics of the University

In 1967, Hiroshima-Denki Institute of Technology was established. It was comprised of the two Departments of Electrical Engineering and Electronic Engineering. Later the same year, the Department of Mechanical Engineering was opened. Since then the Institute has endeavored to develop its facilities for the advancement and growth of the students' education.

The Institute is located midway between Kure and Hiroshima. Up-to-date industrial technology is openly researched at the Institute and utilized in the academic curriculum. In this way, students can develop into open, honest young men as well as technologically creative contributors to society. This is all in accordance with the school ideal that states that, "The Institute is always ready to translate the words trust, cooperation, and practice into action. "

The planning center of the Institute is the education foundation of Hiroshima-Denki Gakuen. This educational foundation is composed of the Hiroshima-Denki Institute of Technology, the Hiroshima Junior College of Automotive Engineering, and the Senior High School attached to Hiroshima-Denki Institute of Technology.

The Institute is characterized by close relationships between staff and students. Each class is assigned two instructors who not only provide academic education but also social education. They are available to the student for counselling and advice concerning the personal problems a student may have as well as academic ones. Through this close contact, students develop into well-rounded persons able to play active roles in society.

UNDERGRADUATE PROGRAMS

Faculty of Engineering (Freshmen Enrollment: 330)
   Department of Electrical Engineering
Automatic Control, Computer Engineering, Electrical Machinery, Electrical Measurement, Electric Circuits, Electric Power Engineering, Electromagnetism, Electronic Circuits, Solid State Electrophysics
   Department of Electronic Engineering
Circuit Analysis, Circuit and Electronics, Communication Systems, Computer Network and Data Base, Computer Organization, Computer Programming, Control, Digital Electronic Circuits, Digital Logic, Electrochemistry, Electromagnetic Radiation and Transmission, Information Theory, Microwave Circuits, Operations Research, Radar and Television, Solid State Devices, Solid State Electronics, Sound and Vibration, Theory Modern Control Theory
   Department of Mechanical Engineering
Applied Mechanics and Mechanical Vibration, Engineering Materials and Processing, Fluid Mechanics and Fluid Machinery, Scientific Measurement and Control Engineering, Strength of Materials and Fracture Control, System Engineering and Production Control, Thermodynamics and Energy Conversion

Foreign Student Admission

Qualifications for Applicants
   Standard Qualifications Requirement
Examination at the University
   Applicants must take an entrance examination consisting of a written examination.
Documents to be Submitted When Applying
   Standard Documents Requirement

＊

Research Institutes and Centers
The Information Center
For Further Information
Undergraduate Admission
Admission Office, The Hiroshima-Denki Institute of Technology, 6-20-1 Nakano, Aki-ku, Hiroshima-shi, Hiroshima 739-03 ☎ 082-893-0381 ext. 266

Hiroshima Institute of Technology
(Hiroshima Kogyo Daigaku)

2-1-1 Miyake, Saeki-ku, Hiroshima-shi,
Hiroshima 731-51   ☎ 0829-21-3121

Faculty
   Profs.   57   Assoc. Profs.   47
   Assist. Profs.   Full–time   26; Part–time   81
   Res. Assocs.   3
Number of Students
   Undergrad.   3, 684
Library   141, 475 volumes

Outline and Characteristics of the University
   Hiroshima Institute of Technology was founded by Noboru Tsuru as an institution where the motto, "To educate is to love" can be practiced. Tsuru is the fourth son of the late Torataro Tsuru, who originally conceived the vision of a comprehensive school system of Tsuru Gakuen (educational foundation), who founded in 1896 the private high school, Surigakkai (Institute for Mathematics and Sciences), and over the next 60 years devoted his life to the promotion of secondary and post-secondary education by private institutions.

   The Institute is the flagship of the Tsuru Gakuen which was approved by the Japanese government in 1957. It was started as a post-secondary technical school, received accreditation as a two-year college in 1961 and as a four-year college in 1963. At first, the Institute consisted of two departments, Electronics and Electrical Engineering. Later, in response to the needs of the society and the industry, it added the department of Mechanical Engineering in 1964, which was followed further by the departments of Civil Engineering (1965), Architecture (1965), and Industrial Engineering (1966).

   The Institute is located in Hiroshima, the very symbol of world peace, resulting from its tragic past as the first city destroyed by the Atomic Bomb. The main campus is in western part of the city. Placed on the slope of a hill with abundant greenery, it commands a spectacular view of both the Seto Inland Sea and the Miyajima Island, one of the so-called three most beautiful sceneries of Japan. In addition, the Institute operates two sub-campuses: one a 20, 000 m² campus in natural forest setting, with several facilities for overnight seminars, sports events, field work and other events; another campus which consists of two five-storied buildings, located almost next to Peace Park, the center of the city, where international conferences and seminars can be held.

The Institute aims at fostering and sending out to the society the engineers who are keenly aware of various human concerns and would make contributions toward the development of technology and its industrial use which best meets societal needs without degrading human dignity. Since its inception, the Hiroshima Institute of Technology has been striving to nurture young people who are always conscious of God and serve fellow human beings.

UNDERGRADUATE PROGRAMS

Faculty of Engineering (Freshmen Enrollment: 940)
Department of Architecture
Architectural Design Course
Architectural Engineering Course
Architectural Design, Architectural Planning, Building Equipment, Form & Composition, Reinforced Concrete, Structural Mechanics
Department of Civil Engineering
Concrete Engineering, Hydraulics, Environmental Engineeing, Planning, Soil Mechanics, Structural Engineering, Surveying, Water Resources Steel Structure
Department of Electrical Engineering
Energy Conversion Engineering, Information Engineering, Materials Engineering
Department of Electronics Engineering
Electron Devices Engineering, Information Engineering
Department of Industrial Engineering
Management Control, Management Science, Production Engineering, System Engineering and Management Information
Department of Mechanical Engineering
Comprehensive Machinery Course
Electronic Machinery Course
Combustion Engineering, Control Engineering, Dynamics, Electronic Circuits, Fluid Mechanics, Materials Science, Measurements Engineering, Thermodynamics

Foreign Student Admission
Qualifications for Applicants
Standard Qualifications Requirement
Examination at the University
There will be no separate special entrance examination for foreign students. Applicants from abroad must take the same entrance examinations as required for Japanese students.

1. Selection procedure
Selection of successful candidates will be based upon a comprehensive evaluation of the results of scholastic examination described below and the contents of application documents.
(Note: Admission may be denied to those who possess health problems which may seriously interfere with normal participation in laboratory and field work.)

2. Scholastic examination
(1) Subjects: Mathematics (mathematics I, algebra, geometry, and fundamental basic analysis), Science (physics or chemistry. In each subject, appropriate parts of Science I will be included.), and Foreign language (English I and English II)
(2) Examination date: February 5, 1989
Documents to be Submitted When Applying
Standard Documents Requirement
All application documents must be sent by mail to the Entrance Examination Office between Januray 14 and January 27, 1989. (No in-person application will be accepted.)

*

Research Institutes and Centers
Central Computer Center, Institute for Engineering Research
For Further Information
Undergraduate Admission
Entrance Examination Office, Hiroshima Institute of Technology, 2-1-1 Miyake, Saeki-ku, Hiroshima-shi, Hiroshima 731-51 ☎ 0829-21-3121 ext. 234, 235, 236

Hiroshima Jogakuin College
(Hiroshima Jogakuin Daigaku)

4-13-1 Ushita-Higashi, Higashi-ku, Hiroshima-shi, Hiroshima 732   ☎ 082-228-0386

Faculty
Profs.   28   Assoc. Profs.   21
Assist. Profs.   Full–time   7; Part–time   43
Number of Students
Undergrad.   1, 419
Library   100, 972 volumes

Outline and Characteristics of the College
Hiroshima Jogakuin College is one of the time-honored Christianity-based institutions for research and superior education for women in the western half of Japan. The college itself is the main body of Hiroshima Jogakuin whose founding dates a full century back to 1886 when Nannie B. Gaines, sent from Southern Methodist Episcopal Church of America, launched a series of schools from kindergarten up to junior college—the first and the only kind in this locality before the war. Currently the College enrolls

some 1, 400 young women in its two departments: the Faculty of Literature offering a B. A. degree, and the Junior College offering courses in home economics. The Faculty of Literature has two wings, one for American and English language and literature, the other for Japanese language and literature, annual matriculation for the former being 120 and for the latter 100. The Junior College annually admits 210 into three branches of home economics. Academic ceremonies and weekly worship are observed in Christian tradition. A variety of extracurricular activities are subsidized by school funds. All courses except drills and advanced lectures in English literature are taught in Japanese.

The Department of English and American Literature and Language inherits its pre-war tradition of realism in learning foreign language through actual contact with native English speaking teachers. In 1949, the College was reorganized to become the first of its kind in this prefecture under the new constitution and school laws. A sequence of capable American women teachers came and inspired the students in the post-war decades until 1967, when the Department of Japanese Language and Literature was added to complete the Faculty. Ever since, the College has been offering opportunities in two aspects of literary culture, the students' own and that of the world.

The campus, surrounded by residential quaters north of downtown, is easy of access both from Hiroshima Station and from the business centers.

UNDERGRADUATE PROGRAMS

Faculty of Literature (Freshmen Enrollment: 220)
Department of American and English Literature
Bible as Literature, English and American Literary Criticism, English and American Literature, English Grammar, English Language, English Phonetics, History of English
Department of Japanese Literature
Calligraphy, Chinese Classics, Chinese Literature, History of Japanese Literature, Japanese Grammar, Japanese Language, Japanese Linguistics, Japanese Literature, Japanese Phonetics, Japanese Stylistics, Medieval Poetics, Modern Poetry, Poets and Novelists of Meiji Era

Foreign Student Admission
Qualifications for Applicants
Standard Qualifications Requirement
The College is open exclusively for women students who have attended two years or more of college level education.
Examination at the College
Special interview may be prescribed for assessing fluency in Japanese.
Documents to be Submitted When Applying
Standard Documents Requirement
＊

For Further Information
Undergraduate Admission
Registrar, Registrar's Office, Hiroshima Jogakuin College, 4-13-1 Ushita-Higashi, Higashi-ku, Hiroshima-shi, Hiroshima 732 ☎ 082-228-0386 ext. 234

Hiroshima Shudo University
(Hiroshima Shudo Daigaku)

1717 Otsuka, Numata-cho, Asa–Minami-ku, Hiroshima-shi, Hiroshima 731-31 ☎ 082-848-2121

Faculty
Profs. 73 Assoc. Profs. 62
Assist. Profs. Full–time 9; Part–time 189
Number of Students
Undergrad. 5, 287 Grad. 58
Library 361, 704 volumes

Outline and Characteristics of the University

Hiroshima Shudo University is a private institution whose history dates back 250 years to the founding of the Asanohan School during the Edo period. After the Meiji Restoration (1868), the name of the school was changed several times, but it was finally established as a modern-style school in 1905 under the name of Shudo Independent Middle School. Due to educational reforms in 1947, this Middle School was reorganized into a new-style senior high school and a new junior high school was established.

The University was first established as a two-year evening junior college for commercial studies in 1952. Day courses at the college were established in 1956. In 1960, Hiroshima College of Commerce was set up with Faculty of Commercial Sciences and a four-year degree course in the Department of Business Studies. In 1963, Department of Business Administration was added to meet the demands of a rapidly changing society in need of new academic and financial expertise. At the same time, the staff was increased and facilities updated. In 1969, Department of Management Science was established to carry out research and to provide instruction in Information and Computer Management, specializing in the fields of economics and business management. In 1973, the Faculty of Humanities and Sciences was established, including Psychology, Sociology, Education, and English Language and Literature.

The motivation behind the establishment of the new faculty was the theme "A University for the Future". Such a development was unusual at that time and the Faculty of Humanities and Sciences at Shudo was unique in its constitution. It was at this time also that the name of the College was changed to Hiroshima Shudo University.

In 1974, the whole University moved from the Kannon campus to the new Numata campus and was equipped with improved facilities. The University stressed the best of traditional educational philosophies whilst introducing new and progressive ideas. The University added the Faculty of Law in 1976; the first in the Chugoku or Shikoku districts of Western Japan. During this early period the University began its deep commitment to the development of its academic facilities, achieving a high standing in the field of education and research. The undergraduate courses were firmly established and a graduate school was set up, offering a Master's degree in Business Studies (1971), and then a doctorate (1973).

From 1978, a Master's degree for either a Psychology or English literature major was available, and from 1981 a doctorate degree program was established. In the same year, a Master's degree was offered in the Department of Legal Research. Then, in 1984 a Master's degree for a Sociology or an Education major was established. All these programs are at present being offered by Hiroshima Shudo University.

UNDERGRADUATE PROGRAMS

Faculty of Commercial Sciences (Freshmen Enrollment: 560)

Department of Business Administration
Applied and Industrial Psychology, Auditing Administrative Accounting, Business Administration, Business Management and Organization, Business Statistics, Business Structure, Corporation Finance, Cost Accounting, Economic Policy, Financial Analysis, Industrial Management, Labor Administration, Marketing Management, Personnel and Labor Management, Small and Medium-sized Enterprizes, Tax Accounting, Theory of Industry

Department of Business Studies
Accounting, Advertising, Bookkeeping, Business Communication, Commerce, Commodities Science, Economics, Foreign Trade, History of Commerce, History of Economics, Industrial Bookkeeping, Insurance Economics, Insurance Management, International Economics, Marketing, Modern Economics, Monetary Theory, Stock Market Theory, Trade Practices, Transport Economics, Urban Economics Geography

Department of Management Science
Corporation Finance, Data Processing, Econometrics, Exploratory Calculation of Demand, Matrix Accounting, Modern Economics, Numerical Analysis, Operations Research, Production Management, Systems Theory

Faculty of Humanities and Sciences (Freshmen Enrollment: 285)

Department of Education
Comparative Education, Education, Educational Law, Educational Organization, Educational Process, Educational Research, Higher Education, History of Education, Infant Education, Social Education (Adult Education), Sociology of Education

Department of English Language and Literature
Bible and Biblical Literature, Communication, English and American Culture, English and American Literature, English Grammar, English Language, English Phonetics, English Studies, History of American Literature, History of English Literature, Linguistics

Department of Psychology
Applied and Industrial Psychology, Clinical Psychology, Development Psychology, Educational Psychology, Learning and Motivation, Physiological Psychology, Psychiatry, Psychology, Social Psychology, Statistics for Behavioral Sciences

Department of Sociology
Analysis of Modern Society, Cultural Anthropology, History of Sociology, Industrial Sociology, Regional Sociology, Sociological Theories, Sociology, Sociology of Religion, Sociology of the Family

Faculty of Law (Freshmen Enrollment: 250)

Department of Legal Research
Administrative Law, Civil Law, Civil Procedure Law, Commercial Law, Constitutional Law, Criminal Law, Criminal Procedure Law, Criminal Psychology, Criminology, Foreign Law, History of Law, History of Political Thought, International Law, International Private Law, International Relations, Judicial System, Labor Law, Legal Philosophy, Legal Sociology, Public Administration, Tax Law

Foreign Student Admission

Qualifications for Applicants
Standard Qualifications Requirement

Examination at the University
To be admitted to the university, applicants must pass the entrance exam which consists of an interview and a written exam.

The date of the entrance exam is subject to change each year, but is generally held between February and March.

Documents to be Submitted When Applying
Standard Documents Requirement

Foreign applicants should consult the International Affairs Office at the earliest possible date prior to the intended date of admission. The academic and other qualifications of each student will be considered, and details of the application will be decided by the University's Admission Committee. Students will be normally enrolled in April.

Application Period: February 25-March 7 (the case of 1986)

Qualifications for Transfer Students
Should there be available space, students from foreign institutions may transfer to Hisroshima Shudo University and enter the second and third year courses. This is on condition that the applicants pass the entrance examination especially arranged for them.

Examination for Transfer Students

To be admitted to the university, applicants must pass the entrance exam which consists of an interview and a written exam.

The date of the entrance exam is subject to change each year, but is generally held between February and March.

Documents to be Submitted When Applying
Standard Documents Requirement
Same as procedure for undergraduates.

GRADUATE PROGRAMS

Graduate Division of the Faculty of Commercial Sciences (First Year Enrollment : Master's 20, Doctor's 5)
Divisions
Business Administration, Business Studies
Graduate Division of the Faculty of Humanities and Sciences (First Year Enrollment : Master's 20, Doctor's 5)
Divisions
Education, English Language and Literature, Psychology, Sociology
Graduate Division of the Faculty of Law (First Year Enrollment : Master's 5)
Division
Legal Research

Foreign Student Admission
Qualifications for Applicants
Master's Program
Standard Qualifications Requirement
Doctor's Program
Standard Qualifications Requirement
Examination at the University
Master's Program
Foreign applicants must take the entrance examination, oral and written, which is normally administered between February and March.
Doctor's Program
Same as Master's program.
Documents to be Submitted When Applying
Standard Documents Requirement
Foreign applicants should consult the International Affairs office at the earliest possible date prior to the intended date of admission. The academic and other qualifications of each student will be considered, and details of the application will be decided by the University's Admission Committee. Students will be normally enrolled in April.
Application Period: February 21-March 5 (the case of 1986)

*

Research Institutes and Centers
Computing Center, Experimental Research Center, Human Rights Research Center, Institute for Advanced Studies
Facilities/Services for Foreign Students
1. Health Service Center
A well-qualified staff of physician assists with the care, health and medical needs of all the university students, staff and faculty members. Health care is provided, free of charge, not only for full–time students but also for auditors, short-term research students, foreign students and foreign scholars and visitors. All students and staff members are urged to take advantage of the various health examiniations regularly offered, free of charge, by the Center in order to maintain and promote good health.
2. International Exchange Committee
The International Exchange Committee was set up in order to promote exchange between overseas universities and research institutes and Hiroshima Shudo University. The International Exchange Committee's aim is to improve the level of academic research and education and to facilitate academic exchange.
Special Programs for Foreign Students
The Japanese language courses at Shudo have been instituted in order to help foreign students. The aim of the courses are to assist those students whose mother tongue is not Japanese so they can acquire a command of Japanese as a foreign language. The content of the course is to some extent flexible and depends upon the students concerned, such as the country of origin of the students, the first language, age, personal and educational history, motivation and purposes, aims and period of study in Japan.

The Japanese as a Foreign Language course would include, for example, note-taking practice, the use of reference material, participation in discussion with university teaching staff and students, and the writing of reports (thesis) or examination scripts in Japanese.
Elementary Japanese Language I, II
Intermediate Japanese language III, IV
Advanced Japanese Language V, VI
Elements of Japanese Culture and Custom
As for foreign students (undergraduate), credits for general education subjects, foreign languages and physical education may be satisfied, up to 22 credits, with credits earned in Japanese Languages and Japanese Studies courses.
For Further Information
Undergraduate and Graduate Admission
International Affairs Section, Public Relations and Planning Office, Hiroshima Shudo University, 1717 Otsuka, Numata-cho, Asa–Minami-ku, Hiroshima-shi, Hiroshima 731-31 ☎ 082-848-2121 ext. 374

Hiroshima University of Economics

(Hiroshima Keizai Daigaku)

5-37-1 Gion, Asa Minami-ku, Hiroshima-shi,
Hiroshima 731-01 ☎ 082-871-1000

Faculty
    Profs. 30   Assoc. Profs. 25
    Assist. Profs. Full-time 18; Part-time 63
Number of Students
    Undergrad. 3,459   Grad. 8
Library 135,800 volumes

Outline and Characteristics of the University

The Hiroshima University of Economics has its campus in the City of Hiroshima which is known as the city of international peace and culture. It was established in 1967 by the Ishida Gakuen, an educational foundation, whose history dates back to 1907 when Yonesuke Ishida first founded the Ishida Gakuen School in Hiroshima City. Unfortunately, however, the original school was totally destroyed by the atomic bomb in 1945.

The university first opened the Department of Economics in its Faculty of Economics. In 1974, the Department of Business Administration was added. In 1979, the Graduate School of Economics (Master's Program) was opened.

The campus occupies an area of about 600,000 m² on the hillside of Mt. Takeda, and commands a serene view of the Ota River to the east and the center of Hiroshima City to the south. In addition to facilities for academic and administrative purposes, there is a full-size ball park, a sports ground that is qualified for official international track and field games, and tennis courts for all season usage.

The spirit of foundation of this institute is "Harmony is to be esteemed" adopted from the precept of Prince Shotoku. Thus, the educational guidelines here are: be constructive instead of indulging in vain speculations, be strict to ourselves and lenient to others, fulfil our respective responsibilities, and help and encourage one another.

UNDERGRADUATE PROGRAMS

Faculty of Economics (Freshmen Enrollment: 700)

Department of Business Administration

Auditing, Banking, Bookkeeping, Business Enterprise, Cost Accounting, Data Processing, Financial Management, Financial Statements, Foreign Trade, History of Business Administration, Industrial Relations, Insurance, International Business Administration, Labor Management, Management Analysis, Management Control, Management Organization, Managerial Accounting, Multinational Business Management, Personnel Management, Policy of Business Administration, Production Control, Sales Management, Small Business, Systems Analysis, Tax Accounting, Transportation, Wage and Salary Administration

Department of Economics

Agricultural Economics, Comparative Economic Systems, Econometrics, Economic Fluctuation, Economic History, Economic Policy, Economics of Industry, Economic Statistics, History of Economic Doctrines, History of Modern Economics, International Economics, Labor Economics, Macroeconomics, Microeconomics, Money and Banking, Public Economics, Public Finance, Regional Economies, Theoretical Economics, Theory of Income and Employment, World Economy

Foreign Student Admission

Qualifications for Applicants
    Standard Qualifications Requirement
Examination at the University
    Applicants must take the same entrance examination applied to Japanese applicants, which is basically a written examination.
Documents to be Submitted When Applying
    Standard Documents Requirement

GRADUATE PROGRAMS

Graduate School of Economics (First Year Enrollment : Master's 10)

Division
Economics

Foreign Student Admission

Qualifications for Applicants
Master's Program
    Standard Qualifications Requirement
Examination at the University
Master's Program
    Applicants must follow the same procedure as Japanese applicants and take a written and oral examination.
Documents to be Submitted When Applying
    Standard Documents Requirement

*

Research Institutes and Centers

Information Processing Center, The Institute for the Regional Economies

For Further Information

Undergraduate and Graduate Admission
Admissions Office, Hiroshima University of Economics, 5-37-1 Gion, Asa Minami-ku, Hiroshima-shi, Hiroshima 731-01 ☎ 082-871-1000

Hokkaido Institute of Pharmaceutical Sciences
(Hokkaido Yakka Daigaku)

7–1 Katsuraoka-cho, Otaru-shi, Hokkaido 047–02
☎ 0134–62–5111

Faculty
  Profs. 17 Assoc. Profs. 8
  Assist. Profs. Full–time 8; Part–time 19
  Res. Assocs. 42
Number of Students
  Undergrad. 874 Grad. 18
Library 45, 547 volumes

Outline and Characteristics of the University

The Hokkaido Institute of Pharmaceutical Sciences was founded in 1974 by The Hokkaido Shoshi Gakuen Foundation for Education. It aims at contributing to the public welfare through research and education in pharmaceutical sciences. The graduate school was opened, offering a Master's Program in 1978, and a Doctor's Program in 1980, over a two-years period.

One of the principal objectives of the Institute is to cultivate men of talent not only in the field of development, evaluation, and management of newly discovered medical supplies, but also in the field of sanitation sciences involving food and environmental sanitation. This is based upon the fact that protecting human life from pollution has become one of the important duties of a pharmacist. Another objective is to conduct humanizing education so as to create compassionate pharmacists, well-rounded in character, for it is the Institute's belief that a pharmacist's mission is deeply related with human society and human life. As part of the program, the Institute places emphasis upon good human relationships between teachers and students.

The campus is located on a hill halfway between Otaru (a main seaport) and Sapporo (the fifth largest city in Japan) in the western part of Hokkaido. The 120, 000 m² campus is especially blessed with natural beauty and tranquility, accompanied by a fine view of Ishikari Bay in the Japan Sea on one side, and surrounding mountains on the other. This makes daily life for students comfortable and enjoyable.

UNDERGRADUATE PROGRAMS

Faculty of Pharmaceutical Sciences (Freshmen Enrollment: 160)
  Department of Biopharmacy
Biochemistry, Chemical Hygiene, Clinical Biochemistry, Environmental Hygiene, Microbiology, Toxicology
  Department of Pharmacy
Analytical Chemistry, Medicinal Chemistry, Organic Chemistry, Pharmaceutics, Pharmacognosy, Pharmacology, Radiobiology

Foreign Student Admission
  Qualifications for Applicants
  Standard Qualifications Requirement
  Examination at the University
  Foreign applicants must take the same entrance examination as Japanese applicants. It is a written examination in mathematics, English, and either chemistry or biology.
  Documents to be Submitted When Applying
  Standard Documents Requirement

GRADUATE PROGRAMS

Graduate School of Pharmaceutical Sciences (First Year Enrollment : Master's 12, Doctor's 3)
  Division
Biopharmaceutical Sciences

Foreign Student Admission
  Qualifications for Applicants
Master's Program
  Standard Qualifications Requirement
Doctor's Program
  Standard Qualifications Requirement
  Examination at the University
Master's Program
  Applicants must take an entrance examination consisting of a written and an oral examination in biochemistry and either English or German.
Doctor's Program
  Applicants must take a written and an oral examination in major.
  Documents to be Submitted When Applying
  Standard Documents Requirement
                    *
Research Institutes and Centers
Herbal Garden, Laboratory Animal House, Radio-Isotope Center
For Further Information
  Undergraduate and Graduate Admission
School Affairs Division, Hokkaido Institute of Pharmaceutical Sciences, 7–1 Katsuraoka-cho, Otaru-shi, Hokkaido 047–02 ☎ 0134–62–5111 ext. 208

Hokkaido Institute of Technology
(Hokkaido Kogyo Daigaku)

419–2 Maeda, Teine, Nishi–ku, Sapporo–shi, Hokkaido 006 ☎ 011–681–2161

Faculty
  Profs. 54 Assoc. Profs. 34

Assist. Profs.   Full–time   26; Part–time   67
Res. Assocs.   18
Number of Students
    Undergrad.   3, 217
Library   92, 461 volumes

Outline and Characteristics of the University

Hokkaido Institute of Technology was founded in April, 1967. The Institute started with two departments, the Department of Mechanical Engineering and the Department of Managerial Engineering. The Institute was established for the purpose of training capable engineers to power the industrial and social development of Hokkaido. There was also great demand in the community for such engineers. The Institute opened its Department of Electrical Engineering in 1968, the Departments of Civil Engineering and Architecture in 1972, and the Department of Applied Electronics in 1986. The Institute now boasts six technical departments and has achieved substantial success in placing excellent engineers in the forefront of every industrial field. One of the salient characteristics of the Institute is its special educational and research programs devoted to improving the life and industry of the people who live in the frigid and snowy climate of the northern region. This aspect of research at H. I. T. is highly esteemed both at home and abroad.

April, 1967 Foundation of Hokkaido Institute of Technology. Inauguration of the Departments of Mechanical Engineering and Managerial Engineering.

April, 1968 Inauguration of the Department of Electrical engineering.

April, 1972 Inauguration of the Departments of Civil Engineering and Architecture.

April, 1978 Foundation of the Computing Center.

April, 1980 Foundation of the Cold Region General Research Center.

April, 1986 Inauguration of the Department of Applied Electronics.

It is said that universities should be dedicated not only to the furthering of technical knowledge but also to the cultivation of persons of wisdom, intelligence and culture. H. I. T. is a university for selfmotivated individuals. The motto of the Institute, "Shoshi, "—"To develop and value our will"—, expresses this aim. The Institute is devoted to the improvement of the industry and society of Japan.

UNDERGRADUATE PROGRAMS

Faculty of Engineering (Freshmen Enrollment: 720)
    Department of Applied Electronics
    Department of Architecture
    Department of Civil Engineering
    Department of Electrical Engineering
    Department of Managerial Engineering
    Department of Mechanical Engineering

Foreign Student Admission

Qualifications for Applicants
    Standard Qualifications Requirement
    You are expected to arrange for a sponsor who will be responsible for your school expenses and personal affairs. The sponsor must be a Japanese national, live in Japan, and be a financially independent adult.

Examination at the University
    1. A short essay in Japanese.
    2. An interview in Japanese.

Besides the two items mentioned above, we will, if necessary, require wtitten examinations, examinations in practical skills, or a sample of your work on a specified subject.

*

For Further Information

Undergraduate Admission
Student Admissions Section, Student Admissions Office, Hokkaido Institute of Technology 419–2, Maeda, Teine, Nishi–ku, Sapporo–shi, Hokkaido 006
☎ 011–681–2161 ext. 327

Hokkaido Tokai University
(Hokkaido Tokai Daigaku)
5–1–1–1 Minami–sawa, Minami–ku, Sapporo–shi,
Hokkaido 005   ☎ 011–571–5111

Faculty
    Profs.   52   Assoc. Profs.   32
    Assist. Profs.   Full–time   21; Part–time   40
Number of Students
    Undergrad.   1, 051
Library   110, 000 volumes

Outline and Characteristics of the University

Hokkaido Tokai University was established in 1977 as a four–year school. It is the only private university devoted to Art and Technology in Japan. It was originally established in 1972 as a Junior College of Art and Industry, an institute that the society of industries in Asahikawa city strongly desired.

In the spring of 1988, the two schools constituting the new Sapporo campus of Hokkaido Tokai University were inaugurated. These Schools, the School of International Cultural Relations and the School of Engineering, along with the School of Art and Engineering in Asahikawa, were founded with the goal of enhancing the development potential only of Hokkaido, but also the whole of Japan and its neighboring countries.

The School of International Cultural Relations (Sapporo Campus) aims to train specialists in international cultural studies and international communications. By focusing on comprehensive and comparative study of various cross-cultural features, institutions and languages, while pursuing the goals of international understanding and harmony, the graduates will be able to engage in any job in the international community.

The school emphasizes the acquisition of English, and the development of comprehensive international knowledge through practical training and seminars. It is necessary for students to grasp the various situations in the modern world in order to deepen their knowledge of foreign cultures. With a view to facilitating this aim, coursework in subjects such as Japanese Culture, International Economics, International Relations and other related subjects are required of every student.

The School of Engineering (Sapporo Campus) was established to cope with the rapid development of contemporary sciences and technology. In the fields of Bioscience and the Marine sciences, an interdisciplinary approach has enabled us to solve a number of problems and to create a number of innovations. The school aims to foster this appoach by encouraging students in the application of electronics to these fields, and by the formation of close and effective networks among the departments. As for curriculum, each student is required to take Life Science, Electronic and Information Technology, Information Processing Engineering, and Fundamental Laboratory Work as common special subjects.

In order to build persons of harmonious character, students are required to take a certain number of credits in the fields of humanities, social sciences and natural sciences. These subjects are particularly significant in that they enable students to broaden their views, develop their personalities, and acquire good judgement. In these classes students will be taught the fundamental knowledge and methods which will constitute the foundation of their specialized studies.

The comprehensive subject 'Contemporary Civilization' is offered to all the students as a required subject. This is a very important series of lectures which the Tokai Educational System Offers in all its universities, colleges, and high schools. A number of distinguished senior professors of Hokkaido Tokai University, Tokai University and Kyushu Tokai University, including Chancellor Matsumae himself, are in charge of these lectures on the fundamental problems of contemporary civilization. This is the core subject in the arts and sciences, and will enabe students to comprehend the significance of studying humanities, social sciences, and natural sciences. It is also designed to give them motivation for the specialized subjects of their major.

UNDERGRADUATE PROGRAMS

School of Art and Technology (Asahikawa Campus: Freshmen Enrollment: 160)
  Department of *Architecture*
  Department of Design
School of Engineering (Sapporo Campus: Freshmen Enrollment: 160)
  Department of Biosciences and Technology

  Department of Electronic and Information Engineering
  Research Institute for Higher Education Programs
  Foreign Languages, Liberal Arts and Sciences, Physical Education
  Department of Marine Sciences and Technology
School of International Cultural Relations (Sapporo Campus: Freshmen Enrollment: 120)
  Department of International Cultural Relations
  Comparative Cultures, Intercultural Communication

Foreign Student Admission
  Qualifications for Applicants
    Standard Qualifications Requirement
  Examination at the University
    Written Examinations and Interview.
  1. Applicants will b? tested in English and Japanese, and will be interviewed. Art and technology applicants will take a practical skills test; Cultural Relations applicants will be tested on Japanese culture; Engineering applicants will be tested on mathematics and science.
  2. The entrance examinations will be held at the Yoyogi Campus of Tokai University in Tokyo, and at the Sapporo and Asahikawa Campuses of Hokkaido Tokai University.
  3. Date of Entrance Examinations: Saturday, February 4, 1989 for the School of Art and Technology and the School of International Cultural Relations; and Sunday, February 5, 1989 for the School of Engineering.
  Documents to be Submitted When Applying
    Standard Documents Requirement

＊

Research Institutes and Centers
Electronics Center, Research Institute for the Study of Life and Culture in the Northern Sector
For Further Information
  Undergraduate and Graduate Admission
Admissions Office, Hokkaido Tokai University 5-1-1 Minami-sawa, Minami-ku, Sapporo, Hokkaido 005
☎ 011-571-1111

Hokkaigakuen Kitami University
(Hokkaigakuen Kitami Daigaku)
235 Hokko, Kitami-shi, Hokkaido 090
☎ 0157-22-2721

Faculty
  Profs. 15   Assoc. Profs. 7
  Assist. Profs. Full-time 4; Part-time 18
Number of Students
  Undergrad. 860
Library 70, 000 volumes

Outline and Characteristics of the University
  Hokkaigakuen Kitami University was estab-

lished in Kitami City, in eastern Hokkaido, in 1977. It aims to provide an education which builds character and develops to the fullest the various potentials of young people who will create the society of the future.

Kitami University is part of the Hokkaigakuen organization, which is centred in Sapporo, and has a history of 103 years. Hokkaigakuen was founded on the pragmatic principles and indomitable spirit of Hokkaido's pioneer tradition, and continues to its original of training students who can contribute to the economic progress and overall development of Hokkaido. It has made continual efforts to adapt its education to modern needs and to expand and improve its facilities, so that it now ranks as the largest and best equipped private university in Hokkaido.

Kitami University maintains the same tradition, but is located in eastern Hokkaido, a region noted for its magnificent scenery and its rich land and sea resources. From the outset, this region has been developed with international rather than solely Japanese concepts in mind. The education and research undertaken at Kitami University seeks to reflect these regional characteristics. Within its Faculty of Commerce, a field of study selected as most appropriate for preparing students for the rapidly changing contemporary world, courses are offered in commerce and distribution, management and accountancy, and economics and development. The university is expanding its facilities in order to establish itself as a base to contribute to the economic development of its region and as a center for promoting greater international awareness.

Hokkaigakuen Kitami Women's Junior College was established in 1977 and offers management, secretarial, and international studies courses within its Department of Management. It aims to provide women, especially but not exclusively those from the eastern Hokkaido region, with the opportunity and the facilities to pursue a high level of education so that they can acquire skills and personal qualities which will enable them to contribute creatively to the society of the future.

UNDERGRADUATE PROGRAMS

Faculty of Commerce (Freshmen Enrollment: 150)
  Department of Commerce
Commerce and Distribution Course Management and Accountancy Course Economics and Development Course

*

For Further Information
  Undergraduate Admission
Entrance Examination Section, Hokkaigakuen Kitami University, 235 Hokko, Kitami-shi, Hokkaido 090 ☎ 0157-22-2721

Hokkaigakuen University
(Hokkaigakuen Daigaku)
4-1-40 Asahi-machi, Toyohira-ku, Sapporo-shi, Hokkaido 062   ☎ 011-841-1161

UNDERGRADUATE PROGRAMS

Faculty of Economics (Freshmen Enrollment: 450)
  Department of Business Administration
  Department of Economics
Faculty of Economics (**Evening Course**) (Freshmen Enrollment: 240)
  Department of Business Administration
  Department of Economics
Faculty of Engineering (Freshmen Enrollment: 280)
  Department of Architectural Engineering
  Department of Civil Engineering
  Department of Electronics and Information Engineering
Faculty of Law (Freshmen Enrollment: 345)
  Department of Law
  Department of Law (*Evening Course*)

GRADUATE PROGRAMS

Graduate School of Economics (First Year Enrollment : Master's 15)
  Division
Economic Policy
Graduate School of Law (First Year Enrollment : Master's 7)
  Division
Law

Hokuriku University
(Hokuriku Daigaku)
Ho-3, Kanakawa-cho, Kanazawa-shi, Ishikawa 920-11   ☎ 0762-29-1161

Faculty
  Profs. 40   Assoc. Profs. 25
  Assist. Profs. Full-time 18; Part-time 23
  Res. Assocs. 54
Number of Students
  Undergrad. 1, 104   Grad. 19
Library 84, 022 volumes

Outline and Characteristics of the University
  Hokuriku University was founded in 1975 through private funds. It is situated in the eastern suburbs of Kanazawa, one of the oldest and prettiest cities in Hokuriku District, and at present has the

Faculty of Pharmacy. The shortest period of study is four years, during which both general education coursework and specialized education coursework is to be completed. Hokuriku University also has a graduate school which offers a two–year Master's course (established in 1979) and a three-year Doctor's course (established in 1983).

Systematic education in Kanazawa dates back to the Tokugawa era. Maeda Tsunanori (1643-1724), the fifth daimyo of Kanazawa, took the lead in educational advancements. His ambitions were fulfilled when a school named Meirindo was established by a succeeding daimyo in 1792. Maeda Tsunanori is said to have led a fruitful life, "loving nature and revering life". The University is determined to develop students who will continue to promote the ideals of this feudal lord so that they, too, may love nature, revere life, support the future of Japan, and contribute to the cultural development of the world.

As a first step, the University founded the Faculty of Pharmacy, because this field of science parallels one of the school's ideas--reverence for life. Hokuriku University thus aims to train pharmacists or pharmaceutical experts who can contribute to medical treatment, health education, and the betterment of the environment, through the study of pharmaceutical sciences.

In 1987, Hokuriku University newly established the Faculty of Foreign Languages, aiming to train competent people who can contribute to an internationalizing society and world peace.

UNDERGRADUATE PROGRAMS

Faculty of Foreign Languages (Freshmen Enrollment: 160)
   Department of Chinese
   Department of English
School of Pharmacy (Freshmen Enrollment: 220)
   Department of Pharmaceutical Sciences
Analytical Chemistry, Bioorganic Chemistry, Medicinal Chemistry, Organic Chemistry, Pharmaceutical Physical Chemistry, Pharmaceutics, Pharmacognosy, Pharmacology, Radiopharmaceutics, Synthetic Organic Chemistry
   Department of Public Health Sciences
BioChemistry, Environmental Hygiene, Hygienic Chemistry, Microbiology, Pharmacology, Physiological Chemistry

Foreign Student Admission
   Qualifications for Applicants
   Standard Qualifications Requirement
   Examination at the University
   A written examination (consisting of Japanese, Mathematics, Physics, Biology, Chemistry, English) conducted by the University and an interview are required.
   Documents to be Submitted When Applying
   Standard Documents Requirement

A document attesting to the applicant's ability to pay tuition and other necessary expenses is also required.
   All documents should be completed in Japanese.

GRADUATE PROGRAMS

Graduate School of Pharmacy (First Year Enrollment : Master's 20, Doctor's 5)
   Divisions
Bio-functional Pharmacy, Hygienic Environmental Sciences, Medicinal Chemistry, Medicinal Resources Chemistry, Pharmacy and Pharmacology

Foreign Student Admission
   Qualifications for Applicants
Master's Program
   Standard Qualifications Requirement
Doctor's Program
   Standard Qualifications Requirement
   Examination at the University
Master's Program
   A written examination conducted by the University and an interview are required
Doctor's Program
   Same as Master's program.
   Documents to be Submitted When Applying
   Standard Documents Requirement
                         *
Research Institutes and Centers
Center of Instrumental Analysis, Medicinal Plant Garden, The Creative Research Laboratory of Medicine (Biochemical Activities/Drug Evaluation)
For Further Information
   Undergraduate and Graduate Admission
Educational Affairs Division, Hokuriku University, Ho-3, Kanakawa-cho, Kanazawa-shi, Ishikawa 920-11 ☎ 0762-29-1161 ext. 207

Hokusei GakuenUniversity
(Hokusei Gakuen Daigaku)

3–1, Oyachi Nishi 2–chome, Shiroishi-ku, Sapporo-shi, Hokkaido 004   ☎ 011–891–2731

Faculty
   Profs. 37   Assoc. Profs. 18
   Assist. Profs. Full–time 10; Part–time 105
Number of Students
   Undergrad. 2, 272   Grad. 31
Library 105, 030 volumes

Outline and Characteristics of the University
   Hokusei Gakuen University is one of seven schools operated under the auspices of the Board of Directors of Hokusei Gakuen. It was begun as a girls' high school in 1887 by Sarah C. Smith. The University itself was established in 1962 with a Faculty of Literature composed of Departments of English

and Social Work. Three years later, the Faculty of Economics was added, and in 1980 postgraduate courses in all departments were established. Sine 1987 Department of Management Information has been newly added to the Faculty of Economics.

Founded on Christian principles, Hokusei Gakuen University is committed to the pursuit of the development of the individual, of society, and of internationalism. In an age of materialism, when mere intellectualism is overemphasized, only education based on the Bible can provide students with deeper resources and values to restore their true humanity. Voluntary chapel services are open to the entire college community daily, a Chaplain serves as a faculty member, both required and elective classes in Christian studies are included in the curriculum, and all official activities of the school year are conducted in the framework of Christian services. Through open lectures and seminars, the University seeks to serve the larger public community. The University has been active in international exchange programs. In 1989 it has a total of 15 sister colleges and universities in the United States and China.

Located in a residential area on the southern side of Sapporo, Hokusei Gakuen University is at the Oyachi exit of the Hokkaido Expressway and a seven minute walk from the Oyachi subway station. Facilities on the 111, 385 square meter campus include a four-story combined classroom and administration boilding, an eight story building for faculty offices and Information Center, a chapel seating 400 persons, a two-story library and a three-story student center which includes a cafeteria, meeting rooms and student supply store. The gymnasium is equipped for basketball, volleyball and judo; the campus includes six outdoor tennis courts, a practice field for soccer and football, a baseball diamond and archery range. A conference and seminar facility with overnight accommodations is located on the campus.

UNDERGRADUATE PROGRAMS

Faculty of Economics (Freshmen Enrollment: 250)
  Department of Economics
  General Economics Course
Economic History and Geography, Economic Theories and Policies, Statistics
International Economics Course
Comparative Economis Systems, Internatinal Economics, International Trade and Finance
Public Economics Course
National and Regional Economics, Public Finance and Administration, Public Policy
  Department of Management Information
  Accounting Information Course
Accounting Information Systems, Accounting Principles, Auditing, Managerial Accounting, Tax Accounting
Information Systems Course
Computer Programming, Information Network, Information Theory, Management Science, Management Systems
Management Course
Business Ilistory, Financial Management, Managerial Economics, Marketing Organizatin Theory
Faculty of Literature (Freshmen Enrollment: 240)
  Department of English
  Language Course
Communication, English Education, English Linguistics, Linguistics, Phonetics, Public Speaking
Literature Course
American Literature, American Novel, American Poetry, English Literature, English Novel, English Poetry, History of English Literature
  Department of Social Work
  Psychology Course
Clinical Psychology, Developmental Psychology, Psychological Methodology and Laboratory Work, Psychology of Personality, Social Paychology
Social Work Course
Health, Life Social Survey, Practicum Theory and The History of Social Work, Problems of Aging the Handicapped Childhood

ONE-YEAR GRADUATE PROGRAMS

One-Year Graduate Course of Literature (Enrollment 20)
English Literature, Social Work
One-Year Graduate Course of Economics (Enrollment 10)
Economics

*

For Further Information
  Undergraduate and Graduate Admission
Entrance Examination Section, Hokusei Gakuen University 3-1, Oyachi Nishi 2-chome, Shiroishi-ku, Sapporo-shi, Hokkaido 004 ☎ 011-891-2731

Hosei University
(Hosei Daigaku)

2-17-1 Fujimi, Chiyoda-ku, Tokyo 102
☎ 03-264-9315

Faculty
  Profs. 382   Assoc. Profs. 76
  Assist. Profs. Full-time 11; Part-time 1, 255
  Res. Assocs. 62
Number of Students
  Undergrad. 26, 636   Grad. 464
Library 1, 330, 000 volumes

Outline and Characteristics of the University
Hosei University traces its history back over 100 years to the foundation of the Tokyo Hogakusha, or Tokyo School of Law, in the heart of Tokyo in 1880. In 1889, the institution merged with the Tokyo Futsu Gakko, or Tokyo School of French Studies, and was

renamed Wafutsu Horitsu Gakko, or Tokyo School of Japanese–French Law. In 1903, it was given its present name, Hosei University.

The genesis of Hosei University began as Japan was beginning to adopt principles of democracy, and when the interest of its citizens in modern thought on law and civil rights was on the rise. In this social setting, Hosei's distinguished faculty offered fresh ideas based on the liberal tradition of French jurisprudence and had significant impact on modern Japanese legal theory and practice. Throughout its long history, Hosei's many graduates have been thinkers and leaders guided by the university's motto: "Liberty and Progress."

At present, the university consists of a graduate school and six departments: Law, Letters, Economics, Engineering, Social Sciences, and Business Administration, with a total enrollmemt of approximately 27, 000 students. The university is situated on three campuses. The newest campus occupies 220 acres of land in the Tama region of the greater Tokyo metropolitan area. In 1984, the Departments of Economics and Social Sciences were relocated there to begin a new program of quality education emphasising maximum communication between students and teaching staff.

In keeping with the long and well–established tradition of international exchange at Hosei, the university exchanges scholars and students with universities from all over the world. At present, 282 students from 14 different nations are presently enrolled in Hosei's graduate and undergraduate programs.

UNDERGRADUATE PROGRAMS

Faculty of Business Administration (Freshmen Enrollment: 650)

Department of Business Administration
Accounting, Business Administration, Business Administration Psychology, Business Analysis, Business Management, Business Organization, Business Sociology, Commerce, Comparative Accounting, Cost Control, Finance, History of Business Management, History of Industrial Development, History of Management in Japan, International Business Administration, International Trade, Labor Economics, Labor Management, Management, Managerial Finance, Marketing, Monetary Economics, Office Management, Organized Action, Production Control, Public Enterprise, Public Finance, Structure of Enterprise, Tourism Industry

Faculty of Economics (Freshmen Enrollment: 700)

Department of Economics
Agricultural Economics, American Economy, Comparative Economic Systems, Econometrics, Economic Geography, Economic History, Economic Policy, Economics, Economics of Education, Economic Statistics, Economy of Developing Countries, Economy of Modern AsianCountries, Economy of Socialism,

European Economy, Finance, History of European Economy, History of Japanese Economy, History of Oriental Economy, History of Social Economic Thought, Industrial Economics, Industrial Economics, International Economics, International Finance, Japanese Economy, Labor Economics, Local Finance, Macro–Economics, Mathematical Economics, Micro–Economics, Money and Banking, Public Economics, Social Security, Statistics, Tertiary Industry

Faculty of Economics (Evening Course) (Freshmen Enrollment: 400)

Department of Commerce
Accounting, Auditing, Business Administration, Commerce, Commercial Mathematics, Cost Accounting, Economics of Industry, Labor Management, Management, Management Accounting, Management Analysis, Structure of Enterprises

Department of Economics
Same as the day curriculum.

Faculty of Engineering (Freshmen Enrollment: 780)

Department of Architecture
Architectural Design, Architecture, Building Construction, Building Economics, Building Equipment, Building Interior, Building Materials, City Planning, Community Design, Design of Building Elements, Earthquake Resistant Structures, Environmental Design, Foundation Engineering, History of Architecture, Landscape Architecture, Planning and Management of Building Construction, Reinforced Concrete Structures, Space Structures, Steel Structures, Strength of Materials, Structural Analysis, Structural Design, Theory of Building Organization, Timber Construction, Town Planning, Urban Design

Department of Civil Engineering
Administration in Public Works, Applied Hydrology, Aseismic Design, Bridge Design, Civil Engineering Materials, Construction Engineering, Design Method of Steel Structures, Design of Reinforced Concrete Structures, Engineering Geology, Engineering Survey, Hydraulics, Hydrology, Numerical Methods in Civil Engineering, Philosophy of Engineering, Regional Planning, Soil and Foundation Engineering, Soil Mechanics, Structural Mechanics, Transportation Engineering, Water Supply and Sewerage Works

Department of Electrical Engineering
Antenna and Propagation, Applied Electronics, Automatic Control Systems, Circuit Theory, Communication Engineering, Computer Engineering, Computer Programming, Digital Circuit Theory, Electric Machines and Design, Electromagnetism, Electronic Circuits, Electronics, Energy Conversion Theory, High Voltage Engineering, Information Theory, Materials Engineering, Physics of Semiconductors, Power Generation and Transformation, Power Systems Engineering, Power Transmission and Distribution, Quantum Electronics, Semiconductor Devices, Solid State Physics

Department of Industrial and Systems Engineering
Analysis and Design of Production Systems, Applied

Probability Theory, Applied Statistics, Behavioral Science, Business Administration, Control Engineering, Engineering Economy, Environmental Engineering, Ergonomics, Financial Management, Industrial Accounting, Industrial and Systems Engineering, Industrial Economics, Industrial Psychology, Information Processing, Marketing, Mathematical Statistics, Office Management, Operations Research, Personnel Management, Production Planning and Control, Quality Contnol, Small Business Management, Social Engineering, Systems Design, Systems Engineering, Work Measurement

Department of Instrument and Control Engineering

Aeronautical and Space Instrumentation, Applied Optics, Computer Science, Computer Structure, Control Devices, Control Engineering, Design of Instrument, Dynamics, Electrical Measurements, Electronic Circuits, Electronic Devices, Electronic Measurements, Industrial Measuring Equipments and Instrumentation, Information Processing, Information Theory, Nuclear Engineering, Operations Research, Radiation Measurements, Science of Measurements, Semiconductor Engineering, Sensor Physics, System Approach, System Engineering, Theory of Vibrations

Department of Mechanical Engineering

Aircraft Engineering, Atomic Power Engineering, Automatic Engineering, Automobile Engineering, Control Engineering, Deformation Mechanics, Dynamics of Machines, Elasticity, Engineering Thermodynamics, Fluid Machinery, Fluid Technology, Friction and Lubrication Engineering, Heat Power, Heat Technology, Hydraulics, Machine Design and Drawing, Machine Elements, Machine Tool Operation, Machine Tool Technology, Material Science, Measurements of Mechanical Engineering, Mechanical Engineering, Mechanical Vibration, Mechanism, Metal Technology, Non–Metallic Material, Planning and Design of Machine Systems, Plastic Working, Powder Technology, Production Management, Quantum Mechanics, Refrigerator and Air–Conditioning, Rheology

Faculty of Law (Freshmen Enrollment: 650)

Department of Law

Administrative Law, Bankruptcy Law, Civil Law, Civil Procedure, Commercial Law, Comparative Law, Constitutional Law, Criminal Law, Criminal Policy, Criminal Procedure, Economic Law, Educational Law, Environmental Law, Foreign Legal Systems, International Law, International Private Law, Jurisprudence, Labor Law, Legal History, Modern Journalistic Law, Philosophy of Law, Social Welfare Law, Sociology of Law, Taxation Law

Department of Political Science

Administrative Law, Administrative Management, Administrative Processes, Comparative History of Political Thoughts, Comparative Politics, Economic Policy, History of International Politics, History of Japanese Political Thought, History of Japanese Politics, History of Politics, International Politics, Local Governments, Mass Communication, Political Culture, Political Processes, Political Science, Politico–Sociology, Public Administration, Public Finance, Public Policy, Social Policy, Theory of Political Awareness, Urban Policy

Faculty of Law (**Evening Course**) (Freshmen Enrollment: 240)

Department of Law

Same as the day curriculum.

Department of Political Science

Same as the day curriculum.

Faculty of Letters (Freshmen Enrollment: 500)

Department of English

Applied Linguistics, English and American Literature, English Language, History of American Literature, History of English Literature, Linguistics

Department of Geography

Applied Geography, Biogeography and Soil Geography, Cartology, Climatology, Cultural Geography, Geography, Geography of America, Geography of Asia, Geography of Europe, Geography of Japan, Geology, Geomorphology, Historical Geography, History of Geography, Human Geography, Mathematical Geography, Natural Geography, Oceanography and Limnology, Physical Geography, Social and Economic Geography

Department of History

Archaeology, Comparative History of Thoughts, European History, History, History of Chinese Literary Arts, History of European Arts, History of European Philosophy, History of Japanese Arts, Japanese Archaeology, Japanese History, Japanese Study of Diplomatics, Oriental History, Palaeography

Department of Japanese

Calligraphy, Chinese Classics, History of Chinese Literary Arts, History of Japanese Arts, History of Japanese Language and Linguistics, History of Japanese Literary Arts, History of Japanese Literary Criticism, History of Japanese Performing Arts, Japanese Grammer, Japanese Linguistics, Japanese Literary Arts

Department of Philosophy

Clinical Psychology, Comparative History of Thought, Cultural Anthropology, Ethics, Folklore, History of Culture, History of European Philosophy, History of Japanese Thought, History of Oriental Thought, History of Social Thought, Language and Culture, Logic, Mass Communication, Philosophy, Publication Culture, Science of Arts, Science of Religions, Social Psychology, Sociology

Faculty of Letters (**Evening Course**) (Freshmen Enrollment: 200)

Department of Education

Adult and Youth Education, Adult Education, Audio–Visual Education, Correspondence Education and Open Schools, Educational Administration and Finance, Educational Curriculum, Educational Psychology, Educational Sociology, History of Adult Education, History of Education, Library

Management Theory and Library Planning, Library Science, Moral Education, Museum Studies, Pedagogy, Philosophy of Education, Physical Education and Recreational Education, Psychology, Teaching Method, Vocational Guidance

Department of English
Same as the day curriculum.

Department of Japanese
Same as the day curriculum.

Faculty of Social Sciences (Freshmen Enrollment: 500)

Department of Applied Economics
Distribution Economics, Economic Development, Economics, Finance, History of Social and Labor Movement, Industrial Organization, International Economics, International Organization, Japanese Economy, Labor Economics, Labor Management, Management, Money and Banking, Problems of Small Business, Public Administration, Self–Governing Communities, Social Policy, Society and Economics (America, Europe, East Europe & Soviet, Middle East & Africa, Asia, Latin America), Socio–Economic History, Union

Department of Sociology
Advertising, Broadcasting, Educational Sociology, Family Sociology, History of Social Thought, History of Sociology, Industrial Sociology, Mass Communication, Political Sociology, Regional Sociology, Social Change, Social Consciousness, Social Education, Social Pathology

Faculty of Social Sciences (**Evening Course**) (Freshmen Enrollment: 100)

Department of Applied Economics
Same as the day curriculum.

Foreign Student Admission
Qualifications for Applicants
    Standard Qualifications Requirement
1. Those who have acquired an international baccalaureate may also apply.
2. Applicants must be 18 years of age or over.
Examination at the University
1. Written Examination: Japanese, English, Mathematics (Applicants for the Department of Engineering only)
2. Interview (those who passed the written examination)
Documents to be Submitted When Applying
    Standard Documents Requirement
Applicants must submit the following documents as well between the beginning of December and the middle of December.
1. The scores of the Japanese Language Proficiency Test and General Examination for Foreign Students. (For only those who elected to take these tests.)

Qualifications for Transfer Students
    There is no special entrance consideration for foreign students. In principle, only those who have enrolled 1 or 2 years at 4–year university or who have graduated from a 2–year college are qualified.
Examination for Transfer Students
    Foreign Languages, Thesis in specialized field of study, Mathematics and Physics (For those who apply for the Department of Engineering.) and Interview.
Documents to be Submitted When Applying
    Standard Documents Requirement

GRADUATE PROGRAMS

Graduate School of Engineering (First Year Enrollment : Master's 50, Doctor's 6)
Divisions
Construction Engineering, Electrical and Electronic Engineering, Mechanical Engineering

Graduate School of Humanities (First Year Enrollment : Master's 44, Doctor's 10)
Divisions
English, Geography, Japanese, Japanese History, Philosophy

Graduate School of Social Sciences (First Year Enrollment : Master's 100, Doctor's 20)
Divisions
Economics, Political Science, Private Law, Sociology

Foreign Student Admission
Qualifications for Applicants
Master's Program
    Standard Qualifications Requirement
Doctor's Program
    Standard Qualifications Requirement
Examination at the University
Master's Program
    Examinations are carried out by each division. They consist of both written examination and interview. Subjects for the written examination are:
1. Thesis of specialized study
2. Foreign Languages
3. Interview (those who have passed the written examination)
Doctor's Program
    The same as requirements for the Master's Program, with the addition of a monograph in the specialized field of study.
Documents to be Submitted When Applying
    Standard Documents Requirement
    Personal Information Form for Interview is to be submitted together with other documents.

*

Research Institutes and Centers
Athletic Research Center, Boissonade Institute of Modern Law and Politics, Center for Business and Industrial Research, Computer Center, Institite of Okinawan Studies, Institute of Comparative Economic Studies, Japan Statistical Research Institute, Nogami Memorial Noh Theater Research Institite, Ohara Research Institute for Social Sciences, Re-

search Center of Ion Beam Technology

Facilities/Services for Foreign Students
1. Open a conversation room
2. Students of Hosei University International Student Friendship Association voluntarily aid foreign students.
3. One or two faculty members in each faculty are appointed as advisors to foreign students in their respective departments.
4. A tutorial system is available.
5. Field trips, speech contests, sports festivals, parties and coffee hours are held on occasion.

Special Programs for Foreign Students

For foreign students, the Japanese Language is considerd as a first or second foreign language.

For Further Information

Undergraduate and Graduate Admission
International Center, Hosei University, 2–17–1 Fujimi, Chiyoda–ku, Tokyo 102 ☎ 03–264–9315

Hoshi University
(Hoshi Yakka Daigaku)

2–4–41, Ebara, Shinagawa–ku, Tokyo 142
☎ 03–786–1011

Faculty
Profs. 22   Assoc. Profs. 15
Assist. Profs.   Full–time 6; Part–time 25
Res. Assocs. 38
Number of Students
Undergrad. 1, 197   Grad. 88
Library 73, 600 volumes

Outline and Characteristics of the University

The founder of this school, Hajime Hoshi, was the first to succeed in producing important alkaloids such as morphine, cocaine, quinine and atropine within the country on an industrial scale.

Born in 1873, Hajime Hoshi journeyed to the United States in 1894 to study statistics, and graduated from Columbia University's graduate school. Upon returning to Japan in 1911, Hoshi created the Hoshi Pharmaceutical Company.

Hoshi Pharmaceutical Business School, intended for pharmacy owners, was opened in 1922.

In 1941, in accordance with Japan's old education policy, the Hoshi Pharmaceutical College was created and the education system was modified to the normal school system.

Immediately after the Second World War, the school's campus and facilities were requisitioned by American troops stationed in Japan. However, in 1946 the education system began to advance again with the implementation of co–education measures. The Hoshi College of Pharmacy was created in compliance with the new educational policy.

Since that time, the facilities have continued to improve with the passing years. A graduate school was created in 1969. In 1982, the Radio–active Chemistry Laboratory was built. And the Institute of Medicinal Chemistry was organized. And as a result, the school's name was changed to Hoshi University.

Continuing in the pioneer spirit of the founder, this school has a rich educational environment and a fine faculty which is among the best in the academic world. Long years of dedicated work have been rewarded with high esteem from both industrial and academic circles.

The present President, Tetsuji Kametani, Doctor of Pharmacy, was the head of the Pharmaceutical Society of Japan from April, 1983 until March, 1985. The Chairman of the Board of Directors is Kokichi Otani, Doctor of Engineering. At present the teaching staff numbers 106 and the employees, 46.

UNDERGRADUATE PROGRAMS

Faculty of Pharmaceutical Sciences (Freshmen Enrollment: 240)

Department of Hygienic Pharmacy
Analytical Chemistry, Biochemistry, Clinical Chemistry, Hygienic Chemistry, Microbiology, Physical Chemistry

Department of Pharmacy
Drug Manufacturing Chemistry, Inorganic Chemistry, Organic Chemistry, Pharmaceutics, Pharmacognosy, Pharmacology

Foreign Student Admission

Qualifications for Applicants
Standard Qualifications Requirement
Examination at the University
Applicants must take an entrance examination consisting of written tests for chemistry, mathematics and English.
Documents to be Submitted When Applying
Standard Documents Requirement

GRADUATE PROGRAMS

Graduate School of Pharmaceutical Sciences (First Year Enrollment : Master's 28, Doctor's 8)

Divisions
Analytical Chemistry, Applied Pharmacology, Biochemistry, Biological Activity Study, Biopharmaceutical Chemistry, Clinical Chemistry, Drug Manufacturing Chemistry, Hygienic Chemistry, Instrumental Analysis, Microbiology, Organic Chemistry, Pharmaceutical Chemistry, Pharmaceutics, Pharmacognosy, Pharmacology, Reaction Organic Chemistry, Synthetic Organic Chemistry

Foreign Student Admission

Qualifications for Applicants
Master's Program
Standard Qualifications Requirement
Doctor's Program

Standard Qualifications Requirement
Examination at the University
Master's Program

The examination is usually given in September and/or March. It may consist of a written and oral examination plus an interview and is given only after the applicants have passed the first–stage procedure for admission. In the written examination, the applicants are required to answer 8 problems (more than 2 but less than 4 problems from each group shown below) in addition to an English and a Japanese examinations. The Japanese examination is held at the interview.

Group 1 (Analytical Chemistry, Pharmaceutics, Pharmaceutical Chemistry, Instrumental Analysis)
Group 2 (Organic Chemistry, Pharmacognosy, Drug Manufacturing Chemistry, Biopharmaceutical Chemistry, Synthetic Organic Chemistry, Reaction Organic Chemistry)
Group 3 (Biochemistry, Hygienic Chemistry, Pharmacology, Microbiology, Clinical Chemistry, Biological Activity Study, Applied Pharmacology)
Two problems are given per subject.
Doctor's Program

An oral examination related to the Master's thesis of the applicant is given in addition to an English and a Japanese written examinations.

Documents to be Submitted When Applying
Standard Documents Requirement

Application forms are available at the Graduate School Office. Applicants are required to submit the specified application documents to the Office. The deadline for receiving application is fixed. (The First Application Period: August 15 to August 20 and/The second Application period is undecided.)

*
Research Institutes and Centers
Institute of Medicinal Chemistry
For Further Information
Undergraduate and Graduate Admission
Registrar, Division of Registry, Hoshi University, 2–4–41, Ebara, Shinagawa–ku, Tokyo 142
☎ 03–786–1011 ext. 204

Hyogo College of Medicine
(Hyogo Ika Daigaku)

1-1 Mukogawa-cho, Nishinomiya-shi, Hyogo 663
☎ 0798-45-6111

Faculty
    Profs.　44　　Assoc. Profs.　51
    Assist. Profs.　Full–time　64; Part–time　30
    Res. Assocs.　207
Number of Students
    Undergrad.　701　　Grad.　80
Library　131, 139 volumes

Outline and Characteristics of the College

Hyogo College of Medicine is located in Nishinomiya, an education-oriented city. Nishinomiya is situated between Osaka, the second largest city in Japan and Kobe, an international city. Beside Mt. Rokko to the west and the Muko River to the east, the College offers a splendid environment for education.

Hyogo College of Medicine was founded in April, 1972 by the late Shigeki Morimura who devoted his whole life to the establishment of a solid basis for the college. In April, 1978 the Graduate School of Medicine was added.

The spirit of the foundation, the education policy and characteristics are as follows: service to the welfare of society, deep love toward mankind, profound scientific understanding of human beings, consistent education for six years on the basis of a complete academic year system, enhancement of the students' spirit toward medicine, consolidation of clinical practice, adoption of a united curricula, promotion of central research projects cooperating with basic medicine—clinical medicine, emphasis on international exchanging program, and medical treatment related to the region.

UNDERGRADUATE PROGRAMS

Faculty of Medicine (Freshmen Enrollment: 100)
Department of Medicine
Anatomy, Anesthesiology, Bacteriology, Biochemistry, Clinical Pathology, Clinical Psychiatry, Dentistry and Oral Surgery, Dermatology, Emergency Medicine, Genetics, Hospital Pathology, Hygiene, Immunology and Medical Zoology, Internal Medicine, Legal Medicine, Neurosurgery, Nuclear Medicine, Obstetrics and Gynecology, Ophthalmology, Orthopedics, Otorhinolaryngology, Pathology, Pediatrics, Pharmacology, Physiology, Public Health, Radiology, Science and Behavior, Surgery, Thoracic Surgery, Urology

GRADUATE PROGRAMS

Graduate School of Medicine (First Year Enrollment : Doctor's 60)
Divisions
Internal Medicine, Pathology, Physiology, Social Medicine, Surgery

*
For Further Information
Undergraduate and Graduate Admission
Educational Affairs Section, Educational Affairs Department, Hyogo College of Medicine, 1-1 Mukogawa-cho, Nishinomiya-shi, Hyogo 663
☎ 0798-45-6111 ext. 6162

Ibaraki Christian College
(Ibaraki Kirisuto–kyo Daigaku)

6–11–1 Omika–cho, Hitachi–shi, Ibaraki 319–12
☎ 0294–52–3215

Faculty
  Profs. 41   Assoc. Profs 11
  Assist. Profs. Full–time 7; Part–time 73
Number of Students
  Undergrad. 1, 135
Library 66, 265 volumes

Outline and Characteristics of the College

Ibaraki Christian College was founded in 1967 to offer higher education influenced by the Christian spirit. It consists of the Faculty of Literature which has a Bible Department, an English Department and a Pedagogy Department. The Bible Department consists of a Bible and Theology Program, a Culture and Thought program, and a Social Welfare program. The English Department consists of an English and American Literature program, an English Linguistics program, and a Living English program. The Pedagogy Department does not offer any programs.

At present, approximately 1, 100 students are enrolled.

Ibaraki Christian College is located in Hitachi, which is famous for the Hitachi Electrical Company. It takes 2 hours from Tokyo to reach the campus which enjoys abandant greenery, and a view of the Pacific Ocean from the school buildings.

The college was originally established in 1947 as the Religious Institute, the Shion Gakuen attachd to the Taga Church of Christ, by missionaries from the United States and their Japanese friends who strongly felt the need for higher education. In 1948, it started its Senior High School Division as a foundation. Between 1949 and 1950, it changed its name to "Ibaraki Christian College" which included the new Ibaraki Christian High School and the Ibaraki Christian Junior College.

In 1955, Dr. Logan Fox, in Japan as a missionary and receiving instructions in counseling from Carl Rogers, opened the Counseling Center. Today, it is called the Counseling Research Institute and offers counseling seminars and private counseling.

As our institute was partly founded by foreign missionaries, it is natural to meet foreign teachers while you are on our campus. In October 1974, we opened the exchange program between Ibaraki Christian College and Oklahoma Christian College in Oklahoma, U. S. A. Every year certain numbers of students from each school participate in study, play and research. These students deepen understanding between the different cultures. To help them understand the Japanese language and culture more deeply we offer Japanese Language Course at the Language-Culture Research Center. Not only the students from Oklahoma but also people from Asia and other countries are studying the Japanese Language there.

We additionally opened auditor programs for aged people in Hitachi, called "the Silver Auditors. " They can choose courses among the 67 regular courses. 19 Silver Auditors are studying this year together with the young students in those courses.

In 1986, we set up the Nature Study Center at Juo in north part of Ibaraki to experience laboring, planting, farming and living in nature. Every year, students often go there to experience these activities.

In 1987, we celebrated the 20th anniversary of our college. At that time, we reconfirmed our commitment to our founding spirit, to accept truth, to understand the suffering of others, and to serve our community faithfully through education.

UNDERGRADUATE PROGRAMS

Faculty of Literature (Freshmen Enrollment: 200)
  Department of Bible
Bible and Theology
History of Christianity, History of Christian Thought, History of Old/New Testament Thought, Philosophy of Religion, The Old/New Testament Ideas
Culture and Thought
Archaeology History between the Testament, History of the Western Mind, History of Western/Japanese Culture, Introduction to General Philosophy
Social Welfare
Field Practice of Social Welfare Aid Skill, History of Christianity, History of Social Work, Principles of Social Walfare, Social Welfare Aid Skill, Studies on Aged People/Disabled Persons/Child/Welfare
  Department of English
English and American Literature, English Linguitics, Living English
  Department of Petagogy
Christian Education, Educational/Social/Linguistic/Developmental Psychology, Juvenile Culture, Physical Training, Studies in Elementary School Subjects

Foreign Student Admission
  Qualifications for Applicants
  Standard Qualifications Requirement
  Examination at the University
  1. Same as for Japanese
  2. Interview.
  Documents to be Submitted When Applying
  Standard Documents Requirement

*
Research Institutes and Centers
Counseling Research Institute, Language-Culture Research Center
For Further Information

Undergraduate Admission
Admision Office, Ibaraki Christian College 6-11-1 Omika-cho, Hitachi-shi, Ibaraki 319-12 ☎ 0294-52-3215 ext. 451

International Budo University
(Kokusai Budo Daigaku)

841 Aza Monomizuka, Shinga, Katsuura-shi, Chiba 299-52   ☎ 0470-73-4111

Faculty
    Profs. 25   Assoc. Profs. 10
    Assist. Profs. Full–time 16; Part–time 39
    Res. Assocs. 23
Number of Students
    Undergrad. 1, 993
Library 22, 900 volumes

Outline and Characteristics of the University

International Budo University was founded in April 1984 as a four-year university. The University consists of one faculty, the Faculty of Physical Education. This faculty includes two departments: the Department of Budo and the Department of Physical Education.

The characteristics of education are as follows: 1. Thorough training in and specialized knowledge of budo, athletics, sports, and recreation within the framework of the spirit of budo. 2. Promotion of scientific research into budo. 3. Proficiency in foreign languages through the use of language laboratory facilities. 4. Development of an international perspective through an internationally-focused curriculum.

It is the aim of International Budo University not only to develop budo skills but also to cultivate highly qualified international budo leaders with both strong backgrounds in academic subjects and thorough training in the philosophy and spirit of budo. Our program provides, in addition to budo training and other athletic training, a complete university curriculum, with courses in language, international studies, and comparative culture. Thus, the objectives of education are as follows. 1. To produce budo and physical education instructors with excellent fundamental training in sports science and sports medicine. 2. To cultivate the spirit of budo in people of ability whose widened perspectives will enable them to play a useful role in an increasingly international society. 3. To produce instructors in budo, physical education, sports and recreation for regional and community organizations and for private enterprise. 4. To train health and physical education teachers for junior and senior high schools.

The University is an institution dedicated to fostering excellence in all who come to its campus. It works to achieve this through a curriculum designed to meet the needs and interests of general education, budo and general athletics. The University is also concerned with students as individuals, and seeks to bring them into close contact with a faculty which is devoted to both excellence in training and to the needs of the individual. The University offers a unique opportunity for budo students from abroad to study, train, and live with their Japanese counterparts.

International Budo University is located in the city of Katsuura, in Chiba Prefecture, just 70 kilometers (2 hours) southeast of Tokyo. A growing seaside resort and an important fishing port, Katsuura, population 25, 700, combines city comfort with a small-town atmosphere. The city, nestled between the beautiful ocean beaches and the rolling green hills of Chiba, provides an excellent living environment.

International Budo University's campus, situated just north of the city, overlooks Katsuura and the Pacific Ocean. The campus itself affords numerous outdoor recreational activities and also provides easy access to the surrounding countryside. The International Budo University campus, beautiful, quiet, and inspiring, is an ideal site for training and study.

UNDERGRADUATE PROGRAMS

Faculty of Physical Education (Freshmen Enrollment: 400)
    Department of Budo
Basketball, Budo, Gymnastics, Handball, History of Judo, History of Kendo, Judo, Kendo, Kyudo, Naginata, Physical Education, Recreation and Camping, Rugby, Soccer, Sports, Swimming, Teaching Method of Judo, Teaching Method of Kendo, Teaching Method of Sports, Track and Field, Volleyball

Foreign Student Admission
    Qualifications for Applicants
        Standard Qualifications Requirement
    Examination at the University
        Applicants must take an entrance examination consisting of a written exam and an interview.
    Documents to be Submitted When Applying
        Standard Documents Requirement
        Application forms are available at the Admissions Office in early Sept. All applicants are required to submit the specified documents to the Admissions Office by the following specified dates.
Application Date of Entrance Examination for Recommended Students: November 17, 1988, November 29, 1988.
Date of Entrance Examination for Recommended Students: December 6, 1988
Application Date of General Entrance Examination: January 23, 1989-February 8, 1989
Date of General Entrance Examination: February 15 and 16, 1989

*

For Further Information

Undergraduate Admission

Admissions Office, International Budo University, 841 Aza Monomizuka, Shinga, Katsuura-shi, Chiba 299-52 ☎ 0470-73-4111

International Christian University
(Kokusai Kirisutokyo Daigaku)

3-10-2 Osawa, Mitaka-shi, Tokyo 181
☎ 0422-33-3131

Faculty
    Profs. 63   Assoc. Profs. 45
    Instructors Full-time 26
                Part-time 83
    Res. Assocs. 27
Number of Students
    Undergrad. 1,993   Grad. 203
Library 342,633 volumes

Outline and Characteristics of the University

ICU was founded in June, 1949 by a group of Christians in Japan and abroad who were concerned about the low morale of the Japanese people after World War II. Support for the project came primarily from Japanese and American Christian businessmen who shared the concern to establish such a school.

ICU has devoted its energies towards fulfilling the goals of being a truly international school. Its fundamental aims are (1) teaching how to lead a life of service based on Christian values, (2) communicating the spirit of friendship and mutual understanding which extends beyond cultural and national boundaries, and (3) imparting a knowledge that is broad in scope and highly academic in content. These principles have guided the direction of both the four year Liberal Arts College and the Graduate programs. Within the College are the divisions of Humanities, Social Sciences, Natural Sciences, Languages, and Education. A student may also choose to be an interdivisional major--an individual program of studies spanning two or more of these categories. There are six College-wide programs: Physical Education, General Education, Freshman English, Japanese Language, Computer Science, and Teacher Certification. The Graduate School consists of three divisions: Education, Public Administration, and Comparative Culture. Each division has programs leading to the master's and doctorate degrees.

ICU is also international in that Japanese and English are the common languages in use among the campus community, in both casual and formal situations. Degree-seeking students are required to undergo intensive study in the language they are lacking so that they will be able to take courses and do assignments in either language.

As part of ICU's commitment and efforts to promote international education and understanding, one-year reciprocal exchange programs with institutions abroad have been developed. ICU is currently conducting this program with twenty-one institutions in six countries.

ICU operates on a trimester system. The school year begins in April. However, students coming from outside the Japanese school system are admitted in September, completing three terms of study by the following June. Commencement is held twice a year, in March and June.

The campus is located on a spacious wooded site in suburban Mitaka, about one hour by public transportation from central Tokyo. From Mitaka station, on the rapid Chuo line, there are several buses whose routes are in the ICU vicinity. One bus, marked "ICU, " has its terminus within the campus.

UNDERGRADUATE PROGRAMS

College of Liberal Arts (Freshmen Enrollment: 450)
Division of Education
Educational Technology and Communication (Mass Communication, Audiovisual Education, Computer Application in Education), Education (Philosophy of Education, History of Education, Comparative Education, Educational Administration, Curriculum and Instruction), Psychology (Statistics, Research Methods, Developmental Psychology, History of Psychology, Mental Health)
Division of Humanities
Art and Archaeology (Eastern Art, Western Art, Japanese Archaeology), Literature (Classics, American Literature, English Literature, French Literature, German Literature, Japanese Literature), Music (History of Western Music, Musicology, Ethnomusicology-Japanese Music), Philosophy and Ethics (Western Philosophy, Logic, Religion and Philosophy in Japan, Values and Ethics in Japan), Religion (Biblical Studies, History of Christianity, Theology, Comparative Religion, Science of Religion)
Division of Languages
Communication (Rhetorical Communication, Speech Communication, Intercultural Communication, Conference Interpreting in Theory and Practice, Journalism), English Language (History of English Language, English Grammar, English Teaching), French Language (History of French Language, French Grammar, Projects in French Translation), Japanese Language (History of Japanese Language, Japanese Grammar, Teaching of Japanese as a Foreign Language), Linguistics (Phonology, Historical Linguistics, Grammar, Semantics, Fieldwork of Linguistics, Sociolinguistics)
Division of Natural Sciences
Biology (Plant Biology, Animal Biology, Cell Biology, Biochemistry, Molecular Genetics, Animal Physiology, Entomological Physiology, Plant Field Study, Marine Field Study), Chemistry (Analytical Chemistry, Organic and Inorganic Chemistry, Physical Chemistry, Environmental and Archaeological

Chemistry), Mathematics (Analysis, Algebra, Geometry, Computer Science), Physics (General Physics, Quantum Mechanics, Structure of Matter, Solid State Physics, Biophysics, Macromolecular Physics, Solar Energy, Electronics Geology)

Division of Social Sciences

Economics and Business Administration (Economic Theory, Economic Policy, Economic Development, History, Econometrics, Banking and Finance, International Economics, Business Administration, Labor Problems, Business in Japan, Economic Geography), History (Asian History, Western History, American History), Political Science (Government and Politics, Public Administration and Law, International Law and Politics, Comparative Politics, Japanese Constitution and Laws), Sociology and Anthropology (Sociological and Anthropological Theories, Methods of Social Research, Field Training in Anthropology, Japanese Society, Folk Culture in Japan, Social Structure in Japan)

Foreign Student Admission

Qualifications for Applicants

Standard Qualifications Requirement

ICU accepts students from abroad under the category of "English-Speaking Applicants." This category is for those students who are able to take college level courses in English and have been attending school outside of the Japanese educational system at least two years prior to application. Prospective freshmen must receive one of the following recognized certifications of their academic qualifications: a High School diploma or certificate, GCE A Level passes, or some equivalent official notice. Successful English-Speaking Applicants are to be admitted in September.

Note: For April admission, there is no special consideration for those educated in a non-Japanese school system.

Examination at the University

Documentary screening for English-Speaking Applicants. Refer to the booklet, "Information for English-Speaking Applicants"

Documents to be Submitted When Applying

1. Completed ICU application form
2. Completed ICU health report form
3. Official transcript of high school and, or university record
4. Certification of Graduation or prospective graduation. This is required of prospective freshmen only.
5. Official report of grades on the educational certificate examinations and, or the specified aptitude and achievement tests. This may vary according to the applicant's previous education; for example:
   US-educated: Four College Board Test scores: SAT plus three subjects from different areas of ACHs.
   British-educated: At least five passes (two must be A'Level) in the General Certificate of Education.
   German-educated: Abitur
   French-educated: Baccalaureat, etc.
   For details of requirements for each category, refer to the ICU information booklet.
6. Proof of English proficiency, e. g. TOEFL. This is required of non-native English-speakers only.
7. Three letters of recommendation, one each from the following:
   1) High School principal (in case of prospective transfer students, dean or academic advisor)
   2) an instructor
   3) one person (other than a relative)
8. Application fee
9. *Gaikokujin Torokuzumi Shomeisho* including *Zairyu Shikaku* and *Zairyu Kikan*. This is required of residents in Japan only.

All of these materials must reach the ICU Admissions Office by the deadline (April 15 for 1989 admission). The screening of completed applications will be conducted in late April through mid-May.

Qualifications for Transfer Students

As one of the categories under "English-Speaking Applicants," ICU accepts transfer students from colleges or universities abroad. Prospective transfer students must be those who have completed at least one year of college or university work outside of the Japanese educational system.

Examination for Transfer Students

The same application procedures as prospective freshmen.

Documents to be Submitted When Applying

Same as prospective freshmen.

ONE-YEAR GRADUATE PROGRAMS

One-Year Postgraduate Course of Education
(Enrollment: 25)
Audio Visual Education, Educational Philosophy, Educational Psychology, English Teaching, Science Teaching

Foreign Student Admission

Qualifications for Applicants

Graduates of universities, as defined under Article 52 of the School Education Law or equivalent, must present the following qualifications

1. Completion of undergraduate work, i. e., schooling of 16 years or more, including college.
2. Satisfaction of the requirements in English and Japanese (reading, aural-oral, and written) sufficient to carry on academic work and to understand lectures in both languages.
3. Completion or expected completion of Teacher Certification.

Examination at the University

Applicants for *Senko-ka* (1-Year Postgraduate Program) student status must follow the same application procedures as those applying to the Graduate School, Division of Education through April Admission procedures for Japanese-speaking applicants.

GRADUATE PROGRAMS

Graduate School Division of Comparative Culture (First Year Enrollment : Master's 25, Doctor's 10)
Division
Comparative Culture
Graduate School Division of Education (First Year Enrollment : Master's 40, Doctor's 14)
Divisions
Methodology of Education, Principles of Education
Graduate School Division of Natural Science (First Year Enrollment: Master's 10)
Graduate School Division of Public Administration (First Year Enrollment : Master's 32, Doctor's 12)
Division
Public Administration

Foreign Student Admission
Qualifications for Applicants
Master's Program
Standard Qualifications Requirement

Applicants who have completed their undergraduate work outside of the Japanese educational system are eligible for documentary screening. Those who succeed in the documentary screening process are admitted in September.

Qualifications for regular students who matriculate as M.A. degree seekers are as follows:

1. Completion or expected completion of undergraduate work, i.e. schooling of 16 years or more including college or equivalent at an accredited educational institution outside of the Japanese educational system.
2. Outstanding scholastic ability, as demonstrated in undergraduate studies.
3. Completion of three requirements in Language:
   English:
   All applicants must have competence in English (reading, aural-oral, and written) sufficient to carry on academic work and to understand lectures given in English.
   Japanese:
   Those applicants whose native language is not Japanese are required to show evidence of acceptable competence in the language or to attain this through Japanese language study after their entrance. For those with little or no proficiency in Japanese, this will mean approximately one additional year.
   Second Foreign Language:

Applicants with Japanese or English as their native language are required, in addition, to attain competence in the other of these as their first foreign language, and to have an acceptable level of study in a second foreign language: French, German, Chinese, Russian, or Spanish. Those whose native language is neither Japanese nor English must have one of these as their first foreign language and the other as their second foreign language.

4. Special requirements in the Division of Education: Applicants for this division must have completed 10 or more units of courses in education. However, applicants who do not meet this requirement may be admitted on condition that they complete the requirement by the end of their first year of enrollment. Further qualifying requirements are stipulated for certain fields of study in the Division of Education.
   Educational Psychology:
   to have completed at least 15 units of psychology (preferably educational psychology), plus an undergraduate thesis in psychology (preferably educational psychology), or 20 or more units of psychology (preferably educational psychology).
   English Teaching:
   to have completed 20 or more units of English language, English and American literature and linguistics.
Doctor's Program
   Standard Qualifications Requirement

Applicants who have completed their graduate work at the M.A. level outside of the Japanese educational system will be screened on the basis of their submitted documents. Those who succeed in this documentary screening process are admitted in September.

Examination at the University
Master's Program
Documentary screening. Refer to the booklet, "M. A. Course Information for Applicants Abroad".
Doctor's Program

Refer to the booklet, "Doctoral Course Information for Applicants Abroad. " However, students wishing to enter doctoral courses should, before making application, choose the area in which they intend to specialize from among the specific areas for that school year, and then confirm whether guidance for their selected field of study is available. Applicants should, before making application, contact the desired research advisor concerning the availability of specific research guidance (residents in Japan must see him/her) and obtain his/her consent to become the applicant's advisor if the applicant is admitted.

Documents to be Submitted When Applying
Applicants for M.A. courses are required to submit the following materials:

1. Completed ICU Graduate School application form
2. Completed ICU health report form
3. Completed ICU applicant's card
4. Official transcript of university record (undergraduate program)
5. Two or more confidential references, one of which should testify to the applicant's knowledge of Japanese (according to the specified requirements). The other should be written by the student's academic advisor at the institution previously attended.
6. Applicants from those countries which offer national certificates of their own for graduate work are required to take the examinations for the certificate concerned, the results of which are to be sent to the Admissions Office. Division of Education and Public Administration: Applicants from countries that do not offer any national certificate of their own graduate work are required to take the General Test of the Graduate Record Examinations (GRE) administered by the Educational Testing Service (Princeton, N. J. 08541, U. S. A.).
7. Other applicants whose native language is not English are required to take the Test of English as a Foreign Language (TOEFL).
8. Application fee
9. For applicants to the Division of Comparative Culture: Senior Thesis (two copies).
   (a) As a substitute for the senior thesis: one academic paper written by the applicant in case there is no thesis requirement by the university (two copies).
   (b) Additional academic paper (s) if any (two copies).
   (c) English summary of the thesis or academic paper (s) in case these are written in a language other than English (two copies).
   N. B.: If the thesis or academic paper (s) is written in a language other than Japanese or English, a translation may be required in addition to the English summary.
10. *Gaikokujin Torokuzumi Shomeisho* including *Zairyu-shikaku* and *Zairyu-kikan*. This is required of residents in Japan only.
    Deadline date (May 1 for 1989 admission).
    For application documents for the Doctoral Course, refer to the booklet, "Doctoral Course Information for Applicants Abroad."

*

Research Institutes and Centers

Computer Center, Institute for the Study of Christianity and Culture, Institute of Asian Cultural Studies, Institute of Educational Research and Service, Integrated Learning Center, Sacred Music Center, Social Sciences Research Institute

Facilities/Services for Foreign Students

Students receive assistance from the ICU administration to find off-campus housing, if desired. There are also Counseling Center services where the foreign student may freely discuss personal needs in English.

Special Programs for Foreign Students

Japanese Language Program:

Intensive Japanese
Advanced Japanese
Special Japanese
   Japan Studies Program:

Courses are grouped into Japanese History, Art and Literature; Japanese Society, Religion, Education and Communication; and Japanese Politics, Economics and International Relations.

For Further Information

Undergraduate and Graduate Admission

Admissions Office, International Christian University, 3-10-2 Osawa, Mitaka-shi, Tokyo 181 ☎ 0422-33-3058, 3059, 3061

International University of Japan
(Kokusai Daigaku)

Yamato-machi, Minamiuonuma-gun, Niigata 949-72
☎ 0257-77-1111

Faculty
   Profs. 13   Assoc. Profs. 13
   Assist. Profs. Full–time 6; Part–time 20
   Res. Assocs. 4
Number of Students
   Grad. 184
Library   61, 100 volumes

Outline and Characteristics of the University

Since 1983 the International University of Japan (IUJ) has established a position unique in Japan as an institution dedicated to offering postgraduate programs in International Relations in which all courses are given in English. In 1988, IUJ started an MBA program under the Graduate School of International Management in collaboration with the Amos Tuck School of Business Administration, Dartmouth College.

The major aim of IUJ is to train professionals with a broad international outlook. IUJ's emphasis on both the academic and practical aspects of scholarly research is intended to deepen its students' understanding of international issues and enhance their capacity to deal with the problems of our times through a combination of integrated interdisciplinary and regional studies.

IUJ recognizes that the creation of a truly international environment on campus is essential for realization of its goals. To this end IUJ has adopted a policy of inviting foreign scholars as visiting professors and as occasional lecturers. It has established affiliations with educational and research institutions overseas. IUJ also invites distinguished scholars, government officials and businessmen to give seminars or participate in symposiums.

IUJ encourages the enrollment of foreign students. The dormitory system and the fact that a large number of staff reside on campus provide students with opportunities to meet Japanese and foreign scholars not only during lectures but also in the course of their daily lives.

All students, Foreign or Japanese, at International University of Japan must live in the residential college unless there are extenuating circumstances.

Its objective is to create an environment that is rather rare in Japan, enabling foreign students from all over the world, their colleagues from Japanese corporations, young people with various experiences in many areas, to interact with each other not only in the classroom, but in all aspects of daily life, and in this way to deepen their mutual understanding presently 184 students, including 76 young men and women from 27 foreign countries, live together under the same roof. The Campus has living facilities for both single and married students.

IUJ actively encourages the enrollment of graduates with practical experience in society. It is hoped that the teaching and research program will help these people to deepen their understanding of the contemporary world and further develop their professional skills. It is also hoped that they will play an active role in international society upon graduation.

GRADUATE PROGRAMS

Graduate School of International Management (First Year Enrollment : Master's 50)
Graduate School of International Relations (First Year Enrollment: Master's 100)
Divisions
East and Southeast Asian Studies, International Economics, International Management, International Politics, Japanese Studies, Middle Eastern Studies, North American Studies

Foreign Student Admission
Qualifications for Applicants
Master's Program
Standard Qualification Requirement
Examination at the University
Master's Program
There are two types of selection procedures. One for residents of Japan (Japanese and Non-Japanese) and the other for residents of foreign countries (Japanese and Non-Japanese).
Residents of Japan:
Acceptance decisions will be based on the results of the Entrance Examination of the University and on the documents submitted.
Residents of Foreign Countries:
Acceptance decisions will be based on a consideration of all submitted documents.
Nature of examination (Residents of Japan On-

ly)
1. TOEFL:
2. Essay Examination: Either in Japanese or in English
3. Interviews: in English.
Documents to be Submitted When Applying
Standard Documents Requirement
Residents of Japan (Japanese and Non-Japanese)
1. Completed Application Form and Application Card.
2. Official Score Report for GMAT
3. Essay Test: in English on a topic to be specified on the application form.
4. Official Transcript: A transcript completed and sealed by the appropriate authority of the university from which the applicant has graduated or will be graduating.
5. Letter of Recommendation: A letter of recommendation written on the designated form by the major professor (university) or a superior (company, government or public office) of the applicant.
6. Medical Examination Report
7. Application Fee: ¥30, 000
8. Envelope for Sending Examination ID Card
9. Alien Registration Certificate (Foreign Residents of Japan only)
Residents of Foreign Countries (Japanese and Non-Japanese)
1. Application Form and Application Card completed in English
2. Official Score Report for GMAT
3. Study and Research Plan
   Official Score for TOEFL
4. Essay Test in English on topics to be specified on the application form.
5. Official Transcript: A transcript completed and sealed by the appropriate authority of the university from which the applicant has graduated or will be graduating.
6. Two Letters of Recommendation: Two letters of recommendation written on the designated form by professors (universities) and/or superiors (companies, governments or public offices) and others who are familiar with the applicant's academic qualifications.
7. Medical Examination Report
8. Certificate of Graduation: Certificate of Graduation from the last school attended or an official letter from the university you are now attending stating your expected graduation date.

*
Research Institutes and Centers
The Center for Japan-U. S. Relations, The Institute of Middle Eastern Studies
Special Programs for Foreign Students
Most of the lectures and seminars are offered in English.
At the present time, introductory Japanese lan-

guage courses are offered for foreign students. We organize one to two weeks intensive field trips in Japan for students from abroad.

For Further Information

Graduate Admissions

Admissions & Curriculum Division, International University of Japan, Yamato-machi, Minamiuonuma-gun, Niigata 949-72 ☎ 0257-77-1111 ext. 441

Iwaki Meisei University
(Iwaki Meisei Daigaku)

5–5–1 Chuodai–Iino, Iwaki–shi, Fukushima 970
☎ 0246–28–5415

Faculty
    Profs. 53   Assoc. Profs. 23
    Assist. Profs. Full–time 8; Part–time 22
    Res. Assoc. 8
Number of Students
    Undergrad. 1, 174
Library 50, 050 volumes

Outline and Characteristics of the University

Iwaki Meisei university was inaugurated with a fresh and lively spirit, in April, 1987 with the great mission of fostering talented persons as leaders of the 21st century and of answering the demands of the time by creating new art, science and culture. It is located in Iwaki, on its way to becoming one of Japan's major cities, bridging the metropolitan area and the southern part of the Northeastern District. I. M. U. stands on the spiritual ground of Meisei Gakuen Institute, with over 60 years of history and tradition, and of Meisei University, founded over 20 years ago.

Meisei Gakuen's eternal principles in education is based on the spirit of "harmony", from which originates humanism. These are the principles of study and life at the university by which students are educated so as to be "scientific and moral-minded and trusted by the rest of the world". Iwaki Meisei University has been conceived and inaugurated with this spirit, principle and objective.

All students in the science and engineering college are required to master the computer; those in the humanities college are trained in the use of computers and practice on them.

The harmonious fusion of science and engineering in the college of science and engineering enables students to study subjects in an interdisciplinary manner.

Classes are kept small, in order to achieve a more humanistic education.

Physical education offers the chance of training on the university's yacht "Echo" in a natural ocean setting.

UNDERGRADUATE PROGRAMS

College of Humanities (Freshmen Enrollment: 180)

Department of English and American Literature

Bible Studies, Communication through Foreign Languages, Comparative Literature, Composition, Computer Operation, Conversation, Current English, Customs and Manners of English and American People, English, English and American Culture, English and American Literature, English Philology, Grammar, History in American Literature, History in English Literature, Latin, Linguistics, Monographic Lecture in English and American Literature, Phonetics, Studies of Juvenile Literature

Department of Japanese Literature

Chinese Literature (Fiction), Comparative Literature (Japan and Orient), History of Chinese Literature, History of Japanese Language, History of Japanese Litarature, History of Japanese Thought, Introduction to Comparative Literature, Introduction to World Literature, Japanese and Japanese Classical Literature, Japanese and Japanese Modern Literature, Japanese Expression, Japanese Grammar, Japanese Language (Rhetoric), Monographic Lecture in Japanese Literature, Monographic Lecture in Waka, Practice in Computer Operations, Reading, Reading in Classical Chinese Literature (Shi–sho), (Poetry), Studies in Literature (Manuscript), (Ancient Documents)

Department of Sociology

Community Studies, Community Welfare, Comparative Culture, Computer Activities, Cultural Anthropology, Elementary Sociological Studies, Family Sociology, Field Research, Gerontology, Group and Organization Studies, History of Sociology, Industrial and Labor Sociology, Industrial Economy, International Affairs, Labor Relations, Mass-Communication, Mass Society Studies, Methodology of Social Research, Methodology of Social Welfare, Population Problems, Principles of Sociology, Social History, Social Security, Social Statistics, Social Thouhgt, Social Welfare, Social Welfare Administration, Sociological Theories, Sociology Seminar, Urban Sociology

College of Science and Engineering (Freshmen Enrollment: 240)

Department of Electronic Engineering

Biological Engineeing, Communication Engineering, Control Engineering, Drawing for Electrical Engineering, Electrical Acoustics, Electrical Circuitry, Electric Wave Engineering, Electronic Circuitry, Electronic Engineering, Electronic Materials Engineering, Electronic Measurement Engineering, English for Electrical Engineering, Exercise in Electronic Computer, Experiments in Electronic Engineering, Fundamental Mathematics for Electronics, Fundamentals of Electronic Properties of Materials, General Survey of Electronic Properties of Materials, General Theory of Atomic Energy Engineering, General

Theory of Computers, General Theory of Robot Engineering, History of Science and Technology, Image Engineering, Information Engineering, Information Theory, Introduction to Atomic Physics, Mathematical Statistics, Mechatronics, Micro–electronics, Power Electronics, Quantum Electronics, Regulations for Electrical Engineering, Robot Engineering, Sensor Engineering, Solid Electronics, Systems Engineering, Theory of Automatic Control, Theory of Energy Conversion, Theory of Transient Phenomena

Department of Fundamental Science
Atomic Nuclei•Atomic Energy, Atomic Physics, Biochemistry, Biology, Controls, Cytology of Organisms, Electronic Computer, Electronic Measurement, Electron Microscopy, English for Sciene, Fundamental Mathematics, Fundamental Science, Genetics, History of Chemistry, Industrial Chemistry, Information Theory, Inorganic Chemistry, Instrumental Analysis, Molecular Biology, Molecular Genetics, Molecular Physics, Optics, Oraganic Chemistry, Photochemistry, Physical Chemistry, Physiology, Polymer Science, Quantum Chemistry, Quantum Mechanics, Radiation Chemistry, Radiation Physics, Radioisotope Experiments, Statistical Mechanics, Thermodynamics

Department of Materials Science
Applied Opics, Atomic Nuclei•Atomic Energy, Atomic Physics, Automatic Control, Computers, Electrical Circuitry, Electro-magnetism, Electromagnetism, Electronic Circuitry, Electronic Computer, Electronic Materials, Electronic Measurement, Electronic Properties of Materials, Energy Conversion, English for Material Science, Fundamental Mathematics, Information Theory, Inorganic Chemistry, Material Science, Material Science, Material Science, Mechanics, Mechanics, Molecular Biology, Optics, Organic Chemistry, Physical Chemistry, Physics of Properties of Materials, Quantum Chemistry, Quantum Electronics, Quantum Mechanics, Sensor, Thermodynamics•Statistical Mechanics

Department of Mechanical Engineering
Analysis, Automatic Control, Control Engineering, Control Engineering, Cutting Engineering, Dynamics of Machines, Electronic Computer, Electronic Computers, Electronic Engineering, Energy Machine Engineering, Engineering Dynamics, Engineering Materials, Engineering Mathematics, English for Mechanical Engineering, Exercise in Strength of Materials, Fluid Dynamics, Fluid Dynamics, Fuel and Combustion, Fundamental Machine Design, Internal Combustion Engines, Machine Design, Machine Design and Drawing, Machine Elements, Machine Shop Practice, Machine Tools, Mathematical Statistics, Measurements in Engineering, Mechanical Engineering, Mechanical Engineering, Mechanism, Mechatronics, Precision Engineering, Production Engineering, Refrigeration Engineering, Robot Engineering, Robot Engineering, Strength of Materials, Systems Engineering, Thermodynamics, Thermodynamics, Vehicle Engineering, Vibration Engineering, Weld-

ing Engineering

Foreign Student Admission
Qualifications for Applicants
Standard Qualifications Requirement
Examination at the University
A written examimation and an interview
1.   Written Examination
College of Science and Engineering: English, Mathematics, Science and Japanese
College of Humanities: English, Japanese and Social studies
2.   Interview
Documents to be Submitted When Applying
Standard Documents Requirement
The application form and prospectus of registration will be available from early August.

*

Research Institutes and Centers
Computer Center, Dynamics Control Research Center, Low-Temperature Physics and Engineering Research Center, Mark Twain Collection Research Center for Mark Twainiana

Services for Foreign Students
Undergraduate
Foreign Language Subjects
1.   1st and 2nd year course (credit) (required): Japanese Language.
2.   3rd and 4th year course (no credit) (required): Japanese Language.

For Further Information
Undergraduate Admission
Entrance Examination Section, Administration Division, Iwaki Meisei University, 5–5–1 Chuodai–Iino, Iwaki–shi, Fukushima 970 ☎ 0246–29–5111 ext. 219

Iwate Medical University
(Iwate Ika Daigaku)

19–1 Uchimaru, Morioka-shi, Iwate 020
☎ 0196–51–5111

Faculty
Profs.   62   Assoc. Profs.   53
Assist. Profs.   Full–time   93; Part–time   283
Res. Assocs.   253
Number of Students
Undergrad.   1, 018   Grad.   199
Library   182, 604 volumes

Outline and Characteristics of the University
Shunjiro Mita founded Iwate Medical School, a private school of medicine in 1901. His purpose was to provide more physicians and medical facilities to the north-eastern region of Japan, particularly for the benefit of the people living in Iwate Prefecture. In 1912, the school had to close because of a change in the Japanese medical education system. Fortunate-

ly, however, the school was able to re-open in 1928, since there was a growing national need for more medical services. The school grew to college status in 1947, when Sadanori Mita became the first president. The graduate course was established in 1960, then the school of Dentistry and premedical course were added in 1965. In October, 1980, the Iwate Critical Care and Emergency Center and a new expansion of the University Hospital were completed. In March, 1983, the graduate course in dentistry was inaugurated. With the most advanced facilities and qualified staff this school still continues to develop further in order to provide better medical care to local residents.

The motto of the founder of this school was "to train every student to be a man of sincerity while at the same time being a man of medicine." This ideal has been pursued by all subsequent presidents. The incumbent president, Tsutomu Ohhori, was elected in 1988. The incummbent chairman of the Board of Directors is Dr. Toshisada Mita.

UNDERGRADUATE PROGRAMS

Faculty of Dentistry (Freshmen Enrollment: 80)
Department of Dentistry
Biochemistry, Dental Pharmacology, Dental Radiology, Dental Technology, Internal Medicine, Operative Dentistry, Oral Anatomy, Oral Biochemistry, Oral Diagnosis, Oral Microbiology, Oral Pathology, Oral Physiology, Oral Surgery, Orthodontics, Pedodontics, Preventive Dentistry, Prosthetic Dentistry
Faculty of Medicine (Freshmen Enrollment: 80)
Department of Medicine
Anatomy, Anesthesiology, Bacteriology, Biochemistry, Clinical Pathology, Dermatology, Hygiene and Public Health, Internal Medicine, Laboratory Medicine, Legal Medicine, Neurology, Neurosurgery, Obstetrics and Gynecology, Ophthalmology, Orthopedic Surgery, Otolaryngology, Pathology, Pediatrics, Pharmacology, Pharmacy, Physiology, Plastic Reconstructive Surgery, Psychiatry, Radiology, Surgery, Urology

Foreign Student Admission
Qualifications for Applicants
Standard Qualifications Requirement
Examination at the University
Applicants must take an entrance examination consisting of a written examination and an interview. All answers must be written in Japanese.
Documents to be Submitted When Applying
Standard Documents Requirement

GRADUATE PROGRAMS

Graduate School of Dentistry (First Year Enrollment : 18)
Division
Basic and Clinical Dentistry

Graduate School of Medicine (First Year Enrollment : 25)
Divisions
Internal Medicine, Pathological Medicine, Physiological Science, Social Medicine, Surgical Medicine

Foreign Student Admission
Qualifications for Applicants
Doctral Program
Graduate School of Dentistry:
1. Applicants must have graduated from a School of Medicine or Dentistry.
2. Applicants for Clinical Dentistry are required to have passed the National Board Examination for Medical or Dental Practice.
3. Applicants who have graduated from the School of Dentis.ry are also allowed to select a Basic Dentistry Course.
Graduate School of Medicine:
1. Applicants must have graduated from a School of Medicine or Dentistry.
2. Those who apply to the Departments of Social Medicine, Internal Medicine, or Surgical Medicine must have a Japanese license for medical practice, or have passed the National Medical Board Examination of Japan.
3. Those who graduated from a dental school (dental college or faculty of dentistry) can apply only to the Departments of Physiological Science and Pathological Medicine.
Examination at the University
Two foreign languages (English and German) plus the Department subject to which the applicant is applying. All answers must be written in Japanese.
Date of Examination: March 1,
Acceptance Notification Date: March 8 (School of Medicine), March 10 (Dentistry)
Documents to be Submitted When Applying
Standard Documents Requirement
Dead line: 2 months prior to the date of examination. Applicants who are working for a company or public office must have the official approval of the supervisor or administrator.

*

For Further Information
Undergraduate and Graduate Admission
Admissions Office, Iwate Medical University, 19–1 Uchimaru, Morioka-shi, Iwate 020 ☎ 0196–51–5111 ext. 3222

Japan College of Social Work
(Nihon Shakai Jigyo Daigaku)

3–1–30 Takeoka, Kiyose–shi, Tokyo 150
☎ 03-402-7507

Faculty
Profs.   16   Assoc. Profs.   3

Assist. Profs.   Full–time   3; Part–time   23
Res. Assocs.   3
Number of Students
Undergrad.   517
Library   76, 690 volumes

Outline and Characteristics of the College

Japan College of Social Work has always played a pioneering and innovative role in the field of social welfare research and education for 40 years since its establishment. Its comprehensive remodeling project for the new university has worked out, and a new, big campus has been set up at Kiyose City, Tokyo since April, 1989.

The important features of education envisioned are gradual introduction of professional curriculum subjects into freshman and sophomore subjects ("wedge-shaped progress"), and tutorial guidance in seminars, social work practicum and graduation thesis. Under this system students obtain helpful instruction and chances of developing their research and studies. In order to help students perform effective fieldwork, the Guidance Center for Fieldwork is set up. The objective of the center is to organize affiliated and designated fieldwork agencies and facilities and to provide students with systematized instruction of social work practice.

Application for Graduate School has been submitted to the Ministry of Education.

UNDERGRADUATE PROGRAMS

Department of Social Welfare (Freshmen Enrollment: 150)

Child Welfare Division (Social Welfare Administration Course, Commonity Development Course)

Social Work Division (Family Welfare Course, Welfare for the Handicapped Course, Welfare for the Elderly Course)

Chid Welfare, Community Welfare, History of Social Welfare, Institutional Care, Interntional Social Welfare, Judicial Welfare, Medical Social Work, Nursery Teaching, Psychology, Public Assistance, Recreation, Rehabilitation, Social Education, Social Security, Social Survey and Research, Social Welfare, Social Welfare Legislative Systems, Social Work Methods, Welfare for the Aged, Welfare for the Disabled, Welfare for Women

Foreign Student Admission

Qualifications for Applicants

Standard Qualifications Requirement

Applicants must have taken the Japanese Language Proficiency Test.

Examination at the College

1. Review of submitted application files
2. Written examination: (a.) English, (b.) Essay (in Japanese)
3. Oral interview

Documents to be Submitted When Applying

Standard Documents Requirement

The Scores of the Japanese Language Proficiency Test

*

Research Institutes and Centers

The Clinical Counseling Center for Children, The Family Counseling Center, The KODOMO GAKU-EN Facilitiy for Mentally Handicapped Children, The Social Work Research Institute

For Further Information

Undergraduate Admission

Administrative Staff, General Affairs Division, Japan College of Social Work, 3-1-30 Takeoka, Kiyose-shi, Shibuya-ku, Tokyo 150 ☎ 03-402-7507 ext. 15

The Japanese Red Cross College of Nursing

(Nihon Sekijuji Kango Daigaku)

4-1-3 Hiroo, Shibuya-ku, Tokyo 150
☎ 03-409-0875

Faculty
Profs.   14   Assoc. Profs.   5
Assist. Profs.   Full–time   6; Part–time   51
Res. Assocs.   5
Number of Students
Undergrad.   60
Library   23, 113 volumes

Outline and Characteristics of the College

The Japanese Red Cross College of Nursing was originally established in 1890 as the Japanese Red Cross Nursing School. Since then it was renamed several times and became the Japanese Red Cross Central Junior College of Nursing in 1966. As the progress of medical science has resulted in making nursing more scientific, it was reorganized and became the Japanese Red Cross College of Nursing. The College is located near the center of Tokyo and the Japanese Red Cross Medical Center, a hospital for the students' practical training, is situated within the same campus.

Based on the Red Cross banner of humanity, the objectives of the College are to train nurses and promote the study of nursing, thus serving the welfare of mankind. To obtain these objectives, a variety of general education, languages, physical education classes and subjects related to the Red Cross are organized systematically. In view of the worldwide character of the Red Cross, English is compulsory.

UNDERGRADUATE PROGRAMS

Faculty of Nursing (Freshmen Enrollment: 50)

Department of Nursing

Adult Nursing, Fundamental Nursing, Midwifery,

Mother and Child Nursing, Nursing Education, Pediatric Nursing, Public Health Nursing

*

For Further Information
Undergraduate Admission
Administrative Office, The Japanese Red Cross College of Nursing, 4-1-3 Hiroo, Shibuya-ku, Tokyo 150 ☎ 03-409-0875

Japan Lutheran Theological College
(Nihon Ruteru Shingaku Daigaku)

3-10-20 Osawa, Mitaka-shi, Tokyo 181
☎ 0422-31-4611

Faculty
 Profs. 12 Assoc. Profs. 4
 Assist. Profs. Full–time 5; Part–time 34
Number of Students
 Undergrad. 182
Library 53, 000 volumes

Outline and Characteristics of the College
The Japan Lutheran Theological College was originally established as the Japan Lutheran Seminary in Kumamoto City in 1909. Two years later it became the Theological Department of Kyushu Gakuin, and in 1916 it was recognized as a Professional School, moving to Tokyo in 1925. It received official accreditation as a Theological College in 1964. Until 1976, the school specialized in theological education for ministers, especially of the Lutheran Church, and was accordingly very small in scope.

In 1976, a second course, in Christian Social Work, was established, and since that time the school has become truly co-educational and has grown to its present size. Recently, in December 1986, the Social Work course was approved by the Ministry of Education as a Department of Social Work which started from April, 1987. Concurrent with this, the entire program of the school is now recognized as a Faculty of Literature, a move which will enhance the social standing of the school.

The Japan Lutheran Seminary, which offers a two-year course in specialized theological study for ministers in the Lutheran Church, exists side-by-side with the Theological College on the same campus. College graduation is a pre-requisite for entering the Seminary.

There is a strong emphasis on field work in both the theological and social work areas. Practical experience is provided at churches, and at hospitals, homes for the elderly, and care centers for the physically and mentally disabled. Nearly 80% of the graduates work in social welfare institutions. Typical graduation thesis topics include the following: "Scouting for Autistic Children," "The Church and

the Mentally Ill," "Feelings and Opinions of Filipino Youth."

The school maintains international exchange programs with several institutions overseas and always has students from abroad enrolled. Although all regular course work is conducted in Japanese, almost all faculty members are bi-lingual and can provide individualized instruction in English, or in some cases in German.

Inasmuch as each entering class is limited to 35 students, the high proportion of faculty to students is one of the chief positive points of the academic program. Students also appreciate the family-like atmosphere and the social interaction within the student body.

The school campus is located in the Tokyo suburb of Mitaka, adjacent to two other institutions of Christian higher education. The environment is extraordinarily quiet, clean and park-like.

UNDERGRADUATE PROGRAMS

Faculty of Literature (Freshmen Enrollment: 35)
 Department of Social Welfare
(Freshman Enrollment: 30)
Child Welfare, Clinical Psychology, Community-based Social Services, Community Organization, Correctional Services, Counseling, Financial Management, Group Therapy, History of Social Welfare, Mental Health, Nursing, Public Assistance, Recreation, Social Casework, Social Group Work, Social Welfare and Social Security System, Social Welfare in Various Countries, Welfare for the Aged, Welfare for the Disabled, Youth Services
 Department of Theology
(Freshman Enrollment: 5)
Christian Ethics, Christian Mass Communication, Dogmatics, Ecumenism, Evangelism and Pastoral Care, Historical Theology, History of Christianity in Japan, Homiletics, Lutheran Confessions, New Testament Exegesis, Old Testament Exegesis, Old Testament History, Pastoral Psychology and Pastoral Counseling, Philosophy of Religion, Theology, Theology of Liturgy

Foreign Student Admission
 Qualifications for Applicants
  Standard Qualifications Requirement
 Examination at the College
For applicants outside Japan, an interview and examination is required. If Japanese language competency is insufficient, the applicant will be required to take additional language study outside the regular curriculum of JLTC.

For applicants living in Japan, the same procedures which apply to ordinary Japanese students are to be followed.

For foreign students formally recommended by a church or educational institution standing in special relationship to JLTC, separate regulations for admission shall be applied.

Documents to be Submitted When Applying

Standard Documents Requirement

Letter of recommendation from church to which applicant is related.

Qualifications for Transfer Students

At least two years of study completed at an accredited college or university.

Examination for Transfer Students

For applicants outside Japan: study of the application documents and the report of the personal interview

For applicants in Japan: a personal interview, the test for Japanese language proficiency, the study of these data and the application documents.

If application documents are received later than Nov. 30, the applicant is required to go through the same selection process as ordinary Japanese applicants.

Documents to be Submitted When Applying

Standard Documents Requirement

Letter of recommendation from church to which applicant is related.

*

Research Institutes and Centers

Luther Research Institute, Personal Growth and Counseling Center

Facilities/Services for Foreign Students

Dormitories (Men 38, Women 18), School cafeteria.

Special Programs for Foreign Students

Guided readings courses in English.

For Further Information

Undergraduate Admission

Office of Academic Affairs, Japan Lutheran Theological College, 3-10-20 Osawa, Mitaka-shi, Tokyo 181 0422-32-2949

Japan Women's College of Physical Education

(Nihon Joshi Taiiku Daigaku)

8-19-1 Kitakarasuyama, Setagaya-ku, Tokyo 157
☎ 03-300-2251

Faculty

Profs. 22   Assoc. Profs. 7
Assist. Profs. Full–time 3; Part–time 31
Res. Assocs. 11

Number of Students

Undergrad. 1, 307

Library 73, 000 volumes

Outline and Characteristics of the College

Japan Women's College of Physical Education, one of the oldest colleges of physical education for women in Japan, has a history of over 60 years since its establishment in 1922 by Tokuyo Nikaido.

In 1913 Nikaido, associate professor at Ochanomizu Women's University, was sent to England by the Japanese Government. For two years she studied physical education at Kingsfield College, London, where she was especially favored by Madame Oesterberg, President of the College. Under the influence of this great teacher, she was convinced that physical education would lead to the personal happiness and social welfare of women. After returning to Japan she was eager to establish what she called "Queensfield" (in contrast to Oesterberg's "Kingsfield"). The realization of her energies was Nikaido Gymnastic Private School. It was renamed Japan Women's College of Physical Education (three-year course) in 1925, and became, for the first time in Japan, the female teacher training college of physical education qualified by the Ministry of Education. After World War II, in 1950, with the educational system reformed, the College became Japan Women's Junior College of Physical Education (two-year course). In addition to the Junior College, Japan Women's College of Physical Education (four-year course) was established in 1965 in response to the increasing need for physical education in the country. The population of the students increased from 40 in 1922 to 2, 200 in 1986. There are several students from abroad.

Nowadays, health and physical fitness is widely recognized as an important factor of human well-being, so that what is required of the students in physical education, is a good understanding of the human body and its physical performance as well as their excellent physical abilities. Japan Women's College of Physical Education and Japan Women's Junior College of Physical Education contribute greatly to the growing demands in physical education, sports and recreation, by educating qualified specialists and conducting scientific researches.

Japan Women's College of Physical Education offers a four-year course leading to the Degree of Bachelor of Physical Education. In addition, the College offers a preparatory program for obtaining teacher's licenses of health and physical education for junior and senior high school. Approximately 95% of the students receive teacher's licenses; some of them succeed in finding employment in schools, some get jobs as instructors or trainers in community sports or recreational activities.

Japan Women's Junior College of Physical Education consists of Physical Education Course and Kindergarten Course. The former is the preparation for the teacher's license of junior high school in health and physical education and the latter is the preparation for the teacher's licenses of kindergarten and nursery school.

The campus is located not far from Shinjuku, one of the busiest centers in Tokyo (20 minutes distant westward from Shinjuku, via the Keio Line), and surrounded by some of the remaining natural beauties of the old Musashino Plain, making student life both convenient and comfortable.

UNDERGRADUATE PROGRAMS

Faculty of Physical Education (Freshmen Enrollment: 250)
Department of Physical Education

Foreign Student Admission
Qualifications for Applicants
Standard Qualifications Requirement
Examination at the College
The same entrance examination as Japanese applicants, However, special consideration for admitting foreign students will be given according to the conditions of application.
Documents to be Submitted When Applying
Standard Documents Requirement

Qualifications for Transfer Students
Transfer to the 3rd-year:
1. Those who have completed all junior college work.
2. Those who have attended lectures at a university/college for more than two years, and taken more than 62 credits.
Examination for Transfer Students
Same as freshman applicants.
Documents to be Submitted When Applying
Standard Documents Requirement

*

For Further Information
Undergraduate Admission
Entrance Examination Section, Student Division, Japan Women's College of Physical Education, 8-19-1 Kitakarasuyama, Setagaya-ku, Tokyo 157 ☎ 03-300-2251 ext. 312, 370

Japan Women's University
(Nihon Joshi Daigaku)

2-8-1 Mejirodai, Bunkyo-ku, Tokyo 112
☎ 03-943-3131

Faculty
    Profs. 97   Assoc. Profs. 37
    Assist. Profs. Full–time 7; Part–time 424
    Res. Assocs. 52
Number of Students
    Undergrad. 4, 775   Grad. 160
Library   377, 700 volumes

Outline and Characteristics of the University
Japan Women's University was established in April, 1901, as the first private liberal arts college for Japanese women. At that time, Japan had been just emerging out of the old feudal ideas and customs, and the status of women was low. However, Rev. Jinzo Naruse firmly believed that the strength of a nation should depend largely on the intelligence and understanding of its women, and worked hard to found Japan Women's University with the assistance of his sympathizers.

Rev. Naruse endeavored to give each student a deep consciousness of great responsibility as a person, as a woman, and as a member of a nation. He also emphasized the philosophy of education which he expressed in the three principles, "True Conviction, " "Creativity" and "Cooperation and Service". His motive of founding the University and three principles of education have been highly respected by all the successors of Japan Women's University.

Today, Japan Women's University has two faculties and two graduate schools: Home Economics and Humanities. In Japan, since it is unique to have 12 departments in a women's university, many young women have gathered from all over Japan to learn at Japan Women's University ever since its establishment.

The Educational Foundation of Japan Women's University has a senior high school, a junior high school, an elementary school and a kindergarten. The University has a correspondence course in the Faculty of Home Economics to give an opportunity for higher education for working women. However, these days, many graduates have entered this course of continuing education. This correspondence course has become an institution for life-long education.

Japan Women's University is situated in Bunkyo Ward, the educational and cultural center of Tokyo. The Mejiro Campus also has the head office of the Educational Foundation, the alumnae association, "Ofukai" (Cherry-Maple Association) and the dormitories. The Mejiro Campus is located in a quiet neighborhood, conducive to higher study and research. There is another campus in Nishi-Ikuta, Kawasaki, Kanagawa Prefecture. The Nishi-Ikuta Campus is mainly used by Senior and Junior High School students.

UNDERGRADUATE PROGRAMS

Faculty of Home Economics (Freshmen Enrollment: 520)
Department of Child Studies
Child Education, Child Health, Child Psychology, Children's Literature, Child Welfare
Department of Clothing
Construction of Clothing, Dyeing and Finishing, Fabric Care Science, Function and Hygiene of Clothing, History of Costume, Textile Formative Science, Textile Materials
Department of Food and Nutrition
Biological and Nutritional Chemistry, Cookery, Cookery Science, Food Chemistry, Food Microbiology, Nutritional Education, Nutrition for the Elderly and Child, Pathophysiological Nutriology, Physiological Aspect of Nutrition, Public Nutrition
Department of Household Economics
Accounting, Business Management, Consumer Eco-

nomics, Consumers' Policy/Cooperative, Economic History of Japan/Europe, Economic Policy, Economic Statistics of Japan, Female Workers' Problem, Home Management, Industrial Structure, Labor Law, Macroeconomics, Microeconomics, Political Economy, Public Finance, Social Policy

Department of Housing

Dwelling and Life Style, House Planning, Housing Design, Materials and Structural System

Department of Sicences for Home Economics: Section I

Chemistry Major Analytical Chemistry, Biopolymer Chemistry, Inorganic Chemistry, Organic Chemistry, Physical Chemistry

Mathematics Major Algebraic Topology, Analytic Functions, Calculus, Computer, Differential Geometry, Functional Analysis, General Topology, Linear Algebra, Statistics

Physics Major Atomic Physics, Dynamics, Electromagnetism, Experimental Solid State Physics, Theoretical Solid State Physics

Department of Sicences for Home Economics: Section II

Animal Ecology and Behavior, Animal Embryology and Physiology, Biochemistry, Cell Biology, Microbiology and Genetics, Floriculture and Plant Breeding, Plant Morphology, Plant Physiology

Faculty of Humanities (Freshmen Enrollment 480)

Department of Education

Educational Field, Humanistic Field, Psychological Field

Department of English

American Culture, American History, English and American Literature, English Linguistics, History of American Literature, History of English Literature

Department of History

Archaeology, Contemporary World History, Ethnology, Geography, Japanese History, Method of History, Occidental History, Oriental History

Department of Japanese

History of Japanese Language, History of Japanese Literature, Japanese Language, Japanese Literature

Department of Social Welfare

Foundation of Social Problems, Methods of Social Work, Social Welfare, Social Welfare Policies

Foreign Student Admission

Qualifications for Applicants

Standard Qualifications Requirement

Examination at the University

Written tests of Japanese and English and/or an Interview

Documents to be Submitted When Applying

Standard Documents Requirement

1. Certificate of Japanese language proficiency issued by a Japanese language school or an equivalent institution
2. If the applicant has taken the Japanese Language Proficiency Test and/or General Examination for Foreign Students, the results of these tests.
3. If the applicant has had higher education after she graduated from high school, Certificate of college/university graduation or course completion and Transcript of school record from college/university.

GRADUATE PROGRAMS

Graduate School of Home Economics (First Year Enrollment : Master's 40)

Divisions

Child Studies, Clothing, Food and Nutrition, Housing

Graduate School of Humanities (First Year Enrollment : Master's 40, Doctor's 12)

Divisions

Education, English Language and Literature, Japanese Language and Literature, Social Welfare

Foreign Student Admission

Qualifications for Applicants

Master's Program

Standard Qualifications Requirement

Doctor's Program

Standard Qualifications Requirement

Examination at the University

Master's Program

The same procedure as Japanese applicants. Applicants for the Graduate School of Literature & Humanities are permitted to choose one language under "Foreign Language."

Doctor's Program

Same as Master's program.

Documents to be Submitted When Applying

Standard Documents Requirement

1. Bachelor's/Master's Thesis, or its copy
2. If the applicant is employed, Letter of Assent by her employer to her application for the Graduate School of Japan Women's University
3. If the person is a foreign applicant, Certificate of Japanese language proficiency issued by a Japanese language school or an equivalent institution.

*

Research Institutes and Centers

Computation Laboratory, Institute for Child Study, Institute for Education for Women, Rural Life Research Institute

Special Programs for Foreign Students

Japanese Language, Japan Studies

For Further Information

Undergraduate and Graduate Admission

Admission Office, Academic Affairs Section, Academic & Educational Department, Japan Women's University, 2-8-1 Mejirodai, Bunkyo-ku, Tokyo 112 ☏ 03-943-3131 ext. 354, 287

Jichi Medical School
(Jichi Ika Daigaku)

3311–1 Yakushiji, Minamikawachi-machi,
Kawachi-gun, Tochigi 329–04   ☎ 0285–44–2111

Faculty
    Profs. 55   Assoc. Profs. 45
    Assist. Profs. Full–time 103; Part–time 97
    Res. Assocs. 292
Number of Students
    Undergrad. 634   Grad. 31
Library 158, 792 volumes

Outline and Characteristics of the University

Jichi Medical School established in April, 1972, is sponsored by all the prefectural governments of Japan. The fundamental principle of the school is to nurture humane and highly competent clinical doctors who are willing to undertake the difficult task of solving the problem of the imbalance in medical care and treatment between remote and urban areas.

Jichi Medical School has several characteristics. All the students, for example, are enthusiastic and highly qualified. They come from all over Japan. Some come from as far as Hokkaido and Okinawa, and a unique six-year integrated curriculum is offered. In addition, they are expected to return to their own prefectures to practice. Finally, school expenses are loaned to all the students for six years, and the students are exempt from these fees if they finish the task of working at public hospitals or clinics appointed by the governor of each prefecture for a fixed period, generally nine years, after their graduation from the school.

The educational aims of the school are the cultivation of humane doctors, the training of competent clinical doctors with a medical knowledge of the highest level, a six-year integrated program achieving complete harmony between general and professional education, personality development through close contact between students and staff, and fostering doctors who devote themselves to the medical care and welfare of the rural districts.

UNDERGRADUATE PROGRAMS

Faculty of Medicine (Freshmen Enrollment: 100)
    Department of Medicine
Anatomy, Anesthesiology, Biochemistry, Biology, Cardiology, Chemistry, Clinical Immunology, Clinical Pathology, Clinical Pharmacology, Dental & Oral Clinic, Dermatology, Endocrinology & Metabolism, Environmental Health, Gastroenterological Surgery, Gastroenterology, General Surgery, Hematology, Legal Medicine, Medical Biology & Parasitology, Microbiology, Neurology, Obstetrics & Gynecology, Ophthalmology, Orthopedics, Otorhinolar-yngology, Pathology, Pediatrics, Pharmacology, Physics, Physiology, Psychiatry, Public Health, Radiology, Respiratory Disease, Surgical Neurology, Thoracic & Cardiovascular Surgery, Urology, Virology

GRADUATE PROGRAMS

Graduate School of Medicine (First Year Enrollment : Doctor's 25)
    Divisions
Community Medicine, Environmental Health, Human Biology

Foreign Student Admission
    Qualifications for Applicants
Doctor's Program
    Standard Qualifications Requirement
    Examination at the University
Doctor's Program
    The same entrance examination as the Japanese students.
    Written tests in two foreign languages, oral tests in specialized fields, health examination, school records, etc.
    Examination date: in March.
    Documents to be Submitted When Applying
    Standard Documents Requirement

＊

Research Institutes and Centers
Experimental Animal Center, Information and Training Center for Community Medicine
For Further Information
    Undergraduate and Graduate Admission
Admissions Office, Jichi Medical School, 3311–1 Yakushiji, Minamikawachi-machi, Kawachi-gun, Tochigi 329–04 ☎ 0285–44–2111 ext. 3312

Jikei University School of Medicine
(Tokyo Jikei–kai Ika Daigaku)

3-25-8 Nishi–shinbashi, Minato–ku, Tokyo 105
☎ 03-433-1111

Faculty
    Profs. 105   Assoc. Profs. 94
    Assist. Profs. Full–time 460
    Res. Assocs. 974
Number of Students
    Undergrad. 738   Grad. 36
Library 240, 121 volumes

Outline and Characteristics of the University

The Jikei Uiversity School of Medicine is one of the oldest medical schools in Japan. It was founded in 1881 by Kanehiro Takaki, general of the naval surgeon and baron in his later years, as the Sei–i–kai Medical School.

Since Takaki was a graduate of St. Thomas's Hospital Medical School in London, British medicine was taught instead of German medicine which was the main trend in all of the other medical schools in Japan. With the expansion of the faculty and hopital, Sei–i–kai Medical School was renamed as the Jikei University School of Medicine in 1921.

The Jikei University is located in the heart of Tokyo and has about 2,418 beds including four branch University Hospitals.

The number of beds is the largest among University Hospitals in Japan, making it possible to give substantial bed–side education for undergraduates and graduates.

UNDERGRADUATE PROGRAMS

Faculty of Medicine (Freshmen Enrollment: 120)
Department of Medicine
Anatomy, Anesthesiology, Bacteriology, Biochemistry, Cardiovascular Surgery, Dermatology, Hygiene, Internal Medicine, Laboratory Medicine, Legal Medicine, Neurosurgery, Nutrition, Obstetrics & Gynecology, Ophthalmology, Orthopedic Surgery, Otorhinolaryngology, Parasitology, Pathology Pediatrics, Pharmacology, Physiology, Plastic Surgery, Psychiatry, Public Health, Radiology, Rehabilitation Medicine, Surgery, Urology

Foreign Student Admission
Qualifications for Applicants
Standard Qualifications Requirement
1. Those who have received the International Baccalaureate and are 18 years or older may also apply.
2. Japanese Language Proficieny Test and General Examination for Foreign Students.
Examination at the University
A written exam and an interview.
Documents to be Submitted When Applying
Standard Documents Requirement
Following documents are also required.
1. Certificates of the Japanese Language Proficiency Test and General Examination for Foreign Students.
2. A certificate of Graduation from the Japanese language school the applicant attended.
Application forms are available at the Admissions Office early December. Application deadline: Feb. 7

GRADUATE PROGRAMS

Graduate School of Medicine (First Year Enrollment : Doctor's 66)
Divisions
Internal Medicine, Pathology, Physiology, Social Medicine, Surgery

*
For Further Information
Undergraduate and Graduate Admission
Admissions Office, Jikei University School of Medicine, 3-25-8 Nishi–shinbashi, Minato–ku, Tokyo 105
☎ 03-433-1111

Jissen Women's University
(Jissen Joshi Daigaku)
4-1-1 Osakaue, Hino-shi, Tokyo 191
☎ 0425–85–0311~5

Faculty
  Profs. 57 Assoc. Profs. 17
  Assist. Profs. Full–time 6; Part–time 119
  Res. Assocs. 3
Number of Students
  Undergrad. 3,007 Grad. 34
Library 227,567 volumes

Outline and Characteristics of the University

Jissen Girls' School has a history of almost 90 years since its establishment in 1899. The University was approved in 1949. Utako Shimoda, the founder of the school, was often heard to remark, "The nature of a woman should be pure and full of affection." Women should have the strength of a mountain, the purity of spring water and the gentleness and grace of a swan in flight. Such qualities blend together to mold women capable of rectifying the social injustices with which they have been saddled.

It was Shimoda's earnest hope that the girls entering this educational institution would leave with those very qualities. Girls strong enough to tackle the most difficult of problems, yet soft enough to melt the hardest of hearts. Girls capable of thinking, educating, meeting the times head on and always willing to better themselves and work for a world a little more peaceful and humane.

So, when Shimoda decided on establishing a school for women, she gave ample consideration not just to an institution that would give women a place to receive a good, sound, challenging and fruitful education but also a place where young girls could blossom into full-fledged women in all their grace and dignity.

Our University is made up of two Faculties, Literature and Domestic Science, with five areas of study. The Faculty of Literature is made up of the Department of Japanese Literature, the Department of English Literature, and the Department of Aesthetics & Art History. The Faculty of Domestic Science consists of the Department of Food Science and the Department of Clothing Science. In accordance with the spirit of the Fundamentals of the Education Act, all departments are specially geared for a university level of education for women, with teaching and research being directed towards the technical arts and sciences. The aim of our university is to cultivate the intellectual, moral and practical faculties of our students, with emphasis being given to developing students of sound character, with educational credentials which are such that they will be able to uphold Japan's long and valued traditions and be of benefit to society in general. Students successfully completing the course requirements will be awarded a Bachelor of Arts or a Bachelor of Domestic Science degree.

Being small in size, our University has the advantage of maintaining friendly relationships between teachers and students.

Our University offers the three Graduate Schools of Japanese Literature, English Literature and Nutrition. Instructions and research guidance by a very competent teaching staff is one asset of which our University can boast. Students successfully completing all the requirements of the master's course will be awarded a Master's Degree. In 1969, a doctor's course for Japanese Literature majors was established and has attracted much attention as a place where students can carry out unique and challenging research.

UNDERGRADUATE PROGRAMS

Faculty of Domestic Science (Freshmen Enrollment: 300)
Department of Clothing Science
Cleaning, Clothing Hygiene, Clothing Materials, Domestic Science, Dress Design, Dressmaking, Dyeing Chemistry, Function of Clothing, Studies on Fibers
Department of Food Science
Dietetics Supervision Major
Chemistry of High Polymers, Cooking, Dietetics, Domestic Science, Food Chemistry, Food Hygiene, Food Management, Food Manufacture & Preservation, Microbiology, Nutritional Guidance, Physiology & Pathology, Public Hygiene
Food Studies Major
Cooking, Cooking Theory, Dietetics, Domestic Science, Family Economics, Food Chemistry, Food Hygiene, Food Manufacture & Preservation, Home Management, Physiology
Faculty of Literature (Freshmen Enrollment: 400)
Department of Aesthetics & Art History
Aesthetics, Cultural History, Culture, Folk Entertainment, Folklore, History of Japanese Fine Arts, History of Oriental Fine Arts, History of Western Fine Arts
Department of English Literature
American Writers, English Linguistics, English Literature, English Poetry, English Women Novelists, History of American Literature, History of English Literature, Shakespeare
Department of Japanese Literature
Calligraphy, Chinese Philosophy & Literature, Comparative Literature, History of Japanese Fine Arts & Culture, History of Japanese Literature, Japanese

Linguistics, Japanese Literature

Foreign Student Admission
Qualifications for Applicants
Standard Qualifications Requirement
Those who have received the International Baccalaureate and are 18 years or older are also eligible to apply.
Examination at the University
A written exam and interview.
Date: November. This special examination is, however, not applicable to those foreign students who have finished a high school in Japan: they must take the same entrance examination in February as the Japanese students.
Documents to be Submitted When Applying
Standard Documents Requirement
Application forms are available at the Administrative Office from late September.

Qualifications for Transfer Students
1. Those who have graduated from a junior college in Japan or are due to do so by March 31 of the year of application.
2. Those who have completed 14 years of education or equivalent.
Examination for Transfer Students
The same written and oral exam plus an interview as Japanese applicants Date: February.
Documents to be Submitted When Applying
Standard Documents Requirement
Application forms are available at the Administrative Office from January.

GRADUATE PROGRAMS

Graduate School of Domestic Science (First Year Enrollment : Master's 6)
Division
Food Science & Nutrition
Graduate School of Literature (First Year Enrollment : Master's 16, Doctor's 3)
Divisions
English Literature, Japanese Literature

Foreign Student Admission
Qualifications for Applicants
Master's Program
Standard Qualifications Requirement
Doctor's Program
Standard Qualifications Requirement
Examination at the University
Master's Program
Same as Japanese applicants a written and oral exam plus an interview. Date: February.
Doctor's Program
Same as Master's program.
Documents to be Submitted When Applying
Standard Documents Requirement
Application forms are available at the Adminis-

trative Office from early December.

*

Research Institutes and Centers
The Literary Materials Research Institute
For Further Information
Undergraduate and Graduate Admission
Administrative Office, Jissen Women's University, 4-1-1 Osakaue, Hino-shi, Tokyo 191 ☎ 0425–85–0311

Jobu University
(Jobu Daigaku)
634 Toyazuka-machi, Isesaki-shi, Gumma 372
☎ 0270–32–1011

Faculty
   Profs. 26   Assoc. Profs. 17
   Assist. Profs. Full–time 15; Part–time 48
Number of Students
   Undergrad. 1, 943
Library 62, 000 volumes

Outline and Characteristics of the University
   Jobu University was founded in 1986 by the late Sadao Mitsumata. At present, Kenichi Mitsumata, who has been in foreign countries for ten years, is the chairman of the board of directors. The university has two campuses. The Department of Commercial Science is in Isesaki City and the Department of Management and Information Science is in Shin-machi, both of which are about 55 miles north of Tokyo.
   Being small in size, the students become closely acquainted with their professors and the university has the advantage of maintaining friendly relationships between students and professors. Education at the university places its emphasis on seminars and courses of study pursued through discussions. Another characteristic is the fact that the university has always been on good terms with local communities.
   Our university is open to foreign youths willing to contribute to international relationship through better understanding. We always provide careful counseling as well as academic assistance.

UNDERGRADUATE PROGRAMS

Faculty of Commercial Science (Freshmen Enrollment: 200)
   Department of Commercial Science
   Course of Commercial Science and AccountingAccounting, Bookkeeping, Business Administration, Business Morphology, Business Organization, Business Organization, Commercial Law, Communication and Transportation, Economic History, Economic Policy, Economics, Economics of Commerce, Economic Statistics, Finance, Financial Management, Financial Management, History of Commerce,

History of Economic Principles, Information Science, Insurance, International Economics, Marketing, Monetary Theory, Programing, Programing Language, Small and Medium Businesses, Statistics, System Engineering, Tax Law
Faculty of Management and Information Science (Freshmen Enrollment: 200)
   Department of Management and Information Science
   Course of Information ProcessingAccounting, Algebra, Business Management, Business Morphology, Communication and Transportation, Computer Science, Cost Accounting, Economics, Financial Management, History of Business Management Theory, History of Economy, Industrial Engineering, Information Engineering, Information Management, Information Mathematics, Information Retrieval, Information Science, Insurance, International Economy, Japanese History of Business Management, Management Mathematics, Marketing, Mathematical Statistics, Operating System, Personnel Management, Planned Economy, Programing, Programing Language, Small and Medium Businesses, System Engineering

Foreign Student Admission
   Qualifications for Applicants
   Standard Qualifications Requirement
   Examination at the University
   The same entrance examination as Japanese applicants. A written test and an interview. Special considerations, however, will be given to foreign applicants according to the conditions of application.
   Documents to be Submitted When Applying
   Standard Documents Requirement
   The application form and the prospectus of registration will be available from early September.
   Applications period: November 1.

   Qualifications for Transfer Students
   Those who have finished the course of liberal arts (two years) in a Japanese university.
   Examination for Transfer Students
   Written examinations and an interview
   Documents to be Submitted When Applying
   Standard Documents Requirement
*
Facilities/Services for Foreign Students
   The professor in charge or student office will take part in consultation.
For Further Information
   Undergraduate Admission
Admission Office, Planning and Information Division, Jobu University, 270 Shin-machi, Tano-gun, Gumma 370-13 ☎ 0274–42–1183 ext. 333

Josai University
(Josai Daigaku)

1–1 Keyakidai, Sakado-shi, Saitama 350–02
☎ 0492–86–2233

Faculty
   Profs.   59   Assoc. Profs.   58
   Assist. Profs.   Full–time   23; Part–time   176
   Res. Assocs.   38
Number of Students
   Undergrad.   6, 927   Grad.   53
Library   320, 000 volumes

Outline and Characteristics of the University

   Josai University was founded in the spring of 1965. The former Chancellor, the late Mikio Mizuta, a liberal statesman and advocate of humanism, founded this place of education on the principle that "the pursuit of studies is not for the sake of studies in themselves but as a means towards the formation of virtues." Consequently, the whole University is dedicated to educating young minds so that they may find what they can do for the world, both in the present and in the future. This creed has over the years evolved into an academic tradition, which has served to send forth a wealth of capable talent into the world.

   The spacious campus is continually filled with students enthusiastic both to learn and become involved in extracurricular activities. Their energy contributes to a beaming academic atmosphere. A graduate school has been established in the economics and pharmacy departments, with many Master's and Doctor's degree students graduating every year.

   The campus of Josai University extends over about 270, 000m², almost inconceivably spacious for people accustomed to urban life, and is surrounded by forests and streams in a natural setting. The path lined with keyaki, the well known symbol of Josai University, and the main university building surrounded by fresh verdure give a never forgotten impression. Many students decide to enter Josai, smitten by the fresh atmosphere bubbling with vitality.

   It is only one hour from Ikebukuro. Its environment of irreplaceable value where studies and sports prevail is far different from the hustle and bustle of the city. City dwellers that have scant opportunities to enjoy nature have the chance to experience the change of the four seasons, considering the academic years here as one of life's luxuries.

UNDERGRADUATE PROGRAMS

College of Economics (Freshmen Enrollment: 800)
   Department of Business Administration
Auditing, Bookkeeping, Business Analysis, Business Organization, Commercial Science, Cost Analysis, History of Management, Human Organization, Industrial Psychology, Management, Managerial Accounting, Managerial and Labor Relations, Marketing, Modern Enterprise, Personnel Management, Programming, Quantitative Methods for Business Management, Small Business, Tax Accounting
   Department of Economics
Business Fluctuations, Econometrics, Economic Geography, Economic Policies, Economics, Financial Policy, History of Economics, History of Economics in the Western World, History of Economic Thoughts, International Economics, Labor Economy, Management Analysis, Mathematics for Economics, Technology and Industry, Transportation, Urban Problems

College of Pharmacy (Freshmen Enrollment: 240)
   Department of Pharmaceutics
   Department of Pharmacy
Analytical Chemistry in Pharmacy, Analytical Physics, Biochemistry, Cosmetics, History of Pharmacy, Medicinal Botany, Microbiology, Pathology, Pharmaceutical Chemistry, Pharmaceutical Manufacturing, Pharmacology, Physical Chemistry in Pharmacy, Physiology, Radiochemistry

College of Science (Freshmen Enrollment: 160)
   Department of Chemistry
Analytical Chemistry, Biochemistry, High Polymer Chemistry, Inorganic Chemistry, Isomer Chemistry, Organic Chemistry, Physical Chemistry, Surface Chemistry
   Department of Mathematics
Algebra, Calculus, Computer and Mathematics, Geometry, Linear Algebra, Mathematical Statistics, Mathematics in Computer, Statistics, Topology

Foreign Student Admission
   Qualifications for Applicants
      Standard Qualifications Requirement
   Examination at the University
   1.   Selection by examination papers.
   2.   Selection by a thesis and interview in Japanese.
   Documents to be Submitted When Applying
      Standard Documents Requirement

GRADUATE PROGRAMS

Graduate School of Economics (First Year Enrollment : Master's 10)
   Divisions
Economic Policy, Economics
Graduate School of Pharmacy (First Year Enrollment : Master's 24, Doctor's 6)
   Division
Pharmacy

Foreign Student Admission
   Qualifications for Applicants
Master's Program

Standard Qualifications Requirement
Doctor's Program
   Standard Qualifications Requirement
   Examination at the University
Master's Program
   A written examination and an interview.
Doctor's Program
   1. Foreign language (English or German)
   2. Explanation of Master's thesis and questions
   Documents to be Submitted When Applying
   Standard Documents Requirement
   Applicants belonging to government offices or private companies must submit Permit for Examination from the employer.

*

Research Institutes and Centers
Center for Inter-Cultural Studies and Education, Information Processing Center, Instrumentation Center, Isotope Center
For Further Information
Undergraduate and Graduate Admission
Entrance Examination and Publicity Section, Josai University, 1-1 Keyakidai, Sakado-shi, Saitama 350-02 ☎ 0429-86-2233

Juntendo University
(Juntendo Daigaku)

2-1-1 Hongo, Bunkyo-ku, Tokyo 113
☎ 03-813-3111

Faculty
   Profs. 79   Assoc. Profs. 71
   Assist. Profs. Full-time 132; Part-time 94
   Res. Assocs. 329
Number of Students
   Undergrad. 1,242   Grad. 119
Library 208,666 volumes

Outline and Characteristics of the University
   The history of the University dates back to 1838, when Taizen Sato (1804-1872), after having studied Dutch medicine in Nagasaki (1835-1838), founded a private school in Edo (now Tokyo). While teaching medicine, he opened his library to many medical personnel so that they could make use of it. In 1843, Sato was invited to Sakura (in present Chiba Prefecture) by a feudal lord. He settled there and conducted classes in medicine. He named the private school there Juntendo. A large number of students came from all over the country to study at Juntendo. This was the origin of today's University.
   The University, as successor to the Juntendo Medical School and as a leader in introducing European medicine to Japan, is mindful of its long history and tradition and continues to strive to attain high goals.
   The University consists of the School of Medicine and the School of Health and Physical Educa-

tion.
   The School of Medicine, conscious of its proud history and long tradition, always strives toward the ideal relationship between medicine and its practitioners and educates the students with this intent. The length of study at the School of Medicine is six years. The first two years are spent in the premedical school at Inba, while the next four years are at the medical school in Hongo.
   The School of Health and Physical Education aims to train leaders in health and physical education with a background in medical science through constant and close communication with the School of Medicine. Juntendo can claim this as a truly unique feature of the University.
   The objectives of the University are to educate students to be good doctors and physical educators with sufficient knowledge of medicine through the cooperation of both schools; to cultivate doctors and physical educators who are both able and knowledgeable, who have a mature character, and who are eager to continue educating themselves throughout their lives; to educate students who have an active interest in programs of postgraduate education and in meeting the needs of society.
   The University Hospitals include Juntendo Hospital, situated in Bunkyo-ku, Tokyo; Juntendo Izunagaoka Hospital, located in Tagata District, Shizuoka; and Urayasu Hospital in Urayasu City, Chiba. These hospitals provide educational facilities for undergraduate clinical training and graduate medical training.
   Juntendo University Hospital, the oldest and one of the largest medical institutions in Japan, provides the latest medical treatment and services, with 1,020 beds, of which 15 are for psychoneurotic patients. There are 2,356 hospital staff members and, on an average day, Juntendo treats nearly 2,430 outpatients and 874 inpatients.

UNDERGRADUATE PROGRAMS

School of Health and Physical Education (Freshmen Enrollment: 280)
Department of Health Education
Administration of Physical Education, Anatomy, Apparatus Gymnastics, Athletics, Ball Games, Basic Movements, Biochemistry and Nutrition, Combatives, Environmental Health, Exercise Physiology, Health Care Administration, Health Education, Medical Science, Physical Education, Physiology, Psychology, Recreation, Sociology, Sports Medicine
School of Medicine (Freshmen Enrollment: 90)
Department of Medicine
Anatomy, Anesthesiology, Bacteriology, Biochemistry, Blood Transfusion, Clinical Pathology, Dermatology, Forensic Medicine, Hygiene, Immunology, Internal Medicine (Cardiology, Gastroenterology, Respiratory Diseases, Nephrology and Rheumatology), Medical Care Administration, Medical Educa-

tion, Medical History, Neurology, Neurosurgery, Obstetrics and Gynecology, Ophthalmology, Orthopaedic Surgery, Otorhinolaryngology, Parasitology, Pathology, Pediatrics, Pediatric Surgery, Pharmacology, Physiological Chemistry, Physiology, Plastic Surgery, Psychiatry, Public Health, Radiology, Surgery, Thoracic Surgery, Urology

GRADUATE PROGRAMS

Graduate School of Health and Physical Education (First Year Enrollment : Master's 21)
  Divisions
Environmental Health, Health Care Administration, Physical Education, School Health, Science of Coaching, Science of Physical Fitness, Sports Medicine
Graduate School of Medicine (First Year Enrollment : Doctor's 31)
  Divisions
Medicine, Pathology, Physiology, Social Medicine, Surgery

*

Research Institutes and Centers
Medical Ultrasonic Research Center
For Further Information
  Undergraduate and Graduate Admission
Administrative Office, Juntendo University, 2-1-1 Hongo, Bunkyo-ku, Tokyo 113 ☎ 03–813–3111 ext. 3220

Kagawa Nutrition College
(Joshi Eiyo Daigaku)

3-9-21 Chiyoda, Sakado-shi, Saitama 350–02
☎ 0492–83–2126

Faculty
  Profs. 34   Assoc. Profs. 19
  Assist. Profs. Full–time 2; Part–time 20
  Res. Assocs. 28
Number of Students
  Undergrad. 1, 283   Grad. 10
Library 57, 514 volumes

Outline and Characteristics of the College
  Kagawa Nutrition College or Joshi Eiyo Daigaku was founded in 1961 by Kagawa Eiyo Gakuen, an Educational Foundation with Aya Kagawa as its Chairperson of the Board of Directors. At the time of its foundation, the College comprised the Faculty of Home Economics including a Food and Nutrition Course in it. The Faculty was revised and renamed the Faculty of Nutrition in 1965. This was the first of its kind offered in private colleges in Japan. An Evening Course was added in 1967, and the Graduate Faculty of Nutrition Sciences was founded in 1969. The Food and Nutrition Course was renamed

the Division of Applied Nutrition. And the Department of Nutrition Sciences was formed under the Undergraduate Faculty of Nutrition, consisting of two divisions; Applied Nutrition, mentioned above, and Nutrition Sciences in 1974. In 1980 the Department of Health and Nutrition was founded with the same Faculty.
  Kagawa Nutrition College offers its students a technical, professional training as well as knowledge of high standard in the field of nutrition sciences. They receive the foremost information of our time in health and nutrition through lectures, experiments and practices. Thus they can start their life in society, upon graduation, by being their communities' model in leading a healthy life through their own diet and other disciplines, whether they are dietitians, nutritionists, teachers or medical technologists.
  The campus is situated in Sakado, Saitama Prefecture, a city of 50, 000 people, 33 km away from Tokyo. Being small in size and open for women, the College has enjoyed friendly relationshps between teachers and students. This continues even after the students have graduated. They visit their former teachers asking·for up to date technical advice. The unique field of study also attracts much attention in the local communities. The College tries to serve this interest through various seminars and the open-house at the annual College festival.

UNDERGRADUATE PROGRAMS

Faculty of Nutrition (Freshmen Enrollment: 300)
  Department of Health and Nutrition
Adult Health, Clinical Nutrition, Epidemiology, Food Science and Nutrition Administration, Health Care Management, Human Ecology, Hygiene, Maternal and Child Health, Nutrition, Public Health Nutrition
  Department of Nutrition Sciences
  Division of Applied Nutrition
Food Sciences, Health Sciences (Environmental Health, Food Administration, Epidemiology, Health Administration), Human Physiology, Nutrition Sciences, Practical Nutritional Activities, Theory of Cooking
  Division of Nutrition Sciences
Basic Nutritional Sciences, Food Sciences, Human Life Studies, International Nutrition Sciences, Science of Physical Exercises

Foreign Student Admission
  Qualifications for Applicants
  Standard Qualifications Requirement
  1. Those who do not possess Japanese nationality.
  2. Those who are 18 years of age or older and have obtained the legal Baccalaureate
  3. Those who have taken the Japanese Language Proficiency Test (Level I) and General Examination for Foreign Students (Science).

4. Those who have stayed in Japan over two years or completed their high school education in Japan must follow the same admission procedure as Japanese applicants.
Examination at the College
An interview
Date : February 14. Place : Komagome Campus.
Documents to be Submitted When Applying
Standard Documents Requirement
Following documents are also required.
1. Certificates or certified true copy of the legal Baccalaureate Qualification, if applicable.
2. Certificates of the Japanese Language Proficiency Test and General Examination for Foreign Students.
Application Period : January 23 to February 3, 1989.
Announcement of Successful Applicants : February 18.
Period of Entrance Procedures : February 20 to 27.

Qualifications for Transfer Students
Those who have completed the undergraduate studies at a college or a junior college abroad
Examination for Transfer Students
The same as freshman enrollment.
Documents to be Submitted When Applying
Standard Documents Requirement

GRADUATE PROGRAMS

Graduate Faculty of Nutrition Sciences (First Year Enrollment : Master's 10)
Division
Nutrition Sciences

Foreign Student Admission
Qualifications for Applicants
Master's Program
Standard Qualifications Requirement
Applicants must be non-Japanese
Examination at the College
Master's Program
A written examination and an intrview.
Date: January 24 and 25. Place: Sakado Campus.
Announcement of Successful Applicants: January 27. Period of Entrance Procedures: Jan. 31 to Feb. 10.
Documents to be Submitted When Applying
Standard Documents Requirement
Following documents are also required.
1. A letter of recommendation by the embassy or legation in Japan of the country concerned, or by an organization deemed proper by the College authorities.
2. A personal history with the record of all job experiences.
3. A letter of permission for the applicant's application from the superviser of her working office or from the dean of the applicant's graduate school if she is currently enrolled.

Application Period: January 12 to 20, 1989

*

For Further Information
Undergraduate and Graduate Admission
Admissions Office, Kagawa Nutrition College, 3–9–21 Chiyoda, Sakado-shi, Saitama 350–02 ☎ 0492–83–2126

Kagoshima Keizai University
(Kagoshima Keizai Daigaku)

8850 Shimofukumoto-cho, Kagoshima-shi, Kagoshima 891-01 ☎ 0992-61-3211

Faculty
Profs. 30   Assoc. Profs. 39
Assist. Profs. Full–time 22; Part–time 66
Res. Assoc. 1
Number of Students
Undergrad. 3, 480
Library 182, 958 volumes

Outline and Characteristics of the University
Kagoshima University of Economics and Sociology was originally established as Kagoshima Higher School of Commerce in 1932. Thereafter, in accordance with the reorganization of the Academic Institute in 1950, it was renamed as Kagoshima Junior College of Economics. Then, in April of 1960, it was reorganized into Kagoshima College of Economics, consisting of two Departments: the Department of Economics and the Department of Business Administration. In 1982, to celebrate the Anniversary of half a century since its establishment, the Faculty of Sociology consisting of the Department of Industrial Sociology and the Department of Social Welfare was opened.

The University campus counting nearly 330, 000 m² is wider than most of the other campuses in Kyushu. It provides an enjoyable learning environment, allowing the students to pursue extra- as well as inner-curricular activities on the campus of the green field under a clear and clean sky, facing Mt. Sakurajima across Kagoshima-bay.

UNDERGRADUATE PROGRAMS

Faculty of Economics (Freshmen Enrollment: 400)
Department of Business Administration
Accounting, Business Economics, Commerce
Department of Economics
Economic History, Economics, Political Economy
Faculty of Sociology (Freshmen Enrollment 240)
Department of Industrial Sociology
Industrial Sociology, Mass Communication, Social Survey
Department of Social Welfare
Methods of Social Welfare, Social Security, Social Welfare

Foreign Student Admission
  Qualifications for Applicants
    Standard Qualifications Requirement
                    ✳
Research Institutes and Centers
Institute for Regional Studies
For Further Information
  Undergraduate Admission
Entrance Examination Information Section, Educational Office, Kagoshima University of Economics and Sociology, 8850 Shimofukumoto-cho, Kagoshima-shi, Kagoshima 891-01 ☎ 0992-61-3211 ext. 209

Kagoshima Women's College
(Kagoshima Joshi Daigaku)

1904 Uchi, Hayato-cho, Aira–gun, Kagoshima
899-51   ☎ 0995-43-1111

UNDERGRADUATE PROGRAMS

Faculty of Literature (Freshmen Enrollment: 200)
  Department of English Literature
  Department of Human Relations
  Department of Japanese Literature

Kamakura Women's College
(Kamakura Joshi Daigaku)

1420 Iwase, Kamakura–shi, Kanagawa 247
☎ 0467–44–2111

Faculty
  Profs. 33   Assoc. Profs. 6
  Assist. Profs. Full–time 24; Part–time 26
  Res. Assocs. 14
Number of Students
  Undergrad. 959
Library   76, 617 volumes

Outline and Characteristics of the College
  On April 1, 1989, Keihin Women's College was renamed as Kamakura Women's College.
  Kamakura Women's College was named for the old cultural city of Kamakura and reorganized in order to complete the plan for a continuous education from Kindergarten to College and contribute to the cultural development of Kamakura.
  The College was established in 1959. It presently consists of the Faculty of Home Economics which is composed of two department, the Department of Child Study and the Department of Domestic Science.
  It was originally founded in 1943 as the Keihin

Women's Domestic and Physical Science School. Subsequently, the following college and schools were added: a junior college (Domestic Science Course and Child Study Course), a senior high school, a junior high school, a primary school, and a kindergarten. The primary school was founded in 1951 and the others in 1950. At present, they are located on the same campus. There are 3, 771 people directly associated with the school: 959 college students, 904 junior college students, 1, 176 senior high school students, 413 junior high school students, 225 primary school children, 94 kindergarteners, and 212 faculty and staff members. This situation enables close communication between teachers and students, and gives the campus a homey atmosphere.
  The College is known as a women's college that maintains Japanese culture. The fundamental spirit of the College is "to live on gratitude and service". The College lays much stress on aesthetics and culture, and also pays attention to musical education. The College Chorus is active at home as well as abroad.
  The College is located in Kamakura City which adjoins the southern part of Yokohama City (population 3, 137, 287). Kamakura was the military capital of Japan during the Medieval period. Kamakura (population 176, 328) is now famous for its long history and natural beauty. A large number of foreigners visit this ancient city. Kamakura Women's College is the only one in Kamakura City.

UNDERGRADUATE PROGRAMS

Faculty of Home Economics (Freshmen Enrollment: 230)
  Department of Child Study
  Child Culture and Nursery Nurses Training Program
  Kindergarten Teachers Training Program
  Primary School Teachers Training Program
Childhood Diet, Childhood Health, Child Psychology, Child Welfare, Clinical Psychology, Nursing, Pedology, Social Welfare, Teaching Materials Survey, Theories in Education
  Department of Domestic Science
  Administrators of Ordinary Dieticians Training Program
  Domestic Science Teachers Training Program
Biochemistry, Clothing Material, Cookery Science, Dietary Counseling, Dress Making, Home Design, Home Economics, Home Management, Home Science, Mental Hygiene, Microbiology, Nutrition, Pathology, Physiology
                    ✳
For Further Information
  Undergraduate Admissions
Instruction Department, Kamakura Women's College, 1420 Iwase, Kamakura–shi, Kanagawa 247
☎ 0467–44–2111

Kanagawa Dental College
(Kanagawa Shika Daigaku)

82 Inaoka–cho, Yokosuka–shi, Kanagawa 238
☎ 0468–25–1500

Faculty
    Profs. 33   Assoc. Profs. 21
    Assist. Profs. Full–time 37; Part–time 95
    Res. Assocs. 144
Number of Students
    Undergrad. 976   Grad. 56
Library 102, 055 volumes

Outline and Characteristics of the College
Kanagawa Dental College, located in the center of the beautiful seacoast known as Shonan, is favored by mountains, seas, and a mild climate, providing an appropriately quiet atmosphere in which to study. To date, the college has sent into the world nearly 3, 000 graduates. Considering the short history of the College, which was established in 1964, the number of graduates bears witness to the fact that the College has observed its educational ideals: pride in accomplishment and the mastering of advanced academic principles and techniques.

Under the old system of education, Nihon Women's Dental School was the first dental school to offer training to females. Subsequently, the school adopted a co–educational system and was established as the present Kanagawa Dental College.

The College takes aim toward the future, pursuing new ideals in dental education. In so doing, the College hopes to fulfill society's growing interest and concern for dental service, conduct educational activities conducive to the advancement of dentistry, and contribute to the development of dental research. The College offers a liberal arts and sciences course, and basic sciences and clinical course. From an educational point of view, these three courses should be synthetically and organically linked with each other, thereby producing a well–rounded curriculum. This curriculum takes six years to complete and promises to produce dentists well–equipped to handle the challenges of society.

UNDERGRADUATE PROGRAMS

Faculty of Dentistry (Freshmen Enrollment: 160)
    Department of Dentistry
Anatomy, Anesthesiology, Biochemistry, Dental Diagnostics, Dental Engineering, Dental Pharmacology, Endodontics, Histology, Internal Medicine, Legal Medicine, Oral Anatomy, Oral Bacteriology, Oral Biochemistry, Oral Histology, Oral Hygienics, Oral Pathology, Oral Physiology, Oral Surgery, Orthodontics, Pediatric Dentistry, Periodontics, Physiology, Prosthetic Dentistry, Radiology, Restorative Dentistry, Sitology, Surgery

Foreign Student Admission
    Qualifications for Applicants
        Standard Qualifications Requirement
    Examination at the College
        There being no special entrance examination system for foreign student at the college, applicants are required to take the regular entrance exam conducted by the college.
    Documents to be Submitted When Applying
        Standard Documents Requirement
        Documents pledging to observe school regulations, and attesting to the student's ability to pay the tuition and other necessary expenses are also required. (These are the attached forms prescribed by the college.)

GRADUATE PROGRAMS

Graduate School of Dentistry (First Year Enrollment : Doctor's 18)
    Divisions
Basic Dentistry, Clinical Dentistry

Foreign Student Admission
    Qualifications for Applicants
Doctor's Program
    1. A graduate of a dental college of the faculty of dentistry at a university.
    2. A graduate of a medical college or the faculty of medicine at a university.
        (In this case applicants must have majored in Oral Surgery of Basic Dental Science or Clinical Dental Science at a college, university.)
    3. Those who have graduated from a college, university in a foreign country and are proven equivalent to the above mentioned articles.
    Examination at the College
Doctor's Program
    Past records about subjects of special written tests on two foreign languages (among English, German and French), and both written and oral tests on subjects of special study.
    Documents to be Submitted When Applying
        Standard Documents Requirement
        A document pledging to observe the school regulations

*

Research Institutes and Centers
College Hospital
For Further Information
    Undergraduate and Graduate Admission
Administrative Office, Faculty of Dentistry Admission Office, Kanagawa Dental College, 82 Inaoka–cho, Yokosuka–shi, Kanagawa 238
☎ 0468–25–1500 ext. 204

Kanagawa Institute of Technology

(Kanagawa Koka Daigaku)

1030 Shimo–ogino, Atsugi–shi, Kanagawa 243–02
☎ 0462–41–1211

Faculty
    Profs. 75   Assoc. Profs 40
    Assist. Profs. Full–time 15; Part–time 109
    Res. Assocs. 25
Number of Students
    Undergrad. 33, 420
Library 104, 000 volumes

Outline and Characteristics of the University

Ikujiro Nakabe, a major figure in the development of the Japanese fishing industry, always embraced high ideals and aspired to improve Japanese education as well. He believed that "sending talented people out into society for the growth of the nation will lead to the prosperity of humankind; for this reason, equal opportunity in education must be made a reality." Inheriting this conviction, Mr. Kenkichi Nakabe, former chairman of the board of directors of the institute, established the Nakabe Scholarship Fund. In April 1963, during the postwar period of economic growth, he founded the predecessor of the Kanagawa Institute of Technology, Ikutoku Technical High School.

The Japanese economy since that time has developed rapidly, requiring talented people with knowledge of more advanced technology. In January 1975, the high school became Ikutoku Industrial College, to meet the demands of the time. Then in 1986, the Department of Mechanical Systems Engineering and the Department of Information and Computer Engineering were established to meet the needs of an information-oriented society. In April 1988, the college, renamed Kanagawa Institute of Technology, made a new start.

As this history shows, the school has always grown with the times, while the educational ideology of training "engineers who will make an immediate practical contribution to society on the job site" has remained the same since its establishment. Finally, we are now aiming at training engineers with emphasis on the future need for increasingly advanced technology for processing and disseminating information.

UNDERGRADUATE PROGRAMS

Faculty of Engineering

Department of Computer Science
Analog Circuits, Business Data Processing, Communication Engineering, Computer Control, Computer Networks, Computer Systems, Control Engineering, Data Communications, Data Structures, Digital Circuits, Electrical Equipment Control, Electric Circuit Theory, Electronic Computers, Electronic Measurements, Image Information Processing, Information Mathematics, Information Theory, Introductory Artificial Intelligence, Introductory Information Mathematics, Language Processors, Logical Design, Machine Language, Mechanical Engineering, Microprocessor Applications, Numerical Analysis, Operations Ressarch, Pattern Information Processing, Peripheral Devices, Programming, Simulation Technology, System Program, Systems Engineering

Department of Electrical Engineering
Electrical and Electronic Engineering Course
Algebra, Analysis, Applied Electromotion, Colloquium, Control Engineering, Electrical and Electronic Experimentation, Electrical Measurements, Electric Circuit Theory, Electric Device Design and Illustration, Electric Generation Engineering, Electric Generation Equipment Engineering, Electric Machinery, Electric Materials, Electric Power Systems Engineering, Electric Power Systems Engineering, Electrochemistry, Electromagnetic Measurement, Electromagnetic Theory, Electronic Circuits, Electronic Computers, Electronic Devices, Geometry, Lighting and Electric Heating, Logical Design, Mathematics for Electricity, Modern Physics, Numerical Analysis, Physics Laboratory, Power Distribution Engineering, Power Electronics, Programming, Regulation and Installation of Electrics, Statistics, Telecommunications Engineering, Transmission Circuit Networks

Telecommunications Course
Acoustic Engineering, Algebra, Analysis, Applied Electronics, Colloquium, Control Engineering, Electric and Electronic Experimentation, Electric Circuit Theory, Electric Machinery, Electric Materials, Electric Power Systems Engineering, Electromagnetic Measurement, Electromagnetic Theory, Electronic Computers, Electronic Device Design and Illustration, Electronic Devices, Electronic Measurements, Geometry, Introduction to Information Theory, Logical Design, Mathematics for Electricity, Modern Physis, Numerical Analysis, Physics Laboratory, Programming, Radio Engineering, Statistics, System Programming, Telecommunications Engineering, Transmission Circuit Networks

Department of Industrial Chemistry
Industrial Chemist Course
Algebra, Analysis, Analytical Chemistry, Analytical Chemistry Laboratory, Biochemistry, Bionics, Biophysical Chemistry, Catalytic Chemistry, Chemical Engineering, Chemical Engineering Laboratory, Chemical Industry Economics, Chemical Reaction Engineering, Chemical Thermodynamics, Computer Science, Device Design and Drawing, Electrical Engineering, Electromagnetic Materials, Fermentation Engineering, General Chemistry Laboratory, Geometry, Industrial Inorganic Chemistry, Industrial Or-

ganic Chemistry, Inorganic Chemistry, Inorganic Reactions, Instrumental Analysis, Introduction to Biotechnology, Introduction to Environmental Engineering, Introduction to Fine Chemicals, Introductory Chemical Engineering, Material Science, Mechanical Engineering, Metallic Materials, Modern Physics, New Materials, Numerical Methods in Industrial Chemistry, Organic Chemistry, Patent Law, Physical Chemistry, Physical Chemistry Laboratory, Physics Laboratory, Polymer Chemistry, Process Physical Chemistry, Production Engineering, Quantum Chemistry, Statistics, Synthetic Chemistry Laboratory, Synthetic Organic Chemistry, Transport Phenomena

Material Chemistry Course

Algebra, Analysis, Analytical Chemistry, Analytical Chemistry Laboratory, Biochemistry, Bionics, Biophysical Chemistry, Catalytic Chemistry, Ceramic Materials, Chemical Industry Economics, Chemical Reaction Engineering, Chemical Thermodynamics, Computer Science, Electrical Engineering, Electromagnetic Materials, Fermentation Engineering, General Chemistry Laboratory, Geometry, Industrial Inorganic Chemistry, Industrial Organic Chemistry, Inorganic Chemistry, Inorganic Reactions, Instrumental Analysis, Introduction to Biotechnology, Introduction to Environmental Engineering, Introduction to Fine Chemicals, Introductory Chemical Engineering, Materials Chemistry, Material Science, Mechanical Engineering, Metallic Materials, Modern Physics, New Materials, Numerical Methods in Industrial Chemistry, Organic Chemistry, Patent Law, Physical Chemistry, Physical Chemistry Laboratory, Physics Laboratory, Polymer Chemistry, Polymer Materials, Process Physical Chemistry, Production Engineering, Quantum Chemistry, Statistics, Synthetic Chemistry Laboratory, Synthetic Organic Chemistry

Department of Mechanical Engineering

Energy Engineering Course

Production Engineering Course

Algebra, Analysis, Applied Thermodynamics, Automatic Control, Automatic Production Machines, Automotive Engineering, Computer Design and Drawing, Computer Programming, Elasticity of Plastic Solids, Electric Power Engineering, Energy Engineering, Environmental Presservation, Ergonomics, Factory Tours, Flow Mechanics and Workshop, Fluid Dynamics, Fluid Engineering, Fluid Machinery, Geometry, Heat Control Engineering, Heat Transfer Engineering, Industrial Dynamics, Industrial Mathematics, Instrumentation Technology, Internal Combustion Engines, Introduction to Chemical Engineering, Introduction to Electrical Engineering, Machinery, Machinery Mathematics, Machine Tools, Material Dyanmics, Materials Engineering, Mechanical and Electrical Engineering, Mechanical Design, Mechanical Design and Drawing, Mechanical Drawing, Mechanical Dynamics, Mechanical Technology, Modern Physics, Nuclear Engineering, Numerical Analysis,

Patent Law, Pattern Processing Workshop, Physics Laboratory, Plastic Solids Processing Technology, Precision Processing Technology, Production Engineering, Refrigeration and Air Conditioning, Resource Engineering, Special Lectures in Mechanical Engineering, Statistics, Steam Engineering, Strength of Materials, Technological Theory, Thermodynamics

Department of Mechanical Systems Engineering

Algebra, Analysis, Applied Computer Programming, Automated Production Systems, Computer-Aided Design (CAD), Computer-Aided Manufacturing (CAM), Computer Graphics, Computer Programming, Control Engineering, Electric and Electronic Circuits, Flow Mechanics and Workshop, Fluid System Engineering, Geometry, Heat Transfer Systems Engineering, Instrumentation Electronics, Material Dynamics, Material Engineering, Mathematics for Systems, Mechanical Design and Drawing, Mechanical Drawing, Mechanical Dynamics, Mechanical System Engineering, Mechanical Systems Design, Mechanical Systems Engineering, Mechanical Systems Workshop, Mechanical Technology, Microcomputers, Microprocessor Applications, Modern Physics, Numerical Analysis, Numerical Control, Numerical Dynamics, Physics Laboratory, Robotics, Sensors, Simulation Engineering, Statistics, System Engineering, Thermodynamics and Workshop, Thermo System Engineering, Vibration System Engineering

Foreign Student Admission

Qualifications for Applicants

Standard Qualifications Requirement

12 years education elsewhere. "Recommended Applicants" must provide a letter of recommendation.

Examination at the University

Recommended Applicants : mathematics, short essay writing, interview.

General Admissions Applicants : mathematics, English and science (either physics or chemistry).

Qualifications for Transfer Students

Applicants must be : (1) graduates of a technical high school by March 1989, or (2) graduates of a junior college by March 1989, or (3) officially recognized as having an education equivalent to or above (1) or (2).

Examination for Transfer Students

Mathematics and English and special subjects determined by the department they are applying to, as follows :

Department of Mechanical Engineering : Strength of materials, thermodynamics and hydraulics

Department of Electrical Engineering : Electromagnetism and electric circuits

Department of Industrial Chemistry : Organic chemistry, inorganic chemistry and physical chemistry

*

For Further Information
Undergraduate Admission
Entrance Exam Division, Office of Educational Affairs, Kanagawa Institute of Technology, 1030 Shimo–ogino Atsugi–shi, Kanagawa 243–02 ☎ 0462–41–1211

Kanagawa University
(Kanagawa Daigaku)

3–27–1 Rokkakubashi, Kanagawa–ku, Yokohama–shi, Kanagawa 221 ☎ 045–481–5661

Faculty
    Profs. 161   Assoc. Profs. 103
    Assist. Profs. Full–time 14; Part–time 353
    Res. Assocs. 39
Number of Students
    Undergrad. 12, 462   Grad. 82
Library   480, 767 volumes

Outline and Characteristics of the University
    The history of Kanagawa University starts with Yoshimori Yoneda's 1928 founding of Yokohama Academy. Yoneda, with fortitude, manliness and progressiveness as his principles, founded the academy to train trustworthy men of ability.
    Yokohama Academy became Yokohama College in accordance with an ordinance regarding Professional Schools in 1929. In 1949, the college was changed to Kanagawa University in conformity with Japan's educational system reform.
    Yokohama College started with two programs-- the law program and commercial economy. In 1930, the commercial economy program was divided into the higher commercial program and the trade program. The college thus had three programs, including the law program. These three programs became the present Faculty of Law and Faculty of Economics.
    In 1939, three engineering programs--mechanical engineering, electronics, and industrial management--were established. These were the predecessors of the present Faculty of Engineering. Yokohama College thus became a composite professional school with three engineering programs and three programs in law and economics. Yokohama College, the foundation of Kanagawa University, turned out its last graduates in 1951.
    Kanagawa University first started with two faculties (the Faculty of Commerce and Economics and the Faculty of Engineering) with five courses of study, and the night school's faculty of commerce and economy with two courses. In 1950, the University was reorganized into the two faculties of commerce and economics, and its night school respectively to the Faculty of Law and Faculty of Economics.
    In addition, the University was provided with a junior college which had programs in commerce, law. mechanical engineering, and electrical engineering. Then in 1959, the Faculty of Engineering was provided with a program in applied chemistry and a night school which had a program in mechanical engineering and a program in electrical engineering, effectively replacing the engineering programs at the junior college.
    In 1965, the Faculty of Foreign Languages was established. The faculty had a program in English Language and Literature and a Spanish Language course. In the same year the Faculty of Engineering was provided with a program in architecture. Thus our University grew to have four day faculties with ten programs and three night faculties with five programs and a junior college.
    In 1967, a graduate school was established and the degree of master and doctorate were offered in the fields of law, economics and engineering. In 1971, the graduate school established a graduate course of engineering for the degree of master.
    A Faculty of Business Admmistration and a Faculty of Science are in the process of being established and should be opened in 1989.

UNDERGRADUATE PROGRAMS

Faculty of Economics (Freshmen Enrollment: Day 590, Evening 280)
    Department of Economics
    Department of Trade
Accounting, Agricultural Economics, American Economy, Asian Economy, Auditing, Banking, Bookkeeping, Business Administration, Chinese Economy, Commerce, Cost Accounting, Current Trading Issues, Econometrics, Economic Fluctuation, Economic Geography, Economic History, Economic Philosophy, Economic Statistics, Economic Theory, European Economy, Financial Accounting, Foreign Exchange, Foreign Trade Theory, History of Commerce and Economics, Industrial Sociology, Insurance, International Finance, Japanese Economy, Labor Economics and Management, Latin American Economy, Local Finance, Management, Managerial Accounting and Finance, Marine Insurance and Transport, Marketing, Marketing and Trading, Merchandise, Modern Economics, Monetary Theory, Public Finance, Securities Markets, Small Businesses, Soviet Economy, Tax Accounting, Trade Policy, Transport, West Asian Economy

Faculty of Engineering (Freshmen Enrollment : Day 720, Evening 160)
    Department of Applied Chemistry
Analytical Chemistry, Biochemistry, Chemical Engineering, Electrophysics, Environmental Chemistry, Industrial Chemistry, Industrial Inorganic Chemistry, Inorganic Chemistry, Metallurgy, Microbiological Engineering, Organic Chemistry, Physical Chemistry, Polymer Chemistry, Quality Control, Solid State Chemistry, Theory of Functions
    Department of Architecture

Air Conditioning, Architectual Materials, Architectual Planning and Design, Building Equipment, Building Erection, City Planning, Disaster Prevention Engineering, Electrical Equipment, Environmental Engineering, Facilities Design, Fire Prevention & Fire Fighting Facilities, Foundation Structure, History of Architecture, Plumbing and Sanitation Engineering, Reinforced Concrete Construction, Steel Frame Structure, Visual Design

Department of Electrical Engineering

Acoustic Engineering, Applied Mathematics, Circuit Design and Theory, Communication Systems, Computer Organization, Computing Systems, Educational Technology, Electrical Control and Design & Drawing, Electrical & Electronic Materials, Electrical Measurements, Electric Machinery and Devices, Electromagnetics, Electromagnetic Waves & Circuits, Electronic Measurements, Electronics, Electronics Design, High Voltage Engineering, Information & Communication Theory, Linear Algebra, Power Generation, Power Transmission and Distribution, Programming Languages, Pulse & Logic Circuits

Department of Industrial Management

Conveyance Management, Cost Management, Equipment Management, Factory Planning, Human Engineering, Industrial Accounting and Management, Industrial Psychology, Information Management, Labor Management, Management Engineering and Organization, Manufacturing Process Management, Marketing, Material Management, Mathematical Statistics, Method Engineering, Operations Research, Pollution Management, Production Control and Engineering, Quality Control, Safety Management, Sales Management

Department of Mechanical Engineering

Automatic Control, Computer Aided Design and Analysis, Computers and Mechanical Engineering, Design of Machine Elements, Engineering Analysis, Fluid Dynamics and Machine, Heat Transfer, Industrial Dynamics, Internal Combustion Engine, Lubrication Engineering, Machine Design and Tool, Manufacturing Processing, Materials and Vibration, Materials Science & Engineering, Mechanical Drawings, Mechanical Dynamics, Mechanical Engineering, Mechanics of Plastic Solids, Mechanism, Mechatronics, Oil Hydraulic Engineering, Plasticity Engineering, Strengths of Materials, Thermodynamics

Faculty of Foreign Language (Freshmen Enrollment: 275)

Deperdment of Chinese

Chiaese Politics and Economics, Chinese Culture, Chinese Literature, Chiness Language, History of Chinese Science and Technology, Modern Chinese History

Department of English

American History, American Literature, British and American Society and Culture, British History, Comparative Cultures and Literature, English Linguistics, English Literature, History of American Literature, History of English Literature, History of the English Language, Literary Criticism, Phonetics

Department of Spanish

Comparative Literature, History of Latin American Literature, History of Spanish Literature, History of the Spanish Language, Spanish and Latin American Culture, Spanish and Latin American Intellectual History, Spanish Language, Spanish Literature

Faculty of Law (Freshmen Enrollment : Day 350, Evening 100)

Department of Law

Administrative Law, Bankruptcy Law, Civil Law, Commercial Law, Constitution, Criminal Law, Criminology, European Political History, Family Law, Foreign Law, History of Political Thought, Insurance Law, International Law, International Relations, Japanese Political History, Labor Law, Law of Civil Procedure, Law of Criminal Procedure, Law of Property, Law of Public Control of Business, Legal History and Philosophy, Political Science, Principles of Legal Obligation, Public Administration and Finance, Sociology of Law, Tax Law

Foreign Student Admission

Qualifications for Applicants

Foreign students are admitted through the same entrance examination procedure as Japanese students. The University also has special acceptance agreements with a number of overseas universities, and is currently preparing improved entrance procedures, to take effect in 1989.

GRADUATE PROGRAMS

Graduate School of Economics (First Year Enrollment : Master's 10, Doctor's 4)

Division

Economics

Graduate School of Engineering (First Year Enrollment : Master's 20)

Divisions

Applied Chemistry, Architecture and Building Engineering, Electrical Engineering, Mechanical Engineering

Graduate School of Law (First Year Enrollment : Master's 8, Doctor's 3)

Division

Law

Foreign Student Admissions

Qualifications for Applicants

Master's Program

    Standard Qualifications Requirement

Doctor's Program

    Standard Qualifications Requirement

Examination at the University

Master's Program

Graduate School of Economics:

    1.   Those applicants who have already entered Japan: preliminary interview based on their ex-

planation of research plans, and their language transcripts, written examination in Japanese on the applicants' major subject and in Japanese language (composition) in other foreign languages (if the applicants' research plan so warrants.)

2. Those applying from outside Japan: (a preliminary screening) explanation of research plans and their language transcripts and also a record of their Japanese language studies and, in their own hand, a statement of their reasons for wanting to enter the University, with a letter of recommendation attached.

Graduate School of Engineering:
1. Those applicants who have already entered Japan: a preliminary interview based on their explanation of research plans written and oral examinations.
2. Those applying from outside Japan: a preliminary screening based on explannation of research plans and also a personal history and a statement of their reasons for wanting to enter the University and a written examination

Graduate School of Law:
1. Written and oral examinations.
2. The written examinations are based on the applicants' major subject and language subject.
3. The test of the major subject requires applicants to summarize some literature on law or politics.
4. For the language test, applicants must select one language (English, German, or French) and complete the test questions in Japanese.
5. The focus of the oral examination will be to determine whether or not applicants have the ability to listen and speak during lectures and seminars at this graduate school.

Doctor's Program
Graduate School of Economics:
1. Applicants who have already entered Japan must have their master's thesis examined, take an oral examination and language proficiency test (composition and another foreign language).
2. Applicants from outside Japan: the preliminary selection described above and the second selection

Graduate School of Law:
The same procedures as those for the master's program.

Documents to be Submitted When Applying
Standard Documents Requirement
Graduate School of Economics (Master's Program):
1. Letter of approval from the applicant's supervisor if the applicant is employed (applicants from overseas only).
2. A statement of the applicants' reasons for wanting to enter the University, written in their own hand, with a letter of recommenda-

tion attached.
3. A record of Japanese language studies.
Graduate School of Economics (Doctor's Program):
1. A copy of the master's thesis or a copy of a paper equivalent in quality to a master's thesis.
2. A synopsis of the above paper.
3. Letter of approval from the applicant's supervisor if the applicant is employed.
Graduate School of Law (Master's & Doctor's Programs):
1. A record of Japanese language studies and a certificate of Japanese language proficiency.
2. An explanation of research plans by applicants to the master's program; and a copy of the master's thesis or a paper equivalent in quality to the master's thesis and its summary in Japanese by applicants to the doctorate program.
3. A letter of recommendation by the applicant's embassy or consulate in Japan, if applicable.

*

Research Institutes and Centers
Center for Foreign Language Studies, Information Processing Center, Institute for Humanities Research, Institute for Legal Studies, Institute for the Study of Japanese Folk Culture, Institute of Economics and Foreign Trade, Institute of International Business Institute of Technological Research, Research Institute for Information and Knowledge

For Further Information
Undergraduate and Graduate Admission
Entrance Examination Center, Kanagawa University, 3-27-1 Rokkakubashi, Kanagawa-ku, Yokohama-shi, Kanagawa 221 ☎ 045-481-5661 ext. 240

Kanazawa College of Economics
(Kanazawa Keizai Daigaku)

10-1 Ushi, Gosho-machi, Kanazawa-shi, Ishikawa 920   ☎ 0762-52-2236

Faculty
    Profs. 22   Assoc. Profs. 10
    Assist. Profs. Full-time 11; Part-time 38
Number of Students
    Undergrad. 2, 001
Library 56, 809 volumes

Outline and Characteristics of the College
Kanazawa College of Economics was founded in 1967 as part of Inaoki Educational Institution which is composed of a college, women's junior college, junior and senior high school and kindergarten.

Inaoki Educational Institution aims at consecutive education from lower to higher education. At the time of foundation in 1967, the College started with the Department of Economics, and in 1971 the evening course was established. Subsequently, in

1973 the Department of Commerce was set up. At present, the College has a freshmen enrollment of 300 and plus, the 100 for the evening course.

The educational philosophy of the College may be seen in its objectives. They are to fully acquaint our graduates with the vital economic facts of life as they relate both to the business community and to our society as a whole; to help our graduates become better human beings, at ease with their fellow members of the community; and to enlarge our graduates' individual horizons, and make them more aware of today's problems, not only economic but social and political as well.

It should be apparent by our educational philosophy that on top of emphasizing professional competency in business, the College recognizes the need to equip students with a well-rounded general education so they may become more useful citizens.

UNDERGRADUATE PROGRAMS

Faculty of Economics (Freshmen Enrollment: 300)
  Department of Commerce
Accounting, Bookkeeping, Business Management, Commercial Policy, Finance, History of Commerce, Management, Management Accounting, Marketing, Marketing Management, Personnel Management, Transportation Economics
  Department of Economics
Econometrics, Economic Policy, Fiscal Policy, History of Economics, History of Economic Theory, History of Japanese Economy, History of Western Economy, International Economics, Social Policy, Statistics, Theory of Economics

Foreign Student Admission
  Qualifications for Applicants
    Standard Qualifications Requirement
  Examination at the College
  1. Japanese and English—same as the regular Entrance Examination
  2. Interview
  Documents to be Submitted When Applying
    Standard Documents Requirement

  Qualifications for Transfer Students
    The same qualifications specified for undergraduate admission. In addition, they must have finished a two-year Liberal Arts course in either Japanese or foreign colleges or universities.
  Examination for Transfer Students
    Same as for freshman admission.
  Documents to be Submitted When Applying
    Standard Documents Requirement
                    *

Research Institutes and Centers
Center for Data Processing, Economics Institute, Human and Cultural Research Institute
For Further Information
  Undergraduate Admission

Instructions Division, Administrative Office, Kanazawa College of Economics, 10-1 Ushi, Gosho-machi, Kanazawa-shi, Ishikawa 920
☎ 0762-52-2236 ext. 211

Kanazawa Institute of Technology
(Kanazawa Kogyo Daigaku)
7-1 Ogigaoka, Nonoichi-machi, Ishikawa 921
☎ 0762-48-1100

Faculty
  Profs. 97   Assoc. Profs. 41
  Assist. Profs. Full–time 40; Part–time 29
  Res. Assocs. 16
Number of Students
  Undergrad. 6, 376   Grad. 90
Library 270, 000 volumes

Outline and Characteristics of the University
Kanazawa Institute of Technology, located in the suburbs of Kanazawa, is a coeducational, nonsectarian, privately-owned institution of technology and science and is the largest single-faculty university in Japan. The Institute was founded in 1957 as a school for radio technology engineers and developed into university status through several enlargements and renovations. Since becoming a university in 1965 it has continued to grow steadily, starting from the two Departments of Electrical Engineering and Mechanical Engineering, and gradually increasing to the present eight departments. The Graduate School of Engineering offers Doctorate and Master's programs in mechanical engineering, electronics and electrical engineering, civil engineering, and information and computer engineering. In addition, there are Master's programs in managerial engineering and in architecture. The undergraduate Faculty of Engineering consists of eight departments: mechanical engineering, electrical engineering, managerial engineering, civil engineering, architecture, electronics, information and computer engineering, and mechanical systems engineering. The Mechanical Systems Engineering Department was added in April, 1986. In addition, courses in philosophy, history, law, economics, psychology, ethics, mathematics, physics, chemistry, physical education, and foreign languages are taught under the Department of Liberal Arts.

Three slogans--"Produce a well-rounded graduate, " "Be technically innovative, " and "Respond to the needs of industry"--express the goals of education and research at Kanazawa Institute of Technology. Kanazawa itself is an old city of 430, 000 people, on the Japan Sea coast 300 kilometers northwest of Tokyo. Kanazawa is a traditional town, proud of its past, its crafts, its renowned cuisine, and its magnificent Japanese garden, Kenrokuen, a legacy of its old culture.

Throughout its history, Kanazawa Institute of Technology has had a high reputation for its progressive applications of computer and information technology to education and research. Its CAI (Computer Assisted Instruction) laboratory, in particular, was the first such facility to be installed in Japan, and is now acknowledged to be the most advanced.

Various facilities are attached to the Institute to aid its efforts in education, research, and management, including the Library Center, the Computer Center, the Educational Technology Center, the Anamizu Bay Seminar House, and the Amaike and Hakusan Athletic Centers. The Library Center, which is the latest addition, is an ambitious 21, 000m^2 structure that houses a fully automated library, an advanced audio-visual facility, an international conference room, and other modern facilities.

UNDERGRADUATE PROGRAMS

Faculty of Engineering (Freshmen Enrollment: 1, 230)

Department of Architecture
Architectural Design, Architectural Planning, Construction Engineering, Environmental Engineering in Architecture, Residential Environment Planning, Structural Engineering
Department of Civil Engineering
Civil Engineering, Conventional Design and Construction, Environmental Engineering, Materials and Construction, Structural Engineering, Systematic Design and Construction
Department of Electrical Engineering
Electrical Machinery Engineering, Electric and Electronic Materials, Electric Control Engineering, Electric Power Engineering, Electromagnetism, Electronics
Department of Electronics
Applied Information Sciences, Circuits and Systems, Communication Systems, Electronic Elements and Devices, Electronic Material Physics, Electronics
Department of Information and Computer Engineering
Computer Engineering, Computer Hardware, Computers and Communication, Computer Software, Information Engineering, Information Processing
Department of Managerial Engineering
Human Systems, Industrial Administration, Information Systems, Production Engineering, Statistical Engineering, Systems Engineering
Department of Mechanical Engineering
Fluids Engineering, Materials Science and Technology, Mechanical Vibrations and Applied Vibrations, Production Engineering and Production System, Strength of Materials and Mechanical Design, Thermal Engineering and Tribology
Department of Mechanical Systems Engineering
Control Engineering, Design Engineering, Energy Transformation Engineering, Instrumentation Engi-

neering, Materials System Engineering, Solid Mechanics

Foreign Student Admission
Qualifications for Applicants
Standard Qualifications Requirement
Examination at the University
Same as Japanese students (written exams and an interview)
Documents to be Submitted When Applying
Standard Documents Requirement
JLPT score

GRADUATE PROGRAMS

Graduate School of Engineering (First Year Enrollment : Master's 62, Doctor's 21)
Divisions
Architecture, Civil Engineering, Electrical and Electronics, Information and Computer Engineering, Managerial Engineering, Mechanical Engineering

Foreign Student Admission
Qualifications for Applicants
Master's Program
Standard Qualifications Requirement
Doctor's Program
Standard Qualifications Requirement
Examination at the University
Master's Program
Same as Japanese students (written exams and an interview)
Doctor's Program
The same procedure as the Master's program.
Documents to be Submitted When Applying
Standard Documents Requirement
JLPT score

*

Research Institutes and Centers
Computer Center, Electronic Device System Laboratory, Instructional Technology Center, Laboratory for Applied Computer Science, Laboratory for Basic Foreign Language Education, Laboratory for Environmental Science, Laboratory for Information Science, Laboratory for Instructional Technology, Laboratory for Structural Engineering, Materials System Research Laboratory, Urban Planning Research Laboratory

Facilities/Services for Foreign Students
The university will assist students in finding suitable lodging near the campus.
For Further Information
Undergraduate and Graduate Admission
International Affairs Office, Kanazawa Institute of Technology, 7-1 Ogigaoka, Nonoichi-machi, Ishikawa 921 ☎ 0762-48-1100 ext. 475

Kanazawa Medical University
(Kanazawa Ika Daigaku)

1-1 Daigaku-cho, Uchinada-machi, Kahoku-gun, Ishikawa 920-02 ☎ 0762-86-2211

Faculty
    Profs. 56   Assoc. Profs. 46
    Assist. Profs. Full–time 73; Part–time 116
    Res. Assocs. 240
Number of Students
    Undergrad. 675   Grad. 61
Library 140, 219 volumes

Outline and Characteristics of the University
    Kanazawa Medical University was founded in 1972 aiming at producing doctors with both medical proficiency and humanity.
    The campus is located on Uchinada dunes in the suburbs of Kanazawa City, overlooking the Sea of Japan and Kahoku Lagoon on either side and commanding a distant view of the Tateyama and Hakusan mountain ranges.
    The Kanazawa Medical University Hospital is constantly up-grading its facilities, equipment and capacity since it was opened in 1974 and now has 1, 020 beds.
    The Graduate School of Medicine was established in 1982, and in 1983 the Institute of Human Genetics and the Institute of Tropical Medicine were founded.
    Our university has emphasized the need to train students in small groups. In the first academic year, two small group seminars are held every week in which three to four students come to a teacher's office to conduct readings, discussions or laboratory work. The 'A' seminar teacher also acts as an adviser and gives advices on life on campus as well as academic problems. In the second and third years a medical study seminar is held every week in which six to seven students conduct laboratory work, readings or discussions mainly on such elementary medical subjects as anatomy, physiology and biochemistry.

UNDERGRADUATE PROGRAMS

Faculty of Medicine (Freshmen Enrollment: 100)
    Department of Medicine
Anatomy, Anesthesiology, Biochemistry, Clinical Pathology, Dermatology, Gerontology, Hygiene, Internal Medicine, Legal Medicine, Medical Zoology, Microbiology, Neuropsychiatry, Neurosurgery, Obstetrics and Gynecology, Ophthalmology, Oral Surgery, Orthopedic Surgery, Otolaryngology, Pathology, Pediatrics, Pediatric Surgery, Pharmacology, Physiology, Plastic and Reconstructive Surgery, Public Health, Radiology, Serology, Surgery, Thoracic and Cardiovascular Surgery, Urology

Foreign Student Admission
    Qualifications for Applicants
    Standard Qualifications Requirement
    Examination at the University
    The same as Japanese students.
    Documents to be Submitted When Applying
    Standard Documents Requirement

GRADUATE PROGRAMS

Graduate School of Medicine (First Year Enrollment : Doctor's 35)
    Divisions
Internal Medicine, Pathology, Physiology, Social Medicine, Surgery

Foreign Student Admission
    Qualifications for Applicants
Doctor's Program
    Standard Qualifications Requirement
    Examination at the University
Doctor's Program
    Written examinations in Japanese and one foreign language (English, French or German).
    Documents to be Submitted When Applying
    Standard Documents Requirement
                    *
Research Institutes and Centers
Institute of Human Genetics, Institute of Tropical Medicine
For Further Information
    Undergraduate and Graduate Admission
Section of General Affairs, Kanazawa Medical University, 1-1 Daigaku-cho, Uchinada-machi, Kahoku-gun, Ishikawa 920-02 ☎ 0762-86-2211 ext. 2411

Kanazawa Women's University
(Kanazawa Joshi Daigaku)

10 Sue–machi, Kanazawa–shi, Ishikawa 920–13 ☎ 0762–29–1181

Faculty
    Profs. 12   Assoc. Profs 3
    Assist. Profs. Full–time 6; Part–time 15
Number of Students
    Undergrad. 362
Library 79, 460 volumes

Outline and Characteristics of the University
    Kanazawa Women's University is the only university for women on the coast of the Japan Sea. Kanazawa Women's University was established in April 1987, but it carries on the long history of Kanazawa Women's Junior College. The junior college has performed for over forty years an important role in the education of women in the Hokuriku district. Kanazawa Women's University was established to

expand knowledge, promote education and cultivate the best characteristics of young women today. The spirit behind its foundation is "Love and Reason". "Love, " like the compassion of God or the mercy of Buddha, is a heart which loves all things. "Reason" means the ability to distinguish between what is good and what is bad. The goals of this university are to foster this "Love" and "Reason" in women's education and to encourage women to contribute to culture in Japan which is facing an era of internationalization.

Kanazawa Women's University is a liberal arts university with departments in Japanese Literature and English & American Literature. The University maintains an Institute of Information Processing, Oguchi Seminar House at the foot of Mt. Hakusan, and a dormitory. Computer education is one of the subjects which is emphasized in the curriculum. The entire school has nearly three hundred personal computers, thirty-three of which are available for use by university students. Special subjects, which both students majoring in Japanese literature and those majoring in English & American literature may register for, are also emphasized. For example, Comparative Literature, Children's Literature, Information Processing and so on.

The university is situated on a hill named Seishoudai in the southeastern part of kanazawa. The natural beauty of famous Sai River, abundant greenery and rolling hills provide a peaceful and scenic environment for study. Nearly half of the students attending the university are from Ishikawa Prefecture. The rest of the students are from all over Japan, from Akita to Okinawa. Kanazawa is one of only two major cities which were not destroyed in World war II. Since many historical monuments, rows of old houses and the old streets remain, students from other cities can experience the atomosphere of traditional Japan in Kanazawa.

UNDERGRADUATE PROGRAMS

Faculty of Literature (Freshmen Enrollment: 140)
Department of English & American Literature
American Literature (Poems, Novels, Critics), American Studies, Cross-Cultural Understanding, English Linguistics, English Literature (Plays, Novels).
Department of Japanese Literature
Chinese Classical Literature, History of Japanese Arts, Japanese Linguistics, Japanese Literature (Ancient, Medieval, Modern, Contemporary)

Foreign Student Admission
Qualifications for Applicants
Standard Qualifications Requirement
Final decision on all applications will be made on a case-by-case basis.

*

For Further Information

Undergraduate Admission
Director of Administration, Division of Entrance Examinations, Kanazawa Women's University, 10 Sue–machi, Kanazawa–shi, Ishikawa 920–13 ☎ 0762 –29–1181 ext. 712

Kanda University of International Studies
(Kanda-gaigo Daigaku)

1–4–1 Wakaba, Chiba–shi, Chiba 260
☎ 0472–73–1233

Faculty
Profs.　29　　Assoc. Profs　8
Assist. Profs.　Full–time　14; Part–time　48
Res. Assocs.　3
Number of Students
Undergrad.　600
Library　42, 143 volumes

Outline and Characteristics of the University
Kanda Gaigo Daigaku (Kanda University of International Studies) is a small private university dedicated to the pursuit of excellence in international studies, particularly in the study of foreign languages. At present these include English, Chinese, Spanish and Korean.

The university, accredited by the Japan Ministry of Education in December, 1986, is located at Makuhari in Chiba Prefecture. It is approximately 45 minutes by train from the centre of Tokyo, and the campus is near the Makuhari Beach and a yacht harbor.

The university enrolled its first students in April 1987. The first year saw a total of 300 students: 200 English majors, 60 Chinese, 20 Spanish and 20 Korean majors. Total enrollment is projected to reach 1, 200 in four years.

The curriculum is characterized by an approach to language which recognizes the three aspects of language study, proficiency and sensitivity to the culture of the language studied.

Our staff is international in character with professors coming not only from Japan, but also from the United States, Canada, Australia, Indonesia, China, Spain and Korea.

UNDERGRADUATE PROGRAMS

Faculty of Foreign Languages (Freshmen Enrollment: 300)
Department of Chinese
Chinese Business Correspondence, Chinese Composition, Chinese Conversation, Chinese Economy, Chinese General Chair, Chinese Linguistics, Chinese Literature, Chinese Society, History of China, History of Chinese
Department of English

American History, American Literature, British and American Literature, British and American Studies, British Literature, Business English, Comparative Study of Japanese, Current English, English and American Culture, English General Chair, English Grammar, English Linguistics, English Phonology, History of English Literature, Oceanian English Cultural Studies, Speech Communication

Department of Korean
History of Korean Literature, Korean Composition, Korean Conversation, Korean Culture, Korean General Chair, Korean Linguistics, Korean Literature, Korean Politics and Economy

Department of Spanish
Business Spanish, Current Spanish, General Condition of Modern Spain, History of Japanese and Spanish Cultural Exchange, History of Latin America, Spanish Composition, Spanish Conversation, Spanish General Chair, Spanish Grammar, Spanish History, Spanish Linguistics, Spanish Phonetics

*
Research Institutes and Centers
Bureau of Physical Culture, Inter-Cultural Communication Institute, Language Teaching Institute
For Further Information
Undergraduate Admission
Undergraduate Admissions, Admissions Office, Kanda University of International Studies, 1-4-1 Wakaba, Chiba-shi, Chiba 260 ☎ 0472-73-1233

Kansai Medical University
(Kansai Ika Daigaku)

1 Fumizono-cho, Moriguchi-shi, Osaka 570
☎ 06-992-1001

UNDERGRADUATE PROGRAMS

Faculty of Medicine (Freshmen Enrollment: 100)
Department of Medicine

GRADUATE PROGRAMS

Graduate School of Medicine (First Year Enrollment : Doctor's 50)
Divisions
Internal Medicine, Pathology, Physiology, Social Medicine, Surgery

---

Kansai University
(Kansai Daigaku)

3-3-35 Yamate-cho, Suita-shi, Osaka 564
☎ 06-388-1121

Faculty

Profs. 359   Assoc. Profs. 90
Assist. Profs. Full-time 32; Part-time 770
Res. Assocs. 45
Number of Students
Undergrad. 23,059   Grad. 601
Library 1,452,771 volumes

Outline and Characteristics of the University
Kansai University was founded as Kansai Law School in November 1886 in the large commercial city of Osaka. Its founders were six judicial officers who were in the service of the then Osaka Court of Appeal.

In the early years of the Meiji Period, the Ministry of Justice established its own law school. Western legal concepts, including the concept of human rights, were introduced to Japan by distinguished foreign scholars. The founders of Kansai University had all studied at this law school under the French jurist Boissonade de Fontarabie. The idea of individual rights and legal processes independent of the central government were new to Japan. Long after their study with Boissonade, the founders continued to feel these concepts were vital to the new Japan. They felt it their duty to popularize jurisprudence in order to inspire people with the idea of independent judiciary and human rights.

From this desire came the idea of founding a Law School. They then sought and received the assistance and cooperation of Kojima Korekata, their superior (later the Chief Justice of the Supreme Court), and Doi Michio, President of the Osaka Chamber of Commerce and Industry.

Thus Kansai Law School made its start as the first law school located in Osaka. The founders taught that law belongs to common citizens and that the citizens should protect themselves by law. Thereupon were born the academic traditions of the love of justice and freedom. Since then the institution has diversified and developed steadily thanks to the support and trust extended by the general public.

In 1905, the institution was renamed Kansai University. In 1922, the main campus was moved to present site in Suita, a suburb of Osaka, thus paving the way for later growth. With the reformation of the educational system in Japan after the Second World War, Kansai University moved over to the new-system university incorporating the four faculties of law, letters, economics, and commerce in an attempt to expand the scope for teaching.

Graduate School was established in 1950. Faculty of Engineering was founded in 1958, followed by Faculty of Sociology in 1967.

Evening classes are taught at a separate campus located in the Tenroku area of Osaka. For many years after the University was founded, it remained primarily a night school for adults. The Tenroku Campus continues to embody this important tradition dating from the earliest years of Kansai University.

At present, Kansai University has six faculties in the day course and five faculties in the evening course, plus the Graduate School with its respective faculties. The University, with its attached senior high school, junior high school, and kindergarten, has a total student body of twenty odd thousand.

UNDERGRADUATE PROGRAMS

Faculty of Commerce (Freshmen Enrollment: Day 660, Evening 80)

Department of Commerce

Accounting, Asian Economy, Auditing, Banking, Business Administration, Business Finance, Business History, Commerce, Commercial Policy, Co-operative Societies, Cost Accounting, Economic Policy, European and American Economy, Financial Accounting, Financial Statements Analysis, Foreign Exchange, History of Commerce, Industrial Relations, Insurance and Risk Management, International Trade, Latin American Economy, Management Accounting, Management Information Systems, Managerial Economics, Marketing Theory, Non-Life Insurance, Production Management, Public Finance, Public Utility Economics, Sales Management, Securities Analysis, Shipping, Soviet Economy, Stock Market, Study of Merchandise, Tax Accounting, Transportation Economics

Faculty of Economics (Freshmen Enrollment: Day 660, Evening 130)

Department of Economics

Agricultural Economics, Agricultural Economics of China, American Economic History, Commercial Economics, Econometrics, Economic Development, Economic Geography, Economic History, Economic History of Europe, Economic History of Japan, Economic Policy, Economics, History of Economic Theory, History of Economic Thought, Industrial Economics, Industrial Structures, International Economics, International Monetary Economics, Labor Economics, Macro Economic Dynamics, Macro Economics, Monetary Economics, Planned Economy, Public Economics, Public Finance, Statistics

Faculty of Engineering (Freshmen Enrollment: 1, 010)

Department of Applied Chemistry

Applied Biochemistry, Industrial Organic Chemistry, Inorganic Chemistry of Materials, Physical Chemistry, Polymer Chemistry

Department of Architecture

Architectural and Urban Planning, Architectural Design, Architectural Environmental Engineering, Architectural History, Building Materials, Environmental Engineering, History of Japanese Architecture, Structural Dynamics, Structural Mechanics

Department of Chemical Engineering

Biochemical Engineering, Chemical Engineering, Extraction Engineering, Fuel Technology, Mass Transfer, Physical Chemistry, Unit Operation

Department of Civil Engineering

Coastal Engineering, Construction Materials, Engineering Geology, Sanitation Engineering, Soil Mechanics, Structual Mechanics, Transportation Engineering

Department of Electrical Engineering

Computation Engineering, Computer Control Engineering, Electrical Circuits and Machinery, Electroacoustics, Electronic Circuits, Plasma Engineering, Power Electronics, Quantum Electronics

Department of Electronics

Digital Computers, Electrical Circuits, Electrical Materials, Electromagnetic Theory, Electronic Circuits, Information Theory, Microwave Electronics, Semiconductor Materials

Department of Industrial Engineering

Human Engineering, Management Engineering, Numerical Analysis, Personnel Administration, Quality Control, Reliability Engineering, Systems Engineering

Department of Mechanical Engineering I

Applied Physics, Aviation Engineering, Dynamics of Machinery, Engineering Materials, Manufacturing Processes, Manufacturing Technology

Department of Mechanical Engineering II

Analysis of Experimental Data, Applied Mathematics, Control Engineering, Fluid Mechanics, Mechanical Designing and Drawing, Thermal Engineering

Department of Metallurgical Engineering

Analytical Chemistry, Chemical Metallurgy, Ferrous Materials, Foundry Engineering, Foundry Materials, Metal Processing, Non-ferrous Metallic Materials, Physical Metallurgy, Plastic Theory of Metals, Welding Engineering

Faculty of Law (Freshmen Enrollment: Day 660, Evening 130)

Department of Law

Administrative Law, American Law, Chinese Legal History, Civil Law, Commercial Law, Constitutional Law, Criminal Law, International Law, Japanese Legal History, Labor Law, Private International Law, Tax Law

Department of Politics

Diplomatic History, History of European Politics, History of Japanese Politics, History of Political Theories, Legal Philosophy, Political and Governmental Organization, Political Philosophy, Political Psychology, Political Theory, Public Administration, Theory of Political Process

Faculty of Letters (Freshmen Enrollment: Day 660, Evening 80)

Department of Chinese Literature

Chinese Literature and Chinese Language, Chinese Philology, History of Chinese Literature, History of Chinese Philosophy

Department of Education

Clinical Psychology, Development Psychology, Educational Psychology, Educational Sociology, Pedagogy, Public Administration of Education

Department of English Literature

American Literature, British and American Drama,

British and American Poetry, British and American Poetry, British and American Prose, English Philology, History of English Literature, Middle English, Modern English Literature, Phonetics

Department of French Literature

French Philology, History of French Literature, Medieval French Literature, Modern French Literature

Department of German Literature

Contemporary Literature and Romanticism in Germany, Dramaturgy, German Linguistics, German Literature, German Literature of the Storm and Stress Period, German Poetic Realism, Old Middle High German Language and Literature

Department of History and Geography

Anthropology, Archaeology, Documents of Chinese History, Documents of Western History, European History, Geography, Islamic History, Japanese History

Department of Japanese Literature

Ancient Japanese Literature, History of Japanese Literature, Japanese Philology, Medieval Japanese Literature, Modern Japanese Literature

Department of Philosophy

Aesthetics and History of Art, History of Japanese and Oriental Art, History of Medieval Western Philosophy, History of Religion, Philosophy

Faculty of Sociology (Freshmen Enrollment: Day 660, Evening 80)

Department of Sociology

Industrial Psychology Course

Industrial Sociology Course

Mass Communication Course

Sociology Course

Clinical Psychology, Communication and Systems Theory, Consumer Psychology, Cultural Authropology, Experimental Psychology, Family Sociology, Human Engineering, Industrial Education, Industrial Sociology, Mass Communication, Mass Communication Industry, Occupation and Health, Personality, Psychometrics, Social Discrimination, Social Problems, Social Psychology, Social Psychology and Group Dynamics, Social Research, Social Welfare, Social Welfare Policy and Planning, Sociology of Education, Theoretical Sociology, Urban Sociology, Vocational Guidance

Foreign Student Admission

Qualifications for Applicants

Standard Qualifications Requirement

Examination at the University

A written exam and an interview.

Subjects of the Entrance Examination:

Faculties of Law, Letters, Economics, Commerce, Sociology: English, Japanese (Composition) and Interview.

Faculty of Engineering: English, Japanese (Composition), Mathematics, Physics, Chemistry and Interview.

Documents to be Submitted When Applying

Standard Documents Requirement

Application deadline: the last day of November

In addition to the standard documents, following documents are also to be submitted.

1. Written pledge of the person who will pay the applicant's tuition and other fees.
2. Other documents deemed necessary by the appropriate faculty.

GRADUATE PROGRAMS

Graduate School of Commerce (First Year Enrollment : Master's 40, Doctor's 10)

Divisions

Commerce, Financial Accounting

Graduate School of Economics (First Year Enrollment : Master's 50, Doctor's 5)

Division

Economics

Graduate School of Engineering (First Year Enrollment : Master's 230, Doctor's 43)

Divisions

Applied Chemistry, Architecture, Chemical Engineering, Civil Engineering, Electrical Engineering, Electronics, Mechanical Engineering, Metallurgical Engineering

Graduate School of Law (First Year Enrollment : Master's 60, Doctor's 10)

Divisions

Private Law, Public Law

Graduate School of Letters (First Year Enrollment : Master's 108, Doctor's 17)

Divisions

Chinese Literature, Education, English Literature, French Literature, Geography, German Literature, Japanese History, Japanese Literature, Philosophy

Graduate School of Sociology (First Year Enrollment : Master's 30, Doctor's 6)

Divisions

Industrial Sociology, Social Psychology, Sociology

Foreign Student Admission

Qualifications for Applicants

Master's Program

Standard Qualifications Requirement

Doctor's Program

Standard Qualifications Requirement

Examination at the University

Master's Program

The Primary Examination:

Examination of application documents.

The Secondary Examination:

Examination on scholastic knowledge (written examinations in Japanese and in subject (s) deemed necessary by the appropriate graduate school.) and on the character of applicants. (an oral examination.)

Doctor's Program

The same as the Master's program.

Documents to be Submitted When Applying

Standard Documents Requirement

Other documents deemed necessary will be specified by the Graduate School.

Research Institutes and Centers
Center for Archaeological Studies, Information Processing Center, Institute of Economic and Political Studies, Institute of Human Rights Studies, Institute of Industrial Technology, Institute of Legal Studies, Institute of Oriental and Occidental Studies

Facilities/Services for Foreign Students
The International Affairs Division provides the foreign students with a special room for their various activities; various consultations as well as medical assistance and financial aid are also available.

Special Programs for Foreign Students
Courses in Japanese are provided for the freshmen foreign student as one of the subjects for General Education.

For Further Information
Undergraduate Admission
Admissions Division, Kansai University, 3-3-35 Yamate-cho, Suita-shi, Osaka 564 ☎ 06-388-1121 ext. 3134
Graduate Admission
Graduate School Office, Kansai University, 3-3-35 Yamate-cho, Suita-shi, Osaka 564 ☎ 06-388-1121 ext. 3923

Kansai University of Foreign Studies
(Kansai Gaikokugo Daigaku)

16-1 Kitakatahoko-cho, Hirakata-shi, Osaka 573
☎ 0720-56-1721

Faculty
    Profs. 50   Assoc. Profs. 18
    Assist. Profs. Full–time 27; Part–time 88
    Res. Assoc. 1
Number of Students
    Undergrad. 4, 557   Grad. 27
Library 236, 424 volumes

Outline and Characteristics of the University
The University's main objective is to provide promising young people with the skills necessary to function in a sophisticated international environment and to make their own contribution to international understanding. The institution provides a broad range of educational opportunities for internationally minded individuals wishing to enhance their personal development and help them achieve their desired scholastic goals.

Kansai University of Foreign Studies Originated in 1945 as a small language school established amid the smoldering ruins of post-war Japan. The founder, Takako Tanimoto hoped to create an institution which would stress cosmopolitanism. The first class enrolled only eight students.

Now the institution is composed of Kansai University of Foreign Studies, a four-year undergraduate program leading to a B. A. in English or Spanish; Kansai Junior College of Foreign Languages, a two-year program in English; The Graduate School, both master's and doctoral programs in English, and Languages and Cultures, emphasizing linguistical approaches through cultural anthropological perspectives; Kansai University of Foreign Studies Hawaii College, a two-year program in American Studies; The Asian Studies Program open to international students to help them gain first-hand knowledge and experience on Japan, East Asia and the Japanese language.

The Asian Studies Program provides students from abroad with no background in Japanese an opportunity to study and obtain practical knowledge of Japan. The Program offers courses in both Spoken and Reading & Writing Japanese from basic to advanced levels, as well as a variety of academic courses ranging from studio art courses to the social sciences. All classes in the Program are conducted in English. The Asian Studies Program begins in September and ends in May. Homestay is a core part of the Program and is arranged on a semester basis.

The University's educational vision has been to create an institution with a new educational philosophy, and its curriculum, stressing the importance of studying abroad (both out-bound and in-bound) is unique.

The University has student exchange programs with 61 colleges and universities in the United States, two in Australia and one in Spain. Each year approximately 700 students participate in the study abroad programs designed by the University.

The Asian Studies Program alone welcomes more than 250 students annually representing approximately 100 institutions mainly from the USA. Since its inception in 1972, the Program has enrolled over 1, 000 students from the USA, Canada, South East Asia, Australia, Europe, and Africa. Among the universities of foreign studies in Japan, Kansai University of Foreign Studies is the largest and most comprehensive.

Another feature of the University is its Ph. D. program in English, and Languages and Cultures. Only one third of the institutions of higher learning in Japan have been authorized to offer programs leading to a doctoral degree.

The University is located in the City of Hirakata (population 370, 000), midway between the commercial center of Osaka and the ancient capital of Kyoto.

UNDERGRADUATE PROGRAMS

College of Foreign Languages (Freshmen Enrollment: 1, 000)
The School of American and English Languages
American-English Literary Works, American Stud-

ies, British Studies, Comparative Culture, Comparative Grammar, Comparative Literature, English Morphology, English Syntax

The School of Spanish Language

History of Spanish Language, Latin American Studies, Linguistics Philosophy, Spanish Literary Works, Spanish Morphology, Spanish Phonetics, Spanish Studies, Spanish Syntax

Foreign Student Admission

Qualifications for Applicants

Standard Qualifications Requirement

Examination at the University

Written English Examination including Oral Comprehension Test and Written Japanese Examination including Japanese Classics.

Documents to be Submitted When Applying

Standard Documents Requirement

Qualifications for Transfer Students

Eligibility is determined on a case-by–case basis for transfer admissions to the Course of American and English Languages.

Examination for Transfer Students

Written English Examination and Japanese Interview

Documents to be Submitted When Applying

Standard Documents Requirement

GRADUATE PROGRAMS

Graduate School of Foreign Studies (First Year Enrollment : Master's 35, Doctoral 6)

Divisions

English, Languages and Cultures

Foreign Student Admission

Qualifications for Applicants

Master's Program

Standard Qualifications Requirement

Doctoral Program

Standard Qualifications Requirement

Examination at the University

Master's Program

Department of English:

Written English Examination, Essay and Oral Examination

Department of Languages and Cultures: Written Examination in either English, German, French or Spanish; Essay and Oral Examination

Doctoral Program

Department of English: Written English Examination, Written Examination in one of the following languages: German, French or Spanish; Essay and Oral Examination

Department of Languages and Cultures: Written Examinations in two of the following: English, German, French and Spanish; Essay and Oral Examination

Documents to be Submitted When Applying

Standard Documents Requirement

*

Research Institutes and Centers

Audio-visual Education Center, Intercultural Research Institute

Facilities/Services for Foreign Students

The Tanimoto Memorial Hall for International Education (classrooms, language laboratories, study room, student lounge, faculty offices, ceramics studio, Center for International Education)

Seminar House (international students' dormitory; co-ed, single & double Japanese-style rooms with accommodations for 62, kitchens, laundry, lounges, study and meeting rooms)

The library has a special English language Asian Studies collection (10, 000 volumes) including 1, 845 Ph. D. dissertations specifically related to East Asia. This collection represents one of the largest available English language resource centers on Asia. Supplementary materials is available through an extensive inter-library loan program.

Special Programs for Foreign Students

The Asian Studies Program offers a wide variety of academic courses on Japanese language, Japan and East Asia. It offers language courses in Spoken Japanese, and Reading & Writing; and more than 25 elective courses such as Modern Japanese Politics, Japanese Economic Development, Japanese Style Management, Sociology of Contemporary Japan, Cross-cultural Communication, Introduction to Japanese History, Survey of Modern Japanese History, Traditional Japanese Literature, Survey of Japanese Art, Comparative Legal Institutions, Aspects of Japanese Painting from 1350 to 1850, Ceramic Techniques, etc. Besides these academic courses the Program offers homestay as a core unit of the students' exposure to Japanese culture.

The University offers one of the most ideal locations to explore various sectors of Japan. It is midway between Osaka, the nation's second largest industrial metropolis and Kyoto, boasting, many of Japans historical treasures and cultural assets. Nara and Uji are also within easy access. Our locational advantage makes possible a wide range of opportunities from visits to structures dating back several hundred or even a thousand years to modern facilities and institutions. For instance, the Survey of Japanese Art class makes trips to ancient tombs in Asuka, mountain temples in Nara, and museums in Kyoto, while students in Economics, Management may visit the world's leading trading companies and advertising agencies. Those in Law and Politics may find themselves visiting government offices. Field trips offer priceless opportunities to put into a real life context the ideas presented in the classroom.

Eligibility for Admission to The Asian Studies Program:

1. Applicants must have completed at least 12 years of education, or the equivalent. It is also preferable that the applicant has spent a year or more at a college level institution.

2. Each applicant is evaluated on the basis of his/her educational interests and probable success as indicated by academic records. In addition, applicants whose overall academic focus will benefit from courses in the Program are given preference.

3. Whether or not the applicants have knowledge of the Japanese language does not affect their application evaluation.

Necessary Documents for Admission

1. Application for Admission
2. Housing Questionnaire
3. Transcripts of record and explanation of the grading system (transcripts should be from all universities, colleges attended)
4. Three letters of recommendation
5. Certificate of Health
6. Confidential Financial Questionnaire
7. 10 photographs
8. A non-refundable processing fee of US 20. 00dollars
9. Since all courses, except Japanese language, are conducted in English, those whose native language is not English are required to submit evidence of their English proficiency. (e. g. TOEFL score)

Deadlines:

For Fall Enrollment: June 10
For Spring Enrollment: November 30

For further information, write to Center for International Education.

For Further Information

Undergraduate and Graduate Admission

Admissions Office, Kansai University of Foreign Studies, 16-1 Kitakatahoko-cho, Hirakata-shi, Osaka 573 ☎ 0720-56-1721 ext. 322, 323, 324

Kanto Gakuen University
(Kanto Gakuen Daigaku)

200 Fujiaku, Ohta–shi, Gunma 373
☎ 0276–31–2711

Faculty
　　Profs. 37　　Assoc. Profs 11
　　Assist. Profs. Full–time 10; Part–time 16
　　Res. Assocs. 2
Number of Students
　　Undergrad. 2, 338　　Grad. 25
Library 101, 938 volumes

Outline and Characteristics of the University

Kanto Gakuen University was established in 1976 on the site of the Ohta campus of Kanto Junior College (the main campus of which is located) in Tatebayashi City. It was originally founded as a Faculty of Economics with only one Department of Economics. The Department of Management and the Graduate School of Economics (master's pro-

gram) were added in 1981.

The University is located in the garden city of Ohta, a high technology industrial center in northern Kanto district, and aims to become a cultural center in this district. A remarkable characteristic of the University is computer training for all students, to qualify them for active participation in an information-oriented society. The study of computers is the main subject at the University. A second feature of the University is its large collection of valuable publications on European classical economics, such as first editions of Adam Smith and John Locke at Matsudaira Memorial Library, which will supply the intellectual resources for the cultural development of the region. The campus is situated in a wooded area, enjoying a view of distant Mt. Akagi. In this beautiful environment the campus offers a place for mutual friendship between all students. In addition, student housing is provided by the community.

UNDERGRADUATE PROGRAMS

Faculty of Economics (Freshmen Enrollment: 400)
Department of Economics
Economic History, Economic policy, Finance, International Econmics, Public Economy, Public Finance, Social Policy, Statistics, Theoretical Economics
　Department of Management
Discourse on Firms, Financial Management, Foreign Exchange, History of Management, International Management, Labour Management, Management Engineering, Marketing, Principles of Management, Securities Market (As mentioned above, the study of Computers is compulsory for all students in both Departments), Study of Computer Accounting

Foreign Student Admission
　Qualifications for Applicants
　　Standard Qualifications Requirement
　Examination at the University
Same as for Japanese (Now the seperate exam for foreign applicants is being scheduled.)
　Documents to be Submitted When Applying
　　Standard Documents Requirement

GRADUATE PROGRAMS

Graduate School of Economics (First Year Enrollment : Master's 10)
　Division
Economics

＊

Research Institutes and Centers
Matsudaira Memorial Institute for Economics and Culture
For Further Information
　Undergraduate and Graduate Admission
Kanto Gakuen University, 200 Fujiaku, Ohta–shi, Gunma 373 ☎ 0276–31–2711

Kanto Gakuin University
(Kanto Gakuin Daigaku)

4834 Mutsuura-cho, Kanazawa-ku, Yokohama-shi, Kanagawa 236   ☎ 045-781-2001

Faculty
  Profs. 108   Assoc. Profs. 61
  Assist. Profs. Full-time 18; Part-time 375
Number of Students
  Undergrad. 9, 171   Grad. 82
Library 400, 000 volumes

Outline and Characteristics of the University

The history of Kanto Gakuin University dates back to 1884, when the American Northern Baptist Board opened the Yokohama Baptist Seminary. A. A. Bennett, the first principal of the Seminary, felt it vitally necessary to give theological and systematic training to Japanese preachers. He started weekly Bible lectures at his home four years before the first training course. The following year, the course was expanded to daily two-hour classes. These daily sessions were the fundamental program until the establishment of the Yokohama Baptist Seminary.

The missionary group of that period then founded in 1895 the Tokyo Baptist Academy in Tsukiji, as a boys' middle school. Five years later, the Tokyo Baptist Academy moved from Tsukiji to Ushigome, and took the new name, Tokyo Gakuin. In 1905 a college department was added. Although it was separate from the Yokohama Baptist Seminary, the college of Tokyo Gakuin functioned as a preparatory course for the Seminary.

The Yokohama Baptist Seminary was renamed as the Japan Baptist Seminary, and in 1919, it was merged with Tokyo Gakuin and became the Tokyo Gakuin School of Theology.

With the acquisition of a favorable site in Yokohama, the middle school department of Tokyo Gakuin was closed, and in January 1919 it became the Kanto Gakuin Middle School (Mabie Memorial Boys' School) at Miharudai, Yokohama. In 1927, the Theological department of Tokyo Gakuin closed the Tokyo campus, moved to Yokohama and became a part of Kanto Gakuin. The departments were systematically united under the newly established educational foundation.

Subsequently, the organization of Kanto Gakuin has changed several times. Just after World War II, there were the Schools of Engineering, Economics, and the Middle School. Under the new School Education Law, issued after the war, the schools of Engineering and Economics became the Colleges of Kanto Gakuin University. This institution has developed into today's K. G. U., acquiring its present site in Mutsuura in the southern part of Yokohama, and adding the college of Humanities.

In 1976, the University entered into a formal agreement of international cooperation with Linfield College, McMinnville, Oregon, U. S. A.

At present, the University consists of two Graduate Schools (Economics and Engineering), two Advanced Courses (Economics and Engineering), three Colleges (Humanities, Economics and Engineering) and two Night Schools (Economics and Engineering).

UNDERGRADUATE PROGRAMS

College of Economics (Freshmen Enrollment: 400)
  Department of Business Administration
Advertising, Budget Control, Business Administration, Business History, Commercial Science, Corporate Planning, Cost Accounting, Financial Analysis, Financial Auditing, Financial Management, Foreign Exchange, Harbor Policy, Information Management, Insurance, International Business Management, International Finance, Labor Management, Management, Management Organization, Managerial Accounting, Marine Insurance, Marketing, Marketing Research, Medium and Small Enterprises, Merchandising, Practical Trade, Production Control, Securities, Tax Accounting, Transportation, Types of Business Enterprises
  Department of Economics
Agricultural Economy, Banking, Econometrics, Economic Geography, Economic History, Economic History of Japan, Economic Planning, Finance, History of Social Economics, Industrial Economics, Industrial Fluctuation, International Economics, International Trade, Japanese Economic Theory, Local Government Finance, National Income, Political Economics, Socialist Economics, Social Policy, Statistical Economics, Theory of Panics, World Economic Theory

College of Economics (**Night School**) (Freshmen Enrollment: 150)
  Department of Economics
  Business Administration Course
Business Administration, Business History, Cost Accounting, Financial Analysis, Financial Auditing, Financial Management, Foreign Exchange, Harbor Policy, Industrial Psychology, Insurance, International Business Management, Labor Management, Management, Management Organization, Marketing, Merchandise, Study of Public Utilities, Trade, Transportation Economy
  Economics Course
American Economic Theory, Asian Economic Theory, Banking, Economic History, Economic History of Japan, European Economic Theory, History of Economics, History of Economic Thought, Industrial Fluctuation, International Trade, Japanese Economic Theory, Local Government Finance, Political Economy, Science of Finance, Social Policy, Theory of Panics, World Economic Theory

College of Engineering (Freshmen Enrollment: 380)

Department of Architectural Environmental Engineering

Air Conditioning Systems, Architectural Planning, Building Code and Architectural Administration, Building Construction and Materials, Building Process, Electrical Building Systems, Environmental Analysis Chemistry, Environmental Control, Environmental Control System Process, Environmental Design, Heating Systems, History of Architecture, Reinforced Concrete Structure, Structural Building Design, Urban Design, Waste Disposal, Water Supply and Drainage Systems

Department of Architecture

Architectural Design, Architecture, Building Construction, Building Construction Design & Drawing, Building Construction Systems Analysis and Planning, Building Materials, City Planning, Construction Engineering, History of Architecture, Landscape Architecture, Photoelastic Principles, Planning Analysis, Soil Mechanics and Foundation Engineering, Steel Structural Vibrations, Structural Design, Structural Engineering, Structural Mechanics

Department of Civil Engineering

Bridge Engineering, Civil Engineering Administration, Civil Engineering Analysis, Civil Engineering Drawings, Coastal Engineering, Engineering Materials, Explosive Engineering, Fluid Dynamics, Geotechnical Engineering, Highway Engineering, Hydraulics, Hydrology, Ocean Engineering, Prestressed Concrete Structure, Railway Engineering, Reinforced Concrete Structures, Soil and Rock Mechanics, Soil Engineering, Structural Mechanics, Traffic Engineering, Urban Planning, Wastewater Engineering, Water Engineering, Water Resources Engineering, Water Supply Engineering

Department of Electrical Engineering

Acoustical Engineering, Communication Engineering, Design of Electrical Machinery and Apparatus, Digital Computer, Electrical Circuits, Electrical Engineering, Electrical Machines, Electrical Measurements, Electric Power Applications, Electrochemistry, Electromagnetic Waves, Electro–Magnetism, Electron Devices, Electronic Circuits, Electronic Measurements, Energy Engineering, Geometrical Graphics, High Voltage Engineering, Information Technology, Information Theory, Power Engineering, System Engineering, Transmission Engineering

Department of Industrial Chemistry

Analytical Chemistry, Applied Electrochemistry, Catalytical Chemistry, Chemical Engineering Design, Flow and Transport Phenomena, Fundamental Chemical Engineering, Industrial Chemistry, Industrial Inorganic Chemistry, Industrial Materials, Industrial Organic Chemistry, Industrial Polymer Chemistry, Inorganic Chemistry, Instrumental Analysis, Metal Finishing, Micro–biological Engineering, Organic Chemistry, Organic Synthetic Chemistry, Physical Chemistry, Pollution Control Chemistry, Polymer Chemistry, Quantum Chemistry, Radiation Chemistry, Reaction Kinetics, Unit Operation

Department of Mechanical Engineering

Auto Control Systems, Automotive Engineering, Engineering Analysis, Experimental Stress Analysis, Fluid Machinery, Gas Dynamics, Hydrodynamics, Internal Combustion Engine, Machine Design, Machine Elements, Machine Mechanism, Machinery Dynamics, Machinery Materials, Machine Tools, Material Strength, Measurement Engineering, Mechanical Engineering, Metal Processing, Non–Ferrous Metallography, Operations Research, Refrigeration Engineering, Solid Mechanics, Steam Prime Movers, Thermodynamics, Welding Technology

College of Engineering (Night School) (Freshmen Enrollment: 200)

Department of Architecture–Civil Engineering

Architecture Course

Architectural Equipment Engineering, Architecture, Building Construction Systems Analysis and Planning, Building Materials, Environmental Control, Landscape Architecture, Planning Analysis, Reinforced Concrete Structure, Structural Engineering, Structural Mechanics, Waste Disposal

Civil Engineering Course

Bridge Engineering, Civil Engineering Administration, Engineering Materials, Geotechnical Engineering, Highway Engineering, Hydraulics, Hydrology, Ocean Engineering, Reinforced Concrete Structures, Seismology, Soil Engineering, Structural Mechanics, Traffic Engineering, Urban Planning, Wastewater Engineering, Water Engineering, Water Supply Engineering

Department of Electrical Engineering

Electrical Circuits, Electrical Engineering Materials, Electrical Machinery and Apparatus Design, Electrical Machines, Electrical Measurements, Electric Illumination and Electric Heating, Electricity and Magnetism, Electric Power Applications, Electrochemistry, Electro–Magnetism, Energy Engineering, Information Technology, Microwave Engineering, Solid State Physical Electronics

Department of Industrial Chemistry

Analytical Chemistry, Chemical Engineering Design, Industrial Inorganic Chemistry, Industrial Organic Chemistry, Inorganic Chemistry, Instrumental Analysis, Metal Finishing Engineering, Organic Chemistry, Physical Chemistry, Pollution Control Chemistry, Reaction Kinetics, Unit Operation

Department of Mechanical Engineering

Automatic Control Systems, Automotive Engineering, Engineering Analysis, Experimental Engineering, Experimental Stress Analysis, Fluid Machinery, Gas Dynamics, Heat Transmission Engineering, Hydraulics, Hydrodynamics, Internal Combustion Engine, Machine Design, Machine Elements, Machine Materials, Machine Mechanisms, Machinery Dynamics, Machine Tools, Manufacturing Processes, Material Strength, Measurement Engineering, Metal Processing, Non–Ferrous Metallography, Refrigeration

Engineering, Steam Prime Movers, Thermodynamics, Welding Technology

College of Humanities (Freshmen Enrollment: 300)
Department of English and American Literature
Children's Literature, English and American Literature, English Grammar, English Linguistics, English Phonetics, History of American Literature, History of English Language, History of English Literature, Translation
Department of Sociology
Child Welfare, Counseling, Family Sociology, History of Social Welfare Thought, History of Sociology, Industrial Sociology, International Organization, International Relations, Mass Communication, Public Assistance, Recreation, Rehabilitation, Social Anthropology, Social Change, Social Education, Social Groups, Social Investigation, Social Psychology, Social Security, Social Welfare, Sociology, Sociology of Knowledge, Sociology of Religion, Theory of Personality, Urban Sociology, Welfare for the Aged

Foreign Student Admission
Qualifications for Applicants
Standard Qualifications Requirement
Those who have received an International Baccalaureate and are 18 years or older may also apply.
Applicants must take the Japanese Language Proficiency Test (in the year of application) and the General Examination for Foreign Students.
Examination at the University
A written exam and an interview.
Documents to be Submitted When Applying
Standard Documents Requirement
Following documents are also required.
1. Baccalaureate Certificate (and of the performance results), if applicable.
2. Japanese Language Proficiency Certificate issued by the Japanese language school (s) applicants attended.
3. Certificates of the Japanese Language Proficiency Test and General Exam for Foreign Students.

ONE-YEAR GRADUATE PROGRAMS

One-Year Graduate Course in Economics (Enrollment 15)
Business Administration
One-Year Graduate Course in Engineering (Enrollment 20)
Architectural Environmental Engineering, Architecture, Civil Engineering, Electrical Engineering, Industrial Chemistry, Mechanical Engineering

Foreign Student Admission
Qualifications for Applicants
Standard Qualifications Requirement
Examination at the University
Applicants must follow the same procedure as Japanese applicants and undergo an interview.

GRADUATE PROGRAMS

Graduate Economics Institute (First Year Enrollment : Master's 5, Doctor's 2)
Divisions
Economics, History of Economics, History of Social Economics
Graduate Engineering Institute (First Year Enrollment : Master's 36, Doctor's 11)
Divisions
Architecture, Civil Engineering, Electrical Engineering, Industrial Chemistry, Mechanical Engineering

Foreign Student Admission
Qualifications for Applicants
Master's Program
Standard Qualifications Requirement
Doctor's Program
Standard Qualifications Requirement
Examination at the University
Master's Program
The same written examination, an English test and an interview as Japanese applicants.
Doctor's Program
The same written examination, an interview and one of five foreign language tests: English, German, French, Russian and Chinese. Applicants cannot choose their native language as Japanese applicants.
Documents to be Submitted When Applying
Standard Documents Requirement
Applicants for the Doctor's program must submit a copy of their Master's thesis and a letter from their faculty advisor for acceptance.

*
Research Institutes and Centers
Computer Center, Counseling Center, Cultural Science Research Institute, Economic Institute, International Center, Japanese Protestant History Institute, Osawa Memorial Institute of Architectural-Environmental Engineering, Technical Institute
For Further Information
Undergraduate and Graduate Admission
Admissions Office, Kanto Gakuin University, 4834 Mutsuura-cho, Kanazawa-ku, Yokohama-shi, Kanagawa 236 ☎ 045-781-2001 ext. 204

Kawamura Gakuen Women's University
(Kawamura Gakuen Joshi Daigaku)
Sageto 1133, Abiko-shi, Chiba 270-11
☎ 0471-83-0111

Faculty
Profs. 14   Assoc. Profs. 9
Assist. Profs. Full-time 8; Part-time 11
Res. Assocs. 7

Number of Students
    Undergrad.   240
Library   19, 000 volumes

Outline and Characteristics of the University

Kawamura Gakuen Women's University was established in 1988 as a four year women's university. It was established in connection with the Kawamura Gakuen, which has a long and respected history of more than 60 years in women's education.

At present the University has a Faculty of Liberal Arts consisting of three Departments. These are the Departments of English Language and Literature, Psychology and History. All Departments are located on the University Campus in Abiko.

The Abiko Campus, located some 40 minutes from the center of Tokyo, is a peaceful and attractive learning environment. The campus buildings are spacious and elegantly designed. Abiko has a long cultural history, and the beauty of its natural surroundings has attracted numerous artists and writers. The University Campus located to the North West of Abiko is in close vicinity to the famous scenic spots of the Tega Numa and Tonegawa Rivers.

The University aims at providing a well-rounded, fully international education for women, firmly based on the guiding principles of Kawamura Gakuen's founder Fumiko Kawamura. Fumiko Kawamura stressed the importance of integrated humanistic education for women emphasizing the principles of social contribution, responsibility, and gratitude.

UNDERGRADUATE PROGRAMS

Faculty of Liberal Arts (Freshmen Enrollment: 200)

Department of English Language and Literature
American Writers, Business English, Commercial English, Composition, Conversation, Current English, English Writers, Grammar, History of American Literature, History of English Literature, International Affairs, Language, Literature, Oral English, Phonetics, Reading Class in English and American Literature, Specialist English

Department of History
Archaelogy, Geographical Studies, Historical Studies, Historiography, History of Women's Education, Domestic Life, Science and Technology, Religion, Japanese Art, Oriental Art, Occidental Art, Music, Calligraphy, the Performing and Applied Arts, Japanese History, Japanese History, Manuscript Studies, Occidental History, Oriental History, Social History, Women's History

Department of Psychology
Aesthetics, Artistic Studies, Child Psychology, Christianity, Clinical Psychology, Comparative Behavioural Studies, Comparative Literature, Comparative Psychology, Consumer Behaviour, Consumer Psychology, Contemporary Society, Counselling, Cultural Anthropology, Delayed Development, De-

velopmental Clinical Psychology, Developmental Psychology, Domestic Economy, Educational Psychology, Experimental Psychology, Family Studies, Folklore, Fundamentals of Economics, History of Education, History of English Language, History of Legal System, History of Psychology, Infant Psychology, Information Processing, Introduction to Italian, Juvenile Law and Delinquency, Law, Linguistics, Mass Communication Theory, Mental Disorders, Mental Health, Oriental Religions, Paleology, Personality Studies, Philosophy, Principles of Writing, Psychiatry, Psychological Statistics, Psychology, Psychology of Anti-social and Criminal Behaviour, Psychology of Learning, Psychology of Perception, Social Psychology, Social Welfare, Survey of Political Studies, Survey of Social Sciences, Theory of Domestic Education, Topography, World History

*

For Further Information
Undergraduate Admission
Division Head, Education Division, Education Affairs Department, Kawamura Gakuen Women's University, Sageto 1133, Abiko–shi, Chiba 270–11
☎ 0471–83–0111

Kawasaki Medical School
(Kawasaki Ika Daigaku)
577 Matsushima, Kurashiki-shi, Okayama 701-01
☎ 0864-62-1111

Faculty
    Profs.   61   Assoc. Profs.   45
    Assist. Profs.   Full–time   117; Part–time   8
    Res. Assocs.   125
Number of Students
    Undergrad.   820   Grad.   95
Library   120, 411 volumes

Outline and Characteristics of the University

Kawasaki Medical School is the oldest of those private medical schools founded in postwar Japan. It was established in Kurashiki City in 1970 in accordance with the following principles: liberal humanity, sound body and profound knowledge. The school is committed not only to training reliable clinicians as specialists who apply theoretical analyses and techniques they have acquired, but also to training medical researchers to contribute to the rapid progress taking place in medical science.

A consistent medical education with a solid curriculum is provided throughout the students' six years of study. All undergraduate students are required to live in dormitories during their first two years. This collective life in the dormitory ensures the cultivation of an independent spirit and the formation of good friendships.

One of the outstanding institutions at Kawasaki

Medical School is the Medical Museum, which aims to facilitate the understanding of medical theories and techniques through audiovisual systems. There the latest information and materials regarding all the fields of medical science are available. The Medical Museum provides all medical students, medical researchers and clinicians with opportunities for independent study, and is also open to the public for health education.

The school is located in an area of historical and industrial significance. The role of this area in early Japanese history was substantial, as can be seen in exhibits in city museums. Industrially, the city is already well known for its Mizushima industrial area; it further occupies the attention of the whole nation as the gateway to further development of western Japan, with the 1988 completion of the Seto Ohashi Bridge which links the main island of Honshu with Shikoku.

UNDERGRADUATE PROGRAMS

Faculty of Medicine (Freshmen Enrollment: 120)
Department of Medicine
Administration of Hospital, Anatomy, Anesthesiology, Biochemistry, Dermatology, Emergency Medicine, Family Practice Hygiene, Inspection & Diagnosis, Internal Medicine, Legal Medicine, Medical Engineering, Microbiology, Neurosurgery, Obstetrics & Gynecology, Ophthalmology, Oral Surgery, Orthopedics, Otorhinolaryngology, Parasitology, Pathology, Pediatrics, Pharmacology, Physiology, Plastic Surgery, Primary Care Medicine, Primary Health Care and Preventive Medicine Psychiatry, Public Health, Radiology, Rehabilitation, Surgery, Urology

GRADUATE PROGRAMS

Graduate School of Medicine (First Year Enrollment : Doctor's 50)
Divisions
Biochemistry, Environmental Medicine, Morphology, Physiology, Tissue Culture and Immunology

*

Research Institutes and Centers
Animal Experimental Research Center, Biochemistry Center, Computer Center, Electron Microscopy Center, Environmental Research Center, Laboratory Animal Center, Physiological Function Research Center, R. I. Center, Tissue Culture Center

For Further Information
Undergraduate and Graduate Admission
Academic Affairs Section, Office of School Affairs, Kawasaki Medical School, 577 Matsushima, Kurashiki-shi, Okayama 701-01 ☎ 0864-62-1111 ext. 3140

Keiai University
(Keiai Daigaku)
1-5-21 Anagawa, Chiba-shi, Chiba 260
☎ 0472-51-6363

UNDERGRADUATE PROGRAMS

Faculty of Economics (Freshmen Enrollment: 200)
Department of Economics

Keio University
(Keio Gijuku Daigaku)
2-15-45 Mita, Minato-ku, Tokyo 108
☎ 03-453-4511

Faculty
 Profs.　472　　Assoc. Profs.　238
 Assist. Profs.　Full–time　202; Part–time　1, 3 24
 Res. Assocs.　398
Number of Students
 Undergrad.　23, 415　　Grad.　1, 915
Library　2, 301, 039 volumes

Outline and Characteristics of the University
Keio University is a private, coeducational university which was founded in 1858 by Yukichi Fukuzawa, a highly recognized intellectual leader in Japanese history. It is the oldest institution of higher learning in Japan. Since its establishment, Keio has adhered to the principle of fostering independence and self-respect along with academic excellence.

Since 1898 Keio has maintained an integrated system of education beginning at the elementary school level. This system now consists of an Elementary School, two Junior High Schools, three Senior High Schools, and a University.

In the University, there are at present five Faculties: Letters, Economics, Law, Business & Commerce, and Science & Technology, together with the School of Medicine and the University Correspondence School. In addition, there are eight Graduate Schools: Letters, Economics, Law, Human Relations, Business & Commercé, Medicine, Science & Technology, and Business Administration. Various research institutes and centers have also been established. Keio University is generally regarded as one of the most important centers of learning in Japan and has educated many of the leading figures in various fields.

Keio University has two campuses in Tokyo. Mita Campus, which is located in the southern part, has been the main campus since 1871, and houses the Specialized Courses of the Faculties of Letters, Economics, Law, and Business & Commerce as well as the Graduate Schools of Letters, Economics, Law, Human Relations, and Business & Commerce. Shinanomachi Campus, which is located in the central part, is the campus for the Specialized Course of the School of Medicine, the Graduate School of Medicine and the University Hospital.

Furthermore, there are a few campuses clustered in the Hiyoshi district of Yokohama City, which are allocated for the General Education of all undergraduate students, the Specialized Course of the Faculty of Science & Technology, the Graduate School of Science & Technology, and the Graduate School of Business Administration.

Keio University has, from the earliest days of its history, promoted interchange with academic institutions in other parts of the globe. The first foreign scholars to be invited to Keio came from the United States in 1872, and Keio became in 1881 the first modern institution of higher learning in this country to admit foreign students. Keio has over 150 visiting scholars during the 1987-88 academic year, 100 part-time teachers and nearly 450 students as of May 1988, from other parts of the world attending the university. Recently, the number of foreign scholars, teachers and students in Keio University has been increasing rapidly year by year.

We at Keio are extremely proud that our founder, Yukichi Fukuzawa, should be regarded as one of the foremost internationally-minded figures in our country's history. Accordingly, the promotion of international understanding has always been something of a tradition here at Keio.

UNDERGRADUATE PROGRAMS

Faculty of Business and Commerce (Freshmen Enrollment: 1, 000)

Department of Business and Commerce
Accounting, Auditing, Business Administration, Business Economics, Business Finance, Commercial Economics, Commercial Management, Cost Accounting, Econometrics, Economic Geography, Economic History, Economic Policy, Economics of Commerce, Economics of International Transport, Economics of Public Utilities, Economic Statistics, Economic Theory, Economic Theory, Hisotry of Business Management Theories, History of Accounting Theory, History of Distribution, History of Economic Thought, Industrial History, Industrial Organization, Industrial Psychology, Industrial Relations, Industrial Sociology, Insurance, Insurance Management, International Economics, International Finance, International Investment, Labor Economics, Management, Management Accounting, Marketing, Modern Economic History of Japan, Monetary Economics, Public Finance, Regional Economics, Sampling Methods, Security Economics, Sociology of Management, Transport Economics, Transport Policy, World Economics

Faculty of Economics (Freshmen Enrollment: 1, 200)
Department of Economics
Agricultural Economics, Bookkeeping, Contemporary Capitalism, Contemporary Japanese Economy, Development Economics, Development of Japanese Capitalism, Econometric Methods, Econometrics, Economic Development, Economic Geography, Economic Growth and Fluctuations, Economic History, Economic History of Asia, Economic History of Japan, Economic History of Pre-Modern Japan, Economic History of the West, Economic Policy, Economics, Economic Socialism, Economics of Developing Countries, Economic Statistics, Financial Economics, History of American Economy, History of Economic Thoughts, History of English Labor Movement, History of Japanese Economic Thoughts, History of Japanese Labor Movement, History of Modern Economic Thoughts, History of Modern European Economy, History of Modern Japanese Socioeconomic Thoughts, Industrial Economics, Industrial Organization, Industrial Sociology, International Finance, International Trade, Japanese Trade and Trade Policy, Laber Economics, Mathematical Economics, Mathematical Methods in Economic Analysis, Monopolistic Capitalism, National Income and Income Analysis, Planned Economy, Population Problems, Price Theory, Public Economics, Public Finance, Region Conceptual Framework, Resource Economics, Social Policy, Statistical Methods for Historical Research, Theory of Games, Urban History in Cultural-Social and Economic Aspects, Urban Sociology, World Economy

Faculty of Law (Freshmen Enrollment: 1, 200)
Department of Law
Administrative Law, Antitrust Law, Aviation Law, Bankruptcy Law, Civil Law, Civil Procedure, Commercial Law, Constitutional Law, Criminal Law, Criminal Policy, Criminal Procedure, Criminology, Foreign Law (English-American, German, French), History of Legal Thoughts, International Business Transactions, International Law, Jurisprudence, Labor Law, Law on Judicial Process, Legal History, Legal Medicine, Legal Sociology, Legal Studies, Medical Law, Private International Law, Security Law, Victimology

Department of Political Science
Area Studies (Africa, Australia, China, England, Korea, Latin America, Middle East, South East Asia, U.S.S.R.), Comparative Politics, Contemporary Democracies, Contemporary International Politics, Contemporary Political and Sociological Theories, Developmental History of Mass Communication, History of Japanese Foreign Policy, History of Modern Political Thoughts, Industrial Society, International Communication, International Relations, Japanese Political History, Japanese Politics, Mass Communication, Mathematical Political Science, Political Behavior, Political Economic Systems, Politi-

cal Philosophy, Political Power, Political Science, Political Thoughts, Public Administration, Quantitative Political Science

Faculty of Letters (Freshmen Enrollment: 700)

Department of History

Anthropology, Archaeology, Asian History, Ethnology, Geography, Japanese History, Methods of Historical Study, Paleography, Philosophy of History, Western History

Department of Library and Information Science

Bibliography, History of Books and Libraries, Information Processing Technology, Information Retrieval, Information Systems, Library and Information Science, Management of Information Systems, Organization of Recorded Materials, Reference and Information Service, Reference and Information Sources, Selection of Recorded Materials

Department of Literature

American Literature, Chinese Classics, Chinese Linguistics, Chinese Literature, Chinese Philosophy, English Linguistics, English Literature, English Phonetics, French Linguistics, French Literature, German Linguistics, German Literature, History of American Literature, History of Chinese Literature, History of English Language, History of English Literature, History of French Literature, History of German Literature, History of Japanese Literature, Japanese Linguistics, Japanese Linguistics, Japanese Literature, Linguistics, Old and Middle English

Department of Philosophy

Aesthetics, Aesthetics and Science of Arts, Christianity, Ethics, History of Asiatic Fine Arts, History of Fine Arts, History of Western Fine Arts, History of Western Music, History of Western Philosophy and Ethics, Logic, Methodology of Sciences, Moral Ideas in Japan, Music History, Ontology, Oriental Ethics, Philosophy, Science of Arts, Theory of Knowledge

Department of Sociology, Psychology, Education and Human Sciences

Behavioral Biology, Behavioral Science, Behavior Analysis, Biopsychology, Clinical Psychology, Cognitive Psychology, Cognitive Science, Communications, Community Psychology, Cultural Anthropology, Cultural Sociology, Culture and Mental & Behavior Disorders, Developmental Psychology, Educational Administration, Educational Psychology, Education & Society, Epistemology, Family & Kinship Organization, General Psychology, History of Education, History of Educational Studies, History of Psychology, History of Sociological Theories, History of Thoughts on Man, Human Behavior, Human Biology, Human Development through Life, Human Sciences, Human Social Relations and Network, Individual Social Behavior, Japanese Society, Labor and Industrial Relations, Logic, Nerve Physiology, Personality Theory and Personality Assessment, Philosophical Studies on Man, Philosophy of Science, Psychiatry, Psychoanalysis, Psychology of Perception, Psychometrics, Social Psychology, Social Systems Theory, Sociology, Sociology of Religion, Urban Sociology

School of Medicine (Freshmen Enrollment: 100)

Department of Medicine

Anatomy (Anatomy, Histology and Embryology), Anesthesiology, Clinical Science, Dentistry, Dermatology, Gynecology and Obstetrics, History of Medicine, Hospital and Medical Administration, Internal Medicine (Internal Diagnostics, Internal Medicine, Clinical Studies), Legal Medicine, Medical Chemistry, Medical Studies, Microbiology (Microbiology and Clinical Microbiology), Ophthalmology, Orthopedics, Otorhinolaryngology, Parasitology, Pathology, Pediatrics, Pharmacology, Physiology, Plastic Surgery, Preventive Medicine and Public Health, Psychiatry, Radiology, Surgery, Urology

Faculty of Science and Technology (Freshmen Enrollment: 840)

Department of Administration Engineering

Administration Engineering, Algorithms, Applications of Computer, Applied Statistcs, Business Administration, Computer Engineering, Data Communication, Econometrics, Economy Engineering, Experimental Design, Human Engineering, Human Factors, Industrial Engineering, Industrial Psychology, Information Engineering, Information System, Management Control, Managerial Accounting and Economics, Marketing Research and Investigation, Mathematical Economics, Mathematical Statistics, Mathematical Statistics, Mathematics for Administration Engineering, Numerical Analysis, Operations Research, Process Simulation, Production Planning and Control, Quantitative Psychology, Reliabilty Engineering, Sample Survey Theory, Software Engineering, Stochastic Processes, Systems Engineering

Department of Applied Chemistry

Analytical Chemistry, Applied Chemistry, Applied High Polymer Chemistry, Applied Synthetic Chemistry, Biochemical Industry, Chemical Analysis, Chemical Engineering, Chemical Kinetics, Chemical Reaction Engineering, Chemistry of Catalytic Reactions, Chemistry of Oil and Fat Products, Electrochemical Engineering, Electrochemistry, Electronic Materials, Energetics for Organic Chemistry, Environmental Chemistry, Industrial Inorganic Chemistry, Industrial Materials, Industrial Synthetic Polymer Chemistry, Inorganic Chemstry, Metal Chemistry, Natural Polymer Chemistry, Organic Chemistry, Physical Chemistry, Polymer Science, Quantum Chemistry, Radiochemistry, Solid State Chemistry, Stereo Chemistry of Organic Compounds, Surface Chemistry, Synthetic Polymer Chemistry, Unit Operations, Unit Reaction of Organic Chemistry

Department of Chemistry

Analytical Chemistry, Biochemistry, Bioorganic Chemistry, Chemical Dynamics, Chemical Education, Chemical Evolution, Chemistry, Chemistry of Catalysis, Chemistry of Energy Sources, Chemistry of Natural Resources, Chemistry of Radioactive Compounds, Chemistry of Solution, Coordination Chemistry, Information Science for Chemistry, Inorganic Chemistry, Material Chemistry, Molecular Design, Molecular Spectroscopy, Natural Product Chemistry, Organic Chemistry, Photochemistry and Radiation Chemistry, Physical Chemistry, Physical Properties of Polymers, Reaction Mechanism in Organic Chemistry, Solid State Chemistry, Statistical Thermodynamics, Structural Chemistry, Structural Organic Chemistry, Structural Polymer Chemistry, Surface Chemistry, Synthetic Polymer Chemistry

Department of Electrical Engineering
Applied Mathematics, Biological Engineering, Communication Engineering, Computer Algorithms, Computer Architecture, Computer Systems Organization, Control Engineering, Design Practice of Electric Motors and Transformers, Digital Systems, Electrical Engineering, Electrical Engneering, Electrical Machines, Electric and Electronic Measurements, Electromagnetism, Electronic Circuits, Electronic Devices, Electronic Physics, Energy Conversion Technology, Gaseous Electronics, High Energy Engineering, Industry and Management of Electric Facilities, Information Engineering, Laws & Regulations on Electric Power, Machine Control, Material Science, Modern Control Theory, Network Theory, Non-Arithmetic Information Processing, Numerical Analysis, Operating System, Optical Engineering, Plasma Engineering, Power Electronics, Power System Control Engineering, Power Transmission, Programming Languages, Quantum Electronics, Quantum Mechanics, Radio Engineering, Radio Probing, Solid State Electronics, Wave Electronic

Department of Instrumentation Engineering
Analysis by Physical Method, Applied Acoustics, Applied Optics, Atomic Power Engineering, Computer Engineering, Control Engineering, Digital Circuits, Digital Data Processing, Electronic Computing Method, Industrial Instrument, Information Engineering, Instrumentation Engineering, Life Science, Linear Mathematics, Materials Science of Semiconductor, Mathematical Physics, Modern Control Theory, Nuclear Radiation Detection and Its Application, Physics of Magnetism, Plasma Physcis, Process Analysis, Process Control Theory, Process Instrumentation, Quantum Electronics, Quantum Mechanics, Servomechanism, Simulation, Solid State Physics, Solid State Science in Extreme Conditions, Statistical Mechanics, Statistical Methods, Stochastic Processes, Systems Control, Telemetering

Department of Mathematics
Advanced Calculus, Algebra, Applications of Computer, Applied Statistics, Complex Analysis, Computer Theory, Data Analysis, Design of Experiments, Differential Equations, Finite Mathematics, Functional Analysis, Geometry, Information Processing, Informations, Information Science, Mathematical Logic, Mathematical Statistics, Mathematics, Multivariate Analysis, Numerical Analysis, Operational Mathematics, Probability and Statistics, Probability Theory, Real Analysis, Statistical Model Theory, Statistics, Stochastics Processes, System Programming, Time Series Analysis

Department of Mechanical Engineering
Aero-Space Engineering, Air Conditioning, Analytical Dynamics, Applied Elasticity and Plasticity, Applied Thermodynamics, Atomic Power Engineering, Automobile Engineering, Combustion, Computer Application in Industry Field, Control Engineering, Dynamics of Machines, Electronic Engineering, Engineering Materials, Engineering Science for Energy, Fluid Machinery, Gas Turbine, Heat Transfer, History of Technology, Human Engineering, Hydrodynamics, Industrial Design, Industrial Management, Internal Combustion Engine, Machine Design, Machine Design and Drawing, Machine Elements, Machine Tool, Material Engineering, Mathematics for Industrial Applications, Mechanical Engineering, Mechanical Vibration, Metal Working, Numerical Analysis, Plastic Working of Metals, Polymer Science and Technology, Production Planning Control, Production Technology, Quantum Mechanics, Rheology, Steam Power Engineering, Strength of Material, Systems Engineering, Transport Phenomena, Unit Operation of the Chemical Industry

Department of Physics
Applied Electromagnetism, Applied Physics, Astrophysics, Atomic Physics, Biophysics, Dynamics of Continuous Media, Electricity and Magnetism, Electricity and Magnetism, Elementary Particle Physics, Experimental Physics, Geophysics, Mathematical Physics, Mathematics in Physics, Mechanics, Molecular Physics, Nuclear Physics, Nuclear Reactor Physics, Optics, Physics, Plasma Physics, Quantum Electronics, Quantum Mechanics, Solid State Physics, Statistical Mechanics and Thermodynamics, Statistical Physics, Stochastic Processes, Theory of Relativity

Foreign Student Admission
Qualifications for Applicants
  Standard Qualifications Requirement
Examination at the College
1. Different screening/admission system from that used for Japanese applicants.
2. Japanese language test, written and oral examinations. The subjects for written examinations vary according to the respective faculty.
3. The exception to the above (1.) is as follows: The applicants for the Faculties of Letters, Law, Business & Commerce and the School of Medicine who have stayed in Japan over two years or have been registered with a Japanese college/university for more than a year as a regular student must take the same kind of examinations that are required of Japanese applicants. However, they are not required to take a Japanese language test.
4. Applicants for the School of Medicine who are not in the above exception category (3.) must take a Japanese language test as well as the same kind of examinations that are required

of Japanese applicants. However, they are exempt from the short essay test.

5. The dates for the examinations also vary with the respective faculty. The School of Medicine gives the examinations from January through March while all the other faculties give them in January.

6. As the prerequisite for the application, the Faculties of Letters, Economics, Business & Commerce and Science & Technology require their applicants to take the Japanese Language Proficiency Test and General Examination for Foreign Students.

7. For further details, please refer to Gaikokujin Ryugakusei Nyugaku Shiken Yoko (Gakubu) which is available from the International Center, Keio University.

Documents to be Submitted When Applying
Standard Documents Requirement
Additional Documents to be submitted:

1. Letter of Reference
2. It is desirable that those foreign students who have taken a national/international standard examination for college entrance or its equivalent in their own countries include the results in their application.

Application deadline:
Applicants residing outside of Japan: middle October
Applicants residing in Japan: middle November

Academic year starts on the first of April:
Foreign students are admitted in April. A special Japanese language program offered at the International Center admits foreign students in April and September.

Applicants who have passed the entrance examinations should complete procedures for admisssion on the dates designated by the respective faculty.
School of Medicine: middle March
Other Faculties: early February

For further details, please refer to Gaikokujin Ryugakusei Nyugaku Shiken Yoko (Gakubu).

GRADUATE PROGRAMS

Graduate School of Business Administration (First Year Enrollment : Master's 70)
Division
Business Administration

Graduate School of Business and Commerce (First Year Enrollment : Master's 30, Doctor's 20)
Divisions
Commercial Science, Management and Accounting

Graduate School of Economics (First Year Enrollment : Master's 70, Doctor's 15)
Divisions
Economic History, Economic Policy, Economics, Economic Theory

Graduate School of Human Relations (First Year Enrollment : Master's 40, Doctor's 11)
Divisions
Education, Psychology, Sociology

Graduate School of Law (First Year Enrollment : Master's 150, Doctor's 30)
Divisions
Civil Law, Political Science, Public Law

Graduate School of Letters (First Year Enrollment : Master's 95, Doctor's 21)
Divisions
Chinese Literature, English and American Literature, French Literature, German Literature, History, Japanese Literature, Library and Information Science, Philosophy

Graduate School of Medicine (First Year Enrollment : Doctor's 68)
Divisions
Internal Medicine, Pathology, Physiology, Preventive Medicine, Surgery

Graduate School of Science and Technology (First Year Enrollment : Master's 365, Doctor's 57)
Divisions
Administration Engineering, Applied Chemistry, Chemistry, Electrical Engineering, Instrumentation Engineering, Mathematics, Mechanical Engineering, Physics

Foreign Student Admission
Qualifications for Applicants
Master's Program
Standard Qualifications Requirement
Doctor's Program
Standard Qualifications Requirement
Applicants for the Graduate School of Medicine must meet one of the following qualifications:

1. have graduated or are to graduate from (undergraduate) programs in Medicine or Dentistry
2. have completed a Master's Program or are eligible for a Master's Degree in a discipline other than Medicine or Dentistry where they have taken courses necessary for a prospective major in the Graduate School of Medicine
3. have completed 18 years of school education abroad, the last part of which is either in Medicine or Dentistry

Applicants for a clinical program in the Graduate School of Medicine have to meet additional qualifications. For such details, please refer to Daigakuin Nyugaku Shiken Yoko which is available from the Academic Affairs Office.

Examination at the University
Master's Program

1. Applicants should take both written and oral examinations. The subjects for the examinations vary according to the respective major. However, all the applicants must take a Japanese language test.
2. The Graduate School of Business Administration gives the same kind of examinations that

are required of Japanese applicants. These consist of written and oral examinations. Applicants can take them either in October, or in winter (late February through March). For further details, please refer to Daigakuin Kei-eikanri Kenkyuka Shushikatei Boshu Yoko, which is available from the Graduate School of Business Administration, Keio University, 1960 Hiyoshi-honcho, Kohoku-ku, Yokohama-shi 223.

3. The examination dates vary according to the respective graduate school. The Graduate School of Science & Technology gives the examinations in January, while all the other graduate schools except for Graduate School of Business Administration give them in September and October.

Doctor's Program

1. Foreign students applying for a Doctor's Program in any graduate school are basically expected to take the same kind of examinations that are required of Japanese applicants with some minor alterations to the screening criteria.

2. The examinations usually consist of written and oral examinations. The subjects for the examinations vary according to the respective major.

3. The date for the examinations is March for all the graduate schools.

4. For further details, please refer to Daigakuin Nyugaku Shiken Yoko.

Documents to be Submitted When Applying

Standard Documents Requirement

Additional documents to be submitted:

Master's Program:

Letter of Reference to be filled out by a person who knows the applicant very well

Doctor's Program:

1. Statement of Research Areas and Goals

2. Personal History

3. Paper (Master's Thesis or other paper comparable to Master's Thesis) and its summary either in Japanese or English for applicants for the Graduate Schools of Economics, Law, Human Relations, Business & Commerce, and Science & Technology.

4. Some applicants for the Graduate Schools of Science & Technology, and Medicine should submit additional documents. Please refer to Daigakuin Nyugaku Shiken Yoko.

Application deadline:

Master's Program:

Graduate School of Science & Technology

Applicants residing outside of Japan: end of August

Applicants residing in Japan: end of October

Graduate School of Business Administration: either early October or middle February (twice a year)

Other Graduate Schools

Applicants residing outside of Japan: end of May

Applicants residing in Japan: end of August

Doctor's Program:

Graduate School of Science & Technology: middle February

Graduate School of Medicine: late February and early March

Other Graduate Schools: early February

*

Research Institutes and Centers

Business School, Center for Area Studies, Computer Center, Electron Microscope Laboratory, Fukuzawa Memorial Center for Modern Japanese Studies, Institute for Communications Research, Institute of Audio-Visual Language Education, Institute of Cultural and Linguistic Studies, Institute of Information Science, Institute of Nutritional Research, Institute of Oriental Culture, Institute of Physical Education, International Center, Ise Keio Hospital in Mie Prefecture, Keio Economic Observatory, Pharmaco Chemical Research Institute, Teacher Training Center, Tsukigase Rehabilitation Center in Shizuoka Prefecture, University Hospital

Facilities/Services for Foreign Students

1. Keio University has an International Center, a mainstay for its international educational interchange. The International Center administers various faculty and student exchange programs. It provides, in addition to the above, the programs described below. The International Center houses a Student Common Room where foreign and Japanese students are encouraged to cultivate mutual understanding and friendship.

2. The Faculty of Science & Technology gives supplementary lessons of mathematics, physics and chemistry for its freshmen.

3. Counseling services are provided for foreign students for such matters as academic, personal, interpersonal, financial, and career concerns as well as for cross-cultural adjustment at the International Center.

4. The International Center, in cooperation with KOSMIC, a voluntary Keio student group, holds various educational/recreational events throughout the year. Among these are a freshmen camp, dance parties, and discussion meetings.

Special Programs for Foreign Students

1. The International Center offers a special Japanese language program for those foreign students who are interested in studying Japanese. The applicants for this program must meet one of the following qualifications:

(1) have completed a four-year college/university education abroad and want to pursue graduate study at Keio University

(2) are either currently registered with or graduated from a four-year college/university

abroad and want to engage in Japanese studies

This Japanese program is independent of undergraduate and graduate programs described above. For further details, please refer to a brochure of Japanese Language Course available from the International Center.

2. Several courses on Japanese studies which center around politics, economics, society and culture of Japan are available through the International Center. These courses are designed for foreign students and are offered in English.

3. For the purpose of helping freshmen and sophomores with their English, some courses are offered. The number of these courses varies according to the respective faculty.

For Further Information
Undergraduate and Graduate Admission
International Education Division, International Center, Keio University, 2-15-45 Mita, Minato-ku, Tokyo 108 ☎ 03–453–4511 ext. 2310, 2322, 2323, 2373

Keisen Jogakuen College
(Keisen Jogakuen Daigaku)

2–10–1 Minamino, Tama–shi, Tokyo 206
☎ 0423–76–8215

Faculty
    Profs. 16   Assoc. Profs. 4
    Assist. Profs. Full–time 6; Part–time 7
Number of Students
    Undergrad. 212
Library 61, 476 volumes

Outline and Characteristics of the College

Keisen Jogakuen College began classes in April, 1988. With its establishment Keisen Jogakuen, founded in 1929, adds a four-year college to its junior high school, senior high school and junior college. The college's Faculty of Humanities includes a Department of Japanese Studies and a Department of British and American Studies.

Since Keisen Jogakuen began fifty-nine years ago, the spirit of Christianity has provided a firm foundation for the school's many educational programs. Founder Michiko Kawai's call for schools which educate women to think globally and independently is further fulfilled by Keisen Jogakuen College's foreign language programs and classes in cross-cultural comparative studies.

To help students attain a cosmopolitan outlook, the college also continues the Keisen tradition of receiving both foreign students and student returnees from abroad. Students are further called upon to avail themselves of various work/study-abroad opportunities. With native speakers employed as full-time faculty members, the school also hopes to provide students with the very best in foreign language education.

As freshmen, students take a broad selection of core courses. This continues with more freedom in selecting classes into the sophomore year. From the third year students begin more focused studies. In the fourth year this culminates in the required thesis, a product of student work in small seminar classes. Also, to help students learn from as broad a spectrum of acadmic disciplines as possible and thus extend their paticular scholary interests, all classes are open for auditing by students. In these and other ways, Keisen Jogakuen College provides a comprehensive, interdisciplinary and international environment for higher education.

Following the policy declared in the college's prospectus, the doors to the college are also held wide open to members of the local community. As part of the surrounding community's cultural development Keisen Jogakuen College aims to be a center for adult and continuing education.

With these educational goals and policies, Keisen Jogakuen College is a place where both the search for Christian truth and the pursuit of specialized academic knowledge can coexist in order to produce women of an international and independent spirit.

UNDERGRADUATE PROGRAMS

Faculty of Humanities (Freshmen Enrollment: 160)
British and American Studies
American History, Biology, British-American Climate and Topography, British History, Chemistry, Chinese, Christianity, Comparative Cultural Studies, English, Fine Arts, French, General Education Seminar, German, Health and Physical Education, History, Horticulture, Human Geography, Indonesian, Japanese, Korean, Life Science, Linguistics, Literature, Peace Studies, Pedagogy, Politics, Thai
Japanese Studies
Biology, Chemistry, Chinese, Chrisitanity, Comparative Cultural Studies, English, Fine Arts, French, General Education Seminar, German, Health and Physical Education, History, Horticulture, Human Geography, Indonesian, Japanese, Japanese Climate and Topography, Japanese History, Korean, Life Science, Linguistics, Literature, Peace Studies, Pedagogy, Politics, Thai

Foreign Student Admission
Documents to be Submitted When Applying
    Standard Documents Requirement
    Those applicants who possess the International Baccalaureate Certificate are required to present (1) the IB Diploma (2) transcripts of the final exams for the 6 courses.

*

Special Programs for Foreign Students

Japanese Language Course: Introductory/Intermediate/Advanced•Japanese State of Affairs. All Courses in the Dept. of Japanese Culture
For Further Information
Undergraduate Admission
Director of Admissions, Admissions Office, Keisen Jogakuen College, 2–10–1 Minamino, Tama–Shi, Tokyo 206 ☎ 0423–76–8215

Kinjo Gakuin University
(Kinjo Gakuin Daigaku)
2-1723 Omori, Moriyama-ku, Nagoya-shi, Aichi 463
☎ 052-798-0180

Faculty
  Profs. 33   Assoc. Profs. 13
  Assist. Profs. Full–time 7; Part–time 125
Number of Students
  Undergrad. 1,803   Grad. 15
Library 212,378 volumes

Outline and Characteristics of the University
  Kinjo Gakuin was first established as a private Christian school for women in 1889 by Annie E. Randolph and R. E. McAlpine, missionaries of the Presbyterian Church, USA. Today it is the oldest and largest women's university in Central Japan.
  The school is located on three campuses with a total enrollment of over 6,000 students. Kinjo Gakuin Junior High School with 1,200 students and the Kinjo Gakuin Senior High School with 1,500 students are located only two blocks from each other near the center of Nagoya, which gives the students the advantage of separate campuses and yet the closeness that make cooperative activities possible. Kinjo Gakuin Junior College with 1,400 students, the University with 1,600 students, Graduate School with 12 students as well as the Kindergarten with 140 students are on the University campus, about 45 minutes from downtown Nagoya.
  Kinjo Gakuin Junior College has three departments. In the Literature Department are courses in Japanese literature, English literature and social studies. The Home Economics Department has courses in food and clothing and the Child Nurturing Department provides training in early childhood development and guidance.
  Kinjo Gakuin University has two departments, the Literature Department offering courses in Japanese literature, English literature and social studies, and the Home Economics Department offering courses in home economics and child training. Studies in Japanese literature, English literature and Sociology are offered in the graduate school.
  Kinjo Gakuin provides a quality Christian education for women. The school is rooted in the firm belief that only in the context of faith in Jesus Christ can young women develop their full potential. There-

fore, the school seeks to maintain an education system that integrates Christian faith and academic achievement.
  The school maintains a high educational standard. In addition, the school tries to instill in its students a sense of Christian commitment, community responsibility and international understanding. In this Christian environment students learn and grow during their formative school years.

UNDERGRADUATE PROGRAMS

Faculty of Home Economics (Freshmen Enrollment: 160)
  Department of Child Education
  Department of Home Economics
Faculty of Literature (Freshmen Enrollment: 240)
  Department of English Literature
  Department of Japanese Literature
  Department of Social Science
                    *
For Further Information
  Undergraduate Admission
Admissions Office, Kinjo Gakuin University, 2-1723 Omori, Moriyama-ku, Nagoya-shi, Aichi 463
☎ 052-798-0180

Kinki University
(Kinki Daigaku)
3-4-1 Kowakae, Higashi-Osaka-shi, Osaka 577
☎ 06-721-2332

Faculty
  Profs. 360   Assoc. Profs. 247
  Assist. Profs. Full–time 188; Part–time 676
  Res. Assocs. 404
Number of Students
  Undergrad. 22,810   Grad. 368
Library 900,000 volumes

Outline and Characteristics of the University
  Kinki University was founded in 1924 in eastern Osaka, Japan's second largest city. Its door was open to as many students as possible, including students from other countries. From that time on, many hopeful young men and women have successfully studied many fields. Because of the university's relative youth and the dynamic spirit which has characterized the school since its foundation, Kinki University is today renowned throughout Japan for its progressive attitude towards education.
  With its sights set firmly on the future, Kinki University has done everything possible to establish an academic atmosphere that will lead students towards the enhancement of society and the creation of a new and enlightened era of human achievement.
  For example, Kinki University was the first in Japan to construct a nuclear reactor and nuclear re-

search laboratory. This laboratory and the research projects conducted there have had great influence, not only on the university, but on society in general.

Kinki University also led the way in marine life research by establishing an "Underwater Farm" where saltwater fish breeding and artificial incubation are studied. This is today one of the world's most advanced projects of its kind.

The Kinki University Medical Department and affiliated hospital were established in 1974. They are today extremely modern in terms of both architecture and facilities. The hospital wards and conference rooms are heated and cooled by an advanced solar energy system, the first of its kind in Japan. The system also supplies the building with hot water. Quiet, virtually maintenance-free, and highly economical, the system is an excellent example of the way in which valuable resources can be husbanded through wise and efficient management.

These are just a few of the ways in which Kinki University has established its reputation for innovation and originality.

In addition to its normal undergraduate curriculum, Kinki University has a graduate school for doctoral and master's degrees in law, business, science, engineering, medicine, and pharmacy. Numerous other reseach organizations and facilities are maintained at the university such as the Asian Medical Research Center and the Marine Products Research Center. Additional facilities include a spacious Student Center, a large, modern library, and a Memorial Hall with a seating capacity of over 10, 000 people.

The major credit for Kinki University's success can be attributed to its underlying principles. More than other institutions of higher learning, Kinki University prides itself on its forward-looking attitude. As mankind enters a sophisticated new age characterized by high technology and unprecedented international, cultural, and artistic exchange, Kinki University will continue to pave the way with innovative ideas, concepts, and educational methods in keeping with the times.

UNDERGRADUATE PROGRAMS

Faculty of Agriculture (Freshmen Enrollment: 400)
Department of Agricultural Chemistry
Agricultural Chemicals, Agricultural Processing Technology, Environmental Pollution, Enzyme Chemistry, Fermentation Chemistry, Fertilizer Science, Fertilizer Technology, Fiber Chemistry, Plant Nutrition, Soil Science, Wood Chemistry, Zymurgy
Department of Agriculture
Agricultural Cooperation Theory, Agricultural Entomology, Citrus Growing, Crop Science, Farm Machinery, Farm Management Economics, Farm Survey, Floriculture, Forage Crop Science, Industrial Crop Science, Livestock Hygiene, Olericulture, Plant Cultivation, Plant Pathology, Pomology, Reproduction in Farm Animals, Soil Science, Tropical Crop Science
Department of Fisheries
Applied Fisheries Physics, Aquiculture, Fish-Diseases, Fisheries Chemistry, Fisheries Civil Engineering, Fisheries Cooperation Theory, Fisheries Economics, Fisheries Management Economics, Fisheries Microbiology, Fisheries Politics, Fresh and Marine Water Science, Limnology, Planktology
Department of Nutrition
Agricultual Food Products, Animal Food Products, Fermented Food Products, Fish Food Products, Food Analysis, Food Chemistry, Food Economics, Food Hygienics, Food Materials, Food Physical Chemistry, Food Preservation, Food Processing, Horticultural Food Products, Nutritional Chemistry, Public Hygienics
Faculty of Economics and Business Administration (Freshmen Enrollment: Day 1, 300; Evening 450)
Department of Business Administration
Administrative Accounting, Bookkeeping, Business Administration, Business Management, Business Management, Cost Accounting, Finance Administration, Forms of Business Organization, Fund Raising, History of Business Management, History of Business Philosophy, Labor Administration, Management Information Systems, Managerometrics, Production Administration, Public Enterprise Management, Sales Management, Tax Accounting
Department of Commerce
Accounting, Advertising, American and European History of Commerce, Auditing, Banking, Bookkeeping, Business Analysis, Commercial Policy, Commercial Science, Commodity Exchange, Financing, Foreign Exchange, Fund Raising, Insurance, International Accounting, International Financing, International Marketing, International Tourist Industry, International Trade, Japanese Commercial History, Japanese Foreign Trade, Life Insurance, Marketing, Marketing Research, Merchandizing, Securities Market, Transportation
Department of Economics
American Economy, Chinese Economy, Communal Economy, Cooperative Association, Econometrics, Economic Geography, Economic History, Economic History of Japan, Economic Methodology, Economic Policy, Economic Principles, Economic Sociology, Economics of Europe, Economics of South East Asia, Economics of Transportation, Economics of U. S. S. R. , Economic Statistics, Farm Economics, Finance, History of Economic Thought, Industrial Economics, Industrial Organization, International Economics, International Financing, International Trade, Regional Economics, Urban Policy
Faculty of Jurisprudence (Freshmen Enrollment: Day 500; Evening 160)
Department of Law
Anglo-American Law, Civil Law, Civil Procedure, Constitution, Criminal Law, Economic Law, Economic Policy, History of Foreign Affairs, History of

Political Affairs, History of Political Thought, International Law, International Politics, Japanese Legal History, Law of International Organization, Philosphy of Law, Private International Law, Public Administration, Public Finance, Real Estate Registration Law, Social Policy, Social Security Law

Department of Management Law

Administrative Law, Bankruptcy Law, Business Law, Commercial Law, Company Law, Industrial Property Law, Insurance and Maritime Commercial Law, International Business Transactions Law, Labor Law, Law for Lease of Land and House, Law of Family and Inheritance, Law of Obligations, Law of Realty, Real Estate Registration Law, Securities Law, Tax Law

Faculty of Medicine (Freshmen Enrollment: 100)

Department of Medicine

Anatomy, Anesthesiology, Bacteriology, Clinical Pathology, Cranial Nerve Surgery, Dermatology, Hospital Management, Hygiene, Internal Medicine, Legal Medicine, Obstetrics and Gynecology, Open-Heart Surgery, Ophthalmology, Otorhinolaryngology, Pathology, Pediatrics, Pharmacology, Physiology, Plastic Surgery, Psychiatry, Radiation Medical Science, Surgery, Urology

Faculty of Pharmacy (Freshmen Enrollment: 120)

Department of Pharmacy

Biochemistry, Chinese Medicinal Pharmacy, Forensic Chemistry, Functional Morphology, Hospitalpharmaceutics, Hygienic Chemistry, Manufacturing Pharmacy, Microbiology and Immunology, Natural Products Chemistry, Pathology, Pharmaceutical Botany, Pharmaceutical Chemistry, Pharmacognosy, Pharmacology, Pharmaco-Physical Chemistry, Pharmacopoeia, Public Hygienics, Toxicology

Faculty of Science and Technology (Freshmen Enrollment: Day 1, 180; Evening 100)

Department of Applied Chemistry

Catalytic Chemistry, Chemical Industrial Management, Industiral Physical Chemistry, Industrial Analytical Chemistry, Industrial Inorganic and Physical Chemistry, Industrial Organic Chemistry, Industrial Polymer Chemistry, Industrial Terpene Chemistry, Material Chemistry, Metal Chemistry, Natural Organic Chemistry, Organic Metal Chemistry, Synthetic Organic Chemistry

Department of Architecture

Architectural Surveying, Architecture, Architecture Economics, Art and Figure for Architecture, Concrete Structure, Environmental Sanitation Engineering, Environment Engineering for Architecture, History of Architecture, Steel Structure, Structural Design, Urban Design

Department of Chemistry

Analytical Chemistry, Biochemistry, Chemical Engineering, Chemical Thermodynamics, Electro Chemistry, Enviromental Chemistry, Geochemistry, High Polymer Chemistry, High Polymer Solid State Physics, Inorganic Chemistry, Organic Chemistry, Physical Chemistry, Quantum Chemistry, Radio Chemistry

Department of Civil Engineering

Bridge Engineering, City Planning, Concrete Engineering, Design of Structure, Determinate Structures, Harbor Engineering, Highway Engineering, Hydraulics, Railway Engineering, Reinforced Concrete Engineering, River Engineering, Sewerage and Sewage Disposal, Soil Mechanics, Surveying, Water Power Engineering, Water Supply and Treatment

Department of Electrical Engineering

Applications of Electric Power, Control Engineering, Electrical Engineering Design and Drawing, Electrical Measurements, Electric Circuits, Electric Machinery, Energy Conversion Engineering, Physics of Electrical Materials, Transient Electric Phenomena

Department of Electronic Engineering

Acoustics, Circuit Theory, Electromagnetism, Electronic Circuits, Electronic Engineering, Electronic Machinery, Electronic Materials, Gas Electronics, Information Theory, Measurements in Electronic Communication Engineering, Microwave Engineering, Physics of Electronic Materials, Radio Engineering, System Engineering, Wire Communication Engineering, Wire Communication Engineering

Department of Management Engineering

Censor Engineering, Cost Control, Human Engineering, Information System, Materials Management, Operations Research, Personnel Management, Plant Engineering, Plant Layout, Production Control, Production Management, Quality Control, Robotics

Department of Mathematics and Physics

Algebra, Analysis, Analysis of Material Structure, Applied Mathematics, Differential Equations, Electromagnetism, Electronics, Elemental Particle Physics, Fluid Dynamics and Elasticity, Information Mathematics, Linear Algebra, Nuclear Physics, Optics, Physical Mathematics, Quantum Mechanics, Relativity, Solid State Physics, Statistical Mechanics, Topology

Department of Mechanical Engineering

Air Conditioning, Automatic Control, Combustion, Engineering Dynamics, Engineering Heat Transfer, Engineering Materials, Engineering Mechanics, Fluid Dynamics, Fluid Machinery, Internal Combustion Engine, Machine Design, Machine Tool, Manufacturing Processes, Measurement Engineering, Mechanical Drawing, Mechanisms, Metal Working, Steam Engineering, Strength of Materials, Structural Dynamics, Thermodynamics, Vacuum Engineering, Welding Engineering

Department of Metallurgical Engineering

Foundry Engineering, Heat Resistant Alloys, Heat Treatment, Iron and Steel, Iron Metallurgy, Metal Finishing, Metallography, Metallurgical Thermodynamics, Metal Physics, Metal Surface Chemistry, Metal Working, Non-Ferrous Alloys, Non-Ferrous Metallurgy, Powder Matallurgy, Refractory Materials, Solid State Physics, Welding

Department of Nuclear Engineering

Health Physics, Nuclear Fuel Engineering, Nuclear Physics, Plasma Engineering, Radiation Chemistry, Radiation Ecology, Radiation Engineering, Radiation Measurement, Radiation Shielding Engineering, Reactor Chemistry, Reactor Engineering

Foreign Student Admission

Qualifications for Applicants

1. Graduation from high school under the school education system in their country.
2. Qualification for enrollment in a university in their country.
3. Completion of 12 or more years of schooling outside of Japan.
4. Education equivalent to the above.

Documents to be Submitted When Applying

1. Application form (Kinki University Form)
2. Examination Voucher
3. Personal Information Sheet
4. Official Transcript from applicant's high school.
5. Graduation Certificate of expected Graduation Certificate from the applicant's high school.
6. Letter of Recommendation from principal of the applicant's high school.
7. Certificate of Alien Registration
8. Guarantee form
9. Japanese Language Certificate
10. Health Certificate

Application documents must be submitted to the Kinki University International Communication Center.

Application Period: October 1-31.

Examination at the University

First Screening: Document screening

Second Screening: Written Examination of Japanese Language proficiency, English and special subjects required by each Faculty, and Interview (if necessary, an interview with the guarantor)

Examination Date: January 13-14.

Announcement of Sucessful Applicants: January 30.

Note 1: An applicant who does not know Japanese sufficiently may be admitted to enter the Japanese Language Course.

Note 2: Documents and examination fee will not be returned or refunded.

GRADUATE PROGRAMS

The Department of Agriculture (First Year Enrollment : Master's 13)

Divisions

Agricultural Chemistry, Agriculture

The Department of Chemistry (First Year Enrollment : Master's 10, Doctor's 3)

Division

Chemistry

The Department of Commerce (First Year Enrollment : Master's 20, Doctor's 5)

Division

Commerce

The Department of Engineering (First Year Enrollment : Master's 22, Doctor's 9)

Divisions

Applied Chemistry, Architecture, Civil Engineering, Electronic Engineering, Mechanical Engineering

The Department of Law (First Year Enrollment : Master's 10, Doctor's 5)

Division

Law

The Department of Medicine (First Year Enrollment : Doctor's 45)

Divisions

Internal Medicine, Pathology, Physiology, Public Health and Hygiene, Surgery

The Department of Pharmacy (First Year Enrollment : Master's 8, Doctor's 5)

Division

Pharmacy

Foreign Student Admission

Qualifications for Applicants

1. Graduation (or expected graduation by the time of enrollment) from university.
2. Completion (or expected completion by the time of enrollment) of 16 or more years of schooling in non-Japanese schools.
3. Recognition by the Minister of Education.
4. Recognition by Kinki University graduate school as having educational equivalent to the above.

Documents to be Submitted When Applying

1. Application form or Examination Voucher (Kinki University Form)
2. Graduation Certificate or expected Graduation Certificate from the last school the applicant attended.
3. Official Transcript of the last school the applicant attended.
4. Letter of Recommendation from either president, dean or an academic advisor of the last school the applicant attended.
5. Health Certificate
6. Photo
7. Certificate of Alien Registration
8. Guarantee form
9. Japanese Language Certificats
10. Study plan

Application Period: October 1, (Sat.)-October 31, (Mon.) 1988.

Application documents must be submitted to the Kinki University International Communication Center.

Examination at the University

First Screening: Document screening

Second Screening: Written Examination and an Interview.

Examination Date: January 13, (Fri.)-January 14,

(Sat.) 1989.

Announcement of Successful Applicants: January 30, (Mon.) 1989.

Note 1: An applicant who does not know Japanese sufficiently may be admitted to enter the Japanese Language Course.

Note 2: Documents and examination fee will not be returned, once they are submitted.

*

Research Institutes and Centers

Atomic Energy Research Laboratory, Educational Research Laboratory, Environmental Science Research Laboratory, Ethnology Research Laboratory, Experimental Farm, Fisheries Research Laboratory, Food Science Research Laboratory, Hypertension Research Laboratory, Labor Problems Research Laboratory, Legal and Political Science Research Laboratory, Life Science Research Laboratory, Occupational Science Research Laboratory, Oriental Medicine Research Laboratory, World Economics Research Laboratory

Facilities/Services for Foreign Students

Lounge for overseas students

Trip in summer

Christmas party

Special Programs for Foreign Students

Japanese Language Course for Foreign Students.

For Further Information

Undergraduate and Graduate Admission

International Communication Center, Kinki University, 3-4-1 Kowakae, Higashi-Osaka-shi, Osaka 577 ☎ 06-721-2332 ext. 2722

Kitasato University
(Kitasato Daigaku)

5-9-1 Shirokane, Minato-ku, Tokyo 108
☎ 03-444-6161

Faculty

    Profs. 178   Assoc. Profs. 121

    Assist. Profs.   Full-time 279; Part-time 321

    Res. Assocs. 626

Number of Students

    Undergrad. 6, 322   Grad. 293

Library 376, 521 volumes

Outline and Characteristics of the University

Kitasato University is a private educational institution and obtains financial assistance from Kitasato Gakuen Foundation. The establishment of both the Kitasato Gakuen and University in 1962 commemorated the semicentennial of the founding of the Kitasato Institute. Shibasaburo Kitasato, founder of the Institute is a world-famous scholar , particularly in the field of bacteriology.

The Kitasato University mottos originated from

Kitasato's brilliant medical achievements and his philosophy are (1) the pioneer spirit, (2) requital of kindness, (3) wisdom culminating in practice and (4) the inflexible spirit.

In 1962 the School of Hygienic Sciences was first established. It was comprised of the Faculty of Chemistry and Faculty of Hygienic Technology.

Thereafter the following several schools have been established.

1964   School of Pharmaceutical Sciences. It comprised Faculty of Pharmaceutical Sciences.

1965   Added Faculty of Pharmaceutical Technology to the School of Pharmaceutical Sciences.

1966   School of Animal Sciences. It comprised Faculty of Veterinary Medicine and Faculty of Zootechnology.

1967   Added Faculty of Industrial Hygiene to the School of Hygienic Sciences.

1970   School of Medicine.

1972   School of Fisheries Sciences. It comprised Faculty of Aquacultural Sciences and Faculty of Marine Food Chemistry.

1978   Changed the names from School of Animal Sciences and Faculty of Zootechnology to School of Veterinary Medicine and Animal Sciences and Faculty of Veterinary Medicine and Animal Sciences.

1986   School of Nursing.

1988   Added Faculty of Biosciences to the School of Hygienic Sciences.

Since 1967, the Graduate Schools consisted of Master's and Doctor's programs were opened within each School except for the School of Nursing. Today, the University enrolls more than 6, 600 students and a full-time faculty of 1, 200 and is composed of six Schools, five Graduate Schools, two Departments of Intensive Studies, four Research Institutes and two University Hospitals.

The Shirogane campus (25, 255m²) is located in Minato-ku, Tokyo, and there are the Administrative Office of the University and School of Pharmaceutical Sciences, providing a gymnasium and tennis courts.

The Sagamihara campus (367, 016m²) is located in Sagamihara City, Kanagawa Prefecture near Tokyo, and there are the Schools of Hygienic Sciences, Medicine, Nursing and two University Hospitals. There are a students club house, and a number of athletic fields, containing tennis courts, a baseball field, an American football field, etc. Gymnasiums for Kendo, Judo and others are also available.

The Sanriku campus (629 ha.) is located in Sanriku-cho, Iwate Prefecture, facing the Pacific Ocean and there is the School of Fisheries Sciences. Recreation Center and the Freshwater Fish Culture Station attached to the School of Fisheries Science are located in Tadami-cho, Fukushima Prefecture.

The Towada campus (38 ha.) is located in Towada City, Aomori Prefecture at the northernmost part of the Honshu and there is the School of Veterinary

Medicine and Animal Sciences. The School maintains the Yakumo Farm (369 ha.) in Yakumo-cho, Hokkaido and the Ojika Farm (86 ha.) in Ojika-cho, Miyagi Prefecture.

UNDERGRADUATE PROGRAMS

School of Fisheries Sciences (Freshmen Enrollment: 160)
Faculty of Aquacultural Sciences
Aquacultural Sciences, Ecology and Environmental Sciences, Fish Pathology, Fish Physiology and Genetics
Faculty of Marine Food Chemistry
Aquatic Microbiology, Food Hygiene, Marine Biological Chemistry, Marine Food Chemistry, Science and Technology of Fishery Produce
School of Hygienic Sciences (Freshmen Enrollment: 340)
Faculty of *Biosciences*
Analytical Cytology, Cell Biology, Functional Morphology, Genetical Biochemistry, Hemogenetics, Laboratory Animal Science, Microbiology, Molecular Biology
Faculty of Chemistry
Analytical Chemistry, Biological Chemistry, Industrial Chemistry, Organic Chemistry, Physical Chemistry
Faculty of Hygienic Technology
Biophysics, Clinical Chemistry, Hematology, Immunology, Microbiology, Pathology, Physiology
Faculty of Industrial Hygiene
Environmental Health, Fundamental Chemistry, Health Administration, Mental Health, Public Health, Radiation Science, Sanitary Engineering
School of Medicine (Freshmen Enrollment: 120)
Faculty of Medicine
Anatomy, Anesthesiology, Autopharmacology, Biochemistory, Clinical Laboratory Medicine, Dermatology, Embryology, Emergency Medicine, Histology, Hygiene and Community Medicine, Internal Medicine, Legal Medicine, Medical Chemistry, Microbiology, Molecular Biology, Neurosurgery, Obstetrics and Gynecology, Ophthalmology, Orthopedics, Osteology, Otorhinolaryngology, Parasitology, Pathology, Pediatrics, Pharmacology, Physical Biochemistry, Physics (Radiant Rays), Physiology, Plastic Surgery, Psychiatry, Radiology, Surgery, Thoracic Surgery, Urology
School of Nursing (Freshmen Enrollment: 100)
Faculty of Nursing
Adult Nursing, Clinical Psychology, Community Health Nursing, Epidemiology, Family Sociology, Geriatric Nursing, Health Management, Health Statistics, Maternal and Child Health Management, Maternal Health Management, Maternal Nursing, Medical Legislation, Medical Nursing, Medical Sociology, Mental Health, Midwifery, Nursing, Nursing Administration, Nursing Art, Nursing Education, Pediatric Nursing, Psychiatric Nursing, Public Health, Surgical Nursing

School of Pharmaceutical Sciences (Freshmen Enrollment: 240)
Faculty of Pharmaceutical Sciences
Analytical Chemistry, Clinical Pharmacology, Clinical Pharmacy, Hospital Pharmacy, Hygienic Chemistry, Microbiology, Pharmaceutics, Pharmacognosy and Phytochemistry, Pharmacology, Physiological Chemistry, Public Health
Faculty of Pharmaceutical Technology
Immunology and Virology, Microbial Chemistry, Organic Synthetic Chemistry, Pharmaceutical Chemistry, Pharmaceutical Technology, Physical Chemistry, Physical Pharmacy, Radioisotope Research
School of Veterinary Medicine and Animal Sciences (Freshmen Enrollment: 340)
Faculty of Animal Sciences
Animal Breeding and Reproduction, Animal Feeding and Management, Animal Nutrition, Environmental Science, Science of Animal Products
Faculty of Engineering for Animal Husbandry
Agricultural Machinery, Grassland Reclamation, Grassland Science, Structures and Environment Engineering, Water Utilization for Animal Husbandry
Faculty of Veterinary Medicine
Experimental Pathology, Poultry Diseases, Veterinary Anatomy, Veterinary Hygiene, Veterinary Infectious Diseases, Veterinary Internal Medicine, Veterinary Microbiology, Veterinary Parasitology, Veterinary Pathology, Veterinary Pharmacology, Veterinary Physiological Chemistry, Veterinary Physiology, Veterinary Public Health, Veterinary Radiology and Radiation Biology, Veterinary Reproduction, Veterinary Surgery

Foreign Student Admission
Qualifications for Applicants
Standard Qualifications Requirement
Examination at the College
Foreign applicants are required to take the same entrance examination as Japanese applicants.
Documents to be Submitted When Applying
Standard Documents Requirement

GRADUATE PROGRAMS

Faculty of Fisheries Sciences (First Year Enrollment : Master's 6, Doctor's 3)
Division
Fisheries Sciences
Faculty of Hygienic Sciences (First Year Enrollment : Master's 10, Doctor's 3)
Divisions
Health Sciences, Hygienic Sciences
Faculty of Medicine (First Year Enrollment : Doctor's 76)
Divisions
Clinical Medicine, Pathological Sciences, Physiological Sciences, Socio-medical Sciences, Surgical Medi-

cine

Faculty of Pharmaceutical Sciences (First Year Enrollment : Master's 20, Doctor's 10)

Division

Pharmaceutical Sciences

Faculty of Veterinary Medicine and Animal Sciences (First Year Enrollment : Master's 10, Doctor's 6)

Divisions

Animal Sciences, Engineering for Animal Husbandry, Veterinary Medicine

Foreign Student Admission

Qualifications for Applicants

Master's Program

Standard Qualifications Requirement

Doctor's Program

Standard Qualifications Requirement

Examination at the University

Master's Program

Foreign applicants must take the same examinations as Japanese applicants.

Doctor's Program

Same as Master's program.

Documents to be Submitted When Applying

Standard Documents Requirement

*

Research Institutes and Centers

Bioscience Research Center, Medicinal Research Laboratory (Chemical Division), Research and Development Center of Hygienic Sciences, Veterinary Medical Research Institute

For Further Information

Undergraduate and Graduate Admission

Administrative Office, Kitasato University, 5-9-1 Shirokane, Minato-ku, Tokyo 108 ☎ 03–444–6161 ext. 3064

Kobe College
(Kobe Jogakuin Daigaku)

4-1 Okadayama, Nishinomiya-shi, Hyogo 662
☎ 0798-52-0955

Faculty
Profs. 51   Assoc. Profs. 25
Assist. Profs. Full–time 8; Part–time 200
Res. Assocs. 2

Number of Students
Undergrad. 2, 278   Grad. 25

Library 240, 000 volumes

Outline and Characteristics of the College

Kobe College has, through its long history of more than 100 years, cherished the great traditions which our predecessors have built in the face of many hardships. Our college has based its character education on Christian principles as exemplified by its motto: "Love thy God, love thy neighbour. " As

the oldest institution of higher education for women in western Japan, it has contributed greatly to the improvement of the position of women in our country. Kobe College has always endeavoured to promote international understanding through English education of a high quality and active international exchange. We must uphold these fine traditions.

To uphold traditions in the true sense, however, does not mean that we merely idealize the past and adhere to the old. As the Bible says, "be ye transformed by the renewing of your mind" (Romans 12: 2), we must renew and transform our traditions so that they revitalize our college in its second century.

Character building through Christianity now encounters difficulties in this age of secularization and mass society. With a renewed conviction that Christian character education should be at the core of education for a true human being, we must make every effort to develop our own education for today's needs and tomorrow's ideals.

Women's education has come to have a somewhat different meaning from that of 100 years ago. We have served to improve women's position and tried to liberate women as full human beings, and now we must form a clearer concept of the uniqueness of women. Paying attention to the recent issue of lifelong education, we must consider seriously the characteristics of the best educational foundation for women who will continue learning throughout their lives. It is the opportunity and duty of Kobe College, founded by women for women, to perform these tasks actively. Our role in furthering international understanding should also be expanded to promote studies of and exchanges with other Asian countries.

We ask for God's help and the cooperation of our many friends in maintaining the traditions of Kobe College and renewing its development as it moves into its second century.

UNDERGRADUATE PROGRAMS

School of Home Economics (Freshmen Enrollment: 110)

Department of Child Development Studies

Child Dietetics, Childhood Education, Child Welfare, Drawing and Handicraft, Early Childhood Education, Educational Anthropology, Family Education, Health Management of Children, Juvenile Culture, Juvenile Literature, Maternal Health Management, Mental Hygiene of Children, Physical Education, Problems of Handicapped Children, Psychology of Personality, Theory of Child Development

Department of Food and Nutrition Studies

Applied Microbiology, Biochemistry, Biophysical Chemistry, Enzyme Chemistry, Food Chemistry, Food Economics, Food Hygiene, Food Materials, Food Processing and Preservation, Health Administration, Nutrition Chemistry, Nutritive Physiology, Organic Chemistry, Pathological Nutrition, Public Health, Public Nutrition, Theory of Food Prepara-

tion
School of Literature (Freshmen Enrollment: 320)
Department of English
American Drama, American Novels, American Poetry, American Studies, British Drama, Contemporary American Literature, Contemporary English Literature, English Novels, English Prose & Poetry, History of American Literature, History of English Literature, History of the English Language, Linguistics, Middle English, Phonetics, Practical Criticism, Public Speaking, Rhetoric, Shakespeare, The Bible as Literature
Department of Inter-Cultural Studies
Archaeology, Comparative Culture: Comparative Psychology, Comparative Education, Comparative Religion, Comparative Sociology, Cultural Anthropology, Cultural Sociology, Ethics, French Literature, German Literature, History, History of Japanese Art, History of Japanese Culture, History of Japanese Thought, History of Oriental Culture, History of Western Art, History of Western Culture, Japanese Culture, Japanese Language and Literature, Philosophy, Problems of Humanity, Social Psychology, Social Psychology, Social Welfare, Sociology, Topography, Western Culture

School of Music (Freshmen Enrollment: 47)
Department of Music
Acoutics, Cembalo, Chamber Music, Chorus, Church Music, Composition, Conducting, Ensemble, Folk Music, Harp, History of Art Song, History of Opera, Keyboard Harmony, Musicology, Orchestra, Organ, Percussion Instruments, Piano, Stringed Instruments, Voice, Wind Instruments

Foreign Student Admission
Qualifications for Applicants
Standard Qualifications Requirement
Women only.

Those who have attended senior high school for more than one year in Japan and graduated, or those who have approved to have achieved the same or a better academic performance expected for a senior high school graduate.
Examination at the College
1. The First Examination:
Documents (The result will be sent to her address in Japan by the end of November.)
2. The Second Examination:
Achievement tests (Japanese, a foreign language required in the department of the applicant's choice, and other subjects), interview, and physical examination. (Full details will be given with the notification of the applicant's passing of the first examination.) Those who have failed in the second examination may audit classes in conformity to the auditor regulation.
Documents to be Submitted When Applying
Standard Documents Requirement
Period of Application: October 3–October 14, 1988.

Qualifications for Transfer Students
1. Women only.
2. Those who have completed the first-year curricula and are now enrolled in the second-year courses at a university, or those who have completed the second-year curricula at a university.
3. Those who have graduated from a two-year junior college or are expected to graduate in March, 1989.
4. Those who have graduated from a technical college or are expected to graduate in March, 1989.
5. Those who have been approved to have the same or better academic ability as those of the above.
Examination for Transfer Students
1. The First Examination:
Documents (The result of the first examination will be sent to the Japanese address of the applicant in November.)
2. The Second Examination:
Full details will be sent to the Japanese address of the applicant with the notification of her passing the first examination. Upon receipt of the second examination fee, Kobe College will send the examination registration card to the Japanese address of the applicant.
3. Notice on Certification:
Those who wish to obtain the license of dietitian from the Department of Food and Nutrition Studies must be transfers from a university authorized as an institution for training dietitians.
Documents to be Submitted When Applying
Standard Documents Requirement
Following documents are also required.
1. Curriculum vitae (not necessary for those who are currently enrolled in a university or college).
2. Permission to apply for the transfer examination from the university or college in which the applicant is currently enrolled (not necessary for those who have graduated or are expected to graduate by March, 1989).
3. The applicant who is currently enrolled in a university or college should indicate all the courses and credits she is now taking (not necessary when the certificate of the school records contains this information).
4. Titles of textbooks and brief descriptions of all the courses that the applicant has taken and is now taking, to be written by the applicant in Japanese or English on sheets of B5-format (18 cm×25. 5 cm).
5. Certificate of TOEFL grade (the Department of English only).
6. A recorded cassette tape of the applicant's performance in her major field. Any musical piece of the applicant's choice, 10 to 15 min-

utes long (the Department of Music only).
Period of Application: October 3-October14, 1988.

GRADUATE PROGRAMS

Graduate School of Literature (First Year Enrollment : Master's 15)
Divisions
English, Japanese Cultual Studies, Sociology and Social Welfare

Foreign Student Admission
Qualifications for Applicants
Master's Program
   Standard Qualifications Requirement
   Women only.
Examination at the College
Master's Program
   The foreign students qualified in the preliminary screening by documents can take the entrance examination with Japanese students. It is usually given in March.
   Subjects of entrance examination:
English Major: English and American Literature, English Linguistics, English, Alternative of French or German and Interview
Sociology and Social Welfare Major: Sociology, A Thesis Examination, Alternative of English, French and German, and Interview
Japanese Cultural Studies Major: Japanese Cultural-Studies, A Thesis Examination, Alternative of English, French and German, and Interview
   Documents to be Submitted When Applying
   Standard Documents Requirement
   The following documents are required in addition to the common ones.
   1. A personal history
   2. Identification documents issued by the home government or embassies and legations in Japan
NB: As to the research plan, only the applicant's own hand writing in Japanese is accepted.

*

Research Institutes and Centers
Kobe College Institute for Women's Studies, Kobe College Research Institute
Facilities/Services for Foreign Students
   Dormitory
The dormitory of Kobe College is considered an integral part of the school's educational facilities rather than a mere lodging house. Participating in numerous educational and recreational activities, students live together in an atmosphere which promotes democracy and Christianity. This kind of group–life experience enriches the students' college years and provides invaluable training for the future home life and social involvement of the residents.
   Social Hall
The Social Hall is used for the purpose of club activities as well as a place for staff members and students

to relax and chat with each other.
   Rokko Seminar House
Rokko Seminar House, situated at the summit of Mt. Rokko, provides an ideal setting for training camps, seminars and recreational activities.
Special Programs for Foreign Students
Elementary Japanese (Grammar, Reading, Chinese Character)
Intermediate Japanese (Grammar, Composition, Reading)
Advanced Japanese
For Further Information
   Undergraduate and Graduate Admission
Admission Office, Kobe College, 4-1 Okadayama, Nishinomiya-shi, Hyogo   662   ☎ 0798-52-0955 ext. 542

Kobe–Gakuin University
(Kobe–Gakuin Daigaku)

518 Arise, Ikawadani-cho, Nishi-ku, Kobe-shi,
Hyogo 673   ☎ 078-974-1551

Faculty
   Profs. 91   Assoc. Profs. 48
   Assist. Profs.   Full–time 13; Part–time 143
   Res. Assocs. 23
Number of Students
   Undergrad. 8, 051   Grad. 46
Library 344, 671 volumes

Outline and Characteristics of the University
   Kobe-Gakuin University is a young university, which celebrated its 20th anniversary in 1986. The Faculty of Nutrition was established in 1966, and the Faculties of Law, Economics, and Pharmaceutical Sciences followed successively.
   Though so young, Kobe-Gakuin Unviersity is a full-grown university. All four faculties of Kobe-Gakuin University have graduate schools with master's and doctoral programs. The Faculties of Nutrition and Pharmaceutical Sciences have produced three graduates with doctoral degrees. Faculty members of Kobe-Gakuin University are excellent, and educational and research facilities such as libraries and laboratories are well-equipped for graduate studies.
   Kobe-Gakuin University offers a well-balanced curriculum in the arts, social sciences, and natural sciences. Reaching beyond the usual liberal-arts program offered by most small-scale private universities, Kobe-Gakuin University has a variety of departments based on both the natural and social sciences, with interdepartmental and interdisciplinary research activities at the very core of the program. Student education is carried out in an atmosphere of extensive professor-student interaction and friendship.
   Kobe-Gakuin University emphasizes small-group education. In order to avoid the ill-conceived practice of "mass-production education, "the Uni-

versity groups students into laboratories in the departments of natural sciences, and into small-group seminars in the departments of social sciences. The system thus allows each teacher to instruct personally 20 to 30 students for a perios of two to three years. Kobe-Gakuin University has dozens of such seminars and laboratories in which true education can be achieved with personal, small-group instruction.

Kobe–Gakuin University believes that the classroom and laboratory are not the only settings for real university life. Kobe–Gakuin University emphasizes extracurricular and club activities in both cultural and athletic fields and encourages the well-rounded development of the student's character. Practical application of our philosophy can be seen in our entrance examination system in which the extracurricular records of the applicants are evaluated as an influential factor for admission.

Kobe–Gakuin University is a distinctive university. We hope that many students will be attracted to our campus.

UNDERGRADUATE PROGRAMS

Faculty of Economics (Freshmen Enrollment: 700)
Department of Economics
Accounting, Agricultural Economics, Auditing, Bookkeeping, Business Administration, Business Cycle, Business History, Business Management, Cost Accounting, Econometrics, Economic Development, Economic History, Economic Planning, Economic Policy, Economics, Economic System, European Economic History, Financial Management, History of Business Administration, History of Economic Doctrines, History of Economic Thought, History of Modern Economics, Industrial Organization, International Business Administration, International Economics, International Monetary Economics, Japanese Economic History, Japanese Economy, Labor Economics, Labor Management, Land Economics, Local Public Finance, Management Engineering, Marketing, Modern Enterprise, Money and Banking, Public Enterprise, Public Finance, Risk and Insurance, Securities, Small Business, Social Policy, Social Security, Statistics, System of National Accounts, Traffic Economics
Faculty of Law (Freshmen Enrollment: 700)
Department of Law
Administrative Law, Anglo-American Law, Civil Law, Commercial Law, Comparative Politics, Constitutional Law, Contemporary Politics and Diplomacy, Criminal Law, Criminology, Eastern Legal History, Economic Law, History of Political Thought, International Area Studies, International Law, International Organizations, International Politics, Japanese Legal History, Japanese Politics and Diplomacy, Labor Law and Social Security Law, Law of Civil Procedure, Law of Corporate Finance, Law of Criminal Procedure, Local Government Law, Philosophy of Law, Political Theory, Private

International Law, Public Administration, Tax Law, Third World Politics, Western Legal History
Faculty of Nutrition (Freshmen Enrollment: 100)
Department of Nutrition
Administration on Feeding Service, Environmental Hygiene, Epidemiology, Exercise Nutrition, Food and Nutritional Science, Food Chemistry and Analysis, Food Economics, Food Hygiene, Food Preparation, Food Science and Technology, Management of Feeding, Maternal Nutrition, Nutrient Enrichment of Foods, Nutrition, Nutritional Chemistry, Nutritional Pathology, Nutritional Physiology, Nutrition Education, Nutrition Management, Pediatric Nutrition, Public Health Nutrition, Science of Cookery, Senile Nutrition, Therapeutic Nutrition
Faculty of Pharmaceutical Sciences (Freshmen Enrollment: 180)
Department of Biopharmacy
Department of Pharmacy
Biochemistry, Chemical Hygiene, Chemistry, Clinical Physiology, Forensic Chemistry, Functional Morphology, Inorganic Pharmaceutical Chemistry, Medicinal Chemistry, Medicinal Phytochemistry, Microbiology, Organic Chemistry, Organic Pharmaceutical Chemistry, Pathology, Pharmaceutical Analysis, Pharmaceutical Analysis, Pharmaceutical Botany, Pharmaceutical Industry, Pharmacognosy, Pharmacology, Pharmacopeia Japonica, Pharmacy Administration, Pharmacy Jurisprudence, Physical Pharmacy, Physiological Chemistry, Radiopharmacy, Toxicology

Foreign Student Admission
Qualifications for Applicants
  Standard Qualifications Requirement
Examination at the University
Examination of application forms and an interview.
Date: February 7
Documents to be Submitted When Applying
  Standard Documents Requirement
1. Certificate of Japanese language proficiency certified on the prescribed form by a Japanese language school.
2. A letter stating the reason for application written in Japanese (about 800 words) by the applicant himself/herself. The topic must be (A) a motive or a reason to apply for admission to Kobe–Gakuin University or (B) applicant's goals upon admission to the University.
3   JLPT score

Qualifications for Transfer Students
  As a general rule, a transfer student can be admitted to the equivalent year of the Faculty of Pharmaceutical Sciences.
Examination for Transfer Students
  Documents and an individual interview including a test for Japanese language proficiency. In addition, one of the following examinations will be given,

depending upon the level at which the applicant expects to enter.

1. A basic examination on natural sciences, for an applicant to be admitted into the junior year.
2. An examination on subjects of general education with emphasis on English, for an applicant to be admitted into the sophomore year.

Documents to be Submitted When Applying
Standard Documents Requirement
1. JLPT score
2. A letter of recommendation from the diplomatic and/or consular office in Japan and any other documents which may be of advantage to the applicant.

GRADUATE PROGRAMS

Graduate School of Economics (First Year Enrollment : Master's 10, Doctor's 5)
Division
Economics
Graduate School of Food and Medicinal Sciences (First Year Enrollment : Doctor's 4)
Division
Food and Medicinal Sciences
Graduate School of Law (First Year Enrollment : Master's 10, Doctor's 5)
Division
Law
Graduate School of Nutrition (First Year Enrollment : Master's 8)
Division
Nutrition
Graduate School of Pharmaceutical Sciences (First Year Enrollment : Master's 12)
Division
Pharmaceutical Sciences

Foreign Student Admission
Qualifications for Applicants
Master's Program
    Standard Qualifications Requirement
    Applicants must take the Japnese Language Proficiency Test and General Examination for Foreign Students.
Doctor's Program
    Standard Qualifications Requirement
    Other requirements are the same as those for the Master's Program.
Examination at the University
Master's Program
Graduate School of Law and Economics:
    Selected by both a written examination and an interview.
Graduate School of Pharmaceutical Sciences:
    Selected by a Japanese language examination conducted through interview, a written examination, and an oral examination.
Doctor's Program

Graduate School of Law and Economics:
    Selected by a written examination, an oral examination on the applicant's Master's thesis, and an interview.
Graduate School of Food and Medicinal Sciences:
    Selected by both an oral presentation (Japanese is preferred although English can be accepted) by an applicant of his/her Master's thesis or of equivalent research work, and an interview.
Documents to be Submitted When Applying
Standard Documents Requirement
            *
Special Programs for Foreign Students
Undergraduate foreign students are also required to take 8 credits of Japanese language and 12 credits of Japanese studies coursework, which can replace the foreign language and general education credit requirements respectively.
For Further Information
Undergraduate and Graduate Admission
Admissions Office, Kobe–Gakuin University, 518 Arise, Ikawadani-cho, Nishi-ku, Kobe-shi, Hyogo 673 ☎ 078-974-1551 ext. 2170~3

Kobe Kaisei (Stella Maris) College
(Kobe Kaisei Joshi Gakuin Daigaku)

2-7-1 Aotani-cho, Nada-ku, Kobe-shi, Hyogo 657
☎ 078-801-2277

Faculty
    Profs. 18   Assoc. Profs. 5
    Assist. Profs. Full–time 8; Part–time 37
    Res. Assocs. 5
Number of Students
    Undergrad. 860

Outline and Characteristics of the College
    Stella Maris Women's College was established by the Franciscan Missionaries of Mary, a Catholic religious congregation of women founded in France in 1877 by Helen de Chappotin de Neuville. This large international congregation has over 9, 000 Sisters working in countries in all five continents (including communist countries). They are engaged in various types of apostolates such as education, social welfare, medical services, and pastoral ministry in local churches.
    The Sisters came to Japan at the close of the nineteenth century. They started their work by caring for lepers in Kumamoto, Kyushu. They established their first primary and secondary level school for girls in 1946 in Kobe just after World War Ⅱ.
    Nine years later, in 1955, they opened a two-years college specializing in English. Then in 1962, a Home Economics Department was added. The English Department was expanded into a four-year

course in 1965. At the same time the four-year French Literature Department was added. Thus the Franciscan Missionaries of Mary are able to offer a complete education beginning at the primary school level and continuing through a four-year college program for those wishing to major in either English or French Literature.

The spirit of Stella Maris College is based upon a Catholicism characterized by love of both God and of neighbor, universality, social justice, and service. The college aims to provide an over-all spiritual and intellectual education. Great emphasis is placed upon the value of the individual student. In order to give the student in-depth help in her major field of research, the enrollment is kept fairly small. Each student may thus receive close supervision from her teachers. In the French and English Departments, during the first two years the students are given an opportunity for language mastery. The last two years are devoted to small group work organized according to the topics of research chosen by the students.

The two-year Home Economics Department program offers a number of courses, some of which are required, and others of which are elective. Among those subjects offered are such courses as cooking, sewing, weaving, embroidety, and dyeing.

UNDERGRADUATE PROGRAMS

Faculty of Literature (Freshmen Enrollment: 80)
  Department of English Literature
  Department of French Literature
                    *
For Further Information
  Undergraduate Admission
Admissions Office, Kobe Kaisei (Stella Maris) College, 2-7-1 Aotani-cho, Nada-ku, Kobe-shi, Hyogo 657 ☎ 078-801-2277

Kobe Women's College of Pharmacy
(Kobe Joshi Yakka Daigaku)

4-19-1 Motoyamakita-machi, Higashinada-ku, Kobe-shi, Hyogo 658   ☎ 078-453-0031

Faculty
    Profs. 25   Assoc. Profs. 10
    Assist. Profs. Full-time 20; Part-time 32
    Res. Assocs. 29
Number of Students
    Undergrad. 1, 218   Grad. 10
Library   69, 134 volumes

Outline and Characteristics of the College
    Kobe Women's College of Pharmacy has sprung from Kobe Women's School of Pharmacy estab-

lished in 1930, which was renamed Kobe Women's College of Pharmacy in 1932. In 1949, the College of Pharmacy was raised to the status of the present College of Pharmacy with the official reforms in the educational system. The College, as is understood from its name, aims to provide women with professional knowledge and highly specialized techniques concerning the pharmaceutical sciences so that they can establish themselves and contribute to society as trained women pharmacists after graduation. The number of alumnae has so far reached over 9, 000 in total. Many of them have cut prominent figures as career women in various occupations or academic research fields.

The College has two departments: Department of Pharmaceutical Science and Department of Biopharmaceutical Science. The latter was opened in 1965, anticipating the future demands for new pharmaceutical studies and education. At the time of graduation, students acquire the following qualifications: 1. eligibility requirements for the national examinations for pharmacist; 2. eligibility requirements for the national examinations for clinical technologist; 3. the license of medical technologist. The Graduate School started offering a two-year Master's program in 1967. Later a three-year Doctor's program was opened in 1979 for those who intend to carry out further studies and to acquire the Doctor's Degree. The Graduate School is coeducational. At present, however, female students outnumber male students.

So as to facilitate the gathering of sufficient data on research at home and abroad, the College Library is equipped with an information retrieval system by way of telephone network. The well–kept Botanical Garden for medicinal herbs is located on the campus and serves as one of the indispensable facilities of the College. The student dormitory which is able to accommodate more than 230 students is also located on the campus. At the top of Mt. Rokko stands a recreational facility called Seminar House, which is frequently used as a place for promoting mutual friendship between teachers and students or among students themselves.

In order not only to present fruitful results of pharmaceutical studies to society but also to inspire the pharmacists' interest in advanced knowledge, the College annually offers, as an extra-curricular program, the academic lectures known as CEP (Continuing Education in Pharmacy) to the alumnae.

The campus is situated at the eastern end of Kobe, an international port city noted for its exoticism and women's new fashion. The campus is in the midst of a quiet residential area. The view from the campus is splendid, with the urban areas and the Bay of Osaka far below. Many students are from the Kinki District, mainly from Osaka and Hyogo Prefectures, and many of the rest are from the western parts of Japan.

UNDERGRADUATE PROGRAMS

Faculty of Pharmacy (Freshmen Enrollment: 240)
Department of Biopharmaceutical Science
Department of Pharmaceutical Science
Biological Chemistry, Clinical Chemistry, Hygienic Chemistry, Inorganic Pharmaceutical Chemistry, Medicinal Chemistry, Microbiology, Organic Pharmaceutical Chemistry, Pharmaceutical Analysis, Pharmacognosy, Pharmacology, Pharmacy, Physical Chemistry, Physiology, Public Health, Radiation Chemistry

Foreign Student Admission
Qualifications for Applicants
    Standard Qualifications Requirement
    Women applicants only.
Examination at the College
    Examinations and a personal interview
Documents to be Submitted When Applying
    Standard Documents Requirement

GRADUATE PROGRAMS

Research Division in Pharmacy (First Year Enrollment: Master's12, Doctor's 6)
Divisions
Pharmaceutical Chemistry, Pharmacognosy, Medicinal Chemistry, Pharmaceutical Analysis, Radiation Chemistry, Hygienic Chemistry, Biological Chemistry, Pathological Biochemistry, Pharmacy, Pharmacology

Foreign Student Admission
Qualifications for Applicants
Master's Program
    Standard Qualifications Requirement
    Male students may also apply.
Doctor's Program
    Standard Qualifications Requirement
    Male students may also apply.
Examination at the College
Master's Program
    The following examinations are given.
    1. Examinations in two specialized subjects: one of them should be the major subject of an applicant. The other is elective.
    2. Foreign languages: English and German.
    A personal interview is also held.
Doctor's Program
    The following examinations are given.
    1. An oral examination mainly concerning the Master's thesis of an applicant.
    2. Foreign languages: English and German.
Documents to be Submitted When Applying
    Standard Documents Requirement
                        *

For Further Information
Undergraduate Admission

Dean of Instruction Department, Instruction Department, Kobe Women's College of Pharmacy, 4-19-1 Motoyamakita-machi, Higashinada-ku, Kobe-shi, Hyogo 658 ☎ 078-453-0031 ext. 310, 311
Graduate Admission
Head of Graduate School, Instruction Department, Kobe Women's College of Pharmacy, 4-19-1 Motoyamakita-machi, Higashinada-ku, Kobe-shi, Hyogo ☎ 658 078-453-0031 ext. 310, 311

Kobe Women's University
(Kobe Joshi Daigaku)
2-23-1 Nakayamate-dori, Chuo-ku, Kobe-shi, Hyogo 650   ☎ 078-231-1001

Faculty
    Profs. 65   Assoc. Profs. 26
    Assist. Profs. Full–time 17; Part–time 69
    Res. Assocs. 16
Number of Students
    Undergrad. 2,632   Grad. 50
Library 101,501 volumes

Outline and Characteristics of the University
    Kobe Women's University is run by Yukiyoshi Educational Institution, founded in 1941. The University's predecessor was Kobe Women's Junior College, established in 1951. This developed into Kobe Women's University in 1966. A graduate school was opened in 1984.
    The University seeks to nurture her female students, taking into account their natural characteristics, thereby bringing their abilities to the fore so that they may contribute to world peace and the welfare of mankind.
    The objectives and ideals of the school are to nurture women endowed with human feelings; raise capable women for the social services; encourage self-discipline; nurture religious sentiment; and raise women who can lead their contemporaries.

UNDERGRADUATE PROGRAMS

Faculty of Home Economics (Freshmen Enrollment: 140)
Department of Nutrition
Department of Nutrition Administrator Training
Faculty of Literautue (Freshmen Enrollment 380)
Department of Education
Department of History
Department of Literature
English Literature, Japanese Literature

Foreign Student Admission
Qualifications for Applicants
    Standard Qualifications Requirement
Examination at the University
    Applicants are required to have a fair knowl-

edge of Japanese.
Documents to be Submitted When Applying
Standard Documents Requirement
Application should be presented by the end of January.

Qualifications for Transfer Students
Applicants should have a proficiency in Japanese.
Examination for Transfer Students
Written examination and oral examination (interview).

GRADUATE PROGRAMS

Graduate School of Home Economics (First Year Enrollment : Master's 8)
Division
Food and Nutrition
Graduate School of Literature (First Year Enrollment : Master's 16)
Divisions
Education, English Literature, Japanese History, Japanese Literature

Foreign Student Admission
Qualifications for Applicants
Master's Program
Standard Qualifications Requirement
Examination at the University
Master's Program
Written examination in the major and oral examination (interview).
Documents to be Submitted When Applying
Standard Documents Requirement
Application deadline: the end of January.
∗
For Further Information
Undergraduate and Graduate Admission
Administrative Office, Kobe Women's University, 2-1 Aoyama, Higashisuma, Suma-ku, Kobe-shi, Hyogo 654 ☎ 078-731-4416 ext. 130

Kogakkan University
(Kogakkan Daigaku)

1704 Kodakujimoto-cho, Ise-shi, Mie 516
☎ 0596-22-0201

Faculty
Profs. 23   Assoc. Profs. 25
Assist. Profs. Full–time 6; Part–time 42
Res. Assocs. 3
Number of Students
Undergrad. 1, 539   Grad. 13
Library 151, 174 volumes

Outline and Characteristics of the University
Kogakkan University, one of the nation's oldest

universities, is located in Ise City, which is situated in Central Japan. Ise City is the site of Ise Jingu, the Grand Shrine of Ise, where the sun-goddess revered as the divine foundress of the Imperial Family is enshrined. The shrine stands in the green-shrouded sanctuary of the Ise-Shima National Park, exactly as it did when it was founded about 1700 years ago. It is visited by large numbers of people from all over the country. The nature of the shrine is best expressed by a remark of Arnold J. Toynbee, who visited it in 1967: "Here, in this Holy place, I feel the underlying unity of all religions. "

Kogakkan University originated in 1882 as a Shinto priest training institute in the library of the Ise Jingu which already had a history of more than two centuries. The initial guidelines of the University are clearly stated in the princely edict of 1900 by Prince Kuninori: "To elucidate and pursue the ethics and teachings rooted in our traditions through the study of the Japanese classics and thereby to contribute to a more complete development of Japanese culture. "

Our university aspires to become the moral and spiritual, as well as academic, center of Japan. It is symbolically situated in the "Holy place" of Ise, the so-called "spiritual home" of the Japanese, pursuing the study of what may be seen as our native virtues, or the spirit of the nation which dwells at the heart of the Japanese classics.

Our university is small consisting of a single Faculty of Literature. We have the Graduate School of Literature (Master's and Doctor's Programs), Graduate Course for Shinto Studies, the Shinto Institute and the Historiographical Institute. The only undergraduate faculty is made up of four independent departments: Education, Japanese History, Japanese Literature, and Shinto. The first department is a course for training elementary school teachers in Japan, and the other three are devoted to methodical research, with critical and annotative expositions of the Japanese classics as a central concern. Though the major fields of study may vary, they are identical in pursuing the essence of Japanese culture and traditions. As for graduate students, they are given the priviledge of free use of the Jingu Bunko, a vast treasure–house of precious documents and materials on Shinto, ancient history and literature of Japan. The two research institutes, situated in the district of long history and traditions, are actively collecting various kinds of historical materials and conducting specialized research.

UNDERGRADUATE PROGRAMS

Faculty of Literature
Department of Education
Education, Educational Administration, Educational Psychology, Educational Sociology, History of Education, Methodology of Education, Moral Education, Philosophy of Education
Department of Japanese History

Historical Geography, Historical Science, History of Japanese Thoughts, Japanese History, Paleography, World History

Department of Japanese Literature
Calligraphy, Chinese Literature, History of Japanese Literature, Japanese Grammar and Rhetoric, Japanese Linguistics, Japanese Literature

Department of Shinto
History of Shinto, Science of Religion, Shinto and Shinto Ritual, Shinto Classics, Shinto Services and Observances, Shinto Studies, Shinto Theology

Foreign Student Admission
Qualifications for Applicants
Standard Qualifications Requirement
Considerable proficiency in understanding and writing Japanese and a certain amount of preliminary knowledge about Japanese history, literature and culture in general.
Documents to be Submitted When Applying
Standard Documents Requirement

ONE-YEAR GRADUATE PROGRAMS

Postgraduate Course for Shinto Studies (Enrollment 10)
Shinto Studies

GRADUATE PROGRAMS

Graduate School of Literature (First Year Enrollment : Master's 10, Doctor's 4)
Divisions
Japanese History, Japanese Literature

*

Research Institutes and Centers
Historiographical Institute, Shinto Institute
For Further Information
Undergraduate and Graduate Admission
Instruction Section, Kogakkan University, 1704 Kodakujimoto-cho, Ise-shi, Mie 516
☎ 0596-22-0201 ext. 243

Kogakuin University
(Kogakuin Daigaku)
1-24-2 Nishi-shinjuku, Shinjuku-ku, Tokyo 163
☎ 03-342-1211

Faculty
    Profs. 82   Assoc. Profs. 48
    Assist. Profs. Full-time 63; Part-time 150
    Res. Assocs. 26
Number of Students
    Undergrad. 5, 134   Grad. 111
Library 183, 000 volumes

Outline and Characteristics of the University
Kogakuin University will commemorate its cen-

tennial in 1987. Credit for originating its concept of providing young people with a combined knowledge of modern technology and Japanese traditional techniques goes to Koki Watanabe, the then president of Tokyo Imperial University, who founded Koshu Gakko, the first Japanese technical training school, the predecessor of Kogakuin University in 1887.

Rechristened as Kogakuin Daigaku in 1949 under the new system of education, Kogakuin University is presently comprised of seven departments: Mechanical Engineering, Production Planning and Management System Engineering, Industrial Chemistry, Chemical Engineering, Electrical Engineering, Electronic Engineering (divided into two courses of study; Electronic Engineering and Information Engineering) and Architecture. Its education and research programs are conducted efficiently under the guidance of a teaching staff selected from the upper levels of the academic and industrial worlds.

Education at Kogakuin University, carried out with the aid of well-furnished laboratories and an extensive fieldwork system, is especially arranged so as to contribute to the promotion of highly-advanced science and technology and to maintain a good balance between "theory" and "practice. " This fact is well represented in the following Kogakuin University slogan: " ... to educate students to become engineers with high-level knowledge and skills in science and technology as well as to provide the educational background and sound judgement needed in today's high-tech. society ... "

Recently Kogakuin University has mapped out future plans for a new type of university to cope with the needs of a newly internationalized and information-oriented society. Kogakuin University is now referred to as a typical "double-nucleus" urban type of school with a good balance between its two campus locations--in Shinjuku, a city sub-center district, and in Hachioji, a suburb of the Metropolis.

UNDERGRADUATE PROGRAMS

Faculty of Engineering (Freshmen Enrollment: 920)
Department of Architecture
Architectural Design, Architectural Theory, Architecture Drawing, Aseismatic Engineering, Building Construction, Building Construction, Building Economics, Building Equipment, Building Materials, Building System Planning, Calamities Proof Engineering, City Planning, Computer Aided Design of Architecture, Construction Method, Construction Planning, Construction System Engineering, Design of Building Equipment, Environmental Engineering, Environmental Equipment, Equipment Engineering, Experimentation of Building, History of Architecture, Housing Planning, Landscape Architecture, Materials Science in Building, Reinforced Concrete Structure, Soil Engineering, Steel Structure, Structural Analysis, Structural Design, Structural Experiment, Structural Mechanics, Structural Theory,

Working Detail

Department of Chemical Engineering

Analytical Chemistry, Biochemical Engineering, Chemical Energy Engineering, Chemical Engineering, Chemical Engineering, Chemical Engineering Thermodynamics, Chemical Equipment and Plant Design, Chemical Equipment Drawing, Chemical Process Economics, Chemical Reaction Engineering, Engineering Materials, Information Processing, Inorganic Chemical Industry, Inorganic Chemistry, Instrumental Analysis, Instrumental and Control Engineering, Mathematics for Chemical Engineering, Mechanical Operations in Chemical Engineering, Organic Chemical Industry, Organic Chemistry, Physical Chemistry, Physical Chemistry, Pollution Prevention Technology, Powder Technology, Process Engineering

Department of Electrical Engineering

Acoustic Engineering, Communication Engineering, Control Engineering, Design Engineering of Electrical Machinery, Digital Electronic Computers, Electrical Experiments, Electrical Materials, Electrical Measurements, Electrical Power Generation and Transformation Engineering, Electrical Power Transmission and Distribution Engineering, Electric Circuit Theory, Electricity and Magnetism, Electric Machinery, Electric Railway, Electric Utility Industry Law and Control for Electric Institution, Electrochemistry, Electronic Circuit Theory, Electronic Materials Science, Electronics, Electronics Measurements, High Voltage Engineering, Illuminating and Electric Heating Engineering, Information Processing, Mechanics, Medical Engineering, Motor Control Engineering, Radio Wave Transmission Engineering, Transient Phenomena

Department of Electronic Engineering

Electronic Engineering Course

Information Engineering Course

Acoustic Engineering, Communication Engineering, Communication System Engineering, Computer Engineering, Control Engineering, Data Communication, Electrical Materials, Electrical Measurements, Electric Circuit Theory, Electro-magnetism, Electromechanics, Electronic Circuit Theory, Electronic Devices, Electronic Engineering, Electronic Materials Science, Electronics Measurements, High Voltage Engineering, Information Processing, Information Processing, Information Theory, Integrated Circuit Applications, Medical Engineering, Numerical Methods, Optoelectronics, Radio Wave Transmission Engineering, Solid State Electronic Devices, Transient Phenomena

Department of Industrial Chemistry

Analytical Chemistry, Applied Mineral Chemistry, Chemical Engineering, Comprehensive Biochemistry, Electrochemistry, Engineering Materials, Environmental Chemistry, Industrial Chemistry, Industrial Inorganic Chemistry, Industrial Organic Chemistry, Information Processing, Inorganic Chemistry, Natural High Polymer Chemistry, Organic Chemistry, Organic Reactions, Photochemistry, Physical Chemistry, Planning Technology, Polymer Chemistry, Radiochemistry, Solid-state Chemistry, Structural Organic Chemistry, Synthetic Chemistry of Polymers, Synthetic Organic Chemistry

Department of Mechanical Engineering

Applied Analysis, Applied Mechanical Engineering, Applied Physics, Control System Technology, Electro-mechanics, Fluid Engineering, Fluid Engineering, Fluid Machine, Group Technology, Heat Transfer, Highpolymeric Materials, Industrial Engineering, Information Processing, Instrumentation Engineering, Internal Combustion Engine, Machine Design, Mechanical Engineering, Mechanical Technology, Mechanical Vibrations, Metal Cutting, Metallic Materials, Nuclear Engineering, Numerical Method, Planning Technology, Plastic Working of Metals, Precision Machinery, Quantum Mechanics, Steam Energy Technology, Strength of Materials, System Engineering, Testing Method of Materials, Welding Technology

Department of Production Planning and Management System Engineering

See the listing above.

Foreign Student Admission

Qualifications for Applicants

Standard Qualifications Requirement

Examination at the College

Same as for Japanese (a written examination, an interview)

Documents to be Submitted When Applying

Standard Documents Requirement

GRADUATE PROGRAMS

Graduate School of Engineering (First Year Enrollment : Master's 28, Doctor's 12)

Divisions

Architecture, Electrical Engineering, Industrial Chemistry, Mechanical Engineering

Foreign Student Admission

Qualifications for Applicants

Master's Program

Standard Qualifications Requirement

Doctor's Program

Standard Qualifications Requirement

Examination at the University

Master's Program

Same as for Japanese

Entrance Examination Subjects: Mathematics, Foreign Language (English or German. Applicants for the Mechanical Engineering Division may choose French), Specialized Subjects, Interview and Oral Examination.

Doctor's Program

Same as for Japanese

Entrance Examination Subjects: Mathematics (Mechanics is included for applicants for the Mechanical Engineering Division.), Foreign Language (English or German. Applicants for the Mechanical Engineering Division must choose two foreign languages from among English, German of French.), Specialized Subjects (Applicants for the Mechanical Engineering Division are exempted), and Oral Examination.

Documents to be Submitted When Applying
Standard Documents Requirement

*

Research Institutes and Centers
The Computer Center
For Further Information
Undergraduate Admission
Kyomu-bu Nyushi-ka, Kogakuin University, 1-24-2 Nishi-shinjuku, Shinjuku-ku, Tokyo 163 ☎ 03–342–1211 ext. 348, 450
Graduate Admission
Kyomu-bu Gakumu-ka, Kogakuin University, 1-24-2 Nishi-shinjuku, Shinjuku-ku, Tokyo 163 ☎ 03–342–1211 ext. 217

Koka Women's College
(Koka Joshi Daigaku)

38 Kadono-cho, Nishi-Kyogoku, Ukyo-ku,
Kyoto-shi, Kyoto 615   ☎ 075-312-1783

Faculty
    Profs.   13   Assoc. Profs.   10
    Assist. Profs.   Full–time   2; Part–time   90
    Res. Assocs.   2
Number of Students
    Undergrad.   946
Library   73, 809 volumes

Outline and Characteristics of the College
Koka Women's College is an institute belonging to Koka Joshi Gakuen (Koka Women's Complex of Education), which educates women from kindergarten through four-year college. Established first in 1944, Koka Women's Vocational College was then reorganized into a junior college in 1950 and, in 1964, added a four-year college composed of two departments: English and American Literature, and Japanese Literature.

Located north of the Hankyu Railway Line's Nishi-Kyogoku Station, it takes only seven minutes from the station to the college. Near the Katsura River, one can enjoy such famous places as Arashiyama and Katsura Detached Palace, making Koka Women's College a place that stands amid splendid surroundings.

The school's name, "Koka" (literally, Light and Flower), was taken from a Buddhist sutra, propagating the teachings of acquiring the way of seeing fathomless life and light, which, in turn, indicates a way to purify our daily life and live in a world of equality. The fundamental principle of learning at Koka

Women's College is the education of students so they will practice this principle in their daily lives.

The central principle of the Department of English and American Literature is the appreciation and annotation of literary works. To this purpose, the department concentrates on organizing many classes composed of the least possible number of students, and aims for the fulfillment of the ideal Bachelor's thesis. All in all, the department intends to cultivate the humanity of generous minds through the learning of a wide range of European cultures centering upon English and American literary works.

UNDERGRADUATE PROGRAMS

Faculty of Literature (Freshmen Enrollment: 160)
Department of English and American Literature
English and American Literature, English Linguistics and Philology, English Phonetics, History of English and American Literature, Scenes and Manners of Great Britain and America
Department of Japanese Literature
Calligraphy and History of Calligraphy, Chinese Characters, History of Japanese Literature, Japanese Grammar, Japanese Linguistics, Scenes and Manners of Japan

*

For Further Information
Undergraduate Admission
Admissions Office, Koka Women's College, 38 Kadono-cho, Nishi-Kyogoku, Ukyo-ku, Kyoto-shi, Kyoto 615 ☎ 075-312-1783

Kokugakuin University
(Kokugakuin Daigaku)

4-10-28 Higashi, Shibuya-ku, Tokyo 150
☎ 03-409-0111

Faculty
    Profs.   130   Assoc. Profs.   54
    Assist. Profs.   Full–time   12; Part–time   433
    Res. Assocs.   4
Number of Students
    Undergrad.   10, 858   Grad.   135
Library   812, 303 volumes

Outline and Characteristics of the University
Kokugakuin University originally started as the Institute for the Study of Japanese Classics, or Koten Kokyu-sho, in 1882. At that time the Institute was located at Iidamachi, Tokyo.

It is quite evident that the Institute made a great contribution to the teaching and studying of the cultural and religious heritages of Japan. Eight years later, when it was re-named Kokugakuin, it became a three-year college for male students only, where history, literature and law were taught as well as Japanese classics. In 1904, Kokugakuin took another step and became a university, with two-year preparatory, three-year undergraduate, and two-year graduate courses.

With the continual increase in the number of students, Kokugakuin had to leave the rather small campus at Iida-machi, and moved in 1923 to a much larger site in Shibuya, Tokyo, where Kokugakuin is still located. Just before relocation, the official recognition as a university had been granted to Kokugakuin by the government under the University Act of 1919.

After World War II, Kokugakuin renewed its educational system, as all Japanese universities did. It should be noted that Kokugakuin was the first co-educational university in Japan. Recognizing brilliant female students is one of the merits Kokugakuin can be proud of. Also to be noted, Kokugakuin offered evening courses to students who had to work for a living in the day. The graduate school with a two-year Master's course and three-year Doctor's course was established for advanced studies on various topics in literature, law and economics.

By the end of 1966 Kokugakuin University was what it is now, with the three Faculties of Literature, Law, and Economics with their respective evening courses, and the Graduate school. Its academic activities now range from the studies of Japanese culture and religion, which is as ever the central part of Kokugakuin's activities, to social studies, which will enable the university to develop in the changing modern world.

University activities are now flourishing on three different campuses. Most of the teaching is conducted in Shibuya, where are situated the Administrative Center, the Main Library and the Museum. Subjects such as foreign languages, general education subjects, and physical education are taught to undergraduate students as Shin-Ishikawa in Yokohama. The baseball ground and other facilities on Hachioji Campus are for the students who enjoy extracurricular activities.

UNDERGRADUATE PROGRAMS

Faculty of Economics (Freshmen Enrollment: 500)
Department of Economics
Accounting, Agricultural Economics, Auditing, Bookkeeping, Business Administration, Business Finance, Business History, Business Management, Business Organization, Capital Market, Commercial Sciences, Contemporary Economy, Contemporary Japanese Economy, Econometrics, Economic Anthropology, Economic Geography, Economic History, Economic Planning, Economic Policy, Economics, Economics of Developing Countries, Economics of Transport, Fiscal Policy, Foreign Economic Affairs, History of Economic Doctrines, History of Management and Administrative Sciences, History of Modern Economics, Industrial Economics, Industrial Relations, International Economics, International Finance, International Trade, Japanese Eco-

nomic History, Labor Economics, Local Finance, Management Analysis, Modern Economics, Monetary Economics, National Economic Accounting, Public Finance, Socialist Economy, Social Policy, Statistics, Theory of Business Cycle, Theory of Money, Western Economic History

Faculty of Law (Freshmen Enrollment: 500)
Department of Law
Administrative Law, Antitrust Law, Bankruptcy Law, Civil Law, Civil Procedure, Commercial Law, Comparative Law, Constitutional Law, Criminal Law, Criminal Procedure, Criminology, Economic Policy, History of Diplomacy, History of Japanese Political Thought, History of Japanese Politics, History of Western Political Thought, History of Western Politics, International Law, International Politics, International Private Law, Japanese Economic History, Labor Law, Legal History of Europe, Legal History of Japan, Local Government, Philosophy of Law, Philosophy of Politics, Political Institutions, Politics, Politics, Public Administration, Social Policy, Tax Law, Western Economic History

Faculty of Letters (Freshmen Enrollment: 750)
Department of History
Archaeology, Archaeology of Foreign Countries, Bibliography, Cultural Anthropology, Descriptive Geography, Diplomatics, Diplomatics, Eastern History, Explanatory Bibliography, Historical Archaeology, Historical Geography, Historiography, History of Arts, History of Japanese Buddhism, History of Japanese Culture, Japanese History, Physical Geography, Shinto Archaeology, Topography, Western History

Department of Literature
Calligraphy, Chinese Classics, Chinese Linguistics, Classic Drama in Japan, Comparative Literature, Foreign Linguistics, Foreign Literature, History of Chinese Calligraphy, History of Chinese Classics, History of Chinese Thought, History of Foreign Literature, History of Japanese Calligraphy, History of Japanese Language, History of Japanese Literature, History of Japanese Philology, History of the Study of Japanese Literature, Japanese Language, Japanese Literature, Japanese Philology, Japanese Phonetics, Linguistics, Mass Communication, Structure of Chinese Ideograms

Department of Philosophy
Aesthetics, Buddhism, Christianity, Comparative Philosophy, Ethics, History of Chinese Thought, History of Indian Thought, History of Japanese Ethics, History of Japanese Thought, History of Literary Thought, History of Religious Thought, History of Social Thought, History of the Western Philosophy, History of Western Ethical Thought, Modern Philosophy, Philosophy, Philosophy of Language, Philosophy of Law, Philosophy of Politics, Philosophy of Science, Religious Philosophy

Department of Shinto
History of Japanese Religions, History of Shinto, History of Shinto Shrines, Liturgical Practices, Mis-

sionary Studies in Shinto, Norito (Shinto Prayer), Religious Laws and Regulations, Religious Utensils and Garments in Shinto, Sectarian Shinto, Shinto Archaeology, Shinto Classics and Documents, Shinto Rites, Shinto Theology

Foreign Student Admission

Qualifications for Applicants
    Standard Qualifications Requirement
Examination at the University
    Same as for Japanese
Documents to be Submitted When Applying
    Standard Documents Requirement
Application Period:
    January 10 to February 2
    February 15 to February 25 (Evening Course)
Date of Examination:
    Faculty of Letters: February 16
    Faculty of Law: February 15
    Faculty of Economics: February 17
    Evening Course: March 10
Announcement of Successful Applicant:
    Faculty of Letters: February 25
    Faculty of Law: February 24
    Faculty of Economics: February 27
    Evening Course: March 16
Period for Entrance Procedure:
    Faculty of Letters: February 25 to March 4
    Faculty of Law: February 24 to March 3
    Faculty of Economics: February 27 to March 6
    Evening Course: March 16 to March 23

GRADUATE PROGRAMS

Graduate School of Economics (First Year Enrollment : Master's 10, Doctor's 5)
    Division
Economics
Graduate School of Law (First Year Enrollment : Master's 10, Doctor's 5)
    Division
Law
Graduate School of Letters (First Year Enrollment : Master's 90, Doctor's 24)
    Divisions
Japanese History, Japanese Literature, Shinto

Foreign Student Admission

Qualifications for Applicants
Master's Program
    Standard Qualifications Requirement
Doctor's Program
    Standard Qualifications Requirement
Examination at the University
Master's Program
    Same as for Japanese (written tests on specialized subjects and foreign language, and an interview)
Doctor's Program
    Same as Master's Program

Documents to be Submitted When Applying
    Standard Documents Requirement

*

Research Institutes and Centers
The Institute for Japanese Culture and Classics
For Further Information
    Undergraduate Admission
Admission Office, Kokugakuin University, 4-10-28 Higashi, Shibuya-ku, Tokyo 150 ☎ 03-409-0111 ext. 243
    Graduate Admission
Graduate Office, Kokugakuin University, 4-10-28 Higashi, Shibuya-ku, Tokyo 150 ☎ 03-409-0111 ext. 251

Kokushikan University
(Kokushikan Daigaku)
4-28-1 Setagaya, Setagaya-ku, Tokyo 154
☎ 03-422-5341

Faculty
    Profs. 134   Assoc. Profs. 84
    Assist. Profs. Full-time 56; Part-time 366
    Res. Assocs. 10
Number of Students
    Undergrad. 12, 714   Grad. 65
Library 400, 000 volumes

Outline and Characteristics of the University

Kokushikan was established some seventy years ago in Tokyo. The first school, Kokushikan Gijuku (Kokushikan Public School) was inaugurated in 1917, since which time, steady and continual improvements were made. 1953 saw the opening of a Short Course University, and in 1958, the Department of Physical Education in the university reform. Various faculties such as those of Political Science and Economics, Engineering, Law, Literature and a Post Graduate School have been added in the intervening years, to produce a composite university with around 13, 000 students today.

The university is organized into six faculties, a Junior College and a Graduate School. The six faculties offer four-year programs of instruction leading to the professional degree of bachelor in the respective academic disciplines. In addition, the curricula provide students with standard qualifications in teaching, research and civil service. Kokushikan University has created a unique supervisor system to assist in student guidance, and through this system, has the advantage of maintaining close relationships between teachers and students.

The Faculty of Political Science and Economics-Day Session, established in 1961, consists of three departments: the Department of Political Science, Department of Economics and Department of Business Administration. This faculty, as well as the other five faculties, provides a program for obtaining teaching certification for junior high schools and senior high schools.

The Faculty of Political Science and Economics-Evening Session, founded in 1965, offers a program of study to meet the growing demand of working students who make use of the evening sessions to acquire their degree. The program offered will lead to the same degree and qualifications as that provided by the daytime curriculum. Management Science is not offered in the evening.

The Faculty of Physical Education came into existence in 1958 and offers programs of sports physiology, personal and social hygiene, advanced gymnastic theory, practice in various sports and martial arts, scientific research and physiological measurements. This Faculty has always maintained a high level of accomplishment in terms of their success in sports and martial arts contests in both national and international arenas.

The Faculty of Engineering, established in 1963, offers a program within four departments to prepare students for a career in engineering development and research.

The Faculty of Law, founded in 1966, exposes students to the legal issues of our society while keeping abreast of the current international trends of legal development. A special awareness is placed on the historical growth of law, an appreciation of the interrelationship of law and society, and the ability to use law as an implement of social control and development.

The Faculty of Literature was founded in 1966. It offers students an opportunity for specialized studies directed to develop the student's knowledge within the liberal arts and human sciences with an emphasis on oriental history and Japanese literature. The curriculum also provides qualification in social education supervision and library and museum science.

Kokushikan Junior College, founded in 1953, offers a two year study program broadly based on liberal arts. Teaching certification for junior high schools can be obtained in the Junior College.

The Setagaya campus is situated in a very quiet and pleasant environment, with an abundance of greenery, in one of Tokyo's residential areas. Shrines and temples, some dedicated to famous personages in Japanese history such as Yoshida Shoin and Ii Naosuke, are located near the school. Such historical surroundings lend themselves to an atmosphere conducive to academic endeavor.

The Tsurukawa campus, which includes the Junior College, is located in a rich natural setting in the Tama Hills some 40 minutes by train from the center of Tokyo to the southwest. This campus is also situated in an ideal environment in which students can devote themselves to their studies.

Other important factors about the university are that it is always on good terms with the local community by taking part in cultural and educational activities, and has played an important part in teaching and developing the Japanese Martial Arts on an international level.

UNDERGRADUATE PROGRAMS

Faculty of Engineering (Freshmen Enrollment: 160)
Department of Architectural Engineering
Basic Design, Building Laws and Regulations, Building Structure, City Planning, Drawing, Environmental Engineering, General Methods of Construction, Japanese Architectural History, Planning, Structural Dynamics, Structural Materials
Department of Civil Engineering
Bridge Engineering, City Planning, Concrete Engineering, Construction Methods, Drawing, Earthquake Engineering, Explosives Engineering, Harbor Engineering, Hydraulics, Hydrography, Railway Engineering, Road Engineering, Soil and Foundation Engineering, Structural Dynamics, Surveying, Water Pollution
Department of Electrical Engineering
Applied Mathematics, Circuit Theory, Communications Theory, Electrical Chemistry, Electrical Measurements, Electrical Physics, Electric Transmission and Distribution, Electromagnetics, Electronic Computer, Engineering of Semi-Conductors, High-Voltage Engineering, Operations Research, Programming Language
Department of Mechanical Engineering
Automatic Control, Casting, Control Theory, Drawing, Elasticity, Fluid Engineering, Freezing and Air-Conditioning, Heat Transfer, Industrial Thermodynamics, Machine Design, Materials Dynamics, Material Testing, Nuclear Engineering, Numerical Analysis, Operations Research, Plasticity, Program Linguistics, Transition Phenomena, Welding
Faculty of Law (Freshmen Enrollment: 200)
Department of Law
Administrative Law, Anglo-American Law, Bankruptcy Law, Civil Law, Civil Procedure, Commercial Law, Constitutional Law, Criminal Law, Criminal Procedure, Criminology, French Law, German Law, History of Legal Thought, Intangible Property Law, International Law, International Private Law, Japanese Legal History, Labor Law, Philosophy of Law, Sociology of Law, Tax Law, Western Legal History
Faculty of Literature (Freshmen Enrollment: 300)
Department of Education
Administration of Physical Education, Audio-visual Education, Educational Finance, Educational History, Educational Psychology, Educational Sociology, Ethics, Guidance of Youth and Adults, Japanese Educational History, Methodology of Education, Moral Education, Oriental Ethics, Pedagogy, Philosophy of Education, School Administration, Studies in Teaching Materials
Department of History and Geography
Air Photographs, Developmental Geography, Foreign History, Geographical Inspections, Japanese

History, Land Surveying Maps, Oriental History, Paleography, Topography

Department of Literature

Calligraphy, Chinese Philosophy, Chinese Poetry, History of Chinese Contemporary Literature, History of Japanese Literature, Introduction to the Japanese Language, Japanese Grammar, Japanese Linguistics, Japanese Literature

Faculty of Physical Education (Freshmen Enrollment: 150)

Department of Physical Education

Anatomy, Coaching Theory, Gymnastics, Individual Health, Kinesiology, Management and Administration of Physical Education, Motor Disturbance and First Aid, Nutrition, Physical Education, Physical Measurements, Physical Motion, Physiology, Preventive Medicine, Public Health, Sociology of Physical Education, Theory of Genetic Development, Training Theory

Faculty of Political Science and Economics (Freshmen Enrollment: 450)

Department of Business Administration

Accounting, Bookkeeping, Commercial Law, Economic Fluctuation, Finance Administration, History of Management, Industry Survey, Insurance, International Trade, Labor Management, Management, Management Theory, Production Management, Programming, Smaller Enterprises

Department of Economics

Economic History, Economic Policy, Economic Principles, Finance, Insurance, International Economics Relations, Japanese Economic History, Management Theory, Marketing, Mass Media Theory, Modern Economics, Science of Finance, Social Policy, Western Economic History

Department of Political Science

Administrative Law, Constitutional Law, History of Politics, Information Systems, International Law, International Politics, International Relations, Japanese Political History, Political Institutions Theory, Political Philosophy, Politics, Public Administration, Western Political History

Faculty of Political Science and Economics (**Evening Course**) (Freshmen Enrollment: 350)

Department of Economics

Accounting, Commercial Structures, Economic Law, Economic Policy, Economics, Energy Economics, History of Economics, International Economics, International Finance, Japanese Economic History, Science of Finance, Security Marketing, Statistics, Tax Law, Theory of Marketing Research, Western Economic History

Department of Political Science

Administrative Law, Commercial Law, Constitutional Law, Finance, History of Politics, International Law, International Politics, Japanese Political History, Labor Problems, Legal Systems, Political Systems, Politics, Public Administration, Western Political Theory

Foreign Student Admission

Qualifications for Applicants

Standard Qualifications Requirement

Examination at the University

Same as for Japanese. However, special consideration can be given by certain departments by providing a special examination for foreign students which consists of an English language examination and essay.

Documents to be Submitted When Applying

Standard Documents Requirement

Qualifications for Transfer Students

Foreign students who wish to transfer into Kokushikan University must first have their credits completed. The grading system, under which these credits were given at the schools they attended or graduated from, must be compared with and authorized by this university. They may then take the transfer student examination.

Keeping the above mentioned requirement in mind, the applicant should visit the university and consult with the persons in charge of this matter.

Examination for Transfer Students

Departmental exam.

Documents to be Submitted When Applying

Standard Documents Requirement

GRADUATE PROGRAMS

Graduate School of Economics (First Year Enrollment : Master's 20, Doctor's 10)

Divisions

Economics, Finance, History of Economics, International Economics

Graduate School of Political Science (First Year Enrollment : Master's 20, Doctor's 10)

Divisions

Administration Science, International Politics, International Relations, Political History and Thought

Foreign Student Admission

Qualifications for Applicants

Master's Program

Standard Qualifications Requirement

Doctor's Program

Standard Qualifications Requirement

Examination at the University

Master's Program

Same as for Japanese (a written examination, an interview and a medical examination.)

Doctor's Program

Same as Master's program.

Documents to be Submitted When Applying

Standard Documents Requirement

*

Research Institutes and Centers

Center for Information Science, Institute for Cultural Studies of Ancient Iraq, Institute for Research on Martial Arts and Ethics, Institute for the Study of

Politics, Institute for the Study of Religion and Culture

Facilities/Services for Foreign Students

The International Relations section helps to guide and counsel foreign students during their stay at the university. Foreign students regularly contact this office for these services.

There is a scholarship program as well as tutoring, home-stay and cultural exchange programs. Assistance funds for medical care are also provided to the students.

Foreign students regularly contact the International Relations section in order to take advantage of the counselling service available there.

Special Programs for Foreign Students

In the College of General Education, located on the Tsurukawa campus, a Japanese language class as well as a "Things Japanese" class are conducted in order to help foreign students reduce possible difficulties in their studies and in their daily life. Students are advised to contact their supervisor or the International Relations section in order to make the best use of this program.

For Further Information

Undergraduate Admission

International Relations section, Education Management Dept., Kokushikan University, 4-28-1 Setagaya, Setagaya-ku, Tokyo 154 ☎ 03-422-5341 ext. 318, 319, 320, 325

Graduate Admission

International Relations section, Graduate School Office, Kokushikan University, 4-28-1 Setagaya, Setagaya-ku, Tokyo 154 ☎ 03-422-5341 ext. 318, 319, 400, 401

Komazawa University
(Komazawa Daigaku)

1-23-1 Komazawa, Setagaya-ku, Tokyo 154
☎ 03-418-9562

Faculty
  Profs. 200   Assoc. Profs. 61
  Assist. Profs. Full-time 24; Part-time 506
  Res. Assocs. 5
Number of Students
  Undergrad. 14,996   Grad. 176
Library 725,000 volumes

Outline and Characteristics of the University

Komazawa University was originally established as a private school named "SENDANRIN" in 1952 by the Soto Sect of Zen Buddhism to promote the practice of Zen and the study of Buddhist philosophy and Chinese literature. On October 15, 1882, this school was refounded, reorganized, and renamed "Soto-shu Academy". The name was changed again to "Komazawa University" in 1925 when it was reorganized as a modern college in which students from

the public sector could enroll. In 1949, with the educational reforms proceeding World War II, eight faculties, 12 departments, a graduate school, and the evening session of a school were instituted: Faculties of Buddhist Studies, Arts and Sciences, Economics, Law, Business Management, Foreign Languages, and Health & Physical Education; Departments of Zen Buddhism, Buddhism, Japanese Literature, English and American Literature, Geography, History, Sociology, Economics, Commerce, Law, Politics, and Business Management; Graduate School of Humanities, Economics, Commerce, Law, and Business Management; the evening course of Economics, Business Management, and Law. Now our university has about 780 teaching faculty and 17,300 students including night school students.

The philosophy of education of Komazawa University is based on the spirit of Zen, which has had a great influence on Japanese culture as well as constituting the backbone of Asian thought for many centuries. The essence of the Zen spirit is realized in one's attitude that states "personal practice and pursuit of learning" must be united together. Therefore, the fundamental educational philosophy of our university is to educate each student in such a way that he can earnestly not only contribute to society but also find his inner self. The educational philosophy is realized by the following practical, main principles: "Confidence" which is one's basic readiness to live progressively; "Sincerity" which is one's pure mind in pursuit of universal truth; "Respect" which through one's innocent modesty esteems the personality of others with the dignity of life; "Compassion" which is one's all-pervasive mental attitude of contributing to others altruisticly.

Our university furnishes six research institutes-- Institutes of Zen Buddhism, Buddhist Economics, Applied Geography, Jurisprudence, Population Studies, and Mass Communications. The Institute of Zen Buddhism was established upon the request of scholars not only in Japan but from many other foreign countries of the world. The Zen Research Institute, where the Zen Meditation Hall is furnished, was completed in 1975 and has already received many visitors from abroad.

There are now about 100 foreign students including graduate students from foreign countries. Two Japanese Language Courses, Basic and Advanced, are offered for the foreign students.

UNDERGRADUATE PROGRAMS

Faculty of Arts and Sciences (Freshmen Enrollment: 520)

Department of English and American Literature
American Literature, Culture in England and America, English Language, English Linguistics, English Literature, History of English and American Literature

Department of Geography

Cartography, Climatology, Economic Geography, Ethnological Geography, Geography, Geomorphology, History of Geography, Human Geography, Oceanography, Hydrology, Physical Geography, Population Geography, Quantitative Geography, Settlement Geography, Soil Geography, Transportation Geography, Urban Geography

Department of History

Ancient Practices and Usages, Archaeology, Asian History, Buddhist Fine Art History, Ethnology, History of Philosophy, Japanese History, Methods of Historical Study, Occidental History, Oriental History, Palaeography, Topography

Department of Japanese Literature

Chinese Classics, History of Japanese Linguistics, History of Japanese Literature, Japanese Culture, Japanese Language, Japanese Literature

Department of Sociology

Psychology Course

Behavior Theory of Learning, Clinical Psychology, Mass Theory, Personality Psychology, Psychiatry, Psychological Statistics, Psychometric Method

Social Welfare Course

Administration of Social Welfare Operation, History of Social Welfare, Legislation of Social Welfare, Social Welfare

Sociology Course

Family Sociology, History of Sociology, Industrial Sociology, Legal Sociology, Mass Communication, Religious Sociology, Rural Sociology, Social Policy, Social Research, Social Statistics, Sociology of Religion, Urban Sociology

Faculty of Buddhist Studies (Freshmen Enrollment: 150)

Department of Buddhism

Buddhism, Buddhist Scriptures, History of Buddhism, History of Buddhist Doctrine

Department of Zen Buddhism

History of Zen Buddhism, History of Zen Buddhist Thought, Soto Zen Scriptures, Zen Buddhism

Faculty of Business Management (Freshmen Enrollment: 300)

Department of Business Management

Accounting, Business History, Business Management, History of Business Theory, Industrial Bookkeeping and Cost Accounting, Labor Management, Management Accounting, Management Control, Managerial Finance

Faculty of Business Management (Evening Course) (Freshmen Enrollment: 150)

Department of Business Management

Accounting, Business Management, Economics

Faculty of Economic Science (Freshmen Enrollment: 500)

Department of Commerce

Accounting, Commerce, Finance, History of Commerce, Policy of Commerce, Trade

Department of Economics

Economic History, Economic Policy, Economics, Political Economy

Faculty of Economics (**Evening Course**) (Freshmen Enrollment: 150)

Department of Economics

Accounting, Economic History, Economic Policy, Political Economy

Faculty of Law (Freshmen Enrollment: 500)

Department of Law

Administrative Law, Bankruptcy Law, Civil Law, Civil Procedure Law, Commercial Law, Constitutional Law, Criminal Law, Criminal Procedure Law, Economic Law, Environment Pollution Law, Industrial Property Law, International Law, Labor Law, Legal History, Legal Philosophy, Social Security Law, Tax Law

Department of Politics

Comparative Politics, History of Diplomacy, History of Japanese Politics, History of Political Thought, International Politics, Political Sociology, Political System, Politics, Public Administration

Faculty of Law (**Evening Course**) (Freshmen Enrollment: 150)

Department of Law

See the listing for Day Course.

Foreign Student Admission

Qualifications for Applicants

Standard Qualifications Requirement

First Grade Japanese Language Proficiency Testresult.

Examination at the University

A written exam and an interview. The contents of the written exam are as follows; (subject to change)

Faculty of Buddhist Studies (February 10, 1987)

Dept. of Zen Buddhism, Dept. of Buddhism: Essay in Japanese, English language

Faculty of Arts and Sciences (February 13, 1987)

Dept. of Japanese Literature: Foundation of Japanese Literature, Dept. of English & American Literature: English-Japanese Translation, Dept. of Geography, Dept. of History, Dept. of Sociology: Essay in Japanese

Faculty of Economics (February 11, 1987)

Dept. of Economics, Dept. of Commerce: Essay in Japanese, English language

Faculty of Law (February 10, 1987)

Dept. of Law, Dept. of Politics: Essay in Japanese, English language

Faculty of Business Management (February 12, 1987)

Dept. of Business Management: Essay in Japanese, English language

Documents to be Submitted When Applying

Standard Documents Requirement

1. JLPT score
2. Essay in Japanese (written in the prescribed forms)

Subject: "Reason for Applying for Komazawa University" (800-1200 characters)

GRADUATE PROGRAMS

Graduate School of Business Management (First Year Enrollment : Master's 5, Doctor's 2)
Division
Business Management
Graduate School of Commerce (First Year Enrollment : Master's 5, Doctor's 2)
Division
Commerce
Graduate School of Economics (First Year Enrollment : Master's 5, Doctor's 2)
Division
Economics
Graduate School of Humanities (First Year Enrollment : Master's 45, Doctor's 17)
Divisions
Buddhism, English Literature, Geography, Japanese History, Japanese Literature, Psychology, Sociology
Graduate School of Law (First Year Enrollment : Master's 10, Doctor's 4)
Divisions
Private Law, Public Law

Foreign Student Admission
Qualifications for Applicants
Master's Program
    Standard Qualifications Requirement
Doctor's Program
    Standard Qualifications Requirement
Examination at the University
Master's Program
    Written exams on specialized subjects, foreign languages, and interviews;
Graduate School of Humanities
Division of Buddhism: Questions on Zen Buddhism or Buddhism (One subject should be chosen.), and English
Division of Japanese Literature: Questions on Japanese Linguistics and Japanese Literature, and English
Division of English Literature: Japanese-English and English-Japanese translation of thesis on English and American Literature, and English
Division of Geography: Questions on Geography in general and English
Division of Japanese History: Questions on Outlines of Japanese History
Division of Sociology: Questions on Sociology in general and English
Division of Psychology: Questions on Psychology in general, and English, German/or French
Graduate School of Business Management
Division of Business Management: Business Administration, Economics Accounting, and English
Graduate School of Law
Division of Public Law: Constitutional Law, Criminal Law or International Public Law, and English or German

Division of Private Law: Civil Law, Civil Procedure Law, Commercial Law or Legal History, and English or German
Graduate School of Economics
Division of Economics: Economis in general, Statistics, History of Economics, Economic Policy or Science of Public Finance, and English
Graduate School of Commerce
Division of Commerce: Accounting (including Bookkeeping), and English
Written Exam Date: February 25, 1987
Interview Test Date: February 26, 1987
Doctor's Program
    Written exams on specialized subjects, foreign languages, and interviews;
Graduate School of Humanities
Division of Buddhism: Questions on Zen Buddhism or Buddhism (One subject should be chosen.), English, and Comprehension of Buddhist Sutra and Zen books written in Chinese
Division of Japanese Literature: Questions on Japanese Linguistics and Japanese language in general and English, German, French or Chinese
Division of English Literature: Japanese-English and English-Japanese translation of dissertation on English & American literature, the trend of thoughts in English and American literature, and German or French
Division of Geography: Questions on Geography in general and English, German or French
Division of Japanese History: Questions on Outlines of Japanese History, English, and Comprehension of Historical Materials in Chinese
Division of Sociology: Questions in Sociology and English, German or French
Division of Psychology: Questions on Psychology in general and English, German or French
Graduate School of Business Management
Division of Business Management: Business Administration, Economics or Accounting and English, German or French
Graduate School of Law
Division of Public Law: English and German
Division of Private Law: English and German
Graduate School of Economics
Division of Economics: Two languages from among English, German, French, Russian, Chinese and Spanish
Graduate School of Commerce
Division of Commerce: English and German or French
Written Exam Date: February 25, 1987
Interview Test Date: February 26, 1987
Documents to be Submitted When Applying
    Standard Documents Requirement
    Following documents are also required.
1. Essay in Japanese (written in the prescribed forms)
        Subject: "Research Project after Graduate

School Enrollment" (1200-2000 characters)

2. Certificate for one's Japanese language ability issued by President of one's last university or one's academic advisor.

3. Master's dissertation (only for those who apply for Doctor's Program)

*

Research Institutes and Centers

The Research Institute of Applied Geography, The Research Institute of Buddhist Economics, The Research Institute of Jurisprudence, The Research Institute of Mass Communications, The Research Institute of Population Studies, The Research Institute of Zen Buddhism

Facilities/Services for Foreign Students

Bus Hike program is organized in July to promote cultural exchange and to strengthen mutual understanding between foreign students and the faculty, staff members and Japanese students.

Rooms free of charge are available for exchange students from sister universities with which an Educational Agreement is established.

Special Programs for Foreign Students

Basic Japanese Language Elective Course: every Saturday.

Advanced Japanese Language Elective Course: every Tuesday.

For Further Information

Undergraduate and Graduate Admission

Chief Clerk for Entrance Exams, Admission Section of Information Bureau, Komazawa University, 1-23-1 Komazawa, Setagaya-ku, Tokyo 154 ☎ 03-418-9562

Konan University

(Kônan Daigaku)

8-9-1 Okamoto, Higashinada-ku, Kobe-shi, Hyogo 658   ☎ 078-431-4341

Faculty
    Profs. 122   Assoc. Profs. 40
    Assist. Profs.   Full–time 19; Part–time 298
    Res. Assocs. 1
Number of Students
    Undergrad. 7,749   Grad. 98
Library   611,013 volumes

Outline and Characteristics of the University

The predecessor of Konan University, Konan High School, was one of only a few private high schools under the old system of education in Japan. Founded in 1923 by Hachisaburo Hirao as a seven-year course of study, Konan quickly became well-known for its remarkable characteristics and was soon vying for fame with the best among public high schools. This tradition of excellence continued to be upheld after Konan evolved in 1951 into the present university with five faculties.

It was the earnest desire of the founder that educators abandon the ill-conceived practice then common in Japanese education of setting intellectual training above all else. Hirao insisted that they instead aim at the development of personality wherein both moral and physical training receive equal emphasis alongside intellectual pursuits.

Educators, Hirao believed, should help pupils cultivate their individual personalities and acquire spiritual independence. In the more than 60 years since the formation of the Konan educational institute, these ideals of the founder have nourished and thrived in Konan, though influenced by the changing times.

The characteristics of Konan students are said to include a broad perspective, independent judgement, capacity for execution, internationalism, and a humane and likeable personality. On the Konan campus, it is hoped that these qualities will be refined through intensive study in concert with participation in campus activities.

In March of 1951, Konan University was founded with a Faculty of Liberal Arts and Sciences. Classes began the following month. The Faculty of Economics was established one year later. The first graduation ceremony at Konan University was held in March of 1955. Two years later, separate Faculties, one of Liberal Arts and another of Sciences, were established to replace the former Faculty of Liberal Arts and Sciences.

In 1959, a Department of Information Systems and Management Science was established in the Faculty of Science. One year later, the Faculties of Law and Business Administration were established. Two years after that, in 1962, in the Faculty of Science, the Department of Applied Physics and Applied Chemistry were established. The Department of Applied Mathematics was established in the same faculty two years later.

The year 1964 also saw the founding of the Graduate School of Konan University, with master's degrees offered in the Humanities for Japanese, English, and Applied Sociology, and in Natural Science for Physics, Chemistry and Biology. Doctoral courses were offered in Humanities for English and in Natural Science for Physics. The following year, the Department of Social Science was established with master's degrees in Economics, Law, and Business Administration.

A ceremony celebrating the 50th anniversary of the foundation was held in April of 1969. The following year, a Department of German was established in the Faculty of Liberal Arts. The same year, doctoral degree courses in Humanities for Japanese and Applied Sociology, and in Social Science for Business Administration were established. In 1979, as the 60th anniversary of the foundation was celebrated, the new library building was dedicated and opened. And in May, 1984, the Institute for Interdisciplinary Studies was opened.

UNDERGRADUATE PROGRAMS

Faculty of Business Administration (Freshmen Enrollment: 300)

Department of Business Administration

Auditing, Business Finance, Business History, Business Management, Consumer Behavior, Cost Accounting, Financial Accounting, Financial Institutions, Foreign Trade, Insurance, International Accounting, International Business, International Marketing, Management and Organization, Management Systems, Managerial Accounting, Managerial Economics, Marketing Management, Money and Banking, Personnel Management and Labor Relations, Science History of Business Administration, Small Business, Tax Accounting

Faculty of Economics (Freshmen Enrollment: 300)

Department of Economics

Agricultural Economics, Comparative Economic Systems, Contemporary Capitalism, Econometrics, Economic Growth and Fluctuation, Economic History, Economic Policy, Economics, Economics of Developing Countries, Economics of Planning, Economics of Transportation, History of Economic Thought, History of European and U. S. Economy, History of Japanese Economic Thought, History of Modern Economics, History of the Japanese Economy, Industrial Economics, International Economics, International Finance, Labor Economics, Local Public Finance, Monetary Economics, Monetary Policy, Public Finance, Urban Economics

Faculty of Law (Freshmen Enrollment: 300)

Department of Law

Administrative Law, Anti-Trust Law, Civil Law, Commercial Law, Comparative Constitutional Law, Comparative Law, Constitutional Law, Criminal Law, Criminal Policy, Criminal Procedure, History of European Law, History of Foreign Policy, History of Japanese Law, History of Political Thought, International Law, International Politics, Labor Law, Local Government, Political Administration, Political History, Political Process, Political Science, Sociology of Law, Tax Law

Faculty of Liberal Arts (Freshmen Enrollment: 300)

Department of English

American Literature, English Linguistics and Grammar, English Literature, History of American Literature, History of English Literature

Department of Japanese

Chinese Literature, History of Japanese Literature, History of the Japanese Language, Japanese Language, Japanese Literature

Department of Sociology

Clinical Psychology, Comparative Culture, Cultural Anthropology, Ethics, Experimental Psychology, Folklore, Geography, History of Japan, History of Philosophy, History of the Occident, History of the Orient, Industrial Psychology, Industrial Sociology, Language and Culture, Mass Communication, Mental Health, Occidental Culture, Philosophy, Psychological Testing, Religion, Social Problems, Social Psychology, Social Survey, Social Welfare, Western Civilization, World History

Faculty of Science (Freshmen Enrollment: 270)

Department of Applied Chemistry

Biochemistry, Chemical Engineering, Colloid Chemistry, Coordination Chemistry, Industrial Inorganic Chemistry, Industrial Organic Chemistry, Metal Technology, Radiochemistry, Synthetic Organic Chemistry

Department of Applied Mathematics

Algebra, Analysis, Applied Mathematics, Automata Theory, Combinatorial Mathematics, Complex Analysis, Computers and Information Processing, Functional Analysis, Functional Equations, Geometry, Linear Algebra, Numerical Analysis, Theory of Probability, Topology

Department of Applied Physics

Acoustics and Electroacoustics, Applied Physics, Computer and Information Processing, Electronics, Instrumentation Technology, Optics, Quantum Mechanics, Strength of Materials, System Engineering, Thermodynamics

Department of Biology

Cytology, Developmental Biology, Ecology, Genetics, Microbiology, Molecular Biology, Physiological Chemistry, Physiology, Regulation in Organisms

Department of Chemistry

Analytical Chemistry, Biochemistry, Biochemistry of Microorganisms, Coordination Chemistry, Inoganic Chemistry, Organic Chemistry, Physical Chemistry, Polymer Chemistry, Structural Inorganic Chemistry

Department of Information Systems and Management Science

Accounting Data Processing, Applied Probability, Business Management, Engineering in Information Processing, Information Processing Systems, Information Theory, Management Information Systems, Management Science, Operations Research, Statistics

Department of Physics

Atomic and Molecular Physics, Atomic and Molecular Spectroscopy, Elasticity and Fluid Dynamics, Electricity and Magnetism, Nuclear Physics, Quantum Mechanics, Solid State Physics, Space Physics, Statistical Mechanics, Structural Inorganic Chemistry, Theory of Function, Theory of Relativity

Foreign Student Admission

Qualifications for Applicants

Standard Qualifications Requirement

Examination at the University

Regular entrance examinations, except for auditors or research students.

Documents to be Submitted When Applying

Standard Documents Requirement

GRADUATE PROGRAMS

Graduate School of Humanities (First Year Enroll-

ment : Master's 16, Doctor's 7)
Divisions
Applied Sociology, English, Japanese
Graduate School of Natural Science (First Year Enrollment : Master's 14, Doctor's 3)
Divisions
Biology, Chemistry, Physics
Graduate School of Social Science (First Year Enrollment : Master's 30, Doctor's 3)
Divisions
Business Administration, Economics, Law

Foreign Student Admission
Qualifications for Applicants
Master's Program
　　Standard Qualifications Requirement
Doctor's Program
　　Standard Qualifications Requirement
Examination at the University
Master's Program
　　Applicants must take the regular entrance examination, except for auditors or research students.
Doctor's Program
　　Same as Master's program.
Documents to be Submitted When Applying
　　Standard Documents Requirement
＊
Research Institutes and Centers
Computer Center, Institute for Interdisciplinary Studies, Konan-Illinois Center
Facilities/Services for Foreign Students
　　Konan-Illinois Center
Special Programs for Foreign Students
　　Konan-Illinois Program, L. L. Program.
For Further Information
Undergraduate and Graduate Admission
Admission Office, Konan University, 8-9-1 Okamoto, Higashinada-ku, Kobe-shi, Hyogo 658
☎ 078-431-4341 ext. 239, 221

Konan Women's University
(Konan Joshi Daigaku)

6-2-23 Morikita-cho, Higashinada-ku, Kobe-shi, Hyogo 658　☎ 078-431-0391

Faculty
　　Profs. 58　　Assoc. Profs. 16
　　Assist. Profs.　Part–time 115
　　Res. Assocs. 1
Number of Students
　　Undergrad. 2, 829　　Grad. 83
Library　228, 746 volumes

Outline and Characteristics of the University
　　The University, with a history of about 60 years, was founded in 1920 as Konan Girls' High School. Konan Women's Junior College was established in 1955, and then Konan Women's University

in 1964. Currently, the Faculty of Letters consists of four departments: Japanese Language and Literature, English Language and Literature, French Language and Literature, and Human Relations, while the Junior College consists of two departments: English and Domestic Science, which is composed of the Section of Food and Nutrition and the Section of Domestic Science.
　　The University is situated in the eastern part of Kobe City. The campus extends on a beautiful hill at the foot of the verdant Rokko Mountains and commands a beautiful view of Osaka Bay extending from Kii Peninsula to Awaji Island. From the front gate, the road is lined with camphor trees which are representative ones in Hyogo Prefecture. On the campus there are metasequoias, cedars, pines, gingkoes, and maples giving pleasant shades.
　　All students lead a full university life on the same campus, and live up to the college traditions of cultivating sincerity, respecting individuality, and instilling independence and creativity.

UNDERGRADUATE PROGRAMS

Faculty of Letters (Freshmen Enrollment: 680)
　　Department of English Language and Literature
American Culture and Society, English and American Literature, English Culture and Society, English Grammar, English Linguistics, History of American Literature, History of English Literature, History of the English Language, Juvenile Literature in English
　　Department of French Language and Literature
French Culture, French Linguistics, French Literature, History of French, History of French Literature
　　Department of Human Relations
Adolescent Psychology, Audio-Visual Education, Clinical Psychology, Cultural Anthropology, Educational Philosophy, Educational Psychology, Educational Sociology, Educational System, History of Education, History of Social Thoughts, History of Sociology, Medical Psychology, Methodology of Education, Pedagogy, Science of Man, Social Education, Social Psychology, Sociology
　　Department of Japanese Language and Literature
Chinese Literature, History of Japanese Literature, History of the Japanese Language, Japanese Language, Japanese Linguistics, Japanese Literature

Foreign Student Admission
　　Qualifications for Applicants
　　Standard Qualifications Requirement
　　Examination at the University
　　Applicants are screened by papers, a written examination (an essay in Japanese), and interview.
　　Documents to be Submitted When Applying
　　Standard Documents Requirement

GRADUATE PROGRAMS

Graduate School of Letters (First Year Enrollment :

Master's 30, Doctor's 12)

Divisions

English Language and Literature, French Language and Literature, Japanese Language and Literature, Pedagogy, Psychology, Sociology

Foreign Student Admission

Qualifications for Applicants

Master's Program

Standard Qualifications Requirement

Women only.

Doctor's Program

Standard Qualifications Requirement

Women only.

Examination at the University

Master's Program

Examination in academic subjects (specialized subject and one foreign language).

Doctor's Program

No examination is given to any applicant who has finished a master's program at our university.

Documents to be Submitted When Applying

Standard Documents Requirement

*

Facilities/Services for Foreign Students

The university has two dormitories.

For Further Information

Undergraduate and Graduate Admission

Publicity Division, Department of Instruction, Konan Women's University, 6-2-23 Morikita-cho, Higashinada-ku, Kobe-shi, Hyogo   658

☎ 078-431-0391 ext. 236

Koriyama Women's College

(Koriyama Joshi Daigaku)

3-25-2 Kaisei, Koriyama-shi, Fukushima 963

☎ 0249-32-4848

Faculty

Profs. 28   Assoc. Profs. 29

Assist. Profs. Full–time 17; Part–time 75

Res. Assocs. 29

Number of Students

Undergrad. 1, 507

Library 60, 000 volumes

Outline and Characteristics of the College

Koriyama Women's College is part of the Koriyama Kaisei Gakuen complex, consisting of the women's college, a girls senior high school, and a kindergarten. The college has both a senior college and junior college division. The school was founded in 1947 as the Koriyama Girls Technical School, and in 1950 was up-graded to Koriyama Women's Junior College with the establishment of a Home Economics department. This was the first women's junior college in Japan. In 1957, the attached girls senior high school was established as part of Kaisei Gakuen College, and today is the largest girls private senior high school in Tohoku. The senior college four-year Home Economics program was begun in 1966.

Since the founding of the junior college division, over 13, 000 graduates have entered almost all levels of society as teachers, specialist advisors, social workers, company workers, house-wives, and so on. In the Fukushima area of Japan, the students have become especially well-known in the fields of kindergarten education and food nutrition and dietetics. With the recent addition of the Japanese Cultural History department, our attention to general education in the fields of language, history, science, and so forth, and other academic innovations, Koriyama Women's Junior College has been a leader in the advancement of educational ideas throughout Japan.

The basic two-year courses in Early Childhood Development, Food Nutrition, Japanese Cultural History, Home Economics, Music, and Art each allow the students to obtain fully certified graduation certificates. Students can also take additional courses which will allow them to qualify for a variety of teaching certificates up to the junior high school level, licenses and certificates in dietetics and nutrition, and, in the case of Japanese Cultural History majors, necessary licenses and certificates for high levels of employement in libraries, museums, and social education centers. All junior college graduates have direct transfer rights to the senior college division.

The senior college division consists of two faculties: Humanistic Living and Food Nutrition. The purpose of the senior college program is to develop new ideas concerning home economics and food nutrition in order to meet the demands of our current daily lives. The College seeks to find basic philosophies for our lives, and to systematize them scientifically. It is from this point of view that the education programs promote the spirit of respect, responsibility, and freedom, and emphasize the establishment of individualism in conjunction with harmony with others. Home economics and dietetics programs should dedicate themselves to bettering people's lives and social culture more and more. Thus the programs aim not only at high levels of academic and scientific education, but at "humanistic" education as well.

The school is located in the center of Koriyama city, next to Kaisei Park. The campus, with its ancient pine trees, lovely gardens, and beautiful cherry trees, creates the kind of environment essential for clearness of thought, appreciation of nature and society, and high levels of academic achievement. The quiet and peaceful Shinshian tea ceremony rooms, the Japanese cultural museum which contains many cultural and historical artifacts from throughout Japan, and the Plateau Nature campus at Ishimushiro Atami village at the foot of Mount Adatara combine with a variety of festivals, athletic and cultural clubs, the school's observatory with the largest privately owned telescope in Tohoku, one of the most modern language laboratories, and other academic facilities to provide the students with the highest degree of academic and humanistic development.

Founding the college under the best natural environment--clear air, bright sunshine, and evergreen trees--the school has devoted itself to realizing the ideal of respect for human beings, thinking about and caring for everything in our daily lives. In that way, the college contributes to the harmony of mankind and peace in the world.

UNDERGRADUATE PROGRAMS

Faculty of Home Economics (Freshmen Enrollment: 100)

Department of Food Nutrition
Food Management Course
Food Nutrition Course
Clinical Nutrition, Cooking Science, Cultural History of Food Life, Food Chemistry, Food Economy, Food Hygiene, Food Material, Food Processing & Preservation, Food Supply Management, Nutrition, Nutritional Instruction, Nutritional Physiology & Biochemistry, Pathological Nutrition, Public Health, Public Nutrition

Department of Humanistic Living
Budget Management, Child Welfare, Cloth Arrangement, Cloth Composition, Clothing Design and Patterns, Clothing Hygienics, Clothing Materials, Clothing Science, Coloring Chemistry, Color Processing, Family and Social Home Economics, Family Education, Family Relations, Family Welfare, Fiber Processing, Food Nutrition and Human Development, History of Clothing, History of Life, Home Economics, Home Management, Institutional Management, Life Art, Merchandise Distribution, Social Security, Social Welfare, Welfare for the Aged

Foreign Student Admission
Qualifications for Applicants
Standard Qualifications Requirement
Examination at the College
Same as for Japanese. However, special consideration will be given according to the conditions of application.
Documents to be Submitted When Applying
Standard Documents Requirement

Qualifications for Transfer Students
Persons who have completed all junior college work or are due to complete it in March of the year of application.
Examination for Transfer Students
Same as for Japanese. However, special consideration will be given according to the conditions of application.
Documents to be Submitted When Applying
Standard Documents Requirement
*
Research Institutes and Centers
Center for Educational Research

For Further Information
Undergraduate Admission
Admission Office, Faculty of Home Economics, Koriyama Women's College, 3-25-2 Kaisei, Koriyama-shi, Fukushima 963 ☎ 0249-32-4848 ext. 213

Koshien University
(Koshien Daigaku)

10-1 Momijigaoka, Takarazuka-shi, Hyogo 665
☎ 0797-87-5111

Faculty
  Profs. 26   Assoc. Profs. 11
  Assist. Profs. Full-time 15; Part-time 37
  Res. Assocs. 14
Number of Students
  Undergrad. 1, 188
Library 43, 000 volumes

Outline and Characteristics of the University
Koshien University, founded in 1967, is a private university with two Faculties: the Faculty of Nutrition and the Faculty of Business Administration and Information Science. It is a member school of Koshien Gakuin, a comprehensive private educational institution ranging from kindergaden to university. The University strives to provide a highly professional education with emphasis on the well - rounded development of the student's personality, as described by the University's motto: "Ungrudging Effort, Harmonious Cooperation, and Absolute Sincerity. "

The University is located on a picturesque hill overlooking a magnificent stretch of Takarazuka City situated between Osaka and Kobe. Koshien University is one of the two four - year institutions in the City of Takarazuka. The Campus is surrounded by the verdant Rokko Mountains and has very easy access through a well-developed public and private transportation network, to Osaka, Kobe, Kyoto, Nara and other major neighbouring cities.

Faculty of Nutrition was established in 1967 with the aim of training students to be administrative dieticians equipped with clinical inspection technologies and expertise in improving dietetics, and also to be hygienic laboratory technicians. The Faculty is one of only three faculties (Eiyo Gakubu) in Japan providing similar nutrition courses.

Faculty of Business Administration and Information Science was added to the University in 1986 for the purpose of acquainting students with the latest management strategies, including managerial information processing technology.

Center for Education in Information Processing is equipped with the most up - to - date computer system. Computer - related courses are offered to students.

UNDERGRADUATE PROGRAMS

Faculty of Business Administration and Information Science (Freshmen enrollment: 200)
 Department of Business Administration and Information Science
Accounting, Artificial Intelligence, Bookkeeping, Business Administration, Business Management, Business Organization, Computer Science, Financial Management, Information Network System, Information Processing, International Management, Management Information Systems, Marketing, Office Automation, Operations Research
Faculty of Nutrition (Freshmen Enrollment: 100)
 Department of Nutrition
Administration in Mass Feeding, Anatomy and Physiology, Biochemistry, Clinical Nutrition, Cooking Science, Dietary Habits and Science, Exercise physiology, Food Economics, Food Hygiene, Food Processing, Food Science, Health Administration, Microbioloby, Nutritional Science, Nutrition Guidance, Pathology, Public Health, Public Health Nutrition

*

Research Institutes and Centers
Center for Education in Information Processing
For Further Information
 Undergraduate Admission
Admissions Office, Koshien University, 10-1 Momijigaoka, Takarazuka-shi, Hyogo   665
☎ 0797-87-5111

Koyasan University
(Koyasan Daigaku)

Koyasan, Koya-cho, Ito-gun, Wakayama 648-02
☎ 0736-56-2921

UNDERGRADUATE PROGRAMS

Faculty of Letters (Freshmen Enrollment: 140)
 Department of Buddhism
 Department of Esoteric Buddhism
 Department of Humanities
English and American Literature, Japanese History, Japanese Literature, Philosophy
 Department of Sociology
Social Welfare, Sociology

GRADUATE PROGRAMS

Graduate School of Letters (First Year Enrollment : Master's 10, Doctor's 6)
 Divisions
Buddhism, Esoteric Buddhism

The Kumamoto Institute of Technology
(Kumamoto Kogyo Daigaku)

4-22-1 Ikeda, Kumamoto-shi, Kumamoto 860
☎ 096-326-3111

Faculty
 Profs. 60   Assoc. Profs. 58
 Assist. Profs. Full-time 25; Part-time 67
 Res. Assocs. 22
Number of Students
 Undergrad. 3, 393   Grad. 33
Library 65, 750 volumes

Outline and Characteristics of the University

Since ancient times, Kyushu has served as one of the main doors through which culture from the Continent and other countries entered Japan. Today, Kyushu is known as the "High-Tech Island" of Japan because of the high concentration of the latest technologies there, supplying about 40% of all integrated circuits (I. C.) and ultra L. S. I. products made in Japan.

Our Institute is situated in Kumamoto, called the "City of Trees", in the center of Kyushu. From here, one can see the volcanic smoke rising from Mt. Aso, which is the biggest caldera in the world.

The Kumamoto Institute of Technology was established in 1967, originating from the Kimigafuchi Educational Foundation set up in 1949. The graduate school was opened in 1982.

Being a general college with only the Faculty of Engineering, the Institute can adapt to the remarkable progress being made by electronics, fine ceramics and biotechnology in present-day society. The Institute consists of eight departments: Electronic Engineering, Electrical Engineering, Industrial Chemistry, Mechanical Engineering, Civil Engineering, Architecture, Structural Engineering and Applied Microbial Technology.

Since its establishment, the Institute, as a private institution, has been future oriented in its research and the systematic promotion of new knowledge. With the constant advances made in the technological fields, the Institute plans to continue progressing into the 21st century.

UNDERGRADUATE PROGRAMS

Faculty of Engineering (Freshmen Enrollment: 750)
 Department of Applied Microbial Technology
Applied Microbiology, Environmental Microbial Technology, Food Microbial Technology, Microbial Chemistry, Microbial Genetic Technology
 Department of Architecture
Architectural Materials and Building, Architectural

Planning and Design, Architectural Structure and Construction, History of Architecture and Design
Department of Civil Engineering
Highway Engineering, Soil Engineering, Structural Engineering, Water Engineering
Department of Electrical Engineeing
Basic Electricity, Electric Application, Electric Machinery, Electric Power Engineering
Department of Electronic Engineering
Basic Electronics, Electronic Circuits, Electronic Measurement Control Engineering, Information and Communication Engineering
Department of Industrial Chemistry
Chemical Engineering, Environmental Engineering, Inorganic Industrial Chemistry, Organic Industrial Chemistry, Polymer Chemistry
Department of Mechanical Engineering
Applied Mechanical Engineering, Fluid Engineering, Mechanical Design, Mechanical Processing, Thermal Engineering
Department of Structural Engineering
Aeronautical Engineering Course
Construction Technology Course
Ship and Ocean Technology Course
Design and Construction, Fluid Engineering, Structural Engineering, Welding Engineering

Foreign Student Admission
Qualifications for Applicants
Standard Qualifications Requirement
Examination at the University
Submitted documents, the Japanese language proficiency.
Documents to be Submitted When Applying
Standard Documents Requirement

Qualifications for Transfer Students
Transfer students are required to have graduated from a recognized university or junior college.
Examination for Transfer Students
Academic career and credits achieved (the credits will be approved by the Faculty Council).
Documents to be Submitted When Applying
Standard Documents Requirement

GRADUATE PROGRAMS

Graduate School of Technology (First Year Enrollment : Master's 15)
Divisions
Applied Microbiology and Technology, Structural Engineering

Foreign Student Admission
Qualifications for Applicants
Master's Program
Standard Qualifications Requirement
Examination at the University
Master's Program
Documents, a written examination for the Japa-

nese language proficiency.
Documents to be Submitted When Applying
Standard Documents Requirement
*

For Further Information
Undergraduate and Graduate Admission
The Entrance Examination Division, The Kumamoto Institute of Technology, 4-22-1 Ikeda, Kumamoto-shi, Kumamoto 860 ☎ 096-326-3111 ext. 1404, 1415

Kumamoto Univeristy of Commerce
(Kumamoto Shoka Daigaku)

2-5-1 Oe, Kumamoto-shi, Kumamoto 862
☎ 096-364-5161

Faculty
Profs. 47   Assoc. Profs. 24
Assist. Profs. Full–time 12; Part–time 102
Res. Assoc. 1
Number of Students
Undergrad. 5, 025
Library 340, 000 volumes

Outline and Characteristics of the University
The predecessor of Kumamoto University of Commerce, the Institute of Oriental Language, was founded in 1942. It expanded to Kumamoto Institute of Foreign Language in 1945. It developed into Kumamoto Junior College with three programs (Social Relations, Commerce and Foreign Language). The Commerce Course became the independent 4-year Kumamoto University of Commerce in 1954. Kumamoto University of Commerce started with the Faculty of Commerce, offering a regular program and a night program.

The Department of Economics was established in the Faculty of Commerce in 1964. The Faculty of Economics was established in 1967. The Department of Management was established in the Faculty of Commerce in 1984. Kumanoto University of Commerce now has two Faculties and three Departments, and also the Graduate School of Commerce, established in April, 1988.

Kumamoto University of Commerce has valued independence, freedom and cooperation since its foundation. This spirit continues to be highly respected today. Every student at Kumamoto University of Commerce is taught to become a person who will contribute to the local Community. The student is encouraged not only to work for Kumamoto but also for Japan, and to be an internationally minded person as well in this era of internationalism.

Kumamoto University of Commerce is in the center of Kumamoto City, famous for its abundant greenery and the city where the Kumamoto Prefectural Office is located.

UNDERGRADUATE PROGRAMS

Faculty of Commerce (Freshmen Enrollment: 600)
Department of Commerce
Accounting, Bookkeeping, Business Finance, Commerce, Commercial Policy, Cost Accounting, Economic Law, Foreign Trade, Marketing, Market Research, Securities Market, Small and Medium-sized Business
Department of Management
Banking, Business Administration, Business Morphology, Commercial Law, Computer Programming, Decision Making, History of Business, Management, Management Science, Personnel Administration
Faculty of Commerce (**Evening Course**) (Freshmen Enrollment: 280)
Department of Commerce
See the listing in Day Course.
Faculty of Economics (Freshmen Enrollment: 430)
Department of Economics
Economic History, Economic Policy, Economics, Economic Theory, Public Finance, Statistics

GRADUATE PROGRAMS

Graduate School of Commerce (First year Enrollment: Master's 5)
Divisions
Accounting, Commerce, Finance, History of Commerce and Commercial Policy, Management

Foreign Student Admission
Qualifications for Applicants
Standard Qualifications Requirement
At least eight years of education must have been completed abroad.
Examination at the University
Applicants residing in Japan: Essay in Japanese and Interview.
Applicants not residing in Japan: Application forms submitted to the Admissions Division. Those who are admitted must write essay in Japanese and have an interview by the end of March.
Documents to be Submitted When Applying
Standard Documents Requirement
Certificate of Japanese Language Proficiency.

∗

Research Institutes and Centers
The Computer Center, The Institute of Economics and Business, The Institute of Foreign Affairs
Facilities/Services for Foreign Students
Foreign Students Lounge is provided.
Courses in Japanese are Provided for freshmen foreign students as one of the General Education Course subjects.
For Further Information
Undergraduate and Graduate Admission

Admissions Division, Educational Affairs Bureau, Kumamoto University of Commerce, 2-5-1 Oe, Kumamoto-shi, Kumamoto 862 ☎ 096-364-5161 ext. 211

Kunitachi College of Music
(Kunitachi Ongaku Daigaku)

5-5-1, Kashiwa-cho, Tachikawa-shi, Tokyo 190
☎ 0425-36-0321

Faculty
   Profs. 80   Assoc. Profs. 80
   Assist. Profs.   Full-time 46; Part-time 173
Number of Students
   Undergrad. 3,581   Grad. 53
Library   194,000 volumes

UNDERGRADUATE PROGRAMS

Faculty of Music (Freshmen Enrollment: 660)
Department of Composition
Department of Instrumental Music
Keyboards (Piano, Organ), Percussion, String Instruments, Wind and Brass Instruments
Department of Music Education
Early childhood education
Department of Musicology
Department of Vocal Music

Foreign Student Admission
Qualifications for Applicants
Standard Qualifications Requirement
   1.   Japanese fluency
   2.   Japanese Language Proficiency Test
Examination at the University
1st Stage : Screening of application forms and Japanese Language Proficiency Test results.
2nd Stage : Only applicants who have passed the 1st Stage will be required to take an examination in their major field. A secondary piano examination, and an interview. The Department of Music Education, however, requires an examination in both Voice and Piano, plus an interview.
No tapes will be accepted for judging.
Documents to be Submitted When Applying
Standard Documents Requirement
Admissions notifications are made in April.
Application deadline : early December.
Announcement of successful 1st stage applicants : end of January.
Date of 2nd stage examinations : same as for Japanese Applicants (end of February).

GRADUATE PROGRAMS

Graduate School of Music (First Year Enrollment : Master's 36,)
Divisions

Composition, Instrumental Music, Music Education, Musicology, Vocal Music

Foreign Student Admission
Examination at the University
Master's Program

Date of the entrance examination : November. Performance, written and oral examinations plus an interview.

Documents to be Submitted When Applying
Standard Documents Requirement

1) Certification of personal character.

2) Permission to apply. (If the applicant is serving at a public office or a business firm, from the head of their section. If enrolled at another graduate school, institution or facility, from the president of that school.)

3) A personal reference from the public office of the applicant's domicile.

4) Certification of Japanese language ability (Certified by a Japanese Language school or a public institute).

5) Foreign applicant's record (a printed form provided by Kunitachi).

*

Research Institutes and Centers
Electronic Music Studio, Research Institute
For Further Information
Undergraduate Admission
Admissions Office, Kunitachi College of Music, 5–5–1, Kashiwa–cho, Tachikawa–shi, Tokyo 190 ☎ 0425–36–0321 ext. 307, 308
Graduate Admission
Graduate School Admissions Office, Kunitachi College of Music, 5–5–1, Kashiwa–cho, Tachikawa–shi, Tokyo 190 ☎ 0425–36–0321 ext. 281, 282

Kurume Institute of Technology
(Kurume Kogyo Daigaku)

2228 Kamitsu-machi, Kurume-shi, Fukuoka 830
☎ 0942-22-2345

Faculty
Profs. 25   Assoc. Profs. 18
Assist. Profs. Full–time 18; Part–time 34
Res. Assocs. 20
Number of Students
Undergrad. 1, 511
Library 66, 500 volumes

Outline and Characteristics of the University
Kurume Institute of Technology opened as a technical college in 1971 after ten years as a technical junior college. The Institute has four departments at the present time: Architecture and Equipment Engineering, Electronics and Information Engineering, Mechanical Engineering, and Mechanical Engineering of Transportation. In addition to course-work

done in these departments, the Institute also includes a special two-year course of study in automotive engineering. There is also the Educational Center for Information Processing affiliated with the Institute, and Intelligence Engineering Laboratory has been opened.

The Institute presently has a faculty of 130 and a student body of 1, 400 in the four departments as well as 200 more enrolled in the automotive engineering course. K. I. T. finds that small class size and high standards of academic excellence produce creative and inspired students. In this way the Institute aspires to be a service to its community.

K. I. T. is situated in a beautiful natural environment in Kurume City located in southern Fukuoka Prefecture, Kyushu. The city is known for its rich historical past as a once prosperous castle town and contains, in its modern setting, a first-rate library and a well-known art gallery. Officially designated plans are underway to transform Kurume into a "technopolis" with international urban planning rich in cultural facilities and high-tech industries.

UNDERGRADUATE PROGRAMS

Faculty of Engineering (Freshmen Enrollment: 250)
Department of Architectural Equipment Engineering
Air Conditioning and Sanitation Engineering, Architectural Environmental Engineering, Architectural Function and Planning, Structural Engineering
Department of Electronics and Information Engineering
Electronic Control, Electronics and Information, Electronic Systems, Information Processing
Department of Mechanical Engineering
Electronic Machinery, Fluid Mechanics, Manufacturing Technology, Material Mechanics, Strength of Materials, Thermal Engineering
Department of Transport Mechanical Engineering
Dynamics of Transport Vehicles, Fuel and Lubrication Engineering, Transport Electrical Engineering, Transport Vehicle Design and Drafting, Transport Vehicle Engines, Transport Vehicle Structure

Foreign Student Admission
Qualifications for Applicants
Standard Qualifications Requirement
Examination at the University
By special selections.
Documents to be Submitted When Applying
Standard Documents Requirement
*
Research Institutes and Centers
Educational Center for Information Processing
For Further Information
Undergraduate Admission
Instruction Division, Student Office, Kurume Institute of Technology, 2228 Kamitsu-machi, Kurume-shi, Fukuoka 830 ☎ 0942-22-2345

Kurume University
(Kurume Daigaku)

67 Asahi-machi, Kurume-shi, Fukuoka 830
☎ 0942-35-3311

Faculty
  Profs.   87   Assoc. Profs.   63
  Assist. Profs.   Full-time   94; Part-time   285
  Res. Assocs.   81
Number of Students
  Undergrad.   4,069   Grad.   97
Library   350,071 volumes

Outline and Characteristics of the University

Kurume University is a private university consisting of the Faculty of Law, the Faculty of Commerce and the School of Medicine. Originally established in 1928 as Kyushu Medical School, it was renamed as Kyushu Higher Medical School in 1943. College status was achieved with the reorganization of the Japanese educational system in 1946, and the name was again changed to Kurume Medical College. University status was achieved in 1950 with the establishment of the Faculty of Commerce and with Kurume Medical College being reorganized as the University School of Medicine. The Graduate School of Medicine was established in 1956. In 1975 the Faculty of Commerce was reorganized and attained its present structure consisting of the Division of Commercial Sciences and the Division of Economics. The Faculty of Law was established in 1987

In the Faculty of Commerce, the Division of Commercial Sciences emphasizes the practical aspects of the business world, while the Division of Economics emphasizes theoretical research. Most of the courses offered in the two divisions are interchangeable, and students are allowed a wide range of curricular choices. The four-year program consists of a two-year core in the liberal arts and sciences and a subsequent two-year professional training in the student's chosen major field.

The aim of the School of Medicine from its beginning has been to produce medical practitioners with high capabilities and humanitarian values. Sixty years of school history have proved that the aim was right and has been effectively achieved. More than 6,600 graduates have actively participated in the field of medical practice, and also in the medical sciences. The school has a six-year educational program consisting of a two-year premedical program and a four-year medical program. Each class is composed of approximately 120 students. A four-year graduate program which leads to the degree of Doctor of Medical Science (D. M. S.) is offered to Medical graduates. Basic and clinical faculties conduct research studies in the laboratories of 33 departments and the five major institutes. Their achievements have received high evaluation by domestic and foreign workers in the biomedical sciences.

UNDERGRADUATE PROGRAMS

Faculty of Commerce (Freshmen Enrollment: 500)
  Department of Commercial Sciences
Accounting, Auditing, Bookkeeping, Business Science, Commercial Sciences, Cost Accounting, Financial Statement, Foreign Trade, Industrial Psychology, Management, Management Accounting, Management Consulting, Management Planning, Marine Transportation, Marketing Management, Personnel Administration, Production Management, Tax Accounting
  Department of Economics
Agricultural Economics, Econometrics, Economic Geography, Economic Policy, Economics, Economics of Developing Countries, Finance, History of Economic Theories, History of Economy, International Economics, International Money and Banking, Marxian Economics, Money and Banking, Public Finance, Theory of Economic Fluctuation

Faculty of Law (Freshmen Enrollment: 250)
  Department of Law and Politics
Administrative Law, Area Study, Author Law, Civil Law, Constitutional Law, Criminal Law, Hiostory of Political Science, International Law, International Politics, Law of Procedure, Legal History, Legal Theory of Law, Media Law, Philosophy of Law, Political Science, Social Law, Sociology of Law

School of Medicine (Freshmen Enrollment: 120)
Anatomy, Anesthesiology, Bacteriology, Biochemistry, Clinical Endocrinology and Metabolism, Dermatology, Gynecology and Obstetrics, Immunology, Internal Medicine, Legal Medicine, Neuropsychiatry, Ophthalmology, Oral Surgery, Orthopedic Surgery, Otorhinolaryngology, Parasitology, Pathology, Pediatrics, Pharmacology, Physiology, Public Health, Radiology, Surgery, Urology, Virology

Foreign Student Admission
  Qualifications for Applicants
    Standard Qualifications Requirement
  Examination at the University
    Same entrance examination as Japanese applicants (a written exam and an interview)
  Documents to be Submitted When Applying
    Standard Documents Requirement
    In addition applicants should submit a name card and an applicant identification tag (both are specified by the university), and the receipt for examination fee.
    Application Period:
Faculty of Commerce; usually the last 10 days in November
School of Medicine; usually the last 20 days in January

GRADUATE PROGRAMS

Graduate School of Medicine (First Year Enrollment : Doctor's 62)
Divisions
Internal Medicine, Pathological Science, Physiological Science, Social Medicine, Surgery

Foreign Student Admission
Qualifications for Applicants
Doctor's Program
1. Applicants are required to have graduated from a school of medicine or dentistry in Japan.
2. Applicants are required to have completed an 18-year course of education (the last segment of which must be medical or dental) outside Japan, or
3. Applicants are required to have the scholastic attainment equivalent or superior to that of a graduate from a school of medicine or dentistry in Japan.
4. Those who have graduated from a Master's Program of a non-medical or non-dental university school can apply for Physiological Science, Social Medicine or Pathological Science of the Doctor's Program, but cannot apply for Internal Medicine or Surgery.
Examination at the University
Doctor's Program
A written exam and an interview Date: the first or second week of March.
Documents to be Submitted When Applying
Standard Documents Requirement
The applicants who have a medical license are expected to submit a copy of the certificate.

*

Research Institutes and Centers
Center for Experimental Animals, Institute of Brain Diseases, Institute of Cardiovascular Diseases, Institute of Comparative Studies of International Cultures and Societies, Institute of Industrial Economy, Isotope Institute for Basic and Clinical Medicine
For Further Information
Undergraduate Admission
Educational Affairs Department, Administrative Office of the School of Commerce, Kurume University, 1635 Mii-machi, Kurume-shi, Fukuoka 830 ☎ 0942-44-2160
Undergraduate and Graduate Admission
Instruction Department, Administrative Office of the School of Medicine, Kurume University, 67 Asahi-machi, Kurume-shi, Fukuoka 830 ☎ 0942-35-3311 ext. 722, 0942-44-4259

Kwansei Gakuin University
(Kwansei Gakuin Daigaku)
1-1-155 Uegahara, Nishinomiya-shi, Hyogo 662
☎ 0798-53-6111

Faculty
    Profs. 236   Assoc. Profs. 36
    Assist. Profs. Full–time 15; Part–time 550
    Res. Assocs. 11
Number of Students
    Undergrad. 13, 714   Grad. 292
Library 960, 000 volumes

Outline and Characteristics of the University
Kwansei Gakuin, one of the leading private schools in Japan, is an educational complex consisting of a university of 15, 000 students with junior and senior high schools of 1, 500. These three units are linked together through a central administrative system which integrates the total program.

Kwansei Gakuin was founded in Kobe, September 28, 1889, by the Methodist Episcopal Church, South, under the direction of Walter Russell Lambuth, both for general education and for ministerial training.

The purpose from the beginning has been to provide for Japanese youths an education based on Christian principles and ideals, incorporating the best in Japanese life and culture.

Looking toward our second century, emphasis is being placed on international relations and exchanges of students and faculty with institutions abroad. As one concrete step towards this goal, a Seminar House accommodating 130 has been built in a rural setting 20 miles from the campus and is available for use by groups from abroad seeking to study and promote international understanding.

UNDERGRADUATE PROGRAMS

School of Business Administration (Freshmen Enrollment: 550)
Accounting, Business Administration, Commerce
School of Economics (Freshmen Enrollment: 600)
Economic History, Economic Policy, Economic Theory
School of Law (Freshmen Enrollment: 550)
Department of Law
Basic Law, Criminal Law, Private Law, Public Law
Department of Political Science
Political Science, Public Administration
School of Literature (Freshmen Enrollment: 515)
Department of Aesthetics
Aesthetics, Science of Arts
Department of Education
Education, Educational Psychology
Department of English

American Literature, English Linguistics, English Literature
  Department of French
French Linguistics, French Literature
  Department of German
German Linguistics, German Literature
  Department of History
Geography, Japanese History, Occidental History, Oriental History
  Department of Japanese
Japanese Linguistics, Japanese Literature
  Department of Philosophy
Ethics, Philosophy
  Department of Psychology
Psychology
School of Science (Freshmen Enrollment: 100)
  Department of Chemistry
Biology, Chemistry
  Department of Physics
Mathematics, Physics
School of Sociology (Freshmen Enrollment: 400)
  Department of Sociology
Industrial Sociology, Mass Communications, Social Welfare, Theoretical Sociology
School of Theology (Freshmen Enrollment: 20)
Historical Theology, New Testament, Old Testament, Pastoral Theology, Systematic Theology

Foreign Student Admission
  Qualifications for Applicants
    Standard Qualifications Requirement
    In addition to the above qualifications, a prospective student for the School of Theology needs to have received baptism.
  Examination at the University
Application Period: Oct. 1-21
Examination Date: Nov. 8
    School of Theology: English-Japanese translation, essay and interview. A second entrance examination on March 12 and 13.
    School of Humanities: English-Japanese translation and interview.
    School of Sociology: Interview.
    School of Law: One foreign language (Engilsh, French, German), essay and interview.
    School of Economics: English-Japanese translation, essay and interview.
    School of Commerce: English-Japanese translation, essay and interview.
    School of Science: English-Japanese translation, mathematics, physics, chemistry and interview.
    A prospective student for the School of Humanities may be able to take French or German in place of English. Those who wish this testing arrangement need to inquire at the Admission Office.
    A prospective student whose health certificate is unsatisfactory will be required to take a medical examination after the interview.
  Documents to be Submitted When Applying
    Standard Documents Requirement

    In addition to the standard documents, the University requires:
1. The School of Theology requires a letter of recommendation by the Pastor of his/her church.
2. For reference, students may attach the score report of a unified examination of the following kinds:
    (1) U. S. A.: Scholastic Aptitude Test (SAT) Achievement Tests (three subjects)
    (2) Great Britain: General Certificate of Education (GCE) 5 subjects (two of them should be A level)
    (3) France: Baccalaureate
    (4) West Germany: Abitur
    (5) International Baccalaureate (IB) score reports of final examinations for six subjects
    (6) Other countries: Score reports for unified examinations. Subject matters to be taken include 4 subjects. Attach official documents with it.
    A prospective student needs to submit application documents by Sept. 9, 1986 to be examined by the University before Oct. 1, 1986.

GRADUATE PROGRAMS

Graduate School of Business Administration (First Year Enrollment: Master's 30, Doctor's 3)
  Divisions
Business Administration
Graduate School of Economics (First Year Enrollment: Master's 30, Doctor's 3)
  Division
Economics
Graduate School of Humanities (First Year Enrollment: Master's 64, Doctor's 20)
  Divisions
Aesthetics, Education, English, French, German, Japanese, Japanese History, Occidental History, Philosophy, Psychology
Graduate School of Law (First Year Enrollment: Master's 45, Doctor's 6)
  Divisions
Basic Law, Political Science, Private and Criminal Law
Graduate School of Science (First Year Enrollment: Master's 20, Doctor's 10)
  Divisions
Chemistry, Physics
Graduate School of Sociology (First Year Enrollment: Master's 12, Doctor's 4)
  Divisions
Social Work, Sociology
Graduate School of Theology (First Year Enrollment: Master's 10, Doctor's 2)
  Division
Biblical Theology

Foreign Student Admission

Qualifications for Applicants
Master's Program
 Standard Qualifications Requirement
 A prospective student for the Graduate School of Theology needs to have received baptism.
Doctor's Program
 Standard Qualifications Requirement
 A prospective student for the Graduate School of Theology needs to have received baptism.
 Examination at the University
Master's Program
 There is no separate system for foreign student etrance examinations in the Graduate School of Humanities.
Doctor's Program
 Same as the Master's program.
 Documents to be Submitted When Applying
 Standard Documents Requirement
 In addition to the standard documents, the Graduate School of Theology requires a letter of recommendation by the Pastors of his/her church.
 Application period: Oct. 1 to 21

Research Institutes and Centers
Information Processing Research Center, Institute for Integrated Educational Research and Development, Institute of Industrial Research
Facilities/Services for Foreign Students
 International Center acts as a coordinator for foreign students.
For Further Information
 Undergraduate and Graduate Admission
Admission Division, Kwansei Gakuin University, 1-1-155 Uegahara, Nishinomiya-shi, Hyogo 662 ☎ 0798-53-6111 ext. 3032

Kwassui Women's College
(Kwassui Joshi Daigaku)

1-50 Higashi-Yamate-machi, Nagasaki-shi, Nagasaki 850   ☎ 0958-22-4107

Faculty
 Profs. 15   Assoc. Profs. 10
 Assist. Profs. Full–time 3; Part–time 17
Number of Students
 Undergrad. 513
Library 121, 692 volumes

Outline and Characteristics of the College
 The origin of Kwassui Women's College goes back to 1879 when two woman missionaries, appointed by the Women's Missionary Society of American Churches, started the educational and evangelical work in Nagasaki, the only port opened for foreign countries for about 300 years during the Tokugawa Shogunate regime. In the first year of Kwassui Girl's School, there were only one student and two teachers.

The school made rapid development and in 1889 it had an enrollment of 190 students. The fact is remarkable when one considers that the system of Japan's compulsory education was set up in 1886 and very few girls could even go to primary school. Kwassui has been highly valued from the point of women's education in Japan because it gave first in Japan an American college-level education to its students. The school was accredited by the authorities as a college in 1919 and it also has the honor of having sent the first woman member to the Japanese Cabinet. The name of the alumna is Masa Nakayama, who served as Minister of Health and Welfare. Under the new system, Kwassui was formally approved by the Ministry of Education as a junior college in 1952 and as a senior college in 1981.

The basis of Kwassui Women's College is on a faith in God in Protestant Christianity. It aims at fostering the "whole woman" with Christian spirit to serve both God and man. The "competent woman" is also pursued through academic training and study on one's own initiative. An international mind, service to the community, and life-long learning are being emphasized in today's Kwassui education.

Today's Kwassui has four schools: a junior and senior high school, junior college and senior college. Kwassui Women's College has only one faculty with two departments: department of English literature and department of Japanese literature. Enrollment of college this year is 513, the teaching staff has 28 full-timers and the number of the office staff is 25.

UNDERGRADUATE PROGRAMS

Faculty of Literature (Freshmen Enrollment: 100)
 Department of English Literature
English Bible, English Grammar, English Language, History of English Language, History of English Literature
 Department of Japanese Literature
History of Japanese Language, History of Japanese Literature, Japanese Grammar, Japanese Literature

*

Facilities/Services for Foreign Students
 Some four or five British and American teaching staff are always on campus.
 A very modern, Western style, well-furnished dormitory is available.
For Further Information
 Undergraduate Admission
Genaral Affairs Section, Kwassui Women's College, 1-50 Higashi-Yamate-machi, Nagasaki-shi, Nagasaki 850 ☎ 0958-22-4107 ext. 206

Kyorin University
(Kyorin Daigaku)

6-20-2 Shinkawa, Mitaka-shi, Tokyo 181
☎ 0422-47-5511

Faculty
    Profs. 103   Assoc. Profs. 52
    Assist. Profs. Full–time 59; Part–time 83
    Res. Assocs. 194
Number of Students
    Undergrad. 2, 764   Grad. 70
Library   250, 000 volumes

Outline and Characteristics of the University

Kyorin University is a new private university that has two campuses, one in Mitaka (58, 379 m²) and the other in Hachioji (130, 415 m²), both in the western suburb of the Tokyo Metoropolitan area.

Kyorin University has its origin in the Mitaka Shinkawa Hospital opened in 1953 by Shinyu Matsuda. The Hospital soon became a large local general hospital in Mitaka City (Western suburb of Tokyo) to which Kyorin College of Medical Technology was added in 1966. Through Matsuda's effort, the govenment in 1970 approved Kyorin, Gakuen's establishment of a new medical school, Kyorin University School of Medicine. In 1975, Kyorin University School of Nursing was also approved. In 1979, Kyorin College of Medical Technology moved to the vast Hachioji campus and became a larger institution for paramedical education, Kyorin University School of Allied Health with two departments, Medical Technology and Health Sciences.

The year 1984 was a new epoch in the history of Kyorin University. Aiming at a fully integrated higher education curriculum, the Faculty of Social Science was established at the Hachioji campus. Education there covers the areas of Economics, Law, Political, Business and Commercial Sciences, offered in the interdisciplinary curricula.

In 1988, as the second step to promote the integrated higher education for humanity the Faculty of Foriegn Languages was established at the Hachioji Campus. It is composed of the Departments of English, Chinese and Japanese.

The School Name "Kyorin" literally means "a forest of apricot trees" that symbolizes a benevolent medical practitioner in ancient China (ca. 220-280 A. D.). The spirit of Kyorin has, Matsuda says, much in common with the philosophy of "Pursuit of Truth, Goodness and Beauty. " The spirit and the philosophy have been always stressed as the school mottos not only in medical education but also in education at all other schools of our university.

UNDERGRADUATE PROGRAMS

School of Allied Health (Freshmen Enrollment: 100)
Department of Health Sciences
Adult Health, Biochemistry, Environmental Health, Epidemiology, Health Administration, Health Education, Health Sociology, Human Ecology, International Health, Mental and Child Health, Mental Health, Microbiology, Nutrition, Parasitology, Related Laws & Regulations
Department of Medical Technology
Analytical Chemistry, Biotechnology, Clinical Biochemistry, Clinical Cytology, Clinical Genetics, Clinical Hematology, Clinical Immunology, Clinical Microbiology, Clinical Physiology, Laboratory Techniques, Medical Electronics, Public Health
Faculty of Foreign Languages (Freshmen Enrollment: 220)
Department of Chinese
Business Chinese, Chinese Classics, Chinese Composition, Chinese Conversation, Chinese Grammar, Chinese Language, Chinese Phonetics, Creative Writing in Chinese, Current Chinese, History of China, History of Chinese Literature, Listening Chinese, Outline of Chinese Literature, Translating Chinese into Japanese
Department of English
American Society. History of European Social System, American Studies, Business English, Comparative Cultures, Creative Writing in English, Current English, English Composition, English Conversation, English Grammar, English Language, English Literature, English Phonetics, History of England and America, History of English, Languages and Cultures, Listening English, Social Linguistics, Translating English into Japanese
Department of Japanese
Comparative Linguistiecs, History of Japan, History of Japanese, History of Japanese, History of Socioal Conditions in Japan, History of Teaching Japanese, Japanese Culture, Japanese Grammar, Japanese Language, Japanese Literature, Japanese Phonetics, Japanese Semantics, Japanese Vocabulary, Materials and Tools for Teaching Japanese, National System of Japanese, Practice Teaching, Rating of Ability in Japanese, Teaching Method of Japanese
School of Medicine (Freshmen Enrollment: 90)
Anatomy, Anesthesiology, Biochemistry, Chest Surgery, Clinical Pathology, Dermatology, Emergency Medicine, Forensic Medicine, Geriatrics, Hospital Administration, Hygiene, Internal Medicine, Microbiology, Neuropsychiatry, Neurosurgery, Obstetrics & Gynecology, Ophthalmology, Orthopedics, Otorhinolaryngology, Parasitology, Pathology, Pharmacology, Physiology, Public Health, Radiology, Surgery, Urology
Faculty of Social Sciences (Freshmen Enrollment: 300)
Administrative Management Course

Administrative Law, Administrative Science, Civil Law, Civil Procedure, Criminal Law, Criminal Procedure, History of Japanese Politics, Local Administration, Local Finance, Political Process, Political Psychology, Social Security, Sociology of Community and Region, Tax Law, Trial Procedure
Business Information Course
Accounting, Business History, Business Information System, Consumer Information, Forms of Enterprise, History of Business Administration, Information Industry, Information Legislation, Information Management, Information Media, Management, Management Engineering, Management Theory, Marketing, System Engineering
International Politics and Economics Course
Area Studies (Asia, China, Europe, the Americas), Comparative Politics, Diplomatic Policy, Economic Development, Foreign Laws, History of Western Politics and Diplomacy, International Business, International Economics, International Finance, International Investment, International Politics, International Resources, Law of International Transactions

Foreign Student Admission
Qualifications for Applicants
Standard Qualifications Requirement
Examination at the College
Written tests and a brief interview.
Documents to be Submitted When Applying
Standard Documents Requirement
Application forms are available at the administrative office of each school or can be requested by mail.
1. School of Medicine: 6-20-2 Shinkawa, Mitaka-shi, Tokyo 181 (☎ 0422-47-5511)
2. School of Allied Health: 476 Miyashita-cho, Hachioji-shi, Tokyo 192 (☎ 0426-91-0011)
3. Faculty of Social Science: 476, Miyashita-cho, Hachioji-shi, Tokyo 192 (☎ 0426-91-5351)
4. Faculty of Foreign Languages: 476 Miyashita-cho, Hachioji-shi, Tokyo 192
Application Deadline (subject to change):
School of Medicine: January 30
School of Allied Health: February 6
Faculty of Social Science: February 16
Faculty of Foreigr Languages: February 8

GRADUATE PROGRAMS

Graduate School of Allied Health (First Year Enrollment : Master's 7, Doctor's 4)
Divisions
Adult Health, Clinical Microbiology, Clinical Pathology, Epidemiology, Health Administration, Human Ecology, Molecular Biology
Graduate School of Medicine (First Year Enrollment : Doctor's 62)
Divisions
Clinical Medicine, Internal Medicine, Pathological Sciences, Physiological Sciences, Social Medicine,

Surgical Sciences

Foreign Student Admission
Qualifications for Applicants
Master's Program
Standard Qualifications Requirement
Doctor's Program
Standard Qualifications Requirement
Examination at the University
Doctor's Program
In the Graduate School of Medicine, no special selection system is offered for the foreign students. Applicants must follow the same procedure as Japanese applicants and sit for a written examination and have an interview and somatoscopy.
Documents to be Submitted When Applying
Standard Documents Requirement

*

For Further Information
Undergraduate and Graduate Admission
Division of Business Administration, Kyorin University, 6-20-2 Shinkawa, Mitaka-shi, Tokyo 181 ☎ 0422-47-5511 ext. 666

Kyoritsu College of Pharmacy
(Kyoritsu Yakka Daigaku)

1-5-30 Shibakoen, Minato-ku, Tokyo 105
☎ 03-434-6241

Faculty
Profs. 16　　Assoc. Profs. 16
Assist. Profs. Full-time 8; Part-time 40
Res. Assocs. 32
Number of Students
Undergrad. 820　　Grad. 23
Library 41, 000 volumes

Outline and Characteristics of the College
Kyoritsu College of Pharmacy has a history of over 50 years since its foundation in 1930 as Kyoritsu Women's Professional School of Pharmacy. Over the years various changes were introduced such as the system reform, and expansion of the departments. In 1949, it was given its present name, Kyoritsu College of Pharmacy by the post-war educational system reform. Since its foundation, only women have been accepted as undergraduate students. Now, it is the only Women's College of Pharmacy in the eastern part of Japan. In 1986, the Graduate School was established and both men and women are enrolled as graduate students.
The main campus of Kyoritsu College of Pharmacy is located in the heart of the metropolitan Tokyo, Shibakoen. The second campus is located in Urawa, the southern part of Saitama Prefecture. On campus, there are facilities for physical education and an herbical garden.

UNDERGRADUATE PROGRAMS

Faculty of Pharmaceutical Sciences (Freshmen Enrollment: 160)
Department of Biological Pharmacy
Biochemistry, Biology, Hygienic Chemistry, Microbiology, Pharmaceutics, Pharmacology, Toxicology
Department of Pharmaceutical Sciences
Analytical Chemistry, Bionucleonics, Medicinal Chemistry, Organic Chemistry, Pharmacognosy, Physical Pharmaceutical Chemistry

GRADUATE PROGRAMS

Graduate School of Pharmaceutical Sciences (First Year Enrollment : Master's 15, Doctor's 3)
Divisions
Analytical Chemistry, Biochemistry, Hygienic Chemistry, Medicinal Chemistry, Microbial Chemistry, Organic Chemistry, Pharmaceutics, Pharmacognosy, Pharmacology, Physical Chemistry

*

For Further Information
Undergraduate and Graduate Admission
Administrative Office, Kyoritsu College of Pharmacy, 1-5-30 Shibakoen, Minato-ku, Tokyo 105 ☎ 03–434–6241 ext. 231

Kyoritsu Women's University
(Kyoritsu Joshi Daigaku)

2-2-1 Hitotsubashi, Chiyoda-ku, Tokyo 101
☎ 03–237–2433

UNDERGRADUATE PROGRAMS

Faculty of Arts and Letters (Freshmen Enrollment: 300)
Department of Arts
Department of Literature
Faculty of Home Economics (Freshmen Enrollment: 240)
Department of Art for Home Life
Department of Clothing
Department of Foods

GRADUATE PROGRAMS

Graduate School of Arts and Letters (First Year Enrollment : Master's 20)
Divisions
Dramatic Arts, English Literature, Japanese Literature
Graduate School of Home Economics (First Year

Enrollment : Master's 16)
Divisions
Clothing, Foods

Kyoto Gakuen University
(Kyoto Gakuen Daigaku)

Otani Nanjo, Sogabe-cho, Kameoka-shi, Kyoto 621
☎ 07712-2-2001

UNDERGRADUATE PROGRAMS

Faculty of Economics (Freshmen Enrollment: 500)
Department of Business Administration
Department of Economics
Faculty of Law (Freshmen Enrollment: 160)

Kyoto Pharmaceutical University
(Kyoto Yakka Daigaku)

5 Misasaginakauchi-cho, Yamashina-ku, Kyoto-shi, Kyoto 607 ☎ 075-581-3161

Faculty
Profs. 27 Assoc. Profs. 16
Assist. Profs. Full–time 6; Part–time 45
Res. Assocs. 61
Number of Students
Undergrad. 1, 560 Grad. 64
Library 65, 769 volumes

Outline and Characteristics of the University
The Kyoto Pharmaceutical University (KPU) is a private and independent university and is one of the oldest pharmacy schools in Japan. It grants a four–year Bachelor of Science in Pharmacy degree. KPU was originally founded as the Pharmacy division of the Kyoto German School in 1884 and became an independent pharmacy school at the high school level for men in 1892. In response to the increased demand for scientific education, it was elevated to a three–year pharmacy college for men in 1919. In 1949, it became coeducational and offered a four–year undergraduate curriculum. In 1965, a graduate school leading to the degree of Master of Science in Pharmacy was inaugurated. Providing a number of required facilities and equipments, the expanded graduate programs for Doctor of Philosophy in Pharmacy in 1977 was subsequently created.

KPU consists of the Main Campus, the South Campus, the Female Student Dormitory and the Athletic Ground, all of which are in close proximity to each other. Its total land area is about 50, 000m² (12. 5 acres). In addition, it has Medicinal Plant Garden (3. 2 acres), the Hohrai Seminar House and an experimental forest (5. 4 acres).

KPU is located in the eastern suburb of Kyoto, an excellent place for study. It is a cultural center and the ancient capital of Japan. It is easily accessible by public and private transportation from the other parts of the city and also from many neighboring cities in Kyoto, Osaka, Hyogo, Nara and Shiga prefectures.

UNDERGRADUATE PROGRAMS

Faculty of Pharmaceutical Sciences (Freshmen Enrollment: 360)

Department of Pharmaceutical Biology

Analytical Chemistry, Biochemistry, Chemistry, Clinical Biochemistry, Medicinal Chemistry, Microbiology, Organic Chemistry, Pathological Biochemistry, Pharmaceutics, Pharmacognosy, Physical Chemistry

Department of Pharmaceutical Chemistry

Analytical Chemistry, Biochemistry, Hygienic Chemistry, Medicinal Chemistry, Microbiology, Natural Product Chemistry, Organic Chemistry, Physical Chemistry, Synthetic Organic Chemistry

Department of Pharmaceutical Sciences

Analytical Chemistry, Biochemistry, Clinical Biochemistry, Hygienic Chemistry, Medicinal Chemistry, Microbiology, Organic Chemistry, Pharmaceutics, Pharmacognosy, Physical Chemistry, Plant Source Sciences

Foreign Student Admission

Qualifications for Applicants

Standard Qualifications Requirement

Examination at the University

General Entrance Examination (1) and Special Entrance Examination (2) are carried out early February and in November, respectively. The former is for regular applicants in Japan, the latter is for applicants who are specially recommended by high schools recognized by the university.

Documents to be Submitted When Applying

Standard Documents Requirement

Application forms are available at the Admission Office early December for (1) and are given from the school master in October for (2). All applicants are required to submit the specified application documents to the Admission Office by the dates named.

GRADUATE PROGRAMS

Graduate School of Pharmaceutical Sciences (First Year Enrollment : Master's 26, Doctor's 8)

Division

Pharmaceutical Sciences

Foreign Student Admission

Qualifications for Applicants

Master's Program

Standard Qualifications Requirement

Doctor's Program

Standard Qualifications Requirement

Examination at the University

Master's Program

The examination is usually given in August. It consists mainly of a written examination and interview.

Doctor's Program

The examination is usually given in March. It consists mainly of a written examination and interview.

Documents to be Submitted When Applying

Standard Documents Requirement

*

Research Institutes and Centers

Center for Clinical and Pharmaceutical Informations

For Further Information

Undergraduate and Graduate Admission

Admission Office, Kyoto Pharmaceutical University, 5 Misasaginakauchi-cho, Yamashina-ku, Kyoto-shi, Kyoto 607 ☎ 075-581-3161 ext. 207

Kyoto Sangyo University
(Kyoto Sangyo Daigaku)

Motoyama, Kamigamo, Kita-ku, Kyoto-shi, Kyoto 603   ☎ 075-701-2151

Faculty
    Profs.   171   Assoc. Profs.   103
    Assist. Profs.   Full–time   22; Part–time   144
Number of Students
    Undergrad.   11, 808   Grad.   19
Library   495, 473 volumes

Outline and Characteristics of the University

Our educational goals are to train men of principles who, having the power of introspective self-discipline, are capable of shouldering the responsibilities of tomorrow's society. We also aim at educating future leaders with internationally respected opinions who can confidently take an active part in the international arena. These objectives cannot be achieved unless these people, however noble-minded they may be, exhibit great knowledge and skill.

In order to realize these educational ideals, Kyoto Sangyo University was founded in January, 1965 as a co-educational university consisting of the Faculties of Economics and Science. In 1967, the Faculties of Law, Business Administration, and Foreign Languages were added. In 1969, the Department of Computer Sciences, unique at the undergraduate level in Japan, was added to the Faculty of Science.

In the same year the Divisions of Economics and Science of the Graduate School were founded. In addition to these, the Graduate Division of Foreign Languages (two areas of concentration: Chinese and Linguistics) was set up in April, 1977. The Graduate School has a five-year program, except for the Graduate Division of Foreign Languages, which now offers only a two-year program. The first two-year program is equivalent to a normal two-year Master's Course and the following three-year program is exclusively for the Doctor's Course. Furthermore, the one year postgraduate diploma course (*Senkoka*) was founded in 1971. And Faculty of Engineering was newly founded in 1989.

At present, the University has an Undergraduate School which consists of the College of General Liberal Arts and Science Education, five Faculties with thirteen Departments, and a Graduate School with four Divisions. The University also has six institutes: the Research Institute for World Affairs and Cultures, the Research Institute for Computer Sciences, the International Institute for Linguistic Sciences, the Research Institute for National Land Utilization and Development, and the Research Institute for Modern Physical Education. Additionally there are the Computer Center, the Language Laboratory Center, the Health Administration Center, and the Library. To assist the students with career preparation, several professional preparatory courses have been open to all since a few years ago.

Our university makes every effort to maintain a faculty of superior ability, to improve and perfect research equipment and educational facilities, and to constantly innovate educational methods to keep abreast of the ever-progressing society.

UNDERGRADUATE PROGRAMS

Faculty of Business Administration (Freshmen Enrollment: 570)

Department of Business Administration
Accounting, Auditing, Business Administration, Business History, Business Organization, Business Policy, Business Psychology, Business Sociology, Business Statistics, Consumer Behavior, Corporation Finance, Financial Management, Foreign Trade, Industrial Organization, Information System of Business Administration, Insurance Administration, International Business Management, International Trade, Management, Marketing, Marketing Management, Operations Research, Organizational Behavior, Personal Management and Labor Relations, Production Control, Sales Management

Faculty of Economics (Freshmen Enrollment: 570)
Department of Economics
Agricultural Policy, Development Economics, Econometrics, Economic Analysis, Economic Anthropology, Economic Development, Economic Dynamics, Economic Geography, Economic Growth, Economic History, Economic Policy, Economics of Commercial Distribution, Economic Statistics, Economic Theory, Fiscal Policy, History of Economic Thought, Industrial Organization, Industrial Sociology, Internaitonal Investment, International Economics, International Finance, Japanese Economy, Japanese Industry, Labor Economics, Monetary Economics, Monetary Policy, National Income, Public Finance, Small and Medium Enterprises, Social Policy, World Banking Systems

Faculty of Engineering (Freshmen Enrollment: 100)

Department of Biotechnology
Advanced Molecular Biotechnology, Animal Breeding Technology, Biochemical Technology, Biochemistry, Biology Laboratory, Biophysics, Biostatistics, Biotechnology·Molecular Biotechnology Laboratory, Cell Technology, Chemistry, Chemistry Laboratory, Computer Programming, English Course in Biotechnology, Introduction to Biology, Introduction to Calculus, Introduction to Chemistry, Introduction to Genetics, Introduction to Medicine and Biology, Introduction to Molecular Biotechnology, Microbiology, Molecular Biology, Molecular Biotechnology, Molecular Physics, Plant Breeding Technology, Polution Genetics, Research in Biotechnology·Molecular Biotechnology Laboratory

Department of Information and Communication
Algebra and Geometry, Biological Informatics, Calculus, Coding Theory, Computer Architecture, Computer Graphics, Computer Hardware, Computer Networks, Database Theory, Data Communications, Digital and Analog Communication Systems, Digital Switch Matrix, Distributed Processing, Electromagnetic Radiations and Antenna Technology, Electromagnetism, Electronic Circuits, Exercises in Programming, Fiber-optic Communications, General Physics, Image Processing and Simulation, Introduction to Communications Engineering, Introduction to Information Engineering, Introduction to Numerical Methods, Knowledge Engineering, Laboratory in Information and Communication Engineering, Mathematical Statistics, Mathematics of Neurodynamics, Mathematics of Nonlinear Phenomena, Numerical Analysis, Optical Engineering, Optoelectronic Devices, Satelite Communications, Seminar in Information and Communication Engineering, Simulation Theory, Software Engineering, Theory of Algorithms, Theory of Automata and Languages

Faculty of Foreign Languages (Freshmen Enrollment: 300)
Chinese Language Department
Chinese Culture, Chinese Language, Chinese Linguistics, Chinese Literature
English Language Department
American Culture, American Literature, British Culture, English Language, English Linguistics, English Literature
French Language Department
French Culture, French Language, French Linguistics, French Literature
German Language Department
German Culture, German Linguistics, German Literature
Department of Linguistics
Indonesian Language Course
Indonesian Culture, Indonesian Language, Indone-

sian Linguistics, Indonesian Literature
   Italian Language Course
Italian Culture, Italian Language, Italian Linguistics, Italian Literature
   Linguistics Course
Comparative Linguistics, Linguistics, Problems of Language
   Slavic Languages Course
Russian Language, Slavic Culture, Slavic Linguistics, Slavic Literature
   Spanish Language Course
Spanish Culture, Spanish Language, Spanish Linguistics, Spanish Literature
Faculty of Law (Freshmen Enrollment: 560)
   Department of Law
Administrative Law, Anglo-American Law, Asian Politics, Bankruptcy Law, Civil Law, Civil Procedure, Code of Civil Enforcement, Commercial Law, Constitution, Criminal Law, Criminal Procedure, Criminology, Economic Law, German Law, History of Foreign Policy, History of Political Thought, International Law, International Organization, International Politics, Japanese Legal History, Legal Theory of State, Local Government Law, Oriental Legal History, Philosophy of Law, Political History, Political Theory, Public Administration, Roman Law, Study of Government, Tax Law, Western Legal History
Faculty of Science (Freshmen Enrollment: 120)
   Department of Computer Sciences
   Computer Communication Course
Computer Communication, Computer Communication Engineering
   Information Processing Course
Computer Architecture, Information Processing, System Program
   Information Science Course
Algorithm Theory, Computer Language Theory, Computer Sciences
   Mathematical Science Course
Computer Sciences, Mathematical Analysis, Numerical Analysis
   System Design Course
Computer Sciences, Data Base Theory, Information Management
   System Science Course
Computer Sciences, Mathematical Programming, System Theory
   Department of Mathematics
Algebra, Algebraic Geometry, Analysis, Complex Variable, Differential Equations, Functional Analysis, Functional Equations, Geometry, Mathematical Logics, Mathematical Statistics, Probability Theory, Theory of Riemann Surfaces, Topology
   Department of Physics
Analytical Dynamics, Astrophysics, Atomic Physics, Earth Science, Electromagnetics, Fluid Dynamics and Elasticity, General Physics, Mathematical Physics, Molecular Physics, Nuclear Physics, Optics, Polymer Science, Quantum Mechanics, Relativity, Solid

State Physics, Space Physics, Statistical Mechanics

Foreign Student Admission
   We do not have special entrance examinations or any study courses for overseas students at present. Therefore all overseas applicants have to take the same entrance examinations as Japanese students.

ONE-YEAR GRADUATE PROGRAMS

   Same as freshman admission

GRADUATE PROGRAMS

One-Year Graduate Course of Foreign Languages (Enrollment: 20)
Chinese, English, French, German, Linguistics

Foreign Student Admission
Graduate Schoolof Economics (First Year Enrollment: Master's 10, Doctor's 5)
   Division
Economics
Graduate Schoolof Foreign Languages (First Year Enrollment: Master's 6)
   Divisions
Chinese, Linguistics
Graduate Schoolof Law (First Year Enrollment: Master's 10, Doctor's 5)
   Division
Law
Graduate Schoolof Science (First Year Enrollment: Master's 10, Doctor's 6)
   Divisions
Mathematics, Physics

Foreign Student Admission
   Same as freshman admission
   Examination at the University
Master's Program
   One or two written foreign language examination(s) and two written examinations in major and related subjects besides an interview.
Doctor's Program
   Two written foreign language examinations and an oral examination in a master's thesis and major and related subjects.
   Documents to be Submitted When Applying
   Standard Documents Requirement
                    *
Research Institutes and Centers
Accounting Profession Center, Computer Center, Data Processing Specialist Center, Health Administration Center, Institute for Computer Sciences, Institute for Modern Physical Education, Institute for National Land Utilization and Development, Institute for World Affairs and Cultures, International Institute for Linguistic Sciences, Legal Profession Center, TeachingProfession Center
For Further Information

Undergraduate and Graduate Admission

Office of Admissions, Kyoto Sangyo University, Motoyama, Kamigamo, Kita-ku, Kyoto-shi, Kyoto 603 ☎ 075-701-2151

Kyoto Seika University
(Kyoto Seika Daigaku)

137 Kino, Iwakura, Sakyo-ku, Kyoto-shi, Kyoto 606
☎ 075-702-5199

Faculty
    Profs. 31   Assoc. Profs. 12
    Assist. Profs. Full–time 10; Part–time 68
Number of Students
    Undergrad. 972
Library 92, 178 volumes

Outline and Characteristics of the University

Originally, Kyoto Seika University was founded in 1968 as a two-year college with two departments—the English Department and the Fine Arts Department. The Fine Arts Faculty of Kyoto Seika University, which offers a four-year undergraduate program, was inaugurated in 1979. Presently, the Fine Arts Faculty consists of two departments—the Formative Art Department and the Design Department. The former has five programs on oil Painting, Japanese Painting, Sculpture, Printmaking, and Ceramics. The latter has four programs on Visual Design, Urban Living Design (Architecture and City Planning), Textile Design, and Cartoon Graphics.

The campus is nestled in the northern hillside of Kyoto City, on the old road to Kurama Temple. Surrounded by hills and fields, it still enjoys the richness of old Kyoto's rural area.

"Freedom and Self-government" is the motto of the university. It was advocated by one of the founders, Seiichi Okamoto, and is persistently cherished by the faculty and administrative office members, as well as by the students. In this uniquely liberal atmosphere, the main emphasis of the Fine Arts Faculty is the pursuit of both the traditional and the modern. Taking advantage of its location in Kyoto, and this city's thousand year tradition, students are required to take a period of practice work in studios of master-craftsmen.

Kyoto Seika University is currently preparing a new Faculty of Humanities (B. A. program), which is scheduled to commence in April 1989, replacing the present Junior College. Education Ministry approval of this faculty is expected to be finalised in Decembher 1988, and full details of enrollment will be announced shortly thereafter.

The new Faculty of Humanities will at first consist of one department, the Department of Humanities, in which the student will be able to pursue courses in either Traditional Japanese Culture or Comparative Cultures. The University expects the new Faculty's annual freshman intake to include approximately 10 overseas students, and will also welcome short-term international exchange students.

UNDERGRADUATE PROGRAMS

Faculty of Fine Arts (Freshmen Enrollment: 240)
    Department of Design
Cartoon Graphics, Textile Designg, Urban Living Design (Architecture and City Planning), Visual Communication Design
    Department of Formative Art
Ceramics, Japanese Painting, Oil Painting, Printmaking, Sculpture

Foreign Student Admission
    Qualifications for Applicants
    Standard Qualifications Requirement.
It is desirable that foreign students pass the second grade of the Japanese Language Proficiency Test.
    Examination at the University
    1. Practical skills.
    2. A written examination of the applicant's Japanese language ability.
    Date: December 15, 1988.
    Documents to be Submitted When Applying
    Standard Documents Requirement
Application Period: November 18 to December 6.
                            *
Special Programs for Foreign Students
    For foreign students who need assistance in Japanese language , the university offers a basic Japanese course and an intermediate course.
For Further Information
    Undergraduate Admission
International Exchange Section, Kyoto Seika University, 137 Kino, Iwakura, Sakyo-ku, Kyoto-shi, Kyoto 606☎ 075-702-5199

Kyoto Tachibana Women's University
(Kyoto Tachibana Joshi Daigaku)

34 Oyake Yamada-cho, Yamashina-ku, Kyoto-shi, Kyoto 607 ☎ 075-571-1111

Faculty
    Profs. 28   Assoc. Profs. 5
    Assist. Profs. Full–time 4; Part–time 96
Number of Students
    Undergrad. 1, 500
Library 65, 352 volumes

Outline and Characteristics of the University

Tachibana Women's University is a four-year institution of higher education. The University's history dates back to 1902 when Takeo Nakamori founded Kyoto Girls' Handicraft School near the Imperial Palace in Kyoto. In 1910, the school's name was changed to Kyoto Girls' Handicraft High School in conjunction with Kyoto Girls' Commercial High School.

The present university was established in 1967 under the motto of "Nobiliter et Veraciter" (for nobility and truth), chosen by the first president Saburo Takada, a noted Japanese philosopher.

Our University is located in the eastern part of Kyoto, one of the most beautiful cities in Japan. It offers students both a quiet atmosphere for study and a chance to visit many places of historical interest.

In our college there are three departments: the English department (English Language, and English and American Literature); the Japanese department and the History department. In each department "face-to-face" education is put into practice. The advantages of this small university are personal education and guidance as well as the development of close student-teacher relationships.

Our new library, with its state of the art language laboratory and audio-visual rooms, was built in March, 1986. Students can use this modern library to improve their studies and gain a scholastic advantage.

There are four full-time native-speaking instructors in the English department. Thus students have the opportunity to bridge the cross-cultural communication gap and discover the similarities and differences between Japanese and English.

The Japanese Department offers students a broad education in Japanese language and literature. Also of interest to students from abroad are courses which take a comparative approach, vis. Western society, to Japanese culture. 60% of the students attending the university are from districts outside the Kyoto area, so there are many opportunities to hear a wide variety of dialects on campus.

The History department is divided into Japanese and World History courses, enabling students to learn about nations all over the world, from Southeast Asia and China to Europe and America.

UNDERGRADUATE PROGRAMS

Faculty of Letters (Freshmen Enrollment   300)
   Department of English Language and English and American Literature
English and American Literature, English Language
   Department of History
Contemporary History, Japanese History, Oriental History, Western History
   Department of Japanese Language and Literature
Japanese Language, Japanese Literature

Foreign Student Admission
   Qualifications for Applicants
   Standard Qualifications Requirement

Japanese Language Proficiency Test results.
   Examination at the University
   An interview in Japanese
   Date: October 25, January 18
   Documents to be Submitted When Applying
   Standard Documents Requirement
   Certificate of Admission will be sent to successful applicants on November 1, January 26
   Registration deadline: the end of February.

*
Facilities/Services for Foreign Students
   The dormitories with Japanese students, Rooming houses.
   Advisor system for foreign students: A full-time advisor and a clerk are stationed at the Academic Affairs Office (Kyomu–ka) to offer guidance and management.
Special Programs for Foreign Students
   Foreign students in the General Education Program can take special lectures on Japanese and Japanese affairs.
For Further Information
   Undergraduate Admission
Entrance Examination Section, Academic Affairs Division, Tachibana Women's University, 34 Oyake Yamada-cho, Yamashina-ku, Kyoto-shi, Kyoto 607
☎ 075-571-1111 ext. 221

Kyoto University of Foreign Studies

(Kyoto Gaikokugo Daigaku)

6 Saiin-Kasame-cho, Ukyo-ku, Kyoto-shi, Kyoto 615
☎ 075-322-6012

Faculty
   Profs.   56   Assoc. Profs.   25
   Assist. Profs.   Full–time   18; Part–time   176
Number of Students
   Undergrad.   3, 683   Grad.   31
Library   323, 437 volumes

Outline and Characteristics of the University
   The university was founded by Dr. and Mrs. Ichiro Morita in May 1947 as Kyoto School of Foreign Studies. As was only natural so shortly after the end of the Second World War, the most pressing need was international understanding based on goodwill between Japan and other countries of the world. It was with this fact in mind that, three years later in 1950, the school was upgraded to Kyoto Junior College of Foreign Languages, and later still, in 1959, to the Kyoto University of Foreign Studies of four year course. Since then the number of departments have increased and now there are the Departments of English and American Studies, Spanish Studies, French Studies, German Studies, Brazilian-Portuguese Studies, and Chinese Studies. The one-year Postgraduate

Course, whose graduates are authorized to apply for the Grade 1 High School Teacher's License, was founded in 1956.

In 1971, the School of Graduate Studies was instituted, covering all the departments of the undergraduate course except for Chinese Studies. The one year course of Japanese Studies for Foreigh Students was instituted in 1980.

Besides the aforementioned, the Kyoto University of Foreign Studies has, as its affiliated institutions, Kyoto Preparatory School and Kyoto Nishi High School. The former was founded in 1954, while the latter in 1957.

The university's motto "Pax Mundi per Linguas", World Peace through Languages, is mirrored in the curriculum, which stresses the building of character and the heightening of potential through the medium of foreign language learning.

The university library has a collection of over 300, 000 volumes including 40, 000 volumes at its Asia Library. Approximately 180, 000 of the collection are in Western languages.

In particular the university library is known for the rare, old books that number several thousand including a number of incunabula and old maps, manuscripts and autographed letters. Of them the following may deserve special mention.

A quarto edition of "Romeo and Juliet";
The first edition of Johnson and Steevens' "Plays of William Shakespeare";
Nearly 1, 000 volumes of Samuel Johnson's works before 1850 including almost every edition of his "Dictionary of the English Language";
Original copies of Charles Dickens' "Pickwick Papers" and other works and his autographed letters;
A large number of dictionaries and encyclopaedias including over 2, 000 of those published in Europe between the 16th and the 19th century;
Works on Japanology written by Jesuit missionaries and other foreigners residing in Japan before the Meiji Restoration of 1867; and
About 500 works in Japanese, either printed or in manuscript, issued before 1880.

UNDERGRADUATE PROGRAMS

Faculty of Foreign Languages (Freshmen Enrollment: 650)
Department of Brazilian-Portuguese Studies
Brazilian Politics and Economics, Brazilian-Portuguese Linguistics, Brazilian-Portuguese Literature, Brazilian-Portuguese Phonetics, Current Affairs of Brazil and Portugal, History of Brazilian-Portuguese Culture, History of Brazilian-Portuguese Literature
Department of Chinese Studies
Chinese Classics, Chinese Current Affairs, Chinese Economics, Chinese Literature, Chinese Phonetics, Chinese Politics, Chinese Politics and Economics, History of Chinese Culture
Department of English and American Studies

Current Affairs of England and America, English and American Literature, English Linguistics, English Phonetics, History of English and American Culture, History of English and American Literature, History of English Language, Phonetics
Department of French Studies
Current Affairs of France, French Civilization, French History, French Literature, French Phonetics, History of French Culture, History of French Language, History of French Literature, History of French Thoughts
Department of German Studies
Current Affairs of Germany, German Linguistics, German Literature, German Phonetics, German Syntax, History of German Culture, History of German Literature
Department of Spanish Studies
Current Affairs of Iberoamerica, Current Affairs of Latin-America, Current Affairs of Spain, History of Latin-American Literature, History of Spanish Culture, History of Spanish Language, History of Spanish Literature, History of the Relations between Japan and Europe, Latin, Latin-American Politics and Economics, Spanish Linguistics, Spanish Literature, Spanish Phonetics

Foreign Student Admission
Qualifications for Applicants
Standard Qualifications Requirement
Examination at the University
Same as the examination for Japanese applicants.
Subjects: English, Japanese and Short Essay.
Date of Examination
1. Dept. of English and American Studies: Feb. 11
2. Other Departments: Feb. 10
Announcement of Successful Applicants: Feb. 20
Period of Enrollment Procedures: Feb. 20-27
Documents to be Submitted When Applying
Standard Documents Requirement
Application Period: January 10-27

Qualifications for Transfer Students
So far only the graduates of the Kyoto Junior College of Foreign Languages are eligible to take the examination for the transfer to either sophomore or junior of the University.

ONE-YEAR GRADUATE PROGRAMS

One-Year Graduate Course of Foreign Languages (Enrollment 20)
English and American Studies

Foreign Student Admission
Qualifications for applicants
Standard Qualifications Requirement
Examination at the University
Same as the examination for Japanese appli-

cants

GRADUATE PROGRAMS

Graduate School of Foreign Languages (First Year Enrollment : Master's 30)
Divisions
Brazilian-Portuguese Studies, English and American Studies, French Studies, German Studies, Spanish Studies

Foreign Student Admission
Qualifications for Applicants
Master's Program
    Standard Qualifications Requirement
Examination at the University
Master's Program
Date: March 10
Announcement of Successful Applicants: March 15
    Documents to be Submitted When Applying
    Standard Documents Requirement
    Report written by the dean or the professor in charge of the applicant and sealed by the same (form prescribed)
Application Period: February 23-March 2
Period for Enrollment Procedures: March 16-23
                              *
Research Institutes and Centers
Asia Library, Data Processing Institute, Foreign Language Institute, Hispano-American Institute, Mexico Research Center, Natural Science Laboratory, Research Center of Brazilian Culture, Research Institute of Health and Physical Education, Research Institute of Human Rights, Research Institute of Islamic Culture

Special Programs for Foreign Students
    The course in Japanese studies for overseas students was instituted in 1980.
It is designed to provide instruction in the Japanese language and related subjects for foreign students.
    The subjects offered at the Course are:
1. Required subjects:
    Japanese language I-VI
2. Elective subjects:
    States of Affairs in Japan I & II
    Tradition, Culture, Politics, and Economics of Japan
    The Department of International Exchange is the administrating office of the Course.
    The term of the Course is one year starting in April. This is for the foreign students who intend to seek entrance to Kyoto University of Foreign Studies or any other Japanese university but whose knowledge of Japanese language is not sufficient to enable them to engage in academic work.
For Further Information
Undergraduate and Graduate Admission
Section of Entrance Examination, Department of Education Affairs, Kyoto University of Foreign

Studies, 6 Saiin-Kasame-cho, Ukyo-ku, Kyoto-shi, Kyoto 615 ☎ 075-322-6035

Kyoto Women's University
(Kyoto Joshi Daigaku)

35 Kitahiyoshi-cho, Imakumano, Higashiyama-ku, Kyoto-shi, Kyoto 605   ☎ 075-531-7030

Faculty
    Profs.   56   Assoc. Profs.   28
    Assist. Profs.   Full-time   9; Part-time   234
Number of Students
    Undergrad.   3, 472   Grad.   31
Library   423, 684 volumes

Outline and Characteristics of the University
    Kyoto Women's University, located at the foot of the rolling hills framing the eastern part of Kyoto, is one of Japan's leading private institutions of higher learning for women. Its location places it veritably in the heart of the vast repository of Japan's proud cultural, artistic and religious heritages. Within a few minutes' walk of the campus are some of the city's best known Buddhist temples and the National Museum. Also easily accessible are scores of Buddhist temples, Shinto shrines, gardens and architectural masterpieces for which Kyoto is well known all over the world.
    The University officially made its start in 1949 under the postwar education system. It comprises two faculties, Literature and Home Economics, and a graduate program. The University has a total enrollment of some 3, 200 students coming from all over the country, testifying to its high academic standards and proud history and tradition.
    The University's history dates back to 1901 when a girls' high school, forerunner of the University, was established in the firm belief that education for women is one of the foremost tasks in the building of modern Japan and that nurturing in the students a Buddhist view of the world and humanity should be at the basis of the school's education. In 1920, Kyoto Women's College was established, crowning decades of efforts to provide higher education to women at a time when such an institution was out of favor in a male-dominated society.
    Throughout its history, the school's guiding principle has been that women play a crucial role in both family and school education and that providing adequate education to women holds the key to the future of the nation. It is in keeping with this principle that since its establishment, the University has made every possible effort to offer education and research of high standards to its students.
    The educational basis of the University is the truth as revealed by Shinran (1173-1262), one of Japan's foremost Buddhist masters to whom the foundation of the Jodo-Shinshu (School of Pure Land

Buddhism) is attributed. The ultimate truth revealed by Shinran is the reality that all beings are equally important without any discrimination. Shinran's soteriological structure, therefore, points to the very basis of education which aims at the final value of human existence.

The University and its affiliated institutions ranging from elementary school to junior college have turned out upwards of 100, 000 graduates. The University's graduates, fully equipped with advanced knowledge and modern skills and a keen awareness of and sensitivity to religious and spiritual values, are active in various professional fields throughout the country.

UNDERGRADUATE PROGRAMS

Faculty of Home Economics (Freshmen Enrollment: 200)

Department of Food Science
Cookery Science, Food Hygiene, Food Science, Nutrition
Department of Pedology
Child Culture, Child Education, Child Health Care, Child Psychology
Department of Textile and Clothing
Chromatics & Designing, Clothing Maintenance, Clothing Materials, History of Costumes, Hygienics on Clothing, Theory of Dressmaking
Faculty of Literature (Freshmen Enrollment: 400)
Department of Education
Elementary Education, Music Education
Department of English
Department of Japanese
Department of Oriental History
Japanese History, Oriental History

Foreign Student Admission
Qualifications for Applicants
Standard Qualifications Requirement
Foreign residents of Japan are not eligible for admission. This does not apply to those foreign residents who can prove that they came to Japan for the purpose of studying.
Examination at the University
A written exam and an interview.
Documents to be Submitted When Applying
Standard Documents Requirement
Following documents are also required:
1. A letter of recommendation by the principal of the last school attended, containing reference to the applicant's ability in Japanese.
2. Certificates of the school and the applicant's qualifications issued by the government of the applicant's country or by a Japanese diplomatic mission.

GRADUATE PROGRAMS

Graduate School of Home Economics (First Year

Enrollment : Master's 18)
Divisions
Food Science, Pedology, Textile and Clothing
Graduate School of Literature (First Year Enrollment : Master's 12)
Divisions
English, Japanese, Oriental History

Foreign Student Admission
Qualifications for Applicants
Master's Program
Standard Qualifications Requirement
Examination at the University
Master's Program
School of Literature: written tests in a foreign language and the proposed field of speciality and an oral test on Bachelor's thesis.
School of Home Economics: written tests in a foreign language and the proposed field of speciality and an oral test in the field of speciality.
Documents to be Submitted When Applying
Standard Documents Requirement
Applicants for the Graduate School of Literature are required to submit a copy of Bachelor's thesis or an equivalent thesis.

*

Research Institutes and Centers
The Institute of Religion and Culture
For Further Information
Undergraduate and Graduate Admission
Admissions Office, Kyoto Women's University, 35 Kitahiyoshi-cho, Imakumano, Higashiyama-ku, Kyoto-shi, Kyoto 605 ☎ 075-531-7054

Kyushu Kyoritsu University
(Kyushu Kyoritsu Daigaku)

1-1 Jiyugaoka, Yahata/nishi-ku, Kitakyushu-shi, Fukuoka 807 ☎ 093-691-3331

Faculty
    Profs. 42   Assoc. Profs. 32
    Assist. Profs. Full–time 12; Part–time 115
    Res. Assocs. 7
Number of Students
    Undergrad. 2, 278
Library 68, 000 volumes

Outline and Characteristics of the University
Kyushu Kyoritsu University is situated in the north-west section of Kita Kyushu city, an industrial community of more than one million citizens. Founded as one of the universities called the Fukuhara Gakuen in 1965, the university began courses in the Faculty of Economics. In addition to courses offered during the day, evening courses were opened for working persons in 1966. In 1967, the Faculty of Engineering offered programs to meet the needs of the times. The Faculty of Engineering has six depart-

ments; Mechanical Engineering, Electrical Engineering, Civil Engineering, Architecture, Land Development, and Environmental Chemistry.

Since that time the university has gradually expanded, having a large campus which comprises an area of approximately 40 acres. On campus stand university buildings, laboratories for the Faculty of Engineering, offices, gymnasium, and grounds for various club activities. The purpose of Kyushu Kyoritsu University is to produce educated men equipped to use their abilities productively and wisely, and also to provide its students with an intellectual challenge and chance for scholarly and professional growth, based on the school discipline "Jiritsu shogyo" meaning to cultivate trustworthy and reliable persons.

The University operates on the semester system. Currently the University enrolls approximately 3,000 students including some students from foreign countries. The Library gives students the chance to develop their intellectual interests and abilities under favorable conditions. Kyushu Kyoritsu University's library is relatively a compact one, having about 100,000 volumes, but its new library gives an added dimension to the University's academic goals of research and services for students.

UNDERGRADUATE PROGRAMS

Faculty of Economics (Freshmen Enrollment: 350)
Department of Economics
Econometrics, Economic History, International Economics, International Finance, Macroeconomics, Microeconomics, Monetary Economics, Public Finance, Statistics
Department of Management
Business Administration, Business Analysis, Business History, Elementary Accounting, Financial Accounting, Financial Management, Management Accounting, Marketing, Organization Theory, Personnel Management

Faculty of Engineering (Freshmen Enrollment: 320)
Department of Architecture
Architectural Acoustics, Architectural Design, Architectural History, Building Materials, Planing, Reinforced Concrete Engineering, Strength of Materials, Structural Design, Town Planing
Department of Civil Engineering
City Planning, Civil Engineering Geology, Foundations of Soil Mechanics, Harbor Engineering, Hydraulics, Railway Engineering, River Hydraulics and Works, Road Engineering, Structural Mechanics
Department of Electric Engineering
Computer System, Electrical Communication Engineering, Electrical Machine Theory, Electrical Materials, Electromagnetism, Electronic Circuit Theory, High Voltage Engineering, Lighting and Furnace, Micro Computer, Semiconductor Engineering, System Program
Department of Environmental Chemistry

Bioorganic Chemistry, Ecological Genetics, Environmental Analytical Chemistry, Environmental Chemistry, Environmental Microbiology, Environmental Toxicology, Hygienic Chemistry, Radiation Chemistry
Department of Land Development
Computer, Construction Machinery, Hydraulics, Hydraulic Works, Irrigation and Drainage Engineering, Soils Engineering
Department of Mechanical Engineering
Automatic Control, Engineering Mechanics, Heat Transfer, Hydrodynamics, Instrumentation, Machine Design, Machine Tool, Strength of Materials, Thermodynamics

*

For Further Information
Undergraduate Admission
Admissions Office, Kyushu Kyoritsu University, 1-1 Jiyugaoka, Yahata Nishi-ku, Kitakyushu-shi, Fukuoka 807 ☎ 093-691-3331

Kyushu Sangyo University
(Kyushu Sangyo Daigaku)

2-3-1 Matsukadai, Higashi-ku, Fukuoka-shi, Fukuoka 813   ☎ 092-681-1831

Faculty
    Profs. 117   Assoc. Profs. 84
    Assist. Profs. Full–time 41; Part–time 317
    Res. Assocs. 17
Number of Students
    Undergrad. 10,532   Grad. 62
Library 318,557 volumes

Outline and Characteristics of the University
Founded in 1960, Kyushu Sangyo University is a private co-educational institution whose philosophy is to provide students with a well-balanced education, emphasizing both modern technical knowledge and intellectual development, which will enable students to cope successfully with today's technology-oriented world community.

Our faculty and staff are very enthusiastic and work very hard to give all students the individual guidance and assistance they need to become truly independent and best suited to function well in our scientifically and technologically advanced society. This philosophy of education requires strong co-operation between university and industry, therefore, great importance is attached to practical applications of new knowledge and theories.

The university has five undergraduate faculties with 14 departments, and three graduate schools with nine divisions. The faculties are Commerce, Management, Engineering, Art and Evening School of Commerce. The graduate schools are Economics, Engineering and Art. The university is located in the north-eastern part of Fukuoka city in Kyushu.

UNDERGRADUATE PROGRAMS

Faculty of Art (Freshmen Enrollment: 420)
Department of Design
Animation, Ceramics, Design Analysis, Display, Dyeing, Experimental Photography, Furniture, Illustration, Interior Planning, Metals, Printing Art, Silk Printing, Systems Engineering, Typography, Visual Communication, Weaving
Department of Fine Arts
Carving, Clay Modeling, Dessin, Fresco, Japanese Style Painting, Mosaic, Oil Painting, Pottery, Printmaking, Welding
Department of Photography
Advertising Photography, Cinematography, Color Photography, Document Photography, Graphic Arts, History & Aesthetics of Photography, Photographic Applied Science, Photographic Materials, Photographic Processing, Photography as Art, Photomechanics, Portrait Photography
Faculty of Commerce (Freshmen Enrollment: 700)
Department of Commerce
Evening School of Commerce (Freshmen Enrollment: 200)
Department of Commerce
Accounting, Bookkeeping, Business Administration, Business Law, Commerce, Finance, Foreign Trade, Industrial Economics, Managerial Accounting, Marketing, Multinational Corporation
Department of Economics
Accounting, Bookkeeping, Business Administration, Cost Accounting, Economic History, Economic Policy, Economics, Finance, Personnel Administrations, Social Policy, Social Thoughts, Statistics, World Economics
Faculty of Engineering (Freshmen Enrollment: 500)
Department of Architecture
Architectural Design & History, Architectural Engineering, Building Science, Earthquake Engineering, Structural Engineering
Department of Civil Engineering
Geophysic Engineering, Hydraulic Engineering, Structural Engineering
Department of Electrical Engineering
Communication Theory and Systems, Electrical Machinery, Electric Power Engineering, Electronic Properties of Matter, Information Processing and Computer Science, Instruments and Control System
Department of Industrial Chemistry
Applied Physical Chemistry, Environmental Chemistry, Inorganic Industrial Chemistry, Organic Structural Chemistry, Organic Synthetic Chemistry
Department of Mechanical Engineering
Fluid Mechanics, Heat Transfer, Industrial Planning and Design, Machine Tools, Machining, Strength of Materials
Faculty of Management (Freshmen Enrollment: 300)
Department of Industrial Management

Accounting, Business Management Theory, Computer Science, Information Management, Management, Management Science, Marketing, Production Management, Statistics
Department of International Management
Business History, Business Management Theory, International Business Studies, International Economics, International Management Strategy, International Relations, Management

Foreign Student Admission
Qualifications for Applicants
    Standard Qualifications Requirement
Examination at the University
    Preliminary screening based on the submitted application materials. Successful applicants can take the secondary screening. (Interview and essay) Those who apply for the departments of Fine Arts and Design are required to take the test of practical skills.
Documents to be Submitted When Applying
    Standard Documents Requirement
    Applicants are also required to submit:
"Statement of purpose", a hand written essay in Japanese

GRADUATE PROGRAMS

Graduate School of Art (First Year Enrollment : Master's 14)
Divisions
Design, Fine Arts, Photography
Graduate School of Economics (First Year Enrollment : Master's 10)
Division
Economics
Graduate School of Engineering (First Year Enrollment : Master's 40)
Divisions
Architecture, Civil Engineering, Electrical Engineering, Industrial Chemistry, Mechanical Engineering

Foreign Student Admission
Qualifications for Applicants
Master's Program
    Standard Qualifications Requirement
Examination at the University
Master's Program
    Applicants will be synthetically screened on the basis of the scholastic ability test, all documents, the Japanese language ability and an interview.
    Those who apply for the divisions of Fine Arts, Design and Photography are required to take the test of practical skills.
Documents to be Submitted When Applying
    Standard Documents Requirement
    Those who apply for the divisions of Fine Arts, Design and Photography are required to submit the applicant's own works.

Research Institutes and Centers

Information Processing Center, Institute of Industrial Management

Special Programs for Foreign Students

The following special courses are offered for foreign students: Japanese Language, Japanese Culture, Japanese Politics & Economics and General Affairs of Japan.

For Further Information

Undergraduate and Graduate Admission

Public Information Section, Section of Registrar and Admissions, Kyushu Sangyo University, 2-3-1 Matsukadai, Higashi-ku, Fukuoka-shi, Fukuoka 813 ☎ 092-681-1831 ext. 276, 227

Kyushu Tokai University
(Kyushu Tokai Daigaku)

223 Toroku, Oe-machi, Kumamoto-shi, Kumamoto 862　☎ 096-382-1141

Faculty
　　Profs.　79　　Assoc. Profs.　45
　　Assist. Profs.　Full–time　27; Part–time　90
　　Res. Assocs.　5
Number of Students
　　Undergrad.　3, 032　　Grad.　14
Library　129, 672 volumes

Outline and Characteristics of the University

Kyushu Tokai University aims to develop well-rounded individuals who, with a broad understanding of history and the present world, will strive to become better citizens and to create a better world. The educational opportunities available at the university are in keeping with its spirit, based on a respect for the individual and on a humanistic rather than materialistic interpretation of history.

Kyushu Tokai University was founded in 1973 with the establishment of the School of Engineering. In 1980, at the urging of the community, the University added a School of Agriculture with two departments, agriculture and animal science. The Graduate School of Agriculture was established in 1984, with aims to ameliorate agricultural desolation and the precipitous fall in self-sufficient food producion.

In 1986, the Department of Information and System Engineering was established to meet the need for training in computer software use and engineering. The Institute of Industrial Science and Technical Research, the Agricultural Research Institute, and the Information Development Technology Center, along with the expanded courses and schools, are presently conducting studies to contribute to the advancement of the sciences. The education of idealistic technical young men, who manifest humanity, originality, and a broad mental horizon — that is the mission of the University.

UNDERGRADUATE PROGRAMS

School of Agriculture (Freshmen Enrollment: 140)
　Department of Agronomy
Agricultural Economies, Appied Botany Pomology, Crop Science, Entomology, Farm Management, Plant Breeding and Genetics, Plant Pathology, Soil Science, Vegtable and Ornamental Horticulture
　Department of Animal Science
Animal Anatomy and Histology, Animal Breeding, Animal Feeding, Animal Management, Animal Reproduction, Biological Chemistry, Chemistry and Technology of Animal Products, Embryology, Grassland Science

School of Engineering (Freshmen Enrollment: 500)
　Department of Architecture
Architectural Design and Drawing, Building Construction Methoods, Building Equipment, Building Execution, Building Materials, Coloration, Engineering Geology, Environmental Engineering, History of Architecture, Reinforced Concrete Construction, Seismic Enginnering, Steel Frame Construction, Structual Dynamics, Town Planning Building Codes
　Department of Civil Engineering
Agricultural Land Engineering, Bridge Engineering, Civil Engineering Geology, Civil Works Management, Concrete Engineering, Disaster Prevention Engineering, Earthquake Resistance Engineering, Explosive Engineering, Foundation Engineering, Geophysical Prospecting, Harbor and Coast Engineering, History of Civil Engineering, Hydraulics, Programing, Reinforced Concrete, Road Engineering, Rural Planning, Sanitation Engineering, Soil Engineering, Traffic Engineering, Water Quality Engineering, Water Resources Engineering
　Department of Electrical Engineering
Atomic Energy, Electrical Communications Engineering, Electrical Drawing, Electrical Equipment Standard and Management, Electrical Measurements, Electrical Power Plant and Substation, Electrical Property of Materials, Electric Circuits, Electricity and Magnetism, Electric Machinery, High Voltage Engineering, Transient Phenomena Theory
　Department of Electronics and Information Technology
Automatic Control, Communication Apparatus, Communication Engineering, Data Communication, Design of Computer System, Digital Computer, Electrical Measurement, Electromagnetic Wave Theory, Electromagnetism, Electronic Circuits, Electronic Devices, Image Engineering, Information Theory, Programming Languages, Pulse and Digital Circuits, Radio Engineering, Satellite Communication, Transmission Circuits
　Depertment of Information and System Engineering
Accounting Systems, Business and Manufacturing Information Systems, Computer Architecture, Cost Engineering, Database Systems, Date Communica-

tion Systems, Factory Automation Systems, Information Psychology, Information Theory, Introduction to Computer Science, Introduction to Information Systems Engineering, Measurement and Control Engineering Reliablility of Computer Programming, Operations Research, Programming Languages, Programming Techniques. Systems Engineering, Seminar on Data Processing, Seminar on Image Processing, Social Information Systems, System Design to Computrer Software, Systems Analisis and Design, System Simulation

Department of Management Engineering

Accounting, Bookkeeping, Business Analysis, Business Management, Business Organization, Computer Science, Cost Engineering, Decision Making, Distributive Economics, Economic Engineering, Industrial Civilization, Industrial Engineering, Industrial Psychology, Information Management, Information Management Systems, Management Accounting, Marketing, Marketing Research, Measurement and Control Systems, Personnel Management, Production Management, Quality Control, Small Business Management, Statistics

Department of Mechanical Engineering

Automotive Engineering, Dynamics of Machinery, Engineering Materials, Engineering Plasticity, Fluid Machinery, Fluid Mechanics, Heat Energy Engineering, Industrial Mechanics, Industrial Thermodynamics, Instrumentation Engineering, Internal Combustion Engines, Machine Design, Machine Tools, Machining Technology, Mechanism, Motor Vehicle Maintenance, Strength of Materials

Foreign Student Admission

Qualifications for Applicants

Standard Qualifications Requirement

Examination at the University

Screening of the Date: documents, written examinations (Japanese, English, Mathmatics, and Science), and an interview.

the end of November and early February.

Documents to be Submitted When Applying

Standard Documents Requirement

The application periods for

The first examination: Throughout November.

The second examination: Throughout January.

Note: Applicants who have studied Japanese at a Japanese language school or other institutions are required to submit a certificate of their language proficiency.

Results of the examination will be sent to each successful candidate about half a month after the examination

GRADUATE PROGRAMS

Graduate School of Agriculture (First Year Enrollment : Master's 16; Doctor's 4)

Courses

Agronomy, Animal Science

Foreign Student Admission

Qualifications for Applicants

Master's and Doctor's

Standard Qualifications Requirement

Japanese Language Proficiency Test and the General Examination for Foreign Students

Examination at the University

Master's and Doctor's

A special selective examination system.

Documents to be Submitted When Applying

Standard Documents Requirement

The application deadline: in September or in March.

*

Research Institutes and Centers

Agricultural Research Institute, Institute of Industrial Science and Technical Research, Technical Center of Knowledge and Information Developments

For Further Information

Undergraduate Admission

Office of Entrance Examination, Kyushu Tokai University, 223 Toroku, Oe-machi, Kumamoto-shi, Kumamoto 862 ☎ 096-382-1141

Graduate Admission

Education and Student Division, Kyushu Tokai University, Kawayo, Choyo-son, Aso-gun, Kumamoto 869-14 ☎ 09676-7-0611

Kyushu Women's University
(Kyushu Joshi Daigaku)

1-1 Jiyugaoka, Yahata, Nishi-ku, Kitakyushu-shi, Fukuoka 807 ☎ 093-691-0591

Faculty

Profs. 26   Assoc. Profs. 12

Assist. Profs. Full-time 7; Part-time 22

Res. Assoc. 13

Number of Students

Undergrad. 600

Library 64, 417 volumes

Outline and Characteristics of the University

In conformity with the Fundamentals of the Educational Act and the School Education Act, the Fukuhara Academy was founded in 1947 by Dr. Gunzo Fukuhara, who recognized the importance of higher education for women.

Along with its founder's lofty ideals, the Academy is endowed with the geographical advantage of lying in Kitakyushu, a city of one million people abundant in natural beauty, sun and greenery.

Over the years the academy has developed into a comprehensive academic institution, embracing 5 kindergartens, 2 high schools, Kyoritsu University, Kyushu Women's Junior College, and Kyushu Women's University, taking full advantage of its position as a private educational organization.

1962—Founding of Kyushu Women's University with the Department of Home Economics : Home Economics, and Nutrition and Food Programs.

1965—Established 2 new literature departments : Japanese and English.

1980—Established a sister-school relation with St. Cloud State University in Minnesota, U. S. A.

UNDERGRADUATE PROGRAMS

Faculty of Home Economics (Freshmen Enrollment: 50)
Department of Home Economics
Faculty of Liberal Arts (Freshmen Enrollment: 100)
Department of English Literature
Department of Japanese Literature

Foreign Student Admission
Qualifications for Applicants
Standard Qualifications Requirement
Students from countries which have diplomatic relations with Japan.
Students who have been deemed to have finished education equivalent to or higher than Japanese high school.
Transcript and statement of objectives
Personal Interview
Written Examination
Review of General Japanese Ability
Documents to be Submitted When Applying
Standard Documents Requirement
＊
For Further Information
Undergraduate Admission
Administrative Office, Kyushu Women's University, 1-1 Jiyugaoka, Yahata, Nishi–ku, Kitakyushu–shi, Fukuoka 807 ☎ 093–691–3331

Matsumoto Dental College
(Matsumoto Shika Daigaku)

1780 Hirooka, Gobara, Shiojiri-shi, Nagano 399-07
☎ 0263-52-3100

Faculty
    Profs. 29   Assoc. Profs. 15
    Assist. Profs.   Full-time 30; Part-time 83
    Res. Assocs. 80
Number of Students
    Undergrad. 752
Library 93, 562 volumes

Outline and Characteristics of the College
Matsumoto Dental College is a private, coeducational, six-year dental school. Approximately 10 km. south of Matsumoto City (pop. 197, 000) in Nagano Prefecture, the school is located in the center of Japan and is easily accessible from all major cities. Express train service from Tokyo is less than three

hours, from Nagoya approximately two hours, and air service from Osaka is only one hour and fifteen minutes.

The school was opened in 1972 by Yasushi Yagasaki. In founding the college, Yagasaki created a professional school in the highest sense. His goal was to provide the young dental student with a scholarly atmosphere that would foster the true meaning of higher education, as well as promote democratic values and an international consciousness. This combination of ideals allows Matsumoto Dental College to offer a unique environment in which there is opportunity for well-rounded intellectual, social, and cultural development.

In keeping with the founder's intentions, the school has a distinctively international flavor. Each year foreign guest lecturers, researchers, students and visitors come to the college from a variety of countries not only in Asia, but from throughout the world. Matsumoto Dental College has particularly close ties with Indiana University through its sister school affiliation, established in 1985. In addition, the college sponsors a yearly U. S. summer study-travel program. In order to facilitate international exchange, the college maintains an Office of External Affairs staffed by foreign native speakers of English.

In planning the school, special care was given to the choice of location and layout. Matsumoto and its surroundings are among the most naturally beautiful areas in Japan. A historic castle town, Matsumoto is surrounded by the Japan Alps, a 3, 000 meter high range of snow capped peaks.

The campus comprises a spacious and attractive 198, 000m² south of Matsumoto in Shiojiri City. An integral part of the campus is the large and attractive library, completed in 1985. Instructional facilities include the main building, plus separate lecture and practicum buildings. The college operates a hospital, also located on the campus.

In addition, the school offers a wide variety of outdoor athletic facilities, such as track and field, baseball, football, tennis, and golf practice, plus extensive indoor facilities and a heated pool. Winter sports enthusiasts can find excellent skiing and skating within a short distance of the campus.

UNDERGRADUATE PROGRAMS

Faculty of Dentistry (Freshmen Enrollment: 120)
Department of Basic Dentistry
Anatomy, Biochemistry, Community Dentistry, Dental Anatomy, Dental Pharmacology, Dental Technology, Histology, Hygiene, Microbiology, Oral Anatomy, Oral Biochemistry, Oral Histology, Oral Microbiology, Oral Pathology, Oral Physiology, Pathology, Pharmacology, Physiology
Department of Clinical Dentistry
Complete and Partial Prosthodontics, Crown and Bridge Prosthodontics, Dental Anesthesiology, Dental Radiology, Dentistry for the Handicapped, Endo-

dontics, General Prosthodontics, Operative Dentistry, Oral and Maxillofacial Surgery, Oral Diagnostics and Surgery, Oral Medicine, Orthodontics, Pedodontics, Periodontics

Foreign Student Admission
Qualifications for Applicants
Standard Qualifications Requirement
Examination at the College
Written exams in English, Mathematics or Natural Science, plus a short essay in Japanese.
Documents to be Submitted When Applying
Standard Documents Requirement

Qualifications for Transfer Students
Persons who have completed 16 years of education at overseas institutions in preparation for advanced studies, or those who will have completed 16 years of such education by March 31, 1989, are eligible to apply for admission as foreign transfer students.
Applications will not be accepted from persons who will have reached the age of 45 years on or before April 1, 1989.
Examination for Transfer Students
A short essay in Japanese and a personal interview.
Documents to be Submitted When Applying
Standard Documents Requirement

*

For Further Information
Undergraduate Admission
Senior Associate Dean, Matsumoto Dental College, 1780 Hirooka, Gobara, Shiojiri-shi, Nagano 399-07 ☎ 0263-52-3100

Matsusaka University
(Matsusaka Daigaku)

1846 Kubo-cho, Matsusaka-shi, Mie 515
☎ 0598-29-1122

Faculty
   Profs. 25   Assoc. Profs. 13
   Assist. Profs. Full–time 4; Part–time 36
Number of Students
   Undergrad. 1, 534
Library 59, 419 volumes

Outline and Characteristics of the University
Matsusaka University is a young university established in 1982, with the unanimous support of the city government and the people of Matsusaka. Though new, Matsusaka University is one of the many educational establishments under the Umemura Educational Institution, whose origin can be traced back to the foundation of Chukyo Commercial School in Nagoya City in 1923. Ever since, the Institution has developed and matured to the point

where it now includes two universities, one women's junior college, three high schools, one junior high school and one kindergarten. These schools are located at the three campuses in Nagoya City and Toyota City in Aichi Prefecture and in Matsusaka City in Mie Prefecture.

Matsusaka University consists of one faculty, Political Science and Economics. Its uniqueness is found in the interlinked study of political science and economics. The faculty has two courses, comparative and regional. The former offers students comparative studies in international politics and economics, while the latter aims to examine regional politics and economics in relation to those of the central government. Besides its distinctive curriculum, Matsusaka University is proud of its academic staff, which is composed of many eminent scholars from major universities throughout the nation as well as from governmental research institutions. Since the zeal of Matsusaka citizens played an important role in the establishment of Matsusaka University, it aims to be an academic and research institution open to the public and wishes to contribute to the development and prosperity of the area.

Matsusaka City is situated squarely in the center of Mie Prefecture, which is itself in the center of the Main Island, Honshu. The large cities of Nagoya and Osaka as well as the ancient capitals of Kyoto and Nara are close at hand. The area is renowned not only for its abundance of historic sites and monuments but also for its natural beauty, with the alluring Ise-Shima National Park to the south of Matsusaka City. Matsusaka University itself is located on a wooded low hill in the southern part of Matsusaka City, an ideal learning surroundings for the students.

UNDERGRADUATE PROGRAMS

Faculty of Political Science and Economics (Freshmen Enrollment: 300)
   Department of Political Science and Economics
*

For Further Information
Undergraduate Admission
Admissions Office, Matsusaka University, 1846 Kubo-cho, Matsusaka-shi, Mie 515 ☎ 0598-29-1122 ext. 251

Matsuyama University
(Matsuyama Shoka Daigaku)

4-2 Bunkyo-cho, Matsuyama-shi, Ehime 790
☎ 0899-25-7111

Faculty
   Profs. 81   Assoc. Profs. 27
   Assist. Profs. Full–time 18; Part–time 103
Number of Students

Undergrad. 5, 384   Grad. 19
Library 452, 000 volumes

Outline and Characteristics of the University

Matsuyama University is a private, independent, coeducational university with colleges of economics, business administration, humanities, and law; graduate schools of economics and business administration; and also a junior college for working people within the community. The University traces its origin to the Matsuyama Technical School of Commerce which was founded in 1923 by Chojiro Nitta, a prosperous businessman of the time, who felt the need for an advanced school where the best possible business education of the local youth might be secured. In 1949, having received full accreditation by the Ministry of Education, the institution acquired university status under the current name of Matsuyama University. Other memorable dates in the University's history are as follows: 1952, addition of the Junior College; 1974, establishment of the Faculty of Humanities; 1988, establishment of the Faculty of Law.

Since its birth 64 years ago, Matsuyama University has always been known for its intellectual vigor and its emphasis on relevant aspects of learning, its close relationship between students and faculty members, its searching examination of values, and its cohesive educational programs as solid foundations for success in personal, professional, and civic life. To meet the challenges of an ever changing world, the University attempts to develop a community in which learning and teaching will flourish and create a campus environment in which innovative student life may support academic goals. True to its three-fold credo of "truth, faith, and use, " the University seeks to foster research in various areas of knowledge and to relate it to current needs and future concerns of society. Above all, the University is devoted to the education of the whole person through integrated programs in general education, career preparation, and campus life.

While encouraged to publish and conduct research, the faculty is primarily committed to teaching and the informal discussions with individual students. Equally significant, all full-time faculty members serve as advisors.

Over the decades, Matsuyama University graduates have entered various walks of life. Distinguished businessmen, public servants, teachers, and accountants who live throughout Japan all share common roots here in the University community, which is unique in heritage, character, and location. In short, we believe Matsuyama University is a private academic institution dedicated to the quality of life of its members for generations to come.

UNDERGRADUATE PROGRAMS

Faculty of Business Administration (Freshmen Enrollment: 400)

Department of Business Administration

Accounting, Advertising, Auditing, Bookkeeping, Business History, Business Management, Commerce, Cost Accounting, Financial Accounting, Financial Management, Financial Statements Analysis, History of Commerce, History of Management, Insurance, International Trade, Management, Management Control, Management Science, Managerial Accounting, Marketing, Merchandising, Organizational Theory, Personnel Management, Tax Accounting, Transportation and Communication

Faculty of Economics (Freshmen Enrollment: 400)

Department of Economics

Econometrics, Economic History, Economic Planning, Economic Policy, Economics, Economics of Agriculture, Economics of Industry, Economics of Transportation, Economic Statistics, Finance, Foreign Economic Affairs, History of Economics, Industrial Structure, International Economics, International Finance, Mathematical Economics, Political Economy, Public Finance, Theory of Market Prices, Trade Cycles

Faculty of Humanities (Freshmen Enrollment: 220)

Department of English Language and English and American Literature

American Literature, English Grammar, English Linguistics, English Literature, English Phonetics, History of American Literature, History of English Literature, History of the English Language

Department of Sociology

Economic Sociology, Family Sociology, History of Sociology, Industrial Sociology, Mass Communication, Methods of Social Research, Occupational Sociology, Political Sociology, Regional Sociology, Rural Sociology, Sociology, Sociology of Religion, Urban Sociology

Faculty of Law (Freshmen Enrollment: 200)

Department of Law

Administrative Law, Bankruptcy Law, Civil Law, Commercial Law, Constitutional Law, Criminal Law, Economic Law, Foreign Law, History of law, International Law, International Private Law, Labor Law, Law of Civil Procedure, Law of Criminal Procedure, Law of Education, Local Government Law, Philosophy of Law, Tax Law

Foreign Student Admission

Qualifications for Applicants

Standard Qualifications Requirement

Examination at the University

The Education Affairs Committee selects applicants with reference to grades, qualifications, personality, and condition of health. The names of those applicants selected by the committee are referred to the relevant Faculty for discussion. The final decision rests with the President.

Documents to be Submitted When Applying

Standard Documents Requirement

GRADUATE PROGRAMS

Graduate School of Business Administration (First Year Enrollment : Master's 10, Doctor's 2)
Division
Business Administration
Graduate School of Economics (First Year Enrollment : Master's 10, Doctor's 4)
Division
Economics

*

Research Institutes and Centers
Research Institute for Economics and Business Administration
For Further Information
Undergraduate and Graduate Admission
Admission Office, Matsuyama University, 4-2 Bunkyo-cho, Matsuyama-shi, Ehime 790 ☎ 0899-25-7111

Meiji College of Oriental Medicine
(Meiji Shinkyu Daigaku)

Hiyoshi-cho, Funai-gun, Kyoto 629-03
☎ 07717-2-1181

Faculty
 Profs. 15 Assoc. Profs. 10
 Assist. Profs. Full–time 17; Part–time 25
 Res. Assocs. 13
Number of Students
 Undergrad. 494
Library 30, 400 volumes

Outline and Characteristics of the College
Meiji College of Oriental Medicine was founded in 1983 as the first and only higher educational institute specializing in acupuncture and moxibustion.

Acupuncture and moxibustion, both of which have a history and tradition of thousands of years since their appearance in China, were introduced to Japan in the sixth century, about 1500 years ago. It can be found in the second volume of "Ishinpo", the oldest medical encyclopedia in existence in Japan, which reports these procedures as the main therapeutics of that time.

In recent years, interest in acupuncture and moxibustion has grown considerably, resulting in a concomitant rise in its development. It is now studied with great interest in various medical faculties and dental colleges in Japan. International conferences and symposia and scientific research around the world bear witness to this fact.

The College offers a unique curriculum. The education systematically integrates the traditional Oriental therapy with modern medicine. This is in large part due to the realization that an indispensable ingredient in the growth and development of the techniques and theories of acupuncture is the scientific knowledge of today's medicine. Detailed acupuncture therapy and techniques are taught and developed at the college. This will foster competent acupuncturists who will eventually be contributing members of medical staffs.

1927 Meiji Vocational School of Acupuncture and Moxibustion founded
1959 Meiji Special School of Acupuncture and Moxibustion opened
1961 Renamed to Meiji Special School of Acupuncture, Moxibustion, and Bonesetting
1978 Meiji College of Acupuncture and Moxibustion (Meiji Shinkyu Tankidaigaku) established
1983 Meiji College of Oriental Medicine (Meiji Shinkyu Daigaku) opened
1987 Meiji College of Oriental Medicine Hospital opened

UNDERGRADUATE PROGRAMS

Faculty of Acupuncture and Moxibustion (Freshmen Enrollment: 100)
Department of Acupuncture and Moxibustion
Anatomy, Basic Acupuncture & Moxibustion, Diagnostics of Acupuncture & Moxibustion, Hygiene, Oriental Herbal Medicine, Oriental Medicine, Pathology, Pharmacognosy, Pharmacology, Physiology, Study of Acupuncture Points, Therapeutics of Acupuncture & Moxibustion.

Foreign Student Admission
Qualifications for Applicants
 Standard Qualifications Requirement
 Japanese Language Proficiency Test (JLPT), General Examination for Foreign Students (GEPS),
Examination at the College
 An Interview
 A Short Article Test
Documents to be Submitted When Applying
 Standard Documents Requirement
*
Research Institutes and Centers
Research Institute of Oriental Medicine
For Further Information
Undergraduate Admission
Department of General Affairs, Meiji College of Oriental Medicine, Hiyoshi-cho, Funai-gun, Kyoto 629-03 ☎ 07717-2-1181 ext. 303

Meiji College of Pharmacy
(Meiji Yakka Daigaku)

1–35–23 Nozawa, Setagaya–ku, Tokyo 154
☎ 03–424–1001

Faculty
 Profs. 33 Assoc. Profs. 12
 Assist. Profs. Full–time 14; Part–time 34
 Res. Assocs. 70
Number of Students
 Undergrad. 1, 780 Grad. 56
Library 114, 379 volumes

Outline and Characteristics of the College

In the 33rd year of the Meiji era (1900), the Bill 'to separate pharmacy from medical practice' was introduced in the Imperial Diet. But it was rejected because the number of pharmacists then was too small, and so it was impossible to realize the ideal represented by the Bill.

The setback induced Shigenobu Onda to establish a new pharmaceutical college for the development of pharmacy and the education of pharmacists. This was the predecessor of the Meiji College of Pharmacy.

Since that time, some modifications have taken place, but the College has kept the original ideal through these years.

It has turned out many of the leading pharmacists of the country who respond to social demands in contributing to the advancement of the health and welfare of mankind.

UNDERGRADUATE PROGRAMS

Faculty of Pharmacy (Freshmen Enrollment: 360)
 Department of Bio–Pharmacy
 Department of Pharmaceutical Chemistry
 Department of Pharmaceutical Science
Analytical Chemistry, Analytical Organic Chemistry, Applied Microbiology, Biochemistry, Biological Products Chemistry, Cosmetic Chemistry, Fermentation Chemistry, Food Hygiene Chemistry, Food Science, Hygiene Chemistry, Inorganic Chemistry, Medical Chemistry, Microbial Products Chemistry, Microbiology, Natural Products Chemistry, Organic Chemistry, Pathological Biochemistry, Pathology, Pharmaceutical Botany, Pharmaceutical Chemistry, Pharmaceutical Physical Chemistry, Pharmaceutical Synthetic Chemistry, Pharmaceutical Technochemistry, Pharmaceutics, Pharmacognosy and Phytochemistry, Pharmacology

GRADUATE PROGRAMS

Graduate School of Pharmaceutical Sciences (First

Year Enrollment : Master's 20, Doctor's 10)
 Division
Pharmaceutical Sciences

Foreign Student Admission
 Qualifications for Applicants
Master's Program
 Standard Qualifications Requirement
Doctor's Program
 Standard Qualifications Requirement
 Examination at the College
Master's Program
 Tests on their comprehension ability in Japanese, their major field, foreign languages (English and Germany) and personal interview. All the examination questions are given in Japanese.
Doctor's Program
 An oral examination about a report or thesis prepared during the Master's program.
 Documents to be Submitted When Applying
 Standard Documents Requirement
*

For Further Information
 Undergraduate Admission
Entrance Examination Section, Administrative Office, Meiji College of Pharmacy, 1–35–23 Nozawa, Setagaya–ku, Tokyo 154 ☎ 03–424–1001 ext. 611
 Graduate Admission
Instruction Division, Meiji College of Pharmacy, 1–35–23 Nozawa, Setgaya–ku, Tokyo 154 ☎ 03–424–1001 ext. 604

Meiji Gakuin University
(Meiji Gakuin Daigaku)

1–2–37 Shirokanedai, Minato–ku, Tokyo 108
☎ 03–448–5110

Faculty
 Profs. 151 Assoc. Profs. 59
 Assist. Profs. Full–time 33; Part–time 525
Number of Students
 Undergrad. 11, 689 Grad. 87
Library 490, 000 volumes

Outline and Characteristics of the University

Meiji Gakuin is widely acknowledged as one of the oldest Christian schools in Japan, though the official date of her founding, 1877, is considerably later than that of other Christian schools. That determination lies in what one accepts as her true birthdate.

The name Meiji Gakuin was first used in 1886, when Union Theological School and Union College, joint projects of the Presbyterian and Reformed Church Missions of the United States, united with a Japanese–English Preparatory School and settled on the present campus site at Shirokanedai. But each of these institutions already had respectably long histories. For example, Union Theological School, the founding of which is the official birthdate of Meiji Gakuin, traces its lineage to the Bible classes started by Samuel R. Brown soon after his arrival in 1859. Union College is the descendant of various schools associated with other famous pioneer missionaries. These include: Martin Wyckoff's Senshi Gakko (1881); the John Ballagh Gakko (1873); Yokohama schools of the Presbyterian and Reformed Missions, respectively; and Rev. Christopher Carrothers' private Tokyo College (1881).

However, the lineage goes back even further to 1861 when the Japanese government sent nine boys to Japan's first Protestant missionary, James C. Hepburn, for instruction in English and science. From those classes the Hepburn Juku was established in 1863. Thus, the true beginning of Meiji Gakuin can be traced back well before the official 1877 date.

By 1886, Meiji Gakuin offered a four–year general arts course, a three–year theology course, and a two–year preparatory course. By the late 1920s, the general and preparatory courses had acquired middle school and high school status with English, Social Work, and Commerce departments. A radical change in structure came in 1930, when the theology department merged with Rev. Masahisa Uemura's Tokyo Theological School. Another merger came in 1933 when Meiji Gakuin merged with Steele Academy (Tozan Gakuin) in Nagasaki. By 1941, Meiji Gakuin had an enrollment of 1, 700 students.

Several dislocations occurred during World War II, but in 1949 Meiji Gakuin reorganized to meet new government regulations, adopting a structure much like that of today. The postwar expansion and increased enrollment necessitated a radical renovation of the old campus and its facilities. In 1952, through the cooperative efforts of Toru Matsumoto of Meiji Gakuin and Luman Shafer in New York, Meiji Gakuin undertook a ten–year building program, which was made possible by a half–million dollar grant from the Presbyterian and Reformed Churches and by the acquisition of property adjacent to the campus.

In 1955, Meiji Gakuin embarked on another long–range program devoted to rebuilding the present campus and developing a new campus away from the heart of the city. In 1963, that plan was realized when Meiji Gakuin opened a second senior high school with new sports facilities in Higashi Murayama, a suburb in western Tokyo. In 1968, the junior high school also moved to Higashi Murayama.

Because of limited space on the Shirokane campus and an enrollment of over 10, 000, Meiji Gakuin in 1980 purchased a spacious tract of land in Totsuka, Yokohama. The university hoped that building a new campus in this quiet environment would recreate the atmosphere which made the 'Hill of Shirokane' so famous in Meiji Gakuin's early years. The new campus for first and second year instruction opened in April 1985.

Today, Meiji Gakuin University has a Faculty of General Education, a Faculty of Literature, with departments of English Literature and French Literature, a Faculty of Economics with departments of Economics and Commerce, a Faculty of Sociology and Social Work, and a Faculty of Law. The Faculty of International Studies at the Yokohama campus began classes in April 1986.

The unique Christian philosophy, which has guided Meiji Gakuin in the past and which influences her present and will mold her future, is that a university should strive to nurture young people who, while continuing to ponder the central question of Christianity (i. e. the meaning of human existence), respect others, have the ability to choose their own path in life, and devote themselves to the promotion of international understanding and peace. With this preparation, Meiji Gakuin graduates have gone on to enter and make significant contributions to many different fields.

UNDERGRADUATE PROGRAMS

Faculty of Economics (Freshmen Enrollment: 560)
Department of Commerce Courses
Accounting, Advertising, Auditing, Bookkeeping, Business Administration, Business History, Business Organizations, Business Planning, Commerce, Commercial Policy, Commodities, Cost Accounting, Economic Geography, Economics of Transportation, Finance Accounting, Finance Management, Financial Statements Analysis, Foreign Trade, History of Accounting, History of Business Administration, History of Commerce, Information Management, Insurance, Insurance Against Loss, International Finance, Labor Management, Management Accounting, Marketing, Marketing Research, Money and Banking, Physical Distribution, Production Management, Securities Market, Structures of Enterprises, Tax Accounting
Department of Economics Courses
Agricultural Policy, Commercial Policy, Econometrics, Economic Change and Development, Economic Growth, Economic History of Asia, Economic History of Japan, Economic History of Western Europe, Economic Policy, Economics, History of Economics, History of Economic Thought, History of Political Economics, History of Social Thought, Industrial Organization, Industrial Policy, International Economics, International Finance, Labor Economics, Local Public Finance, Marxist Economics, Mathematics in Economics, Modern Economic Analysis, Money and Banking, National Income Theory, Population Problems, Public Finance, Socialist Economics, Social Policy, The American Economy, The Chinese Economy, The Japanese Economy, The World Economy
Faculty of International Studies (Freshmen Enrollment: 200)
Department of International Studies Courses
Agricultural and Rural Issues, Area Development,

Area Economics, Area Finance, Buddhist Culture, Christian Culture, Comparative Art, Comparative Cultures, Comparative Politics, Energy Resources, Environmental Economics, Ethnology, History of Comparative Economics, History of International Politics, History of Political Thought, Information Sociology, International Economics, International Finance, International Politics, International Welfare Administration, Islamic Culture, Issues of Developed and Developing Countries, Japanese Culture, Japanese Politics, Mass Communication, Modern Civilization, Modern Literature, Modern Religion, Multinational Enterprises, Political Principles, Socialist Economics, Sociology of Art and Literature, Sociology of Politics, World Order

Faculty of Law (Freshmen Enrollment: 500)

Department of Law Courses

Administrative Law, Anglo–American Law, Canon Law, Civil Law, Civil Procedure, Commercial Law, Comparative Constitutional Law, Conflicts in Law, Constitutional Law, Contract Law, Corporate Law, Criminal Law, Criminal Procedure, Criminology, Economic Law, Family Law, German Civil Law, History of Political Thought, History of Politics and Diplomacy, Industrial Property Law, International Law, International Relations, Japanese Legal History, Labor Law, Law of Drafts and Checks, Maritime Insurance and Shipping Law, Philosophy of Law, Politics, Property Law, Public Administration, Social Security Law, Sociology of Law, Tax Law, Trust Law, Western Legal History

Faculty of Literature (Freshmen Enrollment: 440)

Department of English Literature Courses

American Literary Criticism, Chiristianity, English Grammar, English Language, English Literary Criticism, English Literature, English Phonetics, History of American Literature, History of English Literature, History of the English Language, Linguistics, Phonemics, Pragmatics, Semantics

Department of French Literature Courses

French Language, French Linguistics, French Literary Criticism, French Literature, History of French Literature, History of the French Language

Faculty of Sociology and Social Work (Freshmen Enrollment: 400)

Department of Social Work Courses

Administration of Social Welfare, Child Welfare, Clinical Psychology, Community Organization, Counseling Handicapped Children, Family Social Work, History of Social Thought, History of Social Work, Medical Social Work, Mental Health, Pathology and Health of Handicapped Children, Personality Development, Psychology of Handicapped Children, Public Assistance, Social Pathology, Social Policy, Social Research, Social Security, Social Welfare, Social Welfare Ideology, Social Welfare Legislation, Study of Children with Speech Impediments, Welfare for the Aged, Welfare for the Mentally Handicapped, Welfare for the Physically Handicapped

Department of Sociology Courses

Criminal Sociology, Cultural Anthropology, History of Sociology, Industrial Sociology, Mass Communication, Methods of Social Education, Rural Sociology, Social Education, Social Pathology, Social Psychology, Sociology, Sociology of Education, Sociology of Religion, Sociology of the Family, Urban Sociology

Foreign Student Admission

Qualifications for Applicants

Standard Qualifications Requirement

Japanese Language Proficiency Test (Level 1) and General Examination for Foreign Students.

Examination at the University

Faculty of Literature: Foreign language (English or French), short essay in English, French or Japanese, and an interview

Faculty of Economics, Faculty of International Studies,

Faculty of Law: lnterview

Faculty of Sociology and Social Work (Sociology): Short Essay in Japanese, (Social Work) Interview

Documents to be Submitted When Applying

Standard Documents Requirement

GRADUATE PROGRAMS

Graduate School of Arts (First Year Enrollment : Master's 12, Doctor's 2)

Division

English Language and Literature

Graduate School of Economics (First Year Enrollment : Master's 25)

Divisions

Commerce, Economics

Graduate School of Law (First Year Enrollment : Master's 15, Doctor's 5)

Division

Law

Graduate School of Sociology and Social Work (First Year Enrollment : Master's 20, Doctor's 5)

Divisions

Social Work, Sociology

Foreign Student Admission

Qualifications for Applicants

Master's Program

Standard Qualifications Requirement

Acceptance of foreign students is presently under consideration.

*

Research Institutes and Centers

Christian Research Institute, Foreign Language Institute, General Education Faculty Institute, Institute of Linguistic and Cultural Studies, Institute of Sociology and Social Work, International Peace Research Institute Meigaku (PRIME), Law Research Institute,

Research Institute of Economics and Industry

For Further Information

Undergraduate and Graduate Admission

Center for International Cooperation in Education (CICE), Meiji Gakuin University, 1–2–37 Shirokane-dai,

Minato–ku, Tokyo 108 ☎ 03–448–5152

Meiji University
(Meiji Daigaku)

1–1, Kanda Surugadai, Chiyoda–ku, Tokyo 101
☎ 03–296–4545

Faculty
    Profs. 398   Assoc. Profs. 113
    Assist. Profs. Full–time 52; Part–time 888
    Res. Assocs. 47
Number of Students
    Undergrad. 32, 409   Grad. 739
Library 1, 150, 000 volumes

Outline and Characteristics of the University

Meiji University was established in 1881 as a private, coeducational and nonsectarian institution and is well known as one of the oldest leading universities.

Meiji University has three campuses.

The Izumi campus offers lower division courses for the Schools of Law, Commerce, Political Science and Economics, Literature, and Business Administration.

The Surugadai campus offers upper division courses for the above-mentioned schools; evening sessions; graduate courses; and Junior College courses.

The Ikuta campus offers both undergraduate and graduate courses for the School of Engineering and the School of Agriculture.

The University maintains the highest level of education, providing its students with professors and facilities best suited to ensure a good education. and the systematic research and study of natural and social phenomena.

Meiji has developed into a major university consisting of Schools of Law, Commerce, Political Science and Economics, Literature, Engineering, Agriculture and Business Administration, as well as a Women's Junior College.

In addition, each of these seven schools has a graduate program, and the Schools of Law, Commerce, Political Science and Economics, and Literature offer evening sessions for working students.

There are eight noteworthy attributes of the different Schools. The School of Law has educated many prominent legal professionals; the School of Commerce has been highly appreciated as a pioneer in commercial science in Japan; the School of Political Science and Economics has sent out competent persons into the economic world; the School of Literature's staff is made up of leaders in both literary and academic circles; the School of Engineering is equipped with modern facilities; the School of Agriculture seeks to reform agricultural structures in Japan; the School of Business Administration was the first of its kind at a private university; and the Women's Junior College has played a pioneering role in women's education in Japan.

All of these Schools are able to meet the students' educational requirements.

Meiji University celebrated its centennial anniversary in 1980. The university has taken this opportunity to expand its academic programs, especially international programs, to offer our faculty and students a more international vision.

Meiji University strives in all departments to improve its educational and research systems so that it can continue to handle the new issues of our evolving society.

UNDERGRADUATE PROGRAMS

School of Agriculture (Freshmen Enrollment: 550)

Department of Agricultural Chemistry

Agricultural Products Utilization Technology, Animal Nutrition, Arable Soils, Biological Chemistry, Chemistry of Fertilizers, Chemistry of Natural Products, Fermentation Food Technology, Food Chemistry, Food Engineering, Food Hygiene, Food Preservation, Management of Food Quality, Marine Products Utilization Technology, Microbiology, Nutritional Chemistry, Pesticide Chemistry, Plant Nutrition, Science of Feedstuff, Technology of Chilling and Cold Storage, Zymurgy

Department of Agricultural Economics

Agribusiness, Agricultural Associations, Agricultural Cooperative Insurance, Agricultural Cooperatives, Agricultural Credit, Agricultural Labor Science, Agricultural Marketing, Agricultural Policy, Agricultural Statistics, Comparative Agriculture, Farm Management, Farm Products Market, Planning of Land Utilization, Rural Planning, Rural Sociology, Utilization of Agricultural Products

Department of Agriculture

Division of Agricultural Engineering and Landscape Architecture

Agricultural Machines, Farm Land Conservation, Geotechnical Science, Hydraulic Engineering, Irrigation and Drainage, Land Reclamation, Landscape Architecture, Plant Materials and Planting, Pump, Reinforced Concrete Engineering, Urban Planning

Division of Agronomy

Agricultural Meteology, Applied Entomology, Crop Plant Physiology, Crop Science, Floricultural Science, Horticultural Science, Pest Control, Plant Breeding, Plant Pathology, Soil Amelioration, Storage and Processing of Agricultural Products

Division of Animal Production

Animal Breeding, Animal Reproduction, Grassland

Science, Hygiene of Livestock, Livestock Management, Livestock Physiology, Processing of Animal Products, Stock Farm Practicum

School of Business Administration (Freshmen Enrollment: 650)

Department of Business Administration

Accounting, Auditing, Budgetary Control, Business History, Business Management, Business Organization, Cost Management, Financial Management, Forms of Business Enterprise, International Management, Labor Management Relations, Management Theories, Marketing, Office & Administrative Management, Personnel Administration, Production Management, Public Utility Economics, Wage & Salary Administration

School of Commerce (Freshmen Enrollment: Day 1, 000, Evening 450)

Department of Commerce

Department of Industrial Administration

Accounting, Bookkeeping, Business Management, Commerce, Corporation Finance, Cost Accounting, Economic Development, Economic History, Economic Policy, Economics of Transportation, Economic Theory, Foreign Trade, Industrial Management, Industrial Marketing, Industrial Organization, Industrial Psychology, Insurance Science, International Finance, Japanese Economy, Labor Management, Management Acocunting, Marketing Management, Monetary Economics, Overseas Marketing, Production Management, Public Finance, Sales Management, Shipping, Tax Accounting, Warehouse Management, World Economy

School of Law (Freshmen Enrollment: Day 900, Evening 280)

Department of Law

Administrative Law, Anglo–American Law, Bankruptcy Law, Civil Law, Civil Procedure, Commercial Law, Comparative Constitutional Law, Constitution, Criminal Law, Criminal Procedure, Economic Law, French Law, German Law, History of Legal Thought, International Law, Labor Law, Legal History, Securities Law, Social Security Law, Tax Law

School of Literature (Freshmen Enrollment: Day 620, Evening 300)

Department of History and Geography

Archaeology Course

Asian History Course

European History Course

Geography Course

Japanese History Course

Department of Literature

Anglo–American Literature Course:

American Literature, English Language, English Linguistics, English Literature

Dramatics Course:

Broadcasting, Cinematography, Dramatic Production, Dramatics, History of Japanese Drama, History of Western Drama, Stage Design, Theatrical Production, Theory of Acting

French Literature Course:

French Language, French Linguistics, French Literature, History of France

German Literature Course:

German Language, German Linguistics, German Literature, History of German Literature

Japanese Literature Course:

Chinese Literature, Folklore, History of Japanese Arts, History of Japanese Drama, History of Japanese Literary Thought, History of Japanese Thought, Japanese History, Japanese Language, Japanese Linguistics, Japanese Literature

Literary Arts Course (Evening Division Only):

Chinese Literature, Cinematography, Criticism, Drama, Fiction, History of German Literature, History of Japanese Literature, History of Russian Literature, History of Western Drama, Japanese Literature, Major English Writers & Their Works, Major French Writers & Their Works, Major German Writers & Their Works, Major Russian Writers & Their Works, Poetry, Theory of Arts

School of Political Science and Economics (Freshmen Enrollment: Day 1, 000, Evening 440)

Department of Economics

Accounting, Bookkeeping, Business Management, Cooperatives, Econometrics, Economic Geography, Economic Growth & Fluctuations, Economic History, Economic Policy, Economics, Economics of Transportation, Economic Statistics, Economic Systems, History of Economics, History of Economic Thought, Industrial Organization, International Economics, Labor Problems, Linear Economics, Local Finance, Marxian Economics, Modern Economics, Money & Banking, Population Studies, Public Finance, Social Security, Theory of Small Business

Department of Political Science

Comparative Governments & Politics, Comparative Sociology, Diplomatic History, History of Japanese Political Thought, History of Political Theory, International Politics, Journalism, Local Government, Mass Communication, Political History, Political Philosophy, Political Science, Political Systems, Politics in Soviet Russia, Process of Government, Public Administration, Regional Development, Social Relations, Theories of State, Urban Politics and Public Policy

School of Science and Technology (Freshmen Enrollment: 950)

Department of Architecture

Air Conditioning, Architectural Design and Decoration, Architectural Environment, Architectural Planning, Architecture, Building Economy, Building Materials, History of Architecture, Plumbing, Regional Planning, Soil Engineering, Structural Design, Structural Mechanics

Department of Electrical Engineering

Computer Scinece, Control Engineering, Electrical and Electronic Materials, Electrical and Electronic Measurements, Electrical and Electronic Physics, Electric Circuits, Electric Machinery, Electromagnetism, Power Generation and Substation Engineering,

Power Transmission and Distribution Engineering

Department of Electronics and Communication

Computer Science, Control Engineering, Electromagnetism, Electron Devices, Electronic Circuits, Electronic Materials, Information Engineering, Information Processing Engineering, Solid State Electronics, Systems Engineering, Telecommunication Engineering, Transmission of Information

Department of Industrial Chemistry

Analytical Chemistry, Chemical Engineering, Chemical Process Control, Chemical Process Design, Chemical Safety Engineering, Inorganic Chemistry, Inorganic Industrial Chemistry, Organic Chemistry, Organic Industrial Chemistry, Physical Chemistry, Polymer Technology

Department of Information Sciences

Department of Mathematics

Department of Mechanical Engineering

Control Engineering, Engineering Thermodynamics, Fluid Mechanics, Hydraulics, Instrumentation Engineering, Machine Design Engineering, Manufacturing Processes of Machine, Mechanical Dynamics, Mechanical Engineering Experiment, Strength of Materials

Department of Physics

Department of Precision Engineering

Control Engineering, Experimental Engineering, Instrumentation Engineering, Machine Design Engineering, Mechanical Dynamics, Precision Measurement, Precision Metal Working, Production Systems Engineering, Robotics

Foreign Student Admission

Qualifications for Applicants

Standard Qualifications Requirement

Applicants must come to Japan before September 16 of the previous year of admission and study Japanese for not less than three months at a language school in Japan.

Examination at the University

1. First Screening: Screening of the submitted documents
2. Second Screening: Japanese language test (reading, listening and writing)
3. Third Screening: A written examination and interview

Documents to be Submitted When Applying

Standard Documents Requirement

1. Preregistration

    Applicants must preregister.

    Period of Preregistration: September 16 to September 30.

2. Application Period: October 11 to October 18

3. Other Documents Required

    (1) Certificate of Japanese Language Ability: A prescribed form will be provided by Meiji University. Certification from a proper Japanese language institution is required.

    (2) Letter of Guarantee with Guarantor's Employment Certificate

(3) Japanese Composition

The theme is given in the "Guide for Admission of Foreign Students."

(4) Three self-addressed envelopes

(5) Examination Fee: ¥30, 000.

Only those applicants who have passed the first screening are required to pay the examination fee.

Applicants will not be allowed to take the examination for the evening division of the university.

GRADUATE PROGRAMS

Graduate School of Agriculture (First Year Enrollment : Master's 26, Doctor's 2)

Divisions

Agricultural Chemistry, Agricultural Economics, Agriculture

Graduate School of Business Administration (First Year Enrollment : Master's 25, Doctor's 5)

Division

Business Administration

Graduate School of Commerce (First Year Enrollment : Master's 35, Doctor's 6)

Division

Commerce

Graduate School of Law (First Year Enrollment : Master's 50, Doctor's 12)

Divisions

Civil Law, Public Law

Graduate School of Literature (First Year Enrollment : Master's 50, Doctor's 14)

Divisions

Dramatic Arts, English Literature, French Literature, Geography, German Literature, History, Japanese Literature

Graduate School of Political Science and Economics (First Year Enrollment : Master's 50, Doctor's 8)

Divisions

Economics, Political Science

Graduate School of Science and Technology (First Year Enrollment : Master's 81, Doctor's 20)

Divisions

Architecture, Electrical Engineering, Industrial Chemistry, Mechanical Engineering

Foreign Student Admission

Qualifications for Applicants

Master's Program

    Standard Qualifications Requirement

Doctor's Program

    Standard Qualifications Requirement

Examination at the University

Master's Program

1. First Screening: Screening of the submitted documents
2. Second Screening: Japanese language test (reading, listening and writing)
3. Third Screening: Subject and Interview

(Examination Subject for each applicant differs according to the period of his/her residence in Japan.)

Doctor's Program

The screenings for Doctoral Courses differ with departments and applicants. Please contact the Office of International Programs for further information.

Documents to be Submitted When Applying

Standard Documents Requirement

1. Preregistration

Applicants must preregister.

Preregistration Period:

Applicants residing abroad: August 1 to August 31

Applicants residing in Japan: September 16 to September 30

2. Application Period

Applicants residing abroad: September 1 to September 30

Applicants residing in Japan: October 11 to October 18

3. Other Documents Required

(1) Certificate of Japanese Language Ability

A prescribed form will be provided by Meiji University. Certification from a proper Japanese language institution is required.

(2) Letter of Guarantee with Guarantor's Employment Certificate

(3) A copy of the summary of master's thesis (those who apply for the doctoral course)

(4) Passport (to be produced at the time of application)

(5) Three self-addressed envelopes

(6) Examination Fee: ¥30, 000

Only those applicants who have passed the first screening are required to pay the examination fee.

*

Research Institutes and Centers

Center for International Programs, Information Science Center, Institute of Cultural Science, Institute of Science and Technology, Institute of Social Sciences

Facilities/Services for Foreign Students

Counselling Room, Outdoor Education Program, Freshman Orientation Program

Special Programs for Foreign Students

Japanese Language and culture classec are offered in the undergraduate lower division course. Japanese Language supplementary classes begin at the end of July.

For Further Information

Undergraduate and Graduate Admission

Office of International Programs, Meiji University, 1–1, Kanda, Surugadai, Chiyoda–ku, Tokyo 101 ☎ 03–296–4144, 4140

Meijo University
(Meijo Daigaku)

1-501 Shiogamaguchi, Tenpaku-ku, Nagoya-shi, Aichi 468   ☎ 052-832-1151

Faculty
Profs.   150   Assoc. Profs.   100
Assist. Profs.   Full–time 84; Part–time   497
Res. Assocs.   60
Number of Students
Undergrad.   14, 944   Grad.   161
Library   527, 000 volumes

Outline and Characteristics of the University

The founding spirit of Meijo University is to develop individual trustworthiness, impartiality, technical skills and general academic knowledge, and encourage personal creativity with an eye to the future. This educational policy has been cultivated through a tradition of academic freedom since its founding.

Meijo University began in 1926 with its establishment as Nagoya Higher Technical School. In 1949, the school was reorganized into its present form under post-war educational programs. It consists of five faculties: law, commerce, science and technology, agriculture, and pharmacy. Each faculty has a graduate school and junior college. In the last 30 years, Meijo University has grown to become one of the largest and leading private universities in Japan.

The University, recently expanded with a new library, research and classroom buildings, administers an agricultural farm and sports and extra-curricular facilities for its students of nearly 15, 000. Foreign students now number over 70 from 10 countries. The campus is ideally situated in Nagoya, a metropolis in central Japan which offers easy access to the nation's main educational, cultural, and recreational centers.

The University strives for close faculty-student relations. Special faculty advisors provide assistance whenever necessary during the first two years. In the later years, seminar professors assume this role to ensure completion of the student's goals.

The graduates of Meijo University now number more than 80, 000, many of whom lead distinguished careers in various professions throughout the world.

UNDERGRADUATE PROGRAMS

Faculty of Agriculture (Freshmen Enrollment: 240)

Department of Agricultural Chemistry

Analytical Chemistry, Animal Products, Applied Microbiology, Biological Chemistry, Pesticide Chemistry, Plant Nutrition and Fertilizer, Plant Products, Science of Food and Nutrition, Soil Science

Department of Agricultural Science

Animal Husbandry, Applied Entomology, Crop Science, Farm Management and Economics, Genetics and Breeding, Horticultural Science, Landscape Architecture, Plant Pathology

Faculty of Commerce (Freshmen Enrollment: 500)

Department of Commerce

Auditing, Bookkeeping, Business Finance, Business History, Business Management, Commercial Policy, Cost Accounting, Labor Relations, Managerial Accounting, Securities Market, Transportation

Department of Economics

Agricultural Economics, Economic Geography, Economics, History of Economics, History of Labor Movements, Industrial Economics, International Economics, Labor Economics, Money and Banking, Public Finance, Statistics

Faculty of Law (Freshmen Enrollment: 450)

Department of Law

Administrative Law, Civil Law, Commercial Law, Constitutional Law, Economic Law, International Law, Japanese Legal History, Labor Law, Legal Philosophy, Private International Law

Faculty of Pharmaceutics (Freshmen Enrollment: 240)

Department of Pharmaceutical Science

Biochemistry, Chemical Pharmacology, Clinical Biochemistry, Hygienic Chemistry, Pharmaceutics, Pharmacognosy, Pharmacology

Department of Pharmaceutical Technology

Analytical Chemistry, Instrumental Analytical Chemistry, Natural Products Chemistry, Organic Manufacturing, Pharmaceutical Analysis, Physical Pharmacy, Synthetic Medicinal Chemistry

Faculty of Science and Engineering (Freshmen Enrollment: 680)

Department of Architecture

Architectural Designing, Art Studies, Building Construction, Building Materials

Department of Civil Engineering

Civil Engineering Construction, Civil Engineering Materials, Foundation Engineering, Sea & River Engineering, Structural Mechanics, Traffic Engineering

Department of Electrical and Electronic Engineering

Electrical and Electronic Engineering, Electrical Engineering Materials, Electronics, Information Engineering, Wireless Communication Engineering

Department of Mathematics

Algebra, Analysis, Applied Mathematics, General Topology, Geometry

Department of Mechanical Engineering

Factory Management, Fluid Mechanics, Manufacturing Technology, Mechanics of Machinery, Thermodynamics

Department of Transport Machine Engineering

Aeronautical Engineering, Automobile Engineering, Fluid Mechanics, Machine Design and Production Engineering, Transport Machine Engines

Foreign Student Admission

Qualifications for Applicants

Standard Qualifications Requirement

The Faculty of Pharmacy does not accept those who are color blind.

Examination at the University

Selection is made by the appropriate Faculty.

Faculty of Law:

An oral examination in Japanese, and elementary knowledge related to the applicant's fields of interest.

Faculty of Commerce:

An interview and a written examination in elementary knowledge of Japanese and English.

Faculty of Science and Technology, Faculty of Agriculture, and Faculty of Pharmacentics:

An oral examination in Japanese, and elementary knowledge related to the applicant's fields of interest.

Documents to be Submitted When Applying

Standard Documents Requirement

No changes to another faculty or department will be permitted, once applications have been received.

GRADUATE PROGRAMS

Graduate School of Commerce (First Year Enrollment : Master's 20)

Division

Commerce

Graduate School of Engineering (First Year Enrollment : Master's 26)

Divisions

Architecture, Civil Engineering, Electrical and Electronic Engineering

Graduate School of Law (First Year Enrollment : Master's 15, Doctor's 8)

Division

Law

Graduate School of Pharmacy (First Year Enrollment : Master's 18, Doctor's 10)

Division

Pharmaceutics

Foreign Student Admission

Qualifications for Applicants

Master's Program

Standard Qualifications Requirement

Doctor's Program

Standard Qualifications Requirement

Examination at the University

Master's Program

In the graduate schools a special examination system is adopted for foreign students:

1. An oral examination in the Japanese language, and elementary knowledge related to the applicant's fields of interest.
2. Applicants unable to obtain a departure permit for the entrance examination will be judged on required documents.

Doctor's Program
Same as Master's program.
Documents to be Submitted When Applying
Standard Documents Requirement

*

Research Institutes and Centers
Analytical Center, Experimental Farm, International Exchange Center, Pharmaceutical Information Center

Facilities/Services for Foreign Students
The International Exchange Center provides orientation and covnseling services for foreign students and scholars after their arrival at the University.
Facilities:
1.   International Exchange Room
The International Exchange Room was established in 1983 for the purpose of promoting mutual understanding between foreign students and Japanese students, as well as fostering mutual friendship among foreign students.
2.   Foreign Students' Dormitory
The dormitory, Shimada Ryo, was established in 1983 for foreign students and visiting scholars from abroad to provide comfortable university living quarters at low cost.
Services:
Every May the university holds an overnight outing during which the President and other faculty members share the company of students.
This outing gives them an oportunity to hear students' ideas and requests, serving also as an example to the students.
Special Programs for Foreign Students
Japanese studies course for foreign students:
The Faculties of Law, Agriculture and Pharmaceutics have established Japanese Studies courses taught in Japanese.
These courses for foreign students are alternatives to the second foreign language requirement. The courses are: Outline of Japanese Society, Japanese Culture, Japanese Composition, and Reading Comprehension in Japanese.
For Further Information
Undergraduate and Graduate Admission
Application for admission must be made on official forms, which will be furnished on request.
Office for Admissions, Meijo University, 1-501 Shiogamaguchi, Tenpaku-ku, Nagoya-shi, Aichi 468 ☎ 052-832-1151 ext. 2220

Meikai University
(Meikai Daigaku)
1-1 Keyakidai, Sakado-shi, Saitama 350-92
☎ 0492-85-5511

UNDERGRADUATE PROGRAMS

School of Dentistry (Freshmen Enrollment: 160)
Department of Dentistry
Faculty of Economics (Freshmen Enrollment: Day 200, Evening 120)
Department of Economics
Faculty of Langvages and Cultures (Freshmen Enrollment: Day 190, Evening 120)
Department of Chinese
Department of English
Department of Japanese

GRADUATE PROGRAMS

Graduate School of Dentistry (First Year Enrollment : Doctor's 18)
Division
Dentistry

Meisei University
(Meisei Daigaku)
2-1-1 Hodokubo, Hino-shi, Tokyo 191
☎ 0425-91-5111

Faculty
Profs.   130   Assoc. Profs.   17
Assist. Profs.   Full–time   13; Part–time   106
Res. Assocs.   44
Number of Students
Undergrad.   6, 890   Grad.   100
Library   450, 000 volumes

Outline and Characteristics of the University
The pursuit of truth and the fostering of mature personalities form the basis of a university and its academic endeavors. With this in mind, Kuju Kodama founded Meisei University to share his pedagogical philosophy of harmony among people and harmony between the animate and inanimate forces of the world.
Such a philosophy requires an educational system that uses the world as a classroom. Teachers are facilitators, prompting respect and understanding from students. The professor and the student interact so that the student will grow into a full-fledged member of the universe with a strong understanding of morality and science, concommitant to world peace and cultural advancement. Since its founding in 1964, Meisei University has furthered this philosophy, nurtured through the years by the educational endeavors of the Meisei Educational Institute.
The University's complex interdisciplinary structure has two colleges of science, engineering and humanities and a division of correspondence course. The College of Science and Engineering en-

compasses pure (physics and chemistry) and applied sciences (engineering); the College of Humanities consists of English literature and language, sociology, psychology, pedagogy and economics; and the Division of Correspondence Course is a Japanese version of an open university.

In terms of post graduate education, the science and engineering oriented faculties offer five master's and five doctoral courses, while the humanities-oriented faculties offer four master's and four doctoral degrees.

To render extensive logistics support to the well-organized undergraduate and graduate educational framework, the University management pays particular attention to the enrichment of laboratory facilities, field work programs, libraries and data processing systems. The Kodama Memorial Library houses many remarkable rare books and special collections, that is, one of the world's largest and most prestigious William Shakespeare Collections including 9 First Folios and the largest collections of Abrahaw Lincoln and Civil War outside the USA, Tokyo Lincoln Center. The Information Science Research Center takes full advantage of a high–capacity computer system for the planning of tommorow's education. And, the Meisei University Press is a singificant instrument to implement Mitsuo Kodama's conviction of open and equitable lifelong education based on equal opportunities for everybody.

These facilities, coupled with thorough educational and research programs, ensure the formation of students who will contribute toward cultural improvement and mutual understanding among the people of the world. Health, sincerity and enthusiasm are the guiding words for Meisei's educational ideals.

The principles guiding the Meisei Educational Institute since 1923 are the harmonious oneness of matter and mind, respecting one's own self equally with others, and following the idea of the ceaseless creative development of the universe; education is, in the true sense of the word, developing sincerity of mind by using everything in the universe as educational materials, and the nurturing of individual personalities, to develop natural talents and abilities, leads to individuals who can contribute to the civilization and peace of the world; intimate personal contact between professors and students is essential in effective education.

Such relationships are a characteristic feature of education at Meisei University.

UNDERGRADUATE PROGRAMS

College of Humanities (Freshmen Enrollment: 800)
Department of Economics
Accounting, Agricultural Policy, Bookkeeping, Business Administration, Business Cycle and Growth, Commerce, Cost Accounting, Economic Geography, Economic History, Economic Policy, Economics of Developing Countries, Fiscal Policy, History of Economic Doctrines, History of Economic Thoughts, History of Japanese Economy, History of Oriental Economy, History of Western Economy, Industrial Policy, International Economics, International Management, International Relations, Japanese Economy, Labor Economics, Local Public Finance, Macroeconomics, Microeconomics, Money and Banking, Public Finance, Small Business, Social Policy
Department of English Language and English and American Literature
American Literature, English and American Affairs, English Grammar, English Literature, English Philology, English Phonics, History of American Literature, History of English Language, History of English Literature, History of Western Art, History of Western Thought, Philology
Department of Psychology and Pedagogy
Pedagogy Course
Audio–Visual Education, Curriculum, Educational Administration and Finance, Educational Philosophy, Educational Psychology, Educational Systems, Educational Theory of Art, Educational Theory of Science, History of Japanese Education, History of Western Education, Industrial Psychology, Method of Education, Moral Education, Pedagogy, Pedagogy of Infant
Psychology Course
Behavior Analysis, Child Psychology, Clinical Psychology, Comparative Psychology, Developmental Psychology, Experimental Psychology, History of Psychology, Mental Health, Perception, Psychology, Psychology of Learning, Psychology of Personality, Social Psychology, Teaching–Learning Process
Department of Sociology
Broadcasting Culture, Civic and Rural Sociology, Education Sociology, History of Western Thought, Labor Control, Methods of Social Research, Professional Guidance, Social Philosophy, Social Statistics, Social Welfare, Sociology, Sociology of Mass Society

College of Science and Engineering (Freshmen Enrollment: 710)
Department of Chemistry
Analytical Chemistry, Biochemistry, Chemical Industry, Chemistry, Chemistry of Biosubstances, Electrochemistry, Environmental Chemistry, High Polymer Chemistry, Inorganic Chemistry, Instrumental Analysis, Isotope Chemistry, Molecular Structure, Organic Chemistry, Physical Chemistry, Quantum Chemistry
Department of Civil Engineering
Applied Mechanics, Bridge Engineering, Concrete Engineering, Construction Machinery, Construction Materials, Design and Drawing of Civil Engineering, Execution of Civil Engineering Work, Harbor Engineering, Hydraulics, Hydrology, Railway Engineering, Regional and City Planning, Reinforced Concrete Engineering, River Engineering, Road Engineering, Sanitation Engineering, Soil Engineering,

Soil Engineering, Surveying, Urban Transportation, Water Resources Engineering

Department of Electrical Engineering

Automatic Control Systems, Communication Engineering, Communication Network, Computer Engineering, Design of Electric Machines, Electrical Circuits, Electrical Transient Phenomena, Electric and Electronic Drawing, Electric Materials, Electric Measurements and Instrumentation, Electric Power Engineering, Electric Power Engineering, Electric Wave Engineering, Electromagnetism, Electronic Circuit, Electronic Computer, Electronic Engineering, Energy System, High Voltage Technology, Picture Processing, Power Electronics, Solid State Electronics

Department of Mechanical Engineering

Automatic Control Technology, Cargo Machine, Construction Machine, Cutting Machining, Descriptive Geometry, Dynamics, Elasticity Engineering, Fluid Dynamics, Fuel and Combustion, Heat Transfer Technology, Industrial Engineering, Industrial Materials, Industrial Thermodynamics, Instrument Technology, Internal Combustion Engine, Machine Elements, Machine Tool Practice, Machining, Mechanical Design and Drawing, Mechanical Dynamics, Mechanical Engineering, Mechanics, Plasticity Engineering, Pneumatic Machine, Precision Machine, Refrigeration Engineering, Rolling Stock Engineering, Steam Power Engineering, Strength of Materials, Vibration Technology, Welding Engineering

Department of Physics

Analytical Dynamics, Astronomy, Atomic Physics, Automatic Control, Biological Physics, Cosmic Rays, Cosmology, Elastic Dynamics, Electromagnetism, Elementary Particles, Experimental Physics, Linear Algebra, Mathematical Physics, Modern Physics, Nuclear Physics, Nuclear Radiation Physics, Optics, Plasma Physics, Quantum Mechanics, Real Analysis, Solid State Physics, Statistical Thermodynamics

Foreign Student Admission

Qualifications for Applicants
Standard Qualifications Requirement
Examination at the University
Applicants must take an entrance examination consisting of a written examination and an interview.
A. Written examination
College of Science and Engineering: English and Mathematics
College of Humanities: English and Japanese
B. Interview
Documents to be Submitted When Applying
Standard Documents Requirement
The application form and the prospectus of registration will be available from early October.

GRADUATE PROGRAMS

Graduate School of Humanities (First Year Enroll-

ment : Master's 40, Doctor's 12)
Divisions
English and American Literature, Pedagogy, Psychology, Sociology
Graduate School of Science and Engineering (First Year Enrollment : Master's 50, Doctor's 25)
Divisions
Chemistry, Civil Engineering, Electrical Engineering, Mechanical Engineering, Physics

Foreign Student Admission

Qualifications for Applicants
Master's Program
Standard Qualifications Requirement
Doctor's Program
Standard Qualifications Requirement
Examination at the University
Master's Program
Applicants must take an entrance examination consisting of a written examination and an interview.
A. Written examination
1. Subject of Major
2. Foreign Language
(select   one; English, German, French, Chinese)
B. Interview
Doctor's Program
Applicant must take an entrance examination consisting of a written examination and an interview.
A. Written examination
1. Subject of Major
2. Foreign Language
(select   two; English, German, French, Chinese)
B. Interview
Documents to be Submitted When Applying
Standard Documents Requirement

*

Research Institutes and Centers

High Resolution Analytical Electron Microscopy Research Center, Information Science Research Center, Post–War Educational History Research Center, Shakespeare Research Center for Shakespeariana, Taro Cosmic Ray Laboratory, Tokyo Lincoln Center for Lincolniana

Special Programs for Foreign Students

Undergraduate
Foreign Language Subjects
1. The 1st and 2nd year course for credit (required): Japanese Language
2. The 3rd and 4th year course not for credit (required): Japanese Language
Graduate
1. Master's Program
The 1st and 2nd year course not for credit (required): Japanese Language Seminar
2. Doctor's Program
The 1st, 2nd and 3rd year course not for credit (required): Japanese Language Seminar

For Further Information

Undergraduate and Graduate Admission

Entrance Examination Section, Admission Division, Instruction Office, Meisei University, 2–1–1 Hodokubo, Hino–shi, Tokyo 191 ☎ 0425–91–5111 ext. 216

Mimasaka Women's College
(Mimasaka Joshi Daigaku)

32 Kamigawara, Tsuyama–shi, Okayama 708
☎ 0868–22–7718

Faculty
    Profs. 12   Assoc. Profs 7
    Assist. Profs. Full–time 6; Part–time 19
    Res. Assoc. 1
Number of Students
    Undergrad. 205
Library 82, 180 volumes

Outline and Characteristics of the College

The tradition and roots of Mimasaka Women's College go back to 1915, when local initiatives established a sewing high school in Tsuyama. The institution developed into a college in 1967, when it added the faculty of domestic science as well as an attached kindergarten. As it developed, the College has responded to the wider demands of the society. For example, in 1981 it changed its faculty into one with two departments, Food Science and Child Science. These two departments now provide advanced female education.

Although the college has not yet had overseas students, Mimasaka's students have always been come from a wide area. The College has a hall of residence called Kaede to accommodate these students.

UNDERGRADUATE PROGRAMS

Faculty of Domestic Science (Freshmen Enrollment: 80)
    Department of Child Science
    Department of Food Science

Foreign Student Admission
    Examination at the College
    Mimasaka Women's College is anxious to ensure that no student from overseas begins a course with adequate Jananese ability.
    A Japanese language test, an interview

*

For Further Information
    Undergraduate Admission
The Head of the Registrar, Mimasaka Women's College, 32 Kamigawara, Tsuyama–shi, Okayama, 708 ☎ 0868–22–7718

Minami Kyushu College
(Minami Kyushu Daigaku)

6307 Tayoshi, Miyazaki-shi, Miyazaki 880
☎ 0985-51-6307

Faculty
    Profs. 25   Assoc. Profs. 12
    Assist. Profs. Full–time 13; Part–time 34
Number of Students
    Undergrad. 1, 296
Library 44, 307 volumes

Outline and Characteristics of the College

Minami Kyushu College was establised in 1967 as the Faculty of Horticulture, consisting of two Departments: Horticulture and Landscape Architecture. The College also has its own research farm. The main objectives of the school are to help students build character, develop their individuality, and acquire practical learning.

In 1976, the Department of Agricultural Economics was established, followed by the Department of Food Science and Technology in April, 1986. Thus, both research and education have been substantially reinforced with the establishment of the four departments.

The campus is located in Takanabe-cho, 30 km. north of Miyazaki-shi. Situated on the quiet and green hills, the campus commands a good view of the Pacific Ocean, with its ideal environment for learning.

At present, 1296 students from throughout Japan are enrolled in the College, devoted to their studies and research with a view to becoming competent members of the future society. In addition, the College has made efforts to contribute to the cultural and economic development of the adjoining communities to meet their demands.

UNDERGRADUATE PROGRAMS

Faculty of Horticulture (Freshmen Enrollment: 200)
    Department of Agricultural Economics
Accounting, Agricultural Cooperatives, Agricultural Law, Agricultural Marketing, Agricultural Policy, Economic Policy, Farm Bookkeeping, Farm Management, Farm Management, Public Finance, Rural Development, Rural Sociology, Statistics & Agricultural Statistics
    Department of Food Science and Technology
Biophysics, Cell Biotechnology, Chemistry of Organic Analysis, Ecological Management, Food Chemistry, Food Hygiene, Food Processing, Marketing of Horticultural Products, Microbial Chemistry, Molecular Genetics, Nutritional Chemistry, Olericulture, Plant Protection Law, Pomology, Preservation of Food, Radiation Chemistry

Department of Horticulture

Agricultural Dynamics, Agricultural Management, Agricultural Meteorology, Biostatistics, Farm Machinery, Fertilizer Science, Floricultural Science, Foreign Agriculture, Fruit Science, Genetics, Plant Breeding, Plant Husbandry, Plant Pathology, Plant Physiology, Propagation of Horticultural Crops, Rural Law, Soil Improvement, Structural Horticulture, Study of *Bonsai*, Tropical Agriculture, Vegetable Crop Science, Vegetable Ecology

Department of Landscape Architecture

City & Regional Planning, Environmental Planning, Graphics for Landscape Architecture, Harmful Insect Science, History of Landscape Architecture, Landscape Conservation, Landscape Engineering, Landscape Gardening, Landscape Structure Materials & Construction, Natural Open Space Planning, Planning of Sightseeing Places, Plant Materials & Planting Design, Plant Physiology, Policy of Environmental & Open Space Planning, Soil Science, Theory of Design, Urban Open Space Planning, Vegetable Ecology

Foreign Student Admission

Qualifications for Applicants

Standard Qualifications Requirement

Foreign applicants are requested to take both the Japanese Language Proficiency Test and the General Examination for Foreign Students and submit the records to the College.

Examination at the College

Applicants are selected by examination of documents and personal interviews.

Date of Interview: February 28, 1989

Announcement of Successful Applicants: March 7, 1989

Documents to be Submitted When Applying

Standard Documents Requirement

Application form and the campus prospectus will be available from July 1, 1988.

Period for Application: January 10-February 20, 1989

Period for Entrance Procedure: March 7-17, 1989

*

Research Institutes and Centers

College Farm, Laboratory of Food Irradiation and Preservation, Plant Cell Research Laboratory

For Further Information

Undergraduate Admission

Entrance Examination Section, Administrative Office, Minami Kyushu College, Hibarigaoka, Takanabe-cho, Koyu-gun, Miyazaki 884 ☎ 0983-23-0793

Miyagi Gakuin Women's College

(Miyagi Gakuin Joshi Daigaku)

9-1-1 Sakuragaoka, Sendai-shi, Miyagi 981
☎ 022-279-1311

UNDERGRADUATE PROGRAMS

Faculty of Liberal Arts (Freshmen Enrollment: 320)
　Department of English Literature
　Department of Home Economics
　Department of Japanese Literature
　Department of Music

Miyazaki Sangyo-Keiei University

(Miyazaki Sangyo-Keiei Daigaku)

100 Maruo, Furujo-cho, Miyazaki-shi, Miyazaki 880
☎ 0985-52-3111

Faculty
　Profs.　16　　Assoc. Profs.　4
　Assist. Profs.　Full-time　19; Part-time　18
　Res. Assoc.　2
Number of Students
　Undergrad.　609
Library　35, 235 volumes

Outline and Characteristics of the University

Miyazaki Sangyo-Keiei University opened in 1987, and offers degrees in law and business administration. The university grew out of what was originally the Nishu Bookkeeping School. Licensed as the Oyodo Gakuen in 1953, its name was changed to Miyazaki Chuo High School in 1963. Miyazaki Sangyo-Keiei University was founded in order to advance the educational goals of the high school, and to help meet the educational needs of our community in this age of increasing diversification and internationalization of knowledge.

We seek to broaden our students' minds and to lead them to make practical contributions, both to Japanese society and to the world at large. Our curriculum has been designed with these principles in mind. We believe that by mastering the basic concepts of law and business management, and by learning how to solve problems through the exercise of these disciplines, our graduates will be able to make positive contributions to our shared future.

The university is located close to downtown Miyazaki City, and is surrounded by woods and ponds. It is an ideal environment for studying.

Miyazaki Prefecture is currently attempting to

promote the growth and diversification of its economy by attracting new hi-tech industries to our area. At Miyazaki Sangyo-Keiei University we are committed to the success of these efforts, and in that regard, are cooperating with other universities in the prefecture to provide the educational resources necessary for the growth and development of our community.

UNDERGRADUATE PROGRAMS

Faculty of Business Administration (Freshmen Enrollment: 100)
Department of Business Administration
Faculty of Law (Freshmen Enrollment: 100)
Department of Law

Foreign Student Admission

Qualifications for Applicants
Standard Qualifications Requirement
Applicants to the university must be able to understand Japanese and must have graduated from high school. The equivalency of the above must be approved by the university.
Examination at the University
Admissions decisions will be based on the applicant's personal history and on an interview.
Documents to be Submitted When Applying
Standard Documents Requirement
Transfer students should submit the following documents when applying for admission to the university:
1)   a personal history with a photo
2)   a written guarntee that tuition fees will be paid in full
Note: The school year begins in April, and students will be admiited only at the beginning of the school year.

*

For Further Information

Undergraduate Admission
Chief, Study Management, Student Affairs, Miyazaki Sangyo-Keiei University, 100 Maruo, Furujo–cho, Miyazaki–shi, Miyazaki 880 ☎ 0985–52–3111 ext. 113

Morioka College
(Morioka Daigaku)

4–1–5 Kuriyagawa, Morioka–shi, Iwate 020–01
☎ 0196–41–2139

Faculty
　　Profs. 24　　Assoc. Profs 19
　　Assist. Profs. Full–time 12; Part–time 34
　　Res. Assoc. 2
Number of Students
　　Undergrad. 1, 543
Library 74, 416 volumes

Outline and Characteristics of the College
Morioka College, founded in 1981, is a coeducational, four-year college. It is now composed of three departments, the Department of English, the Department of Japanese, and the Department of Juvenile Education. At present, a total of 1, 534 students are studying at Morioka College. The educational principles of Morioka College are based on Christianity and the promotion of sound individual and social values. These principles guide students to a significant college life.

Morioka College was founded as part of the educational institution Seikatsu-Gakuen, established in Morioka by Mrs. Taiko Hosokawa 35 years ago. It now also consists of three kindergartens, a cooking school, and a junior college. Some 35 years ago, Mrs. Hosokawa, realizing that the mortality rate of infants in Iwate prefecture was the highest in Japan decided to start teaching local girls and housewives about nutrition. This was the beginning of the"Seikatsu-Gakuen"institution.

UNDERGRADUATE PROGRAMS

Faculty of Humanities (Freshmen Enrollment: 300)
Department of English
American Literature, Bible and Literature, British Literature, English Linguistics, English Phonetics, History of American Literature, History of British Literature, History of the English Language, Journalism. , Practical English, Public Speaking
Department of Japanese
Art History, Chinese Classics, History of Calligraphy, History of Chinese Literature, History of Japanese Literature, Japanese Grammar, Japanese Language, Japanese Literature, Literature of the Tohoku area, Research on Literary Relics
Department of Juvenile Education
Adolescent Psychology, Educational Psychology, History of Japanese Education, History of Western Education, Juvenile Art, Juvenile Athletics, Juvenile Civilization, Juvenile Literature, Juvenile Music, Juvenile Pedagogy, Juvenile Psychology

Foreign Student Admission

Examination at the University
Full-Time Students: Written examination on English and Japanese and an interview.
Auditing Students: Submisssion of transcripts and an interview
Qualifications for Transfer Students
　　1. Graduates of universities or four-year Colleges.
　　2. Graduates of two-year junior colleges.
　　3. Those who have finished at least two years of college or university.

Examination for Transfer Students
　　1. English Department: English (to be written

in Japanese) and interviews.

2. Japanese Department: Essay examination on some Japanese topics and interviews.

3. Juvenile Education: Essay examination on some topics of juvenile education and interviews.

*

Services for Foreign Students
Women's Dormitory
For Further Information
Undergraduate Admission
Registrar, Office of Registrar, Morioka College, 5-4-1 Kuriyagawa, Morioka-shi, Iwate 020-01 ☎ 0196-41-2193 ext. 213

Mukogawa Women's University
(Mukogawa Joshi Daigaku)

6-46 Ikebiraki-cho, Nishinomiya-shi, Hyogo 663
☎ 0798-47-1212

Faculty
    Profs. 88   Assoc. Profs. 36
    Assist. Profs. Full-time 24; Part-time 273
    Res. Assocs. 53
Number of Students
    Undergrad. 4, 813   Grad. 77
Library 336, 660 volumes

Outline and Characteristics of the University

Mukogawa Women's University is a part of Mukogawa Gakuin, a privately endowed institution for women which consists of a kindergarten, a girls' junior high school, a girls' senior high school, a women's university including a women's junior college division, and graduate schools.

Mukogawa Gakuin was founded in 1939 as Mukogawa Girls' High School by the late Chancellor Kiichiro Koe who had been greatly inspired by British private school education. The school had an initial enrollment of 165 and a staff of 13. Mukogawa Gakuin has made remarkable development since then, adding Mukogawa Women's College in 1946, Mukogawa Women's Junior College in 1950, and the Graduate Schools for Master's programs in 1966. The initial Women's College with its two departments has developed to include four faculties and ten departments, a junior college division with seven departments, and three graduate schools. The present total enrollment is about 10, 000. Though young in years, the university enjoys the prestige of being one of the few leading educational institutions for women with comprehensive and academically distinguished programs.

What has made possible such remarkable progress in a short time is our persevering devotion to not only a superior academic program but also to a warm and close association between faculty and students and to the discipline vital to the student's sound

intellectual growth and character development. Mukogawa's educational principles mentioned above stem from our founding philosophy which says, "Mukogawa aims at fostering the growth and development of capable women who are endowed with high intelligence, refined sensibility and noble virtues as the builders of a peace-loving nation and society. "

The educational ideals also help our students realize their identity in a way that demonstrates the richness of Japanese cultural accomplishments and the traditional virtues of Japanese women. As a private institution, Mukogawa is proud of its unique programs, both academic and nonacademic, to achieve the foregoing ideals. Freshman and junior retreats at the suburban campus with faculty advisers, a year-round freshman seminar with faculty advisers, and a special one month Winter Study Period afford the program greater flexibility to achieve its aims. In addition, highly active extra-curricular programs contribute diversity and vitality to the campus.

The achievement of the foregoing ideals of Mukogawa Women's University is aided by its geographical and socio-cultural advantages. Mukogawa commands a spectacular view of Osaka Bay to the south and the scenic Rokko Mountains to the north. Our name derives from the historic Muko River which flows nearby, bringing many natural forces into harmony. Another of Mukogawa's advantages is that it is situated in Nishinomiya, an expanding residential and college town between Kobe and the Osaka-Kyoto district. Students enjoy easy access to Kobe, a port city renowned for its cosmopolitan life; to Osaka, a vital business and cultural center second only to Tokyo; and to Kyoto, world famous for its traditional values.

UNDERGRADUATE PROGRAMS

Faculty of Home Economics (Freshmen Enrollment: 170)
    Department of Food Science
Applied Microbiology, Biochemistry, Cooking Science, Dietician Training, Environment and Health Care, Food Hygienics, Food Science and Processing, Home Economics, Nutrition, Nutrition for the Ill
    Department of Textiles and Clothing Sciences
Chemistry of Clothing Materials, Climatology of Clothing, Clothing Construction, History of Clothing, Housing Design, Living and the Environment, Science of Textile Dyeing, Testing of Textile Goods
Faculty of Letters (Freshmen Enrollment: 550)
    Department of Education (*Elementary School Teacher Training*)
Educational Administration, Educational Psychology, Education of Handicapped Children, Geography, Health Care and Physical Education, History, History of Education, Home Economics, Japanese, Mathematics, Moral Education, Philosophy of Education

Department of English
American Civilization, American Literature, British Civilization, English Grammar, English Linguistics, English Phonetics, History of American Literature, History of English Literature, Medieval and Early Modern English Literature, Modern English Literature

Department of Human Relations
Clinical Psychology, Human Relations, Information Science, Integrated Study of Man, Natural History, Psychology of Personality, Science of Recreation, Theories on Man and Society, Theories on Modern Society

Department of Japanese
Calligraphy, Chinese Literature, History of Calligraphy, History of Chinese Literature, History of Drama, History of *Haikai*, History of Japanese Civilization, History of Japanese Fine Arts, History of Japanese Literature, Japanese Grammar, Japanese Linguistics, Japanese Literature

Department of Physical Education
Care and Prevention of Athletic Injuries, History of Japanese Physical Education, Outdoor Activity Programs, Physical Education for the Handicapped, Physiology and Anatomy, Science in Sports Training, Sociology of Physical Education, Sports Psychology

Faculty of Music (Freshmen Enrollment: 40)
Department of Instrumental Study
Accompaniment, Acoustics, Chamber Music, Composition, Harmony, Instrumental Repertoire, Orchestration, Piano Ensemble, Piano Repertoire and Piano Techinique, Theory and History of Instrument Conducting, Violin Repertoire and Violin Technique

Department of Voice
Choral Conducting, Chorus, German Lieder, Harmony, History of Music, Italian Song Literature, Japanese Song Literature, Musical Aesthetics, Opera, Psychology of Music

Faculty of Pharmaceutical Sciences (Freshmen Enrollment: 180)
Department of Bio-pharmaceutical Sciences
Biochemistry, Cell Biology, Clinical Chemistry, Hygienic Chemistry, Microbiology, Pharmacology, Physiological Chemistry

Department of Pharmaceutical Sciences
Analytical Chemistry, Medicinal Chemistry, Organic Chemistry, Pharmaceutical Chemistry, Pharmacognosy, Physical Chemistry, Radiochemistry

Foreign Student Admission
Qualifications for Applicants
Standard Qualifications Requirement
Examination at the University
Foreign applicants must pass a preliminary paper screening and a final examination consisting of a written examination and an interview.
The result of the preliminary screening is reported to the applicant by the end of December (for spring semester applicants) or by the end of June (for fall semester applicants); thereupon the applicant will take the final examination and interview.
The written examination covers specific subjects determined by the pertinent department. Both the written examination and the interview are given in Japanese except in special cases.
Documents to be Submitted When Applying
Standard Documents Requirement
Foreign applicants must submit the required documents and the Entrance Examination Fee by October 31st for the spring semester preliminary paper screening or by May 31st for the fall semester preliminary screening.

Qualifications for Transfer Students
Same as those for undergraduate applicants.
Examination for Transfer Students
Same procedures as those for undergraduate applicants.
Documents to be Submitted When Applying
Standard Documents Requirement

ONE-YEAR GRADUATE PROGRAMS

One-Year Graduate Course in Letters (Enrollment: 15)
Education
One-Year Graduate Course in Music (Enrollment: 10)
Music

Foreign Student Admission
Qualifications for Applicants
Standard Qualifications Requirement
Examination at the University
Same procedures as those for undergraduate applicants.

GRADUATE PROGRAMS

Graduate School of Home Economics (First Year Enrollment : Master's 18)
Divisions
Food Science, Textiles and Clothing Sciences
Graduate School of Letters (First Year Enrollment : Master's 24)
Divisions
English Language and Literature, Japanese Language and Literature
Graduate School of Pharmaceutical Sciences (First Year Enrollment : Master's 12)
Division
Pharmaceutical Sciences

Foreign Student Admission
Qualifications for Applicants
Master's Program
Standard Qualifications Requirement
Examination at the University
Master's Program

Same as undergraduate applicants.
Documents to be Submitted When Applying
Standard Documents Requirement
Same as undergraduate applicants.

*

Research Institutes and Centers
Mukogawa Research Institute for Early Childhood Education, Mukogawa Research Institute for Linguistic and Cultural Studies, Mukogawa Research Institute of Education

For Further Information
Undergraduate and Graduate Admission
Admissions Office, Mukogawa Women's University, 6-46 Ikebiraki-cho, Nishinomiya-shi, Hyogo 663
☎ 0798-47-1212 ext. 285, 286

Musashi Institute of Technology
(Musashi Kogyo Daigaku)

1-28-1 Tamazutsumi, Setagaya-ku, Tokyo 158
☎ 03-703-3111

Faculty
    Profs. 61   Assoc. Profs. 55
    Assist. Profs. Full-time 42; Part-time 174
    Res. Assocs. 20
Number of Students
    Undergrad. 4, 454   Grad. 235
Library 189, 700 volumes

Outline and Characteristics of the University
The Musashi Senior Engineering School was founded in 1929 to promote science and technology based on justice, freedom, and self-government. This founding spirit has been passed down to faculty members, students, and alumni for more than 60 years. The Musashi Senior Engineering School was subsequently renamed the Musashi Engineering College and then the Musashi Institute of Technology in 1949.

The Musashi Institute of Technology was organized around three departments: Mechanical Engineering, Electrical Engineering, and Architecture. After experiencing monetary hardships because of inflation and the maintenance of costly experimental facilities, the school turned to Keita Goto, then president of the Tokyu Electric Train and Transportation Corporation. After Goto became the managing director of the Institute, the school was placed under the Goto Ikueikai (Goto Educational Association). At the same time Shuji Yagi, ex-President of Osaka National University, was made president of MIT.

The institute was then expanded from three departments to seven: Mechanical Engineering, Manufacturing Engineering (later combined with Mechanical Engineering), Electrical Engineering (later renamed Electrical and Electronic Engineering), Electrical Communication Engineering (later renamed Electronics and Communication Engineering), Architecture, Civil Engineering and Industrial Engineering. Various laboratories were added, including the Nuclear Research Institute at Ozenji, Kawasaki City, in Kanagawa Prefecture. After Ryonosuke Yamada, ex-President of Shizuoka National University, became President of MIT, Graduate School of Engineering was established in 1966 in Mechanical Engineering, Mechanical Production Engineering, and Architecture.

In 1968, a doctoral program was established in the same fields. In addition to these programs, a master's course in Civil Engineering was set up in 1972, followed in 1981 by a doctoral program in Civil Engineering and master's programs in Industrial Management and Nuclear Engineering.

In 1978, Kaoru Ishikawa, Professor Emeritus of the University of Tokyo, became President of MIT. As of 1987 the number of MIT graduates totaled 32, 000. Most of these graduates have dedicated themselves to working for a better Japan as well as for a better world.

MIT is located in a valley of the Tama River which acts as the boundary between Metropolitan Tokyo and Kanagawa Prefecture. The campus is set among such green, quiet towns as Den'en Chofu, Oyamadai and Kaminoge. Students can look out of classrooms on to a large campus with trees and greenery and study in a tranquil environment, with little noise and air pollution. On very fine days, Mt. Fuji can be seen from the tops of campus buildings, towering above the Tanzawa Mountains on far side of the Tama River.

Liberal Arts subjects are taught on the same campus which makes it possible for faculty members and students to have easy access to one another. MIT, then, has an ideal environment. Furthermore, the campus is within a comparatively short distance of factories in the Keihin industrial area, one of the greatest industrial areas of Japan. Thus field trips can be easily made to a great number of factories and other industrial plants.

The main campus of MIT is composed of about 20 buildings in an area of 65, 000 m². The Ozenji Campus, which houses the Nuclear Research Center, is located in Kawasaki City, Kanagawa Prefecture.

The research laboratories have been greatly improved since the various graduate schools opened.

A walk around the campus takes one pass the basketball court, tennis courts, a swimming pool, and a big gymnasium surrounded by flowerbeds, trees, and a clock-tower rising from a small pond.

UNDERGRADUATE PROGRAMS

Faculty of Engineering (Freshmen Enrollment: 790)
    Department of Architecture
Architectural Planning, Building Materials and Construction, Environment and Building Services, Structural Engineering of Building
    Department of Civil Engineering

Civil Planning, Construction Management, Hydraulics and River Engineering, Structural Mechanics

Department of Electrical and Electronic Engineering

Computer & Signal Processing, Electrical Machines, Electrical Measurement & Control, Electric Power Engineering, Electron Circuit, Electron Materials/Physical Properties, Fundamentals of Electrical Engineering, Nuclear Engineering

Department of Electronics and Communication Engineering

Communication Engineering, Electronics, Electronics Communication Apparatus, Fundamentals of Electronics & Communication Engineeing, Measurement & Control Engineering

Department of Industrial Engineering

Cost Control & Accounting, Engineering Statistics, Human Engineering, Human Management, Manufacturing Engineering, Production Engineering, System Engineering

Department of Mechanical Engineering

Machine Design & Drawing, Manufacturing Processing, Materials Science & Engineering, Mechanical Engineering Analysis, Thermal and Fluid Engineering

Foreign Student Admission

Qualifications for Applicants

Standard Qualifications Requirement

Examination at the University

The same entrance examination for Japanese students: a written exam and an interview

Documents to be Submitted When Applying

Standard Documents Requirement

GRADUATE PROGRAMS

Graduate School of Engineering (First Year Enrollment : Master's 74, Doctor's 27)

Divisions

Architecture, Civil Engineering, Electrical Engineering, Industrial Engineering, Manufacturing Engineering, Mechanical Engineering, Nuclear Engineering

Foreign Student Admission

Qualifications for Applicants

Master's Program

Standard Qualifications Requirement

Doctor's Program

Standard Qualifications Requirement

Examination at the University

Master's Program

A written and oral exam plus an interview. Date: September and/or March.

Doctor's Program

Same as Master's program.

Documents to be Submitted When Applying

Standard Documents Requirement

*

Research Institutes and Centers

Atomic Energy Research Laboratory, Information Processing Center

For Further Information

Undergraduate and Graduate Admission

Entrance Admissions Section, Musashi Institute of Technology, 1–28–1 Tamazutsumi, Setagaya–ku, Tokyo ☎ 03–703–3111 ext. 229

Musashino Academia Musicae
(Musashino Ongaku Daigaku)
1–13–1 Hazawa, Nerima–ku, Tokyo 176
☎ 03–992–1121

Faculty
Profs. 84   Assoc. Profs. 84
Assist. Profs. Full–time 94; Part–time 237
Number of Students
Undergrad. 4, 020   Grad. 144
Library 142, 000 volumes

Outline and Characteristics of the College

The Musashino Academia Musicae consists of the Graduate School of Music (whose authorized number for admission is 50) and the Undergraduate Department of Music (whose authorized number for admission is 735). The former consists of the five Majors of Instrumental Music, Voice, Composition, Musicology, and Music Education while the latter consists of the same five Faculties.

This college was founded in 1929 as the Musashino Music School. It has two campuses; Ekoda in the urban district of Tokyo and Iruma in the suburbs of Tokyo. The former has nurtured its tradition for just 60 years since its foundation, while the latter (opened in 1972) covering 450, 000 m^2 of a green, natural environment. Both contribute much to the further advancement of music education.

This college has to date put forth many excellent graduates including those occupying important positions in Japan's world of music education.

Since this college was founded through the cooperation of the founder, teachers, students and other parties concerned, "Harmony" is the spirit of Musashino.

As its policy of education, the school emphasizes the development of humanity as well as the study of musical art rather than typical inclination to stress the mastering of practical skills, a pitfall of musical instruction. Everything, not only formal education but also extracurricular education and students' voluntary activities, follows this educational policy.

This college is actively engaging in such performance activities as wind and string instruments, chorus, opera, and wind ensemble which are periodically held within and without Japan. In addition, internationally renowned musicians and performers are invited as guest professors to hold not only usual lessons but also special lectures and concerts. In order to foster such activities, both campuses respectively have concert halls equipped with full-scale organs for effective utilization.

Furthermore, both campuses have unique facilities, which are museums of musical instruments, where efforts are being made to collect and preserve musical instruments, their accessories, and materials connected with music of all areas and ages for the sake of contributing to the development of musical culture as a whole as well as to the education of students. Meanwhile, these museums are the largest in Japan and world–famous with many valuable collections.

UNDERGRADUATE PROGRAMS

Faculty of Music (Freshmen Enrollment: 735)
Department of Composition
Department of Instrumental Music
Keyboard Instruments (Piano and Organ), String Instruments, Wind and Percussion Instruments
Department of Music Education
Department of Musicology
Department of Voice

Foreign Student Admission
Qualifications for Applicants
Standard Qualifications Requirement
Department of Musicology and Music Education have no special admission for foreigners.
Examination at the College
Audition (for the applicant's major instrument only), Japanese composition test, and documentary examination.
Documents to be Submitted When Applying
Standard Documents Requirement
Essay on "My reason for applying for Musashino Academia Musicae and how to utilize its education" in Japanese.
Application period: Oct. 15-Nov. 20

Qualifications for Transfer Students
Completion of two or more years in a course specialized in music at a foreign university, collge or a junior college after finishing a 12–year regular course of education in a foreign country, or the equivalent.
Examination for Transfer Students
Same as freshman applicants.
Documents to be Submitted When Applying
Same as freshman applicants

GRADUATE PROGRAMS

Graduate School of Music (First Year Enrollment : Master's 50)
Divisions
Composition, Instrumental Music, Music Education,

Musicology, Voice

Foreign Student Admission
Qualifications for Applicants
Division of Musicology has no special admission for foreigners.
Master's Program
  Standard Qualifications Requirement
  Examination at the College
Master's Program
Instrumental Music Major, Voice Major and Composition Major: Audition (Instrument Major applicants only "for applicant's voice/major instrument only), Composition practice (Composition Major only) and an interview.
Music Education Major: Audition (instrument or voice), short essay (in Japanese language on "My view of Music Education") and interview.
  Documents to be Submitted When Applying
  Same as freshman applicants

Research Institutes and Centers
Education and Culture Research Center
Facilities/Services for Foreign Students
1. Help to find off–campus accommodation.
2. Annual holding of a round table conference for the purpose of communication with teaching administrative staff and of the advancement of studies.
Special Programs for Foreign Students
The Faculty of Music holds Japanese language courses for freshmen, sophomores and juniors respectively.
For Further Information
Undergraduate and Graduate Admission
Academic Affairs Section, Academic Affairs Division, Musashino Academia Musicae, 1–13–1 Hazawa, Nerima–ku, Tokyo 176 ☎ 03–992–1121 ext. 245

Musashino Art University
(Musashino Bijutsu Daigaku)
1–736 Ogawa–cho, Kodaira–shi, Tokyo 187
☎ 0423–41–5011

UNDERGRADUATE PROGRAMS

College of Art and Design (Freshmen Enrollment: 570)
Department of Architecture
Department of Industrial/Interior and Craft Design
Department of Japanese Painting
Department of Painting
Department of Scenography, Display and Fashion Design
Department of Science of Design

Department of Sculpture
Department of Visual Communication Design

GRADUATE PROGRAMS

Graduate School of Art and Design (First Year Enrollment : Master's 28)
Divisions
Design (Visual Communication Design, Industrial, Interior and Craft Design, Scenography/Display and Fashion Design, Architecture, Science of Design), Fine Arts (Japanese Painting, Painting, Printmaking, Science of Art and Design, Sculpture)

Musashino Women's College
(Musashino Joshi Daigaku)

1-1-20 Shin-machi, Hoya-shi, Tokyo 202
☎ 0424-68-3111

Faculty
    Profs.　24　　Assoc. Profs.　5
    Assist. Profs.　Full-time　6; Part-time　131
    Res. Assocs.　9
Number of Students
    Undergrad.　1, 408
Library　131, 706 volumes

Outline and Characteristics of the College

In 1924, Junjiro Takakusu, the world famous scholar of Buddhism, established Musashino Women's Academy with the help of Nishi Honganji Temple. He reaffirmed his faith that the education of women was the cultivation of the mothers of life and the supreme law of Buddha. He wished the spirit of Buddha for the young, and compassion for women's hearts. In the chaotic state of those days, he aimed at real human education through the spirit of Buddhism. M. W. C. celebrated its 60th anniversary in 1984 and Takakusu's aim is still actively pursued at our college. We hope that every student considers what a real human being is, appreciating the grace of nature in the campus surrounded by trees of the Musashino Area.

In 1945, our sister school, Chiyoda Women's Institute which suffered damage from war, moved to the area of Musashino. In 1949, its administration was transferred to the M. W. A. Foundation. In 1950, when reform of the educational system took place, M. W. A. grew and blossomed into a junior college, and four-year college beginning with a two-year course in 1965. In 1977, the two-year course added the department of education for children, and another special course in 1982 so that education would be more complete.

Located in the western suburbs of Tokyo, M. W. C. has a 100, 000m² campus with some classroom buildings, an administration building, library, two gymnasiums, a Koundai or gathering place, three dining halls, a dormitory, a playground, tennis courts, volley-ball courts and a swimming pool. About one hundred species of trees and many carefully tended lawns flourish all over the campus. As Doppo Kunikida wrote, "Freedom exists in the forest." Recently many colleges in the heart of Tokyo tend to move to the suburbs for the purpose of seeking a better environment. Our campus, which has many trees and flowers, is quiet even though it is conveniently near the city. Such an educational environment is precious for a college, especially a women's college for the students can quietly study literature, art, science and religion, but whenever necessary, they can easily get back out into the active world.

UNDERGRADUATE PROGRAMS

Faculty of Literature (Freshmen Enrollment: 200)
Department of English and American Literature
Department of Japanese Literature

Foreign Student Admission
Qualifications for Applicants
    Standard Qualifications Requirement
Applicants must be women.
Examination at the College
    Written exams and an interview. Guides to the College and application guides are available at Kyomu-ka (Registration Office) by the end of October. Date: the middle of February.
Documents to be Submitted When Applying
    Standard Documents Requirement
An identification or recommendation from the Embassy.

Qualifications for Transfer Students
    There are no separate regulations for foreign students at the College. Applicants are required to fulfill the qualifications both for foreign students and Japanese transfer students. Qualifications are as follows.
  1. Those who have finished or will finish a Junior College.
  2. Those who have finished or will finish two years of a College or a University.
NB. Applicants must intend to continue and complete the same or similar course in Japan.
Examination for Transfer Students
    written exams (foreign language and applicant's major field) and an interview. Date: mid February. The guide is available at the Registration Office by the end of October.
Documents to be Submitted When Applying
    Standard Documents Requirement

＊

Research Institutes and Centers
Cross Culture Center, Institute of Buddhist Culture Research, Noh Research Center

Facilities/Services for Foreign Students
1. The Cross Culture Center
    This Center is founded to promote cultural exchanges between Japan and foreign countries and give advice to students who want to study abroad or foreign students who want to study at the College. The Center also collects materials and information about colleges and universities and research institutions in foreign countries.
2. Foreign Student Adviser
    Professors from their respective courses advise and help foreign students in their study and daily life.

Special Programs for Foreign Students
Japanese

For Further Information
Undergraduate Admission
Undergraduate Affairs Division, Musashino Women's College, 1–1–20 Shin–machi, Hoya–shi, Tokyo 202 ☎ 0428–62–3111 ext. 222

Musashi University
(Musashi Daigaku)
1–26 Toyotama–Kami, Nerima–ku, Tokyo 176
☎ 03–991–1191

Faculty
　Profs. 61　　Assoc. Profs. 21
　Assist. Profs. Full–time 3; Part–time 239
Number of Students
　Undergrad. 3, 658　　Grad. 27
Library 343, 731 volumes

Outline and Characteristics of the University
　Musashi High School, the forerunner of Musashi University, was founded in 1922 by Kaichiro Nezu for the purpose of offering an outstanding education in an intimate setting. The 1949 educational reform resulted in the establishment of a modern four–year university, together with an affiliated senior high school and junior high school. Musashi University opened with a Faculty of Economics containing Department of Economics, and this was followed in 1959 by the formation of a Department of Business Administration. In 1969, the University was reorganized to accommodate a Faculty of Humanities comprising three departments: Western Culture, Japanese Culture, and Sociology. The same year saw the establishment of the Master's Program in Economics. The Doctoral Program in Economics was created in 1972, and the Master's Program in the Humanities in 1973.
　Musashi University is a small university with only two Faculties and more or less 3, 500 students. In spite of its small size, the campus is large, with traces of the Musashi Plain preserved even today in tranquil surroundings.

　A special feature of Musashi University is its bright, free and relaxed atmosphere within the academic traditions of a modestly sized university. To ensure this, Musashi University has maintained the traditions of Musashi High School, following its policy of admitting a limited number of superior students, and thereby avoiding the pitfalls of mass education as much as possible for a private institution.
　Above all, Musashi takes greatest pride in its seminar system, which forms the basis of all teaching in the University, and in its thorough education and guided research, resulting in much personal contact, both inside and outside the classroom, between teachers and students.
　Musashi University has inherited the three founding principles from the days of the old Musashi High School. One of these is the desirability of developing the student's character in the hope that on leaving the University he will not be afraid to stand on his own feet and think for himself. This forms the cornerstone of Musashi's educational philosophy.

THREE FOUNDING PRINCIPLES
　To produce individuals dedicated to the ideal of uniting the cultural values of East and West.
　To produce individuals equal to the challenge of acting on the world stage.
　To produce individuals capable of independent thought and research.

UNDERGRADUATE PROGRAMS

Faculty of Economics (Freshmen Enrollment: 400)
Department of Business Administration
Bookkeeping, Business Administration, Business Information Systems, Business Management, Business Mathematics, Business Organization, Commercial Law, Enterprise, Financial Accounting, Financial Management, Labor Management, Management Accounting, Production Management, Programming, Sales Management
Department of Economics
Administrative Law, Banking, Case Economics, Case Industries, Econometrics, Economic Policy, Economics, Economic Statistics, Finance, History of Economics, International Economics, Social Policy
Faculty of Humanities (Freshmen Enrollment: 350)
Department of Japanese Culture
Calligraphy, Classical Chinese Literature, History of Fine Arts in Japan, History of Japanese Drama, History of Japanese Thought, Japanese and Chinese Cultural Comparisons, Japanese Folklore, Japanese History, Japanese Linguistics, Japanese Literature, Modern Japanese Culture, Paleography
Department of Sociology
Advertisement, Community Sociology, Comparative Sociology, Comparative Urban Development, Group Dynamics, History of Journalism, Labor–Management Relations, Organization Theory, Political Sociology, Problems of Environmental Pollution, Social Behavior, Social Pathology, Social Psychology, So-

cial Research, Social Stratification, Social Structure and Change, Social Theory, Sociology, Sociology of Business Administration, Sociology of Education, Sociology of Welfare, Theory of Groups

Department of Western Culture

American Literary History, American Literature, American Studies, Ancient European History, British Literary History, Classical European Literature, Comparative Culture, English Linguistics, English Literature, English Studies, French Linguistics, French Literary History, French Literature, French Studies, German Linguistics, German Literary History, German Literature, German Studies, History of European Thought, Medieval European History, Modern European History

Foreign Student Admission

Qualifications for Applicants
Standard Qualifications Requirement
Examination at the University
The same entrance examination as Japanese applicants.
Documents to be Submitted When Applying
Standard Documents Requirement
Application Period: January 17 to February 1.

GRADUATE PROGRAMS

Graduate School of Economics (First Year Enrollment: Master's 10, Doctor's 5)
Division
Economics
Graduate School of Humanities (First Year Enrollment: Master's 30)
Divisions
English Language and British & American Literature, French Language and Literature, German Language and Literature, Japanese Language and Literature

Foreign Student Admission

Qualifications for Applicants
Master's Program
Standard Qualifications Requirement
Doctoral Program
Standard Qualifications Requirement
Examination at the University
Master's Program
Date: beginning of October and March (School of Economics), mid March (School of Humānities)
Doctoral Program
Date: the middle of March (for the School of Economics).
Documents to be Submitted When Applying
Standard Documents Requirement

*

For Further Information

Undergraduate Admission
Admissions Office, Musashi University, 1–26 Toyotama–Kami, Nerima–ku, Tokyo 176 ☎ 03–991

–1191 ext. 115
Graduate Admission
Administrative Office of each school, Musashi University, 1–26 Toyotama–Kami, Nerima–ku, Tokyo 176 ☎ 03–991–1191 ext. 193 (Economics), 203 (Humanities)

Nagano University
(Nagano Daigaku)

Shimonogo, Ueda–shi, Nagano 386–12
☎ 0268–38–2350

Faculty
    Profs. 22   Assoc. Profs 12
    Assist. Profs.   Full–time 11; Part–time 31

Number of Students
    Undergrad. 1, 304
Library 67, 225 volumes

Outline and Characteristics of the University

Nagano University is located in the Shioda-daira Basin, with the nearby mountain ranges such as Mt. Asama, the Utsukushi-ga–hara Heights, and the Suga-daira Heights forming a natural backdrop. In the southern suburb of Ueda City, pop. 120, 000, the third largest in Nagano Prefecture, the Shioda-daira Basin is famous for its many historic Shinto Shrines and Buddhist Temples. Established in 1966 as the first private four-year University in Nagano Prefecture, it has continued to serve the community for twenty-two years.

The University has established the following goals: (1) To form an ideal campus suitable for academic study by taking advantage of its natural environment. (2) To allow the students to develop to their highest potential by limiting enrollment in each department to devote more resources on each student. (3) To provide the students with a solid foundation to understand society as well as professional and technical education. (4) To put into practice the theory and knowledge acquired by interacting with the local community.

These goals are still kept alive at Nagano University.

The University consists of three departments under the Faculty of Social Sciences: Department of Industrial Society, Department of Industry-Information Science, and Department of Social Work.

Faculty of Social Sciences: —The aims of this faculty is to provide an interdisciplinary study of societies in an internationalized, post-industrial, information and service oriented age with aging populations.

Department of Industrial Society: —Today's society faces the problems such as a rapidly aging society and international trade friction. The goal of this department is to analyze these problems utilizing the basic curriculum as a foundation. After the third year each student is expected to choose from one of the three courses offered. These are the Sociology, Business Admistration, and Economic Courses.

Department of Industry-Information Science: —Today, it is said that information, not materials or energy, changes society. This department provides computer training to be able to analyze current trends in the economic and business world. It also seeks to interface the social sciences and information sciences.

Department of Social Work: —This department does basic research in the social sciences as well as training in social work. Practical experience in social work and professional seminars are offered to second year students and above. This department requires that students receive training in local child guidance clinics, homes for the handicapped, mentally handicapped home, hospitals, and the other like institutions, so that they can benefit the local community after graduation.

UNDERGRADUATE PROGRAMS

Faculty of Social Sciences
Department of Industrial Society
Accounting, Civil Law, Family Sociology, Fundamentals of Management, Industrial Sociology, Introduction to Digital Computing, Introduction to Sociology, Marketing, Modern Economics, Organizational Theory, Principles of Political Economy, Rural-Urban Sociology, Social Policy, Social Psychology, Social Research Methods, Social Statistics, Socio-Economic History
Department of Industry and Information Sciences
Accounting, Factory Automation, Fundamentals of Management, Industrial Sociology, Information Mathematics, Information Network, Information Sciences, Introduction to Digital Computing, Mechanism and Electronics, Office Automation, Organizational Theory, Programming, Simulation, Systems Design
Department of Social Work
Child Welfare, Clinical Psychology, Counseling, Introduction to Sociology, Law System of Social Security, Mental Hygiene, Methodology of Social Welfare, Outline of Medicine, Principles of Social Welfare in Industrial Societies, Public Assistance, Social Research Methods, Social Security, Theory and Practice of Gerontology in Modern Society, Theory of Medical Social Work, Welfare for the Mentally Handicapped, Welfare for the Physically Handicapped

For Further Information
Undergraduate Admissions.
Admissions Office, Nagano University, Shimonogo,

Ueda–shi, Nagano 386–12 ☎ 0268–38–2350

Nagasaki Institute of Applied Sciences
(Nagasaki Sogo Kagaku Daigaku)
536 Aba–machi, Nagasaki–shi, Nagasaki 851–01
☎ 0958–39–3111

Faculty
    Profs. 37   Assoc. Profs. 34
    Assist. Profs. Full–time 14; Part–time 99
    Res. Assoc. 15
Number of Students
    Undergrad. 2, 114   Grad. 13
Library 95, 693 volumes

Outline and Characteristics of the College
Nagasaki Institute of Applied Sciences is in Nagasaki Prefecture, located in the western extremity of Japan.

Historically, Nagasaki flourished as the country's sole "window" to the outside world, introducing the western knowledge and other aspects of foreign culture to the people of Japan, and greatly contributing to the birth of modern Japan. Nagasaki is one of the most famous tourist cities in Japan, retaining its exotic atmosphere and offering many historical sights.

The college was originally established as the Special School for Naval Architecture, and grew into a 4-year college in 1965. It now has 5 programs : Mechanical Engineering, Electronic Engineering, Architecture, Administrative Technology as well as our traditional Naval Architectural Engineering program. We train our students and further expect them to acquire information techniques and methods outside of their own specialities. We are proud of being a rare private college that sends excellent engineers into the highly technological, information-based Japanese society. We also have a Postgraduate School and Engineering Research Program (Master's Course).

We have accepted foreign students, mainly from Southeast Asian countries, with more than two hundred students having graduated from Nagasaki Institute up to the present. The college also has a one year Japanese Language Course for foreign students so that they may acquire Japanese and study Japanese culture and affairs to enable them to study at a Japanese college.

UNDERGRADUATE PROGRAMS

Faculty of Engineering (Freshmen Enrollment: 350)
Department of Administrative Technology
Business Course, Business Management, Information Engineering, Mathematical Engineering, Production Engineering
Department of Architecture
Architectural Design & History, Environmental Engineering, Housing Course, Structural Engineering, Urban-Community Planning
Department of Electrical Engineering
Electric Machinery & Apparatus, Electric Power & Application, Electronic Engineering, Electronic Engineering Course, Fundamentals of Electrical Engineering
Department of Mechanical Engineering
Applied Mechanics, Computer Science & Control Engineering Course, Fluid Engineering, Machining & Materials, Thermal Engineering
Department of Naval Architectural Engineering
Construction, Strength, Optimization of Construction, Design, Outfitting, Modernization of Design, Marine Engineering Course, Propulsive Performance, Numerical Hydrodynamics, Seakeeping, Manoeuvring Quality, Simulation Technique, System Engineering Course

Foreign Student Admission
Examination at the University
  Mathematics
  Japanese: Composition
  Interview : In Japanese

GRADUATE PROGRAMS

Gradnate School of Engineering (First Year Enrollment: Master's 20)
Fluid Engineering, Structural Engineering

Foreign Student Admission
Examination at the University
Master's Program
  The entrance examination is usually given in September and March and covers mathematics (Algebra, Analysis, Geometry, Theory of Functions) a foreign language (English, French, German) and a professional subject (Strength of Materials or Structual Mechanics (structural Engineeing program) or Hydrodynamics Hydraulics (Fluid Engineering Program) The examination also includes an interview in Japanese.

*

Research Institutes and Centers
Computer Science Center, Nagasaki Institue for Peace Culture, Technical Research Laboratory, The Institute of Regional Sciences
Services for Foreign Students
We help male students to find private lodgings. Our college provides a dormitory for female students. Each room is 7. 7 m² and has a bed and a closet. We help students join local home-stay activities on occasion.
Special Programs for Foreign Students
"Japanese Culture", "Japan Today"
For Further Information
Undergraduate Admission
Admission Office, Nagasaki Institute of Applied Sciences, 536 Aba–machi, Nagasaki–shi, Nagasaki 851–01 ☎ 0958–39–3111ext. 2222, 2223
Graduate Admission
Graduate Admission Office, Nagasaki Institute of Applied Science, 536 Aba–machi, Nagasaki–shi, Nagasaki 851–01 ☎ 0958–39–3111ext. 3027

Nagoya College of Music
(Nagoya Ongaku Daigaku)

7–1 Inabaji–cho, Nakamura–ku, Nagoya–shi, Aichi
453   ☎ 052–411–1111

Faculty
  Profs. 25   Assoc. Profs. 15
  Assist. Profs. Full–time 8; Part–time 87
  Res. Assoc. 1
Number of Students
  Undergrad. 949   Grad. 21
Library 162, 200 volumes

Outline and Characteristics of the College
  Our college was established to foster the Buddhist teachings of Doho Wakei. We try to make the teachings of Doho, expounded by Saint Shinran, relevant to the present day. The teachings of Doho encourage the pursuit of science and truth from a global viewpoint, and encourage us to promote the welfare of human society by working hand in hand with our fellows.
  Our college aims to teach students the theory of music as art as well as practical techniques necessary to attain a professional level of performance. We also try to foster an awareness of the rich variety of human social experience by the cultivation of religious sentiment. Our school is a college of music established as part of the educational system of Doho Gakuen. On this basis, our college values and pays close attention to liberal arts classes as well as subjects of specialized study. We view these classes as absolutely necessary to prevent students from becoming imitative and excessively mechanical in their music. They awaken and nurture the students insight into the harmony, strength and variety of the human spirit from which comes the creativity and spontaneity which is the essence of the art of music. We are also working to complete our facilities in order to make advanced studies possible.
  1965   Establishment of NAGOYA JUNIOR COLLEGE OF MUSIC approved.

1965   Celebrated the 45th anniversary of the founding of the Doho Gakuen and the opening of NAGOYA JUNIOR COLLEGE OF MUSIC.

1966   Visited Higashi Honganji in Kyoto for first training program there.

1967   Held the first graduation concert at Chuden Hall. Held the first graduation ceremony.

1970   Study tour to Hawaii in celebration of the 5th anniversary of the founding of the college.

1971   Held the first of the periodic concerts at Chuden Hall.

1975   Celebrated the 10th anniversary of the founding of the college.

1975   Concert tour and training tour in the U. S. A.

1976   Establishment of NAGOYA COLLEGE OF MUSIC approved.

1977   Held the first of the periodic orchestral concerts.

1978   First European study tour for art of music.

1982   Held a Gamran Concert: Indonesian Music and Dance, at Aichi Bunka Kodo.

1987   Established the graduate school of NAGOYA COLLEGE OF MUSIC.

UNDERGRADUATE PROGRAMS

Faculty of Music (Freshmen Enrollment: 200)
Department of Composition
Department of Instrumental Music
Department of Music Education
Department of Vocal Music

Foreign Student Admission
Qualifications for Applicants
    Standard Qualifications Requirement
Official identification either from the Minister of Education of his/her own country or from the ambassador to Japan should be submitted. The name of his/her guarantor (who actually lives in Japan and, in case of necessity, can pay for all of his/her necessary expenses in Japan and transportation fees back home) is required.
Examination at the University
Examination Procedure 1. Examination of the documents including JLPT (division: the 1st class) results. 2. Only those who pass the examination above can take the second examination (practical technique and interview). Notes: The second examination will be held during the examination for Japanese applicants. The result of each exmination will be mailed to the applicants.

GRADUATE PROGRAMS

Graduate School of Music (First Year Enrollment : Master's 12,)
Divisions
Composition, Instrumental Music (Piano, Flute and

Violin), Music Education, Vocal Music

Foreign Student Admission
Examination at the University
Master's Program
    1.   Written examination required of all applicants:
    i.   One foreign language out of 4 languages (English/German/French and Italian)
    ii.   The History of European Music
    2.   Examination on Practical Technique in major field

* * *

For Further Information
Undergraduate and Graduate Admission
Admissions Office (Kyomu–Ka), Nagoya College of Music 7-1 Inabaji–cho, Nakamura–ku, Nagoya–shi Aichi 453 ☎ 052–411–1111 ext. 432

Nagoya Economics University
(Nagoya Keizai Daigaku)

61-1 Uchikubo, Inuyama-shi, Aichi 484
☎ 0568-67-0511

Faculty
    Profs.   30   Assoc. Profs.   13
    Assist. Profs.   Full–time   6; Part–time   12
    Research Associate   1
Number of Students
    Undergrad.   1, 478
Library   138, 844 volumes

Outline and Characteristics of the University
    Nagoya Economics University, formerly Ichimura Gakuen University, was founded in 1979 by Ichimura Educational Instiute in order to educate and, more importantly, to equip students with practical business abilities. Nagoya Economics University consists of one faculty and two departments--the Faculty of Economics, the Department of Consumer Economics (established in 1979) and the Department of Business Administration (established in 1983).
    One of the most important characteristics of Nagoya Economics University is its environment. The campus is located in Inuyama City 25 kilometers north of Nagoya. In its vicinity one of the most beautiful rivers in Japan, the Kiso River; the oldest existing castle in Japan, Inuyama Castle; and the famous museum-town, Meiji Mura which collects monuments and buildings of the Meiji period. Augmenting the traditional and cultural surroundings of the University is the natural beauty of the area. The campus, covering approximately 500, 000 m^2, is situated on the top of a hill overlooking a wide stretch of pastoral hills and vales untouched by urban life. In spring, the Japanese nightingales rest among the white cherry blossoms and pink peach blossoms. In autumn,

the fields turn golden in anticipation of the harvest. All these things provide an ideal environment for studying. However, the aesthetic surroundings are not the main reason why anyone should study here. The first and foremost feature of the University is the professional education offered.

The Department of Consumer Economics is the one only educational facility of its kind in Japan. Up until now, it has been widely believed that production should take precedence over all else. But it is now clear that this belief should be modified. The presence and consciousness of the consumer should be given more consideration. Nagoya Economics University had the foresight to anticipate such a transition and established the pioneering faculty of Consumer Economics in 1979. By offering this course of study, the University hopes to educate students accordingly and thereby make a significant contribution to society.

UNDERGRADUATE PROGRAMS

Faculty of Economics (Freshmen Enrollment: 250)
Department of Business Administration
Accounting, Bookkeeping, Business Administration, Business History, Business Management, Business Organization, Cost Accounting, Finance, Labor Management, Marketing, Theory of Economics
Department of Consumer Economics
Commodity Science, Consumer Economics, Consumer Education, Consumer Policy, Distribution Economy, Economic History, Economic Policy, Economics, Finance, Prices, Statistics

Foreign Student Admission
Qualifications for Applicants
Standard Qualifications Requirement
Examination at the University
Foreign applicants are admitted in special cases if they pass the screening test
Documents to be Submitted When Applying
Standard Documents Requirement
*
Research Institutes and Centers
Research Institute for Consumer Affairs
For Further Information
Undergraduate Admission
Admission Office, Nagoya Economics University, 61-1 Uchikubo, Inuyama-shi, Aichi 484 ☎ 0568-68-0490

Nagoya Gakuin University
(Nagoya Gakuin Daigaku)

1350 Kamishinano-cho, Seto-shi, Aichi 480-12
☎ 0561-42-0350

Faculty
　　Profs. 42　　Assoc. Profs. 25

　　Assist. Profs. Full–time 7; Part–time 53
Number of Students
　　Undergrad. 3, 467
Library 209, 000 volumes

Outline and Characteristics of the University
Nagoya Gakuin University dates back to 1887 when F. C. Klein, an American-Methodist Protestant missionary, founded the Nagoya Anglo-Japanese College in Nagoya. The College was founded to teach the principles of Christianity and provide an educational experience. In 1906, the College assumed the new name of Nagoya Gakuin. Nagoya Gakuin University was established in 1964 as a private coeducational four-year institution, based on Christian principles as reflected in its school motto: "Reverence to God-Love to Person. " The main campus was moved to the present site of Seto in 1967.

Nagoya Gakuin University conducts research through its Institute and Centers: namely, the Institute of Industrial Sciences, Center for Foreign Language Education and Research, and Center for Information Processing.

The campus, situated high on a hilltop covering 300, 000 m², overlooks Seto City (population: 125, 000). The surroundings offer a pleasant retreat and an expansive landscape of forest green. Seto City has been a famous pottery center for more than 1, 000 years. The richness of the traditions connected with this folk-craft is still very much alive and visible. Although the campus is within rural environs, it still has all the advantages of being near one of Japan's largest cities, Nagoya. The campus can be reached in an hour by railway and bus from downtown Nagoya.

Since its foundation, Nagoya Gakuin University has been active in promoting exchange programs and has exchanged a number of students and professors with universities in the United States.

UNDERGRADUATE PROGRAMS

Faculty of Economics (Freshmen Enrollment: 750)
Department of Business Administration
Bookkeeping, Business Finance, Commerce, Commercial Law, Commercial Policy, Corporation Law, Cost Accounting, History of Commerce, Insurance, Internal Auditing, Labor Management, Law of Property, Management Accounting, Marketing, Principles of Economics, Securities, Statistics, Study of Commodities, Transportation
Department of Economics
Commercial Law, Economic Dynamics, Economic History, Economic Policy, Economics, History of Economic Doctrine, International Economics, Japanese Economy, Law of Property, Modern Economics, Monetary Policy, Money and Banking, Public Finance, Statistics
Faculty of Foreign Studies (Freshmen Enrollment: 200)

Department of Chinese

Area Studies, Chinese Culture, Chinese Language, Chinese Literature, History of China, History of Chinese Language

Department of English

American Literature, Area Studies, British Literature, English Grammar, English Language, English Phonetics, History of English Language, Simultaneous Translation

Foreign Student Admission

Qualifications for Applicants

Standard Qualifications Requirement

Examination at the University

The same entrance examination as Japanese applicants.

Documents to be Submitted When Applying

Standard Documents Requirement

Application period: January

✳

Research Institutes and Centers

Center for Foreign Language Education and Research, Centerfor Information Processing, The Institute of Industrial Sciences

Special Programs for Foreign Students

The Institute for Japanese Language and Culture, established in 1989, provides intensive training in Japanese for the very beginner to the advanced student of the language. The institute also provides courses in Japanese culture and society.

For Further Information

Undergraduate Admission

Admission Division, Nagoya Gakuin University, 1350 Kamishinano-cho, Seto-shi, Aichi 480-12 ☎ 0561-42-0339

Nagoya University of Commerce and Business Administration

(Nagoya Shoka Daigaku)

Sagamine, Nisshin-cho, Aichi-gun, Aichi 470-01
☎ 05617-3-2111

Faculty
    Profs. 34   Assoc. Profs. 10
    Assist. Profs. Full–time 22; Part–time 71
Number of Students
    Research Associate 2
    Undergrad. 3, 152
Library 276, 815 volumes

Outline and Characteristics of the University

Nagoya University of Commerce and Business Administration originated from a private institution of higher education founded in 1935 by Yuichi Kurimoto, a pioneer in education in Japan. The original institution developed into a two-year college in 1950, which was expanded to form a four-year, single-fac-

ulty, undergraduate university in 1953. At that time, the Faculty of Commerce comprised the Department of Commerce and the Department of Business Administration. In April 1984, still within the Faculty of Commerce, the Department of Decision Science and Management Information Systems was established, followed in 1985 by the Department of International Economics. A graduate school is scheduled to be established by 1990.

The University's student body is limited in size, encouraging all students to develop their own individual identities. The University also encourages an international outlook. Many faculty members have studied and worked abroad, and various programs are offered for students to travel and study overseas, while foreign language courses form an important part of all degrees. Computers are used extensively throughout the campus and a new Intelligent Centre, the first of its kind in Japan, was completed in the spring of 1988. This is pioneering a new concept of teaching method, combining the use of computer-assisted instruction, audio-visual materials and satellite television transmission in classrooms designed to promote student/lecturer interaction and debate. The Intelligent Centre workshop also offers students free access to computer facilities for private study.

Originally located in downtown Nagoya, the University moved in 1968 to the current, beautifully landscaped and wooded 200 acre campus, located in the countryside 40 minutes east of the city's center. The Language, Information and Computer Centers, and the affiliated women's junior college, are all located on this site, which provides a wide range of facilities for sports and club activities in addition to an exceptional learning environment. The majority of students commute daily from their homes in the area.

Nagoya, a city of 2 million people, ranks as one of Japan's leading industrial cities. It is the center of a thriving industrial and commercial community of approximately 6. 5 million inhabitants, and forms, together with Tokyo and Osaka, the heart of the nation's economic activity. In addition to its traditional light industries of ceramics and textiles, new chemical and heavy industries such as iron and steel, shipbuilding and auto-manufacturing have developed at tremendous rates, making this port city one of the most important in Japan. Nagoya also plays an important role as a base for tourism, since in addition to its many local attractions, it forms a convenient starting point for the exploration of central Japan which is abundant in mountains, rivers, hot springs and many resorts of scenic beauty and traditional crafts.

UNDERGRADUATE PROGRAMS

Faculty of Commerce (Freshmen Enrollment: 943)

Department of Business Administration

Accounting, Auditing, Cost Accounting, Factory

Management, Finance, History of Management Studies, Industrial Relations, International Accounting, International Management, Management Analysis, Management Policy, Management Strategies, Managerial Accounting, Organization Theory, Personnel Management, Production Management, Tax Accounting

Department of Commerce

Commerce, Commercial Policy, Domestic Marketing, Finance, Foreign Exchange, History of Commerce, History of Trade, Insurance, International Banking, International Business, International Communications, International Marketing, International Security Market, Trade Policy

Department of Decision Science and Management Information Systems

Accounting Information Systems, Computer Models, Computer Programing, Data Base Applications, Decision Theory, Factory Automation, Linear Programing, Operating Systems, Production Models, Statistics, Systems Analysis, System Simulation

Department of International Economics

American Studies, Asian Economic Development, Asian Economic History, Asian Studies, Direct Foreign Investment, Econometrics, Economic Development, Economic Policy, European Economic History International Business, European Studies, History of Economics, International Economic Geography, International Economics, International Economic Statistics, International Finance, International Industrial Systems, International Marketing, International Relations, International Resources, International Security Market, Labor Economics, Mathematical Economics, Middle East Studies, Trade Theory, World Demography

Foreign Student Admission

Qualifications for Applicants

Standard Qualifications Requirement

Examination at the University

An interview to show their competence in their major field of interest, as well as on general topics.

Documents to be Submitted When Applying

Standard Documents Requirement

ONE-YEAR GRADUATE PROGRAMS

One-Year Graduate Course of Commerce (Enrollment: 10)

Commerce

Foreign Student Admission

Qualifications for applicants

Standard Qualifications Requirement

Examination at the University

A written examination in Japanese to test the students's proficiency in their first foreign language and major area of study.

*

Research Institutes and Centers

Center for Decision Science, Center for International Economics, Language Center

For Further Information

Undergraduate and Graduate Admission

The President, Nagoya University of Commerce and Business Administration, Sagamine, Nisshin-cho, Aichi-gun, Aichi 470-01 ☎ 05617-3-3002

Nagoya University of Foreign Studies
(Nagoya Gaikokugo Daigaku)

57 Takenoyama, Iwasaki, Nisshin–cho, Aichi–gun, Aichi 470–01 ☎ 05617–4–1111

Faculty
　　Profs. 15　　Assoc. Profs. 5
　　Assist. Profs. Full–time 9; Part–time 5
　　Res. Assoc. 4
Number of Students
　　Undergrad. 242
Library 19, 678 volumes

Outline and Characteristics of the University

The Nakanishi Educational Trust has, since its inception forty years ago, stressed the importance of giving priority to the individual talents of its students. We are confident that Aichi Women's Junior College and the various colleges of further education which constitute the Trust continue to produce graduates who are able to make a very real contribution towards the enrichment of the society in which they are active.

As we approach the twenty-first century, the world around us is becoming increasingly more complex, and the cultural, political, and economic role which Japan is required to play on the international stage is seen as an important and exacting one.

The university consists of a single faculty, and this is divided into three departments: Britsh and American Studies, French Studies, and Chinese studies. In all of the courses of each department emphasis is laid on the acquisition of practical knowledge of modern spoken languages.

It goes without saying that the study of foreign languages cannot be divorced from a proper understanding of the cultures which have fostered the languages. The university aims to give its students ample opportunity to become familiar with all aspects of the culuture of the country or countries whose ianguage they are studying, and hopes to achieve this aim by means of a system of integrated small classes.

UNDERGRADUATE PROGRAMS

Faculty of Foreign Studies (Freshmen Enrollment: 200)

Department of British and American Studies

Area Studies, British and American Culture, Communication and Speech, English Composition English Grammar, English for Commerce, English Phonetics, English Set Texts, English Shorthand, English Typewriting, Graduation Thesis, History of British and American Literature, History of the English Language, History of Western Thought, Inter-Cultural Communication, Methodology of Interpretation, Methodology of Translation, Modern Economic Relations, Oral English, Outline of British and American Literature, Outline of English Linguistics, Topics in British and American English

Department of Chinese Studies

Chinese Set Texts, Chinese Composition, Chinese Grammar, Chinese Conversation, Language Laboratory, Chinese, Chinese Area Studies (Geography, History), Current Chinese, Fukien Dialect, Graduation Thesis, History of Chinese Literature, History of the Chineese Language, Outline of Chinese Linguistics, Outline of Modern Chinese Literature, Study of Chinese Culture, Study of Chinese Linguistics, Study of Chinese Literature

Department of French Studies

French Area Studies (Language, Culture, Economics, Sociology, Outline of French Linguistics, Outline of French Culture, Study of French Linguistics, Study of French Literature, French for Commerce, Current French, Economics of Europe, Graduation Thesis, French Composition, French Grammar, French Set Texts, Language Laboratory French

*

For Further Information

Undergraduate Admission

Nagoya University of Foreign Studies 57 Takenoyama, Iwasaki, Nisshin-cho, Aichi-gun, Aichi 470-01 ☎ 05617-4-1111

Nagoya University of the Arts
(Nagoya Geijutsu Daigaku)

281 Kumanosho, Shikatsu-cho, Nishikasugai-gun, Aichi 481 ☎ 0568-24-0315

Faculty
   Profs. 32 Assoc. Profs. 25
   Assist. Profs. Full-time 25; Part-time 116
Number of Students
   Undergrad. 1, 574
Library 49, 573 volumes

Outline and Characteristics of the University

Nagoya University of the Arts was established in 1970 with two faculties—the Faculty of Fine Arts and the Faculty of Music.

Our school is the only private university that has two artistic Faculties, Fine Arts and Music, in central Japan. Our principal object is the cultivation of creative students. Therefore, in both the Faculty of Fine Arts and the Faculty of Music, the general edu-

cation course is not arranged in the same way as most other universities.

The general education subjects, the fundamental education subjects and the professional education subjects are taught in conjunction with each other from the first academic year.

In the Faculty of Fine Arts the creative work is done chiefly with the atelier as its focal point. In the Faculty of Music the creative ability of students is cultivated through individual guidance with individual lessons as its focal point. These are the distinctive features of professial education at the University. The school is located in a northern suburban area of Nagoya.

A graduate school and research institutes are in the planning stages and are scheduled to open in the near future. These additions will further improve what is already considered a fine institute for the arts.

UNDERGRADUATE PROGRAMS

Faculty of Fine Arts (Freshmen Enrollment: 180)
   Department of Design
Ceramics Design, Industrial Design, Metal Design, Space Design, Textile Design, Visual Design
   Department of Painting
Japanese Painting, Oil Painting
   Department of Sculpture
Sculpture
Faculty of Music (Freshmen Enrollment: 160)
   Department of Instrumental Music
Piano, Strings, Wind and Percussion
   Department of Music Education
History of Music, Musicology
   Department of Vocal Music
Classical Songs, Opera, Vocalism, Vocal Music

Foreign Student Admission

Qualifications for Applicants
   Standard Qualifications Requirement
   Those who have received the International Baccalaureate and are 18 years or older may also apply.
   All foreign applicants must have recommendations issued from their own diplomatic establishments abroad.
Examination at the University
   The same entrance examination as Japanese applicants.
Documents to be Submitted When Applying
   Standard Documents Requirement

*

For Further Information

Undergraduate Admission

Dean of School Affiars, Department of Educational Affairs, Nagoya University of the Arts, 281 Kumanosho, Shikatsu-cho, Nishikasugai-gun, Aichi 481 ☎ 0568-24-0315

Nagoya Women's University
(Nagoya Joshi Daigaku)

4-30 Shioji-cho, Mizuho-ku, Nagoya-shi, Aichi 467
☎ 052-852-1111

Faculty
    Profs.   33   Assoc. Profs.   12
    Assist. Profs.   Full–time   14; Part–time   36
    Res. Assocs.   17
Number of Students
    Undergrad.   1, 216
Library   119, 384 volumes

Outline and Characteristics of the University

The history of this university begins with Nagoya Girls' School founded in 1915. In 1950 Nagoya Jogakuin Junior College (now Nagoya Women's Junior College) was annexed, and in 1964, Nagoya Women's University was established. Thus, during the past 70 plus years, our institute has developed into quite a large school with a university, a junior college, two junior and senior high schools and a kindergarten.

Haruko Koshihara, founder of this institution, decided that "kindness" was to be the school precept. This ideal represents humanity in the broad sense and friendship, love, and the pursuit of learning in the narrow sense. With this belief, the University has set its aim at education based on academic research and highly developed vocational abilities. Further, it aims to cultivate enlightened human beings who will contribute greatly to the society with the care and affection that is representative of Nagoya Women's University.

UNDERGRADUATE PROGRAMS

Faculty of Home Economics (Freshmen Enrollment: 110)
    Department of Home Economics
    Food Science Course   Nutritional Science Course
Faculty of Literature (Freshmen Enrollment: 150)
    Department of English philology and Literature
    Department of Japanese Literature
    Department of Juvenile Education

Foreign Student Admission
    Qualifications for Applicants
    Standard Qualifications Requirement
    Examination at the University
    Screening of the documents, an interview and a written essay.
    Documents to be Submitted When Applying
    Standard Documents Requirement
Application Period: Nov. 1 to Nov. 18, 1988.
Selection Date: Nov. 27, 1988.

*

Research Institutes and Centers
Educational Research Institute, Institute of Domestic Science
For Further Information
    Undergraduate Admission
Admission Office, Nagoya Women's University, 4-30 Shioji-cho, Mizuho-ku, Nagoya-shi, Aichi 467
☎ 052-852-1111 ext. 211

Nakamura Gakuen College
(Nakamura Gakuen Daigaku)

5-7-1 Befu, Johnan-ku, Fukuoka-shi, Fukuoka 814
☎ 092-851-2531

Faculty
    Profs.   24   Assoc. Profs.   10
    Assist. Profs.   Full–time   6; Part–time   38
    Res. Assocs.   16
Number of Students
    Undergrad.   1, 074
Library   94, 398 volumes

Outline and Characteristics of the College

Nakamura Gakuen College was established in 1965. Haru Nakamura, the foundress of the College, is a heroin who dedicated her whole life to education. Her great personality and enthusiasm for education have been widely praised by many people and inherited by the younger generation in this area. And her noble life is introduced into the textbooks of elementary school.

The College adopts the principle that effective learning is achieved by having a small number of students in lecture, experimentation and in-service training. And great emphasis is placed on in-service training outside of the College, an effective practical way of education.

One of the purposes at college is "physical training" as well as "spiritual training". At the same time, specialist training is also emphasized for infant education and food and nutrition study. At present 1, 100 students are enrolled. Most of them are from various regions of Kyushu Island. 90% of them are female students. We have some international students from Mexico, Taiwan and Korea. As internationalization is widely demanded, the students from abroad are expected to increase judging from geographical convenience.

Fukuoka City is the center of industry and transportation in Kyushu Island. Adjacent to the college, Oohori Park called "The Oasis for the Citizens" is located at the center of this town along with the Fukuoka City Museum and the remains of Fukuoka Castle built by Nagamasa Kuroda, the representative warrior of Edo Era. There are also a number of scenic spots and places of historic interest reflecting the culture and history of Fukuoka.

UNDERGRADUATE PROGRAMS

Faculty of Home Economics (Freshmen Enrollment: 230)
Department of Child Education
Course of Child Study
Course of Primary Education
Department of Food and Nutrition
Course of Food Science
Course of Nutrition
Foreign Student Admission
Qualifications for Applicants
Standard Qualifications Requirement
1. Applicants are required not to possess Japanese nationality.
2. Applicants who passed the Japanese Language Proficiency Test and/or those applicants who have no difficulty with the Japanese language.
Examination at the College
1. Essay or composition in Japanese.
2. Interview
3. Other necessary items
Test results are sent to each applicant by mail.
Documents to be Submitted When Applying
Standard Documents Requirement

All applicants must submit recommendations by appropriate organizations admitted by the College and/or by such official insitutions as Japanese Ambassadors.

*

Research Institutes and Centers
Research Institute of Nutrition Science
For Further Information
Undergraduate Admission
Admission Office, Nakamura Gakuen College, 5-7-1 Befu, Johnan-ku, Fukuoka-shi, Fukuoka 814
☎ 092-851-2531 ext. 221

Nanzan University
(Nanzan Daigaku)

18 Yamazato-cho, Showa-ku, Nagoya-shi, Aichi 466
☎ 052-832-3111

Faculty
  Profs. 96   Assoc. Profs. 72
  Assist. Profs. Full–time 31; Part–time 236
  Res. Assocs. 2
Number of Students
  Undergrad. 5, 272   Grad. 86
Library 440, 742 volumes

Outline and Characteristics of the University
Nanzan University traces its origins back to Nanzan Middle School, founded in 1932 by Rev. Joseph Reiners, a Divine Word Missionary, to provide Catholic education to Central Japan. In 1946 Nanzan College of Foreign Languages was estab-

lished, and in 1949 it evolved into Nanzan University with the Faculty of Arts and Letters. Since then it has added four more Faculties of Foreign Languages, Economics, Business, and Law. It also has a Graduate School, three research institutes, and four area-studies centers to foster its academic goals.

Nanzan is one of the twelve Catholic Universities in Japan. As an educational institution, it aims to combine the principles of Christian Humanism with the achievement of academic excellence. The motto of the university, Hominis Dignitati (For Human Dignity), is a living challenge to instill both a respect for the truth and an understanding of the dignity of all men and women in the world. To bring these ideals to life for the students, Nanzan stresses within its academic milieu the spirit of internationalization, on the one hand, and an increased understanding of the local society, on the other hand.

To accomplish its educational goals the university maintains a high teacher–student ratio for personalized education, provides courses on Christian Thought and Western Culture for international understanding, puts emphasis on the teaching of foreign languages, and shows through literature and history the persistence of traditonal Japanese values and customs in the process of modernization. Furthermore, the teaching faculty is unique because of the large number of foreign teachers and of Japanese teachers who have been trained both in Japan and abroad.

Since its founding Nanzan has enjoyed the firm support of the local community. Originally the university was developed as a service to the people of Nagoya, the largest city in Central Japan. Many of the graduates remain in the Nagyoa area, either finding jobs with corporations in the region or taking teaching positions. Open lectures and workshops are held for interested groups in the Nagoya region, and special classes are also open to the public.

UNDERGRADUATE PROGRAMS

Faculty of Arts and Letters (Freshmen Enrollment: 270)
Department of Anthropology
Cultural Anthropology, Ethnology, Folklore
Department of Education
Child Psychology, Clinical Psychology, Comparative Education, Developmental Psychology, Educational Administration & Finance, Educational Guidance, Educational Psychology, Educational Research, Experimental Psychology, History of Education, Industrial Psychology, Philosophy of Education, Psychology of Adolescence, Psychology of Personality, Social Psychology, Sociology of Education, Testing and Statistics
Department of English Language and Literature
British & American Thought, English Grammar, English Language, English Linguistics, English Literature, English Philology, English Phonetics, History

of American Literature, History of English Literature

Department of French Language and Literature
French Language, French Linguistics, French Literature, French Phonetics, French Thought, History of French Culture, History of French Language, History of French Literature

Department of German Language and Literature
German Culture, German Language, German Literature, German Philology, German Studies, German Thought, History of German Culture, History of German Literature, History of Germany, Studies of Theater

Department of Japanese Language and Literature
Calligraphy, Chinese Classics, History of Japanese Language, History of Japanese Literature, Japanese Literature, Japanese Philology

Department of Philosophy
Ethics, History of Ancient Philosophy, History of Medieval Philosophy, History of Modern Philosophy

Department of Theology
Biblical Languages, Canon Law, Church History, Dogmatic Theology, Fundamental Theology, History of Philosophy, Holy Scripture (Old Testament, New Testament), Liturgy, Metaphysics, Moral Theology, Patrology, Practical Theology, Science of Religion

Faculty of Business Administration (Freshmen Enrollment: 250)

Department of Information Systems
Business Finance, Business History, Communication Systems, Computers and Society, Data Structures and Data Base Management, Decision Analysis, Econometrics, Human Resources Management, Industrial Organization, Information Processing, Information Science, Information Systems, Information Systems Auditing, Management Information Systems, Management Systems, Marketing, Mathematical Statistics, Multivariate Analysis, Statistical Data Analysis, Statistical Methods, Stochastic Models in Operations Research, System Design, Systems Analysis

Department of Management
Accounting, Auditing, Business, Business Finance, Business History, Business Statistics, Corporate Accounting, Cost Accounting, Financial Accounting, Financial Institutions, Financial Statement Analysis, Human Resources Management, Industrial Organization, Industrial Relations, Industrial Sociology, International Accounting, International Business, Investments, Management, Managerial Accounting, Marketing, Marketing Management, Market Structure, Operations Research, Organizational Psychology, Organization Theory, Principles of Economics, Systems Theory for Management, Tax Accounting

Faculty of Economics (Freshmen Enrollment: 240)

Department of Economics
Econometrics, Economic Ethics, Economic Fluctuations, Economic History of Europe, Economic History of Japan, Economic Policy, Economics, Economics of Development, Economic Statistics, Economic Systems, History of Economics, History of Economic Thought, History of Modern Ecomonics, International Economics, International Finance, Japanese Economy, Labor Economics, Money & Banking, Public Finance, Regional Economics, Social Philosophy in Economics, Social Security, Welfare Economics

Faculty of Foreign Languages (Freshmen Enrollment: 230)

Department of British and American Studies
American Culture, American Diplomacy, American Economy, American Judiciary, American Literature, American Politics, British & American Literature, British & American Society, British & American Thought, English Language, English Linguistics, English Phonetics, History of America, History of Britain & British Commonwealth, History of the English Language, Religion in America, Teaching English as a Foreign Language

Department of Japanese Studies
History of Japanese, History of Japanese Literature, International English, Japanese Culture, Japanese Linguistics, Japanese Literature, Methodology of Foreign Language Teaching, Structure of Japanese, Teaching Japanese as a Foreign Language

Department of Spanish Studies
Brazilian Portuguese, Journalistic Spanish, Latin American Culture, Latin American Economy, Latin American History, Latin American Politics, Spanish Culture, Spanish History, Spanish Language, Spanish & Latin American Judiciary, Spanish & Latin American Literature, Spanish Phonetics

Faculty of Law (Freshmen Enrollment: 240)

Department of Law
Administration, Administrative Law, Anglo-American Law, Bankruptcy Law & Law of Company Reorganization, Civil Procedural Law, Commercial Law & Law of Commercial Acts, Constitutional Law, Corporation Law, Criminal Law, Criminal Procedural Law, Economic Law, German Law, History of Japanese Legal System, History of Legal System, Ibero Law, International Law, International Private Law, International Relations, International Trade Law, Labor Law, Law of Bill & Check, Law of Enterprise Accounting, Law of Execution, Law of Family & Succession, Law of Obligations, Law of Real Right, Maritime Law & Insurance Law, Philosophy of Law, Political History, Political Theory, Sociology of Law, Tax Law

Foreign Student Admission

Qualifications for Applicants
   Standard Qualifications Requirement
   Applicants must have high scholastic aptitude as well as sufficient proficiency in Japanese and English.

   Those who have an International Baccalaureate diploma and are 18 years of age or older as of April 1 of the year of entrance to the University are also eligible to apply.

Examination at the University

The entrance examinations will be given in the following subjects:

1. Japanese
2. English
3. Mathematics (applicants to the Department of Information Systems only)

Documents to be Submitted When Applying

Standard Documents Requirement

Following documents are also required.

1. Three letters of recommendation
2. Valid TOEFL scores or the result of the English proficiency test if the applicant is not a native speaker of English. (Nanzan University's TOEFL institutional code number is 9477.)
3. The result of the Japanese Language Proficiency Test or an official certificate of Japanese language proficiency

Qualifications for Transfer Students

The applicant must have completed at least one year of college level education abroad and have all the qualifications required for freshman admission.

Examination for Transfer Students

Similar to those given to freshman applicants.

Documents to be Submitted When Applying

Standard Documents Requirement

The same documents required of freshman applicants.

GRADUATE PROGRAMS

Graduate School of Arts and Letters (First Year Enrollment : Master's 28, Doctor's 10)

Divisions

Cultural Anthropology, English Literature and Linguistics, French Literature and Linguistics, German Literature and Linguistics, Theology

Graduate School of Business Administration (First Year Enrollment : Master's 15, Doctor's 5)

Division

Management

Graduate School of Economics (First Year Enrollment : Master's 15, Doctor's 5)

Division

Economics

Graduate School of Law (First Year Enrollment : Master's 15)

Division

Law

Foreign Student Admission

Qualifications for Applicants

Master's Program

Standard Qualifications Requirement

Doctor's Program

Standard Qualifications Requirement

Examination at the University

Master's Program

1. Written and oral examinations of the subjects in the field of specialization. The subjects will be determined by the graduate department.
2. English
3. Foreign language other than English

Doctor's Program

Same as Master's program.

Documents to be Submitted When Applying

Standard Documents Requirement

*

Research Institutes and Centers

Anthropological Museum, Center for American Studies, Center for Australian Studies, Center for Japanese Studies, Center for Latin American Studies, Institute of Anthropology, Nanzan Institute for Religion and Culture, The Center for Management Studies, The Institute for Social Ethics

Facilities/Services for Foreign Students

Nanzan University waives the half tuition/maintenance fee for all undergraduate and graduate foreign students.

Special Programs for Foreign Students

Nanzan University receives approximately 200 foreign students from over 20 different countries each year. The majority of foreign students study at the Center for Japanese Studies (CJS). The CJS has a faculty advising system for them. All full-time CJS students are assigned to a faculty advisor. There are six faculty advisors and each of them has a group of 20 students. The faculty advisors are available to the students not only for problems related to their studies but also for social and/or personal problems.

The CJS assists the students in locating accommodations since there is no on-campus residence hall for them. The majority of the CJS students stay with Japanese host families.

Undergraduate foreign students must take eight credits of Japanese which can be counted as a part of foreign language requirement.

Up to 16 credits of required general education subjects can be replaced by the credits earned in the courses of Japanese Language and Japanese Studies.

The Center for Japanese Studies (CJS), established in 1974, offers a one-year program for foreign students who wish to study Japanese language and culture. The academic year of CJS starts in September and ends in May of the following year. A special five-week summer intensive Japanese language program is also offered.

For Further Information

Undergraduate and Graduate Admission

Office of Admissions, Nanzan University, 18 Yamazato-cho, Showa-ku, Nagoya-shi, Aichi 466 ☎ 052-832-3111 ext. 234 Fax052-833-6156

Nara Sangyo University
(Nara Sangyo Daigaku)

3-12-1 Tatsunokita, Sango-cho, Ikoma-gun, Nara
636 ☎ 0745-73-7800

Faculty
Profs. 32
Associate Professor 12
Assist. Profs. Full–time 15; Part–time 48
Number of Students
Undergrad. 1, 911
Library 50, 000 volumes

Outline and Characteristics of the University

Nara Sangyo University aims to train leaders for active participation in the economic world of the 21st century, and businessmen with expertise in economics, business administration and law. The university was founded in 1984, with high expectations and support from various circles in the Kyoto-Osaka-Kobe districs and Nara Prefecture. In 1987 the university added, according to the original plan, a Faculty of Law to stand alongside the Faculty of Economics. This is the first such undertaking in Nara Prefecture and promises good results. In cooperation with the surrounding community, the university offers a unique education that enables students to acquire the practical and specialized knowledge and skills on which regional prosperity depends. Moreover, the university endeavors to train talented people to accommodate the social changes attendant upon internationalization, information systems development and ongoing technical innovation.

The university's educational philosophy stresses not only instruction in applied economics, business administration and law, but training that prepares students for an active business life in a rapidly changing world. The university thus offers a well-balanced curriculum in the liberal arts and specialized subjects. In addition, it offers educational activities and programs as part of a well-rounded education.

UNDERGRADUATE PROGRAMS

Faculty of Economics (Freshmen Enrollment: 360)
Department of Business Administration
Accounting, Business Administration, Commerce, History of Business Administration, Management Engineering, Theory of Enterprise
Department of Economics
Economic History, Economic Policy, Financial Theory, Public Finance, Theoretical Economics
Faculty of Law (Freshmen Enrollment: 200)
Department of Law
Administrative Law, Constitutional Law, Criminal Law, History of Law, Political History, Political Science

Foreign Student Admission
Qualifications for Applicants
Standard Qualifications Requirement
Documents to be Submitted When Applying
Standard Documents Requirement
*
For Further Information
Undergraduate Admission
Admissions Office, Nara Sangyo University, 3-12-1 Tatsunokita, Sango-cho, Ikoma-gun, Nara 636
☎ 0745-73-7800

Nara University
(Nara Daigaku)

1230 Horai-cho, Nara-shi, Nara 631
☎ 0742-44-1251

UNDERGRADUATE PROGRAMS

Faculty of Humanities (Freshmen Enrollment: 310)
Department of Cultural Properties
Archaeology, Art History, Conservation, Museology
Department of Geography
Department of History
Department of Japanese Literature
Faculty of Socioresearch (Freshmen Enrollment: 180)
Department of Industrial Sociology
Department of Sociology

Nihon Fukushi University
(Nihon Fukushi Daigaku)

Okuda, Mihama-cho, Chita-gun, Aichi 470-32
☎ 0569-87-2211

Faculty
Profs. 52 Assoc. Profs. 25
Assist. Profs. Full–time 4; Part–time 270
Number of Students
Undergrad. 5, 439 Grad. 12
Library 320, 000 volumes

Outline and Characteristics of the University

Nihon Fukushi University was founded in 1953 by Shugaku Suzuki, a Buddhist priest of the Nichiren-sect, to improve and develop social work in Japan. Originally established as the Chubu Junior College of Social Work, it was expanded and renamed as Nihon Fukushi University in 1957. Since then the University has experienced rapid growth and played a pioneering role in cultivating a new generation of social workers. It is at present composed of two Faculties, the Faculty of Social Welfare, which has two divisions (Day and Evening) and the Faculty of Economics, which was established in 1976. The Graduate School of Social Welfare offering the Degree of Master of Arts was started in 1969. And in 1983 the whole university moved from Nagoya to a new site in Mihama-cho.

The two aims of the University are to carry out research to contribute to the development of knowledge and to prepare students for professions which require well–disciplined abilities to analyze social problems and to meet the needs of the people. Consequently, the University makes it a principle to give students seminars in small groups on general education as well as on specialized subjects. Among other characteristics of the University is the fact that it has always been on good terms with the local communities, and has played an important part in their cultural and educational activities.

The campus is located in the countryside close to the city of Nagoya, one of the great industrial and commercial areas of Japan, and it is beautifully situated upon a gently sloping hill overlooking the sea. This creates an enjoyable learning environment and also allows students to pursue a variety of extra-curricular activities on campus. On the site there is a gymnasium where indoor sports such as volleyball and basketball can be played, together with an outdoor athletics field and several tennis courts. As the majority of the students are from other parts of the country, there are two dormitories and other sufficient lodgings to accommodate the students. As a result, a new University Town has been brought into being in this area.

UNDERGRADUATE PROGRAMS

Faculty of Economics (Freshmen Enrollment: 300)
  Department of Economics
Agricultural Economics, Bookkeeping, Contemporary Economics, Economic Fluctuations, Economic Policy, Economic Theory, History of Economics, History of Social Thought, Industrial Economics, International Economics, Labor Law, Public Finance, Small Enterprises, Social Policy, Statistics, Technological Theory
Faculty of Social Welfare (Freshmen Enrollment: Day Division 400, Evening Division 200)
  Department of Social Welfare
Administration and Finance of Local Governments, Civil Law, Developmental Psychology, History of Social Wefare Development, Living Conditions, Medical Service Welfare, Social Policy, Social Problems, Social Welfare, Social Welfare Methodology, Urban Problems

GRADUATE PROGRAMS

Graduate School of Social Welfare (First Year Enrollment : Master's 5)

Division
Social Welfare

Research Institutes and Centers
Research Institute of Social Science
For Further Information
  Undergraduate and Graduate Admission
Administration Office (Information Division), Nihon Fukushi University, Okuda, Mihama-cho, Chita-gun, Aichi 470-32 ☎ 0569-87-2211 ext. 211

Nihon University
(Nihon Daigaku)
4-8-24 Kudan-Minami, Chiyoda-ku, Tokyo 102
☎ 03-262-2271

Faculty
  Profs. 920   Assoc. Profs. 506
  Assist. Profs. Full–time 595; Part–time 2, 1 94
  Res. Assocs. 651
Number of Students
  Undergrad. 66, 724   Grad. 1, 805
Library 3, 780, 686 volumes

Outline and Characteristics of the University

Nihon University was founded on October 4, 1889 by Count Akiyoshi Yamada who was then the Japanese Minister of Justice. Yamada was an outstanding disciple of Shoin Yoshida, one of the main intellectual forces behind the Meiji Restoration. Yamada travelled in Europe and America to study various legal systems. Striving to equip Japan for its role as a modern nation, he codified the basic elements of civil, commercial and criminal law, thus establishing the Japanese judicial system on a firm foundation. Yamada and the successive presidents of Nihon University inherited the spirit of Shoin Yoshida, a man who was always on the people's side and strove to liberate them from the yoke of the feudal system. The Japanese Law School adopted the name Nihon Daigaku (Nihon University) in 1903 and 17 years later, acquired university status under the University Ordinance of 1920.

Nihon University is the largest university in Japan. It is composed of 14 graduate schools, a post baccalaureate course, 14 colleges, a correspondence division, a junior college with eight departments, numerous research institutes, and 23 senior high schools.

The school buildings cover 1, 069, 170 m², while school property is estimated at over 30, 000, 000 m². It has always been Nihon University's policy to shun empty uniformity and to foster on its campuses a spirit of autonomous creativity and an atmosphere conducive to the development of the student's individuality. While being a traditionally Japanese institution, Nihon University nevertheless is cosmopolitan in its pursuit of truth. As the 21st century nears, Nihon University seeks to further develop its academic potential and at the same time to develop a unique approach to education and scholarship.

UNDERGRADUATE PROGRAMS

College of Agriculture and Veterinary Medicine (Freshmen Enrollment: 1, 410)

Department of Agricultural Chemistry

Analytical Chemistry, Biochemistry, Biophysics, Chemistry of Agricultural Chemicals, Enzyme Chemistry, Feed Science, Fermentation Technology, Food Chemistry, Food Hygiene, High Molecular Chemistry of Living Matter, Instrumental Analytical Chemistry, Microbial Genetics, Nutritional Chemistry, Organic Chemistry, Physical Chemistry, Physiological Chemistry of Microorganisms, Plant Nutrition and Fertilizer, Plant Physiology and Plant Biochemistry, Radiochemistry and Radiation Chemistry, Soil Science, Utilization of Microorganisms

Department of Agricultural Engineering

Agricultural Hydrology, Agricultural Structures, Applied Hydraulic Engineering, Bridge Engineering, Dam Construction Engineering, Farm Machinery, Farm Pumps, Farm Tractor Engineering, Foundation Engineering, Hydraulics, Irrigation and Drainage, Land Disaster Prevention Engineering, Landscape Engineering, Land Use Planning, Prime Mover, Reclamation Engineering, River and Coastal Engineering, Road Engineering, Rural Planning, Soil Engineering, Soil Physics, Soil Science

Department of Agriculture

Agricultural Chemicals, Agricultural Marketing, Agricultural Meteorology, Agricultural Policy, Agrobiology, Applied Entomology, Farm Management, Floriculture, Food Crop Science, Forage Crop Science, Forest Aesthetical Engineering, Horticulture under Structure, Industrial Crop Science, Land Reclamation, Landscape Management, Landscape Planning, Plant Breeding, Plant Ecology and Crop Production, Plant Materials and Planting, Plant Nutrition and Fertilizer Science, Plant Pathology, Pomology, Soil Science, Tropical Horticulture, Urban and Regional Planning, Vegetable Crop Science

Department of Animal Science

Animal Anatomy, Animal Breeds and Varieties, Animal Embryology, Animal Husbandry Mechanics, Animal Hygiene, Animal Management, Animal Nutrition, Animal Physiology, Animal Rearing, Animal Reproduction, Animal Science, Chemistry of Animal Product, Economics of Animal Industry, Grassland Science, Livestock Farming, Location in Animal Industry, Management of Animal Industry, Manufacture Mechanics of Animal Product, Marketing of Animal Industry, Microbiology of Animal Husbandry, Policy of Animal Industry, Poultry Breeding and Reproduction, Poultry Management, Poultry Nutrition, Science of Animal Breeding, Science of Animal Feeding, Science of Animal Products, Science of Feed Crop, Science of Laboratory Animals

Department of Applied Biological Science

Analysis of Cellular Responese, Animal Cell Biology, Applied Virology, Biochemical Molecules, Cell Chemistry, Cell Organization, Development Biology of Differentiation, General Breeding, Metabolic Regulation, Molecualr Microbiology, Molecular Breeding, Molecular Genetics, Molecular Immunology, Nucleic Acid Chemistry, Photosynthesis, Physiology of Animal Reproduction, Physiology of Plant Reproduction, Plant Cell Biology, Plant Growth Regulation, Protein Chemistry, Structural Analysis of Genes

Department of Fisheries

Algology, Aquaculture and Fish Propagation, Environment of Aquaculture, Fish Behavior, Fish Diet, Fish Diseases, Fisheries, Fisheries Economics, Fisheries Food Industry, Fisheries Laws, Fisheries Management, Fisheries Microbiology, Fisheries Oceanography, Fisheries Pharmacology, Fisheries Production, Fisheries Resource, Fishing Instrumentation, Genetics and Breeding of Aquatic Organism, Histology and Embryology of Aquatic Animal, Ichthyology, International Fisheries, Limnology, Macromolecular Colloid Chemistry, Marine Food Chemistry, Marine Industrial Chemistry, Marine Inorganic Chemistry, Marine Synecology, Marketing of Marine Products, Pathology of Aquatic Animal, Physiology of Aquatic Animal, Planktology, Population Dynamics, Seed Production for Aquaculture, Utilization of Marine Products

Department of Food Economics

Agricultural Economy, Agricultural Policy, Cooperatives, Crop Production, Economy of Consumption, Farm Management, Food Dietetics, Food Economy, Food Industries, Food Life, Food Merchandising, Food Policy, Food Production and Technology, Food Resource Development, History of Food Culture, Location Theory of Food Industries, Market Food, Packaging, Rural Sociology

Department of Food Technology

Cold Chain System, Food Administration, Food Analysis, Food Chemical Engineering, Food Hygiene, Food Manufacturing Technology, Food Microbiology, Food Preservation, Food Refrigeration, Food Science and Chemistry, Materials for Food Packaging, Mechanical Engineering for Food, Microstructure of Food, Nutritional Chemistry of Food, Nutritional Physiology and Biochemistry, Packaged Food, Physiochemical Properties of Food, Raw Materials of Food

Department of Forestry

Adhesives and Coating Materials for Wood, Chemistry of Forest Products, Dendrology, Erosion Control, Forest Administration, Forest Aesthetics, Forest Climatology, Forest Ecology, Forest Engineering, Forest Entomology, Forest Geography, Forest Hydrology, Forest Machinery, Forest Management, Forest Mensuration, Forest Organization, Forest Pathology, Forest Policy, Forest Recreation and Tourism, Forestry, Forest Soil Science, Forest Tree Physio-Chemistry, Forest Valuation, Forest Zoology, Gardening, Grassland Management, Greening Technology, Logging, Physics of Wood Materials, Pulp, Silviculture, Timber Marketing, Tree Breeding, Tree Physiology, Tropical Forestry, Wood Chemistry, Wood Physics, Wood Preservation, Wood Structure, Wood Technology

Department of Land Development
Agricultural Commodity Trade, Agricultural Economics, Agricultural Management, Agricultural Marketing, Area Development Policy, Comparative Agricultural History, Development Engineering, Economic Geography, Farm Management, Industrial Constitution, International Coopernation, Plant Nutrition and Fertilizer Science, Plant Protection, Soil Science, Tropical Agriculture, Tropical Animal Husbandry, Tropical Crop Science, Tropical Forestry, Tropical Horticulture

Department of Veterinary Medicine
Animal Ecology, Animal Genetics, Bacteriology, Fish Diseases, Hygiene, Medical Zoology, Nutrition, Radio-biology, Veterinary Anatomy, Veterinary Environmental Hygiene, Veterinary Histology and Embryology, Veterinary Hygiene, Veterinary Infectious Diseases, Veterinary Internal Medicine, Veterinary Microbiology, Veterinary Microbiology and Immunology, Veterinary Obstetrics and Reproduction, Veterinary Pathology, Veterinary Pharmacology, Veterinary Physiological Chemistry, Veterinary Physiology, Veterinary Public Health, Veterinary Radiology, Veterinary Surgery, Veterinary Virology

College of Art (Freshmen Enrollment: 600)

Department of Broadcasting
Acoustic Psychology, Advertising, Announcing, Audience Survey, Broadcasting, Broadcasting Advertising, Broadcasting Education, Broadcasting Laws & Regulations, Broadcasting Systems, Broadcasting Technology, History of Broadcasting, History of Fashion and Ornament, Information Industry, Linguistic Psychology, Mass Communication, Musical Engineering, Radio Direction, Radio & TV Commercials, Radio & TV News Reporting, Radio & TV Programming, Radio & TV Scripts, Radio & TV Technology, TV Direction, TV Lighting, TV Stagesetting & Designing, Writing for Radio & TV

Department of Cinema
Acting, Analysis of Film Works, Animation, Camerawork, Communication, Computer Art, Direction of Acting, Editing Method, Elocution, Film Acting, Film Appreciation & Criticism, Film Art, Film Direction, Film History, Film-Making, Film Music, Film Production, Film Techniques, Film & Video Editing, Foreign Film History, History of Documentary Films, Image Art, Image Media, Image Psychology, Japanese Dance, Japanese Film History, Musical Vocalization, Photographic Optics, Scenario, Scenario Analysis, Social History of Cinema, Sound Recording, Study of Film Works, Video Art, Western Dance

Department of Dramatics
Acting, Concept of Theatre Art, Creative Choreography of Modern Dance, Dance, Drama, Folk Performing Arts, History and Development of Theatre, History of Foreign Theatre, History of the Japanese Dance, History of the Japanese Theatre, History of the Performing Arts, History of Western Dance, Noh and Kyogen, Play Directing, Play Production, Playwriting, Practices in Production Management, Stage Lighting, Stage Management, Study of Scenery, Theory of Theatrical Education, TV Performing Arts

Department of Fine Arts
Advertising Art, Advertising Design, Architectural Planning, Construction of Fine Arts, Design, Figure Drawing, Fine Arts Techniques, Graphic Design, History of Advertising Design, History of Fine Arts, Housing and Gardening, Illustration, Industrial Design, Lettering and Typography, Living Space Design, Oil Painting, Package Design, Philosophy of Fine Arts, Printmaking, Product Planning, Sculpture, Serigraphy, Study of Life Environment, Television Advertising, Theory of Color, Visual Communication Design, Visual Design

Department of Literary Arts
Biography, Comparative Literature, Genre Literature, History of American Literature, History of English Literature, History of French Literature, History of German Literature, History of Japanese Literature, History of Mass Communication, Japanese Classical Literature, Journalism, Juvenile Literature, Linguistics, Literary Composition, Literary Criticism, Poetry, Studies of Advertisement, Studies of Drama, Studies of Editing, Studies of Magazine, Studies of Media, Studies of Newspaper, Studies of Novel, Survey of Literature, Theory of Literature, Translation in Literature

Department of Music
Accompaniment, Acoustics, Chamber Music, Choral Music, Composition, Conducting Technique, Counterpoint and Fugue, Ear Training, Electronic Music, Ensemble for Education, Ethnomusicology, Gagaku, Harmony, Histories of Musical Genres, History of Music, Keyboard Music, Musical Forms, Musical Pedagogy, Musicology, Music Therapy, Opera, Orchestra, Orchestration, Solfege, String Music, Vocal Music, Wind and Percussion Music

Department of Photography
Advertising Photography, Applied Photography, Basic Photography, Film and TV, History of Photography, Newspaper Photographs, Optics, Philosophy of Photography, Photo-Editing, Photographic Chemistry, Photographic Process, Photo-Journalism, Photomaterials, Photomechanics, Photosensitivity, Portrait Photography, Printings, Reportage Photography, Sensitometry, Study and Critique of Photographic Works, Theory of Color, Visual Education

College of Commerce (Freshmen Enrollment: 1, 200)

Department of Accounting

Accounting, Auditing, Bookkeeping, Business Analysis, Business Organization, Business Planning, Cost Accounting, Cost Management, Economic Geography, Economic Statistics, Financial Economics, Financial Institutions, Financial Management, History of Accounting Theories, Industrial Psychology, Industrial Sociology, Information Management, Insurance, Management Audit, Production Control, Small Business Problems, Tax Accounting, Theoretical Economics

Department of Business Administration

Business Administration, Business Organization, Cost Management, Distribution Economy, Economic Policy, Financial Economics, Financial Management, History of Economic Theories, Industrial Sociology, Information Management, Labor Economics, Management, Management Economy, Market Research, Personnel Management, Production Control, Public Finance, Sales Management, Small Business Problems, Theoretical Economics

Department of Commerce

Business Cycles, Business History, Commerce, Commercial Policy, Co-operation, Distribution Economy, Economic Geography, Economic Statistics, Financial Economics, Financial Institutions, Foreign Trade, History of Economic Theories, Industrial Psychology, Information Management, Insurance, International Economics, International Finance, Management Economy, Marketing, Market Research, Merchandising, Ocean Transportation & Harbor Management, Products Planning, Public Finance, Sales Management, Securities Market, Small Business Problems, Theoretical Economics, Tourist Industry, Transportation

School of Dentistry (Freshmen Enrollment: 140)

Department of Dentistry

School of Dentistry at Matsudo (Freshmen Enrollment: 135)

Department of Dentistry

Anesthesiology, Biochemistry, Clinical Pathology, Complete Denture Porsthodonitcs, Complete Denture Prosthodontics, Comprehensive Dental Science, Crown & Bridge Prosthodontics, Crown & Bridge Prosthodontics, Dental Anatomy, Dental Law, Dental Law, Dental Material, Dental Materials, Dental Pharmacology, Dental Pharmacology, Dental Public Health, Dental Radiology, Dental Radiology, Dentistry for the Handicapped, Dermatology, Endodontics, Endodontics, General Medicine, General Surgery, Gynecology, Histology, Histology, Operative Dentistry, Oral Anatomy, Oral Anatomy, Oral Bacteriology, Oral Biochemistry, Oral Biochemistry, Oral Diagnosis, Oral Diagnostics, Oral Histology, Oral Histology, Oral Hygiene, Oral Microbiology, Oral Microbiology, Oral Pathology, Oral Pathology, Oral Phsiology, Oral Physiology, Oral Radiology, Oral Surgery, Oral Surgery, Orthodontics, Orthodontics, Otorhinolaryngology, Partial Denture, Pedodontics, Pedodontics, Periodonotology, Periodontology, Physiology, Pidiatrics, Preventive Dentistry, Public Health, Removable Partial Denture Prosthodontics

College of Economics (Freshmen Enrollment: Day 1, 300, Evening 200)

Department of Economics

Accounting, Agricultural Economics, American Economy, American History of Economics, Business Cycles, Chinese Economy, Commercial Economics, Computerization, Econometrics, Economic Development, Economic Policy, Economics, Economics of Welfare, Economic Statistics, Finance, Financial Systems, Fisheries Economics, Foreign Trade, History of Economics, History of Japanese Economy, History of Social and Economic Thought, Industrial Economics, Industrial Organization, International Economics, Japanese Economy, Labor Economics, Local Public Finance, Mathematics for Economics, Monetary Policy, National Income, Population, Russian Economy, Social Policy, Social Security, Taxation, Theory of Money

Department of Industrial Management

Accounting, Auditing, Bank Accounting, Business Consultation, Business Management, Business Statistics, Cooperations, Cost Accounting, Economic Geography, Economic Policy, Economics of Circulation, Financial Institutions, Financial Management, Foreign Exchange, Foreign Trade, Form of Business Enterprise, History of Business Management, Industrial Efficiency, Industrial History, Industrial Problems, Industrial Psychology, Industrial Relations, Industrial Sociology, Industrial Structure, Industry, Insurance, Labor Management, Management Accounting, Management Organization, Management Science, Marketing Management, Money and Finance, Personnel Management, Production Control, Public Enterprises, Public Relations, Securities Market, Small Enterprises, Transportation

College of Engineering (Freshmen Enrollment: 1, 030)

Department of Architecture

Architectural Design, Architectural Equipment, Architectural Planning, Building Construction Method, Building Materials, Building Production, Building Regulations, City Planning, Dwelling House Planning, Environmental Technologies in Architecture, Ergonomics, Foundation Engineering, History of Architecture, Interior Planning, Prevention and Protection Engineering for Town and Building, Reinforced Concrete Structure, Steel Structure, Structural Vibration

Department of Civil Engineering

Applied Mechanics, Aseismatic Engineering, Bridge Engineering, City Planning, Civil Engineering, Coastal Engineering, Construction Machines, Environmental Protection Engineering, Erosion Control Engineering, Geological Engineering, Highway Engineering, Hydraulics, Material of Construction, Railway Engineering, Reinforced Concrete Engineering, River Engineering, Sewerage Engineering, Soil Engineering, Soil Mechanics, Theory of Errors, Water

Works Engineering

Department of Electrical Engineering
Communication Engineering, Digital Circuit, Electrical Machines, Electrical Measurements, Electrical Power Institution and Management, Electrical Properties of Matter, Electricity and Magnetism, Electric Materials, Electro-Acoustics, Electronic Circuits, Electronic Measurements, Electronic Tube Engineering, High Voltage Engineering, Illuminating Engineering, Information Processing, Microwave Engineering, Optoelectronics, Power Application, Power Station and Substation Engineering, Radio and Electronic Application, Semiconductor Engineering, Transmission and Distribution of Electrical Energy, Transmission Lines and Networks

Department of Industrial Chemistry
Analytical Chemistry, Biological Chemistry, Chemical Engineering, Chemical Industry, Chemical Plant Design, Corrosion Prevention, Electrochemistry, Inorganic Chemistry, Inorganic Industrial Chemistry, Inorganic Materials, Nuclear Reactor Chemistry, Organic Chemistry, Organic Industrial Chemistry, Organic Materials, Organic Synthesis, Physical Chemistry, Polymer Chemistry, Quantum Chemistry

Department of Mechanical Engineering
Aeronautics, Automotive Engineering, Control Engineering, Dynamics of Machinery, Engineering Materials, Engineering Mechanics, Engineering of Instrumentation, Fluid Dynamics, Fluid Machinery, Heat Transfer, Hydraulic Device Design, Information (System) Engineering, Internal Combustion Engine, Machine Elements, Mechanical Technology, Mechanic Design, Non-Destructive Inspection, Nuclear Engineering, Powder Technology, Production Management, Properties of Solids, Public Nuisance Prevention Engineering, Refrigeration and Air Conditioning, Steam and Turbine, Theory of Flow and Fracture of Solids, Tribology, Vibration Engineering, Welding Technology

College of Humanities and Sciences (Freshmen Enrollment: 1, 750)

Department of Applied Mathematics
Algebra, Applied Analysis, Applied Mathematics, Applied Statistics, Calculus, Complex Analysis, Computer Mathematics, Computer Science, Differential Equations, General Topology, Geometry, Linear Algebra and Geometry, Mathematical Statistics, Numerical Analysis, Probability, Real Analysis, Statistics

Department of Applied Physics
Acoustics, Analysis, Analytical Dynamics, Applied Material Physics, Applied Optics, Applied Physics, Atomic Physics, Automatic Control, Differential Equations, Electricity and Magnetism, Electronic Circuit Theory, Electronics, Experimental Physics, Graphics, Mathematical Methods in Physics, Mechanics, Nuclear Physics, Nulear Engineering, Optics, Physics, Quantum Mechanics, Quantum Mechanics, Statistical Mechanics, Statistical Mechanics, Thermodynamics

Department of Chemistry
Analytical Chemistry, Biochemistry, Chemical Engineering, Chemistry, Electrochemistry, Environmental Chemistry, Industrial Chemistry, Inorganic Chemistry, Organic Chemistry, Physical Chemistry, Resource Chemistry, Synthetic Chemistry

Department of Chinese Literature
Chinese Characters, Chinese Classics, Chinese Language, Chinese Literary Works by Japanese, Chinese Literature, Chinese Thought

Department of Earth Science
Earth Sciences, Economic Geology, Geochemistry, Geology, Geomorphology, Geophysical Prospecting, Geotechnics, Historical Geology, Limnology, Mineralogy, Paleontology, Petrology, Photogeology, Photogrammetry, Quaternary Research, Soil Mechanics, Stratigraphy, Structural Geology, Submarine Geology, Surface Deposits, Water Resources

Department of Education
Adult Education, Class Management, Comparative Education, Curriculum Making, Educational Evaluation, Educational Methodology, Educational Psychology, Educational Sociology, Educational System and Administration, Educational Technology, History of Japanese Education, History of Western Eduation, Pedagogy, School Management, Science of Education, Status of Education, Theory on Teaching Profession

Department of English Literature
English and American Literature, English Grammar, English Linguistics, English Phonetics, History of American Literature, History of English Literature, Literary Writers, Oral English

Department of Geography
Cartography, Economic Geography, Geography, Historical Geography, Human Geography, Physical Geography, Population and Settlement Geography, Regional Analysis, Regional Geography of Japan, Regional Geography of World, Urban Geography

Department of German Literature
German Grammar, German Language, German Literature, German Topography, History of German Literature, Phonetics of German Language

Department of History
History of Asia, History of Europe and America, History of Japan, Theory and Methodology on History

Department of Japanese Literature
History of Japanese Language, History of Japanese Literature, Japanese Language, Japanese Literature, Japanese Philology

Department of Mathematics
Algebra, Calculus, Complex Analysis, Computer Mathematics, Differential Equations, Elements of Calculus, General Topology, Geometry, Linear Algebra and Geometry, Mathematical Logic, Probability, Real Analysis, Statistics

Department of Philosophy
Contemporary Philosophical Thoughts, Ethics, History of Japanese Thought, History of Oriental

Thoughts, History of Religions, History of Western Thoughts, Philosophy

Department of Physical Education

Administration of Health Education, Administration of Physical Education, Biomechanics, Health Education, History of Physical Education and Sports, Measurement and Evaluation in Sports, Physical Education (American Football, Basketball, Camping, Dance, Gymnastics, Handball, Judo, Kendo, Rugby, Skating, Soccer, Sumo, Swimming, Table Tennis, Tennis, Track and Field, Volleyball), Physiology of Exercise, Public Health, Safety Education, Sport Psychology, Sport Sociology, Teaching Method

Department of Physics

Analysis, Analytical Dynamics, Atomic Physics, Atomic Structure of Matter, Differential Equations, Diffraction Crystallography, Electricity and Magnetism, Electrodynamics, Experimental Physics, Geophysics, Mathematical Methods in Physics, Mechanics, Nuclear Physics, Optics, Physics, Polymer Physics, Quantum Mechanics, Relativity, Statistical Mechanics, Theoretical Physics, Thermodynamics

Department of Psychology

Applied Psychology, Clinical Psychology, Development Psychology, Experimental Psychology, General Psychology, History of Psychology, Physiological Psychology, Psychological Experiments, Psychological Statistics, Psychological Testing, Psychology of Learning, Psychology of Personality, Psychometrical Measurement, Psychotherapy, Social Psychology

Department of Sociology

History of Sociology, Industrial Sociology, Labor Problems, Regional Sociology, Social History, Social Pathology, Social Psychology, Social Statistics, Social Work, Sociological Research, Sociology, Sociology of Family

College of Industrial Technology (Freshmen Enrollment: 1, 400)

Department of Architectural Engineering

Applied Mechanics, Architectural Design, Architectural Economics, Architectural Equipments, Architectural History, Architectural Planning, Architecture and Architectural Engineering, Building Construction, Building Materials, Designing Theory, Disaster-proof Engineering, Earthquake Engineering, Environmental Design, Environmental Engineering, Foundation Structure, Specification and Cost Estimation, Structural Analysis, Structural Design, Structural Planning, Town and Country Planning

Department of Civil Engineering

Aseismatic Engineering, Bridge Engineering, City Planning, Civil Construction Materials, Civil Construction Methods, Civil Engineering Design, Civil Engineering Planning, Concrete Engineering, Construction Machineries, Design of Experiment, Engineering of Hygienics, Geotechnical Engineering, Harbor Engineering, Highway Engineering, History of Civil Engineering, Hydraulics, Maintenance Control, Measurements and Experiments, Railway Engineering, Reinforced Concrete Engineering, River Engineering, Rock Mechanics, Sanitation Engineering, Structural Mechanics, Tunnel Engineering

Department of Electrical Engineering

Applied Electro Dynamics, Applied Electronics, Communication Engineering, Computer, Electrical Machine Design and Drawing, Electrical Materials, Electrical Measurements, Electric Machinery, Electric Power Distribution, Electric Power Generation, Electric Waves and Antennas, Electroacoustics, Electrochemistry, Electromagnetism, Electronic Circuits, Electronic Devices, Electronic Measurements, Electrothermics, High Voltage Engineering, Illuminating Engineering, Information Theory, Logic Circuits, Management for Electric Installations, Microwaves, Optical Electronics, Pulse Circuits, Solid State Electronics, Transient Phenomena, Transmission Lines and Networks

Department of Industrial Chemistry

Analytical Chemistry, Biological Chemistry, Biotechnology and Bioengineering, Catalysis, Chemical Engineering, Chemistry and Industry of Oil and Fat Products, Chemistry of Inorganic Materials, Chemistry of Natural Polymers, Chemistry of Organic Materials, Chemistry of Polymer Synthesis, Color Chemistry, Electrochemistry, Environmental Chemistry, Fuel Chemistry, Industrial Electrochemistry, Information Chemistry, Inorganic Chemistry, Inorganic Industrial Chemistry, Organic Chemistry, Organic Synthesis, Petrochemistry, Physical Chemistry, Physical Chemistry of Polymers, Quantum Chemistry, Radiation Chemistry, Surface Chemistry

Department of Industrial Engineering and Management

Behavioral Sciences, Control Engineering, Cost Accounting, Cost Engineering, Factory Consulting, Factory Planning, Financial Management, Human Engineering, Industrial Engineering and Management, Industrial Engineering in Process Industry, Industrial Location Planning, Industrial Safety and Hygiene, Industrial Social Psychology, Information Engineering, Instrumentation Engineering, Management, Management Accounting, Manufacturing Engineering and Application, Marketing, Motion and Time Study, Operations Research, Personnel Management and Labor Relations, Production Control, Production Control Systems, Production Management, Quality Control, Reliability Engineering, Small Business Administration, Systems Engineering, Technical History of Industries, Work Measurement

Department of Mathematical Engineering

Algebra, Analysis, Analysis of Structure Systems, Analytical Dynamics, Computational Mechanics, Computer Programing, Data Base, Descriptive Geometry, Fundamental Mathematics, Geometry, Image Processing, Information Processing, Information Theory, Modern Mathematics, Multivariate Analysis, Numerical Analysis, Numerical Approximation Method, Statistical Analysis, Thermodynamics and Statistical Mechanics

Department of Mechanical Engineering

Aeronautical and Astronautical Engineering, Automatic Control, Automotive Engineering, Computer Programming, Controlling Devices and Machinery, Electric Machinery, Engineering Materials, Engineering Mechanics, Environmental Engineering, Fluid Machinery, Fluid Mechanics, Foundry and Forging, Heat Transfer Engineering, Internal Combustion Engine, Machine Design and Drawing, Machine Elements, Machining, Manufacturing Process, Measurements Engineering, Mechanical Technology, Mechanics of Machines, Plasticity, Precision and Unconventional Machining, Refrigeration and Air Conditioning, Steam and Gas Turbine, Steam Boiler, Strength of Materials, Thermodynamics, Welding Engineering

College of International Relations (Freshmen Enrollment: 300)

Department of Intercultural Relations

American Culture, American Literature Studies, Buddhism Culture, Chinese Culture, Chinese Literature Studies, Christian Culture, Comparative Culture, Comparative Ethnology, Comparative Linguistics, Comparative Literature, Cultural Anthropology, Cultural Psychology, Eastern Philosophy, European Culture, European Literature Studies, French Culture, German Culture, History of Intercultural Relations, History of Social Thought, History of the Reception of Foreign Culture, Islamic Culture, Japanese Cultural History, Japanese Culture, Japanese Literature Studies, Modern American History, Modern Chinese History, Modern Culture, Modern Thought, Western Philosophy

Department of International Relations

American and European Economy, American Studies, Asian and Oceanian Studies, East European Studies, International Organization, International Politics, International Relations, Latin American Studies, Middle East and African Studies, West European Studies

College of Law (Freshmen Enrollment: Day: 1, 400: Evening: 600)

Department of Business Law

Administrative Law, Business Accounting Law, Business Law, Civil Law, Commercial Law, Criminal Law in Socio-Economics, Economic Law, Economics, International Transaction and Related Law, Labor Law, Management Administration, Public Relations, Security Market, Social Security, Taxation

Department of Journalism

Broadcasting, Comparative Journalism, Ethics in Journalism, Film-Making and Play-Production, History of Journalism, Journalism, Mass Communication, Newspaper Editing, Newspaper Management and Legislation, Public Opinion Research, Public Relations

Department of Law

Administrative Law, Anglo-American Law, Bankruptcy, Civil Law, Civil Procedure, Commercial Law, Comparative Law, Constitutional Law, Copyright Law, Criminal Law, Criminal Procedure, Criminology, Economic Law, Economic Policy, German Law, History of Legal Thoughts, Insurance Maritime Law, International Law, International Private Law, Labor Law, Legal History, Legal Medicine, Patent Law, Philosophy of Law, Public Finance, Social Policy

Department of Management and Public Administration

Administrative Management, Analysis of Business, Business Administration, Business Management, Business Morphology, Economic Law, Economic Policy, Finance Management, Finance of Local Government, Industrial Structure, International Economics, Labor Law, Labor Management, Local Government, Marketing, Office Management, Parliamentary System, Patent Law, Personnel Management, Public Administration, Public Finance, Social Security, Taxation, Theory of Wages, Urban Problem

Department of Political Science and Economics

Administrative Law, Civil Law, Constitutional Law, Criminal Law, Economic History, Economic Policy, Economics of Finance, History of Diplomacy, History of Economic Thoughts, History of Political Thoughts, History of Politics, International Law, International Politics and Economics, Local Government, Monetary Theory, Parliamentary System, Philosophy of Politics, Political Science, Public Finance, Social Policy, Social Security, Taxation, Theory of Wages

School of Medicine (Freshmen Enrollment: 120)

Department of Medicine

Anatomy, Anesthesiology, Anthropology, Biochemistry, Clinical Pathology, Dermatology, Embryology, Forensic Medicine, Gynecology, Histology, Hospital Administration, Human Genetics, Hygiene, Immunology, Internal Diagnosis, Internal Medicine, Microbiology, Neurology, Neurosurgery, Obstetrics, Ophthalmology, Orthopedics, Osteology, Otorhinolaryngology, Pathology, Pediatrics, Pharmacology, Physiology, Psychiatry, Public Health, Radiology, Surgery, Urology, Venereology

College of pharmacy (Freshmen Enrollment: 180)

Department of Biopharmacy

Advanced Pharmacognosy, Bioassay, Biochemistry, Clinical Chemistry, Cosmetic Chemistry, Forensic Chemistry, Genetic Engineering, Hyginic Chemistry, Immunology, Instrumental Analysis, Introduction to Clinical Medicine, Introduction to Hospital Pharmacy, Introduction to Pharmacy, Microbiology, Organic Chemistry, Pathology, Pharmaceutical Analysis, Pharmaceutical Jurisprudence, Pharmaceutics, Pharmacognosy, Pharmacology, Pharmacy Economies, Physical Chemistry of Pharmaceuticals, Physiology and Anatomy, Public Health, Radiochemistry, Toxicology

Department of Pharmacy

College of Science and Technology (Freshmen Enrollment: 2, 020)

Department of Aerospace Engineering

Aeronautical Engineering, Aerospace Technology, Aircraft Design, Aircraft Instruments and Equipments, Control Engineering, Design and Graphics, Engineering Mechanics, Flight Dynamics, Fluid Mechanics, Heat Transfer, Helicopter Engineering, High-Speed Aerodynamics, Internal Combustion Engines, Space Flight Dynamics, Strength of Materials, Structural Mechanics of Aircraft, Thermodynamics, Vibration Engineering

Department of Architecture

Architectural Design, Architectural Planning, Building Construction, Building Economics, Building Equipment, Building Materials, Building Regulations, Building Works, City Planning, Design of Building Structures, Disaster Prevention Planning, Earthquake-Resistant Structures, Environmental Engineering, History of Architecture, Real Estate Management, Regional Development Planning, Reinforced Concrete Structures, Soil and Foundation Engineering, Steel Structures, Structural Dynamics, Structural Mechanics

Department of Civil Engineering

Aseismatic Engineering, Bridge Engineering, City Planning, Civil Engineering, Coastal Engineering, Construction Materials, Construction Method, Geology and Soil Engineering, Harbor Engineering, Highway Engineering, Hydraulics, Hydrology, Infrastructure Planning and Management, Power Station Engineering, Regional Planning, Reinforced Concrete Engineering, River Engineering, Sabo Engineering, Sewerage Engineering, Soil Mechanics, Tunnel Engineering, Waterworks Engineering

Department of Electrical Engineering

Communication Engineering, Design of Electrical Machines and Tools, Electrical Engineering, Electrical Machines, Electrical Measurements, Electrical Properties of Materials, Electric Circuits, Electro-Acoustics Engineering, Electrochemistry, Electromagnetic Fields and Waves, Electromagnetism, Electronic Computer, Electronic Devises, Heat and Electrical Engineering, High Voltage Engineering, Light and Electronic Engineering, Logic Circuits, Network Analysis and Synthesis, Nuclear Engineering, Power Station and Subpower Station Engineering, Power Transmission and Distribution, Pulse Circuits, Ultrasonic Engineering

Department of Electronic Engineering

Antennae and Propagation, Artificial Intelligence and Pattern Recognition, Cable Communication Engineering, Computer Architecture, Computer Hardwares, Computer Software, Control Engineering, Control Theory, Electrical Properties of Materials, Electric Circuit, Electric Discharge, Electric Power Engineering, Electromagnetic Waves, Electromagnetism, Electron Device and Integrated Circuit Technology, Electronic Circuit, Electronic Engineering Materials, Electronic Measurement, Electronics and Information Science, Electronics & Electric Power Engineering, Engineering of Information Processing in the Information Network System, Image Processing and Pattern Recognition, Information Theory, Logic Circuits, Microwave Engineering, Optical Engineering, Pulse Digital Circuits, Pulse Fundamentals, Radio Communication Engineering, Robot Engineering, Semiconductor Engineering, Sonic and Ultrasonic Engineering, Switching Engineering, Systems Engineering, Traffic Electronics

Department of Industrial Chemistry

Analytical Chemistry, Applied Physical Chemistry, Bio Engineering, Chemical Engineering, Chemical Engineering Kinetics, Chemical Plant Engineering, Electrochemistry, Industrial Chemistry, Industrial Management, Industrial Materials, Inorganic Chemistry, Inorganic Industrial Chemistry, Instrumental Analysis, Materials Science, Organic Chemistry, Organic Industrial Chemistry, Physical Chemistry, Polymer Chemistry, Polymer Science, Quantum Chemistry, Safety Engineering, Statistical Thermodynamics

Department of Mathematics

Algebra and Geometry, Algorithmic Science, Analysis, Complex Analysis, Computer, Differential Equations, Differential Geometry, Information Mathematics, Information Science, Mathematical Statistics, Mathematics, Modern Analysis, Numerical Analysis, Probability and Statistics

Department of Mechanical Engineering

Air Conditioning, Automatic Control, Automotive Engineering, Engineering Mechanics, Fluid Machinery, Fluid Mechanics, Gas Dynamics, Heat Transfer, Hydraulics, Instrumentation, Internal Combustion Engines, Machine Design, Machine Elements, Machine Tools, Mechanical Technology, Metals and Alloys, Plasticity Engineering, Steam Power, Strength of Materials, Structural Mechanics, Theory of Elasticity, Theory of Machining, Thermodynamics, Vibration Engineering

Department of Oceanic Architecture and Engineering

Architectural Planning, Coastal Environment Development, Coastal Ocean Facility Planning, Development Planning in Urban Coastal Area, Marine Architecture Design, Ocean Concrete Structure, Ocean Construction Material Studies, Ocean Construction Technology, Ocean Ecology, Ocean Environment Engineering, Ocean Facility Planning, Oceanic Architecture Installation, Oceanic Architecture Planning, Oceanographic Instrumentation Engineering, Oceanographic Instrumentation Engineering, Oceanography, Ocean Space Utilization and Planning, Ocean Steel Structure, Ocean Structural Design, Ocean Structural Mechanics, Ocean Wave Dynamics, Off Shore Shell Structure Dynamics, Sea Bed Engineering

Department of Pharmacy

Agricultural Chemicals, Bioassay, Biochemistry, Chemistry of Microbiological Preparations, Clinical

Chemistry, Cosmetic Chemistry, Disease Biochemistry, Forensic Chemistry, Hygienic Chemistry, Medicine Manufacturing Engineering, Microbiology, Pharmaceutical Analysis, Pharmaceutical Botany, Pharmaceutical Chemistry, Pharmaceutical Chemistry of Hormones, Pharmaceutical Economics, Pharmacognosy, Pharmacology, Pharmacopoeia, Pharmacy, Pharmacy Administration, Plant Chemistry, Public Health, Radio-Chemistry, Toxicology

Department of Physics

Astronomy, Atomic Physics, Biophysics, Computer Calculus, Condensed Matter Physics, Electricity and Magnetism, Electronics, Elementary Particles, Fluid Dynamics, Low Temperature Physics, Mathematical Methods of Physics, Measurements in Physics, Mechanics, Nuclear Physics, Plasma Physics, Quantum Mechanics, Relativity, Statistical Physics, Theory of Heat, Vibration

Department of Precision Mechanical Engineering

A. C. Circuits, Automatic Control, Cutting Engineering, Engineering Mechanics, Fluid Machinery, Fluid Mechanics, Heat Transfer, Information Engineering, Instrumentation, Kinematics of Machines, Machine Design, Machine Elements, Machine Shop Technology, Material Engineering, Mechanical Technology, Optical Engineering, Plastic Forming, Precision Machinery Engineering, Prime Movers, Production Control, Strength of Materials, Thermodynamics, Vibration Engineering

Department of Transport Civil Engineering

Airport Engineering, City Planning, Engineering Materials, Environmental Engineering, History of Traffic Engineering, Hydraulics, National Development and Planning, Operations Research, Pavement Engineering, Physical Distribution, Psychology, Physiology for Traffic Engineering, Railway Engineering, River and Coastal Engineering, Systems Engineering, Traffic Control, Traffic Engineering, Transportation Engineering, Transportation Management, Transportation Planning, Transport Economics

Foreign Student Admission

Qualifications for Applicants

Standard Qualifications Requirement

Those who have passed or who expect to pass the Ministry of Education's Examination for university admission may also apply.

Examination at the University

1st Examination: Screening of documents

2nd Examination

College of Law: (1) written test (Japanese), (2) foreign language test (English, German or French) excluding one's native language, and (3) oral interview

College of Humanities and Sciences: (1) language tests (Japanese and English), (2) oral interview, and (3) performance test (Dept. of Phys. Ed. only). Applicants to the College of Humanities and Sciences will be required to take the Japanese Language Proficiency Examination Administered by the Association of International Education, Japan.

College of Economics: (1) written test (including Japanese composition), and (2) oral interview

College of Commerce: (1) written examinations (Japanese and English), and (2) oral interview

College of Art: (1) Those who apply to the Departments of Cinema (Acting Course), Fine Arts, Music, and Drams (Stage, Japanese Dance, Western Dance and Acting Courses) will be rgquired to perform. Those who apply to other Departments will be required to write essay or composition, and (2) to have an oral interview

College of International Relations: (1) Japanese essay, and (2) oral interview (in Japanese and English)

College of Science and Technology: (1) written examinations (Mathematics, English and Japanese), and (2) oral interview

College of Industrial Technology: (1) written examination (Mathematics and English), and (2) Japanese composition, (3) oral interview

College of Engineering: (1) written examinations (Mathematics, and English or Japanese), (2) oral interview

College of Agriculture and Veterinary Medicine: written test (language examination exempted), and (2) oral interview

College of Pharmacy: (1) written examinations (Chemistry field and Japanese), and (2) oral interview

Documents to be Submitted When Applying

Standard Documents Requirement

Those applying to the Department of Fine Arts, Drama (Stage) of the College of Art should submit two exhibits. Subject of exhibits is open, but exhibit should be portable. Photographs of exhibits will not be accepted. The submitted exhibits will not be returned.

Application Dates: From September 24 to October 2, 1987

GRADUATE PROGRAMS

Graduate School of Agriculture (First Year Enrollment : Master's 70, Doctor's 17)

Divisions

Agricultural Chemistry, Agricultural Economics, Agricultural Engineering, Agriculture, Animal Science, Fisheries, Food Technology

Graduate School of Art (First Year Enrollment : Master's 20)

Division

Literary Arts

Graduate School of Business Administration (First Year Enrollment : Master's 90, Doctor's 13)

Divisions

Accounting, Business Administration, Commerce

Graduate School of Dentistry (First Year Enrollment : Doctor's 42)

Divisions

Basic Dentistry, Clinical Dentistry

Graduate School of Dentistry at Matsudo (First Year Enrollment : Doctor's 40)

Division

Dentistry

Graduate School of Economics (First Year Enrollment : Master's 30, Doctor's 6)

Division

Economics

Graduate School of Engineering (First Year Enrollment : Master's 50, Doctor's 10)

Divisions

Architecture, Civil Engineering, Electrical Engineering, Industrial Engineering, Mechanical Engineering

Graduate School of Industrial Technology (First Year Enrollment : Master's 70, Doctor's 21)

Divisions

Architecture and Architectural Engineering, Civil Engineering, Electrical Engineering, Industrial Chemistry, Management Engineering, Mathematical Engineering, Mechanical Engineering

Graduate School of International Relations (First Year Enrollment : Master's 10)

Division

International Relations

Graduate School of Law (First Year Enrollment : Master's 75, Doctor's 15)

Divisions

Political Science, Private Law, Public Law

Graduate School of Literature and Social Sciences (First Year Enrollment : Master's 140, Doctor's 30)

Divisions

Chinese Literature, Education, English Literature, German Literature, History, Japanese History, Japanese Literature, Oriental History, Philosophy, Psychology, Sociology

Graduate School of Medicine (First Year Enrollment : Doctor's 64)

Divisions

Internal Medicine, Pathology, Physiology, Social Medicine, Surgery

Graduate School of Science and Technology (First Year Enrollment : Master's 250, Doctor's 62)

Divisions

Aerospace Engineering, Architecture, Civil Engineering, Electrical Engineering, Electronic Engineering, Geography, Industrial Chemistry, Mathematics, Mechanical Engineering, Oceanic Architecture and Engineering, Physics, Precision Mechanical Engineering, Transport Civil Engineering

Graduate School of Veterinary Medicine (First Year Enrollment : Doctor's 2)

Division

Veterinary Medicine

Foreign Student Admission

Qualifications for Applicants

Master's Program

Standard Qualifications Requirement

Applicants who have graduated from or who ex-

pect to graduate from a Japanese university after completing 12 years of schooling in their native country must in principle take the entrance examinations with Japanese students.

Applicants will not be accepted if they have graduated from international schools in Japan that are not recognized by the Ministry of Education.

Doctor's Program

Standard Qualifications Requirement

For Schools of Medicine, Dentistry, and Dentistry at Matsudo, applicants must have completed 18 years of education (the final degree should be in either the medical or dental fields at a foreign university) or expect to meet such a requirement by March 31, 1989.

Those applying to the Schools of Dentistry and Dentistry at Matsudo must have passed the Japanese National Examination for Dentistry.

Applicants to the Doctor's Program who have graduated or expected to graduate from a Japanese Master's Program must in principle take the entrance examinations with Japanese applicants.

Examination at the University

Master's Program

1st Examination: Screening of documents

2nd Examination:

Graduate School of Law: (1) written test (including the major in Japanese), (2) foreign language test (English, German or French) (excluding one's native language), and (3) oral interview

Graduate School of Literature and Social Sciences: (1) language test (Japanese and English), (2) written test in major field, and (3) oral, interview, Those who apply to Graduate School of Literature and Social Sciences will be required to take the Japanese Language Proficiency Test administered by the Association of International Education, Japan.

Graduate School of Economics: (1) essay and written test (Japanese), and (2) oral interview

Graduate School of Business Administration: (1) written test (essay in Japanese), (2) language test (English), and (3) oral interview

Graduate School of Art: (1) essay or composition in Japanese, (2) oral interview

Graduate School of International Relations: (1) Japanese essay, and (2) oral interview (in Japanese and English)

Graduate School of Science and Technology: (1) written examination (major field and Japanese), and (2) oral interview

Graduate School of Industrial Technology: (1) written examination (major field and English), and (2) oral interview

Graduate School of Engineering: oral interview in the major

Graduate School of Agriculture: (1) written test (essay in Japanese and English), and (2) oral interview

Doctor's Program

1st Examination: Screening of documents

2nd Examination:

Graduate School of Law: (1) written test (including the major in Japanese), (2) foreign language test (English, German or French) (excluding one's native language), and (3) oral interview

Graduate School of Economics: (1) essay and written test (Japanese and English), and (2) oral interview

Graduate School of Business Administration: (1) written test in major field, (2) language test (English), (3) foreign language test (German, French or Japanese) (excluding one's native language), and (4) oral interview

Graduate School of Science and Technology: (1) written examination (major field and Japanese), and (2) oral interview

Graduate School of Industrial Technology: (1) written examination (major field and English), and (2) oral interview

Graduate School of Engineering: oral interview in the major

Graduate School of Agriculture: (1) written test (essay in Japanese and English), and (2) oral interview

School of Medicine: Appliants should inquire directly to the Graduate School for details.

School of Dentistry: Applicants should inquire directly to the Graduate School for details.

School of Dentistry at Matsudo:

Applicants should inquire directly to the Graduate School for details.

Documents to be Submitted When Applying
Standard Documents Requirement
Application Dates: From September 24 to October 2, 1987

Research Institutes and Centers
Accounting Research Institute, Art Institute, Atomic Energy Research Institute, Comparative Law Institute, Dental Research Center, Economic Science Research Institute, Institute of Business Research, Institute of Information Science, Institute of Information Sciences, Judicial Institute, Law Institute, Mishima Research Institute of Science for Living, Political Science and Economics Institute, Population Research Institute, Regional Research Institute of Agriculture in the Pacific Basin, Research Institute of Agriculture and Veterinary Medicine, Research Institute of Commerce, Research Institute of Educational Systems, Research Institute of Engineering, Research Institute of Industrial Technology, Research Institute of International Relations, Research Institute of Medical Science, Research Institute of Moral Civilization, Research Institute of Oral Science, Research Institute of Science and Technology, Research Institute of Sciences, Research Institute of Veterinary Medicine, Shimoda Marine Laboratory, The Institute of Humanities and Social Sciences, The Institute of Natural Sciences

Special Programs for Foreign Students
Japanese Language classes (beginning to advanced levels) are offered to foreign students registered at Nihon University.

For Further Information
Undergraduate and Graduate Admission
International Division, Nihon University, 4-8-24 Kudan-Minami, Chiyoda-ku, Tokyo 102 ☎ 03-262-2271 ext. 260, 261, 263, 264

Niigata College of Pharmacy
(Niigata Yakka Daigaku)
5-13-2 Kamishin'ei-cho, Niigata-shi, Niigata 950-21
☎ 025-269-3171

Faculty
Profs. 16   Assoc. Profs. 11
Assist. Profs. Full–time 10; Part–time 16
Res. Assocs. 22
Number of Students
Undergrad. 400
Library 23, 324 volumes

Outline and Characteristics of the College
Niigata College of Pharmacy, founded in 1977 on the coast of the Japan Sea, is one of the youngest private institutions in Japan, aiming to conduct research and educational activities to qualify students for a pharmaceutical career and promote the public welfare by exercising an influence on behalf of humanity. In carrying out this aim, emphasis is placed on pharmaceutical science worthy of being called life science.

The College has designed its curriculum with a two-fold purpose: to develop in all students the capacity for leadership in the clinical practice of pharmaceutics and to provide opportunities for as many students as possible to prepare themselves for careers in research and teaching in the various branches of basic, clinical and social medicine.

The College consists of two departments: Pharmaceutical Sciences and Biopharmaceutical Sciences, with approximately 400 students and 75 faculty members. Rather small in size and scale, the College has the advantage of promoting friendly relationships between teachers and students.

In the four-year course leading to the Bachelor of Science in Pharmacy, all first-year students are required to take the necessary credits from the general education.

Students are expected to make balanced selections among the subjects they learn, taking into consideration their own interests and what is needed for their future specialized studies.

In the second and third year, students proceed to specialized education in which classes are structured as seminars, labs, and practical application studies. Students in both departments are required to take the same subjects except for a few electives. In the fourth year students are divided into several small groups and assigned to a supervising professor who acts as his or her adviser throughout the student's program of study. The appointment is determined primarily by the student's particular area of interest. Special training for research and seminars for the graduation thesis are held in the senior class.

Graduates are awarded qualifications to take the National Examination for the Pharmacist's License.

The campus is located within a few minutes' walk of the sea in the city of Niigata, which is a most important port town on the coast of the Japan Sea. The College is favored with natural beauty, looking out across the sea to Sado Island. This makes for an enjoyable learning environment and also enables students to pursue a variety of extracurricular activities on campus.

UNDERGRADUATE PROGRAMS

Faculty of Pharmaceutical Sciences (Freshmen Enrollment: 100)

Department of Biopharmaceutical Sciences
Biochemistry, Environmental Chemistry, Health Chemistry, Microbiology, Pharmaceutical Analytical Chemistry

Department of Pharmaceutical Sciences
Medicinal Chemistry, Pharmaceutical Chemistry, Pharmaceutical Technochemistry, Pharmaceutics, Pharmacognosy and Phytochemistry, Pharmacology, Physical Chemistry, Radio pharmaceutics, Toxicology

Foreign Student Admission
Qualifications for Applicants
Standard Qualifications Requirement
Examination at the College
Applicants are required to take the same written examination as Japanese applicants.
Documents to be Submitted When Applying
Standard Documents Requirement

*
For Further Information
Undergraduate Admission
Entrance Examination Section, Niigata College of Pharmacy, 5-13-2 Kamishin'ei-cho, Niigata-shi, Niigata 950-21 ☎ 025-269-3171 ext. 350

Niigata Sangyo University
(Niigata Sangyo Daigaku)

4730 karuigawa, Kashiwazaki-shi, Niigata 945–13
☎ 0257–24–6655

Faculty
Profs. 17 Assoc. Profs. 5
Assist. Profs. Full–time 6; Part–time 9
Number of Students
Undergrad. 378

Outline and Characteristics of the University
Niigata Sangyo University is a newly–estab-

lished University founded in April, 1988. At present it has a single Faculty of Economics. The University is rather small in scale, but offers various and substantial subjects; for example, Computer Programming, Marketing, Operations Research, Money and Banking, Systems Engineering, and Econometrics (for a complete list of subjects, see below). By studying these and the required subjects, it is hoped the student will not only acquire a wide-ranging knowledge and understanding of basic economic theories and problems, but also develop the ability to independently utilize the analytical tools of economics to solve current issues. The student will also learn to apply accouting and management theory to the actual practice of business. Our Faculty of Ecomomics is a new type that can fully respond to the demands of the increasingly varing and changing modern world.

Kashiwazaki City, where the University campus is located, is the fourth largest city in Niigata Prefecture, with a population of approximately 86, 000. As the city faces the the Sea of Japan to the west, beautiful sunsets may be enjoyed at the coast. The natural beauty of the area around the city provides a pleasant environment for student life.

We have now only one foreign stuedent, from Taiwan, but we earnestly hope that more students will come to study from around the world. Our academic and administrative staff are ready to welcome you.

UNDERGRADUATE PROGRAMS

Faculty of Economics (Freshmen Enrollment: 200)
Department of Ecomomics
Accounting Economics, Area Economy, Area Sociology, Auditing, Bookkeeping, Civil Law, Commercial Law, Computer Operation, Computer Programming, Cost Accounting, Distributive Economics, Econometrics, Economic Policy, Filing Control, Finance, Financial Management, General Theory of Industry, History of Economic Theory, History of Economy, Industral Economics, Industrial Geography, Japanese Economy, Management Information, Marketing, Operations Research, Principles of Economics, Statistics, Systems Analysis, Systems Engineering, Traffic Economics
Foreign Student Admission
Qualifications for Applicants
Standard Qualifications Requirement
Certification from a Japanese Language school in Japan or elsewhere or working knowledge of Japanese.
Examination at the University
1. Japanese Language Proficiency Test.
2. General Examiniation for Foreign Students.
3. Interview.
NB. The examinination will be held in November.

Documents to be Submitted When Applying
Standard Documents Requirement
1. Preferably, a Certificate of Graduation from a Japanese Language School in Japan or elsewhere.
2. School begins in April.
Qualifications for Transfer Students
Same as for Freshman Applicants.
Examination for Transfer Students
Same as the Entrance Examination.
Documents to be Submitted When Applying
Standard Documents Requirement
Same as for Freshman Applicants.

*

For Further Information
Undergraduate Admission
Student Division, Niigata Sangyo University, 4730 karuigawa, Kashiwazaki-shi, Niigata 945-13
☎ 0257-24-6655

Nippon Bunka University
(Nippon Bunka Daigaku)

977 Katakura-cho, Hachioji-shi, Tokyo 192
☎ 0426-36-5211

UNDERGRADUATE PROGRAMS

Faculty of Law (Freshmen Enrollment: 200)
Department of Law

Nippon Bunri University
(Nippon Bunri Daigaku)

Ichigi, Oita-shi, Oita 870-03
☎ 0975-92-1600

Faculty
　Profs.　58　　Assoc. Profs.　28
　Assist. Profs.　Full-time　15; Part-time　54
　Res. Assocs.　2
Number of Students
　Undergrad.　3, 507
Library　150, 000 volumes

Outline and Characteristics of the University
　Nippon Bunri University, with its two Schools of Engineering, and Business and Economics stresses both academic and industrial education. In this spirit, the university has, since its foundation, educated thousands of young people, providing them with knowledge and expertise in specialized fields of study and yet emphasizing their individual growth. It is a source of pride that Nippon Bunri University has maintained an unbroken tradition of education aimed not at training technicians and managers to aid just the development of the Japanese economy but at fostering globalists conscious of the well-being of humanity as a whole.

　In 1967, Oita Institute of Technology was established (School of Engineering, School of Electoral Engineering, School of Civil Engineering, Architecture). In 1968, Industrial Engineering and Industrial Chemistry were established. Subsequently, Aeronautics and Naval Architecture were established in 1974 and 1975 respectively. In 1982, the School of Business and Economics was established and the Oita Institute of Technology changed its name to Nippon Bunri University.

UNDERGRADUATE PROGRAMS

School of Business and Economics (Freshmen Enrollment: 300)
Department of Business
Auditing, Banking, Business Administration, Business Management, Commercial Management, Commercial Policies, Cost Accounting, Distribution, Economics, Financial Management, Financing, Insurance, International Economics, International Trade, Labor Management, Life Insurance, Management Engineering, Management Information Systems, Management Mathematics, Managerial Accounting, Marketing, Marketing Management, Market Research, Transportation
Department of Economics
Agricultural Economy, Business Cycle Theory, Commercial Economy, Econometrics, Economic Growth Theory, Economic Policies, Economic Statistics, History of Economics, Industrial Economy, Industrial Organizations, International Financing, Money, Transportation Economy, World Economy
School of Engineering (Freshmen Enrollment: 540)
Department of Aeronautics
Aerodynamics, Aeroengine, Aircraft Control, Aircraft Design, Aircraft Design and Casewriting, Aircraft Equipment, Aircraft Laws and Regulations, Aircraft Maintenance, Aircraft Manufacturing Technique, Aircraft Quality Control, Aircraft Structural Analysis, Aircraft Structure, Gasdynamics, Structure of Rocket, Theory of Aircraft Vibration, Thermodynamics
Department of Architecture
Architectural Environmental Engineering, Building Faciliities, Building Materials, Building Operation, City Planning, Earthquake Engineering, Ferro-concrete Structures, General Structures, Steel-frame Structures, Structural Dynamics
Department of Civil Engineering
Applied Mechanics, Coastal Engineering, Environmental Engineering, Explosives, Foundation Engineering, Geological Engineering, Hydraulics, Materials of Construction, Port and Harbor Engineering, Power Generation Hydraulics, Pre-stressed Concrete, Railroad Engineering, Reinforced Concrete Engineering, River Engineering, Road Engineering,

Rock Mechanics, Soil Mechanics, Structural Mechanics

Department of Electrical Engineering

Communication Engineering, Electrical Acoustic Engineering, Electrical Machinery and Appliances, Electrical Materials, Electric Applied Instrumentation, Electric Circuit Theory, Electric Illuminating/Electric Heating Engineering, Electric Instrumentation, Electric Transportation Engineering, Electrochemistry, Electromagnetics, Electronic Applied Engineering, Electronic Circuits, Electronic Computers, Electronic Computer Software, Electronic Engineering, Electronic Instrumentation, Electronic Instrumentation Equipment, High Voltage Engineering, Power Generation/Transformation Engineering, Power Transmission/Distribution Engineering, Semiconductor Engineering, Transmission Circuits Theory, Wire Communications

Department of Industrial Chemistry

Agricultural Chemicals, Analytical Chemistry, Biochemistry, Chemical Engineering, Electrochemistry, Environmental Chemistry, Inorganic Chemistry, Inorganic Industrial Chemistry, Mathematical Chemistry, Organic Chemistry, Organic Industrial Chemistry, Physical Chemistry, Polymer Chemistry, Quantum Chemistry, Radiochemistry, Reaction Engineering, Solid Chemistry, Theoretical Organic Chemistry

Department of Industrial Engineering

Business Analysis, Cost Accounting, Cost Management, Economic Efficiency Engineering, Environmental Control, Group Dynamics, Industrial Accounting, Industrial Management, Industrial Psychology, Information Engineering, Labor Management, Marketing research, Materials Control, Production Engineering, Quality Control, Regional Economy, Systems Engineering, Theory of Administration

Department of Mechanical Engineering

Air-conditioning, Automotive Engineering, Dynamics of Machinery, Engineering Materials, Engineering Mechanics, Fluid Machinery, Hydraulics, Hydrodynamics, Instrumentation Engineering, Internal Combustion Engines, Mechanism, Plastic Working, Refrigeration Technics, Steam Power, Strength of Materials, Thermodynamics, Vibration Problem

Department of Naval Architecture

Construction of Ship, Hydrodynamics, Hydrostatic Calculation of Ship, Ship Equipment, Ship Motion, Ship Propulsion, Ship Resistance, Ship Vibration, Stability of Ship, Strength of Ship Construction

Foreign Student Admission

Qualifications for Applicants
  Standard Qualifications Requirement
Examination at the University
  Screening by documentation:
  1. Application form
  2. Letter of Recommendation
  3. School record and other certificates
Documents to be Submitted When Applying
  Standard Documents Requirement

Qualifications for Transfer Students
  Graduate of junior college or equivalent school, or university.
Examination for Transfer Students
  Screening by documentation:
  1. Application form
  2. School record
  3. Certificate of graduation
Documents to be Submitted When Applying
  Standard Documents Requirement

*

Special Programs for Foreign Students

Educational Foundation, Nippon Bunri University has Japanese Language Institute for forign students. This institute provides Japanese Language courses: one year program (begins in April) and one –year–and–half program (begins in October).

For Further Information

Undergraduate Admission
Student Office, Nippon Bunri University, Ichigi, Oita-shi, Oita 870-03 ☎ 0975-92-1600

Nippon College of Physical Education
(Nippon Taiiku Daigaku)

7-1-1 Fukazawa, Setagaya-ku, Tokyo 158
☎ 03-704-7001

Faculty
  Profs. 57   Assoc. Profs. 31
  Assist. Profs. Full–time 12; Part–time 72
Number of Students
  Undergrad. 5, 845   Grad. 62
Library 186, 712 volumes

Outline and Characteristics of the College

The history of Nippon College of Physical Education began when founder, Tokichiro Hidaka established the Taiikukai in 1891, and a gymnastics practice school at Kojimachi-ku, Iida-machi in 1893.

Educating instructors for the purpose of improving physical fitness among its citizens during the regression period of the Meiji era parallelled the national policy of that time: to build an economically prosperous country and to establish a strong military. This eventually progressed to Nippon College of Physical Education. Ever since, our mission has been consistently directed toward educating physical education instructors and we have ungrudgingly strived to accomplish this goal.

Our college closely adheres to the spirit of the Fundamental Law on Education. It's purpose is to devote our efforts toward the improvement of the citizen's health and physical education culture and to train educated instructors with a wide range of practical, intellectual and moral knowledge, as well as concise up-to-date education.

Our school especially emphasizes the spirit of simplicity, fortitude and unity along with stressing practical physical training. In this way, students become highly qualified physical education instructors.

UNDERGRADUATE PROGRAMS

Faculty of Physical Education (Freshmen Enrollment: 1, 190)
Department of Health Education
Health Administration, Health Education, Hygiene, Physiology of Physical Education
Department of Martial Arts
Combativies, Judo, Kendo, Sumo
Department of Physical Education
Administration of Physical Education, Aquatics, Ball Games, Dance, History of Physical Education, Kinesiology, Measurement and Evaluation in Physical Education, Physical Education, Psycology of Physical Education, Study of Gymnastics, Track and Field
Department of Physical Recreation
Outdoor Education, Recreation, Sports Sociology, Training

Foreign Student Admission
Qualifications for Applicants
Standard Qualifications Requirement
Examination at the College
Applicants will be given an achievement test equal to the level of a Japanese high school curriculum, a language proficiency test, an interview and a medical examination.
Documents to be Submitted When Applying
Standard Documents Requirement

Qualifications for Transfer Students
Graduates or expected graduates of universities, junior colleges, or professional high schools (including foreign universities and junior colleges).
Examination for Transfer Students
Selection will be made after examining essays and interviews. Currently, the college only examines applications that have been recommended by professors from this college.
Documents to be Submitted When Applying
Standard Documents Requirement

ONE-YEAR GRADUATE PROGRAMS

One-Year Postgraduate Course of Physical Education (Enrollment: 20)
Health Education, Physical Education, Recreation, Sports Sociology

Foreign Student Admission
Qualifications for Applicants
Standard Qualifications Requirement

Examination at the College
Examinations are compiled from the fields of:
Foreign language (English or German), applicant's major and an interview

GRADUATE PROGRAMS

Graduate School of Physical Education (First Year Enrollment : Master's 25)
Divisions
Health Education, Methodology of Physical Education, Physical Education, Physical Fitness, Physical Recreation

Foreign Student Admission
Qualifications for Applicants
Master's Program
Standard Qualifications Requirement
Examination at the College
Master's Program
Examinations are compiled from the fields of:
Foreign Language (English, German or French), applicant's major and an interview.
Documents to be Submitted When Applying
Standard Documents Requirement
Following documents are also required.
1. A certificate referring to the applicant's proficiency in Japanese.
2. A Letter of Recommendation from the residing embassy of his/her country.

Research Institutes and Centers
Physical Institutes and Laboratories, Sports Training Center
Facilities/Services for Foreign Students
1. For those who require boarding facilities, the college offers one section of the student dormitory (admission is limited).
2. A meeting room for foreign students.
3. An annual social gathering.
For Further Information
Undergraduate and Graduate Admission
Educational Affairs Section, Educational Affairs Division, Nippon College of Physical Education, 7-1-1 Fukazawa, Setagaya-ku, Tokyo 158 ☎ 03-704-7001 ext. 208 or International Division ☎ 03 (704) 7638, 7639

The Nippon Dental University
(Nippon Shika Daigaku)

1-9-20 Fujimi, Chiyoda-ku, Tokyo 102
☎ 03-261-8311

Faculty
    Profs. 63   Assoc. Profs. 62
    Assist. Profs. Full–time 113; Part–time 253
    Res. Assocs. 270
Number of Students

Undergrad. 1,694   Grad. 100
Library   156,000 volumes

Outline and Characteristics of the University

The Nippon Dental University has the longest history of any private or public dental college in Japan. It has graduated 15,303 dentists, which is equivalent to one fifth of the total number of dentists in Japan's history. The Nippon Dental University is the biggest institution of undergraduate dental education and has excellent programs in undergraduate and graduate education, research and patient treatment.

When the Japanese Dental Law was enacted in 1906, special regulations concerning the "Accreditation of Public and Private Dental Colleges" came into force. In 1907, the first certified dental school based on these regulations was established by Ichigoro Nakahara. In 1947, it became Nippon Dental College; then in 1952, it began a six-year dental program including a two-year pre-dental curriculum. In 1960, the College added a four-year graduate program. In 1968, Nippon Dental College started Dental Technician Program and in 1971, added Dental Hygiene Program. These programs are offered within the School of Dental Technology.

Nippon Dental College started its second School of Dentistry in Niigata in April, 1977. Then, the College changed its name to The Nippon Dental University (N.D.U.). In April, 1983, the School of Dental Hygiene at Niigata accepted its first class. Junior College at Niigata, Dental Hygiene Program is to be established in April, 1987.

UNDERGRADUATE PROGRAMS

School of Dentistry at Tokyo (Freshmen Enrollment: 160)
Department of Dentistry
School of Dentistry at Niigata (Freshmen Enrollment: 120)
Department of Dentistry
Anatomy, Anatomy, Anesthesiology, Anesthesiology, Biochemistry, Complete Denture, Crown and Bridge, Crown and Bridge, Dental Materials Science, Dental Materials Science, Dental Pharmacology, Endodontics, Endodontics, General Dentistry, Histology, Internal Medicine, Internal Medicine, Microbiology, Operative Dentistry, Operative Dentistry, Oral Anatomy, Oral Anatomy, Oral and Maxillofacial Surgery, Oral and Maxillofacial Surgery, Oral Biochemistry, Oral Microbiology, Oral Pathology, Oral Physiology, Oral Radiology, Orthodontics, Orthodontics, Otorhinolaryngology, Partial and Complete Denture, Partial Denture, Pathology, Pedodontics, Pedodontics, Periodontics, Periodontology, Pharmacology, Physiology, Preventive and Community Dentistry, Preventive and Community Dentistry, Radiology, Surgery, Surgery

GRADUATE PROGRAMS

Graduate School of Dentistry (First Year Enrollment : Doctor's 18)
Divisions
Basic Dental Science, Clinical Dental Science

Foreign Student Admission

Qualifications for Applicants
Doctor's Program
   Standard Qualifications Requirement
Examination at the University
Doctor's Program
1. Subject of special study. (The course the applicant wants to go in for.)
2. Foreign language. (English and French, or English and German, and Japanese.)
3. Interview. (Japanese and English)
4. Medical examination
Documents to be Submitted When Applying
   Standard Documents Requirement

*

Research Institutes and Centers

Dental Research Institute at Tokyo, General Research Institute at Niigata

For Further Information

Undergraduate and Graduate Admission
Dean of Educational Affairs, The Nippon Dental University, 1-9-20 Fujimi, Chiyoda-ku, Tokyo 102 ☎ 03-261-8311 ext. 251
Undergraduate Admission
School of Dentistry at Niigata: The Nippon Dental University, 1-8 Hamaura-cho, Niigata-shi, Niigata 951 ☎ 025-267-1500

Nippon Institute of Technology
(Nippon Kogyo Daigaku)

4–1 Gakuendai, Miyashiro-machi, Minamisaitama-gun, Saitama 345   ☎ 0480–34–4111

Faculty
   Profs. 49   Assoc. Profs. 28
   Assist. Profs. Full–time 37; Part–time 101
   Res. Assocs. 4
Number of Students
   Undergrad. 3,552   Grad. 77
Library   132,788 volumes

Outline and Characteristics of the University

One of the best features of N. I. T. is that the Institute usually admits persons who have a strong desire to learn a higher level of science and technology beyond the foundation of the courses of technical high schools. This policy creates a student body that strives for the advancement of modern technology. Up-to-date and ideal course programs have been developed since the year of establishment, in order to effectively educate and prepare students for practical engineers.

Different from usual courses in other universities in Japan, N. I. T. offers new and unique course programs so that students may avoid the mere repetition of similar exercises and trainings already taken at technical high schools. Advanced courses in laboratory work, technical training, mechanical design, and such are thought important. Students are assigned many hours of work to better their technical ability. General Education Courses are opened throughout the four year course work for the degree in order to give the student a solid all-round education.

UNDERGRADUATE PROGRAMS

Faculty of Engineering (Freshmen Enrollment: 720)
Department of Architecture
Architectural Design and Planning, Building Materials, City Environment Engineering, Engineering of Earthquake Proof Construction, Environmental Engineering, Geotechnical Engineering, History of Architecture, Materials and Structures, Planning of Building Construction, Regional Planning, Reinforced Concrete Structures, Rural Planning, Structural Design, Structural Planning, Urban History
Department of Electrical and Electronics Engineering
Applied Systems Analysis, Components and Control, Computer, Electric Applications, Electric Discharge Phenomena and Applications, Electric Machines, Electric Material and Magnetics, Electric Materials, Electric Railway, Electric Technology, Electromagnetic Theory, High Voltage Engineering, Information Processing, Instrumentation and Measurement, Materials Science and Engineering, Optics, Power Applications, Rehabilitation Engineering, Semiconductors, Ultrasonics and Instrumentation
Department of Mechanical Engineering
Air-conditioning, Applied Mechanics, Automation, Biomechanics, Control Engineering, Drilling, Heat Engine, Hydraulic Engineering, Machine Design, Machine Elements, Machine Work, Metals and Alloys, Plastic Working, Welding
Department of Systems Engineering
Casting Engineering, Control Engineering, Data Analysis, Data Processing, Electromagnetics, Engineering of Electronic Materials, Information Mathematics, Mathematical Planning, Opto-electronics, Quality Control, Technology of Metal Surface

Foreign Student Admission
Qualifications for Applicants
Standard Qualifications Requirement
Examination at the University
Applicants must take an entrance examination, consisting of a written examination and an interview, and the Japanese language proficiency tests given in the entrance examination.
Documents to be Submitted When Applying

Standard Documents Requirement

GRADUATE PROGRAMS

Graduate School of Engineering (First Year Enrollment : Master's 24, Doctor's 4)
Divisions
Architecture, Electrical Engineering, Mechanical Engineering

*

Research Institutes and Centers
Building Engineering Center, Electrical Laboratories Center, Health Care and Physical Education Center, Information Technology Center, Institute of Industrial Education, Machining and Processing Center, Materials Testing Center, Museum of Industrial Technology, Ultra High Voltage Laboratory
Facilities/Services for Foreign Students
N. I. T. is planning to offer Japanese courses at the Institute of Language for Foreigners in the near future.
Special Programs for Foreign Students
Japanese language programs will contain the following: Technical exercises and Laboratories.
For Further Information
Undergraduate and Graduate Admission
Office of Educational Affairs, Nippon Institute of Technology, 4–1 Gakuendai, Miyashiro-machi, Minamisaitama-gun, Saitama 345 ☎ 0480–34–4111 ext. 246

Nippon Medical School
(Nippon Ika Daigaku)
1-1-5 Sendagi-cho, Bunkyo-ku, Tokyo 113
☎ 03-822-2131

Faculty
    Profs. 54   Assoc. Profs. 87
    Assist. Profs. Full–time 111; Part–time 95
    Res. Assocs. 481
Number of Students
    Undergrad. 625   Grad. 145
Library 183, 460 volumes

Outline and Characteristics of the College
The history of Nippon Medical School (NMS) can be traced back to 1876. The school was established as "Saiseigakusha" and was located in Yushima, Tokyo. The first dean was Yasushi Hasegawa, a man who contributed much to the introduction of Western medical techniques to Japan.

In 1903, Saiseigakusha was closed down for unknown reasons with the unfortunate result that its students lost their places. A man named Kenzo Isobe resolved to settle this state of affairs by establishing a new medical school to take the place of Saiseigakusha. His efforts were rewarded the following year with the foundation of Private Nippon Medical

School in Awaji-cho, Kanda, Tokyo. The school was later moved to Sendagi-cho, Hongo, Tokyo, where it has stood for the last three quarters of a century. The movement of the school to Sendagi ties in with the purchase of Private Tokyo Medical School which had previously occupied the site.

In the final year of the Meiji Era (1912), the Ministry of Education recognized Shiritsu Nippon Igaku-ko as an official medical school and renamed it "Nippon Igaku Senmon Gakko". At the same time, NISG Hongo Hospital was opened. These developments established both the school and the hospital in the Japanese medical world. Both were destined to function as a connecting point between the medical bureaucracy and medical care, and medical science and medical technology. The guiding spirit of the school has always been "Surmount the self and serve the public", a motto which reflects the Japanese concept of harmony within society, and to a wider extent, within nature.

In the latter part of the Taisho era, a second hospital, NISG Iida-cho Hospital, was built in Iida-cho, Tokyo. It suffered heavy damage during its construction in the Great Kanto Earthquake of 1923. In 1926, NISG was officially recognized as a medical college and was renamed "Nippon Ika Daigaku" (NMS), its present name. At this time, the pre-medical course was set up in Maruko, Kawasaki. Iida-cho and Hongo hospitals were renamed NMS First and Second Hospitals. In addition, NMS Third Hospital was established on a site next to the Maruko school building. Little is officially recorded about the wartime activities of the school or its doctors. It is known, however, that more than 80% of its buildings were exposed to successive air raids. Most of the professors and students carried on their work at Tsuruoka, Yamagata.

After the war, the professors and students returned to Tokyo. Along with the rapid reconstruction of the towns and cities of Tokyo, Nippon Medical School also soon regained its position in society and its perspective.

Large scale reconstruction has taken place since the end of the War. On the School's enlarged site at Sendagi, the building for the study of basic medicine was erected in 1957, that for the graduate course in 1961 and the main building of NMS Hospital (formerly NMS Second Hospital) was completed in 1963.

At Shin Maruko, Kawasaki, the building for the basic science course was constructed next to the renamed Second Hospital in 1961. This enabled a complete six-year education in basic science, basic medicine and clinical medicine. Nippon Medical School's fourth and latest hospital, NMS Tama-Nagayama Hospital, was opened in 1977. It is located in the south western part of Tokyo. Naturally, NMS First Hospital continues its operations at Iidabashi in central Tokyo. The Central Building and library were completed at Sendagi in 1974 to celebrate the 70th anniversary of the school.

In step with the rapid progress of medical science and technology, all the courses and departments at the School and at its hospitals are being enlarged, modernized and reorganized. The Critical Care Unit at NMS Hospital in Sendagi (the first in Japan to be officially approved by the Ministry of Welfare) is especially well-equipped to meet the needs of the time. Finally, the project for the enlargement of NMS Hospital in Sendagi, started in 1983 in commemoration of the 80th anniversary of Nippon Medical School, has complated in 1986.

UNDERGRADUATE PROGRAMS

Faculty of Medicine (Freshmen Enrollment: 100)
Department of Medicine
Anatomy, Anesthesiology, Biochemistry, Clinical Pathology, Dermatology, Emergency and Critical Care Medicine, Hygiene and Public Health, Internal Medicine, Legal Medicine, Microbiology and Immunology, Neuropsychiatry, Neurosurgery, Obstetrics and Gynecology, Ophthalmology, Orthopedics, Otorhinolaryngology, Pathology, Pediatrics, Pharmacology, Physiology, Radiology, Surgery, Urology

Foreign Student Admission
Qualifications for Applicants
Standard Qualifications Requirement
Examination at the College
There are some openings for foreign students and entrance examinations will be given at the discretion of the School.
Documents to be Submitted When Applying
Standard Documents Requirement

Qualifications for Transfer Students
There are some openings for foreign transfer students.
Examination for Transfer Students
Entrance examinations will be given at the discretion of the college.
Documents to be Submitted When Applying
Standard Documents Requirement

GRADUATE PROGRAMS

Graduate School of Medicine (First Year Enrollment : Doctor's 248)
Divisions
Anatomy, Anesthesiology, Biochemistry, Clinical Pathology, Dermatology, Emergency and Critical Care, Hygiene and Public Health, Internal Medicine, Legal Medicine, Microbiology and Immunology, Neuropsychiatry, Neurosurgery, Obstetrics and Gynecology, Ophthalmology, Orthopedics, Otorhinolaryngology, Pathology, Pediatrics, Pharmacology, Physiology, Radiology, Surgery, Urology

Foreign Student Admission

Qualifications for Applicants
Doctor's Program
    Standard Qualifications Requirement
    Applicants for Clinical Medicine courses should hold a Japanese Medical Practitioner's License.
    Examination at the College
Doctor's Program
    Some paper examinations will be given. However Admission will depend mainly upon academic record, personality and physical health.
    Documents to be Submitted When Applying
    Standard Documents Requirement
    Other necessary documents will be requested on admission.

*

Research Institutes and Centers
Institute for the Study of Geriatric Diseases, Institute for the Study of Vaccines
Facilities/Services for Foreign Students
    Hall of Residence for Foreign Students is available.
For Further Information
    Undergraduate and Graduate Admission
The Teaching Affairs Division, Educational Affairs Department, Nippon Medical School, 1-1-5 Sendagi-cho, Bunkyo-ku, Tokyo 113 ☎ 03-822-2131

Nippon Veterinary and Zootechnical College

(Nippon Juichikusan Daigaku)

1-7-1 Kyonan-cho, Musashino-shi, Tokyo 180
☎ 0422-31-4151

Faculty
    Profs. 32   Assoc. Profs. 16
    Assist. Profs. Full–time 21; Part–time 55
    Res. Assocs. 23
Number of Students
    Undergrad. 1, 109   Grad. 137
Library 70, 003 volumes

Outline and Characteristics of the College
    Nippon Veterinary and Zootechnical College has its origin in the Civil Veterinary School chartered by the Tokyo Metropolitan Government. It has remained as a private school since its establishment in 1881, and now is a division of the Nippon Foundation for Medical Education, Inc.
    The objective of this school is to contribute to the welfare and cultural enhancement of mankind, based on the principles of the Japanese Constitution. Our mission is to offer academic training for the students in the fields of veterinary medicine, animal husbandry, and food science and technology, as well as performing research and professional services in related fields. Equally important is our commitment in developing wellrounded individuals through intellec-

tual as well as physical training.
    The campus is conveniently located in a western suburb of Tokyo, a half-an-hour ride by train from the downtown. The location provides an excellent environment for studying and maintaining a large number of animals within campus, while being easily accessible to the downtown Tokyo area where some public and private research institutions are located.
    The School of Veterinary Medicine and Animal Husbandry which offers undergraduate education is divided into four Departments; Departments of Veterinary Medicine, Animal Husbandry, Food Science and Technology, and Liberal Arts. Undergraduate students are required to take general education courses offered by the Department of Liberal Arts during the first two years. For those students majoring in animal husbandry or food science and technology, professional courses are offered during the following two-year period. The graduates of these courses will receive bachelor's degree in agricultural science. The undergraduate students majoring in veterinary medicine take another four-year professional education program after general education. Upon successful completion, they will receive the D.V.M. degree which is one of the prerequisites for taking the National Board Examination for Veterinary Licensing. The Graduate School currently offers both Master's and Doctor's courses in the Veterinary Science for degrees equivalent to M.S. and Ph.D.
    The school employs a semester system with the semesters commencing April and October. The student enrollment is 585 in the Departments of Animal Husbandry, and Food Science and Technology, and 661 in the Department of Veterinary Medicine (including graduate students). The alumni association has almost 12, 000 active members and is one of the largest of its kind in the veterinary and animal science field.

UNDERGRADUATE PROGRAMS

School of Veterinary Medicine and Animal Husbandry (Freshmen Enrollment: 180)
    Department of Animal Husbandry
Agricultural Economics, Animal Breeding, Animal Nutrition and Feeding, Livestock Management
    Department of Food Science and Technology
Dairy Science, Food Chemistry, Food Hygiene, Food Machine, Meat Science
    Department of Veterinary Medicine
Animal Reproduction, Fish Disease, Laboratory Animal Science, Radio Veterinary Medicine Veterinary Anatomy, Veterinary Clinical Pathology, Veterinary Hygiene, Veterinary Internal Medicine, Veterinary Microbiology, Veterinary Parasitology, Veterinary Pathology, Veterinary Pharmacology, Veterinary Physiological Chemistry, Veterinary Physiology, Veterinary Public Health, Veterinary Surgery, Wild Animal Medicine

Foreign Student Admission

Qualifications for Applicants
Standard Qualifications Requirement
Examination at the College
Applicants are required to take the written tests.
Documents to be Submitted When Applying
Standard Documents Requirement

GRADUATE PROGRAMS

Graduate School of Veterinary Science (First Year Enrollment: Doctor's 5)
Division
Veterinary Science

Foreign Student Admission

Qualifications for Applicants
Doctor's Program
Standard Qualifications Requirement
Examination at the College
Doctor's Program

The regular examination is given in March. It consists of written and oral examinations. For foreign students who wish to start the semester in April and October, the examination is given in March and September, respectively.

The test for foreign students consists of an oral examination.

Documents to be Submitted When Applying
Standard Documents Requirement

*

Research Institutes and Centers
Laboratory of Molecular Oncology, University Farm, Veterinary Medical Teaching Hospital
For Further Information
Undergraduate and Graduate Admission
Educational Affairs Office, Nippon Veterinary and Zootechnical College, 1-7-1 Kyonan-cho, Musashino-shi, Tokyo 180 ☎ 0422-31-4151 ext. 220

Nishikyushu University
(Nishikyushu Daigaku)

4490-9 Hirayama, Osaki, Kanzaki-machi, Kanzaki-gun, Saga 842 ☎ 0952-52-4191

UNDERGRADUATE PROGRAMS

Faculty of Home Economics (Freshmen Enrollment: 150)
Department of Food and Nutrition
Department of Social Welfare

Nishinippon Institute of Technology
(Nishinippon Kogyo Daigaku)

1633 Aratsu, Kanda-cho, Miyako-gun, Fukuoka 800-03 ☎ 09302-3-1491

Faculty
Profs. 16 Assoc. Profs. 29
Assist. Profs. Full–time 8; Part–time 53
Res. Assocs. 9
Number of Students
Undergrad. 1, 888
Library 88, 214 volumes

Outline and Characteristics of the University

Nishinippon Institute of Technology was founded in 1967 by the Educational Foundation of Nishinippon Kogyo Gakuen in order to meet the growing and diversified demands of Kitakyushu, the local community noted as the marufacturing center of northern Kyushu.

In 1967, there were two departments, Mechanical Engineering and Electrical Engineering, and the next year NIT added two other departments, Civil Engineering and Architecture. The following 18 years have seen the successive establishment of various educational facilities such as a multipurpose gymnasium, a geotechnical research institute, and an information processing center.

The completion of those facilities and the emphasis on character building, combined with a technical education, have raised NIT up to a prominent position among the colleges of this field in western Japan. In 1983, the Department of Electrical Engineering, consisting of two courses, Electric Power and Electronics, added a third, Computer Science. Correspondingly, the information processing center was enlarged to keep pace with the advent of the information age.

Since its foundation, NIT has been consistent in its educational policy, aiming at the development of creative ability based on a complete mastery of fundamental technical skill. As a result, NIT has been successful in producing and sending out into the world graduates highly equipped with the creative and technical skills needed by engineers. To fulfill the requirements of a thorough mastery of technical knowledge and practical skills, a method of education peculiar to this institution has been introduced and put into practice under the institute's name, the NIT System. In this system, emphasis is placed on the ability and aptitude of individual students, and courses of study are diversified in accordance with the learning level of each student.

Concurrently with the development of technical skills, the institute also places much importance on the formation of character. NIT believes that character is an essential factor in the cultivation of refined manners based on humaneness and sound sentiments marked by a strong individuality and an enterprising spirit not to be daunted in the presence of formidable difficulties. It is to this fulfillment that each of the students is expected to strive for so that he may have his own share in the leading role to be played by Japan in an international society.

UNDERGRADUATE PROGRAMS

Faculty of Technology (Freshmen Enrollment: 320)
Department of Architecture
Architectural History, Architectural Planning, Building Equipment, Building Materials, City Planning and Urban Design, Construction Methods, Environmental Engineering, Housing, Structural Design and Mechanics
Department of Civil Engineering
Bridge Engineering, City Planning, Civil Engineering Planning, Concrete Engineering, Foundation Engineering, Hydraulics, Industrial Explosives, Reinforced Concrete Engineering, River Engineering, Road Engineering, Soil Mechanics, Structural Materials, Structural Mechanics, Surveying
Department of Electrical Engineering
Communication Engineering, Computer Organization, Computer Programming, Electrical Circuit, Electromagnetic Energy Conversion, Electromagnetism, Electronic Circuit, Electronic Devices, Power Engineering
Department of Mechanical Engineering
Computer Technology, Control Engineering, Engineering Thermodynamics, Field Work of Machine and Metal, Fluid Mechanics, Machine Design and Drawing, Material Science, Mechanical Engineering, Strength of Material

*

Research Institutes and Centers
Geotechnical Research Institute, Information Processing Center
For Further Information
Undergraduate Admission
Instruction Division, Nishinippon Institute of Technology, 1633 Aratsu, Kanda-cho, Miyako-gun, Fukuoka 800-03 ☎ 09302-3-1491 ext. 246

Nisho-Gakusha University
(Nisho-Gakusha Daigaku)

6 Sanban-cho, Chiyoda-ku, Tokyo 102
☎ 03-261-7407

Faculty
    Profs. 38   Assoc. Profs. 18
    Assist. Profs. Full–time 8; Part–time 58
Number of Students
    Undergrad. 1,912   Grad. 37

Library   130,000 volumes

Outline and Characteristics of the University
Nisho-Gakusha School for the Study of Chinese Classics was founded by Chusyu Ki Mishima in 1877. In 1928, this school was raised to the status of college and named Nisho-Gakusha College, in which the students majored in Japanese and Chinese classics. In 1949, conforming to the education system reform, this college was reorganized into Nisho-Gakusha University, which is composed of the Faculty of Literature. This faculty consists of two departments: the Department of Japanese Literature and the Department of Chinese Literature.

The basic principle that underlies its academic activities is the pursuit of Oriental studies and by doing so, help sustain and enhance Japanese culture. In order to promote this principle, what is basic to all is the understanding and recognition of our own culture. As a matter of fact, before the Meji era, our cultural basis was Chinese culture, namely, the Chinese classics. Its influence upon Japanese culture is so enormous that Japanese culture and Chinese culture are inseparable. Thus, it is the educational policy of this university to give the students an opportunity to fully study Chinese literature as well as Japanese literature. This is the chief characteristic of this university. Thus, graduates from this university show a tendency to become teachers of Japanese in various parts of the nation. The number is on the increase every year.

In addition to the above-mentioned, the university has two chairs: the Chair of Calligraphy and the Chair of Current Chinese. The former is for those who want to become teachers of calligraphy, and the latter for those who intend to engage in trade with China.

The freshmen and sophomores study subjects for general education, foreign languages, physical education, and basic majors on the campus located at Shonan, Chiba. The juniors and seniors concentrate of their majors on the campus located at Chiyoda-ku, Tokyo.

UNDERGRADUATE PROGRAMS

Faculty of Literature (Freshmen Enrollment: 400)
Department of Chinese Literature
Chinese Language, Chinese Literature, Chinese Literature and Philosophy, Chinese Literature in Japan, Chinese Philology, Contemporary China, History of Chinese Literature, History of Oriental Philosophy, Modern Chinese Culture
Department of Japanese Literature
Comparative Literature, Dramatic Literature, History of Japanese Literature, History of Japanese Philology, History of Modern Japanese Thought, History of the Japanese Language, Japanese Buddhism, Japanese Literature, Japanese Philology, Juvenile Literature, Linguistics

Foreign Student Admission
Qualifications for Applicants
Standard Qualifications Requirement
Examination at the University
Foreign students must take the same entrance exam as Japanese applicants.
Documents to be Submitted When Applying
Standard Documents Requirement

GRADUATE PROGRAMS

Graduate School of Literature (First Year Enrollment : Master's 10, Doctor's 4)
Divisions
Japanese Literature, Science of Studying China

Foreign Student Admission
Qualifications for Applicants
Master's Program
Standard Qualifications Requirement
Doctor's Program
Standard Qualifications Requirement
Examination at the University
Master's Program
For applicants majoring in Japanese Literature, examinations in English, Chinese Classics and majors related to the Japanese language and Japanese literature and oral quiz are given.
For applicants majoring in the Science of Studying China, examinations in English, Current Chinese, and majors related to the Science of Studying China and an oral quiz are given.
Doctor's Program
Examinations in the same subjects as Master's Program and an oral quiz are given.
Documents to be Submitted When Applying
Standard Documents Requirement
Following papers are also to be submitted.
Applicants for admission to the Master's Program should submit:
1. graduation thesis or its equivalent
2. its summary written in less than 1, 200 characters.
Applicants for admission to the Doctor's Program should submit:
1. master's thesis
2. its summary written in less than 1, 200 characters.

*

Research Institutes and Centers
The Institute for Oriental Studies, The Institute of the Doctrines of Wang Yang-ming
For Further Information
Undergraduate and Graduate Admission
Entrance Examination Section, instruction Division, instruction Office, Nisho-Gakusha University, 6 Sanban-cho, Chiyoda-ku, Tokyo 102 ☎ 03-265-3758

Notre Dame Seishin University
(Notre Dame Seishin Joshi Daigaku)
2-16-9 Ifuku-cho, Okayama-shi, Okayama 700
☎ 0862-52-1155

Faculty
Profs.   40   Assoc. Profs.   17
Assist. Profs.   Full–time   17; Part–time   89
Res. Assocs.   4
Number of Students
Undergrad.   2, 014
Library   169, 072 volumes

Outline and Characteristics of the University
Notre Dame Seishin University with its educational ideal based on Christianity pursues truth, goodness and beauty fostering in each student the desire to be a real liberal person through education and research, providing opportunities to pursue the significance of living.
In 1944 Okayama Seishin Women's School was established. In 1949 Notre Dame Seishin University, Faculty of Arts and Science (Department of English Literature, Department of Home Economics) was established. In 1952 structure changed by the establishment of a new faculty. Faculty of Literature (Department of English Literature, Department of Japanese Literature), Faculty of Home Economics (Department of Home Economics) were established. In 1964 Department of Child Welfare in the Faculty of Home Economics was opened. In 1965 Department of Foods and Human Nutrition in the Faculty of Home Economics and Attached Kindergarten were opened.
In the Faculty of Literature and the Faculty of Home Economics, the number quota every year is 390. The total enrollment is about 2, 000. As attached institutions, Notre Dame Seishin University has Christian Research Center, Library, Kindergarten and Elementary School. As sister schools, Notre Dame Seishin University has Notre Dame Junior College and five schools in or outside Okayama Prefecture.

UNDERGRADUATE PROGRAMS

Faculty of Home Economics (Freshmen Enrollment: 210)
Department of Child Welfare
Department of Foods and Human Nutrition
Department of Home Economics
Faculty of Literature (Freshmen Enrollment   180)
Department of English Language and Literature
Department of Japanese Language and Literature

Foreign Student Admission
Qualifications for Applicants
Standard Qualifications Requirement

Female of foreign nationality.

Examination at the University

Selection of foreign students corresponds to the recommendation examination.

For residents in Japan: examination of written documents, interview, and short thesis.

For residents outside Japan: examination of written documents

Documents to be Submitted When Applying

Standard Documents Requirement

Following documents are also required.

1. Document written by the applicant explaining the reasons why she would like to study abroad.
2. Certificates of the Japanese Language Proficiency Test
3. Documents guaranteeing sufficient continued financial support

*

Research Institutes and Centers

Child Clinic Institute, Christian Research Center, Institute of Human Studies, Institute of Life Style Culture, Research Institute for Informatics and Science

Facilities/Services for Foreign Students

Foreign students are given priority to live in the boarding school.

For Further Information

Undergraduate Admission

Section of International Exchange, Administration Office, Notre Dame Seishin University, 2-16-9 Ifuku –cho, Okayama-shi, Okayama 700 ☎ 0862-52-1155 ext. 507

Notre Dame Women's College
(Notorudamu Joshi Daigaku)

1 Minami-Nonogami-cho, Shimogamo, Sakyo-ku, Kyoto-shi, Kyoto 606 ☎ 075-781-1173

Faculty
  Profs. 16   Assoc. Profs. 15
  Assist. Profs. Full–time 7; Part–time 47
  Res. Assocs. 5
Number of Students
  Undergrad. 1, 097
Library 89, 578 volumes

Outline and Characteristics of the College

Notre Dame Women's College is a four-year college approved by the Ministry of Education in March 1961. It is based on the spirit of Catholicism as well as on the fine traditions of Japanese culture. The college aims to contribute to the promotion of Japanese culture through professional research and by providing higher education for women. The religious congregation of the School Sisters of Notre Dame is the primary founder of the college. This congregation was established by Mother Mary Theresa Gerhardinger in Bavaria in 1833. From the very

beginning the congregation devoted itself to education and achieved a swift and lasting growth throughout the world.

In 1948 the congregation undertook its first educational endeavors in the Orient. The former president, Sister Mary Eugenia, together with three other religious sisters came from the Motherhouse of the Southern Province in St. Louis, Missouri, to Kyoto, where they decided to establish the center of their educational works.

After three years' preparation a junior high school was inaugurated in 1952, a senior high school in 1953 and a primary school in 1954. At the request of many, Notre Dame Women's College (the Department of English Language and Literature) was opened in March 1961. Since April 1963, when the Department of Cultural Living was set up to expand the curriculum, the college has been making continual progress as a general educational institution for women.

The goal of the college is to educate students to be women of "virtue and knowledge"—as the international motto of the School Sisters of Notre Dame states—that is, to be women with a deep religious sense who, at the same time, respect the traditional culture of Japan while striving to become women with an international view and are independent, responsible and cooperative.

UNDERGRADUATE PROGRAMS

Faculty of Literature (Freshmen Enrollment: 140)

  Department of Cultural Living

Aesthetics, Clothing Practice, Clothing Theory, Food Chemistry, Food Hygiene, Food Practice, History of Art, History of Clothing, Home Management, Physical Clothing, Psychology

  Department of English

Communication Arts, English and American Literature, Linguistics

Foreign Student Admission

  Qualifications for Applicants

  Standard Qualifications Requirement

  In our college, a"foreign student"means only a student recommended by an ambassador or by the authority of some public organization, who is admitted through the entrance examinations (administered in the Japanese language). At present no other system for foreign students is provided.

*

For Further Information

Undergraduate Admission

Dean of Registrar, Registrar's Office, Notre Dame Women's College, 1 Minami-Nonogami-cho, Shimogamo, Sakyo-ku, Kyoto-shi, Kyoto 606 ☎ 075-781-1173

Obirin University
(Obirin Daigaku)

3758 Tokiwa-cho, Machida-shi, Tokyo 194–02
☎ 0427–97–2661

Faculty
    Profs. 43   Assoc. Profs. 20
    Assist. Profs. Full–time 15; Part–time 115
    Res. Assocs. 2
Number of Students
    Undergrad. 2, 825
Library 246, 000 volumes

Outline and Characteristics of the University

Obirin University is the mainstay of Obirin Gakuen which consists of an attached secondary education school system, and a Junior College. The junior high school, women's high school, and post-graduate English language course were established in 1946. Four years later, the English language course was expanded to create the Junior College English Department. 1955 saw the inauguration of the Home Economics Department in the Junior College.

The University was founded in 1966 with the inauguration of the Departments of English and Chinese. Then, the Economics Department in 1970 and the Commerce Department in 1972 were added to form the Economics Faculty. Thus, the Literature and the Economics Faculties today form the pillars of Obirin University.

All parts of Obirin Gakuen are integrated on one campus. A total of 5, 820 students from secondary school through College students are members of the Obirin family. Also foreign students regularly come to Obirin to study Japanese language and culture.

The school is committed to the founding principle: "Raising Internationally-Minded Citizens with Christian Ideals." All of the institution's activities are dedicated to realizing these ideals.

Yasuzo Shimizu, Obirin's founder, spent 30 years in China from 1916 to 1945 administering Chungchen School in Peking, a school devoted to educating Chinese girls and propagating Christianity. Obirin's unique name can be traced to a different international strand in Shimizu's life: his years at his alma mater, Oberlin College, in the United States. Thus, considering the founder's active background in China and the United States, it is only natural that the school from its founding be dedicated to international understanding.

In the western suburbs of Tokyo, the 243, 000 m² campus is situated at the Tama foothills. The clear air and natural surrounding make it conducive to study. In fact, from the classrooms one can enjoy a view of Mt. Fuji and the Tanzawa mountain range in the distance.

UNDERGRADUATE PROGRAMS

Faculty of Economics (Freshmen Enrollment: 400)
Department of Commerce
Accounting, Analysis of Management, Bookkeeping, Business Trade, Commerce, Commercial Policy, Finance/Inspection, Financial Labor Management, Foreign Exchange, History of Commerce, Insurance, International Commerce, Japanese Commercial History, Management, Marketing, Medium and Minor Enterprises, Merchandising, Personnel/Labor Management, Public Relations, Taxation and Business Accounts, The Securities Market, Trade Relations, Transportation
Department of Economics
Agricultural Policy, Business Fluctuation Theory, Econometrics, Economic History, Economic Policy, Economics, Finance, Financial Theory, Geography of Economics, History of Japanese Economics, Income Theory, Industrial Organization, Industrial Policy, Industrial Systems, International Economic Theory, International Finance, Labor and Management, Modern Economics, Philosophy of Economics, Society and Politics, Statistics, Technological Theory

Faculty of International Studies (Freshman Enrollment: 200)
  American Studies Major
American Diplomacy, American Economy, American History, American Intellectual History, American Literature and Cultural Climate, American Politics, American Social History, Contemporary American Society, Principles of American Studies, Seminar in American Studies
  Asian Studies Major
Anglo-Asian Cultures in Asia, Asian Education, Asian Ethnic Groups and History, Asian Language and Literature, Asian Politics and Economics, Asian Politics and Society, Asian Religoin and Thought, Nature and Culture in Asia, Principles of Asian Studies, Seminar in Asian Studies
  Comparative Culture Major
Buddhist Cultures Islamic Cultures, Christian Cultures, Comparative Education, Comparative Ethnography, Comparative Sociology, Crass-Cultural Communications, Cultural Anthropology, Principles of Comparative Culture, Psychological Anthropology, Select Topics in Comparative Culture, Seminor in Comparative Culture, Social Psychology
  Foundation Courses
Introduction to Communications, Introduction to Comparative Culture, Introduction to Human Relations, Introduction to Information Science, Introduction to International Economics, Introduction to International Relations, Introduction to Linguistics, Japanese History, Theory of Area Studies
  International Relations Major
Comparative Society, Economic Policy, Ethnographic Studies, Fieldwork in International Relations, His-

tory of International Relations, International Economics, International Law, International Organizations, International Politics, Multinational Corporations, Regional Development, Select Topics in International Relations, Seminar in International Relations

Japanese Studies Major

Cultural Studies on Japan, History of Japanese Language, Japanese Art, Japanese Economy, Japanese Education, Japanese Intellectual History, Japanese Literature, Japanese Phonetics, Japanese Politics, Japanese Religions and Thought, Japanese Society, Modern Japanese History, Principles of Japanese Linguistics, Principles of Japanese Studies, Seminar in Japanese Studies, Teaching Japanese as a Foreign Language

Faculty of Literature (Freshmen Enrollment: 250)

Department of Chinese

Calligraphy, Chinese History, Chinese Language, Chinese Linguistics, Chinese Literary History, Chinese Literature, Chinese Thought

Department of English

American Literature, American Studies Christian Literature, Comparative Literature, English andAmerican Drama, English Linguistics, English Literature, English Phonology, English Poetry, History of the English Language, Linguistics, Literary Criticism

*

Research Institutes and Centers

Center for International Studies, English Literary Society, Society for Industrial Economics

For Further Information

Undergraduate and Graduate Admission

Admissions Office, Obirin University, 3758 Tokiwa-cho, Machida-shi, Tokyo 194–02 ☎ 0427–97–2661

Ohtani Women's College
(Ohtani Joshi Daigaku)

Shigakudai, Nishikiori, Tondabayashi-shi, Osaka 584   ☎ 0721-24-0381

Faculty
    Profs.   32   Assoc. Profs.   28
    Assist. Profs.   Full–time   9; Part–time   107
    Res. Assocs.   3
Number of Students
    Undergrad.   2, 282   Grad.   18
Library   150, 000 volumes

Outline and Characteristics of the College

The origin of Ohtani Women's College can be traced back to 1909, when Ohtani Girls' School was founded by the Reverend Ryoshu Sato at the Nanba Branch Temple in the City of Osaka. The aim of the college has been to educate and encourage young girls to be aware of their religion and their position in this present society and to fulfil their roles in bringing up the next generation.

Ohtani Women's College opened for instruction at Shigakudai, Nishikiori, Tondabayashi in 1966. Tondabayashi is situated in the outskirts of Osaka and provides a good environment for students. The College then consisted of just two departments: Japanese and English. The Department of Childhood Education was established in 1970, and enrollment and facilities started growing steadily. When instruction began at the graduate level in Japanese and English studies in 1975, the College had grown to be about six times the size of the faculty and the student body of the early days.

Ohtani college students will be able to immerse themselves in college-level academic work and build the foundations of their general education. The Graduate School offers programs leading to the Master's and Ph. D. degrees. Thus the College today is a modern college embracing not only undergraduate but graduate instruction. Students and faculty members all work together to deepen their knowledge with a view to applying it in the service of their fellow man and society.

UNDERGRADUATE PROGRAMS

Faculty of Literature (Freshmen Enrollment: 480)

Department of Childhood Education

Fine Arts, Health and Physical Education, Home Economics, Japanese, Mathematics, Music, Natural Sciences, Pedagogy, Psychology, Social Sciences

Department of English

English and American Literature, History of English and American Literature, Linguistics, Philology

Department of Japanese

History of Japanese Literature, History of Japanese Songs, Japanese Folklore, Japanese Literature

*

For Further Information

Undergraduate Admission

Administrative Office, Ohtani Women's College, Shigakudai, Nishikiori, Tondabayashi-shi, Osaka 584 ☎ 0721-24-0381

Okayama College of Commerce
(Okayama Shoka Daigaku)

2-10-1 Tsushima-Kyo-machi, Okayama-shi, Okayama 700   ☎ 0862-52-0642

Faculty
    Profs.   24   Assoc. Profs.   17
    Assist. Profs.   Full–time   10; Part–time   49
    Res. Assoc.   1
Number of Students
    Undergrad.   2, 533
Library   142, 832 volumes

Outline and Characteristics of the College

Okayama College of Commerce was founded in

1965. It has one faculty, and the faculty consists of two departments. One is the Department of Business Administration and the other is the Department of Commerce. Each Department is divided into five courses. The student is expected to receive intimate instruction, since the College is a small one. It has the advantage of maintaining friendly relationships between teachers and students. Another important aspect is that it has always been on good terms with the local communities and has done its share in many activities.

The campus is situated in the west section of the City of Okayama, about four kilometers from the center of the City. Okayama is an important transportation center of the Chugoku District and has a population of about 600,000. Moreover, Okayama and the surrounding area in which the college is located are especially favored by natural beauty, a mild climate and the absence of most types of natural disasters. The campus lies in the surburbs, amongst tranquil surroundings. The environment of the College is an ideal one.

The following ideals are those that have existed since the College's founding: (1) to train students to be persons who serve society with fairness and broad vison, (2) to train students to be persons who have passion and a fighting spirit toward truth and academia, (3) to train students tobe persons who have a realistic interest in industry and cultural intelligence.

UNDERGRADUATE PROGRAMS

Faculty of Commerce (Freshmen Enrollment: 450)
Department of Business Administration
Accounting, Bookkeeping, Information Science, Management and Organization Theory, Private Law
Department of Commerce
Commercial History, Commercial Policy, Economics, General Theory of Commerce, Marketing

Foreign Student Admission
Qualifications for Applicants
Standard Qualifications Requirement
Applicants are required to take the Japanese Language Proficiency Test and the General Examination for Foreign Students.
Examination at the College
Japanese, Interview.
Documents to be Submitted When Applying
Standard Documents Requirement
*
Research Institutes and Centers
Research Institutes for Economics and Management
Facilities/Services for Foreign Students
College club-house (Accommodations: 20).
For Further Information
Undergraduate Admission
Secretary General, College Office, Okayama College of Commerce, 2-10-1 Tsushima-Kyo-machi, Okayama-shi, Okayama 700 ☎ 0862-52-0642

ext. 203

Okayama University of Science
(Okayama Rika Daigaku)
1-1 Ridai-cho, Okayama-shi, Okayama 700
☎ 0862-52-3161

Faculty
　　Profs.　106　　　Assoc. Profs.　53
　　Assist. Profs.　Full-time　48; Part-time　66
　　Res. Assocs.　12
Number of Students
　　Undergrad.　4,753　　　Grad.　115
Library　187,231 volumes

Outline and Characteristics of the University

At the establishment of Okayama University of Science in 1964, with its two departments, the Department of Applied Mathematics and the Department of Chemistry, we have aimed at leading the fields of both science and technology in education and research through an interdisciplinary approach to learning. Since then we have endeavored to meet the demands of the ever-changing and ever-developing world of science education by adding new departments of study—Applied Chemistry in 1966, Mechanical Science and Electronic Science in 1975 Biological Chemistry in 1988—to our university curriculum, and by establishing a graduate school for a master's degree in 1975 and a doctor's degree in 1978.

With the remarkable innovations in technology, we find that the research and development of high technology and the preparation of young men and women who can actively contribute to these technological fields is especially urgent in Okayama where we are presently involved in the planning and realization of Kibi Heights Technopolis. In order to meet these demands, we have separated the Departments of Applied Chemistry, Mechanical Science and Electronic Science from the College of Science and established a new College of Engineering in 1986. This will enable an integrated, interdisciplinary study of both science and technology from the vantage point of both the scientist and the engineer.

Okayama City, which grew up as a castle town, is now rapidly developing into a megalopolis with its neighboring city Kurashiki. Situated on the Seto Inland Sea, we enjoy a mild climate and the beautiful Inland Sea with its many islands. Along with the sea, this area, long known for its agricultural products, boasts large areas of spreading fields and gardens. "Kibiji" road which has been used since ancient times can still be viewed in the city. Okayama University of Science is located in this city blessed with both a wide range of industrial opportunities and yet an area rich in natural beauties. The University campus, situated on the top of a hill surrounded by pine groves, commands a grand view of the entire city.

UNDERGRADUATE PROGRAMS

College of Engineering (Freshmen Enrollment: 447)

Department of Applied Chemistry

Applied Chemistry Course

Analytical Chemistry, Applied Chemistry, Chemical Engineering, Chemistry of Resources, Gene Engineering, Industrial Analytical Chemistry, Industrial Biochemistry, Industrial Chemistry, Industrial Physical Chemistry, Inorganic Chemistry, Inorganic Industrial Chemistry, Organic Chemistry, Organic Industrial Chemistry, Physical Chemistry, Polymer Chemistry, Structural Organic Chemistry

Developmental Chemistry Course

Air Quality Protection, Analytical Chemistry, Biochemistry, Environmental Chemical Engineering, Environmental Chemistry, Environmental Ecology, Environmental Physiology, Inorganic Chemistry, Instrumental Analysis, Organic Chemistry, Physical Chemistry, Radio Chemistry, Water Quality Protection

Department of Electronic Engineering

Electronic Engineering Course

Electronic Materials and Devices, Optical and Electromagnetic Wave Engineering, Quantum Electronics, Quantum Physics, Radiation Physics, Semiconductor Engineering, Solid State Electronics, Solid State Physics

Information/Systems Course

Communication System, Computer Mathematics, Control Engineering, Digital Circuit for Computer, Information System, Network Theory, Optical and Electromagnetic Wave Engineering, Software Engineering

Department of Mechanical Engineering

Fundamental Mechanical Engineering Course

Atomic Energy, Energy Conversion, Fluid Mechanics, Fundamental Mechanical Engineering, Material Mechanics, Material Properties, Mathematical Planning, Mechanical Dynamics, Numerical Analysis, Physical Measuring, Plasticity Mechanics, Production Control, Simulation, Thermodynamics

Industrial Mechanical Engineering Course

Control Engineering, Electromechanics, Fluid Machines, Heat Engines, Industrial Mathematics, Industrial Mechanical Engineering, Instruments Control, Kinematics of Machinery, Machine Work, Material Science for Machine, Mechanical Dynamics, Plasticity Processing, Precision Processing, Strength of Materials

College of Science (Freshmen Enrollment: 728)

Department of Applied Mathematics

Information Processing Course

Algebra, Combinatorial Mathematics, Data Structures, Electronic Computer Mathematics, Functional Analysis, Geometry, Graph Theory, Information Processing Language, Language Theory, Linear Algebra, Linear Programing, Mathematical Statistics, Simulation, Statistics, System Theory

Mathematics Course

Algebra, Analysis, Analysis, Electronical Computer Mathematics, Functional Analysis, Geometry, Graph Theory, Information Processing Language, Linear Algebra, Mathematical Statistics, Probability, Simulation, Statistics, Time Series Analysis

Department of Applied Physics

Atomic Physics, Censor System, Computer Mathematics, Low-Temperature Physics, Molecular Physics, Optical Physics, Physics of Fluids, Quantum Physics, Radiation Physics, Semiconductor Physics, Statistical Physics

Department of Biochemistry

Analytical Chemistry, Animal Physiology, Applied Microbiology, Biochemistry, Biochemistry, Bioorganic Chemistry, Biophysical Chemistry, Biopolymers Theory, Chemical Ecology, Cytology, Environmental Biochemistry Ecology, Enzymology, Experimental Method of Isotope, Experiments in Biochemistry, Experiments in Biochemistry Cytobiochemistry, Experiments in Fundamental, Gene Control Theory, Inorganic Chemistry, Instrumental Analysis, Introduction to Immunology, Introduction to Physiological Active Materials, Metobolic Regulation, Microbiology, Moleqular Physiology, Molequrar Genetics, Natural Products Chemistry, Organic Chemistry, Pathology, Physical Chemistry, Plant Physiology, Structual Theory for Organic Natural Products, Vital Information Theory

Department of Chemistry

Analytical Chemistry, Biological Chemistry, Bioorganic Chemistry, Catalytic Reaction Chemistry, Chemical Thermodynamics, Inorganic Chemistry, Interface Chemistry, Material Chemistry, Organic Chemistry, Organic Reaction Chemistry, Photochemistry, Physical Chemistry, Solid State Chemistry, Synthetic Inorganic Chemistry, Synthetic Organic Chemistry, Synthetic Polymer Chemistry

Department of Fundamental Natural Science

Algebra, Analysis, Analytical Chemistry, Anthropology, Biochemistry, Cosmic Physics, Ecology, Education Methodology, Electricity and Magnetism, Engineering of Education, Geochemistry, Geology, Geometry, Geoscience, Inorganic Chemistry, Mineralogy, Morphology, Numerical Mathematics, Organic Chemistry, Philosophy of Science Education, Physical Anthropology, Physics, Prehistory, Quantum Physics, Science Education, Statistics, Taxonomy, Topological Analysis

Foreign Student Admission

Qualifications for Applicants

Standard Qualifications Requirement

Examination at the University

Foreign applicants must undergo an interview and take the Japanese language proficiency test.

Documents to be Submitted When Applying

Standard Documents Requirement

GRADUATE PROGRAMS

Graduate School of Science (First Year Enrollment : Master's 49, Doctor's 7)
Divisions
Applied Mathematics, Applied Physics, Chemistry, Electronic Science, Fundamental Natural Science, Materials Science, Mechanical Science, System Science

Research Institutes and Centers
Central Research Center, Health Care Center, Hiruzen Research Institute, Information Processing Center, Instrumental Analysis Center, Machinery Working Center, Water Quality Control Center

Facilities/Services for Foreign Students
International House #1~#3 (Accomodation: #1–15, #2–One Family, #3–22)

Special Programs for Foreign Students
Japanese Language Class:
Special Classes in the Japanese language are offered at one of the affiliated schools of the University. These classes are for foreign students studying at the University or for those who have matriculated in the University.

For Further Information
Undergraduate and Graduate Admission
Admission Office, Department of Planning and Admission, Okayama University of Science, 1-1 Ridaicho, Okayama-shi, Okayama 700 ☎ 0862-52-3161 ext. 225

Okinawa Kokusai University
(Okinawa Kokusai Daigaku)

276-2 Ginowan, Ginowan-shi, Okinawa 901-22
☎ 09889-2-1111

Faculty
    Profs.　53　　Assoc. Profs.　13
    Assist. Profs.　Full–time　21; Part–time　52
Number of Students
    Undergrad.　3, 518
Library　121, 174 volumes

Outline and Characteristics of the University
Okinawa Kokusai University was founded on February 24, 1972 through the official recognition of the then Ryukyuan Government. When Okinawa was still under the U. S. administration, there were two private universities: Okinawan University and Kokusai University. But a study conducted in connection with the Okinawa reversion to the Japanese administration revealed that both universities had legal problems concerning accreditation standards set by Japanese law. As a result, the two universities worked toward a merger, and on February 24, 1972 the Ryukyuan Government officially approved the merger.

On April 23, Okinawa Kokusai University proclaimed its opening to the public as a university dedicated to the community. Then on May 15, when Okinawa was reverted to Japan, the University was recognized by the Japanese Government as a university. The Government took special measures to grant an endowment of one billion yen. With this aid as the core fund, the University further obtained a special long-term loan totalling 440 million yen from the Japan Private University Promotion Foundation. Now the University owns a total land space of 107, 857 m^2 and a total building space of 24, 485, 61 m^2.

Okinawa consists of over 60 islands replete with trees and flowers under the subtropical sun. It attracts over 2 million tourists a year from all over Japan and from overseas. Also situated at the crossroads of Asian nations, it functions as a meeting place for various cultural exchanges. Already many Asian nationalities stay, together with the 50, 000 Americans on military bases, and the Okinawa International Center was opened last year to train specialists from neighboring countries.

At present, the university has 15 foreign students and three full-time American teachers. It also administers the Southern Islands Cultural Institute which promotes research on Okinawa and the areas adjacent to it.

UNDERGRADUATE PROGRAMS

Faculty of Commerce and Economics (Freshmen Enrollment: Day 200, Evening 100)
Department of Commerce
Accounting, Auditing, Bookkeeping, Business History, Business Policy, Cost Accounting, Financial Management, History of Management, Information Management, Insurance, Management, Management Analysis, Management Controllership, Manufacturing Bookkeeping, Marketing Management, Marketing Research Methods, Money and Banking, Personnel Management, Public Finance, Retailing, Tax Accounting, Theory of Consumer's Behaviour, Transportation

Department of Economics
Agricultural Economics, Econometrics, Economic Development, Economic History, Economic History of Japan, Economic Policy, Economic Policy, Economics, Economics of Business Cycles, Economics of Fisheries, Economics of Socialism, Economics of Tourism, Economic Statistics, Environmental Economics, Foreign Economic Affairs, History of Economic Thought, Industrial Economics, International Economics, International Finance, Money and Banking, National Income Theory, Regional Economics, Social Security

Faculty of Law (Freshmen Enrollment: Day 100, Evening 50)
Department of Law
Administrative Law, Anglo-American Law, Bank-

ruptcy, Civil Executive Law, Civil Law, Civil Procedure, Commercial Law, Comparative Constitutional Law, Constitutional Law, Corporation Law, Criminal Law, Criminal Procedure, Criminology, Diplomatic History, Economic Law, Environmental Law, History of Legal Thought, International Law, International Politics, International Private Law, Judicial Process, Labor Law, Legal History, Legal Philosophy, Legal Sociology, Local Government Law, Politics, Social Security Law, Tax Law

Faculty of Letters (Freshmen Enrollment: 190)

Department of English Literature

Comparative Study of Japanese and English, English and American Children's Literature, English and American Literature, English and American Poetry, English Language, English Poetry, History of American Literature, History of English, History of English Literature, Linguistics, Medieval English Literature, Modern American Novels, Modern English Novels, Semantics, Shakespeare, Speech

Department of Japanese Literature

Chinese Literature, Folklore, History of Japanese Language, History of Japanese Literature, History of Okinawa, Japanese Expression Method, Japanese Grammar, Japanese Language, Japanese Literature, Japanese Phonetics, Okinawan Dialects, Okinawan Literature

Department of Sociology

Archaeology, Cultural Anthropology, Ethnology, History of Cultural Anthropology, History of Sociology, Journalism, Social Anthropology, Social Pathology, Social Psychology, Social Welfare, Sociology, Sociology of Family

Foreign Student Admission

Qualifications for Applicants

Standard Qualifications Requirement

Examination at the University

1. Personal interview
2. Japanese language proficiency examination

Documents to be Submitted When Applying

Standard Documents Requirement

In addition, certification of proficiency in Japanese (which must be completed by an instructor of Japanese, a diplomatic or consular official of Japanese government, or other qualified persons) must be submitted.

Research Institutes and Centers

The Southern Islands Cultural Institute

Facilities/Services for Foreign Students

The Foreign Student Reception Subcommittee takes care of the foreign students' academic problems, and the Students Affairs Department has solid programs to help them out in their life in Japan.

Special Programs for Foreign Students

1. Japanese
2. Method of Japanese Expression
3. Japanese Society
4. Natural Environment in Japan

For Further Information

Undergraduate Admission

Academic Affairs Section, Okinawa Kokusai University, 276-2 Ginowan, Ginowan-shi, Okinawa 901-22 ☎ 09889-2-1111 ext. 303

Osaka College of Music
(Osaka Ongaku Daigaku)

1-1-8 Shonai-Saiwai-machi, Toyonaka-shi, Osaka
561 ☎ 06-334-2131

Faculty
  Profs. 81   Assoc. Profs. 37
  Assist. Profs. Full–time 3; Part–time 268
  Res. Assocs. 2
Number of Students
  Undergrad. 1, 370   Grad. 56
Library 81, 165 volumes

Outline and Characteristics of the College

Osaka College of Music consists of the faculty of music and the graduate school. The former has Departments of Composition (composition and musicology), Vocal Music, Instrumental Music (piano, organ, strings, winds, percussion, Japanese traditional music). The latter has Composition Course (composition and musicology), Vocal Music Course (opera and Lied), and Instrumental Music Course (piano and strings). It has also a one-year graduate program.

This institution was founded by Koji Nagai with the ideals that it should be a center of music in the western area of Japan. By integrating all arts related to music, it might ultimately be a forum for creation of the source of new development of music and opera.

The predecessor of this institution was Osaka Music School established in 1915. In 1958, it was reorganized as Osaka College of Music offering a four-year course of undergraduate education. The Graduate School was added in 1968. Today it is indeed an integrated institution for music education.

This institution offers curricula that encourage the students to learn not only Western music but also Japanese traditional music and ethnomusicology. The students acquire a broad and deep knowledge of these arts.

Moreover, as the center of music activity in western Japan, the graduates and many other musicians, educators and researchers utilize its library, museum of musical instruments, music research institute and other facilities.

Concerts and clinics are given on campus almost everyday by visiting foreign musicians, faculty members and students. Seminars on music are regularly open to the general public as well.

The campus is located in Osaka, the second largest city in Japan, at a commutable distance from

Kyoto, Nara, and Kobe. In fact, Osaka College of Music stands where the history of Japan exists in harmony with modern civilization.

UNDERGRADUATE PROGRAMS

Faculty of Music (Freshmen Enrollment: 225)
Department of Composition
Composition Course
Analysis, Composition, Instrumentation, Theory of Composition
Musicology Course
Aesthetics on Music, Ethnomusicology, Harmony, History of Music, Musicology
Department of Instrumental Music
Japanese Traditional Music, Organ, Percussion Instrument, Piano, Stringed Instrument, Wind Instrument
Department of Vocal Music
Chorus, Histrionics, Opera, Vocal Ensemble

Foreign Student Admission
Examination at the College
1. Japanese language proficiency test (oral, writing, reading)
2. Examination relating to the department selected
3. Performance test

Qualifications for Transfer Students
The applicant must be a graduate of the department of music (the music course included) of a junior college, college or university.
Examination for Transfer Students
Same as the undergraduate procedure.

ONE-YEAR GRADUATE PROGRAMS

One-Year Graduate Course of Music (Enrollment: 10)
Composition, Instrumental Music, Vocal Music

Foreign Student Admission
Qualifications for Applicants
The applicant must be a graduate of a college or university of music or the equivalent (as approved by Osaka College of Music).
Examination at the College
Same as the undergraduate procedure.

GRADUATE PROGRAMS

Graduate School of Music (First Year Enrollment : Master's 10)
Divisions
Composition, Lied, Musicology, Opera, Piano, Strings

Foreign Student Admission
Qualifications for Applicants

Master's Program
Standard Qualifications Requirement
Examination at the College
Master's Program
Same as the undergraduate procedure.
Documents to be Submitted When Applying
Standard Documents Requirement

＊

Research Institutes and Centers
Museum of Musical Instruments, Music Research Institute
For Further Information
Undergraduate and Graduate Admission
Entrance Examination Division, Osaka College of Music, 1-1-8 Shonai-Saiwai-machi, Toyonaka-shi, Osaka 561 ☎ 06-334-2131 ext. 171

Osaka College of Physical Education
(Osaka Taiiku Daigaku)

1558–1 Oaza Noda, Kumatori-cho Sennan-gun, Osaka 590–04   ☎ 0724-53-7070

Faculty
Profs. 23   Assoc. Profs. 24
Assist. Profs. Full–time 13; Part–time 47
Res. Assocs.
Number of Students
Undergrad. 1, 586
Library 70, 000 volumes

Outline and Characteristics of the College
Osaka College of Physical Education, a part of the Namisho Educational Institution, was founded in 1965 to establish the new field of physical education. Namisho Educational Institution has a history of 67 years since its establishment in the great industrial and commercial area of Osaka in 1921 as Naniwa Commercial School and now has a senior high school, a junior high school, and a kindrgarten as well.

Revolutionary advances in scientific technology have made an urbanized and industrialized living enviroment and brought forth in magnified form a lack of physical exercise, man's estrangement from natural biological rhythms. Health can not be maintained with only a small amount of exercise. Quite a few peoplo, though young, are afflicted with lumbago or stiff shoulders. From the very nature of the things, a strong interest in health and physical fitness has grown. Moreover, the two days off work policy and longer life-spans have increased considerably the demand for physical fitness, sports and recreation.

Courses for training physical educators for schools have already been established in universities and colleges of physical education in Japan. The college aims to train sports, physical fitness and recreation leaders and instructors for industries and communities and one of the most important functions of it is to give the students highly-specialized knowledge and techniques of physical training to meet the demands of the times. The college accordingly has three courses of School Physical Education, Industry Physical Education, and Community Physical Education.

UNDERGRADUATE PROGRAMS

Faculty of Physical Education (Freshmen Enrollment: 200)
  Department of Physical Education
Community Physical Education Course
Industry Physical Education Course
School Physical Education Course

ONE-YEAR GRADUATE PROGRAMS

One-Year Graduate Course of Physical Education (Enrollment: 10)
Physical Education

*

For Further Information
  Undergraduate and Graduate Admission
Admissions Office, Osaka College of Physical Education, 1558-1 Oaza Noda, Kumatori-cho Sennan-gun, Osaka 590-04 ☎ 0724-53-7070

Osaka Dental University
(Osaka Shika Daigaku)

1-47 Kyobashi, Higashi-ku, Osaka-shi, Osaka 540
☎ 06-943-6521

UNDERGRADUATE PROGRAMS

Faculty of Dentistry (Freshmen Enrollment: 160)
  Department of Dentistry

GRADUATE PROGRAMS

Graduate School of Dentistry (First Year Enrollment : Doctor's 20)
  Divisions
Clinical Dentistry, Dental Basic Sciences

Osaka Electro-Communication University
(Osaka Denkitsushin Daigaku)

18-8 Hatsu-cho, Neyagawa-shi, Osaka 572
☎ 0720-24-1131

Faculty
  Profs. 60   Assoc. Profs. 26
  Assist. Profs. Full–time 32; Part–time 94
Number of Students
  Undergrad. 3, 976
Library   132, 629 volumes

Outline and Characteristics of the University
  The university was founded in 1961 for the purpose of carrying out education and research related to electronics and electronic engineering. At present the university consists of seven departments: Electronics, Electro–Communication Engineering, Solid State Electronics, Electro-Mechanics, Management Engineering, Precision Engineering, and Applied Electronics. They are closely concerned with the new innovative progress in modern engineering and scientific technologies.
  The university constitution has been organized to include new developing fields in electronic engineering and computer technology so that students can acquire the most advanced knowledge in each department. The curriculum is carefully arranged for the students to be able to master their own course in each department and, in addition, to learn the basic technique as an electronic engineer.
  The purpose of the university's education does not reside in the nurturing of technicians but also in the cultivating of an independent individual with a creative mind and a self-conscious social responsibility. The liberal arts course is organized under the principle of academic freedom so that each free individual can find, according to the guidance of the teachers, his way to wisdom and virtue.

UNDERGRADUATE PROGRAMS

Faculty of Engineering (Freshmen Enrollment: 840)
  Department of Applied Electronics
  Department of Electro-Communication Engineering
  Department of Electro-Mechanics (Mechatronics)
  Department of Electronics
  Department of Management Engineering
  Department of Precision Engineering
  Department of Solid State Electronics

Foreign Student Admission
  Qualifications for Applicants
    Standard Qualifications Requirement
  Examination at the University
  1. Examination in Academic Subjects: Mathematics (Mathematics I, Algebra, Geometry, Basic Analytics, Differential Calculus, Integral Calculus), Sciences (Physics, which includes the area of the subject matter in Science I) and English
       The name of the above-mentioned subjects correspond to those of the same subjects authorized in Japanese senior high schools.

2. Interview

Note: It is desirable that the applicant should have taken the Japanese Language Proficiency Test and General Examination for Foreign Students.

Documents to be Submitted When Applying

Standard Documents Requirement

The applicant must submit a letter of recommendation issued by a Japanese diplomatic establishment abroad or the diplomatic establishment of the applicant's country in Japan.

Qualifications for Transfer Students
1. Transfer students must be either college graduates or have a college education of more than one year.
2. Transfer students must be graduates of junior colleges or higher professional schools corresponding to those institutions in the school system in Japan.

Examination for Transfer Students
1. Examination in Academic Subjects: Mathematics, Physics, and English
2. Interview

Documents to be Submitted When Applying

Standard Documents Requirement

The applicant must submit a letter of recommendation issued by a Japanese diplomatic establishment abroad or the diplomatic establishmant of the applicant's country in Japan.

*

Research Institutes and Centers

Education Center for Information Processing, Electronics Fundamental Research Center, Information Science Center

For Further Information

Undergraduate Admission

Admission Division, Osaka Electro-Communication University, 18-8　Hatsu-cho, Neyagawa-shi, Osaka 572 ☎ 0720-24-1131 ext. 3221

Osaka Gakuin University
(Osaka Gakuin Daigaku)

2-36-1 Kishibe-Minami, Suita-shi, Osaka 564
☎ 06-381-8434

Faculty
Profs.　86　　Assoc. Profs.　58
Assist. Profs.　Full–time　19; Part–time　133
Research Associate　3
Number of Students
Undergrad. 7, 197　　Grad. 30
Library　454, 000 volumes

Outline and Characteristics of the University

Osaka Gakuin University, founded in 1963 by the late Taneo Shirai, is a coeducational institution of higher learning located in Suita City, a suburb of Osaka. It contains the Graduate Schools and the Faculties of Commerce, Economics, Foreign Languages, Law, and Division of Correspondence Education.

The brief history of the Faculties including the Graduate Schools is as follows: (1963) The Faculty of Commerce was established; (1967) The Graduate School of Commerce was established and began offering the Master's Program; (1969) The Doctor's Program was offered; (1970) The Faculty of Economics was added, and the Division of Correspondence Education was established; (1974) The Faculty of Law and the Faculty of Foreign Languages were added and the Graduate School of Economics was established and began offering the Master's Program; (1976) The Doctor's Program was offered.

The University provides an education based on the Founding Spirit: "This institution, by means of higher education and scholarly research, aims to develop human resources with the practical ability and broad vision to serve society at large as well as to contribute to the peace and welfare of mankind. "

UNDERGRADUATE PROGRAMS

Faculty of Commerce (Freshmen Enrollment: 550)
Department of Business Administration
Business Administration, Business Diagnosis, Business Management, Business Statistics, Commercial Marketing, Diagnosis of Enterprise, Factory Management, Financial Management, Information System, Information Theory, Labor Management, Management of Business Enterprise, Management of Manufacturing Industry, Management of Tourism, Marketing Research, Metric Management, Morphology of Enterprise, Personnel Management, Production Management, Transportation Management

Department of Commerce
Accounting, Auditing, Business Analysis, Commercial Bookkeeping, Commercial Economics, Computer Accounting, Cost Accounting, Distribution Theory, Financial Accounting, Financial Management, History of Commerce, International Trade, Management Accounting, Management of Commercial Enterprise, Merchandising, Tax Accounting, Theory of Money, Trade Policy, Trade Practice, Trust and Security

Faculty of Economics (Freshmen Enrollment: 550)
Department of Economics
Agricultural Economics, Business Fluctuations, Econometrics, Economic Geography, Economic History, Economic History, Economic Philosophy, Economic Policy, Economics of Business Enterprise, Economic Statistics, Finance, Financial Economics, Fundamental Economics, History of Economic Theory, Industry Economics, International Economics, Labor Economics, Manufacturing Industry Economics, National Income Analysis, Public Finance, Security Economics, Small Business Administration, Social Welfare Policy, Theory of Economic Growth,

Theory of Taxation, Trust Economics

Faculty of Foreign Languages (Freshmen Enrollment: 200)

Department of English Language

American Literature, English Language, English Linguistics, English Literature, English Phonetics, History of American Literature, History of English Language, Histoy of English Literature

Department of German Language

German Grammar, German Linguistics, German Literature, German Syntax, Historical Survey of Germany, History of German Language, History of German Literature

Faculty of Law (Freshmen Enrollment: 200)

Department of Law

Administrative Law, Bill and Check Act, British and American Law, Civil Affair Executive Law, Civil Procedure Act, Claim Act of General, Code of Criminal Procedure, Commercial Law, Constitutional Law, Contract Act, Corporation Act, Criminal Policy, European Laws, Execution Act, French Law, German Law, Industrial Property Act, International Law, International Law in Time of Peace, International Politics, International Private Law, Japanese Civil Law, Labor Law, Law of International Institutions, Legislation History, Philosophy of Law, Political History, Political Science, Real Property Registrational Law, Science of Administration, Tax Law, Trust Act

GRADUATE PROGRAMS

Graduate School of Commerce (First Year Enrollment : Master's 30, Doctor's 20)

Division

Commerce

Graduate School of Economics (First Year Enrollment : Master's 30, Doctor's 20)

Division

Economics

*

For Further Information

Undergraduate Admission

Admissions Section, General Affairs Office, Osaka Gakuin University, 2-36-1 Kishibe-Minami, Suita-shi, Osaka 564 ☎ 06-381-8434 ext. 1133

Graduate Admission

Admissions Office of Graduate School, Osaka Gakuin University, 2-36-1 Kishibe-Minami, Suita-shi, Osaka 564 ☎ 06-381-8434 ext. 1232

Osaka Institute of Technology
(Osaka Kogyo Daigaku)

5-16-1 Omiya, Asahi-ku, Osaka-shi, Osaka 535
☎ 06-952-3131

Faculty

    Profs. 80   Assoc. Profs. 56

    Assist. Profs. Full–time 71; Part–time 234

    Res. Assocs. 2

Number of Students

    Undergrad. 9, 170   Grad. 120

Library   309, 539 volumes

Outline and Characteristics of the University

The Osaka Institute of Technology has a history of over 60 years since it was founded in 1922 as Kansai Kogaku Senshu Gakko. In 1949, the Institute firmly established the present organization as a four-year college. The Institute consists of the Faculty of Engineering comprising seven departments of Applied Chemistry, Architecture, Civil Engineering, Electrical Engineering, Electronic Engineering, Industrial Management and Mechanical Engineering, including daytime and evening courses. The Graduate School of Engineering founded in 1965 offers six Master's Programs and five Doctor's Programs.

Since 1952, 50, 324 students have graduated from the Institute and 570 students from the Graduate School since 1967. Those graduates have been remarkably active in various fields throughout Japan and abroad. For example, the number of graduates, who have reached high positions of management in stock-listed companies, occupies 36th place out of all the private and public universities in Japan, and has the number four ranking in private colleges with a single faculty of science or engineering.

As a result of innovations in recent years, the field of engineering has been diversified and subdivided. So as to cope with this trend, the Institute aims to develop the fundamental scholastic ability of the students through the education offered in each department, and to cultivate the applicability and the rich creativity based on the knowledge of specified fields. Especially the research for Bachelor's Thesis made under an individual guidance of the professor is the essence of the Institute's education.

Omiya Campus, the main campus, is located on the banks of the Yodo River adjacent to Shirokita Park in the north-eastern section of Osaka City. The campus being 25 minutes away from the city center by bus or subway is conveniently situated. Hirakata Campus of 135, 000 m^2 area is situated at the border of Hirakata and Yawata Cities about 25km away from Omiya Campus, where the Institute has various facilities for experimental research and athletic fields.

In response to the internationalization of science

and culture, the Institute devotes its efforts to opening its gates wide to receive foreign students. To this purpose, a foreign students admission system was established in 1984. Although the number of students making use of this system still remains rather small, foreign students can be eligible for admission as undergraduates, graduates, research students or auditors. They can select courses to suit the purpose of their studies, the duration of their stay in Japan and their scholastic abilities.

UNDERGRADUATE PROGRAMS

Faculty of Engineering (Freshmen Enrollment: Daytime 780, Evening 780)
Department of Applied Chemistry
Applied Electrochemistry, Applied Physical Chemistry, Industrial Analytical Chemistry, Industrial Inorganic Chemistry, Industrial Organic Chemistry (Fuel Chemistry, Surface Active Agents and Natural and Synthetic High Polymers), Material Science of High Polymers, Polymer Science, Thermodynamics and Reaction Rate
Department of Architecture
Architectural History and Design, Architectural Planning and City Planning, Building Materials and Construction, Environmental Engineering, Structural Engineering
Department of Civil Engineering
Bridge Engineering, Concrete Engineering, Disaster Prevention Engineering, Environmental Engineering, Foundation Engineering, Hydraulics, Sanitary Engineering, Soil Mechanics, Structural Mechanics, Transportation Engineering
Department of Electrical Engineering
Automatic Control Engineering, Computer, Electrical Machinery, Electrical Measurements, Electric Circuit Theory, Electricity and Magnetism, Electric Power Generation, Transmission and Distribution, Electronic Circuits and Devices, Solid State Electrophysics, Transient Circuit Analysis
Department of Electronic Engineering
Alternating Current Theory, Communication Engineering, Electric·Electronic Circuit Engineering, Electric·Electronic Measurements, Electromagnetism, Electronic Computer Engineering, Logic Circuit Engineering, Programming Language, Quantum Electronics, Semiconductor
Department of Industrial Management
Behavioral Science, Economy Engineering, Information Engineering, Management System by Computer, Marketing, Mathematical Planning, Operations Research, Production Management, Stochastic Processes, Systems Engineering
Department of Mechanical Engineering
Analysis of Plastic Deformation in Metal Processing, Dynamics of Mechanical System, Engineering Measurement, Hydrodynamics, Machine Elements, Mechanical Drawing, Strength of Materials, Technical Thermodynamics

Foreign Student Admission
Qualifications for Applicants
Standard Qualifications Requirement
Examination at the University
As a rule, the selection process depends on the application documents alone. The decision is made by the Faculty Council. However, as for foreign residents in Japan, a written examination may also be required for slection.
Successful applicants (except foreign residents in Japan) must come to the Institute on the specified date to take an achievement test, health check and personal interview. The achievement test may consist of either oral or written questions in subjects considered necessary by the Department.
Documents to be Submitted When Applying
Standard Documents Requirement
The application forms and the prescribed examination fee by October 27 of the preceding year. The Application forms are available at the General Affairs Section in August.
Announcement of the results: the end of December the middle of February.

GRADUATE PROGRAMS

Graduate School of Engineering (First Year Enrollment : Master's 43, Doctor's 15)
Divisions
Applied Chemistry, Architecture, Civil Engineering, Electrical Engineering, Industrial Management, Mechanical Engineering

Foreign Student Admission
Qualifications for Applicants
Standard Qualifications Requirement
Examination at the University
Same as undergraduate program.
Documents to be Submitted When Applying
Standard Documents Requirement
Application procedure is same as undergraduates.

*

Research Institutes and Centers
CAD Research Center, Central Research Laboratory (Joint Research Cen- ter, Computer Center), Machine Shops, New Material Research Center, Structure Research Center, Yawata Laboratory
Special Programs for Foreign Students
After Admission, the special course in the Japanese language is offered for foreign students as an extracurricular program.
For Further Information
Undergraduate and Graduate Admission
General Affairs Section, Osaka Institute of Technology, 5-16-1 Omiya, Asahi-ku, Osaka-shi, Osaka 535
☎ 06-952-3131 ext. 3053

Osaka International University
(Osaka Kokusai Daigaku)

3–50–1, Sugi, Hirakata-shi, Osaka 573–01
☎ 0720–58–1616

Faculty
Profs. 19   Assoc. Profs. 5
Assist. Profs. Full–time 8; Part–time 38
Res. Assoc. 2
Number of Students
Undergrad. 1, 000
Library 31, 000 volumes

Outline and Characteristics of the University

Osaka International Uviversity was established in April, 1988 and is located in Hirakata City in the eastern suburb of Osaka. At present it consists of only one faculty, Management and Computer Science, but it will add another faculty and a graduate schoool of business in a few years.

OIU's curriculum is designed to train students for competence in (1) the English language, (2) basic programming skills and (3) the fundaments of management, particularly for international businesses Courses on area studies, therefore, are offered on some Asian countries such as Korea, China and Indonesia, as well as on the United States.

Students are offered two program options: (a) International Information Management and (b) International Business Management. In the former they are expected to develop advanced skills in computer programming and information management, whereas in the latter they are to acquire expertise in international business administration. Both programs emphasize English language training which is provided mostly by native speakers. Some seminars and courses are given in English to selected students.

As one of the newest universities in Japan, OIU is equipped with up-to-date facilities in computer science education, satelite TV programs and audio-visual class rooms. The library system is computerized and offers easy access to unique materials and facilities. The school is housed in immaculate brick buildings, and the new campus enjoys abundant greenery. Classes are kept small to maximize the effectiveness of the teaching and opportunities for inter action between students and instructors.

OIU has an independent research institute, the Institute of International Relations. It carries out research on international political economy, area studies, and international business administration, and regularly invites scholars from abroad as well as from other Japanese universities. Researchers in the Institute will have close ties with teachers in the university so as to make their contributions in academic research available to the instructors in the Faculty of Management and Computer Science. The Institute as well as the library will collect relevant information and materials in the research areas mentioned and serve as a resourse center for researchers and business in the Osaka area. The Institute also serves as the Secretariat for the East Asian Economic Association and publishes the Semiannual Asian Economic Journal jointly with the Center of Asian Studies at the University of Hong Kong.

UNDERGRADUATE PROGRAMS

Faculty of Management and Computer Science (Freshmen Enrollment: 180)
Department of Management and Computer Science

Foreign Student Admission
Qualifications for Applicants
Standard Qualifications Requirement
Foreign students will be admitted after 1990. The requirements will be announced later.

*

Research Institutes and Centers
Institute of International Relations
For Further Information
Undergraduate Admission
Manager, Entrance Examination and Publicity Room, Osaka International University, 3–50–1, Sugi, Hirakata–shi, Osaka 573–01 ☎ 0720–58–1616 ext. 1200

Osaka Medical College
(Osaka Ika Daigaku)

2-7 Daigaku-machi, Takatsuki-shi, Osaka 569
☎ 0726-83-1221

Faculty
Profs. 35   Assoc. Profs. 28
Assist. Profs. Full–time 62; Part–time 242
Res. Assocs. 184
Number of Students
Undergrad. 640   Grad. 132
Library 156, 000 volumes

Outline and Characteristics of the College

Osaka Medical College was founded in Takatsuki in 1927 as Osaka Higher Medical College, the first five-year higher school of medicine in Japan. Osaka Higher Medical College became a college under the old system of education in 1946, and under the new system in 1952. In 1959, the Graduate School was opened. In 1965, the Premedical Course was added.

The successive presidents have aimed at training able doctors. The graduates have totalled 6, 423. They actively work as clinicians, research scientists, and educators.

Osaka Medical College Hospital is highly

equipped with technical facilities. The Hospital has bed accommodations for more than 1, 000 in-patients. The College has excellent educational facilities for basic and clinical research, and has an excellent faculty. The College is fully prepared to offer advanced medical education.

UNDERGRADUATE PROGRAMS

Faculty of Medicine (Freshmen Enrollment: 100)
Department of Medicine
Anatomy, Anesthesiology, Clinical Pathology, Dermatology, General Gastrointestinal Surgery, Hygiene and Public Health, Internal Medicine, Legal Medicine, Medical Chemistry, Microbiology, Neuropsychiatry, Neurosurgery, Obstetrics and Gynecology, Ophthalmology, Oral Surgery, Orthopedic Surgery, Otorhinolaryngology, Pathology, Pediatrics, Pharmacology, Physiology, Plastic Surgery, Radiology, Thoracic and Cardiovascular Surgery, Urology

GRADUATE PROGRAMS

Graduate School of Medicine (First Year Enrollment : Doctor's 54)
Divisions
Internal Medicine, Pathological Science, Physiological Science, Social Medicine, Surgery

Foreign Student Admission
Qualifications for Applicants
Doctor's Program
    Standard Qualifications Requirement
    Documents to be Submitted When Applying
    Standard Documents Requirement
    1. A Medical License.
    2. A Letter of Approval. (Those who are in employment must obtain their supervisor's approval.)

*

For Further Information
Undergraduate and Graduate Admission
Instruction Section, General Affairs Division, Osaka Medical College, 2-7 Daigaku-machi, Takatsuki-shi, Osaka 569 ☏ 0726-83-1221 ext. 619

Osaka Sangyo University
(Osaka Sangyo Daigaku)

3-1-1 Nakagaito, Daito-shi, Osaka 574
☏ 0720-75-3001

Faculty
    Profs.   72   Assoc. Profs.   43
    Assist. Profs.   Full–time   20; Part–time   186
    Res. Assocs.   3
Number of Students
    Undergrad.   5, 830   Grad.   14

Library   205, 500 volumes

Outline and Characteristics of the University
Osaka Sangyo University and its Junior College originated in the Osaka Railway School. The parent school was founded in 1928 by Genzaburo Sejima who recognized the indispensability of the joint development of transportation and industry for future industrial and economic society. He accordingly determined to provide for the full development of railway staff and industrial personnel. Thus was begun the academic tradition of education and research on traffic and transportation.

The institution developed as follows over the next 40 years: Osaka First Railway School (1938); Osaka Railway High School (1949); Osaka Transportation Junior College (1950); Department of Automobile Engineering added to the Junior College (1962).

In 1965, Osaka Sangyo University (the then Osaka Transportation University) was founded, incorporating the faculty of business management and the faculty of engineering (day and evening courses), with its departments of mechanical engineering and mechanical engineering for transportation. Since then, thanks to the support and trust extended by the general public and the Ministry of Education, the institution has developed steadily to its present university status. In 1988, the Graduate School of Engineering consisting of the Division of Electrical Engineering and Electronics and the Division of Civil Engineering, was newly founded.

The institution aims to cultivate personnel able to contribute to the industrial society of the 21st century. Since its foundation, the primary concern of the institution has been to offer a rounded education and to encourage creativity in addition to training in the transportation and industry areas. Accordingly, it has established its own academic traditions and contributes to society as an educational functionary capable of adapting to the age of rapid social development.

Pursuant to the institution's founding spirit—in Sejima's words, "Greatness for the Masses"—, the staff gives educational consideration to the development of the abilities and natural talents of students. With an excellent academic staff and a constant exchange among students, the University devotes itself to helping students realize humanity and creativity; individuality based on self-confidence; a deep and profound consideration of life; and internationalization and a broad world-view. With the integration of our moral, intellectual and physical education, we aim to cultivate a modern, harmonious and practical industrial citizen, with innovative ideas and a sound mind capable of contributing to the development of a new, 21st century industrial society and the well-being of its people.

In 1988, our University concluded a partnership agreement with Bayerische Julius-Maximilians-Universität Würzburg.

The institution is situated north-east of Osaka at the foot of the Ikoma Mountain, in one of the most ecologically viable areas of the Osaka District.

UNDERGRADUATE PROGRAMS

Faculty of Business Management (Freshmen Enrollment: 450)

Department of Business Management

Business Administration Course and Transportation Business Administration Course

Accounting, Bookkeeping, Business Economics, Business Finance, Business History, Cost Accounting, Economics of Urban Transportation, Financial Statements, History of Accounting Theories, History of Transportation Business, Hotel Management, Marine Transportation, Marketing Management, Personnel and Human Resource Management, Physical Distribution, Theory of Leisure Behavior, Tourism, Tourism Development

Faculty of Economics (Freshmen Enrollment: 300)

Department of Economics

Economics Course and Industrial Economics Course

Economic Geography, Economic History, Economic Policy, Economics, History of Modern Economics, Industrial Economics, International Economics, Labor Economics, Marine Transportation, Money and Credit Finance, Physical Distribution, Pricing in Transportation, Public Finance, Trade Cycle, Transportation Economics, Urban Transportation

Faculty of Engineering (Freshmen Enrollment: 510)

Department of Civil Engineering

Bridge Engineering, Civil Engineering, Highway Engineering, Hydraulics, Materials of Construction, Planning Theories and Methods in Civil Engineering, Reinforced Concrete Engineering, River Engineering, Sanitation Engineering, Soil Machanics, Structural Mechanics, Surveying

Department of Electrical Engineering and Electronics

Computer Technology, Electrical Engineering and Electronics, Electric Circuit Analysis, Electric Machine, Electromagnetics, Electronic Circuits, Electronic Control, Instrumentation, Programming, Semiconductor Electronics, Solid State Physics of Electrical Engineering, System Engineering, Theory of Control, Transmission Theory of Communication

Department of Mechanical Engineering

Descriptive Geometry, Dynamics, Electrical Engineering, Engineering Drawing, Engineering Materials, Engineering Mechanics, Fluid Mechanics, Heat and Thermodynamics, Kinematics of Machine, Machine Design, Manufacturing Processes, Strength of Materials

Department of Mechanical Engineering for Transportation

Applied Electricity, Automobile Engineering, Automobile Service, Automotive Engineering, Dynamics,

Energy and Thermodynamics, Engineering Materials, Engineering Mechanics, Hydrodynamics, Machine Design, Vehicle Engineering, Vehicle Engines

Faculty of Engineering (**Evening Course**) (Freshmen Enrollment   140)

Department of Mechanical Engineering

See listing for Day Course.

Department of Mechanical Engineering for Transportation

See listing for Day Course.

Foreign Student Admission

Qualifications for Applicants

Standard Qualifications Requirement

Examination at the University

A written examination, and an interview.

Documents to be Submitted When Applying

Standard Documents Requirement

1. Certificate on Japanese language proficiency.
2. Letter of recommendation issued by Japanese embassy (legation) abroad or foreign embassy (legation) in Japan.
3. Curriculum vitae in the applicant's own hand in Japanese.

At the time of application, applicants are required to present themselves at the University to receive explanations of the application forms and accompanying documents.

Qualifications for Transfer Students

1. Applicants who have graduated from a university or recognized as having scholarship equivalent.
2. Applicants who have graduated from a junior college or senior professional school.
3. Applicants who have finished two years of university coursework (Applicable only for transfer admisson to the Junior College of this University).

Application procedures for Transfer Students

Same as the procedures for undergraduate applicants.

Documents to be Submitted When Applying

Standard Documents Requirement

Same as undergraduate application.

GRADUATE PROGRAMS

Graduate School of Engineering (First Year Enrollment: Master's 20)

Divisions

Civil Engineering, Electrical Engineering and Electronics

Foreign Student Admission

Qualifications for Applicants

Standard Qualifications Requirement

Examination at the University

A written examination, and an interview.

Documents to be Submitted When Applying

Same documents as those for undergraduate application.

✳

Research Institutes and Centers

Academic Information Processing Center, The Institute for Industrial Research

Facilities/Services for Foreign Students

The Chamber of International Exchanges Committee assists foreign students to attain their objectives, and promotes international friendship through exchanges with foreign students.

Members of the Foreign Students Committee elected from the academic staff and the administrative staff of this University handle the reception and care of the foreign students while at the University, giving them guidance for the betterment of their studying conditions and living.

Special Programs for Foreign Students

Japanese Language as a second Foreign Language Subject in the General Education Course.

For Further Information

Undergraduate and Graduate Admission

University Administrative Department, Osaka Industrial University, 3-1-1 Nakagaito, Daito-shi, Osaka 574 ☎ 0720-75-3001

Osaka Shoin Women's College
(Osaka Shoin Joshi Daigaku)

4-2-26 Hishiyanishi, Higashi-Osaka-shi, Osaka 577
☎ 06-723-8181

Faculty
    Profs. 28   Assoc. Profs. 28
    Assist. Profs. Full–time 2; Part–time 134
    Res. Assocs. 12
Number of Students
    Undergrad. 1, 796
Library 191, 327 volumes

Outline and Characteristics of the College

Osaka Shoin Women's College is one of the oldest women's college in Japan. Originally established in 1925 as the Shoin Women's College.

In 1949 it was renamed as Osaka Shoin Women's College under the new system of education with the faculty of arts and science. A special study program was established the same year. The Faculties are the Department of Japanese Language and Literature, Department of English and American Literature, Department of Food Science, Department of Clothing Science and Department of Child Study. These are the undergraduate courses leading to Bachelor of Arts degree.

Osaka Shoin Women's College has a beautiful campus with many camphor-trees. This makes for an enjoyable learning environment and also allows students to pursue a variety of extra-curricular activities on campus. Osaka is the second biggest city in Japan in population next to Tokyo. Despite its size, the city has retained much of its natural beauty. Nara, the oldest capital in Japan, and Kyoto, the second oldest capital, are neighboring cities, so students are able to enjoy these ancient cities while they study at Osaka Shoin Women's College.

UNDERGRADUATE PROGRAMS

Faculty of Liberal Arts (Freshmen Enrollment: 380)

Department of Child Study

Adolescent Psychology, Child Care, Child Protection, Juvenile Clinical Psychology, Juvenile Hygienics, Juvenile Psychology, Mental Hygiene, Methods of Juvenile Behavior and Growth, Mother-Child Health, Nursing, Pediatrics, Pedology, Psychiatric Testing, Psychometric Method, Psychotherapy, Social Welfare

Department of Clothing Science

Chemical Analysis of Dyeing, Chromatology, Clothing Hygienics, Clothing Styles, Decoration Display, Design, Dressmaking, History of Decorative Arts, Organic Chemistry, Spinning and Weaving, Study of Clothing, Study of Clothing Merchandise

Department of English and American Literature

American Literature, English Linguistics, English Literature, English Phonetics, History of American Literature, History of English Language, History of English Literature

Department of Food Science

Applied Microbiology, Biochemistry, Cooking Science, Dietetics, Food Chemistry, Food Sanitation, Food Science, History of Food, Nutritional Chemistry, Nutritional Physiology, Organic Chemistry, Technology of Processing and Preservation of Foods

Department of Japanese Language and Literature

Expressions in Japanese Language, History of Japanese Literature, History of Japanese Philology, Japanese Literature, Japanese Philology, Japanese Usages

Foreign Student Admission

Qualifications for Applicants

    Standard Qualifications Requirement

Examination at the College

    An entrance examination and a personal interview.

Documents to be Submitted When Applying

    Standard Documents Requirement

✳

Special Programs for Foreign Students

The College offers Japanese lessons for foreign students.

For Further Information

Undergraduate Admission

The Department of Educational Affairs, Osaka Shoin Women's College, 4-2-26 Hishiyanishi, Higashi-Osaka-shi, Osaka 577 ☎ 06-723-8181 ext. 237

Osaka University of Arts
(Osaka Geijutsu Daigaku)

469 Higashiyama, Kanan-cho, Minamikawachi-gun,
Osaka 585 ☎ 0721-93-3781

Faculty
 Profs. 91 Assoc. Profs. 76
 Assist. Profs. Full–time 72; Part–time 369
 Res. Assocs. 27
Number of Students
 Undergrad. 6, 573 Grad. 44
Library 97, 000 volumes

Outline and Characteristics of the University
 The Osaka University of Arts was inaugurated in 1964 as the Naniwa University of Arts, with the Art College composed of the Departments of Fine Arts and Design. The University was given its present name in 1966.
 The ideals of education are high at the University. As a synthesized institution of learning and arts, the University, based on an orderly system and the spirit of freedom, incorporates courses in a way that is possible only at private institutions and seeks to establish a new era of liberal education. The University is designed to encourage creativity in science and technology, industry, transportation, communications, political administration, and other areas of society.
 Of late, the sciences and arts have become fields in which specialization is characterized by sectionalism. This is indeed a deplorable situation. The University avoids this sectionalism at all costs. Rather, it stresses specialization aimed at the synthesis of related fields—often "blind spots" in the sciences and arts—thereby opening new vistas for students.
 In recognition of the role Japan plays in Asia and the world, the University stresses the value of education with an international viewpoint. Therefore, taking the traditions of the various cultures of the world and combining them with the traditions of Japan's science and arts, the University hopes to contribute a new artistic tradition.
 In view of the University's geographical position near the Hanshin industrial zone, it attaches importance to the practical and rational aspects of the sciences and arts.
 Combining all these ideals, the University hopes to create adults who will be well rounded individuals and active, contributing members of society.

UNDERGRADUATE PROGRAMS

Faculty of Arts (Freshmen Enrollment: 900)
 Architecture Department
Architectural Planning, Architecture Planning, Building Structure, Building Structure Dynamics, Construction Design, Environmental Engineering, History of Architectural Construction, Housing Design, Human Engineering, Japanese Architectural History, Landscape Architecture, Materials Study, Modern Architecture, Theory of Construction, Urban Design, Urban Economics, Urban Sociology, Western Architecture History, Work Execution
 Art Planning Department
Art Criticism, Art Industry, Art Planning, Contemporary Art, Editing Technique, Expression Planning, Human Relations, Information Psychology, Public Opinion and Social Survey, Reproduction Art
 Broadcasting Department
Advertising, Broadcasting Acting and Production, Broadcasting Music, Broadcasting Technique, Creative Scenario Writing, Documentaries, Effects, History of Broadcasting, News Reporting, News Reporting, Public Opinion and Social Survey, Radio, Stage Design, Theatrical Arts, TV Announcing, Voice
 Crafts Department
 Ceramics Course
History of Japanese Art, Theory of Ceramics
 Dyeing and Weaving Course
Dyeing, History of Dresses and Their Ornaments, Printmaking, Theory of Dyeing and Weaving, Theory of Patterning, Weaving
 Metalwork Course
Casting, Coating, Crafts Material, Glasswork, Human Engineering, Industrial Design, Metalsmithing, Metalwork, Theory of Metalwork
 Textile Course
Interior Design, Pattern Printing, Textile, Theory of Textile Design, Weaving
 Design Department
 Graphic Design Course
Display, Drafting, Graphic Design, History of Modern Architectural Culture, Photography, Printing, Printmaking
 Industrial Design Course
Ceramics, Display, Electrical Engineering, Glasswork, History of Modern Architectural Culture, Human Engineering, Illumination Study, Industrial Design, Material Science, Materials Dynamics, Mechanical Engineering, Metalwork, Rendering and Drafting, Theory of Urban Planning
 Informational Design Course
Computer Graphics, Display, Drawing, High Technological Art, Illustration, Theory fo Information Design, Typography
 Interior Design Course
Architecture, Coating, History of Interior Design, History of Modern Architectural Culture, Illumination Study, Interior Design, Materials Study
 Environmental Planning Department
Architectural Planning, Color Planning, Environmental Biology, Environmental Engineering, Environmental Planning, Gardening, Green Belt Construction and Management, Indoor Environmental

Planning, Landscape Architecture, Landscape Planning, Plant Life and Culture, Regional Planning, Scenery Protection, Study of Cities, Study of Sunlight, Surveying, System Engineering, Traffic Engineering, Urban Planning

Fine Arts Department

Anatomy for Art, Formative Arts, Glue Coloring, History of Design Printmaking, History of Japanese Fine Arts, History of Oriental Fine Arts, Oil Painting, Painting, Sculpture, Sculpture

Literary Arts Department

Criticism of Theatrical Arts, Drama, Folklore, History of American Literature, History of Calligraphy, History of Folk Literature, History of French Literature, History of Japanese Drama, History of Literature, History of Modern Japanese Literature, History of Western Drama, Literary Arts Study, Literature, Mass Communication Media, Poetics, Syntax, Theatrical Art

Music Education Department

History of Music, History of Music Education, Music Education for Infants, Music Education Method, Music Psychology, Music Score Analysis, Music Theory, Piano Education Method

Musicology Department

Chorus, Ensemble, Keyboard Harmonics, Music Composing, Music History, Musicology, Music Psychology, Music Sociology, Music Technology, Percussion, Piano, String, Vocal, Western Music History, Wind

Music Performance Department

Brass Band, Chorus, Conducting, Dancing, History of Opera, History of Orchestral Music, History of Piano Music, Opera Acting, Orchestral Music, Percussion Instruments, Piano, String Instruments, Vocal, Wind Instruments

Photography Department

Commercial Photography, Creative Photography, hotographic Chemistry, Illumination Study, Image Planning, News Photography, Photograph Colors, Photographic Aesthetics, Photographic Design, Photographic History, Photography, Printing Media

Theatrical Arts Department

Acting, Costume, Creative Dance, Dancing, Drama, Dramatic Reading, Dramaturgy, Effects, History of Japanese Modern Drama, Lighting, Musical, Performance Planning, Stage Arts, Stage Criticism, Stage Music, Stage Performance, Study of Actors, Theatrical Arts

Visual Concept Planning Department

Acting, Animation, Commercial Film Animation, Display of Visual Concepts, Documentary Film, Editing, Film Arts, Film Drama, Film-making Technique, History of Visual Concepts, Lighting, Photography Aesthetic of Visual Concept, Scenario, Sound Effects, Visual Concept Analysis, Visual Design

Foreign Student Admission

Qualifications for Applicants

Standard Qualifications Requirement

Examination at the University

1. Practical technique or aptitude test
2. Thesis or written test
3. Interview
4. Japanese proficiency test

Documents to be Submitted When Applying

Standard Documents Requirement

Certificate of Proficiency in the Japanese language or certificate of attendance at Japanese language school or its equivalent is also required.

Qualifications for Transfer Students

The applicant must have completed or expects to complete two years or more in the courses related to that which he/she wishes to apply for.

Examination for Transfer Students

1. The presentation of works
2. Thesis or written test
3. Practical technique test
4. Interview
5. Japanese proficiency test

Documents to be Submitted When Applying

Standard Documents Requirement

Certificate of Proficiency in the Japanese language or certificate of attendance at a Japanese language school or its equivalent is also required.

Applicants for transfer program must submit works. If it is impossible to mail or bring them, slides will be acceptable.

ONE-YEAR GRADUATE PROGRAMS

One-Year Graduate Course of Arts (Enrollment: 60) Architecture, Crafts, Design, Fine Arts, Literary Arts, Music Education, Music Performance, Musicology, Photography

Foreign Student Admission

Qualifications for applicants

Standard Qualifications Requirement

Documents to be Submitted When Applying

Standard Documents Requirement

Certificate of Proficiency in the Japanese language or certificate of attendance at Japanese language school or its equivalent is also required.

Applicant for the graduate course must submit the graduate works. If it is impossible to mail or bring them, slides will be acceptable. Graduate thesis must be written in Japanese or English. (If not, it must be translated into Japanese or English.)

The graduate course applicant who can not enter Japan by the date of the Entrance Examination will be examined by the presentation of his/her documents and art works or thesis.

The applicant who wishes to be examined by the presentation of documents is to submit his/her art works or thesis as part of the application for admission. Refer to the application pamphlet.

*

Research Institutes and Centers

European and American Centers of the Osaka University of Arts, Osaka Art Center

Facilities/Services for Foreign Students

The University has Meeting Room of Foreign Students.

Special Programs for Foreign Students

The following special classes in Japanese language and Japanese studies are offered for foreign students studying at our school.

Elementary Japanese Language

Intermediate Japanese Language

Japanese Studies

For Further Information

Undergraduate and Graduate Admission

International Student Office, Osaka University of Arts, 469 Kanan-cho, Minamikawachi-gun, Osaka 585 ☎ 0721-93-3781 ext. 501

Osaka University of Commerce
(Osaka Shogyo Daigaku)

4-1-10 Mikuriya Sakae-machi, Higashiosaka-shi, Osaka 577   ☎ 06-781-0381

Faculty

Profs. 50   Assoc. Profs. 26

Assist. Profs. Full–time 14; Part–time 65

Res. Assoc. 1

Number of Students

Undergrad. 3,549

Library 171,900 volumes

Outline and Characteristics of the University

Osaka University of Commerce was originally founded as a high school of commerce in 1928 in its present location of Kawachi in eastern Osaka. In 1949 the high school became Osaka Joto University with the Faculty of Economics. Three years later it became Osaka University of Commerce with the present Faculty of Commerce and Economics. A special one-year graduate program for advanced study in commerce and ecnomics was added to the school curriculum in 1956. Then, in 1959, the Commerce and Economics Faculty was expanded into three separate departments of Economics, Commerce, and Business Administration. Six years later the Trade Department was added. Present student enrollment is about 3,500.

Valuable documents on the commercial history of Osaka are exhibited at the University's Tanioka Memorial Hall established in 1985. Osaka University of Commerce has a sister school, Osaka Women's Junior College. It also has an associated kindergarden on its campus.

"Become a person useful to society" is the motto and educational aim of the Osaka University of Commerce. Japan is undergoing tremendous change, primarily due to her technological innovation and development; her influence is felt the world over. Japa-nese society cannot be isolated from the rest of the world. Thus it must be the goal of a university to educate its students to a broad international view, new value-systems, and a deep understanding of world cultures. Osaka University of Commerce, with its top-level academic leaders, offers a high quality curriculum; seminars put special emphasis on faculty and student interaction.

The University makes a constant effort to keep its academic curriculum flexible and up-to-date, in accordance with the spirit of an ever-changing society. Many of the University's alumni hold leading posts in the community, as living examples of the University's motto to be "useful people."

UNDERGRADUATE PROGRAMS

School of Commerce and Economics (Freshmen Enrollment: 850)

Department of Commerce

Bookkeeping, Commerce, Commercial Economics, Commodity Science, History of Commerce, Industrial Planning, Information Processing, Insurance, Labor Law, Managerial Accounting, Marketing, Money and Credit, Tax Accounting, Theory of Finance, Theory of Minor Business Enterprises

Department of Economics

Economic Geography, Economic History, Economic History of Japan, Economic Policy, Economics, Economic Statistics, History of Economic Doctrines, Industrial Engineering, Information Processing, International Economics, Mathematical Economics, Money and Banking, Public Finance, Social Policy

Department of Management

Accounting, Business Administration, Business Finance, Business History, Commodity Science, Cost Accounting, Industrial Engineering, Information Processing, Information Science, International Finance, Management Analysis, Management and Organization Theory, Management Science, Managerial Accounting, Marketing, Personnel Administration

Department of Trade

Economy of Foreign Countries, History of Western Economics, Information Processing, International Banking, International Business Enterprise, International Finance, International Public Law, International Trade, Managerial Mathematics, Sea Transportation, Trade and Management, Trade Practice

Foreign Student Admission

Qualifications for Applicants

Standard Qualifications Requirement

Documents to be Submitted When Applying

Standard Documents Requirement

Period of application is during the first half of January each year. Dates for entrance examination are February 7 and 8. Admission procedure must be made by the end of March.

ONE-YEAR GRADUATE PROGRAMS

One-Year Graduate Course of Advanced Study in Commerce and Economics (Enrollment: 10)
Commerce, Economics

Foreign Student Admission
Qualifications for Applicants
Applicant must be a graduate from a Japanese university or its equivalent.

∗

For Further Information
Undergraduate and Graduate Admission
Admission and Records, Osaka University of Commerce, 4-1-10 Mikuriya, Sakae-machi, Higashi-Osaka-shi, Osaka 577 ☎ 06-781-0381 ext. 212, 213, 214.

Osaka University of Economics
(Osaka Keizai Daigaku)

2-2-8 Osumi, Higashi-yodogawa-ku, Osaka-shi, Osaka 533 ☎ 06-328-2431

Faculty
    Profs. 61   Assoc. Profs. 27
    Assist. Profs. Full–time 18; Part–time 146
Number of Students
    Undergrad. 6, 343   Grad. 13
Library 446, 993 volumes

Outline and Characteristics of the University
In the early 1930's there were no private higher institutions for commercial studies in Osaka, which was Japan's largest commercial city at the time. Establishment of such an institution providing an opportunity to study commercial affairs was indeed an urgent requirement for the city's future.

As a result, Naniwa Higher School of Commerce was established in 1932. Three years later, in 1935, the school had gone through basic transformation. Iwao Kokusho, who was a professor of Kyoto Imperial University, was appointed as a new principal. Kokusho had greatly contributed to the school not only by serving as principal, but also by donating a large sum of his private assets to the school. Renamed Showa Higher School of Commerce, the school had sufficiently established itself both in terms of its educational content as well as its financial status. It was around then when the long history and tradition of the school had started emerging and its foundation laid for developing into the present university. While the school was renamed Osaka Women's College of Economics and then Osaka College of Economics during and immediately following World War II, with the Education Reform of 1949, the school was reorganized as Osaka University of Economics. The university started out with the Fac-

ulty of Economics. In 1964, the Faculty of Business Administration was added. In 1966, the Master's Program of Economics was established, and in 1968, the Doctor's Program. It is truly a university specialized in economics and related fields.

Since the main campus is located in the center of Osaka, a great commercial city of the nation, the students have constant access to actual business conditions which they can observe and study in detail. The school has intentionally chosen to remain in the central area of the city to be a model for future university.

A new seven-floor school building was constructed in the spring of 1986 to commemorate the 50th anniversary. The building is equipped with advanced facilities such as large-sized computers, computer terminals and innovative audio-visual equipment to meet the needs of the modern information-oriented society. Moreover, the school promotes academic exchange programs with foreign universities. Close to 51, 000 graduates from the university actively contribute to the society not only of Japan but of the world as a whole.

UNDERGRADUATE PROGRAMS

Faculty of Business Administration (Freshmen Enrollment: Day 550, Evening 100)
Department of Businesss Administration
Accounting, Accounting History, Auditing, Banking Business, Bookkeeping, Business Administration, Business Analysis, Business Economics, Business Finance, Business Organization, Commercial Business, Commercial Science, Computer Accounting, Cost Accounting, Distribution, Financial Accounting, Financial Management, Foreign Exchange, Foreign Trade Management, Forms of Enterprise, History of Business Administration, Industrial Management, Industrial Psychology, Industrial Relations, Industrial Sociology, Industrial Technology, Information Management, Insurance, International Business, International Trade, Japanese Business History, Labor Management, Management Accounting, Marketing, Personal Management and Labor Relations, Production Management, Public Utility Economics, Sales Management, Science of Commodities, Securities Market, Small Business, Transport Economics, Wage Form
Faculty of Economics (Freshmen Enrollment: Day 550, Evening 100)
Department of Economics
Agricultural Economics, American Economy, Chinese Economy, Co-operative Society, Developing Countries Economy, Econometrics, Economic Fluctuations, Economic Geography, Economic History, Economic Policy, Economics, Economics of Labor, Economics of Transportation, Economic Statistics, History of Economics, Industrial Economics, Industrial Organization, Industrial Structure, International Economy, International Finance, Japanese Econo-

my, Modern Capitalism, Money and Banking, Philosophy of Economics, Public Finance, Socialist Economics, Social Policy, Social Security, System of National Accounts, Urban Economics

Foreign Student Admission

Qualifications for Applicants
Standard Qualifications Requirement
Examination at the University
Academic record, English and Japanese fluency, and personal interview. Applicants are expected to consult the examination office in advance.
Documents to be Submitted When Applying
Standard Documents Requirement

GRADUATE PROGRAMS

Graduate School of Economics (First Year Enrollment : Master's 20, Doctor's 10)
Division
Economics

Foreign Student Admission

Qualifications for Applicants
Master's Program
Standard Qualifications Requirement
Doctor's Program
Standard Qualifications Requirement
Examination at the University
Master's Program
The same as Japanese students.
1. Thesis: Two subjects out of following four subjects: Principle of Economics, Economic Policy, History of Economy and Business Administration
2. Foreign language: One out of following three languages: English, German, French
3. Interview
Doctor's Program
The same as Japanese students.
1. Oral examination: On specialized area based on one's master's thesis
2. Foreign language: Two out of following five languages: English, German, French, Russian, Chinese (Native language of foreign students inapplicable.)
Documents to be Submitted When Applying
Standard Documents Requirement
A copy of master's thesis along with around 4, 000 letter abstract. (The submitted materials will be returned by mail after admission announcement.)

✳

Research Institutes and Centers
Computation Center, Institute for Research in Economic History of Japan, Institute of Small Business Research, The Institute of Business Administration, The Institute of Industrial and Economic Research
For Further Information
Undergraduate Admission
Admissions Office, Osaka University of Economics,

2-2-8 Osumi, Higashi-yodogawa-ku, Osaka-shi, Osaka 533 ☎ 06-328-2431 ext. 255~258
Graduate Admission
Instruction Division, Instruction Department, Osaka University of Economics, 2-2-8 Osumi, Higashi-yodogawa-ku, Osaka-shi, Osaka 533 ☎ 06-328-2431 ext. 241~244

Osaka University of Economics and Law

(Osaka Keizai Hoka Daigaku)

6-10 Gakuonji, Yao-shi, Osaka 581
☎ 0729-41-8211

Faculty
　　Profs.　43　　Assoc. Profs.　30
　　Assist. Profs.　Full–time　15; Part–time　206
　　Res. Assoc.　1
Number of Students
　　Undergrad.　5, 097
Library　123, 000 volumes

Outline and Characteristics of the University
Osaka University of Economics and Law was established in 1971. The University is located at the foot of Mount Ikoma, in the suburbs of Osaka City which provides an enjoyable environment in which to study.

The philosophy upon which the foundation of the university is based is summed up in the following four statements: building a university that will provide the education to those who will take a leading role in the construction of a society in which humanity takes center stage; educating students so they will play an important role in the field of economics; stressing the importance of the study of foreign languages to prepare students to actively participate on the international scene; encouraging each individual to develop their natural abilities so that they will become worthy citizens of the 21st century.

In order to realize the above mentioned goals, two fields are of particular importance. These two are the two that the University stresses: Economics and Law. The two are closely tied to each other for one must know law in order to understand economics and vice versa. Therefore the University offers a curriculum in which students are permitted to study the fields of Law and Economics simultaneously. The units earned from one Faculty are recognized by the other upon graduation (however, this total should not exceed 24).

The University has promoted academic exchange with foreign institutions. It established a sister-school relationship with Nice University in Frace in 1984, with Peking University in 1986, and with Yan Bian University in China and the University of Hawaii at Manoa in 1987. Further, this year, the University and the Instituite of Oriental Studies of the USSR Academy of Sciences have entered into an agreement for academic exchange.

UNDERGRADUATE PROGRAMS

Faculty of Economics (Freshmen Enrollment: 200)
Department of Economics
Business Administration Program
Economics Program
Faculty of Law (Freshmen Enrollment: 200)
Department of Law
Jurisprudence Program
Legal Study for Management Program

Foreign Student Admission
Qualifications for Applicants
Those who desire to enroll in a first or third year class are required to have completed two year of college level work.

Applicants are required to write a paper on a subject determined by the university and to undergo an interview.
Documents to be Submitted When Applying
Standard Documents Requirement

*

For Further Information
Undergraduate Admission
Admissions Office, Osaka University of Economics and Law, 6-10 Gakuonji, Yao-shi, Osaka 581
☎ 0729-41-8211

Osaka University of Pharmaceutical Sciences
(Osaka Yakka Daigaku)

2-10-65 Kawai, Matsubara-shi, Osaka 580
☎ 0723-32-1015

Faculty
    Profs. 23   Assoc. Profs. 15
    Assist. Profs. Full–time 7; Part–time 25
    Res. Assocs. 43
Number of Students
    Undergrad. 1, 126   Grad. 33
Library 51, 000 volumes

Outline and Characteristics of the University
Osaka University of Pharmaceutical Sciences is one of the oldest private universities of pharmaceutical sciences in Japan. Originally established in 1904 as Osaka Doshu School of Pharmacy, it developed into Doshu Women's College of Pharmacy in January, 1925. It was renamed Teikoku Women's College of Pharmacy in October of the same year. In 1949, it was reorganized as Teikoku College of Pharmacy, and then as Osaka College of Pharmacy in 1950. It was renamed Osaka University of Pharmaceutical

Sciences in 1986.

In 1968, the Department of Pharmaceutical Technology was added to the Department of Pharmaceutical Sciences which had been established in 1950. As for its graduate schools, the Graduate School of Pharmaceutical Sciences (Master's Program) was established in 1975, and Doctor's Program was added in 1984.

Since its foundation in 1904, the University has made steady progress, contributed much to the education and research in the field of pharmaceutical sciences, and produced many competent graduates, who enjoy much popularity among various research institutes, drug manufacturers and other fields of pharmaceutical sciences.

The main campus of the University is located in Matsubara City adjacent to the southern part of Osaka City, Osaka Prefecture. The University can be reached very easily from major cities in the Kansai District, such as Osaka, Kyoto, Kobe, Nara and Wakayama. Very close to the campus are the Medicinal Plant Garden and Noto Athletic Grounds, which allow students to pursue curricular and extra-curricular activities. The majority of the students are from the Kinki District, but people come from every part of Japan.

UNDERGRADUATE PROGRAMS

Faculty of Pharmaceutical Sciences (Freshmen Enrollment: 240)
Department of Pharmaceutical Sciences
Analytical Chemistry, Hygienic Chemistry, Pharmaceutical Chemistry, Pharmacognosy, Pharmacology
Department of Pharmaceutical Technology
Biochemistry, Chemical Microbiology, Pharmaceutics, Physical Chemistry, Radio Pharmaceutical Chemistry, Synthetic and Industrial Chemistry

Foreign Student Admission
Qualifications for Applicants
Standard Qualifications Requirement
The Japanese Language Proficiency Test (JLPT) and General Examination for Foreign Students (GEFS) (Science).
Examination at the University
A written examination, the interview and the examination of the application forms.
Documents to be Submitted When Applying
Standard Documents Requirement

GRADUATE PROGRAMS

Graduate School of Pharmaceutical Sciences (First Year Enrollment : Master's 16, Doctor's 5)
Division
Pharmaceutical Sciences

Foreign Student Admission
Qualifications for Applicants

Master's Program
    Standard Qualifications Requirement
    JLPT.
Doctor's Program
    Standard Qualifications Requirement
    JLPT.
    Examination at the University
Master's Program
    A written examination, an interview and the examination of the application forms.
Doctor's Program
    The same procedure as the Master's Program.
    Documents to be Submitted When Applying
    Standard Documents Requirement

*

Research Institutes and Centers
Center for Experimental Animals
For Further Information
    Undergraduate and Graduate Admission
Admission Office, Osaka University of Pharmaceutical Sciences, 2-10-65 Kawai, Mastsubara-shi, Osaka 580 ☏ 0723-32-1015 ext. 225

Otani University
(Otani Daigaku)

Kamifusa-cho, Kita-ku, Kyoto-shi, Kyoto 603
☏ 075-432-3131

Faculty
    Profs. 34   Assoc. Profs. 14
    Assist. Profs. Full–time 16; Part–time 154
    Res. Assoc. 1
Number of Students
    Undergrad. 2, 449   Grad. 129
Library 520, 000 volumes

Outline and Characteristics of the University

Otani University is a liberal arts college based upon the teachings of Shinran (1173-1262), the founder of True Pure Land Buddhism. It consists of the Faculty of Letters providing undergraduate and graduate instruction.

Otani University has a long history dating back to 1665, when a seminary was established by the Higashi Hongwanji, the head temple of the Higashi Hongwanji branch of the Jodo Shin Sect, as a center for the study of Mahayana Buddhism. Inheriting this long tradition, the Shinshu Daigaku, the precursor of the present university, was established in Tokyo in 1901.

Kiyozawa Manshi (1863-1903), one of the most important Buddhist thinkers of the Meiji period, was the first president of the university. He emphasized the True Pure Land Buddhist faith which underlies all educational and research activities of the university. Furthermore, Sasaki Gessho (1875-1926), the third president, enunciated the necessity of the objective study of Buddhism, free of narrow sectarian

viewpoints. These two themes, Kiyozawa's stress on personal involvement with Buddhism and Sasaki's emphasis on academic and nonsectarian study of Buddhism, continue to be the basis of all learning at Otani University.

Kiyozawa was a central figure in the movement to redefine the character of the True Pure Land Buddhist faith by shifting the emphasis away from institutionalized religion to individual religious consciousness. Soga Ryojin (1875-1971) and Kaneko Daiei (1881-1976) were two of Kiyozawa's prominent students who taught at Otani University and worked to develop Kiyozawa's vision in terms of traditional True Pure Land Buddhist thought. In particular, Soga's interpretation of Dharmakara Bodhisattva and Kaneko's analysis of the Pure Land have fundamentally altered the character of True Pure Land Buddhist philosophy.

Nanjio Bunyu (1849-1927), the second president, pioneered the development of modern Japanese Buddhology. He studied as a young man under Max Muller at Oxford University and introduced modern Sanskrit studies to Japan. He compiled the "Nanjio Catalogue" of Chinese Buddhist texts, the first of its kind published in modern times.

The internationally known D. T. Suzuki (1870-1966) served as chairman of the Department of History of Religions from 1921. Through his extensive writings on Zen and Mahayana Buddhism, Suzuki played a crucial role in fostering the understanding of Buddhism in Europe and America. He also translated into English the Kyogyoshinsho, Shinran's major work, and thereby contributed greatly towards introducing True Pure Land Buddhist thought to the West. Nishitani Keiji (1900-), an exponent of the "Kyoto School" of Japanese philosophy and the leading philosopher of Japan today, is presently a member of the Department of Philosophy.

Otani University was relocated to Kyoto, the ancient capital and cultural center of Japan, in 1911. The Graduate School was established between 1953 and 1955. The True Pure Land Buddhist Comprehensive Research Institute was created in 1981 as a center for advanced and co-operative research within the university. In 1980, Otani began an exchange program with the Buddhist Studies Department of University of Wisconsin-Madison.

UNDERGRADUATE PROGRAMS

Faculty of Letters (Freshmen Enrollment: 480)
    Department of Buddhist Studies
Buddhist Studies Course
Indian Buddhism Studies Course
    Department of History
East Asian Buddhist History Course
East Asian History Course
Japanese Buddhist History Course
Japanese History Course
    Department of Literature

Chinese Literature Course
English Literature Course
German Literature Course
Japanese Literature Course
Department of Philosophy
Ethics Course
History of Religions Course
Western Philosophy Course
Department of Sociology
Education Course
Sociology Course
Department of True Pure Land Buddhism

Foreign Student Admission
Qualifications for Applicants
Standard Qualifications Requirement
Examination at the University
1. English (written test)
2. Japanese (written test) including kanbun
3. Humanities (written test): one out of Ethics, Japanese History and World History
Documents to be Submitted When Applying
Standard Documents Requirement

Qualifications for Transfer Students
The same qualifications as the Japanese students
Examination for Transfer Students
1. Major Subject (written test)
2. Foreign Language (written test): one out of English, German and French
3. Interview
Documents to be Submitted When Applying
Standard Documents Requirement

GRADUATE PROGRAMS

Graduate School of Letters (First Year Enrollment : Master's 40, Doctor's 12)
Divisions
Buddhist Culture, Buddhist Studies, Philosophy, True Pure Land Buddhist Studies

Foreign Student Admission
Qualifications for Applicants
Master's Program
Standard Qualifications Requirement
Doctor's Program
Standard Qualifications Requirement
Examination at the University
Master's Program
1. Major Subject (written test)
Japanese preferred, however examinee may choose to answer in English, German or French.
2. Foreign Language (written test): one out of English, German and French (those who major in Philosophy must choose two). Examinee's native language will not be considered as a foreign language.
3. Interview

Doctor's Program
Same as the Master's program
Documents to be Submitted When Applying
Standard Documents Requirement
*
Research Institutes and Centers
The Shin Buddhist Comprehensive Research Institute
For Further Information
Undergraduate and Graduate Admission
Koho-Nyushi-ka, Otani University, Kamifusa-cho, Kita-ku, Kyoto-shi, Kyoto 603 ☎ 075-432-3131

Otemae College
(Otemae Joshi Daigaku)

6-42 Ochayasho-cho, Nishinomiya-shi, Hyogo 662
☎ 0798-34-6331

Faculty
Profs. 23 Assoc. Profs. 10
Assist. Profs. Full–time 13; Part–time 60
Res. Assocs. 3
Number of Students
Undergrad. 1, 691
Library 60, 488 volumes

Outline and Characteristics of the College
Otemae College was founded in 1966 by the Otemae Corporation for Women's Education, and started academic activities with the Faculty of Letters, comprising three departments: Arts and Aesthetics (including Practical Training Courses in Painting, Dyeing and Design), English and American Literature, and History.

Its founders aimed "to cultivate virtues and accomplishments characteristic of young ladies", and, recently, in view of the progress in arts and sciences in general, another motto, "Study for Life" has been adopted. The core and essence of college education should be scholastic activities and academic research, and we are proud of having on the staff some 48 teachers, highly qualified and with extensive experience, who share a common interest in conscientiously conducting classes and seminars both in liberal arts and advanced studies, in their respective fields. Moreover, they are willing to prepare students for their future, either in home life or as working members of society, by means of an all-round education.

Students from abroad are readily accepted. Projects are under way for strengthening school facilities and accommodations to meet their needs, and thereby providing effective training and instruction for foreign students. Opening special classes in Japanese Language and Culture for students from other cultures are under consideration.

UNDERGRADUATE PROGRAMS

Faculty of Letters (Freshmen Enrollment: 360)

Department of Art
Aesthetics, Formative Arts (Painting, Dyeing and Design), History of Fine Arts
Department of English and American Literature
American Literature, English linguistics, English Literature, International Culture Studies
Department of History
Japanese History, Occidental History, Oriental History

Foreign Student Admission
Qualifications for Applicants
Standard Qualifications Requirement
Examination at the College
The same examination as Japanese applicants, with some exceptions varying with each individual.
The Japanese Language Proficiency Test and TOEFL.

ONE-YEAR GRADUATE PROGRAMS

One-Year Graduate Course of Letters
(Enrollment: 10 each) Art, English and American Literature

Foreign Student Admission
Qualifications for Applicants
Standard Qualifications Requirement
Examination at the College
The same examination as Japanese applicants, with some exceptions varying with each individual.
The test of the Japanese language.
The Japanese Language Proficiency Test and TOEFL.

*

Research Institutes and Centers
Anglo-Norman Research Center, Research Institute of History
Special Programs for Foreign Students
Japanese language classes are under planning.
Foreign students may choose the Japanese language as their second foreign language.
For Further Information
Undergraduate and Graduate Admission
Chairman of Department of English and American Literature, Faculty of Letters, Otemae College, 6-42 Ochayasho-cho, Nishinomiya-shi, Hyogo 662
☎ 0798-34-6331 ext. 10

Otemon Gakuin University
(Otemon Gakuin Daigaku)

2-1-15 Nishiai, Ibaraki-shi, Osaka 567
☎ 0726-43-5421

Faculty
    Profs. 59   Assoc. Profs. 31
    Assist. Profs. Full–time 12; Part–time 182
    Res. Assocs. 2

Number of Students
    Undergrad. 4, 911   Grad. 28
Library 225, 641 volumes

Outline and Characteristics of the University
1888 Otemon Gakuin Institute (formerly Kaikosha) was founded. It was well known for its traditional education, which produced a good number of leading figures in various fields of society.
1966 Otemon Gakuin University was first founded with four separate departments (Economics, Psychology and Sociology, Oriental History, and English and American Language and Literature). The first of these departments constituted the Faculty of Economics, whilst the other three coexisted with the combined Faculty of Letters.
1970 The combined Department of Psychology and Sociology, and the Department of Oriental History were dissolved, forming thereafter separate departments for Psychology, Sociology; and the Department of Oriental History renamed Asian Studies.
1971 The Department of Business Administration was added to the Faculty of Economics.
1973 A Graduate Course in Psychology was created.
1975 A Graduate Course in Sociology was added.
1977 A Graduate Course in Chinese Culture was added. 1979 A Graduate Course in Economics was opened.
1981 The number of freshmen admitted to the five departments was increased.
1984 A Graduate Course in English Literature was created.
1985 A Graduate Course in Business Administration was added.
Otemon Gakuin Institute has aimed at cultivating the student to be:
1. A dignified, democratic person who knows what to do and stands against any act which violates social order and peace.
2. A dedicated person with a delicate sensibility for ethical as well as aesthetic values; and a man and woman of unbending spirit and unfettered heart.
3. A well-rounded person who can contribute positively to the humanities or natural and social sciences.
4. A person not only well-acquainted with Japanese history and culture, but well-versed in his or her native tongue.
5. An internationally minded person who can contribute to the betterment of mankind.
The educational philosophy of Otemon Gakuin University is based upon that of Otemon Gakuin Institute. With the role of universities and colleges being considered ever more important, the University aims at producing dedicated men and women of international spirit, who are equipped with the flexibility to cope with today's fast-changing world.

To this end, a wide variety of curricula are provided. Small-group education and individual attention is the motto of our university; hence seminars are offered from the first year onwards. Moreover, to foster international outlook, various programs for study abroad are provided. In Addition, the Center for Australian Studies has been in operation since 1967, playing a vital role in scholastic and cultural exchange.

UNDERGRADUATE PROGRAMS

Faculty of Economics (Freshmen Enrollment: 600)
Department of Business Administration
Accounting, Advertising, Auditing, Bookkeeping, Business Environment, Business Management, Business Organization, Commercial Science, Distribution Systems, Ergonomics, Financial Management, Insurance, International Business Management, Japanese Business History, Management, Management History, Management Information System, Marketing Programming, Operations Research, Organizational Behavior, Personnel Management, Theory of Business Firms, Trade Management, Traffic and Transportation, Wage and Salary Administration
Department of Economics
Australian Economy, Econometrics, Economic Geography, Economic Growth, Economic History, Economic Policy, Economic Statistics, History of Economic Thought, Industrial Organization, International Economics, International Finance, Japanese Economy, Labor Economics, Local Government Finance, Macroeconomics, Microeconomics, Monetary Economics, Political Economy, Public Finance, Social Policy, Southeast Asian Economy, Trade Policy
Faculty of Letters (Freshmen Enrollment: 400)
Department of Asian Studies
Chinese Culture Course
Chinese Bibliography, Chinese Classics, Chinese History, Chinese Language, Chinese Literature, History of Chinese Thought
Indo-Islamic Culture Course
Arabic, Bengali, Hindi, History of Indian Thought, Indian Culture, Indian History, Islamic Culture, Sanscrit, Urdu
Japanese Culture Course
History of Cultural Exchange, Japanese Folklore, Japanese Geography, Japanese History, Japanese Literature
Department of English and American Language and Literature
Comparative Literature, English and American Literature, English Phonetics, French Literature, German Literature, Greek, History of America, History of England, Histroy of English and American Literature, Latin, Linguistics
Department of Psychology
Clinical Psychology, Developmental Psychology, Educational Psychology, History of Psychology, Industrial Psychology, Personal Psychology, Psycho-

therapy, Social Psychology, Statistical Methods in Psychology
Department of Sociology
Cultural Anthropology, Cultural Sociology, Educational Sociology, History of Sociology, Industrial Sociology, Mass Communication, Political Sociology, Social Anthropology, Social Pathology, Social Research, Social Welfare, Sociology, Sociology of Knowledge, Sociology of Religion, Sociology of the Family, Sociology of the Village, Theoretical Sociology, Theory of Group, Urban Sociology

Foreign Student Admission
Qualifications for Applicants
    Standard Qualifications Requirement
Examination at the University
1. Japanese
2. English
3. Interview
    Date: toward the end of January.
Documents to be Submitted When Applying
    Standard Documents Requirement
    A letter of recommendation or Certificate of Identification issued by the Embassy or Legation in Japan of the country concerned.
    Applications period: the middle of December.
    Announcement of the results: by the middle of January.
    Deadline for Entrance procedures: the middle of February.

GRADUATE PROGRAMS

Graduate School of Economics (First Year Enrollment : Master's 30)
Divisions
Business Administration, Economics
Graduate School of Letters (First Year Enrollment : Master's 20)
Divisions
Chinese Culture, English Literature, Psychology, Sociology

Foreign Student Admission
Qualifications for Applicants
Master's Program
    Standard Qualifications Requirement
Examination at the University
Master's Program
    The same as Japanese applicants. Date: by the middle of March.
Graduate School of Economics and Graduate School of Business Administration: English, Written Examination and Oral Interview
Grduate School of Letters: English, German, French, or Chinese (applicants for the Division of English Literature must choose English), Written Examination and Interview
Documents to be Submitted When Applying
    Standard Documents Requirement

Application period: around the beginning of March.

Announcement of results: by the middle of March.

Deadline for Entrance procedures: the end of March.

*

Research Institutes and Centers
The Center for Australian Studies
Special Programs for Foreign Students
Japanese Language (8 credits are alloted for 2 years).
For Further Information
Undergraduate and Graduate Admission
Admission Section, Instruction Division, Otemon Gakuin University, 2-1-15 Nishiai, Ibaraki-shi, Osaka 567 ☎ 0726-43-5421 ext. 261

Otsuma Women's University
(Otsuma Joshi Daigaku)
12 Sanban-cho, Chiyoda-ku, Tokyo 102
☎ 03-261-9841

Faculty
Profs. 42   Assoc. Profs. 18
Assist. Profs. Full-time 10; Part-time 95
Res. Assocs. 27
Number of Students
Undergrad. 2, 542   Grad. 47
Library 270, 000 volumes

Outline and Characteristics of the University
Situated in the heart of Tokyo, Otsuma Women's University is one of the oldest and most distinguished women's universities in Japan. Kotaka Otsuma, a pioneer in the field of women's education, founded her Ladies Dressmaking and Handicraft Academy in 1908, and this Academy expanded and developed into the Otsuma High School, the Otsuma Vocational College, and finally, in 1949, into the present Otsuma Women's University.

The University in its early stages consisted of only one Faculty of Domestic Science made up of three Departments: Clothing, Nutritional Science, and Homecraft. This Faculty subsequently underwent several phases of development and restructuring, and consists, at present, of the Department of Clothing, the Department of Nutritional Science, and the Department of Pedology.

The Faculty of Literature was added in 1967, consisting of the Departments of Japanese Literature and English Literature.

The Otsuma Women's University Junior College, founded in 1950, offers two-year courses in both the Department of Domestic Science and the Department of Literature.

The Graduate Schools of the University were founded in 1972, the Graduate School of Domestic Science offering courses leading to Master's Degrees in Clothing, Nutritional Science, and Pedology, and the Graduate School of Literature offering courses leading to Master's Degrees in Japanese Literature and English Literature.

The Life Sciences Research Laboratory was set up in 1981, and since 1982 the Graduate School of Domestic Science has offered Doctor's Degrees in Clothing and Environment Studies.

Otsuma Women's University and its students have long been associated with the well-known catchphrase of 'Good Wife, Wise Mother'. In an age when a woman's place was firmly in the home, the University strove to equip young women with the scientific and technical knowledge necessary to play the fullest role possible within the narrow limits defined by a conservative society. In the 40 years since the War, Japanese society has witnessed enormous changes, and women are now active in business, commerce, industry, and every field of social endeavor. Otsuma Women's University has been in the forefront of the movement to reassess and restructure women's education to meet the changing needs of society, and the extent to which it has been successful in this can best be judged by the unmatched job placement and employment records of its graduates.

UNDERGRADUATE PROGRAMS

Faculty of Domestic Science (Freshmen Enrollment: 300)
Department of Clothing
Aesthetics of Dress and Ornament, Clothing and Hygiene, Clothing Materials, Clothing Organization, Color Science, Design, Dressmaking, Dyeing, Fiber Treatment, History of Japanese Dress and Ornament, History of Western Dress and Ornament
Department of Nutritional Science
Catering Management, Consumer Science, Cooking, Environmental Science, Food Chemistry, Food Economics, Food Hygiene, Food Planning Theory, Food Processing and Preservation, History of Food, Nutritional Biology, Nutritional Chemistry, Nutrition Education, Practical Nutrition, Public Nutrition
Department of Pedology
Child Environment, Child Pathology, Child Psychology, Family Education, History of Education, Instruction and Learning, Juvenile Art, Juvenile Culture, Juvenile Literature, Principles of Primary Education, Social Psychology, Social Security
Faculty of Literature (Freshmen Enrollment: 200)
Department of English Literature
Area Studies, Business English, Comparative Literature, English and American Culture, English Grammar, English Literature, English Phonetics, English Poetry, English Pronunciation, History of English Literature, History of the English Language, Shakespeare Studies, Speech
Department of Japanese Literature
Calligraphy, Classical Chinese Literature, Classical

Literature, Comparative Literature, History of Japanese Literature, Japanese Grammar, Japanese Language, Japanese Literature (Ancient, Medieval, Modern, Contemporary), Literary Expression

Foreign Student Admission
   Qualifications for Applicants
     Standard Qualifications Requirement
   Examination at the University
     The same as for Japanese students.
   Documents to be Submitted When Applying
     Standard Documents Requirement

GRADUATE PROGRAMS

Graduate School of Domestic Science (First Year Enrollment : Master's 18, Doctor's 2)
   Divisions
Clothing and Environment Studies, Clothing Science, Nutritional Science, Pedology
Graduate School of Literature (First Year Enrollment : Master's 12)
   Divisions
English Literature, Japanese Literature

Foreign Student Admission
   Qualifications for Applicants
Master's Program
     Standard Qualifications Requirement
Doctor's Program
     Standard Qualifications Requirement
   Examination at the University
Master's Program
     Written examination in the applicant's major subject and one foreign language, and an interview.
Doctor's Program
     Written examination in one foreign language and an oral examination.
   Documents to be Submitted When Applying
     Standard Documents Requirement
     Following documents are also required.
1. If the applicant is currently employed, a certificate of consent issued by her employer. (Master's Program, Doctor's Program)
2. Photocopy of Master's thesis or equivalent, together with copies of any other theses or publications available. (Doctor's Program)
3. Summary of Master's thesis or equivalent. (Doctor's Program)

                       *

Research Institutes and Centers
Child Development Clinic Center, Environmental Color Center, Information Processing Center, Life Sciences Research Laboratory, Morphological Measurement Center, Movement Analysis Center
For Further Information
   Undergraduate and Graduate Admission
Admissions Section, Administrative Office, Otsuma Women's University, 12 Sanban-cho, Chiyoda-ku, Tokyo 102 ☎ 03-261-9841 ext. 221

Rakuno Gakuen University
(Rakuno Gakuen Daigaku)

582-1 Bunkyodai-Midorimachi, Ebetsu-shi, Hokkaido 069 ☎ 011-386-1111

Faculty
   Profs. 37   Assoc. Profs. 31
   Assist. Profs. Full-time 34; Part-time 25
   Res. Assocs. 8
Number of Students
   Undergrad. 2, 286   Grad. 161
Library 144, 291 volumes

Outline and Characteristics of the University
   Believing that Japanese agriculture, and especially dairy farming, needed improvement, Rakuno Gakuen, the only specialized dairy school in Japan, was first established privately in 1933 on the island of Hokkaido. Torizo Kurosawa, widely known as the father of Japanese dairy agriculture, served as one of the primary founders.
   The school has continued to grow with the opening of Nopporo Kino High School in 1942, Rakuno Gakuen Junior College in 1950, and Rakuno Gakuen Senior College (The College of Dairying) in 1960.
   The College of Dairying was renamed Rakuno Gakuen University in 1986. In the Faculty of Dairy Science, the four departments of Dairy Science, Agricultural Economics, Veterinary Medicine, and Food Science were opened 1960, 1963, 1964, and 1988 respectively. The Graduate Schools of Veterinary Medicine and of Dairy Science were initiated in 1981, offering master's programs, and, in the case of Veterinary Medicine, also a doctorate program.
   Currently, our schools foster first-class leaders in the dairy field, technicians, for food economics specialists, and veterinarians. A large number of graduates from our school are now playing important roles throughout the nation.
   In this modern age, we need not only technological innovation but also people to accomplish it. With this goal in mind, instruction at our university features "education through practical studying", learning practical knowledge, and "San'ai Spirit", based on Christianity.
   At our extensive and verdant campus (142 hectares), situated in the suburbs of Sapporo (population-1. 5 mil.), students learn not only theory but also practical knowledge, fully utilizing dairy farms and livestock available here.
   "San'ai Spirit" (love of God, humanity, and earth) was the principle philosophy behind the founding of Denmark, the world's most highly advanced dairy country. Based on this Christian ideal, people awakened with true love and freedom. At Rakuno Gakuen University, talented personnal are being formed under this principle.

UNDERGRADUATE PROGRAMS

Faculty of Dairy Science (Freshmen Enrollment: 460)

Department of Agricultural Economics
Agricultural Accounting, Agricultural Co-operation, Agricultural & Livestock Product Marketing, Agricultural Marketing, Agricultural Policy, Dairy Farm Management, Economics, Farm Management Rural Sociology

Department of Dairy Science
Agricultural Machinery, Agricultural Microbiology, Animal Breeding, Animal Management, Animal Nutrition, Animal Reproduction, Applied Entomology, Crop Breeding, Dairy Farm Management, Forage Crop Science, Soil Science and Plant Nutrition

Department of Food Science
Applied Biochemistry, Applied Microbiology, Food and Nutrition Chemistry, Meat Science, Milk Science

Department of Veterinary Medicine
Animal Health, Epizootiology, Veterinary Anatomy, Veterinary Biochemistry, Veterinary Internal Medicine, Veterinary Microbiology, Veterinary Obstetrics and Gynecology, Veterinary Parasitology, Veterinary Pathology, Veterinary Pharmacology, Veterinary Public Health, Veterinary Radiology, Veterinary Surgery, Veteyinary Pysiology

Foreign Student Admission
Qualifications for Applicants
Standard Qualifications Requirement
Examination at the University
Admission is based on personal history, personality, the physical condition of applicants, proficiency in Japanese, and scholastic ability.
Documents to be Submitted When Applying
Standard Documents Requirement
Qualifications for Transfer Students
Requirements for transfer students, who graduated or withdrew from foreign universities or colleges are as follows: (Applicants must have attended universities or colleges which are regarded as formal school systems in their respective countries and have similar educational aims and curriculum as in Japan.)
1. Third-year (junior) transfers:
Bachelor's degree, junior college graduates or attendance at other universities for at least two years, obtaining the necessary number of class credits as determined by the college.
2. Second-year (sophomore) transfers:
a. Those applicants who do not meet the above qualifications, and who attended other universities (excluding junior colleges) for at least one year must have acquired. the necessary number of class credits prescribed by the University.
b. Second-year transfers to Veterinary Department: Bachelor's degree.

Examination for Transfer Students
Same as freshman applicants.
Documents to be Submitted When Applying
Standard Documents Requirement

GRADUATE PROGRAMS

Graduate School of Dairy Science (First Year Enrollment : Master's 6)
Division
Dairy Science
Graduate School of Veterinary Medicine (First Year Enrollment : Master's 120)
Division
Veterinary Medicine

Foreign Student Admission
Qualifications for Applicants
Master's Program
Standard Qualifications Requirement
Doctor's Program
Standard Qualifications Requirement
Applicants for the clinical program in the Dept. of Veterinary Medicine must have veterinarian's licenses.
Examination at the University
Master's Program
Admission is based on the results of scholastic ability tests, interviews, reports submitted by respective deans, and health certificates.
Doctor's Program
Same as Master's program.
Documents to be Submitted When Applying
Standard Documents Requirement

*

For Further Information
Undergraduate and Graduate Admission
Examination Section, Instruction Department, Rakuno Gakuen University, 582–1 Bunkyodai-Midorimachi, Ebetsu-shi, Hokkaido 069 ☎ 011–386–1112 ext. 2046

Reitaku University
(Reitaku Daigaku)

2-1-1 Hikarigaoka, Kashiwa-shi, Chiba 277
☎ 0471–73–3601

Faculty
Profs.　27　　Assoc. Profs.　20
Assist. Profs.　Full–time　18; Part–time　53
Res. Assoc.　1
Number of Students
Undergrad.　676
Library　206, 269 volumes

Outline and Characteristics of the University
Reitaku University was established in 1959 as a four-year institution of higher education with one

faculty of foreign languages. Education at Reitaku University has been based on the spirit of moralogy expounded by Chikuro Hiroike, who founded a college affiliated with his Institute of Moralogy (devoted to the study and development of moral science) on the same campus in 1935. Reitaku University now has, in its faculty of foreign languages, four departments--English, German, Chinese and Japanese-as well as a one-year course of Japanese language and culture for students from abroad.

Since its establishment, Reitaku has aimed, firstly, at producing persons of moral excellence and reliability. It has also aimed at producing internationally-minded members of society--people with skills and knowledge of foreign languages as well as international viewpoints, who can freely work and exchange opinions with people of the world, in which distances, physical and psychological, are rapidly diminishing.

In April, 1988, Reitaku University inaugurated its fourth department, the Department of Japanese. The most unique feature of this new department is found in its approach to the Japanese language from a world-wide perspective, encouraging the students to deepen and develop their understanding of the nature of language in general, as well as the Japanese language, through programs such as contrastive linguis-tics and field linguistics.

As the Japanese Department consists of an approximately equal number of Japanese and foreign students the chances of international contact and experience on both the linguistic and cultural levels will be abundant.

In order to attain these aims, Reitaku University in contrast to the normal mass-education system in Japan, offers intensive training in languages and other subjects in small classes. It also offers a residential system in which all freshmen, both Japanese and foreign, live on campus together with many of the senior students and some of the teaching staff so that close contact and warm human communication are always attainable in an international atmosphere.

In addition to its educational facilities, Reitaku University has various sporting facilities, such as tennis courts, golf course, baseball diamond and gymnasiums, as well as other facilities including dining hall, restaurant, cafeteria, shop and clinic. Students can, therefore, live a full and meaningful university life, obtaining maximum benefit from all that Reitaku offers.

UNDERGRADUATE PROGRAMS

Faculty of Foreign Languages (Freshmen Enrollment: 200)
Department of Chinese
Chinese Interpretation, Chinese Language, Chinese Literature, Chinese Orthography, Chinese Phonetics, Chinese Studies, Chinese Translation, History of the Chinese Language

Department of English
American Literature, British and American Studies, British Literature, Communication, English Language, English Phonetics, History of the English Language
Department of German
German Language, German Literature, German Studies, History of German Literature
Department of Japanese
Contrastive Linguistics, Field Linguistics, Japanese Culture, Japanese History, Japanese Language, Japanese Language Teaching Methods, Japanese Literature, Japanese Society

Foreign Student Admission
Qualifications for Applicants
1. Applicants must not be Japanese nationals.
2. Applicants must have spent at least 9 out of the 12 years of prescribed school education in a school outside Japan or in an international school.
3. Applicants must meet one of the following qualification:
    (a) Completed 12 years of prescribed school education by March 31, 1989 or to have an equivalent academic background. (Applications will be accepted from those who have completed the prescribed school education in less than 12 years as the result of grade-promotion owing to excellent academic achievement.)
    (b) Acquired international baccalaureate qualification.
    (c) Passed the college entrance examination in the educational system of a country other than Japan.
Examination at the University
Assessment will be on the basis of the application documents, the results of examinations in academic subject, and an interview.
The subjects to be examined are as follows:
1. Chinese, English and German Departments
    English (applicants for the Chinese and German Departments can take Chinese or German instead of English, but applicants for the English Department must take English), Japanese and an interview.
2. Japanese Department
    Japanese and an oral examination in Japanese
Documents to be Submitted when Applying
1. Prescribed Application Documents
2. A Written Pledge (to abide by the laws of Japan and the rules of Reitaku University)
Dates of Examinations
1. Chinese, English, and German Departments
    (1) November 19, 1988
    (2) March 27, 1989
2. Japanese Department
    (1) February 4, 1989
    (2) March 27, 1989

Application Acceptance Periods
1.   Chinese, English and German Departments
    (1) November 4 to 16, 1988 (for November Examination)
    (2) Around March 20, 1989 (for March Examination)
Qualifications for Transfer Students
    Applications for Transfer will be accepted only if there are vacancies in the department the applicant intends to enter. There will be no vacancies for the year 1989.

Facilities/Services for Foreign Students
University Dormitory
Special Programs for Foreign Students
The Course of Japanese Language (one year):
1.   Japanese language (reading, grammar, composition, conversation)
2.   Japanese society and culture (dietary life, housing situations, language, annual events, home life, climate, history, government and politics, economics, social systems, and culture of Japan)
3.   Outline of Japanese language (Japanese language in the world)
For Further Information
Undergraduate Admission
The Educational Affairs Section, Reitaku University, 2-1-1 Hikarigaoka, Kashiwa-shi, Chiba 277 ☎ 0471-73-3690

Rikkyo (St.Paul's) University
(Rikkyo Daigaku)

3-34-1 Nishi Ikebukuro, Toshima-ku, Tokyo 171
☎ 03-985-2204

Faculty
    Profs. 230   Assoc. Profs. 66
    Assist. Profs. Full-time 22; Part-time 522
    Res. Assocs. 15
Number of Students
    Undergrad. 12, 264   Grad. 329
Library 901, 382 volumes

Outline and Characteristics of the University
    Rikkyo University was founded in 1874 by Channing Moore Williams, a bishop of the American Episcopal Church, who was at that time in charge of the Church's work in Japan and China. He had arrived in Japan in 1859 as a young missionary priest, and had spent the first ten years ministering to the foreign community in Nagasaki, while also studying the Japanese language.
    In 1869 Williams moved to Osaka and three years later he founded St. Timothy's School, the earliest educational work of the Anglican-Episcopal Church in Japan. Soon thereafter, he moved to Tokyo, where he planned to establish a private school

to teach Western learning, and to provide at the same time a place where interested Japanese could observe the faith and practices of the Christian religion.
    In February 1874, Williams leased a house in the Tsukiji district of downtown Tokyo. One portion of the house was made into a chapel and the remainder was turned into classrooms. This was the beginning of "St. Paul's College"—the name given to the school by Bishop Williams—and when it started, it is said there were only five students, with a faculty of two other American missionaries assisting the bishop. From this small beginning has developed the large educational institution now known as Rikkyo University.
    During the first few decades of its existence, the school experienced various difficulties; but under the leadership of Bishop Henry St. George Tucker, who had assumed the presidency in 1903, the school was formally established as a college in 1907, with two departments, Literature and Commerce, and an enrollment of 200 students. Moreover, envisioning the College's future need for a more spacious campus, Tucker negotiated for the purchase of a sizeable tract of land in Ikebukuro on the northwestern outskirts of Tokyo.
    In 1918 the College moved to this new location; and the following April when the new academic year began, 104 applicants were admitted to the freshman course. In 1922 the College acquired the status of a university, having Departments of English Literature, Religion, Philosophy, and History, in its College of Arts, and Department of Commerce in its College of Commerce—the latter becoming the College of Economics in 1931. In 1934, the 60th anniversary of its founding, Rikkyo announced long-range development plans; but unfortunately the plan for the initial stage had to be suspended when war broke out in the Far East.
    A great change in the entire educational system of Japan was brought about in the years immediately following the war, and Rikkyo University also underwent substantial changes. The Technical College—which had been added during the war—was discontinued as such; and three Colleges were established, namely, Arts, Economics, and Science, together with the Faculty of General Education. The former preparatory course was abolished, and a four-year undergraduate curriculum was instituted. In the first year under the new system there were about 3, 000 students. For the first time in its history, women were admitted to the University; and since then, the enrollment of women students has steadily increased.
    By 1955 the University's existing facilities were severely taxed by an ever-increasing enrollment; but with the gradual recovery of the Japanese economy, the University entered a decade of spectacular expansion, not only in its physical plant but in its academic curricula as well. The high point of this period was in 1958 and 1959, when two new Colleges of the University came into being, Social Relations, and Law

and Politics. In the same year the University also added to its physical facilities the five–story Law School Building, the Mitchell Memorial Hall (a dormitory for women students), another faculty office building with research and seminar rooms, and a very spacious athletic ground equipped for virtually all intramural and intercollegiate sports.

Earlier, in 1957, as a result of the gift of an atomic research reactor from the American Episcopal Church, the University had established the Rikkyo Institute of Atomic Energy, complete with buildings to house the reactor and all necessary research facilities. In subsequent years three new wings were also added to the existing Science Building. Also during this period of expansion, a spacious modern library was constructed.

The University today is comprised of five undergraduate Colleges (Arts, Economics, Science, Social Relations, and Law and Politics), Faculty of General Education, and Graduate Division offering courses leading to the master's and doctoral degrees in all of the disciplines represented by the various departments of the University.

UNDERGRADUATE PROGRAMS

The College of Arts (Freshmen Enrollment: 595)
  Department of Christian Studies
  Department of Education
  Department of English and American Literature
  Department of French Literature
  Department of German Literature
  Department of History
  Department of Japanese Literature
  Department of Psychology
The College of Economics (Freshmen Enrollment: 850)
  Department of Business Administration
  Department of Economics
The College of Law and Politics (Freshmen Enrollment: 500)
  Department of International Comparative Law
  Department of Law and Politics
The College of Science (Freshmen Enrollment: 100)
  Department of Chemistry
  Department of Mathematics
  Department of Physics
The College of Social Relations (Freshmen Enrollment: 400)
  Department of Industrial Relations
  Department of Social Relations
  Department of Tourism

Foreign Student Admission
  Qualifications for Applicants
    Standard Qualifications Requirement
    Non–Japanese citizens who are 18 years of age or older and who have been granted an International Baccalaureate Diploma, or who expect to receive one by the time of admission are also eligible to apply for admission.

Note that those who fall under one of the following three categories are not eligible to apply for admission as foreign students.

1. Those who have, at the time of application, been in Japan for more than 2 years after the completion of their secondary education.
2. Those who, at the time of application, have been enrolled in a Japanese university as a regular student for more than a year.
3. Those who have completed their secondary education or are expected to do so by the time of admission, at an institution, whether in Japan or abroad, whose curriculum follows or is based on the Japanese educational system.

It should also be noted, however, that those who fall under one of these three categories are eligible to apply for admission by the same admission procedure as Japanese applicants.

Examination at the University
  Applicants to be accepted for admission will be selected on the basis of their applications and supporting documents (without recourse to any entrance examination).

Documents to be Submitted When Applying
  Standard Documents Requirement
Required Documents (Prescribed Forms):
1. Completed application form
2. Completed application cards
3. Two letters of reference, one from each of two faculty members at the school last attended.
4. Completed physical examination form
5. Self–addressed labels
Supporting Documents:
1. Two copies of the applicant's diploma or other certification of graduation or of prospective graduation from the school last attended (or now being attended).
     In the latter case the applicant, if admitted, must submit certification of graduation after admission.
2. Official transcript of academic records from the school last attended.
     If the school last attended is a university or college, the applicant must submit the transcript of his/her secondary educational institution as well.
     Note that those who have completed their secondary education in less than the normally required period of time (e. g., who have skipped a year) must also submit an official document to verify this.
3. Official report of scores on the specified aptitude and achievement tests and/or educational certification specified below.
     Applicants are strongly urged to submit the originals of test reports or certificates and to avoid the use of photocopies as much as possible. Note that if an applicant is currently

residing in Japan and hence cannot submit the required score reports or certificates, he/she is requested to take the General Examination for Foreign Students, and to write the examinee number in the designated place on the application form.

4. Proof of proficiency in Japanese

Either one or the other of the following documents must be submitted:

(a) Score report of the Japanese Language Proficiency Test, 1st level

If an applicant has taken or is going to take this test in 1985, he/she must put the examinee number in the designated place on the application form.

(b) Certificate of proficiency in Japanese issued by a public institution (with an explanation of the criterion of evaluation)

5. Verification of alien registration
6. Application fee

Educational Certification Required of Foreign Applicants

1. USA: (a) Scholastic Aptitude Test (SAT) or American College Test (ACT) and (b) Achievement Test (AT)
2. United Kingdom: General Certificate of Education (GCE)

The certificate must show more than two A–level subjects out of the five subjects.
3. France: Certificate of Baccalaureate
4. West Germany: Certificate of Gymnasium
5. International Baccalaureate: Test results in six subjects of the final IB
6. Other applicants: Those from other countries that offer national certificate programs should submit the test results or the certificate, with an explanation of the criterion of evaluation. Those who cannot submit the score reports of their national certificate program or those from countries that do not offer national certificate programs of their own are expected to submit one of the certificates in 1–5 above.

Those who are currently in Japan may submit the score reports of the General Examination for Foreign Students.

N. B. The certificates of those applicants who fall under one of 2–6 above and who are applying for the College of Science must include the following subject (s):

Dept. of Mathematics: Mathematics
Dept. of Physics: Mathematics and Physics
Dept. of Chemistry: Mathematics and Chemistry

Timetable

1. Application period: December 1–9, 1988
2. Notification of results: February 2, 1989
3. Registration period: February 20–24, 1989

Qualifications for Transfer Students

Insofar as facilities are available, the University will accept applications for admission to the third year level. That is, only those applicants who have completed with full credits either the curriculum of an accredited junior college, or the coursework of the first two years of an accredited university (in which case certain stipulations apply regarding the subjects of the credits held), are qualified to apply.

Examination for Transfer Students

An entrance examination, on dates announced by the University, is required.

Documents to be Submitted When Applying

1. Standard Documents Requirement
2. Application for admission together with an application and entrance examination fee of ¥30, 000
3. Official transcript of all college work completed.

Date: Jan. 26–28, 1989

place: Admissions Office (1989 not yet decided)

GRADUATE PROGRAMS

Graduate School of Arts (First Year Enrollment : Master's 90, Doctor's 28)

Divisions

Education, English and American Literature, French Literature, Geography, German Literature, History, Japanese Literature, Psychology, Systematic Theology

Graduate School of Economics (First Year Enrollment : Master's 60, Doctor's 5)

Division

Economics

Graduate School of Law (First Year Enrollment : Master's 40, Doctor's 5)

Divisions

Civil and Criminal Law, Comparative Law

Graduate School of Science (First Year Enrollment : Master's 21, Doctor's 11)

Divisions

Atomic Physics, Chemistry, Mathematics

Graduate School of Social Relations (First Year Enrollment : Master's 20, Doctor's 5)

Division

Applied Sociology

Foreign Student Admission

Qualifications for Applicants

Master's Program

Standard Qualifications Requirement

Doctor's Program

Standard Qualifications Requirement

Examination at the University

Master's Program

Examination in the program's prescribed subjects is required.

Doctor's Program

Same as Master's program.

Documents to be Submitted When Applying
Standard Documents Requirement

Applicants for the Doctor's Program who have not received their master's degree from Rikkyo University must submit their master's thesis before the examination.

∗

Research Institutes and Centers

Computer Center, Facilities for Asian Area Studies, Institute for American Studies, Institute for Atomic Energy, Institute for Latin American Studies, Institute of Christian Education, Institute of Industrial Relations, Institute of Social Welfare, Institute of Tourism, Psychological and Educational Clinical Center

Center for International Studies

Organized to operate various programs for students, researchers, and faculty members of universities and research instiutes abroad as well as those at Rikkyo University.

Specifically, the Center is responsible for the administration of the following:

1. Establishing and promoting agreements with foreign universities for the exchange of students and faculty
2. Sending and accepting students to and from abroad
3. Conducting Japanese language and Japanology courses for foreign students
4. Sending and accepting faculty members and researchers to and from abroad
5. International public relations and international liaison

Special Programs for Foreign Students

The language courses, however, are not designed nor intended to constitute a full major. As these courses are only of a supplementary nature, applications for admission to Rikkyo for the study of the Japanese language itself as a major cannot be considered.

For Further Information

Undergraduate and Graduate Admission
Admissions Office, Rikkyo University, 3–34–1 Nishi Ikebukuro, Toshima–ku, Tokyo 171 ☎ 03–985–2204

Rissho University
(Rissho Daigaku)

4–2–16 Osaki, Shinagawa–ku, Tokyo 141
☎ 03–492–5262

Faculty
    Profs. 143   Assoc. Profs. 25
    Assist. Profs. Full–time 10; Part–time 319
    Res. Assocs. 7
Number of Students
    Undergrad. 8, 949   Grad. 158
Library 566, 965 volumes

Outline and Characteristics of the University

Rissho University was originally established in 1904 under the name Nichiren Buddhist College. Following the promulgation of the New School Education Law, the establishment of Rissho University was approved and the former Nichiren Buddhist College was made into a division of Rissho University.

The present Rissho University was thus begun in 1949, with the Faculty of Buddhism and the Faculty of Letters. In 1950, the Faculty of Economics and a junior college division were added. In 1961, the Faculty of Business Administration and the Kumagaya Campus were added. The Faculty of Law was founded in 1981. At present, Rissho University is comprised of five faculties, eleven departments, seven reserch institutes, two campuses, a junior college, and a junior and senior high school.

Rissho University was founded to promote Nichiren Shonin's life–long ideal of upholding righteousness. The founding spirit is manifested in the following three vows: to pursue and be devoted to the truth; to honor justice and eliminate evil; and to pray for peace and do one's best for mankind.

The life of Nichiren Shonin was filled with benevolence, based on the consciousness that he was the messenger of the Buddha Sakyamuni. He fought for justice at the risk of his own life and strove for the realization of an ideal world governed by truth. He pledged "to be the eyes of Japan, pillar of Japan and vessel of Japan" and dedicated his life for all of mankind.

The students of this university should learn from Nichiren Shonin's spirit of righteousness, acquire academic and technical knowledge that meets the needs of the times, and contribute to human society.

UNDERGRADUATE PROGRAMS

Faculty of Buddhism (Freshmen Enrollment: Day 140, Evening 40)
Department of General Buddhism
Buddhism, Buddhist and Western Philosophy, Buddhist Arts, Buddhist Literature, Buddhist Literature in Japan, Buddhist Precepts, Comparative Study of Religious Thinking, History of Chinese Buddhism, History of Formed Mahayana Buddhism, History of Indian Buddhism, History of Indian Philosophy, History of Japanese Buddhism, One Vehicle Teaching, Sanskrit MSS of Lotus Sutra, Study of Central Asia, Study of the Silk Road, Ti'en–tai Buddhism, Ti'en–tai's Thought, Vasubandhu's Thought
Department of Nichiren Buddhism
Contemporary Religion, Doctrine of Lotus Sutra, Historical Development of Nichiren Buddhism, Historical Development of the Nichiren Sect, Life of Nichiren, Nichiren Buddhism, Nichiren's Writings, Propagation and Ceremony of the Nichiren Sect
Faculty of Business Administration (Freshmen Enrollment: 300)

Department of Business Administration

Accounting, Business Enterprise, Business History, Business Management, Business Management, Commercial Science, Management Science

Faculty of Economics (Freshmen Enrollment: Day 300, Evening 160)

Department of Economics

Agricultural Economics, Econometrics, Economic History, Economic History of Europe, Economic History of Japan, Economic Law, Economic Mathematics, Economic Policy, Economics, Economic Statistics, History of Economic Theories, History of Modern American Economy, History of Modern Social and Economic Development of Japan, Industrial Organization, International Economics, Labor Economics, Macroeconomics, Marketing Economics, Microeconomics, Modern Economics, Modern Financial Theory, Monetary Economics, Political Economy, Public Economics, Public Finance, Regional Economics, Regional Finance

Faculty of Law (Freshmen Enrollment: 300)

Department of Law

Adiministrative Law, Anglo-American Law, Asian Law, Bankruptcy Law, Business Law, Civil Law, Commercial Law, Constitutional Law, Corporation Accounts Act, Criminal Law, History of Political Thought, Insurance Law, International Law, Labor Law, Law of Administrative Remedy, Law of Civil Procedure, Law of Criminal Procedure, Law of International Business Transaction, Law of Tourism, Local Goverment Act, Mortgage of Companies Property Act, Political Science, Securities and Exchange Act, Tax Act of Business

Faculty of Letters (Freshmen Enrollment: Day 660, Evening 180)

Department of English and American Literature

American Literature, English Grammar, English Literature, History of American Literature, History of English Literature

Department of Geography

Cartography, Climatology, Geographical Data Ana lysis, Geology, Geomorphology, History of Geography, Hydrology and Oceanography, Methodology of Geography, Physical Geography

Department of History

Archaeology, Japanese History, Occidental History, Oriental History

Department of Japanese Literature

History of Japanese Literature, Japanese Language, Japanese Literature

Department of Philosophy

Ethics, History of Philosophy, Philosophy, Psychology

Department of Sociology

Community Organization, Cultural Anthropology, History of Sociology, Industrial Sociology, Method of Social Research, Rural Sociology, Social Casework, Social Group Work, Social Psychology, Social Welfare, Sociology, Sociology of Family, Sociology of Information, Sociology of Religion, Urban Sociology

Foreign Student Admission

Qualifications for Applicants

Standard Qualifications Requirement

Examination at the University

Selective examination of the submitted documents and an interview.

Documents to be Submitted When Applying

Standard Documents Requirement

Application Period: November 1 to November 18.

GRADUATE PROGRAMS

Graduate School of Economics (First year Enrollment: Master's 10)

Division

Economics

Graduate School of Literature (First Year Enrollment : Master's 66, Doctor's 14)

Divisions

Buddhist Studies, English and American Literature, Geography, History, Japanese Literature, Philosophy, Sociology

Foreign Student Admission

Qualifications for Applicants

Master's Program

Standard Qualifications Requirement

Doctor's Program

Standard Qualifications Requirement

Examination at the University

Master's Program

Entrance examination will be given in early March.

1. Written examination in specified subjects.
2. Written examination of a foreign language: English, German or French. Applicants to the Philosophy Dept. must select between English and German.
3. Oral examination.
4. Foreign students are required to have a certain degree of proficiency in Japanese, depending on subject.
5. Foreign students are required to take the interview and, when necessary, a detailed physical examination.

Economics division In addition to above, written examination on Principles of Political Economy.

Doctor's Program

Entrance examination will be given in every March.

1. Written examination in specified subjects.
2. Written examination of foreign languages:
    Buddhist Studies: Sanskrit and English, German or French.
    Geography: English, German, or French.
    English and American Literature: German or French.
    Sociology: English, and either German or French.

History: English plus one (Japanese History--early Japanese documents; Oriental History--Chinese; Occidental History--German or French.)
3. Oral examination.
4. Foreign students are required to have a certain degree of proficiency in Japanese, depending on subject.
5. Foreign students are required to take the interview and, when necessary, a detailed physical examination.

Documents to be Submitted When Applying
Standard Documents Requirement

*

Research Institutes and Centers
Institute for Economic Research, Institute for the Comprehensive Study of Lotus Sutra, Institute for the Nichiren Buddhist Study, Institute of Industrial Management, Legal Institute of Rissho University, The Center of North Saitama Area Studies, The Institute of Humanistic Sciences

For Further Information
Undergraduate Admission
Office of Curricula and Records, Rissho University, 4-2-16 Osaki, Shinagawa-ku, Tokyo 141 ☎ 03-492-6613
Graduate Admission
Graduate School Office, Rissho University, 4-2-16 Osaki, Shinagawa-ku, Tokyo 141 ☎ 03-492-3830

Ritsumeikan University
(Ritsumeikan Daigaku)

56-1 Kitamachi, Tojiin, Kita-ku, Kyoto-shi, Kyoto 603 ☎ 075-463-1131

Faculty
    Profs. 270   Assoc. Profs. 117
    Assist. Profs. Part-time 613
    Res. Assocs. 28
Number of Students
    Undergrad. 20,169   Grad. 231
Library 1,247,511 volumes

Outline and Characteristics of the University
Ritsumeikan University is a private, secular co-educational institution of higher learning. The phrase "Ritsumei" comes from a passage in a book written by Mencius, a great thinker in ancient China, and means "to fulfil one's mission in life"; "kan" means "building. " Originally this was the name of a small private school founded in 1869 by Prince Kinmochi Saionji, an eminent statesman and liberal thinker who later served as the prime minister of Japan.

Today, the University is ranked among the leading private universities of Japan. However, it had quite a modest start. In 1900 its founding father Kojuro Nakagawa, with the encouragement and help of Prince Kinmochi Saionji, opened a small law school devoted to teaching working youths at night. In a few years, the school developed into an institution of higher education with a college of law and economics and a pre-professional school.

Following the end of the Pacific War, the University underwent a new phase of rapid growth. In 1946 the late Dr. Hiroshi Suekawa was appointed president. Suekawa was a prominent thinker of postwar democracy as well as a noted authority on jurisprudence. His efforts to inculcate the spirit of pacifism, democracy, and academic freedom in both teachers and students contributed immeasurably to making the University what it is today.

At present Ritsumeikan University has seven faculties in the day program and five faculties in the evening program. There are also six graduate schools offering courses leading to the Master's and Doctoral degrees. The total enrollment is approximately 20,000 including many foreign students. In recent years the University has increasingly welcomed students from abroad; eventually the number of foreign students is expected to reach several hundred. The campus is situated in a very quiet residential district and is part of the municipal scenic zone. Well-known temples such as Kinkaku-ji, Ryoan-ji, and Toji-in surround the University site, and a fine panorama of Kyoto City can be enjoyed from the upper floors of the campus buildings.

UNDERGRADUATE PROGRAMS

Faculty of Business Administration (Freshmen Enrollment: 630)
Department of Business Administration
Accounting, Administration and Management, Economic Principles, Industry
Faculty of Economics (Freshmen Enrollment: 600)
Department of Economics
Business Administration, Economic History and Analysis of Present Economic Conditions, Economic Policy, Structural Analysis, Theoretical Economics
Faculty of International Relations (Freshmen Enrollment: 160)
Department of International Relations
Area Studies, Comparative Geography, International Cultural Affairs, International Economic Affairs, International Economics, International Political Affairs, International Politics, International Relations, International Society, Japanese Culture, Law and Culture
Faculty of Law (Freshmen Enrollment: 600)
Department of Law
Civil Law, Criminal Law, Fundamental Law, Politics, Public Law
Faculty of Letters (Freshmen Enrollment: 700)
Department of Geography
Cartography, Economic Geography, Geography of Asia, Geography of Japan, Geography of the World, Historical Geography, Human Geography, Physical

Geography, Urban Geography
Department of History
Asian History Course
Japanese History Course
Western History Course
Archaeology, Asian History, Folklore, Historical Geography, History of Fine Arts, History of Historiography, History of Japanese Thought, History of Socio-Economy, History of Western Literature, Japanese History, Mythology, Paleography, Religious History, Western History
Department of Literature
Chinese Literature Course
Chinese Language, Chinese Literature, Chinese Philology, History of Chinese Literature, History of Chinese Philosophy, Philology
English and American Literature Course
English and American Literature, English Language, English Philology, History of American Literature, History of English Literature, History of Western Literature, Philology
Japanese Literature Course
History of Japanese Literature, History of Japanese Thought, Japanese Literature, Japanese Philology
Department of Philosophy
Philosophy Course
Aesthetics and Fine Arts, Ethics, History of Japanese Thought, History of Oriental Philosophy, History of Western Philosophy, Logic, Philosophy, Religion
Psychology Course
Methods of Psychological Study, Psychology, Psychopathology, Social Psychology
Faculty of Science and Engineering (Freshmen Enrollment: 570)
Department of Chemistry
Analytical Chemistry, Biochemistry, Chemical Engineering, Chemical Engineering Design, Earth Science, High Polymer Chemistry, Industrial Inorganic Chemistry, Industrial Organic Chemistry, Inorganic Chemistry, Inorganic Industrial Materials, Organic Chemistry, Organic Synthesis, Physical Chemistry, Quantum Chemistry, Radiochemistry, Science of Polymers, Spectroscopic Aspect of Organic Compounds
Department of Civil Engineering
Bridges, City Planning, Civil Engineering Materials, Civil Engineering Planning, Construction Engineering, Design of Water Works, Earthquake-proof Structural Engineering, Harbors, Highways, Hydraulics, Railways, Rivers, Sanitary and Environmental Engineering, Soil Mechanics, Strength of Structures, Strength of Structures, Surveying
Department of Computer Science and Systems Engineering
Algorithm Theory, Artificial Intelligence, Compiler Construction, Computer Laboratory, Control Engineering, Data Communication, Data Structure, Electronics, Image Processing, Information Engineering, Programming Language, Robotics, Systems Engineering, Systems Programming

Department of Electrical Engineering
Application of Electric Power, Communication Engineering, Computer Software, Control Engineering, Electrical Materials, Electric Circuits, Electric Machines and Apparatus, Electric Measuring Instruments, Electric Power Generation, Electric Power Transmission and Distribution, Electromagnetic Theory, Electromagnetic Wave Theory, Electronic Circuits, Energy Engineering, Gaseous Electronics, Illumination Engineering, Information Processing Systems, Information Theory, Instrumentation and Measurement, Material Electronics, Measurement Systems in Engineering, Microwave Engineering, Network Theory, Numerical Analysis, Power Control Engineering, Power System Engineering, Signal Theory, Solid State Electronics
Department of Mathematics and Physics
Algebra, Analytical Geometry, Atomic Physics, Complex Variables, Crystal Physics, Electromagnetic Theory, Mathematical Analysis, Mathematical Methods in Physics, Mathematical Statistics, Nuclear Physics, Optics, Physics of Fluids, Physics of Matter, Probability and Statistics, Projective Geometry, Quantum Mechanics, Radiation Biology, Radiation Physics, Real Variables, Topology
Department of Mechanical Engineering
Air Conditioning, Combustion Processes, Elasticity, Engineering Mechanics, Fluid Machines, Fluid Mechanics, Heat Transfer, Instrumentation Engineering, Internal Combustion Engines, Machine Design and Drawing, Machine Tools, Manufacturing Processes, Materials Handling Engineering, Materials Science and Engineering, Mechanical Design, Mechanical Vibration, Mechanics of Materials, Mechanisms and Dynamics of Machinery, Plasticity, Precision Engineering, Production Systems Analysis and Design, Steam Power Plants, Strength of Structural Materials, Structural Mechanics, Thermodynamics
Faculty of Social Sciences (Freshmen Enrollment: 700)
Department of Social Sciences
Industry and Labor, Life and Culture, Social Problems, Social Research and Statistics, Sociology, Economics and History

Foreign Student Admission
Qualifications for Applicants
Standard Qualifications Requirement
Examination at the University
Faculties of Law, Economics, Business Administration, Social Sciences and Letters:
1. Japanese (including Listening Comprehension)
2. English
3. Interview
Faculty of International Relations:
1. Japanese (including Listenig Comprehension)
2. English
3. Essay

4.   Interview
Faculty of Science and Engineering:
1.   Japanese (including Listening Comprehension)
2.   English
3.   Mathematics
4.   Interview
Documents to be Submitted When Applying
     Standard Documents Requirement
Application Deadline: November 19

GRADUATE PROGRAMS

Graduate School of Business Management (First Year Enrollment : Master's 20, Doctor's 5)
  Division
Business Management
Graduate School of Economics (First Year Enrollment : Master's 60, Doctor's 10)
  Division
Economics
Graduate School of Law (First Year Enrollment : Master's 50, Doctor's 15)
  Divisions
Civil Law, Public Law
Graduate School of Letters (First Year Enrollment : Master's 105, Doctor's 25)
  Divisions
English and American Literature, European Philosophy, Geography, History, Japanese Literature, Oriental Literary Thought, Oriental Thought, Philosophy, Psychology
Graduate School of Science and Engineering (First Year Enrollment : Master's 25, Doctor's 10)
  Divisions
Applied Chemistry, Civil Engineering, Electrical Engineering, Mechanical Engineering, Physics
Graduate School of Sociology (First Year Enrollment : Master's 15, Doctor's 5)
  Division
Applied Sociology

Foreign Student Admission
  Qualifications for Applicants
Master's Program
     Standard Qualifications Requirement
Doctor's Program
     Standard Qualifications Requirement
  Examination at the University
Master's Program
Those residing outside Japan:
1.   Screening of required documents
Those residing in Japan:
1.   Screening of required documents
2.   Examination in the subject of the applicant's major
3.   Interview
Doctor's Program
     Same as Master's Program.
  Documents to be Submitted When Applying

     Standard Documents Requirement
Application Deadline: December 15
                    *
Research Institutes and Centers
Data Processing Center, Research Institute of Cultural Sciences, Research Institute of Science and Engineering
Facilities/Services for Foreign Students
     Facilities and Equipment:
International Center
International Lounge
Dormitories (residing together with Japanese students)
Foreign Students Section (in the Library)
Audio-Visual Room for studying languages
     Events:
Visiting the homes of Japanese families during vacations
Exchange Picnic (together with Japanese students)
Farewell Party for Graduating Students
Open House of the International Center
Special Programs for Foreign Students
1.   Japanese Language (Reading Comprehension, Conversation, Grammar, Composition)
2.   Japan Studies (Culture, Geography, Nature Economics, Technology)
3.   Chinese
4.   English
For Further Information
  Undergraduate and Graduate Admission
International Center, Ritsumeikan Universiry, 56-1 Kitamachi, Tojiin, Kita-ku, Kyoto-shi, Kyoto 603
☎ 075-463-1131 ext. 2372

Ryukoku University
(Ryukoku Daigaku)

67 Tsukamoto-cho, Fukakusa, Fushimi-ku, Kyoto-shi, Kyoto 612   ☎ 075-642-1111

Faculty
     Profs.   150   Assoc. Profs.   50
     Assist. Profs.   Full–time   11; Part–time   451
Number of Students
     Undergrad.   9, 445   Grad.   311
Library   914, 029 volumes

Outline and Characteristics of the University
     Dating back to 1679, Ryukoku University is one of the oldest institutions of higher education in the world. Like other long established educational institutions, such as Harvard and Oxford, the school originally started as a religious seminary. Ryukoku has been one of Japan's largest liberal arts universities, with Schools of Letters, Economics, Business Administrations and Law, while retaining its original ideal of Buddhism. However, as other modernized educational institutions, the University values interfaith and international communication which as-

sures progress and success in the future of mankind. Presently, Ryukoku has student exchange programs with five foreign universities and special friendship agreements with several other educational institutions abroad.

Ryukoku is located at the center of the ancient capital of Japan, Kyoto. It is famous for being the center of traditional culture and also as a "University Town" with more than 30 institutions of higher education. Nearby metropolises, Osaka, Nara, Kobe and Nagoya, are only one hour away. Kyoto is greatly blessed with the natural beauty of the four seasons which dramatically change the scenery of the city. Nearby mountains are covered with cherry blossom in spring, fresh green in summer, brilliantly colorful leaves in autumn and silvery white snow in winter. Kyoto is one of the rare cities in the world where the progressive urbane life is in harmony with the peaceful beauty of nature.

UNDERGRADUATE PROGRAMS

Faculty of Business Administration (Freshmen Enrollment: 500)
  Department of Business Administration
Accounting, Accounting for Taxation, Auditing, Bookkeeping, Business Analysis, Business History, Business Management, Business Management Administration, Business Orientation, Cooperatives, Cost Accounting, Financial Management, Financial Statements, Forms of Business Enterprise, History of Management Thought, Industrial Management, Labor Management, Management Information Processing, Management Information Systems, Production Management, Small Corporate Management, Socialist Enterprise
Faculty of Economics (Freshmen Enrollment: 500)
  Department of Economics
Agricultural Economics, Banking Systems, Commercial Economics, Comparative Economic Systems, Contemporary Capitalism, Econometrics, Economic Developments, Economic Dynamics, Economic History, Economic Policy, Economics, Fiscal and Monetary Policy, Foreign Economics, History of Economics, History of Japanese Economic Thought, History of Modern Economics, Industrial Economics, Industrial Structure, International Economics, International Monetary Theory, Japanese Economics, Labor Economics, Mathematical Economists, Monetary Theory, National Income, Philosophy of Economics, Political Economy, Public Economics, Public Finance, Regional Economics, Socialist Economy, Statistical Analysis, Transportation Economics, Urban Economics, World Economics
Faculty of Law (Freshmen Enrollment: 500)
  Department of Law
Administrative Law, Civil Law, Civil Procedure, Commercial Law, Constitutional Law, Criminal Law, Criminal Procedure, Criminology, Economic Law, History of Modern Legal Thought, Interna-

tional Law, Labor Law, Law of Socialist States, Legal History, Philosophy of Law, Religious Law, Social Security Law, Sociology of Law
Faculty of Letters (Freshmen Enrollment: 650)
  Department of Buddhist Studies
Buddhism, Buddhist Scriptures, Buddhist Studies, Chinese Buddhism, History of Doctrine in True Pure Land Buddhism, History of Indian Thought, History of Theories in Pure Land Buddhism, Indian Buddhism, Indian Literature, Japanese Buddhism, Pure Land Buddhism, Tibetan Buddhism
  Department of History
  Buddhism History Course
  Japanese History Course
  Oriental History Course
Archaeology, Ethnology, Historical Geography, History of Buddhism, History of Buddhist Culture, History of Chinese Buddhism, History of Chinese Culture, History of European Culture, History of Fine Art, History of Indian Buddhism, History of Japanese Buddhism, History of Japanese Culture, History of True Pure Land Buddhism, History of Turfan Buddhism, Japanese History, Oriental History
  Department of Literature
  English Literature Course
English and American Literature, English Language, History of American Literature, History of English Literature, History of the English Language, Philology, Phonetics
  Japanese Literature Course
Buddhist Literature, Calligraphy, Classical Chinese, History of Chinese Literature, History of Japanese Literature, Japanese Language, Japanese Literature
  Department of Philosophy
  Education Course
Adolescent Psychology, Educational Administration, Educational Methodology, Educational Psychology, History of European Education, History of Japanese Eduction, Religious Education, Social Education, Sociology of Education
  Philosophy Course
Christian Theology, Esthetics, Ethics, History of Chinese Philosophy, History of Philosophy, History of Religion, Modern Philosophical Thoughts, Philosophy of Science, Psychology of Religion
Faculty of Science and Technology (Freshmen Enrollment: 340)
  Department of Applied Mathematics and Informatics
Algorithm, Analytical Mathematics, Analytic Function, Applied Physics, Artifical Intelligence, Automaton, Communication Theory, Computer Graphics, Computer Organizaition, Data Base, Data Processing Structure, Differential Equation/Fourier Analisis, Digital Signal Analysis, Electric Circuit, Electromagnetics, Environmental Science, Function, Graphics, Graph/Network, Human Engineering, Information Theory, Mathematical Information, Mathematical Physics, Model, Numerical Analysis, Operating System, Ordinary Differential Equation, Partial Dif-

ferential Equations, Pattern Recognition, Probability/Statistics, Programming Language, Pyiscs Laboratory, Science Laboratory, Seminor in Mathematics, Software, Survey of Mathematics

Department of Electronics and Informatics
Applied Mathematics, Artificial Intelligence, Automaton, Computer Graphics, Data Base, Data Communications, Electric Circuit, Formal Languages, Graphic Data Processing, Graphics, Graph/Network, Human Engineering, Information Processing in the Nervous System, Integrated Circuit, Introduction to Information, Introduction to Software, LSI Designing, Numerical Analysis, Operating Systems, Pattern Recognition, Programming Language, Robotto Engineering, Software Engineering, Survey of Information, Theory of Interface

Department of Materials Chemistry
Applied Electro Magnetics, Catalytic Chemistry, Chemical Thermodynamics, Electro-chemistry, Electron-Point of Light-Material Engineering, Environmental Chemistry, Functional Ceramics Engineering, Functional Polymar Engineering, Inorganic Structual Chemistry, Instrumental Analysis Chemistry, Material Science Chemistry, Metal Material Science, Organic Structural Chemistry, Polymer Chemistry, Quantitative Analysis Chemistry, Rational Analysis Chemistry, Reaction Engineering, Structural Chemistry, Survay of Information, Survey of Industrial Chemistry, Survey of Inorganic Chemistry, Survey of Mineralogy, Survey of Organic Chemistry, Survey of Quantum Chemistry

Department of Mechanical and System Engineering
Applied Production System, Artificial Intelligence, CAD/CAM, Composite Material Engineering, Digital Signal Analysis, Electric Circuit, Electronic Control, Electronic Device, Electronic Device, Functional Material, Graphics, Human Engineering, Introduction to Information, Introduction to Soft Ware, Material Mechanics, Non-Destructive Testing, Numerical Analysis, Numerical Control, Real-time System, Reliability Engineering, Rheology, Robotics, Sensor Engineering, Structual Mechanics, System Engineering, Theory of Control, Theory of Interface

Faculty of Sociology (Enrollment: 200)
Department of Social Welfare
Basic Seminor of Social Welfare, Buddhist Social Welfare, Children's Welfare, Clinical Psychology, Comparative Social Welfare, Counseling, Development of Social Welfare, Family Welfare, Introduction to Social Welfare, Mental Hygiene, Personality Development, Regional Welfare, Rehabilitation, Social Policy, Social Psycology, Social Psycology, Social Security, Social Survey, Social Welfare Policy, Survey of Sociology, Welfare of Senior Citizens, Welfare of the Handicapped

Department of Sociology
Comparative Culture, Comparative Society, Comunication, Cultural Anthropology, Ecology, Ethnicity, History of Sociology, Introduction to Sociology, Labor and Capital Relation, Mass-communication, Modern Society, Population Problems, Regional Sociology, Seminor of Sociology, Social Consciousness, Social Development, Social Pathology, Social Psychology, Social Survey, Social System, Sociology of Administration, Sociology of Industry, Sociology of Politics, Sociology of Religion, The Family

Foreign Student Admission
Qualifications for Applicants
Standard Qualifications Requirement
Examination at the University
Application documents presented will be screened by a faculty committee. Applicants who are successful in this first screening will be requested to take an examination (second acreening). The contents of the examination differ from faculty to faculty. All applicants will be examined their Japanese language proficiency. Some faculties also examine English and/or basic knowlege of the area of study to be pursued.

Documents to be Submitted When Applying
Standard Documents Requirement
Certificate of Proficiency in Japanese quired. by a qualified person (an instructor, a diplomatic of consular official of the Japanese Government, or such persons)

Qualifications for Transfer Students
As a third-year undergraduate transfer student:
Completion of the first two years or its equivalent of an undergraduate course at an institution of higher education.
Examination for Transfer Students
Same as the procedure for freshman applicants.
Documents to be Submitted When Applying
Standard Documents Requirement
Certificate of Proficiency in Japanese

GRADUATE PROGRAMS

Graduate School of Business Administration (First Year Enrollment : Master's 10, Doctor's 3)
Division
Business Administration
Graduate School of Economics (First Year Enrollment : Master's 10, Doctor's 3)
Division
Economics
Graduate School of Law (First Year Enrollment : Master's 10, Doctor's 5)
Division
Law
Graduate School of Letters (First Year Enrollment : Master's 82, Doctor's 24)
Divisions
Buddhist Studies, English Literature, Japanese History, Japanese Literature, Oriental History, Philosophy, Social Welfare, Sociology, True Pure Land Buddhism

Foreign Student Admission

Qualifications for Applicants

Master's Program

Standard Qualifications Requirement

Doctor's Program

Standard Qualifications Requirement

Examination at the University

Master's Program

Same as for undergraduate applicants.

Doctor's Program

Same as for undergraduate applicants.

Documents to be Submitted When Applying

Standard Documents Requirement

Certificate of Proficiency in Japanese

a detailed plan of study to be undertaken. Only an applicant to the Graduate Program leading to the doctorate needs to sumbit a summary of the thesis submitted for the Master's degree.

*

Research Institutes and Centers

Institute of Buddhist Cultural Studies, Research Institute for Social Science

Facilities/Services for Foreign Students

1. A dormitory for international students
2. International Student Lounge:

Special Programs for Foreign Students

Japanese Culture and Language Program (JCLP):

an ideal one-year preparatory course for students intending to study in a Japanese university. The basic program consists of 20 hours per week of intensive Japanese language study, including optional introductory lectures on various aspects of Japanese thought and society. As for foreign students in the General Education Course, general education subjects, foreign languages and physical education may be replaced, up to 34 credits, by the courses in Japanese Culture and Language Program.

For Further Information

Undergraduate and Graduate Admission

Admissions Section, Office of Academic Affairs, Ryukoku University, 67 Tsukamoto-cho, Fukakusa, Fushimi-ku, Kyoto-shi, Kyoto 612 ☎ 075-642-1111 ext. 240

Ryutsu-Keizai University

(Ryutsu-Keizai Daigaku)

120 Hirahata, Ryugasaki-shi, Ibaraki 301
☎ 0297-64-0001

Faculty

Profs. 39   Assoc. Profs. 17

Assist. Profs. Full–time 14; Part–time 51

Number of Students

Undergrad. 2, 941   Grad. 5

Library 125, 063 volumes

Outline and Characteristics of the University

Ryutsu-Keizai University was founded in 1965. The original funding for the University was made by Nippon Express Company, one of the leading companies of transportation and physical distribution in the world. The principal purpose of the University is to cultivate persons who are expected to contribute to the development of future industry and culture through positive research, and academic study.

Our University has two faculties: Economics (Departments of Economics and Management) and Sociology (Department of Sociology). The Faculty of Economics was opened in 1965 at the same time of the foundation of the University. And in 1973, the Institute of Distribution Studies was founded as a attached research institute. In 1979, a one-year graduate course was opened. Then in 1988, the Faculty of Sociology was newly opened. Through the University extension courses, we have an "Open University" which promotes friendly relations and communication with the local community.

Students from various parts of the world are now studying on campus. They are Chinese, Indonesian, Korean, Malaysian, and people of other Pan-Pacific countries. It is with gratitude that we joined hands with Beijing College of Economics as a sister school in 1985 and with Beijing Materials College in 1988.

Our University has two characteristics. One is its small classes, which we refer to as "Seminars". From freshman to seniors, students belong to a certain seminar of their own choosing. The other is its teaching staff who are highly qualified and have considerable experience in teaching and broad knowledge of their specialities. Thus, each student under the guidance of his advisor enjoys studying his own special interest. There are many seminar classes from which each student selects his own field of study. The University has the added advantage of maintaining warm and friendly relations between its teaching staff and students.

The campus is located in Ryugasaki City, one-hour by train from Tokyo and thirty minutes by car from Tsukuba Academic Community, the biggest center of research and education in Japan. The campus is appropriately surrounded by wide stretches of open fields offering pastoral tranquility for academic research, study, and sports.

UNDERGRADUATE PROGRAMS

Faculty of Economics (Freshmen Enrollment: 600)

Common Subjects in both Departments

Computer Programing, Computer Science, Information Theory, Marketing and Distribution Economy, Physical Distribution, Theory of International Transportation

Department of Economics

Agricultural Economics, Economic Geography, Economic Policy, Economics, History of Economic Doctrines, International Economics, Japanese Economic

History, Labor Problems, Money and Banking, Public Finance, Statistics, Western Economic History
　Department of Management
Accounting, Auditing, Book Keeping, Business Finance, Cost Accounting Management, Managerial Accoounting, Marketing Management, Personal Management, Production Management
Faculty of Sociology (Freshmen Enrollment: 180)
Family Sociology, General Theory of Social Welfare, History of Sociology, Industrial Sociology, Leisure Sociology, Minority Problems, Regional Sociology, Theory of Social Security

Foreign Student Admission
　Qualifications for Applicants
　　Standard Qualifications Requirement
　Examination at the University
　1.　Dictation and listening comprehension of the Japanese language.
　2.　Examination to determine the ability to read and understand Japanese.
　3.　Interview
　Documents to be Submitted When Applying
　　Standard Documents Requirement

ONE-YEAR GRADUATE PROGRAMS

One-Year Graduate Course of Economics (Enrollment: 15)
Economics, Management

Foreign Student Admission
　Qualifications for Applicants
　　Standard Qualifications Requirement
　Examination at the University
　1.　Oral test about basic knowledge
　2.　Interview
　3.　Examination of academic performances (only on the basis of the school record)
　Regular classes begin in April but special admission is possible in October.

＊

Research Institutes and Centers
Academic Society, Computer Information Center, Institute of Distribution Studies
Facilities/Services for Foreign Students
　Special orientation guidance and welcome party
Special Programs for Foreign Students
International Friendship House low-rented dormitory for foreign students.
　1.　Japanese Society and Culture I~III (as subject of general education)
　2.　Japanese Language class
For Further Information
Admission Office, Ryutsu-Keizai University, 120 Hirahata, Ryugasaki-shi, Ibaraki 301 ☎ 0297-64-0001 ext. 43, 45, Fax: 0297-64-0011

Sagami Institute of Technology
(Sagami Kogyo Daigaku)
1-1-25 Tsujido Nishikaigan, Fujisawa-shi, Kanagawa 251　☎ 0466-34-4111

Faculty
　Profs.　31　　Assoc. Profs.　27
　Assist. Profs.　Full-time　16; Part-time　65
　Res. Assocs.　7
Number of Students
　Undergrad.　2, 532
Library　88, 243 volumes

Outline and Characteristics of the University
　Sagami Institute of Technology was founded in 1963. At the time of its foundation the Institute consisted of two departments: the Department of Mechanical Engineering and the Department of Electrical Engineering. In 1968, the Department of Applied Mathematics was. added, and was renamed the Department of Information Science in 1972.
　Attaching great importance to "initiative and responsibility", the Institute aims to groom the student for this new age of high technology. For this purpose, special emphasis is laid on the student's social adjustment and strong sense of challenge, as well as on his practical ability to cope with today's advanced technology.
　Located in the center of the Shonan District, the Institute provides an ideal environment both for academic and extra-curricular activities.

UNDERGRADUATE PROGRAMS

Faculty of Engineering (Freshmen Enrollment: 570)
　Department of Electrical Engineering
　Department of Information Science
　Department of Mechanical Engineering
＊
For Further Information
　Undergraduate Admission
Admissions Office, Sagami Institute of Technology, 1-1-25 Tsujido Nishikaigan, Fujisawa-shi, Kanagawa 251 ☎ 0466-34-4111

Sagami Women's University
(Sagami Joshi Daigaku)
2-1-1 Bunkyo, Sagamihara-shi, Kanagawa 228
☎ 0427-42-1411

UNDERGRADUATE PROGRAMS

Faculty of Liberal Arts (Freshmen Enrollment: 300)

Department of English Literature
Department of Food and Nutrition
Department of Japanese Literature

Saitama Institute of Technology
(Saitama Kogyo Daigaku)

1690 Fusaiji, Okabe-machi, Osato-gun, Saitama
369–02 ☎ 0485–85–2521

Faculty
  Profs. 24   Assoc. Profs. 14
  Assist. Profs. Full–time 16; Part–time 27
Number of Students
  Undergrad. 1, 264
Library 50, 963 volumes

Outline and Characteristics of the University
  The Saitama Institute of Technology (SIT) was established in 1976 by elevating the status of Hijiribashi Technical College to that of an institute of technology.
  The educational policy of this institute is rather unique in comparison with other universities. This institute aims to instruct science and technology through the spirit of Buddhism. Someone may doubt the validity of the relationship between Buddhism and technology. However, upon looking back at the long history of mankind, one can easily see the close relationship between technology and religion. One clear example for this would be the reciprocal advancement in engineering and architecture over centuries as represented by the improvement in construction of the many great temples, cathedrals, churches, and shrines built all over the world.
  In the past, in the process of the establishment of modern physical science, many conflicts arose between scientists and the church. However, this is no longer the case in recent years. Science and technology have progressed rapidly especially with regard to atomic and life sciences. Unfortunately, their remarkable development has placed mankind in a precarious position, for much of the knowledge accumulated is used for research that could lead to the final destruction of the world as we know it today.
  Hence, many have turned their backs on the Western spirit based on modern science and technology and have come to support the Oriental spirit, especially that of Mahayana Buddhism. Many of Buddhist teachings are simple and straight forward. Due to this, they have gained the sympathy of scientists and engineers who realize that Buddhism is the "Science of Humanity" and the "Religion of Wisdom."
  The institute aims to educate through the spirit of Mahayana Buddhism. Moreover, it aims to educate through practical application rather than inapplicable theory.

  The campus is located in the northern part of Saitama Prefecture, and occupies an area of 91, 896 m² where many buildings provide educational facilities on floor space of 17, 853 m². The campus is graced with Japanese gardens with ponds and waterfalls where students enjoy a relaxed and peaceful academic life.

UNDERGRADUATE PROGRAMS

Faculty of Engineering (Freshmen Enrollment: 240)
  Department of Electronic Engineering
  Electronic Engineering Course
  Information Engineering Course
Circuit Engineering, Computer Engineering, Information Science and Technology, Instrumentation and Control Technology, Microwave Engineering, Semiconductor Engineering
  Department of Environmental Engineering
  Bioscience Course
  Material Science Course
Environmental Analysis, Environmental Chemistry, Environmental Preservation, Process Design
  Department of Mechanical Engineering
  Mechanical Science Course
  System Technology Course
Fluid Mechanics, Heat Engineering, Machine Design and Drawing, Mechanical Technology, Mechanics of Solid and Machinery

Foreign Student Admission
  Qualifications for Applicants
  Standard Qualifications Requirement
  Examination at the University
  Applicants must take an entrance examination consisting of a written examination and an interview held on February 14, 1987.
  Documents to be Submitted When Applying
  Standard Documents Requirement
Application Period: January 16 to 31, 1987
*
Facilities/Services for Foreign Students
A meeting room is provided for common use.
For Further Information
  Undergraduate Admission
Student Division, Saitama Institute of Technology, 1690 Fusaiji, Okabe-machi, Osato-gun, Saitama 369–02 ☎ 0485–85–2521 ext. 2142

Saitama Medical College
(Saitama Ika Daigaku)

Moroyama-machi, Iruma-gun, Saitama 350–04
☎ 0492–95–1111

UNDERGRADUATE PROGRAMS

Faculty of Medicine (Freshmen Enrollment: 100)
Department of Medicine

GRADUATE PROGRAMS

Graduate School of Medicine (First Year Enrollment : Doctor's 50)
Divisions
Biological Medicine, Clinical Medicine, Social Medicine

Sakuyo College of Music
(Sakuyo Ongaku Daigaku)

1334-1 Yaide, Tsuyama-shi, Okayama 708
☎ 0868-24-1811

Faculty
    Profs. 22   Assoc. Profs. 17
    Assist. Profs. Full-time 21; Part-time 111
Number of Students
    Undergrad. 556   Grad. 1
Library 77, 710 volumes

Outline and Characteristics of the College

Sakuyo College of Music desires not only to make much of education of religious sentiments with an ideal of mercy and wisdom, but also to promote the formation of pure and harmonious character. The college goes on such a mission as to cultivate those men of ability, who can widely contribute to society, by having them acquire the high culture modern society requires and at the same time high level of knowledge and techniques about their majors.

In 1930, Nobuo Matsuda (School Manager) and Fujiko Matsuda (Director) founded the school which became the basis of this college. In 1964, The Course of Music was established in Sakuyo Junior College, and in 1966, Sakuyo College of Music (four-year college) was established. In 1970, the Course of Music was established. In 1975, the Department of Educational Music, the Course of Educational Music, and the Course of Infant Education were established in the Faculty of Music.

UNDERGRADUATE PROGRAMS

Faculty of Music (Freshmen Enrollment: 95)
Department of Educational Music
Educational Music Major
Department of Music
Composition, Conducting, Japanese Music, Piano, String Instruments, Vocal Music, Wind and Percussion Instruments

Foreign Student Admission
Qualifications for Applicants
    Standard Qualifications Requirement
Examination at the College
    The same as the general candidates with some consideration as to the Japanese language. Speaking ability good enough for daily conversation and attending lectures is required.
Documents to be Submitted When Applying
    Standard Documents Requirement

Qualifications for Transfer Students
    The same as those of general students, although it is only when there are vacancies.
Examination for Transfer Students
    The same as undergraduate candidates.
Documents to be Submitted When Applying
    Standard Documents Requirement
                  *

Research Institutes and Centers
The Center of Study for Public Performance
For Further Information
Undergraduate and Graduate Admission
Section of Entrance Examination, Division of Planning and Information, Sakuyo College of Music, 1334-1 Yaide, Tsuyama-shi, Okayama 708
☎ 0868-24-1811 ext. 127

SANNO College
(Sanno Daigaku)

1573 Kami-kasuya, Isehara-shi, Kanagawa 259-11
☎ 0463-92-2211

Faculty
    Profs. 24   Assoc. Profs. 12
    Assist. Profs. Full-time 14; Part-time 35
    Res. Assocs. 3
Number of Students
    Undergrad. 1, 501
Library 74, 000 volumes

Outline and Characteristics of the College

SANNO College is a new school. It was opened in 1979 to meet the need for specialists versed in the technical skills crucial to the administration of resources, personnel and information in modern business and industry. Its programs are designed for undergraduate education in the ever expanding sciences of management and information processing.

This four-year degree college is a major academic segment of the time-honoured SANNO Insitute of Business Administration in Tokyo which is one of the largest private institutions in Japan in the field of management development and business education. The Institute has a history dating back to the 1920's when Yoichi Ueno as "the pioneer of scientific management in Japan" was active in prewar days. Its supreme mission is to educate businessmen of integrity who will never cease developing their own concepts and ideals of management and business administration, who will not hesitate to acquire further abilities to realize these on the job, and who will dedicate themselves to the happiness and prosperity of mankind.

Thus, SANNO incorporates a unique breadth of activities in one organization, yet it has been able to achieve a highly responsive working integration of all its diversified departments. The most important key to this is the way business theory and practice evolve together through its interwoven functions of education, research and consultation.

SANNO College is located about 30 miles west of Tokyo in a scenic suburban area of archaeological, historical, and religious interest. The campus houses a four-year college with a combined faculty in the sciences of management, business, and information processing and a plan is under way to create a graduate school.

At the College, students may major in either Management or Informatics, but in both cases must take a number of required or elective courses in the other discipline. In addition to classes and seminars, students also receive work-study experience through company internships at one of the more than 100 firms cooperating with SANNO. Such internships are an example of SANNO College's practice of working in close cooperation with industrial and business circles (a rarity among academic institutions in Japan). Most faculty members have extensive business experience and also engaged in regular consultation or other research work that keep them abreast of the needs and changing conditions of the business world. Though the College is still young, its graduates are in great demand by leading Japanese companies.

UNDERGRADUATE PROGRAMS

Department of Management and Informatics (Freshmen Enrollment: 400)
Informatics Major
Management Major
Behavioral Science, Bookkeeping, Business Administration, Business of Commerce, Consumer Behaviors, Cost Accounting, Data Communication System, Decision Analysis, Economic Theory, Financial Management, Forecasting, History of Management Science, Industrial Socio-psychology, Information Management, Information Mathemetics, Information Processing, Information Science, Information Structure, Information System Analysis, International Business Management, International Economics, International Trade, Large-scale Information System, Management Culture, Management Engineering, Management Information, Management Information System, Management of Systems Development, Management Organization, Marketing, Mar-

ket Research, Medium/Small Businesses, Modern Enterprises, Modern Industry, Multi-variate Analysis, Numerical Computation, Operating Systems, Operations Research, Personnel Administration, Physical Distribution, Probability Theory, Production Management, Quantitative Economics, Simulation, Telecommunications Industries

Foreign Student Admission
Qualifications for Applicants
   Standard Qualifications Requirement
1. In the case of an applicant who uses Chinese characters in daily life, a certificate of completion of six months or more of Japanese language education at a Japanese language school is required.
2. In the case of an applicant who does not use Chinese characters in daily life, a certificate of completion of one year or more of Japanese language education at a Japanese language school is required.
3. Such certification will be waived, in both cases, where the student is deemed to have ability in the Japanese language equivalent to or greater than that expected from such study.

Examination at the College
1. The Fundamental School Achievement Test
2. The Japanese Language Fluency Test
3. The Interview Test

Documents to be Submitted When Applying
   Standard Documents Requirement
   An installment plan for the payment of the fees may be attached together.

Qualifications for Transfer Students
1. Must have completed a junior college course as of or before March next year at the time of application,
2. Must have completed a higher technical, professional school course on or before March next year at the time of application,
3. Must have completed the first two years of an undergraduate course by acquiring a total of 62 or more credit units as of or before March next at the time of application, or
4. Have completed an undergraduate bachelor course as of or before March next year at the time of application.

An applicant for transfer as a junior (third-year) student must have acquired at other institutions a total of 62 or more credits for transfer in the category of general education including the following:
a. General subjects: 20 credits or more
b. Foreign languages: 8 credits or more
c. Gymnastic subjects: 2 credits or more,
and up to a total of 16 credits in the category of professional instruction can be accepted for transfer.

An applicant who does not meet the above conditions can not be accepted as a sophomore (second-year) student.

Examination for Transfer Students

A written examination and, or interview will be conducted, as deemed necessary.

Documents to be Submitted When Applying

Standard Documents Requirement

The same procedure as undergraduates.

*

Research Institutes and Centers

Institute of Cross–cultural Studies, Institute of International Management, Institute of Research in Information Sciences

Facilities/Services for Foreign Students

Psychological Counselling Office:

A senior professor of psychology at SANNO College is ready to accept appointments for a person –to–person interview with any foreign student who has personal problems in his/her student life in general.

Foreign Student Advisors' Office:

Foreign students are welcome to visit the teachers in this office to exchange views, make suggestions and/or discuss problems dealing with any aspect of the student life.

Students Counselling Services:

All students, Japanese and non–Japanese, are provided counselling services largely divided into the following three areas:

(a) Course studies, personal aptitude, learning methods, attendance.

(b) Extra–curricular acitivities and way of life.

(c) Employment opportunities, career development.

Special Programs for Foreign Students

Japanese Language–I:

Designed to help foreign students improve their own Japanese communication skills so that they can enjoy smoother exchange with teachers and students.

Japanese Management:

Designed to help foreign students satisfy their interest in Japanese ways of business and management, increase their vocabulary in related fields, and establish an unbiased understanding and insight into Japanese management.

Japanese Society:

An Extensive "learning by experience" live–in program is provided.

Special Lecture on Japanese Management:

A series of visual–aid learning, field visits and comparative analysis sessions will enable foreign students to be exposed to the reality of Japanese industry and business.

For Further Information

Undergraduate Admission

Admission/Testing Center, SANNO College, 1573 Kamikasuya, Isehara–shi, Kanagawa 259–11 ☎ 0463–92–2211 ext. 206

Sapporo Gakuin University
(Sapporo Gakuin Daigaku)

11 Bunkyodai, Ebetsu–shi, Hokkaido 069
☎ 011–386–8111

Faculty
Profs.   63   Assoc. Profs.   32
Assist. Profs.   Full–time 8; Part–time 146
Number of Students
Undergrad. 4, 714
Library   221, 047 volumes

Outline and Characteristics of the University

The University is one of the rapidly growing, private universities in Japan. Originally it started as a small special college then known as Sapporo College of Liberal Arts in June, 1946. The last four decades brought several significant changes, including the attainment of university status in 1968 and the name change from Sapporo College of Commerce to Sapporo Gakuin University in 1984. Today, the University has grown into an institute which enrolls about 4, 430 students altogether.

Academically, our university is divided into four Faculties: Commerce, Humanities, Law, and Commerce II (Evening Faculty). Within these Faculties are six Undergraduate Departments: Commercial Sciences, Economics, Human Sciences (Interdisciplinary Human Studies), English Language and Literature, Jurisprudence, and Commercial Sciences II. The teaching facilities are extensive. In addition to the four existing buildings, a new building, one of the finest in this area, was completed recently in 1986. It is in this building that modern audio-visual equipment, laboratories for psychological studies, staff research rooms, and student study rooms are provided. A new and large sporting field was also opened in 1985, and is some 200 meters away from the main campus.

One of the major features of our university are expressed in its ideals toward learning: academic freedom, creative research, and respect of individual personality. These ideals have been traditionally kept alive since the beginning of Sapporo College of Liberal Arts. Based upon these, our educational approach has been focused on the following three points; giving students professional training, educating the whole man, and assisting them to develop independent research. As a result, the University is gradually gaining a high reputation for its practical approach to learning. And we are rightfully proud of this achievement.

UNDERGRADUATE PROGRAMS

Faculty of Commerce (Freshmen Enrollment: 525)
Department of Commercial Sciences

Department of Economics
Faculty of Commerce (**Evening School**) (Freshmen Enrollment: 100)
Department of Commercial Sciences
Faculty of Humanities (Freshmen Enrollment: 150)
Department of English Language and Literature
Department of Human Sciences
Faculty of Law (Freshmen Enrollment: 200)
Department of Jurisprudence

Foreign Student Admission
Qualifications for Applicants
Standard Qualifications Requirement
Applicants must satisfy one of the following requirements as well:
1. Those who have taken the Japanese Language Proficiency Test and the General Examination for Foreign Students and received satisfactory grades.
2. Those who have completed courses at a Japanese language school.
3. Those who can demonstrate, in one way or another, to have mastery of the Japanese language.
Examination at the University
1. Screening on their scholastic achievement, personal history, character, health, etc.
2. Examination on the Japanese language proficiency in a written, or oral, or some other reasonable test.
Documents to be Submitted When Applying
Standard Documents Requirement
The procedure for the admitted students
1. Completion of payment of school fees and other expenses.
2. Submission of appended papers referring to credentials: (i) certificate of incumbent of guarantor, and (ii) preceding year's certificate of tax payment, or paper of collection of taxes through withholding, of guarantor.
3. (in case the guarantor does not have Japanese citizenship) Submission of certificate of his/her Alien Registration.

*
Research Institutes and Centers
Computer Center
For Further Information
Undergraduate Admission
Public Information and Admissions Office, Sapporo Gakuin University, 11 Bunkyodai, Ebetsu-shi, Hokkaido 069 ☎ 011-386-8111 ext. 321

Sapporo University
(Sapporo Daigaku)
1-3; 3-7 Nishioka, Toyohira-ku, Sapporo-shi, Hokkaido 062 ☎ 011-852-1181

Faculty
    Profs. 57   Assoc. Profs. 20
    Assist. Profs. Full-time 3; Part-time 103
Number of Students
    Undergrad. 4, 001
Library   230, 000 volumes

Outline and Characteristics of the University
Sapporo University begen with one building and two departments, Economics and Foreign Languages, on its present site in Nishioka (West Hill) in 1967. Plans were already in operation for expansion the following year with a Business Administration Department and a Women's Junior College with faculties of English and Japanese literature.

The University's first graduates were those of the Junior College in March, 1970, and the following year saw the first graduates from the Departments of Economics and Foreign Languages. The Business Administration Department graduated its first class in March, 1972, very shortly after the completion of the Sapporo Winter Olympic Games which brought about a boom in sports facilities and which held some events very near to the University campus in Nishioka.

Facilities expanded apace, with completion of a second building, including an auditorium, and a gymnasium. These were expanded and computer facilities added and then, in 1973, a third building was erected, greatly expanding classroom space. The completion of a second gymnasium gave impetus to the physical education and sports programs of the University. Up-to-date language laboratory facilities were first installed in 1976, and have now been expanded into a Language Training Center which includes a second language lab, a complete audio-visual room, and a TV studio.

The University met the eighties with renewed energy, first installing a main-frame computer to handle the vastly increased data involved in modern education, and a new library. With increasing emphasis on the education of women, the Junior College was expanded, adding the faculties of Cultures and Management.

The global outlook of the University was assured with the establishment of sister-school ties with Kearney State College in Nebraska, U. S. A. and a student exchange. Beyond this, foreign seminars and trips sponsored by the University involve more students every year, with over 120 students taking part in one or another overseas program in 1987 alone.

The determination to stay abreast of the times

can be seen in the establishment of the Office Automation Classroom, with 51 personal computers, printers, displays, etc. This is the most modern facility of its kind in Hokkaido.   Sapporo University seeks, not only to keep up with the age, but to lead it, an attitude it continually strives to pass on to its students.

UNDERGRADUATE PROGRAMS

Faculty of Business Administration (Freshmen Enrollment: 300)

Department of Business Administration
Accounting, Auditing, Basic Ecomonics, Bills of Exchange, Bookkeeping, Civil Law, COBOL, Commercial Law, Commercial Law, Company Law, Computer Accounting, Computer Science, Cost Accounting, Data Processing, FORTRAN, Labor Law, Labor Management, Management Analysis, Management Science, Marketing, Principles of Business Administration, Production Management, Tax Law
Faculty of Economics (Freshmen Enrollment: 300)

Department of Economics
Agricultural Economics, American Economy, Commercial Economics, Econometrics, Economic Fluctuation, Economic Geography, Economic History of Japan, Economic Policy, Economics of Regional Development, Economics of Transportation, Economic Statistics, General Economic History, History of Economic Thought, Industrial Economics, International Economics, International Finance, Introduction to Economics, Labor Economics, Local Finance, Mathematical Economics, Mathematical Methods for Economics, Monetary Theory, National Income, Principles of Economics, Public Finance, Seminars in specialized areas, Small Business, Socialist Economy, Social Policy, Special Topics in Economics, Topics in Hokkaido Economy, Western Economic History
Faculty of Foreign Languages (Freshmen Enrollment: 170)

Department of English
Commercial English, English and English Literature, International Communications
Department of Russian
Basic Russian, Cross-cultural Communication, Current Russian, History of Art and Thought, History of the Russian Language, History of Western Culture, International Law, Japanese-Russian Relations, Principles of International Relations, Russian Literature, Soviet Economic Theory, Soviet Russia

*

Research Institutes and Centers
Computer and Office Automation Rooms, Industrial Management Institute, Language Training Center
For Further Information
Undergraduate Admission
Office of Administration, Sapporo University, 1-3; 3-7 Nishioka, Toyohira-ku, Sapporo-shi, Hokkaido 062 ☎ 011-852-1181 ext. 208

Science University of Tokyo
(Tokyo Rika Daigaku)
1-3 Kagurazaka, Shinjuku-ku, Tokyo 162
☎ 03-260-4271

Faculty
    Profs. 294   Assoc. Profs. 101
    Assist. Profs. Full-time 117; Part-time 554
    Res. Assocs. 170
Number of Students
    Undergrad. 17, 619   Grad. 996
Library 486, 271 volumes

Outline and Characteristics of the University
The history of the Science University of Tokyo dates back to 1881, when the founders opened Tokyo Butsurigaku-koshusho (Tokyo School of Science), the predecessor of the present University. The founders set a firm goal: "Development of the nation should be based on the spread of scientific knowledge. " The school was renamed Tokyo Butsuri Gakko (Tokyo Academy of Science) in 1883. Under the New School Education Law in 1949, Tokyo Butsuri Gakko was reorganized into the Science University of Tokyo.

Today, it consists of six Faculties and 29 Departments specializing in fields ranging from Science and Engineering to Pharmaceutical Sciences. As to advanced study, the Master and Doctor Courses have been instituted in the Graduate Schools of Sciences, Pharmaceutical Sciences, Engineering, and Science and Technology. In addition, the graduate course is designed to further educate teachers in Secondary Schools. Since its founding, over 80, 000 graduates from the University have played active roles in many fields which require a professional knowledge of science and technology, including industry, education and public service. The Science University of Tokyo aims at educating promising youth, equipping them with real ability through rigid discipline, to meet the requirements of society and thus to contribute to peace, prosperity and the well-being of mankind.

UNDERGRADUATE PROGRAMS

Faculty of Engineering (Freshmen Enrollment: 450)
Department of Architecture
Architectural Design, Architectural Planning, Building Construction System, Building Materials, Building Safety Planning, City Planning, Environmental Design, Environmental Physics, Environmental Psychology, Fire Protection in Building and City, Structural Engineering, Structural Material, Structural Mechanics, Urban Design
Department of Electrical Engineering
Applied Electronics, Automatic Control, Communi-

cation Systems, Computational Mechanics, Data Acquisition and Processing, Digital Communications, Electrical Machinery and Apparatus, Electric Motor Application and Control, Electronic Materials and Devices, Finite Element Method, High Frequency Measurements, Information Processing, Magnetic Materials and Their Applications, Microwaves, Semiconductor Materials, Semiconductor Materials and Devices, Solid State Electronics, Theory of Fusion Plasma

Department of Industrial Chemistry
Chemical Engineering, Industrial Analytical Chemistry, Industrial Inorganic Chemistry, Industrial Organic Chemistry, Industrial Physical Chemistry, Organic Syntheses

Department of Management Science
Applied Statistics, Business Administration, Cost Management, Data Analysis System, Design and Experiment, Economic Engineering, Ergonomics, Image Processing Engineering, Industrial Relations and Personnel Administration, Information Engineering, Information Recognition Engineering, Information Technology, Management Accounting, Management Organization, Multivariate Analysis, Operations Research, Optimization, Production Management and Engineering, Quality Management and Engineering, Reliability and Maintainability Engineering, Reliability Engineering, Software Engineering, Systems Engineering, Systems Science, Total Quality Management, Work Study

Department of Mechanical Engineering
Automatic Control, Deformation Processing, Dynamics of Mechanical Systems, Engine Engineering, Fluid Mechanics, Machine Manufacturing, Precision Engineering, Solid Mechanics, Thermal Engineering
Faculty of Engineering (**Evening Course**) (Freshmen Enrollment: 240)

Department of Architecture
Department of Electrical Engineering
Department of Management Science
See the course listing in Day Course.
Faculty of Industrial Science and Technology (Freshmen Enrollment: 240)

Department of Applied Electronics
Electronics engineering, Information Machinery, Modern Engineering Sciences, Software and Hardware Applications in Data Processing

Department of Biological Science and Technology
Department of Materials Science and Technology
Faculty of Pharmaceutical Sciences (Freshmen Enrollment: 160)

Department of Pharmaceutical Sciences
Biochemistry, Experimental Pharmacotherapeutics, Hygienic Chemistry, Pathological Physiology, Pharmaceutics, Pharmacognosy, Pharmacology, Pharmacophysical Chemistry, Radiochemistry

Department of Pharmaceutical Techno–Chemistry
Pharmaceutical Analytical Chemistry, Pharmaceutical Chemistry, Pharmaceutical Techno–Chemistry, Physical Chemistry, Phytochemistry, Toxicology

and Microbial Chemistry
Faculty of Science (Freshmen Enrollment: 660)

Department of Applied Chemistry
Analytical Chemistry, Colloid and Surface Chemistry, Environmental Chemistry, Inorganic Chemistry, Laser Photochemistry, Organic Chemistry, Physical Chemistry, Physical Chemistry of Polymer, Polymer Chemistry

Department of Applied Mathematics
Algebra, Algebra and Graph, Applied Analysis, Applied Functional Analysis, Graph and Geometry, Numerical Computation, Numerical Mathematics, Statistical Analysis, Statistics, Stochastic Analysis, Theory of Functions

Department of Applied Physics
Chemical Physics, Crystal Physics, Electronics, Information Processing, Material Science, Quantum Field Physics, Semiconductor Physics, Semiconductors, Solid State Physics, Spectroscopy, Surface Physics

Department of Chemistry
Analytical Chemistry, Biochemistry, Bioinorganic Chemistry, Chemical Dynamics, Computational Chemistry, Coordination Chemistry, Inorganic Chemistry, Inorganic Electrochemistry and Corrosion Science, Inorganic Photochemistry, Organic Chemistry of Natural Product, Organic Stereochemistry, Physical Chemistry, Polymer Chemistry, Quantum Chemistry, Radio Chemistry, Solution Chemistry, Surface Science and Catalysis, Synthetic Organic Chemistry, The Physical Properties of the Solid State of High Polymeric Substances

Department of Mathematics
Algebra, Differential Geometry, Functional Analysis, General Topology, Mathematical Statistics, Numerical Analysis, Theory of Functions, Theory of Numbers, Theory of Probability

Department of Physics
Astrophysics and Space Science, Biophysics and Bio–Medical Engineering, Geophysics, High–Energy Physics, Metal Physics, Physics Education, Solid State Physics and Quantum Electronics, Solid State Spectroscopy, Solid State Theory, Statistical Physics, Theoretical Physics
Faculty of Science and Technology (Freshmen Enrollment: 1, 150)

Department of Applied Biological Science
Applied Enzymology, Biochemistry, Bioorganic Chemistry, Biophysical Chemistry, Brewing Science, Cell Biology, Developmental Biology, Microbial Physiology, Microbial Resources, Microbiological Chemistry, Molecular Genetics, Natural Polymer Chemistry, Physics of Biomolecules, Systematic Microbiology

Department of Architecture and Building Engineering
Architectural Planning, Building Environmental Engineering, Building Equipments, Building Materials, City Planning, Environmental Engineering, Fire Protection Engineering, Structural Engineering,

Structural Mechanics

Department of Civil Engineering

Application of Electronic Computer for Civil Engineering, Application of Remote Sensing, Bridge Engineering, Coastal Engineering, Concrete Engineering, Construction Methods for Public Works, Drawing for Structural Design, Earthquake–resisting Engineering, Engineering of Construction Materials, Environmental Engineering, Hydraulic Engineering, Information Processing for Civil Engineering, Ocean Engineering, Photogrammetry, Practical Patent Engineering, Railway Engineering, Regional Planning, River Engineering, Road Engineering, Sanitation Engineering, Soil Mechanics, Structural Engineering, Structural Mechanics, Traffic Engineering, Transportation Planning

Department of Electrical Engineering

Applied Electrostatics, Biological Instrumentation and Information Processing, Coding Theory, Color Vision, Communication System, Communication Theory, Electric Power System Engineering, Electronic Circuits, Electronic Computer and Micro Computer, Electronic Material, Electronic Properties of Insulator, Electron–Tube Engineering, Engineering in Medicine and Biology, High Voltage Engineering, Image Processing, Integrated Circuits and System, Microwave Engineering, Power Electronics, Radio Communication Engineering, Semiconductor Engineering, Solid State Electronics, Visual Information, Visual Signaling

Department of Industrial Administration

Applied Statistics, Chemical Engineering, Cognitive Science, Computer Science, Control Engineering, Cost Control, Environmental Engineering, Experimental Design, Human Science, Information Engineering, Knowledge Engineering, Management Acccounting, Operations Research and Prediction, Production Control, Production Engineering, Quality Control, Reliability Engineering, Statistics, Systems Control, Systems Engineering, Value Engineering

Department of Industrial and Engineering Chemistry

Chemical Engineering, Electrochemistry, Industrial Analytical Chemistry, Industrial Inorganic Chemistry, Industrial Organic Chemistry, Inorganic Industrial Chemistry, Inorganic Material Chemistry, Instrumental Analysis, Materials Technology, Physical Chemistry, Polymer Chemistry, Synthetic Organic Chemistry, Vacuum Engineering

Department of Information Sciences

Applied Information Theory, Applied Probability, Applied Statistics, Computer Sciences, Information Mathematics, Information Planning, Information Processing, Physical Information Mathematics, Software Sciences

Department of Mathematics

Algebra, Analysis, Complex Analysis, Differential Equations, Geometry, Group Theory, Numerical Analysis, Real Analysis, Statistics, Theoretical Physics

Department of Mechanical Engineering

Applied Mathematics, Control Engineering, Engineering Materials, Experimental Mechanics, Fluid Engineering, Fluid Machine, Fluid Mechanics, Fracture Mechanics, Friction, Hydraulic Engineering, Instrumentation, Lubrication, Materials Science, Mechanical Vibration, Metallurgy, Nuclear Engineering, Photoelasticity, Plasticity, Plasticity of Metal Crystal, Precision Machining, Solid Mechanics, Theory of Machinig, Thermal Engineering, Thermo–Fluid Engineering, Tribology

Department of Physics

Applied Optics, Crystal Growth, Diffraction Crystallography, Laser Spectroscopy, Magnetism, Mass Spectroscopy, Metal Physics, Nuclear Physics, Physics of Snow and Ice, Semiconductors, Solid State Physics, Spectroscopy of Solids, Surface Physics

Faculty of Science (Evening Course) (Freshmen Enrollment: 480)

Department of Chemistry
Department of Mathematics
Department of Physics

See the course listing in Day Course.

Foreign Student Admission

Qualifications for Applicants

Standard Qualifications Requirement

Examination at the University

1st selection:

1st selection will be made, based on the submitted documents.

2nd selection:

Both a written examination in academic subjects including a foreign language (excluding Japanese) and an oral test will be given. Written examinations are given in Japanese. The duration of examination is two days.

Applicants will be informed of dates and content of examinations.

Reference will be made to the results of the Japanese Language Proficiency Test and General Examination for Foreign students. It is, therefore, desirable for an applicant to take these tests.

Documents to be Submitted When Applying

Standard Documents Requirement

Certificate of Proficiency in Japanese Language (prescribed form) is also required. Applicant who have taken the Japanese Language Proficiency Test and General Examination for Foreign Students, must inform the university of his/her test registration numbers.

Procedures of application:

(A) 1st selection

1. Application Period:

   (1) An applicant who resident abroad at the time of application, should send the completed application form by air mail. Applications will be accepted from September 1 to 30, 1988 for academic year 1989.

   (2) An applicant resident in Japan at the time

of application will be informed of the results in Jannary.

(B) 2nd selection

The 2nd selection fee is ¥14, 000 (for1989) due one day before the date of 2nd selection. Applicant will receive an admission ticket to the exammation. Applicant must bring to the examination both the temporary certificate of admission and a passport.

GRADUATE PROGRAMS

Graduate School of Engineering (First Year Enrollment : Master's 31, Doctor's 15)
Divisions
Architecture, Electrical Engineering, Industrial Chemistry, Management Science, Mechanical Engineering
Graduate School of Pharmaceutical Sciences (First Year Enrollment : Master's 50, Doctor's 6)
Division
Pharmaceutical Sciences
Graduate School of Science (First Year Enrollment : Master's 110, Doctor's 10)
Divisions
Chemistry, Mathematics, Physics
Graduate School of Science and Technology (First Year Enrollment : Master's 180, Doctor's 32)
Divisions
Applied Biological Sciences, Architecture and Building Engineering, Civil Engineering, Electrical Engineering, Industrial Administration, Industrial and Engineering Chemistry, Information Sciences, Mathematics, Mechanical Engineering, Physics

Foreign Student Admission
Qualifications for Applicants
Master's Program
    Standard Qualifications Requirement
Doctor's Program
    Standard Qualifications Requirement
Examination at the University
Master's Program
    The same as for undergraduate foreign applicants.
Doctor's Program
    The same as for undergraduate foreign applicants.
    Documents to be Submitted When Applying
    Standard Documents Requirement
    Procedures of application are the same as for undergraduates.
                    ✳
Research Institutes and Centers
The TRD Research Center for Science and Technology
Facilities/Services for Foreign Students
    "The Committee for Foreign Students" is in charge of guidance for "student life and study" for privately financed students registered at each Faculty. In addition, the following services are extended.

1. Appointed Student Advisors give advice on daily life and other matters to 1st and 2nd year foreign students and others.
2. The Committee holds"Evening Gathering for International Communication. "On this occasion both Japanese and foreign students are invited.
    The following services are offered to both foreign and Japanese students.
1. Health consultations
2. Periodical medical examinations
3. Consultations on daily student life
4. Help to make the scholarships offered by outside organizations available.
5. Help in finding boarding.
Special Programs for Foreign Students
    University offers lectures on "Japanese language" and "About Japan."
For Further Information
    Undergraduate and Graduate Admission
Entrance Examination Section, Public Information Division, Science University of Tokyo, 1-3 Kagurazaka, Shinjuku-ku, Tokyo 162
☎ 03-260-4271 ext. 622

Seigakuin University
(Seigakuin Daigaku)
1-1 Tosaki Ageo-shi, Saitama 362
☎ 048-781-0031

Faculty
    Profs. 21   Assoc. Profs. 5
    Assist. Profs. Full-time 9; Part-time 27
Number of Students
    Undergrad. 273
Library 80, 846 volumes

Outline and Characteristics of the University
    The history of Seigakuin University goes back to 1883 when Protestant missionaries of the Christian Church (Disciples of Christ) began mission work, establishing churches and carrying out educational programs. In 1903 Seigakuin Bible College was established followed by Joshi Seigakuin (Women's) Bible School in 1905. Out of these efforts grew Seigakuin (Boys') Junior/Senior High School, Joshi Seigakuin (Girls') Junior/Senior High School, Seigakuin Kindergarten, Seigakuin Elementary School, and Joshi Seigakuin (Women's) Junior College and the attached kindergarten. The Seigakuin School system was rounded out in April of 1988 when Seigaguin University opened its School of Political Science and Economics.
    Seigakuin University strives to educate students in the basic Protestant Christian spirit so that they will be able to"Love God and Serve His People" (the school motto) in the modern where internationalization, high technology and information are rapidly

progressing. On the basis of the Christian spirit and the world view that grows out of that spirit, Seigakuin University seeks to help students develop a correct understanding of Japan and other countries of the world during this time of rapid change, and to educate and nurture students who will master a comprehensive politico-economic approach, capable of a prompt and aggressive response to the various problems of modem society, and promoting world peace and the progress of the human society.

UNDERGRADUATE PROGRAMS

School of Political Science and Economics (Freshmen Enrollment: 200)
Department of Political Science and Economics
Common Basic Course
Christian Social Ethics, Constitution, Economic History, Economic Policy, Labor Economics, Monetary Theory, Political Ideologies, Principles of Economics, Principles of political Science, Problems of Modern Civilization, Public Finance, Social Policy, Social Psychology, Statistics
Comparative Political Science & Economics Courses
Comparative Politics, Comparative Regional Research: America, Europe, The Soviet Union and Eastern Europe, East Asia, Economic Development, International Economics, International Law, International Monetary Theory, International Politics, International Structure, Securities Exchange Market, World Economics
Related Courses
Accounting, Bookkeeping, Civil Law, Commerce, Commercial Law, English for Specialized Purposes, Information Processing, Introduction to Computer Science, Management Engineering, Mass Communication, Minor Enterprises
Sociological Political Science & Economics Courses
Environmental Planning, Governmental Administration, Interpersonal Relations, Japanese Economy, Japanese Politics, Population, Regional Administration, Social Security, Sociology, Welfare Administration

∗

For Further Information
Undergraduate Admission
Admissions Office, Seigakuin University 1–1 Tosaki Ageo–shi, Saitama 362 ☎ 048–781–0031

Seijo University
(Seijo Daigaku)

6-1-20 Seijo, Setagaya–ku, Tokyo 157
☎ 03-482-1181

Faculty
   Profs. 104   Assoc. Profs. 33
   Assist. Profs. Full–time 7; Part–time 206
Number of Students

Undergrad. 4, 252   Grad. 149
Library 408, 095 volumes

Outline and Characteristics of the University
The history of Seijo University dates back to 1917, when Seijo Primary School was founded by Masataro Sawayanagi. In March, 1926, a seven–year high school was authorized by the Ministry of Education and was established in April of the same year. The new School Education Law, enacted in 1949, enabled the high school to acquire university status. Seijo University, as it was renamed, consisted of two faculties, Economics and Science. When the Faculty of Science was closed in 1954, the new Faculty of Arts and Literature was opened in its place in the same year.

In the following three decades, the University has remodelled and expanded steadily. In 1958, the Faculty of Economics was divided into two departments, Economics and Business Administration; the Faculty of Arts and Literature underwent a similar process, and was divided into five departments: Japanese, English, Art Studies, Japanese Folklore (later renamed Cultural History) and Mass-Communication Studies. In 1967, the Graduate School was founded. M. A. programs were offered in Economics and also in Japanese and English. In 1969, the following programs were added: Ph. D. programs in Economics, Japanese, and English; M. A. programs in Japanese Folklore. In 1971, a Ph. D. program was begun in the Japanese Folklore. In 1975, an M. A. program was established in Aesthetics and History of Art. In 1976, the Faculty of Arts and Literature was reinforced by a new department, European Culture, thus encompassing six departments. In the next year, the new Faculty of Law was founded and a Ph. D. program was begun in Aesthetics and History of Art, and in 1981, the same program in Business-Administration. In 1983, a Ph. D. program was added in European Culture. And in the same year, the most recent change was made; M. A. and Ph. D. Courses were renamed Early Ph. D. and Late Ph. D. Courses, respectively.

The University is widely noted for its academic liberalism. Being small in size, it has the advantage of maintaining friendly relationships between teachers and students.

UNDERGRADUATE PROGRAMS

Faculty of Arts and Literature (Freshmen Enrollment: 300)
Department of Art Studies
Aesthetics, Arts and History of Arts, Cinema and History of Cinema, Dramatic Arts and History of Drama, Japanese Art History, Musicology and Music History
Department of Cultural History
Cultural History, Culturology, Folklore, Historical Science, Methodology of History

Department of English
American Literature, English Linguistics, English Literature, History of English Literature
Department of European Culture
French and French Studies, German and German Studies
Department of Japanese
History of Japanese Literature, Japanese Literature, Japanese Philology
Department of Mass-Communication Studies
Ethics of Mass Communications, History of Mass Communications, Mass Communications, Sociopsychology
Faculty of Economics (Freshmen Enrollment: 300)
Department of Business Administration
Accounting, Bookkeeping, Business Administration, Business Management, Commercial Science, Personnel Management, Public Enterprises
Department of Economics
Economic History, Economic History of Japan, Economic Policy, Economic Principles, History of Economics, International Economics, Public Finance, Social Policy, Statistics
Faculty of Law (Freshmen Enrollment: 200)
Department of Law
Civil Affairs, Commercial Law, Criminal Affairs, Economic Law, Foreign Law, Fundamentals of Law, International Law, Public Law, Social Law

Foreign Student Admission
Examination at the University
Foreign applicants must take the same examination as domestic ones.
Documents to be Submitted When Applying
Standard Documents Requirement

GRADUATE PROGRAMS

Graduate School of Economics (First Year Enrollment : Master's 25, Doctor's 7)
Divisions
Business Administration, Economics
Graduate School of Law (First Year Enrollment: Master's 10)
Division
Law
Graduate School of Literature (First Year Enrollment : Master's 60, Doctor's 30)
Divisions
Aesthetics and History of Art, Communication Studies, English Studies, European Culture, Japanese Folk Culture, Japanese Literature

Foreign Student Admission
Qualifications for Applicants
Master's Program
Standard Qualifications Requirement
Doctor's Program
Standard Qualifications Requirement
Examination at the University

Master's Program
Applicants for admission to the Faculty of Economics are required to take both written and oral examinations for two successive days either on October 5 and 6 or on February 1 and 2. Required subjects for the written examination are one foreign language, economics or business administration, and one major subject.

Applicants for admission to the Faculty of Arts and Literature are required to take their examination for the Courses for two successive days on February 27 (Written exam) and 28 (Oral exam). Required subjects for the written examination for the courses of Japanese Literature, English Studies, Communication Studies and European Culture are one foreign language and their major subjects, and those for the Courses of Aesthetics and History of Art and Japanese Folk Culture are two foreign languages and their major subjects.

Applicants for admission to the Faculty of Law are required to take both written and oral examinations on Februaryl. Required subjects are one foreign language and their major Subjects.
Doctor's Program
Application for admission to Late Ph. D. Courses for the Faculties of Economics and Arts and Literature follows the same procedure as Early Ph. D. Courses (Master's Program) described above.

*

Research Institutes and Centers
The Institute of Economic Studies, The Institute of Folklore Studies
For Further Information
Undergraduate and Graduate Admission
Office of Academic Affairs, Seijo University, 6-1-20 Seijo, Setagaya-ku, Tokyo 157 ☎ 03-482-1181 ext. 331

Seikei University
(Seikei Daigaku)

3-3-1 Kichijoji–Kitamachi, Musashino–shi, Tokyo 180 ☎ 0422-51-5181

Faculty
Profs. 126   Assoc. Profs. 34
Assist. Profs. Full–time 7; Part–time 313
Res. Assocs. 51
Number of Students
Undergrad. 6, 400   Grad. 108
Library 429, 448 volumes

Outline and Characteristics of the University
Seikei University was founded in 1949. The University evolved from the old Seikei High School, the origins of which can be traced to a small informal school which was established and named Seikei–en by Haruji Nakamura in 1906. His educational beliefs of helping the students reach their highest potential,

teaching them intimately in small classes, earned a solid reputation as being among the finest private schools in Tokyo. Nakamura's ideals and beliefs are kept alive today in the University's education. The University is presently composed of four Faculties, five Graduate Schools and two Research Institutes. These Faculties and Graduate Schools not only teach students with their well–organized curriculums, but also promote research on interdisciplinary and international levels, cooperating with research institutions abroad.

Pleasant shade is made in many places on campus by various kinds of trees, and the University itself is housed in two classic buildings inherited from the old Seikei High School and twelve contemporary buildings. It is located not far from the center of Tokyo, yet has a quiet environment ideally suited for college education.

UNDERGRADUATE PROGRAMS

Faculty of Economics (Freshmen Enrollment: 400)
   Department of Business
Accounting, Business, Business History, Economics, Management
   Department of Economics
Economic Theory, General Economic History, History of Economic Thought, International Economics, Money and Banking, Public Finance, Theory of Economic Policy
Faculty of Engineering (Freshmen Enrollment: 280)
   Department of Electrical Engineering
Electrical Engineering, Electrical Measurements, Electric Circuit Theory, Electric Power Engineering, Electromagnetic Theory, Electronics and Communication Engineering
   Department of Industrial Chemistry
Analytical Chemistry, Chemical Thermodynamics, Industrial Chemistry, Inorganic Chemistry, Organic Chemistry, Physical Chemistry
   Department of Industrial Engineering
Artificial Intelligence, Computer Applications, Computer Architecture, Computer Programming, Computer Systems, Database, Industrial Engineering, Operations Research, Probability and Statistics
   Department of Mechanical Engineering
Control Engineering, Dynamics of Machinary, Fluid Mechanics, Industrial Materials, Measurement Techniques, Mechanical Design, Mechanical Engineering, Metal Working Practice, Strength of Materials, Thermoengineering
Faculty of Humanities (Freshmen Enrollment: 390)
   Department of Cultural Sciences
Comparative Studies of Culture, Cultural History of Europe, Cultural History of Japan, Mass Communication, Modern Thought
   Department of English and American Literature
English Linguistics, English Literature, History of American Literature, History of English Literature
   Department of Japanese Literature

History of Japanese Literature, Japanese Linguistics, Japanese Literature
Faculty of Law (Freshmen Enrollment: 350)
   Department of Law
Civil Law, Commercial Law, Constitutional Law, Criminal Law
   Department of Political Science
Civil Law, Constitutional Law, History of Political Theory, Political History of Europe, Political History of Japan, Political Science

Foreign Student Admission
   Qualifications for Applicants
   Standard Qualifications Requirement
   Examination at the University
   The same as Japanese students.
   Documents to be Submitted When Applying
   Standard Documents Requirement

GRADUATE PROGRAMS

Graduate School of Business (First Year Enrollment : Master's 6, Doctor's 3)
   Division
Business
Graduate School of Economics (First Year Enrollment : Master's 6, Doctor's 3)
   Division
Economics
Graduate School of Engineering (First Year Enrollment : Master's 32, Doctor's 16)
   Divisions
Electrical Engineering, Industrial Chemistry, Information Sciences, Mechanical Engineering
Graduate School of Humanities (First Year Enrollment : Master's 24)
   Divisions
English and American Literature, Japanese Literature, Western Civilization
Graduate School of Law and Political Science (First Year Enrollment : Master's 12, Doctor's 6)
   Divisions
Law, Political Science

$*$

Research Institutes and Centers
The Center for Asian and Pacific Studies, The Information Processing Center
Facilities/Services for Foreign Students
   The University arranges tutors for foreign students.
Special Programs for Foreign Students
   Supplementary courses at three levels (Elementary, Intermediate, Advanced) in Japanese as a foreign language.
For Further Information
   Undergraduate and Graduate Admission
Office of Academic Affairs, Dept. of Academic Affairs, Seikei University, 3-3-1 Kichijoji–Kitamachi, Musashino–shi, Tokyo 180 ☎ 0422-51-5181 ext. 365

Seinan Gakuin University
(Seinan Gakuin Daigaku)

6-2-92 Nishijin, Sawara-ku, Fukuoka-shi, Fukuoka
814 ☎ 092-841-1311

Faculty
    Profs.   106   Assoc. Profs.   41
    Assist. Profs.   Full–time   19; Part–time   267
Number of Students
    Undergrad.   7, 291   Grad.   46
Library   499, 200 volumes

Outline and Characteristics of the University

Seinan Gakuin University, founded in 1916 as an academy for boys by Charles K. Dozier, a Southern Baptist missionary from the United States, is part of the Seinan Gakuin Educational Foundation. Today it has developed into a coeducational, private university fully accredited by the Japanese Government and still committed to its broad Christian purposes and to education and research of a high academic level.

C. K. Dozier, who later became Chancellor of the Foundation, gave Seinan Gakuin a unique motto in his dying words: "Tell Seinan to be true to Christ. " Edwin B. Dozier, his son and also Chancellor of the Foundation from 1965-1969, left his own words, interpreting and modifying his father's: "Truth and love to God and man. " These mottoes express the ideal and purpose of the University.

With a student body of about 7, 000 and a faculty of nearly 160, and serving an area with a population of 25 million people, the University has two attractive campuses, one near beautiful Hakata Bay, and the other at the foot of the mountains five kilometers away.

Convinced of the importance of training and producing internationally-minded youths, Seinan Gakuin was the first university in West Japan to carry out a systematic exchange program with foreign universities. The University's International Exchange Program Committee plans and promotes the exchange of professors and students.

Besides these exchange students, Seinan Gakuin has over the years accepted other foreign students—several each year—mainly from Asian countries. To be admitted, they must have a certain level of academic standing and be able to cope as regular students with courses taught in Japanese.

As a school dedicated to professional and liberal arts education with a Christian purpose, Seinan Gakuin University thus wishes to accept highly-motivated students, both Japanese and foreign, who want to study here. Seinan Gakuin wishes to train and educate them to become world citizens who will serve and contribute to mankind all over the world.

UNDERGRADUATE PROGRAMS

Faculty of Commerce (Freshmen Enrollment: 300)
    Department of Business Administration
    Department of Commerce
Faculty of Economics (Freshmen Enrollment: 300)
    Department of Economics
    Economics Course
    International Course
Faculty of Law (Freshmen Enrollment: 350)
    Department of Law
Faculty of Literature (Freshmen Enrollment: 480)
    Department of Childhood Education
    Department of English Literature
    Department of Foreign Languages
    English Course
    French Course
    Department of International Cultures
Faculty of Theology (Freshmen Enrollment: 10)
    Department of Theology
    Christian Humanities Course
    Theology Course

Foreign Student Admission

Qualifications for Applicants
    Standard Qualifications Requirement
    Minimum eight years of schooling should be completed outside of Japan.
Examination at the University
    1st Screening: Application materials
    2nd Screening: A written examination (essay in Japanese) and interview in the beginning of March.
Documents to be Submitted When Applying
    Standard Documents Requirement
Application due: The end of January

Qualifications for Transfer Students
    Applicants should have qualification equivalent to 14 years of schooling (Elementary: 6 years, Junior High: 3 years, High: 3 years, Junior College: 2 years). Minimum ten years of schooling should be completed outside of Japan.
Examination for Transfer Students
    Same as freshman application.
Documents to be Submitted When Applying
    Standard Documents Requirement
Application due: The end of January

ONE-YEAR GRADUATE PROGRAMS

One-Year Graduate Course of Commerce (Enrollment:10)
Commerce
One-Year Graduate Course of Economics (Enrollment:10)
Economics
One-Year Graduate Course of Literature (Enrollment:10)
International Cultures

One-Year Graduate Course of Theology (Enrollment: 10)
Theology

Foreign Student Admission
Qualifications for Applicants
Standard Qualifications Requirement
Minimum 12 years of schooling should be completed outside of Japan.
Examination at the University
Same as freshman application.

GRADUATE PROGRAMS

Graduate School of Business Administration (First Year Enrollment : Master's 10, Doctor's 3)
Division
Business Administration
Graduate School of Economics (First Year Enrollment : Master's 7)
Division
Economics
Graduate School of Law (First Year Enrollment : Master's 15, Doctor's 8)
Division
Law
Graduate School of Literature (First Year Enrollment : Master's 15, Doctor's 8)
Divisions
English Literature, French Literature

Foreign Student Admission
Qualifications for Applicants
Master's Program
Standard Qualifications Requirement
Minimum 10 years of schooling (including 4-year university education) should be completed outside of Japan with Bachelor's degree.
Doctor's Program
Standard Qualifications Requirement
Minimun ten years of schooling (including 4-year university education) should be completed outside of Japan with Master's degree.
Examination at the University
Master's Program
Written Exam. in the beginning of October
Interview in the end of February
Doctor's Program
Written Exam.
Oral Exam in the end of February
Documents to be Submitted When Applying
Standard Documents Requirement

✳

Research Institutes and Centers
Computer Center, Faculty Research Institute
Facilities/Services for Foreign Students
Undergraduate and Graduate Programs:
Foreign Students' Room in the Student Union Bldg. Advisory services for foreign students at the Student Affairs Office.

Field trip expenses could be provided partially by request.
International Division:
Common Room is available.
International Exchange Office generally takes charge of exchange students' affairs.
Special Programs for Foreign Students
Qualifications for Applicants: Exchange students only
International Division (1-year program):
A wide range of courses taught mainly in English, which include instruction in the Japanese language, culture, religion, business, economics and history, among others.
For Further Information
☎ 092–841–1311 ext. 3345, 3346
Undergraduate Admission
Admissions Office, Seinan Gakuin University, 6-2-92 Nishijin, Sawara-ku, Fukuoka-shi, Fukuoka 814
☎ 092-841-1311 ext. 3297, 3300, 3324
Graduate Admission
Graduate School Office, Graduate School of Seinan Gakuin University, 6-2-92 Nishijin, Sawara-ku, Fukuoka-shi, Fukuoka 814
☎ 092-841-1311 ext. 3368, 3369

Seisen Women's College
(Seisen Joshi Daigaku)

3-16-21 Higashi Gotanda, Shinagawa–ku, Tokyo
141   ☎ 03-447-5551

Faculty
Profs.   34   Assoc. Profs.   10
Assist. Profs.   Full–time   6; Part–time   97
Number of Students
Undergrad.   1, 533
Library   148, 239 volumes

Outline and Characteristics of the College
Seisen Women's College is a Catholic university –college founded by the Handmaids of the Sacred Heart of Jesus, a Roman Catholic order of religious women that is actively engaged in the education of women the world over. The College has a unique philosophy of education which adapts Christian humanism as taught by the Catholic Church to the needs of Japanese society.
The College was founded in 1935 when Siesen–ryo Gakuin was founded in Azabu, Tokyo for the purpose of providing higher education for female high school graduates. In 1950, the College, then located in Yokosuka City, was formally estabilished as a women's college of university status consisting of two departments: English Literature and Japanese Literature. In 1961 the Spanish Language and Literature Department was added and at that time, the College also instituted a two–year English Language course. In 1962 the College was moved to its present

location in Tokyo to meet the demands of increasing expansion. In 1963 the Department of Christian Cultural Studies was established.

The English Language Institute is a two–year course of studies outside the Division of Humanities and consists of General Education Subjects and a specially designed English Language Program.

The College is located in Central Tokyo which makes the rich variety of cultural facilites of the capital a part of the educational environment. Moreover, the College is doubly blessed in its location in a quiet, hilly district of the city. The campus is renowned for its beautiful azalea garden and the old original building, a formal residence of the feudal Lord Shimazu.

UNDERGRADUATE PROGRAMS

Faculty of Letters (Freshmen Enrollment: 360)
Department of Christian Culture
Basic Theology, Bible Studies, Christian Culture, Christian Doctrine, Ethics, History of Christianity, History of Christianity in Japan, History of Japanese Religions, History of Modern Japanese Thought, History of Oriental Art, History of Oriental Religions, History of Western Art, History of Western Thought, Japanese History, Moral Theology, Philosophy, Science of Religion, Western History
Department of English Literature
American Literature, English Grammar, English Literature, English Phonetics, English Traslation, History of English Linguistics, History of English Literature
Department of Japanese Literature
Calligraphy, Chinese Classics, Chinese Literature, History of Japanese Linguistics, History of Japanese Literature, Japanese Grammar, Japanese Linguistics, Japanese Literature
Department of Spanish Language and Spanish Literature
History of Spanish Language, History of Spanish Literature, Latin American Literature, Spanish Grammar, Spanish Language, Spanish Literature, Spanish Studies

*

For Further Information
Undergraduate Admission
Admission Section, Administrative Office, Seisen Women's College, 3-16-21 Higashi Gotanda, Shinagawa–ku, Tokyo 141 ☎ 03-447-5551 ext. 305

Seiwa College
(Seiwa Daigaku)

7-54 Okadayama, Nishinomiya-shi, Hyogo 662
☎ 0798-52-0724

Faculty
Profs. 13   Assoc. Profs. 4
Assist. Profs.   Full–time 10; Part–time 34

Research Associate 5
Number of Students
Undergrad. 484   Grad. 11
Library 100, 825 volumes

Outline and Characteristics of the College
Seiwa is a college formed as a result of the "holy union"of three earlier schools: Kobe Women's Evangelistic School established in 1880, Lambuth Memorial Bible Training School established in 1888 and Hiroshima Girls' School (Kindergarten Department) established in 1886. Each of these establishments was founded by Christian missionaries for the purpose of training Christian workers, and as these schools grew and then combined, Seiwa College was established.

Seiwa was originally a women's college, but in 1981, on the 100th anniversary of its foundation, it opened its gates to male students, the Graduate School and four-year College becoming co-educational. At present male students number 58, which is about 10% of the total number enrolled in the B. A. and M. A. programs. The Junior College is only for women.

With its motto being "ALL FOR CHRIST", Seiwa's purpose has been, from its very beginning, to educate Christian workers who respect human beings. In order to realize this spirit of our founders, the following three H's sum up our educational objectives:

HEAD—a high academic level
HEART—a heart full of the love of Christ
HEALTH—health in mind and body
Our aim is the full development in each student of these three respective H's and growth towards a harmonious personality.

Our curriculum emphasizes the pursuit of high level studies, at both the theoretical and practical levels, and is closely connected with actual activities in education. The Christian Education Department, unique in Japan, is educating leaders in the field of Christian education capable of contributing to the present-day church and society. The two Early Childhood Education Departements of Seiwa, under the guiding principle of creative education, are training excellent early childhood educators. From these two departments, we are proud of having an employment rate of 100%for our graduates, who are being highly evaluated in their respective working places. The most significant characteristics of these graduates are that more than 10% of them have been in their occupation for over 20 years, and that more than 50% of them are actively engaged in work in a variety of fields where they have assumed various roles of leadership.

The English Department of the Junior College, opened in April 1986, is intended to enhance the English proficiency of our students and bring about a college which is international in spirit. It also has as its purpose the education of good workers who are able to work in an international society while responding to the demands of the local community.

UNDERGRADUATE PROGRAMS

Faculty of Education (Freshmen Enrollment: 100)
Department of Christian Education
Department of Early Childhood Education

Foreign Student Admission
Qualifications for Applicants
Standard Qualifications Requirement
Examination at the College
1. Japanese proficiency.
2. English ability.
Documents to be Submitted When Applying
Standard Documents Requirement
Application due: the end of November.

GRADUATE PROGRAMS

Graduate School of Education (First Year Enrollment : Master's 6)
Division
Early Childhood Education

Foreign Student Admission
Qualifications for Applicants
Master's Program
Standard Qualifications Requirement
Examination at the College
Master's Program
1. Essay on early childhood education and child development
2. English or German
3. Interview
4. University degree certificate
Documents to be Submitted When Applying
Standard Documents Requirement
Evidence of finances

*

Research Institutes and Centers
Clinic for Emotionally Disturbed Children,
The Child Guidance and Research Center
For Further Information
Undergraduate and Graduate Admission
The Instruction Department, Seiwa College, 7-54 Okadayama, Nishinomiya-shi, Hyogo 662 ☎ 0798-52-0724 ext. 210

Sendai College
(Sendai Daigaku)

Minami 2, 2-18 Funaoka, Shibata-machi,
Shibata-gun, Miyagi 989-16 ☎ 0224–55–1121

Faculty
    Profs. 15   Assoc. Profs. 13
    Assist. Profs. Full–time 9; Part–time 19

Res. Assoc. 1
Number of Students
    Undergrad. 1, 095
    Library 33, 400 volumes

Outline and Characteristics of the College

Sendai College, the only college with the faculty of physical education in Tohoku and Hokkaido, was founded in 1967. The object of the college is to study the general concepts and skills of human movement to contribute to the development of physical culture. The pursuit of the knowledge and skills of this field prepares students who intend to become teachers of health and physical education for junior and senior high school education, and experts to lead physical activity programs in industry, hospitals, and other organizations.

The campus is located in Funaoka, about 30 kilometers south of Sendai, and occupies a flat-site of 98, 772m². On the site, stand three gymnasiums, an indoor swimming pool, five tennis courts, an all-weather track and field ground, athletics fields for baseball, soccer and rugby, a handball court and three buildings. These facilities for sports allow students to improve their skills of teaching and sports through curricular and extracurricular activities. They are also involved in indoor sports such as gymnastics, swimming, volleyball, basketball, handball, table-tennis, Judo and Kendo. The college attracts students not only from northern Japan but all parts of Japan. The suburban environment in Funaoka, at the foot of Mt. Zao and the fountain of the Shiroishi river, affords a quiet atmosphere for study. The number of students being limited, each student receives personal attention and expert advice from the staff on college life.

UNDERGRADUATE PROGRAMS

Faculty of Physical Education (Freshmen Enrollment: 250)
Department of Physical Education
Administration of Physical Education, Exercise Physiology, Health Education, History of Physical Education, Injuries and First Aid Methods in Sport, Kinematics, Kinesiology, Measurement and Evaluation in Physical Education, Physical Eduaction, Physical Education Activities Program, Psychology of Physical Education, Sanitary Science, Sociology of Sports

Foreign Student Admission
Documents to be Submitted When Applying
Standard Documents Requirement
Official Certificate of Athletic Activities

*

For Further Information
Undergraduate Admission
Bureau of Student Affairs, Sendai College, Minami 2, 2-18 Funaoka, Shibata-machi, Shibata-gun,

Miyagi 989-16 ☎ 02245–5–1121 ext. 25

Senshu University
(Senshu Daigaku)

8, Kandajimbo-cho, 3-chome, Chiyoda-ku,
Tokyo   101

☎ 03-265-6211

Faculty
    Profs.   235   Assoc. Profs.   59
    Assist. Profs.   Full–time   23; Part–time   366
Number of Students
    Undergrad.   20, 259   Grad.   119
Library   770, 000 volumes

Outline and Characteristics of the University

As one of the leading Japanese universities founded in 1880, Senshu University has educated a vast number of young people for all sectors of society, in the spirit of the founders. The founders were Nagatane Soma, Inajiro Tajiri, Tanetaro Megata and Shigetada Komai. They were all students selected to go to the United States on a mission to acquire new knowledge and technology. They were motivated by their gratitude for this rare privilege and by their ardent desire to impart such knowledge and technology to the new generation of their homeland.

They began to educate and train young people to serve the public good, in a spirit of gratitude, fortitude, sincerity and industry. This original ideal still defines the academic tradition of this university. Currently it has five schools, both undergraduate and graduate, in Economics, Law, Business Administration, Commerce, and Literature. In addition, it has Evening Divisions of Economics, Law, and Commerce for those who wish to work during regular school hours. It has campuses in two places: Kanda in downtown Tokyo and Ikuta in the suburbs. The Kanda campus is in an 18–floor building (three floors underground) surrounded by other buildings in the metropolitan center close to the Imperial Palace. It houses the university headquarters. The Ikuta Campus is located in a green belt area less than 20 km from the Shinjuku metropolitan subcenter. It is amid natural surroundings in which scenery changes from season to season.

Research, educational and athletic facilities are laid out in such a manner as to fit the geographical features of the Tama hills. Ikuta is now the main campus with 75% of the student body.

UNDERGRADUATE PROGRAMS

School of Business Administration (Freshmen Enrollment: 770)
    Department of Business Administration
    Department of Information Control
School of Commerce (Freshmen Enrollment: 850)
    Department of Accounting
    Department of Commerce
School of Commerce (**Evening Course**) (Freshmen Enrollment: 150)
    Department of Commerce
School of Economics (Freshmen Enrollment: 800)
    Department of Economics
School of Economics (**Evening Course**) (Freshmen Enrollment: 150)
    Department of Economics
School of Law (Freshmen Enrollment: 800)
    Department of Law
School of Law (**Evening Course**) (Freshmen Enrollment: 200)
    Department of Law
School of Literature (Freshmen Enrollment: 550)
    Department of English and American Literature
    Department of Humanities
    Department of Japanese Literature

Foreign Student Admission

Qualifications for Applicants
    Standard Qualifications Requirement
    Japanese language proficiency test
Examination at the University
    A short essay and an interview. in mid December.
Documents to be Submitted When Applying
    Standard Documents Requirement
Application Period: late Novermber-early December

GRADUATE PROGRAMS

Graduate School of Business Administration (First Year Enrollment : Master's 20, Doctor's 3)
    Division
Business Administration
Graduate School of Commerce (First Year Enrollment : Master's 15, Doctor's 3)
    Division
Commerce
Graduate School of Economics (First Year Enrollment : Master's 30, Doctor's 3)
    Division
Economics
Graduate School of Law (First Year Enrollment : Master's 40, Doctor's 6)
    Divisions
Private Law, Public Law
Graduate School of Literature (First Year Enrollment : Master's 15, Doctor's 7)
    Divisions
English Literature, Japanese Literature, Philosophy

Foreign Student Admission

Qualifications for Applicants
Master's Program
    Standard Qualifications Requirement
Doctor's Program
    Standard Qualifications Requirement

Examination at the University
Master's Program
A written examination and an interview are given in early December.
Application Period
In Japan: November
From abroad: September– October
Doctor's Program
Same as Master's program.
Application Period
In Japan: February
From abroad: January–February
Documents to be Submitted When Applying
Standard Documents Requirement
Following documents are also required.
1. Certificate of Japanese Language Ability
2. Master's Thesis (Applicants for Doctor's program.)
3. An admission card for further screening
4. An identification card
(From abroad: A copy of Passport)
(In Japan: Alien Registration Certificate)

＊

Research Institutes and Centers
Center for Information Sciences, Imamura Institute of Legal Studies, Institute for Accounting Study, Institute for Commercial Sciences, Institute for the Humanities, Institute of Business Administration, Institute of Information Science, Institute of Law and Political Science, Institute of Social Science, Institute of Sports, Physical Education and Recreation
Special Programs for Foreign Students
An introductory Japanese course will be given in the near future. This course will cover basic Japanese language and information on procedures for university admission.
For Further Information
Undergraduate Admissions
Admission Office, Senshu University 8, Kandajimbo–cho 3–chome, Chiyoda–ku Tokyo 101 ☎ 03–265–6211 ext. 2531, 2532
Graduate Admissions
Administration office, Senshu University 1–1, Higashimita 2–chome, Tama–ku, Kawasaki–shi, Kanagawa 214 ☎ 044–911–7131 ext. 2473

Senzoku Gakuen College ("Music Academy")
(Senzoku Gakuen Daigaku)

290 Hisamoto, Takatsu–ku, Kawasaki–shi, Kanagawa 213 ☎ 044–877–3211

Faculty
Profs. 31   Assoc. Profs. 7
Assist. Profs. Full–time 2; Part–time 335
Number of Students
Undergrad. 1, 150   Grad. 20

Library 97, 581 volumes

Outline and Characteristics of the College
Founded in 1924 as a small private girls' school in Tokyo, Senzoku Gakuen College ("Music Academy") has developed into a full fledged school of music. Wakao Maeda founded the school in the hopes of developing the younger generation through an education that fosters humanity, nobility in character and the spirit to be daring. The school became a high school in 1930. The campus was moved in 1946 to its present site in Kawasaki City. The school added a Junior College in 1962 and the Music College in 1967.

Graduate courses were introduced at the college in 1971. Attached institutions include a Junior High School and High School which offer their own music courses to students who will eventually complete their education at the College. Senzoku Gakuen College also administers two new institutes, the Institute for Operatic Study and the Institute for Choral Research.

The College comprises major courses in composition and musicology, instrumental music, vocal music, and music education. Established by the late Saburo Moroi, noted composer and music educator, the courses aim to provide superior professional training in music in conjunction with a curriculum of liberal arts to ensure the all–round education of the student.

The College actively participates in exchange programs with foreign schools, particularly Hochschule der Künste, Berlin and Hochschule der Musik, München. A tour for the student orchestra and chorus is organized to perform in Europe from time to time.

The main campus in Kawasaki is a conglomeration of institutions with the College Library and a Concert hall where students perform symphonies, operas, ensemble and other music. Indeed, the opportunity to perform in a hall reputed to have the best acoustics in Japan, as well as the other benefits already mentioned, makes the College an ideal place to further one's musical ambitions.

UNDERGRADUATE PROGRAMS

Faculty of Music (Freshmen Enrollment: 150)
Department of Music
Composition and Musicology, Instrumental Music (Piano/Organ/Strimg/Wind and Percussion Instruments), Music Education, Vocal Music

Foreign Student Admission
Qualifications for Applicants
Standard Qualifications Requirement
Examination at the College
1. a) Composition Students: review of a score of the applicant's own musical work.
b) Instrumental and Vocal Students: Test of

the playing or singing a work of his/her free choice at the College, or review of a tape recording of the applicant playing or singing a work of his/her free choice.

c) Music Education Students: Test of the playing or singing a work of his/her free choice at the College, or review of a tape recording of the applicant playing or singing a work of his/hir free choice.

(In either case the score or the tape must be submitted before the examination dates)

2. A personal interview, in which the applicant's Japanese language ability and knowledge of music may be tested.

Documents to be Submitted When Applying
Standard Documents Requirement

Qualifications for Transfer Students
Graduates of a Junior College Department of Music may transfer upon examination to the 3rd year (i. e. 5th semester) of the Faculty of Music.

Examination for Transfer Students
Examination on the applicant's Major under the same conditions as Japanese applicants.

Documents to be Submitted When Applying
Standard Documents Requirement

ONE-YEAR GRADUATE PROGRAMS

One-Year Graduate Course of Music (Enrollment: 10)
Composition and Musicology, Instrumental Music, Vocal Music

Foreign Student Admissions
Qualifications for Applicants
Standard Qualifications Requirement
Examination at the College
Same as for undergraduate applicants.

*

For Further Information
Undergraduate and One-year graduate Admissions
Administration Section, Administrative Office, Senzoku Gakuen College, 290 Hisamoto, Takatsu-ku, Kawasaki-shi, Kanagawa 213 ☎ 044-877-3211 ext. 222

Setsunan University
(Setsunan Daigaku)

17-8 Ikedanaka-machi, Neyagawa-shi, Osaka 572
☎ 0720-26-5101

Faculty
Profs. 94   Assoc. Profs. 52
Assist. Profs. Full-time 39; Part-time 186
Res. Assocs. 26
Number of Students
Undergrad. 5, 405   Grad. 9

Library   230, 000 volumes

Outline and Characteristics of the University
Setsunan University dates back to 1922, when its predecessor, Kansai Kogaku Senshu Gakko (Kwansai Technical Institution), was founded. The school was opened for students having to work during the day, but desirous of studying standard industrial technology courses at night. It was a night school with limited curricula. Since then, the school has expanded gradually and developed until it grew out into the present Osaka Institute of Technology and Setsunan University.

In 1975, the Osaka Technological College Corporation established Setsunan University, aiming to developing it into a full-fledged, multidisciplinary university. At the beginning, the Faculty of Engineering was the single, pioneering faculty established on the basis of its previous experience in technological education. The graduates of both the Osaka Institute of Technology and Setsunan University, Faculty of Engineering have won recognition in various fields.

In 1982, two faculties—the Faculty of International Languages and Cultures and the Faculty of Business Administration and Information Science—were established. In the following year, the Faculty of Pharmaceutical Sciences was established as the fourth faculty.

In 1987, the corporate body was named Osaka Kodai Setsunan Daigaku (Osaka Technological College and Setsunan University). Also in 1988, the Faculty of Low and Graduate School of Pharmaceutical Sciences (Master's Program) were established. Setsunan University is thus being developed as a university with five faculties and one master's program.

Setsunan University believes that the aim of university education should be to foster personal growth in mind, body and spirit. In order to realize this aim, Setsunan University maintains a small teacher-student ratio and academic programs to meet the individual needs of each student. A strong program of extra-curricular activties is also offered. In this age of rapidly developing technology and internationalization, Setsunan University is at the forefront in striving to provide students with the education needed to be successful in today's society.

UNDERGRADUATE PROGRAMS

Faculty of Businese Administration and Information Science (Freshmen Enrollment: 200)
Department of Business Administration and Information Science
Business Administration, Business and Industrial Management, Business Finance, Business History, Economics, Information Control in Business Accounting, Information Processing, Information Science, Labor Administration
Faculty of Engineering (Freshmen Enrollment: 530)

Department of Architecture
Architectural Design and History, Architectural Environmental Engineering, Architectural Planning, Building Construction

Department of Civil Engineering
Coastal and Harbor Engineering, Concrete Engineering, Geotechnical Engineering, Hydraulic Engineering, River Engineering, Structural Engineering, Traffic Engineering, Transportation Engineering, Urban Regional Planning

Department of Electrical Engineering
Communication Engineering, Control and Information Engineering, Electrical Machines Engineering, Electric Power Engineering, Electronic Engineering

Department of Industrial and Systems Engineering
Environmental Management, Industrial Management, Instrumentation Engineering, Production Management, Systems Engineering

Department of Mechanical Engineering
Control Engineering, Fluid Engineering, Materials Engineering, Production Engineering, Thermal Engineering

Faculty of International Languages and Cultures (Freshmen Enrollment: 200)

Department of International Language and Culture
American and European Cultures, Chinese Culture, Chinese Language, English Language, Indonesian Language, International Cultures, Latin-American Culture, Southeast Asian Culture, Spanish Language

Faculty of Law (Freshmen Enrollment: 170)

Department of Law
Civil and Commercial Course
Judicial and Administrative Course

Faculty of Pharmaceutical Sciences (Freshmen Enrollment 180)

Department of Environmental Health Sciences
Air and Water Pollution Control, Enviromental Dynamics, Enviromental Health Sciences, Environmental Analytical Chemistry, Environmental Health Preservation, Food Hygiene, Health Statistics and Epidemiology, Industrial Health, Safely Assessment, Waste Control Engineering

Department of Pharmaceutical Sciences
Biopharmacy, Clinical Chemistry and Pathological Biochemistry, Clinical Pharmacy, Dispensing Pharmacy, Drug Evaluation, Drug Information, Hospital Pharmacy Administration, Preclinical Assessment, Social Pharmacy

GRADUATE PROGRAMS

Graduate School of Pharmaceutical Sciences (Freshmen Enrollment: 18)
Master's program

Foreign Student Admission
Qualifications for Applicants

Standard Qualifications Requirement
Those who have received the International Baccalaureate and are 18 years or older may also apply.

Application to the University
First Selection
Examination of Submitted Documents
Application Period: Oct. 1-31, 1988
Announcement of Successful Applicants: Nov. 10
Second Selection
Examination in Subjects, Interview, etc.
Application Period: Nov. 18-28, 1988
Examination: Dec. 3, 1988
Announcement of Successful Applicants: Dec. 9
Faculty of Engineering: Japanese, English, Mathematics, Interview
Faculty of International Language and Culture: Japanese, English, Essay, Interview
Faculty of Business Administration and Information Science: Japanese, English, Essay, Interview
Faculty of Law: Japanese (Composition), English, Interview

Documents to be Submitted When Applying
Standard Documents Requirement
Period for Entrance Procedure: Dec. 15-23, 1988

Qualifications for Transfer Students
Those who have finished 14 years of school education in foreign countries

Examination for Transfer Students
Examination in Subjects
Application Period: Mar. 1-6, 1989
Date: Mar. 10, 1989
Announcement of Successful Applicants: Mar. 18, 1989
Faculty of Technology: Mathematics, English, Physics, Interview

Documents to be Submitted When Applying
Standard Documents Requirement
Primary Procedure
1. Written Oath and Written Guarantee
2. Certificate of Alien Registration
3. Photograph-sheet (to be used on student identification)
Secondary Procedure
1. Certificate of School Last Attended
2. School registration sheet
3. Form for Individual Student Data
4. Membership-card form for Parents' Association
Period for Entrance Procedure: Mar. 18-23

*

Research Institutes and Centers
Central Research Institute, Research Laboratory for Drug Safety

For Further Information
Undergraduate Admission
Instruction Section, Setsunan University, 17-8 Ikedanaka-machi, Neyagawa-shi, Osaka 572
☎ 0720-26-5101 ext. 210

Shibaura Institute of Technology

(Shibaura Kogyo Daigaku)

3-9-14 Shibaura, Minato-ku, Tokyo 108
☎ 03–452–3201

Faculty
    Profs. 85   Assoc. Profs. 72
    Assist. Profs. Full–time 55; Part–time 195
    Res. Assocs. 18
Number of Students
    Undergrad. 6, 018   Grad. 219
Library 163, 290 volumes

Outline and Characteristics of the University

Since its establishment in 1926, Shibaura Institute of Technology has maintained a high reputation for success in training engineers well equipped to meet the demands of modern industries. It boasts of a large teaching staff competent both in the instruction and advancement of up-to-date technical knowledge in various engineering fields. The Shibaura campus of the Institute, being located almost in the heart of the metropolis and at the very entrance of the Keihin Industrial District--one of the major industrial areas in Japan, is therefore in direct contact with the country's political and industrial center.

At the Omiya campus, for the first two years, students engage in general cultural studies: social, natural, and cultural sciences including health education and physical exercises; and the studies of foreign languages (English, German and Russian, from which students are to choose two). Those humane studies and the various extracurricular activities play an invaluable part in the students' formative period. A wide variety of clubs and circles independently organized by students are active in almost every field from fine arts to athletic sports, and help to make college life more meaningful.

UNDERGRADUATE PROGRAMS

Faculty of Engineering (Freshmen Enrollment: 880)
  Department of Architecture
Design and Execution, Environmental Engineering, Equipment, Planning, Production, Structural Analysis, Structure
  Department of Architecture & Building Engineering
Equipment Design, Execution, Planning, Structural Design
  Department of Civil Engineering
City Planning, Construction of Bridges, Tunnels and Dams, Construction of Dangerous Equipment and Industrial Areas, Disaster Prevention Measures, Road, Traffic and Railroads, Water-power Plant, Water Supply and Sewerage Treatment
  Department of Electrical Communication
Acoustics, Applied Communication, Electrical Measurement, Radio Communication, Wire Telegraphy
  Department of Electrical Engineering
Automatic Control, Electronic Computers and Information, Electronics, Material Science
  Department of Electronic Engineering
Communications Systems, Control Systems, Material Science, Solid State Science
  Department of Industrial Chemistry
Electro-chemistry, High Polymer Chemistry, Organic Physical Chemistry, Petrochemistry, Quantum Chemistry, Radiochemistry, Silic-chemistry, Spectrochemistry, Unit Operation
  Department of Industrial Management
Economics, Industrial Psychology, Sociology, Technical Methods and Analysis
  Department of Mechanical Engineering
Automatic Control, Flow and Fracture of Materials, Fluid Mechanics and Fluid Engineering, Heat Transfer, Machine Design, Machine Tools and Production Engineering, Structural Analysis and Mechanical Vibration, Thermo-Aero Engieering
  Department of Mechanical Engineering II
Conversion and Transfer of Energy, Design Engineering, Machine Element, Machining Technology, Material Engineering, Systems Engineering
  Department of Metallurgical Engineering
Basic Study of Physical Characteristics of Metals, Chemical Study Concerning Corrosion of Metals and their Surface Treatments, Development of Light Metals and Research of their Properties, Development of New Steels and Analysis of their Properties, Study on Techniques of Foundry and Welding
Faculty of Engineering (**Evening Course**) (Freshmen Enrollment: 160)
  Department of Electrical Engineering
  Department of Mechanical Engineering
See the listing for Day Course

Foreign Student Admission
  Qualifications for Applicants
    Standard Qualifications Requirement
The General Examination for Foreign Students.
  Examination at the University
    An interview. Successful applicants are accepted in addition to the prescribed number of Japanese students.
  Documents to be Submitted When Applying
    Standard Documents Requirement
Application period: February 11 to February 14.
Announcement of successful applicants: Feb. 17-Feb. 20.

GRADUATE PROGRAMS

Graduate School of Engineering (First Year Enrollment : Master's 50)
  Divisions
Architecture and Civil Engineering, Electric Communication and Electronic Engineering, Industrial

Chemistry, Mechanical Engineering, Metallurgical Engineering

Foreign Student Admission
Qualifications for Applicants
Master's Program
Standard Qualifications Requirement
Examination at the University
Master's Program
Same as for Japanese a written exam and an interview.
Documents to be Submitted When Applying
Standard Documents Requirement
All application documents must be submitted to the Admission Office of Graduate School with the specified application fee.
Application due: the end of September. Examination Date: in late September.
Announcement of successful applicants: October 1.
Date of second-stage entrance examination: Feb. 27 to Feb. 28.
Announcement of successful applicants: March 1.
Candidates who have been admitted must complete the necessary procedure for admission by the appointed time.

*

Research Institutes and Centers
Computation Center, Research Laboratory of Engineering
For Further Information
Undergraduate Admission
General Affairs Department, Entrance Examination Section, Shibaura Institute of Technology, 3-9-14 Shibaura, Minato-ku, Tokyo 108 ☎ 03–452–3201 ext. 226
Graduate Admission
Office of Graduate School, Shibaura Institute of Technology, 3-9-14 Shibaura, Minato-ku, Tokyo 108 ☎ 03–452–3201 ext. 236

Shikoku Christian College
(Shikoku Gakuin Daigaku)

3-2-1 Bunkyo-cho, Zentsuji-shi, Kagawa 765
☎ 0877-62-2111

Faculty
Profs. 24   Assoc. Profs. 21
Assist. Profs. Full–time 8; Part–time 119
Number of Students
Undergrad. 1, 939   Grad. 11
Library 130, 000 volumes

Outline and Characteristics of the College
Shikoku Christianity Academy was established as a non-accredited school institution in 1950 to provide instruction in Christian studies and liberal arts for college level students. Rev. L. W. Moore, missionary of the Japan Mission of the Presbyterian Church, U. S. , served as the first president. The educational foundation Shikoku Gakuin was established in 1959 and was accredited by the Ministry of Education as a co-educational junior college. Majors were offered in Christian studies and the English language. In 1962, a senior college, Shikoku Christian College was established and received accreditation from the Ministry of Education. The Faculty of Literature with the Departments of English Literature and Christian Studies was started. In 1966, the Department of Social Welfare was added. In 1967, the Department of Christian Studies developed into the Department of Humanities. In 1972 the Graduate School of Social Welfare (Master's Course) was added. In 1973, the Department of Education was added. In 1982, the Deparment of Sociology was added. Starting with fewer than 50 students in 1950, Shikoku Christian College had a student body of 1, 939 at the beginning of the 1988 academic year.

Study and education based on Christian principles, special emphasis on culture and learning, emphasis upon internationalism, a good student-faculty ratio, and a beautiful environment are characteristics of this college. It is stipulated in Article No. 1 of the College Regulations as the educational policy that "Shikoku Christian College, established upon the foundation of the teachings of Christianity as recorded in the Old and New Testaments, has as its purpose the education of young people, cultivating in them the spirit to search for truth and service to God and man. " Each faculty member, except for the General Education Course, serves as an adviser for a group of students with whom he/she meets regularly. He/she is available for counsel and advice on any number of questions related to their studies or college life. Most faculty members live on campus or nearby in town, and they observe"At Home"hours, when students are welcome to visit them at their office or at home with their families. We encourage close faculty-student relationships in various ways both in and out of class. We also have a Study Abroad System for One Year with Han Nam University, Taejon, Republic of Korea, Whitworth College, Spokane, Washington, U. S. A. and University of the Ozarks, Clarksville, Arkansas, U. S. A.

Shikoku Christian College is located in Zentsuji City, a rural city of about 39, 000 in Kagawa Prefecture, in the northern part of the island of Shikoku, in southwest Japan. The climate of Kagawa Prefecture is considered mild with very little snowfall during the winter. Since this region has such good weather with moderate rainfall and plenty of sunshine, vegetables and fruits grown here are unusually sweet and juicy. Zentsuji City is also an historic city. It was civilized early from the Jomon Period and Yayoi Period. Presently, Zentsuji City is developing into a city of culture and education.

UNDERGRADUATE PROGRAMS

Faculty of Literature (Freshmen Enrollment: 400)
  Department of Education
Art and Craft, Audio-Visual Education, Calligraphy, Children's Literature, Developmental Psychology, History of Education, History of Pedagogy, History of Physical Education, Home Economics, Japanese, Mathematics, Moral Education, Music, Musicology, Philosophy of Education, Physical Education, Science, Social Studies, Sociology of Education
  Department of English Literature
Cross-cultural Communication, English and American Dramas, English and American Poetry, English Grammar, English Linguistics, English Novels, English Phonetics, History of American Literature, History of English, History of English Literature, International Affairs, Media Studies, Teaching of English as a Foreign Language, Teaching of Japanese as a Foreign Language
  Department of Humanities
Aesthetics, Archaeology, Buddhism and Christianity, Cultural Anthropology, Dogmatics, Ethics, Ethnology, History of Japanese Thoughts, History of Religion, History of Western Philosophy, Human Relations, Japanese History, Japanese Literature, Oriental History, Philosophy, Social Philosophy, Study of Religion, Western History
  Department of Social Welfare
Child Development, Child Welfare, Clinical Psychology, Community Organization, Correctional Services, Counseling, International Social Welfare, Psychiatry, Psychological Testing, Public Assistance, Public Health, Social Casework, Social Pathology, Social Policy, Social Psychology, Social Security, Social Welfare, Social Welfare and Law, Social Welfare of Handicapped Persons
  Department of Sociology
Comparative Religion, Comparative Sociology, Environmental Issues, History of Social Theory, History of Sociology, Human Rights Issues, Industrial Sociology, Peace Studies, Political Sociology, Social Philosophy, Sociology, Sociology of Family, Sociology of International Relations, Sociology of Law, Sociology of Local Communities, Sociology of Religion

Foreign Student Admission
  Qualifications for Applicants
  Standard Qualifications Requirement
  Examination at the College
  Required documents.
  Documents to be Submitted When Applying
  Standard Documents Requirement
  Certificate of the Japanese Language Proficiency, or certificate made out by an instructor of Japanese language.
Application deadline: the middle of November

Qualifications for Transfer Students
  Those who have graduated from a junior college, or have earned 52 credits or more at a college or university.
  Examination for Transfer Students
  Required documents.
  Documents to be Submitted When Applying
  Standard Documents Requirement
  Same as for freshman-application.

GRADUATE PROGRAMS

Graduate School of Social Welfare (First Year Enrollment : Master's 10)
  Division
Social Welfare

Foreign Student Admission
  Qualifications for Applicants
Master's Program
  Standard Qualifications Requirement
  Examination at the College
Master's Program
  Required documents
  Documents to be Submitted When Applying
  Standard Documents Requirement
  Certificate of the Japanese Proficiency, or certificate made out by an instructor of Japanese language

*

Facilities/Services for Foreign Students
International Exchange Center:
  International Exchange Lounge
  Study Hall for Foreign Students
  International Exchange Office
Special Programs for Foreign Students
Subjects for Foreign Students:
  Japanese (Elementary, Intermediate)
  Japanology I
For Further Information
  Undergraduate and Graduate Admission
Academic Affairs Division, Shikoku Christian College, 3-2-1 Bunkyo-cho, Zentsuji-shi, Kagawa 765
☎ 0877-62-2111 ext. 230

Shikoku Women's University
(Shikoku Joshi Daigaku)

123-1 Ebisuno, Furukawa, Ojin-cho, Tokushima-shi, Tokushima 771-11   ☎ 0886-65-1300

Faculty
  Profs. 52   Assoc. Profs. 35
  Assist. Profs. Full–time 21; Part–time 111
  Res. Assocs. 11
Number of Students
  Undergrad. 1, 924
Library 169, 300 volumes

Outline and Characteristics of the University

Shikoku Women's University was founded by the late chairperson of the board of directors, Katsu Sato, in 1961. At the time of the foundation, it was named Tokushima Junior College of Home Economics. It was renamed Shikoku Women's Junior College after adding the Department of Literature in 1963. In 1966 Shikoku Women's University was established in addition to Shikoku Women's Junior College. At the present time the Colleges of S. W. U. are Literature and Home Economics. The Departments of the Junior College of S. W. U. are Literature, Life Sciences, Children's Education and Music.

The University's goal is to provide modern women with both academic skills and general knowledge so that they will succeed as career women upon graduation and be capable of leading a productive and fulfilling adult life. S. W. U. places emphasis on general education, a special series of cultural lectures, and a program of readings recommended by the faculty.

Shikoku Women's University is located just beside the beautiful Yoshino River which courses down the mountains through scenic Oboke and Koboke Valleys. On its relaxing green campus stand modern, well-equipped buildings. The school commands a wonderful view of the river which reflects the rising and setting sun, and enhances the beauty of the four seasons of the year. In the center of Tokushima can be seen Shiroyama covered with ancient trees. In such delightful surroundings lies the campus of Shikoku Women's University, a quiet place suitable for teaching, contemplation and learning.

UNDERGRADUATE PROGRAMS

College of Home Economics (Freshmen Enrollment: 120)

Department of Home Economics
Nursing and Health Course
Anatomy, Bacteriology, Immunology, Nursing and Health, Nutrition, Physiology, School Health
Science of Clothing Course
Science of Clothing, Statistics, Textiles and Clothing
Training Course for Managing Dietitians
Bacteriology, Dietetics, Nutrition, Social Psycology
Department of Pedology
Children's Education Course
Calligraphy, Geography, History, Hygiene, Japanese Language, Mathematics, Music, Natural Science, Pedology
Pedology Course
Childcare, Cooking, Family Relations, Pedology, Physiology, Psychology, Theory of Social Welfare
College of Literature (Freshmen Enrollment: 90)
Department of English Language and Literature
English Education, English Linguistics, English Literature, English Phonetics, English Poems, English Prose, History of English and American Literature
Department of Japanese Language and Literature

Calligraphy Course
Japanese Literature Course
Calligraphy, Calligraphy Education, Chinese Language and Literature, Culture and Art, History of Japanese Thought, Japanese Education, Japanese Language, Japanese Literature, Japanese Phonetics

Foreign Student Admission

Qualifications for Applicants
Standard Qualifications Requirement
Examination at the University
Scholastic achievement, personality, health and Japanese language comprehension.
Documents to be Submitted When Applying
Standard Documents Requirement
Successful applicants must submit the following papers on the appointed day.
1. A written pledge declaring one's intention to enter this university
2. A personal reference written by one's guarantor in Japan.

*

Facilities/Services for Foreign Students
The Office of International Programs gives help and advice to foreign students.
Special Programs for Foreign Students
Foreign students may spend five weeks in Japanology Program. This is designed to acquaint our foreign students with Japanese history, culture and language. Other students, who are regularly enrolled at S. W. U. and who are on exchange from foreign countries, take regular classes on our campus and may also enroll in special Japanese language classes which are given personally outside of our regular curriculum.
For Further Information
Undergraduate Admission
Admission Office/International Programs Office, Shikoku Women's University, 123-1 Ebisuno, Furukawa, Ojin-cho, Tokushima-shi, Tokushima 771-11 ☎ 0886-65-1300

Shinwa Women's College
(Shinwa Joshi Daigaku)

7-13-1 Suzurandai-kitamachi, Kita-ku, Kobe-shi, Hyogo 651-11   ☎ 078-591-1651

Faculty
   Profs.   20   Assoc. Profs.   15
   Assist. Profs.   Full–time   6; Part–time   90
Number of Students
   Undergrad.   1, 656
Library   113, 876 volumes

Outline and Characteristics of the College

Shinwa Women's College was established in 1966 as an extension of the Shinwa Educational Institution, which has a history of 100 years. The college is now celebrating the 20th anniversary of its foundation. The high morale that was evident at its opening has helped make possible the steady progress since enjoyed by the college. It continues to expand and modernize, so that future prospects look very bright. Suzurandai, where Shinwa Women's College is situated, is a pleasant area in the northwest of the Rokko Mts. in Kobe, and the students enjoy their academic years in an attractive and quiet location.

In the 20 years since its opening, the college has devoted itself to the education of trustworthy and cultured young women, who adapt to the times in which they live. Shinwa Women's College has already seen many of its graduates go out into the world, and has had the pleasure of knowing they are appreciated throughout society. Everyone associated with the college is determined to make every possible effort to consolidate and further its achievements. The college has consistently aimed at promoting character formation, encouraged by active interchange between students and teaching staff.

Shinwa Women's College hopes to educate honest and intelligent young women, and in so doing, meet the demands of modern society.

UNDERGRADUATE PROGRAMS

Faculty of Literature (Freshmen Enrollment: 300)
Department of Children's Pedagogy
Childhood Culture, Educational Psychology, Educational Sociology, Educational System, Infant Education, Juvenile Literature, Physical Training of Childhood, Special Education, Theories of Educational Curriculum
Department of English Literature
English and American Literature, English Linguistics
Department of Japanese Literature
History of Chinese Literature, History of Japanese Literature, Japanese Calligraphy, Japanese Cultural History, Japanese Linguistics, Japanese Literature, Japanese Stylistics, Literary Study of Chinese Poetry, Literary Study of Chinese Prose

*

For Further Information
Undergraduate Admission
Admission Office, Shinwa Women's College, 7-13-1 Suzurandai-kitamachi, Kita-ku, Kobe-shi, Hyogo 651-11 ☎ 078-591-1651 ext. 22

Shirayuri Women's College
(Shirayuri Joshi Daigaku)

1-25 Midorigaoka, Chofu–shi, Tokyo 182
☎ 03-326-5050

Faculty
   Profs. 31   Assoc. Profs. 16
   Assist. Profs. Full–time 5; Part–time 103
Number of Students

Undergrad.   1, 838
Library   120, 000 volumes

Outline and Characteristics of the College
Established in1946 as an institute of higher ducation known as "senmon gakko, " Shirayuri Women's College had two departments: Japanese Literature and English Literature. In 1950 the school was reorganized into a junior college with the two original majors; the French Literature Department was added in 1958. The present four-year college granting Bachelor of Arts degrees in Japanese, French, and English Literature, was established in 1965, and the last junior college students graduated in 1966. A new department of Child Development and Juvenile Culture was added in 1965.

Transfer students may be admitted by departments that have an opening (announced in the annual bulletin).

The college's education is carried on in a Christian spirit, aiming to prepare women for their roles in a progressive society. Our graduates have been accepted in various graduate schools, and have entered various fields: their high employment rate bears witness to their capabilities.

The wooded campus was formerly the site of the Tsumura Juntendo Garden for medicinal herbs. The woodland has remained almost untouched, with Japanese and foreign trees dating back 100 years, The lawns, the various flowers of the season, the ponds all make it unique among college campuses in Tokyo, and yet it is only about 25 minutes by train on the Keio Line from Shinjuku, and about 20 minutes by bus from Mitaka, Kichijoji and Seijo.

Aside from the school buildings and the administratration wing, there is an auditorium for theatrical performances, concerts and other student activities, and a basement gymnasium. The library has a unique audio–visual center equipped for group as well as individual research. The thousands of video tapes, casette tapes, and compact discs are available to both faculty and students who wish to make use of the center.

Facilities for students include the residence hall which accommodates more than 70 students, and the club houses for year–round student activities. Much in demand are the tennis courts which the students use for their own practice as well as for matches with teams from other universities and colleges.

As the college was founded by the Congregation of the Sisters of St. Paul of Chartres of France, there is a distinct French tradition which attracts students to pursue studies concerning France, aside from countries like the United States and England. There is, therefore, an international atmosphere among the faculty and student body.

The course in Library Science was approved by the Ministry of Education in 1982. Certificates for librarians are granted to those who complete the required units.

UNDERGRADUATE PROGRAMS

Faculty of Liberal Arts (Freshmen Enrollment: 400)
Department of Child Development and Juvenile Culture
Adolescent Psychology, Child Psychology, Developmental Psychology, History of Juvenile Culture, History of Juvenile Literature, Juvenile Culture, Juvenile Literature, Psychology, Science of Family Education, Social Psychology
Department of English Literature
Anglo–Saxon Civilization, Comparative Literature, English and American Literature, English Language, English Linguistics, Greek Mythology, History of American Literature, History of England, History of English Literature, History of the English Language, History of the United States, Philology, Phonetics, The Bible in English Literature, Translation from Japanese into English
Department of French Literature
French Civilization, French Grammar, French Language, French Literature, History of the French Language, Translation from Japanese to French
Department of Japanese Literature
Calligraphy, Chinese Literature, History of Japanese Literature, Japanese Grammar, Japanese Language

*

For Further Information
Undergraduate Admission
Admissions Office, Shirayuri Women's College, 1-25 Midorigaoka, Chofu–shi, Tokyo 182 ☎ 03-326-5050

Shitennoji International Buddhist University

(Shitennoji Kokusai Bukkyo Daigaku)

3-2-1 Gakuenmae, Habikino-shi, Osaka 583
☎ 0729-56-3181

Faculty
    Profs.　34　　Assoc. Profs.　15
    Assist. Profs.　Full–time　11; Part–time　67
Number of Students
    Undergrad.　1, 726
Library　114, 713 volumes

Outline and Characteristics of the University

IBU has a history of almost 1, 400 years. It can be traced back to the founding of the Kyoden'in, the first true educational academy in Japan, by Prince Shotoku in 592 A. D. The educational philosophy of IBU is based on the Buddhist spirit of "Harmony" as advocated by Prince Shotoku. Our goal is to pursue his teaching for future generations.

With the demand for world peace always in mind, IBU strives to produce competent world citizens who will be able to cope with internationaliza-tion. Internationally minded people should have pride in their own culture and should be able to find their own way in the international world guided by the spirit of Buddhism. Furthermore, one should be rich, not only in knowledge, but also in personality, in order to function in today's international world. In order to achieve this end, one must be not only physically strong, but also able to function properly in society. In order to broaden international dialogue, one must be equipped with competent skills, such as using foreign languages.

In order to achieve these goals, the university offers religious services to develop the backbone of personal character guided by the spirit of Buddhism. Every Thursday, first year students participate in meditation while second year students study Buddhist sutras.

Classes and lectures are designed in such a way that teacher-student and student-student relationships can be established on an intimate basis through mutual trust and respect. In classroom situations, students are free to voice their opinions and they participate in class actively in order to pursue their academic goals. We believe that this is how any institution of higher learning should be operated.

Being competent in a foreign language is a must, not only in order to pursue one's academic goals, but also to survive in the international world. In the Faculty of Literature, students are required to take foreign languages such as English, German and French to fulfill their general education requirements. The number of hours that the students have to study is double that of any other university in Japan. The most competent teachers, the latest educational facilities and the most modern teaching methods have produced an excellent foreign language program. In the English and Arabic Departments of the Faculty of Literature and the English Department of the Junior College, students are encouraged to improve their language ability through first hand experience overseas in language and cultural programs in Vienna, Hawaii, and other locations throughout the world. These programs provide students with the opportunity to become truly internationally minded world citizens.

Various extracurricular activities are offered in order to enrich college life and develop physical strength (to build strong minds and bodies). The kinds of experiences that students receive through participation in these activities help the students to appreciate the agony of creation and the joy of developing a bright personality.

UNDERGRADUATE PROGRAMS

Faculty of Literature (Freshmen Enrollment: 400)
Department of Buddhism
Chinese and Japanese Laws and Ceremonies, Comparative Ethnology, Comparative Thought and Religion, History of Buddhism in China, History of Bud-

dhism in India, History of Buddhism in Japan, Japanese Culture, Pali, Religion, Sanskrit Laws and Ceremonies, Tendai Buddhism

Department of Education

Anthropology and Education, Art Theory, Calligraphy, Comparative Education, Education, Educational Administration, Educational Psychology, Education and Society, Education of Small Children, History of Education, Japanese, Japanese Language, Mathematics, Morals in Education, Music, Physical Education, School Management, Science, Social Studies, Special Education, Teaching Materials

Department of Language and Culture

Arabic Studies Course

Arabic Culture, Arabic Language, Arabic Literature, Economics in the Middle East, History of Islamic Law, History of Islamic Thought, History of Persia, Islamic Cultures, Semic

English and American Studies Course

Christian Culture, English and American Culture, English and American Literature, English Language, History of England and America, History of the English Language, Linguistics

Japanese Studies Course

Calligraphy, History of Foreign Influence in Japan, History of Japanese Language, History of Japanese Literature, Japanese Civilization, Japanese Culture, Japanese History, Japanese Literature

Department of Sociology

Area Studies, Communication Theory, Comparative Sociology, Cultural Anthropology, Family and Society, Industry and Society, International Relations, Japanese Civilization, Sociological Investigation, Sociological Pathology, Sociological Psychology, Sociology and Religion, Theories in Modern Sociology

Foreign Student Admission

Qualifications for Applicants

Standard Qualifications Requirement

Examination at the University

1. Interview
2. Japanese Proficiency Examination

Documents to be Submitted When Applying

Standard Documents Requirement

*

Research Institutes and Centers

Shitennoji International Buddhist Cultural Research Institute

Facilities/Services for Foreign Students

Library (Section on Japan, Asia, Buddhism, etc. in English)

Special Programs for Foreign Students

Japanese for Foreign Students is offered.

For Further Information

Undergraduate Admission

Foreign Student Advisor, Shitennoji International Buddhist University, 3-2-1 Gakuenmae, Habikino-shi, Osaka 583 ☎ 0729-56-3181

Shoin Women's University
(Shoin Joshigakuin Daigaku)

1-2-1 Shinoharaobanoyama-cho, Nada-ku, Kobe-shi, Hyogo 657 ☎ 078-882-6122

Faculty
Profs. 24   Assoc. Profs. 8
Assist. Profs. Full–time 6; Part–time 71
Res. Assocs. 5
Number of Students
Undergrad. 1, 120
Library 160, 000 volumes

Outline and Characteristics of the University

Shoin was founded in 1892 by English missionaries sent from "Society for the Propagation of the Gospel" as a mission school for girls. In 1949, Shoin established a two-year college and in 1966, a four-year university. In 1980-81, Shoin united its two campuses into one that stands on a conveniently located site lying between the internationally famed Kobe port and Mt. Rokko which towers behind. The new campus boasts of the most modern facilities housed in a campus admired for its architectural beauty and functional utility. Currently, Shoin Women's University serves the academic, personal and spiritual needs of students of all faiths and ambitions.

In terms of English education, Shoin places an emphasis on English as a means of practical communication. With this in mind, Shoin students are given the opportunity to study at our sister universities in the United States: the University of New Hampshire and Hobart & William Smith Colleges in New York State. Further, Shoin provides a variety of extra-curricular activities in both sports and culture. Shoin is proud of its newly built Classic French 18th Century organ, considered the best pipe organ in Japan. Further, Shoin students are active in such diverse activities as skiing, tennis, the Japanese halberd (Naginata), tea ceremony, koto, English Speaking Society, chorus, calligraphy, movie club and folk singing.

Today, Shoin is dedicated to improving the educational and cultural environment of its students with an emphasis on developing a love of their native culture along with an awareness and respect for foreign language, culture and customs.

UNDERGRADUATE PROGRAMS

Faculty of Literature (Freshmen Enrollment: 325)

Department of English and American Literature

Course in Creative Computing

Artificial Intelligence, Computer Assisted Designing, Computer Assisted Instruction, Computer Communication, Computer Literacy, Computer Translation,

Programming Languages (BASIC, PASCAL, C, FORTH, PROLOG etc.), Word Processing (ENGLISH, JAPANESE)

Course in English and American Literature
Bible English, English and American Literature, History of American Literature, History of English, American Culture, History of English Literature, Linguistics, Philology

Department of Japanese Literature
Course in Japanese Literature
Calligraphy, Classical Chinese, Comparative Study of English and Japanese, Contrastive Linguistics, History of Japanese Culture, History of Japanese Language, History of Japanese Literature, Japanese Linguistics, Japanese Literature, Modern Japanese Literary History

Course in Teaching Japanese as a Foreign Language
Contrastive Linguistics, General Linguistics, History of Japanese, Japanese Linguistics, Japanese Phonology, Japanese Syntax, Sociolinguistics, Teaching Methods of Japanese

Foreign Student Admission
Qualifications for Applicants
Standard Qualifications Requirement
Applicants are required to have passed the Japanese Language Proficiency Test (Grade 2), or to have equiralent Japanese Language Ability.

*

Research Institutes and Centers
Institute for Research in Christian Culture
For Further Information
Undergraduate Admission
The Office of Admission, Shoin Women's University, 1-2-1 Shinoharaobanoyama-cho, Nada-ku, Kobe-shi, Hyogo 657 ☎ 078-882-6122

Shokei College
(Shokei Daigaku)

2155-7 Nirenoki, Shimizu-machi, Kumamoto-shi, Kumamoto 860 ☎ 096-338-8840

Faculty
    Profs. 9   Assoc. Profs. 7
    Assist. Profs. Full–time 8; Part–time 22
Number of Students
    Undergrad. 382
Library 28, 422 volumes

Outline and Characteristics of the College
Shokei College was established on May 20, 1975. It has one faculty of Literature, composed of two (Japanese and English Literature) departments. Its origin is traced to 1888 as an attached girls' school to Seiseiko, the present Seiseiko High School. In 1891, the girls' school became independent and was renamed Shokei Girls'School, which continues today as Shokei High School. From this the name "Sho-

Kei"has been the symbol and spirit of our whole educational institution. Its original source is the Chinese classic, "Shi-Kyo" (The Book of Songs).What is meant by it is that even if one is clothed in such a brilliant dress of brocade or silk, one should always put on a plain and simple topcoat over it, and never show off one's clothes. This is a truly modest and humble attitude towards life. The modern mind and education of our college is deeply based on this traditional value of life.

UNDERGRADUATE PROGRAMS

Faculty of Literature (Freshmen Enrollment: 100)
Department of English Literature
American Literature, English Linguistics, English Literature, English Phonetics, History of English Language, History of English Literature, Speech Writing
Department of Japanese Literature
Chinese Calligraphy, Chinese Classics, Cultural History, History of Japanese Language, History of Japanese Literature, Japanese Calligraphy, Japanese Linguistics, Japanese Literature, Japanese Phonetics

Foreign Student Admission
Qualifications for Applicants
Standard Qualifications Requirement
Applicants must be women who are 18 years old or older. Applicants without sufficient ability in Japanese language may be admitted as regular students under special conditions with the consent of the college authorities.
Examination at the College
A written and oral examination in Japanese language (Under special conditions the Japanese examination may be waived.)
Documents to be Submitted When Applying
Standard Documents Requirement
An application form and a college pamphlet will be made available to students from early November. The application should be returned to the college in time for processing before the beginning of the new school year in April.

*

Facilities/Services for Foreign Students
A student hall and a female student dormitory.
For Further Information
Undergraduate Admission
Administrative Office, The Administration Section, Shokei College, 2155-7 Nirenoki, Shimizu-machi, Kumamoto-shi, Kumamoto 860 ☎ 096-338-8840 ext. 100

Shotoku Academy Gifu College of Education
(Shotoku Gakuen Gifu Kyoiku Daigaku)

2078 Takakuwa, Yanaizu-cho, Hashima-gun, Gifu 501-61 ☎ 0582-79-0804

Faculty
Profs. 41   Assoc. Profs. 20
Assist. Profs.   Full–time 12; Part–time 36
Number of Students
Undergrad. 1, 459
Library 57, 798 volumes

Outline and Characteristics of the College

Shotoku Academy, named after Prince Shotoku (A. D. 574-622), was founded in 1963 by a group of Shin Buddhist priests in the Gifu area. Gifu College of Education, established in 1972, is one of several educational institutions in the Academy. Its educational aim is to provide proper training to future school teachers under the slogan of "Flexibility of Mind,"which can be found in the Seventeen Articles of Prince Shotoku.

At the completion of the four-year program, the student shall receive the degree of Bachelor of Education with one of the following combinations of teaching certificates:

1. First-class certificates in elementary school teaching and kindergarten teaching.
2. First-class certificates in elementary school teaching and kindergarten teaching and a second-class certificate in junior high school teaching.
3. A first-class certificate in junior high school teaching and second-class certificates in elementary school teaching and senior high school teaching.
4. First-class certificates in kindergarten teaching, elementary school teaching, and junior high school teaching and a second-class certificate in senior high school teaching.

The four-year program consists of (1) general education, (2) teacher's training, (3) specialized field of study (Early Childhood, Japanese, Mathematics, Music, Social Sciences), and (4) student teaching. The workload of the student varies depending on the type and number of certificates he or she wishes to obtain.

Gifu is located about 30 kilometers north of Nagoya in central Japan. The campus is situated in the southwest suburbs of Gifu City. Its small community environment promotes friendly human relationships and offers a relatively low cost of living.

UNDERGRADUATE PROGRAMS

Faculty of Education (Freshmen Enrollment: 280)
Elementary Education Program
Child Psychology, Developmental Psychology, Educational History, Educational Psychology, Educational Sociology, Junior High School Teaching, Kindergarten Education, Moral and Ethical Education, Pedagogics, School Administration, Teaching Methodology and Teaching Materials (Japanese, Social Sciences, Mathematics, Natural Sciences, Music, Visual Arts, Health and Physical Education, Home Economics)
Secondary Education Program
Developmental Psychology, Educational History, Educational Psychology, Educational Sociology, Moral and Ethical Education, Pedagogics, School Administration, Teaching Methodology (Japanese, Mathematics, Music, Social Sciences)

Foreign Student Admission

Qualifications for Applicants
Standard Qualifications Requirement
Applicants must not possess Japanese nationality.
Applicants are required to take the Japanese Language Proficiency Test and the General Examination for Foreign Students.
Examination at the College
1. Interview for all students.
2. Musical performance (voice, piano and one other instrument) for those wishing to be enrolled in the Secondary Education Program specializing in music.
Date: Feb. 14
Documents to be Submitted When Applying
Standard Documents Requirement
Application forms are available at the Admissions Office starting from July of the preceding year. application period: January 12 and February 2. The application fee (bank transfer only) of 25, 000 yen must accompany every application. The announcement on successful application will be made on February 24.

✳

Facilities/Services for Foreign Students
Information service on private student dormitories
For Further Information
Undergraduate Admission
Office of General Affairs, Gifu College of Education, 2078 Takakuwa, Yanaizu-cho, Hashima-gun, Gifu 501-61 ☎ 0582-79-0804 ext. 112

Showa Academia Musicae
(Showa Ongaku Daigaku)

808 Sekiguchi, Atsugi–shi, Kanagawa 243
☎ 0462–45–1055

Faculty
Profs. 24   Assoc. Profs. 7
Assist. Profs. Full–time 6; Part–time 46
Res. Assocs. 3
Number of Students
Undergrad. 356
Library 62, 910 volumes

Outline and Characteristics of the College

Showa Academia Musicae is a new school established in 1983. It is the product of Keisuke Shimoyagawa and the Tosei Gakuen Educational Foundation. Although this school was only recently established, the Foundation has a deeper background. It established the Showa Academia Musicae Junior College in 1969, and the Tokyo Seisen Music School in 1940.

Although the school is an academy of music, a diversified curriculum is offered to the students to ensure that they will receive a well balanced education. All students are required to take classes in Cultural Science, Social Science, Natural Science, Foreign Languages, Health and Physical Education, and other fundamental studies.

Through this curriculum and the efforts of the Foundation's Chairman of the Board of Directors, Kyosuke Shimoyagawa, the academy's President, Ryozo Okuda, and Dean, Takatoshi Yoshida, the students develop a sound basis for their future careers in music.

UNDERGRADUATE PROGRAMS

Faculty of Music (Freshmen Enrollment: 120)
Department of Composition
Composition, Conducting, Folk Music, Music Aesthetics, Music History, Piano, Theory of Musical Forms
Department of Instrumental Music
Accompaniment, Concert, Counterpoint, European Music History, Folk Music, Harmonics, Keyboard Harmonics, Keyboard Music History, Music Aesthetics, Music Analysis, Piano, Science of Musical Instruments
Department of Vocal Music
Acting, Art of the Stage, Chorus, Counterpoint, Dancing, Drama, Drama History, Elocution, Ensemble, Folk Music, Harmonics, History of Music, History of Opera, Music Aesthetics, Opera, Oratorio, Vocal Music

Foreign Student Admission
Qualifications for Applicants
Standard Qualifications Requirement
Examination at the College
The same as Japanese applicants.
Documents to be Submitted When Applying
Standard Documents Requirement
*

For Further Information
Undergraduate Admission
Student Division, Showa Academia Musicae, 808 Sekiguchi, Atsugi–shi, Kanagawa 243
☎ 0462–45–1055

Showa College of Pharmaceutical Sciences
(Showa Yakka Daigaku)

5-1-8 Tsurumaki, Setagaya–ku, Tokyo 154
☎ 03–426–3381

UNDERGRADUATE PROGRAMS

Faculty of Pharmaceutical Sciences (Freshmen Enrollment: 240)
Department of Bio–pharmacy
Department of Pharmacy

GRADUATE PROGRAMS

Graduate School of Pharmaceutical Sciences (First Year Enrollment : Master's 16)
Division
Pharmaceutical Sciences

Showa University
(Showa Daigaku)

1-5-8 Hatanodai, Shinagawa-ku, Tokyo 142
☎ 03-784-8000

Faculty
Profs. 115   Assoc. Profs. 110
Assist. Profs. Full–time 163; Part–time 128
Res. Assocs. 684
Number of Students
Undergrad. 2, 270   Grad. 308
Library 176, 047 volumes

Outline and Characteristics of the University

Showa University is comprised of the Schools of Medicine, Dentistry and Pharmaceutical Sciences and two associated Schools of Nursing. Close cooperation among the five faculties has proven fruitful in education and research, and the results place Showa University in a very high position among the private medical schools of Japan. In addition to the teaching facilities, Showa University also operates five medical and one dental hospital in Metropolitan Tokyo. These institutions serve their respective neighborhoods with medical and dental services, and in addition, afford teaching and research facilities for the students and staff of the University.

Showa University was founded as Showa Medical College in Tokyo in 1928. After 36 years of steady progress, the School of Pharmaceutical Sciences was established in 1964, and Showa Medical College then became Showa University. The School of Dentistry, the most recent of the Schools, was opened in 1977 to complete the formation of the medical complex. The original building of the Main Hospital is a grand 17-story structure founded in 1980.

With its excellent facilities and organization, the achievements at Showa University is reflected in the superior research of the staff, each in his own particular field of interest. We anticipate a still brighter future with even greater achievements for Showa University and its people.

UNDERGRADUATE PROGRAMS

School of Dentistry (Freshmen Enrollment: 120)
Department of Dentistry
Anesthesiology, Conservative Dentistry, Dental Pharmacology, Dental Radiology, Dental Technology, Hygiene and Oral Health, Oral Anatomy, Oral Biochemistry, Oral Microbiology, Oral Pathology, Oral Physiology, Oral Surgery, Orthodontics, Pedodontics, Prosthetic Dentistry
School of Medicine (Freshmen Enrollment: 120)
Department of Medicine
Anatomy, Anesthesiology, Bacteriology, Biochemistry, Clinical Pathology, Dermatology, Hygiene, Internal Medicine, Legal Medicine, Medical Zoology, Obstetrics and Gynecology, Ophthalmology, Orthopedic Surgery, Otorhinolaryngology, Pathology, Pediatrics, Pharmacology, Physiology, Plastic Surgery, Psychiatry and Neurology, Public Health, Radiology, Surgery, Urology
School of Pharmaceutical Sciences(Freshmen Enrollment: 180)
Department of Biopharmaceutical Science
Biological Chemistry, Hygienic Chemistry, Microbial Chemistry, Physiological Chemistry, Toxicology
Department of Pharmaceutical Sciences
Analytical Chemistry, Pharmaceutical Chemistry, Pharmaceutic Industrial Chemistry, Pharmacognosy and Plant Chemistry, Pharmacology, Pharmacy, Physical Chemistry

Foreign Student Admission
Qualifications for Applicants
Standard Qualifications Requirement
Examination at the University

Same entrance examination as Japanese students.
Documents to be Submitted When Applying
Standard Documents Requirement

GRADUATE PROGRAMS

Graduate School of Dentistry (First Year Enrollment : Doctor's 18)
Division
Dentistry
Graduate School of Medicine (First Year Enrollment : Doctor's 60)
Divisions
Internal Medicine, Pathology, Physiology, Social Medicine, Surgery
Graduate School of Pharmaceutical Sciences (First Year Enrollment : Master's 16, Doctor's 8)
Division
Pharmaceutical Sciences

Foreign Student Admission
Qualifications for Applicants
Master's Program
Standard Qualifications Requirement
Doctor's Program
Standard Qualifications Requirement
Examination at the University
Master's Program
A written and oral exam plus an interview in September.
Doctor's Program
A written and oral exam plus an interview in September and March.
Documents to be Submitted When Applying
Standard Documents Requirement

*

Research Institutes and Centers
Showa University Research Institute for Biomedicine in Florida
Facilities/Services for Foreign Students
Visiting Fellow House (9 rooms)
For Further Information
Undergraduate and Graduate Admission
Admissions Office, Faculty of Education, Showa University, 1-5-8 Hatanodai, Shinagawa-ku, Tokyo 142 ☎ 03–784–8000 ext. 8022

Showa Women's University
(Showa Joshi Daigaku)

1-7 Taishido, Setagaya-ku, Tokyo 154
☎ 03–411–5111

Faculty
    Profs.   64   Assoc. Profs.   26
    Assist. Profs.   Full–time   18; Part–time   88
    Res. Assocs.   11
Number of Students

Undergrad. 2, 070   Grad. 52
Library   260, 165 volumes

Outline and Characteristics of the University

Showa opened its doors for the first time as a private school named Nihon Joshi Koto Gakuin (Japan Women's Secondary Educational Institute) in 1920, with eight students and five faculty members. The school grew out of a round-table conference of energetic young ladies who met to discuss high educational ideals.

This small school is, after more than 60 years, still welcoming young women who want to study and train themselves to be a "light to the world." Our academic traditions are to work diligently and enthusiastically toward this goal. Over the long years, our students and faculty have created a true university of quietude, purity and discipline. This educational endeavor takes place on a campus overflowing with natural beauty. This spirit is reflected in our educational ideals and goals which have developed an independent educational system and curriculum which is unique in Japan.

The Showa Schools cover all courses of study: kindergarten, elementary school, junior and senior high school, junior college, four-year university and graduate school. All schools are located on the 67, 301 m² Tokyo campus. In the university, a great number of free electives have been scheduled based on students' needs and desires. Students may choose from many special, general and foreign language courses, regardless of major.

Our schools have been earnestly striving in the fields of education and research which enable many young women to contribute to this rapidly changing modern world and to cultivate themselves and build their characters as they become capable professionals or home-loving wives and mothers. Toward this goal, we have two faculties: the Faculty of Literature and the Faculty of Domestic Science.

The Faculty of Literature consists of the Department of Japanese Literaure and the Department of English and American Literature. Foreign languages such as German, French and Chinese are also offered in the Department of English and American Literature. Courses from beginning to advanced are available to students in any department. It is a special goal of the Showa Schools to make books the wellspring of knowledge, available in quantity to the students. In particular, the "Modern Literature Library," housed in our Main Library, is a treasure-house of knowledge for the study of modern literature.

The Faculty of Domestic Science consists of two Departments, Living Arts and Living Science. Here, study and research into housing, clothing and food are undertaken through a systematic view of their relationship to humans and their environment. These courses provide a scientific way for women to enjoy a creative life.

Showa Women's Institute Boston, which opened in April of 1988, is officially sanctioned by the State of Massachusetts. Its creative curriculum is intended to prepare women for the international society of the coming 21st Century.

Showa Boston stands on a suburban hill overlooking the entire downtown section of the city. Its 166, 000 m² campus includes dormitory accommodation for 300 students, classrooms, chapel, gymnasium, hall and cafeteria, as well as basketball and tennis courts.

Showa Women's University students enrolled in the Department of English and American Literature receive credits for the semester they spend in Boston during their third year, as do junior college students from the Department of English Language and Literature in their second year. During the summer break, Showa post-secondary students from other departments are given the opportunity to attend a special program in Boston.

A public auditorium on campus, the Hitomi Memorial Hall, is used for school events and also for public broadcasting and general audiences. The ultra-modern, fully-equipped concert hall which seats approximately 2, 400 was completed in 1980. It is well known even overseas through the musical and cultural events held there.

We have two off-campus educational facilities, dormitories where students and teachers can work and study together in a natural setting. The Tomei Retreat Facility sits in a natural forest and commands a fine view of Mt. Fuji. Showa Boshu Dormitory is located in a seaside town in Chiba Prefecture. About 300 students can be accommodated at each retreat facility, and throughout the school year students make one six-day stay there.

Aizu Camping Village, a 200, 000 m² property, is nestled between Mt. Bandai and Lake Inawashiro. The main lodge provides ten rooms and hot springs baths, and there are five adjacent log cabins. Showa students and graduates may use this facility for special sessions or rest and relaxation.

We have three residential dormitories on and off-campus. Foreign students stay with Japanese students in the dorms, where they are able to have many chances to understand college life, to deepen friendship and to practice Japanese conversation effectively.

UNDERGRADUATE PROGRAMS

Faculty of Domestic Science (Freshmen Enrollment: 230)

Department of Living Arts
Color Theory, Design, Domestic Science, Dressmaking Design, Ergonomics, Folklore, History of Clothing, History of Domestic Culture, History of Dwellings, History of Japanese Culture, Museum Science, Planning and Drafting, Structure of Clothing, Structure of Dwellings, Textile Production, Urban Science

Department of Living Science

Dietetics, Domestic Science, Food Chemistry, Food Economics, Food Hygiene, Food Processing and Preservation, High Polymer Chemistry, Microbiology, Nutrition Guidance, Pathological Dietetics, Public Sanitation, School Food Service Management, Statistics

Faculty of Literature (Freshmen Enrollment: 260)

Department of English and American Literature

Comparative Literature, English and American Linguistics, English and American Literature, English Phonetics, History of American Literature, History of English Literature, Intercultural Communication Theory

Department of Japanese Literature

Chinese Literature, Comparative Literature, History of Calligraphy, History of Japanese Literature, History of Japanese Thought, Japanese Linguistics, Japanese Literature, Juvenile Literature, Methods of Expression

Foreign Student Admission

Qualifications for Applicants

Standard Qualifications Requirement

Examination at the University

All departments, except English and American Literature, admit a few foreign students based on the following examinations:

1. Achievement Test in Japanese (Written)
2. Interview (including Japanese conversation test)

Documents to be Submitted When Applying

Standard Documents Requirement

The university guide is available in June and application forms are available around October at the Admissions Office.

GRADUATE PROGRAMS

Graduate School of Domestic Science (First Year Enrollment : Master's 20)

Divisions

Science of Food and Nutrition, Science of Living Design

Graduate School of Literature (First Year Enrollment : Master's 20)

Divisions

English and American Literature, Japanese Literature

Foreign Student Admission

Qualifications for Applicants

Master's Program

Standard Qualifications Requirement

Examination at the University

Master's Program

The same written examination and interview as Japanese applicants.

Documents to be Submitted When Applying

Standard Documents Requirement

The university guide is available in June and ap-

plication forms are avilable from October at the Admissions Office.

*

Research Institutes and Centers

Institute of Modern Culture, Institute of Women's Culture

Facilities/Services for Foreign Students

Dormitory: Foreign students stay in Ryokuseisha Dormitory. Among the facilities and common areas are a lounge, a parlour, a meeting hall, outdoor athletic field of artificial turf, a library, piano practice room, sewing room and Japanese room for flower arranging and tea ceremony lessons.

Living Education, On and Off Campus: Foreign students are expected to interact with their homeroom teachers and classmates outside class in order to deepen their understanding of university life and friendship. When at Tomei Retreat Facility, Boshu Dormitory or in Ryokuseisha Dormitory, they live the same school life as the Japanese students; they thus adapt more quickly to Japanese life and language.

Special Summer Training Program: To help foreign students further master Japanese culture and language, it can sometimes be arranged for them to stay with their classmates' families during summer vacation.

Scholarships: In order to relieve financial burdens and help students concentrate on their studies, scholarships are awarded to selected students.

Special Programs for Foreign Students

Faculty of Literature offers four class hours a week Japanese language programs in three levels, beginning, intermediate and advanced.

For Further Information

Undergraduate and Graduate Admission

Admissions Office, Administration Office, Showa Women's University, 1-7 Taishido, Setagaya-ku, Tokyo 154 ☎ 03-411-5111 ext. 332, 334

Shuchiin College
(Shuchiin Daigaku)

Toji-cho 545 Mibudori 8-Jo sagaru, Minami-ku, Kyoto-shi, Kyoto 601   ☎ 075-681-6513

Faculty
    Profs. 10   Assoc. Profs 7
    Assist. Profs. Full-time 2; Part-time 31
Number of Students
    Undergrad. 196
Library 30, 342 volumes

Outline and Characteristics of the College

Shuchiin College was the first private college in Japan. It was founded in 828 by Kobo Daishi (Saint Kobo). At that time national colleges were opened only for the aristocracy. Kobo Daishi's purpose was to provide equal opportunity in liberal arts education for the common people, a very advanced idea for its time, the college was abolished soon after his death because of the deficiency of the budget. The college was rebuilt in 1881 mainly for the education of the monks of the Shingon sect. Its name was changed several times, then in 1947 after the enactment of the School Education Law, new Shuchiin College was born. Although the college is one of the smallest in Japan, it is an outstanding research and education center for Tibetan and Chinese Esoteric Buddhism.

Kyoto was the capital of Japan over a thousand years, and is an excellent place for study. The college is located in the quiet precinct of Toji (East Temple) near Japan Railways Kyoto Station.

UNDERGRADUATE PROGRAMS

Faculty of Buddhism (Freshmen Enrollment: 40)
Department of Buddhism
Buddhism, Buddhistic Social Welfare, Esoteric Buddhism

*

For Further Information
Undergraduate Admission
Administrative Office, Shuchiin College, Toji cho 545, Mibudori 8–Jo sagaru, Minami–Ku, Kyoto–shi, Kyoto 601 ☎ 075–681–6513

Shujitsu Joshi University
(Shujitsu Joshi Daigaku)

1-6-1 Nishigawara, Okayama-shi, Okayama 703
☎ 0862-72-3185

Faculty
  Profs. 28   Assoc. Profs. 10
  Assist. Profs. Full–time 16; Part–time 36
Number of Students
  Undergrad. 824
Library 77, 706 volumes

Outline and Characteristics of the University

Shujitsu Gakuen is an educational institution with a long history of 84 years since its foundation in 1904. Since then it has steadily expanded and now consists of a junior and senior high school for girls, a junior college and a four-year university for women, all of which have made a notable contribution to education in Okayama.

The name "Shujitsu" derives from an old saying "Kyoka-Shujitsu" which advocates genuine qualities such as steadiness and usefulness rather than mere outward appearance, and is the educational ideal towards which our four schools have been striving to this day.

Shujitsu Josh University (SJU) was established in 1979 as a school of literature consisting of the two departments of Japanese and English literature respectively. In 1985, however, a department of history

was added, and this was the first course of its kind opened at any private college or university throughout the Chugoku and Shikoku Districts.

SJU aims at giving practical education by making the best use of its modern facilities and by opting for small-group classes directed by excellent staff who seek to instil sensitivity, independence, creativity and an international outlook among the students.

SJU has been endeavoring to cultivate mature and resourceful women who will be able to make a useful contribution to the culture and welfare of our society in the future.

UNDERGRADUATE PROGRAMS

School of Letters (Freshmen Enrollment: 200)
  Department of English
English and American Literature, English Linguistics
  Department of History
Archaeology, Cultural History, Geography, Japanese History, Occidental History, Oriental History
  Department of Japanese
Japanese Classics, Japanese Linguistics, Japanese Literature

Foreign Student Admission
  Qualifications for Applicants
    Standard Qualifications Requirement
    1. Regular foreign students (who follow the same four–year curriculum as Japanese students)
    2. Special foreign students sent by some institute (who are permitted to take some special subjects for a certain period)
  Examination at the University
    Interview and examination of submitted papers.
  Documents to be Submitted When Applying
    Standard Documents Requirement

  Qualifications for Transfer Students
    Same as undergraduate applicants.
  Examination for Transfer Students
    Same procedure as undergraduate applicants.
  Documents to be Submitted When Applying
    Standard Documents Requirement

*

For Further Information
  Undergraduate Admission
The Entrance Examination & Advertising Office, the Planning Department, Shujitsu Joshi University, 1-6-1 Nishigawara, Okayama-shi, Okayama 703 ☎ 0862-72-3185 ext. 214

Shukutoku University
(Shukutoku Daigaku)

200 Daiganji-cho, Chiba-shi, Chiba 280
☎ 0472-65-7331

UNDERGRADUATE PROGRAMS

Faculty of Social Welfare (Freshmen Enrollment: 400)
Department of Social Welfare

Soai University
(Soai Daigaku)

4-4-1, Nanko–Naka, Suminoe–ku, Osaka 559
☎ 06-612-5900

Faculty
Profs. 48   Assoc. Profs 9
Assist. Profs. Full–time 7; Part–time 190
Number of Students
Undergrad. 1, 166
Library 150, 119 volumes

UNDERGRADUATE PROGRAMS

Faculty of Music (Freshmen Enrollment 170)
Department of Composition
Department of Vocal Music
Faculty of Humanities (Freshmen Enrollment 100)
Department of Instrumental Music
Department of Japanese Culture
Department of Anglo–America Culture

Soka University
(Soka Daigaku)

1-236 Tangi–cho, Hachioji–shi, Tokyo 192
☎ 0426-91-2211

Faculty
Profs. 140   Assoc. Profs. 40
Assist. Profs. Full–time 21; Part–time 116
Res. Assocs. 12
Number of Students
Undergrad. 5, 355   Grad. 111
Library 552, 519 volumes

Outline and Characteristics of the University
The plan for establishing Soka University was proposed by Daisaku Ikeda, the Honorary President of Soka Gakkai in 1965, and the university was founded in April, 1971. While initially there were only three faculties, the university presently consists of five faculties: Economics, Law, Letters, Business Administration, and Education.

Over and above the faculties, three Graduate Schools with four Divisions of special studies were added in April, 1975. In addition, the Division of Correspondence Education, the Specific Course (In-

stitute of Japanese Language) and Research Institute were opened in April, 1976. In order to fulfill the researchers' goals, the university is open to people from all walks of life, in Japan and abroad. 15 years after the inauguration of the university, as the 15th year commemorative project, an art museum was established in November, 1984, the Soka Women's Junior College in April, 1985, and the Division of Education, Graduate School of Letters in April, 1986. Overseas branch schools were constructed in the U. S. A. (in California) and in France in 1987. The Department of humanity, Faculty of Letters was established in april, 1988.

Soka University actively promotes cultural exchange with overseas universities. So far, agreements for the exchange of professors and students have been made with Moscow State University, Beijing University, Fudan University, Wuhan University, Sofia University, University of Nairobi the Chinese University of Hong Kong, University of Philippines and Sunderland Polytechnic. Agreements for an academic exchange, including an exchange program for students, have been signed with the University of Arizona, Lund University, Chulalongkorn University, Thammasart University, University of Malaya, National University of Singapore, Univérsite René Descartes Paris V, Texas Tech University, University of Glasgo, Paris Chamber of Commerce and the University of Essex. The university is also currently working out agreements with other universities in order to further establish itself as a university open to the world.

The basic concept of Soka University is summarized in the following three mottos advocated by the founder, Daisaku Ikeda: (1) Be the highest seat of learning for humanistic education. (2) Be the cradle of a new culture. (3) Be the fortress for the peace of mankind.

In order to realize the above, student participation, research activity for the creation of new culture, exchange with foreign universities, and admission of foreign students are all actively promoted. The realization of humanistic education arises from the concerted efforts of both faculty and students. Soka University is determined to contribute to mankind.

Soka University sits on the Tama Hills in a suburb of Hachioji City, just west of Tokyo. This location provides an excellent environment for the University —quiet clean, air and lush greenery. The area is free of urban noise and pollution. Modern white school buildings stand on the large campus, which extends 500, 000m². The pond, called"the pond of letters, " is surrounded by a forest, and affords a suitable place for meditation and rest. Such a satisfactory natural environment may be said to be a truly ideal place for study.

UNDERGRADUATE PROGRAMS

Faculty of Business Administration (Freshmen Enrollment: 200)

Department of Business Administration

Accounting, Business Administration, Business History, Commerce, Economics, Law, Management, Management Science

Faculty of Economics (Freshmen Enrollment: 300)

Department of Economics

Accounting, Business Administration, Economic History, Economic Policy, Economic Statistics, Economic Theory, Public Finance, Social Policy

Faculty of Education (Freshmen Enrollment: 130)

Department of Child Education

Child Clinical Psychology, Child Education, Method of Education, Study of Teaching Materials

Department of Education

Educational Administration and Supervision, Educational Psychology, History of Education, Method of Education, Philosophy of Education, Social Education

Faculty of Law (Freshmen Enrollment: 300)

Department of Law

Administrative Law, Bankruptcy Act, Civil Law, Commercial Law, Constitutional Law, Criminal Law, Criminal Procedure Code, Criminology, Economic Law, Foreign Law, History of Law, History of Legal Thought, History of Politics, International Law, Legal Sociology, Philosophy of Law, Politics, Social Labor Law

Faculty of Letters (Freshmen Enrollment: 280)

Department of English Literature

American Literature, English Language, English Literature, History of English Literature, Philology

Department of Humanity

History, philosophy

Department of Sociology

Mass Communications, Methods of Social Studies, Sociology

Foreign Student Admission

Qualifications for Applicants

Standard Qualifications Requirement

Those applicants who arrive in Japan before September must take first the Japanese Language Proficiency Test

Examination at the University

1. Primary screening: Based on the submitted application documents.
2. Secondary screening: Applicants who successfully pass the preliminary screening will be given a written examination and an interview.

Documents to be Submitted When Applying

Standard Documents Requirement

Following documents are also required.

1. An essay on"Soka Daigaku To Watakushi" (Soka University and I), in Japanese.
2. Certificates: a certificate of Japanese language proficiency, a certificate of English language proficiency (e. g. TOEFL, ACT, and SAT), or a certificate of qualification for university admission examination (e. g. ACT, SAT, GCE, and Baccalaureate), are requested only when one of them has already been obtained.
3. Application cards for the Japanese Language Proficiency Test for those applicants in Japan before Sept. 1.

Schedule

1. Application period: November 1–30
2. Primary screening: Early December (the results of screening will be sent to each applicant in late December)
3. Second screening: Late January
4. Announcement of successful applicants: Early February
5. Registration period: Late February–Early March
6. Entrance period: Early April

Qualifications for Transfer Students

1. Transfer into the third year: graduates of four –year universities
2. Transfer into the second year: those who have been enrolled for one year or more at four–year universities, and who have completed 26 academic credits or more. Graduates of junior colleges.

Examination for Transfer Students

Same procedure as freshman applicants.

Documents to be Submitted When Applying

Standard Documents Requirement

See undergraduate requirements.

GRADUATE PROGRAMS

Graduate School of Economics (First Year Enrollment : Master's 20, Doctor's 10)

Division

Economics

Graduate School of Law (First Year Enrollment : Master's 20, Doctor's 10)

Division

Law

Graduate School of Letters (First Year Enrollment : Master's 25, Doctor's 10)

Divisions

Education, English Literature, Sociology

Foreign Student Admission

Qualifications for Applicants

Master's Program

Standard Qualifications Requirement

Doctor's Program

Standard Qualifications Requirement

Examination at the University

Master's Program

Same as the undergraduate

Schedule

    Same as the undergraduate

Doctor's Program

    Foreign students who have received a master's degree or the equivalent in Japan must take the ordinary examination for Japanese students.

Application period: January 20-31

Examination: March 1

Announcement of successful applicants: March 6

Registration period: Mid-March

    Foreign students who have received a master's degree or the equivalent abroad take the examination for foreign students.

    Documents to be Submitted When Applying

    Standard Documents Requirement

    Following documents are also required.

Master's program:

1. Written application of foreign students
2. Certificate of Japanese language proficiency and certificate of English language proficiency (only those who have received them)
3. Application cards for the Japanese Language Proficiency Test for those applicants in Japan before Sept. 1

Doctor's program:

    In addition to the above (1) through (3), one copy of Master's thesis and its summary are required.

*

Research Institutes and Centers

Audio–Visual Education Institute, Computer Science Laboratory, Division of General Culture, Insitute for the Comparative Study of Cultures, Institute of Applied Economics, Institute of Asian Studies, Institute of Information Science, Institute of Peace Studies, Institute of the Japanese Language, Language and Culture Research Center, Preparatory Course for State Examinations

Special Programs for Foreign Students

Institute of the Japanese Language

For Further Information

    Undergraduate and Graduate Admission

International Division, Soka University, 1-236 Tangi –cho, Hachioji–shi, Tokyo 192 ☎ 0426-91-2206

<hr>

Sonoda Gakuen Women's College

(Sonoda Gakuen Joshi Daigaku)

7-29-1 Minami-Tsukaguchi-cho, Amagasaki-shi,
Hyogo 661   ☎ 06-429-1201

<hr>

Faculty

    Profs. 20   Assoc. Profs. 9

    Assist. Profs. Full–time 4; Part–time 45

    Res. Assocs. 3

Number of Students

    Undergrad. 1, 010

Library   125, 200 volumes

Outline and Characteristics of the College

    The College started as a junior college in 1963. Subsequently, Sonoda Gakuen Women's College was founded with the Faculty of Literature in 1966 as an outgrowth of the College's endeavor to promote higher education for women.

    The College's general aims of education are to develop a better understanding of the current state of research and to develop women with an international sense who can play decisive roles in society in the years to come.

    The Faculty of Literature consists of the Department of Japanese Literature and Department of English Literature.

    The Department of Japanese Literature conducts research on every age and field of Japanese literature. It is making a special effort to gather the texts and criticism of Amagasaki born buddhist monk Keichu and Chikamatsu Monzaemon who had a great influence on the literature during and after their times. Its level of research is comparatively high on drama and modern poetry. Its location near Kyoto and Nara is convenient for the study of old texts and ancient arts.

    The Department of English Literature aims to develop international understanding through critical readings of the works of English literature along with the development of practical skills of the English language.

    The college, in addition, has made every effort to be the center of education for the local community. It is now providing several free lectures to people outside campus. It is also attempting to promote international exchange programs with Brisbane College of Advanced Education in Australia, Christchurch Teachers College in New Zealand and the University of the South Pacific in Fiji.

    Though the college is located in urban surroundings, the campus abounds with trees and flowers and enjoys the seasonal change of colors. Its location as a midway point between Osaka and Kobe (20 min. from Osaka and 30 min. from Kobe) lends a great deal of convenience to those who visit the college.

UNDERGRADUATE PROGRAMS

Faculty of Literature (Freshmen Enrollment: 200)

    Department of English Literature

English and American Literature, English Linguistics, English Usage, History of American Literature, History of English, History of English Literature

    Department of Japanese Literature

Ancient Court Manners, Chinese Literature, History of Chinese Literature, History of Japanese, History of Japanese Culture, History of Japanese Literature, Japanese Calligraphy, Japanese Linguistics, Japanese Literature, Oriental History

Foreign Student Admission

Qualifications for Applicants

Standard Qualifications Requirement

Examination at the College

Entrance examination and interview (in the middle of December and in the middle of February).

Documents to be Submitted When Applying

Standard Documents Requirement

*

Facilities/Services for Foreign Students

Three dormitories (female, twin, 143 rooms)

For Further Information

Undergraduate Admission

Dept. of Public Relations, Sonoda Gakuen Women's College, 7-29-1 Minami-Tsukaguchi-cho, Amagasaki-shi, Hyogo 661 ☎ 06-429-1201

Sophia University
(Jochi Daigaku)

7-1 Kioi-cho, Chiyoda-ku, Tokyo 102
☎ 03–238–3111

Faculty

Profs.   276   Assoc. Profs.   105

Assist. Profs.   Full–time   97; Part–time   379

Res. Assocs.   74

Number of Students

Undergrad.   10, 098   Grad.   814

Library   594, 000 volumes

Outline and Characteristics of the University

The main campus of the University is at Yotsuya, in the Kojimachi district of Tokyo. It is situated just inside the outer moat of the old city of Tokyo. The Palace, the Diet, and the Diet Library are within a short walking distance, and central Tokyo can be reached in about twenty minutes, by public transportation.

The Yotsuya Campus occupies about 71, 000 sq. meters of land. A cluster of 15 modern buildings provides an area of about 115, 000 sq. meters of total floor space, comfortably accommodating about 10, 000 students with all necessary facilities. These include cafeterias, libraries, classrooms, lecture halls, laboratories, machine shops, meeting rooms, gymnasium and auditorium. There are also a television center, an audio-visual language laboratory complex, and a psychological clinic. Next to the university is St. Ignatius Church.

The Shakujii Campus is located in Nerima ward. The Faculty of Theology and Graduate Division of Theology are here, and future Catholic priests as well as educators who desire to study Christianity are prepared on this campus.

The Ichigaya Campus is located about ten minutes walk from the Yotsuya Campus. In a quiet residential section, it houses the Faculty of Comparative Culture (including a graduate program), the Year-in-Japan Program, and the Summer Session in Asian Studies.

The Hadano Campus is situated in Kanagawa Prefecture, about two hours by public transportation from the Yotsuya Campus. It covers over 260, 000 sq. meters of land. Here can be found the Junior College, a women's dormitory, Sophia Seminar House, spacious athletic facilities and an athletic clubhouse.

At present Sophia University has 7 faculties with 29 departments in the undergraduate school and 7 graduate divisions with 24 areas of concentration.

In March, 1913, the Japanese Ministry of Education gave permission to the Society of Jesus to establish a new educational institution. Only sixteen students enrolled. This was the very modest start of Sophia University. Difficulties and challenges of all kinds would accompany this Jesuit University in Tokyo throughout the years, but its inner sense of mission has never been lacking.

Sophia University basically owes its establishment to the long-fostered wish of Saint Francis Xavier, the pioneer of mission work in the Orient. During his stay in Japan (1549-1551), Xavier planned to set up an advanced educational institution capable of supplying Japan with the best cultural assets of Western Europe. Owing to the brevity of his stay, his plan could not be realized.

The first period of Sophia University's history is characterized by its economic difficulties. However, a substantial redbrick building was completed in 1914 through the efforts and sacrifices of many. But it was not long before it was extensively damaged by the great Kanto earthquake of Sept. 1923. Sophia's very existence was for a time in doubt, since economic crises both in Europe and the United States cut off much-needed funds. But the University managed to continue operating in wooden makeshift quarters until a new building was completed in 1932.

Another kind of problem troubled Sophia's next period. As a Christian bastion of the West looking for understanding and communication with the East, Sophia University had taken pride in its international character and its liberal spirit. But these were traits that the increasing nationalistic thirties would regard with suspicion and antagonism. The student enrollment dropped by half, and only 32 entrance applications were received for the 'foreign University' in the spring of 1933.

A completely different atmosphere pervades the third and present stage of Sophia's history. It extends from the years immediately after the Second World War until today. An appeal for volunteers, issued throughout the whole Society of Jesus for men to staff the war-ravaged university, was successful, and Jesuits of all nationalities began arriving to join the teaching faculty. These new men, and added financial support, brought about an unprecedented program of expansion. New departments and faculties were inaugurated, while new buildings were raised.

In 1957, for the first time, women students were also admitted.

Besides the obvious improvement in academic standards, one of the reasons that can be thought as operative in the attraction exerted by Sophia on Japanese students is the international trait of its staff and program, –a mark which has characterized the University from its birth. With a faculty composed of Japanese and foreign professors, Sophia proves faithful to its dual mission of bringing to the Orient the learning of the West, and of interpreting for the West the rich and ancient wisdom of the East.

UNDERGRADUATE PROGRAMS

Faculty of Comparative Culture (Freshmen Enrollment: 170)

Department of Comparative Culture
Anthropology and Sociology, Art History, Business and Economics, History, Literature, Philosophy and Religion, Political Science

Department of Japanese Language and Studies
Japanese Language, Japanese Linguistics, Japanese Studies (Anthropology and Sociology, Art History, Business and Economics, History, Literature, Philosophy and Religion, Political Science)

Faculty of Economics (Freshmen Enrollment: 320)

Department of Economics
Agricultural Economics, Business Statistics, Econometrics, Economic and Business Ethics, Economic Development, Economic Policy, Economics, Economics of Transportation, Economic Statistics, Economic Theory, History of Economics, History of Economic Thought, History of European Economy, History of Japanese Economy, Industrial Sociology, Industrial Structure of Japan, International Economics, International Finance, Labor Economics, Marketing, Marketing Survey, Mathematical Statistics, Monetary Economics, Public Finance

Department of Management
Accounting, Auditing, Bookkeeping, Business Ethics, Business Management, Business Organization, Business Statistics, Computer Application, Cost Accounting, Economic Geography, Economics of Transportation, Financial Management, Forms of Enterprises, History of Business, Industrial Organizations, Industrial Relations, Industrial Sociology, Insurance, International Economics, International Finance, International Management, Marketing, Marketing Survey, Modern Industries, Monetary Theory, Organization and Leadership, Personnel Management, Sampling Survey, Stock Exchange

Faculty of Foreign Studies (Freshmen Enrollment: 430)

Department of English Language and Studies
American Area Studies, American Cultural Foundations, American Cultural Patterns, American Literature, American Thought, Art of Translation, Culture & the Individual, English Area Studies, English Grammar, English-Japanese Translation, English Literature, English of the Bible, English Phonetics, English Teaching Methodology, History of England, History of English Criticism, History of English Language, History of English Thought, Intercultural Communication, Japanese-English Translation, Modern American History, Secretarial English, Semantics, Shorthand, Simultaneous Translation, World Literature

Department of French Language and Studies
English-French Translation, French Area Studies, French-Japanese Translation, French Language, French Linguistics, French Literature, French Teaching Methodology, History and Theory of French Literary Criticism, History of France-Japan Cultural Exchange, History of French Language, Japanese-French Translation

Department of German Language and Studies
German Area Studies, German-Japanese Translation, German Language, German Literature, History of German Language, Japanese-German Translation, Modern German Linguistics

Department of Portuguese Language and Luso-Brazilian Studies
Brazilian Literature, Brazilian Studies, Luso-Brazilian Studies, Portuguese Language, Portuguese Linguistics, Portuguese Literature, Portuguese Teaching Methods

Department of Russian Language and Studies
Russian Area Studies, Russian History, Russian Language, Russian Literature, Russian Translation

Department of Spanish Language and Studies
Hispanic Literature, History of Spanish Language, Interpreting in Spanish and Guide Methods, Japanese-Spanish Translation, Latin American Area Studies, Spanish Area Studies, Spanish-Japanese Translation, Spanish Language, Spanish Linguistics

Faculty of Humanities (Freshmen Enrollment: 620)

Department of Education
Audiovisual Education, Childhood Education, Comparative Education, Counseling, Education, Educational Administration, Educational Survey, History of Education, Moral Education, Pedagogy, Philosophy of Education, School Administration, Social Education, Teaching Methods

Department of English Literature
American Literature, Comparative Culture, Comparative Literature, English Cultural History, English Literature, English Philology, General Linguistics, History of American Literary Thought, History of American Literature, History of English Literary Thought, History of English Literature, History of European Literary Thought, History of the English Language

Department of French Literature
French Journalism, French Literature, History of French Civilization, History of French Literature, International Relations

Department of German Literature
Contemporary German Language, German Cultural

Geography, German Literature, German Philology, History of German Thought

Department of History

Archaeology, Cultural History of Japan, Cultural History of the Orient, Economic History of Europe, Economic History of Japan, European History, History of America, History of French Political Thought, History of Japanese Art, History of Japanese Law, History of Philosophy, History of Political Thought, History of Spanish Culture, History of the Church, History of Western Law, Japanese History, Oriental History, Paleography, Philosophy of History

Department of Japanese Literature

Calligraphy, Chinese Literature, Classics, History of Japanese Language, History of Japanese Literature, Japanese Linguistics, Japanese Literature

Department of Journalism

Advertising, Broadcasting, Communication Theory, Comparative Mass Media, Editing, History of Mass Media, Human Behavior & Mass Media, International Communication, Laws & Ethics of Mass Media, Mass Culture, Media, Public Relations, Publishing, Reporting, Television Production, The Cinema, The Japanese Newspaper, The Press & Technology

Department of Philosophy

Buddhist Philosophy, Epistemology, Esthetics, Ethics, History of Ancient Philosophy, History of Christian Thought, History of Philosophy, History of Religions, History of the Church, History of Western Ethics, Logic, Metaphysics, Philosophical Anthropology, Philosophical Problems in Natural Science, Philosophy, Philosophy of Nature, Philosophy of Religion, Political Philosophy, Practical Philosophy, Scholastic Philosophy, Social Philosophy

Department of Psychology

Behavioral Sciences, Child Psychology, Clinical Psychology, Cognitive Psychology, Counseling, Criminal Psychology, Developmental Psychology, Educational Psychology, Experimental Social Psychology, Fundamental Statistics in Psychology, History of Psychology, Industrial Psychology, Mathematical Psychology, Physiological Psychology, Psychiatry, Psychological Methods, Psychological Testing, Psychology, Psychology of Learning, Psychology of Personality, Psychonomic Sciences, Social Psychology

Department of Social Welfare

Case Work, Child Psychopathology, Clinical Psychology, Demography, History of Social Services, Maternal and Child Health, Mental Health, Physically Handicapped Welfare, Public Assistance, Public Health, Reformatory Social Service, Regional Structure, Social Administration, Social Ethics, Social Pathology, Social Security, Social Service, Social Stratification, Social Survey, Social Welfare, Social Work, Welfare of the Aged

Department of Sociology

Communication, Comparative Sociology, Criminal Sociology, Cultural Contacts, Cultural Sociology, Educational Sociology, History of Social Thought, History of Sociology, Industrial Sociology, International Communication, Mass Sociology, Methodology, Organizational Analysis, Political Sociology, Population, Regional Structure, Rural Sociology, Social Psychology, Social Stratification, Sociology of Religion, Sociology of the Family, Sociology of Women, Theory of Social Change, Urban Sociology

Faculty of Law (Freshmen Enrollment: 300)

Department of International Legal Studies

European Law, International Business Law, International Labor Law, International Private Law, International Public Law, Law of International Organizations, Law of International Trade

Department of Law

Administrative Law, Civil Law, Civil Procedure, Commercial Paper, Constitutional Law, Contracts, Corporations, Criminal Law, Criminal Procedure, Family Law, International Law, Labor Law, Politics, Property, Torts

Faculty of Science and Technology (Freshmen Enrollment: 350)

Department of Chemistry

Analytical Chemistry, Applied Microbiology, Biochemistry, Biomacromolecules, Chemical Engineering, Electrochemistry, Geochemistry, Glass Work, History of Chemistry, Industrial Chemistry, Industrial Inorganic Chemistry, Industrial Physical Chemistry, Inorganic Chemistry, Instrumental Analysis, Organic Chemistry, Organic Reaction Mechanism, Organic Synthesis, Petroleum & Petrochemistry, Physical Chemistry, Polymer Chemistry, Quality Control & Planning of Experiments, Radiochemistry, Stereochemistry

Department of Electrical & Electronics Engineering

Acoustics, Applications of Electric Power, Chemical Engineering, Communication Apparatus, Communications Engineering, Communication Systems, Computer Fundamentals, Control Engineering, Electrical Engineering, Electrical Illumination & Heating, Electric Circuit Theory, Electric Power Equipment, Electrochemistry, Electromagnetic Measurements, Electromagnetics, Electromagnetic Wave and Field Theory, Electromagnetic Wave Engineering, Electronic Circuits, Electronic Computation, Electronic Devices, High Tension Engineering, Information Theory, Measurement, Microwave Engineering, Power Generation Engineering, Power Transmission & Distribution, Probability & Statistics, Quantum Mechanics, Radio Regulations, Safety Engineering, Signal Transmission, Solid-State Physics in Engineering, Systems Engineering

Department of Mathematics

Algebra, Analysis, Analytic Functions, Differential Equations, Electronic Computers, Functional Analysis, Geometry, Linear Algebra, Mathematical Investigations, Mathematics, Measure Theory, Numerical Analysis, Probability, Statistics, Topological Space

Department of Mechanical Engineering

Applied Hydraulics, Complex Functions, Control Engineering, Design & Draftsmanship, Differential Equations, Elastic Mechanics, Electric Machinery, Engineering Measurement, Fluid Dynamics, Fluid Mechanics, Heat Engine Engineering, Heat Transfer, Industrial Mechanics, Machine Design, Machine Tools, Materials Engineering, Mechanical Draftsmanship, Mechanical Dynamics, Mechanical Engineering, Mechanism of Machinery, Operations Research, Operators & Transformations, Safety Engineering, Strength of Materials, Structural Mechanics, Vibration, Work by Cutting, Work by Non-cutting

Department of Physics

Atomic and Molecular Physics, Atoms and Particles, Biophysics, Classical and Quantum Optics, Electromagnetism, Electronics, Geophysics, Mathematical Physics, Particle and Nuclear Physics, Physics of Plasma, Physics of Waves, Quantum Mechanics, Quantum Optics, Relativity and Astrophysics, Solid State Physics, Space Physics, Statistical Physics, Statistical Thermodynamics, Theoretical Mechanics, Vacuum and Low Temperature

Faculty of Theology (Freshmen Enrollment: 25)

Department of Theology

Bible Studies, Canon Law, Church History, Historico-Dogmatic-Systematic Theology, Liturgy, Moral Theology, Practical Theology, Science of Religion

Foreign Student Admission

Qualifications for Applicants

Standard Qualifications Requirement

Examination at the University

Japanese proficiency test, foreign language test and a special written test by each department.

Second exam: an interview test.

Faculty of Comparative Culture:

Applicants will be screened on the basis of documents. A notice of acceptance or rejection is sent to all applicants within six weeks after the deadline.

Documents to be Submitted When Applying

Standard Documents Requirement

(Letter of recommendation is not required.)

Applicants to the Department of Comparative Culture, Faculty of Foreign Studies should submit the following documents.

1. Application Form
2. Official Transcripts of all academic institutions attended (high schools and universities).
3. National Certificate Programs
   Those applicants coming under the following categories should submit the appropriate documents:
   a) British-educated applicants must submit an official, certified copy of the General Certificate of Education indicating passes at the Advanced level in at least two subjects.
   b) Hong Kong-educated applicants must submit an official, certified copy of the University of Hong Kong Advanced Level and Matriculation Examination indicating passes in at

least two subjects.
   c) Other Applicants: those from countries that offer national certificate programs, such as the General Certificate of Education, must submit an official, certified copy of test results indicating passes at the Advanced level in at least two subjects. Such applicants are requested to send any official information available describing the educational system of the country and the school last attended.

Copies of the above documents must be certified by an official agency, such as an embassy, consulate, or examining board. Uncertified copies will not be accepted.

4. SAT Scores

Official scores (not student report) of the Scholastic Aptitude Test (SAT).

This test should be taken not more than two years before the application deadline, unless it was taken during high school and is recorded on the high school transcript. In this case the scores should be no more than five years old, and it must be clear that ever since the test was taken, the applicant has been studying in a school in which English is the language of instruction.

N. B. 1 a) The SAT scores are required also in the case of an applicant for degree status who is already attending another university and wants to transfer to Sophia. In this case, if he/she was required to take the test for admission to his/her present university, the applicant need not retake the exam but may have an official copy of the previous scores sent directly from ETS or from the applicant's university.

b) The SAT scores are not required in the case of an applicant who already holds a Bachelor's degree from another university and wants to enter Sophia to obtain another undergraduate degree.

N. B. 2 The SAT scores are not required in the case of an applicant for non-degree status who is already attending, or has attended in the past, another university and wants to attend courses and earn credits at Sophia.

5. TOEFL Scores

For students whose native language is not English, it is necessary to have the official scores (not student report) of the Test of English as a Foreign Language (TOEFL) sent to the Admissions Office.

The test should be taken not more than two years before the application deadline, unless it was taken during high school and is recorded on the high school transcript. In this case the scores should be no more than five years old, and it must be clear that ever since the test was taken, the applicant has been studying in a school in which English is the language of instruction.

Instead of TOEFL either of the following is acceptable:

a) The English Language Test Service's Test. For information, telephone or write the nearest British Council Office.

b) The English Proficiency Test (EPT) which is administered monthly at the Ichigaya Campus. Information and application forms for the EPT may be obtained from the Ichigaya Office.

6. Letters of Recommendation

Letters of recommendation from three teachers and/or officials of school (s) attended by the applicant, who can testify to the academic ability and character of the applicant, should be submitted.

7. Medical Certificate

8. Essay

The applicant should write an essay of approximately 500 words in English giving his/her reasons for wishing to study at Sophia University.

Qualifications for Transfer Students

Transfer applicants should have completed two years college work, otherwise they should follow freshman application procedure. Students are admitted only in April.

Each department in the University will evaluate credits from other universities according to their own regulations. Students are expected to spend at least two years in residence before being granted a Sophia degree. For further information write to the Office of Academic Affairs (Admissions Section).

Faculty of Comparative Culture:

Transfer students are required to attend accredited universities or colleges for at least one school year and have university credits.

Examination for Transfer Students

Japanese proficiency test, a foreign language test and a separate exam by each department.

Final exam: an interview.

Faculty of Comparative Culture:

Applicants will be screened on the basis of documents. A notice of acceptance or rejection is sent to all applicants within six weeks after deadline.

Documents to be Submitted When Applying

Standard Documents Requirement

Faculty of Comparative Culture:

Same procedure as freshman applicants.

GRADUATE PROGRAMS

Graduate School of Economics (First Year Enrollment : Master's 30, Doctor's 4)

Divisions

Economics, Economic Systems and Organizations

Graduate School of Foreign Studies (First Year Enrollment : Master's 60, Doctor's 9)

Divisions

Comparative Culture, International Relations, Linguistics

Graduate School of Humanities (First Year Enrollment : Master's 110, Doctor's 34)

Divisions

Education, English & American Literature, French Literature, German Literature, History, Japanese Literature, Journalism, Sociology

Graduate School of Law (First Year Enrollment : Master's 20, Doctor's 4)

Division

Law

Graduate School of Philosophy (First Year Enrollment : Master's 20, Doctor's 4)

Division

Philosophy

Graduate School of Science and Technology (First Year Enrollment : Master's 92, Doctor's 36)

Divisions

Applied Chemistry, Biological Science, Chemistry, Electrical & Electronics Engineering, Mathematics, Mechanical Engineering, Physics

Graduate School of Theology (First Year Enrollment : Master's 20, Doctor's 4)

Divisions

Systematic Theology, Theology

Foreign Student Admission

Qualifications for Applicants

Master's Program

Standard Qualifications Requirement

Division of Comparative Culture, Graduate School of Foreign Studies:

1. All applicants are required to have a Bachelor's degree from an accredited university with a minimum overall academic rating of better than average, i. e. , "B" (3. 00), in their undergraduate work.

2. The candidate's undergraduate work does not have to coincide with the study area he/she intends to pursue in the Sophia Graduate Program. A candidate can be accepted for any of the study areas offered in the program provided he/she fulfils the prescribed requirements before entering the program. The specific requirements indicated for each study area are the minimum background needed to attend the courses and seminars offered in that particular area and should be completed before applying to the Graduate School.

Doctor's Program

Standard Qualifications Requirement

Examination at the University

Master's Program

First exam: a foreign language test and a written test by each school.

Second exam: an oral exam.

Division of Comparative Culture, Graduate School of Foreign Studies:

Applicants will be screened on the basis of documents. A notice of acceptance or rejection is sent to all applicants.

Doctor's Program

Same as Master's program.

Documents to be Submitted When Applying

Standard Documents Requirement

Instead of the research plan, a copy of the applicant's graduation thesis is required.

Division of Comparative Culture, Graduate School of Foreign Studies:

1. Application form filled out and signed, with two photos attached and application fee.*
2. Statement of purpose (in English, a minimum of 300 words), in which the applicant should explain why he/she wishes to do graduate work at Sophia University and specify as precisely as possible the area of his/her intended studies.
3. Official academic transcript(s) of all previous undergraduate and graduate studies (sent directly by the university, or contained in a sealed envelope with the university's seal imprinted over the flap).
4. A copy of the applicant's B.A. /B.S. (M.A./ M. S.) graduation thesis. (If there was no graduation thesis requirement, a lengthy paper written during the final undergraduate year should be submitted.)
5. Test scores from the Educational Testing Service, that is the Graduate Record Examinations (GRE) for all areas except International Business for which the Graduate Management Admission Test (GMAT) is required.
6. It is the responsibility of the applicant to contact the Educational Testing Service and make arrangements to take the test, and have the scores sent to the Office of the Graduate School. The test should be taken not more than two years before the application deadline.
7. For applicants whose native language is not English, official results of an English proficiency examination. Applicants who are in Japan are requested to take the English Proficiency Test administered at Sophia University, Ichigaya Campus. Applicants who are not in Japan can take instead the Test of English as a Foreign Language (TOEFL), and have the official scores sent to the Office of the Graduate School of Comparative Culture.
8. Three (3) letters of recommendation, two of which should be from professors who have taught the applicant.*
9. Medical certificate.*

*These forms are included in the Sophia University Catalog.

The application with all the necessary documents must be sent to the Graduate Admissions Office by registered mail, and not in person. No application material will be accepted at the office over the counter.

*

Research Institutes and Centers

Computer Center, Counseling Center, Counseling Institute, Iberoamerican Institute, Institute for the Culture of German-Speaking Areas, Institute for the Study of Social Justice, Institute of American and Canadian Studies, Institute of Asian Cultures, Institute of Christian Culture, Institute of Comparative Culture, Institute of International Relations, Institute of Medieval Thought, Institute of Oriental Religions, Kirishitan Bunko, Life Science Institute, Linguistic Institute for International Communication, Luso-Brazilian Center, Monumenta Nipponica, Renaissance Center, Sophia Editorial Office, Spanish Center, Television Center

Facilities/Services for Foreign Students

Counseling Room for Foreign Students

Housing: Two off-campus women's dormitories and one on-campus men's dormitory.

As for homestay and private lodgings, only a limited amount of information is available. This information can be obtained only by coming to the university.

Special Programs for Foreign Students

Foreign students can take the following Japanese language courses for their second foreign language units:

Japanese I (seminar): Emphasis on the "speaking" and "listening".

Japanese II (seminar) Emphasis on the "writing". Students are required to submit a composition each meeting. Only those who have finished Japanese I can register.

Programs offered at Ichigaya Campus:

I. Japanese Language Program:

Japanese Language offerings for non-native speakers of Japanese consist of the following five divisions:

Program A: Basic Japanese Series: Fundamental skills in listening, speaking, reading, and writing the Japanese language in a relatively shorter time than Program B.

Program B: Intensive Japanese Series: All-round skills in listening, speaking, reading, and writing Japanese while pursuing their academic goals.

Program C: Advanced Series: Reading Courses

Program E: Special Japanese Program: A two-year program specially designed for the students who want to devote all their efforts toward the mastery of the Japaness language.

Program D: Japanese Reading and Writing Series

Courses for the students with native or equivalent-to-native fluency in spoken Japanese.

Among the courses listed under our linguistics offering, the following are specially designed for the purpose of helping our students to understand the problems which people encounter in studying Japanese as a foreign language.

Introduction to Linguistics
Applied Linguistics
Structure of Japanese
Introduction to Japanese Linguistics
Japanese Phonology
Japanese Morphophonemics
Japanese Semantics and Syntax
History of the Japanese Language
Japanese Dialectology

II.　Summer Session of Asian Studies:

For the past twenty-six years Sophia University has been running a highly successful Summer Session of Asian Studies for people who genuinely want to learn more about Japan. This is not just a language program, although courses of basic Japanese are offered. Rather, the Summer Session sets out to provide several hundred participants each year with the opportunity of learning about Japan from experts in business, management, literature, art, theater, and religion. In addition, conducted tours and individual sightseeing allow students to see for themselves what sort of life the Japanese lead.

Courses: Basic Japanese, Comparative Asian Industrial Systems, Contemporary China, History of Japan, Management in Japan, Japanese Religions, Survey of Japanese Art, Survey of Japanese Literature, The Rise of Japanese Industry, Topics in Japanese Literature (Theater), Topics in Sociology (Japan)

III.　Institutional Student Exchanges (Year-in-Japan Program):

The Year-in-Japan Program was established at Sophia University more than 15 years ago to meet the need for better communication among peoples and for developing sensitivity to more than one culture. It aims to provide opportunity for a more geographically, culturally, and historically extended education, and hopes to foster for some the inspiration to become in the future specialists in Japanese Studies. Since the University established the exchange student programs, the office of the Year-in-Japan Program has been in charge of the students from abroad. This program has recently been absorbed by the Office of Academic Affairs.

For Further Information

Undergraduate and Graduate Admission

Admissions Section, Office of Academic Affairs, Sophia University, 7-1 Kioi-cho, Chiyoda-ku, Tokyo 102 ☎ 03-238-3167

Faculty of Comparative Culture, Sophia University Ichigaya Campus, 4 Yonban-cho, Chiyoda-ku, Tokyo 102 ☎ 03-238-4000

Graduate School of Comparative Culture, Sophia University Ichigaya Campus, 4 Yonban-cho, Chiyoda-ku, Tokyo 102 ☎ 03-238-4004

St. Andrew's University
(Momoyama Gakuin Daigaku)

237-1 Nishino, Sakai-shi, Osaka 588
☎ 0722-36-1181

Faculty
　　Profs. 64　　Assoc. Profs. 44
　　Assist. Profs.　Part–time 99
Number of Students
　　Undergrad. 5, 818
Library　273, 600 volumes

Outline and Characteristics of the University

Momoyama Gakuin is an insitution founded as a boys' English language school in Osaka on September 4, 1884 by the Church Missionary Society of England. With a tradition and development of more than 100 years, the institution, affiliated with the Anglican Church of Japan, now comprises a university, a junior college and a boys' high school with enrollment totalling approximately 9, 000 students.

In 1959, St. Andrew's University was founded in Osaka in commemoration of the centennial of the Anglican Mission in Japan. The University moved to a new campus site in Sakai in 1971. Since its foundation, St. Andrew's University has produced over 25, 000 graduates and sent them out into the various fields of society.

The purpose of the University is to serve its students and society at large by offering ample opportunity to its faculty and students to pursue the knowledge, wisdom and values of humankind and nature. To achieve its primary objective, the University seeks to establish and maintain the conditions of free, independent inquiry and expression in all fields of study, with emphasis on Christian humanity, democracy and internationalism.

The University offers a wide range of undergraduate programs in both liberal arts and the professional fields, as well as selected programs of interdepartmental interest. It requires every student to take courses in general education and specialized courses in the Faculties of Economics, Sociology, Business Administration, and Letters.

Since its foundation, the University has had an international perspective. For this purpose, foreign language learning has been considered an absolute necessity to promote intercultural understanding among students. At present, a variety of language courses are offered: Chinese, English, French, German, Korean, Russian and Spanish. The International Centre provides summer programs abroad for students in cooperation with the sister institutions in foreign coutries: California State University, Sacramento (U. S. A.), Douglas College (Canada), and Keimyung University (Korea). At present about 40 foreign students are enrolled as regular students at the University.

St. Andrew's University Research Institute and Library provide research opportunities in appropriate areas for students and faculty, continually expanding their reference library, facilities and scope of services.

UNDERGRADUATE PROGRAMS

Faculty of Business Administration (Freshmen Enrollment: 330)
Department of Business Administration
Business Administration and Management, Management Accounting, Management Information System, Marketing, Principles of Accounting
Faculty of Economics (Freshmen Enrollment: 380)
Department of Economics
Economic Policy, Financial Theory, History of Economic Thought, International Economics, Public Finance
Faculty of Letters (Freshmen Enrollment: 160)
Department of English
British and American literature, English linguistics, English studies
Department of Intercultural studies
Area studies, Intercultural studies, Linguistic-Cultural studies
Faculty of Sociology (Freshmen Enrollment: 330)
Department of Sociology
Cultural Sociology, Industrial Sociology, International Relations, Principles of Sociology, Social Research, Social Welfare

Foreign Student Admission
Qualifications for Applicants
Standard Qualifications Requirement
Applicants must not have resided in Japan for more than two years.
Examination at the University
Date: middle of February
Written tests in both Japanese and English, and an interview in Japanese.
If the first language of the applicant is English, he/she is required to take a written test in a foreign language other than English.
Documents to be Submitted When Applying
Standard Documents Requirement
A paper of identification or a letter of recommendation issued by a diplomatic and/or consular office of the country, or its equivalent, of the applicant.
A certificate issued by the school the applicant attended or an equivalent institution approved by St. Andrew's University, showing that the proficiency of the applicant in the Japanese language is sufficient for academic activities at the University.
Application deadline: middle of December (from abroad), beginning of February (in Japan)
Announcement of successful applicants: the end of February. Entrance procedures deadline: the beginning of March.

Qualifications for Transfer Students
1. Applicants must not have resided in Japan for more than two years.
2. Applicants are required to have completed at least two years of standard curricula, or to be due to complete them by March 31 of the year of admission, at a university or a junior college in a foreign country, or its equivalent.
Examination for Transfer Students
Same as freshman applicants.
Documents to be Submitted When Applying
Standard Documents Requirement
Additional documents to be submitted are the same as those for freshman applicants.

*

Research Institutes and Centers
International Centre, St. Andrew's University Research Institute
Facilities/Services for Foreign Students
The International Centre will give necessary academic advice to foreign students, and assist in promoting mutual understanding between foreign students and Japanese students, faculty members, as well as fostering mutual friendship among foreign students themselves.
Special Programs for Foreign Students
Foreign students are required to take a course in Japanese for the first year.
For Further Information
Undergraduate Admission
Educational Affairs Section, St. Andrew's University, 237-1 Nishino, Sakai-shi, Osaka 588 ☎ 0722-36-1181

St. Catherine Women's College
(Sei Katarina Joshi Daigaku)

660 Hojo, Hojo-shi, Ehime 799-24
☎ 0899-93-0702

Faculty
    Profs. 13   Assoc. Profs. 4
    Assist. Profs. Full-time 6; Part-time 26
    Res. Assocs. 3
Number of Students
    Undergrad. 136
Library 54, 348 volumes

Outline and Characteristics of the College
St. Catherine Women's College was just established in April, 1988, in accordance with the Fundamental Law of Education and the School Education Law under the academic juridical person of St. Catherine and the Religious Missionary Sisters of St. Dominic who have founded many educational and social welfare institutions in Japan since 1929, including one junior college, three high schools, seven kin-

dergartens, one hospital and three homes for the aged.

The College is not only the first women's college in Ehime Prefecture in Shikoku, but also the first women's college with a faculty of social welfare in Japan. With its one Faculty, the main purpose of the College is to give the students a true Christian way of life through the education of social welfare that is based upon Catholicism. It also seeks to let the students learn the very meaning of the solemnity of humanity through their services to the mentally and physically handicapped and abandoned aged people in the society. The students will have the chance to experience practical activities and, following the motto of "Sincerity, Purity, and Service", to join campus life which begins and ends with prayers in the spirit of St. Catherine, the patroness of the College. According to the curriculum newly adopted from the Japanese Association of Schools of Social Work, they are expected to acquire the qualifications to take the state examination for the license for social welfare.

The College is located in the suburbs of Hojo city (population, 30,000). The junior college, kindergarten and the aged home are on the same campus. School buses are provided for the students who live in Matsuyama and other areas. A dormitory with 165 rooms is available for the applicants. As the campus is surrounded by beautiful mountains and the Seto Inland Sea, the students can live in a comfortable environment, studying and enjoying themselves in the mild climate.

December 23, 1987: The foundation of St. Catherine Women's College was officially approved. Faculty of Social Welfare, Department of Social Welfare (regular personnel 100 students)

April 1, 1988: St. Cathrine Women's College was started. Kenichi Takahashi took office as the first president. Hisae Kozuma, the chairman of the board of directors, took office as the vice president.

UNDERGRADUATE PROGRAMS

Faculty of Social Welfare (Freshmen Enrollment: 100)
Department of Social Welfare

Foreign Student Admission
Documents to be Submitted When Applying
Standard Documents Requirement
1. A high school diploma is required.
2. Those who have worked at social activities and services over one year after high school, with the recommendation of the head of principal.

*

Services for Foreign Students
Dormitory for foreign students is provided on campus.
For Further Information

Undergraduate Admission
Educational Affairs Department, St. Catherine Women's College, 660 Hojo, Hojo-shi, Ehime 799-24 ☎ 0899-93-0702ext. 131

St. Luke's College of Nursing
(Sei Roka Kango Daigaku)
10-1 Akashicho, Chuo-ku, Tokyo 140
☎ 03-543-6391

Faculty
  Profs. 20   Assoc. Profs 9
  Assist. Profs. Full-time 12; Part-time 48
  Res. Assocs. 11
Number of Students
  Undergrad. 251   Grad. 29
Library 34,451 volumes

Outline and Characteristics of the College
St. Luke's College of Nursing is founded on the spirit of Christianity. Its goal is to produce nurses who have not only acquired skill and knowledge in the science of nursing, but who are also well-rounded individuals.

St. Luke's, therefore, helps its students develop their own inherent talents, improve their intellectual abilities, form moral judgements, and acquire a cast of mind that will enable them to lead their lives with determination and an awareness of social responsibility. Our college helps its students become people of character who respect others as well as themselves, pursue mutual understanding and promote public welfare through active participation in society, without prejudice to any idea or individual.

It is our desire to meet the needs of society by training skilled nurses and to contribute to the overall quality of life and health.

The forerunner of St. Luke's College of Nursing was the High-Grade Nurse Training School, which was founded in 1920 by a Christian missionary physician, Rudolf Bolling Teusler. The aim of Teusler's nursing education program was not only to provide professional training, but also to develop in nurses an appreciation humanity, society and Christianity. From the first having the goal of raising the general level of nursing skils, our school began an advanced course of education unrivaled in Japan at that time. Mrs. Alice C. St. John, an American with an extensive career in nursing and education, was appointed to direct the college. In addition to clinical nursing education, education in preventive medicine and public health nursing (including school hygiene and health education) was also offered.

St. Luke's college is located near Ginza, Akashicho (formerly Tsukiji) near the banks of the Sumida River between Kachidoki Bridge and Tsukuda-Ohashi Bridge. The Tsukiji district was the cradle of modern culture in Japan and today is still rich in historical interest. At the front entrance of our college is a stone monument commemorating the beginning of Western studies in Japan. The first translation of a Western science book, by Ryotaku Maeno, Genpaku Sugita and others, took place here. Near this spot there is also a marble monument commemorating the birthplace of Keio Gijuku (Now Keio Univ.) where Yukichi Fukuzawa started his school of Western studies. Besides it stands a monument marking the site of the former home of Asano Takuminokami.

UNDERGRADUATE PROGRAMS

Faculty of Nursing (Freshmen Enrollment: 60)
Department of Nursing
Adult Nursing, Anatomy, Care of Clinical Emergencies, Child Nursing, Clinical Lab. Medicine, Comprehensive Nursing, Fundamentals of Nursing, Health and Welfare Administration, Health Teaching, Maternal Nursing, Mental Health and Psychiatric Nursing, Microbiology, Nursing Administration, Nursing Education, Nursing Research, Nutrition, Pathology, Pharmacology, Physiology, Population Problems, Public Health, Public Health Nursing, Radiology, School Health

Foreign Student Admission
Documents to be Submitted When Applying
Standard Documents Requirement

GRADUATE PROGRAMS

Graduate School of Nursing (First Year Enrollment : Master's 15, Doctor's 4)
Division
Nursing

Foreign Student Admission
Examination at the University
Master's Program
Based on school report, entrance examination score, short written essay, interview and health report.
(1) Entrance Examination
1. Foreign Language—English (Dictionaries allowed for one section)
2. Major Subject—Subject chosen from area II clinical (please indicate subject on application for admission)
(2) Short Written Essay
(3) Interview
(4) Health Examination by Physician Affiliated with St. Luke's College of Nursing
Doctor's Program
(1) Written Examination
Foreign Language—English (Dictionaries allowed for one section)
Major Subject (General Nursing)
(2) Written Essay

(3) Interview
Documents to be Submitted When Applying
Master's and Doctor's Program
Standard Documents Requirement
＊

Research Institutes and Centers
Annex in Inamuragasaki, for practical training in domestic science, Kamakura
For Further Information
Undergraduate and Graduate Admission
The Instruction Department, St. Luke's College of Nursing 10–1 Akashi–cho, Chuo–ku, Tokyo 104
☎ 03–543–6391~3 ext. 326

St. Marianna University School of Medicine
（Sei Marianna Ika Daigaku）
2–16–1 Sugao, Miyamae–ku, Kawasaki–shi, Kanagawa 213   ☎ 044–977–8111

Faculty
Profs. 67   Assoc. Profs. 67
Assist. Profs. Full–time 96; Part–time 181
Res. Assocs. 303
Number of Students
Undergrad. 687   Grad. 160
Library 131, 059 volumes

Outline and Characteristics of the University
St. Marianna University School of Medicine was founded in 1971 by the late Kamon Akashi, who was a devout catholic. With his strong religious belief, he promoted medical, educational and social welfare enterprises, such as the St. Marianna Association, Toyoko Hospital, St. Marianna Medical Institute, a school of nursing and a nursery school. Based on these noble achievements, this university was established for the purpose of educating doctors, and inculcating in them the credo "Respect for Life".
Therefore, the founding spirit of the university, while centered upon the remarkably developing fields of medical education and research, also aims to train doctors who can serve society with a mission compatible with the credo "Respect for Life", and who will contribute the fruits of their study to the welfare of their fellow human beings.
On its establishment, the Roman Catholic Pope Paul VI, who took a special interest in the university, sent an congratulatory greeting.

UNDERGRADUATE PROGRAMS

Faculty of Medicine (Freshmen Enrollment: 100)
Department of Medicine
Anatomy, Anesthesiology, Biochemistry, Dermatology, Hygiene, Internal Medicine, Laboratory Medicine, Medical Jurisprudence, Medical Zoology, Mi-

crobiology, Obstetrics and Gynecology, Ophthalmology, Orthopedics, Otorhinolaryngology, Pathology, Pediatrics, Pharmacology, Physiology, Plastic and Reconstructive Surgery, Psychiatry, Radiology, Sanitary Science, Surgery, Urology

Foreign Student Admission
Qualifications for Applicants
Standard Qualifications Requirement
Examination at the University
Achievement test interview, physical examination and Japanese language ability test.
Admission is decided on the basis of the results of all tests.
Documents to be Submitted When Applying
Standard Documents Requirement
Application period: October 1-31
Date of Examination: Early February

Qualifications for Transfer Students
In addition to the qualifications for undergraduate Foreign Applicants, they should be attending, or be a graduate of a university.
Examination for Transfer Students
Examination for Transfer Students can be carried out only when there is a vacancy in the year for which application is made. At present, all years are full. Therefore, no examinations for transfer students are being held.
Documents to be Submitted When Applying
Standard Documents Requirement

GRADUATE PROGRAMS

Graduate School of Medical Research (First Year Enrollment: Doctor's 60)
Divisions
Basic Medicine, Clinical Basic Medicine, Clinical Medicine, Social Medicine

Foreign Student Admission
Qualifications for Applicants
Doctor's Program
Standard Qualifications Requirement
Applicants for areas of clinical medicine must have completed or be about to complete 2 years or more of clinical training.
In principle, applicants for areas of basic medicine, clinical basic medicine or social medicine should have a medical licence.
Examination at the University
Doctor's Program
Examination, interview, a Japanese language ability test transcripts of the school records of the last school attended and physical examination. In addition to examinations concerning the applicant's specialty in Japanese or other languages.
Documents to be Submitted When Applying
Standard Documents Requirement
Following documents are also required.

1. A copy of medical licence, if posessed by the applicant.
2. Certificate of completion or expected completion of clinical training, if the applicant has completed or is likely to complete such training.
3. If the applicant is employed, a letter of permission to take examination from the applicant's department chief.

＊
Research Institutes and Centers
Audio Visual Education Center, Electron Microscope Laboratory, Medical Photo Center, Radioisotope Research Institute for Basic Medicine, St. Marianna University Foundation for Experimental Biology and Medicine
For Further Information
Undergraduate and Graduate Admission
Administration Department, St. Marianna University School of Medicine, 2–16–1 Sugao, Miyamae–ku, Kawasaki–shi, Kanagawa 213 ☎ 044–977–8111 ext. 4512, 4513 (Undergraduate), 3113, 3115 (Graduate)

St. Michael's University
(Yashiro Gakuin Daigaku)
5-1-1 Manabigaoka, Tarumi-ku, Kobe-shi, Hyogo 655 ☎ 078-709-3851

Faculty
Profs. 16 Assoc. Profs. 8
Assist. Profs. Full–time 8; Part–time 29
Res. Assocs. 2
Number of Students
Undergrad. 1, 926
Library 60, 965 volumes

Outline and Characteristics of the University
The university is a college of economics founded by Shinsuke Yashiro, Presiding Bishop of the Anglican Church of Japan; the church has taken a prominent role in Japanese Christian Society.
The university, situated on a hill surrounded by nature in Tarumi, was founded in 1968. Its purpose was to be a unique school fostering Christian internationalism among its students.
Having Rikkyo and Momoyama Gakuin Universities as sister schools sharing the same Anglican background, our university is continually striving to fulfill its high Christian goals.
In the first two years students take general economic subjects, but at the beginning of their third year they are required to choose a major from among economics, business administration, foreign trade or tourism.
The educational principle is "Nourishing internationality through the students' whole personality based on Christianity. "

UNDERGRADUATE PROGRAMS

Faculty of Economics (Freshmen Enrollment: 250)
Department of Economics
Business Administration, Economics, Foreign Trade, Tourism

Foreign Student Admission
Qualifications for Applicants
Standard Qualifications Requirement
Applicants are required to apply solely to Yashiro Gakuin University.
Examination at the University
1. Application Period: Nov. 4-18
2. Date of Test: Nov. 28
3. Content of Test: An interview in Japanese
Documents to be Submitted When Applying
Standard Documents Requirement

Qualifications for Transfer Students
Those who have completed two years of college work, or who are due to finish in May of the year of application.
Those who are certified by the university authorities as having the scholastic ability equivalent of the above.
Those who have not completed the university requirements for the third year may be required to start from the second year.
Examination for Transfer Students
1. Application period: Dec. 19-Jan. 18
2. Date of Test: Jan. 26
3. Content of Test: English, Japanese composition, Interview in Japanese
Documents to be Submitted When Applying
Standard Documents Requirement
∗
Research Institutes and Centers
Yashiro Gakuin Research Institute
For Further Information
Undergraduate Admission
Division of Publicity, St. Michael's University, 5-1-1 Manabigaoka, Tarumi-ku, Kobe-shi, Hyogo 655 ☎ 078-709-3851 ext. 209

Sugino Women's College
(Sugino Joshi Daigaku)

4-6-19 Kamiosaki, Shinagawa-ku, Tokyo 141
☎ 03-491-8151

UNDERGRADUATE PROGRAMS

Faculty of Home Economics (Freshmen Enrollment: 100)
Department of Clothing Science

Sugiyama Jogakuen University
(Sugiyama Jogakuen Daigaku)

17-3 Hoshigaoka-motomachi, Chikusa-ku, Nagoya-shi, Aichi 464   ☎ 052-781-1186

Faculty
    Profs. 46   Assoc. Profs. 27
    Assist. Profs.   Full–time 15; Part–time 169
    Res. Assocs. 18
Number of Students
    Undergrad. 2, 810   Grad. 4
Library 184, 162 volumes

Outline and Characteristics of the University
Sugiyama Jogakuen University, founded in 1905 by Masakazu Sugiyama as the Nagoya Women's Sewing School, aimed at providing young women with both higher education and practical domestic training. It has gone through several stages in the 83 years since its establishment. The Sewing School was expanded in 1917 into Sugiyama Higher School for Women, which in turn became Sugiyama Women's Technical School in 1930.

In 1949, the school was transformed into a four-year College which consisted of the Department of Home Economics. This Department was one of the first of its kind in Japan and has produced more than 5, 000 graduates, many of whom are active in various circles in the community. In 1972, the Faculty of Literature, comprised of the Department of Japanese and the Department of English, was added. In 1977 the Graduate School of Home Economics with the Master's Program was established. The most recent addition in 1987 was the Faculty of Human Sciences with three courses of study in Psychology, Sociology and Education. Thus, the present Sugiyama educational system spans every educational level from kindergarten through graduate school.

With only a little over 2, 800 students at the University, it is possible to maintain close contact between teachers and students. Both teachers and students are dedicated to the building of character through the pursuit of intellectual, moral and physical education.

The main Sugiyama campus is conveniently situated in the eastern part of the city of Nagoya along the Higashiyama Subway Line. It sits on one of the highest hills of Nagoya, commanding outstanding views of Higashiyama Park to the west and of the city proper in all other directions. The other campus, in Nisshin, roughly a 15-minute drive to the east of the main campus, currently serves as a large ground where physical education and tennis classes are conducted. And it is on this site that the new Faculty of Human Sciences is built.

The University celebrated its 80th anniversary in 1985. This coincided with the completion of a new gymnasium and the University Hall. With the addition of these new campus facilities, the University moves toward an even fuller realization of its educational ideal and a step closer to its centennial celebration in the near future.

UNDERGRADUATE PROGRAMS

Faculty of Home Economics (Freshmen Enrollment: 300)
Department of Clothing and Textile
Accessory Aesthetics, Designs, Dyeing Chemistry, Fabric Chemistry, Fabric Hygiene, Fabric Structure, History of Clothing, Study of Color, Textile Materials
Department of Food and Nutrition
Dietetics, Food Chemistry, Food Economics, Food Materials and Preparation, High Polymer Chemistry, Microbiology, Nutritional Physiology, Organic Chemistry, Pathology, Physical Chemistry, Public Hygiene, Public Nutrition
Faculty of Human Sciences (Freshman Enrollment: 200)
Course in Education
Continuing Education, Curriculum Development, Educational Administration, Educational Management, Educational Systems, History of Education, Methodology, Pedagogy
Course in Psychology
Behavioral and Clinical Psychology, Child and Adolescent Psychology, Counselling, Educational Psychology, Introduction to Psychology, Mental Health, Social
Course in sociology
Communication, Japanese Society, Labor-Management Relations, Recreation, Social Problems, Social Welfare, Sociometrics, The Community, The Family
Faculty of Literature (Freshmen Enrollment: 200)
Department of English
American and British Language and Culture, American and British Literature, English Linguistics, English Phonetics and Phonology, History of American and British Literature
Department of Japanese
Calligraphy, Chinese Literature, Eastern Philosophy, History of Japanese Language and Literature, Japanese Grammar, Japanese Language and Literature

Foreign Student Admission
Qualifications for Applicants
Standard Qualifications Requirement
Examination at the University
An interview in November,
The entrance examination in early February,
The announcement of accepted applicants within one week after the exam.
Documents to be Submitted When Applying
Standard Documents Requirement
Application forms are available in January.

GRADUATE PROGRAMS

Graduate School of Home Economics (First Year Enrollment : Master's 12)
Divisions
Clothing and Textile, Food and Nutrition

Foreign Student Admission
Qualifications for Applicants
Master's Program
Standard Qualifications Requirement
Examination at the University
Master's Program
A written examination and an interview.
Documents to be Submitted When Applying
Standard Documents Requirement
Application forms and other relevant forms are available in the Admissions Office. Application deadline: in November or in March.

*

Research Institutes and Centers
Center for Educational Research and Training
For Further Information
Undergraduate and Graduate Admission
Admissions Office, Sugiyama Jogakuen University, 17-3 Hoshigaoka-motomachi, Chikusa-ku, Nagoyashi, Aichi 464 ☎ 052-781-1186 ext. 313, 312

Surugadai University
(Surugadai Daigaku)

698 Azu, Hanno–shi, Saitama 357   ☎ 04297–2–1111

Faculty
Profs.　20　　Assoc. Profs　6
Assist. Profs.　Full–time　12; Part–time　19
Res. Assoc.　1
Number of Students
Undergrad.　685
Library　37, 477 volumes

Outline and Characteristics of the College
Surugadai University was founded in 1987. Its ultimate origin can be traced back to 1918 when Tokyo Koto Juken Koshukai (currently Surugadai Yobi Gakko) was established. In 1952 this became Surugadai Gakuen which has established a number of preparatory shools as well as a high school.
The goal of the university is not only to teach students specialized and systematic knowledge of positive law and socioeconomic phenomena but also to help students acquire the ability to respond effectively to various legal issues, and to foster broad international awareness.
1.　Specialized courses in the area of administrative law (administrative remedy law, tax law, local government law, environmental

protection law, etc.).

2. Specialized courses in business-related law (real estate law, accounting law, banking law, securities and exchange law, bankruptcy law, etc.).

3. Courses designed to broaden students' international perspectives (foreign law such as EC and Chinese law, international organization law, comparative politics, etc.) and foreign-language reading seminars.

4. Many courses in related areas, e. g. , political science, economics, information sciences, etc.

5. The progressive introduction of specialized courses from the freshman year, in place of the traditional curriculum in which liberal arts courses are offered in the first two years and specialized courses in the last two years.

6. Two introductory law courses, Principles of Public Law and Principles of Private Law, are offered by a team of veteran professors in the first semester of the freshman year in order to stimulate students' interest in specialized subjects.

7. Basic seminars are also offered in the freshman year in order to teach the fundamental theories and analytical skills necessary for specialized courses and to foster intellecutual communication between faculty and students as well as among students.

8. Liberal arts seminars are also offered in the general education curriculum. These seminars deal with diverse subjects in the areas of humanities, social sciences, and natural sciences.

9. Comprehensive Lecture Series are offered in the general education curriculum. These are team-taught by a number of faculty members in a multi-disciplinary fashion to enhance students' powers of reasoning and comprehension essential to the acquisition of specialized knowledge required by the complex realities of contemporary society.

In order to guide students in their academic planning and give a sense of direction in their learning, one of the following three major programs is chosen, depending upon the students' future career objectives: the judicial program, the administrative program, and the managerial program.

Various seminars are offered, e. g. , liberal arts seminars in general education, basic seminars in the freshman year and specialized seminars in the sophomore through senior years, and foreign-language reading seminars in the junior year. Through participating in seminars students can acquire the ability to engage in active learning and to deal with problems in a holistic manner. The students are also expected to develop communicative, applicative, and creative abilities through the use of independent thinking and investigation of specific issues.

UNDERGRADUATE PROGRAMS

Faculty of Law

Department of Law

Accounting, Administrative Law, Administrative Law, Administrative Remedy Law, Banking Law, Bankruptcy Law, Civil Execution Law, Civil Law (General Provisions/the law of jus in rem), Civil Proceedings Law, Commercial Law (General Rules and Commercial Transactions Company Law Bill and Check Law Maritime and Insurance Law), Comparative Law, Comparative Politics, Constitution (Basic Principles and Government Fundamental Human Rights), Consumer Protection Law, Criminal Policy, Criminal Proceedings Law, Economic Law, Economic Policy, Education Law, Enterprise Accounting Law, Environmental Protection Law, Finance, Foreign-language Reading, Foreign Law (Anglo-American Law), (German Law), (French Law EC Law Chinese Law), General Discussions on Obligations/Itemized Discossions on Obligations/Family and Inheritance Law), History of Political Thought, History of Politics and Diplomacy, Industrial Psychology, Industrial Sociology, Information Management, Intellectual Property Law, International Aviation and Navigation Law, International Law, International Organization Law, International Political History, International Politics, Introduction to Information Processing, Labor Law, Legal History, Legal Philosophy, Local Autonomy Law, Local Community, Medical Affairs Law, Political Theory, Principles of Economic Theory, Private International Law, Private Law, Public Administration, Public Finance, Public Law, Real Estate Law, Securities and Exchange Law, Social Security Law, Tax Law, Tax Law, Trust Law

Foreign Student Admission

Qualifications for Applicants

Standard Qualifications Requirement

(1) Japanese nationality, except in the case of one who possesses dual nationality-both Japanese and that of a foreign country.

(2) completion of a regular 12-year school program or the equivalent in a foreign country.

(3) The applicants must take the 1989 Japanese Language Proficiency Test lst Grade.

(4) The applicants must take the humanities and social science sections of the 1989 General Examination for Foreign Students

Examination at the University

The First Examination: papers.

The Second Examination: results of the Japanese Proficiency Test (lst Grade) and the General Examination for Foreign Students and interviews.

Documents to be Submitted When Applying

Standard Documents Requirement

Those who possess an international baccalaureate must submit an IB diploma and certification of the final test results of the six subjects.

∗

Special Programs for Foreign Students
Japanese as a foreion language
For Further Information
Undergraduate Admission
Admission office, Surugadai University, 698 Azu, Hanno–shi, Saitama 357 ☎ 04297–2–1110

Taisho University
(Taisho Daigaku)
3-20-1 Nishisugamo, Toshima–ku, Tokyo 170
☎ 03-918-7311

Faculty
    Profs. 55   Assoc. Profs. 20
    Assist. Profs.   Full–time 12; Part–time 121
Number of Students
    Undergrad. 2, 761   Grad. 184
Library 258, 667 volumes

Outline and Characteristics of the University
    Taisho University has historical roots in the earliest educational traditions of Japan and offers both Master's and Doctorate degrees in the Faculty of Buddhism and Letters. Unlike the recent trend toward mass education, Taisho emphasizes direct contact and discussion between students and faculty in a family atmosphere.
    There are two institutes annexed to the university, the Institute of Comprehensive Buddhist Studies and the Counselling Institute. Taisho University has two campuses, one in Nishi–sugamo district, Tokyo, and the other an hour and a half away in Matsubuse, Saitama Prefecture.
    The university was jointly established in 1926 by four Buddhist denominations, and this cooperative spirit and concern for nurturing human life to its deepest potential has been a special characteristic of Taisho ever since. Recently this focus on human development has extended into an active sponsorship of international understanding and student exchange.
    Each summer 36 students participate with the University of Hawaii in a program of English conversation and World Religion for course credit. Faculty from the Department of Religion at the University of Hawaii come to Taisho University for two months to prepare students for the three week program in Hawaii. In addition, other foreign scholars and graduate students regularly study and lecture at Taisho University and an exchange program has been established with Donguk University, Seoul, Korea and Honan University of Kai-feng, China.

UNDERGRADUATE PROGRAMS

Faculty of Buddhism (Freshmen Enrollment: 150)
Department of Buddhist Studies
Buddhism, History of Buddhism, Indian Philosophy, Pali, Pure Land Buddhism, Sanskrit, Shingon Buddhism, T'ien–tai Buddhism
Faculty of Letters (Freshmen Enrollment: 520)
Department of History
Archaeology, Art History, Asian History, Bibliography of Asian History, History of Buddhism, History of Japanese Culture, Japanese History, Western History
Department of Literature
Anglo–American Literature, Buddhist Literature, Chinese Classics, English Literature, History of Anglo–American Literature, Japanese Literature, Linguistics, Phonetics
Department of Philosophy
Chinese Literature and Studies, Christianity, Ethics, Hinduism, History of Oriental Culture, Islam, Logic, Religious Sociology, Science of Religion, Western and Asian Philosophy
Department of Social Welfare
Case Work, Gerontological Social Welfare, Life Structure, Regional Social Welfare, Social Security, Social Welfare
Department of Sociology
Buddhist Sociology, Family Sociology, Folklore, History of Sociology, Problems of Youth, Regional Sociology, Social Pathology

Foreign Student Admission
Qualifications for Applicants
    Standard Qualifications Requirement
Examination at the University
    Japanese language capability and background knowledge in their field of study.
Documents to be Submitted When Applying
    Standard Documents Requirement

Qualifications for Transfer Students
    Standard Qualifications Requirement
Examination for Transfer Students
    Japanese language, a foreign language (other than one's mother tongue), and a written essay
Documents to be Submitted When Applying
    Standard Documents Requirement

GRADUATE PROGRAMS

Graduate School of Letters (First Year Enrollment : Master's 50, Doctor's 16)
Divisions
Buddhism, History, Japanese Literature, Religion

Foreign Student Admission
Qualifications for Applicants
Master's Program
    Standard Qualifications Requirement
Doctor's Program
    Standard Qualifications Requirement
Examination at the University
Master's Program

1. Examinations of essay in academic subjects.
2. Japanese language
3. Foreign language (one of English, German, French, and Chinese except for applicant's mother tongue)
4. Thesis
5. Oral exam

Doctor's Program
1. Japanese language
2. Two foreign languages are required in Group A: English, German, French and Modern Chinese, while one of the Group A is among electives in Group B: Classical Chinese, Sanskrit, Tibetan, Pāli, Manuscript of Ancient Japanese and Classical Japanese.
3. Thesis
4. Oral exam

Documents to be Submitted When Applying
Standard Documents Requirement
Essay explaining reasons for applying to Taisho University and proposed program of study.

*

Research Institutes and Centers
Counseling Institute, Institute for the Comprehensive Study of Buddhism

Facilities/Services for Foreign Students
A Faculty advisor will be appointed for consultation, and a welcoming reception and orientation will be provided.

Special Programs for Foreign Students
Two Japanese language classes totalling four hours a week.
A special class for understanding Japanese culture, Japanese History, and daily life.

For Further Information
Undergraduate and Graduate Admission
Planning Department, Division of Entrance Exam, Taisho University, 3-20-1 Nishisugamo, Toshima-ku, Tokyo 170 ☎ 03-918-7311

Takachiho University of Commerce
(Takachiho Shoka Daigaku)

2-19-1 Omiya, Suginami–ku, Tokyo 168
☎ 03-313-0141

Faculty
   Profs. 29   Assoc. Profs. 16
   Assist. Profs. Part–time 66
   Res. Assocs 1
Number of Students
   Undergrad. 2, 283
Library 100, 745 volumes

Outline and Characteristics of the University
In 1903 Tetsuya Kawada founded Takachiho Elementary School in Okubo, Tokyo. This school was the origin of the present Takachiho Gakuen (Takachiho Educational Institution). Takachiho Kindergarten was established in 1907. Takachiho Middle School was established in 1909. Takachiho College of Commerce was established in 1914 at the present location. This school was the first college of commerce in the history of private schools in Japan. Due to the educational reforms enacted by the government in 1950, the school was reorganized as Takachiho University of Commerce. In 1986, the Institution celebrated its 83rd anniversary when the University sent out its 69th graduating class.

The founder established Takachiho Gakuen, which administered a kindergarten, an elementary school, middle school and a college for giving comprehensive education based on the founder's own principles of education which emphasized the formation of sound human character. The philosophy of education at these schools, which has produced many well–known citizens, has been praised by various authorities. To keep in step with modern trends, the following goals have recently been stressed. Motto: "Always keep half step ahead". Goals: (1) A liberal-minded person who follows the golden mean. (2) A courageous person who possesses common sense. (3) A peace-loving person who is international minded.

The mission of the college is to educate persons who are able to work for society with their broad culture, deep professional knowledge, and international views. This aim is pursued on the following principles of education: (1) Creation of good human relations by small–sized classes. (2) Encouragement of both theoretical and practical studies. (3) Cultivation of individuality for self–realization. (4) Development of sociability through extracurricular activities. (5) Appropriate guidance for the students' moral development.

UNDERGRADUATE PROGRAMS

Faculty of Commerce (Freshmen Enrollment: 300)
Department of Commerce
Division of Accounting
Accounting, Auditing, Bookkeeping, Cost Accounting, Financial Accounting, Financial Statements Analysis, History of Accounting, Industrial Bookkeeping, Management Accounting, Tax Accounting
Division of Business Administration
Business Administration, Business Form, Business Mathematics, Business Organization, Decision Making, Entrepreneure's Function, Financial Management, History of European and American Management, History of Japanese Management, Industrial Management, Industrial Psychology, Industrial Sociology, Information Management, Management Theory, Personnel Adiministration, Production Management, Public Corporation, Small and Medium Business Management, Statistics
Division of Commercial Science

Advertising, Banking, Commodity Management, Consumer Behavior, Distribution Management, Foreign Exchange, History of Commerce, Insurance, International Marketing, International Trade, Marketing, Marketing Information System, Marketing Research, Merchandising, Physical Distribution, Policy for Wholesale and Retailing, Practices of International Trade, Real Estate Industry, Securities, Transportation
Division of Economics
Economic Geography, Economic Policy, Economics, Economic Statistics, European Economic History, History of Economic Thought, Industrial Organization, International Economics, Japanese Economic History, Japanese Industry, Labor Economics, Macro–economics, Monetary Economics, Public Finance, Regional Development, Small and Medium Business, Social Policy, World Economic and Business Affairs
Division of Law
Administrative Law, Antitrust Law, Business Law, Civil Law, Constitutional Law, Labor Law, Tax Law

*

For Further Information
Undergraduate Admission
Entrance Examination Section, Admission Division of Instruction Department, Takachiho University of Commerce, 2-19-1 Omiya, Suginami–ku, Tokyo 168 ☎ 03-313-0141 ext. 455

Takarazuka University of Art and Design
(Takarazuka Zōkei Geijutsu Daigaku)

2–1658, Hibarigaoka, Hanayashiki, Takarazuka–shi, Hyogo 665   ☎   0727–56–1231

Faculty
  Profs. 15   Assoc. Profs 3
  Assist. Profs. Full–time 5; Part–time 15
Number of Students
  Undergrad. 300
Library 15, 917 volumes

Outline and Characteristics of the University
  Takarazuka University of Art and Design was founded in 1987 as a four-year college with the Faculty of Formative Arts. The Faculty comprises two departments, the Fine Arts Department and the Design Department. The former has three programs in Western Painting, Japanese Painting and Sculpture. The latter has four programs of Apparel, Visual Design, Interior Design and Product Design.
  The University is situated on a verdant hillside east of Takarazuka City, with a view of the whole city and the Kansai plains. The campus building was designed by André Wogenscky, disciple of the great modern architect Le Corbusier. It is an innovative building in harmony with the natural features of Japan, and is a place where students can devote themselves to their creative activities.
  The university provides its students with extensive knowledge and guidance in such fields as art, science, and technology. It encourages further reserch in specialized academic disciplines, to develop the students' artistic abilities, as well as intellectual, personal and social insight. The faculty at the university believes that through the blending of creative imagination, human understanding and technical skills, the students can become new artists and designers able to contribute to the development of culture and industrial society in Japan and the world.
  The ultimate aim of the university is to educate creative, competent and self–reliant professionals. To accomplish this goal, the university's students are offered a broad and balanced curriculum in both the visual and the liberal arts.

UNDERGRADUATE PROGRAMS

Faculty of Formative Arts (Freshmen Enrollment: 100)
  Department of Design
  Department of Fine Arts

Foreign Student Admission
  Examination at the University
  A completed application, a written Japanese language examination, a vivavoce examination will be given.

*

For Further Information
Undergraduate Admission
Administrative Office, Takarazuka University of Art and Design 2–1658, Hibarigaoka, Hanayashiki, Takarazuka-shi Hyogo 665 ☎ 0727–56–1231 ext. 303

Takushoku University
(Takushoku Daigaku)

3-4-14 Kohinata, Bunkyo–ku, Tokyo 112
☎ 03-947-2261

Faculty
  Profs. 110   Assoc. Profs. 57
  Assist. Profs. Full–time 32; Part–time 179
  Res. Assocs. 29
Number of Students
  Undergrad. 8, 195   Grad. 226
Library 271, 382 volumes

Outline and Characteristics of the University
  Takushoku University is a private university whose history dates back to 1900 when Taiwan Kyokai Gakko was established by Duke Taro Katsura. The next year, Katsura organized the first Katsura

Cabinet and performed his duty as the Prime Minister. The main purpose of the university is to prepare students to take an active role in international society. There are four main faculties of Takushoku University: the Faculty of Commerce which includes Business Administration and Foreign Trade; the Faculty of Political Science and Economics; the Faculty of Foreign Languages which includes English, Chinese and Spanish and Faculty of Engineering. The university also has Graduate School of Economics and Commerce. In 1972 the university began offering special courses in Japanese Language for foreign students. In order to obtain a good command of Japanese, students from other countries must attend a one year preparatory course before proceeding to the University.

Before world war II, Takushoku University had arrangements with colleges, universities overseas for Takushoku students to study abroad. With the advent of the Canadian School of Takudai, students again have the opportunity to study outside Japan while earning credits from Takushoku University. Takushoku University also has overseas schools in Mexico, Taiwan, China and Spain. The Canadian School of Takudai is a cooperative venture between Takushoku University and Vancouver Community College, Continuing Education.

The university is located amid a quiet residential area, a two minutes walk from Myogadani Station on the Marunouchi Line Subway in Tokyo. Walking along the sloping road lined with rich green trees, one can reach the main gate. The location here in Kohinata, Bunkyo–ku brings about the most suitable environment for education. We have another campus in Hachioji city, with an area of 1, 300, 000 m².

UNDERGRADUATE PROGRAMS

Faculty of Commerce (Freshmen Enrollment: 600)
  Department of Business Administration
  Accounting Course
Accounting, Auditing, Business Accounting
Business Administration Course
Business Administration, Business Management
Management Information Course
Business Statistics, Computer Programming, Data Processing System
  Department of Foreign Trade
  Foreign Trade Course
Accounting, Business Administration, International Economics, Political Economy
International Business Course
Accounting, Bookkeeping, Business Administration, Business English, Political Economy
Faculty of Engineering (Freshmen Enrollment: 320)
  Department of Electronic Engineering
  Department of Industrial Design
  Department of Information Engineering
  Department of Mechanical Systems Engineering
Faculty of Foreign Languages (Freshmen Enroll-

ment: 200)
  Department of Chinese Language
Chinese History, Chinese Language, Chinese Linguistics, Chinese Literature
  Department of English Language
English and American Literature, English Language, English Linguistics, Phonetics
  Department of Spanish Language
History of Spain, Spanish Linguistics, Spanish Literature
Faculty of Political Science and Economics (Freshmen Enrollment: 680)
  Department of Economics
  Economics Course
Economic Policy, Economic Statistics, Japanese Economic History, Political Economy, Western Economic History
International Economics Course
Area Studies, International Economics, International Politics, Western Economic History
  Department of Political Science
  International Affairs Course
Area Studies, Diplomatic History of the World, International Politics
Law Course
Administrative Law, Commercial Law, Constitutional Law, Criminal Law , International Law, Law of Civil Procedure, Tax Law
Political Science Course
Administrative Law, History of Political Thought, Japanese Political History, Political Science, Western Political History

Foreign Student Admission
  Qualifications for Applicants
    Standard Qualifications Requirement
  Examination at the University
    First screening: the documents.
    Second screening: written examination in English and Japanese and an interview.
Date: in the mid-February
  Documents to be Submitted When Applying
    Standard Documents Requirement
    Certificate of Japanese Language Ability.
1. Application Period: January 9 to February 8
2. An applicant must bring the required documents to admission office. When circumstances compel it, application by registered mail is acceptable.

Qualifications for Transfer Students
  Prospective applicants are required to meet at least one of the following stipulations:
1. must have completed the two years of university education or junior college course in countries other than Japan.
2. must have the equivalence of 14 years of school education in countries other than Japan.
3. must have completed the preparatory course

in Japanese of Takushoku university after graduating from the junior college course in countries other than Japan.

All transcripts of previous college work must be submitted directly from each prior institution to the admissions office. Admission of any international student applying for admission to the third year of a degree program is based upon evaluation of all materials submitted. The number of credits that are acceptable for transfer will be determined upon registration, through consultation with an academic advisor.

Applicants are required to take the Japanese Language Proficiency Test in the year of application.
Examination for Transfer Students
Those who have completed the one year preparatory course of Takushoku University
Faculty of Commerce and Faculty of Political Science and Economics: Written Examinations (English and Japanese and Interview
Faculty of Foreign Languages: Written Examinations (Japanese and one foreign language from among English, Spanish, Chinese) and Interview

Those who wish to take the examination for transfer students from other colleges and universities are admitted only to the Faculty of Foreign Languages. Examination Subjects of each Department are as follows.
Department of English Language: English and Interview
Department of Chinese Language: Chinese and Interview
Department of Spanish Language: Spanish and Interview

In case students wish to enter the faculty of Foreign Languages such as English, Spanish and Chinese, students must present evidence of having completed a two year course of the same study in each prior institution.
Documents to be Submitted When Applying
Standard Documents Requirement
1. Application Period: January 9–February 12
2. Applicants must bring the required documents to the admission office.

GRADUATE PROGRAMS

Graduate School of Commerce (First Year Enrollment : Master's 30, Doctor's 5)
Division
Commerce
Graduate School of Economics (First Year Enrollment : Master's 30, Doctor's 5)
Division
International Economy

Foreign Student Admission
Qualifications for Applicants
Master's Program
Standard Qualifications Requirement

Doctor's Program
Standard Qualifications Requirement
Examination at the University
Master's Program
Written tests on specialized subjects and two foreign languages, and an interview
Division of International Economy:
1. Written Examination
(1) Core Foreign Language: Japanese I and II
(2) Elective Foreign Language: English, French, Spanish, German, Chinese (One foreign language except native language)
(3) Core Essay on Economics
(4) Elective Essay on one subject from among Economic policy, Japanese Economic History, Western Economic History, International Economy
2. Interview
Division of Commerce:
1. Written Examination
(1) Foreign Language: Same as above
(2) Foreign Language: Same as above
(3) Essay on Special subject
(4) Essay on one subject from among Business Administration, Economics, Accounting, Science of Law, Intoduction to Commercial Science
2. Interview
Doctor's Program
Division of International Economy and Division of Commerce:
1. Written Examination: English and Elective Foreign Language (Chinese, Spanish, French, German, Russian or Japanese)
2. Oral Examination
Documents to be Submitted When Applying
Standard Documents Requirement,
Certificate of Japanese Language Ability
1. Application Period:
First time: October 1–8
Second time: February 19–26
2. Applicants must bring the required documents to Admissions office.

*

Research Institutes and Centers
General Research Institute, Institute for the Study of Japanese Culture (ISJC), Institute of Accounting, Institute of World Studies, Language Research Institute
Facilities/Services for Foreign Students
Students' Dormitory, Counselling Room, Lounge for Foreign Students
Special Programs for Foreign Students
Japanese Language Section for Foreign Students (Ryugakusei Bekka):
In 1972 Takushoku University began offering special courses in Japanese language for foreign students. The university is open to students from any country or any language background who have completed 12 years of formal school. The number of stu-

dents is fixed at 130. The course lasts for the duration of one calendar year. The university's Japanese as a second language program is especially designed to prepare students for successful study at colleges and universities in Japan.

Following the completion of the Japanese program at the Takushoku University students can apply to Takushoku University for regular undergraduate or graduate programs of study and apply to another university in Japan. Admission to the Japanese program does not guarantee admission to regular undergraduate or graduate programs at Takushoku University.

For Further Information
Undergraduate and Graduate Admission
Admission Office, Takushoku University, 3-4-14 Kohinata, Bunkyo–ku, Tokyo 112 ☎ 03-947-2261 ext. 1310

Tama Art University
(Tama Bijutsu Daigaku)

3-15-34 Kaminoge, Setagaya–ku, Tokyo 158
☎ 03-702-1141

Faculty
  Profs. 49   Assoc. Profs. 29
  Assist. Profs. Full–time 9; Part–time 111
  Res. Assocs. 19
Number of Students
  Undergrad. 2, 486   Grad. 60
Library 66, 000 volumes

Outline and Characteristics of the University
Tama Art University was established in 1935 as a private art school. It is now a private university, consisting of five departments: Painting, Sculpture, Design, Architecture and Reseach of Art and Design.

The Graduate School of Fine Arts and Design (Master's program) was established in 1964, consisting of three departments: Painting, Sculpture and Design.

The College campus is located in Hachioji City, Tokyo and the Graduate School is located in Setagaya, near the center of Tokyo.

UNDERGRADUATE PROGRAMS

Faculty of Fine Arts and Design (Freshmen Enrollment: 500)
  Department of Architecture
Architecture
  Department of Design
Craft Design, Graphic Design, Industrial Design, Interior Design, Textile Design
  Department of Painting
Ceramic Art, Japanese Painting, Oil Painting, Print Making

Department of Sculpture
Metal, Plaster, Stone, Wood
  Department of the Research of Art and Design
Interdisciplinary Study in Arts and Design

GRADUATE PROGRAMS

Graduate School of Fine Arts and Design (First Year Enrollment : Master's 22)
  Divisions
Design, Painting, Sculpture
                          ✱
Research Institutes and Centers
Tama Institute of Art Design
For Further Information
  Undergraduate and Graduate Admission
Dean of Students, Students Office, Tama Art University, 3-15-34 Kaminoge, Setagaya–ku, Tokyo 158 ☎ 03-702-1141

Tamagawa University
(Tamagawa Daigaku)

6-1-1 Tamagawa Gakuen, Machida–shi, Tokyo 194
☎ 0427-28-3111

UNDERGRADUATE PROGRAMS

Faculty of Agriculture (Freshmen Enrollment: 160)
  Department of Agricultural Chemistry
  Department of Agriculture
Faculty of Engineering (Freshmen Enrollment: 320)
  Department of Electronic Engineering
  Department of Information and Communication Engineering
  Department of Management Engineering
  Department of Mechanical Engineering
Faculty of Letters (Freshmen Enrollment: 600)
  Department of Arts
Arts Education for Children, Dramatic Arts, Fine Arts, Music
  Department of Education
  Department of English and American Literature
  Department of Foreign Languages
English, French, German

GRADUATE PROGRAMS

Graduate School of Engineering (First Year Enrollment : Master's 14, Doctor's 4)
  Divisions
Electronic Engineering, Mechanical Engineering, Production Development Engineering
Graduate School of Letters (First Year Enrollment : Master's 20, Doctor's 4)

Divisions
Education, English Literature

Teikoku Women's University
(Teikoku Joshi Daigaku)

6-173 Toda-cho, Moriguchi-shi, Osaka 570
☎ 06-902-0791

Faculty
    Profs. 17   Assoc. Profs. 12
    Assist. Profs. Full–time 10; Part–time 2
    Res. Assocs. 12
Number of Students
    Undergrad. 530
Library 78, 483 volumes

Outline and Characteristics of the University
1965 Faculty of Home Economics was opened.
1966 Department of Food Science was started.
1969 Department of Clothing was started.
1972 Department of Child Development was established.
    This university is devoted to the creation of a humanistic educational background for young women.

UNDERGRADUATE PROGRAMS

Faculty of Home Economics (Freshmen Enrollment: 120)
    Department of Child Development
Child Psychology, Child Welfare, Developmental Medicine, Education of Child, Juvenile Culture
    Department of Clothing
Clothing Care, Clothing Construction, Clothing Design, Clothing Materials, Clothing Mechanism and Function
    Department of Food Science
Food Science, Nutritional Science, Public Health, Science of Cooking

*

For Further Information
    Undergraduate Admission
Examination Preparation Room, Teikoku Women's University, 6-173 Toda-cho, Moriguchi-shi, Osaka 570 ☎ 06-902-0791 ext. 308, 309

Teikyo University
(Teikyo Daigaku)

2-11-1 Kaga, Itabashi–ku, Tokyo 173
☎ 03-964-1211

Faculty
    Profs. 226   Assoc. Profs. 146
    Assist. Profs. Full–time 180; Part–time 242
    Res. Assocs. 388
Number of Students
    Undergrad. 13, 284   Grad. 178
Library 540, 000 volumes

Outline and Characteristics of the University
    Teikyo University was founded in 1966 with two faculties, Economics and Literature which consists of two departments, Japanese Literature and English Literature. Since then, the three faculties of Law (1967), Medicine (1971), and Pharmacology (1977), and the three departments of Pedagogy (1973), History (1984), Sociology (1986), Psychology (1988), and International Culture (1988) were added. Besides, the five graduate schools of Medicine (1977), Literature (1979), Pharmacology (1981), Economics (1982), and Law (1983) were added successively. And this spring, the Faculty of Science and Engineering is to be established. Therefore, Teikyo University is now a university consisting of six faculties, seventeen departments and five graduate schools.
    Based on the founding spirit that "Teikyo University aims to foster Japanese citizens who hold the aquisition of an all–round knowledge, the abolishment of prejudice, the giving of one's best effort, and the necessity to render decisions from an international point of view as their fundamental ideals," the University has developed an educational system with complete facilities and an excellent faculty of professors to fulfill these humanitarian goals. Further, Teikyo University places strong emphasis on practical education thereby producing graduates who immediately become influential members of society.

UNDERGRADUATE PROGRAMS

Faculty of Economics (Freshmen Enrollment: 650)
    Department of Economics
Accounting, Administration, Business, Commerce, Econometrics, Economic History, Economics, Finance, International Economics, Labor Economics
Faculty of Law (Freshmen Enrollment: 650)
    Department of Law
Civil Law, Civil Procedure, Comparative Law, Constitutional Law, Criminal Law, Criminal Procedure, Economics of Tourism, Hotel Management, International Politics, Legal History, Political Science, Tourism Laws and Regulations, Tourist Industry, Travel Agency
Faculty of Literature (Freshmen Enrollment: 850)
    Department of Education
Education CourseChild Education, Child Psychology, Educational Administration, Educational Methodology, Educational Psychology, Education of the Handicapped, Philosophy of Education, Psychology of Learning, School Education
    Department of English Literature
English and American Literature, English Linguistics, History of English and American Literature

Department of History

Archaeology, Folklore, Japanese History, Occidental History, Oriental History

Department of International Culture

American Culture Course

Chinese Culture Couurse

European Culture Course

Economics, Government, History of Culture, Law, Literature, Society and International Relaytions

Korea Culture course

Latin-American Course

Russian Culture Course

Department of Japanese Literature

Calligraphy, Chinese Literature, History of Japanese Literature, Japanese Language, Japnese Literature

Department of Psychology

Developmental Behaviour Course

Character Psychology, Child Psychology, Developmental Psychology, Learning Psychology, Life Psychology, Mass Communicatiom

Fundamental pehaviour Course

Comparative Behaviour, Cultural Anthropology, Educational Psychology, Folklore, Mass Communication, Social Psychology

Industrial Psychology Course

History of Social Thought, Language Psychology, Mental Hygiene, Perception Psychology, Recognition Psychology

Faculty of Medicine (Freshmen Enrollment: 120)

Department of Medicine

Anatomy, Anesthesiology, Bacteriology, Biochemistry, Clinical Pathology, Dermatology, Hygienics, Internal Medicine, Legal Medicine, Mental Science, Neurosurgery, Obsterics and Gynecology, Ophthalmology, Orthopedics, Otorhinolaryngology, Parasitology, Pathology, Pediatrics, Pharmacology, Physiology, Public Hygienics, Radiation Chemistry, Surgery, Urology

Faculty of Pharmacy (Freshmen Enrollment: 160)

Department of Biopharmacology

Department of Pharmacy

Biochemistry, Chemical Toxicology, Chemistry, Hygienic Chemistry, Immunochemistry, Organic Chemistry, Pharmacology, Pharmaceutical Analytical Chemistry, Pharmaceutical Synthetic Chemistry, Pharmaceutics, Pharmacognosy

Faculty of Science and Engineering (Freshmen Enrollment: 480)

Department of Machinery and Precision Engineering

Machinery, Man–Machine System, Structure, Installation, Ultra–Precision Processing

Department of Electricity and Electron Engineering

Electron Device, Electricity and Electron Circuit, Electricity and Electron Control, Computer System Engineering, Electon Material

Department of Material Science Engineering

Material Structure, System Planning, Manufacture, Processing, Estimation

Department of Information Science

Information Management, Information System, Computer Science, Programming, Nervous Information Science

Department of Bioscience

Various Subjects Connected with Life Science

Foreign Student Admission

Qualifications for Applicants

Standard Qualifications Requirement

Examination at the University

Same as for Japanese applicants.

Documents to be Submitted When Applying

Standard Documents Requirement

GRADUATE PROGRAMS

Graduate School of Economics (First Year Enrollment : Master's 15, Doctor's 3)

Division

Economics

Graduate School of Law (First Year Enrollment : Master's 15, Doctor's 3)

Division

Law

Graduate School of Literature (First Year Enrollment : Master's 20, Doctor's 10)

Divisions

English Literature, Japanese Literature

Graduate School of Medicine (First Year Enrollment : Doctor's 70)

Divisions

Clinical Medicine, Fundamental Medicine, Social Medicine

Graduate School of Pharmacology (First Year Enrollment : Master's 24, Doctor's 6)

Division

Pharmacology

Foreign Student Admission

Qualifications for Applicants

Master's Program

Standard Qualifications Requirement

Doctor's Program

Standard Qualifications Requirement

Graduate School of Medicine:

Only those who have finished two years of clinical studies after graduation from the Faculty of Medicine can apply to the Clinical Medicine Division.

Only who have acquired a medical licence can apply to the Clinical Medicine Division.

Only those who finished (are to finish) the master course of the sciences adjacent to medicine or dentistry in the graduate school other than medicine or dentistry can apply for the divisions of physiology, pathology and social medicine.

Examination at the University

Master's Program

A written and oral test.

Doctor's Program

A written and oral test (The Law Division requires an oral test only).
Documents to be Submitted When Applying
Standard Documents Requirement

*

For Further Information
Undergraduate and Graduate Admission
(General Information of Faculty of Medicine and Faculty of Science and Engineering) Entrance Examination Section, Head Office, Teikyo University, 2-11-1 Kaga, Itabashi–ku, Tokyo 173 ☎ 03-964-1211
(Economics, Law, Literature) Information Service, Teikyo University, 359 Otsuka, Hachioji-shi, Tokyo 192–03 ☎ 0426–76–8211
(Pharmacy) Information Service, Teikyo University, 1091 Suarashi, Sagamiko-cho, Tsukui-gun, Kanagawa 199–01 ☎ 04268–5–1211

Teikyo University of Technology
(Teikyo Gijutsu Kagaku Daigaku)

2289–23 Uruido, Aza Oyatsu, Ichihara–shi, Chiba
290–01 ☎ 0436–74–5511

Faculty
　Profs. 29　　Assoc. Profs 17
　Assist. Profs. Full–time 8; Part–time 11
　Res. Assocs. 4
Number of Students
　Undergrad. 1, 148
Library 40, 294 volumes

Outline and Characteristics of the University
　We are now in the midst of what Alvin Toffler called "The Third Wave", that is, a highly information-oriented era. It is often said that what has brought about Japan's prosperity today, and what is expected to further her future prosperity, is information industry, or industries based on the information sciences. But as the demand for expert engineers specializing in information is steadily increasing, the supply of qualified specialists is falling grievously short of the demand. In order to meet the urgent needs of the times, Teikyo University Group founded Teikyo University of Technology, with the Faculty of Information Sciences, in April 1987. This university is the first attempt in Japan to concentrate all fields of study related to the information sciences in one faculty.
　With programs in computer hardware, computer software, and computer management, this is an ideal school for students interested both in computers and in economics.
　The computer system, which is one of the largest in any Japanese university, is linked to networks both outside and inside the university. There are more than 180 terminals for student use.
　Emphasis is on the Acquisition of fundamental knowledge in many fields of study, as well as on the mastery of the techniques involved in running computers. Students will also be given a chance to engage in practical field work studies by visiting firms dealing with computers and network systems.
　Our curriculum is calculated to cultivate a wide range of interests in addition to practical knowledge and ability. Students may attend lectures in other Departments, thus enhancing their future career potential. We also plan to have special lectures given by scholars and informed specialists outside of the university.

UNDERGRADUATE PROGRAMS

Faculty of Informatics (Freshmen Enrollment: 440)
Department of Information Engineering
Acoustic Engineering, Bioelectrical Measurements, Communication Engineering, Communication Systems, Computer Engineering, Computer Graphics, Control Engineering, Digital Circuits, Electrical Circuits, Electrical Devices, Electrical Measurements, Electromagnetics, Electromagnetic Wave, Electronic Circuits, Electronic Devices, Electronic Measurements, Electronics, Energy Conversion Engineering, Engineering of Solid State Physics, Industrial Engineering, Information Devices, Information Engineering, Information Mathematics, Information Theory, Integrated Circuits, Management Engineering, Management Science, Mechanical Engineering, Mechatronics, Microcomputer Application, Office Automation, Optoelectronics, Patent Management, Programming, Quantum Engineering, Semiconductor Engineering, Signal Processing, Statistical Mathematics, System Engineering
Department of Information Management
Accounting, Accounting Control, Auditing, Behavioral Science, Book keeping, Business Administration, Business History, Common Subject Processing, Communication Engineering, Computer Accounting, Computer Engineering, Data Base, Econometrics, Economics, Electric Engineering, Electronics Circuits for Information, Ergonomics, Experiment Design, Finance, Financial Management, Industrial Engineering, Industrial Engineering, Industrial Location, Industrial Psychology, Information Systems, Information Theory, Labor Economy, Labor Law, Law and Information, Macroeconomics, Management, Management Control, Management Information, Marketing Research, Mass Communication, Mechatronics, Medical Information Systems, Office Automation, Operations Research, Personal Management, Production Control, Programing, Public Utilities, Regional Economics, Simulation Study, Social Information Systems, Social Psychology, Statistics, Statistics for Management, Theory of the Firm, Transportation, Urban Information Systems
Department of Information Systems
Acoustic Engineering, Applied Algebra, Applied Mathematics, Artificial Intelligence, Cognitive Engineering, Communication Systems, Compilers, Com-

puter Graphics, Control Engineering, Database Management Systems, Data Structures, Electrical Engineering, Electronic Devices, Electronic Engineering, Ergonomics, Experimental Design, Graph Theory, Industrial Engineering, Information Equipment, Information System Engineering, Information Theory, Integrated Circuits, Introduction to Computers, Logical Circuits Design, Management Science, Mathematical Statistics, Numerical Analysis, Operating System, Operations Research, Patent Management, Production Control, Programming, Programming Languages, Quantum Engineering, Semiconductor Engineering, Signal Processing, Simulation, Software Design, Software Engineering, System Engineering

Foreign Student Admission
Qualifications for Applicants
Standard Qualifications Requirement
Japanese Language Proficiency Test and General Examination for Foreign Students results. In case of failure to do so, contact the University Office before applying.
A good command of Japanese.
Examination at the University
1. The written examination: mathematics and science (either physics or chemistry).
2. The interview in Japanese.
Documents to be Submitted When Applying
Standard Documents Requirement
1. Certification of the Japanese Language Proficiency Test and General Examination for Foreign Students.
2. A Certificate of Graduation from the Japanese language
Application deadline: February 3.

*
Research Institutes and Centers
Center for information science and technology
For Further Information
Undergraduate Admission
Head of Student Division, Student Office, Teikyo University of Technology, 2289–23 Uruido, Aza Oyatsu, Ichihara–shi, Chiba 0436–74–5511 ext. 1101

Tenri University
(Tenri Daigaku)

1050 Somanouchi-cho, Tenri-shi, Nara 632
☎ 07436-3-1511

Faculty
    Profs. 78   Assoc. Profs. 52
    Assist. Profs. Full–time 37; Part–time 93
    Res. Assocs. 11
Number of Students
    Undergrad. 2, 819
Library 1, 507, 165 volumes

Outline and Characteristics of the University
The role of Tenri University is to educate those people who anticipate devoting themselves to the realization of the world of *yokigurashi* (joyous life), a world of peace and harmony, based on the Tenrikyo doctrine. In order to fulfill this role, the University upholds its purpose of education that each student develops his natural talent, enhances the level of his culture, and strengthens his faith through the study and practice of the Tenrikyo doctrine, and by personal contact with professors in a favorable environment. For the purpose of nurturing persons who will devote themselves to world salvation, special care is being taken so that every student masters a foreign language, fosters the spirit of internationalism, and acquires culture as a citizen of the world.

Tenri University aims at a type of education which develops personalities that want to devote themselves to the realization of the world of peace and harmony, based upon the doctrine of the Tenrikyo Faith. Its predecessor, Tenri School of Foreign Languages, was founded in 1925 by Shozen Nakayama, the Second Shinbashira, with the intention of educating missionaries in linguistic skills for use in religious and social work overseas. During the 63 years since then, the Institute has developed into a university with facilities of world-wide fame, such as the extensive library and the collections of the Tenri Sankokan (Folklore and Archaeological Museum). These establishments are intended to cultivate the international way of thinking among the students. Today as ever the will of the Founder is vividly alive in our conception of creating international minds with special emphasis on linguistic skills. This is the role of Tenri University.

Tenri School of Foreign Languages (coeducational) was founded in 1925, according to the Private School Act (equal to college) for the purpose of training those who anticipate engaging in overseas missions of Tenrikyo and instructed foreign languages. Tenri Foreign Language College was founded in 1927, according to the College Act, for the purpose of instructing the Tenrikyo doctrine, higher learning, and modern foreign languages to train those who anticipate engaging in overseas missions.

Tenri University was opened in 1949 for the purpose of transmitting knowledge and studying higher arts and sciences, according to the Fundamentals of Education Act and the School Education Act, and based on the Tenrikyo doctrine, to train those who will contribute to the welfare of humanity and the development of culture, and especially who anticipate engaging in world missions of Tenrikyo. It started with the Faculty of Letters and established the Faculty of Foreign Languages in 1952, and the Faculty of Physical Education in 1955. Presently it consists of the three faculties with eleven departments.

UNDERGRADUATE PROGRAMS

Faculty of Foreign Languages (Freshmen Enrollment: 340)
Department of Chinese Studies
Department of English and American Studies
Department of French Studies
Department of German Studies
Department of Indonesian Studies
Department of Korean Studies
Department of Russian Studies
Department of Spanish Studies
Faculty of Letters (Freshmen Enrollment: 100)
Department of Japanese Language and Literature
Department of Religious Studies
Faculty of Physical Education (Freshmen Enrollment: 120)
Department of Physical Education

Foreign Student Admission
Qualifications for Applicants
Standard Qualifications Requirement
Examination at the University
Selected personal documents and test results (a written and oral test). In the case of the Physical Education Department, a performance test will also be included.
Under special circumstances, the written test may be omitted.
Documents to be Submitted When Applying
Standard Documents Requirement
＊
Research Institutes and Centers
Center for Foreign Language Education and Studies, Oyasato Research Institute
For Further Information
Undergraduate Admission
Information Bureau, Tenri University, 1050 Somanouchi-cho, Tenri-shi, Nara 632
☎ 07436-3-1511 ext. 6451

Tezukayama Gakuin University
(Tezukayama Gakuin Daigaku)

1823 Imakuma 2-chome, Osakasayama-shi, Osaka 589　☎ 0723-65-0865

Faculty
Profs.　30　Assoc. Profs.　17
Assist. Profs.　Full–time　5; Part–time　92
Number of Students
Undergrad.　1, 541
Library　160, 592 volumes

Outline and Characteristics of the University
Tezukayama Gakuin was established in 1916. An elementary school was established the following year and a kindergarten the year after that. A girls'

high school was begun in 1925 and following the changes in the Japanese educational system after World War II, a six-three educational ladder was formed. By its 50th anniversary in 1966, Tezukayama consisted of a unified system of schools from kindergarten through the elementary and secondary levels to a two-year junior college for women. Tezukayama Gakuin University was established in 1966 in order to provide a complete system of education for girls, including an undergraduate degree in liberal arts. The principles and purposes for the university are the same as they have been for Tezukayama Gakuin as a whole ever since its founding—to encourage students to seek the truth, to open their eyes to the world, and to develop highly cultured women capable not only of creating their own families but also of participating fully in society and the world.

UNDERGRADUATE PROGRAMS

Faculty of Literature (Freshmen Enrollment: 400)
Department of Aesthetics and Art History
Aesthetics, Calligraphy, Drama, Eastern Art, History of Calligraphy, History of Eastern Art, History of Japanese Art, History of Japanese Civilization, History of Western Art, History of Western Civilization, Japanese Art, Musicology, Plastic Arts, Science of Art, Science of Literature, Western Art
Department of English Literature
Bible in English, Comparative Cultures, English Language, English Literature, English Phonetics, History of English Literature, Linguistics
Department of International Studies
Comparative Literature
Cultural Anthropology
Cultural History of Asia the West Japan Readings in Foreighn Cultures
　(East Asia, North America, Oceania)
Cultural Geography, Cultures throughout the World
Cultures throughout the World
International Society and Social Welfare
International Understanding
Studies in Modern Japanese
Teaching Japanese
Department of Japanese Literature
Chinese Literature, History of Japanese Literature, Japanese Grammar, Japanese Language, Japanese Literature, Japanese Novels, Modern Japanese Poetry, Studies of Japanese Literary Works (Classic, Modern)

Foreign Student Admission
Qualifications for Applicants
Standard Qualifications Requirement
Japanese Language Proficiency Test result.
Examination at the University
1.　Document Review
2.　A written examination, including a short paper in Japanese.
3.　Interview

Documents to be Submitted When Applying
Standard Documents Requirement
Certificate attesting to the applicant's ability to pay tuition and other necessary expenses is also required.

Qualifications for Transfer Students
1. Must have the same qualifications as Japanese students.
2. Must have sufficient proficiency in Japanese.
Examination for Transfer Students
University's regular entrance examination.
Documents to be Submitted When Applying
Standard Documents Requirement
Same as the procedure for undergraduate application.

*

Special Programs for Foreign Students
the Japanese language and culture
For Further Information
Undergraduate Admission
Admissions Office, Tezukayama Gakuin University, 1823 Imakuma2-chome, Osakasayama-shi, Osaka 589 ☎ 0723-65-0865 ext. 135, 136

Tezukayama University
(Tezukayama Daigaku)
7-1-1 Tezukayama, Nara–Shi, Nara 631
☎ 0742–45–4701

Faculty
　　Profs.　34　　Assoc. Profs　18
　　Assist. Profs.　Full–time　9; Part–time　78
　　Res. Assoc.　1
Number of Students
　　Undergrad.　1, 610
Library　170, 000 volumes

Outline and Characteristics of the University
Tezukayama University was founded in 1964 as a women's college to cultivate students with a deep self-awareness, insight of themselves as Japanese, and an international perspective. At the same time the founders sought to develop culture and creative students who are able to respond to the demands of the modern world. To achieve this goal, broad interdisciplinary achievement has been stressed.

It has however been necessary to change the founding educational principles and move toward the reorganization and professionalization of the contents of each major, and the improvement of the quality of education in order to respond to the increasing demands of the present society.

In response to these demands, the Faculty of Economics was established in 1987, and major changes were made in the Faculty of Liberal Arts, including the addition of a major in Information and Society, and the discontinuation of the Modern Soci-

ety and Culture major. At the same time, the university has been made coeducational.

UNDERGRADUATE PROGRAMS

Faculty of Economics (Freshmen Enrollment: 200)
　Department of Economics
Accounting, Commercial Law, Economic History, Economic Policy, Labor Economics, Macroeconomics, Microecomics, Money and Banking, Principles of Economics, Public Finance, Statistics
　Economic Information Major
Computer Accounting, Data Processing, Econometrics, Economic Forecasting, Economic Statistics, Mathematics for Economics, Time Series Analysis
　International Economics Major
Foreign Exchange, International Business Law, International Economics, International Finance, Regional Studies
Faculty of Liberal Arts (Freshmen Enrollment: 260)
　Department of Liberal Arts
British and American Society and Culture Major
English Grammar, English Linguistics, English Phonetics, Economy, Literature, History, Politics, Society & Culture of Great Britain and the United States.
International Relations Major
Comparative Culture, History of Diplomacy, Int'l Economics, Int'l Law, Int'l Politics, Int'l Relations, Occidental Society and Culture, Private International Law
Japanese Society and Culture Major
History of Japanese Culture, Archaeology, Art, Classics, Drama, Economy and Economic Thought, Folklore, History, Modern Literature, Philosophy Political Science and Political Thought of Japan
Infomation and Society Major
Constitution of Japan, Administration Law, Law of Economics, Studies on the System of Modern Society, Studies on the Family, Behavioral Science, Computer Semiotics, Modern Mass Communication, Advertisement Studies, Computer Science in General, Computer Programming

*

For Further Information
Undergraduate Admission
Admissions Office, Tezukayama University, 7–1–1 Tezukayama, Nara-shi, Nara 631 ☎ 0742–45–4701

Toho College of Music
(Toho Ongaku Daigaku)
84 Imaizumi, Kawagoe-shi, Saitama 356
☎ 0492–35–2157

Faculty
　　Profs.　14　　Assoc. Profs.　13
　　Assist. Profs.　Full–time　4; Part–time　49
Number of Students
　　Undergrad.　596　　Grad.　6

Library　27, 641 volumes

Outline and Characteristics of the College

Toho College of Music was established in 1965 in Kawagoe City, Saitama Prefecture. Originally in 1938 Toho Music School was founded on Ohtsuka Campus in Bunkyo-ku, Tokyo. It was raised to Toho Junior College of Music in 1951. Music Institute of Toho was also established in 1985 on Ohtsuka Campus. This college has two attached senior high schools (one at the Kawagoe Campus, and the other at the Ohtsuka Campus) and a Junior high school on Ohtsuka Campus.

"The development of a student into a refined person who appreciates the values of music" is one of the founding goals of this college. The most important purpose in this college is to develop the students' whole personality through musical education. This college gives the students not only techniques and knowledge on music, but also higher liberal arts education. Many graduates are fine musicians and play active roles in many districts of Japan as teachers of music. They contribute to society as sophisticated and sensible citizens.

UNDERGRADUATE PROGRAMS

Faculty of Music (Freshmen Enrollment: 100)
Department of Music
Acoustics, Aesthetics of Music, Chamber Music, Chorus, Counterpoint, Ensemble, Harmony, Keyboard Harmony, Musical Form, Music Education, Music History, Musicology, Orchestral Direction, Piano Literature, Religious Music, Sociology of Music, Solfege

Foreign Student Admission
Qualifications for Applicants
Standard Qualifications Requirement
Examination at the College
Same as for Japanese applicants. However, special consideration will be given according to the conditions of application.
Subjects of examination.
(1) Major (Performance): Piano, Voice or Orchestra, (2) Music Dictation, (3) Music Grammar, (4) Sight-singing, (5) Japanese (treatise), (6) Foreign Language (English or German), and (7) Interview.
Documents to be Submitted When Applying
Standard Documents Requirement
Application Period: January 11–28
Dates of Examinations: February 1–4
Announcement of Accepted Applicants: February 9
Period for Entrance Procedures: February 10–16

ONE-YEAR GRADUATE PROGRAMS

One-Year Graduate Course of Music (Enrollment: 10)
Composition, Instrumental Music, Vocal Music

Foreign Student Admission
Qualifications for Applicants
Standard Qualifications Requirement
Examination at the College
Same as for Japanese applicants. However, special consideration will be given according to the conditions of applications.
Subjects of examination:
Major (Performance): Piano, Voice or Orchestra, Japanese (treatise), and Interview.

*

Research Institutes and Centers
Music Institute of Toho
For Further Information
Undergraduate Admission
Admission Office (Educational Division), Toho College of Music, 84 Imaizumi, Kawagoe-shi, Saitama 356 ☎ 0492–35–2157

Toho Gakuen School of Music
(Toho Gakuen Daigaku)

1-41-1 Wakaba-cho, Chofu-shi, Tokyo 182
☎ 03-307-4101

UNDERGRADUATE PROGRAMS

Faculty of Music (Freshmen Enrollment: 150)
Department of Composition, Conducting and Musicology
Conducting, Music Composition, Musicology
Department of Music Performance
Piano Course
String Instrument Course
Vocal Music Course
Wind and Percussion Course

Tohoku College of Pharmacy
(Tohoku Yakka Daigaku)

4-4-1 Komatsushima, Sendai-shi, Miyagi 981
☎ 022–234–4181

Faculty
　　Profs.　17　　Assoc. Profs.　15
　　Assist. Profs.　Full-time　27; Part-time　30
　　Res. Assocs.　40
Number of Students
　　Undergrad.　1, 784　　Grad.　42
Library　50, 000 volumes

Outline and Characteristics of the College

The origin of the Tohoku College of Pharmacy can be traced back to the Tohoku Professional School of Pharmacy, founded by Giichi Takayanagi in 1939. Since 1917, when the Sendai Professional School of Medicine (now the Faculty of Medicine at Tohoku University) dissolved the department of pharmacy, there had been no professional school of pharmacy in the Tohoku and Hokkaido districts (the northern part of Japan). The Tohoku Professional School of Pharmacy was founded and became Tohoku College of Pharmacy in 1949, meeting the demand for establishment of a professional school of pharmacy.

Our college has achieved a remarkable expansion of facilities in a very short period of time. The Cancer Research Institute was established in 1959, and the Graduate School was founded in 1962 in order to train specialists on pharmaceutical sciences. The most recent additions to our facilities were the Radioisotope Center in 1982, and the Center for Laboratory Animal Sciences in 1984.

Tohoku College of Pharmacy was developed, based upon the principle that every professor and student should have the desire to seek after truth. The words of Takayanagi, engraved on the campus monument, reads, "Portas veritais aperiamus (Let us open the door of the truth). " This precept is the basis on which the education program at our college was founded, with mutual respect between faculty and students.

Our college is located in the northern part of Sendai. The campus is surrounded by natural beauty, particularly during springtime. Students are very comfortable with the verdant trees which can be seen everywhere on our campus. Sendai is one of the most beautiful cities in Japan. The Hirose River, running through the city, changes the scenery according to the season. This environment promotes an atmosphere ideal for academic life.

UNDERGRADUATE PROGRAMS

Faculty of Pharmaceutical Sciences (Freshmen Enrollment: 360)
  Department of Pharmacy
Medicinal Chemistry, Pharmaceuticals, Pharmacognosy, Pharmacology, Pharm-Analysis, Pharm-Chemistry, Radiopharmacy
  Department of Environmental and Hygienic Chemistry
Biological Chemistry, Environmental Hygienic Chemistry, Hygienic Chemistry, Microbiology, Nutritional Chemistry, Physiological Chemistry, Toxicology
  Department of Pharmaceutical Technochemistry
Biological Pharm-Manufacturing, Microbiological Pharm-Manufacturing, Microbiological Pharm-Manufacturing, Pharmaceutics, Pharm-Manufacturing, Pharm-Synthetic Organic Chemistry, Pharm-Technology, Physical Chemistry

GRADUATE PROGRAMS

Graduate School of Pharmaceutical Sciences (First Year Enrollment : Master's 10, Doctor's 5)
  Division
Pharmaceutical Sciences

*

Research Institutes and Centers
Cancer Research Institute, Center for Laboratory Animal Sciences, Radioisotope Center
For Further Information
  Undergraduate and Graduate Admission
Administrative Office, Instruction Division, Tohoku College of Pharmacy, 4-4-1 Komatsushima, Sendai-shi, Miyagi 983 ☎ 022-234-4181 ext. 233

Tohoku Dental University
(Tohoku Shika Daigaku)
31-1 Misumi-do, Tomita-machi, Koriyama-shi, Fukushima 963   ☎ 0249-32-8931

Faculty
  Profs. 35   Assoc. Profs. 21
  Assist. Profs. Full-time 18; Part-time 66
  Res. Assocs. 68
Number of Students
  Undergrad. 720   Grad. 19
Library   99, 870 volumes

Outline and Characteristics of the University

Tohoku Dental University was founded in 1972 as the one and only school for dentistry in the northeastern provinces of Japan, the Tohoku-Hokkaido District. At that time there were few dentists in the Tohoku District. For the purpose of making up the insufficient number of dentists, the University was opened. Its duty was to satisfy the community's dental needs. The founding spirit is to instruct advanced knowledge and techniques of dentistry and to produce humanistic dentists.

The total number of students is 720. The University has a 240, 000m^2 campus, in which many facilities promoting the students' growth in mind and body are provided, such as a 400m-track, tennis courts, a football ground, a baseball ground, an archery range, a Judo hall, a Kendo hall, a Japanese tea ceremony room (Chashitsu), and Japanese gardens.

Since 1972, for 14 years, our school has been contributing to the solution for the lack of dentists by sending 1, 266 graduates into the society. Furthermore, a Graduate School of Dentistry which aims to improve the quality of dentists has been established.

Year by year, in order to advance and develop dentistry to a higher degree, the University has been completing staff and facilities necessary for research studies. Besides the research facilities which each chair possesses, there are eight collaborative research laboratories with large-sized research facilities necessary for high level research studies. These facilities have enabled the University to further research.

As an academic research institution, there is the Tohoku Dental University Society. Publishing its journal, Journal of Tohoku Dental University, four times a year, it has facilitated progressive research. Furthermore, aiming at internationalization, the University is expanding the foreign research and educational staff.

UNDERGRADUATE PROGRAMS

Faculty of Dentistry (Freshmen Enrollment: 120)
 School of Dentistry
Crown and Bridge Prosthodontics, Dental Anaesthesiology, Dental Materials Science, Dental Pharmacology, Dental Radiology, Endodontics, Operative Dentistry, Oral Anatomy, Oral Bacteriology, Oral Biochemistry, Oral Diagnosis, Oral Histology, Oral Pathology, Oral Physiology, Oral Surgery, Oro-Maxillo-Facial Surgery, Orthodontics, Pathology, Pedodontics, Periodontology, Preventive Dentistry, Removable Prothodontics

Foreign Student Admission
 Qualifications for Applicants
  Standard Qualifications Requirement
 Examination at the University
 1. Academic Examination (in Japanese): Mathematics and one science subject (physics, chemistry, or biology)
 2. Oral Examination (in Japanese)
 3. Voluntary Composition Test (in Japanese)
 Documents to be Submitted When Applying
  Standard Documents Requirement

 Qualifications for Transfer Students
 1. Completion of Courses of General Education at the Universities where applicants were enrolled
 2. Qualifications equivalent to the above
 Examination for Transfer Students
 1. Academic examination on the subjects taken in the Courses of General Education applicants studied (in Japanese)
 2. Oral Examination (in Japanese)
 3. Voluntary Composition Test (in Japanese)
 Documents to be Submitted When Applying
  Standard Documents Requirement

GRADUATE PROGRAMS

Graduate School of Dentistry (First Year Enrollment : Doctor's 19)
 Divisions
Dental Anaesthesiology, Dental Materials Science, Dental Pharmacology, Dental Radiology, Operative Dentistry, Oral Anatomy, Oral Bacteriology, Oral Biochemistry, Oral Pathology, Oral Physiology, Oral Surgery, Orthodontics, Preventive Dentistry, Prothodontics

Foreign Student Admission
 Qualifications for Applicants
Doctor's Program
  Standard Qualifications Requirement
 Examination at the University
Doctor's Program
 1. Academic Examination on the subjects to be taken in the program by applicants (in Japanese)
 2. Oral Examination (in Japanese)
 Documents to be Submitted When Applying
  Standard Documents Requirement
  　　　　　*
For Further Information
 Undergraduate and Graduate Admission
Head of Educational Affairs, Educational Division, Tohoku Dental University, 31–1 Misumi-do, Tomita-machi, Koriyama-shi, Fukushima 963 ☎ 0249–32–8931 ext. 439

Tohoku Fukushi University
(Tohoku Fukushi Daigaku)

1–8–1 Kunimi, Sendai-shi, Miyagi 981
☎ 022–233–3111

Faculty
　Profs. 41　　Assoc. Profs. 25
　Assist. Profs. Full–time 5; Part–time 79
　Res. Assocs. 8
Number of Students
　Undergrad. 4, 089　　Grad. 16
Library 124, 180 volumes

Outline and Characteristics of the University

Tohoku Fukushi University was established as the Tohoku Fukushi Junior College in 1958. The Junior College was raised to the status of university in 1962, and the Graduate School was established in 1976. Presently the University is comprised of the Faculty of Social Welfare and the Graduate School of Social Welfare.

Traditionary the University has a spirit of education regarding "fukushi" in Japanese which means "welfare" or "human service" in English. The spirit is rooted in Zen and human nature.

University campuses are located on the stretch of hills in the northwestern part of Sendai City. On the Main Campus, there are The Administration Building, the Library, the Fukujuden Auditorium which doubles as a gymnasium and a student hall, lecture halls and research laboratories, and others.

Two other campuses are well equipped as athletic institutions. There is a large all-weather gymnasium and multi-purpose ball-game ground on the Second Campus, and a baseball park, an athletic field and tennis courts on the Third Campus.

A proverb saying "a sound mind in a sound

body" is also an important guiding principle for students. Curriculums of the University are emphasized on human relations and social welfare. These are so unique in comparison with other universities in Japan that students come from every part of the country to study here.

UNDERGRADUATE PROGRAMS

Faculty of Social Welfare (Freshmen Enrollment: 600)
Department of Industrial Welfare
Food Chemistry, Food Sanitation, Industrial Welfare (Relation between Industry and Welfare, Labor Administration)
Department of Social Education
Institutions for Social Education, Life-long Education
Department of Social Welfare
Practical Social Welfare (Social Work, Casework, Community Organization), Social Welfare Administration (Social Policy, Social Legislation)
Department of Welfare Psychology
Counseling, Developmental Psychology, Psychology of the Handicapped

Foreign Student Admission
Qualifications for Applicants
Standard Qualifications Requirement
The system of admitting students into the University upon recommendation of a high school principal:
The letter of recommendation should meet the qualifications mentioned below:
1. A student who has joined activities of sports or cultural clubs, and produces excellent results in athletic meets or contests held at the regional or national level.
2. A student who has joined social welfare activities on a voluntary or extramural basis, and obtained satisfactory results.
3. A student who achieves remarkable deeds individually.
Examination at the University
Screening of the personal histories and individual interview.
Documents to be Submitted When Applying
Standard Documents Requirement

Qualifications for Transfer Students
1. A student who has finished an academic course of not less than 14 years or with attainments equal or higher than the former.
2. A student who has graduated from a university or left a university before graduation.
Examination for Transfer Students
Screening of the personal histories and individual interview.
Documents to be Submitted When Applying
Standard Documents Requirement

GRADUATE PROGRAMS

Graduate School of Social Welfare (First Year Enrollment : Master's 10)
Division
Social Welfare

Foreign Student Admission
Qualifications for Applicants
Master's Program
Standard Qualifications Requirement
Examination at the University
Master's Program
The University gives examinations in subjects connected with Social Welfare as mentioned below:
1. A thesis examination.
2. A written examination in a foreign language (English, German or French).
3. Individual interview.
Documents to be Submitted When Applying
Standard Documents Requirement

*

Research Institutes and Centers
Research Institute for Administration, Research Institute for Buddhist Social Education, Research Institute for Buddhist Social Welfare
Facilities/Services for Foreign Students
The University Club Seminar House, a 10 minute walk from the Main Campus, offers living quarters for foreign students.
For Further Information
Undergraduate Admission
Entrance Examination Office, Information Division of Planning and Development Department, Tohoku Fukushi University, 1-8-1 Kunimi, Sendai-shi, Miyagi 981 ☎ 022-233-3111 ext. 225
Graduate Admission
Secretariat of the Graduate School, Student Office, Tohoku Fukushi University, 1-8-1 Kunimi, Sendai-shi, Miyagi 981 ☎ 022-233-3111 ext. 211

Tohoku Gakuin University
(Tohoku Gakuin Daigaku)

1-3-1 Tsuchitoi, Sendai-shi, Miyagi 980
☎ 022-264-6411

Faculty
    Profs. 163   Assoc. Profs. 92
    Assist. Profs. Full-time 58; Part-time 108
    Res. Assocs. 7
Number of Students
    Undergrad. 12, 428   Grad. 51
Library 438, 242 volumes

Outline and Characteristics of the University
Tohoku Gakuin University is a century-old institution, affiliated with the United Church of Christ in

Japan. The University was founded in 1886 with six young men as the Sendai Theological Seminary by Masayoshi Oshikawa, one of the first Protestants in Japan, and William E. Hoy, a pioneer missionary of the (German) Reformed Church in the United States. A Preparatory Department was added, and the name changed to Tohoku Gakuin, North Japan College, in 1891. Through continued growth and organizational changes, the school became firmly established as one of the leading Christian schools in the country. After World War II the College became co-educational and in 1949 the institution was expanded into a university.

On the basis of Christianity, Tohoku Gakuin University seeks to provide students with a deep understanding of the spirit of self-sacrifice and feeling of awe toward God, enriching their personalities and intelligence and helping them devote themselves to the welfare of humankind and society. As an expression of the founding spirit, chapel service is held every morning and is attended by both students and school personnel.

Tohoku Gakuin University offers the Bachelor of Arts degree in English, Theology, History, Economics, Commerce, Law, and Liberal Arts and the Bachelor of Science degree in Mechanical Engineering, Electrical Engineering, Applied Physics, and Civil Engineering. The evening school offers the Bachelor of Arts degree in English and Economics. Graduate degrees (M. A., M. S. and Ph. D.) are awarded in English Literature, Linguistics, Economics, Law, Mechanical Engineering, Electrical Engineering, and Applied Physics. In order to facilitate the research of faculty members and students, the University has established institutes for the collection and dissemination of research materials. The new Library of the University was completed in 1984.

The central administrative offices and the university humanities departments for juniors and seniors are located on the 12-acre Tsuchitoi campus near downtown Sendai. The School of Engineering is located on a 29-acre campus in Tagajo about 13 kilometers east of the center of Sendai. The faculty of Liberal Arts, newly established in 1989, is located on a 67-acre campus in Izumi, a northern suburb of Sendai, where all freshman and Sophomores study.

Tohoku Gakuin University is located in Sendai, approximately 350 kilometers (about 217 miles) north of Tokyo, near the Pacific Ocean. Sendai is the capital, of Miyagi Prefecture, with a population of nearly 700, 000, and is the economic and cultural center of northern Japan. It is called "mori no miyako", the city of trees, and recent beautification projects have made it worthy of the name. The JR bullet train links Sendai to Tokyo with a less than two hour ride.

The current university student body is 12, 479. Students come primarily from northern Honshu, but some come from as far south as Okinawa and as far north as Hokkaido. Tohoku Gakuin University is the largest private university in northern Japan and its alumni are active throughout the country and around the world.

The University offers educational exchange programs in collaboration with two sister schools, Ursinus College and Franklin And Marshall College in U. S. A.

UNDERGRADUATE PROGRAMS

Faculty of Economics (Freshmen Enrollment: 700)
Department of Commerce
Accounting, Auditing, Bookkeeping, Cost Accounting, Financial Management, Financial Statement Analysis, Insurance, International Trade, Labor Management, Management, Management Accounting, Marketing, Merchandizing, Operations Research, Organizational Administration, Production Management, Survey of Business, Transportation
Department of Economics
Economic History, Economic Policy, Economics of Agriculture, Economics of Manufacturing Industry, Economics of Small and Medium Business, Economics of Transportation, Economic Statistics, Economic Theory and Analysis, History of Economic Thought, Industrial Organization, International Economics, Japanese Economy, Mathematics for Economics, Money and Banking, National Economic Accounts, Political Economy, Public Economics, Public Finance, Social Policy, Social Security, Tohoku District Economy
Faculty of Economics (**Evening School**) (Freshmen Enrollment 300)
Department of Economics
Accounting, Economic History, Economic Policy, Economics of Agriculture, Economics of Manufacturing Industry, Economics of Small and Medium Business, Economics of Transportation, Economic Statistics, General Economic Theory, History of Capitalism, History of Economic Thoughts, International Economics, Japanese Economic History, Japanese Economy, Management, Marketing, Money and Banking, National Accounts, Public Finance, Social Policy, Social Security
Faculty of Engineering (Freshmen Enrollment: 440)
Department of Applied Physics
Applied Mathematics, Computer Science, Fabrication of Optical Aspherical Surface, High Energy Physics, Magnetic Semiconductors, Metallurgical Engineering, Physical Chemistry, Physical Optics, Physics and Applications of Magnetic Materials, Quantum Electronics, Theoretical Physics, X-ray Crystallography
Department of Civil Engineering
Aseismatic Engineering, Bridge Engineering, Concrete and Reinforced Concrete Engineering, Highway, Railway and Transportation Engineering, Hydraulics, River, Dam and Harbour Engineering, Soil Mechanics, Structural Mechanics, Tunnel and Explosives Engineering, Water Supply, Sewerage and Sani-

tary Engineering

Department of Electrical Engineering

Electrical Machines, Electro-Magnetic Compatibility, Electronic Computers, Electronic Transducers and Systems, Engineering of Electric Power Transmission and Distribution, Engineering of Power Generation and Plants, High Voltage Engineering, Physics and Technology of Semiconductors, Power Application Engineering, Radio Communication Engineering, Telecommunication Engineering, Wire Communication Engineering

Department of Mechanical Engineering

Aeronautical Aerospace Engineering, Dynamics of Machines, Engineering Materials for Machinery, Engineering Thermodynamics, Fluid Mechanics, Fracture Mechanics, Heat Transfer Engineering, Hydraulic Machinery, Internal Combustion Engines, Machine Design, Manufacturing Processing, Mechanics of Machinery, Mechanics of Materials, Pneumatic Machinery, Steam Power Engineering, Theory of Plasticity

Faculty of English (**Evening School**) (Freshmen Enrollment: 50)

Department of English

Christian Literature, Criticism of English and American Literature, English and American Literature, English Bible, English Philology, English Phonetics, History of American Literature, History of English Literature, Linguistics, Modern English and American Drama, Shakespeare

Faculty of Law (Freshmen Enrollment: 300)

Department of Law

Anglo-American Law, Civil Law, Constitutional Law, Criminal Law, Criminal Policy, French Law, German Law, History of Legal Thought, International Law, Labor Law, Law of Civil Procedure, Law of Criminal Procedure, Philosophy of Law, Political Science

Faculty of Letters (Freshmen Enrollment: 510)

Department of Christian Studies (*Theology*)

Christian Education, Christian Ethics, Comparative Religions, Dogmatics, Greek New Testament, History of Christianity, History of Religions, Homiletics, New Testament, Old Testament, Pastoral Psychology, Pastoral Theology, Philosophy of Religion, Practical Theology, Survey of Theology

Department of English

Christian Literature, Criticism of English and American Literature, English and American Literature, English Bible, English Philology, English Phonetics, History of American Literature, History of English Language, History of English Literature, Linguistics, Modern English and American Drama, Shakespeare

Department of History

Archaeology, Cartography, Cultural History, Folklore, Historiography, History of Christianity, Human Geography, Industrial Geography, Japanese History, Oriental History, Paleography, Physical Geography, Political Geography, Regional Geography, Regional Survey, Western History

Faculty of Liberal Arts (Freshman Enrollment: 200)

Foreign Student Admission

Qualifications for Applicants

Standard Qualifications Requirement

The Japanese Language Proficiency Test and the General Examination for Foreign Students results.

Examination at the College

A written examination.

A foreign applicant may be accepted as a special student on the basis of a written examination provided by the University.

School regulations applied to a regular student are applicable to such a student, except those especially established for a foreign student.

Documents to be Submitted When Applying

Standard Documents Requirement

1. A copy of birth certificate.
2. Letters of two guarantors who reside in Japan. (One of them must be a resident in or near Sendai.)

Same procedure as a Japanese student

GRADUATE PROGRAMS

Research Division in Economics (First Year Enrollment : Master's 5, Doctor's 2)

Division

Economics

Research Division in Engineering (First Year Enrollment : Master's 15, Doctor's 6)

Divisions

Applied Physics, Electrical Engineering, Mechanical Engineering

Research Division in Law (First Year Enrollment : Master's 10, Doctor's 2)

Division

Law

Research Division in Letters (First Year Enrollment : Master's 10, Doctor's 3)

Division

English Language and Literature

Foreign Student Admission

Qualifications for Applicants

Master's Program

Standard Qualifications Requirement

Doctor's Program

Standard Qualifications Requirement

Examination at the University

Master's Program

A foreign applicant may be admitted through a written examination conducted by the Research Division Committee in consultation with the Graduate School Committee.

Doctor's Program

Same as Master's program.

Documents to be Submitted When Applying

Standard Documents Requirement

Research Institutes and Centers
Audio-Visual Center, Counseling Center, Institute for Business and Management, Institute for Christian Studies, Institute for Educational Research, Institute for Engineering of Environmental Protection, Institute for English Language and Literature, Institute for General Education, Institute for Sacred Music, Institute for Social Welfare, Institute for Tohoku (North Japan) Culture, Institute for Tohoku (North Japan) Economy

Special Programs for Foreign Students
Japanese Studies Program:

A five-week course from late May through June. The Program intends to provide students with an introduction to Japanese history, culture, language, society and economics for the purpose of developing an understanding of contemporary Japan. The course comprises three weeks of Japanese language instruction and lecture series under the course title, "Japan's Modernization; Succession or Negation of Tradition? " In general, the course is conducted in English and followed by travel in Japan for two weeks.

For Further Information
Undergraduate Admission
Office of Academic Affairs, Tohoku Gakuin University, 1-3-1 Tsuchitoi, Sendai-shi, Miyagi 980 ☎ 022–264-6455

Graduate Admission
Office of the Graduate School, Tohoku Gakuin University, 1-3-1 Tsuchitoi, Sendai-shi, Miyagi 980 ☎ 022–266-4669

General
International Center Office, Tohoku Gakuin University, 1-3-1 Tsuchitoi, Sendai-shi, Miyagi 980

Tohoku Institute of Technology
(Tohoku Kogyo Daigaku)

35-1 Yagiyama-kasumicho, Sendai-shi, Miyagi 982
☎ 022–229-1151

Faculty
    Profs. 49   Assoc. Profs. 50
    Assist. Profs. Full–time 17; Part–time 75
    Res. Assocs. 59
Number of Students
    Undergrad. 3, 344
Library 111, 770 volumes

Outline and Characteristics of the University
Tohoku Institute of Technology (T. I. T.) was founded in 1964. At that time, T. I. T. consisted of two departments: the Department of Communication Engineering and the Department of Electronics. The Department of Architecture was added two years later in 1966. In 1967, the Department of Civil Engineering and the Department of Industrial Design were added.

T. I. T. aims to prepare engineers who have both a thorough grounding in the humanities and a high level of technical knowledge to meet the needs of our rapidly developing information industrial society. Each academic year, 560 students are accepted. The majority of them are from the Tohoku area but others come from every part of Japan. A few foreign students are accepted.

The campus is located in a hilly region near the center of the city of Sendai. The city of Sendai (population 700, 000) is the largest in the Tohoku area with a long history of local culture, commerce and tourism. And it is often called "verdant Sendai" because of its many trees, parks and surrounding hills. Sendai is also home to a wide variety of technical schools, colleges, and universities.

The natural beauty of Sendai makes for a tranquil and comfortable environment which residents and students alike enjoy.

Being small in size, T. I. T. has the advantage of maintaining friendly relationships between professors and students.

UNDERGRADUATE PROGRAMS

Faculty of Engineering (Freshmen Enrollment: 560)
    Department of Architecture
Architectural Planning and Design, Building Materials, Building Structures, Construction (Program and Management), Disaster Prevention of Buildings, Environmental Engineering of Architecture, History of Architecture, Reinforced Concrete Construction, Structural Mechanics, Urban Planning
    Department of Civil Engineering
Concrete & Reinforced Concrete, Earthquake Engineering, Engineering Materials, Execution of Works, Hydraulic Engineering, Sanitary Engineering, Soil Engineering, Steel Structures, Structural Mechanics, Traffic Engineering
    Department of Communication Engineering
Acoustics Engineering, Apparatus of Communications, Communication Theory, Computer Engineering, Data Communications, Electromaganetic Wave Engineering, Information Theory, Information Transmission Engineering, System Engineering, System of Communications
    Department of Electronics
Applied Electronic Measurements, Biomedical Electronics, Electron Devices, Electronic Circuits, Electronics Control Engineering, Fundamentals of Electronics, Quantum Electronics, Semiconductor Devices, Sensor Engineering, Solid State Physics
    Department of Industrial Design
Color Science, Engineering Mechanism, History of Industrial Technology, Human Engineering, Industrial Design, Internal Environments, Materials Science, Product Design, Space Design, Visual Design

Foreign Student Admission
Qualifications for Applicants

Standard Qualifications Requirement
Examination at the University
Japanese language proficiency test by way of an interview in the year of application, general examination for foreign students (Science, Mathematics, English) conducted by T. I. T. Date: mid-February.
Documents to be Submitted When Applying
Standard Documents Requirement
1. A letter of recommemdation by the embassy or legation in Japan of the country concerned, or by an organization deemed proper by T. I. T.
2. A certificate of permission (where applicable) to leave the country concerned, to study abroad.

∗

Research Institutes and Centers
Informatics Laboratory
Facilities/Services for Foreign Students
Male Students' Dormitory of T. I. T. is available.
For Further Information
Undergraduate Admission
Educational Affairs Division, Tohoku Institute of Technology, 35-1 Yagiyama-kasumicho, Sendai-shi, Miyagi 982 ☎ 022–229–1151 ext. 304

Tohoku Living Culture College
(Tohoku Seikatsu Bunka Daigaku)

1–18 Nijinooka, Sendai-shi, Miyagi 980
☎ 022–272–7511

Faculty
Profs. 11   Assoc. Profs. 7
Assist. Profs. Full–time 14; Part–time 33
Number of Students
Undergrad. 321
Library 49, 879 volumes

Outline and Characteristics of the College
The college was founded in 1958 in Sendai City, and it aims to carry out research and educational activities to contribute to the development of the discipline.

The Faculty of Domestic Science consists of two departments: Domestic Science and Living Art. The Department of Domestic Science aims to prepare students for professions which require well-developed knowledge and creativity to meet the demand of society. In the Department of Living Art, they emphasize the learning of fundamental theory and practice of art. The students pursue and create the beauty in many fields such as painting, prints, woodwork, design, ceramic art, dyeing, textile, stained glass, and mosaic.

From Tokyo northward, there is no college except this institution with a four year course on Living Art. Being small in size the college has the advantage

of maintaining intimate relationships between teachers and students.

UNDERGRADUATE PROGRAMS

Faculty of Domestic Science (Freshmen Enrollment: 100)
Department of Domestic Sciecne
Department of Living Art

For Further Information
Undergraduate Admission
Instruction Department, Tohoku Living Culture College, 1–18 Nijinooka, Sendai-shi, Miyagi 980 ☎ 022–272–7511 ext. 281

Tohoku Women's College
(Tohoku Joshi Daigaku)

1–2–1 Toyohara, Hirosaki-shi, Aomori 036
☎ 0172–33–2289

Faculty
Profs. 15   Assoc. Profs. 12
Assist. Profs. Full–time 5; Part–time 44
Res. Assocs. 5
Number of Students
Undergrad. 528
Library 26, 679 volumes

Outline and Characteristics of the College
Shibata Gakuen was founded in 1923 by Yasu Shibata. Since then, the College's motto has been, "Practice education in everyday living." Based on this ideal, the College's field of education has been broadened to include a junior college, a school of dietetics, a girls' high school, and a kindergarten. The founder's zeal for education was inherited by her eldest daughter, Toshi Imamura, under whose guidance Tohoku Women's College was founded in 1969.

Tohoku Women's College has one faculty, the Faculty of Home Economics, which is divided into the Department of Living Science and the Department of Child Science. The College's aim has been to train the students so they may become able women leaders of the future, as well as having the wide range of cultural knowledge required of housewives and mothers in their homes. This is the role that the College has undertaken and fulfilled until the present day.

History has shown that man is most evidently a creative being when he is involved in the improvement of everyday living. When observed from this point of view, the College's educational ideals place it at the starting point of human development. That is, the College holds that education should not merely result in an accumulation of knowledge, but that it should be examined and vitalized by a spontaneous interest and innovation in the practice of everyday living.

This is the spirit that appears in the motto that the founders have strictly adhered to while living alongside the students. It means, "Everyday Living is Education." This spirit has survived the test of time, and has become established in every facet of life at Tohoku Women's College.

UNDERGRADUATE PROGRAMS

Faculty of Home Economics (Freshmen Enrollment: 120)

Department of Child Science
Child Culture, Child Education, Child Literature, Child Mental Hygiene, Child Psychology, Child Sociology, Child Welfare, Education of Handicapped Children, Moral Education, Pedagogy, Social Welfare, Training Course for Kindergarten Teachers, Training Course for Primary School Teachers

Department of Living Science
Arrangement of Clothing, Clothing Design, Clothing Science, Dyeing, Family Relationships, Food Chemistry, Food Hygiene, Food Processing and Preservation, Food Science, Health Education, Home Economics Education, Home Management, Nutritional Biochemistry and Physiology, Nutrition and Food Chemistry, Nutrition Science, Public Hygiene, Textile Materials, Theory of Housing, Training Course for Dietitians, Training Course for High School Teachers of Home Economics

*
For Further Information
Undergraduate Admission
Admissions Section, Instruction Division, Tohoku Women's College, 1-2-1 Toyohara, Hirosaki-shi, Aomori 036 ☎ 0172-33-2289

Toho University
(Toho Daigaku)

5-21-16 Omori Nishi, Ota-ku, Tokyo 143
☎ 03-762-4151

Faculty
  Profs. 111   Assoc. Profs. 93
  Assist. Profs. Full-time 107; Part-time 168
  Res. Assocs. 418
Number of Students
  Undergrad. 2, 945   Grad. 130
Library 217, 239 volumes

Outline and Characteristics of the University

The history of Toho University begins in 1925, when it was founded by the brothers Yutaka and Susumu Nukada as Teikoku Igaku-Yakugaku Senmon Gakko (Imperial Medical and Pharmaceutical College for Women). The educational standards for women in those days were generally not high, especially in the scientific fields such as medicine and

pharmacology. The appeal to establish such a school was answered by the University to meet the needs of the times.

The school performed an important role as a forerunner in the field of higher education in science for women and established a good public reputation. After the educational system was reformed in 1950, the school became a coeducational institution called Toho University which consisted of three faculties: the School of Medicine (Department of Medicine), the School of Pharmaceutical Science (Departments of Pharmaceutics and Hygienic Pharmaceutics), and the Faculty of Science (Departments of Chemistry, Physics, and Biology). The University focuses on thorough education in small groups. The school advocates "Nature, Life and Humanity" as its educational motto, which was the founder's own philosophy in the pioneering days of the school.

The medical school is located in the Omori district of Tokyo and has two training hospitals, one in Omori and the other in Ohashi. The School of Pharmaceutical Sciences and the Faculty of Science are located near Tokyo in Funabashi City, Chiba Prefecture, offering the students a spacious campus and pleasant natural surroundings. The Graduate School of Medicine, of Pharmaceutical Science, and of Physical Science offer master's and doctoral programs.

UNDERGRADUATE PROGRAMS

School of Medicine (Freshmen Enrollment: 100)
Department of Medicine
Anatomy, Anesthesiology, Biochemistry, Clinical Physiology, Dermatology, Diabetes, Hospital Administration, Hygiene, Immunology, Internal Medicine, Legal Medicine, Microbiology, Molecular Biology, Neonatology, Nephrology, Neurosurgery, Obstetrics and Gynecology, Ophthalmology, Oral Surgery, Orthopedics, Otorhinolaryngology, Pathology, Pediatrics, Pharmacology, Physiology, Psychiarty, Psychosomatic Medicine, Public Hygiene, Radiology, Surgery, Thoracic and Cardiovascular Surgery, Urology

School of Pharmaceutical Sciences (Freshmen Enrollment: 220)
Department of Hygienic Pharmaceutics
Analytical Chemistry, Biochemistry, Chemical Hygiene, Clinical Chemistry, Microbiology, Public Health

Department of Pharmaceutics
Pharmaceutical Chemistry, Pharmaceutical Technochemistry, Pharmacognosy, Pharmacokinetics, Pharmacology, Pharmacy, Physical Analytical Chemistry

Faculty of Science (Freshmen Enrollment: 260)
Department of Biology
Biochemistry, Biophysics, Developmental Biology, Ecology, Marine Biology, Physiological Chemistry, Physiology, Taxonomy and Cytology

Department of Biomolecular Science

Bioorganic Chemistry, Biophysical Chemistry, Cell Biology, Molecular Animal Physiology, Molecular Biology, Molecular Plant Physiology

Department of Chemistry

Analytical Chemistry, Applied Chemistry, Biochemistry, Envionmental Chemistry, Inorganic Chemistry, Organic Chemistry, Physical Chemistry

Department of Information Science

Communication and Control, Computer Science, Information Processing

Department of Physics

Combustion Science, Condensed matter State Physics, Fundamental Physics, Physics of Magnetic Preperties Quantum Electronics, Surface Physics

GRADUATE PROGRAMS

Graduate School of Medicine (First Year Enrollment : Doctor's 23)

Divisions

Internal Medicine, Pathology, Physiology, Social Medicine, Surgery

Graduate School of Pharmaceutical Sciences (First Year Enrollment : Master's 18, Doctor's 5)

Division

Clinical Pharmacy

Graduate School of Physical Science (First Year Enrollment : Master's 18, Doctor's 9)

Divisions

Biology, Chemistry, Physics

Foreign Student Admission

Qualifications for Applicants

Master's Program

Standard Qualifications Requirement

Doctor's Program

Standard Qualifications Requirement

Examination at the University

Master's Program

1. Test of the major subjects: Among the 14 test subjects listed below, applicants may choose eight of them.

   Analytical Medical Chemistry, Analytical Pharmaceutical Chemistry, Biochemistry, Chemical Hygiene, Chemistry of Drugs, Environmental Hygiene, Materia Medica, Micro-biochemistry, Pharmaceutical Chemistry, Pharmacognosy, Pharmacokinetics, Pharmacology, Pharmacy, Synthetic Chemistry.

2. Foreign Language Test: Applicants may choose German or French in addition to English.

3. Oral Examination.

Doctor's Program

1. Test of the major subjects.

   For Chemistry course: An essay and an oral examination.

   For Biology course: An oral examination on the applicant's Master's thesis.

2. Foreign Language Test: Applicants may choose German or French in addtion to English.

Documents to be Submitted When Applying

Standard Documents Requirement

Chosasho (Information of the applicant's health, extracurricular activities, etc.).

An applicant who is employed by someone must obtain certification of permission for application from the director of the organization.

*

For Further Information

Undergraduate Admission

Administrative Office, Toho University, 5-21-16 Omori Nishi, Ota-ku, Tokyo 143 ☎ 03-762-4151 ext. 2122

Graduate Admission

Graduate School of Medicine: Administrative Office, Toho University, 5-21-16 Omori Nishi, Ota-ku, Tokyo 143 ☎ 03-762-4151 ext. 2212

Graduate School of Parmaceutical Sciences: Administrative Office, Toho University, 2-2-1 Miyama, Funabashi-shi, Chiba 274 ☎ 0474-72-1141

Graduate School of Physical Science: Administrative Office, Toho University, 2-2-1 Miyama, Funabashi-shi, Chiba 274 ☎ 0474-72-1141

Toin University of Yokohama
(Toin Gakuen Yokohama Daigaku)

1614 Kurogane-cho, Midori-ku, Yokohama-shi, Kanagawa 227 ☎ 045-972-5881

Faculty

Profs. 14   Assoc. Profs. 7

Assist. Profs. Full-time 4; Part-time 5

Res. Assoc. 1

Number of Students

Undergrad. 177

Library 10, 090 volumes

Outline and Characteristics of the University

This private university was established in April, 1988, as part of the Toin Gakuen, an educational institution, in the city of Yokohama. The Toin Gakuen, with its four-point program of "Liberty, Learning, Integrity, and Loyalty" had long been playing a significant educational role, both regional and national, in all its levels extending from kindergarten to senior high school.

The University, in further pursuit of these principles, aims at training young individuals for the international community of science and engineering in the coming new age. To achieve this goal, special curricular emphasis is placed on the theory and application of high technology, on a broad awareness of human affairs, and on intensive, practical language training.

The University currently has one faculty, the

Faculty of Engineering, and plans to expand further. The Faculty consists of two departments: Control and Systems Engineering and Materials Science and Technology. The Department of Control and Systems Enginerring offers courses on a new integrated, interdisciplinary basis, covering the fields of mechanical, electrical/electronic, and computer engineering; the Department of Materials Science and Technology, on the same basis, provides courses designed for research and development of new materials both organic and inorganic, including those that are biologically active.

The University enjoys abundant greenery on its campus on a hill north of the historic Port of Yokahama, well within commuting distance from Yokohama and Tokyo.

UNDERGRADUATE PROGRAMS

Faculty of Engineering (Freshmen Enrollment: 150)
Department of Control and Systems Engineering
Control Analysis, Control Synthesis, Electronics and Control, Information and Control
Department of Materials Science and Technology
Bio-Active Materials, Inorganic Materials and Ceramics, Organic Materials and Polymers, Structure of Materials

Foreign Student Admission
Documents to be Submitted When Applying
Standard Documents Requirement
Inguiries should be made at the University Admissions Office.
For Further Information
Undergraduate Admission
Admission Office, Toin University of Yokohama, 1614 Kurogane-cho, Midori-ku, Yokohama-shi, Kanagawa 227 ☎ 045-972-5881

Tokai University
(Tokai Daigaku)

2-28 Tomigaya, Shibuya-ku, Tokyo 151
☎ 03-467-2211

Faculty
Profs.   597   Assoc. Profs.   342
Assist. Profs.   Full–time   238; Part–time   797
Res. Assocs.   177
Number of Students
Undergrad.   29, 738   Grad.   656
Library   1, 115, 467 volumes

Outline and Characteristics of the University
Tokai University was founded by the current president, Shigeyoshi Matsumae, as the College of Aeronautical Science in 1943. The following year, the College of Electric Waves was also founded, and in 1945, these two colleges were brought together to become the Tokai College of Science. In 1946, the college was recognized as a university by the Ministry of Education, and the name was changed to Tokai University, which was made up of the School of Economics and Humanities, and the School of Science and Technology.

Since its founding, the university has established the School of Engineering, School of Letters, School of Marine Science and Technology, School of Science, School of Political Science and Economics, School of Physical Education, School of Humanities and Culture, School of Medicine, and School of Law, and has grown to become a comprehensive university with seven campuses.

Education at Tokai University aims to develop Well–rounded individuals. The university was founded on the spirit of contributing to the development of a civilization based on humanism, peace, and harmony.

Tokai University's reputation for international activities is among the most impressive in Japan. The University is proud to have several centers and Schools abroad: Tokai University European Center in Denmark, Tokai University Matsumae Budo Center in Austria, Tokai University Boarding School in Denmark

Tokai University has broad academic exchanges with more than 25 universities in Asia, Europe, and the United States, and has had academic exchanges of students, professors, and researchers. Furthermore, the university has been a host to a number of international symposia.

Tokai University has two research and training vessels of which one is used to conduct an overseas educational cruise every year. It has made 20 cruises so far and has contributed greatly to international exchange among students of universities from many parts of the world.

UNDERGRADUATE PROGRAMS

School of Engineering (Freshmen Enrollment: 2, 200)
Department of Aeronautics and Astronautics
Department of Applied Physics
Department of Architectural Engineering
Department of Civil Engineering
Department of Communications Engineering
Department of Control Engineering
Department of Electrical Engineering
Department of Electronics
Department of Electron Optics
Department of Industrial Chemistry
Department of Management Engineering
Department of Metallurgical Engineering
Department of Nuclear Engineering
Department of Precision Mechanics
Department of Prime Mover Engineering
Department of Production Engineering
School of Engineering (**Evening Course**) (Freshmen

Enrollment: 160)
Department of Construction Engineering
Architectural Engineering
Department of Electrical Engineering
Communications Engineering, Electrical Engineering
Department of Mechanical Engineering
School of Humanities and Culture (Freshmen Enrollment: 320)
Department of Arts
Design, Fine Arts, Music
Department of Human Development
Human Welfare Economics, Resources and Environment Science
Department of International Studies
School of Law (Freshmen Enrollment: 300)
Department of Law
School of Letters (Freshmen Enrollment: 850)
Department of Civilization
Asian Studies (Japan, East Asia, South Asia, West Asia), European Studies (Eastern Europe, Western Europe)
Department of English Literature
Department of History
Archaeology, Japanese History, Occidental History, Oriental History
Department of Japanese Literature
Department of Mass Communication
Information Sociology, Mass Media
Department of Nordic Studies
School of Marine Science and Technology (Freshmen Enrollment: 760)
Department of Fisheries
Aquaculture, Resources Exploitation
Department of Marine Civil Engineering
Department of Marine Electronics
Department of Marine Mineral Resources
Department of Marine Science
Department of Nautical Engineering
Department of Naval Architecture
School of Medicine (Freshmen Enrollment: 100)
Department of Medicine
Anatomy, Anesthesiology, Biochemistry, Biomedical Engineering, Cell Biology, Cellular Information Science, Clinical Pathology, Dermatology, DNA Biology, Environmental Medicine and Occupational Health, Health Development, Hospital and Health Care Administration, Immunology, Legal Medicine, Medicine, Microbiology, Molecular Biology, Neurosurgery, Obstetrics and Gynecology, Ophthalmology, Oral Surgery, Orthopedic Surgery, Otorhinolaryngology, Parasitology, Pathology, Pediatrics, Pharmacology, Physiology, Plastic and Reconstuctive Surgery, Psychiatry and Behavioral Science, Public Health, Radiology, Rehabilitation, Surgery, Transplantation, Urology
School of Physical Education (Freshmen Enrollment: 280)
Department of Judo and Kendo
Department of Physical Education

Department of Physical Recreation
School of Political Science and Economics (Freshmen Enrollment: 450)
Department of Business Administration
Department of Economics
Economics, Mathematical Economics
Department of Political Science
Local Government, Political Science
School of Science (Freshmen Enrollment: 320)
Department of Chemistry
Department of Mathematics
Department of Mathematics and Computer Science
Department of Physics

Foreign Student Admission
Qualifications for Applicants
Standard Qualifications Requirement
Enrollment in the Evening Course, School of Engineering is not open to foriegn students.
Examination at the University
Written examinations, and an interview. Date: in early–February.
Subjects:
1. Schools of Letters, Political Science and Economics, Law, Humanities and Culture (except Resources and Environmental Science), Physical Education: Japanese, Japanese Culture and History, and English.
    (Applicants to the School of Political Science and Economics, Department of Mathematical Economics must take an examination in Mathematics in place of Japanese Culture and History.)
2. Other schools and departments: Japanese, Mathematics, Physics, Chemistry and English.
Applicants to the School of Humanities and Culture, Department of Arts, and the School of Physical Education must take additional departmental examinations, auditions, or practicals, respectively.
Documents to be Submitted When Applying
Standard Documents Requirement
Applicants who have studied Japanese at a Japanese language school or other institutions are required to submit a certificate of their language proficiency.
Application period is from mid–January to the end of January.
Results of the examination will be sent to successful candidates by express mail, and to others by regular mail around mid–February.
Applicants who have been accepted for admission will be sent registration forms which are to be returned to the university by the end of February.
Applications from abroad:
The application period for applicants living abroad is from mid–September to the end of October. For those applicants whose government permits them to leave the country only after they can provide proof of their acceptance to an accredited institution

of higher learning, the university will send a letter of admission by mid–December to those applicants who successfully pass the first screening (based on the submitted documents). Upon receiving the letter, the applicants can then begin processing the documents necessary for travel. However, there is a second screening after the applicant arrives in Japan. Only after the applicant has successfully passed the second screening entrance examinations held in mid–February, will the applicant be officially admitted to the university.

Documents to be Submitted When Applying
Standard Documents Requirement

ONE-YEAR GRADUATE PROGRAMS

One–Year Graduate Course of Marine Science and Technology (Enrollment 40)
Navigation

Foreign Student Admission
Qualifications for Applicants
Applicants are required to have scholastic ability equal to or greater than the graduates of Department of Nautical Engineering, School of Marine Science and Technology, Tokai University, and the experience of having been on board a ship for more than six months.
Documents to be Submitted When Applying
Standard Documents Requirement
Application period is from mid–July to the end of July. Applicants are accepted on the basis of the submitted documents, written examinations, and an interview, which are administered at the beginning of August. Announcement of Examination results will be around the end of August. Applicants who have been accepted for admission will be sent forms for registration which are to be returned to the university between the beginning of March and mid–March.

GRADUATE PROGRAMS

Graduate School of Arts (First Year Enrollment : Master's 8)
Musicology, Plastic Arts
Graduate School of Economics (First Year Enrollment : Master's 10, Doctor's 5)
Applied Economics
Graduate School of Engineering (First Year Enrollment : Master's 88, Doctor's 44)
Aeronautics and Astronautics, Applied Science, Architectural Engineering, Civil Engineering, Electrical Engineering, Electronics, Electron Optics, Industrial Chemistry, Management Engineering, Mechanical Engineering, Metallurgical Engineering
Graduate School of Letters (First Year Enrollment : Master's 36, Doctor's 18)
Civilization Studies, English Literature, History, Japanese Literature, Mass Communications
Graduate School of Marine Science and Technolo-gy (First Year Enrollment : Master's 24, Doctor's 12)
Marine Engineering, Marine Resources, Marine Science
Graduate School of Medicine (First Year Enrollment : Doctor's 35)
Ecological and Environmental Medical Science, Functional Medical Science, Medicine, Morphological Medical Science, Surgery
Graduate School of Physical Education (First Year Enrollment : Master's 10)
Physical Education
Graduate School of Political Science (First Year Enrollment : Master's 10, Doctor's 5)
Political Science
Graduate School of Science (First Year Enrollment : Master's 24, Doctor's 12)
Chemistry, Mathematics, Physics

Foreign Student Admission
Qualifications for Applicants
Master's Program
Standard Qualifications Requirement
Doctor's Program
Standard Qualifications Requirement
Requirements for the applicants to the doctor's program of the School of Medicine are as follows.
1. Applicants who are able to demonstrate scholastic ability equal to or greater than the graduates of Tokai University's School of Medicine will be considered for admission to the program.
2. A medical license or the successful completion of the National Medical Examinations soon after matriculation is desired of applicants to the divisions for Morphology, Functional Medical Science, and Ecological and Environmental Medical Science. However, the above does not apply to those applicants who have completed or are expecting to complete a master's program in areas other than medicine or dentistry and who meet the qualifications in (1) above.
3. Applicants to the divisions of Medicine and Surgery must have completed or be completing the two years of clinical internship as stipulated by law.
Examination at the University
Master's Program
Applications for admission must be filed by mid September. In the event that the number of successful applicants for certain courses of study falls short of the prescribed number, additional applications will be accepted for consideration around the end of February.
Entrance examinations consist of an interview and written examinations in the applicant's field of specialization and in a foreign language (English, German, or French).
Notification of acceptance or denial of the appli-

cants who filed for admission by mid–September will be made at the beginning of October. Those who filed for admission in February, will be notified at the beginning of March.

Successful applicants who receive notification of acceptance in October are requested to complete registration procedures by mid–December, and those who receive notification of acceptance in March, by mid–March.

Doctor's Program

Applications for admission must be filed by midSeptember. In the event that the number of successful applicants for certain courses of study falls short of the prescribed number, additional applications will be accepted for consideration around the end of February.

Entrance examinations consist of an interview and written examinations in two foreign languages (English, German, French, Russian, Chinese, or Spanish).

Notification of acceptance or denial of the applicants who filed for admission by mid–September will be made at the beginning of October. Those who filed for admission in February, will be notified at the beginning of March.

Successful applicants who receive notification of acceptance in October are requested to complete registration procedures by mid–December, and those who receive notification of acceptance in March, by mid–March.

Note: Admission to the School of Medicine.

Applicants who possess baccalaureate degrees from fields other than the premedical sciences may apply for admission to the School of Medicine. However, these applicants will be required to take an examination on special subjects. related to the area.

Documents to be Submitted When Applying

Standard Documents Requirement

In addition to the application form which is to be completed by the applicant, applicants must submit the Personal Academic Record form which the university will send to the applicants. This Record must be completed by the applicants's university, enclosed in a sealed envelope, and submitted to the university unopened.

In addition to the application form and the Personal Academic Record form required of applicants to the Master's Program, applicants to the Doctor's Program must submit a copy of their Master's theses and an abstract of their theses. Applicants who file for admission in October and have not completed their theses at the time of application, must submit a report on the progress made on their theses so far.

Note: Admission to the School of Medicine, Division of Internal Medicine and Surgery.

In addition to the above, applicants must submit a certificate of completion or a letter certifying the expected completion date of their clinical internship.

*

Research Institutes and Centers

Affiliated Facilities Computer Center, Ashikaga Memorial Research Center of the Balkan and Asia Minor, Bosei-gakujuku, Health Control Center, International House, International Residence, Matsumae Commemoration Hall, Ocean Research and Training Vessels Tokai University European Center (Copenhagen, Denmark), Okinawa Area Study Center, Research and Information Center, Research Institute of Arts, Research Institute of Basic Scoiology, Research Institute of Civilization, Research Institute of Education, Research Institute of General Medicine, Research Institute of Industrial Science, Research Institute of Law, Research Institute of Oceanography, Research Institute of sports Medicine, Research Institute of Technology Development, Social Education Center, Space Information Center, Strategic Peace and International Research Institute, Tokai University Press, Tokai Unversity Matsumae Budo Center (Vienna, Austria), Tokai University Hospitals

Facilities/Services for Foreign Students

International Hall:

The International Hall is a dormitory for students from overseas. The Hall is located on Shonan Campus and accommodates about 64 people, some of whom are Japanese students who help foreign students adjust to campus life.

Admission Requirements: Foreign students must be enrolled in the Japanese Language Course (one year.)

Number of Residents to Be Admitted: Male 32, Female 32.

Accommodations: Double room 30, Single room 2, Japanese style room 2.

Facilities for common use include a lounge, a reading room, a game room, a kitchen, two bathrooms, a laundry area with washing machines and others.

Fee: ¥120, 000 (per year)

Foreign Student Society:

This self–governing organization is comprised of all the foreign students enrolled in the university. The Foreign Student Society carries out annual programs with the assistance of university officials. Its regular functions include a welcoming party for freshman students by faculty and staff members, participation in the University Festivals, and excursions.

Special Programs for Foreign Students

Japanese Language Course:

This course is open for those who desire to learn Japanese before they enter the university. It commences in April every year and ends in March of the following year. The objective of this course is to enable students to aquire fundamental linguistic ability of elementary and intermediate Japanese through intensive training in listening, speaking, reading, and writing. In addition to instruction in Japanese, orientation lectures are provided in the second semester (beginning in October) to prepare foreign students for university lectures.

Foreign Students Course:

The aim of the Foreign Students Course is to help foreign students aquire sufficient knowledge of Japanese and other fundamental subjects during their first two years (freshman and sophomore years) and to enable them to participate in lectures in their majors on equal terms with Japanese classmates.

For Further Information
Undergraduate and Graduate Admission
International Affairs Section, Tokai University, 1117 Kitakaname, Hiratsuka-shi, Kanagawa 259-12
☎ 0463-58-1211 ext. 2250

Tokai Women's College
(Tokai Joshi Daigaku)
Kirino-cho, Naka, Kakamigahara-shi, Gifu 504
☎ 0583-89-2200

UNDERGRADUATE PROGRAMS

Faculty of Liberal Arts (Freshmen Enrollment: 200)
Department of British and American Studies
Department of Human Relations
Education Course Psychology Course Sociology Course

Tokiwa University
(Tokiwa Daigaku)
1–430–1 Miwa, Mito-shi, Ibaraki 310
☎ 0292–32–2611

Faculty
    Profs. 24   Assoc. Profs. 10
    Assist. Profs. Full–time 8; Part–time 48
Number of Students
    Undergrad. 1,074
Library 91,000 volumes

Outline and Characteristics of the University

Recently, society has had to make great changes due to the impact of scientific advances and technological innovations. With these changes in mind, Tokiwa University was founded in 1983 in order to study the range of Human Sciences in an objective and interdisciplinary fashion. The Faculty is composed of three Departments, Human Relations , Administrations of Human Organization and Communications.

The Department of Human Relations is made up of the three majors designed to study human nature and society, Sociology, Psychology and Education. Here, the students try to employ an analytical approach to the synthetic relationship within the human sciences.

Within the curriculum, the majors are interdisciplinary in order to investigate a variety of phenomena connected with human behaviour. Although lecturers may be given the same titles as in the past, the methods of teaching the human sciences are constantly under active consideration and revision.

Within each major the student can freely select from the wide range of special subjects within the other majors. This allows academic variety and provides the opportunity for a wider and more flexible approach to the human sciences through the study of the special subjects common to all three majors.

Practical and experimental subjects are also encouraged within the department. This calls for prompt and precise statistical and information processing. The computer is of the highest importance in this field and therefore the study of basic computer skills is a compulsory part of the curriculum here.

The Department of Communications approaches the human sciences by studying human society through the role of communications and the media. Communications are important at every level of society. Moreover, communication related technology, including the computer, plays a vital role. The possibilities and services such technology can provide are continually being developed. The Department of Communications concentrates on mastering new systems and techniques, and effective and practical ways of studying a range of areas including audio visual techniques, presentation, communication technology, and media practices. The Audio Visual floor and the Computer Center are well equipped for practical study.

In communication, whatever the medium, information has to be presented clearly, accurately and concisely. All students learn about the general characteristics of communications, the principles of communication, socio-linguistics and mass-communication. In addition, within the department students can research the areas of non-verbal communications, area communications, intercultural communications, and international communications, thereby considering a wide range of communications between both people and nations.

Mito City (population about 233,000) is the present administrative center of Ibaraki Prefecture. During the Edo period it was the seat of the Mito branch of the Tokugawa family. Although their castle was destroyed during the Second World War there still remains several historical relics and cultural properties of the time such as the Kodokan Istitute and Kairakuen park. After the Meiji Restoration in 1868, Mito prospered as the economical, political, cultural and transportation center of the prefecture.

UNDERGRADUATE PROGRAMS

Faculty of Human Science (Freshmen Enrollment: 300)
Department of Administrations of Human Drganization
Department of Communications

Department of Human Relations
Education, Psychology, Sociology

*

For Further Information
Undergraduate Admission
Admissions Office, Tokiwa University, 1–430–1 Miwa, Mito-shi, Ibaraki 310 ☎ 0292–32–2611

Tokoha-Gakuen Hamamatsu University
(Tokoha-Gakuen Hamamatsu Daigaku)

1230 Miyakoda–cho, Hamamatsu-shi, Shizuoka 431–21   ☎ 0534–28–3511

Faculty
    Profs. 18   Assoc. Profs 9
    Assist. Profs.   Full–time 8; Part–time 21
    Res. Assoc. 1
Number of Students
    Undergrad. 266   Grad. 0
Library   18, 900 volumes

Outline and Characteristics of the University
    Tokoha-Gakuen Hamamatsu University, the newest institution of Tokoha Educational Institute opened in 1988. Tokoha Educational Institute was established by Professor Yasuhiko Kimiya in 1946. Since that time the Institute has been developed into one of the most prestigious educational institutions in the Tokai Region. It has 11 schools ranging from kindergarten to university, with a total student enrollment of 8, 900.
    Tokoha-Gakuen Hamamatsu University strives to provide superior undergraduate education in a friendly rural campus atmosphere and promoting the intellectual, social, and ethical development of the student.
    The Faculty of Tokoha-Gakuen Hamamatsu University consists of the department of Business Administration and Informatics. It is the only university with a department of liberal arts in western Shizuoka Prefecture.
    The University, adjacent to the government–designated site for a high technology industrial center, aims at contributing to the industrial and cultural, development of the community as well as producing students able to cope with the highly information-oriented society of the 21st century.
    Hamamatsu City is situated in central Japan, about 250 kilometers west of Tokyo and 250 kilometers east of Kyoto, and within 100 kilometer of a number of the nation's most famous recreation areas. These include Fuji National Park, Hamana Lake, as well as Sakuma Dam, one of the largest in Japan, on the Tenryu River.

UNDERGRADUATE PROGRAMS

Faculty of Administration and Informatics (Freshmen Enrollment 200)
Department of Administration and Informatics
Accounting, Accunting Information System, Auditing, Business Administration, Business Organization, Computer Science, Computer Simmulation, Cost Accounting, Financial Management, Information theory, International Business, Management Accounting, Management Information System, Management Science, Marketing, Programming Language, System Analysis

Foreign Student Admission
    Qualifications for Applicants
    Standard Qualifications Requirement
    1. Applicants must hold the International Baccalaureate.
    2. Applicants must take the Japanese Language Proficiency Test and General Examination for Foreign Students.

    Examination at the University
    A written exam and an interview.
    Documents to be Submitted When Applying
    Standard Documents Requirement
Application deadline: by December 23.

*

For Further Information
Undergraduate Admission
Tokoha-Gakuen Hamamatsu University 1230 Miyakoda–cho, Hamamatsu–shi 431–21 ☎ 0534–28–3511

Tokoha Gakuen University
(Tokoha Gakuen Daigaku)

1000 Sena, Shizuoka-shi, Shizuoka 420
☎ 0542-63-1125

Faculty
    Profs. 36   Assoc. Profs. 18
    Assist. Profs.   Full–time 11; Part–time 55
Number of Students
    Undergrad. 1, 123
Library   58, 500 volumes

Outline and Characteristics of the University
    Tokoha Gakuen University was founded in April, 1980 starting with the Department of Elementary School Education which aims at training students to become elementary school teachers.
    In 1984 the Faculty of Foreign Studies consisting of the Department of English and the Department of Spanish was started with the purpose of fostering students able to cope with the era of internationalization.
    Tokoha Educational Institute was founded by

Professor Yasuhiko Kimiya in 1946. The founder took the name"tokoha" from an old Japanese poem written by Emperor Shomu, which praised the virtue of the tangerine tree (or tachibana). The tree has ever green leaves, even in heavy snows its blossoms are pure and white, giving off a delicate fragrance and its fruit is of a green color loved by all.

The spirit of Tokoha is symbolized by the tangerine tree. The ideal of Tokoha Educational Institute is to foster young peple who love their neighbors, their locality and the nation. The institute also seeks to train students to have a spirit of challenge, courage and healthy bodies and to overcome any difficulty and continue to strive for higher ideals. Tokoha Gakuen University aims at cultivating young men and women with academic ability who recognize their aims in life.

UNDERGRADUATE PROGRAMS

Faculty of Education (Freshmen Enrollment: 100)
Department of Elementary Education
Elementary School Teachers' Traning Course
Faculty of Foreign Studies (Freshmen Enrollment: 120)
Department of English
Language and Liternture Course
International Relations Course
Department of Spanish
Language and Literature Course
Regional Study Course

Foreign Student Admission
Examination at the University
For the admission of foreign students, a special screening system is given, based on:
1. Submitted documents
2. Examination in Academic Subjects
3. Interviews
4. Others
Qualifications for Transfer Students
Transfer students include:
1. Those who have graduted from a university or have taken general requirement subjects and/or left school.
2. Those who have graduated from a junior college.
3. Those who have graduated from technical college.
4. Those who have sussessfully completed fourteen years or more of formal education in foreign countries.

*

Research Institutes and Centers
Juvenile Education Center attached to the Faculty of Education
For Further Information
Undergraduate Admission
Section Chief of School Affairs, School Affiars, Student Division, Tokoha Gakuen University 1000 Sena,

Shizuoka 422 ☎ 0542-63-1121

Tokushima Bunri University
(Tokushima Bunri Daigaku)
1-8 Terashimahon-cho, Tokushima-shi,
Tokushima 770 ☎ 0886-22-0097

Faculty
  Profs. 108   Assoc. Profs. 63
  Assist. Profs. Full-time 40; Part-time 192
  Res. Assocs. 71
Number of Students
  Undergrad. 2, 327   Grad. 50
Library 208, 535 volumes

Outline and Characteristics of the University
Tokushima Bunri University has a history of 93 years. It was founded in 1895 as a women's college by Madame Sai Murasaki. With her aim of improving women's low position in society, she insisted on the independence of women as the founding principle of her institution. It was renamed Tokushima Bunri University when the co-educational Faculties of Pharmaceutical Science and Music, as well as the women's Faculty of Home Economics, were added to meet the demands of the age and the area, while Tokushima Women's College was renamed Tokushima Bunri Junior College. The Graduate School of Pharmaceutical Science was opened and began a master's program in 1979 and a doctoral program in 1981. The Faculty of Literature was established in Shido-cho, Kagawa Prefecture, in 1983. Moreover, in 1987, the addition of a Department of Management and Information Science is projected. As a result of this expansion of faculties and departments, the University may be considered, both nominally and actually, as one of the oldest and largest private universities in the western part of Japan. The University consists of four Faculties: Pharmaceutical Sciences, Home Economics, Music, and Literature. The Junior College is composed of six Departments: Domestic Science, Nursery-School-Teacher Training, Literature, Music Commerce, and Management & Information.

The Tokushima canıpus is located in the southern part of Tokushima City—the center of its culture and education. On the site stand 16 teaching and research buildings, including a twelve-story building housing the Faculty of Pharmaceutical Science. The Kagawa campus, with its newly-established Faculty of Literature, is situated on a hill surrounded by an area of natural beauty and by historical remains. With an area of 100, 000 m², this campus is located in Shido-cho, in the eastern part of Takamatsu City.

The students of both campuses, Tokushima and Kagawa, enjoy the chance to participate in a wide range of clubs and societies as well as the opportunity to study in excellent academic surroundings. 70%

of the students are from Shikoku Island, but the rest come from all parts of Japan. In the summer of 1985, the Great Naruto Bridge over Naruto Channel (noted for its eddying current) was opened. The bridges between Shikoku Island and Honshu Island will make it possible for travellers in the future to take an overland as well as a sea route to visit Shikoku Island. Soon, the number of students from other parts of Japan is expected to increase.

The history of Tokushima Bunri University goes back to 1895, when Madame Sai Murasaki established a women's college with an ideal of improving women's status in society; viz., their liberation. Subsequently the original basis of the university has had to undergo considerable modification in accordance with the demands of society and the times. Thus, it has been expanded to include the co-ed faculties of pharmaceutical sciences and music as well as the women's faculty of domestic science, on the one hand, and to include the women's junior college, on the other.

UNDERGRADUATE PROGRAMS

Faculty of Domestic Science (Freshmen Enrollment: 100)
Department of Domestic Science
Domestic Science CourseAdministration on Feeding Service, Architectonics of Clothing, Child Care and Health, Clothing, Clothing Arrangements, Clothing Materials, Clothology, Consumer Science, Cooking, Domestic Science, Dyeing and Finishing, Food Hygienics, Food Materials, Food Science, Habitation Science, Hygienics on Clothing, Nutritional Science, Nutrition Guidance, Public Health, Social Welfare, Statistics, Textile Chemistry
Department of Juvenile Education
Juvenile Education Course　Pedology CourseChild Culture, Child Psychology, Health Education for Children, Juvenile Education, Nursing, Social Welfare
Faculty of Literature (Freshmen Enrollment: 140)
Department of English and American Literature
Comparative Literature, English and American Literature, English Linguistics, History of English and American Literature
Department of Japanese Literature
Chinese Literature, Comparative Literature, History of Japanese Literature, Japanese Linguistics, Japanese Literature
Faculty of Music (Freshmen Enrollment: 50)
Department of Music
Cembalo Course　Piano Course　Vocal Music Course　Wind, String and Percussion CourseAccompaniment, Chamber Music, Chorus, Composition, Conducting, Counterpoint, Ensemble, Harmonics, History of Music, History of Special Music, Musical Aesthetics, Musical Appreciation, Musical Forms, Musical Theories, Organology, Phonetics, Solfeggio, Vocal Ensemble

Faculty of Pharmaceutical Sciences (Freshmen Enrollment: 200)
Department of Hygienic Pharmacy
Department of Pharmaceutics
Biological Chemistry, Hygienic Chemistry, Medicinal Chemistry, Microbiology, Pharmaceutical Analytical Chemistry, Pharmaceutical Chemistry, Pharmaceutical Physical Chemistry, Pharmaceutical Radio Chemistry, Pharmaceutical Technochemistry, Pharmaceutics, Pharmacognosy, Pharmacology, Physiological Chemistry, Public Health

ONE-YEAR GRADUATE PROGRAMS

One-Year Graduate Course in Music (Enrollment: 6)
Instrumental Music, Vocal Music

GRADUATE PROGRAMS

Graduate School of Pharmaceutical Sciences (First Year Enrollment : Master's 12, Doctor's 4)
Division
Pharmaceutical Sciences

*

Research Institutes and Centers
Research Institute of Pharmacognosy
For Further Information
Undergraduate and Graduate Admission
The General Affairs Officer, Admission Section, Administrative Office, Tokushima Bunri University, 1-8 Terashimahon-cho, Higashi, Tokushima-shi, Tokushima 770 ☎ 0886-22-0097

Tokuyama University
(Tokuyama Daigaku)

843-4-2 Kume-Kurigasako, Tokuyama-shi, Yamaguchi 745　☎ 0834-28-0411

Faculty
　Profs.　26　　Assoc. Profs.　18
　Assist. Profs.　Full–time　10; Part–time　29
　Res. Assocs.　4
Number of Students
　Undergrad.　2, 335
Library　86, 000 volumes

Outline and Characteristics of the University
Tokuyama University was founded in 1971 with the intention of providing the population in the eastern part of Yamaguchi Prefecture a sound educational institution. It was established with substantial financial help from local businesses and Tokuyama City. The motto of the university is to create an ideal place of learning with fresh, lively education principles in the calm countryside environment. The university emphasizes balanced education by developing three aspects of the personality, that is the intellectual, moral and physical.

The university started as a subsidiary institution of Chuo Gakuin. It was subsequently separated from it and became independent in 1974. The institution which started with a department of Economics added the department of Management in 1976. A memorial hall which functions both as a gymnasium and as the general meeting hall, a student hall building and outdoor stage were built in 1981, in commemoration of the university's 10th anniversary. In 1983, a new library building was erected and the administration building was enlarged. Tokuyama Women's College is expected to open in the spring of 1987. It will offer the course of Managerial Information Engineering.

UNDERGRADUATE PROGRAMS

Faculty of Economics (Freshmen Enrollment: 450)
Department of Economics
Agricultural Economy, Econometrics, Economic Change, Economic History, Economic Mathematics, Economic Policy, Economic Statistics, Economic Structure, Foreign Economic Conditions, History of Economics, History of Economic Thoughts, International Economics, International Economy, Local Finance, Public Finance, Social Policy, Social Security
Department of Management
Bookkeeping and Accounting, Business Management, Commerce, Commodity, Corporate Strategy, Financial Management, History of Management, International Management, International Trade, Management, Management Organization, Managerial Accounting, Medium and Small-sized Enterprises, Modern Management and Capitalistic Firms, Personnel Management, Price Formation, Profit Measurement, Sales Management, Tax Accounting

*
Research Institutes and Centers
Computer Center, General Economic Research Institute
For Further Information
Undergraduate Admission
Admission Division, Tokuyama University, 843-4-2 Kume-Kurigasako, Tokuyama-shi, Yamaguchi 745
☎ 0834-28-5302 ext. 213, 214

Tokyo College of Music
(Tokyo Ongaku Daigaku)

3-4-5 Minami Ikebukuro, Toshima–ku, Tokyo 186
☎ 03-982-3186

UNDERGRADUATE PROGRAMS

Faculty of Music (Freshmen Enrollment: 250)
Department of Music
Composition and Conducting, Instrumental Music, Music Education, Vocal Music

Tokyo College of Pharmacy
(Tokyo Yakka Daigaku)

1432-1 Horinouchi, Hachioji–shi, Tokyo 192-03
☎ 0426-76-5111

Faculty
    Profs. 34   Assoc. Profs. 24
    Assist. Profs. Full–time 37; Part–time 40
    Res. Assocs. 43
Number of Students
    Undergrad. 2,050   Grad. 138
Library 80,000 volumes

Outline and Characteristics of the College
Tokyo College of Pharmacy was established in 1880 as Tokyo Pharmaceutists School. The college was once separated into two campuses in central Tokyo, one for the Men's Division at Shinjuku, and the other for the Women's Division at Ueno. However, both campuses were combined and moved to a new campus in Hachioji on the western outskirts of Tokyo in April, 1976. After the move, the two Divisions remained intact, but the other systems of the institution including staff and research activity were unified, thus enabling the College to aim at effective administration of the school while maintaining our educational tradition.

On the new spacious 29 ha. campus stand the school buildings with a total floor space of 37,000 m². The students' practice rooms, located near the regular class rooms in the Education Houses, are separated from the staff's research laboratories, thus making it possible to give students highly systematized and independent lab instruction. The Research Houses contain the professor's offices, research laboratories, and varied special experiment facilities. The staffing as well as the facilities improve from year to year. In college activities, emphasis is placed not only on education but also on high–level research work in the various fields of pharmaceutical sciences.

UNDERGRADUATE PROGRAMS

Faculty of Pharmacy (**Men's Division**) (Freshmen Enrollment: 240)
  Department of Biopharmacy
  Department of Pharmaceutical Sciences
  Department of Pharmaceutical Technology
Biochemistry, Biotechnology for Pharmaceutical Sciences, Hygienic Chemistry, Pathogenic Microbiology, Pharmaceutical Chemistry, Pharmaceutical Laws, Pharmaceutics, Pharmacognosy, Pharmacology, Pharmacopoeia, Public Health, Radiation Physics, Radiochemistry
Faculty of Pharmacy (**Women's Division**) (Freshmen Enrollment 180)

Department of Biopharmacy
Department of Pharmaceutical Sciences

Biochemistry, Biotechnology for Pharmaceutical Sciences, Hygienic Chemistry, Pathogenic Microbiology, Pharmaceutical Chemistry, Pharmaceutical Law, Pharmaceutics, Pharmacognosy, Pharmacology, Pharmacopoeia, Public Health, Radiation Physics, Radiochemistry

Foreign Student Admission

Qualifications for Applicants
Standard Qualifications Requirement
Examination at the College
A documents examination, a written examination and an interview.
Documents to be Submitted When Applying
Standard Documents Requirement
Application Period: April l to September 30.
Scholastic Aptitude Test and Interview: November 26.
Announcement of Final Result: November 29.
Period for Entrance Procedures: Nov. 29~Dec. 7.

GRADUATE PROGRAMS

Department of Clinical Pharmacy (First Year Enrollment : Master's 20)
Division
Clinical Pharmacy
Department of Pharmaceutical Sciences (First Year Enrollment : Master's 50, Doctor's 8)
Divisions
Biochemistry, Dispensing Pharmacy, Hygienic Chemistry, Pharmaceutical Analytical Chemistry, Pharmaceutical Chemistry, Pharmaceutics, Pharmacognosy, Pharmacology

Foreign Student Admission

Qualifications for Applicants
Master's Program
Standard Qualifications Requirement
Doctor's Program
Standard Qualifications Requirement
Examination at the College
Master's Program
A documents examination, a written examination and an interview.
Doctor's Program
The same as the Master's Program.
Documents to be Submitted When Applying
Standard Documents Requirement
The prospectus for registration and the application form are available in March.

∗

Research Institutes and Centers
Central Analytical Center, Hachioji Pharmaceutical Center
For Further Information
Undergraduate and Graduate Admission
Office of General Affairs, Tokyo College of Pharmacy, 1432-1 Horinouchi, Hachioji–shi, Tokyo 192-03 ☎ 0426-76-5111

Tokyo Denki University
(Tokyo Denki Daigaku)

2-2 Kanda–Nishikicho, Chiyoda–ku, Tokyo 101
☎ 03-294-1551

Faculty
   Profs.   117   Assoc. Profs.   65
   Assist. Profs.   Full–time 23; Part–time 239
   Res. Assocs.   60
Number of Students
   Undergrad. 8, 825   Grad.   203
Library   257, 218 volumes

Outline and Characteristics of the University

Tokyo Denki University is located in the heart of Tokyo near Ochanomize Railway Station in Chiyoda-ku. It is one of the oldest engineering universities in Japan. The first President was Dr. Yasujiro Niwa who served as President from April 1949 to March 1974. He was followed by Dr. Toshifusa Sakamoto from April 1974 to March 1982. Dr. Michio Nakano assumed the current presidency in April 1982.

T. D. U. was founded in 1907 as a night-time vocational school offering classes in electrical engineering. In 1939 it was certified as Tokyo Electrical Engineering Higher College and in 1949 formally established as Tokyo Denki University, but with only a Faculty of Engineering. An Evening Junior College providing a two year course in electrical engineering was added in 1950 and later, in 1952, an Evening course was established at the University. In 1958 a three-year Master's Program (Evening Course) was established, and in 1962, a three-year Doctoral Program was established; in 1975, a two-year Masters Program, (Day Course) was established. Over the years T. D. U. has grown from its two departments of Electrical Engineering and Electrical Communication Engineering to its present seven, including Electronic Engineering, Mechanical Engineering, Applied Science, Precision Machinery Engineering and Architecture.

In 1977 the University established the Faculty of Science and Engineering with six departments: Mathmatical Sciences, Systems and Management Engineering, Civil Engineering, Industrial Mechanical Engineering, Information Sciences and Applied Electronic Engineering. Four Master's Degree programs were established in the Faculty of Science and Engineering in 1981 and a Doctoral program in 1983.

UNDERGRADUATE PROGRAMS

First Faculty of Engineering (Freshmen Enrollment: 720)

Department of Applied Science
Applied Chemistry, Chemistry, Control & Measurements, Electrical Engineering, Materials & Solid State Engineering, Physics

Department of Architecture
Architectural Planning, Architectural Productions, Architecture, Building Equipments, Design & Drawing, Design of Architectural Structure, Environment Science on Buildings, History of Architecture, Mechanics of Structure, Planning & Design, Structure & Security, Technique & Management

Department of Electrical Communication Engineering
Acoustical Engineering, Electrical Circuit Theory, Electrical Measurements, Electromagnetism, Electronic Circuit, Electronic Computers, Information Theory & Communication Systems, Materials & Solid State Physics, Radio Engineering, Systems & Control, Wire Communication Engineering

Department of Electrical Engineering
Applied Electrical Engineering, Communication & Imformation Theory, Control & Measurements, Electrical Circuit Theory, Electric Machines, Electromagnetic Theory, Electronic Computers, High Voltage & Electric Discharge, Materials & Solid State, Power System Analysis Electronics, Systems Engineering

Department of Electronic Engineering
Control & Measurements, Electrical Circuits & Devices, Electronic Computers & Information Theory, Electronic Engineering, Solid State

Department of Mechanical Engineering
Control & Measurements, Electrical Engineering, Electronic Computers, Fluid Mechanic Engineering, Machine Design & Drawing, Machine Manufacturing, Statics & Dynamics, Thermodynamics

Department of Precision Machinery Engineering
Control Engineering, Information of Processing, Machine Design, Machining, Materials, Thermodynamics & Fluid Engineering

Second Faculty of Engineering (Evening Course) (Freshmen Enrollment: 360)

Department of Electrical Communication Engineering
Department of Electrical Engineering
Department of Electronic Engineering
Department of Mechanical Engineering
See the listing for the First Faculty.

Faculty of Science and Engineering (Freshmen Enrollment: 560)

Department of Applied Electronic Engineering
Biological Measurement and Control, Biomechanic and Robotic Engineering, Biosignal and Image Processing, Material Science, Medical Electronics, Power Electronics and Electrical Drives, Semiconductor Devices, Solid State Electronics

Department of Civil Engineering
Concrete Engineering, Disaster Prevention Engineering, Environmental Engineering, Foundation Engineering, Hydraulics, Soil Mechanics, Structural Engineering, Structural Mechanics, Surveying, Transportation Engineering, Urban Planning

Department of Industrial Mechanical Engineering
Control Engineering, Dynamics of Machinery, Fluid Machinery, Fluid Mechanics, Heat Transfer, Instrument Technology, Machine Design, Machine Shop Engineering, Strength of Materials

Department of Information Sciences
Algebraic Cycles on Algebraic Varieties, Computational Complexity, Database Theory, Information Theory and Its Applications, Mathematical System Theory, Numerical Analysis, Program Verification, Theory of Computation, Theory of Diffusion Processes, Vector-Valued Stochastic Processes

Department of Mathematical Sciences
Algebraic Geometry, Computer Science, Differential Equations, Functional Analysis, Mathematical Biology, Mathematical Physics, Stochastic Processes

Department of Systems and Management Engineering
Artificial Intelligence and Knowledge Engineering, Boolean Logic and Digital Circuits, Data Base and Communication Systems, Digital Control Theory and Systems Engineering, Digital Servo Systems and Robotics, Human Engineering and Management Systems, Logic Programming and Intelligent Systems, Pattern Recognition and Data Analysis

Foreign Student Admission
Qualifications for Applicants
    Standard Qualifications Requirement
Examination at the University
1. A written test in the Japanese language
2. Examination of applicant's high school record
3. Interview
Documents to be Submitted When Applying
    Standard Documents Requirement

GRADUATE PROGRAMS

Graduate School of Engineering (First Year Enrollment : Master's 3, (Evening) 6, Doctor's 4)
Division
Electrical Engineering

Graduate School of Science and Engineering (First Year Enrollment : Master's 48, Doctor's 13)
Divisions
Applied Systems Engineering, Civil and Structural Engineering, Mathematical Sciences, Mechanical Engineering, Systems Engineering

Foreign Student Admission
Qualifications for Applicants
Master's Program
    Standard Qualifications Requirement
Doctor's Program
    Standard Qualifications Requirement
Examination at the University
Master's Program
    A written and interview test in the Japanese lan-

guage.
Doctor's Program
    The same General Examination as Japanese applicants.
    A written test in the Japanese language and an interview.
    Documents to be Submitted When Applying
        Standard Documents Requirement

*

Research Institutes and Centers
Center for Research (Energy Study Section, Material Study Section, System Study Section), Computer Center
Special Programs for Foreign Students
    Foreign Students may study their specialized course through the help of a tutor, a Japanese graduate student.
For Further Information
    Undergraduate and Graduate Admission
Division of Admission Office, Tokyo Denki University, 2-2 Kanda–Nishikicho, Chiyoda–ku, Tokyo 101
☎ 03-294-1551 ext. 5220

Tokyo Dental College
(Tokyo Shika Daigaku)

2-9-18 Misaki–cho, Chiyoda–ku, Tokyo 101
☎ 03-262-3421

Faculty
    Profs. 42   Assoc. Profs. 38
    Assist. Profs. Full–time 83; Part–time 302
    Res. Assocs. 114
Number of Students
    Undergrad. 970   Grad. 176
Library 119, 825 volumes

Outline and Characteristics of the College
    In 1890, Tokyo Dental College was founded by Kisai Takayama who worked as a dentist in Tokyo after having studied for about six years in San Francisco, U. S. A. In 1907, the government authorized the school first in Japan as an organized dental school. In 1920, the dental school celebrated its 30th anniversary. At that time, the school had 430 students, 43 teachers and the number of our alumni had reached 2, 960 which was 60% of all the dentists in Japan. In 1946, the school was given college status with a three–year preparatory course and a four–year professional course. In 1952, the law was revised and our college became what it is now, a college with a two–year predental course and a four–year professional course. In 1946, a general hospital was established in Ichikawa City as a result of the necessity to have a close relationship between dentistry and other general medical sciences. It is even now a very progressive idea to have a private dental school manage a general hospital. In 1949, the dental hygienists' school was established which was the first one in Japan. In 1958, the graduate school was established. In 1981, the present school buildings were completed on the outskirts of Tokyo. It is a campus of bout 100, 000 m^2 and is the biggest school among the 29 dental schools of Japan.
    At present we have 970 undergraduate students, 176 graduates, 82 students in dental hygienists' school, 277 full–time instructors, and 302 part–time instructors. There are twelve departments in basic science and thirteen in dental clinical science.
    Our dental hospital has 30 beds and serves an average of 571 outpatients a day at Chiba hospital and 300 at Suidobashi hospital. The general hospital in Ichikawa has 264 beds and 700 outpatients a day. The number of alumni is 8, 622.
    Tokyo Dental College has four sister schools. These are the University of Florida, School of Dentistry; the University of Texas, Dental Branch in U. S. A. ; Karolinska Institute; School of Dentistry in Sweden, and Yonsei University, School of Dentistry in Korea. The correlation and cooperation between these schools has produced advanced research findings and educational effects.

UNDERGRADUATE PROGRAMS

School of Dentistry (Freshmen Enrollment: 145)
    Faculty of Dentisity
Anatomy, Biochemistry, Dental Anesthesiology, Dental Technology, Endodontics, Forensic Odontology, General Pathology, Histology, Hygiene, Microbiology, Operative Dentistry, Oral Medicine, Oral Pathology, Oral Surgery, Orthodontics, Pedodontics, Periodontics, Pharmacology, Physiology, Preventive Dentistry, Prosthodontics, Radiology, Social Dentistry

Foreign Student Admission
    Qualifications for Applicants
        Standard Qualifications Requirement
    Examination at the College
        Same as for Japanese: (Mathematics, English, one of these: Biology; Chemistry & Physics), short essay, interview, physical examination and dental attitude tests.
    Documents to be Submitted When Applying
        Standard Documents Requirement

GRADUATE PROGRAMS

Graduate School of Dental Science (First Year Enrollment : Doctor's 48)
    Divisions
Anatomy, Biochemistry, Crown and Bridge Work, Dental Anesthesiology, Dental Technology, Endodontics, Forensic Odontology, Full Denture, General Pathology, Histology, Hygiene, Microbiology, Operative Dentistry, Oral & Maxillofacial Surgery, Oral Medicine, Oral Pathology, Orthodontics, Partial Denture, Pedodontics, Periodontics, Pharmacology,

Physiology, Preventive Dentistry, Radiology, Social Dentistry

Foreign Student Admission
Qualifications for Applicants
Doctor's Program
    Standard Qualifications Requirement
    Examination at the College
Doctor's Program
    Foreign languages (English and German) and examination for majoring subject.
    Documents to be Submitted When Applying
    Standard Documents Requirement
    A copy of dental licence from the Japanese government

*

For Further Information
Undergraduate and Graduate Admission
The Educational Affairs Department, Tokyo Dental College, 1-2-2 Masago, Chiba-shi, Chiba 260
☎ 0472-79-2222 ext. 2360

Tokyo Engineering University
(Tokyo Koka Daigaku)

1404-1 Katakura-cho, Hachioji-shi, Tokyo 192
☎ 0426-37-2111

Faculty
    Profs. 36   Assoc. Profs. 8
    Assist. Profs. Full–time 9; Part–time 2
Number of Students
    Undergrad. 1, 170
Library 21, 000 volumes

Outline and Characteristics of the University
    Tokyo Engineering University was founded in 1986 by the Nippon Denshi Kogakuin Educational Fourdation. The school continues to make a great contribution to society, having supplied more than 85, 000 young engineers through its technical college since 1953.
    The original plan to establish this university was made in the latter half of the 1970's in response to the great social demands for qualified engineers in the field of high technology centered around electronics.
    Tokyo Engineering University, a fairly new institution, has at this time only one undergraduate faculty consisting of the following three departments, each of which enrolls 120 freshmen every year: Department of Electronics, Department of Information Technology, and Department of Mechatronics.
    The university is located in Hachioji, a suburban city 40 kilometers west of Metropolitan Tokyo. Hachioji, which is often referred to as an academic city, can now boast of 20 universities and colleges, providing an excellent environment for students. The campus of this university is 350, 000 m², more

than enough for the present three undergraduate departments, and having sufficient room for future expansion of the university, including graduate schools.

UNDERGRADUATE PROGRAMS

Faculty of Engineering (Freshmen Enrollment: 360)
    Department of Electronics
Communication Engineering, Control Engineering, Electronic Device Engineering, Electronics
    Department of Information Technology
Computer Engineering, Digital Communication Engineering, Information Processing Technology, Information Technology
    Department of Mechatronics
Control Engineering, Instrumentation, Mechatronics, Mechatronic System Engineering

*

For Further Information
Undergraduate Admission
Administration Office, Tokyo Engineering University, 1404-1 Katakura-cho, Hachioji-shi, Tokyo 192
☎ 0426-37-2111 ext. 2011

Tokyo Institute of Polytechnics
(Tokyo Kogei Daigaku)

1583 Iiyama, Atsugi-shi, Kanagawa 243-02
☎ 0462-41-0454

Faculty
    Profs. 35   Assoc. Profs. 14
    Assist. Profs. Full–time 18; Part–time 79
    Res. Assocs. 15
Number of Students
    Undergrad. 2, 282   Grad. 25
Library 53, 505 volumes

Outline and Characteristics of the University
    Tokyo Institute of Polytechnics has a history of over 65 years since its establishment in 1923 as the one and only professional school of photography in Japan. The Institute has always sought beauty and eternal truth during these years. "The fusion of art and technology" has been the educational ideal of the Institute since its founding. The original system of specialized education has been adopted to carry out this ideal and meet the needs of soceity.
    The Institute experienced rapid growth in 1966. Tokyo College of Photography (renamed Tokyo Institute of Polytechnics in 1977) was inaugurated as a four–year college with the Faculty of Engineering containing the Departments of Photographic Engineering and Printing Engineering (renamed Imaging Engineering in 1976). This raise in status was based on the highly acclaimed tradition of photographic education since the founding of the professional school. The Department of Photographic Engineering is,

therefore, the nucleus of the Faculty. Strong emphasis is laid upon educating the technological side of photography and cultivating excellent engineers who will play an active part in the rapidly developing industry of photography. The Department of Imaging Engineering is the one and only department of Japan's private colleges. This unique department provides the fundamental principle and its technological applications concerning the communication, recording and processing of information by visual images.

The Faculty of Engineering was expanded with the establishment of the Departments of Industrial Chemistry and Architecture in 1973 and 1974 respectively. The former department aims at cultivating chemists and chemical technologists who pursue the coexistence of nature and mankind, and the new phase of strictly defined chemical technology. The latter department provides fundamental and synthetic knowledges and techniques concerning architecture and aims at producing capable engineers who can be expected to take an active part in the architectural industry. The rapid development of electronics and its related field was remarkable during the 1970s. The Department of Electronics was added to the Faculty in 1976. The department affords the students the basic knowledge to cope with the expansion of this field and the advanced knowledge and techniques to participate actively in this field in the future.

Tokyo Institute of Polytechnics made progress again with the establishment of the Graduate School of Engineering in 1978. The aim of the Graduate School is to cultivate scientists and technologists who will play leading roles in the world of technology where innovations progress rapidly. The School consists of two divisions; Divisions of Imaging Engineering and Industrial Chemistry. Each division has a master's program. A strictly small enrollment class system, approaching private tutoring is adopted at this School.

Tokyo Institute of Polytechnics aims to assure close, personal attention in teaching, conduct basic and applied research, and provide thorough professional preparation. The Institute continually strives to fulfill these goals year in and year out to ensure the best training possible for the students.

UNDERGRADUATE PROGRAMS

Faculty of Engineering (Freshmen Enrollment: 390)
Department of Architecture
Architectural Planning, Building Construction Method, Building Structure, Environmental Technology in Architecture, History of Architecture, Ventilation and Air Conditioning
Department of Electronics
Active Circuit, Basic Electronics, Computer Engineering, Electrical Communication, Electronic Component, Electronic Physics, Illuminating Engineering, Information Engineering
Department of Imaging Engineering

Electronic Imaging Engineering, Engineering of Graphic Arts, Materials of Imaging Engineering
Department of Industrial Chemistry
Industrial Inorganic Chemistry, Industrial Organic Chemistry, Industrial Physical Chemistry
Department of Photographic Engineering
Applied Optics, Image Analysis and Processing, Image Formation, Optical Instrument, Photographic Chemistry, Photographic Technology

Foreign Student Admission
Qualifications for Applicants
Standard Qualifications Requirement
Examination at the University
Date: in February
Same as for Japanese: written exam.
1. Foreign Language (one of the following three): English, German, or French
2. Mathematics
3. Science: Physics or Chemistry
The physical exam is mainly a color test.
Documents to be Submitted When Applying
Standard Documents Requirement
Deadline: in February.

Qualifications for Transfer Students
1. The applicant who has graduated from a junior college as a science or engineering major or is expected to graduate in March of the year of application.
2. The applicant who has completed two-year college work as a science or engineering major or is expected to complete it by March of the year of application.
3. Other qualifications are the same as those listed for freshman application.
Examination for Transfer Students
Same as for applicants. Date: the end of February a written exam
1. Foreign Languages (one of the following three): English German, or French
2. Mathematics
3. Science: Physics and Chemistry
Documents to be Submitted When Applying
Standard Documents Requirement
Applicants should consult the Instruction Division by mail or in person, submitting their academic records and declaring their desired major before applying. Those successfully screened are admitted into the suitable grade after credit evaluation. They are expected to spend at least two years in residence before being granted a degree.

GRADUATE PROGRAMS

Graduate School of Engineering (First Year Enrollment : Master's 12)
Divisions
Imaging Engineering, Industrial Chemistry

Foreign Student Admission

Qualifications for Applicants

Master's Program

Standard Qualifications Requirement

Examination at the University

Master's Program

Same as for Japanese written exam and an interview. Date: in September and December. Written exam are as follows.

Foreign Languages: English plus German or French Specialized Subjects (any two from the following subjects): Optics, Electromagnetism, Solid State Physics, Physical Chemistry, Organic Chemistry, Photographic Chemistry, Printing Engineering (in the case of the Imaging Engineering major); Physical Chemistry, Inorganic Chemistry, Organic Chemistry, Analytical Chemistry, Biochemistry, Polymer Chemistry, Reaction Chemical Engineering (in the case of the Industrial Chemistry major).

Documents to be Submitted When Applying

Standard Documents Requirement

If the applicant is currently employed or enrolled in another graduate school, a certificate issued by his, her employer or a dean of the graduate school approving the application must be submitted.

Application Deadline: in September or November.

＊

For Further Information

Undergraduate Admission

Admission Office, Tokyo Institute of Polytechnics, 1583 Iiyama, Atsugi-shi, Kanagawa 243-02 ☎ 0462-41-0454 ext. 140

Graduate Admission

Graduate School Section, Instruction Division, Tokyo Institute of Polytechnics, 1583 Iiyama, Atsugi-shi, Kanagawa 243-02 ☎ 0462-41-0454 ext. 150

Tokyo International University
(Tokyo Kokusai Daigaku)

1-13-1 Matoba-Kita, Kawagoe, Saitama 350
☎ 0492-32-1111

Faculty

Profs. 93   Assoc. Profs. 30

Assist. Profs. Full-time 15; Part-time 72

Res. Assocs. 2

Number of Students

Undergrad. 4, 795   Grad. 93

Library 197, 750 volumes

Outline and Characteristics of the University

Tokyo International University (a. k. a. Tokyo Kokusai Daigaku or T. I. U. for short) is one of Japan's fastest growing institutions of higher education. Founded in 1965 by Dr. Taizo Kaneko, T. I. U. was originally a small college emphasizing international commerce and economics. At one time, in fact, the university was named the International College of Commerce and Economics.

Today, T. I. U. is a medium sized university of approximately 4, 800 students and over 130 full time faculty members who teach a broad gamut of subjects. Its two campuses, situated within minutes of each other, cover over 85, 000 square meters and are located in the historical city of Kawagoe, 25 miles northwest of central Tokyo. Due to the university's convenient location, a student may enjoy the fast pace of Tokyo city, or the rarefied atmosphere of a large, forested park--all within a half hour train ride.

At present, T. I. U. offers undergraduate degrees from the schools of Business and Commerce, International Studies and Human Relations. In addition, T. I. U. offers post graduate degrees from its graduate schools of Business and Commerce, International Relations and Sociology.

From the outset, Dr. Kaneko stressed a unique, international approach to education. To that end, immediately after he founded the university, Dr. Kaneko established a sister school relationship with Willamette University, the oldest university in the Western United States. Over the years, numerous exchange programs have flourished: the annual T. I. U. spring seminar at Willamette University, the annual Willamette University fall seminar for Japanese studies at T. I. U. , a long-term study program for T. I. U. students at Willamette University, and an annual exchange of at least one faculty member from either institution.

In 1981, T. I. U. concluded student exchange agreements with Southern Oregon State College and the University of Washington. An annual European Studies Seminar based in England was also begun in 1981. To further enhance the worldwide vision of T. I. U. , a Research Institute of Foreign Studies was recently established along with two special programs for foreign students that concentrate on both Japanese language and culture.

With an eye always looking toward the future, T. I. U. will start a new school of Economics and open its own American compus in 1989.

UNDERGRADUATE PROGRAMS

Faculty of Business and Commerce (Freshmen Enrollment: 850)

Department of Business and Commerce

Accounting, Business Administration, Commerce and Marketing, Economics and Law, International Trade and Finance

Faculty of International Studies and Human Relations (Freshmen Enrollment: 300)

Department of Human Relations

Education, Industrial Relations, Psychology, Science of Man, Sociology

Department of International Studies

Area Studies, Demography, International Business, International Economics, International Law, International Politics, International Relations

Foreign Student Admission

Qualifications for Applicants
    Standard Qualifications Requirement
Examination at the University
    Date: January.
    ability in both English and Japanese. a short essay in Japanese and an interview in Japanese.
Documents to be Submitted When Applying
    Standard Documents Requirement

Qualifications for Transfer Students
    Applicants should be either undergraduate or graduate students or eligible for either level of study.
    Transfer students are admitted on a "space-available" basis.

GRADUATE PROGRAMS

Graduate School of Business and Commerce (First Year Enrollment : Master's 20, Doctor's 3)
    Divisions
Accounting, Business Administration, Commerce and Marketing
Graduate School of International Relations (First Year Enrollment : Master's 20)
    Divisions
Area Studies, International Economics, International Politics
Graduate School of Sociology (First Year Enrollment : Master's 10)
    Division
Applied Sociology

Foreign Student Admission

Qualifications for Applicants
Master's Program
    Standard Qualifications Requirement
Doctor's Program
    Standard Qualications Requirement
Examination at the University
Master's Program
    Date: October and March.
Business and Commerce: ability in English; an essay in Japanese on a topic related to his/her major and an interview in Japanese.
International Relations: Same as above.
Sociology: one of the following languages: English, German, or French, an essay in Japanese on a topic relating to his/her major. an interview in Japanese.
Doctor's Program
    Date: January.
Business and Commerce: Ability in English and one of the follwing languages: German, French, Chinese, Russian or Spanish, an essay in Japanese on a topic relating to his/her major, an interview in Japanese.
Documents to be Submitted When Applying
    Standard Documents Requirement
                    *

Research Institutes and Centers
Research Institute of Foreign Studies, Showa Research Institute
Facilities/Services for Foreign Students
International Center: The center's role is to promote mutual understanding between foreign students and Japanese students. There are four staff members at the center who are available to offer assistance to anyone who may need it.
Student Advisor System: There are about 20 Japanese students available to help foreign students in any way possible.
Special Programs for Foreign Students
    Foreign students enrolled in the undergraduate program may earn up to 22 credits in the Faculty of Business and Commerce and up to 26 credits in the Faculty of International Studies and Human Relations by taking "Japanese Language and Japanese Studies" courses, instead of General Education, Foreign Languages, and Physical Education classes.
For Further Information
    Undergraduate and Graduate Admission
Admissions and Public Relations Division, Tokyo International University, 1–13–1 Matoba-Kita, Kawagoe-shi, Saitama 350 ☎ 0492–32–1111 ext. 220

Tokyo Kasei Gakuin University
(Tokyo Kasei Gakuin Daigaku)

2600 Aihara–cho, Machida-shi, Tokyo 194-02
☎ 0427-82-9811

Faculty
    Profs. 30   Assoc. Profs. 25
    Assist. Profs. Full–time 12; Part–time 27
    Res. Assocs. 13
Number of Students
    Undergrad. 1, 223
Library 138, 215 volumes

Outline and Characteristics of the University
    Tokyo Kasei Gakuin University has two faculities: Home Economics and Humanities. The former includes the departments of Home Economics and of Habitation Science and the latter the departments of Japanese Cultural Studies and of Cultural Arts Studies. The university was founded by the late Mrs. Sumi Ohe in 1923 as the Kasei Kenkyusho (Institute of Home Economics). It was renamed the Tokyo Kasei Senmon Gakko (Tokyo School of Home Economics) in 1927, and the Tokyo Kasei Gakuin (Tokyo Kasei College) in 1963.
    The institution has since developed a four-year grogram concentrating on the study of home economics. In 1988 a new Faculty of Humanities was inaugurated. It provides the opportunity to examine the field of home economics in the context of the Japanese cutural heritage while rataining a truly global perspective, and in addition to acquire practi-

cal training appropriate to the expanding role of women in society. A comprehensive educational center for women, Tokyo Kasei Gakuin University is affiliated with a full range of junior and senior high schools and junior colleges.

As symbolized by its emblem K. V. A., standing for Knowledge, Virtue, and Arts, the fundamental goals of the university are the enrichment of intelligence, the cultivation of moral character, and the pursuit of the arts. These goals reflect the wisdom, personality, and cultural accomplishments of the university's founder, Sumi Ohe.

UNDERGRADUATE PROGRAMS

Faculty of Home Economics (Freshmen Enrollment: 270)
  Department of Home Economics
  Department of Housing and Planning
Faculty of Humanities (Freshmen Enrollment 200)
  Depertment of Cultural Arts Studies
  Depertment of Japanese Cultural Studies
  ✳
For Further Information
  Undergraduate Admission
Entrance Examination Division, Student Office, Tokyo Kasei Gakuin College, 2600 Aihara–cho, Machida–shi, Tokyo 194-02 ☎ 0427-82-9811

Tokyo Kasei Universtiy
（Tokyo Kasei Daigaku）

1–18–1 Kaga, Itabashi–ku, Tokyo 173　☎ 03–961–5 226

Faculty
  Profs. 46   Assoc. Profs 25
  Assist. Profs. Full–time 16; Part–time 51
  Res. Assoc. 10
Number of Students
  Undergrad. 2, 785
Library 176, 998 volumes

Outline and Characteristics of the University

Tokyo Kasei Universtiy, situated in Itabashi, Tokyo, consists of two faculties, the Faculty of Home Economics and the Faculty of Humanities. Each faculty is composed of several dapartments. The former includes the Department of Clothing Science and Fine Arts, the Department of Food and Nutrition and the Department of Juvenile Science. The latter includes the Department of English Language and Literature and the Department of Psychology and Education.

The university has another campus in Sayama, Saitama Prefecture, at which Humanities students study for four years and Home Economics students study for the first two years of their four-year programs.

Tokyo Kasei Junior College is also on the Itabashi Campus. It offers two-year programs in the Department of Clothing Science and Fine Arts, the Department of Food and Nutrition and the Department of Nursing.

Tokyo Kasei University has three attached schools (a kindergarten, a junior and a senior high school) as well as one institute, the Research Institute of Food, Clothing and Housing. The total number of students in all schools of the institution is over 7, 000.

The founder of the institution, Tatsugoro Watanabe, aimed at improving the talents of young ladies and contributing to their independence. He also strove to foster thier creativity through ethical instruction and training in professional skills. These aims are still the university's basic goals.

Soon after the establishment of the present university in 1949, the motto "affection, diligence, intelligence" was adopted to express the above goals. Past and present students have done justice to this motto, and many graduates of the university have entered the teaching profession.

Tokyo Kasei University, originally established as Wayo Saiho Denshujo (Ladies Dressmaking and Handicraft Academy) in 1881, is one of the oldest women's universities in Japan. In 1892 this academy developed into Tokyo Saiho Jogakko; in 1922 into Tokyo Joshi Semmon Gakko; and finally in 1949 into the present Tokyo Kasei Unniversity.

In its early stages the university consisted of the single Faculty of Home Economics. Since then it has undergone several phases of development. Most recently in 1986 the Faculty of Humanities was added, consisting of the Department of English Language and Literature and the Department of Psychology and Education.

The three departments of the Faculty of Home Economics give instruction in clothing and fine arts, nutrition and nursing. Atteniton is paid to both the technical-theoretical basis and professinonal application of these fields.

The two departments of the Faculty of Humanities endeavor to cultivate an international perspective and an intelligent approach to life. This newly established faculty aims above all to train students who can put their knowledge to practical use.

The Department of English Language and Literature emphasizes the development of students' skills in such subjects as Speech and Discussion, Essay Writing, Commercial English and Secretarial English.

The Department of Psychology and Education stresses practical counseling. Thus, classes are offered in such subjects as Counseling Practice, Psychiatric Studies and Industrial Psychology.

Foreign Student Admission
  Qualifications for Applicants
    Standard Qualifications Requirement
    Examination at the University

Same as for Japanese

Faculty of Domestic Sciences and Faculty of Humanities

Compulsory Subject: Composition in the Japanese language

Elective Subject: (One of the following) Japanese History, World History, Chemistry, Biology, General Homemaking-

Faculty of Domestic Sciences only

Applicants for the Food and Nutrition Program must take either Chemistry or Biology.

Documents to be Submitted When Applying

Standard Documents Requirement

Results of the Japanese Language Proficiency Test

Qualifications for Transfer Students

Graduates or those who have finished the senior course of other junior colleges may apply for direct entrance to the second year.

Graduates and those who have finished the junior or senior year of other junior colleges may apply for direct entrance to the third year.

Examination for Transfer Students

Compulsory Subjects: Specialized Subject 1, Foreign Language 1

Elective Subject: (one of the following) Humanities, Natural Sciences, Social Sciences

Interview

*

Research Institutes and Centers

Research Institute of Domestic Science

For Further Information

Undergraduate Admission

Division of Entrance Examinations, Tokyo Kasei University 1–18–1 Kaga Itabashi-ku, Tokyo 173 ☎ 03–961–5226 ext. 290

Tokyo Keizai University
(Tokyo Keizai Daigaku)

1-7 Minami–cho, Kokubunji–shi, Tokyo 185
☎ 0423-21-1941

Faculty

Profs. 76   Assoc. Profs. 30

Assist. Profs. Full–time 7; Part–time 201

Number of Students

Undergrad. 7,066   Grad. 28

Library 371,000 volumes

Outline and Characteristics of the University

The Okura Commerce School, the predecessor of the present Tokyo Keizai University, was established in 1900 by Kihachiro Okura, a financial magnate of the Meiji era. The chief aim of education in the school was to bring up able businessmen who could play an active part in international trade.

In 1919, the name of the school was changed to the Okura College of Commerce. In 1945 during World War II most of the school buildings, situated in Akasaka in the central area of Tokyo, were destroyed, and in 1946 the College moved to the present site in Kokubunji City.

In 1949, as a result of the national educational system reform the College acquired university status and was renamed Tokyo Keizai University. It was then that it began to offer an undergraduate program in economics. In 1950, the Junior College was attached to the University, and in 1964, the undergraduate program of business administration was established.

In 1970, the University started expanding its courses to the graduate level by establishing the master's program in economics. In 1976, its doctoral course was added. The master's and doctor's programs in business administration were first offered in 1978 and in 1986 respectively.

The Kokubunji campus of the University is situated in a quiet residential area. With beautiful parks and historic sites in its vicinity, it provides an excellent setting for school life. In addition to the campus in Kokubunji, the University has a campus in Musashimurayama with first–class physical education facilities for both indoor and outdoor sports.

The education and research programs of Tokyo Keizai University cover a broad area of social science with emphasis on economics and business administration offering a wide range of subjects geared to the various interests of the students. The students have a wide choice from among the subjects offered and thus they can fully satisfy their academic curiosity. There are also many seminars, each consisting of a small number of students so as to enable them to discuss subjects thoroughly among themselves as well as with their professors.

In the Faculty of Economics, students can study the development process, the structure and the future direction of the modern economy. The program offered in the Faculty of Business Administration aims at providing practical education in business, and also at educating students to become businessmen with a worldwide perspective.

The aim of the program of economics in the Graduate School is to give the students more specialized education related to economic theory, history and applied economics. One of the aims of the program of business administration is to provide an opportunity for foreign students to study Japanese business and management.

UNDERGRADUATE PROGRAMS

Faculty of Business Administration (Freshmen Enrollment: Day 500, Evening 250)

Department of Business Administration

See course listing in Faculty of Economics.

Faculty of Economics (Freshmen Enrollment: Day 550, Evening 250)

Department of Economics

Business Administration and Management Accounting, Advertising, Auditing, Bookkeeping, Business Administration, Business Analysis, Business Environment, Business Finance, Business History, Business Management, Business Mathematics, Business Organization, Chemical Industry, Commercial Science, Corporate Finance, Corporate Management, Cost Accounting, Distribution Theory, Financial Statements, Foreign Trade, Forms of Business Organization, History of Business Administration Theories, History of Technology, Industrial Psychology, Industrial Sociology, Information Data Processing System, Insurance, International Business Management, International Finance, Japanese Business History, Labor Management, Machine Industry, Management Engineering, Management Information System, Managerial Accounting, Marketing, Non-Life Insurance, Office Management, Production Management, Public Enterprise, Securities Market, Statistics For Business, Tax Accounting, Tourist Industry, Transportration

Economic History and Economic Theory Agricultural Economics, Business Cycle, Econometrics, Economic Geography, Economic History, Economic History of Japan, Economic Policy, Economics, Economic Statistics, Economic Theory, Finance, Foreign Economic Condition, History of Economic Theories, History of Social Thoughts, Industrial Economics, Industrial Relations, International Economics, Japanese Economic Condition, Local Government Finance, Planned Economy, Public Finance, Small and Medium Enterprise, Socialistic Economics, Social Policy, Social Security, Theoretical sociology

Foreign Student Admission

Qualifications for Applicants
Standard Qualifications Requirement
Examination at the University
Same as for Japanese. Written tests: Three subjects for Day Course (Japanese Language, English Language, and one of the following elective subjects: Politics & Economics, Japanese History, World History, Geography, Bookkeeping & Accounting, and Mathematics) and two subjects for Evening Course: (Japanese Language and English Language).
Documents to be Submitted When Applying
Standard Documents Requirement
Application deadline: in January.

Qualifications for Transfer Students
1. Those who have finished 14 years of education outside Japan or are due to do so by March of the year of application. They must be equivalent to a student who has completed a social science course of a junior college in Japan.
2. Those who have finished 14 years of education outside Japan and obtained a specified number of credits or are due to do so by March of the year of application. They must be equiva-

lent to a student who has finished the first two years of a social science faculty of a four-year university in Japan.
Examination for Transfer Students
Date: in March. same as for Japanese: an essay examination (concerning business administration for the Faculty of Business Administration, and economics for the Faculty of Economics) and an examination in a foreign language (to be chosen from among six languages).
Documents to be Submitted When Applying
Standard Documents Requirement

GRADUATE PROGRAMS

Graduate School of Business Administraion (First Year Enrollment : Master's 10, Doctor's 3)
Divisions
Business Administration
Graduate School of Economics (First Year Enrollment : Master's 10, Doctor's 5)
Divisions
Economics

Foreign Student Admission
Qualifications for Applicants
Master's Program
Standard Qualifications Requirement
Doctor's Program
Standard Qualifications Requirement
Examination at the University
Master's Program
Date: in Ocotober and in March.
An essay examination concerning their major field of study and an oral examination in Japanese. Those who have graduated from a Japanese university, however, are required to take the same examination given to Japanese students. It consists of a written examination (in a foreign language and specialized subjects) and an oral examination.
Doctor's Program
Date: in March. an oral examination concerning their master's thesis and a written examination (under consideration). Those who have finished a Japanese graduate school are required to take the same examination given to Japanese students. It consists of a written test in foreign languages and an oral examination concerning the applicants' Master's thesis.
Documents to be Submitted When Applying
Standard Documents Requirement
✳

For Further Information
Undergraduate Admission
Admission Office, Tokyo Keizai University, 1-7 Minami-cho, Kokubunji-shi, Tokyo 185 ☎ 0423-21-1941 ext. 249
Graduate Admission
Instruction Division, Tokyo Keizai University, 1-7 Minami-cho, Kokubunji-shi, Tokyo 185 ☎ 0423-

21-1941 ext. 230

Tokyo Medical College
(Tokyo Ika Daigaku)

6-1-1 Shinjuku, Shinjuku-ku, Tokyo 160
☎ 03-351-6141

UNDERGRADUATE PROGRAMS

Faculty of Medicine (Freshmen Enrollment: 120)
Department of Medicine

GRADUATE PROGRAMS

Graduate School of Medicine (First Year Enrollment : Doctor's 68)
Divisions
Internal Medicine, Morphological Medicine, Physiological Medicine, Social Medicine, Surgical Medicine

Tokyo Union Theological Seminary
(Tokyo Shingaku Daigaku)

3-10-30 Osawa, Mitaka-shi, Tokyo 181
☎ 0422-32-4185

Faculty
Profs.   12
Assist. Profs.   Full-time   2; Part-time   29
Number of Students
Undergrad.   84   Grad.   65
Library   77, 617 volumes

Outline and Characteristics of the College

Tokyo Union Theological Seminary has a rich tradition that reaches back to the beginnings of the Protestant church movement in Japan. The first Protestant seminary, founded by missionaries in 1877, was known as the Japan Union Seminary. This seminary later became the theological department of Meiji Gakuin University. Another theological department was established at Aoyama Gakuin University in 1889. In 1904, the Rev. Masahisa Uemura founded the Tokyo Shingakusha (Tokyo School of Theology), sometimes described as the first seminary to be independently financed and administered by Japanese Christians.

A quarter-century later, a number of mergers began to take place: the theological school of the Disciples of Christ with the Aoyama Gakuin theological department (1926); the Meiji Gakuin theological department with the Tokyo Shingakusha (1929); and

during World War II, an amalgamation of all Protestant theological schools (Lutheran, Reformed, Methodist, Baptist, Episcopalian, Salvation Army, etc.). The school born of this amalgamation was Tokyo Union Theological Seminary, formally established by the Nihon Kirisuto Kyodan (United Church of Christ in Japan) in 1943.

After World War II, some denominations re-established their own seminaries, but Tokyo Union Theological Seminary continues to carry on the traditions of a union seminary. It endeavors to provide well-trained Christian leaders for Christian churches, schools, and other institutions.

Tokyo Union Theological Seminary is an accredited institution that offers an undergraduate program leading to a bachelor's degree and a graduate school program leading to advanced degrees. Some students enter directly after graduating from high school. These students pursue a four-year college course with a major in theology, and most go on to study two additional years in order to obtain the equivalent of a Master of Divinity degree. The great majority of the students, however, enter the seminary after completing a four-year degree program in another field at some other university. These students study two years to acquire an undergraduate major in theology, then an additional two years to obtain the equivalent of the Master of Divinity degree. The seminary also offers a doctoral program in the fields of biblical studies and systematic theology.

The seminary campus is located in Mitaka, about twelve miles west of downtown Tokyo. The four-acre campus is adjacent to International Christian University, the Japan Lutheran Theological Seminary, and the Middle Eastern Culture Center. The main building, in the shape of a cross, contains the chapel, classrooms, individual faculty office, studies, and administrative offices. A new library, with a spacious reading and reference room, was completed in 1986.

The student body numbers about 165 full-time students. At present about 20% of the students are women, and about 10% are from other countries. Since competence in Japanese language is a requirement of admission, not all foreign stuedents who apply can be accepted, but each year the students body is enriched by the presence of students from other countries, primarily Korea and Taiwan.

UNDERGRADUATE PROGRAMS

Faculty of Theology (First year Enrollment: 35)
Department of Theology
Biblical History, Biblical Studies, Biblical Theology, Christian Education, Christianity, Church History, Ethics, History of Christian Art, History of Doctrine, History of Religions, Pastoral Psychology, Practical Theology, Religious Education Methods, Sociology of Religion, Systematic Theology, Theolo-

gy of Mission

Foreign Student Admission

Qualifications for Applicants

Standard Qualifications Requirement

The applicant must have been a member of a Protestant church for at least a year prior to admission, and must have a clear sense of being called by God to Christian ministry.

The appricant must also successfully complate a standard Japanese Language Proficiency Test (JLPT) either in Japan or abroad.

Examination at the College

Written examinations on Japanese, English, World History, and the Bible. In the case of foreign applicants who received their high school education in Japan, the examination on Japanese consists of a standard language test; for foreign applicants who received their high school education outside Japan, the examination on Japanese consists of a Japanese–language essay. The examination on the Bible covers both the Old and New Testaments.

In addition to these academic examinations, applicants must take a standard psychology test and be interviewed by the faculty.

Documents to be Submitted When Applying

Standard Documents Requirement

Applicants are also required to submit:

1. A letter of recommendation from the pastor of the church to which the applicant belongs.
2. An essay, written by the applicant, on "The Course of my Life as a Christian."

Qualifications for Transfer Students

1. Graduation from a college or university.
2. Recognition that admission, if granted, may be to either the second or third year of the undergraduate program, depending on the applicant's transcript of credits.

Examination for Transfer Students

1. English, French, or German (applicant's choice)
2. An essay written in Japanese
3. World History
4. Old Testament and New Testament
5. A standard psychology test
6. An interview with the faculty

Documents to be Submitted When Applying

Standard Documents Requirement

Other necessary documents are the same as those for freshman applicants.

GRADUATE PROGRAMS

Graduate School of Theology (First Year Enrollment limit: Master's 30, Doctor's 10)

Divisions

Biblical Theology, Systematic Theology

Foreign Student Admission

Qualifications for Applicants

Master's Program

Standard Qualifications Requirement

An undergraduate major in Christian Studies or the equivalent at a college or university, or graduation from a theological school for which university graduation is a prerequisite of admission, or such equivalent qualifications as the faculty agrees to recognize. Applicants must have membership in a Protestant church.

Doctor's Program

Standard Qualifications Requirement

The Master of Divinity degree or equivalent.

Examination at the College

Master's Program

1. English, French, or German (applicant's choice).
2. An academic dissertation.
3. A language connected with the field of specialized study specified by the applicant.
4. The grades previously received by the applicant in courses connected with the field of specialized study.

Doctor's Program

1. Any two of the following languages (applicant's choice): English, French, German.
2. An academic dissertation.
3. A language connected with the field of specialized study specified by the applicant.
4. The grades previously received by the applicant in courses connected with the field of specialized study.

Documents to be Submitted When Applying

Standard Documents Requirement

Applicants are also required to submit:

1. A letter of recommendation from the pastor of the church to which the applicant belongs.
2. An essay, written by the applicant, on "The Course of my Life as a Christian. "

*

Research Institutes and Centers

Asian Missiology Institute, Japan Missiology Institute

For Further Information

Undergraduate and Graduate Admission

Registrar, Tokyo Union Theological Seminary, 3-10-30 Osawa, Mitaka–shi, Tokyo 181 ☎ 0422-32-4185 ext. 205

Tokyo University of Agriculture
(Tokyo Nogyo Daigaku)

1-1-1 Sakuragaoka, Setagaya–ku, Tokyo 156
☎ 03-420-2131

Faculty

Profs. 114   Assoc. Profs. 65
Assist. Profs. Full–time 89; Part–time 176
Res. Assocs. 51

Number of Students
    Undergrad. 6, 434   Grad. 119
Library 300, 000 volumes

Outline and Characteristics of the University

Tokyo University of Agriculture has its origins in an agricultural course established at Tokugawa Ikueiko in 1891 by Takeaki Enomoto, one of the founders of modern Japan. It subsequently became independent and was renamed Tokyo Agricultural School in 1893, Tokyo Agricultural High School in 1901, and Tokyo College of Agriculture in 1911, with Tokiyoshi Yokoi as the founding president. During this period, in spite of the financial difficulty facing private schools, a firm foundation was laid for the rapid development of agricultural research and an educational institution unique in Japan. The university became the only private agricultural university provided for under the University Enactment of 1925. Many graduates have since made a great contribution to the development of the country especially in agriculture and related industries.

Today, the university plays a leading role in agricultural education and research in the country. It is also rapidly gaining an international reputation as a major center for agricultural research through active and continuing academic cooperation with many universities and research institutions abroad. In particular, it acts as the core university for the scientific cooperation program with Southeast Asian countries in the field of agricultural science, commissioned by the Japan Society for the Promotion of Science, under the auspices of the Ministry of Education, Science and Culture. It also has a long-standing relationship as sister school to Michigan State University, USA, to where it sends students regularly. In addition to MSU, three universities, The University of British Columbia in Canada, Beijing Agricultural University in China, and Kasetsart University in Thailand, have joined its sister schools since 1988.

The university's guiding principle in education is the practical application of science and technology in agriculture, ranging from production to marketing and consumption of agricultural products. Emphasis is placed not only on the study of advanced theories but also the experiment and practice of theories and techniques in laboratory and field training. The system operative at this university is the *kenkyushitsu* (laboratory) system. All the students must belong to a *kenkyushitsu* according to their choice of academic specialization in every department and receive close and continuing guidance from a group of academic staff (professor, associate professor, lecturer, and research associate) who are responsible for them in the laboratory. In other words, the *kenkyushitsu* functions as a unit of education and research as well as a society where students cultivate their personal interests and directions. In this way, it is hoped that students acquire not only professional knowledge and skill but also the well-balanced personality necessary for them to make their contribution as leaders in the progress of agriculture and related industries.

The university offers Bachelor of Agricultural Sciences, Master of Agricultural Sciences and Doctorate degrees, and there are more than 6, 600 students studying for their respective degrees. A total of more than 60, 000 students have graduated from this university and they have been very active in various fields both in and outside Japan. With recent technological development, bio–technology has become a popular field in science, and this university is also conducting active and intensive research in this field. In both research and education, Tokyo University of Agriculture continues to play a leading role in Japan.

UNDERGRADUATE PROGRAMS

Faculty of Agriculture (Freshmen Enrollment: 1, 280)
    Department of Agricultural Chemistry
    Department of Agricultural Economics
    Department of Agricultural Engineering
    Department of Agriculture
    Department of Brewing and Fermentation
    Department of Forestry
    Department of International Agricultural Development
    Department of Landscape Architecture
    Department of Nutrition
    Department of Zootechnical Science
Faculty of Bio-Industry (Freshmen Enrollment: 200)
    Deperment of Bio-Production
    Deperment of Food Science
    Deperment of Industrial Management

GRADUATE PROGRAMS

Graduate School of Agriculture (First Year Enrollment : Master's 54, Doctor's 15)
    Divisions
Agricultural Chemistry, Agricultural Economics, Agricultural Science, Food & Nutrition Science, Forestry, Zootechnical Science

*
Research Institutes and Centers
Computer Center, Food Processing Center, NODAI Research Institute, University Farm
For Further Information
    Undergraduate Admission
Admissions Section, Tokyo University of Agriculture, 1-1-1 Sakuragaoka, Setagaya–ku, Tokyo 156
☎ 03-420-2131 ext. 316
    Graduate Admission
Registration Section, Tokyo University of Agriculture, 1-1-1 Sakuragaoka, Setagaya–ku, Tokyo 156
☎ 03-420-2131 ext. 311

Tokyo University of Art and Design

(Tokyo Zokei Daigaku)

3-2707 Motohachioji, Hachioji-shi, Tokyo 193
☎ 0426-61-4401

Faculty
  Profs. 32   Assoc. Profs. 21
  Assist. Profs. Full–time 5; Part–time 81
Number of Students
  Undergrad. 1, 346
Library 32, 350 volumes

Outline and Characteristics of the University

As technology makes great progress, society changes accordingly, and new movements in art emerge. This is partly due to the fact that people, when placed in a situation where conventional social elements become unsuitable, feel compelled to pursue a more appropriate way of living and thinking, and ultimately a new ideal concerning humanity. This is the situation today. Hence, one of the most important questions is how to cultivate men of creative minds, capable of appropriately responding to these challenges of the coming century.

The University responds to this question by cultivating men of creative minds through education and study in the arts and design. In this way, graduates may contribute to the establishment of a new symbiotic world of humanity, technology, cultural tradition, and mature in the next century. This is the principal educational goals of the University.

Tokyo University of Art and Design is located in Hachioji City on the western edge of Tokyo. Hachioji City provides us with the right conditions for the education and studies for the development of art and design. This city is proud of its long history and natural surroundings as well as its reputation as an emerging center for new technology.

The University was established by Yoko Kuwasawa with 135 students in 1966, as the only advanced education center of the Bauhaus movement in Japan. The small scale of the school enabled the faculty to provide proper, deliberate, and intimate guidance to students so they would be motivated to develop their creative talents. This tradition continues at the University. The student enrollment is limited to 1, 300. Consequently, the student–teacher relationship at the Unversity is not simply academic but also very human.

In order to carry out the original educational policy of synthesizing art with technology, the mental world with the material universe, culture with civilization, the university offers a rich interdisciplinary curriculum that is constantly advancing toward the future in response to the demands of society.

The academic level of the university in the past 21 years is highly esteemed in the design world. The active demands in the industrial fields for our graduates, and the steady increase of applicants for admission bear witness to this fact. Indeed, only a few academic institutes can claim the same level of accomplishments as the University.

UNDERGRADUATE PROGRAMS

Faculty of Art (Freshmen Enrollment: 300)
  Department of Design
Advertising, Architecture, Design Management, Dyeing, Editing, Environmental Housing, Equipment Design, Film, Furniture, Photography, Printing, Visual Environment, Weaving
  Department of Fine Arts
Japanese Painting, Lithography, Painting, Sculpture, Stone Sculpture, Three–Dimentional Design, Wood Printing Presentation, Wood Sculpture

Foreign Student Admission
  Qualifications for Applicants
  Standard Qualifications Requirement
  Those who hold the diploma granted by the International Baccalaureate Office and who are 18 years of age or over may also apply.
  Examination at the University
  There are two admission procedures; to pass the entrance examination and to obtain admission by an interview with recommendation of a designated recommender.
  Admission by Written Examination:
application deadline: the end of January. examination on subjects and artistic field Date: at the beginning of February.
  Admission by Interview and Recommendation:
application deadline the beginning of November. the individual interview for selection Date: at the end of November.
  Documents to be Submitted When Applying
  Standard Documents Requirement
  Applicants for interview with a recommendation letter must obtain further information from the Admission Office in October.

*

For Further Information
  Undergraduate Admission
Admission Office, Tokyo University of Art and Design, 3-2707 Motohachioji, Hachioji-shi, Tokyo 193
☎ 0426-61-4401

Tokyo University of Information Sciences

(Tokyo Joho Daigaku)

1200–2 Yatoh–cho, Chiba–shi, Chiba 280–01
☎ 0472–36–1101

Faculty
  Profs. 14   Assoc. Profs. 7
  Assist. Profs. Full–time 15; Part–time 6
Number of Students
  Undergrad. 403
Library 24, 550 volumes

Outline and Characteristics of the University

Tokyo University of Information Sciences, located in Chiba Prefecture in the environs of Tokyo, was established on April 1, 1988 by Tokyo University of Agriculture. Tokyo University of Agriculture was itself established in 1891 by Takeaki Enomoto, an eminent statesman of the Meiji restoration and a key figure in the Meiji Government, serving as Minister of Communications, Minister of Education and Minister of Foreign Affairs. Enomoto's primary objective in founding Tokyo University of Agriculture was to educate and train the very best Japan had to offer to meet the demands of the new era.

Tokyo University of Information Sciences hopes to continue and further the spirit and aspirations of Takeaki Enomoto. At present the University consists of two departments whose primary object is to prepare students for the great demands that will be placed on them in the 21st century especially with regard to Japan's increasing role in world affairs and the trend toward a world-wide information oriented society. In this society, the demand for computer software specialists greatly outruns the supply and so it is vital that Japan make every effort to alleviate this situation. Thus, the primary object of Tokyo University of Information Sciences is to train students in state-of-the-art computer science, while at the same time developing a sense of international-mindedness, adaptability and a keen interest in scholarship.

In the Department of Business and Management Information, emphasis is placed on educating students for top management positions involving the computer sciences. In the Department of Information Systems, the aim is to train students in the finer arts of computer engineering at the managerial level. In order to achieve these goals the University, while employing a faculty of specialists in computer and computer-related sciences, contains the very latest audio-visual facilities as well as 200 computers which students are free to use at any time.

In the future, Tokyo University of information Sciences hopes to become a college open to the community, conducting joint research projects, providing extension classes and so forth.

UNDERGRADUATE PROGRAMS

Faculty of Business Administration and Information Science (Freshmen Enrollment: 290)

Department of Business and Management Information

Accounting Theory and Financial Statements, Analysis of Information Industry, Applied Mathematics for Management Science, Behavioral Sciences, Business Administration, Business Economics, Business History, Business Organization, Civil Law, Commercial Law, Computer Accounting, Computer Systems, Cost Accounting, Distribution, Economic Policy, Economic Theory, Financial Management, Forms of Business Firms, History of Business Management Theory, Industrial Psychology, Industrial Sociology, Information Management, Information Processing, Information Systems Audit, International Business, Introduction to Computer Science, Japanese Business History, Laws pertaining to Information, Management Accounting, Management Analysis, Management Information System, Management Science, Managerial Statistics, Marketing, Mass Communications, Money and Banking, Office Automation, Operations Research, Organizational Behavior, Personnel Management, Principles of Bookkeeping, Principles of Management, Production Management, Programming Languages I (Fortran) and II (COBOL), Quality Control, Sales Management, Small Business, Studies on New Media, Transportation

Department of Information Systems

Accounting Theory and Financial Statements, Advanced Calculus, Analysis of Information Industry, Behavioral Sciences, Business Administration, Business Organization, CAD/CAM Systems, Calculus, Civil Law, Commercial Law, Computer Accounting, Computer Simulation, Computer System, Cost Accounting, Database Management System, Data Communication Systems, Data Structures, Distribution, Economic Policy, Economic Theory, Forms of Business Firms, Image Information Engineering, Imaging Systems, Industrial Psychology, Industrial Sociology, Information Management, Information Processing, Information Systems Audit, Information Theory, Introduction to Computer Science, Japanese Business History, Laws pertaining to Information, Linear Algebra, Management Accounting, Management Analysis, Management Information Systems, Management Science, Marketing, Mass Communication, Mathematical Programming, Money and Banking, Office Automation, Operating Systems, Operations Research, Organizational Behavior, Personnel Management, Principles of Bookkeping, Principles of Management, Probability Theory and Statistics, Production Management, Programmming Languages I (Fortran), II (COBOL), III (UNIX/C) and

IV (Prolog, LISP), Quality Control, Seminar on Computer Science, Software Engineering, Studies on New Media, Systems Design, Transportation

Foreign Student Admission
Qualifications for Applicants
Japanese Language Proficiency Test (first level), General Examination for Foreign Students results.
Examination at the University
Written Examination in subjects given by department.
Interview.

                          *

For Further Information
Undergraduate Admission
Head, School Affairs Division, Entrance Examination Section, Tokyo University of Information Sciences, 1200–2 Yatoh–cho, Chiba–shi, Chiba 280–01
☎ 0472–36–1101ext. 2142

Tokyo Woman's Christian University
(Tokyo Joshi Daigaku)

2-6-1 Zempukuji, Suginami-ku, Tokyo 167
☎ 03-395-1211

Faculty
    Profs. 82   Assoc. Profs. 25
    Assist. Profs. Full–time 7; Part–time 234
    Res. Assocs. 29
Number of Students
    Undergrad. 2, 919   Grad. 36
Library   410, 000 volumes

Outline and Characteristics of the University
    Ever since it was founded in 1918, Tokyo Woman's Christian University has had, as the aims of its education, the principles of Christianity, a liberal arts education, and internationalism. In an age when there was a marked discrimination between the sexes and women had few opportunities for higher education, Tokyo woman's Christian College (as it was called than) made a great contribution to women's education. Now, the sphere of activities for women has widened remarkably, and the traditions of the university are being consolidated as well as remoulded to meet the needs of the present-day world.
    From the beginning this institution had international ties with kindred-spirited Christians abroad. Its history traces back to the 1910 World Missionary Conference held in Edinburgh, where it was decided to open several institutions of higher education for women in the East. The university's first president was Dr. Inazo Nitobe, who wished to serve, in his own words, as "a bridge across the Pacific. " He did much to set the international tone of the university.

Until very recently, the Tokyo Woman's Christian University Cooperating Committee, which was composed of representatives of several Protestant denominations in North America, never ceased to give support, financial as well as spiritual, to the university.

    In 1924, the university moved to its present campus in Zempukuji, Suginami-Ku. The spacious front garden, and the front of the library building, bearing the school motto — "Quaecunque sunt vera" ("Whatsoever things are true") — carved above the entrance, give the campus the proper atmosphere of learning and thoughtful contemplation. At present this campus houses the College of Arts and Sciences, consisting of seven departments, and also the Graduate School, which was established in 1971.

    The university has one more campus — in the Mure area of Mitaka-shi, which was obtained in 1966 and used first for the Junior College Program, which had been a supplement to the university since 1950. The Junior College was reorganized into a new four-year college, and the College of Culture and Communication was founded on this campus in April, 1988. This reorganization was undertaken in order to equip young women with the kinds of skills and knowledge that are needed in an increasingly internationalized world. While the seven depertments of the College of Arts and Sciences are conceived along more or less traditional lines, each of the three departments of the new college emphasizes the interdisciplinary approach.

    Every year the University's graduates who seek jobs are employed by companies, banks, or educational institutions. Some pursue their study further at the graduate school of their own university or at those of other universities of an equally high academic standard. In whatever field they work, the graduates stand high in the estimation of the people around them, bearing eloquent testimony to the success of education at Tokyo Women's Christian University.

    The university welcomes students from abroad. Classes, especially seminars, are very small, enabling teachers and students to get to know each other very well. Classes are conducted in Japanese. It is hoped that a great variety of social and cultural backgrounds will animate campus life and stimulate each student in the pursuit of her academic interests.

UNDERGRADUATE PROGRAMS

College of Arts and Sciences (Freshmen Enrollment: 650)
Department of English
American Literature, Comparative Literature, English Literature, English Philology and Linguistics
Department of History
Japanese History, Occidental History, Oriental History
Department of Japanese Literature
Chinese Literature, Comparative Literature, Japa-

nese Literature, Japanese Philology and Linguistics, Language Data Processing

Department of Mathematics

Algebraic Geometry, Computer Sciences, Functional Analysis, Number Theory, Probability Theory, Topology

Department of Philosophy

Christian Theology, Philosophy

Department of Psychology

Cognitive Psychology, Community Psychology, Developmental Psychology, Psychology of the Mentally Handicapped, Social Psychology

Department of Sociology and Economics

Economics, History of Social and Economic Thought, International Relations, Social Research, Sociology

College of Culture and Communication (Freshmen Enrollment: 250)

Department of Communication

Communication Media, International Communication, Interpersonal Communication, Intra-personal Communication, Mass Communication, Social Communication

Depertment of Cross-cultural Studies

American Culture, Anthropology, Chinese Culture, Comparative Study of Culture, History, Japanesse Culture, Korean Culture, Literature

Department of Languages

Contrastive Study of English and Japanese, English Advanced Skills, English Linguistics, Japanese Linguistics, Teaching of English as a second Language, Teaching of Japanese as a Second Language

Foreign Student Admission

Qualifications for Applicants

Standard Qualifications Requirement

Applicants who plan to take the examination in Japan are required to take the Japanese Language Proficiency Test and General Examination for Foreign Students.

Examination at the University

1. Applicants who cannot come to Japan for the entrance examination are required to submit a short essay in Japanese on an assigned topic.
2. Applicants who are in Japan must take an entrance examination consisting of a written exam and an interview.

Documents to be Submitted When Applying

Standard Documents Requirement

Certificates of the Japanese Language Proficiency Test and General Examination for Foreign Students must be submitted together with other application documents.

Date of Application:

1. Those applying from their home countries:

For the entrance in April, 1989, applications will be accepted from August 1 till September 21, 1988.

2. Those in Japan:

Application will be accepted from November 1 to November 15.

Qualifications for Transfer Students

Those who have finished 14 years of education in foreign countries. (Those who are graduates of junior colleges and vocational schools are not included.)

Examination for Transfer Students

1. Applicants who cannot come to Japan for the transfer examination are required to submit two short essays respectively in Japanese and in a foreign language (either English, German, French, or Chinese which is not their mother tongue).
2. Applicants who are in Japan must take an examination consisting of a written examination and an interview.

Documents to be Submitted When Applying

Standard Documents Requirement

GRADUATE PROGRAMS

Graduate School of Humanities (First Year Enrollment: Master's 24)

Courses

English History, Japanese Literature, Philosophy

Graduate School of Sciences (First Year Enrollment : Master's 6)

Courses

Mathematics

Foreign Student Admission

Qualifications for Applicants

Master's Program

Standard Qualifications Requirement

Examination at the University

Master's Program

1. Applicants are required, to take the selective examinations in Japan, which are administered in early March. The application documents must be submitted to the Registrar's Office between January 10 and February 10 (dates may vary).
2. For those applicants who cannot be in Japan at the time of the examinations because of unavoidable reasons, special consideration will be given except for applicants to the Department of Mathematics, they can take the examinations in their home country by mail. In this case the applicants are required to apply to the Registrar's Office between August 1 and the middle of September (dates may vary).

Documents to be Submitted When Applying

Standard Documents Requirement

The Japanese Language Proficiency Test (JLPT)

Applicants are required to present a copy of their graduation thesis, together with other application documents.

*

Research Institutes and Centers

Center for Women's Studies, Institute for Comparative Studies of Culture

Facilities/Services for Foreign Students

Several dormitory rooms are available for foreign students in the residential halls on campus.

For Further Information

Undergraduate and Graduate Admission

Registrar's Office, College of Arts and Sciences, Graduate Schools Tokyo Woman's Christian University, 2-6-1, Zenpukuji, Suginami-ku, Tokyo 167 ☎ 03-395-1211 ext. 226

College of Culture and Communication

Registrar's Office, College of Culture and Communication, Tokyo Woman's Christian University 4-3-1, Mure, Mitaka-shi, Tokyo 181 ☎: 0422-45-4145 ext. 210

Tokyo Women's College of Physical Education

(Tokyo Joshi Taiiku Daigaku)

620 Tanikawakami, Aoyagi, Kunitachi-shi,
Tokyo 186　☎ 0425-72-4131

Faculty
　　Profs.　26　　Assoc. Profs.　27
　　Assist. Profs.　Full-time　9; Part-time　18
　　Res. Assocs.　2
Number of Students
　　Undergrad.　1, 339
Library　87, 282 volumes

Outline and Characteristics of the College

Tokyo Women's College of Physical Education was founded in 1902, originally called Tokyo Woman's Gymnastics School. Toyo Fujimura, leading founder of the school believed in the boarding school system and herself lived together with the students in the dormitory to educate them in a family atmosphere. Fujimura has, as the aim of education, the development of women leaders in physical education who live in the spirit of sincerity, faith, friendship and humanity. In 1961, the school moved to the present location in Kunitachi City which is known as a cultural and educational city in the suburbs of Tokyo. In 1962 it became the first academic physical education institution of higher education for women in the country. In 1983, in celebrating the 80th anniversary of its founding, the College undertook the over-all reconstruction of school buildings and facilities for physical activities: all weather track and field, various ball game courts, several gymnasiums by event and other modern educational facilities such as music rooms, special rooms, various laboratories, Computer room and a warm water pool.

The College consists of one Faculty of Physical Education and one Department with approximately 1, 500 students. The students are divided into two specialized courses: school physical education course and social physical education course. In order to develop their capacity as physical educators, they are required to take subjects such as the philosophy of physical education and physical performance in their respective field of major.

The student's extra-curricular activities consist of 32 athletic and cultural clubs and circles; among these, rhythmic sport, track and field, soft-ball, handball, fencing and canoeing are internationally active clubs.

UNDERGRADUATE PROGRAMS

Faculty of Physical Education (Freshmen Enrollment　250)

Department of Physical Education

Administration of School Physical Education, Athletic Accidents, Athletic Prescription, Compensations, Curriculum Development, Health Education, Management of School Physical Education, Recreation, Rehabilitation, Social Education

Foreign Student Admission

Qualifications for Applicants

Standard Qualifications Requirement

Examination at the College

Same as for Japanese: Japanese language, English and athletic performance.

Documents to be Submitted When Applying

Standard Documents Requirement

1. A recommendation from the principal of the school the applicant attended or the equivalent.
2. A certificate of the Japanese language proficiency from the principal of the school the applicant attended or the equivalent.
3. An application form prescribed by the college showing a history of athletic activities in which the applicant participated.

Qualifications for Transfer Students

1. Those who have graduated junior colleges.
2. Those who have completed two years of study of four year colleges or universities.
3. Those who can show sufficient ability corresponding to that of applicants who belong to the above (1) or (2).

Examination for Transfer Students

Same as for Japanese: an interview, an essay and athletic performance.

Documents to be Submitted When Applying

Standard Documents Requirement

*

Research Institutes and Centers

Institute of Physical Education for Women

For Further Information

Undergraduate Admission

Educational Affairs Division II, Tokyo Women's College of Physical Education, 620 Tanikawakami,

Aoyagi, Kunitachi–shi, Tokyo 186 ☎ 0425-72-4131 ext. 222

Tokyo Women's Medical College
(Tokyo Joshi Ika Daigaku)

8-1 Kawada-cho, Shinjuku–ku, Tokyo 162
☎ 03-353-8111

Faculty
    Profs.   98   Assoc. Profs.   75
    Assist. Profs.   Full–time 102; Part–time   123
    Res. Assocs.   452
Number of Students
    Undergrad.   635   Grad.   57
Library   137, 844 volumes

Outline and Characteristics of the College

Tokyo Women's Medical College is still, as at the time of its foundation by Yayoi Yoshioka in 1900, the only women's medical school in Japan. Today, there are some 80 other medical schools and departments in Japan, all accepting both male and female students. Although there were a number of women's medical schools in Japan prior to World War II, our school alone has, in accordance with the thinking of its founder, opted to remain an institution exclusively for women at the undergraduate level.

The College has made truly remarkable progress since the end of World War II. A fine nine–story building with the most modern teaching and research facilities and the Heart Institute of Japan (completed 1954) and its hospital (1965) and other pioneering institutions now stand on the Kawada–cho campus. We now have the Institute of Gastroenterology (1965), the Neurological Institute (1971), the Institute of Geriatrics (1975), the Diabetes Center (1975), the Kidney Center (1979), the Institute of Rheumatology (1982), the Institute of Clinical Endocrinology (1984) and the Maternal and Perinatal Center (1984). With the completion of the Central, East and Psychiatric Wings of the Kawada–cho Main Hospital and its Second Hospital in Nishiogu in Tokyo's Arakawa Ward (362 beds), our general hospitals now have a total of around 1, 800 beds. In 1969, the College established an affiliated Junior College of Nursing, and this was followed in 1977 by the School of Nursing and the Second School of Nursing.

We are confident that in all these areas Tokyo Women's Medical College will continue to move forward, indeed, frequently play a pioneering and leading role.

UNDERGRADUATE PROGRAMS

Faculty of Medicine (Freshmen Enrollment: 100)
Department of Medicine

Anatomy, Anesthesiology, Biochemistry, Cardiology, Cardiovascular Surgery, Dermatology, Gastroenterological Surgery, Gastroenterology, Hygiene and Public Health, Internal Medicine, Legal Medicine, Microbiology, Neurology, Neurosurgery, Obstetrics and Gynecology, Ophthalmology, Orthopedic Surgery, Otolaryngology, Parasitology, Pathology, Pediatric Cardiology, Pediatric Cardiovascular Surgery, Pediatrics, Pharmacology, Physiology, Plastic and Reconstructive Surgery, Psychiatry, Radiology, Surgery, Urology

Foreign Student Admission
Qualifications for Applicants
    Standard Qualifications Requirement
    Applicants are required to pass the Japanese Language Proficiency Test or have the equivalent Japanese ability.
Examination at the College
    The first selection: Screening of the papers, the second Selection: a physical examination, and a written exam plus an interview.
Documents to be Submitted When Applying
    Standard Documents Requirement
1. A statement of purpose (one's own handwriting)
2. A certificate of the first level of the Japanese Language Proficiency Test or a certificate of the equivalent.

Qualifications for Transfer Students
    Decided by the faculty council On a case by case basis.

GRADUATE PROGRAMS

Graduate School of Medicine (First Year Enrollment : Doctor's 31)
Divisions
Functional Science, Internal Medicine, Morphology, Social Medicine, Surgery

Foreign Student Admission
Qualifications for Applicants
Doctor's Program
    Standard Qualifications Requirement
Examination at the College
Doctor's Program
    The first selection: Screening of the papers. Second Selection: a written examination on the desired subject, an oral exam.
Documents to be Submitted When Applying
    Standard Documents Requirement
    A certificate of the applicant's Japanese language ability certified by a guidance professor, or equivalent is also required.

*

Research Institutes and Centers
College Hospital, Diabetes Center, Institute of Biomedical Engineering, Institute of Clinical Endocri-

nology, Institute of Gastroenterology, Institute of Geriatrics, Institute of Laboratory Animals, Institute of Rheumatology, Kidney Center, Maternal and Perinatal Center, Medical Research Institute, Neurological Institute, The Heart Institute of Japan

For Further Information
Undergraduate and Graduate Admission
Student Office, Tokyo Women's Medical College, 8–1 Kawada–cho, Shinjuku–ku, Tokyo 162
☎ 03-353-8111 ext. 2212~3

Towa University
(Towa Daigaku)

1-1-1 Chikushigaoka, Minami-ku, Fukuoka-shi, Fukuoka 815   ☎ 092-541-1511

Faculty
    Profs. 18   Assoc. Profs. 14
    Assist. Profs. Full–time 8; Part–time 57
    Res. Assocs. 7
Number of Students
    Undergrad. 1, 303
Library 46, 454 volumes

Outline and Characteristics of the University
    Mankind is witnessing an age in which technological innovation has made rapid progress. This progress has caused a fundamental as well as a structural change in the industrial world and is now bringing in a revolutionary change in the physical and spiritual aspects of life.
    Meanwhile, an increasing awareness of the limitations of the earth's natural resources has caused man to seek out new technology to replace these limited resources. Accordingly, a higher level of international points of views is required in academia and industry. The raison d'être of a university is, therefore, to provide students with the abilities and insights to cope with the ever-changing situation of society, and enable them to become its leaders tomorrow.
    The ideal Towa University is to enroll those serious students and train them to be qualified engineers. They should acquire not only the basics of advanced technology but also the versatile, creative abilities to deal with the foreseeable technological problems of the future.
    Furthermore, in an attempt not to lose sight of the humanistic aspect of life by placing too much emphasis on materialism, the University pays special attention to the general education of the students. A well-rounded education will allow them to sufficiently understand that every problem or difficulty should ultimately be solved through a person's humanity and not his technical capacity.
    Based on the above philosophy, the University concentrates on educating and fostering capable, well-rounded engineers in various techinical fields.

The responsibility to educate is not limited to domestic students but to all students of the world. In order to contribute to the development of Southeast Asia and other developing countries, the University gladly accepts students from these countries and provides them with an education so they may contribute to their own society in the future.

UNDERGRADUATE PROGRAMS

Faculty of Engineering (Freshmen Enrollment: 160)
    Department of Chemistry
Electronic Chemistry, High Polymer Chemistry, High-temperature Chemistry, Non-organic Chemistry, Organic Chemistry, Physical Chemistry
    Department of Construction
Bridge Building, City Planning, Equipment, Geological Engineering, Hydraulics, Materials, River and Ocean Engineering, Soil Mechanics, Structure Dynamics, Surveying, Vibration
    Department of Electric Engineering
Applied Mathematics, Control Engineering, Electric Acoustics, Electricity Theory, Electric Magnetism, Measurement
    Department of Industrial Engineering
Business Management, Cost-price Management, Financial Management, Human Engineering, Industrial Psychology, Information Theory, Labor Management, Marketing, Operations Research, Production Control, Quality Control, System Engineering

Foreign Student Admission
    Qualifications for Applicants
        Standard Qualifications Requirement
    Examination at the University
        A written exam and an interview in Japanese.
    Documents to be Submitted When Applying
        Standard Documents Requirement
                    *
Research Institutes and Centers
The Institue for International Education
Special Programs for Foreign Students
    The University offers a course in Japanese as a foreign language.
For Further Information
    Undergraduate Admission
Towa University, 1-1-1 Chikushigaoka, Minami-ku, Fukuoka-shi, Fukuoka 815 ☎ 092-541-1511

Toyota Technological Institute
(Toyota Kogyo Daigaku)

2-12 Hisakata, Tempaku-ku, Nagoya-shi, Aichi 468
☎ 052-802-1111

Faculty
    Profs. 21   Assoc. Profs. 14
    Assist. Profs. Full–time 1; Part–time 41
    Res. Assocs. 10

Number of Students
     Undergrad. 218   Grad. 51
Library 34, 183 volumes

Outline and Characteristics of the University
     "Respect the spirit of research and creativity, and always strive to stay ahead of the times." These were the guiding ideals of Sakichi Toyoda, one of Japan's best known inventors, who made important contributions to society through his numerous inventions.
     Toyota Technological Institute was founded in 1981 in the city of Nagoya to put these ideals into practice in the field of research and education.
     For its establishment Toyota Motor Corporation donated a sum of 35. 6 billion yen to express its wish to return to society part of the profits it had earned from its business activities.
     T. T. I. has Faculty of Engineering which consists of two departments; Mechanical Systems Engineering and Information and Control Engineering. It also has Graduate School in Engineering (Master's program).
     Education and research at T. T. I. is aimed not only at providing its students technical knowledge of the highest standard but also at developing them into well-rounded human beings.
     An extremely unique feature of T. T. I. is its students. Priority is given to admitting those who have had experience in engineering-related work at an industrial enterprise. This enables T. T. I. to produce "practical-minded technologists" who have the ability to identify existing and potential problems and solving them.
     Another of its characteristics is that only a small number of students are admitted thus enabling the teaching staff and students to maintain close communications with one another. The number of undergraduate students admitted per year is limited to 80 and that for graduate school students 24.
     Although T. T. I. was established by Toyota Motor Corporation, its doors are open to all other industrial companies in Japan. Many Japanese companies have sent or are trying to send employees to T. T. I. for continuing and advanced education.
     T. T. I. believes that the true mission of a university is to serve society by providing advanced education which is conducted in close communication and co-operation with society, thereby preventing the institute from becoming an academic island isolated from the rest of the community.

UNDERGRADUATE PROGRAMS

Faculty of Engineering (Freshmen Enrollment: 80)
     Department of Information and Control Engineering
Computer Systems, Instrumentation and Control Engineering, Picture Signal Processing, Robot Technology, Semiconductor Process Technology, Surface Science and Application, Systems Engineering
     Department of Mechanical Systems Engineering
Design Engineering, Fluid Engineering, Heat Engineering, Macromolecular Materials Science, Materials Processing, Materials Science of Fine Ceramics, Production Engineering, Strength and Fracture of Materials

GRADUATE PROGRAMS

Graduate School of Engineering (First Year Enrollment : Master's 24)
     Division
Basic Production Engineering
                          *
Research Institutes and Centers
CAD Center, Computer Center, Machine Shop, Semiconductor Center
For Further Information
     Undergraduate and Graduate Admission
Admissions Office, Toyota Technological Institute, 2-12 Hisakata, Tempaku-ku, Nagoya-shi, Aichi 468
☎ 052-802-1111

Toyo University
(Toyo Daigaku)
5-28-20 Hakusan, Bunkyo-ku, Tokyo 112
☎ 03-945-7557

Faculty
     Profs. 243   Assoc. Profs. 90
     Assist. Profs. Full–time 71; Part–time 504
     Res. Assocs. 16
Number of Students
     Undergrad. 15, 074   Grad. 203
Library 710, 795 volumes

Outline and Characteristics of the University
     Toyo University originated as a school called Tetsugakukan (Academy of Philosophy), which was founded by Enryo Inoue, whose guiding principle was: "The basis of all learning lies in philosophy." Later, Tetsugakukan Academy was moved to the University's present site. The name of the school was first changed to Tetsugakukan College, and then to Toyo University. The first president of the college was Enryo Inoue, and courses in philosophy, religion, ethics, education, Japanese, and classical Chinese were offered. The academic system has changed, its curriculum improved, and the university has come to manifest a unique academic character.
     The university was restructured in accordance with the New School Education Law which came into effect in 1949. The Faculty of Literature was first instituted, followed by the Faculties of Economics, Law, Sociology, Engineering, and Business Administration. Graduate programs were added to each

faculty and a junior college was established. Toyo University now consists of a graduate school and six undergraduate faculties, each of which is tied to the graduate school programs, one junior college, and two high schools affiliated with the University.

The University has been making efforts to improve its educational, and academic facilities, pursuing its creative goals based on the founder's guiding principle.

UNDERGRADUATE PROGRAMS

Faculty of Business Administration (Freshmen Enrollment: 500)
Department of Business Administration
Department of Commerce
Accounting, Accounting Information System, Administrative Management, Auditing, Business Administration, Business Enterprise, Business Management, Business Policy, Commerce, Cost Management, Data Management, Decision Making in Business Management, Financial Statements Analysis, History and Theories of Management, History of Industry, Industrial Sociology, Information Processing, International Business Management, Management, Management and Labor, Management Engineering, Management Information System, Management & Organization, Management Policy, Managerial Finance, Office Management, Production Management, Small Business Management, Statistics of Business Management

Faculty of Economics (Freshmen Enrollment: 500)
Department of Economics
Accounting, Agricultural Economics, Banking Policy, Business Fluctuation, Econometrics, Economic Geography, Economic History, Economic Planning, Economic Policies, Economics, Economic Statistics, Economy of Developing Countries, Environmental Economics, History of Economic Theories, History of Economic Thoughts, Industrial Economics, International Economy, International Finance, Japanese Economic History, Japanese Economy, Labor Problems, Local Finance, Marxian Economics, Modern Economics, Monetary Policy, Monetary Theories, Natural Resources, Philosophy of Economics, Public Finance, Socialist Economic Thoughts, Social Policies, Survey of Industry, Traffic Economics Corporations, Welfare Economics

Faculty of Engineering (Freshmen Enrollment: 780)
Department of Applied Chemistry
Analytical Chemistry, Applied Physical Chemistry, Biochemical Industry, Catalysis, Chemical Engineering, Complex Chemistry, Environmental Hygine Engineering, Fermentation Engineering, Food Engineering, General Chemistry, Industrial Chemistry, Inorganic Chemical Industry, Inorganic Chemistry, Inorganic Industrial Material, Organic Chemical Industry, Organic Chemistry, Organic Material, Photochemistry, Physical Chemistry, Physical Chemistry, Polymer Chemistry, Production Planning and Control, Quantum Chemistry, Radiation Chemistry, Synthetic Organic Chemistry

Department of Architecture
Architectual Drawing, Architectural Design, Architectural Design and Drawing, Building Acoustics, Building and Housing Economics, Building Construction and Building Systems, Environmental Engineering, Evaluation of Environmental Performance, Fire-proofing of Buildings, History of Architecture, Landscape Architecture, Planning Methodology of Architecture, Steel-frame Structure, Structural Design, Structural Design, Theory of Design, Theory of Structure

Department of Civil Engineering
Bridge Engineering, City Planning, Civil Engineering, Concrete Engineering, Construction Equipments, Construction Methods, Construction Planning and Management, Dam Engineering, Earthquake Engineering, Engineering Geology, Environmental and Sanitation Engineering, Foundation Engineering, Geotechnical Engineering, Harbor Engineering, Highway Engineering, Hydraulics, Materials for Civil Engineering Use, Numerical Methods, Public Work Systems Engineering, Railway Engineering, Reinforced Concrete Structures, River Engineering, Sewerage, Soil Exploration Methods, Steel Structures, Strength of Materials, Structural Engineering, Surveying, Traffic Engineering, Tunnel Engineering, Vibrations of Civil Engineering Structures, Water Supply, Welding Engineering

Department of Electrical Engineering
Applied Electric Power Engineering, Atomic Power Engineering, Basic Electrical Experiments, Design and Drawing of Electric Appliance, Digital Computer, Electric Circuits, Electric Control, Electric Energy Engineering Apparatus, Electric Illumination and Heating, Electric Machinery, Electric Measurement, Electric Power Systems, Electric Railway, Electroacoustics, Electromagnetics, Electromagnetic Wave Engineering, Electronic Components, Electronic Measurements, High Voltage Engineering, Laws and Regulations for Electrical Facilities, Microwave Engineering, Numerical Engineering, Power Plant Engineering, Power Transmission and Distribution, Quantum Electronics, Radio Engineering, Semiconductor, Semiconductor Engineering, Systems Engineering, Wire Communication

Department of Information and Computer Science
Applied Probability Theory, Assembly Languages, Automata Theory, Classical Field Theory, Coding Theory, Complier Construction, Computer Architecture, Computer Memories, Control Theory, Data Communications, Data Structures, Differential and Integral Calculus, Digital Circuits, Digital Signal Processing, Discrete Mathematics, Electric Circuits, Electronic Circuits, Formal Languages, Functional Analysis, Graph Theory, Information and Computer Sciences, Information Theory, Integrated Circuits, Linear Algebra, Logic Design, Mathematical Programming, Microprogramming, Numerical Analysis,

Numerical Methods, Pattern Recognition, Peripheral Equipment, Programming Languages, Pulse Circuits, Simulation, Systems Engineering, Systems Programming

Department of Mechanical Engineering

Automatic Control, Automatic Control, Automation Engineering, Casting Technology, Computer System, Cutting Physics, Deformation and Fracture of Materials, Design of Machine Elements, Drawing of Machinery, Dynamics, Heat Engine, Heat Transfer, Hydraulic Machinery, Hydrodynamics, Industrial Design, Industrial Thermodynamics, Machine Design, Measurement Engineering, Mechanical Dynamics, Mechanics of Fluids, Mechanics of Machinery, Optional Instruments, Organochemical Materials, Plasticity, Precise Measurement and Instruments, Production Management, Quality Control, Robotics, Sensor Technology, Strength of Materials, Surface Engineering, Unconventional Processing, Vibration Engineering, Welding Engineering

Faculty of Law (Freshmen Enrollment: 500)

Department of Law

Administration, Administrative Law, Bankruptcy Law, Basic Jurisprudence, Civil Law, Commercial Law, Commercial Law, Comparative Law, Constitutional Law, Criminal Law, Criminal Policy, Economic Law, Foreign Legal Systems, History of International Politics, History of Legal Thought, Industrial Property Law, International Economic Law, International Relations, Labor Law, Law of Civil Execution, Law of Civil Procedure, Law of Criminal Procedure, Legal History, Legal Philosophy, Politics, Private International Law, Public International Law, Roman Law, Sociology of Law, Tax Law

Department of Managerial Law

Administrative Law, Business Organization, Civil Law, Commercial Law, Criminal Law, Economic Law, Foreign Law of Corporation, Foreign Legal Systems, International Economic Law, International Law, International Relations, Judiciary Law, Labor Law, Labor-Management Relations, Law, Law of Banking and Trust, Law of Civil Execution, Law of Extraordinary Security, Law of Industrial Property, Management, Multinational Enterprises, Private International Law, Social Security Law, Tax Law (Income Tax, Corporation Tax)

Faculty of Literature (Freshmen Enrollment: 520)

Department of Chinese Philosophy and Literature

Chinese Bibliography, Chinese Ideographs, Chinese Literature, Chinese Philosophy, History of Chinese Buddhism, History of Chinese Literature, History of Chinese Philosophy, Influence of Chinese Classics in Language, Translation in Japanese Literature

Department of Education

Adult and Youth Education, Clinical Psychology, Comparative Education, Developmental Psychology, Early Childhood Education, Educational Psychology, Educational Sociology, Educational Statistics, Education in the Family, Education of Feeble-Minded Children, Education of Handicapped Children, Guidance and Moral Education, History of Education, Industrial Education, Law of Education, Learning and Thinking, Mental Health, Mental Measurement, Methodology of Adult Education, Philosophy of Education, Psychology of Personality, Teaching Methods, Women's Problems and Education

Department of English and American Literature

English and American Literature, English Grammar, English Language, English Philology, English Phonetics, European History, European Literature, History of English & American Literture, History of English Thought, Linguistics

Department of History

Archaeology, Eastern History, Historical Documents (Japanese, Eastern and Western), Historical Science, Historical Studies, History of Buddhism, History of Education, History of Japanese Fine Art, History of Japanese Thought, History of Law (Japanese, Eastern and Western), History of Our Time, Japanese Economic History, Japanese History, Learning of Ancient Manuscripts, Sociology, Western History

Department of Indian Philosophy

Buddhism, Esoteric Buddhism, History of Chinese Buddhism, History of Indian Philosophy, History of Japanese Buddhism, Hokke Buddhism, Indian and Buddhist Arts, Learning of Ancient Manuscripts, Pali, Pure Land Buddhism, Religious Sociology, Sanskrit, Tibetan, Zen Buddhism

Department of Japanese Literature

Comparative Literature, Folklore of Japan, Historical Documents of Japan, History of Japanese Buddhism, History of Japanese Calligraphy, History of Japanese Literature, History of the Japanese Language, Japanese Bibliography, Japanese Calligraphy, Japanese Grammar, Japanese History, Japanese Language, Japanese Literature, Sino-Japanese Classics, Sino-Japanese Writing, Survey of Literature, Survey of Philology

Department of Philosophy

Buddhism, Chiristianity, Comparative Philosophy, Ethics, History of European Philosophy, History of Japanese Thought, History of Natural Science, Logic, Outline of Fine Arts, Philosophy, Religion Studies

Faculty of Sociology (Freshmen Enrollment: 400)

Department of Applied Sociology

Library Science Course

Mass Communication Course

Social Psychology Course

Social Welfare Course

Department of Sociology

Broadcasting Science, Clinical Psychology, Criminal Sociology, Cultural Anthropology, Data Control, Educational Sociology, Family Sociology, History of European Philosophy, History of Social Thought, Industrial Sociology, Mass Communication, Medical Social Work, Population Problems, Psychoanalytic Theory and Therapy, Rural Sociology, Social Education, Social Pathology, Social Policy, Social Psychology, Social Statistics, Social Welfare, Social Welfare Administration, Sociological History, Sociological Theory, Sociology, Sociology of Knowledge, Sociology of Labor, Sociology of Law, Sociology of Religion, Urban Sociology, Welfare Sociology

Foreign Student Admission
  Qualifications for Applicants
    Standard Qualifications Requirement
  Examination at the University
    The Entrance Examination and interview is conducted in October at the Hakusan Campus of the University. Applicants for the Engineering Faculty are examined at the Kawagoe Campus of the University in Kawagoe City.
    Examination Subjects:
Undergraduate Faculties (except Faculty of Engineering): Japanese Language, English Language, Interview
Faculty of Engineering:
Japanese Language, English Language, Mathematics, Science (choice of either Physics or Chemistry), Interview
    The Inteview will consist of an Oral examination to evaluate the applicant's ability in spoken Japanese to the extent of being able to pursue his studies satisfactorily, and to evaluate his specialized knowledge.
    The regular examination in the Japanese language will cover hearing, writing and understanding ability.
    The written examination is in Japanese.
  Documents to be Submitted When Applying
    Standard Documents Requirement

GRADUATE PROGRAMS

Graduate School of Business Administration (First Year Enrollment : Master's 10)
  Division
Business Administration
Graduate School of Economics (First Year Enrollment : Master's 10, Doctor's 3)
  Division
Economics
Graduate School of Engineering (First Year Enrollment : Master's 40, Doctor's 20)
  Divisions
Applied Chemistry, Architecture, Civil Engineering, Electrical Engineering, Mechanical Engineering
Graduate School of Law (First Year Enrollment : Master's 20, Doctor's 5)
  Divisions
Private Law, Public Law
Graduate School of Literature (First Year Enrollment : Master's 34, Doctor's 12)
  Divisions
Buddhism, Chinese Philosophy, English Literature, Japanese History, Japanese Literature, Philosophy
Graduate School of Sociology (First Year Enroll-

ment : Master's 20, Doctor's 6)
  Divisions
Applied Sociology, Sociology

Foreign Student Admission
  Qualifications for Applicants
Master's Program
    Standard Qualifications Requirement
Doctor's Program
    Standard Qualifications Requirement
  Examination at the University
Master's Program
    The Written Entrance Examination is conducted in October and March at the Hakusan Campus of the University. The applicants for the Engineering Department are examined at the Kawagoe Campus.
Examination subjects: Essay (in Japanese), Foreign Languages, Interview
Doctor's Program
    Same as Master's program.
  Documents to be Submitted When Applying
    Standard Documents Requirement

*

Research Institutes and Centers
Asia-African Cultural Research Institute, Institute of Asian Studies, Instituteof Economic Research, Institute of Social Relation, Research and Education Center for Informatics, Research Institute of Business Administration, Research Institute of Comparative Law, Research Institute of Industrial Technology
Facilities/Services for Foreign Students
    Advice and assistance are offered to foreign students.
Special Programs for Foreign Students
    Japanese Classes are offered and credits are given.
For Further Information
  Undergraduate and Graduate Admission
Academic Affairs Office, Toyo University, 5-28-20 Hakusan, Bunkyo-ku, Tokyo 112 ☎ 03-945-7240

Tsuda College
(Tsuda Juku Daigaku)

2-1-1 Tsuda–machi, Kodaira–shi, Tokyo 187
☎ 0423-41-5111

Faculty
    Profs. 42   Assoc. Profs. 32
    Assist. Profs. Full–time 1; Part–time 166
    Res. Assocs. 5
Number of Students
    Undergrad. 2, 553   Grad. 72
Library 176, 000 volumes

Outline and Characteristics of the College
    Tsuda College is the outgrowth of a small private school for women opened by Ume Tsuda in the

heart of Tokyo in 1900. The school emphasized the study of English from the beginning, for Tsuda wanted young Japanese women of her day to have direct access to the best in the traditions of Western culture and civilization.

Ume Tsuda was one of the five girls, ranging in age from 7 to 15, who were selected in 1871 by the newly-established Meiji Government to be sent to the United States for study. Tsuda was the youngest in the group, being barely seven years old at the time. In the United States, she remained mostly under the care and tutelage of Charles and Adeline Lanmen in Washington D. C. Tsuda stayed with this typical middle–class American family for eleven years before she came home to Japan. Back in Tokyo, Ume Tsuda took up teaching positions in several schools, including the Peeresses' School, and became increasingly aware of the urgent need for higher education for women in Japan. In 1889, she went back to the United States for further study at Bryn Mawr College, where she specialized in biology.

While at Bryn Mawr, Tsuda started a campaign for a scholarship fund to continue sending Japanese women to America to study. The fund reached the initially set goal of $ 8, 000 in August, 1892, when she came back to Japan and resumed teaching at the Peeresses' School, but she was not yet satisfied. She could not help noticing, in the Japanese educational system of the day, the conspicuous absence of institutions of higher learning for women.

In the spring of 1900, Tsuda resigned from all positions, private and public, to establish a school of her own. A licence for this school was obtained in July from the Ministry of Education and instruction started in September.

The little school, which first opened its doors to fewer than 10 students over 80 years ago, has grown steadily; today it has three undergraduate and graduate departments and has over 2, 500 students. Keeping in mind, however, Ume Tsuda's original concept of ideal education, the college has always remained small, emphasizing quality rather than quantity.

UNDERGRADUATE PROGRAMS

Faculty of Liberal Arts (Freshmen Enrollment: 580)
   Department of English Language and Literature
American Literature, Cultural Studies of Britain, Cultural Studies of the U. S. A, English Language and Linguistics, English Literature
   Department of International and Cultural Studies
Area Studies, Comparative Cultures, Comparative Sociology, International Law, International Politics, International Relations
   Department of Mathematics
Application of Computers, Applied Mathematics, Differential and Integral Calculus, Linear Algebra, Theory of Functions, Topology

Foreign Student Admission

Qualifications for Applicants
   Standard Qualifications Requirement
Examination at the College
   Applicants will be screened on the basis of the application documents regarding qualification.
   Qualified applicants are required to take an entrance examination as follows:
Dept. of English Language and Literature: Japanese composition, English (composition, comprehension and conversation) and an interview
Dept. of International and Cultural Studies: Japanese composition, English composition, history of the world and an interview
Dept. of Mathematics: Mathematics, Composition (Japanese or English) and an inteview
   Documents to be Submitted When Applying
   Standard Documents Requirement
   JLPT and GEFS scores
   Brochure, etc. explaining the curriculum of the last school, from which the applicant graduated is also to be submitted.
   If the documents are not written in English or Japanese, they must be accompanied by an English or Japanese translation thereof which is certified by the public organization.
   Application forms are available at the Admissions Office from late August.
Application period: Oct. 11–Oct. 21
Announcement of the applicants qualified to take the examination: Nov. 25
Examination: Jan. 21
Announcement of successful applicants: Jan. 26
Period for entrance procedures: Jan. 27–March 24

Qualifications for Transfer Students
1. Those who have graduated from junior college, college or university
2. Those who have finished the sophomore year of college or university
3. Those who have graduated from vocational college
4. Those who are considered to have qualifications equivalent to the above
Examination for Transfer Students
   Applicants will be considered case by case.
Documents to be Submitted When Applying
   Standard Documents Requirement

GRADUATE PROGRAMS

Graduate School of International Studies (First Year Enrollment : Master's 10, Doctor's 3)
   Division
International and Cultural Studies
Graduate School of Literary Studies (First Year Enrollment : Master's 10, Doctor's 3)
   Division
English Language and Literature
Graduate School of Mathematics (First Year Enrollment : Master's 5, Doctor's 3)

Division
Mathematics

Foreign Student Admission
Qualifications for Applicants
Master's Program
　　Standard Qualifications Requirement
Doctor's Program
　　Standard Qualifications Requirement
Examination at the College
Master's Program
　　The dates and methods of entrance examination vary from division to division. Entrance examination consists of a written and oral examination or an interview. The examination is usually given in October.
Doctor's Program
　　Same as the Master's program. The entrance examination is usually given in February.
Documents to be Submitted When Applying
　　Standard Documents Requirement
　　Bachelor's or Master's thesis, as the case may be, with an abstract is also required.

✳

Research Institutes and Centers
AudioVisual Center, Computer Center, Institute for Research in Language and Culture, Institute of International Studies, Institute of Mathematics and Computer Science
Special Programs for Foreign Students
Japanese Language Ⅰ, Ⅱ
For Further Information
　　Undergraduate and Graduate Admission
Admission Office, Tsuda College, 2-1-1 Tsudamachi, Kodaira-shi, Tokyo 187 ☎ 0423-42-5120

Tsurumi University
(Tsurumi Daigaku)

2-1-3 Tsurumi, Tsurumi-ku, Yokohama-shi,
Kanagawa 230 ☎ 045-581-1001

Faculty
　　Profs. 48　　Assoc. Profs. 32
　　Assist. Profs. Full-time 30; Part-time 159
　　Res. Assocs. 138
Number of Students
　　Undergrad. 2, 391　　Grad. 54
Library 303, 000 volumes

Outline and Characteristics of the University
　　The origin of the University can be traced back to a Zen Buddhist mission school in 1924.
　　After World War II, in 1953, the school was first promoted to a junior college under the new educational system in Japan. The aim of the fundamental education comes from the merciful disire of Keizan Zenji, the founder of Soji-ji Temple--the grand temple of the Soto Zen Buddhism. In 1963, Faculty

of Literature was added, comprised of the Department of Japanese Literature and English & American Literature. The college was subsequently recognized as a four-year system as Tsurumi University. In 1970, going a new step further, the School of Dental Medicine--a six year program--was founded.
　　Being trained through the cultivation of moral sense and wisdom in the Zen spirit, students are self-respecting and ready to do service in each field as well as their own duties in modernized educational facilities.
　　The campus is situated on the scenic hills of the Soji-ji Temple and its quiet, open surroundings is favorable to the students, health and education as well as for the fostering humanity.

UNDERGRADUATE PROGRAMS

School of Dental Medicine (Freshmen Enrollment: 160)
　　Department of Dental Medicine
Complete Denture, Crown and Bridge Prosthetics, Dental Anesthesiology, Dental Pharmacology, Dental Radiology, Endodontics, Operative Dentistry, Oral Anatomy, Oral Bacteriology, Oral Biochemistry, Oral Pathology, Oral Physiology, Oral Surgery, Orthodontics, Partial Denture, Pedodontics, Periodontics
Faculty of Literature (Freshmen Enrollment: 300)
　　Department of English & American Literature
American Literature, English Grammar and Usage, English Literature, English Philology, English Phonetics, Journalism
　　Department of Japanese Literature
History of Japanese Literature, Japanese Literature

GRADUATE PROGRAMS

Graduate School of Dental Medicine (First Year Enrollment : Doctor's 72)
　　Division
Dental Medicine

✳

For Further Information
　　Undergraduate and Graduate Admission
Administrative Office, Tsurumi University, 2-1-3 Tsurumi, Tsurumi-ku, Yokohama-shi, Kanagawa 230 ☎ 045-581-1001 ext. 202

Ueno Gakuen College
(Ueno Gakuen Daigaku)

4-24-12 Higashi Ueno, Taito-ku, Tokyo 110
☎ 03-842-1021

Faculty
　　Profs. 18　　Assoc. Profs. 8

Assist. Profs.   Full–time 8; Part–time 65
Res. Assoc. 2
Number of Students
  Undergrad. 445   Grad. 4
Library 116, 669 volumes

Outline and Characteristics of the College

The Ueno Gakuen Educational Foundation was Established in 1904 by Zogoro Ishibashi who advocated Jikaku ("Self Awareness") as its founding spirit for the education of women. In 1952, the Foundation established Ueno Gakuen Junior College, Department of Music, to serve as its institution for higher education. This developed into Ueno Gakuen College, Faculty of Music, established in 1958.

Ueno Gakuen College holds as its objective the development in each student of acute sensitivity and refined intelligence. The College seeks those students who are independent and eager to seek for the real aspects of beauty and the meaning of life through their studies, training, performing and their daily lives, both in music and in academic areas.

The Faculty of Music of the College consists of three undergraduate departments: Musicology, Instrumental Music and Vocal Music The Department of Instrumental Music covers piano, wind, string and percussion instruments, guitar harp, organ and early music instruments.

The Junior College consists of the Faculty of Humanities (English Option, Cultural Studies Option), the Faculty of Music and the Faculty of Domestic Science.

UNDERGRADUATE PROGRAMS

Faculty of Music (Freshmen Enrollment: 90)
  Department of Instrumental Music
Bassoon, Cello, Clarinet, Double bass, Flute, Guitar, Harp, Harpsichord, Horn, Lute, Oboe, Organ, Percussion instruments, Piano, Recorder, Trombone, Trumpet, Tuba, Viola, Viola da gamba, Violin
  Department of Musicology
  Department of Vocal Music

Foreign Student Admission
  Qualifications for Applicants
    Standard Qualifications Requirement
    Must be female.
Full ability to read, write, hear and speak Japanese
  Examination at the University
    Same as for Japanese
    an essay (in Japanese), plus English and music subjects. An interview
  Qualifications for Transfer Students
    Third year transfer students only.
    Must be female.
    Must have completed (or be in prospect of completing) the second year of college, music department, or be a graduate (or prospective graduate) of a junior college, music department, or be certified by

the College as having a level of academic ability equal to or higher than the aforementioned.
Full ability to read, write, hear and speak Japanese
  Examination for Transfer Students
    an essay (in Japanese), plus English and music subjects. An interview

One Year Graduate Program

Foreign Student Admission
  Qualifications for applicants
    Standard Qualifications Requirement
    Must be female.
Full ability to read, write, hear and speak Japanese
  Examination at the university
    Same as for Japanese.

The examination covers language (choice of one from English, German and French) and music subjects. Interview is also required.

✳

Research Institutes and Centers
Centre for Performance of Early Music, Institute for the study of Musical Instruments, International Institute for the Study of Comparative Culture, Research Archives for Japanese Music, Ueno Gakuen Centre for Language Studies
Special Programs for Foreign Students
Arranged individually
For Further Information
  Undergraduate Admission
Head, Gakumu–bu, Ueno Gakuen Collge, 4–24–12, Higashi Ueno, Taito–ku, Tokyo 110 ☎ 03–842–1021

The University of East Asia
(Toa Daigaku)

2-1 Ichinomiya-Gakuencho, Shimonoseki-shi, Yamaguchi 751   ☎ 0832-56-1111

Faculty
  Profs. 31   Assoc. Profs. 9
  Assist. Profs.   Full–time 21; Part–time 24
Number of Students
  Undergrad. 1, 602
Library 45, 000 volumes

Outline and Characteristics of the University

When the establishment of the University of East Asia in Shimonoseki City was proposed in 1966, it was recognized that the University was under the obligation to offer a complete education, the duty of the management of a private university.

The aims of the programs are as follows:
1. Distinctive education and studies are offered in response to the future demand of politics, the economy and culture.
2. Practical education and studies should be carried out in order to train men of ability who acquire highly specified techniques in order to

contribute to the development of society.

3. The trustees, faculty members and staff of the office should do their best to fulfill their duty and responsibility. In this educational environment, they must treat instruments and equipments with care and utilize them to their maximum potential. The students should be trained to become stable and healthy persons.

In 1974, the Faculty of Business Management (Business Management Course) and in 1981 the Faculty of Engineering (Mechanical Engineering Department, Food Technology Department and System Engineering Department) were established. Since then the basic educational plans concerning undergraduate and postgraduate education were established.

Shimonoseki City where the University is located has been known as a point of traffic and commercial importance. Shimonoseki also has an historical relation with China and Korea. The city and the surroundings are favored by natural beauty. Being operated on a small scale, the University has the advantage of maintaining amicable relationships between teachers and students.

UNDERGRADUATE PROGRAMS

Faculty of Business Management (Freshmen Enrollment: 200)
  Business Management Course
Accounting, Business Administration, Business Management, Commercial Science, Economics, History of Business Management, Industrial Theory, Law, Management Engineering
Faculty of Engineering (Freshmen Enrollment: 120)
  Food Technology Department
Chemical Engineering, Dietetics, Food Analysis, Microbiology, Production Technology of Food
  Mechanical Engineering Department
Control Engineering, Design and Drafting, Fluid Mechanics, Heat Engineering, Material Engineering, Production Engineering
  System Engineering Department
Control System, Electronics System, Information System, System Theory

Foreign Student Admission
  Qualifications for Applicants
    Standard Qualifications Requirement
  Examination at the University
    Same as for Japanese. Moreover, if applicants have considerable ability for the Japanese language, they will be admitted regardless of enrollement limits.
  Documents to be Submitted When Applying
    Standard Documents Requirement

*

Research Institutes and Centers
Food Technological Laboratory, Management of Information Center, Mechanical Engineering Laboratory, Scientific Research Institute
For Further Information
  Undergraduate Admission
Administrative Office, The University of East Asia, 2-1 Ichinomiya-Gakuencho, Shimonoseki-shi, Yamaguchi 751 ☎ 0832-56-1111

University of Hannan
(Hannan Daigaku)
5-4-33 Amamihigashi, Matsubara-shi, Osaka 580
☎ 0723-32-1224

Faculty
    Profs. 49   Assoc. Profs. 35
    Assist. Profs. Full–time 2; Part–time 104
Number of Students
    Undergrad. 4, 010
Library 151, 969 volumes

Outline and Characteristics of the University

Hannan University will celebrate its 25th anniversary in 1989. Our university is well-established, and as the steady increase in the number of candidates indicates, our university has been growing in value and social estimation every year.

Our university is located near the city of Osaka is which with the completion of the Kansai International Airport, is a major modern economic center. Our university is an excellent one for students who study political economy or commercial science, making preparations for a more international, information-orented era.

We am to develop students into able men and women so necessary for our future. We continually examine and improve both the content and the organizathor of our curriculd. The results of this earnest endeavour, for example, have appeared in 1986, with the establishment of the "Department of Management-In-Information Science, " and in the "Special-Recommendation-Admission-System for Womn", expecfed to begin in 1989. The aim of this system is to meet the needs of women who wish to enter the work world in the near future. Such as ours is uniquely equipped to offer individualized A middle-scale-university such as ours is uniquely equipped to offer individuallzed education and to encourage our students to entrance their ability and humanity. It is this attitude towards education that has, for instance, determined our teaching methods, such as the institution of seminars and regular courses of small numbers of students.

Our university further dedicates itself to freedom and purity. Freedom is the mother of love, and purity the father of Justice.

UNDERGRADUATE PROGRAMS

Faculty of Commercial Science (Freshmen Enroll-

ment: 550)
Department of Commercial Science
Department of Management-Information Science
Faculty of Economics (Freshmen Enrollment: 400)
Department of Economics

*

Research Institute and Center
Institute of Research for Industry and Economy, Research Center for Computer Science
For Further Information
Undergraduate Admission
Admissions Office, University of Hannan, 5-4-33 Amamihigashi, Matsubara-shi, Osaka 580
☎ 0723-32-1224

University of Marketing and Distribution Sciences
(Ryutu Kagaku Daigaku)

3-1, Gakuen–Nishi–machi, Nishi–ku, Kobe–shi, Hyogo 673   ☎ 078–794–3555

Faculty
Profs. 26   Assoc. Profs. 9
Assist. Profs. Full–time 11; Part–time 42
Number of Students
Undergrad. 477
Library 19, 871 volumes

Outline and Characteristics of the University
The University of Marketing and Distribution Sciences is
•Japan's first college where distribution is systematically studied and taught as a science.
•a college which proposes to study the effect of local cultures on the world economy.
•a college of international exchange, where Japan is studied from an international perspective.
The University of Marketing and Distribution Sciences is located in Kobe, an international port city where materials for distribution field study, company study and consumer study are plentiful and easily accessible. Given the present trend toward internationalization in imformation and distribution, Kobe is an ideal place to establish an educational and research institute for distribution.
The University of Marketing and Distribution Sciences' orientation to practice is evident in its educational systems: six programs of study which allow students to prepare their future career, and the off-campus program.
Exchange between related fields of study and flexibility in the structure of faculty and courses make studies at University of Marketing and Distribution Sciences especially effective. The cantral theme of "humanity & practicality" is stressed throughout all courses in both general and major education. Another characteristic of the University of

Marketing and Distribution Sciences' curriculum is that students begin their major programs in their freshman year.

UNDERGRADUATE PROGRAMS

Faculty of Commerce (Freshmen Enrollment: 250)
Department of Business Administration
Accounting, Business Management, Company Study, Comparative History of Administration, Comparative Studies on Labor and Management, Comparative Studies on Top Management, Financial Management, History of Business Administration, International Accounting, International Management, Japanese Management Style, Labor Management, Management Information, Management Organization, Management Science, Management Strategy, Managerial Accounting, Operations Research, Organization Psychology, Organization Sociology, Public Management, Quality Control, Social, Study on Medium and Smaller Enterprises
Department of Distribution
Business Management, Comparative Distribution Systems, Comparative Studies on Consumer Advocacy, Consumer Behavior Analysis, Consumer Issues, Distribution Policy, Distribution Systems, Financial Institutions, History of Distribution, History of Distribution Science, Insurance, International Commodity Market, International Finance, International Management, International Physical Distribution, International Transaction Contracts, Marketing Communication, Marketing Management, Medium and Smaller Enterprises, Overland Transportation, Product Strategy, Retail and Wholesale Systems, Retail Shop Management, Strategy for Physical Distribution, Trading, Transportation

Foreign Student Admission
Examination at the University
Japanese, English, Interview
*
For Further Information
Undergraduate Admission
Head of the instruction section, The instruction section, University of Marketing and Distribution Sciences, 3–1 Gakuen–Nishi–machi, Nishi–ku, Kobe–shi, Hyogo 673 ☎ 078–794–3555ext. 213

University of Occupational and Environmental Health, Japan
(Sangyo Ika Daigaku)

1-1 Iseigaoka, Yahatanishi-ku, Kitakyushu-shi, Fukuoka 807   ☎ 093-603-1611

Faculty
Profs. 47   Assoc. Profs. 47
Assist. Profs. Full–time 40; Part–time 112

Res. Assocs.   120
Number of Students
   Undergrad. 625   Grad. 54
Library   86, 260 volumes

Outline and Characteristics of the University

The extremely rapid development of modern industry has actuated a development based on the materialistic civilization of our society. This is also true in the area of medicine in Japan. It is widely accepted that Japanese medicine has attained a high level.

However, beneath the surface of this industrialized world, the nations' citizens are threatened by an increase of undesirable health problems produced by the complexities of our highly industrialized life. Japan in particular, partly because of rapid industrial expansion, has lagged behind most countries in coping with occupational and general environments, and has allowed many serious problems concerning the life of the working people to develop. This has incited the Ministry of Labor to establish this university for the purpose of promoting occupational medicine and educating physicians and researchers who are to work in the area of occupational medicine.

At this School of Medicine, almost all subjects and courses, not only the subjects concerning occupational medicine, are laying more and more stress upon the problems of health upon which the influence of occupational and general environments exert. The undergraduate courses are designed, therefore, to educate proficient physicians and researchers who possess the foundation necessary for further studies in the graduate courses.

In March of 1984, the school sent out its first class of the School of Medicine, and inaugurated the Graduate School of Medical Science. This graduate school consists of four divisions and twelve sub-divisions, covering a wide range of occupational as well as general medical courses. Occupational medicine is closely related not only to the whole field of medicine but also to other fields such as engineering and economics. Therefore, the school established the Institute of Industrial Ecological Sciences in April of 1986. The School provides a three-month course in fundamental occupational health for graduating students as well as for doctors who have graduated from other medical schools. Upon completion of this three-month fundamental course, students with satisfactory grades are awarded a diploma in occupational medicine. Furthermore, the school has obtained from the government an exemption from the written National Board Examination for certification of Occupational Health Consultant for students completing this course.

This university thus aims at dealing with the health problems rising in an industrialized society, and is becoming a pioneer in the field of medical and health sciences for the 21st century. It is open to anyone who sympathizes with our school spirit, understands our mission, wishes to think and learn by himself or herself and contributes willingly to human society through his or her assistance in the health control of the working class.

UNDERGRADUATE PROGRAMS

School of Medicine (Freshmen Enrollment: 100)
   Department of Medicine
Anatomy and Anthropology, Anatomy and Histology, Anesthesiology, Biochemistry, Dermatology, Environmental Health, Forensic Medicine, General and Abdominal Surgery, Human Ecology, Immunology, Internal Medicine, Medical and Hospital Administration, Medical Zoology, Microbiology, Molecular Biology, Neurology, Neurosurgery, Obstetrics and Gynecology, Ophthalmology, Orthopedic Surgery, Otorhinolaryngology, Pathology and Oncology, Pathology and Surgical Pathology, Pediatrics, Pharmacology, Physiology, Psychiatry, Radiation Biology and Health, Radiology, Rehabilitation Medicine, Thoracic and Cardiovascular Surgery, Urology

Foreign Student Admission
   Qualifications for Applicants
     Standard Qualifications Requirement
   Examination at the University
     Same as for Japanese
   Documents to be Submitted When Applying
     Standard Documents Requirement
     JFSAT score
Students enrolled in a university must present a letter of consent to apply to our university. Instead of this letter of consent students in their last year of university may present proof of their designated date of graduation.

GRADUATE PROGRAMS

Graduate School of Medical Science (First Year Enrollment : Doctor's 40)
   Divisions
Applied Health Sciences, Clinical and Biomedical Informatics, Fundamental Life Science, Medical and Occupational Health Sciences

Foreign Student Admission
   Qualifications for Applicants
Doctor's Program
   Standard Qualifications Requirement
Applicants who apply for admission to the Graduate School are required to have one of the following qualifications:

1. Graduation from a school of Medicine or Dentistry.
2. Completion of graduate studies in other fields than medicine or dentistry and possession of a Master's degree.
3. Recommendation by the Minister of Education, Science and Culture.
4. Completion, at a college or university outside

Japan, of studies equivalent or superior to the academic work required for Master's degree.

5. Applicants for clinical course are required to have a license to practice medicine in Japan and to have at least one year legal clinical training experience.

Examination at the University

Doctor's Program

Date: in October and/or the following February. An interview, written test (Japanese language), oral test (general knowledge exams for fundamental medicine and life sciences)

Documents to be Submitted When Applying

Standard Documents Requirement

*

Research Institutes and Centers

Institute of Industrial Ecological Sciences

The 3 month course in fundamental occupational health prorides the basic knowledge and techniques necessary for graduates of medical schools to work as occupational health physicians.

Facilities/Services for Foreign Students

A limited number of rooms in the Resident Houses of the University

For Further Information

Undergraduate and Graduate Admission

Admission Office, University of Occupational and Environmental Health, Japan, 1-1 Iseigaoka, Yahatanishi-ku, Kitakyushu-shi, Fukuoka 807 ☎ 093-603-1611 ext. 2219 (Undergraduate), 2273 (Graduate)

The University of Okinawa
(Okinawa Daigaku)

747 Kokuba, Naha-shi, Okinawa 902
☎ 0988-32-1768

Faculty
Profs. 10   Assoc. Profs. 23
Assist. Profs. Full–time 6; Part–time 55
Number of Students
Undergrad. 1, 852
Library 42, 558 volumes

Outline and Characteristics of the University

The University of Okinawa is the oldest private university in Okinawa. It originally started from two Faculties (the Faculty of Law, Economics and Business Administration and the Faculty of Letters), but the Faculty of Letters was dissolved in 1974 after Okinawa was returned to Japan in 1972.

Since its establishment in 1961, it has been a great influence on and has contributed much to the development of Okinawa which suffered severe damage in World War II as the only battle ground in Japan. The University has always aimed at keeping pace with the development of Okinawan society in general, for Okinawa has a different history and culture than that of the mainland.

With all its long history and tradition in Okinawa, the University is also dedicated to the unparalleled new educational system. This is the drastic reform of entrance examinations, the introduction of a four-year seminar system, and the invention of a system in which students can study at one of the five other universities on the mainland for one year while enrolled at the University. The reform, which abolished written tests, aims at admitting students with individual and different personalities as smoothly as possible. Entrance examination consists only of a composition and an interview.

As the University is small in size (about 2, 000 students), it can maintain a four-year seminar system from the freshman to senior year. A seminar class is composed of some 20 students and its aim is to make it possible for students to study under the careful guidance of teachers. Its other aim is to create a friendly student-teacher relationship.

In recent years, the University has become more national and international. The number of students from various prefectures has been increasing (158 this year) and 38 foreign students study at the University now. They are largely from Taiwan, Hong Kong and South America. The University of Okinawa is located near the center of Naha, the capital city of Okinawa. Okinawa is world-famous for its beautiful coral sea and attracts more than two million tourists every year.

UNDERGRADUATE PROGRAMS

Faculty of Law and Economics (Freshmen Enrollment: 200)

Department of Economics

Course of Business Administration: Accounting, Bookkeeping, Business Administration, Business Organization Theory, Financial Management, Management Theory, Marketing, Principles of Economics

Course of Economics: Economic History, Economic Policy, Finance, History of Economic Thoughts, International Money and Banking, Japanese Economy, Principles of Economy, Social Policy, Statistics

Department of Law

Administrative Law, Civil Law, Civil Law Procedure, Commercial Law, Company Law, Costitutional Law, Criminal Law, Education and Law, History of Law, Labor Law, Philosophy of Law, Sociology of Law

Foreign Student Admission

Qualifications for Applicants

Standard Qualifications Requirement

Examination at the University

Entrance Examination by Recommendation: Japanese language proficiency test, an interview, a transcript of the school record and a recommendation letter.

General Entrance Examination: same as for Japanese: a written test (composition) and an interview.

Documents to be Submitted When Applying
Standard Documents Requirement

*

Special Programs for Foreign Students
According to the curriculum, foreign students must take Japanese language as a required subject (8 credits) for two years.

For Further Information
Undergraduate Admission
Dean of Academic Affairs, Office of Academic Affairs, The University of Okinawa, 747 Kokuba, Naha-shi, Okinawa 902 ☎ 0988-32-1768

University of the Sacred Heart
(Seishin Joshi Daigaku)

4-3-1 Hiroo, Shibuya-ku, Tokyo 150
☎ 03-407-5811

Faculty
    Profs. 49   Assoc. Profs. 15
    Assist. Profs. Full-time 6; Part-time 229
Number of Students
    Undergrad. 1,909   Grad. 50
Library 239,205 volumes

Outline and Characteristics of the University

The University of the Sacred Heart is a four-year university for women under the school's corporation "Seishin Joshi Gakuin," whose founding body is the Society of the Sacred Heart, a Roman Catholic order of religious women originating about 200 years ago. It takes its name from the Sacred Heart of Jesus Christ in honor of the generous love of the Son of God and Saviour of mankind. Founded at the end of the French Revolution by St. Madeleine Sophie Barat in response to the need for education for young women, the Society devoted itself to educational works. St. Madeleine Sophie desired "to nurture young women who would develop into good wives and wise mothers in the home and distinguished leaders in society." As the concrete result of the educational aims of its founder, the Society has opened more than 200 schools throughout the world up to the present.

The University believes that God has endowed women with many special characteristics. In order to assist the students in developing these and potential for their leadership, creativity, social responsibility, the University makes full use of the advantages of an institution exclusively dedicated to women's education. In designing the school curriculum and in the guidance of student life, for example, there are many instances in which special attention has been paid to reflect the needs and values meaningful to young women today.

The University has earned a unique reputation among Japanese universities due to its international qualities. The student is assisted in regarding the vital problems of today from an international viewpoint, and in pursuing their potential as truly international members of society possessing the liberal education essential to an understanding of the world today. The University also considers the acquisition of foreign languages to be of great importance.

In 1908 five sisters came to Japan from Australia and established the private institution Seishin Joshi Gakuin in Shiba Shirogane Sanko-cho, Tokyo. Seven years later, in 1915, the Seishin Joshi Gakuin Koto Senmon Gakko, a teachers' training college, was established and the founding spirit was given concrete form. With the termination of World War II a new era began, and under the new Japanese educational system, the longed-for establishment of a women's university materialized. In 1948, the former residence and grounds of the Kuninomiya family in Hiroo were purchased, and the campus was established here. At first four Departments were opened in the University's Faculty of Liberal Arts, and the University was very modest in scale. Since that time, the original Departments have been enlarged, a new department and the Graduate School opened, and today the University comprises 70 full-time members, many part-time lecturers, and more than 1,900 students.

The Christian Culture Research Institute sponsored by the University is located on campus.

The University of the Sacred Heart is conveniently located, a mere five minute walk from the Hiroo subway station. The campus of nearly 70,000 m^2 is located in an extensive residential area of Tokyo. Ancient cherry trees, laurel trees, and Himalayan cedars grace the campus, recalling the palace gardens.

UNDERGRADUATE PROGRAMS

Faculty of Liberal Arts (Freshmen Enrollment: 410)
Department of Education
Education Program: Adult Education, Audio-Visual Technical Education, Class Management, Education, Educational Administration, Educational Evaluation, Educational Research, Educational Sociology, Education Technology, History of Education, Methods of Education, Philosophy of Education, Student Guidance
Primary Education Program: Arts and Crafts, Elementary Mathematics, Japanese History, Music, Physical Education, Primary Education, Science, Teaching Program:
Psychology Course: Clinical Psychology, Developmental Psychology, Educational Psychology, Experimental Psychology, Social Psychology
Department of Foreign Language and Literature
American Literature, English Linguistics, English Literature, English Semantics, History of the English Language, Linguistics, Literary Criticism
Department of History and Social Science
History Course Japanese History, Oriental Histo-

ry, Western History

Human Relations Program Comparative Culture, Comparative Religion, Psychology of Personality, Social Anthropology, Social Psychology

Department of Japanese Language and Literature
Chinese Literature, History of Chinese Literature, Japanese Linguistics, Japanese Literature, Juvenile Literature, Linguistic Expression, Linguistics, Oriental Calligraphy

Department of Philosophy
Aesthetics, Art History, Christian Ethics, Christology, Ethics, History of Ancient and Medieval Philosophy, History of Japanese Ethical Thought, History of Modern European Philosophy, History of Social Thought, Logic, Ontology, Philosophy, Study of Cognition

Teacher Certification Program, Museum Curatorial staff Program, Librarian, Library Leacher Program Teacher's Training Program For Teaching Japanese as a Second Language.

Foreign Student Admission
Qualifications for Applicants
Secondary School Diploma, received or anticipated before beginning the college course
Examination at the University
Date: in March and July
written examinations: Japanese and English language.
Interview
Documents to be Submitted When Applying
1. Secondary School Transcript
2. Secondary School Recommendation
3. Health Certifcate
The following documents are also required.
1. TOEFL: Scores of the Test of English as a Foreign Language
2. Either (a) or (b) or (c):
     (a) SAT: Scores of the Scholastic Aptitude Test administered by the College Entrance Eramination Board (CEEB) U. S. A.
     (b) GCE: The General Certificate of Education in England, indicating Passes in five subjects (including one from each of the following three subject groups: Languages Social Sciences, Natural Science or Mathematics). Two of the five passes submitted must be at the Advanced Level.
     (c) IB: International Baccalaureate
N. B. Those whose Japanese is insufficient to follow ordinary courses given in Japanese, will take special language courses organized at the University during a period of probation. This period may not be counted within the four years prescribed for the degree pregram. New students are admitted at the beginning of the first semester, in April.

GRADUATE PROGRAMS

Graduate School of Literary Studies (First Year Enrollment: Master's 20)

Divisions
English Language and Literature, History: Japanese, Japanese Language and Literature, Oriental and Western

Foreign Student Admission
Qualifications for Applicants
Master's Program
B. A. Diploma, received or anticipates before beginning the M. A. course
Examination at the University
Master's Program
1. Written Examination in the major field.
2. Language Examination on one of the following: chinese English, French, German or Spanish.
     Those whose major field is either English Linguistics or English Literature, must choose one of the four other languages mentioned above.
3. Interviews
Documents to be Submitted When Applying
    1. B. A. Transcript
    2. Health Certificate
A copy or a résumé of the Bachelor's thesis is to be submitted as well.

*

Facilities/Services for Foreign Students
1. Student Housing is available. Meals are provided in the cafeteria or in the Undergraduate Residence Hall.
2. Health Insurance
3. Scholarship (partial)

Special Programs for Foreign Students
Japanese Language
Seminar on Japanese Culture

For Further Information
Undergraduate and Graduate Admission
Academic Dean, Division of Admissions, University of the Sacred Heart, 4-3-1 Hiroo, Shibuya-ku, Tokyo 150 ☎ 03-407-5811 ext. 201

Wako University
(Wako Daigaku)

2, 160 Kanai-cho, Machida-shi, Tokyo 194-01
 044-988-1431

Faculty
   Profs. 66   Assoc. Profs. 16
   Assist. Profs. Full-time 5; Part-time 141
   Res. Assocs. 2
Number of Students
   Undergrad. 3, 726   Grad. 19
Library 170, 000 volumes

Outline and Characteristics of the University
Wako University is a private university established by the educational foundation, Wako Gakuen,

in 1966. Wako Gakuen, founded in 1933, has administered five schools: a kindergarten, an elementary, a junior and senior high school, and a university. Wako, as a whole, is a medium–size integrated school, pursuing the ideal of well–coordinated education.

Wako university has inherited the tradition of Wako Gakuen—teachers with creative and scientific spirits making efforts to practice ideal and true education, denying conventionalism and formalism in education.

In contrast to recent trends in Japan, such as mass production, formalism, cramming and commercialism in education, Wako University believes in humanism, and works to develop the personality and potential ability of each student based on modern educational theories and methods.

Therefore, Wako University does not neccessarily seek the top students, those who are always concerned about grades, or who are anxious to enter leading companies after graduating from prestigious universities. It welcomes those youth who value their own beliefs, do their own work enthusiastically, and want to live honestly.

With earnest and energetic students such as these, we hope to make our university a suitable place for their studies and other fruitful experiences.

UNDERGRADUATE PROGRAMS

Faculty of Economics (Freshmen Enrollment: 300)
  Department of Economics
Economic Policy, Economic Statistics, History of Economics, Jurisprudence, Public Finance, Theory of Economics, Theory of Finance
  Department of Management
A Bahavioral Theory of the Firm, Accounting, Business History, Commercial Science, Principles of Business Adimiistration, Theory of Management Administration
Faculty of Humanities (Freshmen Enrollment: 300)
  Department of Art
Aesthetics and Artistic Theory, Art History, Carving, Design, Japanese Painting, Modern and Contemporary Arts, Oil Painting, Plastic Workings, Printing
  Department of Human Science
Cultural Anthropology, Education and Welfare, Human Science, Pedagogy, Phenomenology, Psychoanalysis, Psychology, Sociology
  Department of Literature
Basho, Chinese Novelists in Japan, Classical Literature, Comarative Literature, English and American Literature, English Philology, History of Buddhism, History of Buddhism in China, History of Chinese Literature, History of Drama, History of Literature, Juvenile Literature, Linguistics, Modern and Contemporary Literature

Foreign Student Admission

Qualifications for Applicants
  Standard Qualifications Requirement
Examination at the University
  Same as for Japanese. Recommendation system: qualified students must obtain a letter of recommendation from the foreign school last attended. writing a thesis and an interview test. Regular academic entrance exam: a foreign language, and another subject chosen from among elective subjects.
Documents to be Submitted When Applying
  Standard Documents Requirement
  A certificate of proficiency in Japanese

Qualifications for Transfer Students
  Any applicant who has completed the course of study equivalent to those of universities or junior colleges in Japan can take the test for transfer students. The appropriate academic year for each successful candidate is decided after considering the results of the test.
Examination for Transfer Students
  Same as for Japanese (knowledge of a foreign language, ability to write a thesis, and a favorable result from an interview)
Documents to be Submitted When Applying
  Standard Documents Requirement
  A certificate of proficiency in Japanese

ONE-YEAR GRADUATE PROGRAMS

One–Year Graduate Course of Humanities (Enrollment: 15)
Art, Education, Literature, Psychology, Sociology
One–Year Graduate Course of Economics (Enrollment: 5)
Economics

Foreign Student Admission
  Qualifications for applicants
  Standard Qualifications Requirement
  Examination at the University
  Same as for Japanese graduation thesis (or report in line of a thesis), knowledge of a foreign language, and results from an interview.
  Documents to be Submitted When Applying
  Standard Documents Requirement
                    *
For Further Information
  Undergraduate and Graduate Admission
Office of Admission, Office of Registration and Instruction, Wako University, 2, 160 Kanai–cho, Machida–shi, Tokyo 194–01 ☎ 044–988–1431 ext. 277

Waseda University
(Waseda Daigaku)
1-6-1 Nishi–Waseda, Shinjuku–ku, Tokyo 160
☎ 03-203-4141

Faculty
Profs. 801   Assoc. Profs. 126
Assist. Profs. Full-time 62; Part-time 1,837
Res. Assocs. 133
Number of Students
Undergrad. 42,954   Grad. 2,927
Library 3,100,000 volumes

Outline and Characteristics of the University

Waseda University's history goes back to 1882. In that year, Marquis Shigenobu Okuma, one of the great statesmen of the Meiji Era, established the Tokyo Semmon Gakko to produce good citizens to form the backbone of the new Japan. When the institution acquired university status in 1902, the name was changed to Waseda University.

At the 30th Anniversary Convocation in 1913, Marquis Okuma declared that the aims of the University were to uphold the independence of learning, to promote the practical utilization of knowledge, and to foster good citizenship. Coeducation was introduced in 1939, and in 1949 the four-year college curricula were established in accordance with the new School Education Law. Graduate schools were established under the new educational programs in 1951.

At present Waseda University has nine undergraduate schools, including two evening divisions, offering courses leading to the Bachelor's degree, and six graduate schools with courses leading to the Master's and Doctor's degrees. The University also has three affiliated schools, ten research institutes, two Divisions, the Library, the Theatre Museum, and several other educational and administrative centers.

Waseda University is situated to the northwest of the center of Tokyo with three campuses (Main Campus, Toyama Campus, and Okubo Campus). In 1987, the University opened the Tokorozawa campus to house the newly established School of Human Sciences, total land are is 2,227,000m².

The present total student enrollment is approximately 50,000 including 749 foreign students who represent 30 nations. About 15% of the total enrollment is women. There are about 43,000 undergraduate students including 6,100 who are registered in the evening divisions, and 3,000 graduate students.

Approximately 2,940 academic staff are serving in the various Schools and Institutes of the University. 1,090 teach full-time, while 1,850 teach on a part-time basis. There are about 1,400 administrative staff serving in the various offices of the University.

Waseda University has been actively engaged in international programs and enjoys exchange relationships with overseas institutions of higher learning. Both faculty and students benefit from exchange programs with University of Bonn, Universities of Paris, Moscow State University, Korea University, De La Salle University, the University of Chicago, University of Southern California, Lyon Graduate School of Business Administration, Peking University, Thammasat University, Nankai University, University of Augsburg, the University of Sydney, University of Stirling, University College Dublin, Shanghai Jiao Tong University, Fudan University, Hankuk University of Foreign Studies, McGill University, University of Rome, Indian Academic Institutions the Great Lakes Colleges Association/the Associated Colleges of the Midwest, the California State University System, the Oregon State System of Higher Education, the California Private Universities and Colleges, the University of Toronto and Georgetown University.

Waseda University celebrated its first centennial in October, 1982. In commemoration of this milestone, the university has launched too prinupal centennial projects: the establishment of the School of Human Suences on the new Tokorozawa Campus and the construction of the new fibrary on the main campus to be concpleted in the fall of 1990.

UNDERGRADUATE PROGRAMS

School of Commerce (Freshmen Enrollment: 1,200)
Accounting, Advertising, Auditing, Banking, Bookkeeping, Business History, Business Systems Management, Commercial Mathematics, Commodity Science, Cost Accounting, Economic Geography, Economic History, Economic Policy, Economics, Economic Statistics, Finance & Insurance, Financial Accounting, Financial Management, Financial Statements Analysis, History of Economic Doctrines, Industrial Psychology, Industrial Structure, Insurance, International Trade, Labor Economics, Management, Management Organization, Management Policy, Managerial Accounting, Managerial Mathematics, Managing, Marine Insurance, Marketing, Marketing Management, Mathematical Statictics, Money and Banking, National Income, Nonlife Insurance, Organizational Behavior, Physical Distribution, Public Finance, Securities Valuation, Social Securities, Transportation

School of Education (Freshmen Enrollment: 1,100)
Department of English Language and Literature
English and American Literature, English and American Poetry, English Grammar, English Linguistics, English Phonetics, History of English Literature
Department of Japanese Language and Literature
Ancient Literature, Chinese Literature, Contemporary Literature, Early Medieval Literature, Early Modern Literature, History of Japanese Literature, Japanese Literature, Japanese Philology, Medieval

Literature, Modern Literature, Teaching of Japanese

Department of Pedagogy

Educational Psychology course: Clinical Psychology, Curriculum Psychology, Development Psychology, Educational Psychology, Experimental Psychology, Juvenile Psychology, Psychological Measurement, Psychology, Social Psychology, Statistical Methods of Psychology and Education

Pedagogy Course: Education, Educational Administration, Educational Psychology, Educational Sociology, History of European Education, History of Japanese Education, Methodology of Education, Moral Education, School Education

Physical Education Course: Administration of Physical Education, Athletics, Ball Exercise, Gymnastics, History of Physical Education, Hygienics, Kendo and Judo, Kinesiology, Medical Science of Sports, Physical Education, Physical Measurement, Physiology, Psychology of Physical Education, Skiing and Skating, Sport Sociology, Swimming

Social Education Course: Administration and Finance of Social Education, Educational Communication and Technology, Educational Sociology, History of Social Education, Instructional Technology and Educational Practice, Methodology of Social Education, Social Education

Department of Science

Biology CourseBiochemistry, Biology, Cytology and Histology, Ecology, Embryology, Fraction System, Genetics, Marine Biology, Morphology

Earth Science CourseCelestial Physics, Chemistry, Earth Science, Geological–map Reading, Geomorphology, Geophysics, Historical Geology, Meteorology, Mineral Deposits, Mineralogy, Petrology, Physics, Structural Geology

Mathematics CourseAlgebra, Analysis, Differential and Integral Calculus, Linear Algebra, Mathematics, Probability and Statistics, Theory of Functions, Topology, Vector Space

Department of Social Studies

Geography and History Course: Archaeology, Descriptive Geography, Foreign History, Geography, History, Japanese History, Natural Geography, Topography

Social Science Course: Broadcasting, Diplomacy, Economic History, History of Diplomacy, History of Political Thought, International Relations, Journalism, Political Institutions, Political Science, Political Science and Economics, Public Finance, Social Policies, Sociology

School of Human Sciences (Freshmen Enrollment: 500)

Department of Basic Human Sciences

Comparative Morphology, General Biology, Introduction to Behavioral Science, Introduction to Psychology, Introduction to Sociology, Introduction to Statistics, Natural Anthropology, Social Life Science

Department of Human Health Sciences

Clinical Psychology, Community Welfare, Environmental Psychology, Human Relations, Introduction to Exercise and Health, Introduction to Recreation, Psychosomatic Medicine, Welfare Services

Department of Sports Sciences

Biomechanics, Cultural Theory of Sports, Physical Training and Practice, Social Survey, Sports Management, Sports Psychology, Sports Sociology, Theory of Sports Information

School of Law (Freshmen Enrollment: 1, 200)

Administrative Law, Civil Law, Civil Procedure, Commercial Law, Constitutional Law, Criminal Law, Criminal Procedure, Foreign Law, Foreign Legal Systems, International Law, Labor Law, Philosophy of Law

School of Literature (Freshmen Enrollment: 1, 110)

Department of Archaeology

Archaeology

Department of Asian History

History of Central Asia, History of Chinese Frontier and Central Asia, Modern History of China, Oriental History, Pre–Modern Chinese History

Department of Asian Philosophy

Ancient Chinese Thought, Chinese Thought, Indian Thought, Japanese Thought

Department of Chinese

Chinese Classics, Contemporary Literature, Early Modern–Modern Literature, Study of Early Chinese Poets

Department of Creative Writing

Contemporary Literature, Drama, Modern Literature, Novel, Poetry, Practical Criticism, Rhetoric, Visual Media and Journalism

Department of Dramatic Arts

Cinema, Japanese Drama, Japanese Dramatic Theories, Western Drama

Department of Education

International Problems in Education, Post-WW II Japanese Education, Social Foundations of Education, Studies of Educational Problems

Department of English

Drama, English, Novels, Poetry

Department of French

French Linguistics, 17th and 18th Century Literature, 19th Century Literature, 20th Century Literature

Department of German

Criticism, Drama, Novels, Poetry

Department of History of Art

History of Asian Art, History of European Art, History of Japanese Art

Department of Humanities

Contemporary Thought, Modern Thought, Oriental Classics, Western Classics

Department of Japanese

Ancient Poetry, Ancient Prose, Early Medieval Literature, Early Modern Poetry, Japanese Linguistics, Medieval Poetry, Modern Literature

Department of Japanese History

Ancient Japanese History, Discrimination and Prejudice in Modern Japan, Early Modern Japanese History, Journals in Medieval Japan, Medieval Japanese History, Modern Japanese History, Peasants' Uprising, Taisho Democracy Thought

Department of Philosophy

English and American Philosophy, Ethics & Religious Philosophy, French Philosophy, German Philosophy

Department of Psychology

Behavior Modification, Behavior Theory, Method of Social Survey, Personality Assessment, Psychological Experiment, Theories of Adjustment

Department of Russian

Drama, Novels, Poetry, Russian Linguistics

Department of Sociology

Consumer's Cooperative, Interaction between Local Government and the Public, Migration and Social Change, Modern Japan and Enterprises, Social Pathology and Social Welfare, Sociology, Sociology of Management and Labor, Urban Culture

Department of Western History

Ancient History, Ancient History (West Asia), Irish Issues in Modern History, Medieval History, Mesopotamian Civilization, Modern History, Modern History (Germany), Modern History (Pan-Slavism), Modern History (West Asia)

School of Literature (Evening Division) (Freshmen Enrollment: 510)

Department of Art

History of Japanese Art, History of Oriental Art, Japanese Art, Western Art

Department of English Literature

English Linguistics, Modern English Novels, Modern Novels, 18th Century English Novels, 19th Century English Literature, 19th Century English Poetry

Department of Japanese Literature

Ancient Literature, Medieval Literature, Modern Literature (Novels), Modern Literature (Poetry), Poetry of the Basho School, Reading of Katakoto, Study on Kojiki

Department of Oriental Culture

Ancient Chinese Thought, Early Modern Japanese Society and Culture, History of Sino–Japanese Relation, Medieval Japanese History, Modern Chinese Thought, Modern Japanese History, Politics and Society in Medieval China, The People's Movement in Early Modern Japan, The State Structure in Ancient China

Department of Social Studies

Community and Education, Environmental Psychology, Family and Modern Society, Mass Media and Environmental Problems, Modern Society and Education, Modern Society and Industry, Psychology of Family Society, Social Basis of Education

Department of Western Culture

Ancient Western Culture, Early Modern Western Culture, Medieval Western Culture, Modern Western Culture, Pan-Slavism

School of Political Science and Economics (Freshmen Enrollment: 1, 100)

Department of Economics

Economic Geography, Economic Policy, History of Economics, International Economics, Japanese Economic History, Modern Economic Theory, Monetary Theory, Public Finance, Socialist Economics, Social Policy, Statistical Theory, Theoretical Economics, Western Economic History

Department of Political Science

Administrative Law, Comparative Political Institutions, Constitutional Law, Contemporary Political Thought, History of Politics, International Politics, Japanese Political History, Local Government, Politics, Public Administration, Western Political History

School of Science and Engineering (Freshmen Enrollment: 1, 740)

Department of Applied Chemistry

Chemical Engineering CourseChemical Engineering, Reaction Engineering, Transport Phenomena, Unit Operation

Industrial Chemistry CourseIndustrial Chemistry, Inorganic Industrial Chemistry, Organic Industrial Chemistry

Department of Applied Physics

Applied Physics, Circuit Theory, Electromagnetic Theory, Physics, Statistical Mechanics, Theoretical Physics

Department of Architecture

Architectural Design, Architectural Drawing, Architecture, Architecture Planning, Building Construction, Building Equipment, Building Execution, Building Materials, City Planning, Environmental Planning, Mechanics of Building Structure, Structural Design, Urban Environmental Planning

Department of Chemistry

Analytical Chemistry, Inorganic Analytical Chemistry, Inorganic Chemistry, Instrumental Analysis, Organic Chemistry, Physical Chemistry, Quantum Chemistry

Department of Civil Engineering

Applied Mechanics, Civil Engineering, Concrete Engineering, Construction Materials, Design and Drawing, Hydraulics, Soil Engineering, Soil Engineering, Strength of Materials, Structural Concrete Engineering, Structural Engineering, Structural Engineering, Surveying

Department of Electrical Engineering

Computer Course Electronics CourseComputer Engineering, Electric Circuit Theory, Electronics, Electrostatic & Electromagnetic Theory, Energy Engineering, Solid State Engineering, System Engineering

Department of Electronics and Communication Engineering

Circuit Theory, Communication Engineering, Electric Measurement, Electromagnetic Theory, Electronic Circuit, Electronic Communication, Electronic Devices, Electronic Materials, Information Sciences, Information Theory, Measurement Engineering, Plasma Electronics

Department of Industrial Engineering and Man-

agement
Bookkeeping and Cost Accounting, Economics of Management, Electrical Engineering, Electronic Computation, Factory Management, Industrial Engineering, Industrial Psychology, Mathematical Statistics, Operations Research, Production Planning and Control, Work Measurements
Department of Materials Science Engineering
Metallography, Metallurgical Engineering, Metallurgy, Physical Chemistry of Metals, Physics of Metals, Strength of Metallic Materials
Department of Mathematics
Mathematics
Department of Mechanical Engineering
Electrical Engineering, Engineering Mathematics, Engineering of Metal Working, Engineering Thermodynamics, Machine Design and Drawing, Machine Materials, Mechanics of Fluids, Mechanics of Machinery, Production Technology, Strength of Materials
Department of Mineral Industry
Earth Science, Mineral Industry, Mineralogy and Petrology, Mining, Raw Materials Technology, Strength of Materials
Department of Physics
Analysis of Mathematics, Electromagnetism, Physics, Quantum Mechanics, Statistical Mechanics, Theoretical Physics
School of Social Sciences (Evening Division) (Freshmen Enrollment: 600)
Accounting, Business Management, Civil Law, Constitutional Law, Economics, Methodology of Social Science, Political Science, Public Finance

Foreign Student Admission
Qualifications for Applicants
Standard Qualifications Requirement
Examination at the University
Applicants must take both the Japanese Language Proficiency Test, and the special written examination and interview given by each School at Waseda University. The subjects of the written examinations vary with each School.
Documents to be Submitted When Applying
Standard Documents Requirement
Applicants are required to submit the necessary application documents in November for admission the next April. This application deadline changes slightly from year to year. For more details please contact the International Liaison Office for "The Guide to Admission for Undergraduate Studies" (Japanese edition only) published in August.

Qualifications for Transfer Students
Applicants who wish to transfer to sophomore or junior status must have completed more than four years of university education or the equivalent thereof in countries other than Japan and must be resident in Japan with an appropriate visa.
Examination for Transfer Students

Preliminary screening is made on the basis of the submitted application documents. Those who successfully pass the screening are allowed to take each School's special entrance examination consisting of written examinations and an interview. Applicants must also take the Japanese Language Proficiency Test.
Documents to be Submitted When Applying
Standard Documents Requirement
High School is transcripts are also required.

ONE-YEAR GRADUATE PROGRAMS

One-Year Advanced Teacher's Training Course (Enrollment: 100)
English Language and Literature, Japanese Language and Literature

Foreign Student Admission
Qualifications for Applicants
Standard Qualifications Requirement
Foreign students are not admitted to the Advanced Teacher's Training course.

GRADUATE PROGRAMS

Graduate School of Commerce (First Year Enrollment : Master's 80, Doctor's 40)
Division
Commercial Science
Graduate School of Economics (First Year Enrollment : Master's 80, Doctor's 40)
Divisions
Applied Economics, Theoretical Economics and Economics History
Graduate School of Law (First Year Enrollment : Master's 80, Doctor's 40)
Divisions
Civil Law, Fundamental Legal Studies, Public Law
Graduate School of Literature (First Year Enrollment : Master's 300, Doctor's 150)
Divisions
Arts, Chinese, English, French, German, History, Japanese, Oriental Philosophy, Pedagogy, Philosophy, Psychology, Russian, Sociology
Graduate School of Political Science (First Year Enrollment : Master's 40, Doctor's 20)
Division
Political Science
Graduate School of Science and Engineering (First Year Enrollment : Master's 780, Doctor's 208)
Divisions
Architecture and Civil Engineering, Electrical Engineering, Mathematics, Mechanical Engineering, Minenal Industry and Moterials Engineering Pure and Applied Chemistry, Pure and Applied Physics

Foreign Student Admission
Qualifications for Applicants
Master's Program

Standard Qualifications Requirement

Applicants to the Graduate Schools, except to the Graduate School of Literature, can apply either in Japan or from abroad. The Graduate School of Literature accepts applications only from those who are in Japan during the application period, with an appropriate visa.

Doctor's Program

Standard Qualifications Requirement

Applicants to the Graduate Schools, except to the Graduate School of Literature, can apply either in Japan or from abroad. The Graduate School of Literature accepts applications only from those who are in Japan during the application period with an appropriate visa.

Examination at the University

Master's Program

Preliminary screening is made on the basis of the submitted application documents. Those who successfully pass the screening are allowed to sit for the Japanese Language Test given by Waseda University and to take each Graduate School's special entrance examination consisting of written examinations and an interview. (Those who apply for the Graduate School of Science and Engineering are required to take only an interview.)

Doctor's Program

Same as Master's Program

Documents to be Submitted When Applying

Standard Documents Requirement

Applicants to the Master's Course are required to submit a detailed study plan to Waseda on the university form Supplied. Graduate School of Economics requires this in handwriting in Japanese.

Those applying for the Doctor's Course are required to submit copies of their Master's degree thesis, its summary and/or the proposed research plan. They should be approximately 20 pages in length each. Documents required vary at each Graduate School and exact information is available at the International Center upon request from each prospective applicant.

The following items must be submitted together with other documents.

1. A Certificate of Japanese Language Ability
2. Self–addressed   Envelope (applicants   from overseas only)
3. Self–addressed   Postcard (applicants   from overseas only)
4. An Envelope with the guarantor's address in Japan (applicants from overseas only)

∗

Research Institutes and Centers

Advanced Research Center for Human Suences, Castings Research Laboratory, Center for Informatics, Center for Japanese Language, Editorial Department of the University History, Environmental Safety Center, Extension Center, Institute for Research in Contemporary Political and Economic Affairs, Institute of Comparative Law, Institute of Language

Teaching, Institute of Social Sciences, Science and Engineering Research Laboratory, System Science Institute, The Institute for Research in Business Administration

Facilities/Services for Foreign Students

Extracurricular activities for foreign students; seminar trip, ski school, factory visits etc. provided through the International Liaison Office.

Subsidies to take trips to attend academic meetings and a tutorial allowance for students in the Graduate Course are available.

Special Programs for Foreign Students

Supplementary Study of Japanese:

Newly admitted students whose ability of Japanese is not up to standard are required to attend Japanese language classes for one year during their undergraduate and graduate study. In the case of undergraduate students, Japanese language study credits are recognized as those of a second foreign language and can be a part of the graduation requirements.

Summer Course of Japanese:

Newly admitted students whose ability of Japanese is comparatively low are required to take supplementary special course in Japanese during summer vacation.

Foreign students in the undergraduate schools can take the following special subjects as their part of general education requirements; Legal System in Japan/Japanese Culture I, II/Education in Japan/Japanese Geography/Japanese Industry and Management/Science and Technology in Japan/Industrialization and Environmental Pollution/Japanese Society/Japan Study Seminar. Also, students in the first year of undergraduate studies can take courses in the International Division in English. Credits for these courses can be transferred toward graduation requirements.

Japanese Language Course:

The Intensive Japanese Language Course at the elementary, intermediate and advanced levels and the Advanced Specialized Course in Japanese are offered at the Center for Japanese Language, Waseda University, to provide foreigners wishing to study Japanese or to do research on Japan with intensive instruction in Japanese. These Japanese courses are open to those who have graduated from a university or undergraduate students who are in the third or fourth year at a university and wish to learn the language in order to specialize in Japanese or in Japanese studies. Each course begins in April and is completed in one year. Application deadline is in September for admission the next April. Inquiries should be directed to the Center.

International Division:

The International Division offers a one–year study abroad program at the undergraduate level to students enrolled at foreign universities. The academic year at the Division is from September through June and the language of instruction is English. It gives courses is history, culture and current social conditions of Japan and Asia as well as Japanese language courses. Credits are given for students' academic requirements but no specific degree is awarded. About 90% of the students are from American institutions which have special agreements with Waseda University. Individual students can be admitted by the independent student admission procedure of the Division. Application deadline is in March for admission the next September and further information can be obtained from the International Division office.

For Further Information

Undergraduate and Graduate Admission

Admission Officer of Foreign Students, International Center, Waseda University, 1–6–1 Nishi-Waseda, Shinjuku–ku, Tokyo 160 ☎ 03-203-4141 ext. 2133, 2134.

Wayo Women's University
(Wayo Joshi Daigaku)

2–3–1 Kounodai, Ichikawa-shi, Chiba
☎ 0473-71-1111

Faculty
    Profs. 38   Assoc. Profs 17
    Assist. Profs. Full–time 5; Part–time 49
    Res. Assocs. 20
Number of Students
    Undergrad. 1, 546
Library 172, 000 volumes

Outline and Characteristics of the University

Wayo Women's University was originally founded in 1897 as Wayo Women's Sewing Academy. As a leader in women's education, it has carried out its tradition for over ninety years. In 1928, according to the Statute governing technical colleges, it became a women's technical college. In 1945, during the war, the college was burnt down in Chiyoda-ku, Tokyo. In 1946, the college was moved to Ichikawa City in Chiba Prefecture, which is its present location. With the amendment of the educational statute in 1949, it was renamed as Wayo Women's University, consisting of the school of Domestic Economy.

The junior college was added in 1950, and in 1953, the Department of Domestic Economy was designated as an instituion for training administrative dietitians. In 1961 both the Department of English and American Literature and the Department of Japanese Literature were added to the Department of Domectic Economy, and renamed as the School of Literature and Domestic Economy at Wayo Women's University.

The university's name"Wayo"was derived from the Japanese phrase "Wakon Yosai" which may be translated into English as"Japanese spirit and Western learning".

UNDERGRADUATE PROGRAMS

School of Literture and Domestic Economy (Freshmen Enrollment: 220)
    Department of Clothing
Art History, Child Care, Clothing Assortment, Consumer's Science of Fiber Goods, Domestic Science, Dyeing Chemistry and Theory of Fiber Processing, Family Relations, Fashion Aesthetics, Fiber for Clothing, History of Costumes, History of Dyeing and Weaving, Home Economics, Home Management, Home Nursing
    Department of Domestic Economy
Major in Administrative Dietetics and Food Science Biochemistry, Cookery, Food Chemistry, Food Materials, Food Preservation and Processing, Food Supply Administration, High Polymer Chemistry, Management and Food Economics, Mathematical Statistics, Microbiology, Nutrition, Pathology, Physiology, Sanitation, Social Psychology, Social Welfare
    Department of English and American Literature
Business English, Current English, English, English Compositon, English Conversation, History of English and American Literature, History of English Language, Lecture and Seminar on English Poetry/Drama/Novel and Criticism, Phonetics
    Department of Japanese Literature
Ancient Practices and Usage, Archaeology, Bibliography, Ethnology, Folklore, History of Chinese Literature, Histroy of Japanese Literature, Linguistics, Performing Arts, Religion, Reseach in Japanese Literature, Research in Chinese Literature, Research in Japanese Literature (Nara, Heian, Kamakura and Muromachi, Edo and after Meiji period)

Women's College of Fine Arts
(Joshi Bijutsu Daigaku)

1-49-8 Wada, Suginami-ku, Tokyo 166
☎ 03-382-2271

Faculty
    Profs. 31   Assoc. Profs. 11
    Assist. Profs. Full–time 6; Part–time 113
    Res. Assocs. 23
Number of Students
    Undergrad. 1, 212
Library 140, 000 volumes

Outline and Characteristics of the College

Women's College of Fine Arts was established by Shizu Sato in 1900 as Women's School of Fine Arts with departments of Japanese painting, European style painting, engraving, embroidery, artificial flower and sewing. It was renamed as Women's College of Fine Arts in 1929. Women's College of Fine Arts was reorganized and consolidated under the National School Establishment Law in 1949. Junior College of Fine Arts (two-year course) was established in 1950.

The College has grown with the times and its facilities and faculty members have been renovated. Now it has one faculty and five departments—Oil Painting, Japanese Painting, Design, Dyeing and Weaving, and Science of Plastic Arts.

UNDERGRADUATE PROGRAMS

Faculty of Fine Arts (Freshmen Enrollment: 200)
Department of Industrial Design
Design, Dyeing and Weaving
Department of Painting
Japanese Painting, Oil Painting, Pictorial Printing
Department of Science of Arts
Plastic Arts

Foreign Student Admission
Qualifications for Applicants
Standard Qualifications Requirement
A fairly high ability of Japanese
Examination at the College
Same as for Japanese
1. Written Examination of Japanese and English languages.
2. Technical Examination of painting, sketch, or design.
Date: in February.

*

For Further Information
Undergraduate Admission
Educational Affairs Section, Women's College of Fine Arts, 1-49-8 Wada, Suginami–ku, Tokyo 166 ☎ 03-382-2271 ext. 25

Yachiyo International University
(Yachiyo Kokusai Daigaku)

1–1, Daigaku–cho, Yachiyo–shi, Chiba 276
☎ 0474–88–2111

Faculty
  Profs. 33   Assoc. Profs 10
  Assist. Profs. Full–time 10; Part–time 26
Number of Students
  Undergrad. 308
Library 46, 280 volumes

UNDERGRADUATE PROGRAMS

Faculty of Political Economy (Freshmen Enrollment: 250)
Department of Political Economy

Yahata University
(Yahata Daigaku)

5-9-1 Edamitsu, Yahatahigashi-ku, Kitakyushu-shi, Fukuoka 805 ☎ 093-671-8910

Faculty
  Profs. 45   Assoc. Profs. 17
  Assist. Profs. Full–time 11; Part–time 26
Number of Students
  Undergrad. 2, 699
Library 200, 297 volumes

Outline and Characteristics of the University
Yahata University was founded in 1947 as Tobata College of Law and Economics. It was renamed as Yahata College of Law and Economics when its campus moved to the present University address in late 1948. The College consisted of two departments: the Department of Law and Politics and the Department of Economics. Offering day and evening courses to students, the College played a pioneering role in the teaching of law and economics in Kyushu Island. In 1950, the College was renamed as Yahata University owing to the post-war educational system reform and opened the Department of Law. With the addition of the Department of Business Economics to the Faculty in 1951, the Faculty was renamed as the Faculty of Law and Economics.

The campus is located in the city of Kitakyushu, a great industrial city in Western Japan in the northern part of Kyushu Island.

The University aims to prepare students for professions which require well-balanced knowledge and specialized technology to meet the demands of society. Being small in size, the University has the advantage of maintaining friendly relationships between teachers and students. Among other important aspects of the University is the fact that it has always been on good terms with the local communities and has done its fair share in their cultural, educational, economic and manufacuring activities. Part of the educational facilities as well as some specialized courses are open to the public.

UNDERGRADUATE PROGRAMS

Faculty of Law and Economics (Freshmen Enrollment : Day Course 400, Evening Course 240)
Department of Business Economics
Accounting, Business Administration, Commercial Science, Economic History, Economic Policy, Information Processing, Money and Banking, Public Finance, Social Policy, Statistics, Theoretical Economics, Trade
Department of Law
Administrative Law, Civil Law, Commercial Law, Constitutional Law, Criminal Law, International

Law, International Private Law, Political Science, Procedural Law, Social Law, Tax Law

*

Research Institutes and Centers
Institute of Sociocultural Studies
For Further Information
Undergraduate Admission
Admission Office, Yahata University,
5-9-1 Edamitsu, Yahatahigashi-ku, Kitakyushu-shi, Fukuoka 805 ☎ 093-671-8913 ext. 271

Yamanashi Gakuin University
(Yamanashi Gakuin Daigaku)

2-4-5 Sakaori, Kofu-shi, Yamanashi 400
☎ 0552-33-1111

Faculty
    Profs. 32   Assoc. Profs. 19
    Assist. Profs. Full–time 14; Part–time 33
    Res. Assoc. 1
Number of Students
    Undergrad. 2, 667
Library 200, 000 volumes

Outline and Characteristics of the University

Yamanashi Gakuin University was founded in 1946, for the purpose of educating students so they may contribute to the restoration of Japan and assist in building a democratic natio.. following World War II. Through the course of recent history, Japan has been restored and developed considerably, and Yamanashi Gakuin University has enriched its facilities and faculty in step with the nation. In this sense, the history of Yamanashi Gakuin University parallels the extraordinary advancements of the renewed Japan.

The campus of Yamanashi Gakuin University is located in Kofu Basin, surrounded by Mt. Fuji and the beautiful Japan Alps but only 100 kilometers away (one hour and half by train) from metropolitan Tokyo. Partly because of the small number of students and, of course, university policy, intimate and active communication and relationship among students as well as between students and faculty members of the university exists. This situation ideally eliminates the problems which tend to occur at a large, mass-producing university.

Even though most of its students are from all over Japan, Yamanashi Gakuin University is deeply rooted in and open to the local community. It also has a sister-university relationship with Pacific University in Oregon, U. S. A. Thus, Yamanashi Gakuin University embodies the principles of both local and international community.

UNDERGRADUATE PROGRAMS

Faculty of Commerical Science (Freshmen Enroll-

ment: 250)
    Department of Commercial Science
Bookkeeping, Business Administration, Circulation and Distribution, Commercial Law, Commercial Policy, Cost Accounting, Economics, Financial Studies, Public Accounts Act
    Department of Management Information
Information Management and Utilization, Introduction to Computer Science Programming Language, Principles of Business Administration Principles of Bookkeeping, Business History, Operations Research Financial Management, Principles of Economics, Marketing
Faculty of Law (Freshmen Enrollment: 240)
    Department of Law
Administrative Law, Civil Law, Code of Civil Procedure, Code of Criminal Procedure, Commercial Law, Company Law, Constitutional Law, Criminal Law, Law of Obligations, Status Law

Foreign Student Admission
    Qualifications for Applicants
    Standard Qualifications Requirement
    Examination at the University
    A written examination and an interview.
    Documents to be Submitted When Applying
    Standard Documents Requirement
    Following documents are also required.
1. Certificate of Japanese Language Proficiency Test or its equivalent.
2. Study plan and statement of purpose which should be filled in the prescribed form.

    Qualifications for Transfer Students
    Applicants who are expected to finish or have finished a two–year program at a Japanese university or junior college.
    Examination for Transfer Students
    Interview and an essay test.
    Documents to be Submitted When Applying
    Standard Documents Requirement

*

Research Institutes and Centers
Institute of Social Science
Facilities/Services for Foreign Students
    The Committee for International Educational Exchange Programs is to function as an advisory window for foreign students and gives a dinner party twice a year in order to strengthen and maintain intimate relationship between foreign students and the faculty members of Yamanashi Gakuin University.
For Further Information
    Undergraduate Admission
Public Relations Office, Yamanashi Gakuin University, 2-4-5 Sakaori, Kofu-shi, Yamanashi 400 ☎ 0552-32-7499

Yasuda Women's University
(Yasuda Joshi Daigaku)

6-13-1 Yasuhigashi, Asaminami-ku, Hiroshima-shi,
Hiroshima 731-01 ☎ 082-878-8111

Faculty
  Profs. 23   Assoc. Profs. 13
  Assist. Profs. Full–time 9; Part–time 48
Number of Students
  Undergrad. 1, 508
Library 75, 170 volumes

Outline and Characteristics of the University

Yasuda Women's University is a private institution established in 1966. It was added as the highest academic institution to the Yasuda Institute of Education, which has a history of over 70 years since its establishment in 1915 and has developed into an educational system comprised of two kindergartens, a primary school, a junior and senior high school, a junior college, and a university. Except for the kindergartens and the primary school, which run on a coeducational basis, the Yasuda Institute enrolls only female students and is noted for its excellence in women's education. With tenderness and firmness as its two guiding principles, Yasuda aims at educating its students to become considerate, intelligent, and dependable Japanese citizens.

Yasuda University has only one faculty, the Faculty of Letters, which is comprised of three departments: Japanese Literature, English Language and English and American Literature, and the Primary Education Department. The Department of Japanese Literature offers a special course in the art of calligraphy, which, being a rare course, is one of the important aspects of the University. Students are granted a Bachelor's Degree upon completion of their courses. Certificates for primary and secondary school teachers, social education officers, and librarians are also obtainable by completing additional subjects offered in these areas. Students are requested to wear uniforms during their first two years and also on designated formal occasions.

Yasuda Women's University is located in the north-western part of Hiroshima and is easily accessible from the downtown section of the city. Situated on the slope of a hill, it is favored by natural beauty and affords an exquisite view to the south. Various extra-curricular activities are held year-round on the spacious campus. The Freshmen Orientation Seminar at Etajima, off-campus Summer Camps in the mountains, Sports Day, and the Campus Festival, to name only a few, are among the major annual activities in which the greater part of the University participates. With an enrollment of some 1, 500, the University may not be very large, but has the advantage of maintaining close and friendly relationships between teachers and students.

UNDERGRADUATE PROGRAMS

Faculty of Letters (Freshmen Enrollment: 320)
  Department of English Language and English and American Literature
  Department of Japanese Literature
  Department of Primary Education

*

For Further Information
  Undergraduate Admission
Educational Affairs Section, Administration Office, Yasuda Women's University, 6-13-1 Yasuhigashi, Asaminami-ku, Hiroshima-shi, Hiroshima 731-01 ☎ 082-878-8111 ext. 217

Yokkaichi University
(Yokkaichi Daigaku)

1200 Kayou-cho, Yokkaichi-shi, Mie 512
☎ 0593-65-6588

Faculty
  Profs. 14   Assoc. Profs. 5
  Assist. Profs. Full–time 5; Part–time 11
  Res. Assoc. 1
Number of Students
  Undergrad. 507
Library 24, 455 volumes

Outline and Characteristics of the University

Yokkaichi University opened in April, 1988. It is comprised of two departments of Economics and Management. It is one of Japan's youngest educational establishments and means to be one of the most forward looking.

Its hilltop campus is only a few minutes' drive from the industrial port of Yokkaichi, currently ranking 13th in Japan in value of maunfactured goods exported. Yokkaichi, population 270, 000, is the largest town in Mie Prefecture, and lies at the head of Ise Bay. A little way to the east is the densely urbanized zone around Nagoya. Down the Bay to the south is the unspoilt Ise-Shima Coast, and inland are the Suzuka Mountains.

The University was born out of ten years of joint planning between the locally prominent Akatsuki College (founded 1946) and the City of Yokkaichi. In the past Japanese universities have been rigidly divided into public and private, with little interchange of personnel and ideas between the two sectors. Yokkaichi University is one of a handful of recent foundations which seeks to bridge this gap, combining the solidity of municipal support with the independence and local awareness of a private establlishment.   In practical terms, this means a symbiotic relation between city and university. The city expects then niversity to attract promising young people to the area and train them to cope with tomorrow's problems. For its part, university expects understanding and gooodwill for its academic objectives not only from the city itself, but from local firms. And all parties hope for benefits to accrue from joint research and consultation in matters of local interest.   The university's foundation is also to be seen in a wider context, as one step in the growth of the Suzuka Mountains Academic City Project announced a few years ago by the central government.

As a major port, Uokkaichi has close links with other cities around the world. Partly to support these links, but mainly to encourage the worldwide flow of knowledge for its own sake, the university is currently neogotiating regular joint activities with partner establishments in the United States, West Germany and China. These will include the sending of Japanese students abroad as integral part of their coursework, not in the traditional punitive form of time-consuming extra credit. We also hope to welcome students from abroad to our home campus.

It goes without saying that the Yokkaichi Campus is well equipped with computers, and that students are being trained in their operation. But intelligent computer use involves more than the tricks of the keyboard. It also requires a wide view of problems and the ability to think for oneself.

In the students' main subjects of Economics and Management, a large range of specialized courses helps to make them aware of the complexities of the subject matter before them. In addition, students may choose from a number of general Humanities classes not directly connected with economics at all. For both utilitarian and mind-broadening reasons, a sound ability in English reading and conversation is required, as well as a basic Knowledge of a second language.

UNDERGRADUATE PROGRAMS

Faculty of Economics (Freshmen Enrollment: 280)
Department of Economics
Economic History, Economic Policy, Economic Statistics, Economic Theory, Monetary Economics and Public Finance, Social Policy
Department of Management
Business Management, Forms of Enterprises, History of Business, Management Engineering, Principles of Accounting, Principles of Management

Foreign Student Admission
Examination at the University
The personal histor of the applicant and an interview.

∗
Special Programs for Foreign Students
The University offers an elementary course in the Japanese language and affairs specially for foreign students.

For Further Information
Undergraduate Admission
General Affairs Division Chief, General Affairs Division, Yokkaichi University, 1200 Kayou–cho, Yokkaichi–shi, Mie 512 ☎ 0593–65–6588

Yokohama College of Commerce
(Yokohama Shoka Daigaku)
4–11–1 Higashi Terao, Tsurumi–ku, Yokohama–shi, Kanagawa 230 ☎ 045–571–3901

Faculty
Profs. 29　Assoc. Profs. 18
Assist. Profs. Full–time 3; Part–time 65
Number of Students
Undergrad. 2, 171
Library 71, 819 volumes

Outline and Characteristics of the College
The history of Yokohama College of Commerce traces back to Yokohama First Commercial School founded by Takeo Matsumoto in 1941. He felt that Yokohama should have a school emphasizing the importance of fiduciary relationships in our human society. Since then, its education has been based on his precepts—"Be a reliable man. " The first expansion came in 1966 when Yokohama Junior College of Commerce was founded to meet the demand for higher business education. In 1968, it further developed into the present Yokohama College of Commerce which observed its 20th anniversary in 1986.

In its early years it had the Department of Commerce only, but in 1974 the Department of Foreign Trade and Tourism and Department of Management Information were added. Its rapid expansion is attributable to the prescient curricula, homey atmosphere, and personal attention to individual needs.

Yokohama College of Commerce enjoys its convenient location to various cultural, educational, industrial, and commercial facilities in Tokyo and Yokohama. Foreign students can take advantage of them.

The Department of Commerce centers around the fields of Marketing, Finance, Transportaion, and Insurance. It aims at fostering businessmen with professional knowledge and the capability to function in trading companies, manufacturers, banks, insurance companies, and independent businesses.

The Department of Foreign Trade and Tourism is a very unique one, integrating visible trade with invisible trade (tourism). Students may study hotel management, tourist services, and tourism development, together with international trade theory and practice, international marketing and monetary problems. Today, these two fields are inseparable in our international business world.

The Department of Management Information covers three fields such as management, accounting, and data processing. Students may major in one of them and take the other courses as minors. No business can be successfully operated without knowledgeable persons in these three areas. Instructions in classes are supported by extra–curricula activities in data processing, if the students so desire.

UNDERGRADUATE PROGRAMS

Faculty of Commerce (Freshmen Enrollment: 300)
Department of Commerce
Accounting, Advertising, Auditing, Bookkeeping, Business Administration, Commercial Policy, Commercial Science, Cost Accounting, Economic Geography, Economic History, Economics, Economic Statistics, Finance, Foreign Exchange, Foreign Trade, Insurance, International Economics, International Finance, Japanese Commercial History, Japanese Economic History, Management, Marketing, Merchandising, Public Finance, Sales Management, Securities Market, Small Business Management, Tax Accounting, Tax Law, Transportation
Department of Foreign Trade and Tourism
Bookkeeping, Finance, Foreign Exchange, Foreign Trade, Foreign Trade Policy, Hotel Management, International Economics, International Finance, International Marketing, International Relations, Leisure and Recreation, Marine Insurance, Marketing, Merchandising, Tourism, Tourism Development, Tourism Geography, Tourism Resources, Tourist Business, Tourist Policy, Transportation, Travel Agency
Department of Management Information
Auditing, Business Administration, Business Analysis, Business Mathematics, Computer Networks and Data Communication, Data Processing, Financial Management, Financial Statements, Foreign Trade, Information Management, Information Systems Design, Labor Management, Management, Management History, Management Information Systems, Management Policy, Management Science, Managerial Accounting, Marketing, Office Management, Production Management, Sales Management, Systems Auditing, Tax Accounting
Foreign Student Admission
Qualifications for Applicants
    Standard Qualifications Requirement
    Applicants must have successfully completed at least one year's education of Japanese in a formal language school either in Japan or in their own country.
Examination at the College
1. A multiple–choice examination on Japanese and English (sixty minutes in total).
2. Japanese composition on an assigned subject (sixty minutes).
3. Interview.
Documents to be Submitted When Applying
    Standard Documents Requirement
1. Foreign applicants whose schooling is short of the 12–year requirement must submit a certifi-

cate of successful completion of additional education for the year or years necessary.
2. As all instructions are given in Japanese, every foreign applicant must submit evidence of successful completion of at least one year's study of Japanese in a formal language school either in Japan or in the applicant's own country.
3. Every applicant is required to submit a personal history in Japanese written in the applicant's own hand in the form prescribed by the College.
Application Period: November 28–December 12, 1988
Entrance examination: December 16 and 17, 1988
Announcement of Successful Applicants: December 23, 1988
Period of Entrance Procedures: December 23, 1988–January 13, 1989.

*

Facilities/Services for Foreign Students
1. Foreign students are assigned an advisor who assists them in planning an academic program and arranging a schedule, and provides further guidance with personal problems.
2. At least every two months, a special tour, guided by one of the professors to Japanese gardens, museums, factories, stores and other historic points of interest will be arranged by the foreign student advisor.
Special Programs for Foreign Students
    The College offers Elementary Japanese and State of Affaire in Japan in the first year and Intermediate Japanese in the second year as a foreign language, in the general education curriculum.
For Further Information
Undergraduate Admission
Department of Educational Affairs, Yokohama College of Commerce, 4–11–1 Higashi Terao, Tsurumi-ku, Yokohama–shi, Kanagawa 230 ☎ 045–571–3901 ext. 17

Majors Index

Major Fields of Study by Discipline

Agriculture
Agricultural Chemistry
Agricultural Economics
Agricultural Engineering
Agriculture
Agrobiology
Agronomy
Animal Science (Husbandry)
Fisheries
Food Science and Technology
Forestry
Horticulture
Landscape Architecture
Sericulture
Veterinary Medicine

Engineering
Aeronautical Engineering
Applied Chemistry
Applied Physics
Architecture and Architectural Engineering
Atomic Physics
Chemical Engineering
Civil Engineering
Communication Engineering
Computer Science
Electrical Engineering
Electronic Engineering
Environmental Sciences
Image Science and Engineering
Industrial Chemistry
Industrial Design
Industrial Management Engineering
Information Sciences
Materials Engineering
Mechanical Engineering
Metallurgical Engineering
Mining and Mineral Engineering
Naval Architecture and Marine Engineering
Nuclear Engineering
Precision Engineering
Textile Technology
Urban and Regional Planning

Humanities
Aesthetics and Art History
Anthropology
Archaeology
Area Studies (incl. Japanology)
Buddhism
Child Education (incl. Kindergarten Teacher Training)
Chinese Language and Literature
Culture Studies
Dramatic Arts
Education
English Language and English/American Literature
Fine Arts
Foreign Languages and Literature (except English, Chinese, French, German, Japanese, Spanish and Russian)
French Language and Literature

German Language and Literature
History
Japanese Language and Literature
Linguistics
Music
Philosophy
Psychology
Religion
Russian Language and Literature
Shinto
Social Welfare
Sociology
Spanish Language and Literature
Special Education
Teacher Training
Theology
Tourism

Medical Sciences
Acupuncture and Moxibustion
Dentistry
Health Sciences
Medicine
Nursing
Pharmaceutical Sciences

Natural Sciences
Astronomy
Biology
Botany
Chemistry
Geology
Geosciences
Mathematics
Physics
Zoology

Social Sciences
Accounting
Business Administration and Management
Commerce
Communication Media
Economics
International Economics
International Relations
Law
Mass Communication and Journalism
Political Science
Public Administration

Others
Biochemistry
Bioengineering and Bioscience
Clothing and Textiles (incl. Fashion)
Food and Nutrition Sciences
Geography
Home Economics
Library Science
Physical Education

Engineering (continued)

Kyushu Institute of Technology   *B, M*
Kyusyu Tokai University   *B*
Kyushu University   *B, M, D*
Nagoya Institute of Technology   *B, M, D*
Shizuoka University   *B, M*
Tokai University   *B*
Tokyo Denki University   *B, M, D*
Tokyo Institute of Technology   *B, M, D*
Toyohashi University of Technology *B, M, D*
University of Electro-Communications, The *B, M, D*
University of Osaka Prefecture   *B, M, D*
Waseda University   *B*
Yamanashi University   *B, M*
Yokohama National University   *B, M, D*

Culture Studies

Aichi Gakuin University   *B*
Atomi Gakuen Women's College   *B*
Chiba University   *B, M*
Chubu University   *B*
Daito Bunka University   *B*
Doshisha University   *B, M, D*
Ehime University   *B*
Fukuoka University   *B*
Hirosaki University   *B*
Hiroshima University   *B*
Hokkaido Tokai University   *B*
Ibaraki University   *B*
International Christian University   *M, D*
International University of Japan   *M*
Kagoshima University   *M*
Kobe College   *B, M*
Kobe University   *D*
Kumamoto University   *B, M*
Mie University   *B*
Musashi University   *B*
Nara Women's University   *D*
Nihon University   *B*
Niigata University   *B, M*
Ochanomizu University   *D*
Osaka University   *B, M, D*
Otemon Gakuin University   *B*
Saitama University   *B, M*
Seijo University   *B, M, D*
Seikei University   *B, M*
Seinan Gakuin University   *B*
Seisen Women's College   *B*
Setsunan University   *B*
Shinshu University   *M*
Shitennoji International Buddhist University *B*
Soai University   *B*
Sophia University   *B, M*
Tezukayama University   *B*
Tokai University   *B, M, D*
Tokyo Kasei Gakuin College   *B*
Tokyo University of Foreign Studies   *B, M*
Tokyo Woman's Christian University   *B*
Toyama University   *B, M*
University of Osaka Prefecture   *B, M, D*
University of Shizuoka   *B*
University of Tokyo, The   *B, M, D*
University of Tsukuba   *B*
Waseda University   *B*
Yamaguchi University   *B, M*

Dentistry

Aichi Gakuin University   *B, D*
Asahi University   *B, D*
Fukuoka Dental College   *B, D*

Higashi Nippon Gakuen University   *B, D*
Hiroshima University   *B, D*
Hokkaido University   *B, D*
Iwate Medical University   *B, D*
Kagoshima University   *B, D*
Kanagawa Dental College   *B, D*
Kyushu Dental College   *B, D*
Kyushu University   *B, D*
Matsumoto Dental College   *B*
Meikai University   *B, D*
Nagasaki University   *B, D*
Nihon University   *B, D*
Niigata University   *B, D*
Nippon Dental University, The   *B, D*
Okayama University   *B, D*
Osaka Dental University   *B, D*
Osaka University   *B, D*
Showa University   *B, D*
Tohoku Dental University   *B, D*
Tohoku University   *B, D*
Tokyo Dental College   *B, D*
Tokyo Medical and Dental University   *B, D*
Tsurumi University   *B, D*
University of Tokushima, The   *B, D*

Dramatic Arts

Kyoritsu Women's University   *B, M*
Meiji University   *B, M, D*
Nihon University   *B*
Tamagawa University   *B*
Waseda University   *B*

Economics

Aichi University   *B, M, D*
Akita University of Economics and Law   *B*
Aoyama Gakuin University   *B, M, D*
Asahikawa College   *B*
Asia University   *B, M, D*
Chiba Keizai University   *B*
Chiba University   *B, M*
Chiba University of Commerce   *B, M*
Chukyo University   *B*
Chuo University   *B, M, D*
Daiichi College of Commerce and Industry *B*
Daito Bunka University   *B, M, D*
Dokkyo University   *B*
Doshisha University   *M, D*
Ehime University   *B*
Fuji College   *B*
Fukuoka University   *B, M, D*
Fukushima University   *B, M*
Fukuyama University   *B*
Gakushuin University   *B, M*
Gifu College of Economics   *B*
Hirosaki University   *B*
Hiroshima University   *B, M, D*
Hiroshima University of Economics   *B, M*
Hitotsubashi University   *B, M, D*
Hokkaido University   *B, M, D*
Hokkaigakuen Kitami University   *B*
Hokkaigakuen University   *B, M*
Hokusei Gakuen College   *B*
Hosei University   *B, M, D*
Ibaraki University   *B*
International Christian University   *B*
Iwate University   *B*
Jobu University   *B*
Josai University   *B, M*
Kagawa University   *B, M*
Kagoshima University   *B*

Kagoshima University of Economics and Sociology   *B*
Kanagawa University   *B, M, D*
Kanazawa College of Economics   *B*
Kanazawa University   *B, M*
Kansai University   *B, M, D*
Kanto Gakuen University   *B, M*
Kanto Gakuin University   *B, M, D*
Keiai University   *B*
Keio University   *B, M, D*
Kinki University   *B*
Kitakyushu University   *B, M*
Kobe–Gakuin University   *B, M, D*
Kobe University   *B, M*
Kobe University of Commerce   *B, M, D*
Kochi University   *B*
Kokugakuin University   *B, M, D*
Kokushikan University   *B, M, D*
Komazawa University   *B, M, D*
Konan University   *B*
Kumamoto Univeristy of Commerce   *B*
Kurume University   *B*
Kwansei Gakuin University   *B, M, D*
Kyoto Gakuen University   *B*
Kyoto Sangyo University   *B, M*
Kyoto University   *B, M, D*
Kyushu Kyoritsu University   *B*
Kyushu Sangyo University   *B, M*
Kyushu University   *B, M, D*
Matsusaka University   *B*
Matsuyama University   *B, M, D*
Meiji Gakuin University   *B, M*
Meiji University   *B, M, D*
Meijo University   *B*
Meikai University   *B*
Meisei University   *B*
Musashi University   *B, M, D*
Nagasaki Prefectural University of International Economics   *B*
Nagasaki University   *B*
Nagoya City University   *B, M, D*
Nagoya Economics University   *B*
Nagoya Gakuin University   *B*
Nagoya University   *B, M, D*
Nanzan University   *B, M, D*
Nara Sangyo University   *B*
Nihon Fukushi University   *B*
Nihon University   *B, M, D*
Niigata Sangyo University   *B*
Niigata University   *B*
Nippon Bunri University   *B*
Obirin College   *B*
Oita University   *B, M*
Okayama University   *B, M*
Okinawa Kokusai University   *B*
Osaka City University   *B, M, D*
Osaka Gakuin University   *B, ·M, D*
Osaka Industrial University   *B*
Osaka University   *B, M, D*
Osaka University of Commerce   *B*
Osaka University of Economics   *B, M, D*
Osaka University of Economics and Law   *B*
Otaru University of Commerce   *B*
Otemon Gakuin University   *B, M*
Rikkyo (St. Paul's) University   *B, M, D*
Rissho University   *B*
Ritsumeikan University   *B, M, D*
Ryukoku University   *B, M, D*
Ryutsu-Keizai University   *B*
Saga University   *B*
Saitama University   *B*
Sapporo Gakuin University   *B*
Sapporo University   *B*
Seigakuin University   *B*

Minami Kyushu College *B*
Nagoya University *B, M, D*
Nihon University *B, M, D*
Nippon Veterinary and Zootechnical College
  B
Tohoku University *B, M, D*
Tokyo University of Fisheries *B, M*
University of East Asia, The *B*
Yamaguchi University *B*

Foreign Languages and Literature

Himeji Dokkyo University *B*
Hiroshima University *B*
Hokkaido University *B*
Hokuriku University *B*
Kanda University of International Studies
  B
Kyonin University *B*
Kyoto Sangyo University *B*
Kyoto University *B, M, D*
Kyoto University of Foreign Studies *B, M*
Meikai University *B*
Nagoya University of Foreign Studies *B*
Ochanomizu University *B*
Osaka University of Foreign Studies *B, M*
Setsunan University *B*
Shitennoji International Buddhist University
  B
Sophia University *B*
Takushoku University *B*
Tamagawa University *B*
Tenri University *B*
Tokai University *B*
Tokyo University of Foreign Studies *B, M*
Toyama University *B*
University of the Sacred Heart *B*
University of Tokyo, The *B, M, D*

Forestry

Ehime University *B, M*
Gifu University *B, M*
Hokkaido University *B*
Iwate University *B, M*
Kagoshima University *B, M*
Kochi University *B, M*
Kyoto Prefectural University *B, M, D*
Kyoto University *B, M, D*
Kyushu University *B, M, D*
Mie University *B, M*
Miyazaki University *B, M*
Nagoya University *B, M, D*
Nihon University *B*
Niigata University *B, M*
Shimane University *B, M*
Shinshu University *B, M*
Shizuoka University *B, M*
Tokyo University of Agriculture *B, M*
Tokyo University of Agriculture and Technology *B, M, D*
University of the Ryukyus *B, M*
University of Tokyo, The *B, M, D*
University of Tottori *B, M*
University of Tsukuba *B, D*
Utsunomiya University *B, M*
Yamagata University *B, M*

French Language and Literature

Aichi Prefectural University *B*
Aoyama Gakuin University *B, M, D*
Chiba University *B*

Chuo University *B, M, D*
Dokkyo University *B*
Eichi University *B*
Fukuoka University *B, M*
Gakushuin University *B, M, D*
Hiroshima University *B, M, D*
Kansai University *B, M, D*
Keio University *B, M, D*
Kobe Kaisei (Stella Maris) College *B*
Kobe University *B, M*
Kochi University *B*
Konan Women's College *B, M, D*
Kwansei Gakuin University *B, M, D*
Kyoritsu Women's University *B*
Kyoto Sangyo University *B*
Kyoto University *B, M, D*
Kyoto University of Foreign Studies *B, M*
Kyushu University *B, M, D*
Meiji Gakuin University *B*
Meiji University *B, M, D*
Musashi University *B, M*
Nagoya University *B, M, D*
Nanzan University *B, M, D*
Okayama University *B, M*
Osaka City University *B, M, D*
Osaka University *B, M, D*
Osaka University of Foreign Studies *B, M*
Rikkyo (St. Paul's) University *B, M, D*
Seinan Gakuin University *B, M, D*
Shirayuri Women's College *B*
Sophia University *B, M, D*
Tenri University *B*
Tohoku University *B, M, D*
Tokyo Metropolitan University *B, M, D*
Tokyo University of Foreign Studies *B, M*
University of Osaka Prefecture *B*
University of Tokyo, The *B, M, D*
University of Tsukuba *B, D*
Waseda University *B, M, D*

Geography

Hiroshima University *B, M, D*
Hosei University *B, M, D*
Kansai University *B, M*
Kobe University *B, M*
Kokushikan University *B*
Komazawa University *B, M, D*
Kumamoto University *B, M*
Kyoto University *B, M, D*
Meiji University *B, M, D*
Nara University *B*
Nara Women's University *B, M*
Nihon University *B, M, D*
Ochanomizu University *B, M*
Osaka City University *B, M, D*
Rikkyo (St. Paul's) University *B, M, D*
Rissho University *B, M, D*
Ritsumeikan University *B, M, D*
Senshu University *B*
Tohoku University *B*
Tokyo Metropolitan University *B, M, D*
University of the Ryukyus *B*
University of Tokyo, The *B, M, D*
University of Tsukuba *B, D*
Waseda University *B*
Yokohama City University *B*

Geology

Hiroshima University *B, M, D*
Hokkaido University *B, M, D*
Kagoshima University *B, M*
Kochi University *B, M*

Kumamoto University *B*
Kyoto University *B, M, D*
Kyushu University *B, M, D*
Nihon University *B*
Niigata University *B, M*
Osaka City University *B, M, D*
Shimane University *B, M*
Shinshu University *B, M*
Tohoku University *B*
University of Tokyo, The *B, M, D*
University of Tsukuba *B, D*

Geosciences

Chiba University *B, M, D*
Ehime University *B, M*
Hirosaki University *B, M*
Hokkaido University *B, M, D*
Ibaraki University *B, M*
Kagoshima University *B*
Kanazawa University *B, M*
Kobe University *B, M*
Kyoto University *B, M, D*
Muroran Institute of Technology *B, M*
Nagoya University *B, M, D*
Okayama University *B, M*
Osaka City University *B*
Shizuoka University *B, M*
Tohoku University *B, M, D*
Toyama University *B, M*
University of Tokyo, The *B, M, D*
Waseda University *B*
Yamagata University *B, M*

German Language and Literature

Aichi University *B*
Chuo University *B, M, D*
Dokkyo University *B, M*
Fukuoka University *B*
Gakushuin University *B, M, D*
Hiroshima University *B, M, D*
Hokkaido University *B, M, D*
International Christian University *B*
Kanazawa University *B, M*
Kansai University *B, M, D*
Keio University *B, M, D*
Kobe University *B, M*
Kochi University *B*
Konan University *B*
Kumamoto University *B, M*
Kwansei Gakuin University *B, M, D*
Kyoto City University *B*
Kyoto Sangyo University *B*
Kyoto University *B, M, D*
Kyoto University of Foreign Studies *B, M*
Kyushu University *B, M, D*
Meiji University *B, M, D*
Musashi University *B, M*
Nagoya University *B, M, D*
Nanzan University *B, M, D*
Nihon University *B, M, D*
Okayama University *B, M*
Osaka City University *B, M, D*
Osaka Gakuin University *B*
Osaka University *B, M, D*
Osaka University of Foreign Studies *B, M*
Otani University *B*
Reitaku University *B*
Rikkyo (St. Paul's) University *B, M, D*
Saitama University *B, M, B*
Sophia University *B, M, D*
Tenri University *B*

Materials Engineering

Himeji Institute of Technology   *B, M*
Hiroshima University   *B, M, D*
Kanazawa University   *D*
Kobe University   *D*
Kyoto Institute of Technology   *B, M*
Kyushu Institute of Technology   *B*
Kyushu University   *M, D*
Muroran Institute of Technology   *B, M*
Nagasaki University   *B, M*
Nagoya Institute of Technology   *B, M*
Nagoya University   *M, D*
Okayama University   *D*
Okayama University of Science   *D*
Osaka University   *B, M, D*
Science University of Tokyo   *B*
Technological University of Nagaoka, The   *B, M, D*
Tohoku University   *B, M, D*
Tokyo Institute of Technology   *B, M, D*
Tokyo University of Agriculture and Technology   *B, M*
Toyohashi University of Technology   *B, M, D*
University of Electro-Communications, The   *B, M*
University of Osaka Prefecture   *M, D*
University of Tokyo, The   *B, M, D*
University of Tsukuba   *D*
Yokohama National University   *B, M, D*

Mathematics

Akita University   *B*
Chiba University   *B, M, D*
Chuo University   *B*
Ehime University   *B, M*
Fukui University   *B*
Fukuoka University   *B, M*
Gakushuin University   *B, M, D*
Hirosaki University   *B, M*
Hiroshima University   *B, M, D*
Hokkaido University   *B, M, D*
Ibaraki University   *B, M*
International Christian University   *B, M*
Japan Women's University   *B*
Josai University   *B*
Kagoshima University   *B, M*
Kanazawa University   *B, M, D*
Keio University   *B, M, D*
Kinki University   *B*
Kobe University   *B, M*
Kochi University   *B, M*
Konan University   *B*
Kumamoto University   *B, M*
Kyoto Sangyo University   *B, M, D*
Kyoto University   *B, M, D*
Kyushu University   *B, M, D*
Meiji University   *B*
Nagoya University   *B, M, D*
Nara Women's University   *B, M*
Nihon University   *B, M, D*
Niigata University   *B, M*
Ochanomizu University   *B, M*
Okayama University   *B, M*
Okayama University of Science   *B, M, D*
Osaka City University   *B, M, D*
Osaka Kyoiku University   *B*
Osaka University   *B, M, D*
Osaka Women's University   *B*
Rikkyo (St. Paul's) University   *B, M, D*
Ritsumeikan University   *B*

Saga University   *B, M*
Saitama University   *B, M*
Science University of Tokyo   *B, M, D*
Shimane University   *B, M*
Shinshu University   *B, M*
Shizuoka University   *B, M*
Sophia University   *B, M, D*
Tohoku University   *B, M, D*
Toin University of Yokohama   *B*
Tokai University   *B, M, D*
Tokyo Institute of Technology   *B, M, D*
Tokyo Metropolitan University   *B, M, D*
Tokyo Woman's Christian University   *B, M*
Toyama University   *B, M*
Tsuda College   *B, M, D*
University of the Ryukyus   *B, M*
University of Tokyo, The   *B, M, D*
University of Tsukuba   *D*
Waseda University   *B, M, D*
Yamagata University   *B, M*
Yamaguchi University   *B, M*

Mechanical Engineering

Aichi Institute of Technology   *B, M*
Akita University   *B, M*
Aoyama Gakuin University   *B, M, D*
Ashikaga Institute of Technology   *B*
Chiba Institute of Technology   *B*
Chiba University   *B, M*
Chubu University   *B, M, D*
Daido Institute of Technology   *B*
Dai Ichi University, College of Technology   *B*
Doshisha University   *B, M, D*
Ehime University   *B, M*
Fukui Institute of Technology   *B, M*
Fukui University   *B, M*
Fukuoka Institute of Technology   *B*
Fukuoka University   *B, M*
Gifu University   *B, M*
Gunma University   *B, M*
Hachinohe Institute of Technology   *B*
Himeji Institute of Technology   *B, M*
Hiroshima-Denki Institute of Technology, The   *B*
Hiroshima Institute of Technology   *B*
Hiroshima University   *B, M, D*
Hokkaido Institute of Technology   *B*
Hokkaido University   *B, M, D*
Hosei University   *B, M, D*
Ibaraki University   *B, M*
Iwaki Meisei University   *B*
Iwate University   *B, M*
Kagoshima University   *B, M*
Kanagawa Institute of Technology   *B*
Kanagawa University   *B, M*
Kanazawa Institute of Technology   *B, M, D*
Kanazawa University   *B, M*
Kansai University   *B, M, D*
Kanto Gakuin University   *B, M, D*
Keio University   *B, M, D*
Kinki University   *B, M, D*
Kitami Institute of Technology   *B, M*
Kobe University   *B, M*
Kogakuin University   *B, M, D*
Kokushikan University   *B*
Kumamoto Institute of Technology, The   *B*
Kumamoto University   *B, M*
Kurume Institute of Technology   *B*
Kyoto Institute of Technology   *B, M*
Kyoto University   *B, M, D*

Kyushu Institute of Technology   *B, M*
Kyushu Kyoritsu University   *B*
Kyushu Sangyo University   *B, M*
Kyushu Tokai University   *B*
Kyushu University   *B, M, D*
Meiji University   *B, M, D*
Meijo University   *B*
Meisei University   *B, M, D*
Mie University   *B, M*
Miyazaki University   *B, M*
Muroran Institute of Technology   *B, M*
Musashi Institute of Technology   *B, M, D*
Nagasaki Institute of Applied Science   *B*
Nagasaki University   *B, M*
Nagoya Institute of Technology   *B*
Nagoya University   *B, M, D*
Nihon University   *B, M, D*
Niigata University   *B, M*
Nippon Bunri University   *B*
Nippon Institute of Technology   *B, M, D*
Nishinippon Institute of Technology   *B*
Oita University   *B, M*
Okayama University   *B, M*
Okayama University of Science   *B, M*
Osaka City University   *B, M, D*
Osaka Industrial University   *B*
Osaka Institute of Technology   *B, M, D*
Osaka University   *B, M, D*
Ritsumeikan University   *B, M, D*
Sagami Institute of Technology   *B*
Saga University   *B, M*
Saitama Institute of Technology, The   *B*
Saitama University   *B, M*
Science University of Tokyo   *B, M, D*
Seikei University   *B, M, D*
Setsunan University   *B*
Shibaura Institute of Technology   *B, M*
Shinshu University   *B, M*
Shizuoka University   *B, M*
Sophia University   *B, M, D*
Takushoku University   *B*
Tamagawa University   *B, M*
Technological University of Nagaoka, The   *B, M*
Tohoku Gakuin University   *B, M, D*
Tohoku University   *B, M, D*
Toin University of Yokohama   *B*
Tokai University   *B, M, D*
Tokyo Denki University   *B, M*
Tokyo Engineering University   *B*
Tokyo Institute of Technology   *B, M, D*
Tokyo Metropolitan Institute of Technology   *B*
Tokyo Metropolitan University   *B, M, D*
Tokyo University of Agriculture and Technology   *B, M*
Tokyo University of Mercantile Marine   *B, M*
Toyama University   *B, M*
Toyohashi University of Technology   *B, D*
Toyota Technological Institute   *B, M*
Toyo University   *B, M, D*
University of East Asia, The   *B*
University of Electro-Communications, The   *B, M*
University of Osaka Prefecture   *B, M, D*
University of the Ryukyus   *B, M*
University of Tokushima, The   *B, M*
University of Tokyo, The   *B, M, D*
University of Tottori   *B, M*
University of Tsukuba   *D*
Utsunomiya University   *B, M*
Waseda University   *B, M, D*
Yamagata University   *B, M*

Osaka Women's University *B*
Otani University *B*
Otemon Gakuin University *B, M*
Rikkyo (St. Paul's) University *B, M, D*
Rissho University *B, M, D*
Ritsumeikan University *B, M, D*
Ryukoku University *B, M, D*
Ryutsu-keizai University *B*
Saitama University *B, M*
Shikoku Christian College *B*
Shinshu University *B*
Shitennoji International Buddhist University *B*
Shizuoka University *B*
Soka University *B, M, D*
Sophia University *B, M, D*
St. Andrew's University *B*
Sugiyama Jogakuen University *B*
Taisho University *B*
Tohoku University *B, M, D*
Tokai Women's College *B*
Tokyo Institute of Technology *B, M, D*
Tokyo International University *M*
Tokyo Metropolitan University *B, M, D*
Tokyo Woman's ChristianUniversity *B*
Toyo University *B, M, D*
Tsuru University *B*
University of the Ryukyus *B*
University of Tokyo, The *B, M, D*
University of Tsukuba *B, D*
Waseda University *B, M, D*
Yamaguchi University *B*

Spanish Language and Literature

Aichi Prefectural University *B*
Eichi University *B*
Kanagawa University *B*
Kansai University of Foreign Studies *B, M, D*
Kobe City University of Foreign Studies *B, M*
Kobe College *B, M*
Kyoto Sangyo University *B*
Kyoto University of Foreign Studies *B, M*
Nanzan University *B*
Osaka University of Foreign Studies *B, M*
Seisen Women's College *B*
Setsunan University *B*
Sophia University *B*
Takushoku University *B*
Tenri University *B*
Tokoha Gakuen University *B*
Tokyo University of Foreign Studies *B, M*

Special Education

Aichi University of Education *B, M*
Akita University *B*
Chiba University *B*
Ehime University *B*
Fukuoka University of Education *B, M*
Gifu University *B*
Gunma University *B*
Hirosaki University *B*
Hiroshima University *B, M*
Hokkaido University of Education *B*
Hyogo University of Teacher Education *B, M*
Ibaraki University *B*
Iwate University *B*
Joetsu University of Education *B, M*
Kagawa University *B*
Kagoshima University *B*

Kanazawa University *B, M*
Kobe University *B*
Kochi University *B*
Kumamoto University *B, M*
Kyoto University of Education *B*
Mie University *B*
Miyagi University of Education *B*
Miyazaki University *B*
Nagasaki University *B*
Nara University of Education *B*
Naruto University of Teacher Education *M*
Niigata University *B*
Oita University *B*
Okayama University *B*
Osaka Kyoiku University *B, M*
Saga University *B*
Shinshu University *B*
Shizuoka University *B*
Tokyo Gakugei University *B, M*
Toyama University *B*
University of the Ryukyus *B*
University of Tottori *B*
University of Tsukuba *B, M, D*
University of Wakayama *B*
Utsunomiya University *B*
Yamagata University *B*
Yamaguchi University *B*
Yamanashi University *B*
Yokohama National University *B, M*

Teacher Training

Aichi University of Educaion *B, M*
Akita University *B*
Ashiya University *M*
Bunkyo University *B*
Chiba University *B, M*
Ehime University *B*
Elisabeth University of Music *B*
Fukui University *B*
Fukuoka University of Education *B, M*
Fukushima University *B, M*
Gifu University *B*
Gunma University *B*
Hirosaki University *B*
Hiroshima Bunkyo Women's College *B, M*
Hiroshima University *B, M, D*
Hokkaido University of Education *B*
Hyogo University of Teacher Education *B, M*
Ibaraki University *B, M*
Iwate University *B*
Joetsu University of Education *B, M*
Kagawa University *B*
Kagoshima University *B*
Kanazawa University *B, M*
Keihin Women's College *B*
Kobe University *B, M*
Kochi University *B*
Kumamoto University *B, M*
Kunitachi College of Music *B, M*
Kyoto University of Education *B*
Mie University *B*
Miyagi University of Education *B, M*
Miyazaki University *B*
Mukogawa Women's University *B*
Musashino Academia Musicae *B, M*
Nagasaki University *B*
Nagoya Music College *B*
Nagoya University of the Arts *B*
Nakamura Gakuen College *B*
Nara University of Education *B, M*
Nara Women's University *B*
Naruto University of Teach, Education

B, M
Niigata University *B, M*
Oita University *B*
Okayama University *B, M*
Osaka Kyoiku University *B, M*
Osaka University of Arts *B*
Saga University *B*
Saitama University *B*
Shimane University *B*
Shinshu University *B*
Shizuoka University *B, M*
Shotoku Academy Gifu College of Education. *B*
Teikyo University *B*
Tokoha Gakuen University *B*
Tokyo Gakugei University *B, M*
Toyama University *B*
Tsuru University *B*
University of the Ryukyus *B*
University of the Sacred Heart *B*
University of Tottori *B*
University of Tsukuba *M*
University of Wakayama *B*
Utsunomiya University *B, M*
Yamagata University *B*
Yamaguc University *B*
Yamanashi University *B*
Yasuda Women's University *B*
Yokohama National University *B, M*

Textile Technology

Fukui University *B, M*
Gifu University *B, M*
Gunma University *B, M*
Hokkaido University *B, M, D*
Kyoto Institute of Technology *B, M*
Kyoto University *B, M, D*
Shinshu University *B, M*
Tokyo Institute of Technology *B, M, D*
Tokyo University of Agriculture and Technology *B, M*
Yamagata University *B, M*

Theology

Doshisha University *M, D*
Eichi University *B*
Ibaraki Christian College *B*
Japan Lutheran TheologicalCollege *B*
Kwansei Gakuin University *M, D*
Nanzan University *B, M, D*
Rikkyo (St. Paul's) University *B, M, D*
Seinan Gakuin University *B*
Seiwa College *B*
Sophia University *B, M, D*
Tohoku Gakuin University *B*
Tokyo Union Theological Seminary *B, M, D*

Tourism

Rikkyo (St. Paul's) University *B*
Teikyo University *B*
Yokohama College of Commerce *B*

Urban and Regional Planning

Dai Ichi University, College of Technology *B*
Fukui University *B, M*
Hokkaido University *M, D*
Hokkaigakuen Kitami University *B*
Kagawa University *B*

1988–89 School Fees

Institution	Level	Faculty/Department	Application Fee	Admission Fee	Tuition Fee	Other Fees
National Colleges and Universities						
Standardized Fee	U		12, 000	180, 000	300, 000	
	G		20, 000	180, 000	300, 000	
Local Public Colleges and Universities						
Aichi Prefectural University	U	Foreign Studies, Literature	12, 000	180, 000	300, 000	
Aichi Prefectural University of Fine Arts	U	Art, Music	12, 000	180, 000	300, 000	
	G	Art, Music	20, 000	180, 000	300, 000	
Fukuoka Women's University	U	Home Life Science, Literature	11, 000	300, 000	300, 000	
Fukushima Medical College	U	Medicine	12, 000	720, 000	300, 000	
	G	Medicine	20, 000	180, 000	300, 000	
Gifu Pharmaceutical University	U	Pharmacy	12, 000	360, 000	300, 000	111, 000
	G	Pharmacy	20, 000	360, 000	300, 000	102, 000
Gunma Prefectural Women's College	U	Letters	12, 000	180, 000	336, 000	
Himeji Institute of Technology	U	Engineering	12, 000	270, 000	300, 000	
	G	Engineering	20, 000	270, 000	300, 000	
Hiroshima Women's University	U	Home Economics, Letters	11, 000	180, 000	252, 000	35, 000
Kanazawa College of Art	U	Art	12, 000	300, 000	300, 000	
	G	Art	20, 000	300, 000	336, 000	
Kitakyushu University	U	Economics and Business Administration, Foreign Studies, Literature, Law	12, 000	225, 000	300, 000	79, 750–97, 750
	G	Angro-American Languages and Cultures, Business Administration, Chinese Studies, Law	20, 000	225, 000	300, 000	15, 600–20, 600
Kobe City University of Foreign Studies	U	Foreign Studies	12, 000	200, 000	300, 000	
	G	Foreigh Studies	17, 000	200, 000	300, 000	
Kobe University of Commerce	U	Economics and Business Administration	12, 000	270, 000	300, 000	
	G	Business Administration, Economics	20, 000	270, 000	M:300, 000 D:252, 000	
Kochi Women's University	U	Home Economics, Literature	11, 000	150, 000	252, 000	
Kumamoto Women's University	U	Letters, Living Science	12, 000	264, 000	300, 000	61, 400
Kushiro Public University of Economics	U	Economics	12, 000	200, 000	300, 000	1, 150
Kyoto City University of Arts	U	Arts, Music	11, 000	300, 000	252, 000	83, 150–108, 150
	G	Arts, Music	11, 000	300, 000	300, 000	
Kyoto Prefectural University	U	Agriculture, Letters, Living Science,	11, 000	150, 000	300, 000	23, 150–24, 900
	G	Agriculture, Living Science	18, 000	150, 000	300, 000	5, 550–8, 250
Kyoto Prefectural University of Medicine	U	Medicine	11, 000	260, 000	252, 000	4, 050
	G	Medicine	18, 000	150, 000	252, 000	
Kyushu Dental College	U	Dentistry	12, 000	360, 000	300, 000	
	G	Dentistry	20, 000	360, 000	300, 000	
Nagasaki Prefectural University of International Economics	U	Economics	11, 000	188, 000	300, 000	77, 150
Nagoya City University	U	Economics, Medicine, Pharmaceutical Sciences	12, 000	180, 000	300, 000	78, 000–87, 050
	G	Economics, Medicine, Pharmaceutical Sciences	20, 000	180, 000	300, 000	36, 000
Nara Medical University	U	Medicine	12, 000	650, 000	300, 000	
	G	Medicine	20, 000	650, 000	300, 000	
Okinawa Prefectural College of Fine Arts	U	Fine Arts	12, 000	360, 000	300, 000	150, 000
Osaka City University	U	Business, Economics, Engineering, Law, Letters, Medicine, Science, Science of Living	20, 000	240, 000	300, 000	
	G	Business, Economics, Engineering, Law, Letters, Medicine, Science, Science of Living	20, 000	230, 000	300, 000	

Institution	Level	Faculty/Department	Application Fee	Admission Fee	Tuition Fee	Other Fees
Osaka Women's University	U	Arts and Science	10, 000	170, 000	252, 000	
	G	Literature	16, 000	170, 000	252, 000	
Sapporo Medical College	U	Medicine	12, 000	180, 000	300, 000	206, 000
	G	Medicine	20, 000	180, 000	300, 000	
Shimonoseki City College	U	Economics	12, 000	180, 000	300, 000	75, 000
Takasaki City University of Economics	U	Economics	12, 000	180, 000	300, 000	77, 150
Tokyo Metropolitan Institute of Technology	U	Engineering	12, 000	180, 000	336, 000	17, 900
Tokyo Metropolitan University	U	Economics, Law, Science, Social Sciences and Humanities, Technology	11, 000	150, 000	300, 000	
	G	Humanities, Science, Social Science, Technology	18, 000	150, 000	300, 000	
Tsuru University	U	Humanities	18, 000	140, 000	300, 000	
University of Osaka Prefecture	U	Agriculture, Economics, Engineering, Integrated Arts and Sciences, Social Welfare	12, 000	230, 000	300, 000	
	G	Agriculture, Economics, Engineering, Integrated Arts and Sciences	20, 000	230, 000	300, 000	
University of Shizuoka	U	Pharmaceutical Science, Food and Nutritional Sciences, International Relations, Administration and Informatics	12, 000	180, 000	300, 000	63, 150–94, 900
	G	Pharmaceutical Science	12, 000	180, 000	300, 000	94, 900
Wakayama Medical College	U	Medicine	12, 000	600, 000	300, 000	4, 050
	G	Medicine	18, 000	425, 000	300, 000	4, 050
Yamaguchi Women's University	U	Home Science, Literature	12, 000	180, 000	300, 000	73, 150–99, 900
Yokohama City University	U	Economics and Business Administration, Liberal Arts and Science, Medicine	12, 000	180, 000	300, 000	58, 000
	G	Business Administration, Economics, Medicine	20, 000	180, 000	300, 000	

Private Colleges and Universities

Institution	Level	Faculty/Department	Application Fee	Admission Fee	Tuition Fee	Other Fees
Aichi Gakuin University	U	Commerce, Law, Letters	23, 000	210, 000	35, 000–400, 000	260, 000–310, 000
		Dentistry	30, 000	500, 000	2, 100, 000	6, 500, 000
	G	Commercial, Science, Law, Letters	25, 000	200, 000	360, 000–400, 000	190, 000
		Dentistry	25, 000	400, 000	750, 000	210, 000
Aichi Institute of Technology	U	Engineering	25, 000	250, 000	520, 000	410, 000
	G	Engineering	25, 000	120, 000	520, 000	190, 000
Aichi Medical University	U	Medicine	40, 000	1, 000, 000	2, 000, 000	7, 500, 000
	G	Medicine	30, 000	200, 000	300, 000	200, 000
Aichi Shukutoku College	U	Literature	25, 000	330, 000	440, 000	345, 000–375, 000
Aichi University	U	Law & Economics, Letters	25, 000	200, 000	430, 000	144, 800–159, 800
	G	Economics, Law, Management	25, 000	200, 000	380, 000	114, 800
Aoyama Gakuin University	U	Business Administration, Economics, International Politics, Economics & Business, Law, Literature	30, 000	260, 000	490, 000	199, 400–259, 400
		Science & Engineering	30, 000	260, 000	690, 000	324, 400
	G	Business Administration, Economics, International Politics, Economics & Business, Law, Literature	30, 000	220, 000	290, 000	112, 900
		Science & Engineering	30, 000	220, 000	440, 000	203, 400

Institution	Level	Faculty/Department	Application Fee	Admission Fee	Tuition Fee	Other Fees
Asahikawa University	U	Economics	23,000	150,000	350,000	301,500
Asahi University	U	Dentistry	30,000	500,000	3,500,000	5,000,000
		Business Administration, Law	25,000	150,000	497,000	210,000
	G	Dentistry	20,000	200,000	400,000	
Ashikaga Institute of Technology	U	Engineering	25,000	200,000	620,000	190,000
Ashiya University	U	Education	20,000	300,000	500,000	750,000
	G	Education	20,000	300,000	500,000	450,000
Asia University	U	Business Administration, Economics, Law	25,000	230,000	420,000	200,100
	G	Business Administration, Economics, Law	25,000	230,000	420,000	175,000
Azabu University	U	Veterinary Medicine	25,000	250,000	500,000	
	G	Veterinary Medicine	25,000	200,000–250,000	400,000–600,000	
Baika Women's College	U	Literature	20,000	210,000	350,000	310,000
Baiko Jogakuen College	U	Letters	20,000	200,000	305,000	202,800
	G	Letters	20,000	85,000	156,000	51,500
Beppu University	U	Literature	25,000	220,000	460,000	175,000–205,000
Bukkyo University	U	Letters, Sociology	25,000	120,000	507,000–566,000	232,000
	G	Letters, Sociology	25,000	120,000	460,000	207,500
Bunka Women's University	U	Domestic Economy	30,000	360,000	500,000	414,930–441,930
	G	Domestic Economy	30,000	240,000	500,000	270,000
Bunkyo University	U	Education	25,000	220,000	490,000	280,000
	U	Human Science	25,000	220,000	480,000	280,000
	U	Music Major	25,000	220,000	590,000	280,000
		Information and Communication	25,000	220,000	490,000	380,000
	U	Language and Literature	25,000	220,000	480,000	280,000
Chiba Institute of Technology	U	Engineering	25,000	200,000	620,000	387,000
Chiba Keizai University	U	Economics	20,000	250,000	410,000	261,000
Chiba University of Commerce	U	Commerce & Economics	23,000	217,000	355,800	187,600
	G	Commerce, Economics	23,000	217,000	355,800	187,600
Chikushi Jogakuen College	U	Arts	22,000	260,000	629,650	
Chubu University	U	Business Administration & Information Science	24,000	250,000	520,000	220,000
		Engineering	24,000	250,000	670,000	260,000
		International Studies	24,000	250,000	560,000	220,150
	G	Engineering	24,000	250,000	700,000	260,000
Chukyo University	U	Commercial Sciences, Law, Letters, Physical Education, Sociology Economics	25,000	220,000	415,000	172,500–360,000
	G	(Master's) Commercial Sciences, Law, Letters, Physical Education	25,000	200,000	390,000	155,000–250,000
	G	(Doctor's) Commercial Sciences, Law, Letters, Physical Education	25,000	200,000	300,000	100,000–200,000
Chukyo Women's University	U	Home Economics	23,000	260,000	430,000	341,500–371,500
		Physical Education	23,000	260,000	400,000	371,500
Chuo Gakuin University	U	Commerce, Law	25,000	200,000	475,000	172,650
Chuo University	U	Commerce, Economics, Law, Literature	25,000	240,000	430,000	102,000
		Science & Engineering	25,000	240,000	650,000	222,000
	G	Commerce, Economics, Law, Literature	25,000	240,000	400,000	100,500
		Science & Engineering	25,000	240,000	630,000	210,500
Daido Institute of Technology	U	Engineering	25,000	230,000	650,000	220,000
Daiichi College of Pharmaceutical Science	U	Pharmaceutical Sciences	20,000	500,000	1,700,000	700,000
Dai Ichi University, College of Technology	U	Technology	15,000	50,000	550,000	
Daito Bunka University	U	Economics, Foreign Languages, International Relations, Literature	25,000	170,000	500,000	212,400–213,400

Institution	Level	Faculty/Department	Application Fee	Admission Fee	Tuition Fee	Other Fees
	G	Literature, Economics, Law	25,000	170,000	500,000	210,400–212,400
Doho University	U	Japanese Literature, Social Welfare	25,000	130,000	400,000	260,000
Dohto University	U	Social Welfare, Fine Arts	23,000	300,000	440,000	140,000–240,000
Dokkyo University School of Medicine	U	Medicine	40,000	6,000,000	2,900,000	1,600,000
	G		40,000	2,000,000	600,000	
Dokkyo University	U	Economics, Foreign Languages, Law	25,000	220,000	380,000	150,000
	G	Foreign Languages, Law	25,000	220,000	380,000	150,000
Doshisha University	U	Commerce, Economics, Law, Letters, Theology	30,000	230,000	530,000	134,000–194,000
		Engineering	30,000	230,000	790,000	254,000
	G	Commerce, Economics, Law, Letters, Theology	30,000	180,000	270,000	67,000–127,000
		Engineering	30,000	180,000	410,000	147,000
Doshisha Women's College of Liberal Arts	U	Home Economics	30,000	200,000	518,000–572,000	388,000–419,500
		Liberal Arts (English Dept.)	30,000	200,000	458,000	371,500
		(Music Dept.)	30,000	200,000	640,000	510,000
	G	Home Economics	30,000	160,000	305,000	156,000
		Letters	30,000	160,000	305,000	103,000
Eichi University	U	Liberal Arts	22,000	220,000	445,000	287,150
Elisabeth University of Music	U	Music	30,000	350,000	650,000	620,000
	G		30,000	350,000	650,000	110,000
Ferris Women's College	U	Literature	30,000	350,000	500,000	310,000
Fujita–Gakuen Health University	U	Hygiene	20,000	300,000	500,000	480,000
		Medicine	30,000	500,000	2,000,000	7,000,000
	G	Medicine	20,000	150,000	500,000	300,000
Fuji Women's College	U	Letters	25,000	150,000	370,000	190,000
Fukui Institute of Technology	U	Engineering	25,000	200,000	674,000	130,000
	G	Engineering	20,000	200,000	550,000	210,550
Fukuoka Institute of Technology	U	Engineering	20,000	180,000	500,000	325,000
Fukuoka University	U	Commerce, Economics, Humanities, Law	26,000	176,000	445,000	65,770
		Engineering, Science	26,000	220,000	734,000	94,770
		Medicine	40,000	1,000,000	2,500,000	5,430,770
		Pharmaceutical Sciences	26,000	415,000	1,035,100	231,770
		Physical Education	26,000	329,000	560,800	73,770
	G	Commerce, Economics, Humanities, Law	26,000	30,000	210,000	54,700
		Engineering, Science	26,000	40,000	339,000	83,700
		Medical Science	40,000	200,000	400,000	115,700
		Pharmaceutical Sciences	26,000	40,000	350,000	83,700
Fukuyama University	U	Economics	25,000	200,000	400,000	
		Engineering	25,000	200,000	500,000	
		Pharmaceutical Sciences	25,000	500,000	840,000	
	G	Engineering	25,000	200,000	300,000	
	G	Pharmacy and Pharmaceutical Science	25,000	300,000	300,000	600,000
Gakushuin University	U	Economics, Law, Literature	25,000	320,000	420,000	174,900–234,400
		Science	25,000	320,000	600,000	860,200–910,200
	G	Business Administration, Economics, Humanities, Law, Political Science	25,000	150,000	300,000	85,600
		Science	25,000	150,000	350,000	112,100
Gifu Women's University	U	Home Economics	25,000	300,000	480,000	280,000
		Literature	25,000	300,000	480,000	260,000
Hachinohe Institute of Technology	U	Engineering	20,000	200,000	550,000	258,000
Hachinohe University	U	Commerce	20,000	250,000	370,000	170,000

Institution	Level	Faculty/Department	Application Fee	Admission Fee	Tuition Fee	Other Fees
Hakodate University	U	Academic Affairs	23, 000	140, 000	350, 000	240, 000
Hakuoh University	U	Business Management	20, 000	250, 000	395, 000	243, 000
Hanazono College	U	Letters	25, 000	180, 000	486, 000	182, 400
Higashi Nippon Gakuen University	U	Dentistry	30, 000	500, 000	2, 500, 000	3, 300, 000
		Pharmaceutical Sciences	20, 000	500, 000	800, 000	500, 000
Himeji Dokkyo University	U	Foreign Language, Law	25, 000	250, 000	700, 000	200, 000
Hirosaki Gakuin College	U	Literature	18, 000	170, 000	200, 000	270, 000
Hiroshima Bunkyo Women's College	U	Letters	20, 000	230, 000	320, 000	157, 000–177, 000
	G	Japanese Literature, Pedagogics	15, 000	150, 000	300, 000	57, 000
Hiroshima–Denki Institute of Technology	U	Engineering	20, 000	150, 000	550, 000	310, 000
Hiroshima Institute of Technology	U	Engineering	20, 000	200, 000	670, 000	144, 200
Hiroshima Jogakuin College	U	Literature	22, 000	220, 000	290, 000	229, 800
Hiroshima Shudo University	U,G	Commercial Sciences, Humanities & Sciences, Law	23, 000	200, 000	404, 000	185, 200–215, 200
Hiroshima University of Economics	U,G	Economics	20, 000	140, 000	390, 000	180, 000
	G	Economics	20, 000	140, 000	390, 000	180, 000
Hokkaido Institute of Pharmaceutical Sciences	U	Pharmaceutical Sciences	23, 000	600, 000	940, 000	600, 000
	G	Pharmaceutical Sciences	23, 000	200, 000	570, 000	200, 000
Hokkaido Institute of Technology	U	Engineering	23, 000	180, 000	570, 000	255, 000
Hokkaido Tokai University	U	Design & Architecture	22, 000	160, 000	434, 000	447, 500
		International Cultural Relations	22, 000	160, 000	490, 000	443, 500
		Engineering	22, 000	160, 000	490, 000	463, 000
		Art & Technology	22, 000	160, 000	453, 000	451, 500
Hokkaigakuen Kitami University	U	Commerce	20, 000	100, 000	414, 000	55, 000
Hokuriku University	U	Foreign Language	25, 000	200, 000	400, 000	200, 000
	U	Pharmaceutical Sciences	25, 000	400, 000	900, 000	1, 000, 000
	G	Pharmaceutical Sciences	20, 000	100, 000	300, 000	
Hokusei Gakuen College	U	Economics, Literature	25, 000	150, 000	360, 000	260, 000
Hosei University	U	Law, Letters, Economics, Social Sciences, Business Administration	30, 000	240, 000	430, 000	115, 000–120, 000
		Engineering	30, 000	240, 000	670, 000	245, 000–250, 000
	G	Humanities, Social Sciences	30, 000	240, 000	430, 000	103, 000–105, 000
		Engineering	30, 000	240, 000	670, 000	233, 000–235, 000
Hoshi University	U	Pharmaceutical Sciences	20, 000	976, 900	1, 081, 000	
	G	Pharmaceutical Science	20, 000	100, 000	801, 550	
Hyogo College of Medicine	U	Medicine	30, 000	1, 000, 000	2, 500, 000	6, 800, 000
	G	Medicine	20, 000	200, 000	300, 000	200, 000
International Budo University	U	Physical Education	28, 000	290, 000	550, 000	443, 000
International Christian University	U	Liberal Arts (for September students)	17, 000	280, 000	675, 000	10, 000
International University of Japan	U	International Relations, International Management	30, 000	200, 000	1, 200, 000	
	G	International Management, International Relations	30, 000	200, 000	1, 200, 000	
Iwaki Meisei University	U	Humanities	23, 000	220, 000	300, 000	240, 000
		Science & Engineering	23, 000	250, 000	460, 000	291, 000
Iwate Medical University	U	Dentistry	30, 000	500, 000	2, 000, 000	5, 200, 000
		Medicine	30, 000	800, 000	2, 500, 000	6, 200, 000
	G	Dentistry, Medicine	30, 000	200, 000	850, 000	
Japan College of Social Work	U	Social Welfare	25, 000	180, 000	300, 000	182, 650
Japan Lutheran Theological College	U	Theology	25, 000	160, 000	420, 000	167, 000
Japan Women's College of Physical Education	U	Physical Education	23, 000	280, 000	460, 000	353, 000

Institution	Level	Faculty/Department	Application Fee	Admission Fee	Tuition Fee	Other Fees
Japan Women's University	U	Home Economics, Literature & Humanities	30, 000	270, 000	380, 000	122, 350–124, 100
	G	Home Economics, Literature & Humanities	30, 000	270, 000	380, 000	30, 000
Jichi Medical School	G	Medicine	20, 000	180, 000	300, 000	50, 000
Jikei University School of Medicine	U	Medicine	50, 000	800, 000	1, 800, 000	2, 000, 000
	G	Medicine	10, 000	100, 000	400, 000	
Jissen Women's University	U, G	Home Economics	25, 000	250, 000	430, 000	285, 650
		Literature	25, 000	250, 000	450, 000	287, 400
Jobu University	U	Commercial Science	30, 000	300, 000	540, 000	162, 000
		Management & Information Science	30, 000	300, 000	540, 000	262, 000
Josai University	U	Economics	20, 000	300, 000	300, 000	250, 000
		Science	20, 000	300, 000	400, 000–500, 000	248, 000
		Pharmacology	20, 000	1, 000, 000	700, 000	448, 000
Juntendo University	U	Health & Physical Education	25, 000	200, 000	450, 000	250, 000
		Medicine	40, 000	1, 000, 000	2, 000, 000	7, 500, 000
	G	Health & Physical Education	20, 000	150, 000	300, 000	50, 000
		Medicine	20, 000	180, 000	300, 000	
Kagawa Nutrition College	U	Nutrition	25, 000	200, 000	548, 000	340, 000–360, 000
Kagoshima University of Economics and Sociology	U	Economics, Sociology	22, 000	120, 000	320, 000	115, 150–125, 150
Kamakura Woman's College	U	Home Economics	25, 000	360, 000	500, 000	325, 000
Kanagawa Dental College	U	Dentistry	30, 000	500, 000	2, 200, 000	5, 600, 000
	G	Dentistry	30, 000	400, 000	600, 000	600, 000
Kanagawa Institute of Technology	U	Engineering	24, 000	200, 000	710, 000	345, 000
Kanagawa University	U	Economics, Foreign Languages, Law	25, 000	270, 000	540, 000	170, 000
		Engineering	25, 000	270, 000	670, 000	340, 000
	G	Economics, Law	25, 000	200, 000	350, 000	135, 000
		Engineering	25, 000	200, 000	550, 000	240, 000
Kanazawa College of Economics	U	Economics	25, 000	200, 000	360, 000	
Kanazawa Institute of Technology	U	Engineering	25, 000	200, 000	693, 000	300, 000
	G	(Master's) Engineering	25, 000	200, 000	816, 000	
		(Doctor's) Engineering	25, 000	200, 000	956, 000	
Kanazawa Medical University	U	Medicine	40, 000	2, 000, 000	3, 300, 000	1, 717, 000–7, 069, 000
	G	Medicine	50, 000	200, 000	300, 000	400, 000
Kanazawa Woman's University	U	Literature	20, 000	250, 000	340, 000	350, 000
Kanda University of International Studies	U		25, 000	150, 000	600, 000	200, 000
Kansai University	U	Commerce, Economics, Law, Letters, Sociology	30, 000	260, 000	470, 000	120, 000
		Engineering	30, 000	260, 000	740, 000	260, 000
	G	Commerce, Economics, Law, Letters, Sociology	30, 000	260, 000	450, 000	120, 000–140, 000
		Engineering	30, 000	260, 000	720, 000	260, 000
Kansai University of Foreign Studies	U	Foreign Languages	25, 000	250, 000	570, 000	168, 150
	G	Foreign Languages	25, 000	130, 000	280, 000	123, 000
Kanto Gakuen University	U	Economics	25, 000	317, 000	444, 000	181, 000
	G	Economics	25, 000	317, 000	444, 000	181, 000
Kanto Gakuin University	U	Economics, Humanities	25, 000	230, 000	450, 000	229, 650–234, 650
		Engineering	25, 000	230, 000	660, 000	382, 900
	G	Economics	25, 000	230, 000	443, 000	56, 900
		Engineering	25, 000	230, 000	541, 000	186, 250
Kawamura Gakuen Woman's University	U	Liberal Arts	25, 000	380, 000	500, 000	458, 000
Kawasaki Medical School	U	Medicine	30, 000	1, 000, 000	2, 000, 000	5, 100, 000

Institution	Level	Faculty/Department	Application Fee	Admission Fee	Tuition Fee	Other Fees
	G	Medicine	20, 000	100, 000	300, 000	100, 000
Keio University	U	Business & Commerce, Economics, Law, Letters	30, 000	240, 000	420, 000	85, 350–93, 350
		Medicine	55, 000	240, 000	1, 710, 000	405, 350
		Science & Technology	30, 000	240, 000	670, 000	215, 350
	G	Business Administration	30, 000	210, 000	1, 450, 000	56, 000–57, 600
		Business & Commerce, Economics, Human Relations, Law, Letters	30, 000	220, 000	280, 000	35, 600–58, 600
		Science & Technology	30, 000	220, 000	370, 000	152, 600
		Medicine	30, 000	220, 000	500, 000	242, 600
Kinjo Gakuin University	U	Home Economics, Literature	25, 000	340, 000	420, 000	320, 000
	G	Literature	25, 000	310, 000	330, 000	
Kinki University	U	Agriculture	25, 000	230, 000	860, 000	14, 400
		Business Administration, Juriprudence	25, 000	230, 000	570, 000	15, 300
		Medicine	25, 000	6, 000, 000	4, 100, 000	4, 500
		Pharmacy	25, 000	230, 000	1, 200, 000	15, 400
		Science & Technology	25, 000	230, 000	860, 000	14, 400
	G	Agriculture, Chemistry, Engineering	25, 000	100, 000	550, 000	2, 500
		Commerce, Law	25, 000	100, 000	420, 000	2, 500
		Medicine	25, 000	200, 000	500, 000	2, 500
		Pharmacy	25, 000	100, 000	550, 000	2, 500
Kitasato University	U	Fisheries Sciences	25, 000	250, 000	600, 000	
		Hygienic Sciences	25, 000	250, 000	700, 000	400, 000
		Nursing	25, 000	250, 000	800, 000	300, 000
		Medicine	50, 000	1, 000, 000	2, 000, 000	1, 500, 000
		Pharmaceutical Sciences	25, 000	400, 000	880, 000	500, 000
		Veterinary Medicine & Animal Sciences	25, 000	250, 000	600, 000–750, 000	200, 000–500, 000
	G	Fisheries Sciences	20, 000	200, 000	600, 000	200, 000
		Hygienic Sciences	20, 000	200, 000	500, 000	200, 000
		Medicine	20, 000	200, 000	350, 000	250, 000
		Pharmaceutical Sciences	20, 000	200, 000	350, 000	100, 000
		Veterinary Medicine & Animal Sciences	20, 000	200, 000	600, 000–750, 000	200, 000–450, 000
Kobe College	U	Literature	30, 000	400, 000	790, 000	33, 800
		Music	30, 000	400, 000	1, 537, 000	33, 800
		Home Economics	30, 000	400, 000	859, 000	33, 800
	G	Literature	25, 000	150, 000	336, 500	15, 000
Kobe-Gakuin University	U	Economics, Law	25, 000	280, 000	600, 000	41, 000
		Nutrition	25, 000	400, 000	970, 000	33, 000
		Pharmaceutical Sciences	25, 000	400, 000	1, 220, 000	35, 000
	G	Economics, Law	25, 000	200, 000	460, 000	16, 000–18, 500
		Food & Medicinal Sciences	25, 000	200, 000	600, 000	10, 000
		Nutrition	25, 000	200, 000	560, 000	15, 000
		Pharmaceutical Sciences	25, 000	200, 000	610, 000	36, 000
Kobe Kaisei (Stella Maris) College	U	Literature	25, 000	270, 000	390, 000	492, 000
Kobe Women's College of Pharmacy	U	Pharmacy	25, 000	300, 000	1, 000, 000	
	G	Pharmacy	20, 000	150, 000	500, 000	
Kobe Women's University	U	Home Economics, Letters	20, 000	400, 000	400, 000	124, 000
	G	Home Economics	20, 000	20, 000	400, 000	30, 000
		Lterature	20, 000	20, 000	400, 000	
Kogakkan University	U	Literature	25, 000	200, 000	430, 000	250, 000–270, 000
	G	Literature	25, 000	200, 000	430, 000	100, 000
Kogakuin University	U	Engineering	25, 000	250, 000	850, 000–860, 000	44, 500
	G	Engineering	25, 000	250, 000	809, 000	

Institution	Level	Faculty/Department	Applica-tion Fee	Admission Fee	Tuition Fee	Other Fees
Koka Women's College	U	Literature	23, 000	310, 000	505, 000	140, 000
Kokushikan University	U	Political Science & Economics, Law	25, 000	250, 000	460, 000	
		Literature	25, 000	250, 000	506, 000	
		Engineering	25, 000	250, 000	600, 000	
		Physical Education	25, 000	250, 000	570, 000	
	G	(Master's & Doctor's)	30, 000	400, 000	440, 000–460, 000	
Komazawa University	U	Arts & Sciences, Buddhist Stud-ies, Business Administration, Economics, Law, Literature	25, 000	220, 000	420, 000	178, 000
	G	Business Administration, Com-merce, Economics, Humanities, Literature	25, 000	200, 000	380, 000	175, 000
Konan University	U	Economics, Law, Business Administration, Liberal Arts	25, 000	300, 000	552, 000	150, 000
		Science	25, 000	300, 000	813, 000	150, 000
Konan Women's University	U	Letters	25, 000	300, 000	400, 000	380, 000
	G	Letters	15, 000	150, 000	100, 000	37, 000
Koriyama Women's College	U	Home Economics	25, 000	210, 000	340, 000	230, 000
Koshien University	U	Business Administration & Infor-mation Science	25, 000	300, 000	480, 000	500, 000
		Neutrition	25, 000	300, 000	480, 000	200, 000
Kumamoto Kogyo University	U	Engineering	22, 000	200, 000	590, 000	440, 000
	G	Technology	22, 000	200, 000	1, 050, 000	200, 000
Kumamoto University of Comm-erce	U	Commerce, Economics	25, 000	120, 000	210, 500	74, 800
	G	Commerce	25, 000	120, 000	421, 000	2, 300
Kunitachi Collage of Music	U	Music	36, 000	400, 000	860, 000	535, 000
	G	Music	36, 000	240, 000	840, 000	395, 000
Kurume Institute of Technology	U	Engineering	22, 000	220, 000	830, 000	25, 000
Kurume University	U	Commerce, Law	25, 000	110, 000	410, 000	82, 000
		Medicine	40, 000	500, 000	2, 000, 000	5, 500, 000
	G	Medicine	20, 000	180, 000	300, 000	100, 000
Kwansei Gakuin University	U	Commercial Sciences, Econmins, Law, Literature, Sociology, The-ology	25, 000	294, 000	538, 000	145, 400–156, 900
		Science	25, 000	294, 000	750, 000	303, 900
	G	Business Administration, Eco-nomics, Law, Literature, Sociol-ogy, Theology	25, 000	207, 000	380, 000	92, 000
		Science	25, 000	207, 000	570, 000	232, 000
Kwassui Woman's College	U	Literature	22, 000	250, 000	340, 000	270, 000
Kyorin University	U	Medicine	40, 000	3, 504, 050	2, 000, 000	2, 500, 000
		Health Sciences	25, 000	502, 900	1, 000, 000	300, 000
		Social Sciences, Foreign Langua-ges	25, 000	321, 150	500, 000	280, 000
	G	Medicine	40, 000	4, 440, 050	2, 000, 000	2, 500, 000
		Health Sciences	25, 000	572, 900	1, 000, 000	330, 000
Kyoritsu College of Pharmacy	U	Pharmaceutical Sciences	28, 000	400, 000	800, 000	430, 000–550, 000
	G	Pharmaceutical Sciences	20, 000	50, 000	300, 000	
Kyoto Pharmaceutical University	U	Pharmaceutical Sciences	25, 000	300, 000	1, 100, 000	
	G	Pharmaceutical Sciences	25, 000	100, 000	600, 000	
Kyoto Sangyo University	U	Business Administration, Eco-nomics, Foreign Languages, Law	25, 000	240, 000	471, 000	
		Science	25, 000	240, 000	605, 000	
	G	Economics, Foreign Languages, Law	25, 000	200, 000	454, 000	119, 000
		Science	25, 000	200, 000	573, 000	154, 000
Kyoto Seika University	U	Fine Arts	30, 000	180, 000	897, 000	324, 000
Kyoto Tachibana Woman's Univ-ersity	U	Literature	25, 000	190, 000	690, 000	
Kyoto University of Foreign Stu-dies	U	Foreign Languages	25, 000	250, 000	515, 000	284, 000

Institution	Level	Faculty/Department	Application Fee	Admission Fee	Tuition Fee	Other Fees
Kyoto Woman's University	G	Foreign Languages	25, 000	160, 000	410, 000	90, 000
	U	Economics	25, 000	200, 000	618, 000	35, 700–51, 400
		Literature	25, 000	200, 000	616, 000–694, 000	25, 000–45, 700
Kyushu Kyoritsu University	U	Economics	20, 000	160, 000	300, 000	250, 000
		Engineering	20, 000	200, 000	380, 000	310, 000
Kyushu Sangyo University	U	Art	13, 000	230, 000	575, 000	337, 650
		Commerce	13, 000	170, 000	395, 000	127, 650
		Engineering	13, 000	210, 000	570, 000	249, 000
		Management	13, 000	180, 000	395, 000	132, 650–157, 650
	G	Engineering	13, 000	55, 000–110, 000	515, 000	221, 000
		Art	13, 000	70, 000–130, 000	545, 000	306, 000
	G	Economics	13, 000	40, 000–70, 000	360, 000	101, 000
Kyushu Tokai University	U	Agriculture, Engineering	22, 000	220, 000	515, 000	
	G	Agriculture	22, 000	220, 000	515, 000	
Kyushu Woman's University	U	Home Economics	18, 000	180, 000	310, 000–322, 000	283, 000
		Liberal Arts	18, 000	180, 000	310, 000–326, 000	237, 000–270, 000
Luke's College of Nursing	U	Nursing	25, 000	400, 000	700, 000	630, 000
Matsumoto Dental College	U	Dentistry	30, 000	500, 000	2, 850, 000	6, 340, 000
Matsusaka University	U	Political Science & Economics	22, 000	210, 000	360, 000	190, 000
Matsuyama University	U	Business Administration, Economics, Humanities, Law	24, 000	170, 000	380, 000	100, 000
	G	Business Administration, Economics	24, 000	170, 000	480, 000	
Meiji College of Oriental Medicine	U	Acupuncture & Moxibustion	20, 000	900, 000	600, 000	720, 000
Meiji College of Pharmacy	U	Pharmacy	25, 000	400, 000	870, 000	300, 000
	G	Pharmaceutical Sciences	20, 000	100, 000	550, 000	200, 000
Meiji Gakuin University	U	International Studies	25, 000	260, 000	470, 000	
	U, G	Literature, Economice, Sociology & Social Work, Law	25, 000	260, 000	470, 000	
	G	(Master's & Doctor's)	25, 000	260, 000	450, 000	
Meiji University	U	Business Administration, Commerce, Law, Literature, Political Science & Economics	30, 000	220, 000	410, 000	95, 200–115, 200
		Agriculture	30, 000	220, 000	590, 000–660, 000	195, 300–225, 300
		Engineering	30, 000	220, 000	660, 000	225, 300
	G	Business Administration, Commerce, Law, Literature, Political Science & Economics	30, 000	220, 000	410, 000	85, 000–87, 500
		Agriculture	30, 000	220, 000	590, 000–660, 000	185, 000–225, 000
		Engineering	30, 000	220, 000	660, 000	225, 000–227, 000
Meijo University	U	Agriculture	25, 000	290, 000	475, 000	340, 000
		Commerce, Law	25, 000	240, 000	310, 000	190, 000
		Pharmacy	25, 000	490, 000	710, 000	580, 000
		Science & Technology	25, 000	340, 000	545, 000	300, 000–320, 000
	G	(Master's) Agriculture	27, 000	130, 000	260, 000	280, 000
		(Master's) Commerce, Law	27, 000	130, 000	210, 000	130, 000
		(Master's) Engineering	27, 000	170, 000	300, 000	280, 000
		(Master's) Pharmacy	27, 000	300, 000	340, 000	330, 000
		(Doctor's) Law	30, 000	130, 000	210, 000	170, 000
		(Doctor's) Agriculture	30, 000	130, 000	260, 000	350, 000
		(Doctor's) Pharmacy	30, 000	300, 000	340, 000	410, 000
Meisei University	U	Humanities	25, 000	260, 000	437, 000	279, 300

Institution	Level	Faculty/Department	Application Fee	Admission Fee	Tuition Fee	Other Fees
		Science & Engineering	25, 000	260, 000	482, 000	353, 300
	G	Humanities	25, 000	260, 000	437, 000	187, 000
		Science & Engineering	25, 000	260, 000	482, 000	246, 000
Mimasaka Woman's College	U	Domestic Science	20, 000	220, 000	310, 000	395, 000
Minami Kyushu College	U	Horticulture	25, 000	150, 000	530, 000	230, 000–310, 000
Miyazaki Sangyo–Keiei University	U	Law, Business Administration	25, 000	200, 000	400, 000	350, 000
Morioka College	U	Humanities	22, 000	230, 000	390, 000	311, 500–321, 500
Mukogawa Women's University	U	Home Economics	25, 000	350, 000	628, 000	150, 000
		Music	25, 000	450, 000	852, 000	200, 000
		Pharmaceutical Sciences	25, 000	500, 000	1, 003, 000	280, 000
	G	Letters	15, 000	100, 000	180, 000	
		Home Economics	15, 000	100, 000	300, 000	
		Pharmaceutical Sciences	15, 000	100, 000	330, 000	
Musashi Institute of Technology	U	Engineering	28, 000	250, 000	930, 000	
	G	Engineering	28, 000	250, 000	830, 000	
Musashino Academia Musicae	U	Music	37, 000	460, 000	910, 000	460, 000
	G	Music	24, 000	320, 000	490, 000	130, 000
Musashino Art University	U	Art & Design	25, 000	250, 000	570, 000	103, 500–185, 500
Musashino Women's College	U	Literature	25, 000	240, 000	480, 000	279, 900
Musashi University	U	Economics, Humanities	25, 000	270, 000	460, 000	160, 000
	G	Economics, Humanities	25, 000	250, 000	440, 000	160, 000
Music Academy of Senzoku Gakuen College	U	Music	41, 000	350, 000	850, 000	735, 000
Nagasaki Institute of Applied Science	U	Engineering	22, 000	120, 000	580, 000	260, 000
	G	Engineering	22, 000	120, 000	580, 000	220, 000
Nagoya Economics University	U	Economics	25, 000	300, 000	400, 000	418, 650
Nagoya Gakuin University	U	Economics, Foreign Studies	25, 000	250, 000	455, 000	185, 000
Nagoya Music College	U	Music	35, 000	300, 000	885, 400	350, 000
	G	Music	35, 000	100, 000	300, 000	100, 000
Nagoya University of the Arts	U	Fine Art	30, 000	300, 000	462, 000	
		Music	30, 000	300, 000	580, 000	
Nagoya University of Commerce and Business Administration	U	Commerce	25, 000	150, 000	450, 000	
Nagoya University of Foreign Studies	U	Foreign Studies	30, 000	350, 000	500, 000	400, 000
Nagoya Women's University	U	Home Economics, Literature	25, 000	345, 000	445, 000	320, 000
Nakamura Gakuen College	U	Home Economics	24, 000	230, 000	440, 000	264, 000–275, 000
Nanzan University	U	Arts & Letters, Business Administration, Economics, Foreign Languages, Law	25, 000	250, 000	455, 000	185, 000
	G	Arts & Letters, Business Administration, Economics, Law	25, 000	250, 000	455, 000	170, 000
		Center for Japanese Studies	10, 000		600, 000	30, 000
Nara Sangyo University	U	Economics, Law	23, 000	200, 000	410, 000	200, 000
Nihon Fukushi University	U	Economics, Social Welfare	25, 000	180, 000	380, 000	140, 000
	G	Social Welfare	25, 000	180, 000	380, 000	140, 000
Nihon University	U	Commerce, Economics, Humanities & Sciences, Law, Agriculture & Veterinary Medicine	25, 000	250, 000	400, 000–800, 000	100, 000–720, 000
		Engineering, Industrial Technology, International Relations, Science & Technology	25, 000	250, 000	540, 000–600, 000	200, 000–380, 000
		Art	30, 000	250, 000	750, 000	440, 000–520, 000
		Dentistry	30, 000	500, 000	2, 000, 000	6, 500, 000
		Medicine	40, 000	1, 000, 000	2, 000, 000	6, 800, 000
		Pharmacy	25, 000	400, 000	900, 000	600, 000
	G	Economics, Law, Literature & Social Sciences	25, 000	250, 000	350, 000	100, 000

Institution	Level	Faculty/Department	Application Fee	Admission Fee	Tuition Fee	Other Fees
		Agriculture, Engineering, Industrial Technology, International Relations,	25, 000	250, 000	400, 000–500, 000	160, 000–380, 000
		Science & Technology, Veterinary Medicine	25, 000	250, 000	500, 000	
		Dentistry	30, 000	200, 000	500, 000	
		Art	30, 000	250, 000	650, 000	390, 000
		Medicine	40, 000	200, 000	500, 000	
Niigata College of Pharmacy	U	Pharmaceutical Sciences	25, 000	500, 000	900, 000	800, 000–1, 300, 000
Nippon Bunri University	U	Engineering	22, 000	220, 000	500, 000	290, 000
		Business & Economics	22, 000	220, 000	440, 000	204, 000
Nippon College of Physical Education	U	Physical Education	20, 000	250, 000	380, 000	612, 000
	G	Physical Education	20, 000	250, 000	380, 000	85, 000
Nippon Dental University, The	U	Dentistry	30, 000	500, 000	1, 700, 000	7, 732, 000
	G	Dentistry	20, 000	200, 000	500, 000	200, 000
Nippon Institute of Technology	U	Engineering	22, 000	220, 000	624, 000	353, 100
	G	Engineering	22, 000	220, 000	624, 000	314, 600
Nippon Medical School	U	Medicine	40, 000	2, 000, 000	1, 800, 000	5, 100, 000
	G	Medicine	20, 000	100, 000	300, 000	
Nippon Veterinary and Zootechnical College	U	Veterinary Medicine & Animal Husbandry	25, 000	250, 000–300, 000	510, 000–680, 000	326, 000–604, 000
	G	(Master's) Veterinary Science	20, 000	300, 000	680, 000	450, 000
		(Doctor's) Veterinary Science	20, 000	100, 000	650, 000	450, 000
Nishinippon Institute of Technology	U	Technology	20, 000	200, 000	500, 000	290, 000
Nisho–Gakusha University	U	Literature	25, 000	200, 000	400, 000	228, 150
	G	(Master's) Literature	25, 000	200, 000	240, 000	206, 000
		(Doctor's) Literature	25, 000	200, 000	430, 000	207, 500
Notre Dame Seishin University	U	Literature, Home Economics	20, 000	250, 000	380, 000	228, 000–231, 000
Notre Dame Women's College	U	Literature	25, 000	200, 000	450, 000	388, 000–408, 000
Obirin College	U	Literature	22, 000	240, 000	420, 000	340, 400
		Economics	22, 000	240, 000	370, 000	340, 400
Okayama College of Commerce	U	Commerce	20, 000	130, 000	300, 000	257, 000
Okayama University of Science	U	Engineering	23, 000	200, 000	560, 000	455, 000
		Science	23, 000	200, 000	560, 000	380, 000–390, 000
	G	Science	23, 000	200, 000	560, 000	380, 000
Okinawa Kokusai University	U	Commerce & Economics, Law, Letters	25, 000	120, 000	290, 000	100, 000
		Commerce & Economic, Law, Letters	25, 000	120, 000	290, 000	100, 000
Osaka College of Music	U	Music	30, 000	400, 000	730, 000	680, 000
	G	Music	30, 000	400, 000	730, 000	770, 000
Osaka College of Physical Education	U	Physical Education	30, 000	200, 000	640, 000	323, 000
Osaka Electro–Communication University	U	Engineering	25, 000	200, 000	980, 000	62, 000
Osaka Gakuin University	U	Commerce, Economics, Foreign Languages, Law	25, 000	200, 000	378, 000	723, 000
	G	(Master's) Commerce, Economics	30, 000	490, 000	290, 000	460, 000
		(Doctor's) Commerce, Economics	30, 000	560, 000	390, 000	500, 000
Osaka Industrial University	U	Business Management, Economics	25, 000	320, 000	634, 000	100, 500
		Engineering	25, 000	320, 000	924, 000	100, 500
	G	Engineering	25, 000	320, 000	924, 000	31, 500
Osaka Institute of Technology	U	Engineering	25, 000	200, 000	620, 000	325, 000–330, 000
	G	(Master's) Engineering	25, 000	150, 000	610, 000	130, 000
		(Doctor's) Engineering	25, 000	220, 000	610, 000	130, 000

Institution	Level	Faculty/Department	Application Fee	Admission Fee	Tuition Fee	Other Fees
Osaka International University	U	Management & Information	25, 000	200, 000	780, 000	
Osaka Medical College	U	Medicine	30, 000	1, 000, 000	1, 000, 000	1, 000, 000– 10, 500, 000
	G	Medicine	10, 000	60, 000	100, 000	150, 000
Osaka Shoin Women's College	U	Child Study, Clothing Science, English & American Literature, Food Science, Japanese Language & Literature	22, 000	300, 000	550, 000– 590, 000	145, 250
Osaka University of Economics	U	Economics, Business Administration	30, 000	200, 000	450, 000	173, 600
	G	Economics	30, 000	200, 000	450, 000	177, 000
Osaka University of Economics and Law	U	Economics, Law	20, 000	250, 000	490, 000	308, 000
Osaka University of Arts	U	Arts	30, 000 – 35, 000	250, 000– 300, 000	450, 000– 650, 000	340, 000– 720, 000
Osaka University of Commerce	U	Commerce & Economics	25, 000	180, 000	500, 000	380, 500
	G	One–Year–Graduate Course	25, 000	180, 000	500, 000	
Osaka University of Pharmaceutical Sciences	U	Pharmaceutical Sciences	25, 000	300, 000	900, 000	200, 000
	G	Pharmaceutical Sciences	25, 000	200, 000	400, 000	
Otani University	U	Letters	25, 000	130, 000	542, 000	186, 000
	G	Literathre	25, 000	130, 000	360, 000	120, 000
Otani Women's College	U	Literature	25, 000	300, 000	580, 000	
	G	Literature	25, 000	15, 000	56, 000	
Otemae College	U	Letters	20, 000	260, 000	380, 000	340, 000
Otemon Gakuin University	U	Economics, Letters	28, 000	210, 000	400, 000	205, 000
	G	Economics, Letters	28, 000	210, 000	400, 000	205, 000
Otsuma Woman's University	U	Literature	25, 000	250, 000	550, 000	205, 350
	G	Domestic Science	25, 000	250, 000	550, 000	204, 350– 205, 050
		Literature	25, 000	250, 000	550, 000	203, 400
Otsuma Women's University	U	Domestic Science	25, 000	250, 000	550, 000	207, 100– 221, 100
Rakuno Gakuen University	U	Dairy Science	25, 000	310, 000– 570, 000	325, 000– 925, 000	295, 000– 345, 000
	G	Dairy Science	23, 000	37, 000	445, 000	330, 000
		Veterinary Medicine	23, 000	57, 000	925, 000	345, 000
Reitaku University	U	Foreign Languages	25, 000	230, 000	460, 000	150, 000
Rikkyo University	U	Arts, Economics, Social Relations, Law & Politics	25, 000	280, 000	426, 000	97, 000– 199, 000
		Science	25, 000	280, 000	608, 000	181, 000– 216, 000
	G	Arts, Economics, Social Relations, Law & Politics	25, 000	280, 000	358, 000	64, 000– 105, 000
		Science	25, 000	280, 000	512, 000	87, 000– 122, 000
Rissho University	U	Buddhism, Business Administration, Economics, Law, Letters	25, 000	168, 000	490, 000	103, 000
	G	Literature, Economics	25, 000	167, 000	503, 000	102, 000
Ritsumeikan University	U	Business Administration, Economics, Law, Letters, Social Sciences	25, 000	140, 000	410, 000– 533, 000	111, 000– 144, 000
		Science & Engineering	25, 000	140, 000	615, 000	204, 000– 240, 000
	G	Business Administration, Economics, Law, Letters, Sociology	25, 000	140, 000	289, 000	111, 000
		Science & Engineering	25, 000	140, 000	386, 000	111, 000
Ryukoku University	U	Business Administration, Economics, Law, Letters	30, 000	85, 000	560, 000	160, 000
	G	Business Administration, Economics, Law, Letters	30, 000	150, 000	280, 000	160, 000
Ryutsu-Keizai University	U	Economics	25, 000	180, 000	460, 000	90, 150
	G	Economics	23, 000	78, 000	370, 000	86, 000
Sagami Institute of Technology	U	Engineering	25, 000	250, 000	540, 000	350, 000

Institution	Level	Faculty/Department	Application Fee	Admission Fee	Tuition Fee	Other Fees
Saitama Institute of Technology, The	U	Engineering	25,000	200,000	720,000	260,000
Sakuyo College of Music	U	Music	30,000	250,000	810,000	790,000
SANNO College	U	Management & Informatics	25,000	250,000	535,000	235,000
Sapporo Gakuin University	U	Commerce, Humanities, Law	25,000	150,000	360,000	150,000
Science University of Tokyo	U	Engineering, Science, Science & Technology	25,000	250,000	470,000	221,000–287,000
	U	Industrial Science & Technology	25,000	280,000	520,000	290,000
	U	Pharmaceutical Sciences	25,000	320,000	660,000	417,000
	G	Engineering, Science, Pharmaceutical Sciences, Science & Technology	25,000	250,000	394,000–420,000	242,000–559,000
Seijo University	U	Economics, Arts & Literature, Law	25,000	300,000	460,000	200,000
Seikei University	U	Economics, Humanities, Law	28,000	300,000	500,000	120,000
		Engineering	28,000	300,000	720,000	350,000
	G	(Master's Course) Business, Economics, Humanities, Law	25,000	300,000	400,000	120,000
		(Doctor's Course) Business, Economics, Humanities, Law	25,000	300,000	380,000	120,000
		(Master's) Engineering	25,000	300,000	550,000	330,000
		(Doctor's) Engineering	25,000	300,000	470,000	320,000
Seinan Gakuin University	U	Commerce, Economics, Law, Literature, Theology	25,000	240,000	453,000	
Seisen Women's College	U	Letters	25,000	260,000	465,000	180,000
Seiwa College	U,G	Education	25,000	350,000	390,000	252,000–309,000
	G	Education	25,000	350,000	390,000	
Sendai College	U	Physical Education	24,000	170,000	450,000	450,000
Senshu University	U	Economics, Law, Business Administration, Commerce, Literature	25,000	260,000	440,000	139,700–199,700
	G	Economics, Law, Business Administration, Commerce, Literature	25,000	260,000	440,000	129,000
Senzoku Gakuen College	U	Music	41,000	350,000	850,000	735,000
	G	Music	41,000	230,000	850,000	385,000
Setsunan University	U	Business Administration, Science	25,000	200,000	490,000	190,000
		Engineering	25,000	200,000	520,000	420,000
		International Language & Cultures	25,000	200,000	510,000	195,000
		Law	25,000	200,000	500,000	205,000
		Pharmaceutical Science	25,000	400,000	830,000	700,000
	G	Pharmaceutical Science	25,000	300,000	600,000	100,000
Shibaura Institute of Technology	U	Engineering	25,000	200,000	520,000	280,000
	G	Engineering	25,000	50,000	210,000	40,000
Shikoku Christian College	U	Literature	23,000	280,000	340,000	80,000–120,000
	G	Social Welfare	23,000	260,000	340,000	
Shikoku Women's University	U	Home Economics, Literature	20,000	230,000	360,000	280,000
Shinwa Women's College	U	Literature	20,000	120,000	380,000	375,000
Shirayuri Women's College	U	Liberal Arts	27,000	320,000	380,000	300,000
Shitennoji International Buddhist University	U	Literature	23,000	300,000	539,000	320,000
Shoin Women's University	U	Literature	25,000	300,000	460,000	300,000
Shokei College	U	Literature	18,000	150,000	270,000	140,000
Shotoku Academy Gifu College of Education	U	Education	25,000	200,000	400,000	500,000
Showa Academia Musicae	U	Music	38,000	550,000	800,000	590,000
Showa University	U	Dentistry	30,000	500,000	2,000,000	7,000,000
		Medicine	40,000	500,000	2,000,000	1,000,000
		Pharmaceutical Sciences	20,000	400,000	800,000	700,000
	G	Dentistry, Medicine	20,000	100,000	300,000	400,000
	G	Pharmaceutical Sciences	20,000	100,000	400,000	300,000
Showa Women's University	U	Literature, Domestic Science	30,000	270,000	558,000	200,000
	G	Literature, Domestic Science	23,000	270,000	498,000	
Shujitsu Joshi University	U	Literature	20,000	250,000	680,000	69,000

Institution	Level	Faculty/Department	Application Fee	Admission Fee	Tuition Fee	Other Fees
Shukutoku College	U	Social Welfare	25, 000	180, 000	529, 000	150, 000
Soka University	U	Economics, Law, Letters, Business Administration, Education	25, 000	208, 000	400, 000	160, 650
	G	(Master's) Economics, Law, Letters	25, 000	206, 000	405, 000	110, 500
		(Doctor's) Economics, Law, Letters	25, 000	228, 000	405, 000	110, 500
Sonoda Gakuen Women's College	U	Literature	22, 000	250, 000	800, 000	
Sophia University	U	Comparative Culture	25, 000	250, 000	20, 000 per credit	169, 000
		Theology, Humanities, Law, Economics, Foreign Studies	25, 000	250, 000	480, 000	181, 000–207, 000
		Science & Technology	25, 000	250, 000	694, 000	296, 000–298, 900
	G	Theology, Philosophy, Humanities, Law, Economics, Foreign Studies	25, 000	250, 000	480, 000	206, 000–236, 500
		Science & Technology	25, 000	250, 000	694, 000	344, 000–345, 550
		Comparative Culture	25, 000	250, 000	37, 000 per credit	204, 500
St. Andrew's University	U	Business Administration, Economics, Sociology	25, 000	200, 000	527, 000	102, 000
St. Cathrine Woman's College	U	Social Welfare	20, 000	200, 000	350, 000	360, 000
St. Luke's College of Nursing	G	(Master's & Doctor's)	25, 000	400, 000	700, 000	405, 000
St. Marianna University School of Medicine	U	Medicine	30, 000	1, 000, 000	2, 000, 000	5, 100, 000
	G	Medical Research	30, 000	100, 000	400, 000	
St. Michael's University	U	Economics	25, 000	300, 000	623, 000	360, 000
Sugiyama Jogakuen University	U	Home Economics	25, 000	330, 000	410, 000	351, 200
		Literature, Human Sciences	25, 000	330, 000	400, 000	327, 200–387, 200
Taisho University	U	Buddhism, Letters	25, 000	200, 000	400, 000	
	G	(Master's) Letters	30, 000	200, 000	370, 000	235, 000
		(Doctor's) Letters	30, 000	200, 000	390, 000	235, 000
Takachiho University of Commerce	U	Commerce	22, 000	200, 000	420, 000	150, 000
Takarazuka University of Art and Design	U	Formative Arts	25, 000	400, 000	600, 000	450, 000
Takushoku University	U	Commerce, Political Science & Economics, Foreign Languages	25, 000	200, 000	420, 000–450, 000	
		Technology	25, 000	200, 000	630, 000	
	G	(Master's) Commerce, Economics	30, 000	150, 000	460, 000	
		(Doctor's) Commerce, Economics	30, 000	150, 000	480, 000	
Tama Art University	U	Fine Art & Design	30, 000	250, 000	687, 000	210, 150
	G	Fine Art & Design	25, 000	50, 000–100, 000	687, 000	99, 600
Teikoku Women's University	U	Home Economics	25, 000	250, 000	790, 000	
Teikyo University	U	Economics, Law, Literature	26, 000	500, 000	700, 000	158, 150
		Pharmacology	26, 000	1, 000, 000	1, 100, 000	502, 900
		Medicine	40, 000	1, 500, 000	2, 600, 000	7, 532, 050
	G	Economis, Law, Literature	25, 000	250, 000	640, 000	102, 600–102, 900
		Medicine	30, 000	500, 000	1, 000, 000	
		Pharmacy	25, 000	120, 000	760, 000	390, 000
Teikyo University of Technology	U	Informatics	26, 000	200, 000	600, 000	302, 900–362, 900
Tenri University	U	Foreign Languages, Letters, Physical Education	25, 000	200, 000	380, 000	63, 000
Tezukayama Gakuin University	U	Literature	25, 000	365, 000	551, 000	268, 000

Institution	Level	Faculty/Department	Application Fee	Admission Fee	Tuition Fee	Other Fees
Tezukayama University	U	Liberal Arts, Economics	25, 000	200, 000	855, 000	
The College of Dairying	U	Dairy Science	23, 000	21, 000– 38, 000	595, 000– 1, 740, 000	16, 000– 19, 000
	G	Dairy Science, Veterinary Medicine	23, 000	38, 000	1, 225, 700	19, 000
The Japanese Red Cross College of Nursing	U	Nursing	23, 000	400, 000	650, 000	646, 000
The Kumamoto Institute of Technology	U	Engineering	22, 000	200, 000	550, 000	440, 000
The University of East Asia	U	Business Management	20, 000	120, 000	300, 000	231, 150
		Engineering	20, 000	120, 000	460, 000	332, 900– 352, 900
Tohoku College of Pharmacy	U	Pharmaceutical Sciences	25, 000	650, 000	650, 000	695, 000
Tohoku Dental University	U	Dentistry	30, 000	500, 000	1, 800, 000	6, 700, 000
	G	Dentistry	25, 000	200, 000	500, 000	
Tohoku Fukushi University	U	Social Welfare	23, 000	170, 000	390, 000	152, 000– 187, 000
Tohoku Gakuin University	U	Economics, Law, Letters	25, 000	200, 000	470, 000	172, 000
		Engineering	25, 000	200, 000	635, 000	242, 800
	G	Economics, Law, Letters	25, 000	100, 000	470, 000	168, 500
		Engineering	25, 000	100, 000	635, 000	262, 800
Tohoku Institute of Technology	U	Engineering	22, 000	180, 000	710, 000	165, 000
Tohoku Living Culture College	U	Domestic Science	20, 000	130, 000	310, 000– 330, 000	283, 000
Tohoku Women's College	U	Home Economics	20, 000	170, 000	200, 000	315, 600
Toho Music College	U	Music	30, 000	720, 000	680, 000	100, 000
Toho University	U	Medicine	40, 000	1, 000, 000	3, 088, 000	6, 384, 050
		Pharmaceutical Sciences	20, 000	400, 000	614, 000	844, 900
		Physical Science	20, 000	300, 000	614, 000	674, 900
	G	Medicine	10, 000	1, 000, 000	200, 000	
		Pharmaceutical Sciences	20, 000	150, 000	320, 000	150, 000
		Physical Science	20, 000	100, 000	320, 000	100, 000
Tokai University	U	Humanities & Culture, Engineering, Marine Science & Technology, Science	25, 000	270, 000	562, 000	446, 200– 736, 200
		Law, Letters, Political Science & Economics	25, 000	270, 000	496, 000	435, 200– 446, 200
		Physical Education	25, 000	270, 000	536, 000	484, 200– 508, 200
		Medicine	25, 000	1, 000, 000	2, 148, 000	7, 787, 200
	G	Arts, Engineering, Marine Science & Technology, Science	25, 000	270, 000	562, 000	412, 000– 488, 000
		Economics, Letters, Political Science	25, 000	270, 000	496, 000	404, 000– 412, 000
		Physical Education	25, 000	270, 000	536, 000	412, 000
		Medicine	25, 000	270, 000	445, 000	388, 000
Tokiwa University	U	Human Science	20, 000	200, 000	500, 000	230, 000
Tokushima Bunri University	U	Domestic Science, Literature	20, 000	230, 000	360, 000	280, 000
		Music	25, 000	250, 000	520, 000	740, 000
		Pharmaceutical Sciences	20, 000	400, 000	700, 000	960, 000
Tokuyama University	U	Economics	20, 000	150, 000	336, 000	192, 000
Tokyo College of Pharmacy	U	Pharmacy	25, 000	200, 000	800, 000	267, 000
Tokyo Denki University	U	Engineering	25, 000	210, 000	840, 000	300, 000
		Science & Engineering	25, 000	210, 000	930, 000	300, 000
	G	Engineering, Science & Engineering	25, 000	230, 000	560, 000– 840, 000	300, 000
Tokyo Dental College	U	Dentistry	30, 000	4, 600, 000	2, 300, 000	1, 500, 000
Tokyo Engineering University	U	Engineering	25, 000	220, 000	547, 000	427, 200
Tokyo Institute of Polytechnics	U	Engineering	25, 000	200, 000	670, 000	376, 400
	G	Engineering	20, 000	150, 000	530, 000	181, 550
Tokyo International University	U	Business & Commerce, International Studies & Human Relations	20, 000	200, 000	500, 000	388, 000
	G	Business & Commerce, International Relations, Sociology	24, 000	200, 000	460, 000	210, 000

Institution	Level	Faculty/Department	Application Fee	Admission Fee	Tuition Fee	Other Fees
Tokyo Kasei Gakuin College	U	Home Economics, Humanities	23,000	300,000	460,000	410,000–450,000
Tokyo Kasei University	U	Home Economics	25,000	260,000	480,000	285,000–294,000
		Humanities	25,000	260,000	480,000	286,300–287,000
Tokyo Keizai University	U	Business Administration, Economics	25,000	240,000	440,000	155,400
	G	Business Administration, Economics	25,000	200,000	356,000	118,000
Tokyo Union Theological Seminary	U, G	Theology	25,000	150,000	240,000	70,000
Tokyo University of Art and Design	U	Art	30,000	250,000	704,000	325,000–336,000
Tokyo University of Agriculture	U	Agriculture	25,000	270,000	490,000	293,750–515,250
	G	Agriculture	25,000	270,000	490,000	322,000–571,000
Tokyo University of Information Sciences	U	Business Administration & Informaton Science	25,000	600,000	750,000	
Tokyo Woman's Christian University	U	Arts & Sciences, Culture & Communication	30,000	·240,000	450,000	
	G	Humanities, Sciences	25,000	220,000	420,000	70,000–100,000
Tokyo Women's College of Physical Education	U	Physical Education	25,000	300,000	470,000	300,000
Tokyo Women's Medical College	U	Medicine	30,000	1,500,000	2,580,000	7,844,000
	G	Medicine	20,000	300,000	300,000	402,000
Towa University	U	Engineering	20,000	200,000	640,000	338,000
Toyota Technological Institute	U	Engineering	15,000	180,000	300,000	
	G	Engineering	20,000	200,000	500,000	
Toyo University	U	Literature, Economics, Business Administration, Law, Sociology	25,000	220,000	370,000	117,000
		Engineering	25,000	220,000	570,000	239,000
	G	Literature, Economics, Business Administration, Law, Sociology	25,000	220,000	380,000	102,000
		Engineering	25,000	220,000	580,000	252,000
Tsuda College	U	Liberal Arts	25,000	220,000–240,000	440,000–480,000	12,000
	G	Literary Studies, International Studies, Mathematics	20,000	40,000	344,000–376,000	80,000
Tsurumi University	U	Literature	25,000	270,000	440,000	180,000
		Dental Medicine	30,000	5,000,000	2,500,000	800,000
	G	Dental Medicine	30,000	200,000	600,000	1,000,000
Ueno Gakuen College	U	Music	36,000	545,000	667,000	679,800
University of Hannan	U	Commercial Science, Economics	25,000	120,000	390,000	340,000
University of Marketing and Distribution Sciences	U	Commerce	30,000	300,000	450,000	270,000
University of Occupational and Environmental Health, Japan	U	Medicine	12,000	500,000	650,000	700,000
University of Okinawa	U	Law & Economics	20,000	180,000	300,000	91,650
University of Setsunan	U	Business Administration & Information, International Language & Culture	25,000	200,000	630,000	
		Engineering	25,000	200,000	880,000	
		Pharmaceutical Sciences	25,000	400,000	1,460,000	
University of the Sacred Heart	U	Liberal Arts	25,000	300,000	380,000	270,000
	G	Liberal Arts	25,000	300,000	300,000	260,000
Yokkaichi University	U	Economics	25,000	220,000	400,000	280,000
Wako University	U	Economics, Humanities	25,000	250,000	450,000	199,000–202,000
Waseda University	U	Commerce, Law, Literature, Political Science & Economics	25,000	260,000	460,000–720,000	114,450–284,700
		Education	25,000	260,000	460,000–720,000	112,700–267,700

Institution	Level	Faculty/Department	Application Fee	Admission Fee	Tuition Fee	Other Fees
		Science & Engineering	25, 000	260, 000	720, 000	238, 200–274, 200
	G	Commerce, Economics, Law, Literature, Political Science	25, 000	240, 000	340, 000	83, 000–100, 000
		Science & Engineering	25, 000	240, 000	540, 000	240, 000–264, 000
Women's College of Fine Arts	U	Arts	30, 000	250, 000	687, 000	265, 950–535, 750
Yahata University	U	Law & Economics	26, 000	100, 000	420, 000	112, 000
Yamanashi Gakuin University	U	Commercial Science, Law	25, 000	200, 000	480, 000	260, 000–350, 000
Yasuda Women's University	U	Letters	20, 000	200, 000	320, 000	20, 000
Yokohama College of Commerce	U	Commerce	25, 000	250, 000	430, 000	260, 000

Scholarships

Japanese Government (Monbusho) Scholarships (1988–89)

Types / Specifications	Research (Graduate) Student	In-Service Training for Teachers	Undergraduate Student	Technical College Student	Senshu-gakko Student	Japanese Studies
Qualifications	University graduates	University graduates with 5 years or more experience in the educational field	Those completing secondary school, eligible for entering university in their country			Those in their 3rd or 4th year of university
(Areas covered)	(Southeast Asia, Central & South America)		(Southeast Asia, Oceania, Central & South America)	(Southeast Asia)	(Southeast Asia & Pacific countries)	
Age	under 35		under 22			18 & over
Duration	2 years including language training	18 months including language training	5 years including language training; 7 years for medicine and dentistry	3 years & 6 months including language training	2 years & 6 months including language training	1 school year
Number of applicants to be accepted	1,785	140	110	40	40	150
Monthly allowance	¥177,500		¥134,500			
Tuition, etc.	Exempt from tuition					
Transportation	One round-trip ticket provided					
Research allowance per year (maximum)	¥40,000		¥40,000 for final school year	¥25,000		¥40,000
Arrival allowance						
Housing assistance	¥12,000 in major cities, ¥9,000 in local cities					
Medical fee reimbursement	80% of actual cost					

Scholarships Awarded by Private Foundations

Legend:
- J: Junior College Students
- U: Undergraduate Students
- M: Master's Course Students
- A: Auditors
- S: Special Training College Students
- G: Graduate School Students
- D: Doctorate Course Students
- R: Research Students

Name of Foundation/ Scholarship	Type	Eligibility			Monthly Stipends (Yen)	Duration	Application Period/ Deadline	Number of Grantees	Address/Telephone
		Age	Country Requirements	Other Requirements					
Association of International Education, Japan Honors Scholarships (Gakushu Shoreihi)	S J U M D R	S: Under 30 J: Under 30 U: Under 30 M: Under 35 D: Under 35 R: Under 35		S: 2nd and 3rd year students, Students of the participating schools	S: 45,000 J: 45,000 U: 45,000 M: 65,000 D: 65,000 R: 65,000	1 year	April	S:] J:] 1,700 U:] M:] D:] 800 R:]	Application through University
Arabian Oil Company Ltd. Tokyo Scholarship	U		Saudi Arabia		365,000	5½ years	June–July	4	8F NKK Bldg. 2-18-2 Nishi-shinbashi, Minato-ku, Tokyo 105 ☎ 03-438-1421
Asahi Glass Foundation of Thailand	M	Under 30		Students of the specified schools	80,000	2 years	February–April	3	Application through University
Asia Kyoiku Bunka Koryu Kyokai	M	Under 35	China	Field: Social Science	100,000	2 years	January	10	Application through University
Better Home Welfare Foundation Better Home Goodwill Scholarship	U R M D	Under 30		Students of the specified schools	30,000	Up to Graduation	March–April	17	Application through University
Charitable Trust Yamaha Motor International Friendship Fund	M	Under 30		Prospective freshmen, Students of the specified schools, Field: Engineering	100,000	2 years	December–February	5	Application through University
CWAJ (College Women's Association, Japan), The	R M D			Female graduate school students or female prospective graduate school students, English fluency	Sum: 2,000,000	1 year	September–November	3	B-1 35th Kowa Bldg. 1-14-14 Akasaka, Minato-ku, Tokyo 107
The Daiko Foundation Ikuei Shogakukin	U R M D			Students attending Universities in Aichi	20,000	1 year	May	30	Application through University
Gakubu Shoreikin	U			Students attending Universities in Aichi	Sum: 200,000	1 year	May–December	10 10	Application through University

Name of Foundation/ Scholarship	Type	Eligibility			Monthly Stipends (Yen)	Duration	Application Period/ Deadline	Number of Grantees	Address/Telephone
		Age	Country Requirements	Other Requirements					
Foundation for Asian Management Development, The	R M D		ASEAN & Asia		Sum: 1,600,000	Up to Graduation	March & August	2	Application through University
Foundation for International Information Processing Education (FINIPED)	R M D			Field: Information Science	Sum: 500,000	1 year	December– February	12	Application through University
Hakumon Shogakkai	U M			U: 1st–3rd year students. M: 1st year students. Students attending Universities in Tokyo	Sum: 360,000	1 year	May	10	3F Bldg. #6 Faculty of Science and Engineering, Chuo University 1-13-27 Kasuga, Bunkyo-ku, Tokyo 112
Hashiya Scholarship Foundation Hashiya Scholarship Program	S J U R M D		Indonesia		60,000	Up to Graduation	March– May	8	3-17-9 Higashi Kasai, Edogawa-ku, Tokyo 134 ☎ 03-689-3111 ext. 260
Hattori Kaigai Ryugakusei Ikueikai	U R M D		South East Asia	Students attending Universities in Aichi	50,000	Up to Graduation	February	3	Application through University
Hitachi Scholarship Foundation, The Hitachi Scholarship Program	M D			Graduates of the specified schools in Thailand, Singapore, Indonesia, Malaysia Field: Science & Engineering	M: 180,000 D: 180,000 J: 175,000 & Tuition Travel expenses	M: 2 years D: 3 years	September– December	8	4-6 Surugadai, Kanda, Chiyoda-ku, Tokyo 101 ☎ 03-258-2062
Hokkaido Kankokujin Shogakkai	All		Korea	Students attending Universities in Hokkaido	30,000	1 year	February	5	Application through University ☎ 011-562-4133
Ichikawa International Scholarship Foundation	U M D		Asia	Students attending Universities in Kinki Area	100,000	2 years	November– December	15	Application through University

Name of Foundation/ Scholarship	Eligibility				Monthly Stipends (Yen)	Duration	Application Period/ Deadline	Number of Grantees	Address/Telephone
	Type	Age	Country Requirements	Other Requirements					
Inner-Trip Kokusai Koryu Kyokai	U M D	U: Under 30 M: Under 35 D: Under 35	South-East Asia, Central & South America, etc.	Students of the specified schools	120,000	2 years	June	5	Application through University
INPEX Foundation INPEX Scholarship	M	Under 30	Indonesia	Natural Science Graduates from Universities in Indonesia	150,000	32 months	August–November	6	9F Toranomon 37 Mori Bldg., 3-5-1 Toranomon, Minato-ku, Tokyo 105 ☎ 03-434-1131
Interchange Association (Applying in Taiwan)	R M D	Under 35	Taiwan	Students who will be attending National Universities	177,500	2 years	September– October	55	No. 43, 2nd Section, Chinan Road, Taipei, R.O.C. 3517250
(Applying in Japan)	M D	Under 35	Taiwan	Students or prospective students attending National universities	177,500	2 years	September– October	4	NP Onarimon Bldg. 8F 3-25-33 Nishi Shinbashi, Minato-ku, Tokyo 105 ☎ 03-437-1501~5
Ishizaka Foundation, The Ishizaka Scholarship	M D			Students of the specified schools	100,000	1 year	April	12	Application through University
Iwaki Scholarship Foundation Iwaki Scholarship	U M D		Asia	Field: Medicine, Pharmacy, Chemistry, Students attending Universities in Kanto Area	100,000	2 years	November– December	5	Application through University
Iwatani Naoji Foundation, The Iwatani International Scholarship	M D	M: Under 30 D: Under 35	South-East Asia, East Asia	Field: Natural Science	100,000	1 year	December– January	10	2-10-2 Nagata-cho, Chiyoda-ku, Tokyo 100 ☎ 03-580-2700
Japanese Association of University Women (JAUW), International Scholarship Committee	D			Association of University Women member, Female researcher, Bachelor degree holder	Sum: 700,000	3–6 months	April– June	2	241 Toyama Mansion 7-17-18 Shinjuku, Shinjuku-ku, Tokyo 160
Japan-Korea Cultural Association	U M D		Korea	Students attending Universities in Tokyo area	30,000	1 year	April	*	Application through University

* Scholarships whose duration is longer than one year become available upon graduation of grantees.

Name of Foundation/ Scholarship	Type	Eligibility			Monthly Stipends (Yen)	Duration	Application Period/ Deadline	Number of Grantees	Address/Telephone
		Age	Country Requirements	Other Requirements					
Japan-Oceania Society for Cultural Exchanges	U R M D			Students from the South Pacific University, attending University in Amagasaki City	1,600,000	2–3 months		2–3	Application through University
Japan Securities Scholarship Foundation Educational Awards for Overseas Students	R M	Under 30	Thailand, Malaysia, Indonesia, Philipines, Hong Kong, Taiwan, Korea, China	Field: Social Science, University Graduate or prospective graduate	R: 180,000 M: 180,000 (150,000— during 1 year Japanese Training Period) & Tuition, Travel expenses	R: 2 years M: 3 years (including 1 year Japanese Training Period)	January—July	5	Tokyo Shoken Bldg. 1-5-8, Kayaba-cho, Nihonbashi, Chuo-ku, Tokyo 103 ☏ 03-664-7113
Kaiseikai Foundation, The	U R M D			Field: Music	1,000,000 –2,000,000	1 year	Anytime	1–3	13-2 Kabuto-cho, Nihonbashi, Chuo-ku Tokyo 103 ☏ 03-666-2022
Kamei Memorial Foundation	U M D			Students attending Tohoku University	20,000	Up to Graduation	April—May	5	Application through University
Kambayashi Scholarship Foundation Kambayashi Scholarship	U M D		South-East Asia, East Asia	Students attending Universities in Kanto area	U: 60,000 M: 90,000 D: 90,000	1 year	April	16	Application through University
Kaneko Foundation for International Cultural Communication	U R M D		Circum-pan-Pacific Nations	Students attending Universities in Kanto area U: 3rd and 4th year students Field: Japanese and Japan Studies	50,000	10 months	April—May	10	Application through University
Kashiyama Scholarship Foundation Kashiyama Scholarship	M D	U: Under 30 D: Under 35	Asia, Pacific Nations	U: 1st year student D: 2ndyearstudent	100,000	2 years	April—May	7	3-10-5 Nihonbashi, Chuo-ku, Tokyo 103 ☏ 03-272-2336

Name of Foundation/ Scholarship	Type	Eligibility			Monthly Stipends (Yen)	Duration	Application Period/ Deadline	Number of Grantees	Address/Telephone
		Age	Country Requirements	Other Requirements					
Kawakami Memorial Foundation, The	M	Under 35		Students attending International University of Japan	100,000	2 years	August	2	Application through University
Kinoshita Kinen Jigyodan Kinoshita Scholarship	U M D		South-East Asia	Students of the specified schools	U: 360,000 M: 480,000 D: 600,000	Up to Graduation	March–April	1–4	Application through University
Kitano Lifelong Integrated Education Foundation	R			At least 5 years job experience (Applicants over 30 years old exempted)	50,000 & Tuition, etc.	1 year	May	A: 17 R: 7	1-12-16 Gohongi, Meguro-ku, Tokyo 153 ☏ 03-711-1111
KIWANIS Scholarship Foundation KIWANIS Scholarship	U M D		South-East Asia	Students attending Universities in Osaka-Fu	10,000	1-2 years	April	10	Application through University
Korean Scholarship Association, The	U M D		South and North Korea		U: 18,000 M: 30,000 D: 40,000	1 year	April–May	175	Shinjuku Bldg. 1-8-1 Nishi Shinjuku, Shinjuku-ku, Tokyo 160 ☏ 03-343-5757
Kumahira Scholarship Foundation Kumahira Scholarship	U R M D			Students attending Universities in Hiroshima	50,000	1 year	March–April	50	Application through University
Kobayashi Foundation for Students from Abroad Kobayashi Scholarship	J A U R M D		Asia, Africa, Latin America	Students attending Universities in Okayama	30,000	2 years	April–May	25	Application through University
Kobe International Association Kobe Asia Center Shihi Ryugakusei Shogakukin	M D	Under 35	Asia	Students attending Universities in Kobe City	80,000	1 year	April	10	Application through University

Name of Foundation/ Scholarship	Eligibility				Monthly Stipends (Yen)	Duration	Application Period/ Deadline	Number of Grantees	Address/Telephone
	Type	Age	Country Requirements	Other Requirements					
Kokusai Kyowa Foundation	S U R M D			Students attending Universities in Tokyo	80,000	2 years	December	10	Application through University
Kumamoto Lions Club 337 D Zai Kuma Gaikokujin Ryugakusei Shogakkai	U R M D				10,000	1 year	June		Application through University
M. MAEDA Memorial Trust	M	Under 30		Students of the specified Schools Field: Humanities, Social Science	50,000	2 years	April– May	2–3	Application through University
Maezawa Ikuei Zaidan	U M D			Students attending Universities in Tokyo, U: 1st year students only	20,000	Minimum years required for completion	April– May	10	Application through University
Makita Scholarship Foundation	U M D	U: Under 30 M: Under 35 D: Under 35		U: 3rd and 4th year students M: 2nd year Students D: 2nd and 3rd year students	100,000	2 years	January	20	2-18 Ageba-cho, Shinjuku-ku, Tokyo 162 ☎ 03-260-2788
Meitetsu International Scholarship Association	U M D		Circum-pan-Pacific Nations	Students attending Universities in Aichi Prefecture	80,000	2 years	November– December	10	Application through University
Mitsui Kanagata Shinko Zaidan				Student s of the specified schools	20,000	2 years	June– July	15 –20	Application through University
Morita Scholarship Foundation, The	J U M D			Students attending Universities in Aichi Prefecture	Sum: 1,000,000	1 year	May– July	4	Application through University

Name of Foundation/ Scholarship	Type	Eligibility			Monthly Stipends (Yen)	Duration	Application Period/ Deadline	Number of Grantees	Address/Telephone
		Age	Country Requirements	Other Requirements					
Moritani Scholarship Foundation, The	U M D			Students attending Universities in Tokyo, 1st year students only	U: 20,000 M: 25,000 D: 25,000	Minimum years required for completion	April	40	Application through University
Moriya Foundation	U	U: Under 30	Asia	3rd year students	40,000	2 years	April	15	Teikokushoin, 3-29 Jinbo-cho, Kanda, Chiyoda-ku, Tokyo 101
Nagasaki-Foundation	S J A U R M D	Over 18 Under 30	Asia	Students attending Universities in Nagasaki Prefecture, Students recommended by the government or educational institute of his/her own country	104,000 & Travel Expenses, Tuition, Etc.	1 year		5	2-13 Edo-cho, Nagasaki-shi, Nagasaki 850 ☎ 0958-24-1111/2084
Nagasaki North Rotary Club	U R M D			Students attending Universities in Nagasaki	30,000	Up to Graduation		5	Application through University
Nagoya Lions Club	U M D		Asia	2nd year students, Students attending Universities in Aichi	50,000	6 months		10	Application through University
Nagoya Zonta Club	U R M D			Female students attending Universities in Aichi	30,000	1 year	July	2	Application through University
Nakauchi Ikueikai	U M D			Students attending Universities in Hyogo, Field: Commerce	80,000	2 years		7	Application through University

Name of Foundation/ Scholarship	Type	Eligibility			Monthly Stipends (Yen)	Duration	Application Period/ Deadline	Number of Grantees	Address/Telephone
		Age	Country Requirements	Other Requirements					
Nomura Foundation, The	J U M			J: 2nd year students U: 2nd, 3rd and 4th year students M: 2nd year students Students who have been attending Japanese school over a year	10,000	Minimum years required for completion	April	13	1-11-9 Nishi, Takaido, Suginami-ku, Tokyo 168 ☎ 03-334-7186
Okumura Shogakkai Okumura Scholarship	U M D		Asia, Pacific Nations	Students not holding Doctoral degree, Students attending Universities in Oaska-Fu	U: 30,000 M: 40,000 D: 40,000	Up to Graduation	May	U: 5 M: 3 D: 2	Application through University
Osaka Nagahoribashi Lions Club	M D			Students attending Osaka University	50,000	2 years		3	Application through University
Park Young Koo Scholarship Foundation	M D	M: Under 30 D: Under 35	Korea	Field: Natural Science	70,000	1 year	March– April	19	5F 2nd Chuo Bldg. 3-8-6 Nihonbashi, Chuo-ku, Tokyo 103 ☎ 03-271-3414
Rural Asia Solidarity Association RASA Kenkyuchi Hojo	S J U R M D		Asia		Sum: 100,000	1 year	April– May	10	7-14 Kawada-cho, Shinjuku-ku, Tokyo 162 ☎ 03-358-6233
Sagawa Scholarship Foundation Sagawa Scholarship	U M D	U: Under 27 G: Under 35	South-East Asia	U: 3rd and 4th year students	100,000	2 years	February– April	15	678 Oomandokoro-cho, Bukkoji Sagaru, Karasuma-dori, Shimogyo-ku, Kyoto 600 ☎ 075-371-0818
Sakaguchi Kokusai Ikuei Shogaku Zaidan	U G				80,000	2 years		10	☎ 03-253-8233

Name of Foundation/ Scholarship	Eligibility				Monthly Stipends (Yen)	Duration	Application Period/ Deadline	Number of Grantees	Address/Telephone
	Type	Age	Country Requirements	Other Requirements					
Saneyoshi Scholarship Foundation Saneyoshi Scholarship	M D			Students of the specified schools Field: Science and Engineering	90,000	1–2 years	April–May	10	Application through University
Shundoh International Foundation	M D			Students of the specified schools	100,000	2 years	March	5	Application through University
Takakyu Foundation	A U R M D				A: 100,000 U: 100,000 R: 70,000 M: 70,000 D: 70,000	1 year	August	U: 20 G: 20	1-5-22 Shimo Ochiai, Shinjuku-ku, Tokyo 161 ☎ 03-366-6727
Takugin Shogakkai Takugin Scholarship	D		Asia, Africa	2nd, 3rd & 4th year students, Students attending Universities in Hokkaido	20,000	2 years	April–May	3	Application through University
Theather Company Hikosen International Scholarship	U		China, Taiwan, Korea, South East Asia	Students of the specified schools	20,000	1 year	November–February	4	Application through University
Toa Ryugakusei Ikuyukai	U G		Korea	Students of the specified schools	80,000	1 year	June	23	Application through University
Toka Kyoiku Bunka Koryu Zaidan	U G				80,000	2 years		10	☎ 03-351-3477
Tsuru Torataro Schogakkai Tsuru Torataro Scholarship	S U M D			Students attending Universities in Hiroshima	4,500	Up to Graduation	April	5–6	Hiroshima Kogyo University 275 Miyake, Itsukaichi-machi, Saeki-gun, Hiroshima 731-51 ☎ 0829-21-3121
Tokyu Foundation for Inbound Students Tokyu Scholarship	R M D	M: Under 30 D: Under 35	Asia, Pacific Nations		110,000	2 years	October–December	21	26-20 Sakuragaokacho, Shibuya-ku, Tokyo 150 ☎ 03-461-0844

Name of Foundation/Scholarship	Eligibility				Monthly Stipends (Yen)	Duration	Application Period/Deadline	Number of Grantees	Address/Telephone
	Type	Age	Country Requirements	Other Requirements					
Tokyo YWCA Ryugakusei no Hahaoya Undo / Tokyo YWCA Ryugakusei no Hahaoya Undo Shogakukin	S J U		Asia, Africa, Latin America	U: 1st and 2nd year students	20,000	1–2 years	April	A few	3-1-1 Sadohara-cho, Ichigaya, Shinjuku-ku, Tokyo 162 ☎ 03-268-4462
Yamamura Ikueikai	U			2nd year students, Students attending Universities in Hyogo Prefecture	20,000	3 years, Medical Students: 5 years	April	10	Application through University
Yayasan Asahi Glass Indonesia	M D	M: Under 30 D: Under 35		Students of the specified school	80,000	2 years	February— April	3	Application through University
Yoshida Ikueikai	U M D	Over 20 Under 28		Students of the specified school	150,000	1 year	April— May	10	Application through University
Yoshimoto Shoji Shogakkai	U			Students attending Universities in Fukuoka	Sum: 960,000	2 years	April	20	Application through University
Rotary Memorial Foundation, Inc. Yoneyama Master and Doctor Course Scholarship / Yoneyama Undergraduate Course Scholarship	M D U	Under 40	Nations where Rotary Club exists		120,000 110,000	2 years	November	376 108	8F abc Hall 2-6-3 Shibakoen, Minato-ku, Tokyo 105 ☎ 03-434-8681
Yumoto Ikueikai	U			Students of the specified school	15,000	Minimum years required for completion	May	10	Application through University
ZONTA International Kyoto (I) Shogakukin	U M D			Female Students living in Kyoto and attending Universities in Kyoto-Fu.	50,000	1 year		2	Application through University

Fellowships for Doctoral, Post-doctoral or Professional Researchers

Name and Address of Foundation/Organization	Eligibility	Duration, Conditions and Application Deadline
Institute of Developing Economics 42 Ichigaya-Honmura-cho, Shinjuku-ku, Tokyo 162 ☎ 03-353-4231	Doctoral degree holders in the field of social sciences or other professionals with substantial training and experience in developmental economics or sociology in the developing countries.	Duration: 3-10 months. Conditions: ¥357,000 or ¥396,000/month. One round trip ticket provided. Applications: by May 31 or November 30.
The Japan Foundation Park Bldg., 3-6 Kioi-cho, Chiyoda-ku, Tokyo 102 ☎ 03-263-4497	Professional Fellowship: Academic faculty, writers, or other professionals with substantial training and experience in some aspect of Japanese studies. Dissertation Fellowship: Doctoral candidates in the social sciences, humanities, law or business who have completed all requirements except the dissertation and who wish to conduct dissertation research in Japan.	Duration: 4-12 months (long-term), 2-4 months (short-term) Conditions: ¥300,000 or ¥240,000/month. One round ticket provided. Duration: 4-14 months. Conditions: ¥180,000/month. One round trip ticket provided. Applications: by November 15
The Japan Society for the Promotion of Science Yamato Bldg., 5-3-1 Koji-machi, Chiyoda-ku, Tokyo 102 ☎ 03-263-1721	Short-term Program: Senior scientists and university professors. Long-term Program (Senior): University professors and assistant professors. Long-term Program (Junior): Post-doctoral researchers and other persons of comparable research experience who are 25 years of age or older.	Duration: 14-120 days. Duration: 6-10 months. Duration: 6-12 months. Conditions: ¥240,000-¥300,000/month. One round trip ticket provided. Applications: in May and in September by a host Japanese scientist.
The Matsumae International Foundation 33F Kasumigaseki Bldg., 3-2-5 Kasumigaseki, Chiyoda-ku, Tokyo 100 ☎ 03-581-1070	Those who hold a Doctorate degree or equivalent, or have at least two years of research experience after completion of Master's degree and who are under 40 years old. Naturanl science, engineering and medicine are preferable fields.	Duration: 3-6 months Conditions: ¥200,000-¥300,000/month. One round trip ticket provided. Applications: by August 31 for the following school year

University Scholarships

U = Undergraduate Students
G = Graduates School Students
A = Auditors
R = Research students
J = Japanese Language Program Students

Name of University /Scholarship	Type	Eligibility	Annual Stipends (Yen)	Application Period/ Deadline	Number of Grantees
Bukkyo University	U G		600,000 1,200,000	April 1-15	1988 U :2 G :3
Chubu University	U G		300,000	April	10
Chukyo University Scholarship for International Students	U G		600,000 –900,000	April	15
Special Scholarship for Foreign Undergraduate Students	U		600,000	June	5
Chuo University	U G	U :2nd-4th year students	Half tuition & laboratory fees	June	1988:36
Dokkyo University	U		790,000 & Dormitory Fee	May, November	A few
Doshisha University	U G		60,000-120,000	September	24 or less
Fuji Women's College	U		According to individual needs	Any time	1988:0
Higashi Nippon Gakuen University	U G		400,000	April	1988:1
Hiroshima Shudo University	U G A R		Full tuition	April	1988:9
Hitotsubashi University JOSUIKAI Scholarship	U G		360,000	April	20
Hosei University International Fund Scholarship	U		Tuition & fees	March-April	8
International Budo University	R	Field : Judo and Kendo	210,000	September —December	10

Name of University /Scholarship	Type	Eligibility	Annual Stipends (Yen)	Application Period/ Deadline	Number of Grantees
International Christian University ICU Non-Japanese Student Scholarship (Tuition Scholarship)		Regular students enrolled for at least two terms	1/3, 1/2 or 2/3 full tuition	May	1987:27
International University of Japan					Unfixed
Type1	G		admission fee, tuition, Round-trip travel cost, 100,000 per month	January	
Type2			admission fee. tuition, 100,000 per month		
Type3			admission fee, tuition		
Kansai University	U G		360,000	October	10
Kansai University of Foreign Studies					
Teaching Assistantship		Asian Studies Program students	US$4,400.00	May & October	5-10
Merit Scholarships		Asian Studies Program students	US$2,600.00	2/1-6/10, 9/1-11/30	1988:59
Keio University Scholarships for undergraduates	U				
Category I			Full tuition	April	15
Category II			Half tuition	April	16
Scholarships for graduates	G				
Category I			Full tuition, 41,000& prescribed	April	1988:14
Category II			Full tuition & 41,000	April	1988:24

Name of University /Scholarship	Type	Eligibility	Annual Stipends (Yen)	Application Period/ Deadline	Number of Grantees
Kokushikan University	U G		1,200,000/600,000/360,000	Feburuary	
Komazawa University Centenary Commemorative Scholarship	U G	Exept freshmen	240,000	April 12-May31	7
Alumni Association Scholarship	U		200,000	July	5
Konan Women's University	G		1, 200, 000	April	15
Kwansei Gakuin University	U G		Full or Half tuition	Any time	1988:1
Kyoto Institute of Technology International Cultural Exchange Promotion Fund	U G		60, 000	October	1988:24
Kyushu Institute of Technology Uemura Scholarship		Asian students	20, 000	April	6
Kyushu Tokai University Type1: Type2: Type3:	U G	1st year students	1, 160, 000 515, 000 460, 000		A few
Matsuyama University	U A		Full tuition	April	5 5
Meiji Gakuin University	U		According to individual needs	October	1988:10
Meijo University	U G	Students enrolled before '87	Half tuition	May	Unlimited
Nagasaki Institute of Applied Science Kihara Scholarship	U G J		According to individual needs	June	1988:12

Name of University /Scholarship	Type	Eligibility	Annual Stipends (Yen)	Application Period/ Deadline	Number of Grantees
Nanzan University	U G J	Students of the Center for Japanese Studies	Full or half tuition	U.G : April CJS : May, November	1988:13
Nihon University	U G G U U G U G	Field: Humanities and Sciences Literature & Social Sciences Science & Technology Economics Industrial Technology Industrial Technology Commerce Business Administration	120,000 200,000 200,000 150,000 500,000 600,000 Full tuition Full tuition	September " " April June " April-May "	1987:10 1988:8 1987:4 1987:1 5
Nippon Medical School		Research Associate and Trainee	960,000	February, August	16
Notre Dame Seishin University	U R		600,000	April	Unfixed
Reitaku University Type 1 Type 2 Type 3	U		Tuition Tuition & Room Tuition,Room & Board		A few
Rikkyo University St. Paul's Ladies Club Scholarship	U G	Female student	300,000	October	1
Ritsumeikan University	U G	Except 1st year students	200,000	April	1988:23
Science University of Tokyo	U G		Half tuition	September	Unlimited
Seiwa College	U G		Full tuition	April	1988:3
Shibaura Institute of Technology	U G A R	Students in urgent need	400,000	Any time	1988:0

Name of University /Scholarship	Type	Eligibility	Annual Stipends (Yen)	Application Period/ Deadline	Number of Grantees
Shikoku Women's University International Exchange Scholarship	U A R		According to individual needs	Any time	
Showa Women's University	U G		Full or half Tuition	April	1988:22
St. Andrew's University	U		300,000	Autumn	9
Tokai University Type 1 Type 2	U		Tuition & fees Tuition	April	4 14 for 1st & 2nd year student· 4 for 3rd & 4th year students
Tokyo Keizai University	U	Self-supporting Students	300,000	April	2~3
Tokyo Women's Christian University Foreign Fellowship	U G		Tuition & fees	At the time of entrance application	Several
University of The Sacred Heart	U G		600,000	April	3
Waseda University Okuma Memorial Scholarships	U G	Sophomore & Senior	Tuition150,000–360,000, Tuition and other fees	April April	8 8
Yokohama City University	U G		Half Tuition	April	1988:17

Preparatory Japanese Language Programs associated with the Universities

	Asia University, Special Course for Foreign Students	Daito Bunka University, Japanese Language Program for Overseas Students	Keio University, Japanese Language Course at the International Center	Kinki University, Japanese Language Classes for Foreign Students	Kyorin University, Special Japanese Training Course for Overseas Students	Kyoto University of Foreign Studies, The Course in Japanese Studies for Overseas Students
Address	5-24-10 Sakai, Musashino-shi, Tokyo 180	1-9-1 Takashimadaira, Itabashi-ku, Tokyo 175	2-15-45 Mita, Minato-ku, Tokyo 108	3-4-1 Kowakae, Higashiosaka-shi, Osaka 577	476 Miyashita-cho, Hachioji-shi, Tokyo 192	6 Saiin Kasame-cho, Ukyo-ku, Kyoto 615
Telephone	0422-54-3111	03-935-1111	03-453-4511	06-721-2332	0426-91-0141	075-314-5827
Year Program Established	1954	1977	1964	1970	1988	1981
Faculty — Full-time	0	6	7	9	2	3
Faculty — Part-time	10	4	19	3	4	17
Eligibility	*	*	*	*	*	
Program Length	1 y.	1 y.	6 m.	1 y.	1 y.	1 y.
Application Deadline	Oct. 31	Nov. 15	Oct. 31 / Apr. 30	Oct. 30	Feb. 28	Oct. 31
Program Starting Date	Apr.	Apr.	Apr. / Sep.	Apr.	Apr.	Apr.
Program Size	60	20	80	30	20	30
Class Size	15~20	20	14	23	11	11
Hours/week × Number of weeks	40 × 25	42 × 30	20~30 × 15	48 × 30	32 × 31	40 × 31
Other Subjects — English					○	
Other Subjects — Mathematics					○	
Other Subjects — Science					○	
Other Subjects — Social Science					○	
Application Fee	20,000	28,000	6,500	20,000		
Admission Fee	120,000	150,000	70,000	80,000	100,000	100,000
Tuition	390,000	420,000	180,000	400,000	450,000	400,000
Other Fees	36,000				25,000	
3 largest ethnic groups†	TA HK US	TA CH KO	US WG KO	KO CH TA	TA	CH TA US
Guarantor system	○	○				
Dormitory					M	

* Only open to students seeking entrance into the same University.
† CH=China IN=Indonesia MA=Malaysia TH=Thailand WG=West Germany HK=Hong Kong KO=Korea TA=Taiwan US=United States

Institution / Address	Est.				Dur.	Deadline	Start	Enroll		Class size	20,000	340,000	60,000	10,000					Langs		F
Nagasaki Institute of Applied Science, Japanese Language Course — 536 Aba-machi, Nagasaki-shi, Nagasaki 851-01, 0958-39-3111	1978	2	4		1 y.	Nov. 15	Apr.	10	13	30 ×30	20,000	340,000	60,000	10,000	○	○	○	○	CH MA TA	○	F
Reitaku University, The Course of Japanese Language — 2-1-1 Hikarigaoka, Kashiwa-shi, Chiba 277	1976	10	4		1 y.	Sep. 28	Apr.	60	20	30 ×30		350,000	145,000	22,000	○	○	○	○	TA US CH	○	○
Ryukoku University, Japanese Culture and Language Program — 67 Tsukamoto-cho, Fushimi-ku, Kyoto 612, 075-642-111 ext. 719	1985	1	21		1 y.	Feb. 28 / Aug. 31	Apr. / Sep.	20 / 20	14	24 ×30		487,000	50,000	30,000					CH TA KO		M: 20 F: 20
Soka University, Institute of the Japanese Language — 1-236 Tangi-cho, Hachioji-shi, Tokyo 192, 0426-91-2206	1976	6	8	*	1 y.	Nov. 30	Apr.	20	10	30 ×30			478,500	25,000					US TA CH	○	○
Takushoku University, Japanese Language Section for Foreign Students — 3-4-14 Kohinata, Bunkyo-ku, Tokyo 112, 03-947-2261	1972	0	27		1 y.	Nov. 21	Apr.	130	20	30 ×35		380,000	120,000	10,000	○	○	○	○	TA KO CH	○	
Japanese Language Learning Center					6 m.	Dec. 10 / Jun. 30	Apr. / Oct.	70 / 70	20 / 20		44,500	210,000	50,000								
Tenri University, Special Course for the Japanese Language — 1050 Somanouchi-cho, Tenri-shi, Nara 577, 07436-3-1511	1981	10	1		2 y.	Sep. 30	Apr.	40	10	27 ×72		350,000	70,000	5,000					TA TH IN		
Tokai University, Japanese Language Program — 1117 Kitakaname, Hiratsuka, Kanagawa 259-12, 0463-58-1211	1964	14	30	*	1 y.	Oct. 12	Apr.	60	10 ~25	33 ×35	159,000	393,000	40,000		○	○	○	○	TA CH KO	○	○
Tokyo International University, Japanese Language Program — 1-13-1 Matobakita, Kawagoe-shi, Saitama 350, 0492-32-1111	1982	2	9		1 y.	Oct. 31	Apr.	40	15	30 ×35	60,000	420,000	130,000	20,000					TA KO CH		
Waseda University, Center for Japanese Language, Intensive Japanese Language Course — 1-6-1 Nishi-waseda, Shinjuku-ku, Tokyo 169, 03-203-4141 ext. 5343	1954	5	18		1 y.	Sep. 30	Apr.	30	10	20 ×33	10,000	140,000	5,000	3,000	○	○	○	○	KO CH US		

Study Abroad Programs

	International Christian University	Kansai University of Foreign Studies Asian Studies Program	Konan University Year in Japan Program	Kwansei Gakuin University International Program	Nanzan University Center for Japanese Studies	Sophia University Faculty of Comparative Culture	Waseda University International Division
Courses Available in Japan Studies	Art, Archeology, Modern Literature, Business, History, Society, Religion, Education, Values & Ethics, Social Structure, Philosophy, Politics, Economics, International Relations, Music, etc.	Pacific Rivalry, Politics, Economics, Trading, Marketing, Management, Law, Women, Intercultural communication, Society, History, Literature, Art, Foreign Relations, Ceramics, Brush Painting, etc.	Art, Anthropology, History, Law and Politics, Economics and Business, Literature, Society and Culture, Popular Culture, etc.	(Beginning, Intermediate, Advanced) Japanese, Early History, Religion, Psychology, Management, Social Welfare Issues, Art, Literature, Society, International Trade, Economy & Business.	Business, Economy, Folklore, History, Religions, Linguistics, Literature, Politics, International Relations, Society, Translation, Classical Japanese, Ikebana, Sumie, Hanga, Shodo, etc.	Classical Japanese, Kanbun, Linguistics, Art, Archaeology, Anthropology, Sociology, Religions, Business, Economics, History, Literature, Political Science, Philosophy, Traditions, etc.	Politics, Economics, Society, International Trade, Law, Business, Industrial structure, Geography, Legal Institution, Foreign Policy, History, Religions, Art, Literature, Language & Culture, Islam, etc.
Scholarship Program					O		
Home Stay Program		O	O		O		
Dormitory	O	O	O	O		O	
Guarantor System	O	O	O		O		
Other Fees					60,000		20,000
Tuition	882,000	US$3,800	Total Fee: US$12,000	Total Fee: US$8,000	600,000	50,000 (4 classes)	450,000
Admission Fee	280,000	US$150				250,000	50,000
Application Fee	18,000	US$20			10,000	30,000	5,000
Program Size	84	150 / 150	32	16	40	40	60
Program Starting Date	Sep.	Aug. / Jan.	Sep.	Sep.	Sep.	Apr. / Oct.	Sep.
Application Deadline	Apr. 15			May 16	May 15		Mar. 31
Program Length	1 y.	6 m.	1 y.	1 y.	1 y.	6 m.	1 y.
Faculty — Part-time	14	0	6	2	11	5	13
Faculty — Full-time	11	8	1	0	5	9	0
Year Program Established	1953	1972	1976	1979	1974	1967	1963
Address / Telephone	3-10-2 Osawa, Mitaka-shi, Tokyo 181, 0422-23-3191	16-1 Kitakatahoko-cho, Hirakata-shi, Osaka 573, 0720-51-6751	Univ. of Illinois, Center for East & Pacific Studies 1208 West California, Urbana, IL 61801	Umegahara, Nishinomiya, Hyogo 662, 0798-53-6111	18 Yamazato-cho, Showa-ku, Nagoya 466, 052-832-3123	4 Yonban-cho, Chiyoda-ku, Tokyo 102, 03-238-3521	1-6-1 Nishi-waseda, Shinjuku-ku, Tokyo 169, 03-203-4141

Japanese and English Name List
of Colleges and Universities

Sangyo Ika Daigaku
  University of Occupational and Environmental Health, Japan 644
Sanno Daigaku
  SANNO College 535
Sapporo Daigaku
  Sapporo University 538
Sapporo Gakuin Daigaku
  Sapporo Gakuin University 537
Sapporo Ika Daigaku
  Sapporo Medical College 220
Seigakuin Daigaku
  Seigakuin University 542
Seijo Daigaku
  Seijo University 543
Sei Katarina Joshi Daigaku
  St. Catherine Women's College 578
Seikei Daigaku
  Seikei University 544
Sei Marianna Ika Daigaku
  St. Marianna University School of Medicine 580
Seinan Gakuin Daigaku
  Seinan Gakuin University 546
Sei Roka Kango Daigaku
  St. Luke's College of Nursing 579
Seisen Joshi Daigaku
  Seisen Women's College 547
Seishin Joshi Daigaku
  University of the Sacred Heart 647
Seiwa Daigaku
  Seiwa College 548
Sendai Daigaku
  Sendai College 549
Senshu Daigaku
  Senshu University 550
Senzoku Gakuen Daigaku
  Senzoku Gakuen College Music Academy 551
Setsunan Daigaku
  Setsunan University 552
Shibaura Kogyo Daigaku
  Shibaura Institute of Technology 554
Shiga Daigaku
  Shiga University 127
Shiga Ika Daigaku
  Shiga University of Medical Science 128
Shikoku Gakuin Daigaku
  Shikoku Christian College 555
Shikoku Joshi Daigaku
  Shikoku Women's University 556
Shimane Daigaku
  Shimane University 131
Shimane Ika Daigaku
  Shimane Medical University 130
Shimonoseki Shiritsu Daigaku
  Shimonoseki City College 221
Shinshu Daigaku
  Shinshu University 133
Shinwa Joshi Daigaku
  Shinwa Women's College 557

Shirayuri Joshi Daigaku
  Shirayuri Women's College 558
Shitennoji Kokusai Bukkyo Daigaku
  Shitennoji International Buddhist University 559
Shizuoka Daigaku
  Shizuoka University 136
Shizuoka Kenritsu Daigaku
  Shizuoka Prefectural University 222
Shoin Joshigakuin Daigaku
  Shoin Women's University 560
Shokei Daigaku
  Shokei College 561
Shotoku Gakuen Gifu Kyoiku Daigaku
  Shotoku Academy Gifu College of Education 562
Showa Daigaku
  Showa University 563
Showa Joshi Daigaku
  Showa Women's University 564
Showa Ongaku Daigaku
  Showa Academia Musicae 563
Showa Yakka Daigaku
  Showa College of Pharmaceutical Sciences 563
Shuchiin Daigaku
  Shuchiin College 566
Shujitsu Joshi Daigaku
  Shujitsu Joshi University 567
Shukutoku Daigaku
  Shukutoku University 567
Soka Daigaku
  Soka University 568
Sonoda Gakuen Joshi Daigaku
  Sonoda Gakuen Women's College 570
Sugino Joshi Daigaku
  Sugino Women's College 582
Sugiyama Jogakuen Daigaku
  Sugiyama Jogakuen University 582
Surugadai Daigaku
  Surugadai University 583
Taisho Daigaku
  Taisho University 585
Takachiho Shoka Daigaku
  Takachiho University of Commerce 586
Takarazuka Zo kei Geijutsu Daigaku
  Takarazuka University of Art and Design 587
Takasaki Keizai Daigaku
  Takasaki City University of Economics 223
Takushoku Daigaku
  Takushoku University 587
Tama Bijutsu Daigaku
  Tama Art University 590
Tamagawa Daigaku
  Tamagawa University 590
Teikoku Joshi Daigaku
  Teikoku Women's University 591
Teikyo Daigaku
  Teikyo University 591
Teikyo Gijutsu Kagaku Daigaku
  Teikyo University of Technology 593
Tenri Daigaku
  Tenri University 594

Index

Japanese Colleges
and Universities 1989　　　定価 4,900円 (in Japan)

平 成 元 年 3 月 25 日 発 行

　　　　　　　　　　　監　修　　文　　　部　　　省
©1989　　　　　　　編　者　　財団法人 日本国際教育協会

　　　　　　　　　　　発 行 者　　海 老 原　　熊 雄

　　発 行 所　　丸 善 株 式 会 社
　　郵便番号 103　　東京都中央区日本橋二丁目 3 番10号

印刷・製本　大日本印刷株式会社
Published by **MARUZEN COMPANY, LTD.**
Tokyo, Japan
ISBN4-621-03357-3　C1502